THE

New College Encyclopedia of MUSIC

THE New College Encyclopedia of MUSIC

J. A. WESTRUP
Professor of Music, Oxford University

F. Ll. HARRISON
Senior Lecturer in Music, Oxford University

W · W · NORTON & COMPANY · INC · *New York*

W. W. Norton & Company, Inc. is the publisher of current or forthcoming books on music by Gerald Abraham, William Austin, Anthony Baines, Sol Berkowitz, Friedrich Blume, Howard Boatwright, Nadia Boulanger, Nathan Broder, Manfred Bukofzer, John Castellini, John Clough, Doda Conrad, Aaron Copland, Hans David, Paul Des Marais, Otto Erich Deutsch, Frederick Dorian, Alfred Einstein, Gabriel Fontrier, Karl Geiringer, Harold Gleason, Richard Franko Goldman, Peter Gradenwitz, Donald Jay Grout, F. L. Harrison, A. J. B. Hutchings, Charles Ives, Leo Kraft, Paul Henry Lang, Jens Peter Larsen, Maurice Lieberman, Joseph Machlis, W. T. Marrocco, Arthur Mendel, William J. Mitchell, Douglas Moore, Carl Parrish, John F. Ohl, Vincent Persichetti, Marc Pincherle, Walter Piston, Gustave Reese, Curt Sachs, Adolfo Salazar, Arnold Schoenberg, Denis Stevens, Oliver Strunk, Francis Toye, Donald R. Wakeling, Bruno Walter, and J. A. Westrup.

Library of Congress Catalog Card No. 60-10570

Printed in the United States of America

5 6 7 8 9 0

CONTENTS

PREFACE

The chief difficulty in compiling an encyclopedia of any kind is to decide what to leave out. No doubt this problem does not seriously worry editors who are able to spread themselves over several volumes. But it becomes acute when the material has to be compressed within the covers of a single book. It would have been possible to include more entries in the present volume by reducing the amount of information supplied and by omitting the music examples. But though conciseness in general is a virtue, it can easily reach a point where the elimination of what appears to be unessential leaves little that is of practical value to anyone. As for the music examples, we regard these as indispensable. It is difficult to see how any technical explanation of the elements or the forms of music can be made intelligible without an illustration. To the experienced musician many of our examples may appear superfluous. But it is a basic principle in making an encyclopedia to assume that the reader comes to any article without previous knowledge of the subject.

So far as the biographical entries are concerned, we have made a general distinction between composers who may be presumed to be widely known and others who are less well-known, though without presuming to impose any implied judgment of values on the reader. In the case of composers of the first category we have supplied fairly detailed summaries of their principal works; for those of the second category we have been content to indicate the main fields of composition in which they were active—a method which does not exclude particular mention of works which may be of special interest. The bibliographies, both in the biographical articles and in the technical articles, are admittedly a selection, but we hope they will provide sufficient material to start the reader off on any plan he may have for more detailed study. Though we have naturally given preference to works in English, on the ground that these are likely to be more accessible to the general reader, we have also included a large number of standard works in foreign languages.

The principle on which we have selected musicians for inclusion cannot be stated simply, since each case has had to be decided on its merits. No doubt the specialist on any particular period will be surprised at the omission of persons whom he regards as of considerable importance. Equally, the reader with no specialist knowledge may question the inclusion of musicians of whom he has never heard. But this work is not designed for specialists nor to flatter a reader's ignorance. We believe that every entry in this volume, whether biographical or technical, is likely to be of interest to somebody at some time, and we have tried to provide for this contingency, however remote it may appear.

A large number of foreign words for instruments and for technical terms are included in these pages. The latter may appear unnecessarily numerous. On the other hand, many of them occur in the footnotes to modern editions of classical works published abroad, and recourse to a dictionary does not always tell the reader precisely what they mean. We have also taken into account the fact that many English and American writers today tend to use foreign terms (particularly German terms) in essays on a musical subject. This habit is deplorable; the English language must be a very poor medium for expression if it cannot supply equivalents to German terms (which are, incidentally, often far from precise and not always very good German). But since the practice is now common, it seemed reasonable to offer some assistance towards interpretation.

On the other hand, the number of foreign words indicating tempo or expression has been strictly limited. It would have been quite impossible to include them all, since there is no limit to the directions which a composer may wish to convey in his own language. We have been content to include those which occur most commonly in Italian (traditionally the *lingua franca* of musical expression), French and German. For the rest, particularly those which strain verbosity beyond reasonable limits, the reader must consult a dictionary.

The alphabetical order of entries ignores hyphens and the divisions between separate words. Thus 'Tre corde' follows 'Treble Viol'. This is the only satisfactory method of ensuring that every entry can be found without having to search for it. For this purpose the German *ö* is regarded as indistinguishable from *o*, not as the equivalent of *oe*. In cases where this might create difficulty, *i.e.*, where a German name may be spelled in more ways than one, a cross reference is provided.

With a few unimportant exceptions, the titles of operas are given in the language employed at their first production. Cross references are given under their English titles, if these are in general use, and also under titles in any other foreign language which may be familiar (*e.g.*, 'Coq d'Or', 'Pique-Dame'). The titles of other works (oratorios, symphonies, etc.) are generally given in the language which is most likely to be familiar, with cross references for the English or foreign titles as the case may be.

Pronunciation presented several difficulties. In the first place, it often differs considerably in different parts of the same country. The only possible solution here is to adopt what may be regarded as the standard pronunciation of educated people, as represented in reputable dictionaries. In the second place, pronunciation has varied from one century to another. However, it would have been quite impossible to attempt to record, for example, the various changes that have occurred in the pronunciation of French vowel sounds. All that can be done is to suggest the pronunciation that would be normal at the present day, unless there is any evidence to the contrary (as in the case of 'Dufay', which we know was pronounced as three syllables). Even modern names sometimes present difficulties. One would except 'Koechlin' to be pronounced 'k*e*rsh-lãn', but in fact Frenchmen say 'k*e*rk-lãn'; and M. Darius Milhaud is illogical enough to insist on calling himself not 'mee-lo' but 'mee-yo'. Similar misconceptions sometimes occur with English names: it is not uncommon to hear 'Rubbra' pronounced 'roob′-ra' instead of 'rub′-ra'.

The only completely satisfactory scheme for indicating pronunciation is the use of phonetic symbols; but these inevitably create difficulties for the reader who has neither the time nor the patience to master them. The method used here is to employ English consonants and English vowel sounds in an attempt to provide a near equivalent of the sounds of foreign languages. This attempt can never be wholly successful: there are a number of sounds in foreign languages which have no equivalent in English and which an Englishman can master only with long practice. All we can offer in such cases is an approximation. The guide to pronunciation is unusually detailed, in order to save the reader the trouble of trying to build up the various combinations of letters for himself. Wherever possible familiar English words are used to illustrate the pronunciation both of vowel sounds and of initial consonants. Where a particular combination has no ready-made equivalent in English, we have had to be content with indicating the way in which it is built up.

It is hardly necessary to say that we are heavily indebted to the labours of other writers and editors. Among the encyclopedic works which we have found particularly useful are the late Alfred Loewenberg's *Annals of Opera*, *The International Cyclopedia of Music and Musicians* (revised by Nicolas Slonimsky), *Grove's Dictionary of Music and Musicians* (fifth edition, edited by Eric Blom) and *Die Musik in Geschichte und Gegenwart* (edited by Friedrich Blume). The last of these had only reached the letter G when our final revision was completed, but within these limits it proved invaluable on many points of detail. We have to thank many friends and colleagues for answering questions and providing information.

In particular, we wish to record our indebtedness to Mr. and Mrs. William Webb and Mr. Ralph Leavis, who gave valuable assistance with proof-reading. It is impossible that a work of this kind should be entirely free from errors; but we hope that any that survive will prove to be the result not of carelessness but of inadvertence.

Oxford,
June, 1959.

J. A. W.
F. Ll. H.

GUIDE TO PRONUNCIATION

Vowel Sounds

* In syllables marked thus the *r* must be silent.

† In syllables marked thus the *r* must be well rolled.

The vowel *u* is to be pronounced as in Southern English. It is roughly equivalent to the short *a* in Northern English, *e.g.*, Southern English *bud*=Northern English *bad*.

a like the first *a* in *aha!*

abe as in *babe*

ace as in *face*

ack as in *back*

ade as in *fade*

ague as in *vague*

ah as in *hurrah*

ahb like **a*(r)b* in *barb*

ahd like **a*(r)d* in *hard*

ahf like *alf* in *calf*

ahg like **a*(r)g* in *target*

ahk like **a*(r)k* in *bark*

ahkh like *ahk*, but with guttural termination (as in Scottish *loch*)

ahkt like **a*(r)ked* in *parked*

ahkts like **a*(r)keds* in *parked since*

ahl like *ale* in *morale*

ahlss *ahl* plus *s* as in *sense*

ahm like *alm* in *balm*

ahmss *ahm* plus *s* as in *sense*

ahn like **a*(r)n* in *barn*

ahnd like **a*(r)nd* in *barndoor*

ahnk *ahn* plus *k* as in *kettle*

ahp like **a*(r)p* in *carp*

ahr like *ar* in *car*

ahrr like †*ar* in *car*

ahss like **a*(r)ce* in *farce* (or as *ass* in Southern English *pass*, with long *a*)

aht like **a*(r)t* in *cart*

ahtsh like **a*(r)tsh* in *art shop*

ahv like **a*(r)v* in *carving*

ahz like **a*(r)s* in *parsing*

aimz like *aims*

ain as in *train*

air as in *hair*

aird as in *hair-do*

airg as in *airgun*

airk like *airc* in *hair-cut*

airl as in *fairly*

airm as in *airman*

airn as in *cairn*

airnst as in *cairn-stone*

airr as in *hair-raising*

airrd like †*aired* in *paired*

airrk like †*airc* in *hair-cut*

airrt like †*airt* in *hair-trigger*

airsh like *airsh* in *airship*, but with the lips drawn back

airt as in *hair-trigger*

airv as in *air-vent*

ake as in *take*

aked as in *baked*

ale as in *tale*

ame as in *fame*

an as in *can*

a͡n like *an*, but through the nose

ane as in *mane*

a͡nbr *a͡n* plus *br* as in *brisk*

a͡nt *a͡n* plus *t* as in *tot*

ar as in *car*, but short

arr like *urr* in *curry*

arrb *arr* plus *b* as in *bib*

arrce *arr* plus *s* as in *sense*

arrg *arr* plus *g* as in *gag*

arrk *arr* plus *k* as in *kettle*

arrt *arr* plus *t* as in *tot*

arrts *arr* plus *ts* as in *tots*

art as in *cart*, but short

ast as in *dastardly*

ate as in *mate*

aw as in *saw*

awl as in *bawl*

awr as in *awry*

ay as in *day*

ayth like *aith* in *faith*

aze as in *haze*

ebr as in *February*

eck as in *deck*

ĕck like *eck*, but short (as *ec* in *Alec*)

eckh like *eck*, but with guttural termination (as in Scottish *loch*)

ecks as in *decks*

ee as in *see*

e͝e like *ee*, but with rounded lips

eeb as in *feeble*

e͝eb like *eeb*, but with rounded lips

eece as in *fleece*

e͝ece like *eece*, but with rounded lips

eech as in *speech*

eed as in *need*

e͝ed like *eed*, but with rounded lips

eef as in *beef*

eeg like *eag* in *eager*

e͝eg like *eeg*, but with rounded lips

eek as in *seek*

e͝ek like *eek*, but with rounded lips

e͝eks like *eeks* in *seeks*, but with rounded lips

eekt like *eaked* in *leaked*

eel as in *feel*

e͝el like *eel*, but with rounded lips

eelce like *eels* in *eel-skin*

eem as in *seem*

e͝em like *eem*, but with rounded lips

een as in *green*

e͝ensh as in *greenshank*, but with rounded lips

e͝ent as in *greentail*, but with rounded lips

eep as in *weep*

e͝ep like *eep*, but with rounded lips

eepr as in *knee practice*

eer as in *peer*

e͝er like *eer*, but with rounded lips

e͝ern *e͝er* plus *n* as in *noun*

e͝erst *e͝er* plus *st* as in *state*

eert as in *beer tankard*

eestr like *E str* in *E string*

eet as in *feet*

e͝et like *eet*, but with rounded lips

eeth as in *teeth*

eets as in *meets*

e͝ets like *eets*, but with rounded lips

eev as in *sleeve*

eevr like *evr* in *fev'rish*

eex like *eeks* in *seeks*

eext as in *seeks to*

eez as in *freeze*

e͝ez like *eez*, but with rounded lips

eezh like *eiz* in *seizure*

ĕf like *ef* in *effete*

eff as in *Effie*

eg as in *beg*

egg like *egg*

eh like *eh?*

ehd *eh* plus *d* as in *did*

ehl *eh* plus *l* as in *lull*

ehn *eh* plus *n* as in *noun*

ehr *eh* plus *r* as in *rural*

el as in *melon*

ĕl like *le* in *able*

elce like *else*

ell as in *tell*

elm as in *helmet*

ĕlss *ĕl* plus *s* as in *sense*

elt as in *belt*

ĕlt *ĕl* plus *t* as in *tot*

elts as in *belts*

em as in *hem*

ĕm like *em* in *tell 'em*

emp as in *hemp*

empft *emp* plus *f* as in *fife* and *t* as in *tot*

en as in *men*

ĕn like *en* in *heaven*

ence as in *hence*

ĕnce like *ence* in *prudence*

ĕnd *ĕn* plus *d* as in *did*

eng as in *strength*

enk like *enc* in *hen-coop*

ensh like *ent* in *mention*

ent as in *sent*

ĕnt like *ent* in *urgent*

enz like *ens* in *hens*

ep as in *step*

er as in *bitter*

er as in **bitte(r)*

er see 'yer' under Initial Consonants

erce like *erse* in *terse*

erk like **o(r)k* in *work*

erl as in *Berlin*

err as in *merry*

errd *err* plus *d* as in *did*

errt *err* plus *t* as in *tot*

ert as in *Herbert*

erts like **i(r)ts* in *skirts*

esh as in *mesh*, but with the lips drawn back

esht *esh* plus *t* as in *tot*

esk as in *desk*

ess as in *mess*

ĕss like *ess* in *careless*

est as in *best*

estr as in *vestry*

et as in *bet*

etch as in *wretch*

ets as in *bets*

etsh like *etch*, but with the lips drawn back

ev as in *ever*

ew as in *dew*

ex as in *flex*

eye like *eye*

ez as in *fez*

ezh like *eis* in *leisure*

i as in *pity*

ib as in *nib*

ibe as in *tribe*

ice as in *mice*

iced like *iced*

ick as in *stick*

icks as in *sticks*

id as in *bid*

ide as in *side*

ife as in *life*

ifes as in *lifesaver*
iff as in *tiff*
ig as in *dig*
ike as in *like*
ile as in *pile*
ill as in *fill*
il*sh* like *illsh* in *millshaft*, but with the lips drawn back
ilt as in *gilt*
im as in *whim*
ime as in *lime*
in as in *pin*
ince as in *mince*
ind as in *wind*
ine as in *mine*
ing as in *ring*
ingce like *ings* in *ringside*
ink as in *sink*
int as in *hint*
ip as in *lip*
ire as in *fire*
irr as in *irritate*
irrn *irr* plus *n* as in *noun*
irr*sh* *irr* plus *sh* pronounced with the lips drawn back
ish as in *fish*
i*sh* like *ish*, but with the lips drawn back
iss as in *miss*
ist as in *mist*
it as in *bit*
itch as in *pitch*
ite as in *bite*
ites as in *bites*
its as in *bits*
iv as in *given*
ize as in *size*

o as in *go*
ŏ like *o* in *pot*
oaf as in *loaf*
oast as in *toast*
oat as in *boat*
oats as in *boats*
obe as in *lobe*
oce as in *grocer*
ock as in *dock*
ockh like *och* in Scottish *loch*
ockhs like *ochs* in Scottish *lochs*
od as in *plod*
ode as in *code*
off as in *doff*
og as in *dog*
ogue as in *vogue*
oh like *oh!*
ohn like *one* in *bone*
ohrr *oh* plus strongly rolled *r*
oise as in *noise*
oke as in *spoke*
ol as in *solid*
ole as in *hole*
olf as in *olfactory*
oll as in *doll*
olld as in *doll'd up*
ollk like *ollc* in *dollcart*
ollt as in *doll table*
ollts *ollt* plus *s* as in *sense*
om as in *from*
ome as in *home*
on as in *don*
ŏn̄ like *on*, but through the nose
ŏn̄b *ŏn̄* plus *b* as in *bib*
one as in *tone*
ong as in *song*
onk as in *donkey*
ŏn̄t *ŏn̄* plus *t* as in *tot*
ŏn̄z *ŏn̄* plus *z* as in *zinc*
oo as in *too*
oob as in *too bad*
ŏŏb *oo* as in *foot* plus *b* as in *bib* (or like *ub* in Northern English *blubber*)
oobl as in *too blind*
ooce like *oose* in *loose*
ŏŏd as in *good*
oof as in *hoof*
oog as in *too good*
ook as in *spook* (or as *uke* in American *duke*)
ŏŏk as in *book*
ookh like *ook*, but with guttural termination (as in Scottish *loch*)
ŏŏkh like *ŏŏk*, but with guttural termination (as in Scottish *loch*)
ŏŏks as in *books*
ool as in *fool*
ŏŏm like *um* in *album*
ŏŏmp *ŏŏm* plus *p* as in *pop*
ŏŏn *oo* as in *foot* plus *n* as in *noun* (or like *un* in Northern English *bun*)
ŏŏnd *ŏŏn* plus *d* as in *did*
ŏŏnfts *ŏŏn* plus *ft* as in *raft* and *s* as in *sense*
ŏŏngs *ŏŏ* plus *ng* as in *sung* and *s* as in *sense*
ŏŏnk *ŏŏn* plus *k* as in *kettle* (or like *unk* in Northern English *drunk*)
ŏŏnkt *ŏŏnk* plus *t* as in *tot*
ŏŏnst *ŏŏn* plus *st* as in *test*
ŏŏnt *ŏŏn* plus *t* as in *tot* (or like *unt* in Northern English *hunt*)
ŏŏp *ŏŏ* plus *p* as in *pop* (or like Northern English *up*)
oor as in *moor* (not like *ore* in *more*)
ŏŏr *ŏŏ* plus *r* as in *rural*
oorb as in *poor-box* (see *oor*)
ŏŏrk *ŏŏr* plus *k* as in *kettle*
ŏŏrl *ŏŏr* plus *l* as in *lull*
oorr as in *poor rate* (see *oor*)
ŏŏr*sh* *ŏŏr* plus *sh* as in *ship*, but with the lips drawn back
ŏŏrt *ŏŏr* plus *t* as in *tot*
oosh like *ouche* in *douche*
ŏŏsh like *ush* in *bush*
ŏŏss like *uss* in *puss*
oost as in *boost*
ŏŏst *ŏŏ* plus *st* as in *test* (or like *ust* in Northern English *bust*)
oot as in *boot*
ŏŏth *ŏŏ* plus *th* as in *thick*
oov as in *groove*

ooz as in *ooze*
oozh like *ouge* in *rouge*
op as in *mop*
ope as in *hope*
opf as in *hopfield*
opft *opf* plus *t* as in *tot*
orr as in *horrid*
orrce *orr* plus *s* as in *sense*
orrd *orr* plus *d* as in *did*
orrf *orr* plus *f* as in *fife*
orrk *orr* plus *k* as in *kettle*
orrm *orr* plus *m* as in *mime*
orrn *orr* plus *n* as in *noun*
orrsh *orr* plus *sh* as in *ship*
orrzh *orr* plus *s* as in *leisure*
orrt *orr* plus *t* as in *tot*
osh as in *bosh*
oss as in *moss*
osst like *ost* in *Ostend*
ot as in *hot*
otch as in *botch*
ote as in *note*
otr as in *not really*
out as in *bout*
ov like *of*
ow as in *cow*
owb as in *cow-byre*
owce like *ouse* in *house*
owf as in *cow-field*
owk like *owc* in *cowcatcher*
owkhs like *owk*, but with guttural termination (as in Scottish *loch*), plus *s* as in *sense*
owm as in *cowman*
own as in *town*
owp as in *cowpat*
owr like *our* in *hour*
owst as in *frowsty*
owt like *out*
owz like *ows* in *cows*
oy as in *toy*
oyce like *oice* in *voice*
oyl like *oil* in *boil*
oym as in *toymaker*
oyn like *oin* in *join*
oynd like *oined* in *joined*
oyts like *oits* in *quoits*
oytsh like *oitsh* in *quoit shaker*
oz as in *sozzle*
oze as in *doze*
ozh *o* as in *pot* plus *s* as in *leisure*

(All *u* syllables as in Southern English: see note at beginning)

ub as in *rub*
ubl as in *Dublin*
ubr as in *tub race*
uck as in *duck*
uckh like *uck*, but with guttural termination (as in Scottish *loch*)
uckht *uckh* plus *t* as in *tot*
uckr as in *muckrake*
uckt like *uct* in *duct*
ud as in *mud*
ude as in *nude*
uff as in *muff*
uft as in *tuft*
ug as in *jug*
ulb as in *bulb*
uld like *ulled* in *culled*
ulk as in *sulk*
ull as in *dull*
ullce like *ulc* in *ulcer*
ullm like *ulm* in *culminate*
ullsh as in *dull show*, but with the lips drawn back
ult as in *cult*
ults as in *cults*
ulzh *ull* plus *s* as in *leisure*
um as in *sum*
umpf as in *rump-fed*
un as in *bun*
u͡n like *un*, but through the nose
unce as in *dunce*
u͡nce like *unce*, but through the nose
und as in *under*
u͡nd like *und*, but through the nose
u͡ndr *u͡nd* plus *r* as in *rural*
ung as in *sung*
u͡nk *u͡n* plus *k* as in *kettle*
u͡nl *u͡n* plus *l* as in *lull*
u͡nsh *u͡n* plus *sh* as in *ship*
unt as in *hunt*
u͡nt like *unt*, but through the nose
unts as in *hunts*
u͡nzh *u͡n* plus *s* as in *leisure*
up as in *cup*
upt as in *abrupt*
ur as in *fur*
ur as in **pu(r)sue*
urd as in *curd*
urd *ur* plus *d* as in *did*
urk *ur* plus *k* as in *kettle*
urlts *url* as in **pu(r)loin* plus *ts* as in *Betsy*
urn *ur* plus *n* as in *noun*
u͡rn like urn, but through the nose
urnt *urn* plus *t* as in *tot*
urp as in **su(r)prise*
urr as in *burr*
ursh *ur* plus *sh* as in *ship*
urst *ur* plus *st* as in *test*
urt *ur* plus *t* as in *tot*
ush as in *hush*
uss as in *fuss*
ust as in *dust*
ustr as in *lustral*
ut as in *shut*
utr like *uttr* in *buttress*
uts as in *shuts*
utt as in *butter*
uv like *ove* in *love*
ux like *ucks* in *ducks*
uz as in *buzz*
uzh *u* as in *but* plus *s* as in *leisure*

y as in *cry*
ykh like *yke* in *dyke*, but with guttural termination (as in Scottish *loch*)
ynts like *ints* in *pints*
ysh like *eyesh* in *eye-shade*
ysh like *ysh*, but with the lips drawn back

Initial Consonants

Combinations of consonants which are self-evident are not included in this list.

b as in *big*
bw as in *cobweb*
by like *b* in *beauty*
c as in *cat*
ch as in *church*
crzh *cr* as in *crop* plus *s* as in *leisure*
cv like *ckv* in *brick-van*
cw like *qu* in *quick*
d as in *dog*
dj as in *bad joke*
dv as in *advise*
dy like *d* in *duty*
dz as in *mad zeal*
dzy like *dsy* in *dad's yawn*
f as in *fat*
g as in *get* (never as in *germ*)
gly like *gl* in *wag lute*
gny like *gn* in *big newt*
grw *gr* as in *grim* plus *w* as in *wed*
gw as in *bagwash*
h as in *hot*
j as in *jam*
k as in *kettle*
kh like *k*, but guttural (as in Scottish *loch*)
kny like *kn* in *black news*
l as in *lip*
lw like *llw* in *Millwall*
ly like *l* in *lute*
m as in *make*
my like *m* in *mute*
n as in *noun*
nw as in *unwell*
ny like *n* in *new*
p as in *pay*
pf as in *cupful*
py like *p* in *pew*
r as in *red*
rw *r* plus *w* as in *wed*
ry *r* plus *y* as in *yet* (practically the same as *ri* in *Marian*)
s as in *sit*
scr as in *screw*
scw like *squ* in *squash*
sg like *ssg* in *pressgang*
sh as in *shake*
shl as in *ashling*
shm as in *cashmere*
shn as in *fish-net*
shp as in *fishpond*
shr as in *shrub*
sht as in *washtub*
shtr as in *ash-tree*
shv as in *cash-voucher*
shw as in *fishwife*
sk as in *skate*
sny like *sn* in *it's new*
spy like *sp* in *spew*
sy like *s* in *suit*
t as in *take*
tch *t* plus *ch* as in *church*
tr as in *train*
trw *tr* plus *w* as in *wed*
ts as in *Betsy*
tsv *ts* plus *v* as in *vote*
tsy as in *it's yours*
ty like *t* in *tune*
v as in *vote*
vw like *fw* in *Prince of Wales*
vy like *v* in *view*
w as in *wed*
y as in *yet*
yer *y* followed by an inaudible vowel sound (rather like *i*(*a*) in *Britannia*, pronounced quickly with the final *a* silent)
z as in *zeal*
zh like *s* in *leisure*
zhw *zh* plus *w* as in *wed*
zm like *sm* in *prismatic*

Accent is indicated by the sign ′ placed immediately after the accented syllable. There is no accent for French words.

LIST OF ABBREVIATIONS

A., American
Add., Additional Manuscripts (Brit. Mus.)
Apr., April
Arab., Arabic
Aug., August

b., born
bapt., baptized
B.B.C., British Broadcasting Corporation
B.G., *Bach Gesellschaft*
B.Mus., Bachelor of Music
Brit. Mus., British Museum

c., *circa* (about)
Cal., California
cent., century, centuries
cf., *confer* (compare)
Co., County
Conn., Connecticut
Cz., Czech

D., Dutch
d., died
D.B.E., Dame of the British Empire
D.C., District of Columbia
D.D.T., *Denkmäler deutscher Tonkunst*
Dec., December
dim., diminutive
D. Mus.., Doctor of Music
D.T.B., *Denkmäler der Tonkunst in Bayern*
D.T.Ö., *Denkmäler der Tonkunst in Österreich*

E., English
ed., edited, edition, editor
e.g., *exempli gratia* (for example)
E.D.M., *Erbe deutscher Musik*
E.H., *English Hymnal*
E.M.S., *The English Madrigal School*
E.S.L.S., *The English School of Lutenist Songwriters*
etc., etcetera

Feb., February
fem., feminine
Fl., Flemish
fl., *floruit* (flourished)
foll., following

Fr., French
ft., foot, feet

G., German
Glos., Gloucestershire
Gr., Greek
G.S.M., Guildhall School of Music

H., Hungarian
H.A.M., *Historical Anthology of Music*
Herts., Hertfordshire
H.M.C., *Historical Manuscripts Commission*
H.M.V., His Master's Voice
Hymns A. & M., *Hymns Ancient and Modern*

I., Italian
ibid., *ibidem* (in the same place or work)
i.e., *id est* (that is)
introd., introductory
I.S.C.M., International Society for Contemporary Music

Jan., January

L., Latin
l., line
Lancs., Lancashire
L.C.C., London County Council
Lincs., Lincolnshire
lit., literally

Mass., Massachusetts
Med. Fr., Medieval French
Med. L., Medieval Latin
Mich., Michigan
mod., modern

N., Norwegian
N.H., New Hampshire
N.J., New Jersey
no., number
Northants., Northamptonshire
nos., numbers
Nov., November
nr., near
N.Y., New York State

Oct., October
O.E., Old English
Ont., Ontario
Op., *opus* (work)
op. cit., *opus citatum* (the work already cited)
Oxon., Oxfordshire

p., page
Pa., Pennsylvania
Ph.D., Doctor of Philosophy
pl., plate, plates
plur., plural
Port., Portuguese
pp., pages
prob., probably
Prov., Provençal
pt., part
pts., parts

q.v., *quod vide* (see this entry)

R., Russian
R.A.M., Royal Academy of Music
R.C.M., Royal College of Music
rev., revised

Sept., September
seq., *sequentia* (and the following pages)
ser., series
Sp., Spanish
S.P., *Songs of Praise*
Staffs., Staffordshire

T.C.M., *Tudor Church Music*
tr., trans., translated
U.S.A., United States of America

v., *vide* (see)
vol., volume
vols., volumes

W., Welsh
Wilts., Wiltshire
Wis., Wisconsin

Yorks., Yorkshire

A

A, *E.G.* (*Fr. I.* la). (1) The 6th note (or submediant) of the scale of C major. In the early middle ages the letter A came to be attached to

in preference to other notes, because this had been the lowest note of the two-octave scale system of the Greeks. The practice of using the letters A to G for successive octaves dates from the 10th cent. In Germany it is common to use *A* for A major and *a* for A minor, and similarly with other letters.

is the note (normally given by the oboe) to which an orchestra tunes. By international agreement its pitch is 440 cycles a second. *v.* KEY, NOTATION, PITCH, SCALE.

(2) As an abbreviation *A.* = Alto, Associate.

Aaron (Aron) [ah'-rone], PIETRO: *b.* Florence, *c.* 1490 ; *d.* Venice, 1545. Theorist, who was active as a teacher in Rome. He was one of the most progressive writers of his time, refusing to accept many of the conventions of medieval practice which still survived in the sixteenth century. He recommended, among other things, that accidentals should always be written in the music and not left to the performers. His best known work was *Il Toscanello in musica*, which went into several editions.

Abaco [ah'-bah-co], (1) EVARISTO FELICE DALL': *b.* Verona, July 12, 1675; *d.* Munich, July 12, 1742. Violinist and composer; from 1714 director of the Court music at Munich. Published trio sonatas, violin sonatas and orchestral concertos. Modern editions in *D.T.B.*, i & ix (1).

(2) GIUSEPPE CLEMENS FERDINAND DALL': *b.* Brussels, 1709; *d.* Verona, 1805. Son of (1). Cellist: from 1738 director of the Court music at Bonn. Composed cello sonatas.

Abba-Cornaglia [ahb-bah'-corr-nahl'-yah], PIETRO: *b.* Alessandria (Piedmont), March 20, 1851; *d.* there, May 2, 1894. Composer and historian. Founded a school of music at Alessandria. His compositions include a Requiem and operas.

Abbatini [ahb-bah-tee'-nee], ANTONIO MARIA: *b.* Tiferno, *c.* 1597; *d.* there 1677. Active as a church musician in Rome. Published Masses, psalms, motets and antiphons. Joint composer, with Marco Marazzoli, of one of the earliest known comic operas, *Dal male il bene* (Rome, 1653).

Abbé [a-bay], JOSEPH BARNABÉ SAINT-SEVIN L': *b.* Agen, June 11, 1727; *d.* Paris, July 25, 1803. Virtuoso violinist, a member of the orchestra of the Comédie-Française at the age of 12. Active as teacher and composer. Published music for violin and *Les Principes du violon* (1761).

Abbellimenti [ahb-bell-lee-men'-tee], *I.* Ornaments.

Abbey, JOHN: *b.* Whilton (Northamptonshire), Dec. 22, 1785; *d.* Versailles, Feb. 19, 1859. Organ-builder; lived in Paris from 1826 and built many organs for French cathedrals and churches. Built the first organ in the Paris Opéra for the production of Meyerbeer's *Robert-le-diable* (1831).

Abel [ah'-běl], KARL FRIEDRICH, *b.* Cöthen, Dec. 22, 1723; *d.* London, June 20, 1787. Son of a violinist in the Court music at Cöthen. Court musician at Dresden, 1748-58. Became a distinguished performer on the bass viol and appeared in this capacity in London, where, in association with John Christian Bach, he gave several series of subscription concerts. Published a quantity of instrumental music. His portrait was painted by Gainsborough. There is no evidence that he attended St. Thomas's School, Leipzig, under J. S. Bach (*v.* C. S. Terry, *John Christian Bach*, p. 76).

Abell, John: *c.* 1650-1724. Counter-tenor singer in the service of Charles II and James II. Travelled on the Continent during the reign of William III, returning to England in 1700. His publications include three collections of songs. His reputation as a singer was high (*v.* Evelyn, *Diary*, Jan. 27, 1682).

Abendmusiken [ah'-bĕnt-moo-zeek'-ĕn], *G.* Evening musical performances, in particular those given every autumn in the Marienkirche at Lübeck. They are first mentioned in 1673, when Buxtehude was organist. They consisted of organ solos and a cycle of five church cantatas for voices and instruments, performed on the last Sunday after Trinity, the Sunday next before Advent, and the 2nd, 3rd and 4th Sundays in Advent (*v.* Albert Schweitzer, *J. S. Bach*, vol. i, pp. 76-9). In 1705 Bach (aged 20) obtained leave of absence from Arnstadt (about 230 miles from Lübeck) in order to hear the *Abendmusiken* under Buxtehude. He was so impressed by what he heard that he overstayed his leave.

Abendroth [ah'-bĕnt-rote], HERMANN: *b.* Frankfort-on-Main, Jan. 19, 1883. Conductor. Studied in Munich; director of the Cologne Conservatorium, 1915; conductor of the Gewandhaus Orchestra, Leipzig, 1928.

Abert [ah'-bert], HERMANN: *b.* Stuttgart, March 25, 1871; *d.* there, Aug. 13, 1927. Historian and musicologist. Professor at Halle, 1909; Leipzig, 1920; Berlin, 1923. His publications include studies of Greek and medieval music, a biography of Schumann, and an authoritative study of the life and work of Mozart (based on Jahn).

Abgesang [up'-ger-zung], *G.* "After-song." The concluding portion of a stanza of a MINNESINGER or MEISTERSINGER song. *v.* BAR (3).

Abraham, GERALD ERNEST HEAL: *b.* Newport (Isle of Wight), March 9, 1904. Critic and historian, whose special field is Russian music. Director of the gramophone department of the B.B.C., 1942; professor at Liverpool, 1947. His publications include *Masters of Russian Music* (with M. D. Calvocoressi, 1936), *A Hundred Years of Music* (1938), *Chopin's Musical Style* (1939), *Eight Soviet Composers* (1943). Editor of a series of collective works on Tchaikovsky, Schubert, Sibelius, Schumann, and Handel. General editor, *History of Music in Sound* (H.M.V.).

Ábrányi [ahb'-rahn-yi], (1) EMIL: *b.* Budapest, Sept. 22, 1882. Director of the National Opera at Budapest since 1920 and composer of several operas.

(2) KORNÉL: *b.* Szentgyörgy-Ábrány, Oct. 15, 1822; *d.* Budapest, Dec. 20, 1903. Pianist and composer. Grandfather of (1). A close friend of Liszt, he was active in promoting the cause of Hungarian music, for which purpose he founded a musical journal in 1860. He also translated opera librettos and acted as music critic to several Hungarian papers. His compositions comprise piano music, songs and part-songs. He published a number of biographical, historical and pedagogical works.

Abschiedssymphonie [up'-sheets-zēēm-fo-nee'], *G.* *v.* FAREWELL SYMPHONY.

Absil [up-seel], JEAN: *b.* Peruwelz (Hainaut), Oct. 23, 1893. Composer. Studied at Brussels Conservatoire; since 1923 director of the Musical Academy of Etterbeek. His compositions, which reject traditional harmony, include 5 symphonies, concertos for violin, viola, cello and piano, choral music, and chamber music.

Absolute Music. A term commonly used as the opposite of PROGRAMME MUSIC, to indicate music that has no admitted association with anything outside itself. The great majority of instrumental music comes into this category. The distinction is, however, unsound, since music, being a product of the human mind, can never be wholly divorced from human experience.

Absolute Pitch. The gift of recognizing the pitch of any note that is heard, or of singing any note at the correct pitch without help from an instrument. Though it derives largely from a constant association with music performed at the standard pitch, it is also found in precocious children, and may decline with advancing years. It is particularly useful to singers and conductors but may prove embarrassing when music is transposed. There is no justification for regarding it as a sign of outstanding musical ability.

Abt [upt], FRANZ: *b.* Eilenburg, Dec. 22, 1819; *d.* Wiesbaden, March 31, 1885. Active as conductor of choral societies, and composer of a large quantity of amiable music for solo voices and choirs (particularly male-voice choirs).

Academic Festival Overture. Brahms's *Akademische Fest-Ouvertüre* for orchestra, Op. 80 (1880), written in recognition of the conferment of an honorary Ph.D. on the composer by the University of Breslau in 1879. A number of students' songs are introduced into the score, including "Gaudeamus igitur," with which the piece ends.

A cappella [ah cahp-pell′-lah], *I.* "In the church style." Applied to choral music which is either (1) entirely without accompaniment or (2) without any independent accompaniment. Now used only in the first sense.

Accelerando [ah-tcheh-leh-rahnd′-o], *I.* "Quickening [the time]." Often abbreviated *accel.*

Accent. (1) The rhythm of music, as of verse, is made clear by accent. Where the structure is symmetrical, as in most 18th-cent. music, the accent will recur at regular intervals, *e.g.* in 4/4 time on the first beat of the bar and, with lesser force, on the third; in 3/4 time on the first beat of the bar. But even in 18th-cent. music this is by no means universal:

HANDEL, *Messiah*

This is equivalent to:

i.e. an accent on the word "hath" would distort the rhythm. A further example:

[MOZART, *Sonata in F major, K. 332*

Here the departure from the normal rhythm in the 3rd and 4th bars is made clearer by the alternation of *f* and *p*. Modern composers tend to express such changes of rhythm by altering the lengths of the bars, but this is often quite unnecessary and merely adds to the difficulties of conductors and players. Although bar-lines represent a fundamental rhythm (similar to the scansion of a line of verse), there is no reason why accent should coincide with the "strong" beats, any more than the words in poetry exactly represent the scansion by feet. This distinction is clearly marked in 16th-cent. music. Here, in spite of the absence of bar-lines, there is a fundamental rhythm which governs the treatment of consonance and dissonance, while at the same time the rhythm of any individual phrase pursues an independent course. The opening of Palestrina's *Stabat Mater* is barred in modern editions as follows:

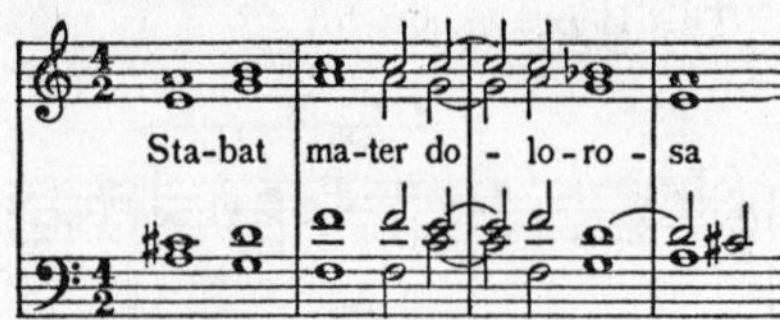

This represents the fundamental rhythm of the piece. But the rhythm of the phrase is more clearly seen if we remove the bar-lines and write:

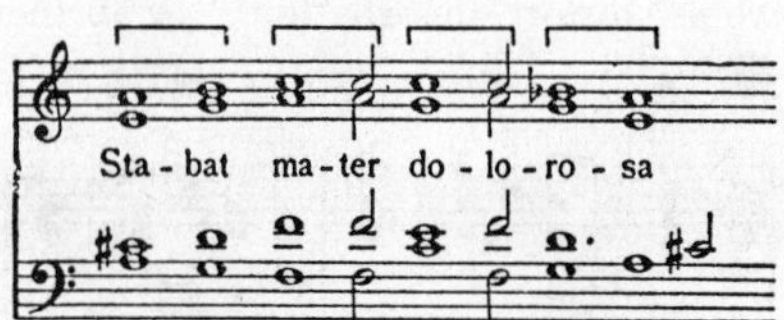

In this example all the voices have the same rhythm; but where the vocal lines are independent of each other we find contrasted rhythms, with the accent occurring in different places in the different voices:

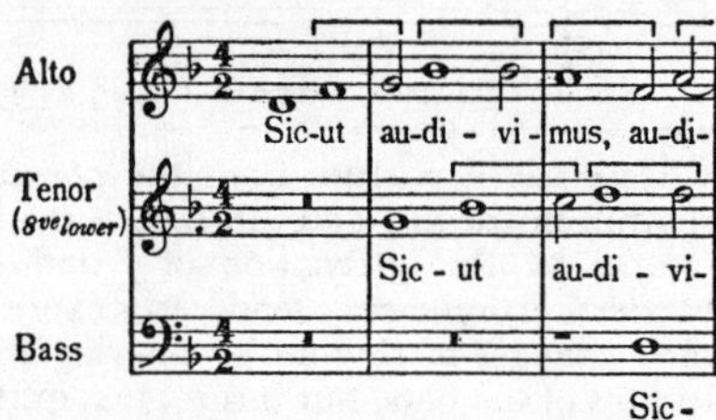

BYRD, *Gradualia, Book I, i, 2*

In such cases intelligent singers will require no signs to show where the accent lies.

Accent signs are properly used to indicate special emphasis, in whatever part of a bar it may be required. Those in current use are: (1) > (2)—(3) ∧ or ∨. Composers are not always consistent in using them; but > normally indicates a strong accent,—stress or pressure, ∧ or ∨ heavy pressure. > and—are written over or under the note, whichever is more convenient; ∧ is written over, ∨ under. These signs indicate relative intensity and may occur in a passage marked *pianissimo*. They are also found, rather unnecessarily, in combination, *e.g.* △, and in association with the sign for *staccato, e.g.* ÷. The following abbreviations also indicate strong emphasis: *sf* or *sfz* (*sforzando*, "forcing"), *sfp* or *fp* (*sforzando piano* or *forte piano*, an accent followed immediately by *piano*), *rf* or *rfz* (*rinforzando* "reinforcing"). The sign *pf*, used by Brahms, has nothing to do with emphasis; it is an abbreviation of *poco forte*, "moderately loud."

(2) *Fr.* [uck-sũ]. An ornament used in French music of the 17th and 18th cent., equivalent to the German NACHSCHLAG.

Acciaccatura [ah-tchahk-tah-too′-rah], *I.* A "crushing" (implying violent pressure). (1) A keyboard ornament current in the 17th and 18th cent. A dissonant ornamental note, of the shortest possible duration, is struck at the same time as the chord which it decorates. The ornamental note is often printed as part of the chord, in which case it is for the interpreter to guess the composer's intention:

BACH, *Partita No. 3*

Here the G♯, in the chord marked *, must be released as soon as it is struck, leaving the A minor chord to sound without further interference. In music in slower tempo it was customary to play the chord arpeggio. The conventional sign for the acciaccatura was an oblique stroke to represent the dissonant note, *e.g.*

As written :

As played :

BACH, *English Suite No. I*

French composers also used the following sign (which now indicates a simple arpeggio) :

As written :

As played :

(2) The name is now applied to the short APPOGGIATURA.

Accidental. A comprehensive term for a SHARP, DOUBLE SHARP, FLAT, DOUBLE FLAT or NATURAL prefixed to a note in the course of a composition. In FIGURED BASS accidentals are placed before or after the figures ; an accidental by itself, without any figure, applies to the third from the bass.

Accompaniment. A subordinate part or parts, most frequently instrumental, added to a principal part or parts. Such accompaniment may be merely a duplication, as often happens with the organ accompaniment of vocal church music, in which case it can be dispensed with at will. More often it is independent, though it may incorporate some details of the principal part or parts. In the 17th and early 18th cent. keyboard accompaniment was normally from FIGURED BASS and hence involved an element of improvisation. With the decline of figured bass such accompaniment was less likely to be purely subordinate. In many 19th- and 20th-cent. songs the accompaniment is at least as important as the vocal line ; such works are rather duets for voice and piano than songs with piano accompaniment. The popular view that an accompanist is a person inferior in skill and importance to the person accompanied has no justification. In the 18th cent. sonatas for violin (or flute) with harpsichord (or piano) were commonly said to be for keyboard instrument with accompaniment, *e.g.* J. C. Bach's Op. 10 : *Six Sonatas, for the Harpsichord or Piano Forte* ; *with an Accompagnament for a Violin.* *v.* ADDITIONAL ACCOMPANIMENTS, OBBLIGATO.

F. T. ARNOLD : *The Art of Accompaniment from a Thorough-Bass* (1931).

Accordion (*Fr.* accordéon, *G.* Ziehharmonika, *I.* fisarmonica). A portable reed organ, invented by Friedrich Buschmann of Berlin in 1822 under the name *Handäoline.* The principle is similar to that of the mouth-organ and the HARMONIUM. Sound is produced by reeds vibrating freely within frames, the air being supplied by a bellows. In the modern accordion (sometimes known as piano-accordion) the right hand plays a keyboard, while the left hand, in addition to operating the bellows, controls a number of press-studs which enable the player to produce a simple harmonic accompaniment. The CONCERTINA is a member of the same family.

Achron [ahkh'-ron], JOSEPH : *b.* Lozdzeye (Lithuania), May 13, 1886 ; *d.* Hollywood, April 29, 1943. Violinist, composer and teacher. Made his first concert tour in Russia at the age of 8. Head of the violin department at Kharkov Conservatoire, 1913-16. Settled in the United States, 1925, and became an American citizen. His compositions include 3 violin concertos. Author of a manual *Über die Ausführung der chromatischen Tonleiter auf der Violine* (1926).

Achtel [uckh'-tĕl], *G.* Quaver.

Acis and Galatea. A masque for soloists, chorus and orchestra, written for the Duke of Chandos by Handel about 1720. Libretto by John Gay. The Italian cantata, *Aci, Galatea e Polifemo* (Naples, 1708) is an entirely different composition, though when Handel revised it for performance in London in 1732 he incorporated parts of the English work.

Acis et Galatée [a-seece ay ga-la-tay]. (Acis and Galatea). Opera with a prologue and three acts by Lully. Libretto by Jean Galbert de Campistron. First performed by the Duke of Vendôme for the Dauphin at Anet, Sept. 6, 1686 and eleven days later in Paris.

Ackerman [uck'-er-mun], ALEXANDER. *v.* AGRICOLA (1).

Ackté [uck'-tay], AÏNO: *b.* Helsinki, Apr. 23, 1876; *d.* Nummela, Aug. 8, 1944. Soprano, sang in opera in Paris, New York and London. She appeared in the title-role of Richard Strauss's *Salome* at the first London performance in 1910.

Acoustic Bass. An organ stop in which the pipes of a 16 ft. pedal stop sound with a rank a fifth above, producing a RESULTANT TONE an octave below the 16 ft. pipes, *i.e.* an artificial 32 ft. effect, which is, however, lacking in clarity.

Acoustics (*Gr.* ἀκούω, I hear). The science of sound. Sound, in music, consists in the impact on the ear of air vibrations set in motion by (1) the vibration of some elastic material, (2) the vibration of an air column in a pipe, or (3) vibrations electrically produced or transmitted. The elastic material may be (*a*) a gut string or wire, set in motion by a bow (violin), or plucked with the fingers (harp) or a plectrum (mandoline) or a quill (harpsichord), or hit with a metal tongue (clavichord) or a hammer (piano); (*b*) a reed or reeds set in motion by air pressure (oboe, clarinet); (*c*) a membrane set in motion by air pressure, such as the vocal chords (human voice) or the lips (brass instruments), or struck with a beater (drums); (*d*) a solid body, set in motion by striking (bells, triangle, xylophone).

The *intensity* of a note is determined by the amplitude of the vibration. Hence force is needed to produce a loud note.

The *pitch* of a note is determined by the frequency of the vibration. A low note vibrates slowly, a high one quickly. The frequency of the vibration may depend (1) on the length, thickness, tension and density of the vibrating material, (2) on the length and density of the air column and the nature of the tube enclosing it, or (3) may be directly produced by electrical processes. Thus, other things being equal, a short string will produce a higher note than a long one, a taut string a higher note than one less taut. A short air column will produce a higher note than a long one: the piccolo is shorter than the flute and so higher in pitch. On the other hand, the clarinet, though approximately the same length as the flute and oboe, is much lower in pitch than either. This is because it has a cylindrical tube stopped at one end (the mouthpiece), whereas the flute, though cylindrical, is open at both ends and the tube of the oboe, though stopped at one end, is conical or expanding. String and wind instruments are differently affected by temperature. A rise in temperature causes strings to expand, so that their tension is relaxed and they drop in pitch; but the expansion of air decreases its density, so that the pitch of wind instruments rises, the expansion of their material not being sufficient to counteract this.

The *resonance* of a note depends on the presence of some auxiliary material or an air column that will vibrate either in sympathy or by direct contact with the original vibrations. Thus the violin owes its resonance to its belly, the oboe to the air column contained in its tube. There is, however, an important difference. In the violin the belly has to vibrate as the strings dictate. In the oboe (as in other wind instruments) the vibrating air column, being of a definite length, controls the vibrations of the reed; so that in this case the resonator determines the pitch.

The *quality* of a note depends on the complex character of the vibrations.

A stretched string does not merely vibrate as a whole. It also vibrates simultaneously in sections, which are in an exact mathematical relationship to the length of the string. These sections are the halves, thirds, quarters, fifths and so on. The halves produce a note an octave higher than the note sounded by the whole string, the thirds a note a twelfth higher, the quarters a note two octaves higher, and so on. The "overtones" sounded by the respective sections fall into a series known as the HARMONIC SERIES. If the principal note or "fundamental" is the series will run as follows:

(The notes marked x are not in tune with our ordinary scale).

The numbers of the series indicate exactly the mathematical relationship between the frequencies of the notes. Thus the ratio between: and is 1 : 2, and 2 : 3, and so on. The sound of the overtones is very much fainter than that of the note produced by the whole string, but without them the note heard by the listener would lose its lustre. The air-column of a wind instrument or an organ pipe also vibrates in sections. If it is stopped at one end, as in some organ pipes, only alternate sections vibrate, so that a stopped pipe produces only Nos. 1, 3, 5, 7 etc. of the harmonic series. Much the same thing happens with the clarinet, with its cylindrical tube stopped at one end. The characteristic tone-quality of instruments is thus due to the extent to which the "upper partials" (the overtones of the harmonic series) are present or absent and to their relative intensity. This makes it possible, in electronic instruments like the Hammond organ, to imitate closely the sound of orchestral instruments by presenting an artificial selection of the appropriate upper partials and giving to each the necessary intensity. In some instruments the overtones do not fall into the harmonic series and are therefore "inharmonic." The result may be a confused but recognizable sound, as in a bell, or one of indeterminate pitch, as in most percussion instruments.

By touching a string lightly at a point half-way from the end the player can prevent the whole string from vibrating while leaving the two halves free to vibrate. A similar result can be achieved by touching the string at other sectional points. The notes so produced are known, for obvious reasons, as HARMONICS. In the same way a wind-player, by increased lip-tension (known technically as "over-blowing"), can split the air column in his instrument into one of its component parts, so that instead of sounding No. 1 of the harmonic series it produces one of the upper partials as its principal note. This is done to a limited degree on wood-wind instruments and extensively on brass instruments. The horn, for example, has a choice of upper partials from the 2nd to the 16th harmonic. This explains why horn-players sometimes seem uncertain about their notes. The higher harmonics lie very close together, so that the selection of the right one by lip-tension calls for considerable skill. The extent to which members of the harmonic series are available on brass instruments depends on the relation between the diameter of the tube and its length. Neither the horn nor the trumpet, being narrow-bored instruments, can sound No. 1 of the series.

When two notes are sounded simultaneously the difference between their frequencies produces a faintly sounding note known as a DIFFERENCE TONE, and this in turn combines with them to produce further difference tones. With a chord of three notes there will be even more difference tones, which may conflict with the notes of the chord. The difference tones set up by the major triad merely confirm the harmony, but the difference tones set up by the minor triad include notes completely alien to the chord :

This explains why the minor triad sounds less smooth and restful than the major triad. An additional reason is to be found in the clashes between the upper partials of notes heard in combination :

There are obvious clashes between the upper partials of the notes of the major triad ; but in the minor triad the third of the chord (emphasized by its 2nd and 4th harmonics) itself clashes strongly with the prominent 5th harmonic of the bass note, *i.e.* in this example E♭, the third of the chord, clashes with E♮, the 5th harmonic of C. Such clashes are apparent in a resonant building. It was a sure instinct that led 16th-cent. composers of church music to avoid ending a piece with a minor chord. They preferred in such cases either to leave the final chord without any third at all or to substitute a major third, the so-called *tierce de Picardie*.

A further result of the combination of two notes is a very much fainter sound produced by the sum of their frequencies and therefore known as a SUMMATION TONE. Difference tones and summation tones are together known as COMBINATION OR RESULTANT TONES. The principle of difference tones is applied in a number of electrical instruments, which by combining two high frequencies produce an audible difference tone which can then be amplified. For a clumsy application of the same principle to organ building *v.* ACOUSTIC BASS, ORGAN.

The science of acoustics is practical. It is responsible for improvements in the manufacture of instruments, in wireless transmission and gramophone recording, and in the building of concert halls. The "acoustics" of a concert hall or theatre are good if the building provides an adequate but not an excessive amount of resonance. Resonance is affected both by the shape of the building and by its material and interior decoration.

H. BAGENAL & A. WOOD : *Planning for Good Acoustics* (1931).
P. C. BUCK : *Acoustics for Musicians* (1918).
J. JEANS : *Science and Music* (1937).
LL. S. LLOYD : *Music and Sound* (1937).
H. LOWERY : *The Background of Music* (1952).
E. G. RICHARDSON : *The Acoustics of Orchestral Instruments and of the Organ* (1929).
A. WOOD : *The Physics of Music* (1943).

Act Tune. A term used in England in the 17th and early 18th cent. to indicate a piece of instrumental music (generally in dance rhythm) performed between the acts of a play. There are a large number of examples in Purcell's music for the theatre. The modern term is the French word *entr'acte*.

Acute. An ornament in 17th-cent. English music. *v.* SPRINGER.

Adagietto [ah-dah-jet'-to], *I.* Slightly faster than *adagio*.

Adagio [ah-dah'-jo], *I.* "At ease," *i.e.* slow. Hence used to describe the slow movement of a symphony, sonata or concerto.

Adagissimo [ah-dah-jee'-see-mo], *I.* Very slow.

Adam [a-dũn], ADOLPHE CHARLES : *b.* Paris, July 24, 1803 ; *d.* there, May 3, 1856. Composer, teacher and critic, most successful as a composer of *opéra comique*. He was the son of a pianist and composer, Jean Louis A., and a pupil of Boieldieu. His attempt to found a new opera house in 1847 was ruined by the Revolution of 1848. Professor of composition at the Paris Conservatoire from 1849. His Christmas part-song *Minuit, Chrétiens* became widely popular.

Adamberger [ahd'-um-bairg-er], JOHANN VALENTIN: *b.* Munich, July 6, 1743; *d.* Vienna, Aug. 24, 1804. Tenor singer and teacher. Sang first in Italy under the name Adamonti, then in Vienna from 1780. Mozart wrote the part of Belmonte in *Die Entführung aus dem Serail* (1782) for him.

Adam de la Hale (Halle) [a-dũñ der la ull]: *b. c.* 1230; *d.* Naples, *c.* 1286. Trouvère and composer, who wrote both solo songs and polyphonic motets and rondeaux. He was nicknamed *le bossu d'Arras* (the hunchback of Arras), but himself denied that he was deformed. In the last years of his life he was in the service of Count Robert II of Artois and followed him to Naples. His dramatic pastoral *Li Gieus de Robin et Marion* (The Play of Robin and Marion), in which popular songs were incorporated, remained in favour long after his death. His works were published by E. de Coussemaker (1872) but more reliable transcriptions are to be found in F. Gennrich's *Rondeaux, Virelais und Balladen* (2 vols., 1921, 1927). An English edition of *The Play of Robin and Marion* has been published by J. B. Beck, with translation by J. M. Gibbon (1928).

Adams, SUZANNE: *b.* Cambridge (Mass.), Nov. 28, 1872; *d.* London, Feb. 5, 1953. Operatic soprano. She made her début in Paris in 1894 and appeared frequently in opera and oratorio both in England and America. She sang the part of Hero in Stanford's *Much Ado about Nothing* (Covent Garden, 1901).

Added Sixth (*Fr.* sixte ajoutée). A term invented by Rameau to describe the addition of a sixth from the bass to the subdominant chord in a plagal cadence, *i.e.* in the key of C major:

He thus distinguished the chord by its function from the same combination of notes followed by the dominant chord:

where he regarded it as the first inversion of the supertonic seventh:

Later theorists have failed to observe this distinction, so that the term "added sixth" no longer has any significance and might with as much, or as little, justification be applied to similar combinations of notes on other degrees of the scale. *v.* CHORD, FIGURED BASS, HARMONY.

Additional Accompaniments. Parts for extra instruments added to the scores of 17th- and 18th-cent. works, which through the employment of a figured bass and modest orchestral resources are thought by a later age to lack fullness. Handel has been the chief victim of this practice, though Bach has also suffered considerably on the Continent. Mozart wrote additional accompaniments for performances of *Messiah* where no organ was available, and further additions were made to these by other hands. Ebenezer Prout's edition (1902), still widely used, was an ineffective compromise between additional accompaniments and a return to the original text. Sir Henry Wood ignored compromise and rescored the whole work. He also applied the same principles to other works by Handel. A common defence of rescoring is that choirs today are much larger than in Handel's time. This is clearly no defence at all, since there is no reason why any of Handel's works should be sung by a large choir. Bach's *St. Matthew Passion* is regularly sung without any additional accompaniments whatever, and there is no reason why Handel's oratorios should not be treated in the same way.

Adélaide, ou Le Langage des Fleurs [a-day-la-eed oo ler lũñ-guzh day fler], *Fr.* (Adelaide, or the Language of the Flowers). *v.* VALSES NOBLES ET SENTIMENTALES.

Adieux, L'Absence et Le Retour, Les [laze a-dyur lup-sũñce ay ler rer-toor], *Fr.* "Farewell, absence and return." The sub-title of Beethoven's *Sonate* *caractéristique* for piano, Op. 81a (1809), dedicated to the Archduke Rudolph, who with other members of the imperial family was obliged to leave Vienna when the city was besieged by the French. The first movement is based on a slow phrase suitable for two horns, over which Beethoven has written *Lebewohl* (farewell):

Adler [ahd′-ler], GUIDO: *b.* Eibenschütz (Moravia), Nov. 1, 1855; *d.* Vienna, Feb. 15, 1941. Historian and musicologist. Professor at Prague, 1885; Vienna, 1898. Founded the institute of musical history at Vienna University and directed it until 1927. His pupils include a large number of distinguished scholars. In 1894 he founded the *Denkmäler der Tonkunst in Österreich* (Monuments of Music in Austria) and acted as general editor of the series for 44 years, as well as editing 16 volumes himself. Author of books on Wagner and Mahler and on methods of historical study in music. His *Handbuch der Musikgeschichte* (1924, 2nd ed. in 2 vols. 1930), with contributions by 47 writers, is indispensable to the student of musical history.

M. CARNER: *Of Men and Music* (1944).

Ad libitum, *L.* "At pleasure." Generally abbreviated *ad lib.* According to the context the performer has complete freedom (1) to interpret a passage as he wishes, without regard for strict time (*I.* a piacere), or (2) to make use of an alternative note or notes provided by the composer, or (3) to improvise. Also applied to a part (generally instrumental) which may be omitted at will or exchanged for another; in this sense the opposite of OBBLIGATO.

Adlung [ahd′-loong], JACOB: *b.* Bindersleben (nr. Erfurt), Jan. 14, 1699; *d.* there, July 5, 1762. Organist at Erfurt from 1727 and teacher. Of his theoretical works the most important is *Musica mechanica organoedi* (2 vols., 1768), (a treatise on the manufacture and care of keyboard instruments): facsimile ed. by C. Mahrenholz (1931). Facsimile ed. of his *Anleitung zur musikalischen Gelahrtheit* (1758) by H. J. Moser (1953).

Admeto, Re di Tessaglia [ahd-meh′-to reh dee tess-sahl′-yah] (Admetus, King of Thessaly). Opera in three acts by Handel. Libretto by Nicola Francesco Haym or Paolo Antonio Rolli (altered version of an earlier Italian text by A. Aureli). First performed, London, Feb. 11, 1727.

A due [ah doo′-eh], *I.* "In two parts." Generally written *a* 2. (1) In wind parts indicates that a single melodic line is to be played by two instruments in unison. (2) In string parts indicates that a passage in two parts is to be played *divisi* (the term normally used today). So also *a* 3 and *a* 4.

Aeolian Mode. (1) In ancient Greek music one of the names given to:

(2) From the 16th cent. onwards applied to:

The tonic (or final) and dominant are marked respectively T and D. *v.* GLAREANUS, GREEK MUSIC, MODE.

Affektenlehre [uff-eck′-tĕn-lay-rer], *G.* A system of musical aesthetics, formulated in Germany in the 18th cent. and widely accepted, according to which compositions were judged by the extent to which they portrayed and aroused specific emotions.

Affettuoso [ahf-fet-too-o′-zo], *I.* "Affectionate," *i.e.* with tender emotion.

Affrettando [ahf-fret-tahnd′-o], *I.* "Hurrying," *i.e.* increasing the speed.

Africaine, L' [la-free-ken] (The African Girl). Opera in five acts by Meyerbeer. Libretto by Augustin Eugène Scribe. First performed, Paris, Apr. 28, 1865.

Agazzari [ah-gah-tsah'-ree], AGOSTINO: *b.* Siena, Dec. 2, 1578; *d.* there, Apr. 10, 1640. Composer of church music, madrigals and the opera *Eumelio* (Rome, 1606). Author of *Del sonare sopra'l basso* (1607), the earliest separate treatise on the playing of FIGURED BASS (reprinted in O. Kinkeldey, *Orgel und Klavier in der Musik des 16. Jahrhunderts*, pp. 216-21; translation in O. Strunk, *Source Readings in Music History*, pp. 424-31).

Agincourt Song. A 15th-cent. carol in celebration of Henry V's victory over the French at Agincourt (1415). It is in English with a Latin refrain (*Deo gracias, Anglia, redde pro victoria*). There are two versions of the music, one at Trinity College, Cambridge (facsimile in J. A. Fuller Maitland, *English Carols of the Fifteenth Century*), the other in the Bodleian Library, Oxford (facsimile in J. Stainer, *Early Bodleian Music*, i, pl. lxvi).

Agitato [ah-jee-tah'-toh], *I.* "Agitated," *i.e.* restless and wild.

Agnus Dei [ahn'-yooss day'-ee], *L.* "Lamb of God." The concluding portion of a musical setting of the Roman Mass, a three-fold petition ending with the words "dona nobis pacem" (grant us thy peace). In a Requiem Mass the petition ends with the words "dona eis requiem sempiternam" (grant them rest eternal) and is followed by *Lux aeterna* (Light eternal).

Agostini [ah-goss-tee'-nee], PAOLO: *b.* Valerano, 1593; *d.* Rome, Oct. 3, 1629. Organist in Rome and prolific composer of church music, some of it for several choirs.

Agréments [a-gray-mũn], *Fr.* Ornaments.

Agricola. Of the musicians who bore this name the most important are:

(1) ALEXANDER: *b. c.* 1446; *d.* Valladolid, *c.* 1506. Flemish composer, a pupil of Ockeghem. He served in succession Charles VIII of France, Lorenzo de' Medici, the Duke of Mantua, and Philip I of Castile. He composed church music and chansons. His real name was Ackermann.

(2) JOHANN FRIEDRICH: *b.* Dobitschen (Saxony), Jan. 4, 1720; *d.* Berlin, Dec. 2, 1774. Organist and composer. He studied under J. S. Bach at Leipzig and Quantz at Berlin, and became court composer to Frederick the Great. His compositions, mostly unpublished, include operas and choral and instrumental works. He married the celebrated soprano Benedetta Emilia Molteni (*b.* Modena, 1722; *d.* Berlin, 1780).

(3) MARTIN: *b.* Schwiebus, Jan. 6, 1486; *d.* Magdeburg, June 10, 1556. Author of several books on music, notably *Musica instrumentalis deutsch*, of which five editions were published (reprinted by R. Eitner, 1896). He also composed hymns, motets and instrumental music. His real name was Sore.

Agrippina [ah-greep-pee'-nah]. Opera in three acts by Handel. Libretto by Vincenzo Grimani. First performed, Venice, Dec. 26, 1709.

Aguilera de Heredia [ah-gee-leh'-rah deh eh-reh'-dee-ah], SEBASTIAN: *b.* 1560-70. Spanish composer who published a volume of settings of the Magnificat for 4-8 voices (1618) and composed Versets and *Tientos* for organ. Examples of his organ pieces have been published in Pedrell's *Antologia de Organistas Españoles*, i (1908) and in Bonnet's *Historical Organ Recitals*, vi (1940).

Agujari [ah-goo-yah'-ree], LUCREZIA: *b.* Ferrara, 1743; *d.* Parma, May 18, 1783. A remarkable soprano, nicknamed "La Bastardella." In a letter of March 24, 1770 Mozart pays tribute to her powers. Her range was remarkable. She was popular in London as well as in Italy. She married the opera composer Giuseppe Colla.

Ahle [ahl'-*er*], JOHANN RUDOLPH: *b.* Mühlhausen (Thuringia), Dec. 24, 1625; *d.* there, July 9, 1673. Organist at St. Blasius Church, Mühlhausen and composer of a large number of works (many of a simple character) for voices and instruments. A selection is published in *D.D.T.*, v. One of his tunes, used for the hymn "Liebster

Jesu, wir sind hier" (Beloved Jesu, we are here), became very popular (*E.H.* 336, *S.P.* 457).

Aiblinger [eye'-bling-er], JOHANN CASPAR: *b.* Wasserburg (Bavaria), Feb. 23, 1779; *d.* Munich, May 6, 1867. Composer and assiduous collector of church music. His only opera, *Rodrigo und Ximene* (Munich, 1821), founded on Corneille's *Le Cid*, was not successful. He lived mainly in Italy, but was for a short time *Kapellmeister* of the Italian opera in Munich.

Aichinger [y*sh*'-ing-er], GREGOR: *b.* Regensburg, 1564; *d.* Feb. 21, 1628. German composer of church music, strongly influenced by the Venetian school of Gabrieli. Selected works are printed in *D.T.B.*, x (1).

Aida [ah-ee'-dah]. Opera in four acts by Verdi. Libretto by Antonio Ghislanzoni and the composer. Written for the celebration of the opening of the Suez Canal. First performed Cairo, Dec. 24, 1871. A story of warfare between Egypt and Ethiopia and the love of Aida, daughter of the Ethiopian king and a slave at the Egyptian court, for Radames, the Egyptian commander-in-chief. For both of them there is a conflict between love and patriotism. Yielding to love, Radames is convicted of treachery through the jealous fury of Amneris, daughter of the Egyptian king. He is sentenced to be buried alive, and Aida, though she had escaped, prefers to share his punishment.

Air, *E. Fr.* (1) A tune.

(2) A song, either for one voice with instrumental accompaniment or for several voices. Common in this sense in the 17th cent., when the normal English spelling was "ayre."

(3) A song or *aria* (*I.*) in an opera or oratorio.

(4) An instrumental piece whose melodic style is similar to that of solo song.

P. WARLOCK: *The English Ayre* (1926).

Air on the G String. An arrangement by August Wilhemj of the second movement of Bach's suite No. 3 in D major for orchestra. The first violin part of the original becomes a solo with accompaniment and is transposed down so as to be suitable for playing on the lowest string of the instrument.

Ais [ah'-iss], *G.* A sharp (A♯).

Aisis [ah'-iss-iss], *G.* A double sharp (A×).

Akademische Fest-Ouvertüre [uck-ud-ay'-mish-*er* fest'-oo-vair-teer-*er*], *G.* *v.* ACADEMIC FESTIVAL OVERTURE.

Akimenko [uck-ee-men'-co], FEODOR STEPANOVICH: *b.* Feb. 20, 1876; *d.* Paris, Jan. 8, 1945. Ukrainian composer, a pupil of Balakirev and Rimsky-Korsakov. He lived for many years in France. His works include a symphony, a violin concerto, an opera, *The Little Mermaid*, chamber music, piano music and songs.

À la hongroise [a la on-grwahz], *Fr.* *v.* ALL' ONGARESE.

Alain [a-lan], (1) JEAN (Johannes Alanus). Late 14th- and early 15th-century composer. The text of his motet 'Sub Arthuro plebs vallata' (printed in *D.T.Ö.*, xl, pp. 9-11) contains references to several English musicians. This has suggested an identification with a composer called Aleyn who is represented in *The Old Hall Manuscript*.

(2) JEHAN ARISTE: *b.* Saint-Germain-en-Laye, Feb. 3, 1911; *d.* Saumur, June 20, 1940. Composer. Studied at the Paris Conservatoire. Organist in Paris, 1935-9. Killed on active service. His compositions, original in idiom and distinguished in execution, include choral works, 3 volumes of organ music, 3 volumes of piano music, chamber music and songs.

B. GAVOTY: *Jehan Alain, musicien français* (*1911-40*) (1945).

Alalá [ah-la-lah'] *Sp.* A type of Galician folk-melody, sung in free rhythm and often ornamented with grace notes. It appears to have melodic affinities with plainsong.

Alaleona [ah-lah-leh'-o-nah], DOMENICO: *b.* Montegiorgio (Piceno), Nov. 16, 1881; *d.* there, Dec. 29, 1928. Composer, conductor and historian. His works include an opera, *Mirra*, to his own libretto (Rome, 1920), and a history of Italian oratorio.

Alanus [a-lah'-nooss], JOHANNES. *v.* ALAIN (1).

Alayrac, D'. *v.* DALAYRAC.

Albanesi [ahl-bah-neh'-zee], LICIA : *b.* Bari, July 22, 1913. Italian soprano, a member of the Metropolitan opera House, New York, since 1940. Naturalised, 1945. She has also sung in opera in Italy, where she made her first appearance in 1935, England, France and Spain.

Albani [ahl-bah'-nee], MARIE LOUISE CÉCILIE EMMA : *b.* Chambly, near Montreal, Nov. 1, 1847 ; *d.* London, Apr. 3, 1930. French-Canadian soprano, whose real name was Lajeunesse. She studied in Paris and Milan, where she made her first appearance in 1870 in Bellini's *La Sonnambula*. She sang frequently in England, both in opera and oratorio, and in many other parts of the world. After her retirement in 1911 she devoted herself to teaching. She published her memoirs under the title *Forty Years of Song* (1911).

Albéniz [ull-beh'-neeth], ISAAC : *b.* Camprodón (Catalónia), May 29, 1860 ; *d.* Cambo-les-Bains (Pyrenees), May 18, 1909. Catalan pianist and composer. He began his career as a child prodigy, then studied at Madrid, Brussels and Leipzig. He wrote a number of operas, including one to an English libretto, *The Magic Opal* (London, 1893), but is now remembered only by his later piano works (notably the suite *Iberia*), which borrow effectively the rhythms and idioms of Spanish popular music.

Albert [dull-bair], EUGÈNE FRANCIS CHARLES D' : *b.* Glasgow, Apr. 10, 1864 ; *d.* Riga, March 3, 1932. Pianist and composer, of French descent on his father's side. He studied at the National Training School for Music (later the Royal College of Music) in London, and appeared as a concert pianist at the age of 16. Having won the Mendelssohn Scholarship he went abroad and studied with Liszt. He settled in Germany and became director of the Berlin Hochschule in 1907. His numerous compositions include 21 operas, of which the most successful were *Tiefland* (Prague, 1903), *Die toten Augen* (Dresden, 1916), and the comic operas *Die Abreise* (Frankfort, 1898) and *Flauto Solo* (Prague, 1905). The use of jazz idioms won for *Die schwarze Orchidee* (Leipzig, 1928) a temporary success. He also composed two piano concertos, a violin concerto, a symphony, chamber music and piano solos. He transcribed several of Bach's organ works and edited piano works by Beethoven and Liszt.

Albert [ull'-bert], HEINRICH : *b.* Lobenstein (Saxony), July 8, 1604 ; *d.* Königsberg, Oct. 6, 1651. Poet and composer, a nephew and pupil of Heinrich Schütz. He published eight collections of *Arien*—sacred and secular songs with German words for one or more voices with accompaniment (reprinted in *D.D.T.*, xii and xiii). An adaptation of the melody of his " Gott des Himmels " was used by Bach in the *Christmas Oratorio* and is in current use (*Hymns A. & M.* 368 (i) and 551). For the original form of the melody *v. E.H.*132 and *S.P.*32 (i).

Albert Herring. Comic opera by Benjamin Britten. Libretto by Eric Crozier (after Guy de Maupassant's short story *Le Rosier de Madame Husson*). First performed, Glyndebourne, June 20, 1947. In the absence of a girl of suitable virtue to be chosen May Queen of the village Lady Billows agrees to crown Albert Herring, a grocer's boy, May King. At the banquet his drink is doctored, and he becomes intoxicated, with disastrous results.

Alberti [ahl-bair'-tee], DOMENICO : *b.* Venice, *c.* 1710 ; *d.* Formie, 1740. Singer, harpsichord-player and composer. In his keyboard sonatas he was addicted to the use of a conventional figuration for the left hand, which, though purely harmonic in effect, suggests the bustle of contrapuntal elaboration :

ALBERTI, *Sonata No. 6 (Op. 1)*

The formula, known as the " Alberti bass," (though it was not invented by him or peculiar to him) became part of the stock-in-trade of late 18th-cent. and early 19th-cent. composers, not excluding Beethoven.

Albertini [ahl-bair-tee′-nee], GIOVACCHINO : *b.* Pesaro, 1751 ; *d. c.* 1812. Opera composer and director of music at the Polish court. His *Don Juan*, to a Polish text, was performed in Warsaw in 1783, four years before Mozart's *Don Giovanni*.

Albicastro [ahl-bee-cust′-ro], HENRICO. Late 17th-cent. Swiss violinist and composer. He wrote a number of sonatas and orchestral concertos. His real name was Weyssenburg.

Albinoni [ahl-bee-no′-nee], TOMMASO : *b.* Venice, June 8, 1671 ; *d.* there, Jan. 17, 1750. A prolific composer and violinist, one of the first composers to write concertos for solo violin. He was much admired by Bach, who wrote two keyboard fugues on themes by him (*B.G.* xxxvi, pp. 173 and 178).

Albion and Albanius. Opera by Grabu with a prologue, three acts and an epilogue. Libretto by John Dryden. First performed, London, June 13, 1685.

Alboni [ahl-bo′-nee], MARIETTA : *b.* Citta di Castello, March 6, 1826 ; *d.* Ville d'Avray, June 23, 1894. Celebrated contralto. She studied Rossini's operas with the composer and was one of the singers at his funeral in Paris in 1868.

Alborada [ull-boh-rah′-dah], *Sp.* (*Fr.* aubade). "Morning song." A form of instrumental music popular in Galicia, where it is played on the bagpipes (*gaita*) with side-drum (*tamboril*) accompaniment. A modern sophisticated example is the *Alborada del gracioso* (The clown's aubade), No. 4 of Ravel's *Miroirs* for piano.

Albrechtsberger [ull′-bre*sh*ts-bairg-er], JOHANN GEORG : *b.* Klosterneuburg (nr. Vienna), Feb. 3, 1736 ; *d.* Vienna, March 7, 1809. Organist, composer and teacher. Appointed court organist in Vienna, 1772. He had a great reputation as a teacher. Beethoven had counterpoint lessons from him during 1794-5 but was not, in Albrechtsberger's opinion, a promising pupil. Albrechtsberger's instrumental works are published in *D.T.Ö.*, xvi (2). He published a text-book entitled *Gründliche Anweisung zur Composition.*

Albumblatt [ull′-bo͝om-blut], *G.* "Album leaf." A title frequently used by 19th-century composers and their successors for a short piece of an intimate character.

Alceste [ull-sest]. (1) Opera in three acts by Gluck. His original setting of Ranieri Calzabigi's Italian libretto was performed at Vienna, Dec. 26, 1767. A revised version, with French adaptation by François du Roullet, was given at Paris, Apr. 23, 1776. The plot is borrowed from the Greek legend of the wife who offers to die in place of her husband, Admetus, and is subsequently restored to life. The dedication of the Italian version of *Alceste*, published in 1769, contains a statement of Gluck's artistic principles, probably written by Calzabigi (*v.* A. Einstein, *Gluck*, pp. 98-100).

(2) Opera by Lully with a prologue and five acts. Libretto by Philippe Quinault. First performed, Paris, Jan. 19, 1674.

Alcestis. *v.* ALKESTIS.

Alchymist, Der [dair ull*sh*′-ee-mist] (The Alchemist). Opera in three acts by Spohr. Libretto by "Fr. Georg Schmidt" (pseud. for Karl Pfeiffer), founded on a story by Washington Irving. First performed, Cassel, Dec. 28, 1830.

Alcina [ahl-chee′-nah]. Opera in three acts by Handel. Libretto by Antonio Marchi (from Ariosto's *Orlando Furioso*). First performed, London, Apr. 27, 1735.

Alcock, (1) JOHN : *b.* London, Apr. 11, 1715 ; *d.* Lichfield, Feb. 23, 1806. Organist of Lichfield Cathedral, 1750-60. Composer of instrumental music, glees and church music. His son John (*c.* 1740-91) was also an organist and composer.

(2) WALTER GALPIN : *b.* Edenbridge, Dec. 29, 1861 ; *d.* Salisbury, Sept. 11, 1947. Organist of Salisbury Cathedral from 1916 and teacher of the organ at the Royal College of Music. He was knighted in 1933.

Aldrich, (1) HENRY : *b.* Westminster, 1647 ; *d.* Oxford, Dec. 14, 1710. Dean of Christ Church, Oxford, from 1689 and Vice-Chancellor of the University, 1692-5. A versatile scholar, whose interests included theology, architecture, philosophy and music. He bequeathed his valuable musical library to his college. His compositions are unimportant, though the three-part catch "Hark! the bonny Christchurch bells" survives in school song-books.

(2) PUTNAM CALDER: *b.* South Swansea, Mass., July 14, 1904. Harpsichordist and musicologist, a pupil of Tobias Matthay and Wanda Landowska. He has held teaching appointments at several American universities and is now associate professor at Stanford University, California. He has appeared frequently as a soloist and has published *Ornamentation in J. S. Bach's Organ Works* (1950).

(3) RICHARD: *b.* Providence (Rhode Island), July 31, 1863; *d.* Rome, June 2, 1937. American music critic. A graduate of Harvard, he served as critic on several papers, becoming eventually music editor of the *New York Times* (1902-23). Among his publications were a volume of reprinted essays, entitled *Musical Discourse* (1928), and a catalogue of his library (1931).

Alembert [da-lūn-bair], JEAN LE ROND D': *b.* Paris, Nov. 16, 1717; *d.* there, Oct. 29, 1783. Philosopher and mathematician, a contributor to the *Encyclopédie* and author of several works on music. He was one of the advocates of that operatic reform which we now associate principally with Gluck.

Alessandri [ah-less-sahn′-dree], FELICE: *b.* Rome, Nov. 24, 1742; *d.* Casalbino, Aug. 15, 1798. Prolific composer of operas and instrumental music. He travelled widely and from 1789-92 was second conductor at the Berlin Opera. His most successful comic opera was *Il vecchio geloso* (Milan, 1781).

Alessandro [ah-less-sahn′-dro]. Opera in three acts by Handel. Libretto by Paolo Antonio Rolli. First performed, London, May 16, 1726.

Alessandro Stradella [ah-less-sahn′-dro strah-dell′-lah]. Opera in three acts by Flotow. Libretto by "W. Friedrich" (Friedrich Wilhelm Riese). First performed, Hamburg, Dec. 30, 1844.

Alexander Balus. Oratorio by Handel. Libretto by Thomas Morell. First performed, London, March 9, 1748.

Alexander's Feast. Ode for soloists, chorus and orchestra by Handel. Words by John Dryden (originally written for St. Cecilia's Day, 1697). First performed, London, Feb. 19, 1736.

Alexandrov [ull-ek-sahn′-droff], ANATOL NIKOLAIEVICH: *b.* Moscow, May 25, 1888. Russian composer. He studied at the Moscow Conservatoire, where he now teaches composition. His works, which are on the whole conservative in style, include two operas, two orchestral suites, piano music, and songs.

Aleyn. *v.* ALAIN (1).

Alfano [ahl-fahn′-o], FRANCO: *b.* Posilipo (nr. Naples), March 8, 1876; *d.* Oct. 27, 1954. Opera composer, educated at Naples and Leipzig. Director of the Liceo Musicale, Bologna, 1919; Liceo Musicale, Turin, 1923. His most successful operas are *Risurrezione* (Turin, 1904) and *La leggenda di Sakuntala* (Bologna, 1921), for the latter of which he wrote the libretto. He completed the third act of Puccini's *Turandot* (Milan, 1926). His other works include two symphonies.

Al fine (ahl fee′-neh], *I.* "To the end." Most commonly in the phrases *da capo al fine* (from the beginning to the end) and *dal segno al fine* (from the sign to the end). *v.* DA CAPO and DAL SEGNO.

Alfonso el Sabio [ull-fon′-so el sah′-bee-o]: *b.* Toledo, Nov. 23, 1221; *d.* Seville, Apr. 4, 1284. Alfonso X, nicknamed "the Wise" (*el Sabio*), king of Castile and León (1252-84). A patron of music and poetry, he compiled a collection of more than 400 *Cantigas de Santa Maria* (hymns to the virgin). The music of these shows the influence of French troubadours but has also specifically Spanish characteristics, in which Moorish influence has been suggested, though without any precise evidence. The miniatures in the manuscripts suggest the use of a wide variety of instruments, though the melodies appear without accompaniment, as in troubadour manuscripts. A facsimile of one of the manuscripts has been published by Julian Ribera y Tarragó, *La Música de las Cantigas* (1922). Modern edition of the *Cantigas* by H. Anglès (1948).

J. B. TREND : *Alfonso the Sage* (1926).

Alfonso und Estrella [ull-fon'-zo ŏŏnt ess-trell'-la] (Alfonso and Estrella). Opera in three acts by Schubert. Libretto by Franz von Schober. First performed, Weimar, June 24, 1854.

Alfvén [ull-vehn'], HUGO : *b.* Stockholm, May 1, 1872. Violinist, composer and conductor. Studied at the Stockholm Conservatoire and in Brussels. Director of music at Upsala University, 1910-39. His works include 5 symphonies, choral works, chamber music, piano pieces and songs.

Algarotti [ahl-gah-rot'-tee], FRANCESCO : *b.* Venice, Dec. 11, 1712 ; *d.* Pisa, May 3, 1764. A widely travelled amateur, with a considerable experience of opera. His essay *Saggio sopra l'opera in musica* (1755) advocates the abandonment of the outworn conventions of early eighteenth-century opera and states principles of reform similar to those expressed in the dedication to Gluck's *Alceste* (1769).

Alkan [ull-kũn], CHARLES HENRI VALENTIN : *b.* Paris, Nov. 30, 1813 ; *d.* there, March 29, 1888. Composer and pianist. He spent his life as a piano-teacher in Paris. His numerous compositions for piano, which demand a high degree of virtuosity and display unusual gifts of imagination, have been largely ignored by pianists, with the exception of Busoni and Egon Petri. His real name was Morhange.

Alkestis. (1) Opera in two acts by Boughton. Libretto from Euripides's tragedy in Gilbert Murray's English version. First produced, Glastonbury, Aug. 26, 1922.

(2) [ull-kest'-iss]. Opera in one act by Wellesz. Libretto by Hugo von Hofmannsthal (based on Euripides's tragedy). First performed, Mannheim, March 20, 1924.

Alla breve [ahl'-lah breh'-veh], *I.* This expression, which defies literal translation, means that the BREVE is to be taken as the standard of mensuration instead of the SEMIBREVE, *i.e.* that the music is to be performed twice as fast as its notation would suggest. In the following example from Handel's *Messiah* the minims are to be treated as though they were crotchets, *i.e.*, there will be two beats in each bar, not four :

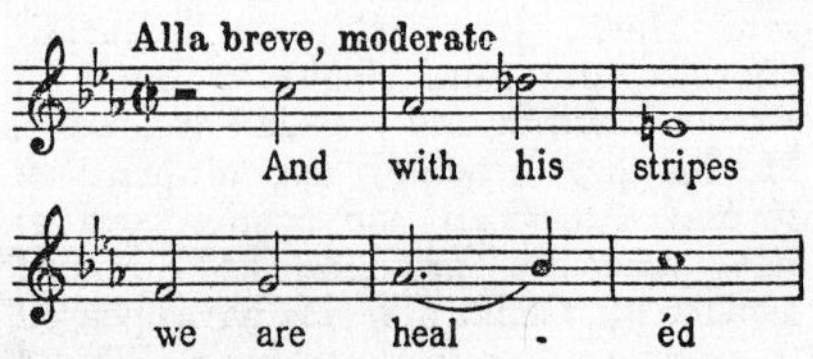

This is the equivalent of :

The term originated in the 16th cent., when the corresponding term *alla semibreve* was also used to indicate that the notes had their normal value. Diminution of note values was represented by alterations in the time-signature. A vertical stroke indicated that the notes had only half their written value. Thus the sign C indicated "imperfect" (or, as we should say, duple) time, in which one breve equalled two semibreves ; but the same sign with a vertical stroke through it, ¢, meant that the two semibreves to a breve became in effect two minims to a semibreve. The other proportional signs became obsolete ; so did the term *alla semibreve.* But the sign ¢ survived as the equivalent of what we should call 2/2, just as C survived as the equivalent of 4/4. (*v.* NOTATION). In the 18th cent. ¢ is the normal time-signature for a piece marked *alla breve.* But even then the term did not necessarily imply two beats in a bar. The following extract from the aria "Es ist vollbracht" in Bach's *St. John Passion* shows it was used simply as an indication of relative speed :

Here *alla breve* means that the crotchet of the 3/4 section is equivalent to the slow quaver of the *Molto adagio*—in other words, the quaver of the 3/4 section is to be taken twice as fast as the quaver of the *Molto adagio*.

Allargando [ahl-larr-gahnd'-o], *I.* "Getting broader," and, in consequence, slower.

Alla tedesca [ahl'-lah teh-dess'-cah], *I.* Short for *alla danza tedesca, i.e.* in the style of the German dance or ALLEMANDE of either type. Beethoven uses *alla tedesca* in the 1st movement of the piano sonata in G major, Op. 79, and *alla danza tedesca* in the 4th movement of the string quartet in B♭ major, Op. 130. Both movements represent the later type of allemande—the *deutscher Tanz* in triple time, current in the late 18th and early 19th cent.

Alla turca [ahl'-lah toorr'-cah]. "In the Turkish style." *v.* JANISSARY MUSIC.

Alla zingarese [ahl'-lah tseen-gah-reh'-zeh], *I.* In the style of gypsy music (from *zingaro,* a gypsy).

Alla zoppa [ahl'-la tsop'-pah], *I.* Lit. "in a limping manner," *i.e.* syncopated. Applied particularly to the rhythm

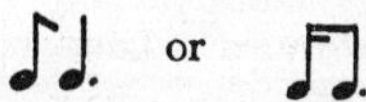

(known also as the "Scotch snap" or the "Lombardy rhythm"), familiar in songs like "Comin' thro the rye" or in pieces like the following:

LISZT, *Hungarian Rhapsody, No. xiv*

Allegretto [ahl-leh-gret'-to], *I.* Diminutive of ALLEGRO, indicating a moderately quick movement.

Allegri [ahl-leh'-gree], GREGORIO: *b.* Rome, 1582; *d.* there, Feb. 17, 1652. A priest who was at first attached to the cathedral of Fermo and in 1629 became one of the Papal singers. He composed a quantity of church music. A nine-part *Miserere*, sung annually in Holy Week in the Sistine Chapel, was greatly prized, though its effect was due more to the method of performance than to the music. *v.* Charles Burney, *The Present State of Music in France and Italy* (1771), pp. 275-281, and Emily Anderson, *The Letters of Mozart and his Family* (1928), p. 187.

Allegro (ahl-leh'-gro), *I.* "Lively." Used to indicate a brisk movement, often in association with other adjectives or qualifying expressions, *e.g. allegro moderato, allegro con brio.*

Allegro, il Penseroso ed il Moderato, L' [lahl-leh'-gro, eel pen-zeh-ro'-zo ed eel mo-deh-rah'-to] (The Lively Man, the Thoughtful Man, and the Moderate Man). Cantata for soloists, chorus and orchestra by Handel. Words compiled from Milton by Charles Jennens, with the addition of *Il Moderato.* First performed, London, Feb. 27, 1740.

Allemande [ull-mũnd], *Fr.* Short for *danse allemande*, " German dance." (1) A moderately slow dance of German origin in duple time, adopted in the 16th cent. by the French, and from them by the English (*E.* almain, alman, almand, *I.* allemanda, tedesca). Described by Thomas Morley (1597) as heavier than the GALLIARD and " fitlie representing the nature of the people, whose name it carieth." Here is a characteristic Elizabethan example from the *Fitzwilliam Virginal Book* (No. LXI) :

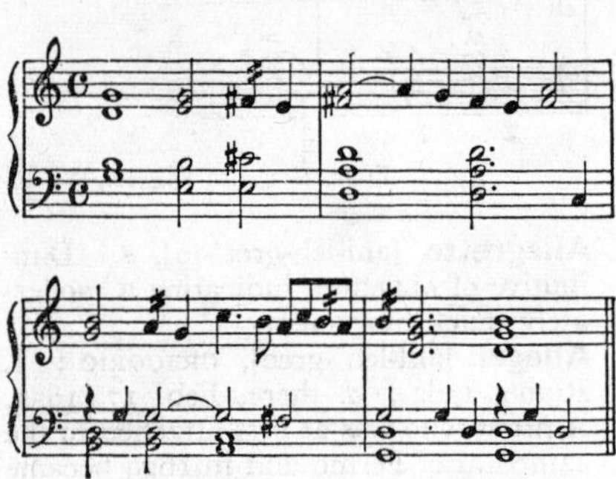

BYRD, *Monsieur's Alman*

In the 17th and early 18th cent. it was normally the first of the four contrasted dances which formed the basis of the SUITE. Composers did not always adhere to the slow tempo. Corelli has allemandes marked *allegro* and *presto*, as well as *largo* and *adagio*. But by the 18th cent. it had settled down into a stylized instrumental form, described by Mattheson as representing " a contented mind that delights in order and calm," *e.g.* :

BACH, *English Suite No. 1*

The initial semiquaver is typical.

(2) A brisk dance in triple time, current in the late 18th and early 19th cent. and still popular among the peasantry of Swabia and Switzerland (*G.* deutscher Tanz, *I.* danza tedesca), *e.g.*

HAYDN, *Trio No. 5 in E♭*

This is the prototype of the WALTZ. No. 3 of Beethoven's *Bagatellen* (Op. 119) is marked *à l'allemande* = ALLA TEDESCA.

Allen, HUGH PERCY : *b.* Reading, Dec. 23, 1869 ; *d.* Oxford, Feb. 20, 1946. Professor at Oxford, 1918-46. Knighted, 1920. Organist, St. Asaph's Cathedral, 1897 ; Ely, 1898 ; New College, Oxford, 1901-18. Director, Royal College of Music, 1918-37. Conductor, Bach Choir, 1907-20. At Oxford he promoted performances of music of all kinds—polyphonic church music, opera, ballet, choral and orchestral works. He was specially active in spreading enthusiasm for the works of Bach.

C. BAILEY : *Hugh Percy Allen* (1948).

Allentando [ahl-len-tahnd′-o], *I.* "Slowing down."

Allin, NORMAN : *b.* Ashton-under-Lyne, Nov. 19, 1884. Bass. Studied at Manchester Royal College of Music. First appeared in opera under Beecham, London, 1916, and has since sung a large number of roles, notably Gurnemanz in *Parsifal.* He was one of the founders and directors of the BRITISH NATIONAL OPERA COMPANY (1922-9).

Allison, RICHARD : *fl.* 1600. Composer. Published *The Psalmes of David in Meter* (1599), a harmonization for voice (or voices) and instruments of the melodies to which the metrical psalms were sung (*v.* PSALTER), and *An Howres Recreation in Musicke* (1606), a collection of madrigals for four and five voices. Modern edition of the latter in *E.M.S.*, xxxiii.

Allmählich [ull′-may-li*sh*], *G.* "Gradual, gradually."

All' ongarese [ahl on-gah-reh′-zeh], *I.* (*Fr.* à la hongroise). In the style of Hungarian (gypsy) music.

All' ottava [ahl lot-tah′-vah], *I.* "At the octave" (above or below). *v.* OTTAVA.

All' unisono [ahl loo-nee′-so-no] *I.* "In unison," *i.e.* two or more instruments are to play the same notes.

Almain, Alman, Almand. *v.* ALLEMANDE.

Almeida [dahl-meh′-ee-dah], FRANCISCO ANTONIO D' : *fl.* 1740. Composer. His comic opera *La Spinalba* (Lisbon, 1739) is the first Italian opera by a Portuguese composer to be preserved intact. The third act of an earlier work, *La pacienza di Socrate* (Lisbon, 1733) has also survived. He also composed church music.

Almenräder [ull′-mĕn-ray-der], KARL : *b.* nr. Düsseldorf, Oct. 3, 1786 ; *d.* Biebrich, Sept. 14, 1843. Bassoon-player, who made considerable improvements in the structure of the instrument, which are described in his *Abhandlung über die Verbesserung des Fagotts.* *v.* Adam Carse, *Musical Wind Instruments* (1939), pp. 196-200.

Almira [ahl-mee′-rah]. Opera in three acts by Handel. Libretto by Friedrich Christian Feustking (based on an Italian libretto by Giulio Pancieri). First performed, Hamburg, Jan. 8, 1705.

Alphorn [ulp′-horrn], *G.* "Alpine horn." A primitive instrument still used by herdsmen in Switzerland and other mountainous countries. It is made of wood, bound with bark, is either straight or slightly curved, with an upturned bell, and may be as much as 10 ft. long. It produces the notes of the HARMONIC SERIES, with certain modifications due to the material of which it is made and its irregular diameter. The practice of yodelling is thought to be an imitation of the sounds of the alphorn.

Also sprach Zarathustra [ull′-zo shprahkh tsa-ra-toost′-ra], *G.* (Thus spoke Zarathustra). Symphonic poem by Richard Strauss, Op. 30, based on Nietzsche. First performed, Frankfort, Nov. 27, 1896.

Alt. (1) In the phrase *in alt*, an English adaptation of the Latin *in alto* (in the height), applied to notes from

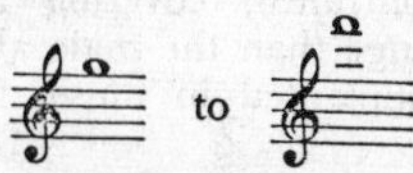

The notes in the octave above are said to be *in altissimo.*

(2) *G.* [ult] = ALTO.

Altenburg (ull′-tĕn-bŏŏrk], (1) JOHANN ERNST : *b.* Weissenfels, June 15, 1734 ; *d.* Bitterfeld, May 14, 1801. Trumpeter and organist. Author of *Versuch einer Anleitung zur heroisch-musikalischen Trompeter- und Pauker-Kunst* (1795 ; reprinted in facsimile, 1911).

(2) JOHANN MICHAEL : *b.* Alach, May 27, 1584 ; *d.* Erfurt, Feb. 12, 1640. Pastor in Erfurt and composer of church music and instrumental works.

Alteration. (1) A conventional augmentation of the value of the breve, semibreve or minim in mensural notation before 1600. *v.* RHYTHMIC MODES, MENSURAL NOTATION.

(2) Chromatic alteration is the raising or lowering of a note of the scale by means of an ACCIDENTAL.

Altflöte [ult'-flurt-er], *G.* Bass flute.

Althorn [ult'-horrn], *G.* A brass instrument of the SAXHORN family.

Altnikol [ult'-nee-kole], JOHANN CHRISTOPH : *b.* Berna, 1719 ; *d.* July 25, 1759. Organist and composer, a pupil and son-in-law of J. S. Bach, whose last composition—the chorale prelude " Vor deinen Thron "—he wrote out from dictation when the composer was on his death-bed.

Alto, *I.* Lit. " high." (1) The highest adult male voice, now employed mainly in church choirs and male-voice choirs. The range of the voice is roughly two octaves, from

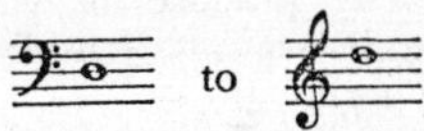

though the lower notes lack resonance. The upper part of the compass is made possible by the cultivation of the FALSETTO voice. In 17th-cent. England the alto (known also as counter-tenor) was popular as a solo voice.

(2) A low female voice (properly called contralto), covering a slightly higher range than the male alto, which it has supplanted in music for mixed voices.

(3) *Fr.* [ull-to] = viola.

(4) Prefixed to the name of an instrument it indicates one size larger than the treble (or soprano) member of the family, *e.g.* alto saxophone.

(5) The alto clef is the C clef (indicating middle C) on the third line of the stave :

It was at one time in general use for any vocal or instrumental part of the appropriate range and was also employed in keyboard music. It is now used only for the viola, for which it is the normal clef.

Altobasso [ahl-to-bahss'-so], *I.* (*Fr.* tambourin du Béarn). A zither with gut strings sounding only the tonic and dominant. *v.* TAMBOURIN (2).

Alto Flute. *v.* BASS FLUTE.

Alto Saxophone. *v.* SAXOPHONE.

Alto Trombone. *v.* TROMBONE.

Altposaune [ult'-po-zown'-er], *G.* Alto trombone.

Alvarez [ull-va-rez], ALBERT RAYMOND : *b.* Bordeaux, 1861 ; *d.* Nice, Feb. 26, 1933. French operatic tenor, whose real name was Gourron. He sang in the first performance of a number of operas, including Massenet's *Thaïs*.

Amadigi di Gaula [ah-mah-dee'-jee dee gow'-lah] (Amadis of Gaul). Opera in three acts by Handel. Libretto probably by John James Heidegger (signature on dedication). First performed, London, June 5, 1715.

Amadis [a-ma-deece]. Opera with a prologue and five acts by Lully. Libretto by Philippe Quinault. First performed, Paris, Jan. 18, 1684. *v.* also AMADIGI DI GAULA.

Amati [ah-mah'-tee]. A family of violin-makers at Cremona in Italy in the 16th and 17th cent. The earliest known is ANDREA (*c.* 1520-80), who established a design and standard of craftsmanship to which his descendants adhered. NICOLO (*b.* Sept. 3, 1596 ; *d.* Aug. 12, 1684), the most celebrated member of the family, was the master of Antonio Stradivari.

Amboss [um'-boss], *G.* Anvil.

Ambros [um'-broce], AUGUST WILHELM : *b.* Vysoké Myto (Bohemiá), Nov. 17, 1816 ; *d.* Vienna, June 28, 1876. A brilliant and versatile musician, who managed to combine his work as historian, composer and pianist with regular employment in the Austrian Civil Service. His *Geschichte der Musik* (4 vols., 1862-81), of which the last volume was compiled from his notes, is a standard work, though the first and fourth volumes have since been extensively revised. It ends with the 16th cent. A fifth volume of examples was compiled after his death, and two volumes by Wilhelm Langhans were added to bring the history down to the 19th cent.

Ambrose : *b.* Trèves, 340 ; *d.* Milan, Apr. 4, 397. Bishop of Milan. He appears to have introduced into the Western Church the Syrian practice of antiphonal singing, as well as encouraging the singing of hymns. None of the melodies of the so-called Ambrosian chant (or plainsong) can be certainly attributed to him.

American Organ. A free-reed keyboard instrument, originally known as the Melodeon, introduced by Mason and Hamlin of Boston (Mass.) about 1860. The principal difference between the HARMONIUM and the American organ is that in the former the air is forced through the reeds, while in the latter it is drawn through by suction. The American organ is nearer in tone-quality to the organ, but is less expressive than the harmonium. It is also made with two manuals and pedals, in which case the air supply has to be provided by a separate hand-blower or by electricity.

Am Frosch [um frosh], *G.* (*Fr.* au talon). With the nut (or heel) of the bow (*i.e.* the end nearer the hand).

Am Griffbrett [um griff′-bret], *G.* (*Fr.* sur la touche, *I.* sul tasto). On the fingerboard (of a string instrument), *i.e.* play near, or actually above, the fingerboard, thus producing a rather colourless tone.

Amico Fritz, L' [lah-mee′-co freets] (Friend Fritz). Opera in three acts by Mascagni. Libretto by " P. Suardon " (pseudonym of Nicolo Daspuro), based on Erckmann-Chatrian's novel. First performed, Rome, Oct. 31, 1891.

Amner, JOHN : *d.* 1641. Organist and choirmaster of Ely Cathedral from 1610. Composed a number of services and anthems, and published *Sacred Hymnes of* 3, 4, 5, *and* 6 *parts, for Voyces and Vyols* (1615).

Amor Brujo, El [el ah-morr′ broo′-ho] (Love, the Magician). Ballet by Falla. First performed, Madrid, Apr. 15, 1915.

Amore [ah-moh′-reh], *I.* " Love." *Con amore*, lovingly.

Amore dei Tre Re, L' [lah-moh′-reh deh′-ee treh reh] (The Love of the Three Kings). Opera in three acts by Montemezzi. Libretto by Sen Benelli (from his play of the same title). First performed, Milan, Sept. 10, 1913.

Amour des Trois Oranges, L' [lamoor day trwahz orr-ũnzh] (The Love for Three Oranges). Comic opera in four acts by Prokofiev. Original Russian text by the composer (from Gozzi's comedy). First performed, Chicago, Dec. 30, 1921.

Amphion Anglicus. A volume of songs by John Blow (1649-1708), published in 1700 with a dedication to Princess Anne.

Am Steg [um shtake], *G.* (*Fr.* au chevalet, *I.* sul ponticello). On the bridge (of a string instrument), *i.e.* play near the bridge, thus producing a glassy, brittle tone.

Anacréon [a-na-cray-õn]. *Opéra-ballet* in two acts by Cherubini. Libretto by R. Mendouze. First performed, Paris, Oct. 4, 1803.

Anche [ũnsh] *Fr.* Reed, reed instrument, reed pipe (in an organ).

Ancia [ahn′-chah], *I.* Reed.

Ancudine [ahn-coo′-dee-neh], *I.* Anvil. Also spelt *incudine.*

Andamento [ahn-dah-ment′-o], *I.*

(1) " Movement."

(2) An 18th-cent. term for a fugue subject of substantial length, which will often fall naturally into two contrasted sections, *e.g.* :

BACH, *48 Preludes & Fugues, Book I, No. 20*

(3) An episode in a fugue.

(4) A movement in a suite (*e.g.* Bonporti's *Invenzioni* for violin and figured bass, No. 7, wrongly ascribed to Bach and called No. 4 in *B.G.* xlv, (1), p. 188).

Andante [ahn-dahn′-teh], *I.* " Going, moving." Generally used today of a moderate tempo, inclining to slowness rather than actually slow. Hence used as the title of a piece or movement in this tempo. *Più andante* means properly " moving more," *i.e.* slightly faster (*v.* the slow movement of Brahms's G major sonata for violin and piano, Op. 78).

Andantino [ahn-dahn-tee′-no], *I.* Diminutive of ANDANTE. An ambiguous term, since it is impossible to know whether it implies a movement slightly faster than *andante* or slightly slower.

An die ferne Geliebte [un dee fair′-ner ger-leep′-ter], *G.* "To the distant beloved." Song-cycle by Beethoven, Op. 98 (1816), words by A. Jeitteles.

André [un′-dray]. A German publishing firm. The family included:

(1) JOHANN : *b.* Offenbach a/M., Mar. 28, 1741 ; *d.* there, June 18, 1799. He also composed a large number of operas, among them *Belmonte und Constanze, oder die Entführung aus dem Serail* (1781), a setting of the libretto which, with modifications and additions, was reset by Mozart a year later.

(2) JOHANN ANTON : *b.* Offenbach, Oct. 6, 1775 ; *d.* there, Apr. 6, 1842. Third son of (1). Like his father he was a composer and also wrote books on harmony, counterpoint and composition. He purchased all Mozart's surviving manuscripts from the composer's widow.

Andreae [un-dray′-ay], VOLKMAR : *b.* Berne, July, 5, 1879. Composer and conductor. Principal of the Zurich Conservatoire. His works include two symphonies, two operas—*Ratcliff* (Duisburg, 1914) and *Abenteuer des Casanova* (Dresden, 1924), chamber music, choral music (including a number of works for male-voice choirs) and songs.

Andriessen [un′-dree-sĕn], WILLEM : *b.* Haarlem, Oct. 25, 1887. Dutch pianist and composer. Director, Amsterdam Conservatorium, 1937 ; The Hague Conservatorium, 1949. His reputation as a teacher is high. His works include a Mass for soli, chorus and orchestra, a piano sonata, a piano concerto and songs.

Andrieu, D'. *v.* DANDRIEU.

Anerio [ah-nehrr′-yo], (1) FELICE : *b. c.* 1560 ; *d.* Rome, Sept. 27, 1614. Composer to the Papal Chapel, 1594-1602. His works include madrigals and church music.

(2) GIOVANNI FRANCESCO : *b.* Rome, *c.* 1567 ; *d.* Graz, June, 1630. Brother of (1). Voluminous composer of sacred music and madrigals.

Anet [a-nay], JEAN-BAPTISTE : *b. c.* 1661 ; *d.* Lunéville (Lorraine), Aug. 14, 1755. Distinguished violinist, who studied with Corelli in Rome. Described by Philippe-Louis Daquin, son of the composer, as the greatest violinist that had ever existed. One of the first violinists to appear at the *Concert spirituel*, founded by Philidor in Paris in 1725. His compositions, apart from the evidence of virtuosity, are unimportant.

Anfossi [ahn-foss′-see], PASQUALE : *b.* Taggia (nr. Naples), Apr. 25, 1727 ; *d.* Rome, Feb. 1797. Opera composer. A pupil of Piccinni, whose influence shows itself in an inclination to sentimentality. Anfossi in turn influenced the young Mozart, particularly through his *La finta giardiniera* (Rome, 1774), the libretto of which was reset by Mozart in the following year (*v.* E. J. Dent, *Mozart's Operas*, 2nd ed., p. 26).

Anglaise [ũn-glez], *F.* Short for *danse anglaise*, English dance. (1) A dance in quick duple time, one of the dances of foreign origin (*cf.* POLONAISE) introduced in the 17th cent. and so incorporated in the SUITE as one of the *Galanterien* or optional dances added to the normal *allemande, courante, sarabande* and *gigue*, *e.g.* :

BACH, *French Suite No. 3*

(2) Also applied to other dances of English origin.

Anglebert [dũn-gler-bair], JEAN HENRY D' : *b.* Paris, *c.* 1628 ; *d.* there, Apr. 23, 1691. Harpsichordist, organist and composer, a pupil of Chambonnières. In the service of the Duc d'Orléans, 1661, and of Louis XIV, 1664. His *Pièces de clavessin* (1689), including both original compositions and transcriptions of works by Lully, is a valuable record of contemporary ornamentation : modern ed. in *Publications de la Société française de Musicologie,* viii.

Anglès [ahn'-glace], HIGINI : *b.* Maspujols (Catalonia), Jan. 1, 1888. Catalan musicologist. Professor of musical history, Barcelona Conservatoire, 1927-33, and subsequently at Barcelona University. Director of the Pontifical Institute of Sacred Music, Rome, since 1947. Among the works he has edited are *El Còdex Musical de Las Huelgas* (3 vols., 1931), *Monumentos de la Música Española* (2 vols., 1941 & 1944), *La Música de las Cantigas del Rey Alfonso el Sabio* (1948), and a complete edition of the works of Morales (1953).

Anglican Chant. A harmonized setting, designed to be used for successive verses of the canticles and psalms in the English Prayer-Book. A *single chant* consists normally of seven bars, unequally divided into three and four, the caesura in the middle corresponding to the colon in the text, *e.g.* :

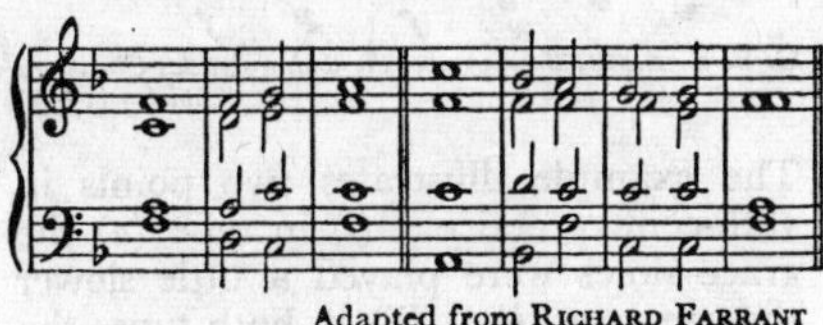

Adapted from RICHARD FARRANT

This is repeated for each verse of the canticle or psalm. A *double chant* serves for a pair of verses, a *triple* or *quadruple chant* for groups of three or four respectively. If a double chant is used for a psalm (or section of a psalm) that has an odd number of verses, the second half of the chant will be repeated for the odd verse. This may be done at the end of psalm (or section) or at any convenient place suggested by the words. Similar modifications may be necessary in the case of triple and quadruple chants, though examples of these forms are not common.

The difficulty of accommodating verses of different lengths to the same tune is solved by treating the first and fourth bars of the single chant, and the first, fourth, eighth and eleventh of the double chant, as reciting notes of indefinite length, *e.g.*:

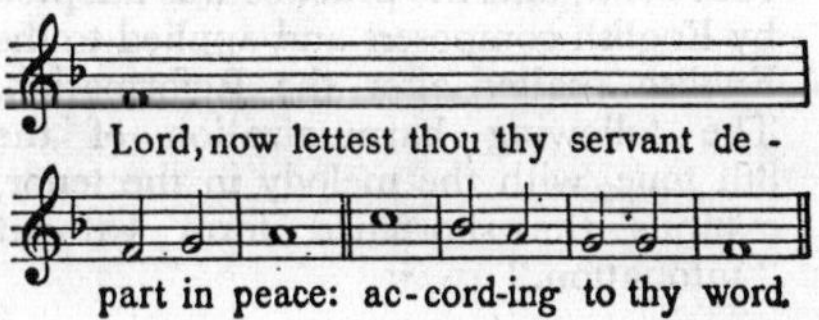

This may easily result in a hurried gabbling of the syllables sung to the reciting notes and a rigid, metrical interpretation of the rest of the chant. Modern practice strives to avoid this by aiming at a flexible rhythm dictated by the natural rhythm of the words and, if necessary, ignores the caesura, making the whole chant continuous. To secure a uniform interpretation from a choir a system of " pointing " is used, indicating how the syllables of each verse are to be allotted to the chant. The publication of psalters with pointing dates from the first half of the nineteenth century, when the cathedral service was beginning to be copied in parish churches. The system of pointing differs from one psalter to another, in accordance with the editors' views on interpretation. Among the devices used in printing the words have been bar-lines, dots, asterisks, accents, heavy type, figures to indicate grouping, and miniature minims and crotchets placed above the syllables.

The Anglican chant is an imitation of the Gregorian tones used for the musical recitation of the psalms in the Roman Catholic Church, *e.g.* :

8th tone, 1st ending

It was the practice to use the complete tone only for the first verse of the psalm: in the others the initial "intonation" was omitted. Harmonizations of the Gregorian tones were current in the 16th cent., and the practice was adopted by English composers and applied to the English psalter after the Reformation. The following harmonization of the 8th tone, with the melody in the tenor, exhibits the shortened form without "intonation."

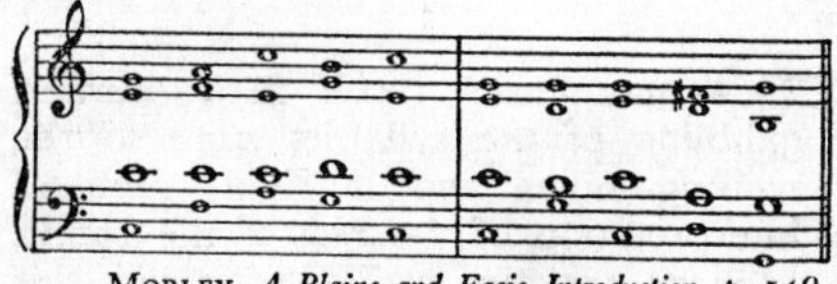
MORLEY, *A Plaine and Easie Introduction, p. 148*

When English composers began writing original chants at the Restoration they took this shortened form as their model and established a type which has remained constant up to the present day.

Anima [ah'-nee-mah], *I.* "Spirit." *Con anima*, with spirit.

Animato [ah-nee-mah'-toh], *I.* "Animated."

Animuccia [ah-nee-moo'-tchah], GIOVANNI: *b.* Florence, *c.* 1500; *d.* Rome, March 25, 1571. *Maestro di cappella* at St. Peter's, Rome, 1555-71. A friend of St. Philip Neri, for whose Oratory he composed *laudi spirituali* (*v.* LAUDA, ORATORIO). Composed also church music and madrigals.

Annibale Padovano [ahn-nee-bah'-lee pah-do-vah'-no]: *b.* Padua, 1527; *d.* Graz, 1575. Organist, St. Mark's, Venice, 1552-66; then in the service of the Archduke Karl at Graz. Composed church music, madrigals and organ music.

Anrooy [un-roh'-i], PETER VAN: *b.* Zalt-Bommel, Oct. 13, 1879. Composer and conductor. Conductor, Gröningen Philharmonic Orchestra, 1905; Arnhem Orchestra Society, 1910; Residence Orchestra, The Hague, 1917-35. He has composed orchestral music, including the Dutch rhapsody *Piet Hein*, chamber music and two cantatas for children's voices. He has been active in organizing children's concerts in Holland.

Anschlag [un'-shlahk], *G.* (1) Lit. "touch," *i.e.* either the way in which a player depresses the keys of a keyboard instrument or the way in which they respond to pressure.

(2) An ornament, sometimes known as the double APPOGGIATURA, consisting of two successive grace notes, one lower than the principal note, the other a second above it. Since *c.* 1750 it has been represented by two small notes, the first of which is played on the beat. The first note is normally either (*a*) a repetition of the preceding note or (*b*) a second below the principal note, *e.g.*:

As written:

As played:

C. P. E. BACH, *Versuch über die wahre Art das Clavier zu spielen (1753)*

The example illustrates two points in 18th-cent. practice: (i) in type (*a*) the grace notes were played a little slower than in type (*b*); (ii) in both types the grace notes were played more softly than the principal note.

Ansermet [ũn-sair-may], ERNEST: *b.* Vevey, Nov. 11, 1883. Conductor. Teacher of mathematics in Lausanne, 1906-10. Began his career as a conductor by directing the Casino concerts at Montreux in 1911. From 1915 associated with Diaghilev's Russian ballet. He has made a reputation as a conductor of modern music, particularly of Stravinsky.

Ansorge [un-zorr′-ger], CONRAD : *b.* Buchwald (Silesia), Oct. 15, 1862 ; *d.* Berlin, Feb. 13, 1930. Composer and pianist. A pupil of Liszt. His works include songs, 3 piano sonatas, chamber and orchestral works, and a non-liturgical Requiem for male chorus and orchestra.

Answer. In the exposition of a FUGUE the answer is a transposition of the subject. In a four-part fugue the second and fourth entries of the subject will normally be transposed and so answer respectively the first and third entries, *e.g.* :

BACH, *48 Preludes & Fugues, Book II, No. 9*

If the transposition of the subject is exact, as in the previous example, the answer is called a " real " answer. If the transposition is modified in some way, whether at the beginning or the end or both, the answer is called " tonal ", *e.g.* :

BACH, *48 Preludes & Fugues, Book I, No. 7*

Antarctic Symphony, *v.* SINFONIA ANTARTICA.

Antheil [an′-tile], GEORGE : *b.* Trenton (N.J.), July 8, 1900; *d.* 2/12/59. An American composer who spent much of his life in France. He won notoriety by the performance in Paris of his *Ballet mécanique* (1925), the score of which includes various mechanical devices for producing sound, among them a number of pianolas. He has written two operas —*Transatlantic* (Frankfort, 1930) and *Helen retires* (New York, 1934), four symphonies, a piano concerto, a violin concerto, chamber music and a quantity of music for films.

Anthem (an English corruption of ANTIPHON). A setting of non-liturgical English words used in the Anglican church services of morning and evening prayer, where its proper place is after the third collect, in accordance with a rubric which first appeared in the Prayer Book of 1662. It derives from the Latin MOTET of the Roman church, but ever since its first appearance at the English Reformation it has developed on independent lines. The introduction of passages for solo voice with accompaniment in the late 16th cent. led to the creation of a type known as the "verse" anthem, in which any section sung by one or more solo voices was technically a "verse." Contrasted with this was the "full" anthem, where the voices supplied all the necessary harmony and there was no independent accompaniment. Restoration composers developed an elaborate type of anthem, in which solo recitative and instrumental interludes played a part, the whole forming a cantata for voices and instruments. In modern practice the anthem is not confined to settings of English words nor to pieces specifically written for the purpose. Latin motets and excerpts from oratorios and similar works are often used.

E. H. FELLOWES : *English Cathedral Music* (1941).

Anthologies. *v.* HISTORY OF MUSIC.

Anticipation. The sounding of a note (or notes) before the chord to which it or they belong, *e.g.* :

BEETHOVEN, *Sonata in C♯ minor, Op. 27, No. 2*

where the first D♭ in the treble is an anticipation of the chord of D♭ in the second bar.

Antiphon. A plainsong setting of sacred words, sung before and after a psalm or canticle in the Latin church service with a view to emphasizing its significance. It was originally a refrain occurring after every verse of the psalm and was so called from the method of performing the psalm, which was antiphonal, *i.e.* by two bodies of singers in alternation. In course of time the refrain was omitted from the body of the psalm and sung only at the beginning and end. A further restriction was the curtailment of the antiphon before the psalm to the first two or three words, leaving the complete melody to be sung when the psalm was over. This is the current practice. The INTROIT and COMMUNION were originally antiphons, but the psalms to which they were attached disappeared from the Mass. The name "antiphon" was also applied to certain processional melodies and to four hymns in honour of the Virgin. Polyphonic settings of such pieces were also known as antiphons, or, in a typically English corruption of the word, as "anthems." Hence the use of the word "ANTHEM" in the Anglican church service to indicate a musical setting independent of the liturgy.

Antiphonal. The book containing the music sung by the choir in the Office of the Roman church, *i.e.* in all services other than the Mass. The choir music for the Mass is contained in the GRADUAL.

Anvil (*Fr.* enclume, *G.* Amboss, *I.* ancudine). An instrument composed of steel bars struck with a hard wooden or metal beater. It is intended to represent the sound of the blacksmith's anvil and has been used for this purpose by several 19th-cent. composers, including Verdi in Act II of *Il Trovatore.* The sound is normally of indefinite pitch, but Wagner in *Das Rheingold* wrote for 18 anvils of three different sizes tuned respectively to

Apel [ah'-pĕl], WILLI : *b.* Konitz, Oct. 10, 1893. Musicologist. Studied mathematics at Bonn, Munich and Berlin. Piano teacher, 1922-8. Lecturer, Longy School of Music, Cambridge, Mass., 1936-43 ; Harvard, 1938-42 ; Boston Centre for Adult Education, 1937-50. Professor, University of Indiana, 1950. His publications include *Musik aus früher Zeit* (2 vols., 1934), *Accidentien und Tonalität in den Musikdenmälern des 15. und 16. Jahrhunderts* (1936), *The Notation of Polyphonic Music, 800-1600* (1942), *Harvard Dictionary of Music* (1944), *Historical Anthology of Music* (with A. T. Davison, 2 vols., 1946 and 1950), and *Masters of the Keyboard* (1947).

Apertum [a-pair'-to͞om], *L.* *v.* OUVERT.

A piacere [ah pee-ah-cheh′-reh], *I.* " At pleasure," the same as AD LIBITUM, indicating that the performer is free to use his own judgment in interpreting the music, without regard for strict time.

Apollonicon. A particularly elaborate type of BARREL ORGAN, provided with keyboards for six performers and fitted with stops designed to imitate the sound of orchestral instruments. It was made by Flight and Robson, organ-builders, and first exhibited in London in 1817.

Apostles, The. Oratorio by Elgar, Op. 49, dealing with the calling of the apostles, the crucifixion and resurrection of Christ, and the ascension. First performed, Birmingham Festival, Oct. 14, 1903. It was intended to be the first part of a trilogy. The second part is *The Kingdom* (1906) ; the third part was never completed.

Appalachia. " Variations on an old slave song with final chorus "—orchestral piece by Delius, originally written in 1896 and revised in 1902.

Appassionato [ahp-pahss-yo-nah′-toh], *I.* " Impassioned." *Sonata appassionata*, the title given (though not by the composer) to Beethoven's piano sonata in F minor, Op. 57.

Appoggiatura [ahp-pod-jah-too′-rah], *I.* (*G.* Vorschlag). Lit. a " leaning." There are three principal forms: (1) The *long appoggiatura*, now known simply as appoggiatura. A note of varying length, alien to the harmony against which it is sounded but subsequently resolving on to a harmony note, *e.g.* :

TCHAIKOVSKY, *Symphony No. 6 in B minor*

where the appoggiaturas are marked *. Here the appoggiatura is anticipated by a harmony note in the previous chord, *e.g.* the D in the treble on the first beat of the bar is prepared by the D in the previous bar. In such cases an appoggiatura is very similar to a SUSPENSION, the only difference being that in a suspension the two D's would have been tied together :

But very frequently an appoggiatura is not anticipated by any harmony note in the previous chord, *e.g.* :

MOZART, *Symphony No. 40 in G minor*

In such cases the effect of the appoggiatura is more striking, because it is unprepared. The systematic use of appoggiaturas over a long period has enriched the harmonic vocabulary, since the chords which they create become familiar and so can be used by themselves without any resolution of the " alien " note (*v.* CHORD).

The length of an appoggiatura is now precisely indicated by the notation, but in the 17th and 18th cent. it was a convention to allow the harmony note to occupy the whole of the time to be shared between it and the appoggiatura, and to indicate the appoggiatura by a stroke or a curve or a note of smaller size. The reason for this was that the appoggiatura was regarded as an ornament and hence subordinate to the main melodic line. The following examples all mean that the C must be less than a minim, to allow room for a preceding B on the beat :

 Appoggiatura

What remains to be determined in such cases is the length of the appoggiatura. In the latter part of the 18th cent. precise rules were formulated for doing this, and the practice arose of showing exactly the value of the small note, *e.g.* :

MOZART, *Violin Sonata in E flat major, K. 380*

is to be played :

Earlier practice, however, was less rigid, and the interpretation of the texts is made more difficult by the fact that the same signs were also used for the short appoggiatura. The following examples from Quantz's *Versuch einer Anweisung die Flöte traversiere zu spielen* (1752) will give some idea of conventional interpretation about the middle of the 18th cent. :

As written :

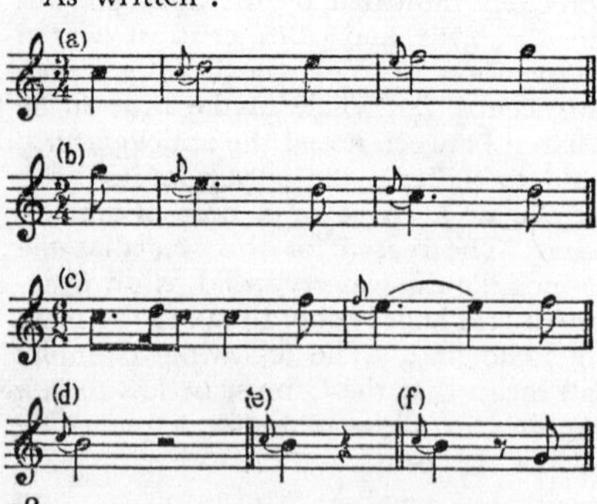

As played :

(2) The *short appoggiatura*, now known inaccurately as the ACCIACCATURA. A very short note of indeterminate length, originally played on the beat (like the long appoggiatura) and indicated by the same signs. Among the cases in mid-18th-cent. music where the appoggiatura is short are : (i) when it precedes short notes, (ii) when it decorates repetitions of the same note, (iii) when it resolves on to a note dissonant with the bass, so that it is itself consonant with the bass :

C. P. E. BACH, *Versuch über die wahre Art das Clavier zu spielen* (1753)

The following passage illustrates both the short appoggiatura (*b*) and the long appoggiatura (*c*), as well as the SLIDE (*a*) :

As written :

As played :

BACH, *St. Matthew Passion*

(The long appoggiatura has not been translated in accordance with Quantz's rules, which do not necessarily apply to Bach). In the latter part of the 18th cent. the practice arose of distinguishing the short appoggiatura by an oblique stroke across the note :

but it was some time before this became universal. In the 19th cent. there was a growing tendency to play the short appoggiatura before the beat, and this is now the normal method of execution, though it is naturally incorrect to apply it to older music. The result of this development is that the short appoggiatura has become similar in execution to the passing appoggiatura.

(3) The *passing appoggiatura*, current in the 18th cent. (though condemned by C. P. E. Bach), occurred normally when the principal notes of a melody formed a sequence of thirds. It was indicated by a curved sign identical with that used for the ordinary appoggiatura, or by a small quaver or semiquaver. Unlike the short appoggiatura, it was played before the beat. In the following example (*a*) is the passing appoggiatura, (*b*) the ordinary long appoggiatura :

As written :

As played :

BACH, *Organ Prelude on "Allein Gott in der Höh sei Ehr"*

Quantz recommends a similar interpretation where the ornamental note precedes a long appoggiatura written in ordinary notation :

As written:

As played :

where the notes marked * are long appoggiaturas.

Appoggiaturas may occur simultaneously in more than one part, *e.g.* :

BEETHOVEN, *Sonata in E major, Op. 109*

In the second bar A, F♯ and D♯ are all appoggiaturas.

The name *double appoggiatura* is sometimes given to the ornament whose German name is ANSCHLAG.

E. DANNREUTHER : *Musical Ornamentation.*
A. DOLMETSCH : *The Interpretation of the Music of the XVIIth and XVIIIth Centuries.*

Apprenti Sorcier, L' [lup-rūn-tee sorrce-yay], *Fr.* (The Prentice Wizard). Symphonic scherzo by Dukas (after a ballad by Goethe). First performed, Paris, May 18, 1897.

Après-Midi d'un Faune, L'. *v.* PRÉLUDE À L'APRÈS-MIDI D'UN FAUNE.

A punta d'arco [ah poon'-tah darr'-co], *I.* With the point of the bow.

Aquin, D'. *v.* DAQUIN.

Arabella [a-rub-ell'-a]. Opera in three acts by Richard Strauss. Libretto by Hugo von Hofmannsthal. First performed, Dresden, July 1, 1933.

Arabesque. In architecture an ornament in the Arabic style. Hence in music (1) decorative treatment of thematic material, (2) a lyrical piece in a fanciful style. In the latter sense first used by Schumann (Op. 18) and subsequently by other composers, including Debussy.

Araja [ah-rah'-yah], FRANCESCO : *b.* Naples, *c.* 1700 ; *d.* there, *c.* 1767. Italian opera composer, resident in Russia 1735-59. His *La forza dell' amore e dell' odio* was the first Italian *opera seria* to be given in St. Petersburg (1736). His *La clemenza di Tito* (St. Petersburg, 1751) was the first opera with a Russian libretto.

Arbeau [arr-bo], THOINOT : *b.* Dijon, 1519 ; *d.* Langres, 1595. The name is an anagram of Jehan Tabourot (J represented by I), a priest who wrote a treatise on dancing, entitled *Orchésographie et traité en forme de dialogue par lequel toutes personnes peuvent facilement apprendre et pratiquer l'honnête exercise des danses* (1589). This includes descriptions of the dances, directions for playing the appropriate instruments, and a number of dance-tunes, some of which were arranged by Peter Warlock in his suite *Capriol.*

> TH. ARBEAU : *Orchesography—a Treatise in the Form of a Dialogue.* Translated by C. W. Beaumont (1925).

Arbos [arr-boce'], ENRIQUE FERNANDEZ : *b.* Madrid, Dec. 25, 1863 ; *d.* San Sebastian, June 3, 1939. Violinist and conductor. A pupil of Vieuxtemps and Joachim. Professor of the violin at the R.C.M., 1894-1916. For many years conductor of the Orquesta Sinfónica, Madrid. He orchestrated the suite *Iberia* by Albéniz. His compositions include a comic opera, *El centro de la tierra* (Madrid, 1895).

Arcadelt [arr-ca-delt'], JACOB : *b. c.* 1514 ; *d.* Paris after 1562. Presumably of Flemish origin. One of the papal singers in Rome, 1540-49 ; from 1555 in the service of the Duc de Guise in Paris. A famous composer of Italian madrigals, he wrote also French *chansons,* motets and masses. The so-called "Ave Maria," transcribed by Liszt, is a 19th-cent. adaptation, with altered harmony, of the *chanson* "Nous voyons que les hommes" (published in 1554). His *chansons* are published in *Smith College Music Archives,* v.

Archduke Trio. Piano trio No. 7 in B♭ major by Beethoven, Op. 97 (1811), dedicated to the Archduke Rudolph.

Arched Viol. A 17th-cent. keyboard instrument designed "to resemble several vyalls played on with one bow" (*v.* Pepys, *Diary,* Oct. 5, 1664). It was not successful.

Archet [arr-shay], *Fr.* Bow (*I.* arco). *Instruments à archet* (or *archets* alone), string instruments.

Archlute (*Fr.* archiluth, *G.* Erzlaute, *I.* arciliuto). A large bass lute, with two necks, one for the stopped strings running over the fingerboard, the other for the independent bass strings (*v.* LUTE). It was much used in the 17th cent. for playing the bass part in concerted compositions, *e.g.* Corelli's Op. 1 was published as *Sonate à tre, doi Violini, e Violone ò Arcileuto, col Basso per l'Organo* (1681).

Arcicembalo [arr-chee-chem'-bah-lo], *I. v.* VICENTINO.

Arciorgano [arr-chee-orr'-gah-no], *I. v.* VICENTINO.

Arco [arr'-co], *I.* (*Fr.* archet, *G.* Bogen). Bow (of a string instrument). *Coll' arco,* with the bow (generally abbreviated to *arco*), as opposed to *pizzicato,* plucked with the finger. *Strumenti d'arco* (or the plur. *archi* alone), string instruments.

Arditi [arr-dee'-tee], LUIGI : *b.* Crescentino (Piedmont), July 22, 1822 ; *d.* Hove, May 1, 1903. Italian composer and conductor, particularly of opera. His waltz-song "Il bacio" (The kiss) achieved an extraordinary popularity. His reminiscences, compiled by Baroness von Zedlitz, were published in 1896.

Arensky [arr-en'-ski], ANTON STEPANOVICH : *b.* Novgorod, Aug. 11, 1861 ; *d.* Tarioki (Finland), Feb. 25, 1906.

Russian composer. Studied at St. Petersburg Conservatoire, where he was a pupil of Rimsky-Korsakov. Teacher of harmony and counterpoint, Moscow Conservatoire, 1883 ; director of the Imperial Chapel, St. Petersburg, 1895-1901. His compositions include 3 operas, 2 symphonies, a violin concerto, cantatas, church music, chamber music, piano solos and songs. In England his best-known works are the piano trio in D minor (Op. 32) and the variations on Tchaikovsky's " Legend " from the second string quartet in A minor (Op. 35). Though he made some use of folk-tunes, his work in general is nearer to the main stream of Western European music than to the ideals of the Russian nationalists.

Argyll Rooms. The name of three successive buildings in London used for the performance of music in the early part of the 19th cent. The first stood in Argyll Street (adjoining Oxford Circus tube station) and was the first home of the Philharmonic Society (now the ROYAL PHILHARMONIC SOCIETY), which was formed in 1813. The second, designed by John Nash, was in Regent Street and from 1818 till 1830, when it was destroyed by fire, was the principal concert hall in London. The third, built on the same site, failed to achieve the same success.

Aria [arr'-yah], *I.* (*E. Fr.* air, *G.* Arie). (1) A song for one or more voices, now used exclusively of solo song. It came into current use in the early 17th cent., when it was used in opera and the chamber CANTATA to describe a symmetrical piece of vocal music, as opposed to the declamatory recitative. The attraction of such pieces for listeners, who were apt to find recitative tedious, was such that by the early 18th cent. the aria completely dominated opera. There were a large number of accepted types, designed to exploit the capabilities of singers and to afford contrast within a single work. Structure had also become stereotyped. The use of a form in which a contrasted middle section is followed by a repetition of the first section—an obvious symmetrical device—had become general. This form was known as the *da capo* aria, since after the middle section the singer began again " from the beginning " (*da capo*). An early English example of this form on a small scale is Belinda's song " Pursue thy conquest, love " in Purcell's *Dido and Aeneas* (1689). From opera the *da capo* aria was transferred naturally to oratorio. In both it was the practice of singers to vary the *da capo* by adding improvised ornaments. The modern habit of shortening a *da capo* by playing only the instrumental introduction, in order to save time, is indefensible, since it destroys the symmetry of the piece.

Since the structure of the *da capo* was primarily musical it did not always harmonize with the words. There were cases where the repetition of the first section weakened the effect made by the words of the middle section. Hence protests were made in the later 18th cent. against the domination of the *da capo* aria in opera as something unnatural. These protests took practical shape in the work of Gluck ; but the principle of using lyrical pieces to intensify the emotion of dramatic situations was not challenged, until Wagner in his later operas demonstrated the possibility of a new continuity, in which set vocal pieces are abandoned and the function of establishing symmetry is assigned to the orchestra.

(2) An instrumental piece of a song-like character, *e.g.* the theme of Bach's *Goldberg Variations.*

Ariadne auf Naxos [a-ri-ud'-nay owf nux'-oss] (Ariadne on Naxos). Opera in one act with prelude by Richard Strauss. Libretto by Hugo von Hofmannsthal. First version, without prelude, designed to follow Molière's *Le Bourgeois Gentilhomme* : Stuttgart, Oct. 25, 1912. Second version, with prelude —a self-contained work : Vienna, Oct. 4, 1916. The main plot is the familiar story of Ariadne, abandoned on Naxos by Theseus and delivered by Bacchus ; but this is interrupted by an intermezzo performed by some of the traditional figures of the Italian *commedia dell' arte*—the idea being to save time by presenting two entertainments simultaneously. The prelude to the second version enabled the opera to be given without any reference to *Le Bourgeois Gentilhomme* by attributing the request for the performance to a Viennese nobleman instead of to Molière's Monsieur Jourdain. Strauss's incidental music to *Le Bourgeois Gentilhomme* is quite independent of *Ariadne auf Naxos*.

Ariane et Barbe-Bleue [arr-yun ay barrb-bler] (Ariadne and Bluebeard). Opera in three acts by Paul Dukas—a setting of the play by Maeterlinck. First performed, Paris, May 10, 1907. Ariadne, the sixth of Bluebeard's wives, opens the forbidden door and releases her five predecessors. Instead of revenging themselves on Bluebeard they show sympathy for him when he is attacked and wounded by the peasants. Ariadne, however, abandons him.

Arianna, L' [larr-yahn'-nah]. Opera with a prologue and eight scenes by Monteverdi. Libretto by Ottavio Rinuccini. First performed, Mantua, May 28, 1608. *v.* LAMENT.

Arie [ah'-ri-er], *G.* Air, aria.

Arietta [arr-yet'-tah], *I.* Diminutive of ARIA. (1) A term in use since the early 17th cent. to indicate a short song, simpler in character and structure than the aria.

(2) An instrumental piece of a similar kind, *e.g.* the theme of the variations which form the second movement of Beethoven's Sonata in C minor, Op. 111.

Ariette [arr-yet], *Fr.* (1) A short aria.

(2) In early 18th-cent. opera a brilliant aria in Italian style, and even with Italian words.

(3) In late 18th-cent. *opéra comique* a song introduced into a scene in dialogue.

Arioso [arr-yo'-zo], *I.* "Like an aria." (1) A piece of recitative which has characteristics demanding a more song-like interpretation than the declamatory style proper to recitative. These characteristics are likely to include an expressive melodic line and rhythmical definition. The change from strict recitative to *arioso* is common in Bach. He also uses the word to describe a piece wholly in this style. A typical example of the latter is No. 31 of the *St. John Passion*—"Betrachte, meine Seel" (Consider, O my soul)—for bass solo accompanied by lute, 2 viole d'amore and continuo.

(2) A short vocal solo in a lyrical style, *e.g.* No. 37 of Mendelssohn's *Elijah*—"Ja, es sollen wohl Berge weichen" (For the mountains shall depart).

(3) In instrumental music a piece similar in style to vocal *arioso*. In the third movement of Beethoven's Sonata in A♭ major, Op. 110, the plaintive melody in A♭ minor is marked *arioso dolente* to distinguish it from the preceding *recitativo*.

Ariosti [arr-yoss'-tee], ATTILIO: *b.* Bologna, Nov. 5, 1666; *d. c.* 1740. Opera composer. After some years in Berlin he came to England and was, with Handel and G. B. Bononcini, one of the musical directors of the Royal Academy of Music—a company for the production of Italian opera which was formed in 1720 and came to an abrupt end in 1728. Among the operas written for London by Ariosti were *Cajo Marzio Coriolano* (1723) and *Teuzzone* (1727). The old story that he collaborated with Handel and Bononcini in writing *Il Muzio Scevola* (1721) is without foundation.

Arlecchino [arr-leck-kee'-no] (Harlequin). Opera in one act by Busoni. Libretto by the composer. First performed (with *Turandot*), Zürich, May 11, 1917.

Arlésienne, L' [larr-laze-yen] (The Girl from Arles). A play of Provençal life by Alphonse Daudet (1840-97), with incidental music for small orchestra by Bizet. First performed, Paris, Oct. 1, 1872. Two suites from the music. which introduces tunes popular in Provence, are played in the concert room. The score includes a saxophone.

Armida [arr-mee'-da]. Opera in four acts by Dvořák. Libretto by "Jaroslav Vrchlický" *i.e.* Emil Bohuš Frida (based on his Czech translation of Tasso's *La Gerusalemme liberata*). First performed, Prague, March 25, 1904.

Armide [arr-meed]. (1) Opera in five acts by Gluck. Libretto by Philippe Quinault (after Tasso). First performed, Paris, Sept. 23, 1777.

(2) Opera with a prologue and five acts by Lully. Libretto by Philippe Quinault (after Tasso). First performed, Paris, Feb. 15, 1686.

Arne, (1) THOMAS AUGUSTINE: *b.* London, Mar. 1710; *d.* there, Mar. 5, 1778. Composer. Educated at Eton and intended for the law, but studied music privately and adopted it as a profession. His first opera was a setting of Addison's *Rosamond* (London, 1733), previously set by Thomas Clayton. His most ambitious work was the opera *Artaxerxes*, to a text adapted by the composer from Metastasio (London, 1762). His comic opera *Thomas and Sally* (London, 1760)—the first English opera with clarinets—has been successfully revived in the present century. In addition to a very large number of works for the stage he also wrote two oratorios and instrumental music. His masque *Alfred* (1740) includes the patriotic song "Rule Britannia." His settings of "Under the greenwood tree," "Blow, blow, thou winter wind" and "When daisies pied" were written for a revival of *As you like it* in 1740, and "Where the bee sucks" for a revival of *The Tempest* in 1746.

H. LANGLEY: *Doctor Arne* (1938).

(2) MICHAEL: *b.* London, 1740; *d.* there, 1786. Son of (1). Singer and composer of dramatic music. His most successful work was the music for Garrick's *Cymon* (1767). He also dabbled in chemistry, attempting to discover the philosopher's stone.

(3) SUSANNA MARIA: *b.* London, 1714; *d.* there, 1766. Sister of (1). Singer and actress. She married Theophilus Cibber, son of Colley Cibber, but the marriage was not a success. Her interpretation of "He was despis'd," which she sang at the first performance of *Messiah* in Dublin in 1742, made a great impression. Handel wrote the part of Micah in *Samson* for her. She enjoyed an equal reputation as a tragic actress.

Arnell, RICHARD ANTHONY SAYER: *b.* London, Sept. 15, 1917. Composer. Studied with John Ireland at the R.C.M. Lived in New York, 1939-47. His compositions include 4 symphonies, the symphonic poem *Lord Byron*, a violin concerto, ballets, two string quartets, and piano music.

Arnold, (1) MALCOLM HENRY: *b.* Northampton, Oct. 21, 1921. Composer, Studied at the R.C.M. Trumpeter in the London Philharmonic and B.B.C. Symphony Orchestras. His compositions include concertos for horn and clarinet, symphony for strings, overture—*Beckus the Dandipratt*, and chamber music.

(2) SAMUEL: *b.* London, Aug. 10, 1740; *d.* there, Oct. 22, 1802. Organist, composer and editor. Organist, Chapel Royal, 1783; Westminster Abbey, 1793. He wrote several oratorios and a great quantity of music for the stage. He also published a subscription edition of Handel's works (incomplete and in many respects inaccurate) and a collection of *Cathedral Music* in four volumes.

Arnold von Bruck. *v.* BRUCK.

Arnould [arr-noo], MADELEINE SOPHIE: *b.* Paris, Feb. 13, 1740; *d.* there, Oct. 22, 1802. Singer and actress. The first Iphigenia in Gluck's *Iphigénie en Aulide* (1774) and the first Eurydice in the Paris version of his *Orfeo*, produced in the same year. She owed her success more to her ability as an actress than to her voice, which was not outstanding. Her portrait was painted by Greuze.

Aron. *v.* AARON.

Arpa [arr'-pah], *I.* Harp.

Arpeggio [arr-peh'-djo] (*I.* arpeggiare, "to play the harp"). (1) The notes of a chord played not simultaneously but in rapid succession, as on the harp. The old English name was "battery." Among the signs in use in the 17th and 18th cent. were the following:

As written:

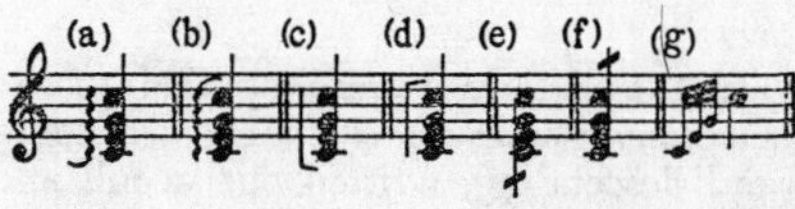

As played :

(*v.* also ACCIACCATURA). A vaguer indication was to mark a chord *arpeggio* and leave the interpretation to the player, who was free to play ascending and descending arpeggios as he wished and to interpolate acciaccaturas. The modern practice is to play all arpeggios ascending and to use one of the following signs (of which the second is the least common) :

The question whether the arpeggio begins before or on the beat is one that now depends on the context. In piano music the following distinction should be observed between chords in which the right and left hands play arpeggios simultaneously and those in which there is a single arpeggio divided between the two hands :

As written :

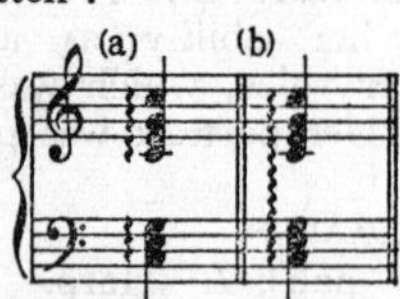

As played :

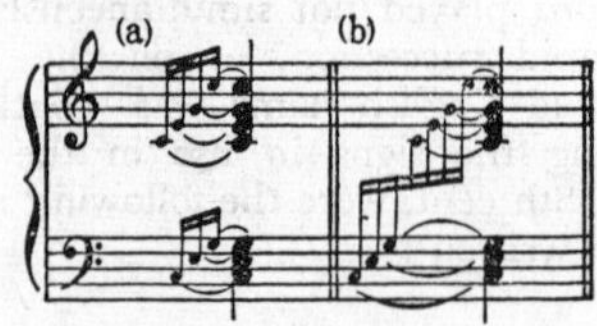

(2) The term is also applied to the successive notes of a chord, ascending and descending, written out in full and performed in strict time. The practice of such passages forms part of the technical training of every singer and instrumentalist.

Arpeggione [arr-peh-djo′-neh], *I.* A sort of bass guitar, played with a bow like the cello. It had six strings, tuned :

It was invented by G. Staufer of Vienna in 1823 but would be forgotten today if Schubert had not written a sonata for arpeggione and piano in 1824 (*Complete works*, series viii).

Arrangement. (1) The adaptation of a piece of music so as to make it suitable for performance by forces other than those for which it was originally composed. The purpose of such an arrangement may be (*a*) to facilitate study or domestic performance, as with the vocal score of an opera or oratorio ; (*b*) to enlarge the repertory of a particular medium, as with organ arrangements of orchestral works ; (*c*) to enable a work written for a large number of performers to be given with more limited resources. In the last of these three cases arrangement is unlikely to involve more than transference from one instrument to another and the omission of unessential details. In the other two cases it involves a modification of the original text. An orchestral score not only has to be compressed if it is to be playable on the piano ; many of its details will also have to be translated into pianistic terms. Conversely, much that is effective on the piano will need considerable adaptation if it is to be equally effective in the orchestra. Arrangers often go far beyond such necessary modification, elaborating details in the original text until they acquire a new significance and adding extraneous material of their own. The criterion of an arrangement is not only technical skill but good taste.

The practice of arrangement is ancient and many composers have arranged their own works. As early as the first half of the 14th century we find examples of organ arrangements of motets in a manuscript from Robertsbridge Abbey, Sussex (*v.* H. E. Wooldridge, *Early English Harmony*, pl. 43-5). Organ arrangements of vocal works occur also in the 15th cent., *e.g.* in the *Buxheim Organ Book* (1470). In the 16th cent. arrangements of vocal works for lute solo or for solo voice with lute accompaniment are very common. In the 18th cent. Bach was particularly active in arranging his own works and those of other composers, *e.g.* Vivaldi's violin concertos, which he arranged for the keyboard. Beethoven arranged his own violin concerto in D major (Op. 61) as a piano concerto. Brahms adopted the unusual course of issuing two of his works in two different forms : the piano quintet in F minor (Op. 34) appeared also as a sonata for two pianos (Op. 34a), and the Variations on a theme of Haydn were published both for orchestra (Op. 56a) and for two pianos (Op. 56b). Howard Ferguson's Partita (1937) is a more recent example of a work issued in two forms—for orchestra (Op. 5a) and for two pianos (Op. 5b).

(2) A harmonized setting, whether for voices or instruments, of an existing melody. Folksong provides obvious material for such treatment, which may range from the provision of a simple piano accompaniment to the most ingenious polyphony. Here too good taste is essential, since a setting that is out of keeping with the character of the melody will deform it instead of enhancing its beauty.

H. F. ELLINGFORD : *The Art of Transcription for the Organ* (1922).

Arrau [arr-ah'-oo], CLAUDIO : *b.* Feb. 6, 1903. Chilean pianist. Having made an early reputation as a child prodigy, he studied in Berlin, where he gave his first recital in Germany in 1914. Taught at Stern's Conservatorium, Berlin, 1925-40. Subsequently opened a school of piano-playing in Santiago, Chile. Now resident in the United States.

Arrieta y Corera [ahrr-yeh'-tah ee corr-eh'-rah], EMILIO : *b.* Puente la Reina (Navarra), Oct. 21, 1823 ; *d.* Madrid, Feb. 11, 1894. Opera composer. Professor of composition, Madrid Conservatoire, 1857 ; director, 1868. Best known by his light opera *Marina* (Madrid, 1855), which was later enlarged into a three-act opera with recitatives (Madrid, 1871)—the first opera to be sung in Spanish at the Madrid Court Theatre.

Ars antiqua, *L.* "The old art" Music of the late 12th cent. and 13th cent., in contrast with ARS NOVA, the music of the 14th cent. The two terms were originally used by early 14th-cent. writers to distinguish the music of the late 13th cent. from that of their own time.

G. REESE : *Music in the Middle Ages* (1940).

Arsis (*Gr.* ἄρσις). (1) Lit. "a raising" (of the hand or foot), hence an up-beat, in contrast to *thesis*, a down-beat. The Romans, however, used *arsis* of a strong accent, and this interpretation was followed not only by medieval theorists but by many modern writers. Hence the use of the word today may easily create confusion, though there is a growing tendency to accept the meaning of the original Greek.

(2) The expression *per arsin et thesin* was formerly applied to imitation by contrary motion, since one part goes up where the other goes down, and vice versa, *e.g.*:

BACH, *The Art of Fugue, Contrapunctus V*

Ars nova, *L.* "The new art." The name of an early 14th-cent. treatise ascribed to Philippe de Vitry. The term was used by theorists of the period to describe the music of their own time in contrast to that of the late 13th cent. (ARS ANTIQUA). It is now generally applied to the whole of 14th-cent. music.

G. REESE : *Music in the Middle Ages* (1940).

Artaria [arr-tah-ree'-ah]. A Vienna music-publishing firm, of Italian origin. Their publications, which began in 1778, included many works by Haydn, Mozart and Beethoven.

Artaxerxes. Opera in three acts by Arne. The libretto is an English adaptation, by the composer, of Metastasio's *Artaserse.* First performed, London, Feb. 2, 1762.

Art of Fugue, The (*G.* Die Kunst der Fuge). A work by J. S. Bach, written in 1749 and published after his death in 1750. The first edition had no sale ; of the second, published with a preface by F. W. Marpurg in 1752, only about 30 copies were sold in four years. In 1756 C. P. E. Bach sold the copper plates for their value as metal.

The work demonstrates by example almost every possible kind of contrapuntal treatment of the following theme :

It consists of 13 fugues (for which Bach uses the term *contrapunctus*), two of which are also inverted, and 4 canons. The published text includes also an unfinished fugue on three subjects (none of which is the subject of *The Art of Fugue*) and the chorale prelude "Vor deinen Thron," which Bach dictated shortly before his death to his son-in-law J. C. Altnikol. The chorale prelude clearly has no connection with *The Art of Fugue,* and there is no evidence that the unfinished fugue was intended to form part of the work, the engraving of which was largely completed before Bach died. It has been shown, however, that the subject of *The Art of Fugue* can be combined contrapuntally with the three subjects of the unfinished fugue and a conjectural completion on these lines is published in Tovey's edition.

The original text is in score, without any indication of the instruments for which it is intended, except that Bach himself provided an arrangement for two harpsichords (with a fourth part added) of Contrapunctus XIII and its inversion. The whole work, however, with the exception of Contrapunctus XII and Contrapunctus XIII and the concluding bars of Contrapunctus VI, can be performed on the keyboard by a single player. Modern transcriptions include one for orchestra by Wolfgang Graeser and another for string quartet by Roy Harris.

D. F. TOVEY : *A Companion to the Art of Fugue* (1931).

Artôt [arr-toh], MARGUÉRITE JOSÉPHINE DÉSIRÉE : *b.* Paris, July 21, 1835 ; *d.* Berlin, Apr. 3, 1907. Soprano. She made her début in opera in Paris in 1858, but her principal successes were won in Italian opera in Berlin. She visited England and Russia, where Tchaikovsky in 1868 fell in love with her and intended to marry her. She was however already engaged to the Spanish baritone Padilla-y-Ramos, whom she married in 1869. On her retirement from the stage she taught singing in Berlin.

Artusi [arr-too'-zee], GIOVANNI MARIA : *b. c.* 1540 ; *d.* Aug. 18, 1613. Canon of San Salvatore, Bologna, 1562. Theorist and composer. His most celebrated work was *Delle imperfettioni della musica moderna* (1600-3), in which he attacked the music of his more advanced contemporaries, particularly Monteverdi.

As [uss], *G.* A flat (A♭).

Asafiev [a-sahf-'yeff], BORIS : *b.* St. Petersburg, July 29, 1884 ; *d.* Moscow, Jan. 27, 1949. Composer and musicologist. Studied at St. Petersburg Conservatoire. After the revolution he took an active part in propagating the official Soviet attitude towards composition. His own compositions were chiefly for the stage. Under the name "Igor Glebov" he was active as a music critic and published several books, mainly on Russian music.

Ases [uss′-ĕss], *G.* A double flat (A♭♭).

Ashton, Hugh. *v.* ASTON.

Aspelmayr [uss′-pĕl-mire], FRANZ : *b.* 1728 ; *d.* Vienna, July 29, 1786. The second German to have a work included in the repertory of the Vienna *Nationalsingspiel*, founded in 1778. This was his opera *Die Kinder der Natur* (1778). Also one of the first Viennese composers to practise the new instrumental style associated particularly with the Mannheim school.

Aspiration [uss-pee-russ-yõn], *Fr.* (*E.* springer, *G.* Nachschlag). An ornament current in the 17th and 18th cent., indicated by various signs :

As written :

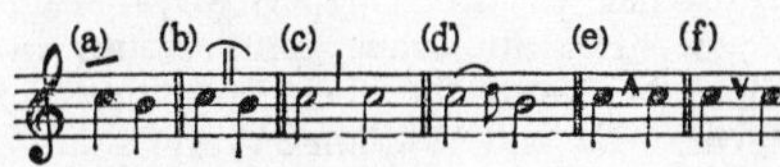

As played :

Assai [uss-sah′-ee], *I.* "Very," *e.g.* *allegro assai*, very fast.

Aston (Ashton), HUGH : *b. c.* 1485 ; *d.* after 1549. Composer. Master of the choristers, St. Mary Newarke Hospital and College, Leicester, *c.* 1525-48. His compositions include a Hornpipe for virginals, which anticipates by a good many years the methods of Elizabethan and Jacobean composers, and some church music (printed in *Tudor Church Music*, x).

Astorga [uss-torr′-gah], EMANUELE GIOACCHINO CESARE RINCÓN, Baron d' : *b.* Augusta (Sicily), March 20, 1680 ; *d.* 1757. Sicilian nobleman (of Spanish descent) and composer. His works include a single opera, *Dafni* (Genoa, 1709), a *Stabat mater* (1707) which appears to have been first performed at Oxford in 1752, and a number of chamber cantatas. An opera dealing with his life by J. J. Albert (1832-1915), was produced at Stuttgart in 1866.

Atalanta [ah-tah-lahn′-tah]. Opera in three acts by Handel (librettist unknown). First performed, London, May 23, 1736.

A tempo [ah tem′-po], *I.* (*Fr.* au mouvement). "In time." Used to restore the normal tempo of a piece after it has been interrupted by a *rallentando*, *allargando*, *a piacere*, etc., or by a section marked to be played at a faster or slower speed than that indicated at the beginning of the piece.

Athaliah. Oratorio by Handel. Libretto by Samuel Humphreys. First performed, Oxford, July 10, 1733.

Atonality. A term often used loosely of any music whose harmony appears unfamiliar, but properly applied to music which rejects traditional tonality, *i.e.* which abandons the use of a tonic or key-centre to which all the notes and chords of a piece are related. Since the mere rejection of traditional methods would not produce intelligible music, Schönberg and his followers have adopted a new method of construction, known as the TWELVE-NOTE SYSTEM, based on artificial relationships of quite a different kind. The term "atonality" is often used of music written in accordance with this system, but as it implies a negation of tonality it is not well chosen to describe something which is anything but negative in character.

G. ABRAHAM : *This Modern Stuff* (1939).
G. DYSON : *The New Music* (1924).

Attacca [aht-tahk′-cah], *I.* "Begin," *i.e.* start the next movement or section without any break. So also *attacca subito*, begin suddenly.

Attacco [aht-tahk′-co], *I.* A short figure used as a subject for imitation in a fugue or other polyphonic composition, *e.g.*:

BACH, *48 Preludes and Fugues, Book II, No. 3*

material was reminiscent of the work of other composers. The composer himself then declared that the reminiscences were deliberate.

Attaingnant [a-tain-yŭn], PIERRE : *d. c.* 1550. French music-publisher, the first in Paris to print from movable types. His publications include a large quantity of *chansons*, motets, masses, lute music and organ music. There are modern editions of *Trente et une chansons musicales* (1529) in *Les Maîtres musiciens de la Renaissance française*, v (1897), four volumes of instrumental music (1530-1) in facsimile (Munich, 1914), and two volumes of organ music in *Publications de la Société française de musicologie*, (1925).

Attaque du Moulin, L' [la-tuck dee moo-lăn] (The Attack on the Mill). Opera in four acts by Bruneau. Libretto by Louis Gallet (based on a story in Zola's *Soirées de Médan*). First performed, Paris, Nov. 23, 1893.

Atterberg [utt'-er-bair-y*er*], KURT : *b.* Gothenburg, Dec. 12, 1887. Composer, conductor and critic. Originally trained as an engineer. Studied music at the Stockholm Royal Academy of Music and in Germany, having been awarded a State grant. Music critic of *Stockholms Tidningen*, 1919. His works include 8 symphonies, concertos for violin, cello, horn and piano, three operas—*Härvard Harpolekare* (Stockholm, 1919), *Bäckahästen* (Stockholm, 1925), *Fanal* (Stockholm, 1934), choral cantatas and miscellaneous orchestral and chamber works. His sixth symphony in C major, Op. 31, won the first prize of £2000 offered by the Columbia Graphophone Company in 1928 to commemorate the anniversary of Schubert's death. It was adversely criticized when it first appeared on the ground that too much of its thematic material was reminiscent of the work of other composers. The composer himself then declared that the reminiscences were deliberate.

Attey, JOHN : *d.* Ross, *c.* 1640. The last of the English lutenist songwriters. His only published work, *The First Booke of Ayres* (1622), includes the well-known "Sweet was the song the virgin sang." The songs in the collection are designed to be sung by four voices with lute, or as solos with accompaniment for lute and bass viol. Modern edition in *E.S.L.S.*, 2nd ser.

At the Boar's Head. Opera in one act by Holst. Libretto by the composer (based on Shakespeare's *King Henry IV*). First performed, Manchester, Apr. 3, 1925.

Attwood, THOMAS : *b.* London, Nov. 23, 1765 ; *d.* Chelsea, March 24, 1838. Organist of St. Paul's Cathedral and composer to the Chapel Royal from 1796. His numerous compositions include anthems for the coronations of George IV and William IV and a large number of works for the stage. He was a favourite pupil of Mozart, with whom he studied in Vienna (1785-7), and a close friend of Mendelssohn, who dedicated to him his three Preludes and Fugues for organ, Op. 37.

Atys [a-teece]. Opera with a prologue and five acts by Lully. Libretto by Philippe Quinault. First performed, Saint-Germain, Jan. 10, 1676.

Aubade [o-bud], *Fr.* (*Sp.* alborada). Morning music, as opposed to serenade, which is properly evening music. Often used as the title of short instrumental pieces.

Auber [o-bair], DANIEL FRANÇOIS ESPRIT : *b.* Caen, Jan. 29, 1782 ; *d.* Paris, May 13, 1871. Opera composer. Director, Paris Conservatoire, 1842. His early years were spent as a clerk in London, where his songs had some success in society. He returned to Paris in 1804 and began to write operas, but without success until the performance of *La Bergère châtelaine* (1820). From 1823 onwards he collaborated with the librettist Augustin Eugène Scribe. He produced in all 45 operas, of which the most successful were *Le Maçon* (1825), *La Muette de Portici*, known in England as *Masaniello* (1828), *Fra Diavolo* (1830), *Le Cheval de bronze* (1835), *Le Domino noir* (1837), *Les Diamants de la couronne* (1841), *Haydée* (1847) and *Le Premier jour de bonheur* (1868). *La Muette de Portici*, was the first of the French romantic "grand operas" of the 19th cent. and is remarkable in that the heroine is dumb. It was much admired by Wagner for its dramatic intensity. Its representation of the spirit of revolt against tyranny was so striking that a performance at Brussels in 1830 precipitated the revolution which established Belgian independence. Apart from this work Auber was at his best in *opéra comique*. His *Fra Diavolo*, dealing with the adventures of English tourists among Italian bandits, is still popular.

CH. MALHERBE : *Auber* (Paris, 1911).

Aubert [o-bair], (1) JACQUES : *b.* Sept. 30, 1689 ; *d.* Belleville, nr. Paris, May 18, 1753. Violinist and composer. A member of the king's band of 24 violins and the Opéra orchestra. Composed a considerable amount of instrumental music for the *Concert spirituel*, as well as ballets for the Opéra and music for the *Théâtre de la foire*.

(2) LOUIS FRANÇOIS MARIE : *b.* Paramé (Ille-et-Vilaine), Feb. 19, 1877. Composer. As a boy he sang at the Madeleine and studied at the Paris Conservatoire, where he was a pupil of Fauré for composition. Before 1900 he appeared frequently as a pianist, but after that date devoted himself almost exclusively to composition. His most important work is the fairy-tale opera *La Fôret bleue* (Geneva, 1913), which was not performed in Paris until 1924. It combines impressionist harmony with considerable melodic charm. His orchestral *Habanera* (1919) has won popularity.

L. VUILLEMIN : *Louis Aubert et son oeuvre* (Paris, 1921).

Aubry [o-bree], PIERRE : *b.* Paris, Feb. 14, 1874 ; *d.* Dieppe, Aug. 31, 1910. Musicologist, whose special field was medieval music. In his book *Trouvères et troubadours* (Paris, 1909) he advocated the interpretation of troubadour melodies in accordance with the rhythm of the words. According to his interpretation, which was also advanced by J. B. Beck and is now widely accepted, the music is to be transcribed in one of the RHYTHMIC MODES. Aubry also published *Les plus anciens monuments de la musique française* (1903), *Estampies et danses royales* (1906), *Le Roman de Fauvel* (1907), *Cents Motets du XIIIe siècle* (3 vols., 1908) and *Le Chansonnier de l'Arsenal* (1909), of which the last remained unfinished at his death.

Au chevalet [oh sher-va-lay], *Fr.* (*G.* am Steg, *I.* sul ponticello). On the bridge (of a string instrument), *i.e.* play near the bridge, thus producing a glassy, brittle tone.

Audran [o-drũn], EDMOND : *b.* Lyons, Apr. 12, 1840 ; *d.* Tierceville, Aug. 17, 1901. Composer, whose reputation rests on a large number of comic operas, of which *La Mascotte* (Paris, 1880) and *La Poupée* (Paris, 1896) were the most popular. He also wrote church music and was for some years organist of a church in Marseilles.

Auer [ow'-er], LEOPOLD : *b.* Veszprém (Hungary), June 7, 1845 ; *d.* Loschwitz, July 15, 1930. Violinist and teacher, a pupil of Joachim. Professor of the violin, Imperial Conservatoire, St. Petersburg, 1868-1917. In 1918 settled in New York, where he continued to teach. His pupils included Mischa Elman, Jascha Heifetz, Efram Zimbalist and Isolde Menges. Published *Violin Playing as I teach it* (1921) and *My Long Life in Music* (1923).

Auf dem Anstand [owf dem un'-shtunt], *G.* "At the hunting station." Symphony No. 31 in D major by Haydn (1765), also known as *Mit dem Hornsignal*, "with the horn call." It includes prominent, and sometimes elaborate, parts for four horns, and opens with a hunting fanfare.

Aufforderung zum Tanz [owf'-forrd-er-oong tsoom tunts], *G.* (Invitation to the Dance). A piano piece by Weber, Op. 65 (1819). It consists of a sentimental introduction, an extended waltz and a reminiscent coda. Generally known in England as "Invitation to the Waltz."

Aufstieg und Fall der Stadt Mahagonny [owf′-shteeg ŏŏnt full dair shtut ma-ha-gon′-ni] (Rise and Fall of the City of Mahagonny). Opera in three acts by Weill. Libretto by Bert Brecht. First performed, Leipzig, March 9, 1930. (Originally a *Singspiel*, first performed, Baden-Baden, 1927).

Augener [ow′-gen-er]. A London music-publishing and printing firm, founded in 1853 by George Augener (*d.* 1915). Publishers of *The Monthly Musical Record* (founded 1871).

Augmentation. The presentation of a theme in notes double the value of those originally assigned to it. In the following example the fugue subject and its augmentation are combined :

BACH, *48 Preludes and Fugues, Book II, No. 2*

v. CANON. The opposite of augmentation is DIMINUTION.

Augmented Interval. The following intervals can be augmented by sharpening the upper, or flattening the lower, note : major second, major third, fourth, fifth, major sixth, major seventh, octave, *e.g.* :

Fourth : Augmented fourth :

Major sixth : Augmented sixth :

The augmented fourth occurs between the fourth and seventh notes of every major scale, *e.g.* :

The other augmented intervals necessitate notes foreign to the key.

Augmented Sixth. *v.* AUGMENTED INTERVAL. The so-called chord of the augmented sixth has three forms hallowed by tradition, known respectively (for no good reason) as Italian, French and German :

Since on keyboard instruments it is impossible to distinguish between the sound of F♯ and G♭ the last of the three may also be treated as a DOMINANT SEVENTH chord (in this case in the key of D♭) :

Such ambiguity appealed particularly to 19th-cent. composers, who exploited it for the purpose of modulation.

The "Italian" sixth originated in the 17th cent. as the result of the combination of two alternative progressions :

(1) 

(2) 

A more pathetic effect was produced by combining the sharpened sixth with the flattened bass :

The frequent use of a chromatically descending bass in movements built on a *basso ostinato* (ground bass) encouraged the adoption of this progression.

Augmented Triad. A chord composed, in its simplest form, of two major thirds, *e.g.*

The notes of the chord can also be rearranged as follows :

v. CHORD, INVERSION.

Augustine (Aurelius Augustinus) : *b.* Tagaste, Nov. 13, 354 ; *d.* Hippo (now Bona, in Algeria), Aug. 28, 430. In his early years taught at Carthage, Rome and Milan, where he was baptised in 384. He returned to Carthage in 388 and was ordained priest in 391, becoming bishop of Hippo in 396. His *Confessiones* and *De civitate Dei* date from the latter part of his life, after his appointment as bishop. The treatise *De musica* was written *c.* 387-9. It deals principally with metre. An English summary has been published by W. J. F. Knight.

Aulin [ow'-leen], TOR : *b.* Stockholm, Sept. 10, 1866 ; *d.* there, March 1, 1914. Violinist and conductor. Founder of the Aulin String Quartet, 1887, and first conductor of the Stockholm Konsertförening (founded 1902). His compositions include 3 violin concertos.

Aulos [ow'-loss] (*Gr.* *αὐλός*). (1) A generic term used by the Greeks for a wind instrument (*L.* tibia).

(2) More particularly a double-reed instrument, with a cylindrical bore, normally played in pairs by a single performer. The double reed was not held between the lips, as in the modern oboe, but inside the mouth. Inflation of the cheeks, which produced the necessary wind-pressure, was controlled by a leather band, called *phorbeia* (*φορβειά*), which passed round the player's head. It is thought that the second *aulos* was used to provide a drone bass, as on the bagpipe. The *aulos* was used in the Greek drama, in musical competitions, at marriage ceremonies and for entertainment. Girls playing the *aulos* were popular at banquets. The tone of the instrument was shrill and penetrating, like that of the medieval shawm.

K. SCHLESINGER : *The Greek Aulos* (1939).

Au mouvement [o moov-mũn], *Fr.* " In time " (*I.* a tempo). *v.* A TEMPO.

Aural Training. The purpose of aural training is to teach pupils to recognize the sounds and rhythms they hear and to write them down on paper. The ability to do this is indispensable for the study of harmony and counterpoint, and no one can properly be called a musician who cannot do it. There are a number of books on the subject, but what the student needs most is constant practice with a good teacher.

B. C. ALLCHIN : *Aural Training.*

Auric [o-reek], GEORGES : *b.* Lodève (Hérault), Feb. 15, 1899. Composer. Studied at the Paris Conservatoire and the Schola Cantorum. He was influenced by Erik Satie and became one of a group of young composers known as *Les Six*, the others being Darius Milhaud, Louis Durey, Arthur Honegger, Francis Poulenc and Germaine Tailleferre (*v.* SIX). His compositions pay tribute both to popular music and to Stravinsky. They include songs, piano music, chamber music, ballets and music for films (including René Clair's *À nous la liberté* and Bernard Shaw's *Caesar and Cleopatra*). He has also been active as a music critic.

Aus der neuen Welt [owce dair noy'-ĕn velt], *G.* *v.* FROM THE NEW WORLD.

Aus meinem Leben [owce mine'-ĕm labe'-ĕn], *G.* (*Cz.* Z mého života). " From my life." The German subtitle of Smetana's string quartet No. 1 in E minor (1876), indicating that the work has autobiographical associations. In particular the sustained high E for the first violin in the last movement alludes to his deafness.

Austin, (1) FREDERIC : *b.* London, March 30, 1872 ; *d.* London, Apr. 10, 1952. Baritone and composer. He sang the solo in the first English performance of Delius's *Sea Drift* (Sheffield,

1908). From 1908 onwards sang in opera under Richter and Beecham and became a member of the Beecham Opera Company in 1915. Artistic director of the BRITISH NATIONAL OPERA COMPANY, 1924. His compositions include orchestral works, incidental music for the stage and a choral setting of *Pervigilium Veneris* (Leeds, 1931). His version of *The Beggar's Opera* (London, 1920), in which he sang as Peachum, was extraordinarily successful.

(2) RICHARD : *b.* Birkenhead, Dec. 26, 1903. Son of (1). Conductor, Bournemouth Municipal Orchestra, 1934-9. Founded the New Era Concert Society, 1947.

Au talon [o ta-lo͞n], *F.* (*G.* am Frosch). With the nut (or heel) of the bow (*i.e.* the end nearer the hand).

Authentic Mode. *v.* MODE.

Ave Maria [ah′-veh mah-ree′-a], *L.* "Hail, Mary!" (1) A prayer to the Virgin in use in the Roman Catholic church, beginning with the salutations of the angel Gabriel and Elizabeth. It has often been set to music.

(2) Among the popular pieces known by this title are (a) "Arcadelt's *Ave Maria*," a transcription by Liszt, with altered harmony, of Arcadelt's *chanson* "Nous voyons que les hommes" (1554); (b) A setting by Schubert, Op. 52, No. 6 (1825) of a translation by P. A. Storck of one of Ellen's songs in Scott's *Lady of the Lake*; (c) a *cantabile* melody superimposed by Gounod on the first prelude, in C major, from Bach's *Das wohltemperirte Clavier.*

Avison, CHARLES : *b.* Newcastle upon Tyne, *c.* 1709; *d.* there, May 9, 1770. Organist and composer. He published a number of instrumental concertos but is now known only by his treatise *An Essay on Musical Expression* (2nd ed., 1753), which, though opinionated, is valuable for the evidence it affords of contemporary taste and practice. He was a pupil of Geminiani, whom he praises warmly in his *Essay*. For his "Grand March" *v.* Robert Browning, *Parleyings with certain people of importance in their day* (1887).

Ayre. *v.* AIR (2).

B

B, *E.* (*Fr. I.* si, *G.* H). (1) The 7th note (or leading note) of the scale of C major. In the 10th cent. a distinction was established between ♭ (*B molle* or *rotundum*, " soft " or " rounded " B), representing B♭, and ♮ (*B durum* or *quadratum*, " hard " or " square " B), representing B♮ (*v.* HEXACHORD). From these two signs the ♭ and ♮ respectively were derived. The modern French and Italian names for the ♭ (*bémol* and *bemolle*) and for the ♮ (*bécarre* and *bequadro*) have a similar origin. The adjectives *molle* and *durum* are also perpetuated in the modern German terms for major and minor—*dur* and *moll*. In the 16th cent. the Germans came to write ♮ as h ; hence in German nomenclature *B* is B♭ and *H* is B♮. *e.g.* " Klarinette in B " means " Clarinet in B♭."

(2) As an abbreviation *B.* = Bass, Bachelor (*B. Mus.* or *Mus. B.* = Bachelor of Music).

Babell, WILLIAM : *b. c.* 1690 ; *d.* Canonbury, Sept. 23, 1723. Composer and performer on the harpsichord and violin. He made a reputation by issuing showy transcriptions for the harpsichord of popular operatic arias, for which Burney had the greatest contempt (*General History of Music*, vol. iv, pp. 648-9). He also published sonatas of his own composition for violin or oboe.

Babin, VICTOR : *b.* Moscow, Dec. 13, 1908. Pianist and composer. He has appeared as a solo pianist and in works for two pianos with his wife, Vitya Vronsky. His compositions are mainly instrumental.

Baborák [bub′-orr-ahk], *Cz.* A Bohemian national dance, consisting of alternating sections in 3/4 and 2/4 time.

Baccaloni [bahk-cah-lo′-nee], SALVATORE : *b.* Rome, Apr. 14, 1900. Operatic bass, who has made his reputation mainly in comic opera. He was a chorister in the Sistine Chapel, Rome, and for some years studied architecture. First public appearance, 1922. Outside Italy he has sung in many other countries, including England and the United States. He excels equally as an actor and as a singer.

Bacchantinnen, Die [dee buckh-unt′-in-něn] (The Bacchants). Opera in two acts by Wellesz. Libretto by the composer (based on Euripides's tragedy). First performed, Vienna, June 20, 1931.

Baccusi [bahk-coo′-zee], IPPOLITO : *b.* Mantua, *c.* 1545 ; *d.* Verona, 1609. *Maestro di cappella*, Mantua cathedral, *c.* 1580 ; Verona, 1592. Composer of Masses, motets and madrigals. He contributed to a number of 16th-century collections, including the *Psalmodia vespertina* dedicated to Palestrina (1592) and *Il trionfo di Dori* (1592), the collection of Italian madrigals which suggested the publication of the English collection *The Triumphes of Oriana*.

Bach [buckh]. A family of Thuringian musicians, active from the 16th to the 18th cent. The most important members (in chronological order) were :

(1) JOHANN CHRISTOPH : *b.* Dec. 8, 1642 ; *d.* March 31, 1703. Organist at Eisenach and composer of instrumental and vocal works, including the motet *Ich lasse dich nicht* (I wrestle and pray), formerly attributed to J. S. Bach. To be distinguished from other members of the family with the same name, including J. S. Bach's elder brother (1671-1721), commemorated by the *Capriccio sopra la lontanza del suo fratello dilettissimo*, and Johann Christoph Friedrich (1732-95), son of J. S. Bach by his second wife (6).

(2) JOHANN MICHAEL : *b.* Aug. 9, 1648 ; *d.* May, 1694. Brother of (1). Organist and parish clerk at Arnstadt. Composed motets and organ music. His youngest daughter, Maria Barbara (1684-1720), was the first wife of J. S. Bach.

(3) JOHANN SEBASTIAN : *b.* Eisenach, March 21, 1685 ; *d.* Leipzig, July 28, 1750. Son-in-law of (2). His father, Johann Ambrosius, was first cousin of (1) and (2). Organist and composer. Choir-boy at Michaelis-Kirche, Lüneburg, 1700 ; violinist in the Weimar court orchestra, 1703 ; organist, Bonifacius-Kirche, Arnstadt, 1703 ; organist, Blasius-Kirche, Mühlhausen, 1707 ; court organist, Weimar, 1708 ; director of music to the court, Cöthen, 1717 ; cantor, Thomasschule, Leipzig, 1723. Married (i) Maria Barbara Bach (*d.* 1720), daughter of (2) ; (ii) Anna Magdalena Wilcken (*d.* 1760). Of his 20 children 10 died in infancy or at birth. His work, vast in bulk, includes every form of music current at the time, except opera. His principal compositions are :

(a) CHURCH MUSIC : Magnificat ; *St. John Passion* (1723) ; *St. Matthew Passion* (1729) ; *Christmas Oratorio* (1734) ; *Mass in B minor* ; 198 cantatas ; 6 motets.

(b) SECULAR CHORAL MUSIC : 23 cantatas.

(c) ORCHESTRA : 6 Brandenburg concertos (1721) ; 4 overtures (or suites) ; 2 violin concertos ; concerto for 2 violins ; concertos for one or more harpsichords ; concerto for harpsichord, flute and violin.

(d) CHAMBER MUSIC : 6 sonatas for solo violin ; 6 suites for solo cello ; flute sonatas ; violin sonatas ; *viola da gamba* sonatas ; *Musicalisches Opfer* (1747).

(e) HARPSICHORD OR CLAVICHORD : 7 toccatas ; chromatic fantasia and fugue ; 15 two-part inventions ; 15 three-part inventions (symphonies) ; 6 French suites ; 6 English suites ; *Das wohltemperirte Clavier* (1722 and 1744) ; 6 partitas (1731) ; Italian concerto (1735) ; Goldberg variations (1742) ; *Die Kunst der Fuge* (probably intended for the keyboard).

(f) ORGAN : 6 sonatas ; 143 chorale preludes ; fantasias, preludes, fugues, toccatas.

The chief influences in Bach's music are the Lutheran chorale, the church and organ music of his predecessors and the contemporary French and Italian styles in instrumental music. In his lifetime he had a great reputation as an organist, but his music was considered by many to be over-elaborate and old-fashioned. He combined extraordinary contrapuntal skill with a mastery of picturesque and passionate expression. His genius required no special stimulus ; it overflowed the channel of his daily employment. His music was written for a practical purpose—for the court orchestra at Cöthen, for the Sunday service at Leipzig, for the instruction of his sons, for the gratification of patrons, and for his own use. Among his didactic works *Das wohltemperirte Clavier* (The Well-Tempered Keyboard) and *Die Kunst der Fuge* (The Art of Fugue) are particularly important. The former supports the argument for EQUAL TEMPERAMENT with two sets of preludes and fugues in all the major and minor keys ; the latter demonstrates with a wealth of ingenuity the possibilities latent in a single fugue subject (*v.* ART OF FUGUE). Both achieve beauty. Bach was a universal musician, whose music has a universal appeal. It is steeped in the flavour of its period, yet belongs to all time. *v.* BACH GESELLSCHAFT.

H. T. DAVID & A. MENDEL : *The Bach Reader* (1945).

J. N. FORKEL : *Johann Sebastian Bach : His Life, Art and Work* (trans. C. S. Terry, 1920).

K. GEIRINGER : *The Bach Family* (1954).

H. GRACE : *The Organ Works of Bach* (1922).

E. & S. GREW : *Bach* (1946).

C. H. H. PARRY : *Johann Sebastian Bach* (2nd ed., 1934).

A. SCHWEITZER : *J. S. Bach* (trans. E. Newman, 2 vols., 1911).

C. S. TERRY : *Bach : a Biography* (2nd ed., 1933).

Bach's Orchestra (1932).

The Origin of the Family of Bach Musicians (1929).

W. G. WHITTAKER : *Fugitive Notes upon some Cantatas and the Motets of J. S. Bach* (1925).

(4) WILHELM FRIEDEMANN : *b.* Weimar, Nov. 22, 1710 ; *d.* Berlin, July 1, 1784.

Eldest son of (3) by his first wife. Organist and composer. Organist, Sophien-Kirche, Dresden, 1733; Liebfrauen-Kirche, Halle, 1746 (resigned 1764). For the latter part of his life he made a living by teaching and giving recitals. He was a remarkable performer on the harpsichord and organ. J. S. Bach's *Clavier-Büchlein vor Wilhelm Friedmann Bach* (which includes the two-part and three-part inventions) was written for his instruction. In spite of his restless temperament his own compositions are considerable in number and of distinguished quality. They include works for harpsichord and organ, trio sonatas, symphonies and cantatas.

(5) CARL PHILIPP EMANUEL: *b.* Weimar, March 8, 1714; *d.* Hamburg, Dec. 15, 1788. Second son of (3) by his first wife. Harpsichordist and composer. Harpsichordist to Frederick the Great, 1740; director of music to the five principal churches of Hamburg, 1767. His music is characteristic of the middle of the 18th cent. in its reaction against the habits of polyphonic writing to be found in his father's work. He himself expressed contempt for mere counterpoint. The essence of his work is taste and refinement, and in particular an understanding of the expressive possibilities of keyboard instruments. He had remarkable skill in improvisation. He wrote a large number of vocal and instrumental works, including two oratorios—*Die Israeliten in der Wüste* (The Israelites in the Wilderness, 1775) and *Die Auferstehung und Himmelfahrt Jesu* (The Resurrection and Ascension, 1787), 50 keyboard concertos, and several collections of keyboard sonatas (*v.* A. Wotquenne, *Catalogue thématique de l'oeuvre de C.Ph.Em. Bach*, 1905). His sonatas show the growth of thematic treatment of contrasted keys, from which classical SONATA FORM developed. The influence of opera is to be detected in his sentimental andantes and in the occasional use of instrumental recitative. His treatise *Versuch über die wahre Art das Klavier zu spielen* (Essay on the proper method of playing keyboard instruments, 2 pts., 1753 & 1762) is a valuable guide to the contemporary style of keyboard-playing and in particular to the interpretation of ornaments. Modern edition by W. Niemann (1925); translation by W. J. Mitchell (1949). For a first-hand account of C. P. E. Bach see C. Burney, *The Present State of Music in Germany* (1773), vol. ii, pp. 244-72.

(6) JOHANN CHRISTOPH FRIEDRICH: *b.* Leipzig, June 21, 1732; *d.* Bückeburg, Jan. 26, 1795. Eldest surviving son of (3) by his second wife. In the service of Count Wilhelm of Schaumburg-Lippe at Bückeburg, first as chamber musician (1750), then as *Konzertmeister* (*c.* 1758). His compositions include oratorios, cantatas, motets, symphonies, keyboard concertos, keyboard sonatas, chamber music and songs. A selection is in course of publication by the Bückeburg Institut für musikwissenschaftliche Forschung. The oratorios *Die Kindheit Jesu* (The childhood of Christ) and *Die Auferweckung Lazarus* (The raising of Lazarus) are printed in *D.D.T.*, vol. lvi, which also includes a thematic catalogue of his works.

(7) JOHANN CHRISTIAN (later known as John Christian): *b.* Leipzig, Sept. 5, 1735; *d.* London, Jan. 1, 1782. Youngest son of (3) by his second wife. Pianist and composer. Studied with C. P. E. Bach in Berlin and with Martini in Bologna. Organist, Milan Cathedral, 1760; composer to the King's Theatre, London, 1762; music-master to Queen Charlotte (wife of George III), 1763. Associated with K. F. Abel in a series of subscription concerts in London. He showed much kindness to Mozart, who visited London as a boy of 8 in 1764, and was popular with the royal family. His works include 11 operas (produced at Turin, Naples, London, Mannheim and Paris), an oratorio, church music, symphonies, piano concertos, chamber music, piano solos and songs. He was the first to play solos on the piano (then a relatively new instrument) in England. His portrait was painted by Gainsborough.

C. S. TERRY: *John Christian Bach* (1929). (includes a thematic catalogue).

Bachelet [bush-lay], ALFRED GEORGES: *b.* Paris, Feb. 26, 1864; *d.* Nancy, Feb. 10, 1944. Composer. *Grand Prix* *de Rome*, 1890. Director of the Nancy Conservatoire, 1919. Conductor at the Paris Opéra, 1914-18. His works, which are few in number and date from the latter part of his life, include three operas—*Scemo* (Paris, 1914), *Quand la cloche sonnera* (Paris, 1922) and *Un Jardin sur l'Oronte* (Paris, 1932).

Bach Gesellschaft [buckh ger-zell'-shuft], *G.* "Bach Society," an organization formed in 1850 to publish a complete edition of the works of J. S. Bach. The last of the 46 volumes was issued in 1900. Its formation was an indirect result of Mendelssohn's pioneer work in reviving the *St. Matthew Passion* in 1829. The *Neue Bach Gesellschaft* (New Bach Society), founded in 1900, has issued performing editions of a large number of Bach's works and since 1904 an annual *Bach-Jahrbuch*, containing important critical articles on various aspects of Bach's works. A new complete edition was initiated by the Johann - Sebastian - Bach - Institut, Göttingen, in 1954.

Bach Trumpet. A modern instrument designed to make practicable for present-day performers the high and florid trumpet parts to be found in the works of Bach and other composers of his time. *v.* TRUMPET.

Backer-Gröndahl [buck'-er-grurn'-dahl], (1) AGATHE URSULA : *b.* Holmestrand, Dec. 1, 1847 ; *d.* Ormöen (nr. Oslo), June 4, 1907. Norwegian pianist and composer. Among those with whom she studied the piano were Kjerulf, Kullak and von Bülow, who had a great admiration for her gifts. Her compositions consist of songs and piano pieces.

(2) FRIDTJOF : *b.* Oslo, Oct. 15, 1885. Son of (1). Pianist and composer, who has done much to make Norwegian music known.

Backfall. A term current in 17th-cent. England for the short APPOGGIATURA, where the ornamental note is one degree of the scale above the principal note. It was written :

 or 

and played :

The *double backfall* was equivalent to the SLIDE taken from above, *i.e.* with two ornamental notes above the principal note :

As written :

As played :

Backhaus [buck'-howce], WILHELM : *b.* Leipzig, March 26, 1884. Pianist. Pupil of Eugène d'Albert. Taught at the Royal Manchester College of Music, 1905.

Bacon, ERNST : *b.* Chicago, May 26, 1898. Pianist, conductor and composer. Studied in Chicago and Vienna. Teacher of the piano, Eastman School of Music, Rochester, N.Y., 1925-8. Director of the School of Music, University of Syracuse, N.Y., since 1945. He has also been active as a solo pianist and as conductor of opera at Rochester. His compositions include two symphonies, the musical play *A Tree on the Plains*, a piano quintet and choral works.

Badinage [ba-dee-nuzh], *Fr.* = BADINERIE.

Badinerie [ba-dee-ner-ee], *Fr.* "Frolic." A term used by 18th-cent. composers for a quick, frivolous movement in duple time, *e.g.* in Bach's suite in B minor for flute and strings. In the SUITE it is one of the optional dances or *Galanterien.*

Badings [bah'-dingce], HENK : *b.* Bandoeng (Dutch East Indies), Jan. 17, 1907. Composer and teacher. Originally a mining engineer but studied composition with Willem Pijper. His works, which are popular in Holland, include three symphonies, a violin concerto, a cello concerto, chamber music, piano works and choral music.

Bagatelle [ba-ga-tell], *Fr.* "Trifle." A short piece, for piano or other instruments. Beethoven published three sets of *Bagatellen* for piano (Op. 33, Op. 119

and Op. 126). The term has often been used since.

Bagpipe (*Fr.* cornemuse, *G.* Sackpfeife, *I.* cornamusa). A reed instrument, with one or more pipes, to which air is supplied from a skin reservoir or bag inflated by the player. It is probably of Asiatic origin, and was introduced to Europe by the Romans in the 1st cent. A.D. In course of time it became popular in every European country. Various forms exist: (1) the bag may be inflated by the player's breath through a pipe or by a bellows held under the arm; (2) the pipes may have single reeds (like the oboe) or double (like the clarinet)—in some types both are found in the same instrument; (3) since the 14th cent. it has been normal for the bagpipe to have not only a pipe with finger holes (sometimes two), called in English the "chanter" (or "chaunter"), on which the melody is played, but also one or more "drone" pipes, each tuned to a single note, which provide a simple and monotonous accompaniment.

In the past the bagpipe has been used as a military instrument and for popular music-making. These two functions survive in Scotland. It was also used in association with other instruments in the 16th cent., and at the courts of Louis XIV and Louis XV an aristocratic type, known as the *musette*, became popular as a result of the fashionable craze for pastoral entertainments (the name *musette* was also given to a type of rustic oboe). But it never became a member of the standard orchestra, and once the French fashion had become obsolete it disappeared from polite society, though musicians might call upon it for special purposes, as Verdi did for the peasants' serenade in the second act of *Otello*. On the other hand two of its characteristics have been widely imitated in instrumental and vocal music: (1) the drone bass, which it shares with the hurdy-gurdy, (2) a melodic ornament of short duration, known as the "cut" or "snap." The piece marked "The bagpipe and drone" in Byrd's *The Battell* (*My Ladye Nevells Booke*, no. 4) is not particularly characteristic, but Elizabethan virginal music generally is rich in examples of the drone bass, and in the 17th and 18th cent. the popularity of the *musette* led to the composition of a large number of pieces bearing the same name, *e.g.*

BACH, *English Suite No. 3*

HANDEL, *Alcina*

The first of these examples illustrates the drone bass, the second the "snap." Another dance of the same period, the LOURE, takes its name from an earlier type of bagpipe current in France. The "Pastoral Symphony" in Handel's *Messiah*, called "Pifa" in the score, is an imitation of rustic Italian bagpipe music, *piva* or *piffero* being one of the Italian names for the instrument. Many composers have written "Pastorales" in the same idiom.

C. SACHS: *The History of Musical Instruments* (1940).

Baguette [ba-get], *Fr.* Drumstick.

Baillot [ba-yo], PIERRE MARIE FRANÇOIS DE SALES: *b.* Passy (Paris), Oct. 1, 1771; *d.* Paris, Sept. 15, 1842. Violinist, distinguished both as a solo-player and in quartets. His compositions include concertos and chamber music.

Bainton, EDGAR LESLIE : *b.* London, Feb. 14, 1880 ; *d.* Sydney, Dec. 8, 1956. Pianist and composer. Principal, Newcastle upon Tyne Conservatoire, 1912 ; director, Sydney Conservatorium, 1934-46. His works include symphonies, symphonic poems, chamber music, choral works and an opera, *The Crier by Night.*

Bairstow, EDWARD CUTHBERT : *b.* Huddersfield, Aug. 22, 1874 ; *d.* York, May 1, 1946. Organist and composer. Organist of York Minster, 1913-46 ; professor at Durham, 1929-46. Knighted, 1932. He had a great influence as a teacher and conductor in the north of England. Author of *Counterpoint and Harmony* (1937).

Bakfark [bock'-forrk], BÁLINT : *b.* Brassó (otherwise Kronstadt), 1507 ; *d.* Padua, Aug. 13, 1576. Hungarian lutenist and composer. In the service of King Sigismundus Augustus of Poland, 1549-66. From his early years he travelled extensively in Europe, visiting France and Italy. His published works for the lute include both original compositions and transcriptions ; modern ed. of his fantasias by O. Gombosi.

Balakirev [ba-lahk'-i-reff], MILY ALEXEIVICH : *b.* Nijny-Novgorod, Jan. 2, 1837 ; *d.* St. Petersburg, May 29, 1910. Leader of the group of Russian nationalist composers known as the *Kutchka* (" The Five "), the others being Borodin, Cui, Moussorgsky and Rimsky-Korsakov. As a boy he owed much to Alexander Oulibishev (author of a three-volume study of Mozart), who gave him the run of his library. He arrived in St. Petersburg in 1855 and began to make his name as a pianist, but preferred to devote himself to teaching. To the other members of the *Kutchka* he gave not only instruction but encouragement. He was the first director of the Free School of Music in St. Petersburg, but the venture was not financially successful and in 1870 he became a railway clerk. For some years he lived a secluded life but later became a school inspector and from 1883-95, when he retired on a pension, was Director of the Court Chapel. His teaching followed the lines of his own education in being founded on the study of the classics. His compositions, which show the influence both of Russian folk-music and of the Romantic composers of Western Europe, particularly Liszt, include two symphonies, two symphonic poems (*Russia* and *Tamara*), an overture to *King Lear*, a piano sonata, an Oriental fantasy, *Islamey*, for piano solo, and a number of songs. Of these *Islamey* is the best known.

M. D. CALVOCORESSI & G. ABRAHAM : *Masters of Russian Music* (1936).
G. ABRAHAM : *Studies in Russian Music* (1935).
On Russian Music (1939).

Balalaika [ba-la-like'-a], *R.* A triangular guitar, of Tartar origin, very popular among the Russian peasantry. It normally has three strings and is made in several sizes.

Balfe, MICHAEL WILLIAM : *b.* Dublin, May 15, 1808 ; *d.* Rowney Abbey (Herts.), Oct. 20, 1870. Violinist, baritone and opera-composer. He began his career as a violinist in the orchestra at Drury Lane. In 1827 he appeared as Figaro in Rossini's *Il barbiere de Siviglia* in Paris. His first opera, *I rivali di se stessi*, was produced at Palermo in 1829. The majority of his 29 operas were written for London. The only one now remembered is *The Bohemian Girl* (1843).

W. A. BARRETT : *Balfe—His Life and Work* (1882).

Balfour Gardiner. *v.* GARDINER.

Ball, GEORGE THOMAS THALBEN : *b.* Sydney, June 18, 1896. Organist. Studied at the R.C.M. Organist, Temple Church, London, since 1923 ; Royal Albert Hall, London, 1933 ; City of Birmingham, 1948. In addition to his regular duties in England he has given a large number of recitals abroad.

Ballad. (1) A narrative song, either traditional or (as in the 19th cent.) specially written in imitation of traditional forms. From the 16th to the 19th cent. the words of ballads, which often dealt with contemporary events, were printed on sheets and sold at fairs, markets and other public gatherings.

(2) A sentimental, drawing-room song of the late 19th and early 20th cent.

(3) An instrumental piece = BALLADE (2).

S. NORTHCOTE : *The Ballad in Music* (1942).

Ballade [ba-lud], *Fr.* (1) A type of medieval French verse in which the refrain comes at the end of the stanza. Ballades were set to music for solo voice by the TROUVÈRES, and in two or more parts, for voices and instruments, by Guillaume de Machaut (14th cent.) and other polyphonic composers of the later Middle Ages.

(2) In the 19th and 20th cent. an instrumental piece, sometimes of considerable length, of a lyrical and romantic character. In some cases the influence of the traditional poetic ballad is strongly marked, *e.g.* in Brahms's Op. 10, No. 1 for piano, which is preceded by the text of the Scottish ballad *Edward*.

Ballad Opera. A type of opera popular in England in the mid-18th cent., in which dialogue was interspersed with songs set to popular tunes. The term "ballad opera" is misleading, since the popular tunes were often taken from the works of well-known composers. The best-known of these works is John Gay's *The Beggar's Opera* (1728), the music for which was arranged by John Pepusch. This has been successfully revived in the 20th cent. in Frederic Austin's edition. There are also more recent versions by Edward J. Dent and Benjamin Britten. The English ballad opera was imitated in Germany and led to the creation of the German *Singspiel*. In England it was succeeded in the latter part of the 18th cent. by a similar form of entertainment in which the music, however, was original, not borrowed.

F. KIDSON : *The Beggar's Opera* (1922).
W. E. SCHULTZ : *Gay's "Beggar's Opera"* (1923).

Ballard [ba-larr]. A French publishing firm, active from the middle of the 16th to the end of the 18th cent. Their publications included the scores of Lully's operas.

Ballata [bahl-lah'-tah], *I.* A 14th-cent. Italian verse-form, in which the refrain occurs at the beginning and end of the stanza. A large number of such poems were set by 14th-cent. Italian composers, notably Francesco Landini.

L. ELLINWOOD : *The Works of Francesco Landini* (1939).

Ballet. A dramatic entertainment presented by dancers in costume with musical accompaniment. Such entertainments existed in the ancient world and the Middle Ages and were an important part of the ceremonial festivities associated with French and Italian courts at the Renaissance. A landmark in the history of French ballet was the production of *Circe*, described as *Balet comique de la Royne* (The queen's dramatic ballet), for the marriage of the Duc de Joyeuse and Margaret of Lorraine at Versailles in 1581. The title does not mean that it was a comic ballet but indicates that it combined dancing (*ballet*) with a dramatic plot (*comédie*) to form an organic whole. As such it was an innovation, consisting not only of dancing and instrumental music, but also of spoken declamation and singing, and hence a forerunner of opera. The *ballet de cour*, as it was called, on account of its association with the French court, was extremely popular in the 17th cent., and led in England to the cultivation of the Jacobean masque. In France spoken declamation was abandoned at the beginning of the 17th cent. in favour of sung recitative. A large number of ballets were composed by Lully (1632-87), himself a dancer as well as a musician, who also joined with Molière to write *comédies-ballets*, a combination of spoken drama and ballet. When Lully turned to writing opera in 1673, it was only natural that he should incorporate ballet in the new form.

The association of ballet with opera continued in the 18th cent., but ballet also maintained its existence as an independent art, in which vocal music was superfluous. It was saved from developing into a conventional medium for virtuosity by Jean Georges Noverre (1727-1810), who published his *Lettres sur la danse et les ballets* in 1760. It was for Noverre that Mozart wrote his ballet *Les petits riens* in Paris in 1778. In the meantime other countries had adopted the French ballet, including Russia, where an Imperial School of Ballet was founded in the 18th cent. Tchaikovsky's *Swan Lake* (1876), *The Sleeping Beauty* (1889) and *Nutcracker* (1892), are evidence of the popularity of ballet in Russia in the 19th cent. It was from Russia that a new reform came at the beginning of the 20th cent. in the work of Sergei Diaghilev (1872-1929), who not only adapted existing music, such as Schumann's *Carnaval*, but also encouraged young composers to write ballets for him. Works like Stravinsky's *Firebird* (1910), *Petrouchka* (1912) and *The Rite of Spring* (1913), and Ravel's *Daphnis et Chloé* (1912) owe their origin to Diaghilev. The more recent revival of ballet in England has similarly led a number of well equipped composers to take an interest in the form, *e.g.* Vaughan Williams with *Job* (1931) and Arthur Bliss with *Checkmate* (1937). The old reproach that ballet music was frivolous and second-rate, though once justified, is no longer true.

The hey-day of ballet as a part of opera was in the latter part of the 19th cent., when it was considered an essential part of the Paris *grand opéra*. Modern taste, however, and the extraordinary development of ballet as an independent art have combined to favour the separation of opera and ballet into distinct categories, though the influence of ballet technique is often to be observed in the production of operas and some modern composers have re-admitted vocal music to the ballet, *e.g.* Stravinsky in *The Wedding* (1923) and Lord Berners in *A Wedding Bouquet* (1937).

C. W. BEAUMONT : *Complete Book of Ballets* (1937 & 1942).

J. G. NOVERRE : *Letters on Dancing and Ballets*, tr. C. W. Beaumont (1930).

H. PRUNIÈRES : *Le Ballet de cour en France* (1914).

S. SITWELL & C. W. BEAUMONT : *The Romantic Ballet* (1938).

Ballett (*I.* balletto). A composition for several voices, mainly homophonic in character, generally with a refrain to the words *fa la*. It originated in Italy at the end of the 16th cent. and is associated particularly with the name of Giovanni Gastoldi. It was imitated in other countries, including England. Thomas Morley, who mentions the ballett in his *Plaine and Easie Introduction to Practicall Musicke* (1597), p. 180, published a set in 1595, of which the best known is " Now is the month of maying." Italian and German editions of Morley's balletts appeared in 1595 and 1609. The refrain *fa la*, which is purely Italian in origin, became domesticated in other countries and in England survived as a symbol of light-hearted gaiety. From the prevalence of this refrain the ballett was often known by the title " fa la." The name " ballett " indicates that the music, which was generally in a lively, square-cut rhythm, was suitable for dancing, as Morley points out. Three of Gastoldi's balletts were adapted in Germany to Lutheran hymns. One of them, " A lieta vita," was fitted to David Spaiser's " O Gott, mein Herre " in 1609, and later in the 17th cent. to " In dir ist Freude," the words of which may be by Johann Lindemann. Bach included a prelude on " In dir ist Freude " in his *Orgelbüchlein* (Little Organ Book).

Balletto [bahl-let′-to], *I.* (1) *v.* BALLETT.

(2) A dance movement in a suite. The term was current in this sense in the 17th and 18th cent.

(3) Ballet.

Balling [bull′-ling], MICHAEL : *b.* Heidingsfeld a/M., Aug. 29, 1866 ; *d.* Darmstadt, Sept. 1, 1925. Conductor. Began as a viola-player and was a member of the orchestra at the Bayreuth Festival Theatre. Taught in New Zealand and founded a music school at Nelson. Succeeded Felix Mottl as conductor at Carlsruhe. Conducted at the Bayreuth Festivals, 1906-14. Succeeded Hans Richter as conductor of the Hallé Orchestra, Manchester, 1912-14. Director of music at Darmstadt, 1919. Editor of the complete works of Wagner, published by Breitkopf & Härtel.

Ballo [bahl′-lo], *I.* Dance. *Tempo di ballo*, in dance time.

Ballo in Maschera, Un [oon bahl′-lo een mahss′-keh-rah] (A Masked Ball). Opera in three acts by Verdi. Libretto by Antonio Somma (founded on Scribe's *Gustave III*). First performed, Rome, Feb. 17, 1859. For political reasons the action was transferred to New England. Riccardo, governor of Boston, who is in love with Amelia, the wife of his secretary, Renato, is the object of a conspiracy. To save him Renato changes cloaks, but discovering his wife's guilty secret joins the conspirators himself and murders Riccardo at a masked ball.

Balmer [bull′-mer], LUC : *b.* Munich, 1898. Swiss composer and conductor. A pupil of Ferruccio Busoni. Conductor at the Lucerne Kursaal, 1928-32 ; Municipal Theatre, Berne, 1934-5 ; Volks-Sinfoniekonzerte, Berne, 1935. His works include orchestral and chamber music and a setting of Petrarch's Sonnet 103 for chorus and orchestra.

Baltzar [bults′-arr], THOMAS: *b.* Lübeck, *c.* 1630 ; *d.* London, 1663. A brilliant violinist who was in the service of Queen Christina of Sweden in 1653 and came to England shortly afterwards, where his virtuosity created a great sensation (*v.* Evelyn, *Diary*, March 4, 1656). Appointed a member of Charles II's private music in 1661. Buried in Westminster Abbey.

Banchieri [bahnk-yeh′-ree], ADRIANO : *b.* Bologna, Sept. 3, 1568 ; *d.* there, 1634. Composer, theorist and poet. Organist of the monastery of S. Michele in Bosco, near Bologna, and founder of the *Accademia de' floridi* in Bologna. His compositions include madrigal dramas (similar to Orazio Vecchi's *L'Amfiparnaso*), concerted instrumental music, organ works (*v.* L. Torchi, *L'arte musicale in Italia*, iii) and church music. He was one of the first writers to give instruction in playing from figured bass in his treatise *L'organo suonario* (2nd ed., 1611).

F.T. ARNOLD : *The Art of Accompaniment from a Thorough-Bass* (1931).

Band. A term once applied to any large-scale group of instrumentalists but now reserved for ensembles other than the concert orchestra. *v.* BRASS BAND, JAZZ BAND, MILITARY BAND, ORCHESTRA.

Bandora. *v.* PANDORA.

Bandurria [bun-door′-ryah], *Sp.* A Spanish instrument of the guitar family, similar to the English CITHER, with six double strings generally played with a plectrum.

Banister, JOHN : *d.* London, Oct. 3, 1679. Violinist. Sent abroad by Charles II in 1661 to study French instrumental music and appointed director of a select band of 12 string-players on his return in 1662. He lost this position in 1667 (*v.* Pepys, *Diary*, Feb. 20, 1667) but remained in the king's service until his death. In 1672 he began a series of public concerts (among the first of their kind) in Whitefriars. His compositions include music for the stage.

Banjo. An American negro instrument of the guitar family. Its body, unlike that of the guitar, consists of a shallow metal drum, covered with parchment on the top side and open at the bottom. Its strings, which vary in number from five to nine, are played either with the fingers or with a plectrum. It is supposed to have been brought to America by slaves from West Africa and to have owed its origin to the activities of Arab traders in Africa. As a result of its introduction into jazz bands a tenor model has been made with four strings, tuned like the viola.

Bantock, GRANVILLE : *b.* London, Aug. 7, 1868 ; *d.* there, Oct. 16, 1946. Composer and conductor. Director of music, The Tower, New Brighton, 1897 ; principal, Birmingham and Midland Institute School of Music, 1900-34 ; professor, Birmingham University, 1908-34. Editor, *New Quarterly Musical Review*, 1893-6. Knighted, 1930. As a conductor he worked untiringly to further the interests of young English composers. As a composer he was very prolific and attracted by the local colour of a number of different countries, from Scotland to China. His works, which are in the Romantic tradition, include :

(a) ORCHESTRA : *Helena* (variations) ; *The Pierrot of the Minute* (overture); *Dante and Beatrice*; *Fifine at the Fair*; *Hebridean Symphony*; *The Frogs* (overture).

(b) CHORUS AND ORCHESTRA: *Christ in the Wilderness*; *Omar Khayyám* (3 parts); *The Great God Pan*; *Song of Songs*; *The Pilgrim's Progress.*

(c) UNACCOMPANIED CHOIR: *Atalanta in Calydon*; *Vanity of Vanities*; *A Pageant of Human Life.*

(d) OPERA: *The Seal-Woman.*

(e) CHAMBER MUSIC: Viola sonata.

(*f*) SONGS: *Sappho* (9 fragments).

Bar. (1) Properly a vertical line drawn across one or more staves of music, now generally known in England as "bar-line" (*Fr.* barre, *G.* Taktstrich, *I.* barra). The original purpose of the bar-line was to guide the eye when music was presented simultaneously on several staves or in TABLATURE. Hence it was used in 16th-cent. keyboard music but was not necessary for the separate parts of concerted music for voices or instruments. When concerted music began to appear in score at the end of the 16th cent. the bar-line was naturally employed there also, and it was found convenient to draw the lines at regular intervals. The increasing rhythmical symmetry of the 17th cent., which became stereotyped in the 18th and 19th cent., led to a false association between the bar-line and ACCENT. As a result, when 20th-cent. composers came to abandon the regular rhythmical periods current in the 18th and 19th cent., they were supposed to be in revolt against the "tyranny of the bar-line." In fact, they submitted to the "tyranny" more wholeheartedly than their predecessors, since they found it necessary to change the length of the bars whenever the rhythm changed. It is more logical, and more practical, to regard the bar-line as a convenient sign of subdivision, which may or may not coincide with the rhythmical accent of the moment. This does not exclude the use of bars of different lengths where the change is appropriate. The essential in all musical notation is that the composer's intentions should be perfectly clear to the performer.

(2) The space between two bar-lines, known in America as "measure" (*Fr.* mesure, *G.* Takt, *I.* battuta). *v.* (1).

(3) *G.* The name commonly given to a song-form borrowed by the German MINNESINGER from the French TROUVÈRES, and used by them and their successors, the MEISTERSINGER. It consists of two *Stollen* (lit. "props"), each set to the same music, and an *Abgesang* ("after-song"), the whole forming a complete stanza or *Gesätz* (*cf.* Wagner, *Die Meistersinger*, i, 3 & iii, 2). The form may be represented by the formula *a a b*. It is quite common, however, for the *Abgesang* to end with part or the whole of the melody of the *Stollen*:

WALTHER VON DER VOGELWEIDE (*c. 1200*)

Here we have the germs of the principle of recapitulation, which in one form or another has played an important part in musical structure, particularly in instrumental music.

Barber, SAMUEL : *b.* Westchester (Pa.), March 9, 1910. Composer. Studied at the Curtis Institute, Philadelphia. Pulitzer Prize, 1935 & 1936. His works, which show a respect for tradition as well as an original mind, include two symphonies, overture to *The School for Scandal*, *Capricorn Concerto* for flute, oboe, trumpet and strings, violin concerto, cello concerto, Adagio for strings, 2 string quartets, cello sonata, *Dover Beach* for voice and string quartet, choral work and songs. The Adagio for strings, adapted from a movement in the first string quartet, has won wide popularity.

Barber of Seville, The. *v.* BARBIERE DI SIVIGLIA.

Barbiere di Siviglia, Il [eel barrb-yeh′-reh dee see-veel′-yah] (The Barber of Seville). Comic opera in two acts by Rossini, originally entitled *Almaviva o sia L'inutile precauzione* (Almaviva, or the Fruitless Precaution). Libretto by Cesare Sterbini (founded on Beaumarchais's *Le Barbier de Séville*). First performed, Rome, Feb. 20, 1816. Count Almaviva, in love with Rosina, the ward of Dr. Bartolo, succeeds with the help of Figaro (the barber of Seville) in defeating the doctor's attempts to separate them and wins his bride. Mozart's *Le nozze di Figaro* (1786) is founded on Beaumarchais's *Le Mariage de Figaro*, which is a sequel to *Le Barbier de Séville*. An earlier adaptation of *Le Barbier de Séville* by Giuseppe Petrosellini, with music by Paisiello, was first performed at St. Petersburg in 1782.

Barbieri [barrb-yeh′-ree], FRANCISCO ASENJO : *b.* Madrid, Aug. 3, 1823 ; *d.* there, Feb. 19, 1894. Composer and musicologist. He began his career as a clarinettist and a café pianist. He wrote a number of comic operas, of a characteristically Spanish type, of which the one-act *Pan y Toros* (Madrid, 1864), dealing with the painter Goya, has proved the most successful. He also edited *Cancionero musical de los siglos XV y XVI*, an important collection of Spanish part-songs of the 15th and 16th cent.

Barbier von Bagdad, Der [dair barr-beer′ fon bug′-dut] (The Barber of Baghdad). Comic opera in two acts by Cornelius. Libretto by the composer. First performed, Weimar, Dec. 15, 1858.

Barbireau [barr-bee-ro], JACQUES : *b.c.* 1408 ; *d.* Antwerp, Aug. 4, 1491. Flemish composer. Master of the choristers, Antwerp Cathedral, from 1447. His compositions include church music and *chansons*.

Barbirolli, JOHN : *b.* London, Dec. 2, 1899. English conductor of Italian origin. Studied at Trinity College of Music and the Royal Academy of Music and began his career as a cellist. First appeared as a conductor in 1925, joining the British National Opera Company in 1926. Conductor, Scottish Orchestra, 1933-7 ; New York Philharmonic-Symphony Orchestra, 1937-40 ; Hallé Orchestra, 1943. Knighted, 1949.

Barblan [barr-blũn], OTTO : *b.* Scanfs (Engadine), March 22, 1860 ; *d.* Geneva, Nov. 19, 1943. Swiss composer, organist and conductor. Studied at Stuttgart Conservatorium. Organist, Geneva Cathedral, from 1887. Conductor, Société de chant sacré, 1892-1938. Teacher of organ-playing and conducting, Geneva Conservatoire. His works include music for the Calven festival play, *Ode patriotique*, Passion according to St. Luke, organ and piano music and partsongs.

Barcarola [barr-cah-roh′-lah], *I.* Barcarolle.

Barcarolle, *E. Fr.* (*G.* Barkarole, *I.* barcarola). From *I.* barca, "boat." Properly a boating-song sung by the gondoliers at Venice, and hence applied to any piece of vocal or instrumental music in the same rhythm (6/8 or 12/8). Familiar examples are Chopin's for piano (Op. 60) and Offenbach's in *Les Contes d'Hoffmann* (1881), which was originally part of *Die Rheinnixen* (1864). Fauré wrote 13 barcarolles for piano. A large number of compositions are in fact barcarolles, though not so described, *e.g.* Schubert's song *Auf dem Wasser zu singen* and some of Mendelssohn's *Lieder ohne Worte* (Op. 19, no. 6, Op. 30, no. 6, Op. 62, no. 5).

Bard. Originally a Celtic minstrel, whose duties included the composition of extempore songs in honour of a patron. In medieval Wales they also had considerable political influence. An early 17th-cent. manuscript of instrumental music, entitled *Musica neu Beroriaeth* (Music of the Britons) and written in TABLATURE (facsimile edition, Cardiff, 1936), purports to record the practice of a much earlier age, but its authority as a record of medieval bardic music is obviously uncertain. The practice of bardic gatherings was revived in the 19th cent. at the Welsh *Eisteddfodau* (plur. of *Eisteddfod*, "session"), which are now very largely musical competition festivals.

P. CROSSLEY-HOLLAND : "Secular Homophonic Music in Wales in the Middle Ages" (*Music & Letters*, Apr. 1942).

A. DOLMETSCH : *Translations from the Penllyn Manuscript of Ancient Harp Music* (1937).

Bardi [barr'-dee], GIOVANNI : *b.* 1534, *d.* 1612. Count of Vernio. A Florentine nobleman, himself a composer, whose house was a meeting-place of poets, musicians and scholars interested in the problem of creating a music-drama on the lines of Greek tragedy. From these gatherings the first operas originated.

Bärenreiter [bay'-rĕn-rite-er]. A firm of music-publishers founded at Augsburg in 1924 by Karl Vötterle and now established at Cassel, with a branch at Basle.

Bargiel [barr'-geel], WOLDEMAR : *b.* Berlin, Oct. 3, 1828 ; *d.* there, Feb. 23, 1897. Teacher and composer, a step-brother of Clara Schumann. Teacher at Cologne Conservatorium, 1859 ; director, Institute of the Maatschappij tot bevordering van toonkunst, Rotterdam, 1865 ; teacher at the Königliche Hochschule für Music, Berlin, 1874. His compositions, which were strongly influenced by Schumann, include a symphony, three orchestral overtures, chamber music, piano music and choral works.

Baritone (*Gr.* βαρύτονος, deep-sounding). (1) A high bass voice, with a range of roughly two octaves from

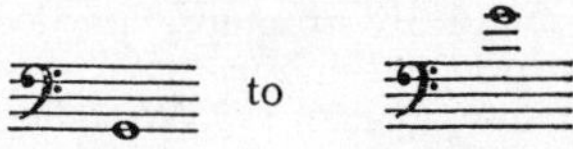

It is much used in operatic music. Sometimes written "barytone."

(2) A brass instrument of the SAXHORN family (*Fr.* bugle ténor, *G.* Tenorhorn, *I.* flicorno tenore). It is built in B♭ at the same pitch as the EUPHONIUM, but has a smaller bore and only three valves. It is used only in wind bands and is written for as a transposing instrument. The written compass is

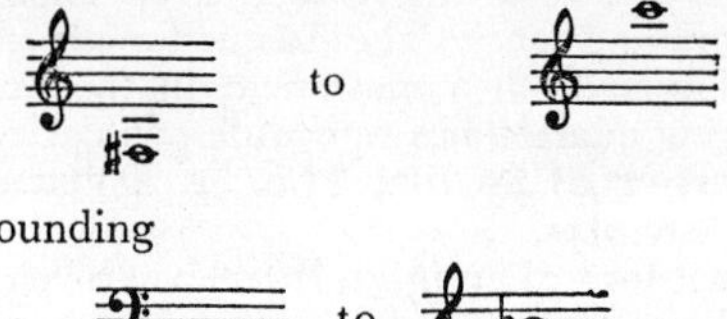

sounding

to

(3) The baritone clef is the F clef on the third line :

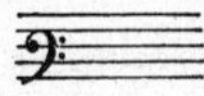

now obsolete.

(4) Baritone oboe. *v.* HECKELPHONE.

(5) Baritone saxophone. *v.* SAXOPHONE.

Barkarole [barr-ca-roh'-ler], *G.* Barcarolle.

Bar-Line. *v.* BAR (1).

Bärmann [bair'-mun], HEINRICH JOSEPH : *b.* Potsdam, Feb. 14, 1784 ; *d.* Munich, June 11, 1847. Clarinet-player, for whom Weber and Mendelssohn wrote pieces. His son Karl (*b.* Munich, 1811 ; *d.* there, May 24, 1885) was also a clarinet-player.

Barnard, JOHN : *fl.* early 17th cent. A minor canon of St. Paul's Cathedral, who published in separate part-books first printed collection of English cathedral music, under the title *The First Book of Selected Church Musick* (1641). A second collection survives in manuscript in the Royal College of Music library. A manuscript score of the contents of the first collection, made from the printed part-books and other sources, is in the British Museum (Add. 30,087).

Barnby, JOSEPH: *b.* York, Aug. 12, 1838; *d.* London, Jan. 28, 1896. Composer, conductor and organist. Studied at the Royal Academy of Music. Organist, St. Anne's, Soho, 1871-86. Precentor of Eton, 1876-92; principal, Guildhall School of Music, 1892-6. Conductor, Royal Choral Society, 1872-96. Knighted, 1892. He did valuable pioneer work in introducing Bach's Passions to English audiences. His numerous compositions are unimportant.

Barnett, (1) JOHN: *b.* Bedford, July 15, 1802; *d.* Apr. 16, 1890. English opera composer, the son of German and Hungarian parents (the father's name was originally Beer) and a second cousin of Meyerbeer. His most important work was *The Mountain Sylph* (London, 1834), the first of a series of English romantic operas by Balfe, Benedict, Wallace and other composers.

(2) JOHN FRANCIS: *b.* London, Oct. 16, 1837; *d.* there, Nov. 24, 1916. Nephew of (1). Pianist and composer. Studied at the Royal Academy of Music and Leipzig Conservatorium. Taught at the Royal College of Music and the Guildhall School of Music. His works include a symphony and other orchestral pieces, chamber music, piano music, and a number of cantatas, among them a setting of Coleridge's *The Ancient Mariner* (1867). He completed Schubert's symphony in E major (sometimes said to be in E minor on account of its opening Adagio) from the composer's sketches. He also published *Musical Reminiscences and Impressions* (1906).

Baron [ba-rone'], ERNST GOTTLIEB: *b.* Breslau, Feb. 17, 1696; *d.* Berlin, Apr. 12, 1760. German lutenist, who held a number of court appointments and published several theoretical works, including the important *Historich-theoretische und practische Untersuchung des Instruments der Lauten* (1727).

Baroni [bah-ro'-nee], LEONORA: *b.* Mantua, 1611. A famous singer, said to have been the mistress of Cardinal Mazarin, who brought her to Paris in 1644 to further his efforts to establish Italian opera at the French court. Her praises were sung by a number of poets, including Milton (*Ad Leonoram Romae canentem*), who met her in Rome in 1638. Her mother, Adriana, and her sister, Catarina, were also well-known as singers.

Baroque (*Port.* barroco, "rough pearl"). Originally "grotesque," but now used as a technical term to describe the lavish architectural style of the 17th and early 18th cent. It has been borrowed by historians of music as a general description of the music of the same period, which may be said to exhibit similar characteristics. A distinction is common between early baroque music (Gabrieli, Monteverdi, Frescobaldi, Carissimi, etc.) and late baroque music (Alessandro Scarlatti, Bach, Handel etc.). The pre-baroque period (late 15th and 16th cent.) is generally called "Renaissance," the post-baroque (late 18th cent. "Rococo."

v. RENAISSANCE MUSIC.

Barra [barr'-rah], *I.* Bar-line.

Barraine [barr-en], ELSA: *b.* Paris, Feb. 13, 1910. Composer, a pupil of Dukas. *Prix de Rome*, 1929. Her compositions include 2 symphonies, ballets and other stage music, chamber music, and music for films and radio.

Barre [barr], *Fr.* (1) Bar-line.

(2) *v.* CAPOTASTO.

Barrel Organ. A mechanical organ, in which air is admitted to the pipes by means of pins on a rotating barrel. It was very common in England in the late 18th and early 19th cent. and was used in village churches, where the provision of interchangeable barrels made it possible to play a limited number of the best-known hymn-tunes. A complete chromatic compass was unusual, so that the choice of keys was restricted. The term was applied incorrectly to the 19th-cent. street piano, also operated by a barrel-and-pin mechanism, and is currently used in this sense.

Bartered Bride, The. *v.* PRODANÁ NEVĚSTA.

Barthélémon [barr-tay-lay-mon͡], FRANÇOIS HIPPOLYTE: *b.* Bordeaux,

July 27, 1741; *d.* London, July 23, 1808. French violinist and composer, active in England (where he was leader of the orchestra at the opera and Marylebone Gardens), Ireland and France. He was associated with Haydn when the latter visited London in 1791-2 and 1794-5. His works include music for the stage, violin sonatas and concertos and a hymn-tune, "Awake, my soul," which is still popular (*E.H.* 257, *S.P.* 25, i).

Bartlet, JOHN: *fl. c.* 1610. Composer of a volume of lute-songs entitled *A Booke of Ayres with a Triplicitie of Musicke* (1606). Modern edition in *E.S.L.S.*, 2nd ser.

Bartók [borr'-toke], BÉLA: *b.* Nagyszentmiklós, March 25, 1881; *d.* New York, Sept. 26, 1945. Hungarian composer and pianist. Began to compose at 9, appeared in public as a pianist at 10. Studied at Royal Hungarian Musical Academy, Budapest, where he became teacher of the piano in 1907. With Zoltan Kodály devoted himself to the study and collection of genuine Hungarian folk music, as opposed to the international gypsy music generally known as "Hungarian." He also studied Roumanian and Slovak folk music. These studies helped to emancipate his creative talent from earlier influences (which included Liszt and Strauss). The great bulk of his work is the product of a highly original mind, which sometimes finds expression in an almost aggressive objectivity. His music is "modern" not in obedience to any fashionable creed or artificial system but in its up-to-date solution of the problems of composition. One becomes conscious of a sincere artist wrestling with the raw material of composition. The result may sometimes be forbidding, but it is always impressive. Bartók was one of the most "professional" composers of our time. He was also a fine pianist. A record of his work as a teacher is to be found in the collection of graded pieces called *Mikrokosmos*. His principal works are:

(a) ORCHESTRA: Rhapsody for piano and orchestra; 2 suites; 3 piano concertos; 2 rhapsodies for violin and orchestra; Music for strings, percussion and celesta; Divertimento for strings; concerto for orchestra; violin concerto.

(b) STAGE: *Duke Bluebeard's Castle* (opera); *The Wooden Prince* (ballet); *The Wonderful Mandarin* (pantomime).

(c) CHAMBER MUSIC: 6 string quartets; 2 violin sonatas; rhapsody for cello and piano; sonata for 2 pianos and percussion.

(d) PIANO: Sonatina; sonata; *Allegro barbaro*; *Mikrokosmos*; bagatelles, sketches, études, &c.

(e) CHORAL: *Cantata profana.*

Also numerous arrangements of folksongs for voices and instruments.

B. BARTÓK: *Hungarian Folk Music*, tr. M. D. Calvocoressi (1931).
E. HARASZTI: *Béla Bartók* (1938).
H. STEVENS: *The Life and Music of Béla Bartók* (1953).

Baryton. (1) *F.* [ba-ree-tōn], *G.* [ba-ri-tone]. Baritone.

(2) *G.* (*I.* viola di bordone). A bowed string instrument in use in Germany during the 18th cent. It originated in the late 17th cent. and became obsolete in the 19th. Its foundation was a bass viol with six bowed strings, but to these were added a large number of additional strings which vibrated in sympathy (as on the VIOLA D'AMORE). As the neck of the instrument was open the sympathetic strings could also be plucked from behind by the player's left thumb. It was a favourite instrument of Prince Nicolas Esterházy, for whom Haydn composed 125 trios for baryton, viola and cello. Burney describes the playing of Andreas Lidl (formerly in Prince Esterházy's service) on the baryton:

> "The late Mr. Lidl played with exquisite taste and expression upon this ungrateful instrument [*i.e.* the bass viol], with the additional embarrassment of base strings at the back of the neck, with which he accompanied himself, an admirable expedient in a desert, or even in a house, where there is but one musician; but to be at the trouble of accompanying yourself in a great concert, surrounded by idle per-

formers who could take the trouble off your hands, and leave them more at liberty to execute, express, and embellish the principal melody, seemed at best a work of supererogation."
(*A General History of Music*, vol. iv, pp. 679-80)

(3) *G.* Short for BARYTONHORN.

Barytone. *v.* BARITONE.

Barytonhorn [ba-ri-tone'-horrn], *G.* Euphonium.

Baskische Trommel [busk'-ish-er trom'-el], *G.* (*Fr.* tambour de basque). Tambourine.

Bass (*Fr.* basse, *G.* Bass, *I.* basso). In general, "low" as opposed to "high." Used particularly of the lowest part of a composition, whether for one or more instruments or for voices —the foundation (*Gr.* βάσις) on which the harmony is built. Also in the following special senses:

(1) The lowest adult male voice, with a range of roughly two octaves, from

to

(2) Prefixed to the name of an instrument it indicates either the largest member of the family or (in cases where a contrabass instrument exists) one size smaller than the largest, *e.g.* bass viol, bass clarinet.

(3) Short for double bass, also (in military bands) for bass tuba.

(4) The bass clef is the F clef on the fourth line:

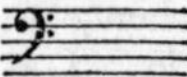

v. FIGURED BASS.

Bassani [bahss-sah'-nee], GIOVANNI BATTISTA: *b.* Padua, *c.* 1657; *d.* Bergamo, Oct. 1, 1716. Organist at Ferrara Cathedral and composer of oratorios, operas, church music and instrumental works.

Bass-Bar. A strip of wood glued inside the belly of members of the viol and violin families immediately under the left foot of the bridge. *v.* VIOLIN.

Bass-Baritone. A term sometimes used to indicate a bass voice with a good command of the higher register.

Bass Clarinet [*Fr.* clarinette basse, *G.* Bassklarinette, *I.* clarinetto basso, clàrone). A single-reed instrument, built an octave lower than the clarinet, with a metal bell turned upwards for convenience. It was formerly made in B♭ and A but is now made only in B♭. The compass is from

to

sounding

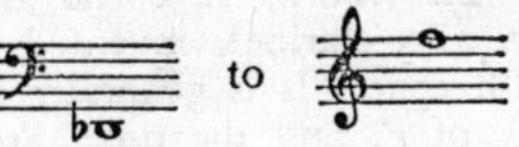

v. TRANSPOSING INSTRUMENTS.
A. CARSE: *Musical Wind Instruments* (1939).

Bass Drum (*Fr.* grosse caisse, *G.* grosse Trommel, *I.* gran cassa). A percussion instrument of indeterminate pitch. It consists of a large wooden shell, cylindrical in shape, covered on one or both sides with vellum. It is normally beaten with a stick having a large felt-covered knob, but it can also be played with timpani sticks if a roll is required (*v.* TIMPANI).

Basse chiffrée [buss sheef-ray], *Fr.* Figured bass.

Basse danse [buss dũnce], *Fr.* Lit. "low dance," so called because the feet were kept close to the ground, in contrast to leaping dances such as the GALLIARD. A court dance current in France in the 15th and early 16th cent. It was moderately slow, in duple or triple time, and was described by Thoinot Arbeau (1588) as "a manner of dancing full of honour and modesty." The *basse danse* was often followed by the *tordion,* a quicker dance, just as the pavane was followed by the galliard. The following example dates from the middle of the 16th cent. (the note values have been halved):

ANON. (*Les Maîtres musiciens de la Renaissance française vol. xxiii, p. 6*)

Basse fondamentale [buss fon͡-da-mun͡-tull), *Fr. v.* FUNDAMENTAL BASS.

Basset Horn [*Fr.* cor de basset, *G.* Bassethorn, *I.* corno di bassetto). An alto clarinet, invented in the late 18th cent. It is generally built in the key of F, and the notes are written a fifth higher than they sound. The compass is from

sounding

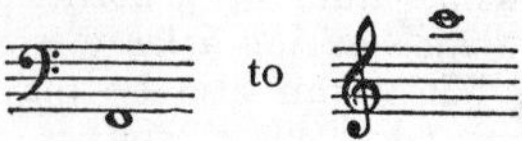

It was used by Mozart (*e.g.* Requiem, *Die Zauberflöte*) and has been revived by Richard Strauss (*Elektra*). The name is probably due to the fact that the shape was originally curved. *v.* TRANSPOSING INSTRUMENTS.

A. CARSE : *Musical Wind Instruments* (1939).

Bass Flute (*Fr.* flûte alto, *G.* Altflöte, *I.* flautone). An instrument built a fourth lower than the normal FLUTE, sometimes known more correctly as the alto flute. The compass is from

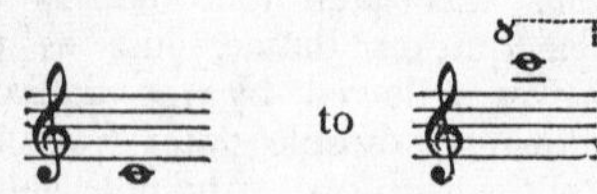

sounding

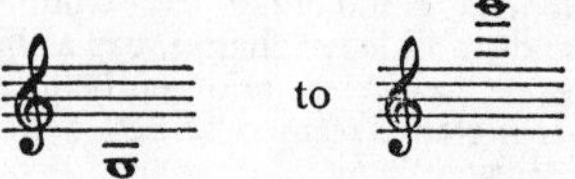

v. TRANSPOSING INSTRUMENTS.

A. CARSE : *Musical Wind Instruments* (1939).

Bass Horn (*Fr.* serpent droit, *G.* Basshorn). An obsolete instrument, dating from the late 18th cent. It consisted of a SERPENT of wood or brass made in the shape of a bassoon. It was also known as the Russian bassoon.

Bassklarinette [buss′-cla-ree-net′-ter], *G.* Bass clarinet.

Basso [bahss′-so], *I.* Bass. *Basso continuo* (lit. " continuous bass "), figured bass, *i.e.* the bass line of a composition marked with figures to indicate the harmonies to be played on a keyboard instrument. *v.* FIGURED BASS. *Basso ostinato* (lit. " obstinate bass "), ground bass, *i.e.* a figure repeated in the bass throughout a composition, while the upper parts change. The lament at the end of Purcell's *Dido and Aeneas* (" When I am laid in earth ") is a good example. *v.* GROUND BASS.

Basso continuo [bahss′-so con-tee′-noo-o], *I. v.* BASSO.

Basson [buss-on͡], *Fr.* Bassoon. *Basson russe*, Russian bassoon.

Bassoon (*Fr.* basson, *G.* Fagott, *I.* fagotto). A double-reed instrument, dating from the 16th cent., with a compass from

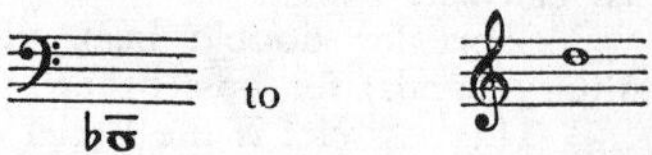

It is made of a wooden tube doubled back on itself, hence the name *fagotto*, a bundle of sticks. The double bassoon (*Fr.* contrebasson, *G.* Kontrafagott, *I.* contrafagotto) is built an octave lower and is made either of wood or of metal. There is a solo for the double bassoon in Ravel's *Ma Mère l'Oye*.

A. CARSE : *Musical Wind Instruments* (1939).
L. G. LANGWILL : *The Bassoon* (in Hinrichsen's *Musical Year Book*, 1947, pp. 426-63).

Basso ostinato [bahss′-so oss-tee-nah′-toh], *I. v.* BASSO.

Bassposaune [buss'-po-zown'-er], *G.* Bass trombone.

Bass Trombone. *v.* TROMBONE.

Basstrompete [buss'-trom-pay'-ter], *G.* Bass trumpet.

Bass Trumpet. *v.* TRUMPET.

Bass Tuba. *v.* TUBA.

Bass Viol. *v.* VIOL.

Bastien und Bastienne [bust-yañ oont bust-yen]. Operetta in one act by Mozart (aged 12). Libretto by F. W. Weiskern from C. S. Favart's *Les Amours de Bastien et Bastienne* (a parody of Rousseau's *Le Devin du Village*). First performed in the garden theatre of Anton Mesmer (inventor of animal magnetism) in Vienna, 1768.

Bataille [ba-ta-yer], GABRIEL : *b. c.* 1575 ; *d.* Paris, Dec. 17, 1630. Lutenist at the French court. A selection from his *Airs de différents autheurs mis en tablature de luth* (Songs by various composers arranged with lute accompaniment, 1608-18) has been published by Peter Warlock.

Bate, STANLEY : *b.* Plymouth, Dec. 12, 1913. Composer and pianist. Studied at the R.C.M., where he won several prizes, and subsequently with Nadia Boulanger and Hindemith. From 1942-9 he was in the United States, where he appeared as soloist in his own works. His compositions include 2 symphonies, 2 piano concertos, 2 violin concertos, harpsichord concerto, cello concerto, piano works and several ballets.

Bateson, THOMAS : *b. c.* 1570 ; *d.* Dublin, March, 1630. Organist successively of Chester and Dublin Cathedrals, and apparently the first B.Mus. of Trinity College, Dublin. Composer of two sets of madrigals (1604 & 1618). Modern edition in *E.M.S.*, xxi & xxii.

Bathe, WILLIAM : *b.* Apr. 2, 1564 ; *d.* Madrid, June 17, 1614. Author of *A Briefe Introduction to the True Art of Musicke* (1584), the first book on the theory of music printed in England, and of *A Briefe Introduction to the Skill of Song* (1600). He was at first in the service of Queen Elizabeth but subsequently became a Jesuit priest.

Baton, RENÉ. *v.* RHENÉ-BATON.

Batten, ADRIAN : *d.* London, 1637. Organist of St. Paul's Cathedral and composer of church music. He compiled an organ score containing a large number of 16th-cent. church compositions, known as the Batten Organ Book (now in St. Michael's College, Tenbury, 791).

Batterie [butt-ree], *Fr.* (1) = BATTERY.

(2) The percussion section of the orchestra.

Battery. A 17th- and 18th-cent. term for ARPEGGIO.

Battishill, JONATHAN : *b.* London, May 1738 ; *d.* Islington, Dec. 10, 1801. Organist and composer of music for the church and stage.

Battle Music. Descriptive pieces dealing with war were popular from the 16th to the 19th cent. They include Jannequin's part-song *La Guerre* (1529, reprinted in H. Expert, *Les Maîtres musiciens de la Renaissance française*, vii), Andrea Gabrieli's *Aria di battaglia* for wind instruments (1590, reprinted in *Istituzioni e monumenti dell' arte musicale italiana*, i), William Byrd's *Battell* for virginals (in *My Ladye Nevells Booke*), Johann Kaspar Kerll's *Battaglia* for harpsichord (17th cent., printed in *D.T.B.*, ii (2),), Kotzwara's *The Battle of Prague* for piano (1788) and Beethoven's *Wellington's Sieg oder die Schlacht bei Vittoria* (Wellington's Victory or the Battle of Vittoria) for orchestra (1813).

Battle of the Huns. *v.* HUNNENSCHLACHT.

Battuta [baht-too'-tah], *I.* (1) "Beat." *A battuta*, in strict time. *Senza battuta*, without any regular beat, *i.e.* in free time (*e.g.* in recitative).

(2) Particularly the first beat in the bar, hence "bar." *Ritmo di tre battute*, three-bar rhythm, *i.e.* every group of three bars forms a rhythmical unit.

Bauer [bow'-er], HAROLD : *b.* New Malden, Apr. 28, 1873 ; *d.* Miami, March 12, 1951. Pianist, of mixed German and English parentage. He was a pupil of Paderewski, and for a time was associated with Thibaud and Casals in the performance of piano trios. He founded the Beethoven Association of New York (1919), a society for the performance of chamber music.

Bäumker [boym'-ker], WILHELM : *b.* Elberfeld, Oct. 25, 1842 ; *d.* Rurich-Aachen, March 3, 1905. Priest and historian. His principal work was *Das katholische deutsche Kirchenlied in seinen Singweisen von der frühesten Zeiten* (3 vols., 1883-91).

Bax, ARNOLD EDWARD TREVOR : *b.* London, Nov. 8, 1883 : *d.* Cork, Oct. 3, 1953. Composer. Studied at the R.A.M. under Frederick Corder. Knighted, 1937. Master of the King's music, 1942. His style is romantic and is powerfully influenced by his affection for Ireland and Irish folklore. His principal compositions are :

(a) ORCHESTRA : 7 symphonies ; *The Garden of Fand* ; *Tintagel* ; *November Woods* ; Overture to a Picaresque Comedy ; cello concerto ; violin concerto.

(b) CHAMBER MUSIC : Nonet ; octet ; string quintet ; oboe quintet ; 3 string quartets ; piano quintet ; trio for flute, viola and harp ; 3 violin sonatas ; sonatas for viola, cello, clarinet and piano ; sonata for viola and harp.

(c) CHORAL WORKS : *Mater ora filium* ; *Of a rose I sing* ; *This worlde's joy* ; *St. Patrick's Breastplate* ; *The Morning Watch*.

(d) PIANO : 4 sonatas.

He has also composed numerous songs and folksong arrangements and has published an autobiography of his early years under the title *Farewell, my Youth* (1943).

Bayreuth [by-royt']. A town in Franconia where Wagner built a festival theatre, provided by public subscription, for the sole performance of his own operas. The first production was the tetralogy *Der Ring des Nibelungen*, performed in 1876. After Wagner's death in 1883 the theatre was controlled in turn by his widow Cosima, his son Siegfried and his daughter-in-law Winifred. Since 1951 it has been managed by his grandsons, Wolfgang and Wieland.

B.B.C. Symphony Orchestra. Founded in 1930 by the British Broadcasting Corporation. In addition to studio broadcasts, which provide its principal activity, it also appears at public concerts, including the Promenade Concerts. Conductors : Adrian Boult, 1930-50 ; Malcolm Sargent, 1950-6 ; Rudolf Schwarz, 1956.

Be [bay], *G.* Flat. So called because the sign for the flat (♭) was originally shaped like a small rounded B. *v.* HEXACHORD.

Beach, AMY MARCY : *b.* Henniker (New Hampshire), Sept. 5, 1867 ; *d.* New York, Dec. 27, 1944. Generally known as Mrs. H. H. Beach (her maiden name was Cheney). American pianist and composer, who showed great precocity as a child. Her compositions include orchestral and choral works, piano pieces and songs.

Bear, The. *v.* OURS.

Bearbeitung [ber-arr'-by-tŏŏng], *G.* Arrangement.

Beard (1), JOHN : *b. c.* 1717 ; *d.* Feb. 5, 1791. English tenor, who sang in many of Handel's oratorios and appeared as Macheath in *The Beggar's Opera*. As a boy he was a chorister in the Chapel Royal. The tenor solos in *Israel in Egypt*, *Messiah*, *Samson*, *Judas Maccabeus* and *Jephtha* were written for him.

(2) PAUL : *b.* Birmingham, Aug. 4, 1901. English violinist. Studied at the R.A.M., where he subsequently taught the violin. Leader, City of Birmingham Orchestra, 1920 ; B.B.C. Symphony Orchestra, 1936.

Beat. (1) The unit of measurement in music, indicated in choral and orchestral works by the motion of the conductor's stick (*Fr.* temps, *G.* Zählzeit, Schlag, *I.* battuta). The number of beats in a bar depends on the time-signature and on the speed of the movement. A movement in 4/4 time may have eight beats if very slow, four if the speed is moderate, two if it is very fast. In exceptional cases there may be only one beat in the bar. This occurs most frequently in very quick movements in 3/4 or 3/8 time.

(2) An old English name for more than one kind of ornament. The following are the signs and explanations given respectively by (a) Christopher Simpson (1659), (b) Purcell (1696), (c) Geminiani (1749) :

Béatrice et Bénédict [bay-a-treece ay bay-nay-deekt] (Beatrice and Benedict). Opera in two acts by Berlioz. Libretto by the composer (based on Shakespeare's *Much Ado about Nothing*). First performed, Baden-Baden, Aug. 9, 1862.

Bebung [bay′-bŏŏng], *G.* A form of VIBRATO used on the clavichord. The finger repeatedly presses the key without releasing it. The metal tangent which presses on the string responds and by slightly increasing the tension of the string produces minute variations of pitch, similar to those produced on the violin by the player's finger. The *Bebung* was indicated by a special sign :

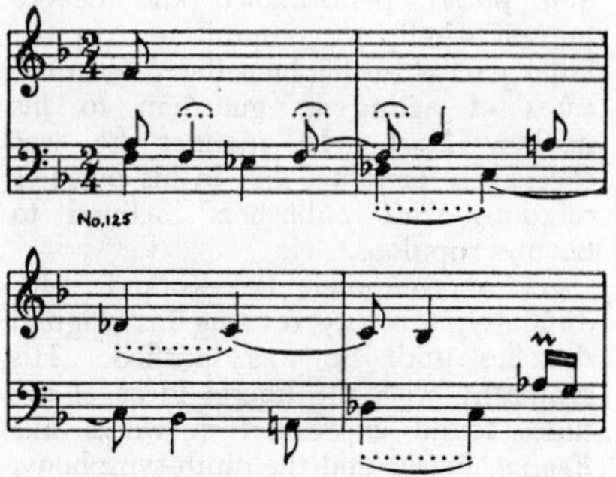

C. P. E. BACH, *Sechs Clavier-Sonaten* (1779).

Bécarre [bay-carr], *Fr.* Natural. (The name is due to the fact that the sign for the natural (♮) was originally a square-shaped B, *i.e.* a *bé carré*. *v.* HEXACHORD.

Bechstein [be*sh*′-shtine]. A firm of piano-makers founded in Berlin by Friedrich Wilhelm Carl Bechstein (1826-1900) in 1856. The Bechstein Hall in Wigmore Street, London, opened by the sons of F. W. C. Bechstein in 1901, became the Wigmore Hall in 1917.

Beck [beck], (1) CONRAD : *b.* Lohn, 1901. Swiss composer. Studied at Zürich, Paris and Berlin. His works include 6 symphonies, concerto for piano, violin, viola, cello, flute and harpsichord, *Der Tod des Oedipus* (chorus and orchestra), *Angelus Silesius* (oratorio), *La Grande Ourse* (ballet), and 4 string quartets.

(2) FRANZ : *b.* Mannheim, Feb. 15, 1723 ; *d.* Bordeaux, Dec. 31, 1809. German composer, a pupil of Johann Stamitz. He moved to France, where he became known as François Beck, and settled at Bordeaux in 1761. He wrote a large number of symphonies, which are important for the early history of the form (one is reprinted in *D.T.B.*, viii (2)). He also wrote music for the stage and for the *Fêtes de la Révolution.*

(3) JOHANN BAPTIST (Jean Baptiste) : *b.* Guebweiler (Alsace), Aug. 14, 1881 ; *d.* Philadelphia, June 23, 1943. Musicologist, who concentrated on the study of the music of the troubadours and trouvères. His publications include *Die Melodien der Troubadours* (1908), *La Musique des troubadours* (1910), *Le Chansonnier Cangé* (1927), *Le Chansonnier du Roy* (1938). He held several posts at American colleges and universities.

Becken [beck′-ĕn], *G.* Cymbals.

Becker [beck′-er], (1) JEAN : *b.* Mannheim, May 11, 1833 ; *d.* there, Oct. 10, 1884. Violinist. Founder and leader of the Florentine Quartet.

(2) HUGO : *b.* Strasbourg, Feb. 13, 1864 ; *d.* nr. Munich, July 30, 1941. Son of (1). Cellist and composer. Member of the Heermann Quartet at Frankfort. Teacher at the Berlin Hochschule. Appeared in piano trios with Ysaÿe and Busoni, also with Flesch and Schnabel.

Becking [beck′-ing], GUSTAV : *b.* Bremen, March 4, 1894 ; *d.* Prague, May 8, 1945. German musicologist, a pupil of Johannes Wolf and Hugo Riemann. Professor, German University of Prague,

1930. Published and edited a number of works on musical history.

Bedford, HERBERT : *b.* London, Jan. 23, 1867 ; *d.* there, March 13, 1945. Composer, author and painter. Husband of Liza Lehmann. His compositions include a one-act opera, *Kit Marlowe*, works for military band and orchestra, chamber music and songs (including unaccompanied songs). Author of *An Essay on Modern Unaccompanied Song* (1923).

Bédos de Celles [bay-do der sell], DOM FRANÇOIS : *b.* Caux, Jan. 24, 1709 ; *d.* Toulouse, Nov. 25, 1779. Benedictine monk. Author of *L'Art du facteur d'orgues* (1766-78), an important work on 18th-cent. organ-building, which also contains valuable information about the interpretation and tempo of music of the period (*v.* A. Dolmetsch, *The Interpretation of the Music of the 17th and 18th Centuries*) ; modern ed. by C. Mahrenholz (1936).

Bedyngham, JOHN. An English composer of church music in the early 15th cent. Some of his compositions are preserved in the so-called Trent Codices (printed in *D.T.Ö.*, vii, xi (1) & xxxi).

Beecham, THOMAS : *b.* St. Helens, Apr. 29, 1879. English conductor. Knighted, 1914 ; succeeded to his father's baronetcy, 1916. First appeared as a conductor in London in 1905. Has been conductor of the New Symphony Orchestra, Beecham Symphony Orchestra, Hallé Orchestra, London Philharmonic Orchestra and Royal Philharmonic Orchestra. Since 1910 has been active in promoting the cause of opera in England and has introduced a large number of unfamiliar works to English audiences. These activities have at various times involved him in financial difficulties, which do not, however, seem to have had any permanent effect. He has conducted in a large number of towns on the Continent, in America and in the Dominions. Apart from his special predilection for the works of Mozart, Handel and Delius (for whom he has done a great deal of pioneer work) his sympathies in general lie with the Romantic composers. He has a remarkable memory and an unusual power of stimulating orchestras to give vivid and subtle performances. He has published the first instalment of his autobiography under the title *A Mingled Chime* (1944).

Bee's Wedding, The. A name given (though not by the composer) to Mendelssohn's *Lieder ohne Worte*, No. 34 in C major.

Beethoven [bate'-hoh-fĕn], LUDWIG VAN : *b.* Bonn, Dec. 16, 1770 ; *d.* Vienna, March 26, 1827. German composer of Flemish descent. His grandfather and father were musicians in the employment of the Elector of Cologne at Bonn. Studied violin, viola, harpsichord and organ. Harpsichord-player in the court orchestra, 1783 ; second court organist, 1784. Sent to Vienna, 1792, where he studied with Haydn and Albrechtsberger and spent the rest of his life. First public appearance in Vienna as composer and pianist, 1795. Though he was friendly with many aristocrats and willing to accept the support of individuals, he rebelled against the 18th-cent. system of patronage, by which a musician was tied to the service of an employer. His increasing deafness forced him to abandon public performance and devote himself wholly to composition. In the latter part of his life he suffered from the cares of acting as guardian to his nephew Karl. In manner he was excessively brusque, and in his business relations with publishers inclined to be unscrupulous.

As a composer he worked with difficulty, tirelessly revising his original sketches until he was satisfied. His sympathy with the liberal ideas of the times found expression in works like *Egmont*, *Fidelio* and the ninth symphony. His music reflects his tempestuousness and the sincerity of his own nature, but with all his rebellion against convention there is also in his work a native simplicity and particularly in middle life an obstinate squareness of rhythm. The tyranny of ideas made him impatient of technical restrictions and he could be merciless to voices and instruments.

He was one of the most original of all composers, and had an enormous influence on the course of 19th-cent. music. His principal compositions are :

(a) ORCHESTRA : 9 symphonies (the last with chorus) ; violin concerto ; 5 piano concertos ; concerto for piano, violin and cello ; overtures—*Coriolan*, *Leonore* Nos. 1, 2 & 3, *Namensfeier* (Name-Day), *Die Weihe des Hauses* (The Consecration of the House) and overtures to works mentioned in (c) ; fantasia for piano, orchestra and chorus ; 2 romances for violin and orchestra.

(b) CHORAL WORKS : 2 Masses (C major and D major) ; oratorio—*Christus am Ölberg* (The Mount of Olives) ; *v.* also (a).

(c) STAGE WORKS : Opera—*Fidelio* ; incidental music to *Egmont*, *König Stephan* (King Stephen), *Die Ruinen von Athen* (The Ruins of Athens) ; ballet—*Die Geschöpfe des Prometheus* (The men created by Prometheus).

(d) CHAMBER MUSIC : Septet ; quintet for piano and wind ; string quintet ; 16 string quartets ; 4 string trios ; serenade for flute, violin and viola ; 6 piano trios ; trio for clarinet, cello and piano ; 10 violin sonatas ; 5 cello sonatas ; horn sonata.

(e) PIANO : 32 sonatas ; 21 sets of variations ; *Bagatellen*.

(f) SONGS : *An die ferne Geliebte* (To the distant beloved—song-cycle) ; *Ah, perfido* (Ah, faithless one—*scena* for soprano and orchestra).

P. BEKKER : *Beethoven* (1925).
E. BLOM : *Beethoven's Pianoforte Sonatas Discussed* (1938).
E. CLOSSON : *The Fleming in Beethoven* (1936).
G. GROVE : *Beethoven and his Nine Symphonies* (1896).
A. C. KALISCHER : *Beethoven's Letters*, 2 vols. (1909).
J. DE MARLIAVE : *Beethoven's Quartets* (1928).
P. MIES : *Beethoven's Sketches* (1929).
M. M. SCOTT : *Beethoven* (1934).
J. W. N. SULLIVAN : *Beethoven—His Spiritual Development* (1927).
A. W. THAYER : *The Life of Ludwig van Beethoven*, ed. H. E. Krehbiel, 3 vols. (1921-5).
D. F. TOVEY : *Beethoven* (1944).

Beggar's Opera, The. A ballad opera by John Gay, first produced in London in 1728. It consists of a play, interspersed with nearly 70 songs set to tunes popular at the time, some of them by well-known composers such as Purcell and Handel. In addition to satirizing the vices of the town it also makes fun of the conventions of Italian opera of the day, *e.g.* the habit of introducing extravagant similes into arias. The songs were arranged for the original production by John Christopher Pepusch, who also composed an overture, in which he utilized the melody of one of the songs. The work has frequently been revived. In the 20th century new editions of the music have been made by Frederic Austin, Edward J. Dent and Benjamin Britten. *v.* BALLAD OPERA, DREIGROSCHENOPER.

F. KIDSON : *The Beggar's Opera : its Predecessors and Successors* (1922).
W. E. SCHULTZ : *Gay's "Beggar's Opera" : its Content, History and Influence* (1923).

Begleitung [ber-glite'-o͞ong], *G.* Accompaniment.

Bègue [ler begg], NICOLAS ANTOINE LE : *b.* Laon, *c.* 1630 ; *d.* Paris, July 6, 1702. Organist and composer. Organist to Louis XIV, 1678. Organ works reprinted in Guilmant's *Archives des maîtres de l'orgue*, vol. ix. He left a manuscript *Méthode pour toucher l'orgue.*

Beinum [fun beh'-no͞om], EDUARD VAN : *b.* Arnhem, Sept. 3, 1901 ; *d.* Amsterdam, April 14, 1959. Conductor. Conductor, Harlem Orchestra, 1927 ; second conductor, Amsterdam Concertgebouw Orchestra, 1931 ; first conductor (with Willem Mengelberg and Bruno Walter), 1938 ; principal conductor since 1945.

Bekker [beck'-er], PAUL : *b.* Berlin, Sept. 11, 1882 ; *d.* New York, March 7, 1937. Writer on music. Some time violinist in the Berlin Philharmonic Orchestra. Active as a music critic from 1906. Intendant, Cassel Opera, 1925 ; Wiesbaden, 1927-32. His most important works, published in English translations, are *Beethoven* (1925), *The*

Story of Music (1927), *Richard Wagner* (1931), *The Changing Opera* (1936).

Belaiev [bay-lyah′-yeff], MITROPHANE PETROVICH: *b.* St. Petersburg (now Leningrad), Feb. 22, 1836; *d.* there, Jan. 10, 1904. Music-publisher, the son of a timber merchant. Founded a publishing firm in Leipzig, 1885, and issued a very large number of works by Russian composers. He also organized concerts of Russian music, both in Russia and at the Paris Exhibition of 1889.

Belime [ber-leem], JEAN. *v.* COEUROY.

Bell (*Fr.* cloche, *G.* Glocke, *I.* campana). The bell used in the orchestra is made in the shape of a tube, hung from a hook and hit with a metal hammer. A complete set of tubular bells normally covers all the notes in an octave.

Bell, WILLIAM HENRY: *b.* St. Albans, Aug. 20, 1873; *d.* Cape Town, Apr. 13, 1946. Composer and conductor. Studied at the R.A.M., where he became teacher of harmony, 1903-12. Principal, South African College of Music, Cape Town, 1912; professor, Cape Town University, 1919-36. His compositions include 2 operas, 2 symphonies, viola concerto, symphonic poems, chamber music and choral works.

Bellaigue [bell-egg], CAMILLE: *b.* Paris, May 24 1858; *d.* there, Oct. 4, 1930. Writer on music. Studied at the Conservatoire. He published biographies of Mozart, Mendelssohn and Gounod and various volumes of musical criticism.

Bell Anthem. The name given to "Rejoice in the Lord alway," an anthem for voices and strings by Purcell (*Purcell Society*, xiv), which begins with repeated descending scales in the bass, suggesting the tolling of bells.

Belle Hélène, La [la bell ay-len] (Fair Helen). Operetta in three acts by Offenbach. Libretto by Henri Meilhac and Ludovic Halévy. First performed, Paris, Dec. 17, 1864.

Bellérophon (bell-ay-roff-on͡]. Opera with a prologue and five acts by Lully. Libretto by Thomas Corneille. First performed, Paris, Jan. 31, 1679.

Bellini [bell-lee′-nee], VINCENZO: *b.* Catania, Nov. 3, 1801; *d.* Puteaux, Sept. 23, 1835. Opera composer. Studied at the Naples Conservatorio. His principal operas are *La Straniera* (1829), *I Capuleti ed i Montecchi* (1830), *La Sonnambula* (1831), *Norma* (1831), *I Puritani* (1835). The main characteristics of his work are elegance and lyrical charm. He was a close friend of Chopin, whose melodic style is often said to have been influenced by Bellini, though without sufficient foundation in fact (*v.* A. Hedley, *Chopin*, pp. 58-9).

Belly (*Fr.* table). The upper part of the soundbox of a string instrument, often known as the table, in imitation of the French term.

Belshazzar. Oratorio by Handel. Libretto by Charles Jennens. First performed, London, March 27, 1745.

Belshazzar's Feast. Oratorio by William Walton. Words selected by Sacheverell Sitwell. First performed, Leeds Festival, Oct. 8, 1931.

Bémol [bay-mol], *Fr.* Flat. The word is a modification of the Latin *B mollis* (soft B). The sign for the flat (♭) was originally a rounded B. *v.* HEXACHORD.

Bemolle [beh-mol′-leh], *I.* Flat (♭). *v.* BÉMOL.

Benda [ben′-da], GEORG (JIŘI) ANTONIN: *b.* June 30, 1722; *d.* Köstritz, Nov. 6, 1795. Czech composer, pianist and oboist. *Kapellmeister* to the Duke of Gotha, 1750-78. He wrote church music, orchestral works, chamber music and operettas and 3 melodramas (*i.e.* spoken plays with instrumental accompaniment), two of which, *Ariadne auf Naxos* (1775) and *Medea* (1775), were extraordinarily successful. The latter was much admired by Mozart (Emily Anderson, *The Letters of Mozart and his Family*, p. 937). Modern edition of *Ariadne auf Naxos* by A. Einstein (1920). Benda's operetta *Der Dorfjahrmarkt* (1775) is printed in *D.D.T.*, lxiv.

Bendl [ben′-d'l], KAREL: *b.* Prague, Apr. 16, 1838; *d.* there, Sept. 20, 1897. Composer. Conductor and founder of the choral society "Hlahol." He wrote orchestral music, choral works, and chamber music, and operas, including *Leila* (1886), *Stary Ženich* (1873), *Černohorci* (1881), *Ditě Tábora* (1892) and *Máti Míla* (1895). When Dvořák was a young man, he gave him a great deal of help and encouragement.

Benedicite, *L.* The canticle known as the "Song of the Three Children," appointed as an alternative to the Te Deum in the Morning Service of the Anglican Church. (Generally pronounced in England "ben-ni-dice'-it-i").

Benedict, JULIUS : *b.* Stuttgart, Nov. 27, 1804 ; *d.* London, June 5, 1885. German composer, a pupil of Hummel and Weber. Conductor, Kärntnerthor Theatre, Vienna, 1823 ; San Carlo, Naples, 1825-34 ; Lyceum Theatre, London, 1836 ; Drury Lane, 1838 ; Her Majesty's Theatre, 1852 ; Harmonic Union, 1852 ; Norwich Festival, 1845-78 ; Liverpool Philharmonic Society, 1876-80. He became a naturalized Englishman and was knighted in 1871. He wrote a large number of instrumental works, oratorios and operas but is remembered today only by *The Lily of Killarney* (London, 1862). He also wrote a life of Weber (1881), which is valuable for its personal reminiscences.

Benedictus, *L.* (1) The second part of the *Sanctus* of the Roman Mass. It begins *Benedictus qui venit in nomine Domini,* "Blessed is he that cometh in the name of the Lord."

(2) The canticle *Benedictus Dominus Israel,* "Blessed be the Lord God of Israel," appointed as an alternative to the Jubilate in the Morning Service of the Anglican Church.

Benet, JOHN. 15th-century English composer, whose works (a Mass, motets and Mass movements) appear principally in Continental manuscripts.

Benevoli [beh-neh'-vo-lee], ORAZIO : *b.* Apr. 19, 1605 ; *d.* Rome, June 17, 1672. Composer. Court musician to the Archduke Leopold Wilhelm in Vienna, 1643-5 ; *maestro di cappella* at the Vatican, 1645-72. Composed a quantity of large-scale church music, some of it for several choirs. His Mass in 53 vocal and instrumental parts, written for the dedication of Salzburg Cathedral in 1628, is printed in *D.T.Ö.*, x (1).

Benjamin, ARTHUR : *b.* Sydney, Sept. 18, 1893. Pianist and composer. Studied at the R.C.M. and taught the piano at Sydney Conservatorium, 1919-21, returning to the R.C.M. as teacher in 1926. His works, which show a lively sense of humour as well as an accomplished technique, include the operas *The Devil Take Her* (1931), *Prima Donna* and *A Tale of Two Cities,* concertino for piano and orchestra, violin concerto, *Overture to an Italian Comedy,* a symphony, chamber music and songs. He has also written a good deal of film music. His *Jamaican Rumba* has become widely popular.

Bennet, JOHN. English composer, who published a set of four-part madrigals in 1599 (reprinted in *E.M.S.*, xxiii). His "All creatures now are merry minded," contributed to *The Triumphes of Oriana* (1601) is one of the best-known of all English madrigals. He also contributed to Ravenscroft's *Brief Discourse* (1614) and wrote five hymn-tunes for William Barley's Psalter.

Bennett, (1) ROBERT RUSSELL : *b.* Kansas City, June 15, 1894. American composer. Studied with Carl Busch and Nadia Boulanger. In addition to film music his works include the opera *Maria Malibran* (1935), *Abraham Lincoln Symphony,* chamber music and choral works, and many orchestrations.

(2) WILLIAM STERNDALE : *b.* Sheffield, Apr. 13, 1816 ; *d.* London, Feb. 1, 1875. English composer. Chorister of King's College, Cambridge. Studied at the R.A.M. Visited Germany at Mendelssohn's suggestion, 1836, and was warmly received by Schumann (*v.* R. Schumann, *Music and Musicians,* 1st & 2nd ser., *passim*). Returned to teach at the R.A.M., 1837. Founded the Bach Society, 1849, and gave the first performance in England of Bach's *St. Matthew Passion,* 1854. Conductor, Royal Philharmonic Society, 1856-66 ; professor, Cambridge, 1856 ; principal, R.A.M., 1866. Knighted, 1871. His works, which are strongly influenced by Mendelssohn, include a symphony in G minor, four piano concertos, overtures —*The Naiads* and *The Woodnymphs, The Woman of Samaria* (oratorio), piano music, choral music and songs.

J. R. STERNDALE BENNETT : *The Life of William Sterndale Bennett* (1907).

Benoît [ber-nwa], (1) CAMILLE : *b.* Roanne, Dec. 7, 1851 ; *d.* Paris, July 1, 1923. Composer and writer on music, a pupil of César Franck. Curator of the Louvre, 1895. His works include the opera *Cléopâtre*, a symphonic poem—*Merlin l'enchanteur*, and *Eleison* for chorus and orchestra. His books include *Souvenirs* (1884) and *Musiciens, poètes et philosophes* (1887).

(2) PIERRE LÉOPOLD LÉONARD (in Flemish, Peter Benoît) : *b.* Harlebeke, Aug. 17, 1834 ; *d.* Antwerp, March 8, 1901. Composer. Studied under Fétis at the Brussels Conservatoire. Conductor at the Bouffes Parisiens, Paris, 1861. Returned to Belgium, 1864, and promoted a national movement which led to the foundation of the L'École Flamande de Musique, Antwerp, 1867, of which he became director. His numerous works include 3 operas, 3 oratorios, and several choral cantatas. He also published books and pamphlets in support of the Flemish national movement.

C. VAN DEN BORREN : *Peter Benoît* (1942).

Bentzon [bent'-son], (1) JØRGEN : *b.* Copenhagen, Feb. 14, 1897 ; *d.* July 9, 1948. Danish composer, a pupil of Carl Nielsen. He also studied at Leipzig Conservatorium with Karg-Elert. His works include orchestral variations, five string quartets, and other chamber compositions.

(2) NIELS VIGGO : *b.* Copenhagen, Aug. 24, 1919. Composer. Studied at Copenhagen Conservatoire. His compositions include 3 symphonies, a piano concerto, chamber music and piano works.

Benucci [beh-noo'-tchee], FRANCESCO : *b. c.* 1745 ; *d.* Florence, Apr. 5, 1824. Operatic bass, who sang Figaro at the first performance of Mozart's *Le nozze di Figaro* at Vienna in 1786. Mozart describes him as a " particularly good " buffo singer (*v.* Emily Anderson, *The Letters of Mozart and his Family*, p. 1263). For his singing of " Non più andrai " *v. Reminiscences of Michael Kelly* (1826), vol. i, p. 259.

Benvenuto Cellini [ben-veh-noo'-to chell-lee'-nee]. Opera in two acts by Berlioz. Libretto by Léon de Wailly and Auguste Barbier. First performed, Paris, Sept. 10, 1838.

Bequadro [beh-cwahd'-ro], *I.* Natural. The name is due to the fact that the sign for the natural (♮) was originally a square-shaped B, in Latin *B quadratum*. *v.* HEXACHORD.

Berceuse [bair-serz], *Fr.* (*G.* Wiegenlied). " Cradle song." A piece suggesting by its rhythm the gentle rocking of a cradle, *e.g.* Chopin's Op. 57 for piano.

Berenice [beh-reh-nee'-cheh]. Opera in three acts by Handel. Libretto by Antonio Salvi. First performed, London, May 29, 1737.

Berezowsky [bair-ez-off'-ski], NICOLAI : *b.* St. Petersburg, May 17, 1900. Composer, violinist and conductor. Musical director, School of Modern Art, Moscow, 1921. Went to the United States, 1922, and became an American citizen. Member of the Coolidge String Quartet, Library of Congress, Washington. His works include 4 symphonies, fantasy for two pianos and orchestra, violin concerto, cello concerto, viola concerto, 2 string quartets and other chamber and orchestral compositions.

Berg [bairk], ALBAN : *b.* Vienna, Feb. 9, 1885 ; *d.* there, Dec. 24, 1935. Composer. A pupil of Schönberg, whom he followed in accepting TWELVE-NOTE MUSIC as a basis for composition, though he used it less rigidly and with more imagination than his master. He also wrote extensively in defence of Schönberg's music. As a teacher he was devoted to his pupils. His principal works are :

(a) OPERAS : *Wozzeck* (1921), *Lulu* (1934).
(b) ORCHESTRA : Three orchestral pieces, chamber concerto for piano, violin and 13 wind instruments, violin concerto.
(c) CHAMBER MUSIC : String quartet, *Lyric Suite* for string quartet.
(d) PIANO : Sonata.

He also wrote a number of songs, with piano and with orchestra.

W. REICH : *Alban Berg* (1937).

Bergamasca [bair-gah-muss'-cah], *I.* (*Fr.* bergamasque). (1) A popular dance-tune, so called from Bergamo in north Italy, current in the 16th and 17th cent. In its simplest form it runs :

Frescobaldi wrote an organ canzona on this theme in his *Fiori musicali* (1635, modern edition by J. Bonnet, p. 88). Other composers used its harmonic scheme as the basis for variations, as with the chaconne or passacaglia. Shakespeare refers to the dance in *A Midsummer Night's Dream*, v, 1.

(2) A 19th-cent. dance in quick 6/8 time, similar to the tarantella.

(3) In Debussy's *Suite bergamasque* for piano the adjective seems to have no special significance. It is obviously suggested by Verlaine's " Clair de lune," which begins :

> Votre âme est un paysage choisi,
> Que vont charmant masques et bergamasques
> Jouant du luth et dansant . . .

It is significant that the third piece in the *Suite bergamasque* is entitled " Clair de lune."

Bergamasque [bair-ga-musk], *Fr.* *v.* BERGAMASCA.

Berger [bairg'-er], LUDWIG : *b.* Berlin, Apr. 18, 1777 ; *d.* there, Feb. 18, 1839. Composer, pianist and teacher. Pupil of Clementi, who took him to St. Petersburg, where he met John Field. Taught the piano in Berlin from 1815. His pupils included Mendelssohn and his sister Fanny, Taubert and Henselt.

Bergerette [bair-zher-et], *Fr.* (*berger*, shepherd). (1) A 16th-cent. dance in brisk triple time.

(2) An 18th-cent. French song dealing with shepherds and shepherdesses.

Berggeist, Der [dair bairk'-giced] (The Spirit of the Mountain). Opera in three acts by Spohr. Libretto by Georg Döring. First performed, Cassel, March 24, 1825.

Berggreen [bairg'-grehn], ANDREAS PETER : *b.* Copenhagen, March 2, 1801 ; *d.* there, Nov. 8, 1880. Composer and teacher. His only opera, *Billedet og Busten* (Copenhagen, 1832) was unsuccessful. He is remembered chiefly for his collections of national songs, school songs and psalm tunes. He was active in promoting music for the working classes. Niels Gade was his pupil.

Bergmann [bairk'-mun], CARL : *b.* Ebersbach, Apr. 11, 1821 ; *d.* New York, Aug. 16, 1876. Conductor. Studied in Breslau, and went to America in 1850. Conductor, Germania Orchestra, New York, 1850-4 ; Handel and Haydn Society, Boston, 1852-4. Conducted concerts of the New York Philharmonic Society, 1855-65 ; sole conductor, 1866-76. He established a new standard of conducting in America, and did much to promote a knowledge of the works of Wagner and Liszt.

Bergomask. *v.* BERGAMASQUE.

Beringer [bair'-ing-er], OSCAR : *b.* Furtwangen, July 14, 1844 ; *d.* London, Feb. 21, 1922. Pianist of German origin, who lived in London from the age of 5. Gave piano recitals at the Crystal Palace, 1859-60. Studied at Leipzig and Berlin with Moscheles, Tausig and others. Returned to England in 1871. Founded an " Academy for the Higher Development of Pianoforte Playing," 1873-97. Gave the first performance in England of Brahms's second piano concerto, 1882. Teacher of the piano, R.A.M., 1885. He wrote a number of piano pieces and songs.

Bériot [bay-ryo], CHARLES AUGUSTE DE : *b.* Louvain, Feb. 20, 1802 ; *d.* Brussels, Apr. 8, 1870. Violinist and teacher. Studied in Paris. Married (1) the singer Maria Malibran, 1836, having lived with her from 1830, (2) Marie Huber, daughter of a Viennese magistrate. Teacher of the violin, Brussels Conservatoire, 1843-52. Became blind in 1858. He was a brilliant performer, with considerable influence on his successors. He published concertos, studies and instruction books. Henri Vieuxtemps was his pupil.

Berkeley, LENNOX RANDAL FRANCIS : *b.* Oxford, May 12, 1903. English composer. Studied with Nadia Boulanger in Paris, 1927-33. His works, which were originally influenced by Stravinsky and show a French regard for clarity and precision, include the oratorio *Jonah*, the operas *Nelson*, *A Dinner Engagement* and *Ruth*, the ballet *The Judgment of Paris*, a *Stabat Mater*, a symphony, concertos for piano, 2 pianos and flute, a violin sonata, 2 string quartets, and piano works.

Berkshire Festival. An annual festival of music founded in 1937 at Tanglewood, Mass., by Koussevitsky. The orchestra is the Boston Symphony. Since 1940 courses have also been held in composition, conducting and performance.

Berlin Philharmonic Orchestra. Founded 1882. Conductors: Franz Wüllner, 1882-5; Joseph Joachim, 1884-6; Karl Klindworth, 1884-6; Hans von Bülow, 1887-95; Artur Nikisch, 1895-1922; Wilhelm Furtwängler, 1922-45.

Berlioz [bairl-yoze], (LOUIS) HECTOR: *b.* La Côte St. André (nr. Grenoble), Dec. 11, 1803; *d.* Paris, March 8, 1869. Composer, and conductor, the son of a doctor. Studied at the Medical School, Paris, 1821. Having turned to music, studied privately with Lesueur, 1823, and then at the Conservatoire, 1826. Won the *Prix de Rome,* 1830, after earlier unsuccessful attempts. Married (1) the Irish actress Henrietta (Harriet) Smithson (*d.* 1854) 1833, from whom he separated in 1842, (2) the singer Marie Recio (*d.* 1862), 1854. Visited Germany, Austria, Russia and England as conductor. An eccentric and sometimes unbalanced personality, whose music, romantic in spirit, ranges from vivid imagination to utter banality. His originality showed itself particularly in his handling of the orchestra. His principal works are:

(a) OPERAS: *Benvenuto Cellini* (1838); *Les Troyens* (The Trojans, 1865-9); *Béatrice et Bénédict* (1862).

(b) ORCHESTRA: *Symphonie Fantastique*; *Harold en Italie* (for viola and orchestra); overtures—*Le Roi Lear* (King Lear), *Le Corsaire, Le Carnaval Romain.*

(c) CHORAL WORKS: *Sara la baigneuse* (Sara the bather), *Roméo et Juliette* (a "dramatic symphony"), *Symphonie funèbre et triomphale, La Damnation de Faust, Grande Messe des Morts* (Requiem Mass), *L'Enfance du Christ* (The Childhood of Christ), *Te Deum.*

He also wrote a "monodrama," *Lélio, ou le Retour à la vie* (Lelio, or the return to life—intended as a sequel to the *Symphonie Fantastique*) for actor, soloists, chorus, pianists and orchestra. The *Symphonie Fantastique* (1830), though his best-known composition, is an early work, largely patched together from previous works, and is not representative.

For a large part of his life Berlioz was active as a critic, and published several volumes on music, in addition to an important *Traité de l'Instrumentation* (1844) and his autobiography (1870), which is not wholly reliable (English trans., ed. by Ernest Newman, 1932). A complete edition of his works was begun by Breitkopf and Härtel in 1900, under the editorship of Charles Malherbe and Felix Weingartner, but was never finished. The last volume to appear was *Béatrice et Bénédict* (vols. xix-xx) in 1907.

J. BARZUN: *Berlioz and the Romantic Century,* 2 vols. (1950)
J. H. ELLIOTT: *Berlioz* (1938).
W. J. TURNER: *Berlioz—the Man and his Work* (1934).
T. S. WOTTON: *Hector Berlioz* (1935).

Bermudo [bair-moo'-do], JUAN: *b.* Ecija (nr. Seville), early 16th cent. Author of an instruction book on music and musical instruments, *Libro llamado Declaración de instrumentos* (1549), which also contains biographical information about Cristobal Morales. He also wrote a second instruction book for the use of a convent of nuns, *El Arte Tripharia* (1550).

Bernacchi [bair-nah'-tchee], ANTONIO: *b.* Bologna, June 23, 1685; *d.* there, March, 1756. Castrato singer, who appeared in several of Handel's operas in London. He was criticized by old-fashioned people for his excessive use of improvised ornamentation. He was for a time in the service of the Elector of Bavaria, and later of the Emperor.

Bernard [bair-narr], ROBERT: *b.* Geneva, Oct. 10, 1900. Composer and critic. Since 1926 resident in Paris, where he became a teacher at the Schola Cantorum. Director of the *Revue Musicale* from 1939-51. His compositions include choral works and orchestral pieces. He has also published several books on music.

Bernardi [bair-narr′-dee], STEFFANO : *b.* Verona ; *d.* before 1638. *Maestro di cappella*, Verona Cathedral, 1615 ; *Kapellmeister*, Salzburg Cathedral, 1628-34. Composed church music, madrigals and instrumental music and published a successful primer of counterpoint (1615). Some of his church music is printed in *D.T.Ö.*, xxxvi.

Bernasconi [bair-nah-sco′-nee], ANTONIA. Operatic soprano, daughter of Andrea B. (1706-84), an opera-composer, who was *Kapellmeister* at Munich. She sang the title-role in the first performance of Gluck's *Alceste* (Vienna, 1767). She also sang the principal soprano role in Mozart's *Mitridate* (Milan, 1770 : *v.* Emily Anderson, *The Letters of Mozart and his Family*, pp. 223 & 261). Twenty years later her powers seem to have declined considerably (*ibid.*, pp. 1133-4).

Berners, LORD (GERALD HUGH TYRWHITT-WILSON) : *b.* Bridgnorth, Sept. 18, 1883 ; *d.* Apr. 19, 1950. Composer, painter and author. In the diplomatic service, 1909-19. Succeeded to the barony, 1918. As a composer, largely self-taught, though he had some encouragement from Stravinsky. His music is often ironical and parodies the conventions of Romanticism, but it is evident that he is himself a Romantic at heart. He was most successful as a composer of ballets. His works include the one-act opera *Le Carrosse du Saint-Sacrement* (Paris, 1924), the ballets *The Triumph of Neptune* (1926), *Luna Park* (1930), *A Wedding Bouquet* (1937) and *Cupid and Psyche* (1939), *Fantaisie espagnole* and Fugue in C minor for orchestra, piano music and songs. He also published two instalments of an autobiography, *First Childhood* (1934) and *A Distant Prospect* (1945).

Bernhard [bairn′-harrt], CHRISTOPH : *b.* Danzig, 1627 ; *d.* Dresden, Nov. 14, 1692. Tenor singer and composer. Entered the service of the Elector of Saxony, 1649. Studied singing in Italy, where he met Carissimi. Vice-*Kapellmeister*, Dresden, 1655 ; cantor, Hamburg, 1664 ; *Kapellmeister*, Dresden, 1674. Some of his Protestant church music is printed in *D.D.T.*, vol. vi.

Bernstein, LEONARD : *b.* Lawrence (Mass.), Aug. 25, 1918. Conductor and composer. Studied at Harvard and the Curtis Institute, Philadelphia. Assistant conductor, New York Philharmonic Orchestra, 1943 ; conductor, New York City Center Orchestra, 1945; music director, N.Y. Philharmonic, 1958. His compositions include two symphonies, a clarinet sonata, ballets, musical comedies (*West Side Story,* 1957), and songs.

Bertolli [bair-tol′-lee], FRANCESCA. Operatic contralto, who sang in several of Handel's operas and oratorios (in English) in London, 1729-37.

Bertolotti [bair-to-lot′-tee], GASPARO DI. *v.* SALA.

Berton [bair-tõ], HENRI MONTAN : *b.* Paris, Sept. 17, 1767 ; *d.* there, Apr. 22, 1844. Composer. Violinist in the Opéra orchestra, 1782. Teacher of harmony at the Paris Conservatoire, 1795. Conductor, Opéra-Comique, 1807. Member of the Institut, 1815. In spite of financial difficulties, due partly to conditions under the Terror, he produced a large number of compositions. His operas, of which *Aline, Reine de Golconde* (Paris, 1803) was the most successful, were translated and performed in other European countries. He also wrote oratorios, cantatas and ballets and published works on harmony and the construction of string instruments.

Bertoni [bair-to′-nee], FERDINANDO GIUSEPPE : *b.* Salo (nr. Venice), Aug. 15, 1725 ; *d.* Desenzano, Dec. 1, 1813. Composer of operas, oratorios and instrumental works, a pupil of Martini. Organist, St. Mark's, Venice, 1752 ; *maestro di cappella*, 1785. His *Orfeo* (Venice, 1776) was a setting of the libretto by Calzabigi which had previously been set by Gluck in 1762. Burney said of him : " Few masters know the mechanical parts of their business better than this worthy professor . . . yet there is sometimes a pacific smoothness in his Music that borders upon languor " (*A General History of Music*, vol. iv, p. 541).

Berwald [behr′-vuld], FRANZ ADOLF :

b. Stockholm, June 23, 1796; *d.* there, Apr. 30, 1868. Swedish composer. Studied the violin with Du Puy, but as a composer was self-taught. Member of the king's orchestra, Stockholm, 1812-28. In Germany, 1829-41; Vienna, 1841-2, where three of his symphonic poems were performed. Teacher of composition at the Stockholm Conservatoire, 1867. His works include three symphonies (two entitled respectively *Symphonie sérieuse* and *Symphonie singulière*), several symphonic poems, concertos for violin, bassoon and piano, chamber music, two operas—*Estrella de Soria* (Stockholm, 1862) and *Drottningen av Golconda*, cantatas, songs and piano pieces. He was not appreciated as a composer in Sweden in his lifetime; his reputation, which is high, dates from the revival of his works in the 20th cent.

Bes [bess], *G.* B double flat (B♭♭).

Besard [ber-zarr], JEAN BAPTISTE: *b.* Besançon, *c.* 1567. A doctor of laws, who was also an accomplished lutenist and composer. In addition to writing works on other subjects he also published an anthology of lute music (including his own compositions), entitled *Thesaurus harmonicus* (1603), and a sequel, *Novus partus sive concertationes musicae* (1617). These are valuable sources for our knowledge of early 17th-cent. lute music. A number of *airs de cour* from *Thesaurus harmonicus* are printed in O. Chilesotti, *Biblioteca di rarità musicali*, vol. vii.

Besseler [bess'-er-ler], HEINRICH: *b.* Dortmund-Hörde, Apr. 2, 1900. Musicologist. Studied at Freiburg, Vienna and Göttingen. Lecturer, Freiburg, 1925; professor, Heidelberg, 1928; Jena 1949-56. Has specialized in the study of medieval music, but has also written a biography of Bach. His most important work is *Die Musik des Mittelalters und der Renaissance* (1931), in E. Bücken's series, *Handbuch der Musikwissenschaft*.

Besson [bess-on͡], GUSTAVE AUGUSTE: *b.* Paris, 1820; *d.* there, 1875. Manufacturer of brass instruments, in which he introduced several improvements. He also constructed in 1890 a contrabass clarinet, described as a *clarinette-pédale*, with a compass an octave below that of the bass clarinet (*v.* A. Carse, *Musical Wind Instruments*, p. 174). This instrument was used by d'Indy in his opera *Fervaal* (1897).

Best, WILLIAM THOMAS: *b.* Carlisle, Aug. 13, 1826; *d.* Liverpool, May 10, 1897. English organist, largely self-taught. Organist, St. George's Hall, Liverpool, 1855. He was famous as a recitalist, with a wide repertory, including a very large number of transcriptions. He wrote instruction books for the organ and edited the complete organ works of Bach (subsequently revised by A. Eaglefield Hull). His compositions are unimportant.

Betz [bets], FRANZ: *b.* Mainz, March 19, 1835; *d.* Berlin, Aug. 11, 1900. Operatic baritone. First appeared on the stage at Hanover, 1856. Royal Opera House, Berlin, 1859-97. Sang Hans Sachs at the first performance of Wagner's *Die Meistersinger* (Munich, 1868) and Wotan at the first performance of *Der Ring des Nibelungen* (Bayreuth, 1876).

Bevin, ELWAY. Organist of Bristol Cathedral, probably from 1587 to 1638, when he was dismissed (*v.* J. E. West, *Cathedral Organists*, 2nd ed., 1921, p. 7). Described in Laud's visitation of 1634 as "a verie olde man, who, having done good service in the church is not now able to discharge the place, but that hee is holpen by some other of the quier" (*H.M.C.*, iv, p. 141). Author of *A briefe and short instruction of the art of musicke* (1631). His Service in the Dorian mode is still sung in cathedrals.

Bewegt [ber-vaked'], *G.* "Moved," *i.e.* with animation (*I.* mosso). *Bewegter*, faster (*I.* più mosso). *Mässig bewegt*, at a moderate speed.

Bezifferter Bass [ber-tsiff'-er-ter buss], *G.* Figured bass.

Bianchi [bee-ahn'-kee], FRANCESCO: *b.* Cremona, *c.* 1752; *d.* Hammersmith, Nov. 27, 1810. Opera composer and conductor. Harpsichordist at the Théâtre Italien, Paris, 1775-8; second *maestro di cappella*, Milan Cathedral, 1783; second organist, St. Mark's, Venice, 1785-93. Subsequently conducted at the King's Theatre, London, and in Dublin. Committed suicide,

1810. Of his numerous operas the most popular was *La Villanella rapita* (Venice, 1783). Sir Henry Bishop was his pupil.

Biber [bee′-ber], HEINRICH IGNAZ FRANZ VON : *b.* Wartenberg, Aug. 12, 1644 ; *d.* Salzburg, May 3, 1704. German violinist and composer. In the service of the Archbishop of Salzburg, 1673 ; vice-*Kapellmeister*, 1680 ; *Kapellmeister*, 1684. His works, which are often of considerable technical difficulty, consist of chamber compositions for various groups of instruments, including sonatas for violin and figured bass. Fifteen of the violin sonatas are associated with incidents in the life of Christ and his mother. There is also a Passacaglia for unaccompanied violin. Biber made considerable use of *scordatura*, *i.e.* modifications of the accepted tuning of the violin. Modern editions of his works in *D.T.Ö.*, v (2) & xii (2) (violin sonatas), xxv (1) (Mass), xxx (1) (Requiem).

Bicinium, *L.* (*bis*, twice, and *canere*, to sing). A term used in Germany in the 16th cent. for a composition for two voices which could equally well, however, be played on instruments, and extended in the early 17th cent. to include purely instrumental music in two parts.

Biggs, EDWARD GEORGE POWER : *b.* Westcliff-on-Sea, March 29, 1906. English organist, an American citizen since 1938. Studied at the R.A.M. He is widely known as a recitalist, particularly for his performances of Bach's works.

Bigot [bee-go], EUGÈNE : *b.* Rennes, Feb. 2, 1888. Conductor and composer. Studied at the Paris Conservatoire. Chorus master, Théâtre des Champs-Élysées, 1913. Conductor, Société des Concerts du Conservatoire, 1923 ; Concerts Lamoureux, 1935 ; Opéra-Comique, 1936. His works include orchestral suites and ballets, chamber music and songs.

Bigot de Morogues [bee-go der morr-og], MARIA (*née* Kiene) : *b.* Colmar, March 3, 1786 ; *d.* Paris, Sept. 16, 1820. Alsatian pianist. Married M. Bigot, librarian to Count Rasoumovsky in Vienna, where she met Haydn and Beethoven (1804-9). Beethoven seems to have been very much attached to her (*v.* A. C. Kalischer, *Beethoven's Letters*, trans. J. S. Shedlock, vol. i, pp. 136-8). In 1809 she and her husband moved to Paris, where Mendelssohn (aged 7) had lessons from her in 1816.

Billington, ELIZABETH (*née* Weichsel) : *b.* London, *c.* 1765 ; *d.* Venice, Aug. 25, 1818. Operatic soprano, a pupil of J. C. Bach. Her father, Carl Weichsel (a native of Saxony), was principal oboe at the King's Theatre, London ; her mother was a singer. First appeared as a pianist, 1774. Married James Billington, a double-bass player (*d.* 1794), 1783. Made her first appearance in opera at Dublin. First appearance at Covent Garden, 1786 ; at San Carlo, Naples, 1794. Returned to England, 1801, and continued to sing in opera and oratorio till 1811. The circumstances of her second marriage are obscure. The publication in 1792 of *Memoirs of Mrs. Billington*, reputed to be letters written to her mother, created a considerable scandal. She was at one time intimate with the Prince of Wales (later George IV). Her manners are said to have been " distinguished by the utmost grossness, and in many instances by the most positive indelicacy," but she was a remarkable singer and had a great reputation on the Continent, as well as in England. Her portrait was painted by Reynolds.

M. SANDS : " Mrs. Billington " (*Monthly Musical Record*, 1944, pp. 33-9).

Billy Budd. (1) Opera in four acts with prologue by Britten. Libretto by E. M. Forster and Eric Crozier (after the story by Herman Melville). First performed, London, Dec. 1, 1951.

(2) Opera in one act by Ghedini. Libretto by Salvadore Quasimodo (after Melville). First performed, Venice, Sept. 8, 1949.

Binary Form. As the name implies, a composition in binary form is one that can be divided into two sections. This division is characteristic of a good deal of early dance music, where the structure is further emphasized by the repetition of each section. Dance forms were frequently employed by 17th-cent. composers, both in keyboard music and in works for instrumental ensemble, and it was natural that they should transfer the form to pieces which had no association with the dance. In 17th-cent. music the first section may end (a) in the tonic key (b) on a half close (c) in a related key, *i.e.* the dominant or (in a piece in a minor key) the relative major. The second section naturally ends in the tonic key. The following is a miniature example, with the first section ending on a half close :

CORELLI, *Op.* 4, *No.* 5

Of the endings of the first section mentioned above the first, in the tonic key, was not wholly satisfactory, because it suggested a premature ending to the piece. The second type of ending, on a half close, was apt to sound indefinite. Hence the standard way of ending the first section came to be the third, *i.e.* the music modulated in the course of the section and the section ended with the establishment of a related key. As a result of this procedure the first part of the second section had to be devoted to a modulation back to the tonic ; and as modulation offered considerable opportunities for development, the second section came to be noticeably longer than the first and the music frequently passed through several keys before reaching the tonic. This was the standard procedure in movements in binary form in the early 18th cent.

Since recapitulation was a feature of the *da capo* aria, composers introduced it also into pieces in binary form, *i.e.* the whole (or a substantial part) of the first section would be repeated at the end of the second section but modified so that what was previously in the related key would now be in the tonic key. An example of this procedure is the prelude in D major from Book II of Bach's *Das wohltemperirte Clavier.* A further development, which occurred in the middle of the 18th cent., was to make the contrast between the two key centres of the first section more vivid by a contrast of thematic material. This procedure was the basis of SONATA FORM as practised by composers in the second half of the 18th cent., though even then there are examples (*e.g.* in Haydn's works) of movements in which there is very little thematic contrast or even none at all. Since the second section of a movement in sonata form was by now considerably longer than the first, the practice of repeating it soon died out. The practice of repeating the first section, however, survived till the end of the 19th cent.

Binchois [bañ-shwa], GILLES : *b.* Mons, *c.* 1400 ; *d.* there (?), Sept. or Oct., 1460. Composer. At first a soldier, then a priest. Chaplain to Philip, Duke of Burgundy, 1430. Also held several canonries. Composed secular part-songs and church music. Modern editions in *D.T.Ö.*, vii, xi, (1), xxvii, (1), xxxi, J. Stainer, *Dufay and his Contemporaries*, C. van den Borren, *Polyphonia Sacra*, J. Marix, *Les Musiciens de la Cour de Bourgogne.*

Bindungszeichen [bin′-dŏŏngss-tsy*sh*-ĕn], *G.* *v.* SLUR (1).

Binet [bee-nay], JEAN : *b.* Geneva, Oct. 17, 1893. Composer. Studied in Geneva, where his teachers included Ernest Bloch. Lived in U.S.A., 1919-23 ; Brussels, 1923-9. His compositions include choral works, orchestral suites based on folk-dances, ballets and chamber music.

Birmingham Orchestra, City of. Founded in 1920. Conductors : Appleby Matthews, 1920-4 ; Adrian Boult, 1924-30 ; Leslie Heward, 1930-43 ; George Weldon, 1946-51 ; Rudolf Schwartz, 1951-57 ; Andrzej Panufnik, 1957-9. Now known as the City of Birmingham Symphony Orchestra.

Bis [beece], *Fr.* " Twice " (*L.* bis). An indication that the passage over which the word is written (generally with a bracket for the sake of clearness) is to be played twice. It is still to be found as a convenient abbreviation in manuscript music, but in printed music is obsolete.

Bisbigliando [beez-beel-yahnd'-o], *I.* " Whispering." Used by Strauss in his *Sinfonia Domestica* to indicate the method of playing a quiet tremolando on the harp, and by Britten in *Peter Grimes* for a background figure on the celesta.

Bischof [bish'-off], MARIE. *v.* BRANDT.

Biscroma [beece-cro'-mah], *I.* Demisemiquaver.

Bishop, HENRY ROWLEY : *b.* London, Nov. 18, 1786 ; *d.* there, Apr. 30, 1855. Composer and conductor. Held a number of appointments as conductor at London theatres and also conducted some of the concerts of the Philharmonic Society (founded 1813). Professor, Edinburgh, 1841-3 ; Oxford, 1848. Knighted, 1842. Conductor, Ancient Concerts, 1843-8. He wrote and adapted a very large number of works for the stage. He is now known only by the songs " Lo, here the gentle lark " (with flute obbligato) and " Home, sweet home " (from the opera *Clari, or the Maid of Milan*, London, 1823).

Bispham, DAVID SCULL : *b.* Philadelphia, Jan. 5, 1857 ; *d.* New York, Oct. 2, 1921. Baritone. Studied in Milan and London. First appearance on the stage in Messager's *La Basoche* (London, 1891). Sang in performances of Wagner's operas at Drury Lane, Covent Garden and Metropolitan Opera House, New York. His best parts were Kurwenal and Beckmesser. He was a strong advocate of opera and song recitals in English. Published his autobiography under the title *A Quaker Singer's Recollections* (1920).

Bitonality. The use of two keys simultaneously, whether indicated by different key signatures or not. The following example illustrates the practice in its simplest form :

VAUGHAN WILLIAMS, *Flos Campi*

It will be noticed that the viola's A♭ and G♭ fit comfortably into the oboe's key as G♯ and F♯. This use of notes which can have two different associations is common in bitonality. However clear the distinction may be between the two keys, the ear instinctively seizes on any points that they may have in common. *v.* POLYTONALITY.

Bittner [bit'-ner], JULIUS: *b.* Vienna, Apr. 9, 1874 ; *d.* there, Jan. 9, 1939. Composer. Of his nine operas, which are popular in style, the most successful was *Das höllisch Gold* (Darmstadt, 1916). He also wrote an Austrian Mass with orchestra for concert performance, ballets, chamber music and songs.

Bizet [bee-zay], GEORGES (christened Alexandre César Léopold) : *b.* Paris, Oct. 25, 1838 ; *d.* Bougival, June 3, 1875. Composer. Studied at the Paris Conservatoire, 1849-57. *Grand Prix de Rome*, 1857. Returned to Paris, 1860. His principal operas are *Les Pêcheurs de perles* (Paris, 1863), *La*

Jolie Fille de Perth (Paris, 1867), *Djamileh* (Paris, 1872) and *Carmen* (Paris, 1875). His other works include incidental music to Daudet's *L'Arlésienne*, the symphonic suite *Roma*, the overture *Patrie*, *Jeux d'enfants* for piano duet (also for orchestra) and an early symphony. Bizet was very successful in introducing local colour, *e.g.* in *L'Arlésienne* (a Provençal story) and *Carmen* (where the background is Spanish). The "realism" of *Carmen* has been much exaggerated: Bizet accepted the traditions of the French operatic stage and applied them to a vulgar subject. Though *Carmen* is now frequently given with the recitatives added by Ernest Guiraud it was originally an opera with dialogue.

Lettres de George Bizet (1907).
G. BIZET: *Lettres à un ami* (1909).
M. COOPER: *Georges Bizet* (1938).
W. DEAN: *Bizet* (1948).
D. C. PARKER: *Georges Bizet—his Life and Works* (1926).

Björling [byur'-ling], JUSSI: *b.* Stora Tuna, Feb. 2, 1911. Swedish tenor, one of a family of singers. Appeared in a quartet with his father and two brothers in America, 1919. Studied at the Royal Opera School, Stockholm, First appeared as Ottavio in *Don Giovanni*, Stockholm, 1930. Has sung also at the Metropolitan Opera, New York, La Scala, Milan, Covent Garden, and other opera houses. He excels in Italian opera.

Blacher [bluckh'-er], BORIS: *b.* New-Chwang (China), Jan. 3, 1903. German composer. Studied in Berlin. Taught at Dresden Conservatorium, 1938-9. Director, Hochschule für Musik, Berlin, since 1954. His music, freely contrapuntal in style, has had a considerable influence on younger musicians. His compositions include a symphony and other orchestral works, a violin concerto, 3 string quartets, piano music, songs and several works for the stage (among them the dramatic oratorio *Romeo und Julia*).

Blamont [bla-mon͡], FRANÇOIS COLIN DE: *b.* Versailles, Nov. 22, 1690; *d.* there, Feb. 14, 1760. Composer, a pupil of Michel de Lalande. *Surintendant* of the royal music, 1719; *Maître de la musique de la chambre*, 1726. His works include ballets, pastorales, cantatas and motets. His *divertissement*, *Le Retour des Dieux sur la Terre*, was written for the marriage of Louis XV in 1725.

Blanche [blun͡sh], *Fr.* Minim.

Blanchet [blun͡-shay], ÉLISABETH-ANTOINETTE. *v.* COUPERIN (5).

Blangini [blahn-jee'-nee], GIUSEPPE MARCO MARIA FELICE: *b.* Turin, Nov. 18, 1871; *d.* Paris, Dec. 18, 1841. Singer, teacher and composer. Very fashionable as a singing-teacher in Paris. Director of music to King Jerome of Westphalia (Napoleon's brother) at Cassel, 1809-14. Wrote numerous operas, of which the most important is *Nephtali ou Les Ammonites* (Paris, 1806).

Blasinstrumente [blahss'-in-stroo-men'-ter], *G.* Wind instruments.

Blavet [bla-vay], MICHEL: *b.* Besançon, March 13, 1700; *d.* Paris, Oct. 28, 1768. Flautist and composer. In addition to works for the flute he also wrote operas and ballets. His *Le Jaloux corrigé* (Berny, 1752) is mainly compiled from arias in Italian comic operas which were being performed at Paris at that time. It is one of the earliest French *opéras-comiques*.

Blaze. *v.* CASTIL-BLAZE.

Blech, HARRY: *b.* London, March 2, 1910. Violinist and conductor. Studied at Trinity College of Music, London, and the Royal Manchester College of Music. Played in the Hallé Orchestra, 1929-30, and the B.B.C. Symphony Orchestra, 1930-6. Leader of the Blech Quartet, 1936-50. Founder and conductor, London Wind Players, 1942; London Symphonic Players, 1946; London Mozart Players, 1949.

Blech [blesh], LEO: *b.* Aachen, Apr. 21, 1871; *d.* Berlin, Aug. 24, 1958. Conductor, a pupil of Humperdinck. Conductor, Aix-la-Chapelle Stadttheater, 1893; Deutsches Landestheater, Prague, 1899; Berlin Opera, 1906. Director, Berlin Opera, 1913-23. Conductor, Berlin Volksoper, 1924; Vienna Volksoper, 1925; Berlin Staatsoper, 1926-37. Guest conductor, Stockholm Opera. Returned to Berlin, 1949. His compositions include symphonic poems, choral works, songs and several operas, of which the one-act

Versiegelt (Hamburg, 1908) has been the most popular.

Blechinstrumente [blehs'-in-stroo-men'-ter], *G.* Brass instruments.

Bliss, ARTHUR : *b.* London, Aug. 2, 1891. English composer. Studied at Pembroke College, Cambridge, and the R.C.M. Served in the 1914-18 war. Taught composition at the R.C.M., 1921. Settled in California, 1923-5. Director of music, B.B.C., 1942-4. Knighted, 1950. Master of the Queen's Music, 1953. His early works, which include *Rout* for soprano and ten instruments (1919) and *Conversations* for five instruments (1919) are largely experimental in character. His mature work, which is still characterized by independence and vigour of expression, is related rather to the English romantic tradition. His principal compositions are :

(a) ORCHESTRA : A Colour Symphony ; concerto for two pianos ; Introduction and Allegro ; Music for strings ; piano concerto ; *Meditations on a theme by John Blow.*

(b) CHAMBER MUSIC : Oboe quintet ; clarinet quintet ; viola sonata ; 2 string quartets.

(c) CHORAL WORKS : *Pastoral* (*Lie strewn the white flocks*) ; *Morning Heroes.*

(d) OPERA : *The Olympians* (London, 1949).

(e) BALLET : *Checkmate* ; *Miracle in the Gorbals* ; *Adam Zero.*

(f) SONGS : Serenade for baritone and orchestra ; 7 American poems.

(g) BRASS BAND : *Kenilworth* suite.

(h) PIANO : Sonata.

Blitheman, WILLIAM : *d.* 1591. English composer, noted as an organist and teacher of John Bull. Gentleman of the Chapel Royal. Examples of his work are in the MULLINER book and the *Fitzwilliam Virginal Book.*

Blitzstein [blits'-tine], MARC : *b.* Philadelphia, March 2, 1905. Pianist and composer, a pupil of Nadia Boulanger and Arnold Schönberg. His works include a piano concerto, orchestral variations, a piano sonata, a string quartet, a choral opera—*The Condemned*, operas, ballets and film music. His light opera *The Cradle will rock* (1936) was very successful in New York.

Bloch [block], ERNEST : *b.* Geneva, July 24, 1880; *d.* July 16, 1959. Composer, pupil of Jacques-Dalcroze. Studied at Brussels Conservatoire, 1897-9 ; Hoch Conservatorium, Frankfort, 1900. Also studied with Ludwig Thuille in Munich. Teacher at the Geneva Conservatoire, 1911-15 ; David Mannes School, New York, 1917. Director, Cleveland Institute of Music, 1920 ; San Francisco Conservatory, 1925-30. His music is typically Jewish in its intensity and conscious pathos, as well as in its love of orchestral colour. It has aroused fanatical enthusiasm, and almost equally fanatical opposition. His principal works are :

(a) ORCHESTRA : Symphony ; *Hiver-Printemps* ; *Israel* ; *Trois poèmes juifs* ; *Schelomo* for cello and orchestra ; concerto grosso ; *America* ; *Helvetia* ; *Voice in the Wilderness* ; *Evocations* ; violin concerto.

(b) CHAMBER MUSIC : 3 string quartets ; suite for viola and piano ; 2 violin sonatas ; piano quintet.

(c) OPERA : *Macbeth* (Paris, 1910).

(d) CHORAL WORKS : Sacred Service.

(e) SONGS : *Historiettes au crépuscule* ; *Poèmes d'automne.*

(f) PIANO : Sonata.

G. PANNAIN : *Modern Composers* (1932).
M. TIBALDI-CHIESA : *Ernest Bloch* (1933).

Blockflöte [block'-flur-ter], *G.* Recorder or beaked flute (*Fr.* flûte-à-bec).

Blockx [blocks], JAN : *b.* Antwerp, Jan. 25, 1851 ; *d.* there, May 26, 1912. Composer. Studied at the Flemish School of Music, Antwerp, and Leipzig Conservatorium. Teacher of harmony, Flemish School of Music (later Royal Flemish Conservatoire), 1886. Director, Royal Flemish Conservatoire, 1902. Like Pierre Benoît, his predecessor as director, he was an enthusiastic supporter of Flemish nationalism. His compositions include a symphony, a symphonic triptych, *Kermisdag* (symphonic poem), 8 cantatas, and 8 operas, of which *De Herbergprinses* (*Princesse d'Auberge*, Antwerp, 1896) and *De Bruid der*

Zee (*La Fiancée de la mer*, Antwerp, 1901) were particularly successful.

Blodek [blod'-eck], VILÉM : *b.* Prague, Oct. 3, 1834 ; *d.* there, May 1, 1874. Flautist and composer. His numerous compositions include the one-act comic opera *V studni* (In the Well—Prague, 1867), which is still performed in Czechoslovakia. In this work there is an *intermezzo sinfonico*—a device which Mascagni used later in his *Cavalleria Rusticana* (1890).

Blom, ERIC WALTER : *b.* Aug. 20, 1888; *d.* April 11, 1959. English critic. Music critic, *Birmingham Post*, 1931-46 ; *Observer*, 1949. Editor, *Music and Letters*, 1937-50, 1954-. His works include *Step-children of Music* (1923), *The Limitations of Music* (1928), *Mozart* (1930), *The Music Lover's Miscellany* (1935), *Beethoven's Sonatas Discussed* (1938), *A Musical Postbag* (1941), *Everyman's Dictionary of Music* (1946). He has also translated a number of works, notably O. E. Deutsch's *Schubert : a Documentary Biography* (1946). He is editor of the fifth edition of Grove's Dictionary.

Blomdahl [bloom'-dahl], KARL-BIRGER: *b.* Växjö, Oct. 19, 1916. Swedish composer, awarded a grant by the State in 1941. His works include chamber music, a concert overture, viola concerto, violin concerto, and 3 symphonies.

Blow, JOHN : *b.* prob. Newark, Feb. 1649 ; *d.* London, Oct. 1, 1708. Composer and organist. Brought up as a chorister in the Chapel Royal. Organist, Westminster Abbey, 1668-79 and 1695-1708 ; Master of the Children, Chapel Royal, 1674-1708 ; Organist, Chapel Royal, 1676-1708 ; Master of the Choristers, St. Paul's Cathedral, 1687-93 ; Composer to the Chapel Royal, 1699-1708. He had several pupils, including Henry Purcell. His music, which though in general less vivid than Purcell's, has a similar independence of convention, includes numerous court odes, anthems, songs, harpsichord solos, and a masque (which is virtually a miniature opera), *Venus and Adonis* (modern edition by Anthony Lewis). He published a collected edition of his songs under the title *Amphion Anglicus* (1700)—an obvious imitation of Purcell's *Orpheus Britannicus*.

H. WATKINS SHAW : *John Blow : a Biography*.

Blume [bloo'-mer], FRIEDRICH : *b.* Schlüchtern (Hesse), Jan. 5, 1893. Musicologist, a pupil of Sandberger, Kretzschmar, Riemann, Schering and Abert. Assistant, Leipzig University, 1921 ; Lecturer, Berlin University, 1923. Professor, Berlin, 1933 ; Kiel, 1934-58. Editor of the complete works of Michael Praetorius (in progress) since 1928, and of the collection of old choral music entitled *Das Chorwerk*. His most important book is *Die evangelische Kirchenmusik* (1931) in Bücken's series, *Handbuch der Musikwissenschaft*. Editor of the encyclopedia *Die Musik in Geschichte und Gegenwart*.

Blumenfeld [bloo'-mĕn-felt], FELIX MICHAILOVICH : *b.* Kovalevska, Apr. 19, 1863 ; *d.* Moscow, Jan. 21, 1931. Pianist and composer, a pupil of Rimsky-Korsakov. Studied at the St. Petersburg Conservatoire ; teacher there, 1885-1918. Conductor, Imperial Opera, St. Petersburg, 1898-1912. His compositions include a symphony, a string quartet, and numerous piano pieces, including 24 preludes.

Blüthner [bleet'-ner]. A firm of piano-manufacturers, founded at Leipzig in 1853 by Julius Ferdinand Blüthner (1824-1910).

B minor Mass. A setting of the Latin text of the Mass for soloists, chorus and orchestra by Bach. The popular title is misleading, since only five of the 24 numbers are in B minor. The *Kyrie* and *Gloria* were written in 1733 to support Bach's application for the title of *Hofcomponist* (court composer) to Frederick Augustus II, Elector of Saxony, who also succeeded his father as King of Poland under the title Augustus III (*v.* H. T. David & A. Mendel, *A Bach Reader*, pp. 128-9). Augustus was a Roman Catholic, but the two movements set by Bach were equally suitable for the Lutheran liturgy. Bach subsequently completed the work by adding settings of the *Credo*, *Sanctus* and *Agnus Dei*. He adapted the following numbers from earlier works :

No. 6 : *Gratias agimus* from Cantata No. 29, *Wir danken dir.*

No. 8 : *Qui tollis* from Cantata No. 46, *Schauet doch und sehet.*

No. 13 : *Patrem omnipotentem* from Cantata No. 171, *Gott, wie dein Name.*

No. 16 : *Crucifixus* from Cantata No. 12, *Weinen, Klagen.*

No. 19 (second part) : *Et exspecto resurrectionem* from Cantata No. 120, *Gott, man lobt dich in der Stille.*

No. 21 : *Osanna* from the secular cantata *Preise dein Glücke.*

No. 23 : *Agnus Dei* from Cantata No. 11, *Lobet Gott in seinen Reichen.*

No. 24 : *Dona nobis pacem* from No. 6, *Gratias agimus.*

In addition to the B minor Mass Bach wrote four other Masses, each consisting of settings of the *Kyrie* and *Gloria* only.

C. S. TERRY : *Bach—the Mass in B minor* (1924).

D. F. TOVEY : *Essays in Musical Analysis*, vol. v (1937), pp. 20-49.

Boatswain's Mate, The. Comic opera in one act by Smyth. Libretto by the composer (founded on a story by W. W. Jacobs). First performed, London, Jan. 28, 1916.

Bobillier [bob-eel-yay], ANTOINETTE CHRISTINE MARIE. *v.* BRENET.

Bocca chiusa [bock'-cah kew'-zah], *I.* Singing with closed lips (*Fr.* bouche fermée).

Boccherini [bock-keh-ree'-nee], LUIGI : *b.* Lucca, Feb. 19, 1743 ; *d.* Madrid, May 28, 1805. Cellist and composer. Studied in Rome. Visited Paris, 1768, where he won a great reputation ; Madrid, 1769, where the Infante Don Luis became his patron. Chamber composer to Friedrich Wilhelm II of Prussia, 1786-97. Returned to Spain, where he suffered neglect and died in poverty. His fertility as a composer was astonishing. His chamber music, though little known today (apart from a single minuet), is important for the history of 18th-cent. music. In addition to his chamber music, symphonies and concertos he also wrote a certain amount of vocal music.

Bodansky [bod-unce'-ki], ARTHUR : *b.* Vienna, Dec. 16, 1877 ; *d.* New York, Nov. 23, 1939. Conductor. Studied at the Vienna Conservatorium. Violinist in the Imperial Opera Orchestra, 1896. From 1900 conductor at Budweis ; chorus master, Vienna Opera, 1903 ; conductor, Mannheim, 1909 ; Metropolitan Opera House, New York, 1915. Conductor, Society of the Friends of Music, New York, 1918-31. He conducted the first London performance of *Parsifal*, Covent Garden, 1914.

Boehm. *v.* also BÖHM.

Boehm [burm], (1) JOSEPH : *b.* Pest, March 4, 1795 ; *d.* Vienna, March 28, 1876. Violinist, a pupil of Rode. After giving several concert tours appointed teacher at Vienna Conservatorium, 1819-48. Member of the Imperial Orchestra, 1821-68. His numerous pupils included Auer, Ernst, Joachim and Reményi.

(2) THEOBALD : *b.* Munich, Apr. 9, 1794 ; *d.* there, Nov. 25, 1881, Flute-player attached to the Munich court and inventor of improved mechanism for the flute, since known as the Boehm system and applied to other instruments, including the clarinet. In the Boehm system an elaborate mechanism allows the holes to be pierced in the correct positions and at the same time to be easily controlled by the fingers (for details *v.* Adam Carse, *Musical Wind Instruments*, pp. 94-9). The effect of this is to facilitate accurate intonation and also the playing of passages in keys that were formerly difficult.

Boëllmann [bwel-mun], LÉON : *b.* Ensisheim (Alsace), Sept. 25, 1862 ; *d.* Paris, Oct. 11, 1897. Composer and organist. Studied at the École Niedermeyer, Paris. Organist, St. Vincent de Paul, Paris, 1881. His compositions include a symphony, *Variations symphoniques* for cello and orchestra, chamber music, church music, and organ music, including the *Fantaisie dialoguée* for organ and orchestra.

Boëly [bwel-ee], ALEXANDRE PIERRE FRANÇOIS : *b.* Versailles, Apr. 19, 1785 ; *d.* Paris, Dec. 27, 1858. Composer and organist. He had a considerable influence on Saint-Saëns and César Franck, and also did much to promote a knowledge of Bach's works in France.

He wrote a large amount of keyboard music and chamber music.

Boethius. [bo-ay-ti-ŏŏss, *E.* bo-eeth′-yŏŏss], ANICIUS MANLIUS SEVERINUS : *b.* Rome *c.* 480 ; *d.* nr. Milan (?), 524. Philosopher and statesman. Consul, 510. *Magister officiorum* at the court of Theodoric at Ravenna, 522. Executed by Theodoric. His best-known work is *De consolatione philosophiae.* His treatise *De institutione musica,* based on Greek sources, was a standard text-book throughout the Middle Ages ; it is included in the Teubner edition of his works, ed. G. Friedlein (1867).

Bogen [boh′-gĕn], *G.* Bow (*I.* arco). In string parts used, like *arco,* to contradict a preceding *pizzicato.*

Bohème, La [la bo-em] (The Bohemians). Opera in four acts by Puccini. Libretto by Giuseppe Giacosa and Luigi Illica (founded on Henri Mürger's *Scènes de la vie de Bohème*). First performed, Turin, Feb. 1, 1896. The story deals with the life of the Latin Quarter in Paris and is particularly concerned with the respective love affairs of Rodolfo and Mimi, and Marcel and Musetta, which are not uniformly happy. Rodolfo and Mimi separate. When they are finally reunited it is too late ; Mimi dies of consumption.

Böhm. *v.* also BOEHM.

Böhm [burm], (1) GEORG : *b.* Hohenkitchen, Sept. 2, 1661 ; *d.* Lüneburg, May 18, 1733. Organist at Hamburg and Lüneburg (from 1698) and composer. His compositions include church music and a large number of works for organ and harpsichord, including chorale preludes and suites. Collected edition of his works by J. Wolgast. Sacred songs in *D.D.T.*, xlv. Some organ pieces in *Alte Meister des Orgelspiels.*

(2) KARL : *b.* Graz, Aug. 28, 1894. Austrian conductor. Studied at the Graz Conservatorium and in Vienna. Chorus master, Graz Opera, 1917 ; conductor, 1918. Conductor, Munich Opera, 1921 ; director, Darmstadt Opera, 1927 ; Hamburg Stadttheater, 1931 ; Dresden State Opera, 1934 ; Vienna State Opera, 1954. Conducted the first performance of Richard Strauss's *Die schweigsame Frau* (Dresden, 1935).

Boieldieu [bwull-dyu*r*], FRANÇOIS ADRIEN : *b.* Rouen, Dec. 16, 1775 ; *d.* Jarcy, Oct. 8, 1834. Opera-composer. Studied with the organist of Rouen Cathedral. His first opera, *La Fille coupable,* was produced in Rouen in 1793. First opera to be performed in Paris was *Les Deux lettres* (1796). Teacher of the piano, Paris Conservatoire, 1798 ; conductor, Imperial Opera, St. Petersburg, 1803-11 ; teacher of composition, Paris Conservatoire, 1817. Of his numerous operas the most successful were *Le Calife de Bagdad* (Paris, 1800) and *La Dame blanche* (Paris, 1825), the latter founded on Scott's *Guy Mannering* and *The Monastery.* He also wrote a certain amount of instrumental music.

Bois [bwa], *Fr.* Wood. *Instruments de bois* (or *bois* alone), woodwind instruments.

Boito [bo-ee′-to], ARRIGO : *b.* Padua, Feb. 24, 1842 ; *d.* Milan, June 10, 1918. Composer and poet. Studied at the Milan Conservatorio, and in France and Germany (with a travelling scholarship). His first opera, *Mefistofele,* was performed at Milan in 1868, without success in spite of the enthusiasm of a minority. After revision it became extremely popular. His second opera, *Nerone,* was not performed until 1924. He is likely to be remembered chiefly for his brilliant librettos, closely modelled on Shakespeare, for Verdi's *Otello* and *Falstaff.*

Bolero [bo-leh′-ro]. A Spanish dance in moderate triple time, the characteristic rhythm being marked on the castanets, *e.g.*

or

The dance has been made particularly popular in the concert room by Ravel's orchestral piece with this title (1928).

Bombard. A double-reed instrument, now obsolete, the bass of the SHAWM family.

Bombardon. A term used in military bands for the bass TUBA.

Bonnal [bon-ull], JOSEPH ERMEND: *b.* Bordeaux, July 1, 1880. Organist and composer. Studied at Bordeaux and the Paris Conservatoire. Organist, St. André, Bayonne, and director of the École Nationale de Musique there, 1921. His compositions include orchestral works, chamber music and organ music.

Bonnet [bon-ay], JOSEPH ÉLIE GEORGES MARIE: *b.* Bordeaux, March 17, 1884; *d.* Ste. Luce-sur-Mer (Quebec), Aug. 2, 1944. Organist. Studied with Guilmant at the Paris Conservatoire. Organist of St. Eustache, Paris, 1906. Well known as a recitalist in Europe and America. Published original compositions for the organ and editions of old organ music, including Frescobaldi's *Fiori musicali*.

Bonno [bon'-no], GIUSEPPE: *b.* Vienna, Jan. 29, 1710; *d.* there, Apr. 15, 1788. Studied at Naples. Composer to the Imperial court at Vienna, 1739; *Kapellmeister*, 1774. His numerous compositions, which include 20 works for the stage and 3 oratorios, survive in manuscript. Mozart speaks of him with affection (*v.* Emily Anderson, *Letters of Mozart and his Family*, p. 1076).

Bononcini [bon-on-chee'-nee], (1) GIOVANNI MARIA: *b.* Modena, Sept., 1642; *d.* there, Nov. 18, 1678. Composer and theorist. Court musician to the Duke of Modena, and *maestro di cappella*, Modena Cathedral. His works include chamber sonatas, solo cantatas and a treatise on counterpoint, *Musico prattico* (1673).

(2) GIOVANNI: *b.* Modena, July 18, 1670; *d. c.* 1755. Son of (1) and brother of (3). Cellist and composer. After holding various posts in Italy, Austria and Germany he came to London in 1720 and was supported by the Duke of Marlborough. Though he wrote operas for the newly founded Royal Academy of Music (a company for performing Italian opera) of which Handel was one of the directors, a rivalry grew up between him and Handel, which was encouraged by his aristocratic supporters for political reasons. The rivalry is commemorated in John Byrom's epigram:

> Some say, compar'd to Bononcini,
> That Mynheer Handel's but a ninny;
> Others aver that he to Handel
> Is scarcely fit to hold a candle.
> Strange, all this difference should be
> 'Twixt Tweedledum and Tweedledee.

(The verb " to tweedle " meant to play an instrument in a trifling manner.) Bononcini left England in 1732 and subsequently lived in Paris, Vienna and Venice. He wrote a large number of operas (several for London), oratorios, cantatas, etc. His one-act opera *Polifemo* (1702) is the first extant opera produced at Berlin (modern edition by G. Kärnbach, 1938).

(3) ANTONIO MARIA: *b.* Modena, June 18, 1675; *d.* there, July 8, 1726. Son of (1) and brother of (2). *Maestro di cappella* to the Duke of Modena, 1721. His works include 20 operas and 3 oratorios. His most successful opera, *Il trionfo di Camilla* (Naples, 1696), was one of the first Italian operas to be given in London, where it was performed (at first in English) in 1706.

Bonporti [bon-porr'-tee], FRANCESCO ANTONIO: *b.* Trent, June, 1672; *d.* Padua, Dec. 19, 1749. Composer of chamber music, including trio sonatas and solo sonatas. Four of his *Invenzioni* for violin and figured bass (1712) were copied by Bach and mistakenly published by the *Bach Gesellschaft* (xlv (1), pp. 172-89).

Boosey. A London firm of music-publishers and manufacturers of musical instruments, founded in 1816 by Thomas Boosey. Since 1930 amalgamated with Hawkes & Son as Boosey & Hawkes, Ltd.

Bordes [borrd], CHARLES: *b.* La Roche-Corbon, May 12, 1863; *d.* Toulon, Nov. 8, 1909. Composer and organist, a pupil of César Franck. Choirmaster, St. Gervais, Paris, 1890; director of the *Chanteurs de St. Gervais*, 1892. One of the founders of the Schola Cantorum. He was an enthusiast for old polyphonic music and did a great deal of work to promote its performance, including the publication of an *Anthologie des maîtres religieux primitifs*. He also made a collection of Basque folksongs for the Ministry of Education, and composed a number of orchestral and choral works and songs.

Bordoni [borr-do'-nee], FAUSTINA : *b.* Venice, 1700 ; *d.* there, Nov. 4, 1781. Soprano, a pupil of Gasparini. First appeared in opera in Venice in 1716, and subsequently in Naples, Florence and Vienna. She was brought to London by Handel in 1726 and sang there for two seasons. She married the composer Johann Adolf Hasse in 1730. Her notorious rivalry with Francesca Cuzzoni in London was satirized in *The Beggar's Opera* (1728).

Bore [bo'-reh], *I.* Bourrée.

Boree. *v.* BOURRÉE.

Borgioli [borr-jo'-lee], DINO : *b.* Florence, Feb. 15, 1891. Operatic tenor and painter. Studied in Florence and first appeared in Milan, 1918. He has sung on several occasions at Covent Garden and Glyndebourne. Now lives in London, where he teaches singing.

Boris Godounov [borr-eece' god-oo-noff]. Opera with a prologue and four acts by Moussorgsky. Libretto by the composer (after Pushkin's *Boris Godounov* and Karamzin's *History of the Russian Empire*). First performed, St. Petersburg, Feb. 8, 1674. The story dates from about 1600. Boris Godounov has murdered Dmitri, heir to the throne, and becomes Tsar. A young monk, Gregory, pretends to be Dmitri, and wins support from the people. Boris, overcome by remorse and terror, entrusts the succession to his son Feodor and dies.

There are three versions of this opera : (1) by Moussorgsky, 1868-9, rejected by the St. Petersburg Imperial Opera in 1870 ; (2) also by Moussorgsky, with revisions, 1871-2, first performed in 1874 ; (3) revised and re-orchestrated by Rimsky-Korsakov, 1896.

Bořkovec [borrzh'-cov-eck], PAVEL : *b.* Prague, June 10, 1894. Composer. A pupil of Suk at Prague Conservatoire. Teacher of composition, Prague Academy, 1946. His compositions include 2 operas (*Satyr* and *Paleček*), a symphony, 2 piano concertos, cello concerto and chamber music.

Borodin [borr-o-dyeen'], ALEXANDER PORPHYRIEVICH : *b.* St. Petersburg (now Leningrad), Nov. 12, 1833 ; *d.* there, Feb. 27, 1887. Composer and scientist. Assistant professor of organic chemistry, Academy of Medicine, St. Petersburg, 1862 ; professor, 1864. Began composing as a boy and was much stimulated by meeting Balakirev in 1862. From 1862-7 wrote his first symphony, which was performed under Balakirev in 1869. His other works, which were not numerous, include 2 more symphonies (the third unfinished), *In the steppes of Central Asia* for orchestra, 2 string quartets, 2 operas—*Bogatyri*, a parody (Moscow, 1867) and *Prince Igor* (completed after his death by Rimsky-Korsakov and Glazounov), and songs. He also published a number of scientific papers. He was one of the most strongly national of all the 19th-cent. Russian composers, drawing his inspiration from Russian folksong and also owing something to Oriental influences.

G. ABRAHAM : *Borodin : the Composer and the Man* (1922).

G. ABRAHAM : *Studies in Russian Music* (1935).

M. D. CALVOCORESSI & G. ABRAHAM : *Masters of Russian Music* (1936).

Borowski, FELIX : *b.* Burton (England), March 10, 1872; *d.* Sept. 6, 1956. American composer, studied at Cologne Cons. Teacher of composition, Chicago Musical College, 1897 ; president, 1916-25. President, Civic Music Association, 1926-32. Lecturer, Northwestern University. He served as music critic to several Chicago papers. His compositions include several symphonic poems, a piano concerto, 3 symphonies, a string quartet, and ballets.

Borrel [borr-el], EUGÈNE : *b.* Lisbon, Aug. 22, 1876. Violinist and musicologist. Studied at the Paris Conservatoire. Teacher of the violin, Schola Cantorum, 1911 ; lecturer in history of music, École César Franck, 1935. Joint founder of the Société Haendel (1909-13), which revived a large number of old choral works. He has edited a number of works for the violin and made a particular study of Oriental music. His books include *L'Interprétation de la musique française de Lully à la Révolution* (1934).

Borren [borr-ĕn], CHARLES JEAN EUGÈNE VAN DEN : *b.* Ixelles, Nov. 17, 1874. Musicologist. Originally studied law and practised as a barrister, 1897-1905. Active as a critic and lecturer on music and painting. Librarian, Brussels Conservatoire, 1919-40. Lecturer, Brussels University, 1926 : Liége, 1927. Founder of the *Pro Musica Antiqua* group, conducted by his son-in-law, Safford Cape. His numerous books include *L'Oeuvre dramatique de César Franck* (1907), *Les Origines de la musique de clavier en Angleterre* (1912, published in English as *The sources of keyboard music in England*), *Les Origines de musique de clavier dans les Pays-Bas* (1914), *Orlande de Lassus* (1920), *Guillaume Dufay* (1925), *Études sur le quinzième siècle musical* (1941). His editions of old music include *Polyphonia Sacra : a continental miscellany of the fifteenth century* (1932) and several of the works of Philippe de Monte.

Hommage à Charles van den Borren : Mélanges (1945).

Børresen [ber'-rĕss-ĕn], AXEL EINAR HAKON : *b.* Copenhagen, June 2, 1876. Danish composer, a pupil of Svendsen. In addition to 3 symphonies, a violin concerto and chamber music, has composed two successful operas, *Den kongelige Gaest* (1919) and *Kaddara* (1921), the latter on an Eskimo subject.

Borwick, LEONARD : *b.* London, Feb. 26, 1868 ; *d.* Le Mans, Sept. 15, 1925. Pianist, a pupil of Clara Schumann. First public appearance, Frankfort, 1889. Well known as a recitalist, excelling particularly in the works of Romantic composers and modern French music.

Borry. *v.* BOURRÉE.

Boschot [bosh-o], ADOLPHE : *b.* Fontenay-sous-Bois, May 4, 1871 ; *d.* Paris, June, 1955. Music critic, who specialized in the study of Berlioz. His books include a life of Berlioz, entitled *Histoire d'un romantique* (3 vols., 1906-13), *Chez les musiciens (du xviii*[e] *siècle à nos jours)* (3 vols., 1922-6), *Mozart* (1935) and *Musiciens poètes* (1937).

Bösendorfer [burz'-ĕn-dorr-fer]. A firm of piano-manufacturers, founded in Vienna in 1828 by Ignaz Bösendorfer (1796-1859).

Bossi [boss'-see], (1) MARCO ENRICO : *b.* Salo, Apr. 25, 1861 ; *d.* at sea, Feb. 20, 1925. Organist and composer. Studied at the Liceo Musicale, Bologna, and the Milan Conservatorio. Organist, Como Cathedral, 1881 ; teacher of organ and theory, Naples Conservatorio, 1891 ; director, Liceo Benedetto Marcello, Venice, 1896 ; director, Liceo Musicale, Bologna, 1902-12 ; director, Academy of St. Cecilia, Rome, 1916-23. In addition to organ works he also wrote operas, choral music, orchestral works and chamber music, and in collaboration with G. Tebaldini published a *Metodo di studio per l'organo moderno* (1893).

(2) RENZO : *b.* Como, Apr. 9, 1883. Son of (1). Studied at the Liceo Benedetto Marcello, Venice, and in Leipzig, where he was a pupil of Nikisch for conducting. Active as a conductor in Germany and Italy. Teacher of composition, Regio Conservatorio, Parma, 1913 ; Conservatorio Giuseppe Verdi, Milan, 1916. His compositions include operas, orchestral works and chamber music.

Boston Symphony Orchestra. Founded at Boston (Mass.) by H. L. Higginson in 1881. Conductors : George Henschel, 1881-4 ; Wilhelm Gericke, 1884-89 and 1898-1906 ; Arthur Nikisch, 1889-93 ; Emil Paur, 1893-8 ; Karl Muck, 1906-8 and 1912-18 ; Max Fiedler, 1908-12 ; Henri Rabaud, 1918-19 ; Pierre Monteux, 1919-24 ; Sergei Koussevitzky, 1924-49 ; Charles Munch, 1949.

Bote & Bock [boh'-ter ŏŏnt bock]. A Berlin firm of music publishers, founded in 1838 by Edouard Bote and Gustav Bock.

Botstiber [boat'-shtib-er], HUGO ; *b.* Vienna, Apr. 21, 1875 ; *d.* Shrewsbury, Jan. 15, 1942. Musicologist. Studied at Vienna University. Assistant in the library of the Gesellschaft der Musikfreunde, 1896. Secretary, Wiener Konzertverein, 1900 ; Gesellschaft der Musikfreunde, 1905 ; Konzerthausgesellschaft, 1913-37. He completed C. F.

Pohl's biography of Haydn by adding a third volume (1927). He also wrote a history of the overture (1913) and edited some volumes of instrumental music for the *Denkmäler der Tonkunst in Österreich.*

Bottesini [bot-teh-see′-nee], GIOVANNI : *b.* Crema, Dec. 24, 1821 ; *d.* Parma, July 7, 1889. Double-bass virtuoso, conductor and composer. Studied at the Milan Conservatorio. In addition to touring widely as a soloist he held various conducting posts. His execution and the beauty of his tone were much admired. His compositions include several operas, of which *Ero e Leandro* (Turin, 1879) was the most successful, and an oratorio, *The Garden of Olivet* (Norwich Festival, 1887).

Bottrigari [bot-tree-gah′-ree], ERCOLE : *b.* Bologna, Aug. 24, 1531 ; *d.* there, Sept. 30, 1612. Author of the dialogue *Il desiderio, overo de' concerti di varii strumenti musicali*, which gives a valuable picture of musical life and practice in an Italian court of the late 16th cent. The first edition (1594) was published under a pseudonym ; facsimile ed. by K. Meyer (1924).

Bouche fermée [boosh fair-may], *Fr.* Singing with closed lips (*I.* bocca chiusa).

Bouchés. *v.* SONS BOUCHÉS.

Bouffons. *v.* GUERRE DES BOUFFONS.

Boughton, RUTLAND : *b.* Aylesbury, Jan. 23, 1878. Opera-composer. Studied at the R.C.M. under Stanford and Walford Davies. Taught at the Midland Institute School of Music, Birmingham, 1904-11. Settled at Glastonbury, in Somerset, with a view to writing a series of operas on the Arthurian legends and establishing a permanent home for their performance. The scheme was never completed, but his two-act opera *The Immortal Hour* was performed there in 1914, followed in subsequent years by other productions. *The Immortal Hour*, produced in Birmingham (1921) and London (1922), was for a time extremely popular, largely on account of its tunefulness and romantic colouring. The later operas, which include *Alkestis* (1922), *The Queen of Cornwall* (1924) and *The Lily Maid* (1934), have been less successful, though the choral drama *Bethlehem* (1915) is still performed by amateurs. Boughton has also written books on Bach and *The Reality of Music* (1934).

Boulanger [boo-lũn-zhay], (1) LILI JULIETTE MARIE OLGA : *b.* Paris, Aug. 21, 1893 ; *d.* Mézy, March 15, 1918. Sister of (2). Studied at the Paris Conservatoire. The first woman to win the *Grand Prix de Rome*, 1913. Her compositions include symphonic poems, cantatas, chamber music and songs.

(2) JULIETTE NADIA : *b.* Paris, Sept. 16, 1887. Composer and teacher. Studied at the Paris Conservatoire. As a teacher of composition she has a great reputation. She has also been active in reviving old music, including the works of Monteverdi.

Boult, ADRIAN CEDRIC : *b.* Chester, Apr. 8, 1889. Conductor. Studied at Christ Church, Oxford, and Leipzig Conservatorium. Joined the staff of Covent Garden, 1914. Conducted the first performance of Holst's *The Planets*, 1918. Conductor, Royal Philharmonic Society, 1918-19. Teacher of conducting, R.C.M., 1919. Conductor, City of Birmingham Orchestra, 1924. Director of music and chief conductor, B.B.C., 1930-41 ; chief conductor, 1941-50. Conductor, London Philarmonic Orchestra, 1950. Knighted, 1937. Has conducted many orchestras in Europe and America. He excels in performances of the classics and of Elgar's works. He has published a short *Handbook on the Technique of Conducting.*

Bourdon [boor-dõn], *Fr.* Lit. "burden." (1) A drone bass, such as that produced on the lowest strings of the HURDY-GURDY.

(2) A soft organ stop, employing stopped pipes generally of 16 ft. tone.

Bourgault-Ducoudray [boor-go-dẽe-coo-dray], LOUIS ALBERT : *b.* Nantes, Feb. 2, 1840 ; *d.* Vernouillet, July 4, 1910. Composer. Studied at the Paris Conservatoire. *Grand Prix de Rome*, 1862. Conducted a choral society in Paris, which revived a large amount of old music, 1869-74. Visited Greece, 1874, and studied church music and folksong. Lecturer in history of music, Paris Conservatoire, 1878-1908. He was one of the first to draw attention to the possibilities for composers of modal and non-European scales. His numerous compositions include 5 operas, only one of which was produced in his lifetime, choral works and orchestral pieces. He also published collections of Greek, Breton, Welsh and Scotch folksongs and wrote a book on Schubert (1908).

Bourgeois [boor-zhwa], LOUIS: *b.* Paris, *c.* 1510. Arranger and composer of hymn-tunes for the Genevan Psalter, 1541-57.

Bourrée [boor-ay], *Fr.* (*E.* borry, boree, *I.* bore). (1) A French dance in brisk duple time, starting on the thir quarter of the bar, *e.g.*:

BACH, *Suites for Cello Solo, No. 3*

It appears to have originated about the beginning of the 17th cent. In the 18th-cent. suite it was one of the *Galanterien*, or optional dances inserted between the SARABANDE and the GIGUE. Two bourrées were often written to form a contrasted pair, as was also done with the MINUET and the GAVOTTE.

(2) A dance in triple time, still current in Auvergne, *e.g.*:

PURCELL (*Purcell Society*, vol. vi, p. 55)

Bow (*Fr.* archet, *G.* Bogen, *I.* arco). Instruments of the viol and violin families are played with a bow, which consists of horse-hair strung on a wooden stick. The name "bow" is due to the fact that the original shape of the stick was convex. The tension of the hair can be varied by means of an adjustable nut attached to one end of the stick. The shape of the bow has varied from time to time. In Bach's day, for example, a slightly convex bow was in use in Germany, so that the playing of chords in works like the unaccompanied sonatas and partitas for solo violin was much easier than it is today. The modern bow was established by François Tourte (1747-1833) at the end of the 18th cent. It is a little longer than the earlier 18th-cent. bows; the stick tapers towards the point (*i.e.* the end furthest from the hand) and is slightly curved towards the hair. The bows used for the viola, cello and double-bass are similar to those used for the violin, but progressively heavier. Cello bows are also shorter, and double-bass bows shorter still.

Bowing. (1) In general the technique of playing a string instrument with a bow.

(2) In particular the method of playing notes or passages, indicated by conventional signs. The sign ⊓ indicates a down-bow, *i.e.* the arm moving from left to right; the sign V indicates an up-bow, *i.e.* the arm moving from right to left. A strong down-bow ensures a good attack; the increased pressure possible with an up-bow, after the bow has already touched the string, helps to produce a steady crescendo. If two or more notes are to be played without changing the direction of the bow, a slur is placed over them, *e.g.*:

ELGAR, *Symphony No. 2*

This passage begins with an up-bow. The D, B♭ and C in the second bar are played with a single down-bow, the D and C following are played with a single up-bow, the E♭ and D at the end of the bar are played with a down-bow and up-bow respectively, and the passage ends with a down-bow on the C in the third bar.

There is normally no perceptible break between two consecutive notes, one of which is played with an up-bow and the other with a down-bow. If a note is to be detached from its neighbour a horizontal stroke is placed above it, *e.g.*:

ELGAR, *Enigma Variations*

It is also possible to detach notes slightly without changing the direction of the bow. This is indicated by combining the slur and the horizontal stroke, *e.g.*:

TCHAIKOVSKY, *Symphony No. 5*

Notes can also be played staccato without changing the direction of the bow; in this case the slur is combined with dots, *e.g.*:

TCHAIKOVSKY, *Symphony No. 6*

Unfortunately composers are not always consistent in their use of these signs, nor are their indications of bowing always practicable. It is one of the duties of the leader of an orchestra, or of a particular section of the strings, to ensure that the bowing marks are adequate and to correct or amplify them where necessary. Some conductors carefully mark the bowing in their scores and then have the marks transferred to the parts. Preparation of this kind contributes a good deal to an effective performance.

The following terms indicate particular methods of using the bow: (a) *col legno*, lit. "with the wood," *i.e.* bouncing the stick on the strings instead of playing with the hair of the bow (*e.g.* Holst, *The Planets, No.* 1, *Mars*); (b) *a punta d'arco*, with the point of the bow; (c) *am Frosch* (*G.*) *au talon* (*Fr.*), with the nut or heel of the bow (*i.e.* the end nearest the hand); (d) *sul tasto* or *sulla tastiera* (*I.*), *sur la touche* (*Fr.*), *am Griffbrett* (*G.*), on the fingerboard, *i.e.* play near, or actually above the fingerboard, thus producing a rather colourless tone; (e) *sul ponticello* (*I.*), *au chevalet* (*Fr.*), *am Steg* (*G.*), on the bridge, *i.e.* play near the bridge, thus producing a glassy, brittle tone; (f) *martellato* (*I.*), *martelé* (*Fr.*), lit. "hammered," heavy, detached up-and-down strokes, played with the point of the bow, without taking the bow from the string; (g) *flautando* or *flautato*, playing like a flute, *i.e.* producing a light, rather colourless tone, which is done by playing gently near the end of the fingerboard; (h) *spiccato*, lit. "clearly articulated," a light staccato played with the middle of the bow and a loose wrist; (i) *saltando* (*I.*), *sautillé* (*Fr.*), allowing the bow to bounce lightly on the string.

Boyce, WILLIAM: *b.* London, *c.* 1710; *d.* Kensington, Feb. 7, 1779. Organist and composer. Chorister of St. Paul's Cathedral and a pupil of Maurice Greene. Organist, Oxford Chapel, Cavendish Square, 1734; St. Michael's, Cornhill, 1736-68; All-hallows, Thames Street, 1749-69. Composer to the Chapel Royal, 1736. Conductor, Three Choirs Festival, 1737. Master of the King's Music, 1755; organist, Chapel Royal, 1758. He suffered from deafness from his youth, and this increased as time went on. His compositions include church music, cantatas and odes, 8 symphonies (modern edition by Constant Lambert), chamber music, and works for the stage. His music for the play *Harlequin's Invasion* (1759) includes the song "Heart of oak," commemorating the British victories of that year, the *annus mirabilis*. He completed a collection of church music begun by Maurice Greene and published it in three volumes under the title *Cathedral Music*. It is still in use.

Boyd Neel Orchesra. *v.* NEEL.

Brace. A vertical line, generally accompanied by a bracket, used to join two or more staves together:

Brade, WILLIAM: *b. c.* 1560; *d.* Hamburg, Feb. 26, 1630. English viol-player and composer, who held several court appointments in Denmark and Germany. He published on the Continent several volumes of concerted instrumental music, mostly dance movements.

Braham, JOHN: *b.* London, March 20, 1777; *d.* there, Feb. 17, 1856. English tenor of Jewish birth (originally Abraham). First appeared at Covent Garden as a boy soprano in 1787. First appearance as a tenor, Drury Lane, 1796. Sang frequently in opera in Italy and Germany, and reappeared at Covent Garden in 1801. He was the original Sir Huon in Weber's *Oberon* (London, 1826). In his later years he lost much money through theatrical speculations. His music for *The Americans* (1811) includes the song "The Death of Nelson." According to Leigh Hunt his voice in Handel's arias "became a veritable trumpet of grandeur and exaltation."

Brahms [brahmss], JOHANNES: *b.* Hamburg, May 7, 1833; *d.* Vienna, Apr. 3, 1897. Composer, son of a double-bass player at the Hamburg Stadttheater. Became an accomplished pianist as a boy, but had to make money by playing in sailors' taverns and dancing saloons. Toured North Germany with the gypsy violinist, Eduard Reményi, 1853. In the same year met Liszt and Schumann, who gave him great encouragement. Settled in Düsseldorf, where Schumann had attempted suicide in 1854, and moved to Bonn, where Schumann died in 1856. Director of music to the Prince of Lippe-Detmold, 1857-9. Conductor of the Singakademie, Vienna, 1863-4; Gesellschaft der Musikfreunde, 1872-5. Vienna was his home, apart from temporary visits and concert tours, from 1863 until his death. His earliest extant works are songs and piano works, including the three piano sonatas (1852-3). His earliest orchestral work is the D minor piano concerto, which in its final form dates from 1858. The earliest chamber music is the first version of the piano trio in B major (1854).

His music reflects both the austerity of his North German home and also the sensuous charm of Vienna. Both these facets of his work are illustrated in one of his best-known compositions, *Ein deutsches Requiem*. He was also influenced by his early expreience of gypsy music and by German folksong. Of all the Romantic composers he was the most successful in reconciling the conflicting claims of lyricism and classical form. His principal compositions are:

(a) ORCHESTRA: 2 serenades; 4 symphonies; 2 piano concertos; violin concerto; concerto for violin and cello; variations on a theme of Haydn; *Academic Festival Overture*; *Tragic Overture*.

(b) CHORAL WORKS: *Ein deutsches Requiem*; *Rinaldo*; Rhapsody (alto solo, male chorus and orchestra); *Schicksalslied* (Song of destiny): *Triumphlied* (Song of triumph); *Gesang der Parzen* (Song of the Fates).

(c) CHAMBER MUSIC: 2 string sextets; 2 string quintets; 3 string quartets; clarinet quintet; piano quintet; 3 piano quartets; 3 piano trios; trio for clarinet, cello and piano; trio for violin, horn and piano; 3 violin sonatas; 2 cello sonatas; 2 clarinet sonatas.

(d) PIANO SOLOS: 3 sonatas; variations (1) on a theme of Schumann (2) on an original theme (3) on a Hungarian theme (4) on a theme by Paganini (two sets); variations and fugue on a theme of Handel; 3 rhapsodies; intermezzi, capriccios, ballades, etc.

(e) PIANO DUET: variations (1) on a theme of Schumann (2) on a theme of Haydn (for 2 pianos); sonata for two pianos (= the piano quintet); *Liebeslieder* waltzes and *Neue Liebeslieder* waltzes (with optional voice parts); Hungarian dances.

(f) ORGAN: 11 chorale preludes.

(g) SONGS: nearly 200 solo songs; duets; folksong arrangements.

Brahms was keenly interested in the revival of old music and edited Couperin's keyboard works for Chrysander's *Denkmäler der Tonkunst.*

J. A. FULLER MAITLAND: *Brahms* (1911).
K. GEIRINGER: *Brahms; his Life and Work* (1936).
J. HARRISON: *Brahms and his Four Symphonies* (1939).
F. MAY: *The Life of Johannes Brahms,* 2 vols. (2nd ed., 1948).
W. MURDOCH: *Brahms—with an analytical study of the complete pianoforte works* (1933).
D. G. MASON: *The Chamber Music of Brahms* (1933).
W. NIEMANN: *Brahms* (1929).
R. SPECHT: *Johannes Brahms* (1930).

Brain, (1) AUBREY HAROLD: *b.* London, July 12, 1893; *d.* there, Sept. 21, 1955. Horn-player. Son of A. E. Brain, a horn-player in the London Symphony Orchestra. Studied at the R.C.M. Played successively with the New Symphony Orchestra, London Symphony Orchestra, Beecham Opera Company, Covent Garden Opera and B.B.C. Symphony Orchestra. Retired, 1945. Teacher, R.A.M., 1923. Ethel Smyth's concerto for violin and horn was written for him.

(2) DENNIS: *b.* London, May 17, 1921; *d.* Hatfield, Sept. 1, 1957. Son of (1) and also a horn-player. Studied at the R.A.M. Principal horn in the R.A.F. Central Band, 1939-45 and since then with the Royal Philharmonic and Philharmonia Orchestras. Among the works specially written for him are Britten's *Serenade* for tenor, horn and strings, and Hindemith's concerto.

Branco [brahn'-coo], (1) LUIS FREITAS: *b.* Lisbon, Oct. 12, 1890. Composer and teacher. Studied in Lisbon, Berlin (with Humperdinck) and Paris. Teacher at Lisbon Conservatoire 1916-39. President of the State Chamber of Music since 1933. His compositions include 5 symphonies, 5 symphonic poems, a violin concerto, an oratorio, chamber music, piano and organ music, and songs. He has also been active as a critic and has published several books.

(2) PEDRO FREITAS: *b.* Lisbon, Oct. 31, 1896. Brother and pupil of (1). Conductor of the State Symphonic Orchestra since 1934. Has conducted frequently in other European countries, including England.

Brand [brunt], MICHAEL. *v.* MOSONYI.

Brandenburg Concertos. Six orchestral concertos written by Bach in 1721 for Christian Ludwig, Margrave of Brandenburg. For the original title and dedication *v.* H. T. David and A. Mendel, *The Bach Reader* (1945), pp. 82-3. The scoring is as follows:

No. 1 in F major: 2 horns, 3 oboes, bassoon, *violino piccolo,* strings and continuo.

No. 2 in F major: trumpet, recorder, oboe, violin, strings and continuo.

No. 3 in G major: 3 violins, 3 violas, 3 cellos, double bass and continuo.

No. 4 in G major: violin, 2 recorders, strings and continuo.

No. 5 in D major: flute, violin, harpsichord, strings (without 2nd violin) and continuo.

No. 6 in B♭ major: 2 violas, 2 bass viols, cello, double bass and continuo.

Brandenburgers, The. *v.* BRANIBOŘI V ČECHÁCH.

Brando [brahnd'-o], *I.* Branle.

Brandt [brunt], MARIANNE: *b.* Vienna, Sept. 12, 1842; *d.* there, July 9, 1921. Austrian mezzo-soprano. Studied in Vienna and Paris. First appeared in *La Juive* at Graz, 1867. Sang frequently in opera in Germany, England and America. Her principal parts were Leonora in *Fidelio*, Brangäne in *Tristan und Isolde,* Kundry in *Parsifal*, Eglantine in *Euryanthe*, Orpheus in Gluck's

Orfeo, Ortrud in *Lohengrin*, Donna Elvira in *Don Giovanni*, Fricka in *Die Walküre*, Erda in *Siegfried* and Amneris in *Aida*. Her real name was Marie Bischof.

Brandts-Buys [brunts′-boyce], JAN : *b*. Zutphen, Sept. 12, 1868 ; *d*. Salzburg, Dec. 8, 1933. Dutch composer. Studied at the Raff Conservatorium, Frankfort. His compositions include 3 piano concertos, chamber music, songs and several operas, of which *Die Schneider von Schönau* (Dresden, 1916), was the most successful.

Brangill. *v.* BRANLE.

Braniboři v Čechách [brun′-i-borr-zhi v'checkh′-ahkh] (The Brandenburgers in Bohemia). Opera in three acts by Smetana. Libretto by Karel Sabina. First performed, Prague, Jan. 5, 1866.

Branle [brûnl], *Fr.* (*E.* brawl, brangill, *I.* brando). Originally, in the 15th cent., a step in the BASSE DANSE (from *branler*, to sway).

(2) Hence a dance with a swaying movement, current in France in the 16th and 17th cent. and popular also in other countries, including England (*cf.* Shakespeare, *Love's Labour's Lost*, iii, 1). It could be sung as well as danced and existed in a variety of forms, *e.g. branle de Bourgogne, branle de Champagne, branle simple, branle double, branle gai*. Some *branles* were in duple time, *e.g.* the *branle simple* :

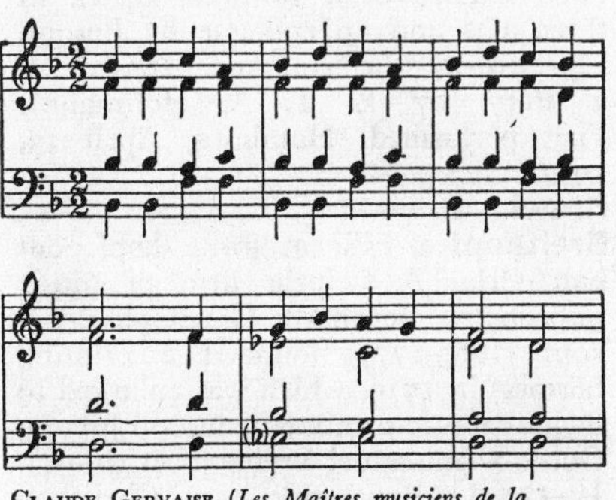

CLAUDE GERVAISE (*Les Maîtres musiciens de la Renaissance française*, xxiii, p. 43)

Others were in triple time, *e.g.* the *branle gai* :

Ibid., p. 76

Brass Band. A band consisting of brass instruments and drums, as opposed to the MILITARY BAND, which includes woodwind instruments. The standard organization in England is : 1 E♭ cornet, 8 B♭ cornets, 1 B♭ flügelhorn (a treble saxhorn), 3 E♭ saxhorns, 2 B♭ baritones, 2 euphoniums, 2 tenor trombones, 1 bass trombone, 2 E♭ bombardons (bass tubas), 2 B♭ bombardons. With the exception of the bass trombone, which is written for at the actual pitch in the bass clef, all the instruments are treated as transposing instruments and their parts are written in the treble clef (even the bombardons). The written note :

will sound :

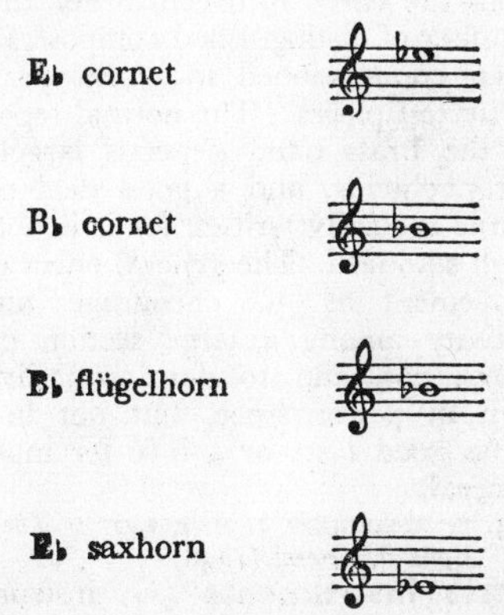

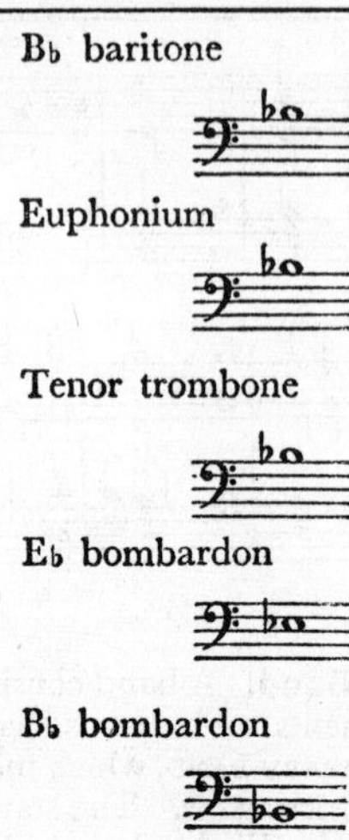

The popularity of the brass band in England dates from the early part of the 19th cent. and is a direct consequence of the invention of valves for brass instruments, which enabled them to play a complete chromatic scale. Brass bands are amateur organizations, generally coached by experts and often receiving material support from the factories and collieries from which the large majority of the players are drawn. There are at present some 5000 brass bands in Great Britain, apart from the Salvation Army, which has more than 1000. Standards of performance, which are extremely high, are maintained by the competition festivals, which date from the early 19th cent. For these a number of distinguished composers have been commissioned in recent years to write test pieces. The normal repertory of the brass band depends largely on arrangements, and a good deal of the music specially written for it is not of a high standard. The general effect of the movement is to encourage musical activity among a large section of the population and to develop individual skill in performance, but not to promote good taste or a love for music in general.

J. F. RUSSELL & J. H. ELLIOT : *The Brass Band Movement* (1936)

Brass Instruments (*Fr.* instruments de cuivre, *G.* Blechinstrumente, *I.* strumenti d'ottone). Instruments made of metal, in which the sound is produced by vibration of the lips, transmitted to a tube by a cup-shaped or funnel-shaped mouthpiece. Usually known in the orchestra simply as "brass." In all instruments of this type successive notes of the HARMONIC SERIES are produced by increased tension of the lips. The intervening notes are produced by lengthening the sounding tube, either with a movable slide (trombone) or with valves which open extra lengths of tubing (all other brass instruments). *v.* BARITONE (2), CORNET, EUPHONIUM, FLÜGELHORN, HORN, SAXHORN, TROMBONE, TRUMPET, TUBA.

A. CARSE : *Musical Wind Instruments* (1939).

Bratsche [brahtsh'-*er*], *G.* Viola. The name is an adataption of the Italian *viola da braccio.*

Braunfels [brown'-felce], WALTER : *b.* Frankfort, Dec. 19, 1882. German composer and pianist. Studied at the Hoch Conservatorium, Frankfort, and in Vienna and Munich. Director of the Hochschule für Musik, Cologne, 1925-33, 1945-50. His compositions, which are romantic in style, include songs, piano music, a Te Deum, and several operas, of which *Die Vögel* (Munich, 1920), based on Aristophanes's *The Birds,* has been the most successful.

Brautwahl, Die [dee browt'-vahl] (The Choice of a Bride). Opera in three acts and an epilogue by Busoni. Libretto by the composer (based on a story by E. T. A. Hoffmann). First performed, Hamburg, April 13, 1912.

Brawl. *v.* BRANLE.

Breitkopf & Härtel [brite'-kopf ŏŏnt hair'-tĕl]. A Leipzig firm of music publishers. Bernhardt Christoph Breitkopf (1695-1777) founded a printing business in 1719, which was enlarged to include music-printing by his son Johann Gottlob Immanuel Breitkopf (1719-94). J. C. I. Breitkopf's son Christoph Gottlob Breitkopf (1750-1800) assigned the business to Gottfried Christoph Härtel (1763-1827). The firm's outstanding achievement is the publication of complete editions (some still incomplete) of the works of the great composers, from Palestrina to Wagner. They have also published a number of works by English composers, including Bantock's *Omar Khayyám* and the original edition of Vaughan Williams's *Sea Symphony*.

Brema [bray'-ma], MARIE : *b.* Liverpool, Feb. 28, 1856 ; *d.* Manchester, March 22, 1925. English mezzo-soprano, the daughter of a German father and an American mother. First appeared on the stage as Lola in the first English production of *Cavalleria Rusticana*, 1891. She sang in Wagner's operas several times at Bayreuth, as well as in Paris and in America. She sang the part of Beatrice in Stanford's *Much Ado about Nothing* (Covent Garden, 1901) and the Angel in Elgar's *The Dream of Gerontius* (Birmingham Festival, 1900). In her later years she taught at the Royal Manchester College of Music. Her real name was Minny Fehrman.

Bremner, ROBERT : *b.* Edinburgh, *c.* 1713 : *d.* London, May 12, 1789. Edinburgh music publisher, who established himself in London in 1762, while retaining his original business in Edinburgh. His publications, which are numerous, are notable for the fine quality of the engraving.

Brenet [brer-nay], MICHEL : *b.* Lunéville, Apr. 12, 1858 ; *d.* Paris, Nov. 4, 1918. Pseudonym of Antoinette Christine Marie Bobillier. Musicologist. She published a large number of historical works, including biographies of Grétry, Palestrina, Haydn and Handel, a history of the symphony before Beethoven, a sketch of the history of the lute in France, *Les Musiciens de la Sainte Chapelle du Palais* (1910), *Musique et musiciens de la vieille France* (1911) and *La Musique militaire* (1917). Her life of Haydn has been translated into English.

Bretón [breh-tone'], TOMÁS : *b.* Salamanca, Dec. 29, 1850 ; *d.* Madrid, Dec. 2, 1923. Composer. Studied at Madrid Conservatorio, and in Rome, Paris and Vienna. Director, Madrid Conservatorio, 1903. Also conducted at the Madrid Opera. An enthusiast for Spanish national music, he wrote a large number of operettas (*zarzuelas*), of which the most successful was *La Verbena de la Paloma* (Madrid, 1894). His other compositions include 9 operas, an oratorio—*El Apocalipsis*, a violin concerto and chamber music.

Bréval [bray-vull], JEAN BAPTISTE : *b.* 1756 ; *d.* Chamouille, 1825. Cellist and composer. First cellist at the Paris Opéra. Teacher at the Conservatoire until 1802. His compositions include orchestral music, chamber music, a comic opera, and an instruction book for the cello, which was also translated into English.

Breve (*L.* brevis, " short "). Originally a short note, introduced in the early 13th cent. when a distinction between the lengths of notes became necessary, it became increasingly longer with the introduction of notes of still shorter value—such as the semibreve (half a breve) and the minim (*L.* minima, " smallest ")—until it was the longest note surviving from the old notation. There is now little need for a note equal to 8 crotchets, but it still occurs in compositions where, in imitation of 16th-cent. practice, the minim is used as the unit of measurement. It is written 𝅜 or 𝅜. *v.* ALLA BREVE, NOTATION.

Bréville [bray-veel], PIERRE ONFROY DE : *b.* Bar-le-Duc, Feb. 21, 1861 ; *d.* Paris, Sept. 23, 1949. Composer, a pupil of César Franck. His compositions, which are chiefly notable for a sensitive lyricism, include a large number of songs, chamber music, choral works, and a three-act opera, *Éros vainqueur* (Brussels, 1910). He was also active as a teacher (at the Schola Cantorum and the Paris Conservatoire) and as a critic.

Brian, WILLIAM HAVERGAL : *b.* Dresden (Staffs.), Jan. 29, 1877. Composer, mainly self-taught. His compositions, some of which demand very large forces and suffer from the extravagance characteristic of the early 20th cent., include a *Gothic Symphony*, an opera—*The Tigers*, comedy overture—*Dr.*

Merryheart, By the waters of Babylon (chorus and orchestra), piano music and songs. He has also been active as a critic.

R. NETTEL : *Ordeal by Music* (1945).

Bridge. (1) (*Fr.* chevalet, *G.* Steg, *I.* ponticello). A piece of wood standing on the belly of string instruments and supporting the strings. In instruments of the viol and violin families it is not fixed to the belly but retains its position through the tension of the strings. It has two feet : the right foot (on the side of the highest string) stands almost over the sound-post ; the left foot, on the other hand, is free to vibrate. The transmission of the vibrations to the belly is assisted by the bass-bar glued inside the belly underneath the left foot of the bridge. *v.* VIOLIN.

(2) A passage in a composition forming a connecting link between two important statements of thematic material and often consisting of a modulation or a series of modulations from one key to another.

Bridge, FRANK : *b.* Brighton, Feb. 26, 1879 ; *d.* Eastbourne, Jan. 10, 1941. Composer, viola-player and conductor. Studied at the R.C.M. For several years a member of the English String Quartet. His compositions include symphonic poems, *A Prayer* for chorus and orchestra, 4 string quartets, string sextet, piano quintet, phantasy quartet for piano and strings, 2 piano trios, violin sonata, cello sonata, works for piano and organ, and songs. His earlier works are in the Romantic tradition ; his later works (including the third and fourth string quartets) turn aside from traditional tonality and are less accessible to the ordinary music-lover.

Bridgetower, GEORGE AUGUSTUS POLGREEN : *b.* Biala (Poland), 1780 ; *d.* London, Feb. 29, 1860. Violinist, the son of an African father and a European mother. First appeared in Paris in 1789, and subsequently played at several concerts in London. He visited the Continent in 1802 and gave the first performance of Beethoven's " Kreutzer " sonata (with the composer) in Vienna in 1803 (see A. W. Thayer, *Beethoven,* ii, p. 299). From that time he lived partly in England and partly on the Continent.

Brigg Fair. Orchestral variations on an English folksong by Delius (1907).

Brinsmead. A firm of piano-manufacturers, founded by John Brinsmead (1814-1908) in London in 1836.

Brio [bree'-o], *I.* " Vigour." *Con brio,* vigorously.

Brisé [bree-zay,] *Fr.* Turn.

British National Opera Company. A company formed in 1922 to perform operas both in London and in the provinces. It came to an end in 1929. Among the operas by English composers produced were Holst's *The Perfect Fool* and *At the Boar's Head,* Boughton's *Alkestis* and Vaughan Williams's *Hugh the Drover.*

Britten, EDWARD BENJAMIN : *b.* Lowestoft, Nov. 22, 1913. Composer and pianist, a pupil of Frank Bridge and John Ireland. Studied at the R.C.M. Active as a composer since childhood and one of the most prolific English musicians of today. His style does not reflect the influence of any single composer but is rather an amalgam of what he has learned from a large number, combined with a resourceful invention of his own and a gift for using familiar materials in a new way. His most important work is the opera *Peter Grimes* (London, 1945), which shows considerable dramatic power. Of his other works the most successful are those for solo voice. His compositions include :

(a) OPERAS : *Peter Grimes* (1945) ; *The Rape of Lucretia* (1946) ; *Albert Herring* (1947) ; *Billy Budd* (1951) ; *Gloriana* (1953) ; *The Turn of the Screw* (1954).

(b) CHORAL WORKS : *A boy was born* ; *Ballad of heroes* ; *Hymn to St. Cecilia* ; *A Ceremony of carols* ; *Rejoice in the Lamb* ; *Saint Nicholas* ; *Spring Symphony.*

(c) ORCHESTRA : Variations on a theme of Frank Bridge (strings) ; *Sinfonia da Requiem* ; *Young person's guide to the orchestra* (Variations on a theme of Purcell) ; piano concerto ; violin concerto.

(d) CHAMBER MUSIC : 2 string quartets ; oboe quartet ; suite for violin and piano.
(e) SONG CYCLES (with orchestra) : *Our hunting fathers* ; *Les Illuminations* ; Serenade for tenor, horn and strings.
(f) SONGS : 7 sonnets of Michelangelo ; *Holy Sonnets of John Donne* ; *A Charm of Lullabies* ; *Winter Words.*

D. MITCHELL & H. KELLER, ed. : *Benjamin Britten* (1953).

Britton, THOMAS : *b.* Rushden, Jan. 14, 1644 ; *d.* London, Sept. 27, 1714. An amateur musician, who carried on a small-coal business in Clerkenwell. His concerts of chamber music, inaugurated in 1678 in a room over his shop, became fashionable. Handel was among the musicians who performed at them. *v.* J. Hawkins, *A General History of the Science and Practice of Music* (1875 ed.), pp. 762, 788-92.

Broadcasting. Public transmission of music by wireless dates from 1920. In England the British Broadcasting Company (B.B.C.) was formed in 1922 and became the British Broadcasting Corporation in 1927. Since music forms only a part of the programmes transmitted by wireless, an account of the methods of transmission has no place in a dictionary of music. Two special points concern the transmission of music : (1) Control in the studio, (2) The effect of broadcasting on public taste and public concert-giving.

(1) Since the performance of music often involves a large number of performers and a number of different instruments, it presents quite different problems from those involved in the broadcasting of the spoken word. The exact placing of the microphones to ensure that the sound is satisfactory to the listener and that the balance is just is a matter of extreme importance, which can only be solved by experiment at rehearsal, since not only the forces employed but also the building in which they perform have to be taken into consideration. It may also be necessary to control the volume of sound during performance, either to ensure that pianissimos are not inaudible or that fortissimos are not excessively heavy, or to adjust the balance where several microphones are used for various sections of the forces taking part. The result of such control may be to create a balance superior to what the ordinary listener would hear in the concert hall, or it may substitute a false balance which misrepresents the composer's intention, *e.g.* if the solo instrument in a concerto is given excessive prominence.

(2) In the early days of broadcasting it was feared that wireless transmission would adversely affect attendances at concert halls. The reverse has proved to be true. Broadcasting has created a new army of music-lovers, who are anxious to hear in the concert hall what they already know through the wireless. The taste of such people is naturally conservative. At the same time, broadcasting has introduced a wealth of unfamiliar music, both of the past and present, to the music-loving public. One can now hear in the course of a single week works which are heard only infrequently (if at all) in the concert hall. The only danger inherent in the broadcasting of music is that listeners may come to regard the broadcast sound as normal.

Broadwood. A firm of piano-manufacturers, founded by Burkat Shudi (1702-73) in London for the manufacture of harpsichords about 1728. John Broadwood (1732-1812), who was employed by Shudi, became his partner in 1770, having married his daughter in the previous year. The firm first began making pianos in 1773. Grand pianos were made from 1781 onwards, and several patents for improvements were taken out in the latter part of the 18th cent. Members of the Broadwood family are still on the board of directors.

Brockway, HOWARD : *b.* Brooklyn, Nov. 22, 1870 ; *d.* New York, Feb. 20, 1951. Composer and pianist. Studied in Berlin. Taught at the Peabody Conservatory, Baltimore, 1903-9, and from 1925 at the Juilliard School of Music, New York. His compositions include a symphony, a violin sonata, a piano quintet and a piano concerto.

Brodsky [brod'-ski], ADOLF: *b.* Taganrog, Mar. 21, 1851; *d.* Manchester, Jan. 22, 1929. Russian violinist. Studied at Vienna Conservatorium. Member of the Vienna opera orchestra, 1868-70. Taught at the Moscow Conservatoire, 1875. Conductor of symphony concerts at Kiev, 1879-81. Toured Europe as a soloist. Taught at the Leipzig Conservatorium, 1883. Leader of Damrosch's symphony orchestra, New York, 1891-4; of the Hallé Orchestra, Manchester, 1895. Succeeded Charles Hallé as principal of the Royal Manchester College of Music. Leader of the Brodsky Quartet.

Broken Consort. *v.* CONSORT.

Broman [broo'-mun], STEN: *b.* Upsala, Mar. 25, 1902. Composer, viola-player and critic. Studied at Prague, Stockholm, Freiburg and Berlin. Music critic of *Sydsvenska Dagbladet* since 1923. His compositions, which are polyphonic in style, include orchestral works, chamber music (including 2 string quartets) and music for Aristophanes's *Lysistrata.*

Bronwen. Opera in three acts by Holbrooke (the last part of the trilogy *The Cauldron of Annwen*). Libretto by Thomas Evelyn Ellis (Lord Howard de Walden). First performed, Huddersfield, Feb. 1, 1929.

Brosa [bro'-sah], ANTONIO: *b.* Canonja (Tarragona), June 27, 1896. Spanish violinist, resident in England for several years before the last war and in the United States from 1940-6. Studied in Barcelona and Brussels. Founder and leader, Brosa Quartet, 1925-38.

Broschi [bross'-kee], CARLO. *v.* FARINELLI.

Brossard [bross-arr], SÉBASTIEN DE: *b. c.* 1654; *d.* Meaux, Aug. 10, 1730. Composer and writer on music. *Maître de chapelle*, Strasbourg Cathedral, 1689; Meaux Cathedral, 1698. His compositions include songs, church music and chamber music. Author of an important *Dictionnaire de musique* (1703), which went into six editions; an English translation appeared in 1740.

Browne, JOHN. The greatest English composer of his day. Nothing is known for certain about his life; he may be the John Browne (*b.* Coventry, Dec. 25, 1452) who was elected King's Scholar at Eton on July 8, 1467. His surviving compositions comprise 7 complete antiphons, two incomplete antiphons and an incomplete Magnificat (all in the Eton choirbook), two carols, and a three-part secular song.

Browning. An English form of instrumental chamber music current at the end of the 16th cent., consisting of variations on the folksong "The leaves be green":

Byrd wrote a five-part "browning" on this theme (*v.* E. H. Fellowes, *William Byrd*, pp. 196-7 and E. H. Meyer, *English Chamber Music*, pp. 112-3).

Bruch [brŏŏkh], MAX: *b.* Cologne, Jan. 6, 1838; *d.* Friedenau, Oct. 2, 1920. German composer of Jewish birth. Studied at Bonn and Cologne, where he taught from 1858-61. Director, Concert-Institution, Coblenz, 1865; *Kapellmeister* to the Prince of Schwarzburg-Sondershausen, 1867-70; director, Liverpool Philharmonic Society, 1880; director, Orchesterverein, Breslau, 1883-90; teacher of composition, Berlin Hochschule, 1892-1910. His compositions include 3 symphonies, 3 violin concertos (of which the first, in G minor, Op. 26, is still one of the most popular works in the repertory), 2 operas, an operetta, choral works (including the cantata *Odysseus*) and chamber music. His setting of the Hebrew melody *Kol Nidrei* for cello and orchestra, Op. 47, is well known.

Bruck [brŏŏk], ARNOLD VON: *b.* Bruck, *c.* 1490; *d.* Linz, *c.* 1554, German composer, for some time *Kapellmeister* to Ferdinand I in Vienna. He wrote a large number of part-songs and motets. For his setting of the chorale "Aus tiefer Not" *v. H.A.M.*, no. 111b (recorded in Decca *Two Thousand Years of Music*).

Bruckner [broo͝k′-ner], ANTON: *b.* Ansfelden, Sept. 4, 1824; *d.* Vienna, Oct. 11, 1896. Composer and organist. Organist, Linz Cathedral, 1856; teacher of theory and organ, Vienna Conservatorium, 1868-91. His compositions, which are romantic in style and characterized by a mixture of homely simplicity and Catholic mysticism, include:

(a) ORCHESTRA: 9 symphonies (the last unfinished).

(b) CHORAL WORKS: 3 Masses; Te Deum; Psalm 150.

(c) CHAMBER MUSIC: String quintet.

Bruckner allowed his friends to make cuts in his symphonies and to alter the orchestration. For long after his death these revised versions were the only ones known to the public. The International Bruckner-Gesellschaft, founded in 1929, promoted a new edition of Bruckner's works in their original form. Bruckner's music is popular in Austria, but is less admired in other European countries, where its naivety and excessive length have proved obstacles to appreciation.

M. AUER: *Anton Bruckner—sein Leben und Werk* (1934).

Brüll [brēēl], IGNAZ: *b.* Prossnitz, Nov. 7, 1846; *d.* Vienna, Sept. 17, 1907. Pianist and composer, who toured Europe as a soloist and also taught in Vienna. His compositions include a symphony, 2 piano concertos, a violin concerto, and several operas, of which *Das goldene Kreuz* (Berlin, 1875) was very popular in Germany.

Brumel [brēē-mel], ANTOINE: late 15th- and early 16th- cent. Master of the choristers, Chartres Cathedral, 1483; Notre Dame, Paris, 1498-1501. Attached to the court of Alfonso, Duke of Ferrara, from 1505. Composer of numerous Masses, printed in the early 16th cent., and polyphonic *chansons*. *v.* H. Expert, *Les Maîtres musiciens de la Renaissance française*, vol. viii.

Brun [broon], FRITZ: *b.* Lucerne, Aug. 18, 1878. Composer and conductor. Studied at Cologne, Berlin and London. Teacher of piano and theory, Dortmund Conservatorium, 1902; teacher of piano, Berne Musikschule, 1903. Conductor of various organizations in Berne since 1909. His compositions include 9 symphonies. He is a great admirer of Bruckner.

Bruneau [brēē-no], ALFRED (christened Louis Charles Bonaventure): *b.* Paris, Mar. 3, 1857; *d.* there, June 15, 1934. Composer and critic. Studied cello at the Paris Conservatoire, where he won the *premier prix* and was also a pupil of Massenet for composition. He won his reputation chiefly as a composer of operas, some of which were considered bold, even crude, when they first appeared. Three of them—*Messidor* (Paris, 1897), *L'Ouragan* (Paris, 1901) and *L'Enfant Roi* (Paris, 1905)—had libretti by Émile Zola. *Le Rêve* (Paris, 1891), *L'Attaque du moulin* (Paris, 1893), *Naïs Miscoulin* (Monte Carlo, 1907) and *Les Quatre journées* (Paris, 1916) were founded on works by Zola. Of Bruneau's works other than operas the most important is the Requiem Mass. He also published three volumes of criticism.

Brunette [brēē-net], *Fr.* A pastoral song of an amorous character, current in the late 17th and 18th cent. Three volumes of *brunettes* were issued (1703-11) by the publisher Christophe Ballard, with the alternative title *petits airs tendres*.

Brustad [brēēst′-ud], BJARNE: *b.* Oslo, Mar. 4, 1895. Norwegian composer and violinist. Studied at Oslo Conservatoire and became a member of the Oslo Philharmonic Orchestra. His compositions, which, in addition to a national flavour, show the influence of Stravinsky, Bartók and the French impressionists, include 2 violin concertos, a symphonic poem—*Atlantis*, and chamber music.

Brustpositiv [broost′-poz-it-eef], *G.* = BRUSTWERK.

Brustwerk [broost′-vairk], *G.* One of the manuals in old German organs, with stops of a quieter tone than those on the Great organ (*Hauptwerk*). Also known as *Brustpositiv*. There is no exact English equivalent.

Buck, PERCY CARTER: *b.* West Ham, Mar. 25, 1871; *d.* Oct. 3, 1947. Composer, organist and writer on music. Studied at R.C.M. and Oxford. Organist, Wells Cathedral, 1896 ; Bristol Cathedral, 1899. Director of music, Harrow School, 1901 ; musical adviser to the L.C.C., 1927-36. Professor at Dublin, 1910 ; London, 1925-36. Knighted, 1937. His compositions are of less importance than his educational works, which include *Unfigured Harmony* (1911, 2nd ed., 1920), *Organ Playing* (1912), *Acoustics for Musicians* (1918), *The Scope of Music* (1924) and *Psychology for Musicians* (1944).

Bücken [beĕk′-ĕn], ERNST : *b.* Aachen, May 2, 1884 ; *d.* Overath, July 28, 1949. Musicologist. Studied at Munich. Lecturer, Cologne University, 1920 ; professor there, 1925. In addition to writing biographies of Wagner and Beethoven for a series called *Die grossen Meister* he also edited an important *Handbuch der Musikwissenschaft*, a lavishly illustrated work in 10 volumes, three of which are by Bücken himself.

Buffo [boof′-fo], *I.* (fem. *buffa*). "Comic." *Opera buffa*, comic opera. The word is now often used as an English adjective, *e.g.* "buffo parts," "buffo singers." As a noun it means a comic actor or singer.

Bugle. A brass instrument with a conical tube and a cup-shaped mouthpiece, used for giving military signals. The regulation bugle of the British Army is in B♭, and as it has no pistons or keys can sound only the notes of the HARMONIC SERIES, *i.e.* :

Of these the first and the last two are not used for bugle calls, so that the working compass is from

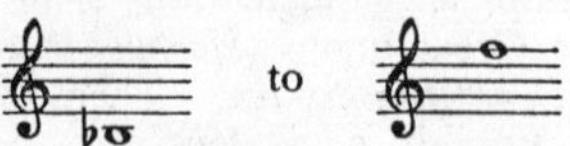

In the early 19th cent. an attempt was made to give the bugle a complete chromatic compass by adding keys (*v.* KEY BUGLE).

Bugle à Clefs [beĕgl a clay], *Fr.* Key bugle.

Bukofzer [boo-coff′-tser], MANFRED : *b.* Oldenburg, March 27, 1910 ; *d.* Berkeley, Cal., Dec. 7, 1955. Musicologist. Studied at Heidelberg, Berlin and Basle. Lecturer, Western Reserve University, Cleveland, 1940. Assistant professor, University of California, 1941 ; associate professor, 1944 ; professor, 1946. His publications include *Geschichte des englischen Diskants und des Fauxbourdons* (1936), *Music of the Baroque Era* (1947) and *Studies in Medieval and Renaissance Music* (1950). He also edited the complete works of Dunstable, *Musica Britannica*.

Bull, (1) JOHN : *b.* 1563 : *d.* Antwerp, Mar. 12, 1628. Organist and composer. Chorister of the Chapel Royal. Organist, Hereford Cathedral, 1582 ; Chapel Royal, 1591 (?). First professor of music, Gresham College, London, 1596-1607. Left England, 1613, and became one of the organists in the Archduke's chapel at Brussels ; organist, Antwerp Cathedral, 1617. His compositions include church music and a large number of keyboard works. Some of the keyboard pieces were published in *Parthenia* (1611), a collection of works by Byrd, Bull and Gibbons. Others have been reprinted in the *Fitzwilliam Virginal Book*, edited by J. A. Fuller Maitland and W. Barclay Squire (2 vols., 1894-9). Some of them require considerable virtuosity and also show individuality in the treatment of harmonic progressions.

(2) [bŏŏl], OLE BORNEMAN : *b.* Bergen, Feb. 5, 1810 ; *d.* Lysø, Aug. 17, 1880. Norwegian violinist, largely self-taught. His determination to become a great virtuoso was the result of hearing Paganini play in Paris. Appeared as a soloist in Paris, 1832, and subsequently toured in Europe and America. In public recitals he displayed his virtuosity almost exclusively in his own compositions, very few of which were published.

S. C. BULL : *Ole Bull—a Memoir* (1886).

Bülow [fon beē′-loh], HANS GUIDO VON :

b. Dresden, Jan. 8, 1830; *d.* Cairo, Feb. 12, 1894. Pianist, conductor and composer. Originally a student of law at Leipzig University. Became a devoted adherent of Wagner after hearing *Lohengrin* at Weimar, 1850. Studied piano with Liszt, 1851. Toured Germany and Austria as a solo pianist, 1853. Teacher of piano in Berlin, 1855-64. Conductor, Munich Opera, 1864; director, Munich Conservatorium, 1867. Married (1) Cosima, daughter of Liszt, 1857; divorced, 1870, after she had left him for Wagner; (2) Marie Schanzer, 1882. *Kapellmeister*, Hanover Court Theatre, 1878; director of the court music to the Duke of Meiningen, 1880-5. Conducted also in England, America and Russia. Conducted first performance of *Tristan und Isolde*, Munich, 1865, and *Die Meistersinger von Nürnberg*, Munich, 1868. As a pianist he had a remarkable repertory and an extraordinary memory. His greatest achievement as a conductor was with the Meiningen Orchestra, which he trained to a high degree of excellence. In addition to his own compositions he made arrangements of some of Wagner's works and edited a large number of piano works by classical composers.

Bund [bŏŏnt], *G.* Fret (on a viol, lute, etc.). *Bundfrei*, "unfretted," a term applied to a CLAVICHORD in which each note has a separate string.

Buononcini. *v.* BONONCINI.

Burgundian School. The name given to a number of composers of the first half of the 15th cent., of whom Guillaume Dufay was the most important. The court of the Dukes of Burgundy at Dijon played an important part in the cultural life of the time, and their territories embraced the Netherlands and Eastern France. Examples of the work of these composers are printed in J. Stainer, *Dufay and his Contemporaries*, C. van den Borren, *Polyphonia Sacra*, J. Marix, *Les Musiciens de la Cour de Bourgogne*.

Burkhard [bŏŏrrk-harrt], WILLY: *b.* Leubringen, Apr. 17, 1900; *d.* Paris, June 1, 1955. Composer. Studied at Berne, Leipzig, Munich and Paris. Teacher of piano and theory, Berne Musikschule (later Conservatorium) until 1937. His compositions, which incline to an austere simplicity and show also a respect for traditional forms, include 2 symphonies, 2 string quartets, "Ulenspiegel Variations" for orchestra, concerto for string orchestra, and several works for chorus and orchestra, among them *Musikalische Übung* (1934), the oratorio *Das Gesicht Jesajas* (1935) and the 93rd psalm (1937).

Burla [boorr'-lah], *I.* Lit. "jest." A short piece of a lively and frolicsome character, *e.g.* Schumann's *Albumblätter*, Op. 124, No. 12.

Burlesca [boorr less'-cah], *I.* (*Fr.* burlesque, *G.* Burleske). = BURLA, *e.g.* the fifth movement of Bach's Partita No. 3 in A minor. Also applied to an extended composition in a playful style, *e.g.* Richard Strauss's *Burleske* for piano and orchestra, Op. 16.

Burlesque [bĕĕr-lesk], *Fr.* *v.* BURLESCA.

Burney, CHARLES: *b.* Shrewsbury, Apr. 7, 1726; *d.* Chelsea, Apr. 12, 1814. English historian and composer. Studied with his half-brother, James Burney, and Arne. Organist, St. Dionis-Backchurch, London, 1749; King's Lynn, 1751-60. Toured Italy, France and Germany (1770-2) to collect materials for his *A General History of Music* (4 vols., 1776-89), the first work of its kind in English, though John Hawkins's *A General History of the Science and Practice of Music* was published in 5 vols. four months after Burney's first volume in 1776. Burney also published an abridged account of his tours—*The Present State of Music in France and Italy* (1771) and *The Present State of Music in Germany, the Netherlands and the United Provinces* (2 vols., 1773). His other works include *An Account of the Musical Performances in Westminster Abbey and the Pantheon in Commemoration of Handel* (1785), *Memoirs of the Life and Writings of the Abate Metastasio* (1796) and musical articles contributed to Rees's *Cyclopaedia* (1802-*c.*1820).

C. BURNEY: *A General History of Music*, ed. F. Mercer, 2 vols. (1935).

F. BURNEY: *Memoirs of Dr. Burney*, 3 vols. (1832).

C. GLOVER : *Dr. Burney's Continental Travels* (1927).
P. A. SCHOLES : *The Great Dr. Burney*, 2 vols. (1948).

Busch [bo͝osh], (1) ADOLF GEORG WILHELM : *b.* Siegen, Aug. 8, 1891 ; *d.* Guildford, Vermont, June 9, 1952. Violinist and composer, leader of the Busch Quartet. Studied at Cologne and Bonn. Leader of the orchestra of the Konzertverein, Vienna, 1912 ; teacher at the Berlin Hochschule, 1918-22. Became a Swiss citizen, 1935. His numerous compositions include a choral symphony, concertos and variations for orchestra, violin concerto, piano concerto, many chamber works, and songs.

(2) FRITZ : *b.* Siegen, Mar. 13, 1890 ; *d.* London, Sept. 14, 1951. Brother of (1). German conductor. Studied at Cologne. Conductor, Riga Stadttheater, 1909 ; director of music, Aachen, 1912 ; conductor, Stuttgart Opera, 1918 ; director, Dresden State Opera, 1922-33. Best known in England as conductor of Glyndebourne Opera, 1934-9. Also conducted at Buenos Aires (Teatro Colón), Copenhagen and Stockholm, and in America.

Bush, ALAN DUDLEY : *b.* London, Dec. 22, 1900. Composer and pianist. Studied at the R.A.M. and with John Ireland, and at Berlin University. Teacher of composition, R.A.M., 1925. His compositions include a piano concerto, a violin concerto, symphonies, *Dialectic* for string quartet, operas and choral works. He has been active in promoting an interest in music among the working classes and is president of the Workers' Music Association, a co-operative society founded in 1936.

Busnois [bee͞-nwa], ANTOINE : *d.* Bruges, Nov. 6, 1492. Composer, a pupil of Okeghem. For some time attached to the court of Charles the Bold of Burgundy and his successor Marie. His compositions include church music and part-songs ; for examples *v. D.T.Ö*, vii, p. 105, *Oxford History of Music*, ii (1932), p. 56.

Busoni [boo-zo′-nee], FERRUCCIO BENVENUTO : *b.* Empoli, Apr. 1, 1866 ; *d.* Berlin, July 27, 1924. Composer and pianist. Appeared as a child prodigy in Vienna at the age of 9. Studied composition with Wilhelm Mayer at Graz. Member of the Accademia Filarmonica of Bologna for composition and piano-playing, 1882 (the youngest to be admitted since Mozart). Teacher of piano, Helsinki Conservatoire, 1889 ; Moscow Conservatoire, 1890 ; New England Conservatory, Boston, 1891-4. Lived in Berlin, 1894-1913, apart from concert tours. Conducted orchestral concerts in Berlin, 1902-9, introducing a number of new works and works performed for the first time in Germany. Director, Liceo Musicale, Bologna, 1913-14. Lived in Zurich, 1915-20, and from 1920 in Berlin. As a pianist he was remarkable not only for his virtuosity but also for his intellectual approach to the problems of interpretation. He had a great admiration for the music of Liszt, but his large repertory included the works of many other composers, including Alkan, Bach, Beethoven, Chopin, Mozart, Schumann and Weber. His compositions, which also provide evidence of his intellectual stature, include the operas *Die Brautwahl* (Hamburg, 1912), *Turandot* (Zürich, 1917), *Arlecchino* (Zürich, 1917) and *Doktor Faust* (completed by Philipp Jarnach, Dresden, 1925), orchestral suites, piano concerto with male-voice chorus, 6 piano sonatinas, *Fantasia contrappuntistica* for piano, chamber music, songs and a large number of arrangements and transcriptions. He wrote the librettos of his operas and also published an essay on aesthetics—*Entwurf einer neuen Aesthetik der Tonkunst* (1907)—and a collection of articles entitled *Von der Einheit der Musik* (1922).

F. BUSONI : *Letters to his Wife* (1938).
E. J. DENT : *Ferruccio Busoni* (1933).
B. VAN DIEREN : *Down among the Dead Men* (1935).

Büsser [bee͞ce-ay], PAUL HENRI : *b.* Toulouse, Jan. 16, 1872. Composer and conductor. Studied at the Paris Conservatoire. *Grand Prix de Rome*, 1893. For some time director of the École Niedermeyer, conductor at the Paris Opéra, and director of the Opéra-Comique. His compositions include several operas, as well as church music, orchestral pieces and songs.

Butterworth, GEORGE SAINTON KAYE: *b.* London, July 12, 1885; *d.* Pozières, Aug. 5, 1916. Composer. Studied at Oxford and the R.C.M. His compositions include two song-cycles on poems from Housman's *A Shropshire Lad*, an orchestral rhapsody with the same title, and an idyll for small orchestra, based on folksongs, *The Banks of Green Willow*. He was killed in action.

Buus [booce], JACHET (Jacques de): *d.* 1565. Flemish composer. Organist, St. Mark's, Venice, 1541-50; organist to Ferdinand I, Vienna, 1553-64. He published a number of important instrumental works (including *ricercari*), both for organ and for instrumental ensembles (*v.* O. Kinkeldey, *Orgel und Klavier in der Musik des 16. Jahrhunderts*, p. 141).

G. SUTHERLAND: "The *ricerari* of Jacques Buus" (*Musical Quarterly*, Oct. 1945).

Buxtehude [books-ter-hoo-der], DIETRICH: *b.* Helsingborg, 1637; *d.* Lübeck, May 9, 1707. Danish composer and organist. Organist at Helsingborg, 1657; Helsingor, 1660; Marienkirche, Lübeck, 1668. At Lübeck he became famous as a player and also as director of the ABENDMUSIKEN, from 1673. His compositions include church cantatas, organ music and sonatas for instrumental ensembles. Modern edition of the organ music (preludes, fugues, chorale preludes) by P. Spitta, 2 vols. (1876-7; new ed. 1952); other ed. by H. Keller and J. Hedar; a selection of church cantatas in *D.D.T.*, vol. xiv; instrumental sonatas in *D.D.T.*, vol. xi. A complete edition of Buxtehude's works was begun in 1925.

A. PIRRO: *Dietrich Buxtehude* (1913).

Byrd, WILLIAM: *b.* Lincoln, 1543; *d.* July 4, 1623. Composer and organist. Organist, Lincoln Cathedral, 1563-72. Gentleman of the Chapel Royal, 1570, and subsequently organist. With Tallis obtained a monopoly of printing and selling music, 1575, which remained his after Tallis's death in 1585. In spite of his appointment at the Chapel Royal he was a Roman Catholic, and was more than once cited as a recusant. His compositions include madrigals, settings of metrical psalms, 3 Masses, Latin church music (notably the two volumes of *Gradualia*, published in 1605 and 1607), English church music, music for viols and pieces for the virginals. The following volumes of *Tudor Church Music* contain works by Byrd:

Vol. ii: English church music
Vol. vii: *Gradualia*
Vol. ix: Masses, motets from *Cantiones Sacrae* (1575), motets preserved in manuscript.

The following works are printed in *The English Madrigal School*, ed. E. H. Fellowes:

Vol. xiv: *Psalmes, Sonets and Songs* (1588).
Vol. xv: *Songs of Sundry Natures* (1589).
Vol. xvi: *Psalmes, Songs and Sonnets* (1611).

Some of his keyboard pieces were printed in *Parthenia* (1611), together with works by Bull and Gibbons. Others have been reprinted in the *Fitzwilliam Virginal Book*, edited by J. A. Fuller Maitland and W. Barclay Squire (2 vols., 1894-9) and *My Ladye Nevells Booke*, edited by Hilda Andrews (1926). The latter consists entirely of Byrd's compositions. A complete edition of Byrd's works is edited by E. H. Fellowes. Byrd excelled in the composition of church music, and particularly music for the Roman Catholic church, where supreme technical mastery is combined with an intimate understanding of the texts and their associations. He is one of the great masters of 16th-cent. polyphony.

E. H. FELLOWES: *William Byrd* (2nd ed., 1948).

Byzantine Music. The music of the Christian church in the Eastern Roman Empire, so called from Byzantium, which was made the capital by Constantine in the 4th cent. with the name Constantinople (now Istanbul). The music of the Byzantine liturgy survives in a notation of ancient origin, which uses NEUMES, though of a different kind from those found in Western manuscripts. These neumes survived in use for many centuries ; the earliest examples date from the 10th cent. A number of correspondences between Byzantine and Gregorian music show that the influence of the Eastern Church on the Western was strong in the early centuries of our era. A further contribution to the West was the organ, though this was used at Byzantium only for secular purposes. The *Monumenta Musicae Byzantinae* (in progress) include a number of facsimiles of manuscripts and several volumes of transcriptions.

E. WELLESZ: *Eastern Elements in Western Chant* (1947).

A History of Byzantine Music and Hymnography (1949).

C

C, *E. G.* (*Fr.* ut, do, *I.* do). (1) The key-note or tonic of the scale of C major.

(2) As an abbreviation = *cantus* (*I.* canto), contralto, *con* (with), *col* or *colla* (with the). *c. B.* = *col Basso*, an indication that the cellos are to play with the double-basses. *C. B.* = *contrabasso* (double-bass). *C. F.* = *cantus firmus* (*I.* canto fermo), *i.e.* a given theme (generally in long notes) to which counterpoints are added (*v.* CANTO FERMO, COUNTERPOINT).

(3) The C clef, an ornamental form of the letter C, indicates middle C or

It may be placed on any line of the stave, and is still so used in some modern library editions of old music, but only the following three positions are used in recent scores :

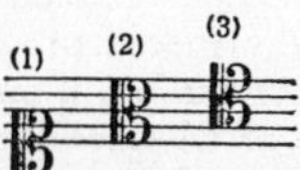

These are (1) soprano clef, still used for the soprano voice in late 19th-cent. German scores ; (2) alto clef, formerly used for the alto voice and alto trombone and in regular use today for the viola ; (3) tenor clef, formerly used for the tenor voice and in regular use today for the tenor trombone and the upper register of the bassoon, cello and double bass. A knowledge of the alto and tenor clefs is indispensable for reading chamber music or orchestral scores. The easiest way to acquire that knowledge is by learning to play an instrument that uses them. A tenor-trombone player today must be able to read alto, tenor or bass clefs with equal facility.

(4) The sign

is a time signature and means that there are four crotchets in the bar (4/4). Its original form was a half circle, indicating "imperfect time" (breve = 2 semibreves), as opposed to the complete circle indicating "perfect time" (breve = 3 semibreves). If a vertical stroke is drawn through the C, thus :

it generally indicates that the minim is to be taken as the unit of measurement (2/2) instead of the crotchet.

v. ALLA BREVE, MENSURAL NOTATION, TIME-SIGNATURE.

Cabanilles [cah-bah-neel'-lyess], JUAN: *b.* Algemesi, Sept. 4, 1644; *d.* Valencia, Apr. 29, 1712. Organist of Valencia Cathedral from 1665 till his death and composer of organ music ; modern ed. by H. Anglès in progress.

Cabaletta [cah-bah-let'-tah], *I.* (1) Formerly a simple operatic aria, with an incisive and continuously repeated rhythm, often found in Rossini.

(2) In later 19th-cent. Italian opera the concluding section of an aria in which the principal emphasis is on an incisive and reiterated rhythm.

The derivation of the word is disputed. It seems unlikely that it has any connection with *caballo*, a horse, nor is it easy to see why it should be regarded as a corruption of *cavatinetta*, diminutive of *cavatina*.

Cabezón [cah-bayth-one'], ANTONIO DE: *b.* Castrillo de Matajudíos, Mar. 30, 1510 ; *d.* Madrid, Mar. 26, 1566. Spanish organist and composer, blind from birth. Organist to Charles V and Philip II. His instrumental works were published posthumously by his son Hernando in 1578 under the title

Obras de musica para tecla arpa y vihuela (Musical works for keyboard, harp and lute); modern edition in F. Pedrell, *Hispaniae Schola Musica Sacra*, iii, iv, vii & viii. The music consists of liturgical pieces and variations on secular songs. It has been suggested that the English virginalists learned the art of variation from Cabezón and his Spanish contemporaries. See also H. Anglès, *La música en la corte de Carlos V* (*Monumentos de la Música Española*, ii, 1944).

Caccia [cah'-tchah], *I.* Lit. "chase" or "hunt."

(1) An early 14th-cent. Italian poem dealing with hunting, fishing or scenes of popular life, set to picturesque and lively music for two voices in canon, generally with a third part (instrumental) providing an independent accompaniment. These pieces seem to have been imitated originally from earlier examples current in France under the name *chace* at the beginning of the century (*v.* H. Besseler in *Archiv für Musikwissenschaft*, vii, p. 251).

W. T. MARROCCO: *The 14th-Century Italian Caccia* (1942).

(2) *Corno da caccia*: *v.* HORN. *Oboe da caccia*: *v.* OBOE.

Caccini [cah-tchee'-nee], (1) GIULIO: *b.* Rome, *c.* 1550; *d.* Florence, Dec. 1618. Italian singer and composer, for many years in the service of the Grand Duke of Tuscany at Florence. A member of the circle of scholars, musicians and poets who met at the house of Count Bardi in Florence and wished to recreate the music and drama of ancient Greece. One result of this movement was the composition of solo songs with figured bass accompaniment, designed to reproduce as completely as possible the accents and emotions of the poetry. Caccini published a number of settings of this type in 1602 under the title *Nuove Musiche* (facsimile edition, 1934). In the preface he declared that it had been his object to write a type of music in which one could, so to speak, talk in music (*in armonia favellare*), allowing mere song to take second place to the words. He also contributed part of the music of Peri's opera *L'Euridice* (Florence, 1600), in which the same principles were practised, and in the same year published a complete setting of the same libretto (modern edition by R. Eitner, *Publikationen der Gesellschaft für Musikforschung*, vol. x), which was performed in 1602.

(2) FRANCESCA: *b.* Florence, Sept. 18, 1588. Daughter of (1). Singer and composer. Her compositions include sacred and secular cantatas for one and two voices, 2 ballets and the opera *La liberazione di Ruggiero dall' isola d'Alcina* (Florence, 1625; modern edition by Doris Silbert, *Smith College Music Archives*, vii).

Cadence. Lit. "a falling" (*L.* cado, "I fall"). The name seems to originate from the fact that in unharmonized melody (*e.g.* plainsong or folksong) it is common for a tune to end by falling to the tonic or keynote (*cf. Twelfth Night*, i, 1: "That strain again! it had a dying fall"). Hence it is applied to a concluding phrase, whether at the end of a section or at the end of a complete melody, and, by a natural transference, to the harmonization of such phrases. A number of conventional formulae for such harmonization have acquired currency at different periods. In consequence "cadence" has come to mean a harmonic progression which suggests a conclusion, if only temporary, irrespective of whether the melody rises or falls or remains stationary. In this matter opinions vary from one period to another: what would have seemed inconclusive, if not unintelligible, at one time may very well appear the opposite a hundred years later. To provide a complete index of cadences would be difficult, since there is hardly any limit to the possible variations; in particular, composers have not been slow to enhance the effect of a final close by interpolating something unexpected at the last moment.

Conventional names have been given to certain simple types of cadential formulae current in the classical and Romantic periods, *e.g.* (in the key of C major or C minor):—

(1) Perfect cadence (or full close)—dominant to tonic:

(2) Imperfect cadence (or half close)—tonic to dominant :

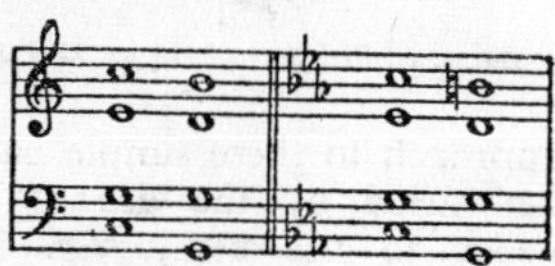

(This will normally occur in the middle of a composition, not at the end—hence the name).

(3) Plagal cadence—subdominant to tonic :

(4) Interrupted cadence—dominant to some chord other than the tonic, *e.g.* :

(This is strictly not a cadence at all, since it is not conclusive ; the name alludes to the fact that the ear is expecting the tonic chord, but the expected cadence is interrupted by the substitution of another chord). The names given above are those most commonly in use in England, but there is no absolute uniformity of nomenclature ; for instance, Nos. 1 and 3 are often referred to as "perfect (authentic)" and "perfect (plagal)," the use of the word "plagal" by itself being in fact an abbreviation.

The following are actual examples of the cadences described above :—

(1) Perfect :

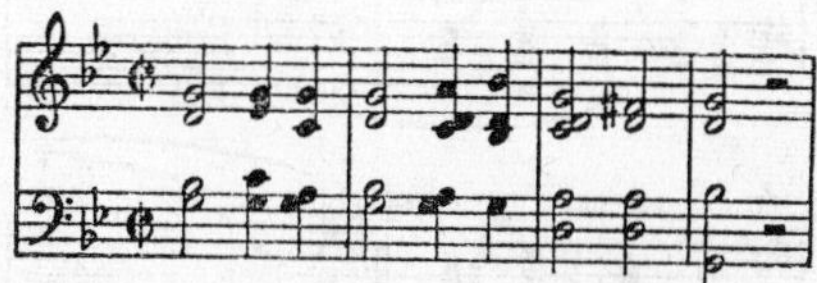

SCHUBERT, *Quartet in D minor*

(2) Imperfect :

BACH, *Partita in B♭ major*

(3) Plagal :

HANDEL, *Messiah*

(4) Interrupted :

BRAHMS, *Ein deutsches Requiem*

Among the many possible modifications of these basic formulae one of the commonest is the substitution of a minor chord for a major, or vice versa, in the plagal cadence, *e.g.*

(1) Subdominant minor in a major key :

BRAHMS, *Symphony No. 3*

(2) Tonic major in a minor key (the so-called *tierce de Picardie*) :

BEETHOVEN, *Quartet in C♯ minor, Op. 131*

The substitution of the tonic major in a perfect cadence in a minor key is also very common :

BACH, *48 Preludes and Fugues, Book I, No. 24*

The approach to these simple cadences can be varied by the use of chords extraneous to the key ; *e.g.* in the perfect cadence :

BEETHOVEN, *Sonata in F minor, Op. 57*

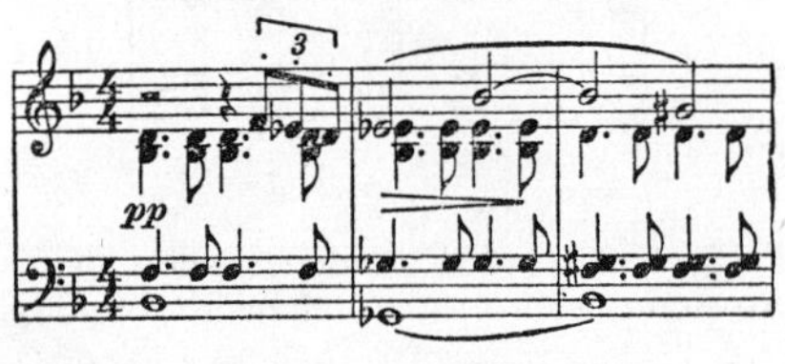

SCHUBERT, *Quartet in D minor*

The revival of interest in modal folksong (*v.* MODES) has led in modern times to the frequent use of a perfect cadence in which the seventh degree of the scale is not sharpened, *e. g.*:

and of other cadences using the same melodic idiom, *e.g.* :

A simple example is the following :

VAUGHAN WILLIAMS, *The Wasps*

This practice contrasts with the medieval and Renaissance practice of sharpening the seventh degree of the modal scales, where necessary, in polyphonic music (*v.* MUSICA FICTA). The use of cadences in the course of a composition played an important part in defining the structure of 16th-cent. motets and madrigals. The sharpening of the seventh in cadences was normal in the Dorian (D to D), Mixolydian (G to G) and Aeolian (A to A) modes. It was unnecessary in the Lydian (F to F) and Ionian (C to C) modes, where the seventh was already sharp, and was avoided in the Phrygian (E to E) mode, where the following typical harmonization of the cadence was adopted (with sharpened third in the final chord, in accordance with normal 16th-cent. practice) :

This cadence, which came to be known as the "Phrygian cadence," survived the break-up of the modal system and was often used as a cadence on the dominant in minor keys, *i.e.* the second chord in the above example would be treated as the dominant of A minor.

The sharpening of the seventh in modal scales did not exclude the use of the flat seventh proper to the mode, either in close juxtaposition to the sharp seventh or simultaneously. This practice is particularly common in English music of the 16th and 17th cents., *e.g.* :

BYRD, *Gradualia, Book I, ii, 3*

PURCELL, *My heart is inditing*

A. CASELLA : *The Evolution of Music, through the History of the Perfect Cadence* (1924).

Cadenza [cah-den'-tsah], *I.* Lit. "cadence." Used to describe the improvisation introduced by operatic singers in the 18th cent. before the final cadence at the end of an aria. The practice was borrowed by soloists in instrumental concertos. In both cases an instrumental *ritornello* normally followed the final cadence for the soloist. The convention was to pause on a $^6_4$ chord on the dominant, *i.e.* in the key of C major :

then embark on the improvisation and conclude with the cadence which had been deferred. In the classical concerto the cadenza occurs most frequently in the first movement ; it is found also in the finale. The player was expected not only to display his virtuosity but also to make allusions to the thematic material of the movement. Although these cadenzas were normally improvised Mozart left written cadenzas for several of his piano concertos. Later composers have left the player no option. In Mendelssohn's violin concerto, Schumann's piano concerto and Elgar's violin concerto—to take only three examples—the cadenza is an integral part of the composition ; in Elgar's work it is actually accompanied by the orchestra. Brahms's violin concerto is an exceptional example of the survival of the old practice of leaving the cadenza to the player. The cadenza in modern works has become in fact an anachronism, since the conditions to which it originally owed its existence no longer exist. The practice of improvising cadenzas to classical concertos has now completely disappeared. Players either write their own beforehand, or use published examples by others. In such cases a disparity of style between the cadenza and the work it is supposed to adorn is often very marked.

Cadman, CHARLES WAKEFIELD : *b.* Johnstown (Pa.), Dec. 24, 1881 ; *d.* Los Angeles, Dec. 30, 1946. American composer, organist and critic. In his compositions he has made use of American Indian themes. His works include orchestral pieces, music for piano and organ, songs and the operas *Shanewis* (New York, 1918) and *A Witch of Salem* (Chicago, 1926).

Cadmus et Hermione [cud-mēēce ay airm-yon] (Cadmus and Hermione). Opera with a prologue and five acts by Lully. Libretto by Philippe Quinault. First performed, Paris, Apr. 27, 1673.

Caffarelli [cahf-fah-rell'-lee] : *b.* Bari, Apr. 12, 1710 ; *d.* Naples, Jan. 31, 1783. The professional name of Gaetano Majorano, a celebrated *castrato* singer. A pupil of Caffaro (from whom he took his name) and Porpora. He had an enormous reputation as an opera singer in Italy, and appeared also in London (in two of Handel's operas) and Paris. He was noted for the beauty of his voice and for his skill in singing embellishments, particularly chromatic scales.

Caix d'Hervelois [cay dairv-lwa] LOUIS DE : *b.* Paris, *c.* 1670 ; *d.* there, *c.* 1760. French player on the *viola da gamba*, in the service of the Duke of Orleans. Published pieces for the *viola da gamba* and for the flute.

Calando [cah-lahnd'-o], *I.* Giving way, both in volume and in speed, a combination of *diminuendo* and *ritardando.*

Caldara [cahl-dah'-rah], ANTONIO : *b.* Venice, 1670 ; *d.* Vienna, Dec. 28, 1736. Italian cellist and composer, a pupil of Legrenzi. Vice-*Kapellmeister* at the Imperial Court, Vienna, 1716. Wrote more than 100 operas and oratorios, church music (including a " Crucifixus " in 16 parts), and chamber music. Modern editions of his church music and secular vocal music in *D.T.Ö.*, xiii (1) & xxxix.

Caletti-Bruni. *v.* CAVALLI.

Calife de Bagdad, Le [ler ca-leef der bug-dud] (The Caliph of Baghdad). Opera in one act by Boieldieu. Libretto by Claude Godard d'Aucour de Saint-Just. First performed, Paris, Sept. 16, 1800.

Callas, MARIA MENEGHINI : *b.* New York, Dec. 3, 1923. Soprano, the child of Greek parents. Studied in Athens, where she made her first appearance during the war. First appeared in Italy at Verona, 1947, in which year she married Signor Meneghini. Since then she has sung regularly in Italy and is also well-known at Covent Garden. Though she has sung in Wagner, she excels in the standard works of the Italian repertory.

Callcott, JOHN WALL : *b.* Kensington, Nov. 20, 1766 ; *d.* Bristol, May 15, 1821. English composer and organist, famous as a writer of glees.

Calvé [cul-vay], EMMA : *b.* Decazeville, Aug. 15, 1858 ; *d.* Millau, Jan. 6, 1942. French soprano, who sang in opera in France, Belgium, Italy, England and America until 1910, when she retired from the stage and appeared only on the concert platform. Her interpretation of the title role of *Carmen* was outstanding.

E. CALVÉ : *My Life* (1922).

Calvocoressi, MICHEL D. : *b.* Marseilles, Oct, 2, 1877 ; *d.* London, Feb. 1, 1944. Critic, of Greek parentage. Educated in Paris. In addition to making numerous translations into French and English, he made a special study of Russian music. His published works include *Musical Criticism* (1923, 2nd ed. 1931), *Masters of Russian Music* (with G. Abraham, 1936), *A Survey of Russian Music* (1944), *Mussorgsky* (completed by G. Abraham, 1946), another larger study of Moussorgsky (1956), and an autobiography, *Musicians' Gallery* (1933).

Cambert [cũn-bair], ROBERT : *b.* Paris, *c.* 1628 ; *d.* London, 1677. French composer and organist, a pupil of Chambonnières. He became associated with the poet Pierre Perrin ; they produced jointly *La Pastorale d'Issy* (1659) and *Pomone* (1671), pioneer works in the history of French opera. Cambert also set *Les Peines et les Plaisirs d'Amour* (1672), libretto by Gabriel Gilbert. After Perrin had fallen out of favour with Louis XIV in 1672 Cambert went to London, where his activities are uncertain.

Cambiata [cahmb-yah'-tah], *I.* Short for *nota cambiata*, changed note. The term, used mainly of 16th-cent. counterpoint, implies the use of a dissonant note where one would normally expect a consonant note. It is currently used in two senses :

(1) Of an accented passing dissonance, *e.g.* :

PALESTRINA, *Suscipe verbum*

In Palestrina's practice it occurs, as here, on the even beats (second or fourth) of the bar and in a descending passage. Other composers show greater freedom in its use, *e.g.* :

BYRD, *Gradualia, Book II*, 20

(2) Of a sequence of notes, also known as "changing note group," which occurs most frequently in the following forms :

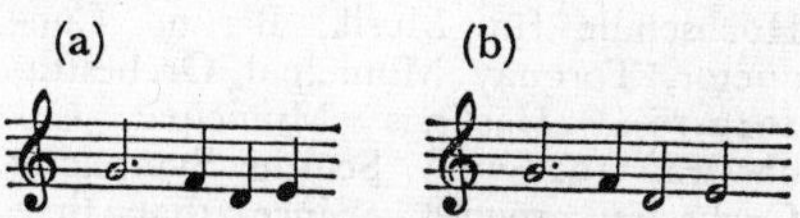

The second note is dissonant with one or more of the other parts, but instead of moving by step to the third note (in accordance with the normal treatment of passing dissonance) it leaps, *e.g.* :

PALESTRINA, *Missa Assumpta est Maria*

(The sequence of notes may occur without any dissonance, but it is not then strictly a *cambiata*).

The following example illustrates both types of *cambiata* :

TALLIS, *Domine, quis habitabit ?*

Camera [cah'-meh-rah], *I.* "Room." Used in the 17th and early 18th cent. to distinguish music suitable for performance in secular surroundings from that suitable for performance in church, *e.g. sonata da camera.* The English term "chamber music" is a literal translation of *musica da camera. v.* SONATA.

Cameron, BASIL : *b.* Reading, Aug. 18, 1884. Conductor. Studied at the Hochschule für Musik, Berlin. Conductor, Torquay Municipal Orchestra, 1912-16 ; Hastings Municipal Orchestra, 1923-30 ; Seattle Symphony Orchestra, 1932-8. Since that time he has regularly acted as assistant conductor of the Promenade Concerts in London.

Campana [cahm-pah'-nah], *I.* Bell. Diminutive, *campanella.*

Campanelli [cahm-pah-nell'-lee], *I.* Glockenspiel.

Campion, THOMAS : *b.* London, Feb. 12, 1567 ; *d.* there, March 1, 1620. Poet and song-writer, a doctor by profession. Educated at Cambridge. Published four books of lute-songs, a fifth in association with Philip Rosseter, and a treatise on counterpoint. He also wrote the music for several court masques. The lute-songs are reprinted in *E.S.L.S.*, 2nd ser., the treatise on counterpoint in the edition of his works by Percival Vivian.

KASTENDIECK, M. M. : *England's Musical Poet, Thomas Campion* (1938).

WARLOCK, P. : *The English Ayre* (1926).

Campra [cũn-pra], ANDRÉ : *b.* Aix-en-Provence, Dec. 4, 1660 ; *d.* Versailles, June 29, 1744. French composer. *Maître de chapelle,* Toulon, 1679 ; Arles, 1681 ; Toulouse, 1683 ; Notre Dame, Paris, 1694. He composed some distinguished church music but is best known by his *divertissements* and operas, of which *L'Europe galante* (1697), *Les Fêtes vénitiennes* (1710) and *Tancrède* (1702) have been published in vocal score in *Chefs-d'oeuvre de l'opéra français.*

Canarie [ca-na-ree], *Fr.* A French dance, current in the 17th cent., which takes its name from the Canary Islands. It is very similar to the gigue, being in 3/8 or 6/8 time, with a persistent dotted rhythm. Examples occur in keyboard works by French and German composers, and in operas, *e.g.* :

PURCELL, *Dioclesian*

Cancrizans. "Crab-like" (*L.* cancer, "crab"). *v.* CANON, RETROGRADE MOTION.

Cannabich [cun'-ub-ish], CHRISTIAN : *b.* Mannheim, Dec. 1731 ; *d.* Frankfort, Jan. 20, 1798. Violinist, composer and conductor, a pupil of Johann Stamitz. Orchestral conductor at Mannheim and Munich. His conducting was much praised by his contemporaries, including Mozart, who described him as "the best conductor I have ever seen" (letter of July

9, 1778). Examples of his instrumental works are in *D.T.B.*, viii (2) & xv-xvi.

Canon (*Gr.* κανών, rule). A polyphonic composition in which one part is imitated by one or more other parts, entering subsequently in such a way that the successive statements of the melody overlap, *e.g.* :

BIZET, *L'Arlésienne*

If the imitation is exact in every detail the canon is "strict"; if it is modified by the introduction or omission of accidentals it is "free." It is common for such compositions to end with a short coda, in which imitation is abandoned, in order to make a satisfactory conclusion. If, on the other hand, each part, on coming to the end of the melody, goes back to the beginning again and repeats, the result is a "perpetual" or "infinite" canon. popularly known as a "round" (*e.g.* "Three blind mice"). Canons are often accompanied by one or more independent parts, *e.g.* :

BACH, *Musikalisches Opfer*

In this example the independent part is a pre-existing melody, the theme given to Bach for improvisation by Frederick the Great. Canons have also been written on a ground bass, *e.g.* :

PURCELL, *Dioclesian, Act III*

The problems to be solved in canonic writing have fascinated composers of all ages, some of whom (particularly in the 15th cent.) have invested the art with mystery by providing only the melody and adding enigmatic instructions for which a solution must be found before the canon can be scored. The part which imitates may begin at the same pitch as the original melody or at an interval above or below it ; hence the terms "canon at the unison," "canon at the fifth," etc. (for examples see particularly Bach's *Goldberg Variations*).

Among the possible varieties of canon are

(1) Canon by inversion, or contrary motion (*canon per arsin et thesin*). The part which imitates is the same as the original melody but upside down, *e.g.* :

CLEMENTI, *Sonata in G major, Op. 40, No. 1*

(2) Canon by augmentation. The part which imitates is in longer notes than the original, *e.g.* :

PURCELL, *Sonatas of III Parts, No. 6*

(This example illustrates also double augmentation).

(3) Canon by diminution. The part which imitates is in shorter notes than the original.

(4) A combination of (1) and (2), or (1) and (3), *e.g.* the following canon by augmentation and inversion :

BACH, *Musikalisches Opfer*

(5) Crab canon (*canon cancrizans*) or retrograde canon. The part which imitates is written backwards, beginning with the end.

(6) Crab canon by inversion. The part which imitates is written backwards and upside down.

Two or more canons may be combined. A simple canon between two parts is called a "canon two in one," because both parts are singing the same melody. If two two-part canons are combined, making four parts in all, the result will be a "canon four in two," *e.g.* :

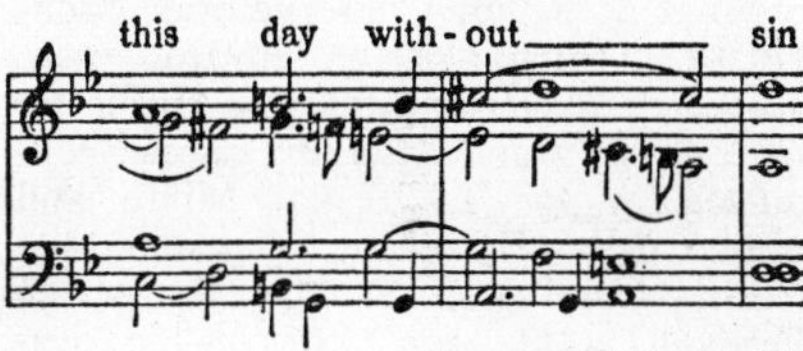

PURCELL, *Te Deum in B♭*

Cantabile [cahn-tah′-bee-leh], *I.* "Singable." Applied to an instrumental piece it indicates that the player should make the music sing.

Cantata (*I.* cantare, "to sing"). Properly a piece which is sung, as opposed to "sonata," a piece which is played. In the early 17th cent. the word was used of extended pieces of secular music, for one or two voices with accompaniment, in which contrasting sections of declamatory recitative and aria were normal. The style of such pieces was similar to that of opera, but they were intended purely for concert performance. In the course of the 17th cent. the cantata was imitated by French, German and English composers. It was also extended to include settings of religious texts and became increasingly elaborate. In Germany the Lutheran chorale was introduced into the cantata as the basis for extended treatment. This type of cantata, written for soloists, chorus and orchestra and owing much to the example of opera, was the model adopted by J. S. Bach, of whose church cantatas nearly 200 survive. The older practice of writing dialogues survives in many of the duets in Bach's cantatas. Bach also wrote a few secular cantatas on the same plan. Since the late eighteenth century the term "cantata" has generally been used for secular or sacred choral works, with or without soloists, accompanied by orchestra, which are similar in conception to the oratorio but less extended.

A. SCHWEITZER : *J. S. Bach*, 2 vols. (1911).
W. G. WHITTAKER : *Fugitive Notes on Certain Cantatas and the Motets of J. S. Bach* (1924).

Cantelli [cahn-tell'-lee], GUIDO : *b.* Novara, Apr. 27, 1920 ; *d.* Orly, nr. Paris, Nov. 24, 1956. Conductor. Studied at Milan Conservatorio. Conductor, Teatro Coccia, Novara, 1943. Interned in Germany during the latter part of the war. After his release conducted at the La Scala, Milan and visited many European cities and New York. Conducted at the Edinburgh Festival, 1950 and 1951. He was generally regarded as likely to develop into one of the great conductors of our time. He lost his life in an aeroplane crash.

Canteloube [cũnt-loob], JOSEPH : *b.* Anonnay, Oct. 21, 1879 ; *d.* Nov. 4, 1957. French composer, active in the collection of folksongs. Studied at the Schola Cantorum. His compositions include instrumental works, songs and the operas *Le Mas* (Paris, 1929) and *Vercingétorix* (Paris, 1933), the former of which was awarded the Prix Heugel.

Canti carnascialeschi [cahn'-tee carr-nah-shah-less'-kee], *I.* Carnival songs : part-songs of a popular character written in the early part of the 16th cent. to be performed at court festivals during the annual carnival. Examples are printed in P. M. Masson, *Chants de Carnaval florentin*, and *Das Chorwerk* (ed. F. Blume), xliii.

F. GHISI : *I canti carnascialeschi* (1937).

Cantiga [cahn-tee'-gah], *Sp.* *v.* ALFONSO EL SABIO.

Canto fermo [cahnt'-o fair'-mo], *I.* (*L.* cantus firmus). "Fixed song." A pre-existing melody used, generally in long notes, as the foundation of a polyphonic composition for voices (with or without instruments), for an instrumental ensemble, or for a keyboard instrument. Plainsong melodies were extensively used in the Middle Ages and later for this purpose. Among the other materials drawn upon by composers were secular songs, Lutheran chorales, scales, and solmization syllables representing the vowels in a verbal text. The practice of using a *canto fermo* survives today mainly in organ pieces based on hymn-tunes. Mozart used a chorale melody as a *canto fermo* in his opera *Die Zauberflöte* (1791). A *canto fermo* in semibreves, to which other parts have to be added, is used in the traditional method of teaching "strict" counterpoint. *v.* COUNTERPOINT, TENOR.

Cantor, *L.* "Singer." Hence the chief singer in a choir, or in cathedrals and collegiate churches and similar establishments the director of the music (in English "chanter" or "precentor"). Though the office of precentor still exists in English cathedrals, and carries with it certain responsibilities, the actual work of training the choir is normally undertaken by the organist. The genitive *cantoris* is used in England to indicate that half of the choir which sits on the same side as the precentor ; the other half, sitting on the dean's side, is called *decani*. This division of the choir is used regularly in the antiphonal chanting of the psalms, and frequently in anthems and services.

Cantus firmus. *v.* CANTO FERMO.

Canzona [cahn-tso'-nah], CANZONE or CANZON, *I.* "Song" (*Fr.* chanson) ;

used either of a vocal piece or of an instrumental piece modelled on a vocal form. In particular:

(1) In the 16th cent. a polyphonic setting of a secular poem, simpler and more popular in style than the madrigal.

(2) The name used in Italy at the same period for the polyphonic French *chanson* (*canzon francese*).

(3) From the 17th cent. a solo song with keyboard accompaniment.

(4) In opera a song of a simple type, in contrast to the normally elaborate *aria*, *e.g.* "Voi che sapete" in Mozart's *Le nozze di Figaro.*

(5) A 16th-cent. transcription for lute or keyboard of a French *chanson.*

(6) An instrumental piece in the same style written for keyboard or an instrumental ensemble (late 16th and early 17th cent.), sometimes described as *canzon per sonar* (for playing) or *da sonar*. From the contrasted sections introduced into such pieces developed the separate movements of the sonata.

(7) An instrumental piece (or movement in a sonata) of a polyphonic character (17th and early 18th cent.).

(8) An instrumental piece or movement in the style of a song, *e.g.* the slow movement of Tchaikovsky's fourth symphony, Op. 36, marked "Andantino in modo di canzone."

Canzonetta [cahn-tso-net'-tah], *I.* (*E.* canzonet). Diminutive of *canzona.*

(1) A short piece of secular vocal music, light in character, for two or more voices, with or without instrumental accompaniment, *e.g.* 16th cent.: Morley's *Canzonets or little short aers to five and sixe voices* (1597); 17th cent.: *canzonetta a 2 voci concertata* and *canzonetta a 4 concertata* in Monteverdi's 7th book of madrigals (1619); 18th cent.: Mozart's *canzonetta* "Più non si trovano" (Metastasio), for 2 sopranos and bass, with 3 basset horns, K.549.

(2) A solo song of a similar character, *e.g.* Haydn's *Six Original Canzonettas* (1794), followed by a second set of 6 in 1795.

(3) An instrumental piece, *e.g.* Buxtehude's keyboard *canzonette* (17th cent.), which are in the same style as CANZONA (6).

Capet [cup-ay], LUCIEN: *b.* Paris, Jan. 8, 1873; *d.* there, Dec. 18, 1928. French violinist and composer, founder of the Capet Quartet. Studied at the Paris Conservatoire, where he taught from 1907. Both as a teacher and a soloist he had a great reputation. His compositions include 5 string quartets, orchestral works, and a setting of Psalm XXIII for soli, chorus and orchestra. He also published a study of bowing, *La Technique supérieure de l'archet* (1916).

Caplet [cup-lay], ANDRÉ: *b.* Le Havre, Nov. 23, 1878; *d.* Paris, Apr. 22, 1925. French composer and conductor. Studied at the Paris Conservatoire. *Grand Prix de Rome*, 1901. Conductor of the Boston Opera, 1910-14. A close friend of Debussy, whose *Children's Corner* he arranged for orchestra. His compositions include orchestral works, chamber music, songs and church music.

Capotasto [cah-po-tust'-o], *I.* "Head (*capo*) of the finger-board (*tasto*)" of a string instrument. Also a mechanical device, consisting of a cross bar of wood, metal or ivory (*Fr.* barre), for shortening all the strings simultaneously and hence raising their pitch. It has the practical advantage of simplifying the performance of pieces in extreme keys. It can be conveniently applied only to instruments with FRETS, to which it can be attached. In cello-playing the thumb is used as a temporary *capotasto* to facilitate playing in the high register.

Cappella. *v.* A CAPPELLA, MAESTRO DI CAPPELLA.

Capriccio [cah-pree'-tcho], *I.* (*F.* caprice). In general a piece in which the composer follows the dictates of fancy. In particular:

(1) In the late 16th and 17th cent. an instrumental piece, fugal in character, similar to the *ricercar*, *fantasia* and *canzona*, though sometimes more fanciful in the choice of themes, *e.g.* Frescobaldi's *Capriccio sopra il cucu* (Capriccio on the cuckoo).

(2) A piece which does not fall into one of the conventional forms of its period, *e.g.* Bach's *Capriccio sopra la lontanza del suo fratello dilettissimo* (Cap-

riccio on the departure of his beloved brother), which consists of several movements with descriptive titles (*B.G.*, xxxvi).

(3) A technical study, *e.g.* Paganini's 24 *capricci* for violin solo, Op. 1.

(4) An original piece of a lively character, *e.g.* the sixth movement of Bach's keyboard *Partita No.* 2 (which might equally well be called an "invention"), or Nos. 1, 3 and 7 of Brahms's *Fantasien*, Op. 116, for piano.

(5) A potpourri or rhapsody, *e.g.* Tchaikovsky's *Capriccio italien*, Op. 45, for orchestra, which is based on popular tunes.

Capriccio [cup-rits'-yo]. Opera in one act by Richard Strauss. Libretto by Clemens Krauss and the composer. First performed, Munich, Oct. 28, 1942.

Cardillac [carr-dee-yuck]. Opera in three acts by Hindemith. Libretto by Ferdinand Lion (based on E. T. A. Hoffman's *Das Fräulein von Scuderi*). First performed, Dresden, Nov. 9, 1926. Revised version, 1952.

Carestini [cah-rest-ee'-nee], GIOVANNI: *b.* Monte Filatrano (Ancona), *c.* 1705; *d.* there, *c.* 1760. Italian *castrato*, with a remarkable contralto voice. First appeared in Rome, 1721. He was in London, 1733-5 and sang in several of Handel's operas. He also sang in Prague, Berlin and St. Petersburg. His compass is said to have been from

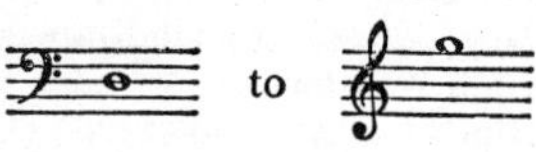

Carey, HENRY: *b. c.* 1690; *d.* Clerkenwell, Oct. 4, 1743. Composer and dramatist. His numerous works include operettas, songs and cantatas. His opera *The Dragon of Wantley*, the music of which was by J. F. Lampe (London, 1737), was a very successful satire on Italian opera. He wrote the words and tune of "Sally in our alley" (part of the tune is used in the scene in the condemned hold in *The Beggar's Opera*). The melody to which the song is now sung is traditional; it became associated with Carey's words in the late 18th cent.

Carillon (ca-ree-yon͡), *Fr.* (1) A set of bells in a church tower, or other public building, played by means of keyboard and pedals, or by automatic mechanism.

F. P. PRICE: *The Carillon* (1933).

(2) = Glockenspiel.

Carissimi [cah-reece'-see-mee], GIACOMO: *b.* Marino, 1605; *d.* Rome, Jan. 12, 1674. Italian composer, active for the greater part of his life in the direction of church music in Rome. He played an important part in the cultivation of the solo cantata, and was one of the first to write extended oratorios which break away from the early 17th-cent. practice of opera on sacred subjects. His oratorios, though often dramatic in treatment, were intended for the church, not for the stage, and therefore include a narrator, who sings in recitative. The oratorios *Jephte*, *Judicium Salomonis*, *Jonas* and *Baltazar* (all with Latin texts) have been published in a modern edition by F. Chrysander. A complete edition of all the oratorios is in course of publication in Italy.

Carl Rosa Opera Company. Founded in 1873 by Carl Rosa (originally Rose), a German violinist, for the performance of opera in English. It has been active mainly in the provinces and has given the first performance of a number of works by English composers.

Carlton, (1) NICHOLAS. Early 17th-cent. English composer, who wrote one of the earliest known examples of a keyboard duet under the title "A Verse for two to play on one Virginal or Organ" (Brit. Mus., Add. 29, 987).

H. MILLER: "The Earliest Keyboard Duets" (*Musical Quarterly*, Oct., 1943).

(2) RICHARD: *b. c.* 1558; *d. c.* 1638. Master of the choristers at Norwich Cathedral. Published a set of five-part madrigals (1601; modern edition in *E.M.S.*, xxvii), remarkable for their free use of dissonance, and contributed to *The Triumphes of Oriana* (1601).

Carmen [carr-men]. Opera in four acts by Bizet. Libretto by Henri Meilhac and Ludovic Halévy (after the story by Prosper Mérimée). First performed, Paris, March 3, 1875. In its original form it included spoken dialogue, which was replaced by recitative written by Ernest Guiraud when it was first given in Vienna, Oct. 23, 1875 (after Bizet's death). The scene is in Seville and in the neighbouring mountains. Carmen, a gypsy girl employed in a cigarette factory, exercises a fatal fascination on Don José, a sergeant of the guard, who allows her to escape after she has been arrested for disorderly behaviour. José joins Carmen and her smuggler friends in the mountains but soon longs to return home. Carmen, wearying of him, transfers her affections to Escamillo, a bull-fighter. At the bull-ring in Seville, where Escamillo has been successful, José makes a last appeal to Carmen. When she refuses he stabs her.

Carnaval [carr-na-vull], *Fr.* (Carnival). A set of 20 piano pieces by Schumann, Op. 9 (1835), bearing the sub-title *Scènes mignonnes sur quatre notes* (Dainty scenes on four notes). The four notes are derived from Asch, the home town of Ernestine von Fricken, with whom Schumann was in love at the time. The letters A S C H can represent either A, E♭ (*G.* Es), C, B (*G.* H) or A♭ (*G.* As), C, B. By a curious coincidence, of which Schumann was aware, these are also the only letters in his own name which can represent notes. *v.* also FASCHINGSSCHWANK AUS WIEN.

Carnaval des Animaux, Le [ler carr-na-vull daze a-nee-mo], *Fr.* (The Animals' Carnival). Satirical suite by Saint-Saëns for 2 pianos, string quintet, flute, clarinet and xylophone, described as a *fantaisie zoologique*. Though composed in 1886 it was not published until 1922 (after his death).

Carnaval Romain, Le [ler carr-na-vull rom-an͡] (The Roman Carnival). Concert overture by Berlioz, Op. 9 (1844), based on material from the opera *Benvenuto Cellini*, Op. 23 (1834-8). The cor anglais solo is derived originally from the early scena *Cléopâtre* (1829).

Carneval [carr'-ner-vull], *G.* *v.* CARNIVAL.

Carnicer [carr-nee'-thair], RAMÓN : *b.* Tárrega, Oct. 24, 1789 ; *d.* Madrid, March 17, 1855. Spanish composer. Active as an organist and teacher in Minorca during the French invasion of Spain. Director, Barcelona Opera, 1820 ; Madrid Opera, 1827 ; teacher at the Madrid Conservatorio, 1830-54. His compositions include Masses, symphonies and operas. His *Don Giovanni Tenorio* (Barcelona, 1822), which like his other operas has an Italian libretto, was the first opera on the Don Juan story to be written by a Spanish composer.

Carnival (*G.* Carneval). Concert overture by Dvořák, Op. 92 (1891) dedicated to the Czech University, Prague. It is the second of a set of three which he originally intended to call *Nature, Life and Love*. The other two are *In Nature's Realm*, Op. 91 (1891) and *Othello*, Op. 93 (1892). *v.* also CARNAVAL.

Carnival Jest. *v.* FASCHINGSSCHWANK AUS WIEN.

Carol (*Fr.* noël, *G.* Weihnachtslied). The word is now used in the same sense as *noël* and *Weihnachtslied* to mean a song for Christmas. In medieval English it meant any song with a burden (or refrain), whether related to the church festivals or not ; in this sense the Agincourt Song is a carol. The music of Christmas carols is drawn from many sources ; principally (1) tradtional folksong (2) secular music in general, including opera (3) tunes specially composed. The practice of setting or arranging carols for two or more voices is as old as the 15th cent. Some of the carol melodies in popular use today, *e.g.* that associated with "Good King Wenceslas," were borrowed in the late 19th cent. from a 16th-cent. hymn-book, *Piae Cantiones* (1582 ; modern edition by G. R. Woodward, 1910). Among modern English collections are *The English Carol Book* (1913 & 1919), *The Cowley Carol Book* (1902 & 1919) and *The Oxford Book of Carols* (1928). The latter includes notes on the words and tunes. Traditional carols are printed in C. Sharp's *English Folk Carols* (1911).

H. BACHELIN : *Les Noëls français* (1927).

J. A. FULLER-MAITLAND : *English Carols of the 15th Century* (1891).

R. L. GREENE : *The Early English Carols* (1935).

Musica Britannica, iv (1952).

E. B. REED : *Christmas Carols printed in the 16th Century* (1932).

Caron [ca-rõn], PHILIPPE. French or Flemish composer of the latter half of the 15th cent., probably a pupil of Dufay. Composed *chansons* and Masses, including one on " L'homme armé " (modern ed. in *Monumenta polyphoniae liturgicae*, ser. 1, i & iii).

Carpani [carr-pah'-nee], GIUSEPPE ANTONIO : *b.* Villalbese, Jan. 28, 1752 ; *d.* Vienna, Jan. 22, 1825. Author of several opera libretti, and translator of French and German operas into Italian. He also translated the text of Haydn's *Creation*. Another product of his admiration for Haydn was the study of his works entitled *Le Haydine* (1812). Henri Beyle published a French adaptation of this, entitled *Lettres écrites de Vienne en Autriche sur le célèbre compositeur Joseph Haydn* (1814), as his own work under the pseudonym C. A. L. Bombet, and in spite of the author's protests issued it again under the pseudonym Stendhal, with the title *Vies de Haydn, Mozart et Metastase* (1817).

Carpenter, JOHN ALDEN : *b.* Chicago, Feb. 28, 1876 ; *d.* there, Apr. 26, 1951. American business man (until his retirement in 1936), who was also active as a composer. His principal teacher was Bernard Ziehn. In spite of his dual activity, there is nothing amateurish about his music. He wrote a jazz pantomime, *Krazy Kat* (1922), and a " ballet of modern American life," *Skyscrapers* (1926). His other ballet, *The Birthday of the Infanta* (1919), is based on a story by Oscar Wilde. His compositions also include 2 symphonies, a violin concerto, chamber music, choral works and songs.

Carreño [carr-rehn'-yo], TERESA : *b.* Caracas, Dec. 22, 1853 ; *d.* New York, June 12, 1917. Venezuelan pianist, a pupil of Rubinstein. She appeared as an opera-singer in the early part of her career. The first of her four husbands was the violinist Émile Sauret, the third the pianist and composer Eugène d'Albert.

Carse, ADAM : *b.* Newcastle upon Tyne, May 19, 1878 ; *d.* Great Missenden, Nov. 2, 1958. Composer and writer on music. Studied at the R.A.M. His numerous compositions include 2 symphonies, but he is best known by his arrangements of old music (particularly early classical symphonies), text-books on the theory of music, and a number of books on the history of the orchestra and orchestral instruments, particularly *Musical Wind Instruments* (1939), *The Orchestra in the 18th Century* (1940), and *The Orchestra from Beethoven to Berlioz* (1948).

Cartan [carr-tũn], JEAN LOUIS : *b.* Nancy, Dec. 1, 1906 ; *d.* Bligny, March 26, 1932. French composer. Studied at the Paris Conservatoire with Paul Dukas. He died before he could completely fulfil the great promise shown by his early works, which include 2 string quartets, a cantata—*Pater Noster*—for soli, chorus and orchestra, and songs.

Caruso [cah-roo'-zo], ENRICO : *b.* Naples, Feb. 25, 1873 ; *d.* there, Aug. 2, 1921. Italian tenor, the most famous of his time. Made his first appearance in Naples, 1894. First sang in London, 1902, and subsequently at the Metropolitan Opera House, New York. He was immensely popular on both sides of the Atlantic. His gramophone records, some of which have been reissued with new accompaniments, give some idea of the power and quality of his voice.

D. CARUSO : *Enrico Caruso* (1945).
P. U. R. KEY & B. ZIRATO : *Enrico Caruso* (1923).

Carver, ROBERT : *b.* 1487. Early 16th-cent. Scottish composer, a monk of Scone Abbey. He composed a number of Masses and motets, including a Mass on the secular song " L'homme armé " (used by many other 15th and 16th-cent. composers) and a motet in 19 parts, " O bone Jesu " (modern editions in *Musica Britannica*, xv.)

Casals [cah-sahlss'], PAU (*Sp.* Pablo) : *b.* Vendrell, Dec. 29, 1876. Catalan cellist, conductor and composer, the son of an organist. Studied at the Madrid Conservatorio and taught at the Barcelona Conservatorio. Appeared as a soloist in Paris and London, 1898 ; in America, 1901. Founded his own orchestra at Barcelona, 1919, and conducted it until 1936. Founded the Prades Festival of chamber music, 1950. His remarkable gifts of execution and interpretation (particularly of Bach's unaccompanied suites) have done more than anything else in the present century to raise the prestige of the cello as a solo instrument. Married (1) the Portuguese cellist Guilhermina Suggia, 1906, (2) the American singer Susan Metcalfe, 1914, (3) Marta Montanez (Puerto Rico), 1957. In addition to his cello-playing and conducting he is also a remarkable accompanist. His compositions include works for cello and a choral work, *La Visión de Fray Martin*. Among his pupils are Cassadó and Eisenberg.

L. LITTLEHALES : *Pablo Casals* (1948).
B. SHORE : *The Orchestra Speaks* (1938).

Casella [cah-zell'-lah], ALFREDO : *b.* Turin, July 25, 1883; *d.* Rome, March 5, 1947. Italian composer, conductor, pianist and critic. Studied at the Paris Conservatoire, where he was a pupil of Fauré for composition. Taught at the Paris Conservatoire, 1912 ; at the Conservatorio di Santa Cecilia, Rome, 1915-23. Took an active part in furthering the cause of modern Italian music and in organizing the *Biennale* festivals at Venice. His music is modern in outlook, eclectic in style. His compositions include :

(a) ORCHESTRA : 3 symphonies ; 2 concertos (string orchestra full orchestra) ; violin concerto ; organ concerto ; cello concerto ; concerto for trio and orchestra.
(b) OPERAS : *La donna serpente* (Rome, 1932) ; *La favola d'Orfeo* (Venice, 1932) ; *Il deserto tentato* (Florence, 1937).
(c) BALLETS : *Il convento veneziano* ; *La giara* ; *La camera dei disegni* ; *La rosa del sogno.*
(d) CHAMBER MUSIC : Cello sonata ; concerto for string quartet (= concerto for string orchestra) ; *serenata* for clarinet, bassoon, trumpet, violin and cello ; *sinfonia* for piano, cello, trumpet and clarinet.
(e) PIANO : Variations on a chaconne ; sonatina ; *Sinfonia, arioso e toccata* ; many shorter works.
(f) SONGS : *L'Adieu à la vie* and *Notte di Maggio* (voice and orchestra) ; various other songs.

Literary works include :

L'evoluzione della musica a traverso la storia della cadenza perfetta (1919 ; Eng. trans. 1924).
Igor Stravinsky (1928).
21 + 26 (1930—autobiography).
Il pianoforte (1937).

He also transcribed a number of works by other composers.

Casimiri [cah-zee-mee'-ree], RAFFAELE : *b.* Gualdo Tadino, Nov. 3, 1880 ; *d.* Rome, Apr. 15, 1943. Choral conductor, composer and musicologist. After holding various posts as teacher and choir director he became director of music at St. John Lateran, Rome, 1911. He was editor of *Rassegna Gregoriana* and also founded two other periodicals, *Psalterium* (1907) and *Note d'archivio* (1924). He founded the *Società polifonica romana* for the performance of church music and toured with them abroad. He also edited a considerable amount of old music, notably a new edition of the works of Palestrina (in progress). His compositions include 2 oratorios, Masses, motets and madrigals. His literary works include studies of Palestrina and Lassus.

Casini [cah-zee'-nee], GIOVANNI MARIA : *b.* Florence, *c.* 1670 ; *d c.* 1715. Italian organist and composer, a pupil of Pasquini. Organist, Florence Cathedral, 1703. Composed church music, including 2 oratorios, and organ works, and being interested in the Greek scales had a harpsichord made with a compass of 4 octaves, each octave consisting of 31 notes. Two of his organ pieces are in L. Torchi, *L'arte musicale in Italia*, iii.

Cassadó [cahss-sah'-doh], GASPAR : *b.* Barcelona, Sept. 30, 1897. Catalan cellist and composer, a pupil of Casals. His compositions include 3 string quartets, a piano trio and a *Rapsodia catalonia* for orchestra.

Cassation (*I.* cassazione). A term used in the 18th cent. for an instrumental suite suitable for performance in the open air and therefore similar to the serenade or divertimento. Mozart wrote two (K. 62-3 & 99), both dating from 1769. The origin of the word is disputed.

Casse-Noisette [cuss-nwa-zet] (Nutcracker). Ballet by Tchaikovsky, Op. 71, based on a fairy tale by E. T. A. Hoffman. First performed, St. Petersburg, Dec. 17, 1892. A concert suite from the ballet was performed earlier, on March 19, 1892: it contains the following numbers:

I. *Ouverture miniature* (Miniature overture).

II. *Danses caractéristiques* (Characteristic dances).
- (a) *Marche* (March).
- (b) *Danse de la Fée-Dragée* (Dance of the Sugar-Plum Fairy).
- (c) *Danse russe Trépak* (Russian dance—Trepak).
- (d) *Danse arabe* (Arab dance).
- (e) *Danse chinoise* (Chinese dance).
- (f) *Danse des Mirlitons* (Dance of the Kazoos).

III. *Valse des Fleurs* (Waltz of the Flowers).

Castanets (*Fr.* castagnettes, *G.* Kastagnetten, *I.* castagnette). A percussion instrument, characteristic of Spain, consisting properly of two shell-shaped pieces of hard wood, joined by a cord, which passes over the thumb, and struck together by the fingers. In the orchestra a modified form is normally used, in which the clappers are attached to a stick. The word "castanet" comes from the Spanish *castañeta*, a diminutive of *castaña*, "chestnut."

Castelnuovo-Tedesco [cust-el-noo-o'-vo teh-dess-'co], MARIO: *b.* Florence, Apr. 3, 1895. Italian composer, a pupil of Pizzetti. His opera *La Mandragola* (Venice, 1926) won a prize offered by the Italian Government in 1925. He left Italy in 1939 for the United States, where he became naturalized. His compositions include 2 piano concertos, 2 violin concertos, several overtures to Shakespeare's plays, sonatas for violin, cello, clarinet and bassoon and other chamber music, piano music and songs. Among the latter are a number of songs from Shakespeare's plays and settings of 27 of the sonnets, all with the original text.

Castil-Blaze [cust-eel-bluz], FRANÇOIS HENRI JOSEPH: *b.* Cavaillon, Dec. 1, 1784; *d.* Paris, Dec. 11, 1857. Writer on music and composer. Studied at the Paris Conservatoire. He adapted (not always scrupulously) a large number of Italian and German operas for the French stage. His critical works include *De l'Opéra en France* (2 vols., 1820), *Dictionnaire de la musique moderne* (1821), *Théâtres lyriques de Paris* (3 vols., 1847-56), *Molière musicien* (2 vols., 1852). His compositions are unimportant.

Castillon [cust-ee-yon͡], ALEXIS DE (Vicomte de Saint-Victor): *b.* Chartres, Dec. 13, 1838; *d.* Paris, March 5, 1873. Composer, a pupil of Franck. Originally intended for the army. One of the founders of the *Société Nationale de Musique* (1871) and its first secretary. His works include a piano concerto (first played by Saint-Saëns in 1872), chamber music and songs. Outside the circle of his fellow-musicians his remarkable gifts were not appreciated.

Castor et Pollux [cust-orr ay pol-lēēks] (Castor and Pollux). Opera in five acts by Rameau. Libretto by Pierre Joseph Justin Bernard. First performed, Paris, Oct. 24, 1737.

Castrato [cust-rah'-toh], *I.* An adult male singer with a soprano or contralto voice, produced by means of an operation on the genital organs before the age of puberty. This has the effect of preventing the voice from "breaking," as it would normally do at that time. In consequence the *castrato* combines a boy's range with the power and capacity of a man. *Castrati* were known in church music in the 16th cent., but their principal field of activity was in Italian *opera seria* in the 17th and 18th cent., when many of them were famous for their virtuosity and the beauty of their voices. The fact that these singers were used regularly for male parts is one of the difficulties that have to be faced in reviving operas of that period.

A. HERIOT: *Castrati in Opera* (1956).

Castro [cust'-ro], (1) JEAN DE: 16th-cent. composer of church music, madrigals and *chansons* (including settings of Ronsard).

(2) JUAN JOSÉ: *b.* Buenos Aires, March 7, 1895. Argentinian composer, a pupil of d'Indy in Paris. His com-

positions include a *Sinfonía Argentina*, a *Sinfonía Bíblica*, ballet music and operas. He has also been active as conductor at the Colón Theatre and at Montevideo. His opera *Proserpina y el extranjero* (Milan, 1952) won the Verdi prize offered by La Scala, Milan, in 1951.

Castrucci [cust-roo'-tchee], PIETRO : *b.* Rome, 1679 ; *d.* Dublin, Feb. 29, 1752. Italian violinist, a pupil of Corelli. He came to England in 1715 and led the orchestra in Handel's opera performances for several years. His compositions include 12 *concerti grossi* and 30 violin sonatas. He died in poverty. His brother Prospero (*d.* 1760), also a violinist, was the original of Hogarth's picture "The Enraged Musician."

Catalani [cah-tah-lah'-nee], ANGELICA : *b.* Sinigaglia, May 10, 1780 ; *d.* Paris, June 12, 1849. Celebrated Italian soprano, who made her first appearance in opera at Venice, 1797. She travelled widely, and in England sang Susanna in the first performance there of Mozart's *Le nozze di Figaro*. In Paris she managed for a time the Théâtre Italien, but without success. Her singing is said to have been remarkable for its execution and beauty of tone but extravagant in the liberties she took with the music. Lord Mount-Edgcumbe (*Musical Reminiscences*, 1825) describes her taste as "vicious."

Catch. A round for three or more voices. The earliest to be printed appeared in Thomas Ravenscroft's *Pammelia : Musicke's Miscellanie, or mixed varietie of Pleasant Roundelayes and delightful Catches* (1609). Catches were also published during the Commonwealth and became still more popular after the Restoration, when they were remarkable not only for the ingenuity shown in their composition but also for the coarseness of their words. Purcell wrote more than 50 (*Purcell Society*, xxii). By the 18th century it had become the custom to introduce puns and other humorous devices into the catch. The most plausible derivation of the word is from the Italian CACCIA.

Catel [ca-tel], CHARLES-SIMON : *b.* Laigle, June 10, 1773 ; *d.* Paris, Nov. 29, 1830. Composer. Studied at the École Royale de Chant. During the Revolution he was active as a composer of military music and works in celebration of the new régime. Teacher of harmony, Paris Conservatoire, 1795 ; inspector of studies, 1810-14. He wrote 10 operas, of which *Les Bayadères* (Paris, 1810) was the most successful, and one in collaboration with three other composers. His *Traité d'harmonie* (1802) was for long a standard text-book.

F. HELLOUIN & J. PICARD : *Un Musicien oublié, Catel* (1910).

Catterall, ARTHUR : *b.* Preston, 1883 ; *d.* London, Nov. 28, 1943. Violinist, a pupil of Hess and Brodsky. Leader, Hallé Orchestra, 1912-25 ; B.B.C. Symphony Orchestra, 1930-6. Founded the Catterall Quartet, 1910.

Cauldron of Annwen, The. A trilogy by Holbrooke consisting of the three operas *The Children of Don*, *Dylan* and *Bronwen*. Libretto by Thomas Evelyn Ellis (Lord Howard de Walden). For the first performances see the separate entries.

Caurroy [co-rwa], FRANÇOIS EUSTACHE DU : *b.* Gerberoy, nr. Beauvais, 1549 ; *d.* Paris, Aug. 7, 1609. French composer. Began his career as a singer in the royal chapel, eventually becoming master of the music. He had a great reputation in his day as a composer. He was one of the group of French composers who experimented in writing music in longs and shorts in imitation of classical scansion. His works include polyphonic vocal music, sacred and secular, and instrumental fantasias. 20 pieces from his *Mélanges de musique* (1610), consisting of *chansons*, *noëls* and *vers mesurés à l'antique* are printed in *Les Maîtres musiciens de la Renaissance française*, xvii (1903).

Caustun, THOMAS : *d.* Oct. 28, 1569. One of the earliest composers to write for the services of the Anglican Church. Anthems and services by him are in John Day's *Certain notes set forth in foure and three parts* (1560) and settings of the metrical psalms in the same publisher's *The whole psalmes in foure parts* (1563).

Cavaillé-Col [ca-va-yay-col], ARISTIDE : *b.* Montpellier, Feb. 2, 1811 ;

d. Paris, Oct. 13, 1899. Member of a firm of organ-builders which still exists, and influential in improving the technique of organ-building in France in the 19th cent.

C. & E. CAVAILLÉ-COL : *Aristide Cavaillé-Col, ses orgues, sa vie, et ses oeuvres* (1929).

Cavalieri [cah-vahl-yeh′-ree], EMILIO DE' : *b. c.* 1550 : *d.* Rome, March 11, 1602. An amateur composer, one of the Florentine *camerata* who were interested in recreating in music the spirit of Greek drama, and one of the first to write the new declamatory solo song with figured bass accompaniment. Of his extant works the most important is *La rappresentazione di anima e di corpo* (1600), a morality play set to music in recitative, interspersed with choruses in the style of popular hymns and instrumental movements ; facsimile edition, 1912. It was first performed in the Oratory of St. Philip Neri (*d.* 1595) in Rome.

E. J. DENT : " La Rappresentazione di Anima e di Corpo " (*Papers read at the International Congress of Musicology*, 1944).

Cavalleria Rusticana [cah-vahl-leh-ree′-ah roost-ee-cah′-nah] (Rustic Chivalry). Opera in one act by Mascagni. Libretto by Guido Menasci & Giovanni Targioni-Tozzetti (founded on a play by Giovanni Verga). First performed, Rome, May 17, 1890. The scene is a Sicilian village. Turiddu, supposed to be in love with Santuzza, has not forgotten Lola, now married to Alfio. Santuzza informs Alfio, who challenges Turiddu to a duel and kills him.

Cavalli [cah-vahl′-lee], PIETRO FRANCESCO : *b.* Crema, Feb. 14, 1602 ; *d.* Venice, Jan. 14, 1676. Italian opera-composer. His real name was Caletti-Bruni, but he took the name Cavalli from his patron Federico Cavalli, mayor of Crema. Became a singer at St. Mark's, Venice (under Monteverdi), 1617 ; second organist, 1640 ; principal organist, 1665 ; *maestro di cappella*, 1668. The opening of the first public opera house in Venice in 1637 gave him the opportunity of writing for the stage. He wrote more than 40 operas, of which the first, *Le nozze di Teti e di Peleo*, appeared in 1639. His *Ercole amante* was specially written for performance in Paris, 1662. Modern edition (incomplete) of *Il Giasone* (1649) in *Publikationen der Gesellschaft für Musikforschung*, vol. xii. The style of his operas, as of Monteverdi's later works, illustrates the growing importance of song (as opposed to recitative) in Italian opera at this time. He also composed some church music.

A. A. ABERT : *Claudio Monteverdi und das musikalische Drama* (1953).

H. PRUNIÈRES : *Cavalli et l'opéra vénitien au xvii*[e] *siècle* (1931).

L'Opéra italien en France avant Lulli (1913).

E. WELLESZ : " Cavalli und der Stil der Venetianischen Oper von 1640-60 " (*Studien zur Musikwissenschaft*, 1913).

Cavatina [cah-vah-teen′-ah], *I.* Diminutive of *cavata* (lit. " extraction ")—a term used in the 18th cent. for an *arioso* section occurring in recitative.

(1) A song in an opera or oratorio which is less elaborate in structure and treatment than the normal *aria*, *e.g.* " Porgi amor " in Mozart's *Le nozze di Figaro.*

(2) An instrumental piece or movement of a similar character, *e.g.* the fifth movement of Beethoven's string quartet in B♭, Op. 130.

Cavazzoni [cah-vah-tso′-nee], (1) GIROLAMO. Son of (2). Published *Intavolatura cioè Recercari Canzoni Himni Magnificat* (1542) for the organ ; extracts in L. Torchi, *L'arte musicale in Italia*, iii.

(2) MARCO ANTONIO : *b.* before 1490 ; *d.* after 1559. Known as Marcantonio Cavazzoni da Bologna, *detto* d'Urbino. He was for a short time organist of Chioggia Cathedral, 1536-7 and later a singer at St. Mark's, Venice. Published *Recerchari, Motetti, Canzoni* (1523) for the organ, dedicated to his patron, Francesco Cornaro ; modern ed. in K. Jeppesen, *Die italienische Orgelmusik am Anfang des Cinquecento* (1943).

Cavendish, MICHAEL : *b. c.* 1565 ; *d.* London, 1628. Composer of lute-songs and madrigals, published in a single volume in 1598. His madrigal " Come gentle swains " was the first work by an English composer to include the refrain " Long live fair Oriana " (borrowed from the English version of Giovanni Croce's

"Ove tra l'herb' i fiori" which was printed in the second book of *Musica Transalpina* in 1597). It was rewritten for inclusion in Morley's anthology *The Triumphes of Oriana* (1601). Modern ed. of the lute-songs in *E.S.L.S.*, 2nd ser.; of the madrigals in *E.M.S.*, xxxvi.

Cazzati [cah-tsah'-tee], MAURIZIO: *b.* Guastalla, *c.* 1620; *d.* Mantua, 1677. Italian composer, who held various posts as *maestro di cappella* at Mantua, Bozolo, Bergamo and Bologna. In addition to a large amount of secular and sacred vocal music he also wrote a number of sonatas for various instrumental combinations which are important for the early history of the form. G. B. Vitali was his pupil.

Cebell. *v.* CIBELL.

Cebotari [seb-ot-ah'-ri], MARIA: *b.* Kishinev, Feb. 10, 1910; *d.* Vienna, June 9, 1949. Russian soprano. Made her first appearance in opera at Dresden, 1930. She sang leading roles in a number of modern operas and also appeared in films.

Cédez [say-day], *Fr.* "Give way," *i.e.* go a little slower.

Celesta. A keyboard instrument invented in 1886 by Auguste Mustel in Paris. The hammers strike steel bars, underneath which are a series of wooden resonators. Its ethereal tone is heard to the best advantage in the higher register. Its written compass is from

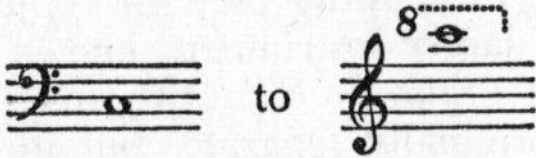

but the actual sound is an octave higher First used in the orchestra by Tchaikovsky in the "Danse de la Fée-Dragée" (Dance of the Sugar-Plum Fairy) in the ballet *Casse-Noisette* (Nutcracker), Op. 71 (1892).

Céleste Pedal. A device invented by Sebastien Érard (1752-1831) for reducing the tone on a piano by damping the strings with a strip of pedal. This method is now obsolete. The modern practice is either to check the impact of the hammers or to move the keyboard slightly to the right (*v.* CORDA).

Cellier, ALFRED: *b.* London, Dec 1, 1844; *d.* there, Dec. 28, 1891. Conductor and composer. After holding posts as a church organist he became conductor at the Prince's Theatre, Manchester, 1871-5, and subsequently at the Opéra-Comique, London, 1877-9. As a composer he was best known by his operettas, particularly *Dorothy* (London, 1886) and *The Mountebanks*, to a libretto by W. S. Gilbert (London, 1892).

Cello. Abbreviation of VIOLONCELLO.

Cembalo [chem'-bah-lo], *I.* (1) Dulcimer. (2) Abbreviation of *clavicembalo. v.* HARPSICHORD.

Cenerentola, La [lah cheh-neh-rent'-o-lah] (Cinderella). Opera in two acts by Rossini. Libretto by Jacopo Ferretti. First performed, Rome, Jan. 25, 1817.

Céphale et Procris [say-full ay prock-reece] (Cephalus and Procris). Opera in three acts by Grétry. Libretto by Jean François Marmontel. First performed, Versailles, Dec. 30, 1773.

Cerone [cheh-ro'-neh], DOMENICO PIETRO: *b.* Bergamo, 1566; *d.* Naples, 1625. Singer at Oristano Cathedral (Sardinia), in the service of Philip II and Philip III of Spain (1592-1603), and finally a priest and singer at the church of the Annunciation, Naples (from 1604). His principal theoretical work, written in Spanish, was *El Melopeo y Maestro* (The Musician and Master), published at Naples in 1613—a voluminous treatise of 1160 pages, which offers not only instruction but also a good deal of information about contemporary music and musicians.

Čert a Káča [chairt a cah'-cha] (The Devil and Kate). Opera in three acts by Dvořák. Libretto by Adolf Wenig. First performed, Prague, Nov. 23, 1899.

Certon [sair-tôn], PIERRE: *d.* Paris, Feb. 23, 1572. French composer, a pupil of Josquin des Prés. Singer at the Sainte-Chapelle, 1532; *magister puerorum* (master of the boys) there, 1542. Wrote Masses, motets and *chansons*. Modern edition of three Masses in H. Expert, *Monuments de la musique française au temps de la Renaissance*, ii (1925).

M. BRENET: *Les Musiciens de la Sainte-Chapelle du Palais* (1910).

Cervelas [sairv-la,] *Fr.* v. RACKET.

Ces [tses], *G.* C flat (C♭).

Ceses [tsess'-ĕss], *G.* C double flat (C♭♭).

Cesti [chess'-tee], PIETRO ANTONIO : *b.* Arezzo, Aug. 5, 1623 ; *d.* Florence, Oct. 14, 1669. Italian opera-composer, who became a Franciscan monk. *Maestro di cappella*, Volterra, 1645-9 ; singer in the Papal chapel, 1659-62 ; vice-*Kapellmeister* to the Imperial court, Vienna, 1666-9. His operas are an important contribution to the development of the *aria* in music-drama. The most elaborate, *Il pomo d'oro*, was written to celebrate the marriage of the Emperor Leopold I to the Infanta Margerita of Spain at Vienna, 1667 ; modern edition in *D.T.Ö.*, iii (2) & iv (2). Modern edition (incomplete) of *La Dori* (Florence, 1661) in *Publikationen der Gesellschaft für Musikforschung*, xii.

Cetera [cheh'-teh-rah], *I.* Cither (or cittern).

Ceterone [cheh-teh-ro'-neh], *I.* A large cither.

Chabrier [shub-ryay], ALEXIS EMMANUEL : *b.* Ambert, Jan. 18, 1841 ; *d.* Paris, Sept. 13, 1894. French composer, largely self-taught. He made his reputation with the vivacious orchestral rhapsody *España* (1883), having previously had two operettas performed. An enthusiastic admirer of Wagner, he wrote two operas, *Gwendoline* (Brussels, 1886, and subsequently in German and French theatres) and *Le Roi malgré lui* (Paris, 1887).

Chace [shuss], *Fr.* v. CACCIA.

Chaconne [shuck-on], *Fr.* (*I.* ciaccona). A stately dance in triple time, which appears to have been imported into Spain from Mexico in the late 16th cent. Like the PASSACAGLIA, from which it is often indistinguishable, it was habitually written in the form of a series of variations on (*a*) a ground bass (*basso ostinato*) or (*b*) a stereotyped harmonic progression. It was particularly popular in the 17th cent., when it occurs frequently in operas and keyboard music. Examples are also found which are chaconnes without being so described, *e.g.* the "Triumphing Dance" in Purcell's *Dido and Aeneas*. The most famous example of type (*b*) is the chaconne in Bach's Partita in D minor for solo violin.

Chacony. A 17th-cent. English version of CHACONNE.

Chadwick, GEORGE WHITFIELD : *b.* Lowell, Nov. 13, 1854 ; *d.* Boston, Apr. 4, 1931. American composer. Studied at Boston, Leipzig and Munich. Teacher of composition, New England Conservatory, Boston, 1880 ; director, 1897. His principal works, which are in the Romantic tradition, are :

(a) OPERAS : *The Quiet Lodging* ; *Tabasco* ; *Judith* ; *The Padrone* ; *Love's Sacrifice*.

(b) CHORAL WORKS : *The Viking's Last Voyage* ; *The Song of the Viking* ; *Lovely Rosabel* ; *Phoenix Expirans* ; *The Lily Nymph* ; *Ecce jam noctis* ; 2 odes.

(c) ORCHESTRA : 3 symphonies ; 6 overtures ; symphonic poems—*Cleopatra, Aphrodite, Angel of Death, Tam o' Shanter* ; serenade for strings ; Symphonic sketches ; sinfonietta ; *Suite symphonique* ; Theme, variations and fugue for orchestra and organ.

(d) CHAMBER MUSIC : 5 string quartets ; piano quintet.

Also songs with orchestra, piano or organ, piano works, organ works, church music and part-songs.

Chair Organ. A term used in England in the 17th and 18th cent. for a small organ (*Fr.* positif) used in conjunction with a larger instrument, known as the "great organ." The two instruments were originally separate, but in course of time became incorporated, the great organ being played from one manual, the chair (or choir) organ from another. It has been supposed that "chair" is a corruption of "choir," but it is just as likely that "choir," used in this sense, is a corruption of "chair." In that case "chair" (often written "chayre") is probably the same as the French *chaire* (*L.* cathedra), though it is not clear why a word meaning a seat, throne or pulpit should be applied to an organ. The explanation that the chair organ was so called because it was placed at the back of the organist's seat (*G.*

Rücknositif) is not convincing. *v.* CHOIR ORGAN.

Chaliapin [shahl-yah'-peen], FEDOR IVANOVICH : *b.* Kazan, Feb. 11, 1873 ; *d.* Paris, Apr. 12, 1938. Russian bass, the son of a peasant. Began to sing in opera at the age of 17, but first won a reputation in Moscow in 1896. Though he sang in Italian opera he was best known for his interpretation of the principal bass parts in Russian opera, particularly Moussorgsky's *Boris Godounov.* He possessed not only a remarkable voice but also an unrivalled sense of the stage. He was well-known, both as an opera-singer and as a recitalist, in England and America.

F. CHALIAPIN : *Pages from my Life* (1927). *Man and Mask* (1932).

Chalumeau [sha-lēē-mo], *Fr.* (1) Generic term for a rustic reed-pipe (*L.* calamellus, dim. of "calamus," a reed, *E.* shawm), in use up to the 18th cent. (*v.* A. Carse, *Musical Wind Instruments*, pp. 148-152).

(2) In the first half of the 18th cent. also used to mean "clarinet."

(3) Now applied to the lower register of the clarinet. *v.* CLARINET, SHAWM.

Chamber Music (*Fr.* musique de chambre, *G.* Kammermusik, *I.* musica da camera). Properly music suitable for a room (*I.* camera) in a house, as opposed to music for a church or theatre. At one time it included vocal as well as instrumental music, *e.g.* Martin Peerson's *Mottects or Grave Chamber Musique* (1630). Now restricted to instrumental works written for a limited number of performers, in which there is only one player to each part. Such music is necessarily intimate in character even though performed (as it is today) in a public concert hall. Characteristic forms are the fantasia or ricercar for viols (16th and early 17th cent.), the trio sonata for two violins and bass with organ or harpsichord (17th and early 18th cent.), and the string quartet for two violins, viola and cello (late 18th cent. to the present day). In addition to the string quartet compositions have also been written (*a*) for fewer or more than four string instruments (string duo, string trio, string quintet, etc.), (*b*) for strings with one or more wind instruments (*e.g.* clarinet quintet = a work for clarinet and string quartet), (*c*) for piano with string or wind instruments (*e.g.* piano trio = a work for piano, violin and cello). There is no foundation for the view that chamber music is the "purest" form of instrumental music, but the limitation of the means employed does present a serious challenge to the composer's invention and necessarily involves a type of composition in which emphasis is laid on clarity of texture. *v.* DUO, TRIO, QUARTET, QUINTET, SEXTET, SEPTET, OCTET, NONET.

W. W. COBBETT : *Cyclopedic Survey of Chamber Music* (2 vols., 1929-30).
H. ULRICH : *Chamber Music* (1948).

Chamber Orchestra. A 20th-cent. term for a small orchestra.

Chambonnières [shūn-bon-yair], JACQUES CHAMPION DE : *b. c.* 1602; *d. c.* 1672. Harpsichordist to the French court under Louis XIII and Louis XIV. His works for harpsichord, published in 1670 though written many years earlier, rank high among the keyboard music of the 17th cent. and had a great influence on younger composers. His pupils included d'Anglebert and Louis Couperin. Modern edition of his works by P. Brunold and A. Tessier (1926).

A PIRRO : *Les Clavecinistes* (1925).

Chaminade [sha-mee-nud], CÉCILE : *b.* Paris, Aug. 8, 1857 ; *d.* Monte Carlo, Apr. 18, 1944. French pianist and composer. Her compositions included orchestral music, chamber music and *Les Amazones* (a *symphonie lyrique* for chorus and orchestra), but her reputation rests on her songs and piano pieces, which though never profound often show considerable charm.

Changing Note. *v.* CAMBIATA (2).

Chanson [shūn-sōn], *Fr.* Song, whether for a single voice or for a vocal ensemble. Also applied, like *air*, to instrumental pieces of a vocal character. The normal word in modern French for a solo song with piano accompaniment is *mélodie.*

Chant. (1) In general, music which is sung in accordance with prescribed ritual or tradition.

(2) In particular, the unaccompanied

vocal music used for the services of the Christian church, *e.g.* Ambrosian chant, Gregorian chant (also known as "plainchant" or "plainsong").

(3) In the Anglican church used only of the music to which the psalms and canticles are sung.

(4) *Fr.* [shũn]. Song, singing, voice.

v. ANGLICAN CHANT, PLAINSONG.

Chanter (also "chaunter"). (1) Part of a bagpipe: the pipe with finger holes on which the melody is played, as opposed to the "drone" pipes, which merely sustain single notes. *v.* BAGPIPE.

(2) Obsolete term for "precentor" in a cathedral.

Chappell. A London firm of music-publishers and piano-manufacturers, founded in 1812 by Samuel Chappell (*d.* Dec. 1834), in association with J. B. Cramer and F. T. Latour.

Charpentier [sharr-pũnt-yay], (1) MARC-ANTOINE: *b.* Paris, 1634; *d.* there, Feb. 24, 1704. French composer, a pupil of Carissimi in Rome. Became director of music to the Jesuits of the *Maison professe* in Paris, and in 1698 director of music at the Sainte-Chapelle. His compositions include two operas—*Les Amours d'Acis et Galatée* (1678) and *Médée* (1693)—and other stage music, several oratorios (a form not otherwise cultivated in France at this time) and a large quantity of church music.

(2) GUSTAVE: *b.* Dieuze, June 25, 1860; *d.* Paris, Feb. 18, 1956. Composer. Studied at Lille Conservatoire and Paris Conservatoire. Won the *Prix de Rome*, 1887. Though he composed instrumental music and songs his reputation rests on the opera *Louise* (Paris, 1900), which adds romantic music to a realistic subject—the life and loves of working-class people in Paris. By the end of 1931 it had had 800 performances in Paris alone. Its successor, *Julien ou la Vie du Poète* (Paris, 1913), failed to achieve the same success and has not been revived. After the production of *Julien* Charpentier virtually abandoned composition.

M. DELMAS: *Gustave Charpentier et le lyrisme français* (1931).

Charton [sharr-tõn], ANNE ARSÈNE. *v.* DEMEUR.

Chasins, ABRAM: *b.* New York, Aug. 17, 1903. Pianist and composer. Studied at the Juilliard Graduate School, New York and the Curtis Institute, Philadelphia, where he subsequently taught the piano, 1926–35. Music director of WQXR, N. Y., since 1947. His compositions include orchestra works, chamber music and piano solos.

Chasse [shuss], **La,** *Fr.* (The Hunt). Title given to two of Haydn's instrumental works containing themes based on a hunting-call idiom: (1) String quartet No. 2 in B♭; (2) Symphony No. 73 in D.

Chaunter. *v.* CHANTER.

Chausson [sho-sõn], ERNEST: *b.* Paris, Jan. 21, 1855; *d.* Limay, June 10, 1899. French composer, a pupil of Massenet and Franck. His compositions, sensitive and romantic in style, include the opera *Le Roi Arthus* (Brussels, 1903), a symphony, *Poème* for violin and orchestra (his best-known work), a concerto for piano, violin and string quartet, a piano quartet, and songs.

Chávez [chah'-vez], CARLOS: *b.* Mexico City, June 13, 1899. Composer and conductor. Director, National Conservatorio, Mexico City, and conductor, Orquesta Sinfónica de México, 1928-52. Much of his work consists of a presentation in modern terms of the characteristic elements of Indian folk music. His compositions include 4 symphonies, a piano concerto, a violin concerto, 3 string quartets and other chamber music, ballets, choral works, piano music and songs.

Chef d'attaque [sheff dut-uck], *Fr.* Leader of an orchestra.

Chef d'orchestre [sheff dorr-kestr] *Fr.* Conductor.

Chekker (*Fr.* eschequier). A keyboard instrument with strings in use in the 14th and 15th cent., described towards the end of the 14th cent. as *isturment semblant d'orguens, qui sona ab cordes* (an instrument like the organ in appearance, which sounds with strings). Its exact nature is unknown, nor has any convincing explanation been given of the name.

Chelard [sher-larr], HIPPOLYTE ANDRÉ JEAN BAPTISTE: *b.* Paris, Feb. 1, 1789;

d. Weimar, Feb. 12, 1861. French opera-composer and conductor. Studied at the Paris Conservatoire under Kreutzer, Gossec, Méhul and Cherubini. Won the *Prix de Rome*, 1811, and studied further in Rome and Naples. Violinist at the Paris Opéra, 1816-27; successively conductor at the Bavarian court at Munich, at Augsburg (1836) and at Weimar (1840), where he was succeeded by Liszt in 1848. Wrote several operas, of which *Die Hermannschlacht* (Munich, 1835) was the most important.

Cherbuliez [shair-bĕĕl-yay], ANTOINE ÉLISÉE: *b.* Mulhouse, Aug. 22, 1888. Swiss musicologist and composer, who began his career as an engineer. Studied music at Zürich, Strasbourg, Meiningen and Jena, where he was a pupil of Max Reger. Played as a cellist in orchestras at Meiningen, Dresden and Berlin, 1913-17. From 1917 active in Switzerland as organist, teacher and conductor. Lecturer, Zürich University, 1923; professor, 1932. He has written a number of historical works, many of them dealing with the history of music in Switzerland. His compositions include chamber music and songs.

Cherubini [keh-roo-bee′-nee], MARIA LUIGI CARLO ZENOBIO SALVATORE: *b.* Florence, Sept. 14, 1760; *d.* Paris, March 15, 1842. Italian composer, a pupil of Sarti at Venice. Visited London, 1784-6, and was appointed composer to the king. Settled in Paris, 1788, and remained there for the rest of his life. Director of the Paris Conservatoire, 1822. Of the 24 complete operas composed wholly by himself 7 belong to his early years in Italy, 2 were written for London, 1 was written for Brescia in 1786, 1 for Turin in the winter of 1787-8, 1 for Vienna in 1806, and 12 for Paris. In the Paris operas he showed, *e.g.* in *Médée* (1797), that the old traditions of *opéra comique* with spoken dialogue were not inconsistent with a tragic subject. His *Les Deux Journées* (1800), known in England as *The Water-Carrier*, is a classic example of the so-called "rescue" opera, inspired by the hazards and heroism of the French Revolution. He was much admired by Beethoven (*v.* A. C. Kalischer, *Beethoven's Letters*, trans. J. S. Shedlock, vol. ii, p. 234), who shows the influence of Cherubini in his own work, *e.g.* in *Egmont* and *Fidelio* (also a "rescue" opera). After 1813 Cherubini devoted himself mainly to church music, including several Masses with orchestral accompaniment. Among his other works are 6 string quartets and 6 piano sonatas. He also published a *Cours de contrepoint et de la fugue* (1835).

E. BELLASIS: *Cherubini* (2nd ed., 1912).

Chester. A firm of music-publishers, founded at Brighton in 1860 and transferred to London in 1915. Publishers of *The Chesterian*.

Chest Voice. The lower "register" of the voice, as distinct from the higher register ("head voice").

Cheval de Bronze, Le [ler sher-vull der brõnz] (The Bronze Horse). Opera in three acts by Auber. Libretto by Augustin Eugène Scribe (*opéra-féerique*). First performed, Paris, March 23, 1835.

Chevalet [sher-va-lay], *Fr.* (*G.* Steg, *I.* ponticello). Bridge of a string instrument. *Au chevalet*, on the bridge, *i.e.* play near the bridge, thus producing a glassy, brittle tone.

Chevillard [sher-vee-yarr], PAUL ALEXANDRE CAMILLE: *b.* Paris, Oct. 14, 1859; *d.* Chatou, May 30, 1923. French conductor, pianist and composer, son of the cellist Pierre Alexandre François Chevillard (1811-77). Studied at the Paris Conservatoire. Son-in-law of Charles Lamoureux, whom he succeeded as conductor of the Concerts Lamoureux, 1897. He played an important part in familiarizing the French public with Russian music. His compositions include chamber music and orchestral works.

Chiavette [kee-ah-vet′-teh]. *I.* Plural of *chiavetta*, diminutive of *chiave* (key, clef). First used by Paolucci (1726-76) to indicate the use of clefs other than those normal for the voices in 16th- and early 17th-cent. music, *e.g.* the use of the tenor clef:

for a bass part instead of

or the use of the G clef on the second line:

for a soprano part in place of the normal

The use of such clefs avoided the necessity for leger-lines, but since notes on leger-lines might well lie outside the effective compass of the voice they were used also to indicate transposition down a fourth or fifth, *e.g.* a soprano part written in the G clef with this compass:

might indicate that it was to be sung at this pitch (which is not necessarily the same as the standard pitch today):

with a similar transposition indicated by the *chiavette* of the other parts. Though the word *chiavette* does not appear before the 18th cent., the principle of transposition when "high clefs" are used is precisely stated by Praetorius in his *Syntagma Musicum*, vol. iii (1619).

A. MENDEL: "Pitch in the 16th and early 17th Centuries," pt. iii (*Musical Quarterly*, 1948, pp. 336-57).

Chickering. The oldest American firm of piano-manufacturers, founded by Jonas Chickering (1798-1853) in 1823. They were pioneers in the use of the iron frame for grand pianos. In 1908 they were merged with the American Pianoforte Company.

Chiesa [kee-eh'-zah], *I.* "Church." Used in the 17th and early 18th cent. to distinguish music suitable for performance in church from that suitable for performance in secular surroundings, *e.g. sonata da chiesa.* *v.* SONATA.

Child, WILLIAM: *b.* Bristol, 1606; *d.* Windsor, March 23, 1697. Organist and composer. Lay-clerk, St. George's Chapel, Windsor; organist, 1632-43 and from 1660. Organist, Chapel Royal, 1660. His compositions consist mainly of church music, which shows an adherence to traditional styles but also accepts the new manner of Restoration music. He published in 1639 *The first set of Psalms of iii voyces, fitt for private chappells, or other private meetings with a continuall Base, either for the Organ or Theorbo, newly composed after the Italian way.*

E. H. FELLOWES: *Organists and Masters of the Choristers of St. George's Chapel in Windsor Castle* (1939).

Children of Don, The. Opera with a prologue and three acts by Holbrooke (the first part of the trilogy *The Cauldron of Annwen*). Libretto by Thomas Evelyn Ellis (Lord Howard de Walden). First performed, London, June 15, 1912.

Children's Corner. The original title of a suite of piano pieces by Debussy (1908), dedicated to his infant daughter. The separate pieces are: *Gradus ad Parnassum* (a satire on technical exercises), *Jimbo's lullaby* (for a toy elephant, who ought presumably to have been called Jumbo), *Serenade of the doll* (a mistake for "Serenade to the doll"), *The snow is dancing*, *The little shepherd* and *Golliwog's cake walk* (including a malicious quotation from *Tristan*). The suite was orchestrated by André Caplet in 1911.

Chilesotti [kee-leh-sot'-tee], OSCAR: *b.* Bassano, July 12, 1848; *d.* there, June 20, 1916. Italian musicologist. Studied law at Padua University. Devoted himself particularly to the history of lute music and published 9 vols. of music from the 16th to the 18th cent. under the title *Biblioteca di rarità musicali*.

Chisholm, ERIK: *b.* Glasgow, Jan. 4, 1904. Composer and conductor.

Studied at Edinburgh University. As conductor of the Glasgow Grand Opera Society from 1930 he directed performances of a number of works not in the normal repertory. He was also active in organizing performances of contemporary music. Professor, University of Cape Town, 1945. In South Africa he has continued his policy of arousing interest in opera and modern music. His compositions include several operas, 2 symphonies, 2 piano concertos, a violin concerto and piano music.

Chitarra [kee-tarr'-rah], *I.* Guitar.

Chitarrone [kee-tarr-ro'-neh], *I.* A large lute. *v.* LUTE.

Chiuso [kee-oo'-zo], *I.* *v.* CLOS.

Choeur [cur], *Fr.* Choir, chorus.

Choir (*Gr.* χορός, *L.* chorus). (1) The place in a cathedral where the singers are stationed.

(2) A body of singers in which there is more than one voice to a part.

(3) In America also a particular section of the orchestra, *e.g.* "brass choir."

(4) Short for CHOIR ORGAN.

Choirbook. A large volume so designed that the separate parts of a choral composition could be read by a number of singers standing in front of a lectern. The music was not written in score : the parts were written separately on two facing pages, using as much or as little space as might be necessary. The system originated on a smaller scale in the 13th cent. It was found to be economical to write out a motet in this way, since the upper parts took up far more space than the slow-moving tenor. The large choirbook was in general use in the 15th cent. and continued to be used in the 16th cent., when printed examples are also found, but its use inevitably declined in favour of the more practical system of separate PART-BOOKS. A modification of the choirbook system, however, persisted in domestic music for voices and instruments, which was often printed with the parts facing various ways, so that a small group of performers could sit round a table and read them.

Choir Organ (*Fr.* positif, *G.* Unterwerk, *I.* organo di coro). In modern use a section of the organ played from the lowest of three or more manuals. It consists generally of quieter stops, some of which will be suitable for solo work, and is frequently enclosed in a box with movable shutters (like the SWELL ORGAN) which enables the player to make a *crescendo* or *diminuendo*. If the organ has no SOLO ORGAN the choir organ may include a powerful reed stop (trumpet or tuba), or alternatively the trumpet stop on the GREAT ORGAN may also be available on the choir organ. This makes it possible to provide a trumpet solo with a heavy accompaniment on the great organ. *v.* CHAIR ORGAN, MANUAL, ORGAN.

Chopin [shop-a͡n], FRYDERYK FRANCISZEK (Frédéric François) : *b.* Zelazowa Wola, Mar 1, 1810 ; *d.* Paris, Oct. 17, 1849. Pianist and composer. Son of a French father, living in Poland, and a Polish mother. Became known as an infant prodigy. Studied with Joseph Elsner at the Warsaw Conservatoire. Gave two concerts in Vienna, 1829, and three in Warsaw, 1830. Visited Vienna, Munich, Stuttgart, 1830-1, arriving in Paris, 1831, where he began to give lessons and appear at concerts, and also made the acquaintance of Liszt, Mendelssohn, Berlioz and Bellini. Began to associate with the female novelist George Sand, 1837 ; lived with her in Majorca, 1838-9, and subsequently in Paris and at Nohant, 1840-6. Broke off this association as a result of a quarrel over family matters, 1847. Toured in England and Scotland, 1848. Died of consumption.

His compositions are almost entirely for the piano. Though he owed something to the example of Field and Hummel, he succeeded in creating an individual art of keyboard-writing, which makes a virtue of the evanescent tone of the instrument and uses melodic decoration as an enrichment of the harmonic texture. He was a master of the art of suggestion, and explored a harmonic territory going far beyond the conventional boundaries of his time. Other influences include the folk-music of Poland, noticeable particularly in the Mazurkas, and the melodic style, often demanding considerable virtuosity, of Italian opera. His playing was incomparable, remarkable both for its delicacy and its intensity and giving a magical significance to passages which his contemporaries found incomprehensible on paper. His principal compositions are:

(a) PIANO & ORCHESTRA: 2 concertos; *Andante spianato* and *Polonaise*; fantasia on Polish airs; *Rondo à la Krakowiak*; variations on "Là ci darem."

(b) PIANO SOLO: 4 *Ballades*; 3 *Écossaises*; 27 *Études*; 3 impromptus; 51 Mazurkas; 19 Nocturnes; 12 *Polonaises*; 25 preludes; 4 scherzos; 3 sonatas; 17 waltzes; *Barcarolle*; *Berceuse*; *Fantaisie* in F minor; *Fantaisie-Impromptu.*

(c) CHAMBER MUSIC: Piano trio; cello sonata; Introduction and *Polonaise* for cello and piano.

(d) SONGS: 17 Polish songs.

G. ABRAHAM: *Chopin's Musical Style* (1939).
A. HEDLEY: *Chopin* (1947).
W. MURDOCH: *Chopin: his Life* (1934).

Chor [cohrr], *G.* Choir, chorus.

Choral. (1) *E.* Adjective used of music involving a chorus, *e.g.* choral cantata. (2) [coh-rahl'], *G.* (i) Plainsong (Gregorian chant). (ii) A hymn-tune of the Lutheran church (*v.* CHORALE).

Chorale [coh-rahl'] (*E.* phonetic spelling of *G.* Choral). A hymn-tune of the Lutheran church. The earliest publications date from 1524. The materials used in Lutheran hymnody in the 16th cent. included (1) adaptations of Latin hymns already in use in the Catholic Church, (2) adaptations of pre-Reformation popular hymns in German, (3) adaptations of secular songs, (4) original hymns. Examples of these four categories are (1) "Nun komm, der Heiden Heiland" (*L.* "Veni, redemptor gentium"), (2) "Christ ist erstanden," (3) "Herzlich thut mich verlangen" (from Hassler's "Mein G'müt ist mir verwirret"), (4) "Ein feste Burg." In the 16th cent. the melodies showed considerable rhythmical freedom, but by the 18th cent. their shape had acquired a four-square symmetry, familiar to us in Bach's harmonizations. Bach made no attempt to preserve the original flavour of the tunes, so that in his hands they become virtually 18th-cent. compositions. The Bach revival in the 19th cent. led to the incorporation of a certain number of Lutheran chorales in English hymn-books, sometimes in a modified form.

The process of adaptation and transformation may be illustrated by one of the best-known of the chorales—"Herzlich thut mich verlangen" (the so-called "Passion Chorale"). The original melody, as it appears in Hassler's *Lustgarten Neuer Teutscher Gesäng* (1601), set to secular words, is:

The following is one of nine harmonizations of the tune made by Bach:

BACH, *St. Matthew Passion*

From the 17th cent. onwards the chorale was used as the basis of two main types of extended music: (1) the church cantata, (2) preludes, partitas or variations for organ. Both served a liturgical purpose, since the congregation would be familiar with the tunes employed, and would relate them to the words associated with them. The majority of Bach's church cantatas use chorales, either in a four-part harmonization, or as the *canto fermo* of a choral movement, or in association with solo voices. For organ works based on chorales *v.* CHORALE PRELUDE.

Hymns Ancient and Modern—Historical Edition (1909).

C. S. TERRY: *Bach's Chorals*, 3 vols. (1915-21).

Bach's Four-part Chorals (1928).

Chorale Prelude. (For pronunciation *v.* CHORALE. The spelling "choral prelude" is misleading because it suggests that "choral" is an English adjective instead of a German noun.) A generic term for a piece of organ music based on a hymn-tune. It originated in Germany in the 17th cent., when it was the custom in the Lutheran church to play on the organ an introduction to the hymn (or chorale) to be sung by the congregation. Various types of treatment were employed. The melody might be used as a *canto fermo*, round which counterpoints were written, or it might appear in ornamented form as a solo with accompaniment, or it might be subjected to fugal treatment or used as a theme for variations. Contrapuntal devices such as canon were also used. All these types of treatment are to be found in Bach's chorale preludes. Among later composers of chorale preludes Reger and Karg-Elert were specially prolific. Chorales have also been used in works which do not strictly fall into the category of chorale preludes, *e.g.* in Mendelssohn's sixth organ sonata, which makes use of the chorale "Vater unser im Himmelreich."

H. GRACE: *The Organ Works of Bach* (1922).

A. SCHWEITZER: *J. S. Bach*, trans. E. Newman, 2 vols. (1911).

S. DE B. TAYLOR: *The Chorale Preludes of J. S. Bach* (1942).

Choral Fantasia. (1) A work by Beethoven for piano solo, chorus and orchestra, Op. 80 (1808), consisting of a theme and variations, with improvisatory introduction for the piano. The words of the choral section are a poem in praise of music by Christoph Kuffner.

E. J. DENT : "The Choral Fantasia" (*Music & Letters*, Apr., 1927).

D. F. TOVEY : *Essays in Musical Analysis*, vol. ii (1935), pp. 133-6.

(2) A setting by Gustav Holst, Op. 51 (1930) of words by Robert Bridges for chorus, organ, brass, strings and percussion.

Choral Symphony. (1) The popular name for Beethoven's ninth symphony in D minor, Op. 125 (1823), the last movement of which consists of a setting of Schiller's ode *An die Freude* (To joy) for soloists, chorus and orchestra. The original title was *Sinfonie mit Schlusschor* (Symphony with final chorus).

D. F. TOVEY : *Essays in Musical Analysis*, vol. ii (1935), pp. 1-45.

(2) A setting of poems by Keats for soprano solo, chorus and orchestra by Gustav Holst, Op. 41 (1924). It is entitled *First Choral Symphony* but had no successor.

(3) Among the works which bear the sub-title "choral symphony" are Granville Bantock's *Atalanta in Calydon* (1912) and *Vanity of Vanities* (1914) for unaccompanied choir.

(4) Symphonies written for chorus and orchestra, though not specifically entitled "choral," include Mahler's eighth symphony (1907), Vaughan Williams's *A Sea Symphony* (1910) and Armstrong Gibbs's *Odysseus* (1939).

(5) Symphonies with choral finales include Liszt's *Eine Faustsinfonie* (1857) and Widor's *Symphonie antique*. Mendelssohn's *Lobgesang* (Hymn of Praise), Op. 52 (1840), is a "symphony-cantata," consisting of three symphonic movements followed by a choral cantata.

Chord. A term normally used of three or more different notes sounded simultaneously. A chord may be represented by only two different notes, but in that case a third note is implied. The classification of chords and their relation to each other forms part of the study of harmony. A *diatonic chord* is one that uses only notes proper to the key. A distinction between consonant and dissonant chords is arbitrary, since different standards of consonance and dissonance have prevailed at different times.

A chord of three notes in which the lowest note is accompanied by the third and fifth above it is known as a *triad*, *e.g.*:

Major triad:

Minor triad:

Augmented triad:

Diminished triad:

Of the diatonic triads in the key of C major, three are major, three are minor and one is diminished:

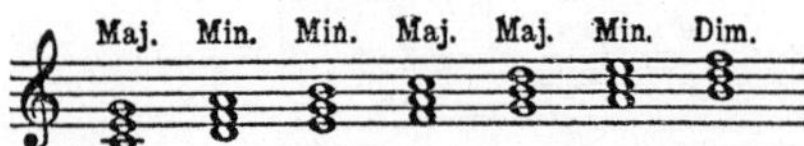

All other triads are chromatic in this key. The range of diatonic triads in a minor key is wider since the minor scale includes both flat and sharp sixths, and both flat and sharp sevenths, *i.e.* in the key of C minor, A♮ as well as A♭, and B♮ as well as B♭ (*v.* MINOR). There are therefore 13 diatonic triad, in a minor key—five major, four minors one augmented, and three diminished:

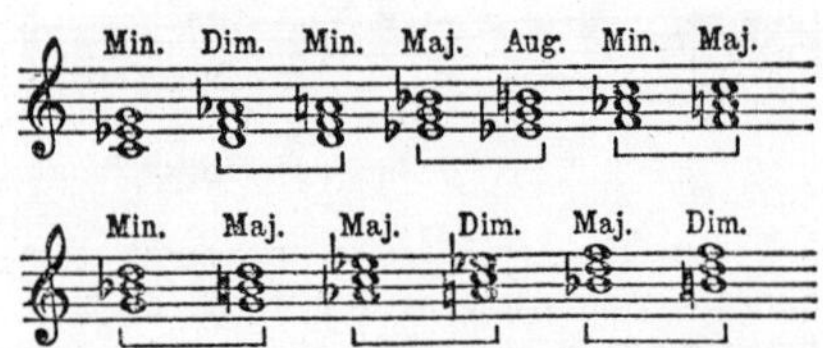

The chords in the above examples are generally said to be in *root position*. Major and minor triads in root position are known as *common chords.* The disposition of the notes above the bass does not affect the nature of the chord. The following are possible versions of the triad of C major in root position :

Where the harmony is in more than three parts it will obviously be necessary to double one or more notes of a triad, either at the unison or at the octave. The following illustrates some possible arrangements of the triad of C major in root position in four, five, six and seven parts :

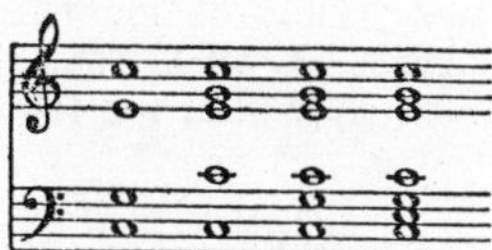

In three-part harmony, and in four-part harmony if the movement of the parts makes it desirable, the fifth of a major or minor triad is often omitted and the bass note doubled :

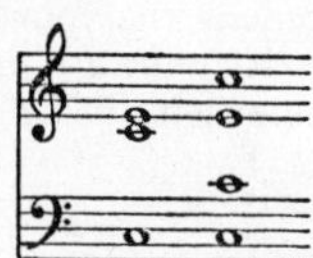

In 16th- and 17th-cent. music for several voices or instruments it is not uncommon to find the third omitted in the final chord, in which case the major third is supplied by the accompanying keyboard instrument or by the natural resonance of the building (*v.* ACOUSTICS, TIERCE DE PICARDIE).

If the notes of a chord in root position are re-arranged so that one of the upper notes becomes the lowest, the result is generally known as an *inversion.* There are only two possible inversions of a triad, *e.g.* :

Root position :

First inversion :

Second inversion :

On a keyboard instrument it is not possible to tell, without the context, whether an augmented triad is in root position or inverted, *e.g.* :

Root position of augmented triad on C :

First inversion of augmented triad on A♭ :

Second inversion of augmented triad on E :

On the piano or organ these three chords are identical. This makes possible a variety of harmonic progressions, *e.g.* :

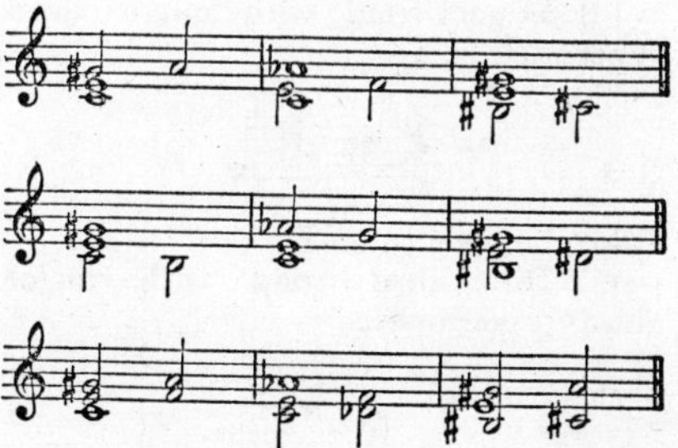

In FIGURED BASS the first inversion of a triad is called a $\begin{smallmatrix}6\\3\end{smallmatrix}$ chord (or more simply, *chord of the sixth*), since its two upper notes are respectively a sixth and a third above the lowest note. Similarly the second inversion of a triad is called a $\frac{6}{4}$ chord. If the sixth in a minor $\frac{6}{3}$ chord is sharpened, *e.g.* if

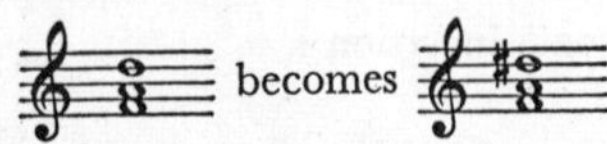

the result is called an *augmented sixth* chord (*v.* AUGMENTED SIXTH). A major $\frac{6}{3}$ chord on the fourth degree of the scale is known as a *Neapolitan sixth* chord (*v.* NEAPOLITAN SIXTH).

If an additional third is added above a triad in root position, thus producing a chord of four notes, the result is called a *chord of the seventh*, because the highest note is a seventh above the lowest. The seventh chords in the key of C major are :

These may be classified as follows :

(1) Major triad with major third superimposed :

(2) Major triad with minor third superimposed :

(3) Minor triad with minor third superimposed :

(also the seventh on D).

(4) Diminished triad with major third superimposed :

All these are *diatonic sevenths*, because they do not involve any note foreign to the key. No. 2 is called the *dominant seventh* chord, because its lowest note is the dominant of the key (*v.* DOMINANT). The introduction of chromatic notes makes possible further combinations, *e.g.* :

Diminished triad with minor third superimposed :

This is known as the *diminished seventh* chord.

In three-part harmony it will be necessary to omit one of the notes of a seventh chord. Since the seventh cannot be omitted, it follows that either the fifth or, less frequently, the third will be omitted. Thus the dominant seventh chord in the key of C major may be represented by one of the following :

The same thing may happen in four-part harmony if the movement of the parts makes it desirable, in which case the bass note will most probably be doubled, *e.g.* :

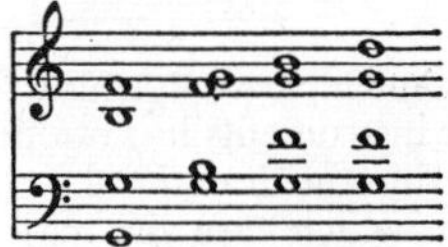

The theory of inversions is applied also to four-note chords. There are three possible inversions of these, *e.g.* :

Root position :

First inversion :

Second inversion :

Third inversion :

On a keyboard instrument the inversions of a diminished seventh chord are indistinguishable from transpositions of the same chord in root position, *e.g.* :

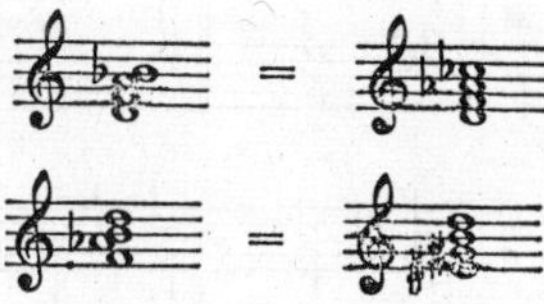

This makes it possible to use any diminished seventh chord as a means of modulating to (and consequently from) any major or minor key, *e.g.* :

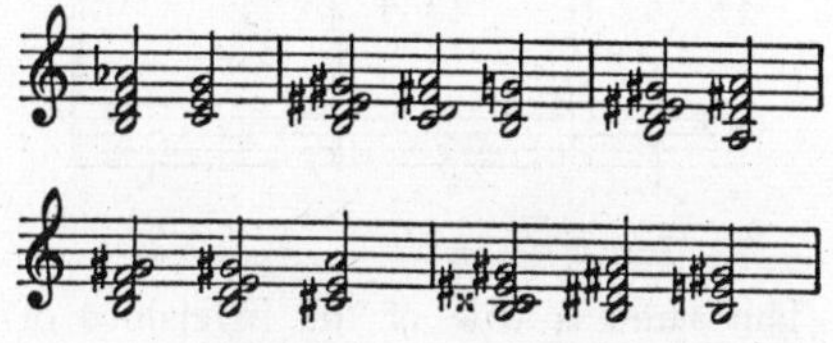

The superimposition of a third on a seventh chord will produce a *chord of the ninth.* A ninth chord with a third added becomes a *chord of the eleventh.* An eleventh chord with a third added becomes a *chord of the thirteenth, e.g.* :

These can also be inverted. A third added to a thirteenth chord does not produce a new chord, since the note added is merely the bass note doubled two octaves higher, *e.g.* :

Inversion and the superimposition of thirds makes it possible to build up the chords described above, but it does not explain their origin or their function. The $\begin{smallmatrix}6\\3\end{smallmatrix}$ chord did not arise from the conscious rearrangement of the notes of the triad. It arose naturally in the Middle Ages from the use of a passing note in three-part writing, *e.g.* in cadences of this kind :

The combination of a sixth and a third proved so attractive that we find English composers of the late 13th and early 14th cent. writing successions of such chords, *e.g.*:

M. Bukofzer, *Geschichte des englischen Diskants, E. 18*

The conception of the $\begin{smallmatrix}6\\3\end{smallmatrix}$ chord as composed of a sixth and third combined explains why in the 16th cent. the diminished triad :

was avoided, because of the diminished fifth between the upper and lower parts, whereas :

(described by later theorists as its first inversion) was freely used.

The $\begin{smallmatrix}6\\4\end{smallmatrix}$ chord also occurred as a result of the free use of passing notes, *e.g.* in the following examples dating respectively from the 13th and 15th cent. :

G. Reese, *Music in the Middle Ages*, p. 334

J. Stainer, *Dufay and his Contemporaries*, p. 64

In 16th-cent. practice this chord was normally used only as the result of a suspension requiring resolution (*v.* SUSPENSION), *e.g.* :

Palestrina, *Missa Assumpta est Maria*

or as a decoration of a perfect cadence, *e.g.* :

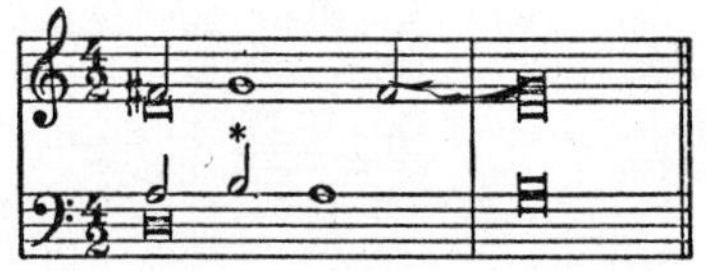
Palestrina, *Ascendens Christus*

Chords other than triads also arose from the practice of using suspensions or passing notes. The following example shows the seventh treated as a dissonance which has to be resolved or can merely occur in passing :

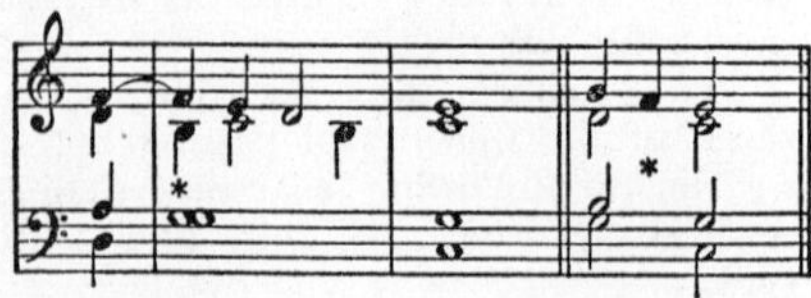

It is evident that in four-part harmony one note will have to be omitted from the chord of the ninth, two notes from the chord of the eleventh, and three notes from the chord of the thirteenth. The resulting four-part chords, though conventionally known as chords of the ninth, eleventh and thirteenth, are not in fact mere selections from the notes of those chords but, like the chord of the seventh, are the product of suspensions or passing notes, *e.g.* :

The same is true of the inversions of four-note chords, *e.g.* :

Familiarity with the sound of chords

produced and of chords in five or more parts and their inversions in this way led to their use as normal elements in a harmonic progression. The use of chromatic notes as suspended dissonances, appoggiaturas or passing notes led to a further extension of the harmonic vocabulary. Chords once regarded as dissonant came to be accepted as concords on to which more strongly dissonant chords could resolve, *e.g.* :

WAGNER, *Tristan und Isolde*

Every chord has a function, but that function may differ according to the context in which it occurs. For example, the $\substack{6\\5\\3}$ chord on the subdominant (or fourth degree of the scale) *i.e.* in the key of C major :

has two distinct functions, resulting from its dual origin (*a*) as a $\substack{6\\3}$ chord sounded simultaneously with a suspended fifth :

(*b*) as a $\substack{5\\3}$ chord against which a passing sixth is heard :

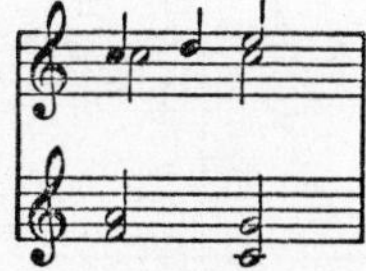

The resulting functions of the chord are :

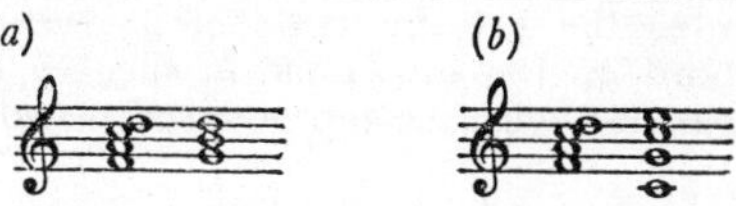

Another illustration is provided by two further forms of the augmented sixth chord, in which a fourth note has been added to the three mentioned above :

The first of these could be regarded as the second inversion of a seventh chord on the supertonic (or second degree of the scale) in the key of A minor, with the top note sharpened :

or as the second inversion of a dominant seventh chord in the key of E major, with the lowest note flattened :

or as the second inversion of a seventh chord on the leading note (or seventh degree of the scale) in the key of C major, with the top note sharpened :

The other augmented sixth could be regarded as the first inversion of a seventh chord on the subdominant in the key of A minor, with the top note sharpened :

or as a diminished seventh with the lowest note flattened :

or as the first inversion of a seventh chord on the supertonic in the key of C major, with the top note sharpened :

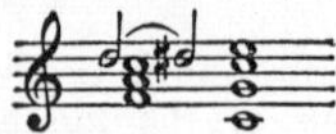

But whatever form of vertical analysis we adopt, these progressions derive in fact from the following simple cadences :

modified by the use of one or more passing notes or anticipations, *e.g.* :

Awareness of chords must go hand in hand with awareness of part-writing, since it is often the individual movement of the parts that determines the chords. The following examples, both from the 17th cent., will make this clear :

MONTEVERDI, *Madrigals, Book V*

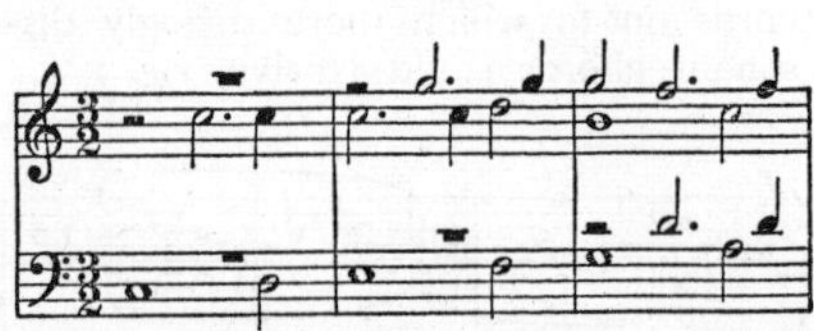

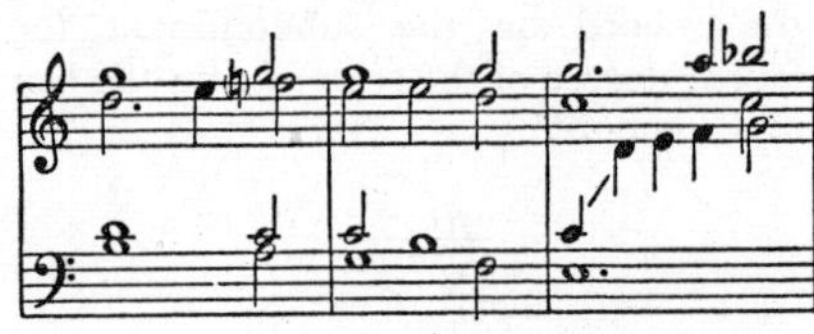

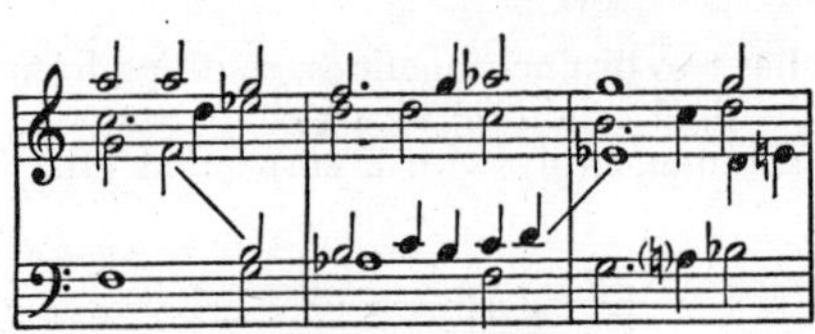

PURCELL, *Dioclesian*

v. HARMONY, INVERSION.

Chorton [cohrr'-tone], *G.* "Choir pitch," *i.e.* the pitch to which church organs in Germany were formerly tuned. This pitch was neither constant nor universal. By the beginning of the 17th century it was generally high in the Protestant churches of North Germany, about a minor third higher than our standard pitch today, though naturally there were local variants. In Prague, on the other hand, it was a tone lower at the same period, *i.e.* about a semitone higher than our standard pitch ; this is the pitch advocated by Praetorius in his *Syntagma Musicum*, vol. ii (1619) and is the actual pitch of the contemporary organ at Frederiksborg in Denmark, which still survives. Elsewhere, *e.g.* in a number of Catholic chapels, a pitch was in use which was a semitone lower than the Prague pitch and a minor third lower than the North German *Chorton*, *i.e.* approximately the same as our standard pitch today. The following table shows approximately the sounds that would be produced in our standard pitch by playing the note

on the different organs mentioned above:

Protestant churches in North Germany :

Prague and Frederiksborg :

Catholic chapels :

The following table shows the notes that would have to be played to sound approximately the note

in our standard pitch :

Protestant churches in North Germany :

Prague and Frederiksborg :

Catholic chapels :

The inconvenience of different pitches for organs, of which those quoted above are merely instances, became much greater when orchestral instruments were used in church music, as happened frequently in the 17th and early 18th cent. The highest of the *Chorton* pitches mentioned above (which Praetorius insists on calling *Kammerton*, or " chamber pitch," in defiance of contemporary German usage) was unsuitable for strings and wood-wind instruments ; and even the second, in which the A is roughly equivalent to our B♭, came to be regarded as too high. According to Quantz, in his *Versuch einer Anweisung die Flöte traversiere zu spielen* (1752), the introduction of a lower pitch for orchestral instruments in Germany was due to the influence of French wood-wind manufacturers. Some of the new organs built in the early 18th cent. were built to the lower pitch, known as *Kammerton*, but the pitch of older organs could not easily be changed. Where older organs were used for the performance of works for voices, organ and orchestra two alternatives were possible : (1) if the high pitch of the organ (*Chorton*) were accepted, the wood-wind parts had to be transposed into a higher key, while the strings had to tune up to the organ ; (2) if the low orchestral pitch (*Kammerton*) were accepted, the organ part had to be transposed down. Both these expedients are found in Bach's cantatas, the former in works written for the ducal chapel at Weimar between 1708 and 1717, the latter in works written for the Leipzig churches between 1723 and 1750.

v. KAMMERTON, PITCH.

A. MENDEL : " Pitch in the 16th and early 17th Centuries " (*Musical Quarterly*, 1948, pp. 28-45, 199-221, 336-57, 575-93).
" On the Pitches in Use in Bach's Time " (*Musical Quarterly*, 1955, pp. 332-54, 466-80).

C. S. TERRY : *Bach's Orchestra* (1932).

Chorus (*Fr.* choeur, *G.* Chor, *I.* coro). (1) A body of singers (male or female or both) in which there are several performers to each part, as opposed to the soloists in an opera, oratorio, cantata or other concerted work. A *semi-chorus* is a smaller body of singers used in association with, or in contrast to, a large chorus.

(2) Music written for a body of singers of this kind.

(3) In a solo song a refrain intended for a number of singers.

(4) Medieval Latin name for the CRWTH.

Choudens [shoo-dũnce]. A Paris firm of music-publishers, founded in 1845 by Antoine de Choudens (*d.* 1888).

Christmas Concerto. A *concerto grosso* by Corelli, Op. 6, No. 8 (1712), entitled *Concerto fatto per la notte di natale* (Concerto made for Christmas Eve). The last movement is a PASTORALE.

Christmas Oratorio (*G.* Weihnachts-Oratorium). (1) A series of 6 church cantatas by Bach (1734), designed to be performed on the three days of Christmas, New Year's Day, the Sunday after New Year's Day, and Epiphany (*B.G.*, v (2)).

(2) The name is sometimes given to Schütz's *Historia der freuden- und gnadenreichen Geburt Gottes und Mariens Sohn Jesu Christi* (1664), printed in the complete edition, supplement I.

Christoph Columbus [crist′-off col-ōōm′-bōōss] (Christopher Columbus). Opera in two parts (27 scenes) by Milhaud. Original French text by Paul Claudel. First performed, in a German version by Rudolf Stephan Hoffman, Berlin, May 5, 1930.

Christus am Ölberge [crist′-ōōss um url′-bairg-er] (Christ on the Mount of Olives). Oratorio by Beethoven, Op. 85 (1802), known in England as *The Mount of Olives*.

Chromatic (*Gr.* χρῶμα, colour). Lit. " coloured," hence " embellished." In particular :

(1) In ancient Greek music used to describe a modification of the diatonic tetrachord (or descending scale of four notes), by which the second note from the top was flattened a semitone :

Diatonic tetrachord :

Chromatic tetrachord :

(2) By a natural transference applied in Western European music to notes foreign to the mode or key, produced by the use of accidentals, whereas " diatonic " refers to notes forming part of the ordinary scale of the mode or key. The sharpened sixth and seventh used in a minor key, *e.g.* in C minor :

were originally chromatic notes, but they became so firmly established as regular alternatives to the sixth and seventh of the diatonic scale :

that they ceased to be regarded as chromatic.

(3) *Chromatic chord* : a chord which

includes one or more notes foreign to the key. A chord which is chromatic in one key may be diatonic in another, *e.g.* the chord of D♭ major is chromatic in the key of C major, where it needs accidentals, but not in the key of A♭ major, where it needs none :

This means that a chord which is merely an embellishment of one key may be an integral part of another, so that after using such a chord it is equally possible to remain in the first key or to modulate to the second, *e.g.* :

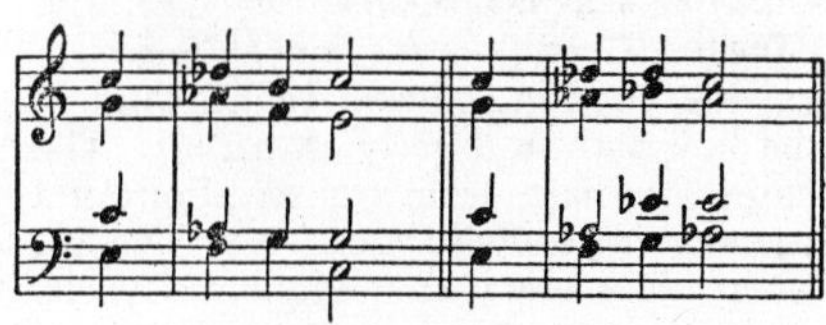

v. CHORD, HARMONY.

(4) *Chromatic harmony* : harmony which makes substantial use of chromatic chords. The use of chromatic notes for melodic purposes does not necessarily produce chromatic harmony, since they may be merely a decoration of diatonic harmony, *e.g.*

MOZART, *Symphony in C major, K.* 551

Contrast the following from the same movement, where the use of a similar melodic progression in four different parts produces chromatic harmony :

MOZART, *Symphony in C major, K.* 551

For the origin and development of chromatic harmony *v.* HARMONY.

(5) *Chromatic instrument* : an instrument whose normal compass includes all the notes of the chromatic scale (*v. infra*). A chromatic compass is now normal on all instruments. Before the invention of valves for the HORN and TRUMPET in the early 19th cent. these instruments were incapable of playing a chromatic scale. The HARP in normal use in the modern orchestra is chromatic in the sense that all the semitones are available, but they cannot be played in rapid succession ; this is possible only on the so-called chromatic harp. The word " chromatic " is also applied to TIMPANI fitted with a mechanical device which makes possible an immediate change of tuning.

(6) *Chromatic scale* : a scale consisting of successive semitones. It is convenient to write this with sharps if it ascends :

and with flats if it descends:

but the application of this principle will depend on the key of the piece. In a flat key, for example, it is obviously simpler in an ascending scale to use the notes which are already flattened by the key-signature and subsequently to sharpen them with naturals, since the naturals would be required in any case: *e.g.* in the key of E♭ it is simpler to write

than

In all such cases the object should be to achieve the maximum of intelligibility with the minimum of trouble.

(7) In 16th-cent. Italy *cromatico* was also used to refer to the use of black notes, *i.e.* notes of smaller value (*croma* is still the word for "quaver" in Italian). Thus *madrigale cromatico* meant a madrigal employing the smaller note values and hence sung at a brisk speed (*v.* A. Einstein, *The Italian Madrigal*, vol. i, pp. 398-401).

Chromatic Fantasia and Fugue. A keyboard work in D minor by Bach, composed *c.* 1720-3 (*B.G.*, xxxvi). The original title is *Fantasia cromatica e fuga*. The adjective refers to the considerable use made of chromatic harmony in the fantasia.

Chrotta. *v.* CRWTH.

Chrysander [crēē-zund′-er], KARL FRANZ FRIEDRICH: *b.* Lübtheen, July 8, 1826; *d.* Bergedorf, Sept. 3, 1901. Historian and musicologist; editor of a complete edition of Handel's works. Studied at Rostock University, and devoted his life to the study of Handel. His biography of Handel (3 vols., 1858-67) remained incomplete at his death. He also published the text of four oratorios by Carissimi and a number of works from which Handel borrowed material.

Church Modes. *v.* MODE.

Chybiński [khēē-been′-ski], ADOLF: *b.* Cracow, March 29, 1880. Polish historian. Studied at Cracow University and Munich. Professor at Lwów (Lemberg), 1921. He has taken an active part in the publication of old Polish music, including the *Monumenta Musices Sacrae in Polonia*, and has written extensively on the history of Polish music and on Polish folksong.

Ciaccona [chahk-co′-nah], *I.* Chaconne.

Cialamello [chah-lah-mell′-lo], *I.* Shawm.

Cibber, SUSANNA MARIA. *v.* ARNE (3).

Cibell (Cebell). A dance form in gavotte rhythm, current in England in the late 17th and early 18th cent. The name originates from transcriptions of a passage in Lully's opera *Atys* (1676), where the scene is the temple of Cybele. The majority of the pieces described as "cibell," however, have no connection with this passage beyond the fact that they imitate the rhythm, which is common in French music of this period.

T. DART: "The Cibell" in *Revue belge de musicologie*, vi (1952), pp. 24-30.

Ciconia [chick-one′-yah], JOHANNES: *b.* Liége, late 14th cent. Composer and theorist, some time canon of Padua. Examples of his works are in *D.T.Ö.*, xxxi, and J. Stainer, *Dufay and his Contemporaries*. (Ciconia, *L.* = stork).

Cid, Der [dair tseet] (The Cid). Opera in three acts by Cornelius. Libretto by the composer. First performed, Weimar, May 21, 1865.

Cid, Le [ler seed] (The Cid). Opera in four acts by Massenet. Libretto by Adolphe Philippe d'Ennery, Louis Gallot and Édouard Blau (based on Corneille's tragedy). First performed, Paris, Nov. 30, 1885.

Cifra [chee′-frah], ANTONIO: *b.* Rome, 1584; *d.* Loreto, Oct. 2, 1629. Prolific composer of church music, who held various appointments in Rome and at Loreto.

Cilèa [chee-leh′-ah], FRANCESCO : *b.* Palmi, July 26, 1866 ; *d.* Varazza, Nov. 20, 1950. Italian composer. Studied at the Naples Conservatorio, where he also taught the piano from 1890 to 1892. Taught at Istituto Musicale, Florence, 1896-1904. Director, Palermo Conservatorio, 1913-16, and subsequently Conservatorio S. Pietro a Maiella, Naples. Composed several operas, of which *Adriana Lecouvreur* (Milan, 1902) was the most successful.

Cimarosa [chee-mah-ro′-zah], DOMENICO : *b.* Aversa, Dec. 17, 1749 ; *d.* Venice, Jan. 11, 1801. Italian opera-composer, the son of a bricklayer. Studied at the Conservatorio Santa Maria di Loreto. His first opera, *Le stravaganze del conte*, was performed at Naples in 1772. He rapidly became one of the foremost opera-composers of the time. He worked mainly in Rome and Naples, but was also for a time in the service of Catherine II of Russia, and subsequently of the Emperor Leopold II in Vienna. His most famous work was the comic opera *Il matrimonio segreto* (Vienna, 1792), which is still performed. In addition to 65 operas he also wrote Masses, oratorios, cantatas, songs, and piano sonatas.

M. TIBALDI CHIESA : *Cimarosa e il suo tempo* (1939).
R. VITALE : *Domenico Cimarosa : la vita e le opere* (1929).

Cimbalom [chim′-ba-lom] (*I.* cimbalo ongarese). A form of DULCIMER used in Hungary. It consists of a series of metal strings which are strung on pegs fixed into a wooden box. The strings are struck with sticks held in the player's hands. It has been used by Stravinsky in *Renard* and *Rag-time*, and by Kodály in the *Háry János* suite.

Cimbasso [cheem-bahss′-so], *I.* Bass tuba.

Cinderella. *v.* CENERENTOLA.

Cinelli [chee-nell′-lee], *I.* Cymbals. The more usual term is *piatti*.

Cinque-Pace (from *Fr.* cinq pas, " five steps "). A term used for the GALLIARD by Elizabethan writers, who adapted it from the French original but apparently pronounced it as an English word, as it is often written " sink-a-pace " (there are several other spellings). *Cf.* Shakespeare, *Much Ado about Nothing*, ii, 1, and *Twelfth Night*, i, 3.

Cinti, La [lah cheen′-tee]. The professional name of Laure Cynthie DAMOREAU.

Cis [tsiss], *G.* C sharp (C♯).

Cisis [tiss′-iss], *G.* C double sharp (C×).

Cistre [seestr], *Fr.* Cither.

Cither, Cithern. *v.* CITTERN.

Cittern (*Fr.* cistre, *G.* Zither, *I.* cetera). Also spelt " cither " and " cithern." A plucked string instrument similar to the LUTE, but with a flat back and wire strings, popular in the 16th and 17th cent. It was played either with a plectrum or with the fingers. The music was written in TABLATURE. In the 18th cent. known in England as the English guitar. The modern German ZITHER is a different instrument.

Clapisson [cla-pee-sõ], ANTOINE LOUIS : *b.* Naples, Sept. 15, 1808 ; *d.* Paris, March 19, 1866. Violinist and composer ; teacher of harmony at the Paris Conservatoire, where his valuable collection of old instruments is preserved. Of his numerous operas the most successful were *La Promise* (Paris, 1854) and *La Fanchonnette* (Paris, 1856).

Clari [clah′-ree], GIOVANNI CARLO MARIA : *b.* Pisa, Sept. 27, 1667 ; *d.* there, May 16, 1754. Italian composer, a pupil of Colonna. Handel, in his oratorio *Theodora* (1749), used materials from some of Clari's vocal duets (*v.* S. Taylor, *The Indebtedness of Handel to Works by other Composers*, pp. 28-30 and supplement No. 4 of Chrysander's edition of Handel's works).

Clarinet (*Fr.* clarinette, *G.* Klarinette, *I.* clarinetto). A single-reed instrument, dating from the late 17th cent. As the tube is cylindrical, the lowest octave is reproduced a twelfth (not an octave) higher by " overblowing," *i.e.* the series :

becomes :

The notes between these two series are produced by opening a thumb-hole and by using keys, which also extend the compass downwards a minor third. The complete compass is :

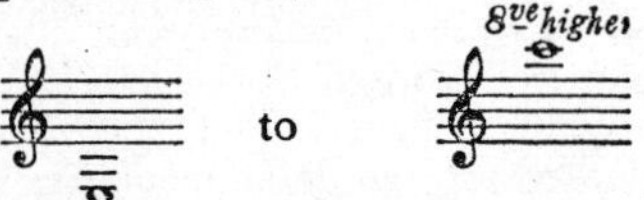

Clarinets were originally made in several sizes, in order to facilitate playing in different keys, and to save the player the trouble of learning a different fingering for each instrument were treated as TRANSPOSING INSTRUMENTS. By Beethoven's time (late 18th and early 19th cent.) only three sizes were in normal use—in C (sounding as written), in B♭ (sounding a tone lower) and in A (sounding a minor third lower). The clarinet in C is now obsolete in the orchestra, though it has been occasionally revived for performances of old music : the B♭ and A clarinets are in regular use, though some players prefer to use only the B♭ clarinet, with an extra key to obtain the extra semitone at the bottom. The sounding compass of the B♭ clarinet is :

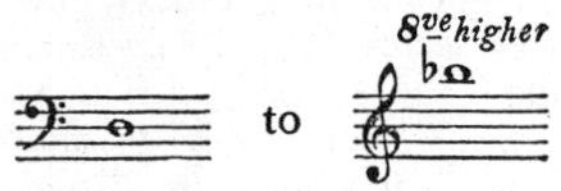

and of the A clarinet :

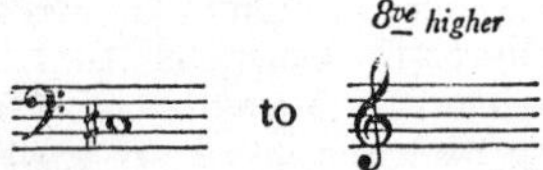

A smaller clarinet in E♭ (sounding a minor third higher than written) is used in military bands and occasionally in the orchestra : a similar instrument in D has also been made for orchestral use. Larger members of the family are the BASSET HORN, the BASS CLARINET and the CONTRABASS OR PEDAL CLARINET. The first of these was in use principally in the late 18th and early 19th cent. ; the last, a 19th-cent. invention, has remained virtually an experiment. Mozart was one of the first composers to realize the expressive possibilities of the clarinet (*e.g.* in his clarinet concerto and quintet for clarinet and strings). Brahms's chamber music includes two sonatas for clarinet and piano, a trio for clarinet, cello and piano, and a quintet for clarinet and strings.

A. CARSE : *Musical Wind Instruments* (1939).
F. G. RENDALL : *The Clarinet* (1954).

Clarinet Quintet. A work, generally in several movements, for clarinet and string quartet. Among the best known examples are those by Mozart (K. 581), Brahms (Op. 115), Reger (Op. 146) and Bliss.

Clarinette [cla-ree-net], *Fr.* Clarinet.

Clarinette basse [cla-ree-net buss], *Fr.* Bass clarinet.

Clarinette d'amour [cla-ree-net da-moor], *Fr.* An alto clarinet in A♭ or G with a bulb-shaped bell (like the *oboe d'amore*), current in the late 18th cent.

Clarinetto [clah-ree-net'-to], *I.* Clarinet. The word is a diminutive of *clarino* (trumpet) and was used originally because the tone of the 18th-cent. clarinet suggested at a distance the sound of the trumpet.

Clarinetto basso [clah-ree-net'-to bahss'-so], *I.* Bass clarinet.

Clarino [clah-ree'-no], *I.* (1) Trumpet. Applied particularly, in the 17th and early 18th cent., to the high register of the trumpet, for which players were specially trained. *v.* TRUMPET.

(2) Clarinet, on account of the similarity of tone in the early 18th cent. The diminutive *clarinetto* is the normal term.

Clarke, (1) JEREMIAH : *b. c.* 1673 ; *d.* London, Dec. 1, 1707. Composer and organist. Chorister in the Chapel Royal. Organist, Winchester College, 1692 ; St. Paul's Cathedral, 1695 ; Chapel Royal, 1704. His compositions include anthems, odes, music for the stage, and harpsichord pieces. Modern editions of harpsichord pieces in J. A. Fuller Maitland, *The Contemporaries of Purcell*, vol. v and *At the Court of Queen*

Anne; they include "The Prince of Denmark's March," which has been falsely attributed to Purcell and is widely known under the title "Trumpet Voluntary."

(2) REBECCA: *b.* Harrow, Aug. 27, 1886. Viola-player and composer, who has spent a large part of her life in America. Studied at the R.C.M. Her compositions include chamber music and songs.

Clarone [clah-ro'-neh], *I.* Bass clarinet.

Classical Music. The term "classical" (vulgarly but ineptly applied to serious, as opposed to popular, music) is used by historians to distinguish music which accepts certain basic conventions of form and structure, and uses them as a natural framework for the expression of ideas, from music which is more concerned with the expression of individual emotions than with the achievement of formal unity, *i.e.* ROMANTIC MUSIC. In practice the term is generally restricted to 18th- and early 19th-cent. music, *i.e.* roughly speaking, from Bach to Beethoven inclusive. In so far as the works of the great masters of this period are constantly performed and may be said to have stood the test of time, they are "classical" also in the sense in which one speaks of the "classics" of literature. The historical distinction, however, is not strictly valid, since many works of the Romantic period (roughly, from 1830 to 1910) show considerable pre-occupation with formal design, while equally Romantic elements are apparent in a good deal of 18th-cent. music, and in 17th-cent. music as well. It would probably be truer to say that the Romantic composers were often self-conscious, whereas the "classical" composers of the 18th cent. were not. Beethoven, in whose work the struggle between formal unity and intensely individual expression is often strongly marked, may be said to stand at the junction of the two periods.

Claudin [clo-dān]. *v.* SERMISY.

Clausula [clow'-sŏŏ-la], *L.* Lit. (1) "close," (2) "clause" or "section." Hence (1) cadence, in music in two or more parts (*cf. E.* full close, half close). *v.* CADENCE.

(2) In the *organa* or polyphonic compositions of the late 12th and early 13th cent. (associated particularly with Notre Dame, Paris) a clearly defined section, complete in itself (also known as *punctum*). Applied by some modern writers particularly to the new metrical sections written by Perotin and his contemporaries (*c.* 1200) to replace similar sections in the older *organa* of Léonin, and hence known as "substitute *clausulae*" (*G.* Ersatzklauseln). The "tenors" of such sections were taken from melismatic portions of the plainsong on which the whole composition was based, *i.e.* portions where there were several notes to one syllable. These notes were arranged in regular rhythm and so formed a metrical framework to which the added counterpoints conformed. These metrical sections formed a contrast to others where the notes of the plainsong were sustained so as to provide a foundation for rhythmically independent counterpoint (*v.* H. Besseler, *Musik der Mittelalters und der Renaissance*, p. 99, G. Reese, *Music in the Middle Ages*, pp. 296 *et seq.*). Perotin's "substitute *clausulae*" were the immediate forerunners of the 13th-cent. MOTET. *v.* PUNCTUM, ORGANUM.

Clausum [clow'-sŏŏm], *L.* *v.* CLOS.

Clavecin [cluv-sān], *Fr.* Harpsichord.

Clavicembalo [clah-vee-chem'-bah-lo], *I.* Harpsichord. Often found in the abbreviated form *cembalo.*

Clavichord (*Fr.* clavicorde, *G.* Clavichord, Klavichord, *I.* clavicordio). A keyboard instrument, first mentioned by this name at the beginning of the 15th cent. It appears to have been a development of the monochord, a scientific instrument consisting of a stretched string of variable length, which was known to the Greeks and has been used for acoustical demonstrations from the Middle Ages to the present day (hence the old names for the clavichord: *Fr.* manicorde, manicordion, *I.* manicordio). In the clavichord, which is oblong in shape, there is a series of stretched strings running roughly parallel with the front of the instrument. The depression of a key presses a small blade of brass (known as a "tangent") against the string. This divides the string into two lengths, one of which is free to vibrate while the other is damped by a piece of cloth. Since the tone is produced by pressure, it can to some extent be controlled by the player, who by repeated pressure on the key can produce minute variations of pitch, similar to the violinist's *vibrato* (*v.* BEBUNG).

In pre-18th-cent. clavichords a single string may do duty for more than one note. If two notes are not likely to be required to sound simultaneously, two tangents can be arranged to operate on the same string—an economical device which reduces the number of strings necessary. A clavichord of this type was called *fretted* (*G.* gebunden). The clavichord with a separate string for each note (*G.* bundfrei) was introduced in the early 18th cent. Clavichords with pedals (like an organ) were also made in the 18th cent. The clavichord was praised by C. P. E. Bach (1714-88) in his *Versuch über die wahre Art das Clavier zu spielen* (1753), and his performance on it elicited the admiration of Burney (*The Present State of Music in Germany*, 1773, vol. ii, p. 269). With the increasing use of the piano the clavichord came to be neglected. It has been successfully revived in the 20th cent. for the performance of old keyboard music, and new compositions have been written for it, *e.g.* Herbert Howells's *Lambert's Clavichord.* Its small tone makes it ineffective in the concert hall, but it is admirable for intimate music-making and for broadcasting.

P. JAMES : *Early Keyboard Instruments* (1930).

Clavier. (1) *Fr.* [cluv-yay]. Keyboard. (2) *G.* [cluv-eer′] (also *Klavier*). (*a*) Keyboard (*cf.* CLAVIERÜBUNG).

(*b*) Keyboard instrument with strings, *i.e.* clavichord, harpsichord or piano. There is nothing in the title of Bach's *Das wohltemperirte Clavier* to show whether the pieces are for clavichord or harpsichord.

(3) *E.* (*a*) Often used by modern writers, particularly Americans, as the equivalent of the German word.

(*b*) A keyboard designed for finger-practice, *e.g.* the Virgil practice clavier, patented in America by A. K. Virgil in 1892. This instrument produces no sound, but the pressure of the keys can be regulated, and a series of clicks, made as the keys rise and fall, enables the ear to detect whether a strict legato is being achieved.

Clavierübung [cluv-eer′-ee-bŏŏng], *G.* Lit. " keyboard practice." The title of a collection of keyboard music by Bach, one of the few works to be published in his lifetime. It was issued in four parts :

Part I (1731): 6 partitas (previously issued separately).

Part II (1735): Italian concerto and overture in the French style (partita in B minor).

Part III (1739): organ prelude in E♭ major, 21 chorale preludes on hymns illustrating the catechism, 4 *duetti* for harpsichord, organ fugue in E♭ major (known in England as " St. Anne's ").

Part IV (1742): Goldberg variations.

v. GOLDBERG VARIATIONS, ITALIAN CONCERTO.

Clef (borrowed from *Fr.* clef, " key ": *G.* Schlüssel, *I.* chiave). A sign used to determine the pitch of a particular line on a stave, from which the pitch of the remaining lines and of the spaces can be deduced. The three clefs now in use:

𝄞 𝄡 𝄢

are ornamental forms of the letters g, c and f (*v.* NOTATION) and represent respectively the notes *g′* (an octave above the fourth string of the violin), *c′* (the so-called " middle C," a fifth below *g′*) and *f* (a fifth below *c′*). Medieval scribes found that letters were more convenient than the coloured lines which were originally used to indicate *c′* and *f*, as their position on the stave could easily be changed. All three clefs were used in a variety of positions until the latter half of the 18th cent. Since that time the position of the G (treble) and F (bass) clefs has been invariable, except in some modern reprints of old music which retain the original positions of the clefs. The G clef is placed on the second line of the stave:

the F clef on the fourth line:

The C clef is placed either on the third line (alto clef) or on the fourth line (tenor clef):

The alto clef, formerly used for the alto voice and the alto trombone, is now used only for the viola. The tenor clef, formerly used for the tenor voice, is now used only for the tenor trombone and for the upper register of the bassoon, cello and double bass.
The C clef on the first line (soprano clef):

was in use in Germany as late as the end of the 19th cent. for the soprano voice, but is now obsolete, except in some modern reprints of old music.

In modern vocal scores, and in solo vocal music, the G clef is also used for the tenor voice, with the understanding (expressed or implied) that the music will sound an octave lower than the written pitch. Modifications of the G clef intended to express this transposition more precisely are:

The first of these is the most satisfactory, since the figure 8 indicates the octave transposition. It is used increasingly in modern editions of old music. For transposition in instrumental notation *v.* TRANSPOSING INSTRUMENTS.

Though the old practice of changing the position of a clef in the course of a composition has been abandoned, there are many occasions when a change of clef is necessary to avoid the excessive use of LEGER LINES. Thus, in keyboard music, where the right hand normally has the treble clef and the left hand the bass, it may be necessary to use the bass clef for the right hand or the treble clef for the left. In music for the viola the treble clef is used instead of the alto when the range of the music makes it desirable. Similarly, the tenor clef is used when necessary for the bassoon, cello and (more rarely) the double bass, and in music for the horn the bass clef may temporarily replace the treble.

Clemens non Papa [clay′-mence nohn pah′-pa], JACOBUS, the Latin name of JACQUES CLÉMENT: *b. c.* 1510; *d. c.* 1557. One of the most distinguished Flemish composers of his time. Little is known of his life, beyond the fact that he worked in Ypres and Dixmuiden. His compositions, which are remarkable for their expressive quality, include polyphonic Masses, motets, *chansons* and Flemish psalms. He is supposed to have added the words " non Papa " to his name to distinguish himself from the poet Jacobus Papa, who lived in Ypres at the same time. The fact that Clemens non Papa can be translated literally as " Clement, not the Pope "may be taken as an example of the delight in double meaning which was common in the 16th cent. The view, formerly expressed, that there was any need to distinguish a Flemish composer from Pope Clement VII is too absurd to be accepted seriously. A complete edition of his works by K. P. Bernet Kempers is in progress.

E. LOWINSKY : *Secret Chromatic Art in the Netherlands Motet* (1946).

Clément [clay-mũn], (1) FÉLIX: *b.* Paris, Jan. 13, 1822; *d.* Jan. 23, 1885. Composer and historian. His principal post was that of organist and director of music at the Sorbonne. His interest in old music took practical shape in the form of a series of performances at the Sainte-Chapelle in Paris. In addition to editions of old church music (including plainsong) and textbooks he published *Histoire générale de la musique religieuse* (1860), *Les Musiciens célèbres* (1868), *Dictionnaire lyrique ou Histoire des opéras* (1869, later issued with supplements and in a revised edition), and *Histoire de la musique* (1885).

(2) JACQUES. *v.* CLEMENS NON PAPA.

Clementi [cleh-men′-tee], MUZIO: *b.* Rome, Jan. 23, 1752; *d.* Evesham, March 10, 1832. Composer and pianist, the son of a silversmith. At the age of 14, having already showed considerable talent as a composer, he was brought to England by Peter Beckford and continued his studies there. His first three piano sonatas, Op. 2, were published in 1773. He also won outstanding success as a performer. After serving as harpsichordist at the Italian Opera in London (1777-80), he toured on the Continent (1781-2). He lived in England from 1782 to 1802, and in 1800 founded a firm of music-publishers and piano-manufacturers (known after his death as Collard & Collard). Travelled on the Continent again, 1802-10, including a visit to St. Petersburg with his pupil John Field. Married (1) Karoline Lehmann (d. 1805), 1804, (2) Emma Gisburne, 1811. He knew personally Haydn, Mozart and Beethoven (all of whom he survived), as well as many other musicians of the time. Mozart's opinion of his playing was unfavourable :

> " He is an excellent cembalo-player, but that is all. He has great facility with his right hand. His star passages are thirds. Apart from this, he has not a farthing's worth of taste or feeling ; he is a mere *mechanicus*." (Jan. 16, 1782, *Letters of Mozart and his Family*, trans. E. Anderson, p. 1181 ; *cf.* pp. 1267-8).

This, however, was before he had developed his later style of playing, characterized by its mastery of cantabile and legato.

His influence on other pianists and composers for the piano was considerable. He did more than anyone to develop a style of writing which exploited the characteristics of the piano, as opposed to the harpsichord. His numerous compositions include symphonies, piano sonatas, and *Gradus ad Parnassum*, a series of piano studies which achieved a remarkable union of technical instruction and artistic expression.

K. DALE : " Hours with Muzio Clementi " (*Music and Letters*, July 1943).

J. S. SHEDLOCK : *The Pianoforte Sonata* (1895).

Clemenza di Tito, La [lah cleh-men′-tsah dee tee′-to] (Titus's Clemency). Opera in two acts by Mozart. Libretto adapted from Metastasio by Caterino Mazzolà. First performed, Prague, Sept. 6, 1791.

Clérambault [clay-rũn-bo], LOUIS NICOLAS: *b.* Paris, Dec. 19, 1676; *d.* there, Oct. 26, 1749. Organist and composer, a pupil of André Raison. He became organist of St. Sulpice, Paris. His compositions include cantatas and works for harpsichord and organ; modern edition of the organ works in A. Guilmant, *Archives des maîtres de l'orgue*, iii.

Cliquot [clee-co], FRANÇOIS HENRI: *b.* Paris, 1728; *d.* there, 1791. French organ-builder, who succeeded his father, uncle and grandfather in this profession. He built organs for a number of churches in Paris, including Sainte-Chapelle, St. Sulpice and Notre Dame, as well as in the provinces. Much of his work survives today.

Cloche [closh], *Fr.* Bell.

Clochette [closh-et], *Fr. v.* GLOCKENSPIEL.

Clock Symphony. The name given to Haydn's Symphony No. 101 in D major. In the slow movement the accompanying instruments suggest the ticking of a clock.

Clos [clo], *Fr.* (*L.* clausum, *I.* chiuso). " Closed." A medieval term used in dance music, and in vocal pieces similar in structure, to indicate a final cadence at the end of a repeated section, in contrast to an intermediate cadence (*Fr.* ouvert, *L.* apertum, *I.* verto) used when the section is performed the first time, *e.g.* :

LANDINI, *Works*, ed. L. Ellinwood, no. *103*

Ouvert and *clos* thus correspond to what is now called " 1st time " (or " 1st ending ") and " 2nd time."

Close. Cadence. *Half close*, imperfect cadence. *Full close*, perfect cadence. *v.* CADENCE.

Closson [closs-ōn], ERNEST: *b.* St. Josse-ten-Noode, Dec. 12, 1870; *d.* Brussels, Dec. 21, 1950. Belgian critic and historian, for many years curator of the collection of musical instruments at the Brussels Conservatoire and lecturer in musical history there and at the Mons Conservatoire. He was also music critic of *L'Indépendance belge.* His publications include *Les Chansons populaires des provinces belges* (1905), *Le Manuscrit dit des Basses Danses de la Bibliothèque de Bourgogne* (1912), *Esthétique musicale* (1921), *L'Élément flamand dans Beethoven* (1928: in English as *The Fleming in Beethoven*, 1936), as well as numerous articles in periodicals.

Coates, (1) ALBERT: *b.* St. Petersburg, Apr. 23, 1882; *d.* Milnerton, nr. Cape Town, Dec. 11, 1953. Conductor and composer, the son of an English father and a Russian mother. Studied science at Liverpool University, and music at Leipzig Conservatorium, where he was in the conducting class held by Artur Nikisch. Conductor, Elberfeld Opera, 1906-8, and subsequently at Dresden and St. Petersburg (1909-14). Settled in England (where he had already appeared as visiting conductor) in 1919; since then appeared frequently as conductor of opera, symphony concerts and festivals. His compositions include the operas *Samuel Pepys* (Munich, 1929) and *Pickwick* (London, 1936).

(2) EDITH MARY: *b.* Lincoln, May 31, 1908. Contralto. Studied at Trinity College of Music. Member of the opera company at Sadler's Wells since 1931, and at Covent Garden since 1946.

(3) ERIC: *b.* Hucknall, Aug. 27, 1886; *d.* Chichester, Dec. 21, 1957. Viola-player and composer. Studied at the R.A.M. Principal viola, Queen's Hall Orchestra, 1912. From 1918 he worked solely as composer. His works, many of which are for orchestra, are light in substance but impeccable in workmanship.

(4) JOHN: *b.* Girlington, June 29, 1865; *d.* Northwood, Aug. 16, 1941. Tenor. Began his career as a baritone in musical comedy. After becoming a tenor sang Claudio at the first performance of Stanford's *Much Ado about Nothing* (London, 1901) and in Elgar's *Dream of Gerontius* at Worcester in 1902. Sang frequently in opera and oratorio, both in England and in the Dominions. After his war service (1914-1919) devoted himself almost entirely to oratorio and song recitals.

Cobbett, WALTER WILSON: *b.* Blackheath, July 11, 1847; *d.* London, Jan. 22, 1937. Business man and amateur violinist, who rendered considerable service to the cause of chamber music by (1) offering prizes for new works by English composers, (2) founding the Chamber Music Association, which is connected with the British Federation of Music Festivals, (3) editing a *Cyclopedia of Chamber Music* (2 vols., 1929).

Cobbold, WILLIAM: *b.* Jan. 5, 1560; *d.* Beccles, Nov. 7, 1639. Organist of Norwich Cathedral until 1608. He harmonized five of the tunes in Thomas East's *The Whole Booke of Psalmes*, 1592 (modern edition by Musical Antiquarian Society, 1844) and contributed a madrigal to *The Triumphs of Oriana*, 1601 (reprinted in *E.M.S.*, vol. xxxii).

Cocks. A London music-publishing

firm, founded in 1823 by Robert Cocks (*d.* 1887) and acquired by Augener in 1898.

Coclicus [cock'-li-cooss], ADRIANUS PETIT: *b.* Flanders, *c.* 1500; *d.* Copenhagen, *c.* 1563. Composer and singer, a pupil of Josquin des Prés. He migrated to Wittenberg in 1545 and became a Protestant. Member of the Chapel Royal, Copenhagen, 1556. His *Compendium musices* (1552) is a valuable exposition of current musical practice (facsimile ed. by M. Bukofzer, 1954), and his collection of psalms entitled *Musica reservata* (1552) is the first known use of that term (*q.v.*) to indicate a particular type of music, suitable for connoisseurs and private occasions.

M. VAN CREVEL: *Adrianus Petit Coclico* (1940).

E. LOWINSKY: *Secret Chromatic Art in the Netherlands Motet* (1946).

Coda [co'-dah], *I.* Lit. "tail" (*L.* cauda). A passage, long or short, at the end of a piece or movement, which extends the ideas which have already received logical or symmetrical expression and brings the work to a satisfying conclusion, *e.g.*:

(1) in a CANON a short concluding passage in which strict imitation is abandoned in order to construct a convincing cadence.

(2) in a FUGUE a similar passage, often based on a PEDAL POINT, which sums up and clinches the arguments already presented by the polyphonic treatment of the subject, and so corresponds roughly to the peroration of a speech or the conclusion of an essay.

(3) In a movement in SONATA FORM a passage added to the end of the recapitulation. In 18th-cent. works the coda was generally short, but in Beethoven was often expanded to a considerable length, *e.g.* in the first movement of the *Eroica* symphony.

Codetta [co-det'-tah,] *I.* Diminutive of CODA. Applied particularly to (1) a short passage forming a tail-piece to a particular section of a composition.

(2) An extension of a fugue subject which serves to delay the next entry, *e.g.*:

BACH, *48 Preludes & Fugues, Book I, No. 16*

Coelho [coo-el'-yoo], RUY: *b.* March 3, 1891. Portuguese composer and critic, a pupil of Humperdinck, noteworthy particularly for his operas, but has also written symphonic poems, chamber music, piano works and songs. His opera *Belkiss* (Lisbon, 1938) was awarded a prize in a Spanish competition.

Coenen [coo'-nĕn], (1) FRANZ: *b.* Rotterdam, Dec. 26, 1826; *d.* Leyden, Jan. 24, 1904. Dutch violinist and composer, a pupil of Vieuxtemps and Molique. After touring in America he became director of the Amsterdam Conservatorium, retiring in 1895.

(2) WILLEM: *b.* Rotterdam, Nov. 17, 1837; *d.* Lugano, March 18, 1918. Brother of (1). Pianist and composer. Settled in London, 1865, and gave chamber concerts devoted to the works of modern composers, including Brahms.

Coeuroy [cur-rwa], ANDRÉ: *b.* Dijon, Feb. 24, 1891. The pseudonym of Jean Belime. French critic and historian. Studied at the École Normale Supérieure, Paris, and in Germany with Reger. Founded the *Revue Musicale* with Henry Prunières, and edited it until 1935. In addition to writing books on music (particularly on modern music) he has translated the texts of foreign works and has himself written opera-librettos.

He has also composed some chamber music.

Colasse [col-uss], PASCAL: *b.* Rheims, Jan., 1649; *d.* Versailles, July 17, 1709. Assistant to Lully and himself a composer of operas, as well as church music. He is said to have helped to write the inner parts (*i.e.* those between treble and bass) of Lully's music.

Colbran [col-brahn'], ISABELLA ANGELA: *b.* Madrid, Feb. 2, 1785; *d.* Bologna, Oct. 7, 1845. Spanish dramatic soprano, with a European reputation, which began to decline after 1815 as a result of uncertain intonation. She was *prima donna* at Milan, Venice, Rome and Naples, and also sang in Vienna, London and Paris. Married Rossini, 1822.

Coleman. *v.* COLMAN.

Coleridge-Taylor, SAMUEL: *b.* London, Aug. 15, 1875; *d.* Croydon, Sept. 1, 1912. Composer. His father was a native of Sierra Leone, his mother was English. Studied violin and composition at the R.C.M., where he had a scholarship for composition and was a pupil of Stanford. He made his reputation with his choral setting of Longfellow's *Hiawatha's Wedding Feast* (1898), still his most popular work, followed by *The Death of Minnehaha* (1899) and *Hiawatha's Departure* (1900). His other compositions include the oratorio *The Atonement* (1903), the cantata *A Tale of Old Japan* (1911), orchestral music, chamber music, and incidental music for the stage. Conductor of the Handel Society, 1904-12.

W. C. BERWICK SAYERS: *Samuel Coleridge-Taylor—His Life and Letters* (2nd ed. 1927).

Colla parte [col'-lah parr'-teh], *I.* "With the part," *i.e.* the accompaniment is to follow any modifications of tempo made by the soloist. *cf.* COLLA VOCE.

Colla punta dell'arco [col'-lah poon'-tah del arr'-co], *I.* With the point (*i.e.* the end furthest from the hand) of the bow.

Coll' arco [col arr'-co], *I.* "With the bow." A term used in string music to contradict the previous designation *pizzicato* (plucked with the finger). Generally abbreviated to *arco.*

Collard. A London firm of piano-manufacturers, originally founded by Clementi. F. W. Collard was one of five partners of the firm in 1802. By 1823 the firm was known as Clementi, Collard and Collard, and after Clementi's death in 1832 as Collard and Collard.

Colla voce [col'-lah vo'-cheh], *I.* "With the voice." The same as *colla parte*, but used exclusively in the accompaniment of a vocal solo.

Collegium Musicum [col-leh'-gi-ŏŏm moo'-si-cŏŏm], *L.* A society for the practice of music, generally associated with a university. The term was in use in Germany in the 17th and 18th cent. and has been revived there in the present century. The purpose of a *collegium musicum* is primarily to study music (particularly old music) by playing it, rather than to give public performances. Its activities form a normal part of musical education in any German university today.

Col legno [col lehn'-yo], *I.* Lit. "with the wood." A direction to string players to bounce the stick of the bow on the string, instead of playing with the hair (*e.g.* Holst, *The Planets*, No. 1, *Mars*).

Colles, HENRY COPE: *b.* Bridgnorth, April 20, 1879; *d.* London, March 4, 1943. Critic and historian. Studied at Oxford and the R.C.M. Assistant music critic to *The Times*, 1906; principal critic, 1911; lecturer, R.C.M., 1919. Edited the third (1927) and fourth (1940) editions of Grove's *Dictionary of Music and Musicians*. His books include *Brahms* (1908), *The Growth of Music* (3 vols., 1912-16), *Voice and Verse* (1928), *Symphony and Drama*: 1850-1900 (vol. vii of the *Oxford History of Music*, 1934), *Walford Davies* (1942) and *Essays and Lectures* (1945). The last includes a memoir by his wife.

Collet [col-lay], HENRI: *b.* Paris, Nov. 5, 1885; *d.* there, Nov. 27, 1951. Composer and historian, who made a particular study of Spanish music. His books include *Le Mysticisme musical espagnol au XVIe siècle* (1913), *Victoria* (1914), *Albéniz et Granados* (1926). He also wrote orchestral music and chamber music.

Collingwood, LAWRANCE ARTHUR: *b.*

London, March 14, 1887. Conductor and composer. Chorister at Westminster Abbey. Studied at Oxford and St. Petersburg Conservatoire. For some years assistant to Albert Coates at the St. Petersburg Opera. Principal conductor, Sadler's Wells Opera, 1931-47. Now music adviser to H.M.V. His compositions include the opera *Macbeth* (London, 1934), a setting of Shakespeare's text.

Coll' ottava [col ot-tah'-vah], *I.* Doubled at the octave (above or below).

v. OTTAVA.

Colman, (1) CHARLES: *d.* July, 1664. Court musician to Charles I and Charles II and one of the composers of the instrumental music in the first English opera, *The Siege of Rhodes* (1656).

(2) CHARLES: *d. c.* 1694. Son of (1). Court musician to Charles II and James II.

(3) EDWARD: *d.* Greenwich, Aug. 29, 1669. Son of (1) and brother of (2). Court musician to Charles II. Sang in *The Siege of Rhodes.* For his wife, also a singer, *v.* Pepys, *Diary*, Oct. 31, 1665.

Colonne [col-on], EDOUARD (originally Judas): *b.* Bordeaux, July 23, 1838; *d.* Paris, March 28, 1910. French violinist and conductor. Studied at the Paris Conservatoire; in the Opéra orchestra, 1858-67. Founder of the Concerts Colonne (at first known as Concert National), 1873, at which a large number of works by French composers (particularly Berlioz) were given. Also conducted at the Opéra, 1891-3, and in other European countries.

Color. *v.* ISORHYTHM.

Coloratura [co-lo-rah-too'-rah], *I.* (*G.* Koloratur). Elaborate ornamentation of the melodic line in music for solo instruments or (more frequently) voices. Arias including such ornamentation occur constantly in 18th- and 19th-cent. opera, particularly in Italy. A coloratura singer is one who specializes in the virtuosity which such arias demand.

Colour. A word used, by analogy with painting, to describe the individual tone-quality of instruments and voices, or their association together, *e.g.* orchestral colour. The many attempts that have been made to relate actual colour to key or to tone-quality are based on pure fantasy.

Combarieu [cõn-barr-yer], JULES LÉON JEAN: *b.* Cahors, Feb. 3, 1859; *d.* Paris, July 7, 1916. Historian. Studied in Paris and in Berlin under Spitta. Lecturer, Collège de France, 1904-10. Inspector general of choral singing in schools. Founded the *Revue Musicale* (1904-12), a different periodical from the later one with the same name founded by Coeuroy and Prunières. His principal publications were *Les Rapports de la musique et de la poésie considérés au point de vue de l'expression* (1894), *La Musique, ses lois, son évolution* (1907; also in English), *Histoire de la musique* (3 vols., 1913-19).

Combination Pedals. (1) Properly a device invented in France for bringing into action several rows of organ pipes by admitting air to the soundboard on which they are placed.

(2) Also used in the same sense as COMPOSITION PEDALS, which control the movement of stops.

Combination Tone. A faint note resulting from sounding two notes simultaneously (known also as *resultant tone*). Combination tones are of two kinds: (1) *difference tones*, resulting from the difference between the frequencies of the notes sounded, (2) *summation tones* (fainter than difference tones), resulting from the sum of their frequencies. In the following examples the two notes which are sounded together are represented by semibreves and the combination tones by black notes:

Difference tones:

Summation tones:

The two notes originally sounded together also combine with the combination tone to produce further combination tones.

If three or more notes are sounded together the number of combination tones will be proportionately increased. *v.* ACOUSTICS.

Come prima [co'-meh pree'-mah], *I.* As at first.

Comes [com'-ace], *L.* "Companion." The name given by older theorists to the second part to enter in a CANON or FUGUE, because it serves as a companion to the first part, known as *dux* (leader), which it imitates.

Come sopra [co'-meh so'-prah], *I.* As above.

Come stà [co'-meh stah], *I.* As it stands, *i.e.* without any modification or ornamentation of the text.

Commer [com'-mer], FRANZ: *b.* Cologne, Jan. 23, 1813; *d.* Berlin, Aug. 17, 1887. Organist and editor of old music. Studied in Cologne and Berlin. He helped to found the Berlin Tonkünstlerverein and the Gesellschaft für Musikforschung (*v.* EITNER). He wrote a certain amount of choral music, including music for two Greek plays, but is best known for his *Collectio operum musicorum Batavorum saeculi XVI*[i] (a collection of music by Netherlands composers, 12 vols.) and *Musica sacra XVI*[i], *XVII*[i] *saeculorum* (26 vols.).

Commodo. An obsolete form of COMODO.

Common Chord. A major or minor triad in root position, *e.g.*:

v. CHORD.

Common Time. Four crotchets in a bar, indicated by the time-signature $\frac{4}{4}$ or C. *v.* C, TIME.

Communion (*L.* communio). An antiphon sung after communion at Mass. Originally an antiphon to the verses of a psalm.

Comodo [co'-mo-do], *I.* "Convenient," *i.e.* at a convenient speed, neither too fast nor too slow. Often combined with *allegro*.

Compenius [com-pay'-ni-ŏŏss]. A firm of organ-builders active in the late 16th and early 17th cent. A Compenius organ built in 1612 still survives at Frederiksborg in Denmark (gramophone records by Finn Vider, H.M.V.).

Compère [cõn-pairr], LOYSET: *d.* St. Quentin, Aug. 16, 1518. Composer, a pupil of Okeghem. Became canon and chancellor of St. Quentin Cathedral. His numerous compositions include Masses, motets and *chansons*.

Competition Festivals. Meetings for competitive performance (with or without prizes) of choral music, songs, chamber music and solo instrumental music. First organised in England by J. S. Curwen at Stratford, East London, 1882 and by Mary Wakefield in Westmorland, 1885; now organised by the British Federation of Music Festivals (1921) and held in all parts of the country. The Welsh Eisteddfod, in its modern form, dates from the early 19th cent., as do the brass band festivals. Similar festivals are also held in the United States and the Dominions.

R. NEWMARCH: *Mary Wakefield—a Memoir* (1912).

Composition Pedals. A set of metal pedals, or buttons operated by the feet, used in the organ to bring into action one or more stops without having to draw them individually by hand. Each pedal, in addition to bringing on the stops which it controls, automatically puts out of action any others which happen to be drawn at the time. In modern organs composition pedals generally operate on pedal stops and couplers, but can also be adjusted to bring on manual stops appropriate to the pedal combinations. The electrical action now in use makes it possible for the player to select his own combinations by means of switches, instead of being compelled to use the builder's selection.

Composition Pistons. These are similar in action to composition pedals, but are placed below the manuals and are controlled by fingers or thumbs. They generally operate on manual stops and couplers, but can also be adjusted to bring on pedal stops appropriate to the manual combinations.

Compound Time. Time in which each beat in the bar is divisible into three, *e.g.*:

as opposed to SIMPLE TIME, in which each beat is divisible into two, *e.g.*:

Comte Ory, Le [ler cônt orr-ee] (Count Ory). Opera in two acts by Rossini. Libretto by Augustin Eugène Scribe and Charles Gaspard Delestre-Poirson. First performed, Paris, Aug. 20, 1828.

Comus. Masque by John Milton, with music by Henry Lawes. First performed, Ludlow Castle, Sept. 29, 1634. An adaptation by John Dalton, with new music by Arne (modern ed. in *Musica Britannica*, iii) was performed in London, March 4, 1738.

Con affetto [con ahf-fet'-to], *I.* With tender emotion.

Con amore [con ah-moh'-reh], *I.* Lovingly.

Con anima [con ah'-nee-mah], *I.* With spirit.

Con brio [con bree'-o], *I.* Vigorously.

Concert. (1) The public performance of music other than opera or church music; in particular a performance by a group of singers or players, as opposed to a RECITAL by a soloist. Until the late 17th cent. such performances were to be heard only at the courts of kings and princes or in the private houses of wealthy patrons. A pioneer of public concerts, which anyone could attend on payment of a charge for admission, was John Banister, who started a series at Whitefriars, London, in 1672. Banister's experiment was imitated by others and led in course of time to more ambitious undertakings, *e.g.* the series of orchestral concerts organized by Salomon in London in the late 18th cent., for which Haydn wrote his "London" symphonies. Similar concerts were organized in France under the title *Concert spirituel*, founded in 1725 by Anne Philidor. The growth of public concerts made it necessary to provide buildings in which they could be given. The oldest hall in Europe specially built for this purpose appears to have been the Holywell Music Room in Oxford, opened in 1748 and still in regular use.

v. PROMENADE CONCERTS, ROYAL PHILHARMONIC SOCIETY.

M. BRENET : *Les Concerts en France sous l'ancien régime* (1900).

J. H. MEE : *The Oldest Music Room in Europe* (1911).

G. PINTHUS : *Die Entwicklung des Konzertwesens in Deutschland bis zum Beginn des 19. Jahrhunderts* (1932).

(2) *Fr.* [côn-sair]. (a) Concert. (b) Concerto.

Concertant, *Fr.* [côn-sair-tûn], **Concertante,** *I.* [con-chair-tahn'-teh].

(1) As an adjective used to describe a work, whether for orchestra or for two or more performers, in which one or more solo instruments are prominent, *e.g.* Mozart's *Symphonie concertante* for violin, viola and orchestra (K.364), Weber's *Grand Duo concertant* for piano and clarinet (Op. 48), Walton's *Sinfonia concertante* for piano and orchestra.

(2) The Italian *concertante*, used as a noun, = *sinfonia concertante*.

Concertato [con-chair-tah'-toh], *I.* = CONCERTANTE. *Coro concertato*, a group of solo singers used to form a contrast to the full choir (17th cent.). *Stile concertato*, the "modern" style of the early

17th cent., in which solo instruments or voices were exploited, with figured-bass accompaniment.

Concertgebouw [con-sairrt'-ger-bow], *D.* Lit. "concert building." An Amsterdam society founded in 1883 for giving public orchestral concerts. The Concertgebouw Orchestra was directed from 1895 to 1945 by William Mengelberg, and until 1959 by Eduard van Beinum.

Concertina. A form of ACCORDION, patented by Sir Charles Wheatstone in 1829. It is hexagonal in shape. Small pistons or studs, placed at each end of the instrument and operated by the fingers, take the place of a keyboard.

Concertino [con-chair-tee'-no], *I.* Diminutive of CONCERTO.

(1) The group of soloists in a *concerto grosso* (17th and 18th cent.).

(2) A work for one or more solo instruments with orchestra, less formal in structure and often shorter than an ordinary concerto (*G.* Konzertstück), *e.g.* Weber's concertino for clarinet and orchestra, Op. 26.

(3) The title given by Stravinsky to a work for string quartet, in which the first violin has a prominent solo part (1920).

Concert-Master, *A.* (*G.* Konzertmeister). The principal first violin (*E.* leader) of an orchestra.

Concerto [con-chair'-to], *I.* (*Fr.* concert, *G.* Konzert).

(1) A work for one or more voices with instrumental accompaniment, either for figured bass or with the addition of other instruments, *e.g.* Banchieri's *Concerti ecclesiastici a 8 voci* (1595), Viadana's *Concerti ecclesiastici a una, a due, a 3 & a 4 voci, con il Basso continuo per sonar nell'organo* (1602). Monteverdi's seventh book of madrigals (1619) is entitled *Concerto,* indicating that it contains vocal pieces with instrumental accompaniment, not madrigals in the conventional sense. This use of the word *concerto* survived till the early 18th cent. It was the name given by Bach to several of his church cantatas.

(2) A work for several instruments, supported by figured bass and offering opportunities for contrast (17th and early 18th cent.), *e.g.* Bach's third Brandenburg concerto. In particular:

(3) *Concerto grosso,* an orchestral work in several movements, in which it was customary to have passages for a group of solo instruments (*concertino*) as a contrast to the *tutti* for the main body (*concerto grosso*). The favourite group of solo instruments consisted of two violins and cello (accompanied, like the *tutti,* by figured bass), but many other combinations are found, *e.g.* in Bach's second Brandenburg concerto, where the solo instruments are trumpet, recorder, oboe and violin.

(4) The solo concerto (*i.e.* for one instrument with orchestra) dates from the early 18th cent., when the violin was the most favoured solo instrument. Keyboard instruments, being used to play the figured bass accompaniment, were not at first thought of as suitable for playing solos in a concerto. Bach's concertos for one or more harpsichords were a novelty at the time, and most of these were transcriptions of violin concertos by himself or other composers. Handel's organ concertos were written for his own use, to provide interludes in his oratorio performances. By the late 18th cent. the solo concerto had become the normal type, and many keyboard concertos were written, *e.g.* by C. P. E. Bach, Haydn and Mozart. Works of the same character for more than one solo instrument were also written, *e.g.* Mozart's concertos for flute and harp (K.299) and for two pianos (K.365). By Mozart's time the figured bass for a keyboard instrument had ceased to be an indispensable part of an orchestral composition, but it was still customary for a harpsichord or piano to play with the orchestra, even in concertos for a keyboard instrument.

The use of a solo instrument had obvious similarities to the use of a solo voice in the operatic aria. Hence contrasts between *ritornelli* for full orchestra and sections where the soloist took command were normal, and opportunities for improvised display were offered at the cadence before the final *ritornello* (*v.* CADENZA). Mozart, however, achieved a much closer integration of the soloist and the orchestra, and there are many places in his piano concertos where the soloist provides the accompaniment to solos by wind instruments in the orchestra. In this respect his example has been followed by many subsequent composers, but not always with the same success. The increased power of the modern piano and the growth of the orchestra have resulted in the composition of concertos in which there seems at times to be a pitched battle between the soloist and the orchestra.

(5) The word *concerto* has also been used by modern composers in a sense similar to (2) above, *i.e.* a composition for an instrumental ensemble, though without the implication of a figured bass, *e.g.* Bartók's concerto for orchestra.

(5) Bach's *Concerto nach Italiaenischen Gusto* (Concerto in the Italian style), popularly known as the *Italian Concerto*, is a work for harpsichord solo, which imitates the style of the solo concerto with orchestra by reproducing the contrast between soloist and *tutti*.

C. M. GIRDLESTONE : *Mozart et ses concertos pour piano*, 2 vols. (1939); also in English (1948).

A. SCHERING : *Geschichte der Instrumentalkonzerts* (2nd ed., 1927).

A. VEINUS : *The Concerto* (1944).

Concerto grosso [con-chair′-toh gross′-so], *I.* (1) In the 17th and early 18th cent. a composition for orchestra in several movements generally with passages for a group of solo instruments to form a contrast with the *tutti*. *v.* CONCERTO (3).

(2) The main body of instruments in a work of this kind, as opposed to the *concertino* of solo instruments..

Concert Overture. A form originating in the 19th cent. and consisting of an orchestral piece similar to the overture to an opera or play but intended purely for the concert room. Beethoven's overtures to *Egmont* and *Coriolan* and his *Leonora No.* 3 overture (originally intended for the opera *Fidelio*), all of which reflect vividly the spirit of the dramas which they introduce, had a considerable influence on the composers of concert overtures, which often have a title and are associated, more or less definitely, with a programme. Typical examples are Mendelssohn's *The Hebrides* (*Fingal's Cave*), Brahms's *Tragic Overture*, Tchaikovsky's *Romeo and Juliet* and Elgar's *Cockaigne*.

Concert Pitch. A conventional term for standard international pitch, according to which the note:

is fixed at 440 cycles a second. Brass bands in England use a higher pitch (*v.* PITCH).

Concert spirituel [cõn-sair spee-ree-tẽe-el], *Fr.* Lit. "sacred concert." An organization founded in Paris in 1725 by Anne Philidor to give concerts on religious festivals when the Opéra was closed. Before long the introduction of secular works made the original title a misnomer. The concerts came to an end in 1791.

Concertstück. *v.* KONZERTSTÜCK.

Concone [con-co′-neh], GIUSEPPE: *b.* Turin, Sept. 12, 1801; *d.* there, June 1, 1861. Teacher and composer, for some years resident in Paris, which he left after the 1848 revolution, becoming court organist at Turin. Best known for his collections of vocal exercises, which are still in use.

Concord. A combination of sounds agreeable to the ear—the opposite of discord. As, however, there have been widely different opinions as to what is agreeable to the ear, not only at different periods but also at one and the same period, any precise definition or list of concords is arbitrary and has no absolute validity. *v.* CONSONANCE, DISCORD.

Conducting. The direction of a performance given by a group of singers or players or both. It involves not only precise indications of speed and dynamics, but also careful preparation to ensure that the balance is correct and that the intentions of the composer are adequately represented. These requirements are not always observed, but a good performance is impossible without them. Unlike the singer or instrumentalist, the conductor has to persuade others to accept his view of the music and so help him to shape it into a unified and convincing whole. The method by which this is achieved varies according to the individual. Some conductors make detailed annotations in the orchestral parts or vocal scores, indicating details of bowing to the string-players or of breathing to the singers, Others rely on verbal instruction at rehearsals and on the impress of a strong personality.

The use of a baton, though at least as old as the 15th cent., did not become the almost universal method of directing a performance until the second half of the 19th cent. Other methods before that time included the hand, a roll of paper, or a violin bow. When a stick was employed it was sometimes used to beat time audibly, *e.g.* at the Paris Opéra in the 17th and 18th cent. Elsewhere in the 18th cent. it was normal for opera to be directed from the harpsichord, which was in any case necessary for playing the recitative, and for symphonies to be directed by the principal first violin (still known in England as " leader " of the orchestra). When the baton was introduced to London by Spohr in 1820 and to Leipzig by Mendelssohn in 1835, it was regarded as a novelty. The increasing complication of orchestral writing and the growth of the forces employed made a clear and visible direction indispensable, and the use of the baton soon became general. Even today, however, there are a few conductors who prefer to dispense with it and use their hands, particularly for choral conducting, though the practice is apt to be disconcerting to players and singers who are not familiar with it.

The original purpose of conducting was simply to keep the performers together, and hence it was very necessary when large forces were employed for church or court festivals. By the latter part of the 18th cent., however, the growing subtlety of orchestral expression called for something more than the mere indication of time. By the middle of the 19th cent. the conductor had become an interpreter. Berlioz, Wagner, von Bülow and Richter showed that a conductor needed to be a consummate musician, with an intimate understanding of every detail of the score and the power to communicate his understanding to others. Hence the rise in the 20th cent. of the " star " conductor, who is worshipped as intensely as the operatic singer in the 18th and 19th cent.

The only satisfactory training for conducting is continual practice, which naturally depends to some extent on opportunity. Among the other indispensable requirements are practical familiarity with orchestral instruments and a knowledge of their capabilities and limitations, ability to read a full score and to hear it mentally, and an intimate knowledge of the style of widely different composers and periods. Methods vary from one conductor to another. The normal practice, however, is to use the right hand for beating time with the baton and the left to indicate entries, dynamics and expression in general. The eyes play an important part in securing the attention of the performers, and for this reason a good conductor uses the score only for reference. To dispense with the score altogether makes a good impression on the audience and may help the conductor to concentrate wholly on the details of performance, but it is liable to cause anxiety to the players, who have reason to fear the consequences of a lapse of memory.

A. CARSE : *The Orchestra in the XVIIIth Century* (1940).
The Orchestra from Beethoven to Berlioz (1940).
A. T. DAVIDSON : *Choral Conducting* (1941).
H. SCHERCHEN : *Handbook of Conducting* (1933).
G. SCHÜNEMANN : *Geschichte des Dirigierens* (1913).
B. SHORE : *The Orchestra Speaks* (1938).

Conductus [con-dŏŏk-tŏŏss], *L.* In the 12th and 13th cent. a metrical Latin song, sacred or secular, for one or more voices. The polyphonic examples are rarely for more than three voices and are generally characterized by simple part-writing, in which all the voices move together. Unlike other polyphonic forms of this period the *conductus* is not usually founded on a pre-existing liturgical melody. The precise meaning of the word, which first occurs in the 12th-cent. musical drama on the subject of Daniel (from Beauvais), is disputed, though its derivation from the verb *conducere* is obvious.

Conforti [con-forr'-tee], GIOVANNI LUCA: *b.* Mileto, *c.* 1560. Singer in the Papal choir. Author of *Breve et facile maniera d'essercitarsi ad ogni scolare . . . a far passaggi* (facsimile edition by J. Wolf, 1922), a valuable source of information about the late 16th-cent. practice of improvised ornamentation in vocal music.

Con fuoco [con foo-o'-co], *I.* With fire.

Consecration of the House, The. *v.* WEIHE DES HAUSES.

Consecutive Intervals. If any interval between two parts, whether vocal or instrumental, is followed immediately by the same interval between the same two parts, the two intervals are described as "consecutive" or "parallel," *e.g.*:

Consecutive thirds:

Consecutive fourths:

Consecutive fifths:

Consecutive fifths and octaves, though frequent in medieval music, came to be avoided in the 15th cent., presumably because they were felt to prejudice the independence of the parts. In the 16th century they were common in popular part-songs, such as the Italian *villanella*, but were avoided in cultured polyphony, whether secular or sacred. This practice established a tradition which was maintained, with occasional exceptions, until the late 19th cent. and is still incorporated in the teaching of elementary harmony, which is based on 18th- and 19th-cent. styles.

In 16th-cent. polyphony it is common to find consecutive fifths which (1) occur by contrary motion, *i.e.* a fifth followed by a twelfth or *vice versa* (generally in music in five or more parts), or (2) are separated by the interposition of a harmony note, or (3) are avoided by a suspension which does not create a dissonance, *e.g.*:

LASSUS, *Salve regina* (*Works, vol. xiii, p.* 125)

PALESTRINA, *Missa Assumpta est Maria*

PALESTRINA, *Stabat Mater*

Consecutive octaves are also found treated in the same way, *e.g.*:

TALLIS, *Lamentations II*

BYRD, *Alleluia, ascendit Deus* (*Gradualia Bk. II*)

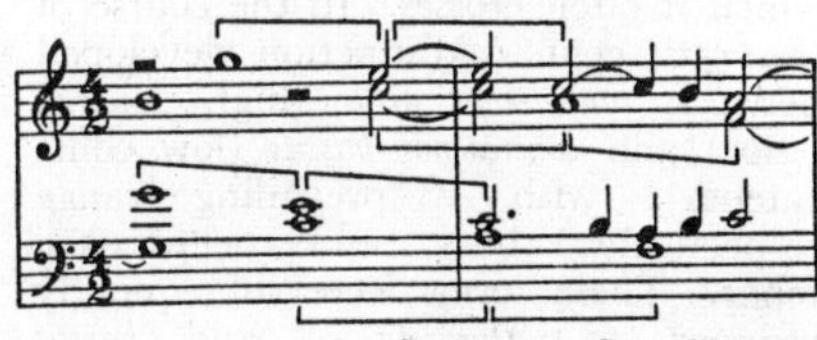

PALESTRINA, *Surge, illuminar*

In the case of contrary motion, however, it is more usual to find a unison proceeding to an octave than an octave proceeding to a fifteenth.

Console. That part of the organ from which the player controls the instrument, *i.e.* the keyboards, pedals, stops, music desk, etc. In modern organs with electrical action it is often placed apart from the rest of the instrument and is sometimes mounted on wheels.

Consonance. Consonance and dissonance provide a valuable contrast in music, one suggesting repose, the other stress. There is, however, no absolute agreement as to which intervals or chords are consonant and which are dissonant. The ear is the final judge, and musicians' ears have reacted in different ways at different periods. Traditionally the major and minor thirds, the perfect fourth, the perfect fifth, the major and minor sixths and the octave are classed as consonant, and all other intervals (*e.g.* the second, the diminished fifth) as dissonant. Various scientific theories have been advanced to justify this distinction, but they are not convincing. In actual fact only the unison and the octave are mathematically consonant; all other intervals are dissonant in a greater or less degree.

Con sordino [con sorr-dee'-no], *I.* "With the mute." *v.* MUTE.

Consort. (1) In the 16th and 17th cent. a chamber ensemble, *e.g.* consort of viols. *Whole consort*, an ensemble of instruments of the same family. *Broken consort*, an ensemble consisting of instruments of different kinds.

(2) Music written for such an ensemble, *e.g.* Morley's *First Booke of Consort Lessons* (1599), written for a broken consort consisting of treble lute, pandora, cittern, bass viol, flute and treble viol.

Con spirito [con spee'-ree-to], *I.* With spirit, lively.

Consul, The. Opera in three acts by Menotti. Libretto by the composer. First performed, New York, March 15, 1950. Magda Sorel is the wife of a member of the resistance movement in an unspecified European state, who has had to flee to escape the secret police. The story, which ends with her suicide, is concerned with her continually frustrated attempts to procure a visa so that she can cross the frontier to freedom. The consul himself is never seen.

Contes d'Hoffman, Les [lay cȏnt doff-mun] (Tales of Hoffman). Opera in four acts by Offenbach. Libretto by Jules Barbier and Michel Carré. First performed, Paris, February 10, 1881 (four months after the composer's death). The orchestration was completed by Ernest Guiraud. The opera represents three episodes in the life of E. T. A. Hoffman (1776-1822), on whose stories the libretto is based. In the first he falls in love with Olympia, a mechanical doll whom he believes to be real. In the second he meets Giulietta in Venice and kills her lover, only to lose her to another. In the third he is in love with Antonia, whose health prevents her from using her beautiful voice. Dr. Miracle induces her to sing and she dies.

Continuo [con-tee′-noo-o], *I.* Abbreviation for *basso continuo* (lit. "continuous bass"), *i.e.* the bass line of a composition marked with figures to indicate the harmonies to be played on a keyboard instrument. *v.* FIGURED BASS. Popular usage today often restricts the term to the keyboard accompaniment of recitative, *e.g.* in Bach's *St. Matthew Passion.* This is quite incorrect. In 17th-cent. and 18th-cent. music the *continuo* is played throughout the work, unless there is any indication to the contrary.

Contrabass. (1) As a prefix indicates an instrument built an octave lower than the normal bass of the family, *e.g.* contrabass trombone.

(2) As a noun = DOUBLE BASS, the largest member of the violin family.

Contrabass Clarinet. Also known as "pedal clarinet." A 19th-cent. invention designed to extend the lower range of the clarinet family. In its present form it dates from 1890. It is built in B♭, an octave below the bass clarinet, and has the following compass:

Written:

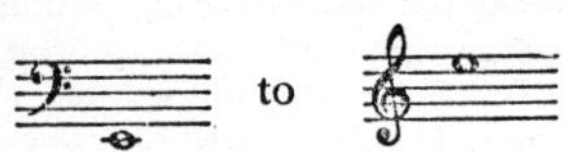

Sounding:

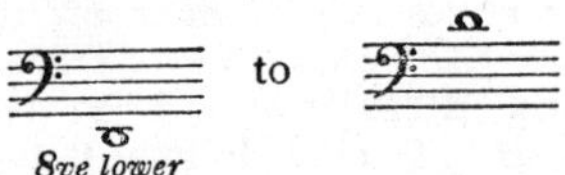

There is a part for it in D'Indy's opera *Fervaal* (1897), but owing to its unwieldy size and the heavy demands it makes on the player it has never become a normal member of the orchestra.

A. CARSE: *Musical Wind Instruments* (1939).

Contrabasso [con-trah-bahss′-so], *I.* Double bass.

Contrabass Trombone. *v.* TROMBONE.

Contrabass Tuba. *v.* TUBA.

Contradanza [con-trah-dahn′-tsah], *I.* Contredanse.

Contrafactum [con-tra-fac′-to͞om], *L.* In medieval music a piece of vocal music in which the original words are replaced by others of a different character. A common practice was to replace sacred words by secular; the reverse process also occurred.

Contrafagotto [con-trah-fah-got′-to], *I.* Double bassoon. *v.* BASSOON.

Contralto. (1) The lowest female voice, with a compass of roughly two octaves, from

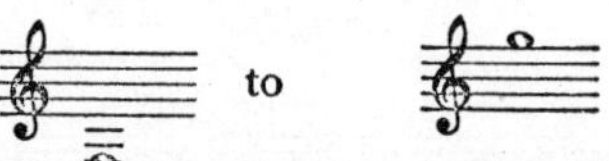

(2) In the 16th and 17th cent. a male alto or countertenor.

Contrapunctus [con-tra-po͝onk′-to͞oss], *L.* (1) Counterpoint. (2) A piece in contrapuntal style, *e.g.* the fugues in Bach's *Die Kunst der Fuge.*

Contratenor. In 14th- and early 15th-cent. music the name for a part with roughly the same range as the tenor, which it often crosses. In the course of the 15th cent. a distinction developed between *contratenor altus* (high contratenor) and *contratenor bassus* (low contratenor), with a prevailing range respectively above and below the tenor. These terms were subsequently reduced to *altus* (alto) and *bassus* (bass).

Contrebasse [co͞n-trer-buss], *Fr.* Double bass.

Contrebasson [co͞n-trer-buss-o͞n], *Fr.* Double bassoon.

Contredanse [co͞n-trer-du͞nce], *Fr.* (*G.* Kontretanz, *I.* contradanza). A corruption of *E.* "country dance." A lively dance popular in France and Germany in the 18th cent. Mozart and Beethoven wrote several (*v.* EROICA SYMPHONY).

Converse, FREDERICK SHEPHERD: *b.* Newtown, Mass., Jan. 5, 1871; *d.* Westwood, June 8, 1940. American composer. Studied at Harvard University and Munich. Taught at New England Conservatory, Boston, 1899-1901; Harvard University, 1901-4 (associate professor, 1904-7). His numerous compositions include 3 symphonies, several symphonic poems, chamber music, and two operas—*The*

Pipe of Desire (Boston, 1906) and *The Sacrifice* (Boston, 1911).

Conzert [con-tsairrt'], *G.* *v.* KONZERT.

Cooke, (1) ARNOLD: *b.* Gomersal, Nov. 4, 1906. Composer. Studied at Cambridge and with Hindemith in Berlin. Teacher of composition, Royal Manchester College of Music, 1933-8; Trinity College of Music, 1947. His *Concert Overture No.* 1 won a prize in the *Daily Telegraph* competition, 1934. He has also written a piano concerto, a piano sonata, a sonata for two pianos and several chamber works.

(2) BENJAMIN: *b.* London, 1734; *d.* there, Sept. 14, 1793. Organist and composer, a pupil of Pepusch. Master of the choristers, Westminster Abbey, 1757; organist, 1762. His compositions include church music, glees, concertos and a number of odes, including a setting of Collins's *Ode on the Passions.*

(3) HENRY: *d.* Hampton Court, July 13, 1672. Singer and composer. Served in the Royalist army during the Civil War, and took part in Davenant's opera *The Siege of Rhodes.* Appointed the first master of the children of the Chapel Royal after the Restoration, where he was extraordinarily successful in re-establishing a standard of performance. Among the boys whom he trained were Blow, Humfrey (who married his daughter) and Purcell. He had a reputation as a singer (*v.* Evelyn's *Diary*, Oct. 28, 1654, Pepys's *Diary*, July 27, 1661.) His compositions are unimportant.

Cooper, JOHN. *v.* COPRARIO.

Coperario, JOHN. *v.* COPRARIO.

Coperto [co-pair'-to], *I.* "Covered." *Timpani coperti*, timpani covered with a cloth in order to mute the sound.

Copland, AARON: *b.* Brooklyn, Nov. 14, 1900. American composer and lecturer, a pupil of Nadia Boulanger. He has played an important part in furthering the interests of contemporary composers in America. His works include 3 symphonies, a piano concerto, several shorter orchestral works, chamber music and ballets.

Coprario (Coperario), JOHN: *d.* 1626. English lutenist and composer, who changed his name from "Cooper" after a visit to Italy. He wrote music for court masques in the reign of James I and also a number of "fancies" (fantasias) for viols (examples in *Musica Britannica*, ix). Facsimile ed. of his *Rules how to compose* by M. Bukofzer (1952).

Coq d'Or, Le [ler cock dorr]. *v.* ZOLOTOY PETOUSHOK.

Cor [corr], *Fr.* French horn, generally known simply as HORN.

Cor anglais [corr ũn-glay], *Fr.* (*G.* Englisch Horn, *I.* corno inglese). English horn. An alto oboe, having a bulb-shaped bell and built a fifth lower than the oboe. The name, which has not been satisfactorily explained, appears first about the middle of the 18th cent., but the instrument existed, in different forms, at least 50 years earlier and was known variously as "tenor hautboy" (*E.*), *oboe da caccia* (*I.*) and *taille* (*Fr.*). "Tenor hautboy" appears in Purcell's *Dioclesian* (1690), *oboe da caccia* and *taille* in Bach's cantatas. The compass of the modern instrument is:

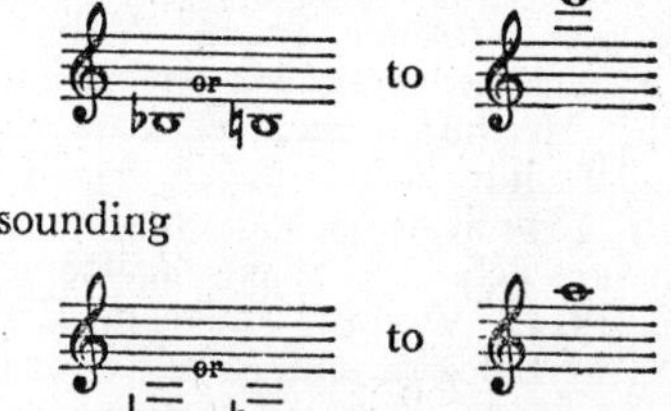

v. TRANSPOSING INSTRUMENTS.

A. CARSE: *Musical Wind Instruments* (1939).

Coranto [co-rahn'-to], *I.* *v.* COURANTE.

Corda [corr'-dah], *I.* String. *Una corda* (in piano music), "one string," *i.e.* use the left-hand pedal, which on grand pianos normally shifts the whole keyboard slightly to the right, so that the hammers can strike only one or two of the two or three strings assigned to each note. The effect is to reduce the volume of sound; on upright pianos the left-hand pedal produces a similar result by bringing the hammers nearer to the keys, so that they strike with less force. There is also another system, now obsolete, which damps the strings with a strip of felt. *Tre corde* (three strings) or *tutte le corde* (all the strings) is an indication that the left-hand pedal is to be released. *v.* MUTE.

Corde [corrd], *Fr.* String. *Instruments à cordes* (or *cordes* alone), string instruments. *Quatuor à cordes*, string quartet.

Cor de basset [corr der buss-ay], *Fr.* Basset horn.

Cor de chasse [corr der shuss], *Fr.* Lit. " hunting horn," 18th-cent. name for the French horn.

Corder, FREDERICK: *b.* London, Jan. 26, 1852; *d.* there, Aug. 21, 1932. Composer and teacher. Studied at the R.A.M. Mendelssohn Scholarship, 1875. Studied further at Cologne under Hiller. Conductor, Brighton Aquarium, 1880. Teacher of composition, R.A.M., 1888. Founded the Society of British Composers (1905-15). His compositions include the opera *Nordisa,* to his own libretto (Liverpool, 1887), several cantatas, orchestral overtures, part-songs and songs. He published *The Orchestra and how to write for it* (1895), *Modern Composition* (1909) and *History of the Royal Academy of Music* (1922). With his wife he translated Wagner's operas into English. His pupils included Bantock, Bax and Holbrooke.

Corelli [co-rell'-lee], ARCANGELO: *b.* Fusignano, Feb. 17, 1653; *d.* Rome, Jan. 8, 1713. Violinist and composer. Studied at Bologna and travelled as a young man in Germany. Returned to Rome about the age of 30 and there enjoyed the patronage of Cardinal Pietro Ottoboni. He had a European reputation as violinist and composer. In his trio sonatas (*sonate da chiesa* and *sonate da camera*), solo violin sonatas and *concerti grossi* he not only showed a talent for vivacious and intimate expression but also helped to establish a characteristic style of writing for the violin both as a solo instrument and in the orchestra. Modern ed. by J. Joachim and F. Chrysander (5 vols.).

Coriolan [cohr-i-o-lahn'] A play by Heinrich Joseph von Collin, for which Beethoven wrote an overture (Op. 62) in 1807.

Cori spezzati [coh'-ree speh-dzah'-tee], *I.* " Divided choirs." A term used of the antiphonal choruses which are a characteristic feature of the style of church music practised by Venetian composers of the 16th and 17th cent. *v.* WILLAERT.

Corkine, WILLIAM. Composer of two sets of lute-songs and instrumental pieces (1610 and 1612). Modern edition of the songs only in *E.S.L.S.*, 2nd ser.

Cornamusa [corr-nah-moo'-zah], *I.* Bagpipe.

Cornamuto torto [corr-nah-moo'-to torr'-to], *I.* Krummhorn.

Cornelius [corr-neh'-li-ŏŏss], PETER: *b.* Mainz, Dec. 24, 1824; *d.* there, Oct. 26, 1874. Composer and writer on music, orginally intended to be an actor. Studied music with Dehn in Berlin. He became a close friend of Liszt and later of Wagner, whom he followed to Munich in 1865. In his literary works he championed the " new music," of which these two composers were the chief representatives. His compositions include a number of songs and part-songs, which are still sung, and three operas—*Der Barbier von Bagdad* (Weimar, 1858), *Der Cid* (Weimar, 1865) and *Gunlöd* (completed by Carl Hoffbauer, Weimar, 1891). The production of *Der Barbier von Bagdad* under Liszt in 1858 aroused such strong opposition that Liszt resigned his position at the Weimar court.

Cornemuse [corrn-mēēz], *Fr.* Bagpipe.

Cornet. (1) A brass instrument with three valves (*Fr.* cornet à pistons, piston, *G.* Kornett, *I.* cornetta), dating from the early 19th cent. Its written compass is from

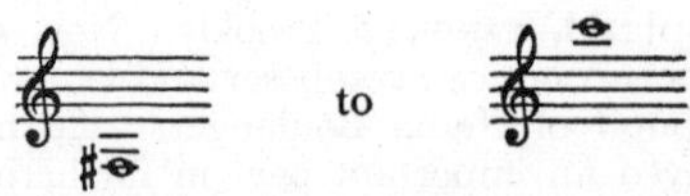

It is normally built in B♭ (*v.* TRANSPOSING INSTRUMENTS), in which case its sounding compass is from

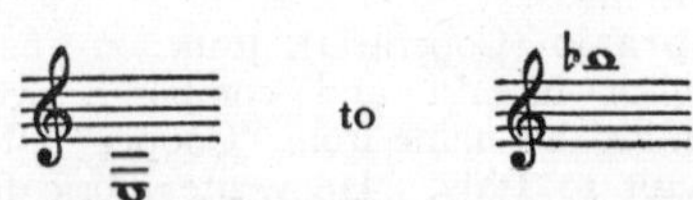

By using a larger CROOK or by turning a switch on the instrument its pitch can be lowered a semitone and it becomes a cornet in A, with a sounding compass from

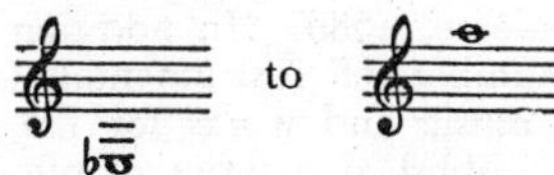

A cornet in E♭ is used in brass bands, with a sounding compass from

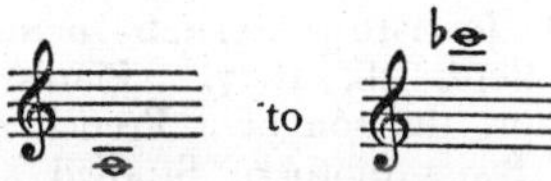

The cornet is a standard instrument in the brass band and military band, where its flexibility makes it particularly suitable for light and rapid passages. In the orchestra it has often been used in addition to the trumpet, *e.g.* in Franck's symphony and Elgar's *Cockaigne* overture, but outside France is not a normal member of the symphony orchestra. In the hands of a good player it is capable of producing a very expressive tone in *cantabile* passages. There is an early example of a cornet solo in Donizetti's opera *Don Pasquale* (Paris, 1843).

A. CARSE : *Musical Wind Instruments* (1939).

(2) An organ stop with several ranks (*i.e.* with several pipes of different pitches for each note, *cf.* MIXTURE), very popular in the 18th cent. for florid solos.

(3) = CORNETT.

Cornet à bouquin [corr-nay a boo-kan͡], *Fr.* The obsolete cornet.

Cornet à pistons [corr-nay a peece-ton͡], *Fr.* The modern cornett.

Cornett (*Fr.* cornet à bouquin, *G.* Zink, *I.* cornetto). A wind instrument, now obsolete, used in the Middle Ages, in the Renaissance period and as late as the early 18th cent. The spelling " cornett " is used to distinguish it from the modern CORNET, an entirely different instrument. The normal type was slightly curved and made of wood, or less frequently of ivory, with holes which were stopped by the fingers. The mouthpiece was cup-shaped. It was made in several sizes, the commonest of which had the compass

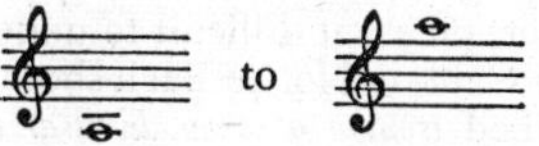

with a possible extension upwards, and served as a treble to the trombone family, with which it was frequently associated. Contemporary accounts and the music written for it indicate that it had a wide range of expression—gentle in *piano*, brilliant in *forte*. Two types of straight cornett also existed—the *cornetto diritto* (*gerader Zink*), which had a detachable mouthpiece, and the *cornetto muto* (*stiller Zink*), where the mouthpiece was an integral part of the instrument.

A. CARSE : *Musical Wind Instruments* (1939).

Cornett-ton [corr-net'-tone], *G.* A pitch used by the German *Stadtpfeifer* in the early 18th cent. It appears to have been the same as CHORTON.

Cornetta [corr-net'-tah], *I.* The modern cornet.

Cornetta a chiavi [corr-net'-tah ah kee-ah'-vee], *I.* Key bugle.

Cornetto [corr-net'-to], *I.* The obsolete cornett.

Cornish, WILLIAM. *v.* CORNYSHE.

Corno [corr'-no], *I.* Horn. In the 18th cent. frequently known as *corno da caccia,* hunting horn.

Corno da caccia [corr'-no dah cah'-tchah], *I.* (*Fr.* cor de chasse, *G.* Waldhorn). Lit. " hunting horn," 18th-cent. name for the French horn.

Corno da tirarsi [corr'-no dah tee-rahrr'-see], *I.* Lit. " slide horn," a term found in a few of Bach's cantatas. The same instrument is implied in a considerable number of other cantatas, where a horn (described simply as *corno*) is required to play a chorale melody in unison with the sopranos—an impossibility on the natural horn of Bach's time. There is no evidence that a horn fitted with a slide existed in Bach's time. Two explanations of the term have been suggested: (a) that it indicates a slide trumpet (*tromba da tirarsi*) played with a horn mouthpiece (*v.* C. S. Terry, *Bach's*

Orchestra, pp. 34-6), (b) that it was simply an equivalent of *tromba da tirarsi* (*v.* C. Sachs, *The History of Musical Instruments*, p. 385.). The latter explanation, however, makes it difficult to understand why in Cantata No. 46 Bach should have prescribed *tromba o corno da tirarsi* (slide trumpet or slide horn).

Corno di bassetto [corr'-no dee bahss-set'-to], *I.* Basset horn. Used by Bernard Shaw as a pseudonym when he was writing musical criticism for the *Star* in 1888-9.

Corno inglese [corr'-no een-gleh'-zeh], *I. v.* COR ANGLAIS.

Cornyshe, WILLIAM: *b. c.* 1468; *d.* 1523. Playwright and composer. Gentleman of the Chapel Royal, 1496; master of the children, 1509. He attended Henry VIII at the Field of the Cloth of Gold, 1520. His compositions consist mainly of secular part-songs and antiphons (examples of the latter in *Musica Britannica*).

Coro [coh'-ro], *I.* Choir, chorus. Also used of a body of instrumental players, *e.g.* Handel's *Concerti a due cori* (concertos for two instrumental ensembles). *v.* also CORI SPEZZATI.

Coronation Concerto (*G.* Krönungskonzert). The name given to Mozart's piano concerto in D major, K.537, composed in 1788, on the ground that he is said to have performed it at Frankfort in 1790, on the occasion of the coronation of Leopold II.

Coronation Mass (*G.* Krönungsmesse). Mozart's Mass in C major, K.317 (1779), said to have been composed in commemoration of the crowning of a miraculous image of the Virgin at Maria Plain, near Salzburg, about 1744.

Correa de Arauxo [corr-eh'-ah deh a-rah'-ook-so], FRANCISCO: *b. c.* 1576. Organist of San Salvador, Seville, 1598-1633. His *Facultad orgánica* (1626) contains 69 compositions for organ; modern ed. in *Monumentos de la Música Española*, vi & xii.

Corregidor, Der [dair corr-ay'-gee-dorr'] (The Corregidor). Opera in four acts by Hugo Wolf. Libretto by Rosa Mayreder (founded on Pedro Antonio de Alarcón's story *El Sombrero de tres Picos*). First performed, Mannheim, June 7, 1896.

Corrente [corr-ren'-teh], *I.* *v.* COURANTE.

Corrette [corr-et], MICHEL: *b.* Rouen, 1709; *d.* Jan. 22, 1795. Organist and composer. He held various organist's posts, the last as organist to the Duc d'Angoulême, 1780. In addition to a large number of instrumental works, church music and works for the stage he also published a series of tutors for instruments and one for singing, and issued an anthology of violin solos under the title *L'Art de se perfectionner dans le violon* (1782).

Cortot [corr-to], ALFRED DENIS: *b.* Nyon, Sept. 26, 1877. Pianist and conductor, the son of a French father and a Swiss mother. Studied at the Paris Conservatoire. Having served as *répétiteur* at Bayreuth, he founded in Paris the Société des Festivals Lyriques, 1902, and conducted performances of Wagner's *Tristan und Isolde* and *Die Götterdämmerung* (the latter for the first time in France). Founded the Société des Concerts Cortot, 1903. Conductor, Concerts populaires, Lille, 1904-7; Société Nationale, 1904. Teacher, Paris Conservatoire, 1907-17. Founded the École Normale de Musique, Paris, 1918. For many years, from 1905, played piano trios with Thibaud (violin) and Casals (cello). His publications include *La Musique française du piano.* He is the owner of a remarkable private library of rare works: the first volume of a catalogue (comprising theoretical works) appeared in 1936.

Così fan tutte [co-zee' fahn toot'-teh]. Comic opera in two acts by Mozart. Full title: *Così fan tutte, ossia La scuola degli amanti* (This is how all women behave, or the School for Lovers). Libretto by Lorenzo da Ponte. First performed, Vienna, January 26, 1790. An elderly philosopher, Don Alfonso, makes a wager with two officers, Ferrando and Guglielmo, that the ladies they love, Fiordiligi and Dorabella respectively, will not remain true to them in their absence. To test the truth of this it is announced that the officers must leave for military service. With the connivance of the maid, Despina, they return disguised as

Albanians and make love to the ladies. When they are rejected they pretend to take poison: Despina, disguised as a doctor, restores them by magnetism. The ladies hearts are softened. Dorabella agrees to marry Guglielmo, and Fiordiligi to marry Ferrando. Alfonso, however, announces that the officers are returning. Guglielmo and Ferrando escape and re-enter in their own persons. The bogus marriage contracts signed by the ladies prove that Alfonso has won his wager.

Costa [coss'-tah], MICHAEL ANDREW AGNUS (originally Michele Andreas Agnus): *b.* Naples, Feb. 4, 1808; *d.* Hove, Apr. 29, 1884. Conductor and composer. Studied at the Real Collegio di Musica, Naples. By the time he was 21 he had already composed several operas and other large-scale works. He first came to England in 1829 and rapidly established himself as a conductor. His appointments included: King's (later Her Majesty's) Theatre, 1832-46; Royal Italian Opera, Covent Garden, from 1847; Philharmonic Society, 1846-54; Sacred Harmonic Society, 1848-82; Handel Festivals, Crystal Palace, 1859-80. Knighted, 1869. His efficiency and discipline appear to have been in striking contrast with the slovenly character of much English conducting at the time: he aroused the enthusiasm not only of the public but also of many distinguished musicians. His compositions for English audiences included two oratorios: *Eli* (Birmingham, 1855) and *Naaman* (Birmingham, 1864).

Costeley [cost-lay], GUILLAUME: *b. c.* 1531; *d.* Feb. 1, 1606. Composer. Organist at the French court. He wrote some keyboard music, but his reputation rests on his polyphonic *chansons*, of which he wrote more than 100; 62 of these are reprinted in H. Expert, *Les Maîtres musiciens de la Renaissance française*, iii, xviii & xix.

Cosyn, BENJAMIN. Organist, Dulwich College, 1622-4; Charterhouse, 1626-43. His manuscript collection of virginal music (mostly by Bull, Gibbons and himself) is an important source for English keyboard music of this period. 25 pieces from it were edited by J. A. Fuller-Maitland and W. Barclay Squire (1923).

Cotton, JOHN (Johannes Cotto). Early 12th-cent. theorist, who was a monk at Afflighem, near Brussels. His *Liber de musica* contains a section on *organum.* Modern ed. by J. Smits van Waesberghe, *Johannis Affligemensis De Musica cum Tonario* (1950). He is thought to have been an Englishman, but this is not universally admitted ; for the arguments see Van Waesberghe's edition, pp. 22-33, L. Ellinwood in *Notes,* Sept., 1951, pp. 650-9, and Van Waesberghe in *Musica Disciplina,* vi (1953), pp. 139-53.

Coulé [coo-lay], *Fr. v.* SLIDE (1).

Counterpoint. (1) The combination of two or more independent parts in a harmonious texture. Independence is of two kinds: (a) melodic, (b) rhythmic. The second of these is more forceful than the first; on the other hand rhythmic independence without melodic characterization is not sufficient to produce counterpoint. The combination of two or more melodic lines results in a series of related chords. The relationship between the notes of each individual chord and the relationship between the chords themselves constitutes HARMONY. Counterpoint is therefore inseparable from harmony; but since it is possible to write a series of chords without melodic or rhythmic interest in every individual part, harmony can exist without counterpoint. On the other hand the conventions of harmony are historically the product of counterpoint (*v.* CHORD), *i.e.* certain conventions of contrapuntal writing resulted in harmonic relationships which became so familiar that they were stereotyped and came to exist in their own right. Harmony is therefore the crystallization of counterpoint. The following examples illustrate the difference between (*a*) treatment which is primarily harmonic, (*b*) treatment which is primarily contrapuntal. In the first a melody is accompanied by two parts which have virtually no melodic or rhythmic interest. In the second each of the three parts has an independent life of its own :

BACH, *St. Matthew Passion*, no. 58

BACH, *St. Matthew Passion*, no. 33

In the earliest known music in parts (late 9th cent.) there is no rhythmic, and hardly any melodic, independence. Every note in one part is accompanied by a single note in the other, and the melodic lines are either wholly, or substantially parallel (*v.* ORGANUM). From these beginnings there developed, in the early Middle Ages, first melodic, and then rhythmic, independence. By the 13th cent. we find a fully mature art of counterpoint (*v.* MOTET), side by side with the preservation of what may well be a popular tradition consisting of simple successions of similar chords without either melodic or rhythmic independence in the parts (*v.* ENGLISH DESCANT). The later history of contrapuntal writing is basically merely a further development of the principles already established. In the 14th century we find a new rhythmic freedom (following the abandonment of the RHYTHMIC MODES), in the 15th the growing use of IMITATION (already familiar in the CANON), which became an integral part of 16th-cent. writing and formed the basis of the 17th-cent. fugue. By the 18th cent. the conception of tonality (or key relationships) as a vital element in the structure of a piece of music had its influence on contrapuntal writing, without weakening its basic principles. This is true also of 19th-cent. music. The present century has seen a marked tendency to free counterpoint from its dependence on traditional harmony and to allow it to develop on its own lines, and in doing so to create new harmonic relationships and to establish new harmonic conventions.

Some forms of composition, *e.g.* canon and fugue, are by their very nature essentially contrapuntal. Others, such as the 16th-cent. motet and madrigal, may be wholly contrapuntal in conception; but it is very common to find a contrast between sections which exhibit counterpoint, in the strict sense of the word, and others in which there is virtually no melodic or rhythmic independence in the parts. Sections of the first type are polyphonic (*v.* POLYPHONY), of the second type homophonic (*v.* HOMOPHONY). Counterpoint, in fact, is not a musical form : it is a manner of organizing musical material which may form the basis of a complete piece or may be used intermittently, as the composer desires. In the later 18th cent. tradition dictated that a considerable amount of church music should be contrapuntal in texture; but contrapuntal methods, even complete fugues, were constantly employed by the best composers in instrumental music as well. To think contrapuntally, to be aware of the potential energy and independence of individual parts is a necessary discipline for any serious composer, whatever style or idiom he may favour.

The teaching of counterpoint was systematised as early as the 16th cent. Zacconi, in his *Prattica di musica* (2 vols., 1592 & 1619) gives a series of examples of two-part counterpoint in which a given melody (or CANTO FERMO) in semibreves is treated in various ways: (1) *nota contra nota* (note against note), with the added part in semibreves also, (2) with the added part in minims, (3) with the added part in crotchets, (4) *contrappunto sincopato*, with the added part in semibreves but a minim's distance after the *canto fermo*, *i,e.* syncopated :

and other varieties which need not be mentioned here. This system of progressive study was the basis of the five "species" or types of counterpoint established by Fux in his *Gradus ad Parnassum* (1725). Fux's method, which consisted of adapting 16th-cent. practice to the harmonic conventions of the 18th cent., became widely accepted as the foundation of what is called "strict" counterpoint. The rediscovery of Bach in the 19th cent. led to a different method of instruction, based largely on his practice, which came to be known as "free" counterpoint. The terms "strict" and "free" are, however, illogical, since art cannot exist without limitations: it is simply a question of deciding what those limitations are to be. The discipline of observing certain conventions is valuable to any student of composition. 20th-cent. teaching, however, inclines more and more to relate such discipline to the works of the great masters. Instead of being forced to obey arbitrary rules and to work mechanically at the solution of problems in one or other of the five "species," the student is encouraged to observe at first hand the methods of the great masters of contrapuntal writing. In this way the study of counterpoint is also the study of history and of style.

If counterpoint is so written that the parts can be interchanged, *e.g.* the treble becoming the bass, and the bass the treble, it is called invertible (*v.* INVERSION). Invertible counterpoint between two parts is called DOUBLE COUNTERPOINT. Where three parts can be so interchanged, each making a suitable bass for the remaining two, the result is TRIPLE COUNTERPOINT. Similarly with four or more interchangeable parts (quadruple, quintuple counterpoint, etc.). A simple calculation will show that the possible permutations increase rapidly according to the number of parts: in double counterpoint there are 2 possible arrangements of the parts, the original and the inversion ; in triple counterpoint there are 6, in quadruple 24, and so on.

(2) A contrapuntal part added to an existing part, *i.e.* part B is said to be a counterpoint to part A.

E. C. BAIRSTOW : *Counterpoint and Harmony* (1937).

K. JEPPESEN : *Counterpoint : the Polyphonic Vocal Style of the Sixteenth Century* (1939).

C. H. KITSON : *The Art of Counterpoint* (2nd ed., 1924).

A. T. MERRITT : *Sixteenth-Century Polyphony* (1939).

R. O. MORRIS : *Contrapuntal Technique in the Sixteenth Century* (1922).

W. PISTON : *Counterpoint* (1947).

Countersubject. A melody which is designed as a counterpoint to the subject (or principal theme) of a FUGUE. Its first appearance is normally in association with the ANSWER (or second statement of the subject), so that it is in fact a continuation of the subject as well as a contrast to it, *e.g.* :

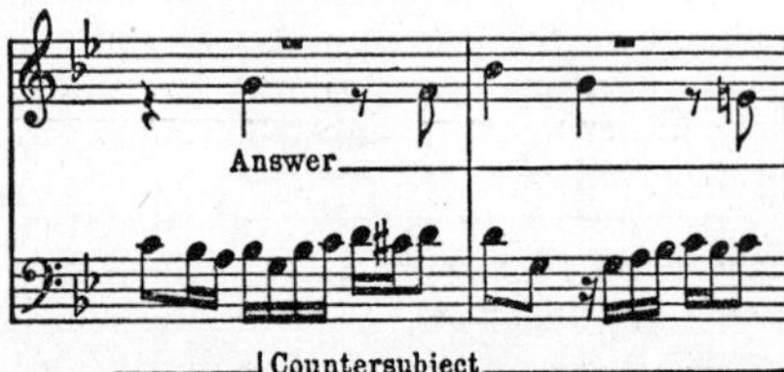

BACH, 48 *Preludes and Fugues, Book II, No.* 16

This association continues regularly until the EXPOSITION is complete. Later appearances of the countersubject in association with the subject are not determined by any hard and fast principle but depend on the inclination of the composer. The countersubject may also supply thematic material for the episodes or intermediate passages which occur between the recurrent appearances of the subject. Since it is convenient to be able to use a countersubject both above and below the subject, it is generally designed so that it makes DOUBLE COUNTERPOINT with the subject.

A countersubject is not essential in a fugue: several of Bach's are without one. Equally there may be more than one countersubject, in which case the additional ones must necessarily enter later than the first: for an example of a fugue with two countersubjects *v.* FUGUE. Cases occur where a countersubject enters simultaneously with the subject at the beginning of the fugue; but here the countersubject has the characteristics of a subject, so that a fugue of this kind may be described as a fugue with two subjects.

Counter-tenor. The highest male voice (also known as alto), produced by using the head register. English composers of the late 17th cent. frequently wrote solos for this voice which demand not only a mastery of expression but also a brilliant, ringing tone.

Country Dance. The name given to a traditional English dance of popular origin. The term first appears in the glossary to Spenser's *Shephearde's Calendar* (1579). The first printed collection was *The English Dancing Master*, published by John Playford in 1651 (modern ed. by L. Bridgewater and H. Mellor, 1933), which was followed by several further editions up to 1728. In the 20th cent. Cecil Sharp enlarged the repertory by collecting surviving examples of folk dances, which he published in *The Country Dance Book* (6 pts., 1909-22). He also revived the practice of folk-dancing and founded the English Folk Dance Society (1911), now amalgamated with the Folk-Song Society as the English Folk Dance and Song Society. A form of English country dance also became popular on the Continent: *v.* CONTREDANSE.

Couperin [coop-rañ], (1) ANTOINETTE-VICTOIRE: *b. c.* 1760; *d.* Paris, 1812. Daughter of (2). Organist, singer and harpist.

(2) ARMAND-LOUIS: *b.* Paris, Feb. 25, 1725; *d.* there, Feb. 2, 1789. Son of (13), whom he succeeded as organist of St. Gervais, 1748. He also held several other organist's posts. Organist to the king at Versailles, 1770; first organist, 1782. He had a great

reputation as a performer. He composed mainly keyboard music.

(3) CÉLESTE-THÉRÈSE: *b.* Paris, 1793; *d.* Belleville, Feb. 14, 1860. Daughter of (8). Organist, singer and pianist.

(4) CHARLES: *b.* Chaumes, Apr., 1638; *d.* Paris, 1678 or 1679. Brother of (6) and (9), father of (7). Succeeded his brother Louis as organist of St. Gervais, 1661.

(5) ÉLISABETH-ANTOINETTE (*née* Blanchet): *b.* Jan., 1729; *d.* May 25, 1815. Wife of (2). Organist and pianist, who continued active to the end of her life.

(6) FRANÇOIS: *b.* Chaumes, Apr., 1630; *d. c.* 1700. Brother of (4) and (9), uncle of (7). Organist and violinist.

(7) FRANÇOIS (le grand): *b.* Paris, Nov. 10, 1668; *d.* there, Sept. 12, 1733. Son of (4). Organist and composer, pupil of his father (4) and his uncle François (6). Organist of St. Gervais, 1685 till his death. Organist to the king at Versailles, 693. He taught several children of the royal family. He excelled as a composer of keyboard music, works for instrumental ensemble, secular songs and church music. His harpsichord music, arranged in *ordres* (or suites) is a model of refinement, skill and charm; many of the pieces bear fanciful titles (Couperin called them portraits) which suggest a romantic imagination, disciplined however by a scrupulous regard for formal symmetry.

An argument between the organists of Paris and the corporation of minstrels (*Confrérie de Saint-Julien des Ménestriers*) provoked the composition of the satirical and descriptive suite *Les Fastes de la grande et ancienne Mxnxstrxndxsx* (*i.e. Ménestrandise*): *v.* FASTES. Couperin also exercised his talent for description and irony in his chamber music, *e.g.* in *Le Parnasse ou l'Apothéose de Corelli* (1724) and its companion the *Apothéose de Lully* (1725), where he imitates the style of Corelli and Lully respectively. His church music is noble, dignified and profoundly impressive. He also published *L'Art de toucher le clavecin* (1716)—an instruction book, dedicated to the young Louis XV, which is valuable not only for the light it throws on contemporary practice in harpsichord playing but also for its grace and humour. A complete edition of Couperin's works is published by the Lyre-Bird Press, Paris, under the direction of M. Cauchie (12 vols.).

(8) GERVAIS-FRANÇOIS: *b.* Paris, May 22, 1759; *d.* there, March 11, 1826. Son of (2). Succeeded his brother Pierre-Louis (14) as organist of St. Gervais, 1789. His duties were interrupted by the Revolution, but he managed to save the organ from destruction and resumed his post in 1795. His compositions include variations on the Revolutionary song, "Ah, ça ira" (1790).

(9) LOUIS: *b.* Chaumes, *c.* 1626; *d.* Paris, Aug. 29, 1661. Brother of (4) and (6), uncle of (7). Viol-player and organist, a pupil of Chambonnières. Organist of St. Gervais, 1653; also a string-player in the royal service. His works survive only in manuscript; modern ed. by P. Brunold (1936). One of the most accomplished keyboard-composers of his time, he was also one of the first French composers to write solo and trio sonatas for strings.

(10) MARGUERITE-ANTOINETTE: *b.* Paris, Sept. 19, 1705; *d. c.* 1778. Daughter of (7). Harpsichordist to Louis XV and teacher of his daughters.

(11) MARGUERITE-LOUISE: *b.* Paris, 1676 (or 1679); *d.* Versailles, May 30, 1728. Daughter of (6). Singer and harpsichordist.

(12) MARIE-MADELEINE: *b.* Paris, Mar. 11, 1690; *d.* Apr. 6, 1742. Daughter of (7). Organist of the Benedictine nunnery at Maubuisson.

(13) NICOLAS: *b.* Paris, Dec. 20, 1680; *d.* there, July 25, 1748. Son of (6), cousin of (7). Succeeded his cousin as organist of St. Gervais, 1733.

(14) PIERRE-LOUIS: *b.* Paris, March 15, 1755; *d.* there Oct. 10, 1789. Son of (2), brother of (8). Succeeded his father as organist of St. Gervais, 1789, but died within the year.

C. BOUVET: *Les Couperins* (1919). *Nouveaux documents sur les Couperins* (1933).

W. MELLERS: *François Couperin and the French Classical Tradition* (1950).

A. PIRRO : *Les Clavecinistes* (1925).
F. RAUGEL : *Les Organistes* (1923).
J. TIERSOT : *Les Couperins* (1926).

Coupler. A device used to augment the resources of the organ. Couplers, which are controlled by stops or tabs, are of three kinds:

(1) Octave and sub-octave couplers, which automatically double in the octave above or below any note which is played.

(2) Manual couplers, which enable the player to combine the resources of two manuals, *e.g.* the Swell to Great coupler automatically transfers to the Great manual all the stops on the Swell.

These couplers also exist as octave and sub-octave couplers, *e.g.* if the Swell to Great sub-octave coupler is drawn, any note played on the Great manual will automatically bring into action the note an octave lower on the Swell.

(3) Pedal couplers (*Fr.* tirasse, *pl.* tirasses). These operate in a similar way to the manual couplers, *e.g.* the Choir to Pedal coupler makes available on the pedals any stops drawn on the Choir manual. Pedal couplers working the reverse way, *i.e.* transferring pedal stops to the manuals, are also found, but they are not part of the normal equipment of an organ.

Courante [coo-rũnt], *Fr.* (*I.* coranto, corrente). Short for *danse courante*, a running dance. A lively dance in triple time, which originated in the 16th cent. and was immensely popular in the 17th and early 18th cent., becoming one of the regular members of the SUITE, the others being the ALLEMANDE, SARABANDE and GIGUE. In the 17th cent. a distinction appears between the Italian *coranto* (or *corrente*) and the French *courante*:

(1) The *coranto* (or *corrente*) is written in $\frac{3}{4}$ (or $\frac{3}{8}$) time, often with quaver (or semiquaver) figuration, *e.g.*:

CORELLI, *Sonate de Camera*, Op. 4, no. 1

The rhythm of the *coranto* also had a strong influence on secular song of this period.

(2) The French *courante* was more subtle. The time alternated between $\frac{3}{2}$ and $\frac{6}{4}$ (*i.e.* between three accents in a bar and two), and in keyboard music the broken-chord texture of lute music was frequently imitated, as in other movements of the suite, *e.g.*:

COUPERIN, *Premier livre de clavecin*, 2e *ordre*

Both types, the Italian and the French, occur in Bach's suites and partitas.

Courvoisier [coor-vwuz-yay], WALTER: *b.* Riehen (near Basle), Feb. 7, 1875; *d.* Locarno, Dec. 27, 1931. Composer.

Began his career as a surgeon, but turned to music in 1902 and studied with Ludwig Thuille in Munich. Teacher, Akademie der Tonkunst, Munich, from 1910. His compositions include the operas *Lancelot und Elaine* (Munich, 1917) and *Die Krähen* (Munich, 1921), choral works (including *Gruppe aus dem Tartarus, Der Dinurstrom, Das Schlachtschiff Temeraire* and *Auferstehung*), various orchestral and chamber works, piano music and numerous songs.

Coussemaker [cooce - muck - er], CHARLES EDMOND HENRI de: *b.* Bailleul, Apr. 19, 1805; *d.* Lille, Jan. 10, 1876. Musicologist. In addition to studying the law he also had lessons in violin, cello and composition. Throughout his life he pursued a legal career, but was also active in the study of medieval music. His most important publications were *Histoire de l'harmonie au moyen-âge* (1852), *Chants populaires des Flamands de France* (1856), *Drames liturgiques du moyen-âge* (1860), *Scriptorum de musica medii aevi nova series* (4 vols., 1864-76, a sequel to Gerbert's *Scriptores*), *L'Art harmonique aux XII*e *et XIII*e *sècles* (1865), *Oeuvres complètes du trouvère Adam de la Halle* (1872). His historical works and transciptions of medieval music have long since been superseded. On the other hand his collection of *Scriptores*, in spite of its numerous inaccuracies, is still indispensable. His compositions are of no significance.

Cousser, JOHANN SIGMUND. *v.* KUSSER.

Coward, HENRY: *b.* Liverpool, Nov. 26, 1849; *d.* Woking, June 10, 1944. Choral conductor. Originally a cutler in Sheffield, then an elementary schoolmaster. Founded the Sheffield Tonic Sol-Fa Association (later the Sheffield Musical Union), 1876. Adopted music as a profession, 1887. Chorus-master, Sheffield Musical Festival, 1895. Toured with his choir in Europe, America and the Dominions. Knighted, 1926. Author, *Choral Technique and Interpretation* (1904).

Cowell, HENRY DIXON: *b.* Menlo Park (California), March 11, 1897. Composer and pianist. Son of an Irish father and an American mother. Studied at the University of California and the Institute of Applied Music, New York. Visited Berlin with a Guggenheim Fellowship, 1931, and studied comparative musicology there. Toured as a pianist in Europe, 1923-33. Teacher at various American institutions; director of the department of composition, Peabody Institute, Baltimore, 1951. Founded the New Music Society, 1927. With Leon Theremin invented the "rhythmicon," an electrical instrument designed to produce different rhythms simultaneously. In 1912 he introduced a new method of playing the piano, using the forearm, elbow and fist: the chords so produced were called "tone clusters." His numerous compositions include an opera, 6 symphonies and a piano concerto. He has also published *New Musical Resources* (1931) and edited *American Composers on American Music* (1933); *Charles Ives & His Music* (1955).

Cowen, FREDERIC HYMEN (originally Hymen Frederick): *b.* Kingston (Jamaica), Jan. 29, 1852; *d.* London, Oct. 6, 1935. Composer and conductor. Studied at the Leipzig Conservatorium and the Stern Conservatorium, Berlin. First known in England as a pianist and composer. Conductor, Norwich Philharmonic Society, 1888-92; Hallé Orchestra, 1896-9; Liverpool Philharmonic Society, 1896-1913; Philharmonic Society (London), 1900-7. He also conducted the Bradford Festival Choral Society and the Scottish Orchestra, as well as the Crystal Palace Handel Festivals from 1903 to the 1914-18 war, and in 1920 and 1923. His gifts as a composer, which found their most effective expression in music of a slight and delicate kind, were not so well suited to large-scale works, of which there were none the less several. His compositions include 4 operas, 7 oratorios, several cantatas, 6 symphonies, 4 overtures, piano concerto, orchestral suites, and nearly 300 songs.

Cox and Box. Operetta in one act by Sullivan. Libretto by Francis Cowley Burnand (from John Maddison Morton's farce *Box and Cox*). First performed, London, May 11, 1867.

Crab Canon (*L.* canon cancrizans). *v.* CANON, RETROGRADE MOTION.

Cracovienne [cra-cov-yen], *Fr. v.* KRAKOWIAK.

Cramer [crah'-mer], JOHANN BAPTIST: *b.* Mannheim, Feb. 24, 1771; *d.* London, Apr. 16, 1858. Son of (2). Pianist and composer, a pupil of Clementi. He had a considerable reputation as a performer and as a teacher. Of his numerous compositions only his studies survive in use. He founded the publishing firm of J. B. Cramer & Co., 1824.

(2) WILHELM: *b.* Mannheim, 1745; *d.* London, Oct. 5, 1799. Violinist. After several years as a member of the Mannheim court orchestra he settled in London, 1772, where he rapidly acquired a reputation as a soloist and as an orchestral leader.

Cras [cra], JEAN ÉMILE PAUL: *b.* Brest, May 22, 1879; *d.* there, Sept. 14, 1932. Composer, a pupil of Duparc. He spent his life in the French navy, becoming eventually a rear-admiral. His compositions include the opera *Polyphème* (Paris, 1922), numerous songs, chamber music and orchestral works.

Creation, The (*G.* Die Schöpfung). Oratorio by Haydn. First performed, Vienna, April 29, 1798. The German text by Baron van Swieten is a translation of an English libretto selected from the Book of Genesis and Milton's *Paradise Lost.* The English version commonly used in this country is an inferior, and sometimes unintelligible, translation from van Swieten's German. A new translation by A. H. Fox Strangways and Steuart Wilson was published in 1932.

Creation Mass (*G.* Schöpfungsmesse). Mass in B♭ by Haydn (1801), No. 11 in the complete edition of the Haydn Society Inc. (No. 4 in Novello's edition in vocal score). So called because two bars of the *Agnus Dei,* at the words "tollis peccata" bear a resemblance to bars 7-8 of the duet for Adam and Eve, "Graceful consort" (Holde Gattin) in *The Creation* (No. 32).

Creatures of Prometheus, The. *v.* PROMETHEUS.

Crécelle [cray-sell], *Fr.* Rattle.

Credo [cray'-doh], *L.* The initial word of the Creed in the Roman Mass—in full, "Credo in unum Deum" (I believe in one God) These opening words were sung by the priest; hence in polyphonic settings of the 15th and 16th cent. the choir regularly begins with the words "patrem omnipotentem" (the Father almighty). This tradition was later abandoned, though the plainsong intonation of the opening words still survives in Bach's Mass in B minor, where it is used as a *canto fermo* for the choir. The length of the Creed influenced its treatment by composers. Examples are found in the 15th cent. of "telescoped" settings, in which different parts sing different words simultaneously, and also of incomplete settings, in which some of the words were omitted. With English composers of the early 16th cent. the practice of omitting some of the words was quite common. The normal solution of the problem in the 16th cent. was to treat certain sections, *e.g.* "Deum de Deo, lumen de lumine" (God of God, light of light), in a simpler, homophonic style, and so save the time that would otherwise be employed in contrapuntal elaboration.

Créquillon [cray-kee-yoñ], THOMAS: *d.c.* 1557. Flemish composer, at one time in the service of Charles V. He was a prolific composer of *chansons* and church music, very few of which are available in modern editions.

Crescendo [creh-shen'-do], *I.* "Increasing," *i.e.* getting louder. Often abbreviated *cresc.* The opposite of *crescendo* is *decrescendo* or *diminuendo.*

Crescendo Pedal. A pedal on the organ which when applied successively adds more and more stops. The name is inappropriate, since a true *crescendo* (a gradual increase of power) cannot be achieved by an artificial increase of resources which necessarily proceeds by stages, however rapidly these may succeed each other.

Creston, PAUL: *b.* New York, Oct. 10, 1906. Composer, of Italian origin, whose baptismal name was Joseph Guttoveggio. Originally a bank clerk, he became a church organist and subsequently devoted himself to composition, teaching and criticism. His compositions include 3 symphonies, a piano concerto, a saxophone concerto, a fantasy for trombone and orchestra, a *concertino* for marimba and orchestra, chamber music, choral works, piano pieces and songs.

Cries of London. Some of the traditional melodies to which itinerant traders in London proclaimed their wares were arranged as rounds or catches by early 17th-cent. composers. More elaborate settings of a series of such melodies, in the form of fantasias for voices and instruments, were made by Weelkes, Gibbons, Dering (modern ed. by J. F. Bridge) and others. Dering also wrote a similar composition on country cries.

J. F. BRIDGE: *The Old Cryes of London* (1921).

Cristofori [creece-to'-fo-ree], BARTOLOMEO: *b.* Padua, May 4, 1655; *d.* Jan. 27, 1731. Harpsichord and piano manufacturer, for many years in the service of the Medici at Florence. In 1709 he invented the characteristic mechanism of the piano—the striking of a string by a mechanically controlled hammer which is immediately forced to rebound or " escape " by means of a " hopper " attached to a spring, while a " damper," withdrawn from the string at the moment of percussion, returns to it and terminates the vibration. *v.* PIANOFORTE.

Critic, The. Opera in two acts by Standford. Libretto by Lewis Cairns James (after Sheridan). First performed, London, Jan. 14, 1916.

Criticism, Musical. The reasoned discussion, in a periodical or book, of public performances or compositions, new or old. Published criticism, in the modern sense of the word, first appeared in Germany in the early 18th cent. with Mattheson's periodical *Critica Musica* (1722-5), which was followed by similar publications by other authors (including Scheibe and Marpurg). In England Charles Avison, in his *Essay on Musical Expression* (1753) suggested that " it might not be altogether foreign to the Design of some periodical Memoir of Literature, to have an Article sometimes, giving an Account and Character of the best musical Compositions " (p. 99), but the suggestion bore no immediate fruit. Musical criticism in daily newspapers was a product of the 19th cent., no doubt in consequence of the increased interest in music taken by the middle classes. In England *The Times* seems to have been the first newspaper to employ a music critic. In Vienna Eduard Hanslick, active as a critic from 1848 onwards, came to exercise a strong influence on opinion, particularly through his support of Brahms and opposition to Wagner. At the same time the lead given by Mattheson and others in the 18th cent. had been followed up by the foundation of musical periodicals in several countries, *e.g.* in France the *Journal de musique française et italienne* (1764), in Germany the *Allgemeine musikalische Zeitung* (1798) and the *Neue Zeitschrift für Musik*, founded by Schumann (1834), in England the *Quarterly Musical Magazine and Review* (1818) and the *Harmonicon* (1823). In the course of the century the number of such periodicals, some devoted to music in general, others to specific aspects of it, increased enormously. Inevitably many of these publications enjoyed only a relatively short life; a few, however, have survived to the present day, among them the *Musical Times* in England (1844), *Le Ménestrel* in France (1833), and the *Neue Zeitschrift für Musik* in Germany (1834).

The function of the critic is to assess values and hence indirectly to maintain standards. The assessment of performances, however valuable for the performers and however instructive for the public, is clearly less important than the assessment of compositions, since creative art endures and performances do not. In both, the essential requisites are the widest possible knowledge, a cultivated taste, and complete sincerity. Attempts have been made to reduce criticism to an exact science. In so far as every critic is an individual human being, with his own private reactions to what he hears, this is clearly an impossibility. Even though there is often general agreement about the value of particular compositions or particular composers, there have been, and still are, many cases of individual critics taking a markedly different line from their colleagues; and there are also plenty of examples of judgments almost universally accepted in one age and universally rejected in the next. The annals of musical criticism are full of exaggerated expressions of enthusiasm for works which now seem to us of very little account. No criticism is universally and permanently valid. On the other hand any criticism which is informed and sincere is valuable, provided we can understand the author's premises. The best critics not only tell us a good deal about themselves; they also stimulate us to form our own judgments.

From the early part of the 19th cent. onwards musical criticism has been a profession in itself. It has, however, often been combined with other musical occupations. Several composers have been active in this capacity, among them Weber, Schumann, Berlioz, Liszt, Wagner, Wolf and Debussy. At the same time composers rarely make the best critics, probably because their affinities with certain kinds of music, however unconscious, are particularly strong. The writings of Wolf and Debussy, for example, are more valuable as an expression of their authors' personalities than as a serious contribution to our knowledge of the period.

Criticism is also part of the function of the historian. This has often been denied, on the ground that history is an objective science, concerned with what has happened and not with its value. On the other hand, since all history is of necessity selective, there must be some criterion for selection; and it is difficult to see how selection can operate without an assessment of values.

M. D. CALVOCORESSI : *The Principles and Methods of Musical Criticism* (2nd ed., 1931).

E. NEWMAN : *A Musical Critic's Holiday* (1925).

O. THOMPSON : *Practical Music Criticism* (1934).

Croce [cro'-cheh], GIOVANNI: *b.* Chioggia, *c.* 1557; *d.* Venice, May 15, 1609. Composer, a pupil of Zarlino. Singer in the choir of St. Mark's, Venice, 1565. Subsequently ordained priest and became second *maestro di cappella* at St. Mark's, *c.* 1595; first *maestro di cappella*, 1603. In addition to a number of Masses, motets and other church compositions he also published several books of madrigals. His madrigal "Ove tra l'herb' i fiori" (modern ed. by L. Benson), originally published in the anthology *Il trionfo di Dori* (1592), was included in Yonge's *Musica Transalpina*, book ii (1597), with the English words "Hard by a crystal fountain." The concluding lines of the Italian poem:

> Poi concordi seguir Ninfe e Pastori,
> Viva la bella Dori.

are represented in the English version by:

> Then sang the shepherds and nymphs of Diana:
> Long live fair Oriana.

This refrain was adopted by Michael Cavendish for his madrigal "Come gentle swains" (1598) and occurs in the madrigals which comprise the English anthology *The Triumphes of Oriana* (1601). Morley, the editor of that collection, included in it his own setting of "Hard by a crystal fountain." *v.* TRIUMPHES OF ORIANA.

Croche [crosh], *F.* Quaver (the word for crotchet is *noire*). *Double croche*, semiquaver.

Croche [crosh], MONSIEUR. An imaginary person invented by Debussy as a mouthpiece for his own critical opinions: see *Monsieur Croche the Dilettante Hater* (1927).

Croft, WILLIAM: *b.* Nether Ettington (Warwickshire), Dec. 1678; *d.* Bath, Aug. 14, 1727. Composer and organist. Chorister of the Chapel Royal. Organist, St. Anne's, Soho, 1700-12; Chapel Royal, 1704; Westminster Abbey, 1708. Master of the Children, Chapel Royal, 1708. He published his doctoral exercise for Oxford (1713), consisting of two odes, under the title *Musicus apparatus academicus*, and a selection of his anthems in two volumes under the title *Musica Sacra* (1724). Keyboard compositions appeared in *A choice collection of ayres for the harpsichord* (1700) and *The Harpsichord Master*, ii & iii (1700-2). As a young man he wrote music for 4 dramatic productions. His setting of the Burial Service, in a simple, syllabic style, is still used at state funerals.

Croma [cro′-mah], *I.* Quaver. Hence the adjective *cromatico*, which not only means " chromatic " but also in the 16th cent. was applied to compositions which made liberal use of black notes. *v.* CHROMATIC (7).

Cromorne [crom-orrn], *Fr.* Krummhorn.

Crook. A piece of tubing inserted into a brass instrument between the mouthpiece and the body of the instrument. The pitch of the instrument varies according to the size of the crook. Thus a horn with an A crook will sound a major third higher than the same instrument with an F crook. In the 18th and early 19th cent., before the introduction of valves or pistons on horns and trumpets the use of crooks was necessary in order to enable these instruments to be played in a variety of keys. A horn in F, for example, was for all practical purposes restricted to the HARMONIC SERIES in that key, *i.e.*:

None of the notes, except A, would have been any use in the key of E. By exchanging his F crook for an E crook the player could produce the same series a semitone lower:

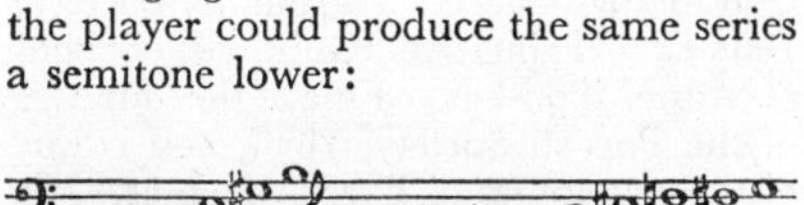

The same principle applied to the trumpet. On the trombone crooks were not required, since the slide made available a complete chromatic compass.

Horn-players today normally confine themselves to a single crook (in F), since notes which are not in the harmonic series can be produced by valves. Occasionally, however, they use smaller crooks (in A or B♭) for 18th-cent. works where the high range of the parts makes their performance hazardous or uncomfortable. To facilitate this change horns are now regularly built in F and B♭ (*i.e.* with two crooks incorporated in a single instrument), with a device enabling the player to switch from one to the other. Trumpets are made in B♭ and A with a switch to change from one to the other. For the high trumpet parts to be found in the works of Bach and Handel and their contemporaries a smaller instrument (in D) is used. *v.* TRANSPOSING INSTRUMENTS.

Cross, JOAN : *b.* London, Sept., 1900. Soprano. Sang in opera at the Old Vic. Theatre from 1924 and at Sadler's Wells from 1931. Director, Sadler's Wells, 1941-5. Member of the English Opera Group, 1946. Founded an Opera School in London, 1948.

Cross Relation. The American equivalent of FALSE RELATION.

Crot. *v.* CRWTH.

Crotch, WILLIAM: *b.* Norwich, July 5, 1775; *d.* Taunton, Dec. 29, 1847. Composer and organist. He was an infant prodigy and gave organ recitals in London at the age of 4. An oratorio, *The Captivity of Judah*, was performed in Cambridge (where he lived for 2 years), 1789. Organist, Christ Church, Oxford, 1790; St. John's College, 1797. Professor, Oxford, 1797, till his death. Principal, R.A.M., 1822-32. He delivered several series of lectures at Oxford and at the Royal Institution, London, which were later published, together with the music used as illustrations. His compositions include the oratorios *Palestine* (1812) and *The Captivity of Judah* (1834: a different work from the early composition mentioned above), an ode on the accession of George IV, anthems and keyboard works. The anthem " Lo, star-led chiefs," which is still sung in cathedrals, is from *Palestine*.

Crotchet (*A.* quarter-note, *F.* noire, *G.* Viertel, *I.* semiminima). The fourth part of a semibreve, represented by the sign ♩. The crotchet rest is either 𝄽 or 𝄾. The word is French in origin, *crochet* = hook. The name was given to it since in the 14th cent. the minim was represented by a lozenge-shaped black note with a stem, and the crotchet was distinguished from it by the addition of a hook at the top of the stem. With the introduction of white notation in the

15th cent. the minim became a white note (𝅗𝅥), and the crotchet adopted the earlier form of the minim (♩). The hooked note (♪) became the quaver—hence the French word for a quaver is *croche*.

Crowd. *v.* CRWTH.

Crüger [cree′-ger], JOHANNES: *b.* Gross-Breese, Apr. 9, 1598; *d.* Berlin, Feb. 23, 1663. Composer and theorist. Studied theology at Wittenberg. Cantor, St. Nicolaus, Berlin, 1622 till his death. In addition to a number of theoretical works he published several collections of Lutheran hymns with music. Many of his settings have remained in use to the present day. Among those which are familiar in England are "Nun danket alle Gott" (Now thank we all our God) and "Jesu, meine Freude" (Jesu, joy and treasure).

Cruit. *v.* CRWTH.

Crwth [crooth]. The Welsh name of a bowed lyre, known in Irish as *crot* or *cruit*, in English as *crowd* and in Latin as *chorus*, which had a considerable vogue in the Middle Ages and survived in Wales as late as the 19th cent. In its later form it had four strings passing over a finger-board (as on the violin) and two additional unstopped strings at the side. It has been argued that the Latin word *chrotta*, which has often been regarded as the same thing as the *crwth*, indicates in fact a form of harp (*v.* C. Sachs, *The History of Musical Instruments*, p. 262).

Csárdás [charr′-dush], *H.* A Hungarian dance, consisting of two alternating sections—the first slow and melancholy (*lassú*), the second fast and vivacious (*friss*). Liszt's familiar *Hungarian Rhapsody* No. 2 provides a characteristic example.

Cucuel [kee-kee-el], GEORGES: *b.* Dijon, Dec. 14, 1884; *d.* Grenoble, Oct. 28, 1918. Historian. Studied with Romain Rolland in Paris. He was active in collecting in Italy materials for the history of 18th-cent. music. His most important works are *La Pouplinière et la musique de chambre au XVIIIe siècle* (1913), *Étude sur un orchestre du XVIIIe siècle* (1913) and *Les Créateurs de l'opéra-comique français* (1914). He served throughout the 1914-18 war and died in a military hospital.

Cui [kee-ee], CÉSAR ANTONOVICH: *b.* Vilna, Jan. 18, 1835; *d.* Petrograd, March 24, 1918. Composer, the son of a French officer who settled in Russia. His mother was Lithuanian. By profession an engineer in the army (becoming eventually Lieutenant-General), he enjoyed the friendship of Balakirev and found time to compose a large number of works, including several operas. Though he was a member of the nationalist group known as "the Five" and was severely critical of other composers, his own works were neither strongly nationalist in feeling nor particularly distinguished. He was primarily a lyrical composer, who was at his best in song and piano pieces.

M. D. CALVOCORESSI & G. ABRAHAM: *Masters of Russian Music* (1936).

Cuivre [kee-eevr], *Fr.* Brass. *Instruments de cuivre* (or *cuivres* alone), brass instruments.

Cuivré [kee-eev-ray], *Fr.* (*G.* schmetternd). "Brassy." An indication to horn-players to play with a harsh, blaring tone.

Cummings, WILLIAM HAYMAN: *b.* Sidbury, Aug. 22, 1831; *d.* London, June 6, 1915. For many years a tenor soloist and teacher at the R.A.M., 1879-96. Conductor, Sacred Harmonic Society, 1885-8. Principal, Guildhall School of Music, 1896-1911. One of the founders of the Purcell Society, 1876, and editor of three volumes of Purcell's works. His valuable library was sold at his death, and went to Japan.

Cundell, EDRIC: *b.* London, Jan. 29, 1893. Conductor and composer. Studied at Trinity College of Music. Began his career as a horn-player. Active as a conductor from 1919. Principal, Guildhall School of Music, 1938. A string quartet won a prize offered by the *Daily Telegraph*, 1933. Most of his compositions are in manuscript.

Cunningham, GEORGE DORRINGTON: *b.* London, Oct. 2, 1878; *d.* Birmingham, Aug. 4, 1948. Organist and choral conductor. Studied at the R.A.M. Organist, Alexandra Palace, 1900 till the 1914-18 war. He also held various church appointments, including St. Alban's, Holborn. City organist, Birmingham, 1924 till his death; University organist and conductor, City Choir, Birmingham, 1926. Both as a performer and as a choral conductor he was outstanding.

Cupid and Death. A masque by James Shirley, with music by Matthew Locke and Christopher Gibbons (modern ed. in *Musica Britannica*, ii). First performed, London, March 26, 1653.

Curtall. The name given in England in the 16th and 17th cent. to a small bassoon. A larger form, corresponding roughly to the modern bassoon, was called *double curtall.* The name seems to derive from the Low German *kortholt* (short wood), the shortness resulting from the folding back of the tube.

Curwen, (1) JOHN: *b.* Heckmondwike, Nov. 14, 1816; *d.* Manchester, May 26, 1880. A Noncomformist minister who founded the Tonic Sol-Fa Association and the publishing firm of J. Curwen and Sons. Published several educational works.

(2) JOHN SPENCER: *b.* Plaistow, Sept. 30, 1847; *d.* London, Aug. 6, 1916. Son of (1). Studied at the R.A.M. He continued his father's work as principal of the Tonic Sol-Fa College and director of J. Curwen and Sons. A pioneer of the competition festival movement, which he started in Stratford, East London, in 1882. His wife Annie (1845-1932) was the author of a piano method which has been familiar to several generations of young pianists.

Curzon [kēer-zōn], EMMANUEL HENRI PARENT DE: *b.* Havre, July 6, 1861; *d.* Paris, Feb. 25, 1942. Archivist and historian. Published a catalogue of all documents dealing with the theatre and music in the Archives Nationales (1899). Translated Mozart's letters and Schumann's critical writings and published biographical studies of Grétry, Meyerbeer, Mozart, Rossini, Thomas, Reyer, Delibes and others, and several bibliographical works.

Custos [cōoss'-toce], *L.* *v.* DIRECT.

Cuzzoni [coo-dzo'-nee], FRANCESCA: *b.* Parma, *c.* 1700; *d.* Bologna, 1770. Operatic soprano. First appeared at Bologna at the age of 16. Engaged by Handel to sing in London and first appeared there in his *Ottone*, 1723. She won great popularity, though her rivalry with Faustina Bordoni led to violent demonstrations in the theatre. She left London in 1728 and sang in Venice, Vienna, Hamburg and Stuttgart. A benefit concert in London in 1751 was not a success. Her last years were miserable.

Cyclic. An adjective which implies some unity between the various sections or movements of an extended work, more particularly the unity which arises from thematic connection of some kind. In the 15th cent. composers began to write Masses with thematic resemblances between the openings of the sections (*Kyrie*, *Gloria*, etc.), or with the same *canto fermo* (plainsong or secular) in all the sections, or with both together. Such Masses are now commonly described by historians as "cyclic" (*v.* MASS). Thematic association also occurs in 16th- and 17th-cent. dance suites. In the symphony it was introduced by Beethoven (in the 5th symphony) and developed further by Romantic composers, such as Mendelssohn, Schumann, Berlioz and Franck. Works of this kind are often said to be in "cyclic" form. It may be questioned, however, whether there is justification for using as a technical term a word whose exact significance is not self-evident..

Cymbals. (1) An old English name for chime-bells, which were used in monasteries and schools in the Middle Ages and often appear in miniatures and sculpture (*Fr.* cymbales, *G.* Zimbeln, *L.* cymbala).

J. SMITS VAN WAESBERGHE : *Cymbala* (*Bells in the Middle Ages*) (1951).

(2) Percussion instruments of great antiquity, still used in the modern orchestra and in military bands (*Fr.* cymbales, *G.* Becken, *I.* piatti, cinelli). They consist of two metal plates, held in the hands and clashed together. An alternative (but unsatisfactory) method is used when there is only one performer to play both the bass drum and the cymbals: one of the cymbals is fixed horizontally on the top of the drum and the other is clashed against it. There are also two ways of

using a single cymbal: (a) hitting it with a stick, hard or soft, in the manner of a gong, (b) performing a roll on it with timpani or side-drum sticks. The two cymbals can also be clashed rapidly together so as to produce a persistent vibration. The range of dynamics, from very soft to very loud, is considerable. It can be further modified by using smaller or larger cymbals, according to the nature of the composition.

(3) Small cymbals were used, like castanets, by dancers in the Ancient World. Berlioz introduced a pair of these (*cymbales antiques*), tuned to two different notes, in the "Queen Mab" scherzo of his *Roméo et Juliette* symphony (1839).

Czaar und Zimmermann [tsahrr o͞ont tsim′-mer-mun] (Czar and Carpenter). Opera in three acts by Lortzing. Libretto by the composer (based on a French play). First performed, Leipzig, Dec. 22, 1837.

Czardas. *v.* CSÁRDÁS.

Czar Saltan. *v.* LEGEND OF THE CZAR SALTAN.

Czar's Bride, The. *v.* TSARSKAYA NEVESTA.

Czerny [chairn′-i], KARL: *b.* Vienna, Feb. 20, 1791; *d.* there, July 15, 1857. Composer and pianist, the son of a Czech piano-teacher who settled in Vienna in 1786. He was taught by his father and Beethoven (see *Beethoven*: *Impressions of Contemporaries*, pp. 25-31). Instead of making a name for himself as a virtuoso he preferred to devote himself to teaching and earned a great reputation. Liszt was among his pupils. He was an astonishingly prolific composer in every form (including church music) and arranged an enormous number of works by other composers for two, four or eight hands, but is now known only by his technical studies, which are still in use. He left in manuscript an autobiography, *Erinnerungen aus meinem Leben.*

D

D. The 2nd note (or supertonic) of the scale of C major. As an abbreviation D. = discantus, doctor, dominant. D. Mus. or Mus.D. = Doctor of Music. *D.C.* = *da capo* (go back again to the beginning). *D.S.* = *dal segno* (go back to the sign). *m.d.* = *mano destra*, *main droite* (right hand). In TONIC SOL-FA **d** = *doh*, the 1st note (or tonic) of the major scale.

Da capo [dah cah'-po], *I.* Lit. "from the head," *i.e.* go back again to the the beginning of the piece. Often abbreviated *D.C.* *Da capo* aria, a song which repeats the first section after an imtermediate section (generally of a contrasted character)—a form very common in 17th- and 18th-cent. opera and oratorio and also imitated in instrumental music.

Dahl [dahl], VIKING: *b.* Osby, Oct. 8, 1895. Composer and critic. Studied in Stockholm, Paris, Munich and Berlin. His works include the opera *Sjömansvisa*, ballets, orchestral and chamber music, piano music and songs. He has also published educational books on music.

Dalayrac [da-lay-ruck], NICOLAS: *b.* Muret, June 13, 1753; *d.* Paris, Nov. 27, 1809. Opera-composer (originally d'Alayrac). He wrote nearly 60 *opéras-comiques*, beginning in 1781 and continuing through the Revolution, of which he was a supporter. Among the most successful were *Les Deux petits Savoyards* (1789), *Adolphe et Clara* (1799), *Maison à vendre* (1800), *Gulistan* (1805) and *Deux Mots* (1806). In 1781 he also wrote a set of string quartets (*quatuors concertants*).

D'Albert. *v.* ALBERT.

Dale, BENJAMIN JAMES: *b.* London, July 17, 1885; *d.* there, July 30, 1943. Composer. Studied at the Royal Academy of Music, of which he became warden in 1936. He made his reputation with a piano sonata in D minor (1902), but his output remained relatively slight. Among his compositions, which are romantic in style and marked by fine craftsmanship, the best known are the suite for viola and piano (1907) and the cantata *Before the paling of the stars* (1912).

Dalibor [dull'-i-borr]. Opera in three acts by Smetana. German libretto by Joseph Wenzig, Czech translation by Erwin Spindler. First performed, Prague, May 16, 1868.

Dall' Abaco. *v.* ABACO.

Dallam, (1) THOMAS. English organ-builder of the early 17th cent. He built organs for King's College, Cambridge (1606) and Worcester Cathedral (1613). He also built a mechanical organ, operated either by keys or by a clock, which Queen Elizabeth sent as a present to the Sultan of Turkey. For Dallam's diary of his journey to Constantinople see *Early Voyages and Travels in the Levant*, ed. J. T. Bent (Hakluyt Society, 1893).

(2) ROBERT: *b.* Lancaster, 1602; *d.* Oxford, May 31, 1665. Probably a son of (1). Built several organs before the Civil War, including York Minster, St. Paul's Cathedral and Durham Cathedral.

(3) RALPH: *d.* Greenwich, 1673. Built organs after the Restoration, including St. George's, Windsor.

Dallapiccola [dahl-lah-pick'-co-lah], LUIGI: *b.* Pisino, Feb. 3, 1904. Composer. Studied at the Florence Conservatorio. His music, much of which is in the twelve-note style, shows a peculiar sensitiveness to instrumental colour. His compositions include the operas *Volo di notte* (Florence, 1940), and *Il prigionero* (Florence, 1950), choral works and chamber music.

G. M. GATTI: "Luigi Dallapiccola" (*Monthly Musical Record*, Feb. 1937).

Dallery [dull-ree]. A family of French organ-builders active in the 18th cent.

Dal segno [dahl sehn′-yo], *I.* "From the sign," *i.e.* go back to a point in the music marked by the sign ·$·. Often abbreviated *D.S.*

Daman. *v.* DAMON.

Dame Blanche, La [la dum blũnsh] (The White Lady). Opera in three acts by Boieldieu. Libretto by Augustin Eugène Scribe (based on Scott's *Guy Mannering* and *The Monastery*). First performed, Paris, Dec. 10, 1825.

Damnation de Faust, La [la danuss-yõn der foast], *Fr.* (The Damnation of Faust). A *légende dramatique* (dramatic legend) for soloists, chorus and orchestra by Berlioz, Op. 24, originally described as *opéra de concert* (concert opera).

The text is an adaptation of Gérard de Nerval's French translation of Goethe's *Faust*, with additions by the composer and Almire Gandonnière. First performed, Paris, Dec. 12, 1846. Adapted for the stage by Raoul Gunsbourg and first performed in this version at Monte Carlo, Feb. 18, 1893.

Damon (Daman), WILLIAM: *d.* 1591. An Italian musician, born in Liége, who came to England about 1564. He was at first in the service of Lord Buckhurst, and then of Queen Elizabeth (see *The Musical Antiquary*, 1912, pp. 118-9). His harmonizations of metrical psalmtunes were published in two editions (1579 & 1591). He also wrote church music (reprint of a "Miserere" in G. E. P. Arkwright, *The Old English Edition*, xxi).

Damoreau [da-mor-o], LAURE CYNTHIE: *b.* Paris, Feb. 6, 1801; *d.* there, Feb. 25, 1863. Operatic soprano, known as La Cinti. First appeared at the Paris Opéra, 1826. Sang the principal roles in several operas by Rossini and Auber. Taught singing at the Paris Conservatoire, 1834-56 and published a *Méthode de chant.* Retired from the stage, 1843, and toured as a recitalist in the United States, Holland, Belgium and Russia, 1843-6. Her maiden name was Montalant.

Damper. A piece of felt, glued to a strip of wood, which covers a piano string and prevents it from vibrating. It is automatically removed from the string when the key is struck and covers it again as soon as the key is released. The right-hand pedal removes the dampers from all the strings and so increases the sonority of the instrument by permitting sympathetic vibration. *v.* ACOUSTICS, PIANOFORTE.

Dämpfer [demp′-fer], *G.* Mute (*I.* sordino). *Mit Dämpfer*, with mute (*con sordino*). *Dämpfer weg*, without mute (*senza sordino*).

Damrosch, (1) LEOPOLD: *b.* Posen, Oct. 22, 1832; *d.* New York, Feb. 15, 1885. Violinist and conductor. Studied medicine at Berlin University, graduating in 1854, then became a professional violinist, playing in the Weimar orchestra under Liszt, 1857. Conductor, Breslau Philharmonic Society, 1858-60; Breslau *Orchesterverein* (which he founded), 1862-71; Arion Male Voice Choir, New York, 1871. Founded in New York the Oratorio Society, 1874, and the Symphony Society, 1878, both of which he conducted. Directed a season of German opera at the Metropolitan Opera House, 1884-5. He was an intimate friend of Wagner and Liszt, who dedicated to him his *Le Triomphe funèbre du Tasse.* He wrote a large number of vocal and instrumental works, including a violin concerto.

(2) FRANK HEINO: *b.* Breslau, June 22, 1859; *d.* New York, Oct. 22, 1937. Son of (1). Chorus-master, Metropolitan Opera House, New York, 1885-91. Active as conductor of choral societies and in the promotion of musical education. Director, Institute of Musical Art, New York, 1904. Author of educational works.

(3) WALTER JOHANNES: *b.* Breslau, Jan. 30, 1862; *d.* New York, Dec. 22, 1950. Son of (1). Assistant conductor, Metropolitan Opera House, New York, 1884; conductor, Oratorio Society, 1885-98 and New York Symphony Society, 1885-94. Founded Damrosch Opera Company, 1894-9. Conductor, New York Philharmonic Orchestra, 1902-3; New York Symphony Orchestra (reorganized), 1903-26. A pioneer of broadcast concerts in America. His numerous compositions include the operas *The Scarlet Letter* (Boston, 1896), *Cyrano de*

Bergerac (New York, 1913) and *The Man without a Country* (New York, 1937).

W. DAMROSCH : *My Musical Life* (1923).

Dandrieu [dūndr-yer], JEAN FRANÇOIS: *b.* Paris, 1682; *d.* there, Jan. 17, 1738. Organist and composer. Published music for harpsichord and organ (including arrangements of *noëls*) and chamber music. Modern edition of organ music in A. Guilmant, *Archives des maîtres de l'orgue*, vii; harpsichord music in H. Expert, *Les Maîtres du clavecin des XVIIe et XVIIIe siècles.*

D'Anglebert. *v.* ANGLEBERT.

Danican [da-nee-cūn], FRANÇOIS ANDRÉ. *v.* PHILIDOR.

Daniel (Danyel), JOHN. Composer of the late 16th and early 17th cent. Brother of the poet, Samuel Daniel. Graduated B.Mus. at Oxford, 1604. Musician to Queen Anne, consort of James I, 1612, and to Charles I, 1625. Published *Songs for the Lute, Viol and Voice* (1606), including the elaborate and pathetic setting, with chromatic harmonies, of " Can doleful notes " ; modern edition in *E.S.L.S.*, 2nd ser.

P. WARLOCK : *The English Ayre* (1926).

Danse Macabre [dūnce ma-cubr], *Fr.* An orchestral piece (Op. 40) by Saint-Saëns (1874), based on verses by Henri Cazalis. It represents Death playing the violin for a dance of skeletons—a legendary conception which goes back to the Middle Ages. Liszt's *Totentanz* for piano and orchestra deals with the same subject.

Dante Symphony (*G.* Eine Symphonie zu Dante's *Divina Commedia*). Orchestral work by Liszt, with female chorus in the final section. There are two movements: I. *Inferno* ; II. *Purgatorio*, leading to *Magnificat.* The work is dedicated to Wagner. First performed, Dresden, Nov. 7, 1857.

Danyel. *v.* DANIEL.

Danza tedesca [dahn'-tsah teh-dess'-cah], *I.* " German dance." *v.* ALLA TEDESCA, ALLEMANDE, DEUTSCHER TANZ.

Daphne [duff'-nay]. Opera in one act by Richard Strauss. Libretto by Joseph Gregor. First performed, Dresden, Oct. 15, 1938.

Daphnis et Chloé [duff-neece ay clo-ay] (Daphnis and Chloe). Ballet by Ravel. Choreography by Michel Fokine. Décor by Léon Bakst. First public performance, Paris, June 8, 1912. The composer subsequently made two substantial excerpts (each continuous) for concert performance, to which he gave the misleading title *Fragments symphoniques* (often absurdly translated " symphonic fragments ").

Da Ponte. *v.* PONTE.

Daquin [da-cān], LOUIS CLAUDE: *b.* Paris, July 4, 1694; *d.* there, June 15, 1772. Organist and composer, a pupil of Louis Marchand. He began his career as a child prodigy, and became organist at the French Chapel Royal, 1739. Published *Premier livre de pièces de clavecin* (1735; modern edition in *Le Trésor des pianistes*, ed. Farrenc, ix), which includes the well-known " Le coucou," and *Nouveau livre de Noëls pour l'orgue et le clavecin* (modern edition in *Archives des maîtres de l'orgue*, ed. Guilmant).

Dardanus [darr-da-nēece]. Opera in five acts by Rameau. Libretto by Charles Antoine Leclerc de La Bruère. First performed, Paris, Nov. 19, 1739.

D'Arezzo. *v.* GUIDO D'AREZZO.

Dargomijsky [dahrr-go-meezh'-ski], ALEXANDER SERGEIVICH: *b.* Toula, Feb. 14, 1813; *d.* St. Petersburg, Jan. 17, 1869. Composer. He was largely self-taught, but received encouragement from Glinka. His first opera, *Esmeralda* (Moscow, 1847), produced eight years after its composition, was not a success. *The Roussalka* (St. Petersburg, 1856) made a much stronger impression. His most individual work is *The Stone Guest* (St. Petersburg, 1872), which was completed by Cui and orchestrated by Rimsky-Korsakov; the text, which is the story of Don Juan, is set to a sort of continuous recitative. Though essentially an amateur he had a considerable influence on the nationalist school of Russian composers, as well as on Tchaikovsky. In addition to his operas he also wrote a number of songs, some of which are satirical, and three characteristic orchestral fantasias.

G. ABRAHAM : *Studies in Russian Music* (1935).
On Russian Music (1939).

Das. For German titles beginning thus, see the second word of the title.

Daughter of the Regiment, The. *v.* FILLE DU RÉGIMENT.

Dauprat [do-pra], LOUIS FRANÇOIS: *b.* Paris, May 24, 1781; *d.* there, July 17, 1868. Horn-player. At the Paris Opéra, 1808-31; teacher at the Conservatoire, 1816-42. In addition to 5 horn concertos and other works for the instrument he published a *Méthode de cor alto et de cor basse,* which was for many years a standard work.

Dauvergne [do-vairn-*yer*], ANTOINE: *b.* Moulins, Oct. 3, 1713; *d.* Lyons, Feb. 12, 1797. Violinist and composer. He became master of the king's chamber music and manager of the Paris Opéra, as well as one of the directors of the Concert Spirituel. After having written a considerable amount of instrumental music he turned his attention to opera in 1752. His one-act *Les Troqueurs* (Paris, 1753) was said to be the first French comic opera in the style of the Italian intermezzo, with recitative instead of dialogue.

Davenant, WILLIAM: *b.* Oxford, Feb. 1606; *d.* London, Apr. 7, 1668. Poet and dramatist. Author of the libretto of the first English opera, *The Siege of Rhodes* (London, 1656).

David [da-veed], FÉLICIEN CÉSAR: *b.* Cadenet, May 13, 1810; *d.* St. Germain-en-Laye, Aug. 29, 1876. Composer. Studied at Aix and the Paris Conservatoire. Of his numerous compositions, which include 2 symphonies and several operas, the one which made his reputation was *Le Désert* for chorus and orchestra (1844), which showed a remarkable gift for oriental colouring—the result of several years' residence in the Near East.

R. BRANCOUR : *Félicien David* (1911).

David [dah′-feet], (1) FERDINAND: *b.* Hamburg, June 19, 1810; *d.* Klosters, July 18, 1873. Violinist, a pupil of Spohr and a friend of Mendelssohn. First appeared at the Gewandhaus concerts, Leipzig, 1825; leader of the orchestra there (under Mendelssohn), 1836; teacher of the violin at Leipzig Conservatorium, 1843. He advised Mendelssohn during the composition of the latter's violin concerto and gave the first performance at Leipzig, 1845. His pupils included Joachim and Wilhelmj. In addition to a large number of compositions, including 5 violin concertos, he published a *Violinschule* and a *Hohe Schule des Violinspiels* (both standard works) and edited numerous works for the violin by older composers.

(2) JOHANN NEPOMUK: *b.* Eferding, Nov. 30, 1895. Composer and organist. Became teacher at the Leipzig Conservatorium, 1934. His compositions include 5 symphonies, chamber works, organ music and choral works.

Davidov [dah′-vid-off], KARL: *b.* Goldingen, March 15, 1838; *d.* Moscow, Feb. 26, 1889. Cellist and composer. Studied at Moscow, St. Petersburg and Leipzig. First appeared at the Gewandhaus concerts, Leipzig, 1859. Principal cello, Gewandhaus orchestra, 1859; St. Petersburg Opera, 1862. Director, St. Petersburg Conservatoire, 1876-86. His compositions include 4 cello concertos; he also wrote a cello tutor.

Davidsbündler [dah′-feets-bēent′-ler], *G.* " Members of the League of David " (*Davidsbund*). An imaginary association invented by Schumann, which was supposed to fight against Philistines in music. The names of some of the members, however, represented real people, including Schumann himself and Mendelssohn (*v.* F. Niecks, *Robert Schumann*, p. 132). A " Marche des Davidsbündler contre les Philistins " occurs in Schumann's *Carnaval*, Op. 9, and he also wrote a set of characteristic dances entitled *Davidsbündlertänze*, Op. 6, and signed with the initials " F " or " E," *i.e.* Florestan and Eusebius (names adopted by the composer to represent two different sides of his personality).

Davies, (1) BENJAMIN GREY: *b.* Pontardawe, Jan. 6, 1858; *d.* Bath, March 28, 1943. Tenor. Studied at the Royal Academy of Music. Appeared frequently in opera, including Stanford's *The Canterbury Pilgrims* (London, 1884) and Sullivan's *Ivanhoe* (London, 1891), but from 1890 devoted himself mainly to oratorio, in which he excelled.

(2) CECILIA: *d.* July 3, 1836. Sister of (5). A singer who made a considerable reputation in Italian opera, both on the Continent and in England. She first appeared in London in 1767, and subsequently visited Paris, Vienna, Milan and Florence. The last 40 years of her life were spent in poverty.

(3) FANNY: *b.* Guernsey, June 27, 1861; *d.* London, Sept. 1, 1934. Pianist, a pupil of Clara Schumann. Her first public appearance in England was in 1885. She excelled in the music of Schumann and Brahms, the latter of whom she knew intimately; but her tastes were catholic, and she included a great deal of early keyboard music in her programmes.

(4) HENRY WALFORD: *b.* Oswestry, Sept. 6, 1869; *d.* Wrington, March 11, 1941. Organist and composer. Chorister at St. George's Chapel, Windsor, and assistant there to Walter Parratt, 1885-90. Studied at the R.C.M.; teacher of counterpoint there, 1895-1903. Organist, Temple Church, 1898-1923; St. George's Chapel, Windsor, 1927-32. Conductor, Bach Choir, 1903-7. Professor, University of Wales, 1919-26. Master of the King's Music, 1934-41. Knighted, 1922. Among his numerous compositions are several works for chorus and orchestra written for various festivals; the most successful of these was *Everyman* (Leeds, 1904). He was active in providing music for the forces in the 1914-18 war and became Director of Music to the Royal Air Force in 1917. He broadcast frequently to schools and to adult listeners, and his gift for simple and lively exposition won him many friends. His *Solemn Melody*, for organ and strings, was written for the celebration of Milton's tercentenary at Bow Church, 1908.

H. C. COLLES: *Walford Davies* (1942).

(5) MARIANNE: *b.* 1744; *d.* 1792. Sister of (2), with whom she toured on the Continent. She made her reputation chiefly as a performer on the glass HARMONICA.

Davison, ARCHIBALD THOMPSON: *b.* Boston, Mass., Oct. 11, 1883. Choral conductor and musicologist. Studied at Harvard. Assistant, Harvard, 1909; organist and choirmaster, 1910; instructor, 1912; assistant professor, 1917; associate professor, 1920; professor of choral music, 1929; professor of music, 1940-54. His published works include *Historical Anthology of Music* (with W. Apel); *Bach and Handel: the Consummation of the Baroque in Music* (1951); *Church Music: Illusion & Reality* (1952).

Davy, RICHARD. English composer of the late 15th and early 16th cent. Organist, Magdalen College, Oxford, 1490-2; subsequently became a priest. Vicar-choral, Exeter Cathedral, 1497-1506. His compositions, mainly for the church, include an incomplete setting of the Passion, six complete and one incomplete antiphons, and one incomplete Magnificat (all in the Eton choirbook), and two carols.

Day, ALFRED: *b.* London, Jan., 1810: *d.* there, Feb. 11, 1849. Homeopathic doctor, who devoted several years to writing a *Treatise on Harmony* (1845) which had considerable influence in its day. It propounds a rigidly vertical analysis of chords, based on acoustics and Rameau's theory of "roots" (*v.* FUNDAMENTAL BASS), but fails to recognise that such an analysis becomes a *reductio ad absurdum* when chords are said to be derived from roots which are not heard and which no one but a fanatical theorist would be likely to imagine. *v.* CHORD, INVERSION (3).

Daza [dah'-thah], ESTEBAN: *b.* Vallodolid. 16th cent. Spanish lutenist. His *Libro de Musica en cifras para Vihuela, intitulado el Parnasso* (1576) contains a number of transcriptions of motets, madrigals and *villancicos*; excerpts in G. Morphy, *Les Luthistes espagnols du XVI*[e] *siècle* (1902).

Death and the Maiden. *v.* TOD UND DAS MÄDCHEN.

Death and Transfiguration. *v.* TOD UND VERKLÄRUNG.

De Bériot. *v.* BÉRIOT.

Debora e Jaele [deh'-bo-rah eh yah-eh'-leh] (Deborah and Jael). Opera in three acts by Pizzetti. Libretto by the composer. First performed, Milan, Dec. 16, 1922.

Deborah. Oratorio by Handel. Libretto by Samuel Humphreys. First performed, London, March 17, 1733.

Debussy [der-bēēce-ee], CLAUDE ACHILLE: *b.* St. Germain-en-Laye, Aug. 22, 1862; *d.* Paris, March 25, 1918. Composer. Studied at the Paris Conservatoire; *Grand Prix de Rome,* 1884. His early compositions, which include *L'Enfant prodigue* (1884) and *La Damoiselle élue* (1888, the text translated from Rossetti's *The Blessed Damozel*) show the influence of Massenet, of which there are also traces in some later works. The first notable signs of an individual style appeared with the string quartet (1893) and the orchestral *Prélude à l'Après-midi d'un faune* (1894), written to illustrate a poem by Mallarmé. The kaleidoscopic harmonies and the shifting tone-colours of these works are the counterpart of the elusive style of the impressionist painters and the symbolists in poetry. Debussy's impressionism became the ruling principle of his work, developed on a large scale in the opera *Pelléas et Mélisande*, a setting of Maeterlinck's play (Paris, 1902), and in orchestral works such as *La Mer* (1905), a set of three seascapes. The same elusive treatment is found in his music for the piano, in which he discovered sonorities to which earlier composers had paid little or no attention. For all its power of suggestion, his music is not vague but shows every sign of precise and methodical workmanship. His later chamber music, written during the 1914-18 war, bears the marks of the ill-health which dogged his final years. His critical writing, though sometimes prejudiced, is frank and witty. His principal compositions are:

(a) ORCHESTRA: *Printemps* (1887); *Prélude à l'Après-midi d'un faune* (1894); *Nocturnes* (1899); *La Mer* (1905); *Images* (1912).

(b) CHAMBER MUSIC: String quartet (1893); cello sonata (1915); sonata for flute, viola and harp (1915); violin sonata (1916-17).

(c) PIANO: *Suite bergamasque* (1905); *Pour le piano* (1901); *Estampes* (1903); *Images* (1905 & 1907); *Children's Corner* (1908); *Preludes* (book i, 1910; book ii, 1913); *Études* (1915); *En blanc et noir* for two pianos (1915).

(d) CHORAL WORKS: *L'Enfant prodigue* (1884); *La Damoiselle élue* (1888); *Le Martyre de saint Sébastien* (1911).

(e) OPERA: *Pelléas et Mélisande* (1902).

(f) SONGS: more than 50.

A. CORTOT: *The Piano Music of Debussy* (1922).

C. DEBUSSY: *Monsieur Croche the Dilettante-hater* (1927).

E. LOCKSPEISER: *Debussy* (1936).

O. THOMPSON: *Debussy, Man and Artist* (1937).

L. VALLAS: *Claude Debussy; his Life and Works* (1933). *The Theories of Claude Debussy* (1929).

Decani [deck-ah'-nee], *L.* Lit. "of the dean," *i.e.* that half of the choir in an English cathedral which sits on the dean's side, as opposed to *Cantoris*, the precentor's side. Alternations between the two halves of the choir are common in English cathedral music of all periods. The abbreviations *Dec.* and *Can.* are in common use for *Decani* and *Cantoris*. The traditional English pronunciation is "deck-ain'-eye."

De Castillon. *v.* CASTILLON.

Déchant [day-shūn], *Fr.* Descant.

Decrescendo [deh-creh-shen'-do], *I.* "Decreasing," *i.e.* getting softer, the opposite of *crescendo*. Often abbreviated *decresc.*

Dedekind [day'-deck-int], CONSTANTIN CHRISTIAN: *b.* Reinsdorf, Apr. 2, 1628; *d.* Dresden, Sept. 1715. Poet and prolific composer of sacred and secular songs. Attached to the Dresden court from 1654 to 1675, first as a singer, then as *Konzertmeister*.

Deering. *v.* DERING.

De Falla. *v.* FALLA.

Defesch [der-fesh'], WILLIAM (Willem): *b.* Alkmaar, Aug., 1687; *d.* London, Jan 3, 1761. Flemish composer. Dismissed from his post as *maître de chapelle* at Notre Dame, Antwerp, he came to London, *c.* 1732, where an oratorio by him was performed. His works include concertos and chamber music, among which are several cello sonatas.

Degrees in Music. These are peculiar to universities in the English-speaking world. At Oxford and Cambridge they date from the 15th cent.; they are now awarded by most English universities. The following degrees are found: Bachelor of Music (B.Mus., Mus.B. or Mus.Bac.), Master of Music (M.Mus. or Mus.M.), Doctor of Music (D.Mus., Mus.D., or Mus.Doc.). At Oxford and Cambridge the B.Mus. is a post-graduate degree: at the former the examination consists only of composition, but is open only to those who have gained first- or second-class honours in the B.A. in music; at the latter it embraces also research and performance. At most other universities the B.Mus. corresponds to the B.A. in arts subjects or the B.Sc. in science. At Durham and London it can be taken externally; elsewhere it involves residence. The D.Mus. is an advanced degree, involving normally composition (sometimes with an examination in the history of music as well); at some universities it is awarded also for research or performance. The M.Mus., which exists only at certain universities, is a degree intermediate between the B.Mus. and the D.Mus.; it is also awarded by the Royal College of Music. The Archbishop of Canterbury has the right to confer the degree of Doctor of Music without examination; such a degree is generally known as a Lambeth degree and is represented by the abbreviation D.Mus. Cantuar. The degrees of B.Litt., M.Litt., Ph.D. (at Oxford D. Phil.) or D.Litt. may be awarded for research in music.

In the United States the degree of D.Mus. was until recently awarded only as an honorary degree. At several universities, however, it is now possible to obtain this degree, or A.Mus.D. (Doctor of Musical Arts), by examination. The qualifications for these degrees and for the degrees of B.Mus. and M.Mus. vary considerably from one university to another. The Ph.D. is awarded, as in England, for research.

In Germany there are no degrees specifically for music, though the Ph.D., which is the normal university degree, can be awarded to students who have passed certain examinations and submitted a thesis. In France and Switzerland the Dr. ès Lettres may be awarded for musical research, as for other subjects studied at an advanced level.

C. F. ABDY-WILLIAMS: *A Short Historical Account of the Degrees in Music at Oxford and Cambridge* (1893).

Dehn [dain], SIEGFRIED WILHELM: *b.* Altona, Feb. 25, 1799; *d.* Berlin, Apr. 12, 1858. Musicologist and teacher. From 1842 he was in charge of the music section of the Royal Library at Berlin. He edited a large number of works of the 16th and 17th cent., as well as several of Bach's works, at a time when these were little known. His theoretical works include *Theoretisch-praktische Harmonielehre* (1840) and *Lehre vom Kontrapunkt* (1859). Among his many pupils were Glinka, Cornelius and Anton Rubinstein.

Deidamia [deh-ee-dah-mee'-ah]. Opera in three acts by Handel. Libretto by Paolo Antonio Rolli. First performed, London, Jan. 21, 1741.

Deiters [dite'-erce], HERMANN: *b.* Bonn, June 27, 1883; *d.* Coblenz, May 11, 1907. Writer on music, by profession a schoolmaster and inspector of schools. He edited the third and fourth editions of Jahn's life of Mozart, and translated and revised Thayer's life of Beethoven. He also wrote a life of Brahms, with whom he was intimate, for Count Waldersee's *Sammlung musikalischer Vorträge* (1880, 1898).

De Koven. *v.* KOVEN.

Delannoy [der-la-nwa], MARCEL FRANÇOIS GEORGES: *b.* Ferté-Alais, July 9, 1898. Composer, mainly self-taught, who began his career as a student of painting and architecture. His works include a symphony and 4 operas, including *Le Poirier de misère* (Paris, 1927) and *Puck* (Strasbourg, 1949).

Delibes [der-leeb], CLÉMENT PHILIBERT LÉO: *b.* St. Germain du Val, Feb. 21, 1836; *d.* Paris, Jan. 16, 1891. Opera-composer. Studied at the Paris Conservatoire. He held various opera and organ posts from 1853 to 1872. His best-known works are the operas *Le Roi l'a dit* (Paris, 1873) and *Lakmé* (Paris, 1883) and the ballets *Coppélia* (1870) and *Sylvia* (1876), which contain a wealth of charming light music.

H. DE CURZON: *Léo Delibes* (1927).

Delius, FREDERICK: *b.* Bradford, Jan. 29, 1862; *d.* Grez-sur-Loing, June 10, 1934. English composer, of German parentage, the son of a wool-merchant. Migrated to Florida as an orange-planter, 1884, but abandoned this for music after a year, making a living as teacher and organist. Went to Leipzig to study at the Conservatorium, 1886, and there met Grieg and Sinding. Went to Paris to live with his uncle, 1888, and settled permanently in France. In Paris he met Strindberg, Gauguin, Florent Schmitt and Ravel, and married the artist Jelka Rosen. An orchestral work, *Sur les cimes* (1892), was performed at Monte Carlo in 1893, followed by *Over the hills and far away* (1895) at Elberfeld in 1897. A concert of his works was given in London in 1899, but it was some time before his music became generally known in England. Many of his compositions had their first performance in Germany—among them the operas *Koanga* (Elberfeld, 1904), *A Village Romeo and Juliet* (Berlin, 1907) and *Fennimore and Gerda* (Frankfort, 1919), the orchestral works *Paris* (Elberfeld, 1901), *Appalachia* (Elberfeld, 1904) and *Brigg Fair* (Basle, 1907), and the setting of Whitman's *Sea-Drift* (Essen, 1906). The growth of Delius's popularity in England was due very largely to Sir Thomas Beecham's enthusiasm and unusually intimate understanding of his music: a Delius festival, organized by Beecham, was given in London in 1929. In his later years Delius became blind and paralysed, but with the assistance of Eric Fenby managed to dictate a number of compositions.

Though he was influenced by Grieg in his earlier days, his work falls into no ready-made category. It is marked particularly by a luscious use of shifting chromatic harmonies and by a style which prefers rhapsody to calculated construction; the basis of his melodic style, however, is diatonic and often shows an affinity with folksong. Like many other Romantic composers of his generation he demands an extravagantly large orchestra. His music is, perhaps, most characteristic when it is intimate, but it is also frequently marked by a robust vigour. His principal compositions are:

(a) ORCHESTRA: *Over the hills and far away* (1895); piano concerto (1897, revised 1906); *Paris* (1899); *Appalachia* (1896; revised, with chorus, 1902); *Brigg Fair* (1907); *North Country Sketches* (1914); concerto for violin and cello (1916); violin concerto (1916); *Eventyr* (1917); cello concerto (1921).

(b) CHORAL WORKS: *Sea-Drift* (1903); *A Mass of Life* (1905); *Songs of Sunset* (1907); *Song of the High Hills* (1912); *Requiem* (1916); *Songs of Farewell* (1930).

(c) OPERAS: *Irmelin* (1892); *Koanga* (1897); *A Village Romeo and Juliet* (1901); *Fennimore and Gerda* (1910).

(d) CHAMBER MUSIC: 3 violin sonatas; cello sonata; 2 string quartets.

C. DELIUS : *Frederick Delius* (1935).
E. FENBY : *Delius as I knew him* (1936).
P. HESELTINE : *Frederick Delius* (1923).

Della Corte [del'-lah corr'-teh], ANDREA: *b.* Naples, Apr. 5, 1883. Historian and critic. Music critic, *La Stampa*, 1919; professor of musical history, Liceo Musicale, Turin, 1926. His books are mainly concerned with the history of Italian opera. He has also published, with Guido Pannain, a *Storia della musica dal 1600 al 1900* (1936).

Deller, ALFRED GEORGE : *b.* Margate, May 30, 1912. Counter-tenor. Lay clerk, Canterbury Cathedral, 1940 ; St. Paul's Cathedral, London, 1947. In addition to his valuable services as a cathedral singer he has done much for the revival of late 17th-cent. English music by his brilliant and expressive performance of the solo music of Purcell and his contemporaries. He has also specialized in the performance of lute-songs of the early 17th cent. and has sung in several works by Handel (including operas). His frequent broadcasts and a number of gramophone recordings have familiarized a wide public with the potentialities of the counter-tenor voice and have encouraged others to follow his example.

Dello Joio, NORMAN : *b.* New York, Jan. 24, 1913. Organist, pianist and composer. He has won a number of awards for composition in America and has also appeared frequently as a solo pianist. His compositions include 3 piano sonatas, chamber music, chamber concertos, orchestral works, choral works and ballets.

Delvincourt [del-vãn-coor], CLAUDE: *b.* Paris, Jan. 12, 1888; *d.* Orbetello, Apr. 5, 1954. Composer. Studied under Widor at the Paris Conservatoire; *Grand Prix de Rome*, 1913. Severely wounded in the 1914-18 war, he lost an eye and did not resume composition until 1922. Director, Versailles Conservatoire, 1932; Paris Conservatoire, 1941. He played an active part in the resistance movement in the 1939-45 war. His compositions, which show a capacity for humour and for vivid colouring, include the oriental ballet *L'Offrande à Siva*, the comic opera *La Femme à barbe*, chamber music and songs. He lost his life in a car accident.

Demeur [der-mer], ANNE ARSÈNE: *b.* Saujon, March 5, 1824; *d.* Paris, Nov. 30, 1892. Operatic soprano, whose maiden name was Charton. She married the flautist Jules Antoine Demeur, 1847. First appeared, Bordeaux, 1842. She had a great reputation on the Continent, in England and in America. She was the Béatrice in Berlioz's *Béatrice et Bénédict* (Baden-Baden, 1862) and the Dido in his *Les Troyens à Carthage* (Paris, 1863).

Demi-semiquaver (*Fr.* triple croche, *G.* Zweiunddreissigstel, *I.* biscroma). Half a semiquaver, or the thirty-second part of a semibreve—in America "thirty-second note." A single demi-semiquaver is written

a group of four

Demiton [der-mee-ton], *Fr.* Semitone.

De Monte *v.* MONTE.

Denkmäler der Tonkunst in Bayern [denk′-may-ler dair tone′-co͝onst in by′-ern] (Monuments of Music in Bavaria). A series supplementary to DENKMÄLER DEUTSCHER TONKUNST. The first volume appeared in 1900.

Denkmäler der Tonkunst in Österreich [denk′-may-ler dair tone′-co͝onst in urst′-er-rysh] (Monuments of Music in Austria). A series of publications of old music, analogous to the *Denkmäler deutscher Tonkunst*, including works by foreign composers written in Austria or found in Austrian libraries. It includes six volumes of 15th-cent. music from the so-called TRENT CODICES, operas by Monteverdi, Cesti and Gluck and two volumes of early 18th-cent. Viennese instrumental music. The first volume was published in 1894. The series was interrupted by the *Anschluss* but resumed after the 1939-45 war.

Denkmäler deutscher Tonkunst [denk′-may-ler doytsh′-er tone′-co͝onst] (Monuments of German Music). A series of publications of old music by German composers, including also works by foreign composers resident in Germany. The first volume was published in 1892; the third did not appear till 1900, after the inauguration of the similar *Denkmäler der Tonkunst in Österreich.* The supplementary series *Denkmäler der Tonkunst in Bayern* started in 1900. With the accession to power of the National-Socialist government in 1933 the two series came to an end and were replaced in 1935 by *Das Erbe deutscher Musik* (The Heritage of German Music), subdivided into two series: (1) *Reichsdenkmale* (National Monuments), (2) *Landschaftsdenkmale* (Provincial Monuments).

Denner [denn′-er], JOHANN CHRISTOPH: *b.* Leipzig, Aug. 13, 1655; *d.* Nuremberg, Apr. 20, 1707. A maker of wood-wind instruments at Nuremberg, who, according to Doppelmayr's *Historische Nachricht von den Nürnbergischen Mathematicis und Künstlern* (1730), "invented" the clarinet about 1700, possibly by improving a less artistic instrument already in existence.

Dent, EDWARD JOSEPH: *b.* Ribston, July 16, 1876; *d.* London, Aug. 22, 1957. Historian and critic. Educated at Eton and Cambridge, where he was a pupil of Charles Wood and Stanford. Fellow of King's College, Cambridge, 1902; music critic, *The Athenaeum*, 1919; professor, Cambridge, 1926-41. President, International Society for Contemporary Music, 1922-38; International Society for Musical Research, 1932-49. His lifelong research work was devoted principally to the study of opera. In his capacity as president of two international societies he also did much to foster relations between musicians of different countries and to arouse a lively interest in the music of our time. To the English public he is best known by his idiomatic and often witty translations of operas (in regular use at Sadler's Wells), which have successfully killed the belief that opera in English is absurd. He was responsible for the revival of many neglected works at Cambridge, including Mozart's *Die Zauberflöte* (1911) and Purcell's *The Fairy Queen* (1920). His books include *Alessandro Scarlatti, his Life and Works* (1905), *Mozart's Operas* (1913; 2nd ed. 1947), *Foundations of English Opera* (1928), *Ferruccio Busoni* (1933), *Handel* (1934). A bibliography of his writings by L. Haward was published in the *Music Review*, Nov. 1946.

Denza [den'-tsah], LUIGI: *b.* Castellamare di Stabia, Feb. 24, 1846; *d.* London, Jan. 26, 1922. Composer of a single opera, *Wallenstein* (Naples, 1876), and more than 500 songs, but remembered only for his Neapolitan song "Funiculì funiculà" (1880), which Richard Strauss borrowed in his orchestral fantasia *Aus Italien* (1887). He was resident in London from 1879, and a teacher of singing at the R.A.M. from 1898.

Der. For German titles beginning thus see the second word of the title.

De Reszke. *v.* RESZKE.

Dering (Deering), RICHARD : *d.* London, March, 1630. English composer, who studied in Italy, possibly because he was an illegitimate child. Organist, English Convent of the Blessed Virgin, Brussels, 1617 ; organist to Queen Henrietta Maria of England, 1625. His motets and *canzonette* were published in Antwerp. A further volume of two-part and three-part motets with *basso continuo* was published in London in 1662. He also wrote music for viols. Modern editions of several motets and *The Cryes of London* by J. F. Bridge.

Des [dess], *G.* D flat ($D\flat$).

De Sabata. *v.* SABATA.

Descant (*Fr.* déchant). A translation of the medieval Latin *discantus*, lit. "a different song."

(1) A melodic line, or counterpoint, added to an existing melodic line (*cantus prius factus*), whether extempore or on paper.

(2) Music in which one or more counterpoints of this kind are added, *i.e.* the art of polyphony. In modern works often spelt "discant" as nearer to the Latin, and also to distinguish it from (5) and (6).

(3) In particular, 13th-cent. polyphony in mensural rhythm, as opposed to the freely melismatic style of 12th-cent. *organa*.

(4) The name "English descant" has been given to English music of the late thirteenth and early fourteenth century written in a simple style based on successions of thirds and sixths. See M. Bukofzer, *Geschichte des englischen Diskants und des Fauxbourdons nach den theoretischen Quellen* (1936). Examples of such music are in A. Hughes, *Worcester Medieval Harmony* (1928).

(5) The upper part of a polyphonic composition (*G.* Diskant). Hence an instrument which plays the upper part, *e.g.* descant recorder, descant viol.

(6) In modern English practice a contrasted melody to be sung simultaneously with one which is already familiar, such as a hymn or folksong; designed particularly for occasions when the voices of trained singers can be combined with those of an audience or congregation, but suitable also for school choirs which can divide into two groups. *v.* COUNTERPOINT, ENGLISH DESCANT, FAUXBOURDON, SIGHT, RECORDER, VIOL.

Descort [dess-corr], *Fr.* *v.* LAI.

Déserteur, Le [ler day-zair-ter], (The Deserter). Opera in three acts by

Monsigny. Libretto by Jean Michel Sedaine. First performed, Paris, March 6, 1769.

Deses [dess'-ĕss], *G.* D double flat (D♭♭).

Désir, Le. *v.* TRAUERWALZER.

Des Knaben Wunderhorn [dess knahb'-ĕn voon'-der-horrn], *G.* (The Boy's Magic Horn). An anthology of German folk poetry, which has been drawn on by several composers, notably Mahler, who set 9 of the poems in his *Lieder und Gesänge aus der Jugendzeit* and a further 12 in *Lieder aus "Des Knaben Wunderhorn."*

Désormière [daze-orrm-yairr], ROGER: *b.* Vichy, Sept. 13, 1898. Conductor and composer. Studied at the Paris Conservatoire. Conductor, Diaghilev Ballet, 1925-30; Opéra-Comique, Paris, 1937; Orchestre National de la Radiodiffusion Française, 1947. He has also composed film music.

Des Prés. *v.* JOSQUIN DES PRÉS.

Dessus [dess-ee], *Fr.* Treble. *Dessus de viole*, treble viol.

Destinn [dess'-tin], EMMY: *b.* Prague, Feb. 26, 1878; *d.* Budějovice, Jan. 28, 1930. Operatic soprano, a pupil of Marie Loewe-Destinn, from who she borrowed her professional name (her real name was Kittl). First appearance, Berlin, 1898; Bayreuth, 1901; London, 1904; New York, 1908. Sang Minnie at the first performance of Puccini's *La Fanciulla del West* (New York, 1910). After the 1914-18 war she changed her name to Destinnova. In addition to her outstanding gifts as a singer and actress she was also a dramatist, poet and novelist.

Destouches [day-toosh], ANDRÉ CARDINAL: *b.* Apr. 1662; *d.* Paris, Feb. 7, 1749. Opera-composer. He became a pupil of Campra, having previously been a sailor and a soldier. His first work, *Issé* (Fontainebleau, 1697), a *pastorale héroïque*, was very successful. He later wrote several operas and ballets, solo cantatas with orchestra, and church music. He was much favoured by Louis XIV and held several posts under him, including the directorship of the opera. Modern editions of *Issé*, *Omphale* (opera) and *Les Éléments* (ballet) in the collection *Chefs d'oeuvre classiques de l'opéra français.*

Dett, ROBERT NATHANIEL: *b.* Drummondsville, Oct. 11, 1882; *d.* Battle Creek, Oct. 2, 1943. Composer and pianist. Studied at Eastman School of Music, Rochester (N.Y.) and in Paris with Nadia Boulanger. Teacher at Hampton Institute, Virginia, from 1913 and director of the choir. His compositions include several choral works, among them the oratorio *The Ordering of Moses* (1937). He was active in the study of negro music and in promoting the interests of negro musicians.

Dettingen Te Deum. A setting by Handel for soli, chorus and orchestra, written to commemorate the victory at Dettingen (June 26, 1743) and first performed Nov. 27, 1743. Much of the music is borrowed or adapted from a *Te Deum* by Francesco Antonio Urio (modern edition by F. Chrysander); for the contrary opinion that Urio's work is actually by Handel see P. Robinson, *Handel and his Orbit* (1908).

Deutsch. *v.* DEUTSCHER TANZ.

Deutsch [doytsh], OTTO ERICH: *b.* Vienna, Sept. 5, 1883. Austrian bibliographer, who has made a special study of Schubert. Librarian of the Hoboken collection of facsimiles of musical manuscripts, Vienna, 1926-35; now resident in Cambridge. Author of *The Schubert Reader: A Life of Franz Schubert in Letters and Documents* (1947; trans. by Eric Blom); *Handel: A Documentary Biography* (1954); ed. the series *Musikalische Seltenheiten;* many articles in music publications.

Deutscher Tanz [doytsh'-er tunts], *G.* (*I.* danza tedesca). "German dance." In the late 18th and early 19th cent. a brisk dance in waltz time, often known simply as *Deutsch* or *Teutsch.* Examples occur in the works of Mozart, Beethoven and Schubert, *e.g.*:

SCHUBERT, *12 Deutsche Tänze*, No. 3

v. ALLEMANDE, LÄNDLER, WALTZ.

Deutsches Requiem, Ein [ine doytsh′-ĕss rake′-vi-em], *G.* (A German Requiem). A memorial cantata (not a Requiem Mass) for soloists, chorus and orchestra by Brahms, Op. 45. The words are compiled from the German Bible. First performance of Nos. 1-3, Vienna, Dec. 1, 1867; of Nos. 1-4, 6 & 7, Bremen, Apr. 10, 1868; of the complete work, Leipzig, Feb. 18, 1869.

Deux Journées, Les [lay der zhoor-nay] (The Two Days). Opera in three acts by Cherubini, known in English as *The Water Carrier*. Libretto by Jean Nicolas Bouilly. First performed, Paris, Jan. 16, 1800.

Development. The exploiting of the possibilities of thematic material by means of contrapuntal elaboration, modulation, rhythmical variation, etc. In a movement in SONATA FORM the development section follows the exposition (in which the principal themes are stated): it may be short or long, may discuss all the themes of the exposition or select from them, may present them whole or break them up into sections; it may also (less frequently) merely continue the general character of the movement without precise reference to any of the themes of the exposition, and may introduce new themes which have not been heard before. There are also compositions, *e.g.* Sibelius's *Tapiola*, in which practically the whole piece is devoted to the development of a simple theme. In symphonic poems development is often influenced by a programme, *i.e.* it not only presents the themes in new ways and new combinations but illustrates episodes in a story at the same time.

The first movement of Mozart's symphony in G minor, K.550, will serve as a simple example of development. The opening theme of the movement is:

The development, represented here in outline, is concerned entirely with this theme:

f
p
f
p
[Recapitulation]

Devienne [der-vyen], FRANÇOIS: *b.* Joinville, Jan. 31, 1759; *d.* Charenton, Sept. 6, 1803. Flautist, bassoonist and composer. As a young man he was in the service of Cardinal de Rohan. First bassoon at the Théâtre de Monsieur, Paris, from 1789 till his death. He played a prominent part in the music of the Revolution, was a member of the band of the Garde Nationale and became teacher of the flute at the Institut National de Musique (known as the Conservatoire from 1795). He wrote several operas, music for the *fêtes nationales*, concertos for flute, bassoon and horn, *sinfonies concertantes* for various wind instruments and orchestra, and an enormous amount of chamber music. He also published a *Méthode de flute théorique et pratique* (1795) which went into several editions.

Devil and Kate, The. *v.* ČERT A KÁČA.

Devil's Trill, The. *v.* TRILLO DEL DIAVOLO.

Devin du Village, Le [ler der-vañ dee vee-luzh] (The Village Soothsayer). Opera in one act by Rousseau. Libretto by the composer. First performed, Fontainebleau, Oct. 18, 1752. A parody by Charles Simon Favart, *Les Amours de Bastien et Bastienne*, was translated into German by Friedrich Wilhelm Weiskern. Weiskern's version was set by Mozart in 1768 under the title *Bastien und Bastienne*.

Devrient [der-freent'], (1) EDUARD: *b.* Berlin, Aug. 11, 1801; *d.* Karlsruhe, Oct. 4, 1877. Operatic baritone, and subsequently theatre director. Librettist of Marschner's opera *Hans Heiling* (Berlin, 1833), in which he sang the title role. His memoirs of Mendelssohn, *Meine Erinnerungen an Felix Mendelssohn-Bartholdy* (1869), include an account of the revival of Bach's *St. Matthew Passion* in 1829, in which he sang the part of Jesus (*v.* H. T. David & A. Mendel, *The Bach Reader*, pp. 377-86).

(2) WILHELMINE. Wife of (1). *v.* SCHRÖDER-DEVRIENT.

Diabelli [dee-ah-bell'-lee], ANTON: *b.* Mattsee, Sept. 6, 1781; *d.* Vienna, Apr. 7, 1858. Founder of a firm of music-publishers and composer. Chorister at Salzburg, where he was a pupil of Michael Haydn. Subsequently educated in Munich and intended for the priesthood, but abandoned the idea and settled in Vienna, 1803. Became partner in Peter Cappi's publishing firm, 1818; after Cappi's withdrawal the firm became Diabelli and Co., 1824. His first independent publication was the *Vaterländische Kunstverein*, variations by 51 composers on a waltz-theme of his own composition, published in two books: book I consists of 33 variations by Beethoven, Op. 120 (previously published, 1823), book II contains single variations by 50 composers, including Czerny, Hummel, Liszt (aged 12 at the time of publication), Moscheles, W. A. Mozart, jun., Schubert and Tomášek, with a coda by Czerny (*v.* O. E. Deutsch, *Schubert—a Documentary Biography*, pp. 348-51). For the theme *v.* WALTZ.

Diabelli Variations. *v.* DIABELLI.

Diamants de la Couronne, Les [lay dya-mūñ der la coo-ron] (The Crown Diamonds). Opera in three acts by Auber. Libretto by Augustine Eugène Scribe and Jules Henri Vernoy de Saint-Georges. First performed, Paris, March 6, 1841.

Diamond, DAVID LEO: *b.* Rochester, N.Y., July 9, 1915. Composer. Studied at the Cleveland Institute, Eastman School of Music (Rochester) and the Dalcroze Institute (New York). His compositions include 4 symphonies, 2 violin concertos, cello concerto, 3 string quartets and other chamber music, and ballets.

Diapason. (1) In Greek and medieval theory, the interval of the OCTAVE, from *Gr.* διὰ πασῶν χορδῶν, "through all the strings [of the lyre]."

(2) *Fr.* [dya-pa-zoñ]. Tuning-fork. *Diapason normal*, concert pitch. *v.* PITCH.

(3) The generic term for a family of flue-pipes on the organ, which provide the substantial foundation of organ tone. *Open diapason* (*Fr.* principal, montre, *G.* Prinzipal): (1) On the manuals normally of 8 ft. pitch, with metal pipes; (2) on the pedals normally of 16 ft. pitch, with wood or metal pipes. The corresponding stop of 4 ft. pitch is generally called Principal or Octave (*Fr.* prestant, *G.* Oktave, Prinzipal 4 Fuss,

Kleinprinzipal). *Double diapason*: a manual stop of 16 ft. pitch, similar to the Bourdon. *Stopped Diapason*: a manual stop of 8 ft. pitch and a mellow flute-like tone; the pipes are the same length as those of a 4 ft. stop, but being closed at one end sound an octave lower (*v.* ACOUSTICS, ORGAN).

Diaphony (*Gr.* διαφωνία). (1) The original Greek word means "dissonance" (the opposite of συμφωνία, "consonance"), and was used in this sense by some medieval writers.

(2) Used generally by early medieval theorists to describe the simple form of polyphony known as ORGANUM. By the 13th cent., when polyphony had become more elaborate, the Latin word *discantus* was generally preferred (*v.* DESCANT).

Diatonic. In the strict sense used of notes proper to a key, *e.g.* in the key of D major the following notes are diatonic and constitute a diatonic scale:

Any other notes involve accidentals (sharps or flats) and are CHROMATIC. In minor keys the sharpened sixth and seventh are in such common use, though not strictly proper to the key, that they are also regarded as diatonic, *e.g.* in the key of D minor the notes:

are added to the proper diatonic scale:

Diatonic chord, a chord composed of notes proper to the key. *Diatonic harmony*, strictly harmony which employs only diatonic chords; more generally, harmony which is predominantly based on diatonic chords and their association. *Diatonic tetrachord*, in ancient Greek music a descending scale of four notes, the successive intervals being a tone, a tone, and a semitone, *e.g.*:

v. CHROMATIC (1), ENHARMONIC (1).

Dibdin, CHARLES: *b.* Southampton, March, 1745; *d.* London, July 25, 1814. Composer. Chorister, Winchester Cathedral, 1756-9; otherwise self-taught. Sang in several theatrical productions in London and elsewhere, and composed a considerable amount of music for the stage, including a number of sea-songs which made his reputation. His "Tom Bowling" was written for an entertainment called *The Oddities* (1789). His literary works include an entertaining and informative *Musical Tour* (1788) and a record of his *Professional Life* (1803).

Dichterliebe [di*sh*'-ter-leeb-er], *G.* (Poet's Love). Cycle of 16 songs by Schumann, Op. 48 (1840). Words by Heinrich Heine.

Dictionaries of Music. *v.* HISTORY OF MUSIC.

Dido and Aeneas. Opera in three acts by Purcell. Libretto by Nahum Tate. First performed, 1689, "at Mr. Josias Priest's Boarding School at Chelsey." Modern edition by E. J. Dent. Aeneas, fleeing from Troy, takes refuge at Carthage, where he falls in love with the queen, Dido. He is impelled, however, by his destiny to leave Carthage for Italy. Dido, deserted by her lover, dies.

Die. For German titles beginning thus see the second word of the title.

Diepenbrock [dee' - pĕn - brock], ALPHONS: *b.* Amsterdam, Sept. 2, 1862; *d.* there, Apr. 5, 1921. Composer, self-taught, who has had a considerable influence on his contemporaries. His compositions include church music, incidental music for plays, and songs.

Dieren [fun deer'-ĕn], BERNARD VAN: *b.* Dec. 27, 1884; *d.* London, Apr. 24, 1936. Composer, the son of a Dutch father and a French mother. Began his career as a scientist, and did not study composition seriously until he was 20.

Settled in London, 1909, as correspondent of the *Nieuwe Rotterdamsche Courant*, and became naturalized. His compositions, much admired by a limited circle, include a *Chinese Symphony* for soli, chorus and orchestra (1914), a comic opera—*The Tailor* (1917), six string quartets and other chamber music, and numerous songs. His style, alternating between elaborate polyphony and impressionism, remains impersonal. His volume of essays, *Down among the Dead Men* (1935), a substantial part of which is devoted to memories of Busoni, is provocative, verbose and sometimes violent.

Dièse [dyez], *Fr.* Sharp (♯).

Dies Irae [dee'-ace ee'-ry], *L.* (Day of wrath). An early 13th-cent. sequence, the words of which are attributed to Thomas of Celano. It forms part of the *Missa pro defunctis*, or Requiem Mass. The plainsong melody begins as follows:

16th-cent. composers who wrote Requiem Masses generally preferred not to set the " Dies Irae " but to leave it to be sung to the plainsong melody. In common with the rest of the Requiem Mass it was set to new music, often of a dramatic character, by later composers, *e.g.* Mozart, Berlioz, Verdi.

The plainsong melody has been used in orchestral and choral works by several modern composers, *e.g.* Berlioz, *Symphonie fantastique* (1830); Liszt, *Totentanz* (1849); Rachmaninov, *Rhapsody on a Theme of Paganini* (1936).

Diesis (*Gr.* δίεσις). (1) In Pythagorean theory the difference between a fourth and two " major " tones (*v.* TONE), *i.e.* a semitone slightly smaller than that of the scale based on the harmonic series. Also known as *limma* (*Gr.* λειμμα).

(2) In Aristotelian theory the quarter-tone of the enharmonic tetrachord. *v.* ENHARMONIC.

(3) In modern acoustics the *great diesis* is the interval between four minor thirds, *i.e.*

$$\left(\frac{6}{5}\right)^4 = \frac{1296}{625}:$$

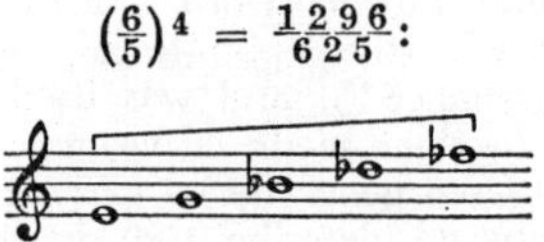

and an octave, *i.e.*

$$\frac{2}{1}:$$

by this reckoning F♭ is sharper than E, and the interval is

$$\frac{1296}{625} \div 2 = \frac{648}{625}$$

The *enharmonic diesis* is the interval between an octave, *i.e.*

$$\frac{2}{1}$$

and three major thirds, *i.e.*

$$\left(\frac{5}{4}\right)^3 = \frac{125}{64}$$

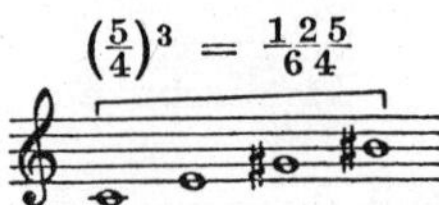

By this reckoning B♯ is flatter than C, and the interval is

$$2 \div \frac{125}{64} = \frac{128}{125}$$

v. HARMONIC SERIES, TEMPERAMENT.

(4) *I.* [dee-eh'-siss]. Sharp (♯).

Dietrich [dee'-tri*sh*], (1) ALBERT HERMANN: *b.* Golk, Aug. 28, 1829; *d.* Berlin, Nov. 20, 1908. Composer, a pupil and friend of Schumann. He collaborated with Schumann and

Brahms in writing a violin sonata for Joachim, 1853: the four movements are (1) Allegro, A minor (Dietrich); (2) Intermezzo, F major (Schumann); (3) Scherzo, C minor (Brahms); (4) Finale, A minor and major (Schumann). Conductor, Bonn, 1855; Oldenburg, 1861-90. His compositions include two operas—*Robin Hood* (Frankfort, 1879) and *Das Sonntagskind* (Bremen, 1886), a symphony, concertos for horn, violin and cello, choral works, piano pieces and songs. In collaboration with J. V. Widmann he published a memoir of Brahms, *Erinnerungen an J. Brahms* (1898; English ed., 1899).

(2) SIXT: *b.* Augsburg, *c.* 1492; *d.* St. Gall, Oct. 21, 1548. German composer. Chorister at Constance, returning there as teacher in the choir-school, 1517. A prominent adherent of the Reformation. Composed a considerable quantity of church music. Five pieces were printed by Glareanus in his *Dodecachordon* (1547; modern ed. in R. Eitner, *Publikationen älterer . . . Musikwerke*, xvi-xviii, 1899). For songs by him published in Georg Rhau's *Newe deudsche geistliche Gesenge* (1544) see *D.D.T.*, xxxiv.

Dieupart [dyer-parr], CHARLES: *d.c.* 1740. Composer, violinist and harpsichordist. Settled in London and took an active part in the introduction of Italian opera to England at the beginning of the 18th cent. He also gave concerts (*v. The Spectator*, nos. 258 & 278) and was in demand as a teacher. He published for the harpsichord *Six suittes de clavessin*, which were clearly known to Bach, who made a copy of No. 6 in F minor (*v.* ENGLISH SUITES).

Diferencia [dee-feh-ren'-thee-ah], *Sp.* In the 16th cent. a variation. Many sets of *diferencias* were written for lute and keyboard instruments by Spanish composers in the latter half of the century, and these are supposed to have influenced English composers in the composition of variations for the virginals.

Difference Tone. A faint note resulting from the difference between the frequencies of two notes sounded simultaneously. *v.* ACOUSTICS, COMBINATION TONE.

Diminished Interval. A perfect or minor interval reduced by flattening the upper note or sharpening the lower, *e.g.*:

Perfect fifth:

Diminished fifth:

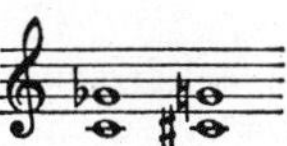

Minor seventh:

Diminished seventh:

On keyboard instruments diminished intervals are indistinguishable from the augmented or major interval immediately below, *e.g.*:

Diminished fifth:

sounds the same as augmented fourth:

Diminished seventh:

sounds the same as major sixth:

The harmonic function of the intervals, however, remains distinct.

Diminished Seventh Chord. A chord composed of three minor thirds, or a diminished triad with a diminished seventh superimposed, *e.g.*

By means of enharmonic changes, *e.g.* writing G♯ for A♭, a chord of this kind can be used as a transition to any major or minor triad, *e.g.*:

Diminished Triad. A minor triad with the fifth flattened, *e.g.*:

Minor triad:

Diminished triad:

The triad on the seventh note of the major scale, *e.g.* in the key of C major :

is the only diminished triad proper to the key; all others require accidentals. In minor keys the same triad occurs if the seventh note is sharpened, and the triad on the second note of the scale is also diminished, *e.g.* in the key of C minor :

Diminuendo [dee-meen-oo-en ′-do], *I.* "Diminishing the tone," *i.e.* getting softer. Often abbreviated *dim.* or *dimin.*

Diminution. (1) The presentation of a theme in notes of smaller value, *e.g.*:

HANDEL, *Messiah*

v. AUGMENTATION, CANON.

(2) In 16th- and 17th-cent. music the ornamentation of a simple melodic line, in vocal or instrumental music, by breaking it up into notes of smaller value. Such ornamentation was often improvised and was applied to the separate parts of a polyphonic composition as well as to solo pieces. We may take as an example the opening o a five-part *chanson* by Lassus (1560):

Complete Works, vol. xiv, p. 29

followed by three different adaptations of the text:

AMMERBACH, *Orgel oder Instrument Tabulatur* (1571)

BASSANO, *Motetti, Madrigali et Canzoni francese . . . diminuiti* (1591)

A. GABRIELI, *Canzoni alla Francese*, book V (1605)

v. DIVISION.

Di molto [dee moll'-to], *I.* "Extremely." *Allegro di molto*, extremely fast.

D'Indy. *v.* INDY.

Di nuovo [dee noo-o'-vo], *I.* "Again." *Poi a poi di nuovo vivente*, gradually getting lively again.

Dioclesian. Opera with dialogue, adapted from Beaumont and Fletcher by Thomas Betterton. Music by Purcell. First performed, London, 1690. The full title is *The Prophetess, or the History of Dioclesian.* Diocles (later Dioclesian), a Roman soldier, fulfils a prophecy by killing the murderer of the late emperor, and becomes emperor himself. Victorious over the Persians, he hands over the empire to his nephew Maximinian. Maximinian, who is jealous of Dioclesian's popularity, attempts to kill him but is prevented by the prophetess, Delphia. The opera concludes with an elaborate masque, designed as an entertainment for Dioclesian.

Diplomas in Music. Certificates of proficiency awarded by colleges of music or accredited bodies after examination in performance, theoretical subjects, composition or teaching. They may also be conferred *honoris causa* on persons who have rendered services to a particular institution or to music in general. Most of them are open to external as well as internal students. There is no absolute consistency in the nomenclature of diplomas: thus the A.R.C.M. (Associate of the Royal College of Music) and L.R.A.M. (Licentiate of the Royal Academy of Music) represent approximately the same standard. Reputable diplomas are those recognized by the Incorporated Society of Musicians. A diploma represents the achievement of a certain standard in a specific branch of music; it is no guarantee of ability in any other branch or of a wide knowledge of music in general. The pursuit of diplomas by persons whose interest in music is confined to examinations is one of the disturbing features of musical life in England.

Direct. A sign rather like an ornamental W, formerly used in manuscripts and printed music, (1) at the end of a line or page, to indicate in advance the pitch of the next note, (2) in the middle of a line, to draw the performer's attention to a change of clef (*L.* custos).

Thus, if the following example were the end of a line, the sign would indicate that the first note of the next line would be D:

Accidentals can be added, exactly as if the sign were an actual note. The practice is now obsolete except in examination papers and incomplete musical quotations in books, where it indicates what the next note would be if it were printed, though without, of course, specifying its duration.

Dirigent [dee-ree-gent′], *G.* Conductor.

Diruta [dee-roo′-tah], GIROLAMO: *b.* Deruta, *c.* 1560. Organist and teacher, a pupil of Zarlino, Porta and Merulo. Organist, Chioggia Cathedral, 1597; Gubbio Cathedral, 1609. One of the foremost players of his time, known today by his elaborate treatise on organ-playing, written in the form of a dialogue, *Il Transilvano* (2 vols., 1597 & 1609). *v.* E. Dannreuther, *Musical Ornamentation*, and O. Kinkeldey, *Orgel und Klavier in der Musik des* 16. *Jahrhunderts* (1910).

Dis [diss], *G.* D sharp (D♯).

Discant. *v.* DESCANT.

Discantus [diss-cahn′-tooss], *L.* Descant. *Discantus supra librum*, "descant on the book," *i.e.* the improvisation of a counterpoint to an existing melody—a practice common from the Middle Ages to the end of the 16th cent. *v.* SIGHT.

Discord. A combination of notes which includes at least one dissonant interval. In popular use applied to music in which the relationship between a series of dissonances is not intelligible to the listener, *e.g.* in the familiar phrase "Modern music is all discord." *v.* CONSONANCE, DISSONANCE.

Disis [diss′-iss], *G.* D double sharp (D×).

Diskant [diss-cunt′], *G.* Soprano, treble. *Diskantmesse*, a modern term for a 15th-cent. Mass in which the plainsong, generally freely embroidered, appears not in the tenor but in the upper part. *Diskantschlüssel*, the soprano clef, *i.e.* the C clef on the first line of the stave:

Dissoluto Punito, Il [eel diss-so-loo′-to poo-nee′-toh] (The Rake Punished). *v.* DON GIOVANNI.

Dissonance. Etymologically a jarring sound. The term is incapable of precise definition, since a jarring sound must be judged by the ear, and not all ears agree. The ways in which dissonance can occur, however, remain constant: (1) by introducing a passing note which is dissonant with the rest of the chord, (2) by tying over, or suspending, from one chord a note which is dissonant with the succeeding chord, (3) as an essential note of the chord. If for the sake of argument we regard the major seventh as dissonant, the following examples will illustrate the three types of dissonance:

Historically type 3 is the result of types 1 and 2, *i.e.* dissonances which are familiar as passing notes or suspensions come in time to be accepted without preparation. A series of unprepared dissonances may create difficulties for the listener, if their relationship is unfamiliar or obscure. *v.* CONSONANCE.

Ditson. An American firm of music-publishers in Boston (Mass.). Originally Parker & Ditson (1832), then Oliver Ditson & Co. (1857), after the name of its founder, Oliver Ditson (1811-88).

Dittersdorf [dit′-erce-dorrf], KARL DITTERS VON: *b.* Vienna, Nov. 2, 1739; *d.* Oct. 24, 1799. Violinist and composer, originally Karl Ditters but ennobled in 1773. After having had experience in the private orchestra of Prince von Hildburghausen and the Imperial Opera, became *Kapellmeister* to the Bishop of Grosswardein, 1765-9, and to the Prince Bishop of Breslau, 1769-95. He was one of the most prolific composers of his time. His numerous compositions include 44 operas—among them the still popular *Doktor und Apotheker* (Vienna, 1786), oratorios, Masses, symphonies, concertos, chamber music and piano sonatas. His symphonies include 12 on subjects from Ovid's *Metamorphoses* (modern ed. of 6 of them, 1899). Modern ed. of various instrumental works in *D.T.Ö.*, xliii (2). His autobiography, *Lebensbeschreibung* (1801; English ed., 1896), though marked by an excess of vanity, is an entertaining picture of 18th-cent. life and music. Michael Kelly recalled hearing a string quartet played by Haydn, Dittersdorf, Wanhal and Mozart (*Reminiscences of Michael Kelly*, vol. i, p. 241).

Divertimento [dee-vair-tee-men′-to], *I.* A term originating in the late 18th cent. for a suite of movements for a chamber ensemble or orchestra, designed primarily for entertainment.

Divertissement [dee-vair-teece-mũn], *Fr.* (1) An entertainment in the form of a ballet, with or without songs, interpolated in an opera or play for the sake of variety.

(2) A fantasia on well-known tunes, *e.g.* Schubert's *Divertissement à la hongroise*, Op. 54, for piano duet.

(3) Divertimento.

Divisi [dee-vee′-zee], *I.* "Divided." A term used in the string parts of orchestral music, indicating that a body of players who normally play the same part, *e.g.* 1st violins, are for the time being to play two or more separate parts. Often abbreviated *div.* The end of the division may be indicated by the abbreviation *unis.*, *i.e.* "in unison."

Division. (1) A term current in England in the 17th and 18th cent. for the ornamental elaboration of a simple melodic line, whether for voice or instrument: *cf.* Shakespeare, *Henry IV Part I*, 3. i. 207:

> Thy Tongue
> Makes Welsh as sweet as ditties highly penn'd,
> Sung by a fair queen in a summer's bower,
> With ravishing division, to her lute.

(2) In particular, a variation on a GROUND BASS, written or improvised. The favourite medium for divisions of this kind in 17th-cent. England was a solo bass viol, accompanied by harpsichord or organ, with a second bass viol playing the bass line; but the practice was not restricted to this combination. The standard work is Christopher Simpson's *The Division Violist* (1659); the 2nd ed. (1667) is entitled *The Division Viol.* John Playford published *The Division Violin* (2nd ed., 1685), "containing a collection of divisions upon several grounds for the treble violin, being the first musick of the kind made publick."

v. DIMINUTION.

Division Viol. A bass viol slightly smaller than the normal size, suitable for playing divisions. "A Viol for Division, should be something a lesser size than a Consort Bass; so that the Hand may better command it" (Christopher Simpson, *The Division Viol*, pp. 1-2).

v. DIVISION, VIOL.

Do [do], *Fr. I.* The note C. In French *ut* is more common.

Dobrowen [do-bro-ven′], ISSAY ALEXANDROVICH: *b.* Nishni-Novgorod, Feb. 27, 1894; *d.* Oslo, Dec. 9, 1953. Russian conductor and composer. Studied at the Moscow Conservatoire and the Vienna Akademie der Tonkunst (with Godowsky). Conductor, Imperial Opera, Moscow, 1919; Grosse Volksoper, Berlin, and Dresden Philharmonic Concerts, 1924; State Opera, Sofia, 1927-8; San Francisco Symphony Orchestra, 1930-5. He appeared as guest conductor in several European countries and in America. His compositions include a piano concerto, in which he appeared as soloist, a violin concerto, piano music and songs.

Doctor und Apotheker [dock'-torr ŏŏnt up-o-take'-er] (Doctor and Apothecary). Opera in two acts by Dittersdorf. Libretto by Gottlieb Stephanie. First performed, Vienna, July 11, 1786.

Dodecachordon [doh'-deck-a-corr'-don], *Gr.* Properly *δωδεκάχορδον*, a book published in 1547 by Heinrich Loris, writing under the name Glareanus. So called because it upholds the theory that there were not eight church modes but twelve (*δώδεκα* = twelve, *χορδή* = string), with examples from polyphonic compositions of the late 15th and early 16th cent. and commentaries on them. German translation by P. Bohn, with transcriptions of the examples, in R. Eitner, *Publikationen älterer . . . Musikwerke*, xvi-xviii, 1899. The four additional modes accepted by Glareanus were the Æolian and Hypoaeolian (with final on A) and the Ionian and Hypoionian (with final on C). *v.* MODE.

Dodecaphonic (*Gr.* *δώδεκα*, twelve, *φωνή*, sound). An unnecessary adjective applied by pretentious writers to music written in the TWELVE-NOTE SYSTEM.

Doh. Anglicized form of the Italian *do* (c). In TONIC SOL-FA the 1st note (or tonic) of the major scale.

Dohnányi [dohkh'-nahn-yi], ERNÖ (formerly Ernst von): *b.* Pressburg (Bratislava), July 27, 1877; *d.* February 9, 1960. Composer and pianist, studied at Budapest. The first of his symphonies was performed in Budapest, 1897; in the same year he made his first public appearance as a solo pianist in Berlin. He has frequently toured in Europe and America. Taught the piano at the Berlin Hochschule, 1905-15; Budapest, 1916-19. President, Budapest Philharmonic Society, 1919. Director of music, Hungarian Radio, 1931. Resident in U.S.A. since 1949. His principal compositions, marked by a Brahmsian romanticism and complete technical competence, are:

(a) ORCHESTRA: 3 symphonies; piano concerto; violin concerto; suite in F♯ minor; *Variations on a Nursery Song* for piano and orchestra; *Ruralia Hungarica.*

(b) OPERAS: *Tante Simona* (Dresden, 1913); *A Vajda Tornya* (The Tower of the Voyvod) (Budapest, 1922); *A Tenor* (The Tenor) (Budapest, 1929).

(c) PANTOMIME: *Der Schleier der Pierrette* (The Veil of Pierrette) (Dresden, 1910).

(d) CHAMBER MUSIC: piano quintet; 3 string quartets; violin sonata; cello sonata.

(e) PIANO: 4 rhapsodies; *Winterreigen*; 5 humoreskes; *Suite in the Olden Style*; variations on a Hungarian folksong.

Doktor Faust [dock'-torr fowst]. Opera by Busoni, completed after his death by Philipp Jarnach. Libretto by the composer. First performed, Dresden, May 21, 1925. Intended to be performed in the manner of a puppet play. Faust, practising magic arts at Wittenberg, summons six spirits, the last of whom, Mephistopheles, persuades him to sign a pact. He pays a visit to the court of Parma, where he displays his magic arts and elopes with the Duchess. By the end of the year agreed on with Mephistopheles he is back in Wittenberg, where he intervenes in a quarrel between Catholics and Protestants. In the street he meets a beggar-woman, who proves to be the Duchess; she gives him their dead child and vanishes. By magic Faust manages to transfer his personality to the dead child. At midnight he dies. From the child's body rises a youth with a green twig in his hand.

Dolce [doll'-cheh], *I.* Sweet, gentle. *Dolcissimo*, very sweet.

Dolcian (also Dulcian, Dulzian). One of the names by which the bassoon was known in the 16th and 17th cent., presumably on account of its gentle tone.

Dolente [do-len'-teh], *I.* Sorrowful.

Doles [doh'-lěss], JOHANN FRIEDRICH: *b.* Steinbach, Apr. 23, 1715; *d.* Leipzig, Feb. 8, 1797. Composer and organist. Studied theology at Leipzig University, and while there became a pupil of Bach.

In 1744 he wrote a cantata, *Das Lob der Musik*, to celebrate the first year of the Leipzig Gewandhaus concerts. Cantor, Freiberg, 1744; St. Thomas's, Leipzig, 1756-89. On the occasion of Mozart's visit to Leipzig in 1789 he performed for his benefit Bach's motet *Singet dem Herrn* (*v.* H. T. David & A. Mendel, *The Bach Reader*, pp. 359-60). In 1790 he dedicated to Mozart and J. G. Naumann his cantata *Ich komme vor dein Angesicht*. Among his other compositions, many of which were popular in his day, are Masses, settings of the Passion, cantatas, motets, songs and harpsichord sonatas.

Dolmetsch, (1) ARNOLD: *b.* Le Mans, Feb. 24, 1858; *d.* Haslemere, Feb. 28, 1940. Violinist and instrument-maker, the son of a Swiss father and a French mother. Studied at Brussels with Vieuxtemps. For a short period taught the violin at Dulwich College. Having begun to collect and repair old instruments, he started making harpsichords and clavichords. He was employed by the firm of Chickering in Boston, 1902-9, and by Gaveau in Paris, 1911-14. Returned to England, 1914, and settled in Haslemere, where he inaugurated in 1925 an annual festival of old music, played on the appropriate instruments, in which the members of his family took part. In addition to keyboard instruments he also made viols, lutes and recorders. The present popularity of the recorder is due entirely to his work. He published a valuable account of *The Interpretation of the Music of the XVIIth and XVIIIth Centuries* (1915), supplemented by a volume of examples.

R. DONINGTON : *The Work and Ideas of Arnold Dolmetsch* (1932).

(2) CARL: *b.* Fontenay-sous-Bois, Aug. 23, 1911. Younger son of (1). Recorder-player. As a boy played at the Haslemere Festivals, and has since become the foremost exponent of his instrument. He succeeded his father as director of the Haslemere Festival, and is managing director of the workshops for making old instruments (Arnold Dolmetsch, Ltd.).

Doloroso [do-lo-ro'-zo], *I.* Sorrowful.

Domestic Symphony. *v.*SYMPHONIA DOMESTICA.

Dominant. (1) The fifth degree of the major or minor scale. *Dominant chord* or *dominant triad*, the triad on the dominant, *i.e.* in the key of C major:

Dominant seventh chord, the dominant triad with the addition of a seventh from the bass:

The convention of harmonizing the melodic cadence:

with the dominant and tonic triads dates from the latter half of the 15th cent. This is the so-called perfect cadence or full close. Its air of finality is due to (1) the melodic cadence, sinking by step to the tonic, (2) the upward semitone progression of the leading note (B to C), (3) the juxtaposition of two major triads. This close relationship between the dominant and tonic triads plays an important part in establishing a new key (*v.* MODULATION). The substitution of the dominant seventh chord for the dominant triad in a perfect cadence :

originated in the introduction of the seventh as a passing or ornamental note :

(2) The name given to the reciting note (properly *repercussio*, *tenor* or *tuba*) of each of the Gregorian psalm-tones, and hence to the degree of the scale in each mode on which this note falls. In the authentic modes the dominant is the fifth degree of the scale, except in the third mode (E to E), where it is the sixth degree, in order to avoid the note B. In the plagal modes it is a third below the dominant of the corresponding authentic mode, except in the eighth mode (D to D), where it is a tone below (C instead of B). *v.* MODE, TONE.

Dompe. *v.* DUMP.

Donalda, PAULINE: *b.* Montreal, March 5, 1884. Operatic soprano, whose real name was Lightstone. Studied in Montreal and Paris. Married (1) Paul Seveilhac (2) Mischa Léon. First appeared, Nice, 1904. Sang subsequently in Brussels, London, New York and Paris.

Donato [do-nah′-to], BALDASSARE: *d.* 1603. Organist, composer and singer. He was a member of the choir of St. Mark's, Venice, in 1550. Appointed *maestro di cappella piccola* there, 1562-5; director of the seminar, 1580; *maestro di cappella*, 1590 (succeeding Zarlino). He published a volume of motets and several books of madrigals. Two of his madrigals were printed, with English words, in Yonge's *Musica Transalpina* (1588). Modern editions in L. Torchi, *L'Arte musicale in Italia*, i and A. Einstein, *The Italian Madrigal*, vol. iii.

Don Carlos [don carr′-loss]. Opera in 5 acts by Verdi. Libretto by François Joseph Méry and Camille du Locle (after Schiller's play). First performed, Paris, March 11, 1867. Don Carlos, heir to the Spanish throne, is betrothed to Élisabeth de Valois. He visits France incognito to see her and falls in love. His father, Philip II of Spain, however, decides to marry her himself. One of her ladies-in-waiting, Princess Eboli, is herself in love with Don Carlos. She discovers his love for Élisabeth and determines to have vengeance. Don Carlos espouses the cause of the Flemings and asks to be appointed governor of Flanders. The king refuses, and Don Carlos, who becomes threatening, is disarmed and imprisoned. Through the intrigue of Eboli, the king discovers that Élisabeth was once in love with Don Carlos. He threatens her but repents of his violence. Rodrigo, associated with Don Carlos in supporting the cause of Flanders, is killed. The crowd demands the release of Don Carlos and is prevented from violence only by the arrival of the Grand Inquisitor. Don Carlos, about to escape to Flanders, takes leave of Élisabeth at a monastery where Charles V is buried. The king and the Grand Inquisitor arrive to arrest him, but a monk dressed like Charles V and presumed to be an apparition saves him from his fate.

Don Giovanni [don jo-vahn′-nee]. Comic opera (*dramma giocoso*) in two acts by Mozart. Full title: *Il dissoluto punito, ossia Don Giovanni* (The Rake Punished, or Don Juan). Libretto by Lorenzo da Ponte (after Giovanni Bertati's *Don Giovanni, ossia Il Convitato di Pietra*); *v. Memoirs of Lorenzo da Ponte*, trans. L. A. Sheppard, pp. 152-7. First performed, Prague, Oct. 29, 1787. The scene is laid in Seville. Don Giovanni, in pursuit of Donna Anna, is surprised by her father, the Commendatore, whom he kills. Donna Anna and her lover, Don Ottavio, vow vengeance. Don Giovanni, having further escaped from the recriminations of a former mistress, Donna Elvira, joins a peasant's wedding party, invites them to his house and attempts to seduce the bride, Zerlina. Donna Anna, having met Don Giovanni again and recognized him, denounces him, in company with Donna Elvira and Don Ottavio, but he makes his escape. Don Giovanni persuades his servant, Leporello, to change clothes with him. In this disguise he gives Masetto, Zerlina's betrothed, a beating. Leporello, being left to escort Elvira, is discovered by Don Ottavio, Masetto, Donna Anna and Zerlina. Donna

Elvira, imagining him to be Don Giovanni, pleads for him, declaring that he is her husband; but he reveals himself, and she joins the others in denouncing him. He escapes and meets Don Giovanni in the cemetery, where there is a statute of the Commendatore. Don Giovanni invites the statue to have supper with him, and the answer is "Yes." Meanwhile Don Ottavio offers Donna Anna marriage, but she begs him to wait. At Don Giovanni's supper Donna Elvira makes a last appeal to him but is anwered with ridicule. The statue arrives and Don Giovanni is dragged down to hell. The remaining characters enter and make an appropriate commentary on the situation.

Doni [do'-nee], GIOVANNI BATTISTA: *b.* Florence, 1594; *d.* there, Dec. 1, 1647. Writer on music. Studied the humanities at Bologna and Rome. Visited Paris, 1621-2; entered the service of Cardinal Barberini in Rome, 1623, with whom he visited again Paris and Madrid. In 1640 returned to Florence, and became professor of rhetoric at the university. He made a special study of Greek music and published *Compendio del trattato de' generi e de modi della musica* (1635), *Annotationi sopra il compendio* (1640) and *De praestantia musicae veteris* (1647). A number of miscellaneous works were published posthumously in 2 vols. in 1763. Extracts from his writings dealing with the early history of opera are printed in A. Solerti, *Le origini del melodramma* (1903).

Donizetti [do-nee-tsett'-tee], GAETANO: *b.* Bergamo, Nov. 29, 1797; *d.* there, Apr. 8, 1848. Opera-composer. Studied at Bergamo and Bologna. His first opera, *Enrico, conte di Borgogna*, was performed at Venice in 1818. A prolific composer, he wrote with a rapidity remarkable even for the early 19th cent.; in consequence, his work, though often charming, is generally superficial, depending to a large extent on the virtuosity of the soloists. His best-known works are the serious operas *Lucrezia Borgia* (Milan, 1833), *Lucia di Lammermoor* (Naples, 1835), *La Favorite* (Paris, 1840) and *Linda di Chamounix* (Vienna, 1842), and the comic operas *L'elisir d'amore* (Milan, 1832), *La Fille du régiment* (Paris, 1840) and *Don Pasquale* (Paris, 1843). The last of these is still frequently performed.

Don Juan [don hoo-ahn']. (1) *v.* DON GIOVANNI.

(2) Symphonic poem by Richard Strauss, Op. 20, after a poem by Nicolaus Lenau. First performed, Nov. 11, 1889.

Don Pasquale [don puss-cwah -leh]. Comic opera in three acts by Donizetti. Libretto by the composer and "Michele Accursi," *i.e.* Giacomo Ruffini (after Angelo Anelli's *Ser Marc' Antonio*). First performed, Paris, Jan. 3, 1843. Dr. Malatesta proposes that Don Pasquale, an elderly bachelor, shall marry his sister, who is in fact nothing of the kind but a young lady beloved of Ernesto, Pasquale's nephew. When the marriage contract has been signed, Norina behaves intolerably and embarks on reckless extravagance. In despair Pasquale asks Ernesto to marry Norina in his place, which is precisely what Dr. Malatesta had intended. The plot has been successful, and Ernesto wins his bride.

Don Quichotte [dō̃ kee-shot] (Don Quixote). Opera in five acts by Massenet. Libretto by Henri Cain (based on Cervantes and Jean Le Lorrain's comedy *Le Chevalier de la longue figure*. First performed, Monte Carlo, Feb. 19, 1910.

Don Quixote. (1) *v* DON QUICHOTTE.

(2) Symphonic poem by Richard Strauss, Op. 35, based on Cervantes' novel. Described as *Fantastische Variationen über ein Thema ritterlichen Charakters* (Fantastic variations on a theme of knightly character). It includes an important part for solo cello. First performed, Cologne, March 8, 1898.

Doppelschlag [dop'-ĕl-shlahk], *G.* The ornament known in *E.* as TURN.

Dopper [dop'-per], CORNELIS: *b.* Stadskanal, Feb. 7, 1870; *d.* Amsterdam, Sept. 18, 1939. Composer and conductor. Studied at the Leipzig Conservatorium. Assistant conductor, Amsterdam Concertgebouw, 1908-31. His compositions, which have a strongly marked national flavour, include several operas, 7 symphonies and other orchestral works (including the *Ciaccona gotica*,

1920), choral works, songs, chamber music (including a prize-winning string quartet, 1914) and piano pieces.

Doppio movimento [dop′-yo mo-vee-men′-to], *I.* Twice as fast.

Doppio pedale [dop′-yo peh-dah′-leh], *I.* " Double pedal," a term used in organ music to indicate that the two feet play simultaneously. An outstanding example is Bach's chorale prelude " An Wasserflüssen Babylon " (Novello ed., book xviii, p. 13).

Doret [do-ray], GUSTAVE: *b.* Aigle, Sept. 20, 1866; *d.* Lausanne, Apr. 19, 1943. Composer and conductor. Studied in Berlin and Paris. Active as conductor in Paris and Switzerland. His compositions include several operas, of which the most successful was *Les Armaillis* (Paris, 1906). He also published essays on music.

Dorfmusikanten-Sextett [dorrf′-moo-zee-cunt′-ĕn-zecks-tet′], *G.* *v.* MUSIKALISCHER SPASS.

Dorian Mode. (1) In ancient Greek music:

(2) From the Middle Ages onwards applied to:

The tonic (or final) and dominant are marked respectively T and D. *v.* GREEK MUSIC, MODE.

Dorian Toccata. The name given to an organ toccata in D minor by Bach (Novello ed., book x, p. 196), presumably because there is no B♭ in the signature. (*v.* DORIAN MODE.)

Dorn [dorrn], HEINRICH LUDWIG EGMONT: *b.* Königsberg, Nov. 14, 1804; *d.* Berlin, Jan. 10, 1892. Composer, conductor, teacher and critic. Studied in Königsberg and Berlin, and held various posts as teacher and conductor. Conductor of the Royal Opera, Berlin (in succession to Nicolai), 1849-69. Schumann studied counterpoint with him at Leipzig, 1830-2 (*v.* F. Niecks, *Robert Schumann*, pp. 106-112). Among his numerous operas was *Die Nibelungen* (Berlin, 1854), written independently of Wagner, of whom he was a severe critic. He published his memoirs and collected essays under the title *Aus meinem Leben* (1870-9).

Dot. (1) Written above or below a note, *e.g.*

(*a*) it normally indicates STACCATO, *i.e.* the following passage:

is played approximately:

(*b*) In 18th-cent. violin music a series of dots with a slur, *e.g.*:

indicates that the notes are to be detached but without changing the bow. The normal notation today is:

(*c*) In 18th-cent. clavichord music a series of dots with a slur, placed over or under a single note:

indicates the BEBUNG, *i.e.* the gently repeated movement of the finger on the key which produces an effect similar to the vibrato of a guitar.

(*d*) In 18th-cent. French music it often

has a rhythmical significance: *v.* 2 (iv) below.

(2) Written after a note it indicates a prolongation of the normal length by one-half. Hence:

In older music the dot was used to indicate such a prolongation not only within a bar but also beyond a bar-line, *e.g.*:

This practice was still used by Brahms but is now obsolete.

The double dot, first suggested by Leopold Mozart in 1756 (*v.* his *Treatise on the Fundamental Principles of Violin Playing*, trans. Editha Knocker, p. 42), indicates a prolongation of the normal length by three-quarters, *e.g.*:

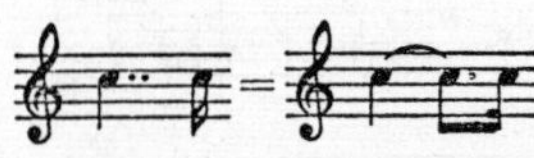

The dot and double dot are also used after rests, though less frequently after semibreve and minim rests than after those for the crotchet, quaver and semi-quaver, *e.g.*:

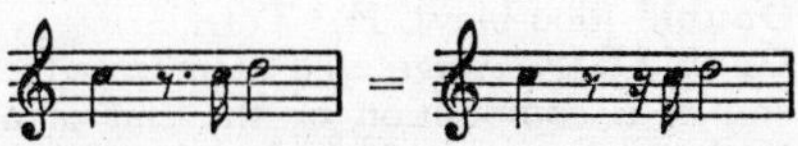

In music of the 17th and early 18th cent. the use of the dot was neither precise nor consistent. A number of theorists of the period deal with the ambiguity and give advice on interpretation. The following points should be noted:

(i) In passages of the following kind:

a dot is assumed after the rest, and the first note loses half its written value, *i.e.* the interpretation is:

A good example of this convention is the chorus "Surely he hath borne our griefs" in Handel's *Messiah.*

(ii) In movements where triplets occur consistently, the rhythm

is generally, though not invariably, to be interpreted as

e.g.:

BACH, *Brandenburg Concerto No. 5*

is to be played:

(iii) In general, however, the value of a dotted note is to be prolonged, and the value of the subsequent note or notes reduced accordingly. This applies particularly to dotted quavers and dotted semiquavers, but it may also apply to dotted crotchets. Much depends on the character and tempo of the piece. It was with the object of providing a precise notation for this convention that Leopold Mozart invented the double dot.

(iv) In French music, and music in the French style, it became the fashion to play successions of quavers or semiquavers (sometimes also crotchets) unevenly, *i.e.* alternately long and short. In certain cases this would mean that

would be played

but the lengthening was not always so considerable, and cannot in fact be exactly represented in notation. Notes which were to be altered in this way were called *notes inégales*, and the rhythm was termed *pointé*. Where alteration of rhythm was not required, the notes often had dots over them, or were marked *notes égales*.

(3) In the notation of late medieval and Renaissance music (roughly from 1300 to 1600) the dot was used (*a*) as in modern notation, to prolong by half the value of an "imperfect" note (*e.g.* a semibreve equal to two minims); (*b*) to clarify, where necessary, the notation of triple time by performing the function of a modern bar-line, *i.e.* by separating off one group of three equal notes (or its equivalent) from another. *v.* MENSURAL NOTATION.

R. T. DART: *The Interpretation of Music* (1951).

Double. (1) *E.* An octave lower, *e.g.* double bassoon, built an octave lower than the bassoon; double diapason, an organ stop sounding an octave lower than the DIAPASON.

(2) *E.* Prefixed to an instrument it may also signify one that combines two instruments in one, *e.g.* double horn, an instrument which combines the essential features of a horn in F and a horn in B♭ alto (*v.* HORN).

(3) *Fr.* [doobl]. An 18th-cent. term for a variation (of an air or dance movement), consisting primarily of melodic ornamentation or new figuration, *e.g.*:

SARABANDE

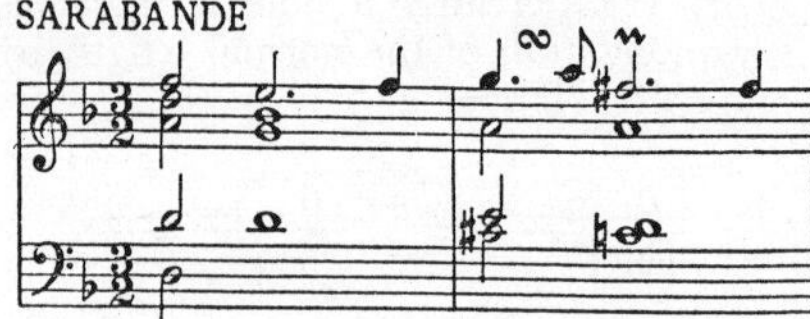

DOUBLE

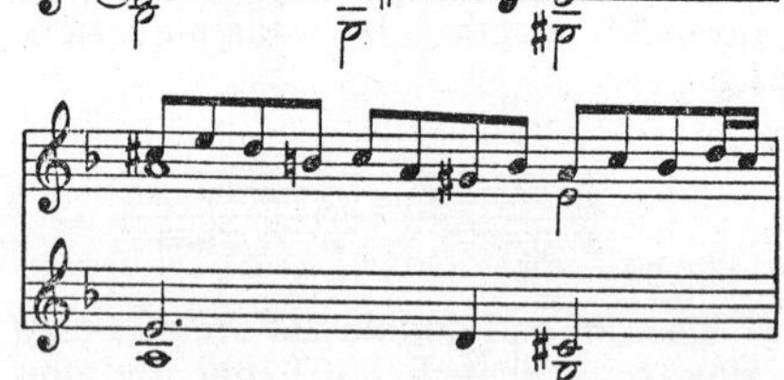

BACH, *English Suite No. 6*

A set of such variations would be labelled Double I, Double II, Double III, etc.

Doublé [doo-blay], *Fr.* Turn.

Double Bar. A sign used to indicate the end of a composition or the end of a section:

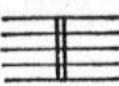

It is not necessarily equivalent to a bar-line, as it may occur in any part of a bar. It is often accompanied by dots indicating that the preceding or succeeding section or both are to be repeated :

Double Bass (*Fr.* contrebasse, *G.* Kontrabass, *I.* contrabasso). The largest bowed string instrument and the foundation of the string ensemble. In shape it differs from the other members of the violin family, being modelled on the old double-bass viol (or *violone*)—the sloping shoulders are a characteristic feature. Music for it is written an octave higher than the real sounds, in order to avoid the constant use of leger lines. The modern instrument has four, sometimes five, strings. If there are four strings they are generally tuned:

(sounding an octave lower), though some players prefer:

If there are five strings they are tuned:

or even:

In orchestral music before about 1800 the parts for cellos and double basses are very largely identical (apart from the difference in pitch), except that the cellos often play without the double basses. In more recent music the association of the two instruments has continued down to the present day, but there has been an increasing tendency to exploit the independence of the cellos. Extended passages for double basses alone, without any other instruments, are relatively uncommon: a good example occurs in the last act of Verdi's *Otello*, where Othello enters to murder Desdemona:

In chamber music the double bass has rarely been used, apart from works for large ensembles, such as Schubert's octet. Examples include Schubert's "Trout" quintet for violin, viola, cello, double bass and piano, Dvořák's quintet in G major for 2 violins, viola, cello and double bass, and van Dieren's quartet No. 4 for 2 violins, viola and double bass.

Double Bassoon (*Fr.* contrebasson, *G.* Kontrafagott, *I.* contrafagotto). A double-reed instrument, of wood or metal, built an octave lower than the BASSOON.

Double Cadence [doobl ca-dünce], *Fr.* Turn.

Double Chant. An Anglican chant consisting of four sections, to which two verses of a psalm or canticle are to be sung. *v.* CHANT.

Double Concerto. A concerto for two solo instruments and orchestra, *e.g.* Brahms's concerto for violin, cello and orchestra, Op. 102.

Double Counterpoint. The name given to invertible counterpoint in two parts. It consists in adding to an existing melody a second melody which will fit equally well above or below the first. In theory the added melody can move up or down any interval to its new position, but in practice the commonest intervals are those of the octave, tenth and twelfth. It is not uncommon for the first melody to move at the same time an octave, or even two octaves, in the opposite direction, either to prevent a crossing of parts, or to make room for additional parts in between. Double counterpoint occurs frequently in fugues, since the COUNTER-SUBJECT may be required to enter above the subject in one place and below it in another.

(a) Double counterpoint at the octave:

BACH, *Two-Part Inventions, No. 9*

(b) Double counterpoint at the tenth:

BACH, *Art of Fugue*

(c) Double counterpoint at the twelfth:

BACH, *Ibid.*

Double croche [doobl crosh], *F.* Semiquaver.

Double Diapason. *v.* DIAPASON (3).

Double Flat. The sign ♭♭, indicating that the pitch of the note to which it is prefixed is to be lowered two semitones, *e.g.* on a keyboard instrument

will sound the same as

v. FLAT.

Double Fugue. (1) Properly, a fugue in which a new theme is introduced in the course of the piece and after being itself treated fugally is finally combined with the original subject, to which it forms in fact a countersubject.

(2) The name sometimes given to a fugue in which the subject and countersubject appear simultaneously at the beginning and are regularly associated throughout the piece. *v.* FUGUE.

Double Reed. Two pieces of cane, the lower and thicker ends being bound round a metal tube, while the upper ends, which are very thin, practically meet, leaving however a small aperture through which the player's breath is forced. This method of tone production is used in the oboe, cor anglais, heckelphone, bassoon, double bassoon and sarrusophone.

Double Sharp. The sign ×, indicating

that the pitch of the note to which it is prefixed is to be raised two semitones, *e.g.* on a keyboard instrument

will sound the same as

v. SHARP.

Double Stop. A chord of two notes played on a bowed string instrument (such as the violin) by using two adjacent strings. The name is applied not only to chords where both the notes are stopped with the finger, but also to those in which one or both can be played on an open string.

Double Tonguing. A means of achieving a rapid articulation of successive notes (particularly repeated notes) on the flute and brass instruments. It consists in articulating alternately the consonants T and K. It is not possible on reed instruments, such as the oboe, clarinet and bassoon, where the mouthpiece is held inside the mouth. *v.* TRIPLE TONGUING.

Double Touch. A system employed by some modern organ-builders, by which a heavier pressure on the keys can be used to bring into action new registration, without the necessity for changing stops. In this way it is possible for a solo and accompaniment to be played on the same manual in two contrasted tone-colours. The system is common on cinema organs.

Dowland, (1) JOHN: *b.* 1563; *d.* Jan. 1626. Composer and lutenist. From 1580 to 1584 in the service of the English Ambassador at Paris, where he became a Roman Catholic. Graduated B.Mus. at Oxford, 1588. Unsuccessful in obtaining a place at the English court in 1594, on account of his religion, he travelled widely on the Continent. His *First Booke of Songes or Ayres* was published in 1597, followed in due course by three further collections. Lutenist to Christian IV of Denmark, 1598-1607. In the service of Lord Walden, 1612; of James I and Charles I, 1612-26. He had a great reputation both as a performer and as a composer. His four books of ayres are the most important English contribution to the literature of the solo song with lute accompaniment; modern ed.: (1) for solo voice and lute, *E.S.L.S.*, 1st ser., (2) songs for 4 voices, with lute, *Musica Britannica*, vi. He also published a collection of instrumental ensemble music, under the title *Lachrimae, or Seaven Teares figured in seaven passionate Pavans* (1605): modern edition by P. Warlock. A number of ensemble pieces and lute solos were published in foreign collections, but much of his lute music survives only in manuscript (see *The Lute Music of John Dowland*, ed. P. Warlock).

(2) ROBERT: *b. c.* 1585; *d.* 1641. Son of (1). Lutenist and composer. Succeeded his father as lutenist to Charles I, 1626. Published *Varietie of Lute-Lessons* (1610) and edited *A Musical Banquet* (1610), a collection of songs in several languages.

R. NEWTON: "English Lute Music of the Golden Age" (*Proceedings of the Musical Association*, 1938-9).

P. WARLOCK: *The English Ayre* (1926).

Draeseke [dray′-zeck-er], FELIX AUGUST BERNHARD: *b.* Coburg, Oct. 7, 1835; *d.* Dresden, Feb. 26, 1913. Composer and writer on music, one of the followers of Liszt. Studied at Leipzig Conservatorium, and held various teaching appointments. In addition to his numerous compositions, which include 4 symphonies and several operas, he wrote treatises on the theory of music and essays on Liszt and Cornelius.

Draghi [drah′-gee], (1) ANTONIO: *b.* Rimini, 1635; *d.* Vienna, Jan. 16, 1700. Composer. In the service of the Imperial Court of Vienna from 1658 onwards (*Kapellmeister* from 1682). One of the most prolific composers of his time, he wrote an enormous number of operas and oratorios, and also some opera librettos. Selected church music in *D.T.Ö.*, xxiii (1).

(2) GIOVANNI BATTISTA: *d. c.* 1710. Italian musician, resident in London in the Restoration period (*v.* Pepys, *Diary*, Feb. 12, 1667). Successively master of Charles II's Italian musicians, organist to Catharine of Braganza, and organist to

James II's Roman Catholic chapel. His compositions include a setting of Dryden's ode for St. Cecilia's day, *From Harmony, from heavenly Harmony.*

Dragonetti [drah-go-net'-tee], DOMENICO: *b.* Venice, Apr. 7, 1763; *d.* London, Apr. 16, 1846. Double-bass virtuoso and composer. As a young man appointed to St. Mark's, Venice. Came to London in 1794, and played in opera and concerts there until his death. Throughout this period he played with the cellist Robert Lindley. He had a great reputation, and was acquainted with both Haydn and Beethoven.

Drdla [derrd'-la], FRANZ: *b.* Saar, Nov. 28, 1868; *d.* Gastein, Sept. 3, 1944. Czech violinist and composer. He wrote two operas, but is best known by his violin solos, some of which have become widely popular.

Dream of Gerontius, The. Oratorio by Elgar, op. 38. Text taken from the poem by Cardinal Newman. First performed, Birmingham Festival, Oct. 3, 1900.

Drehleier [dray'-ly-er], *G.* Hurdy-gurdy.

Dreigroschenoper, Die [dee dry'-grosh-ĕn-ope-er] (The Threepenny Opera). Opera with a prologue and eight scenes, a modern version of John Gay's *The Beggar's Opera*, founded on a German translation by Elisabeth Hauptmann. Lyrics by Bert Brecht (who also used ballads by François Villon and Rudyard Kipling); music by Kurt Weill. First performed, Berlin, Aug. 31, 1928.

Dresden [dress'-dĕn], SEM: *b.* Amsterdam, Apr. 20, 1881; *d.* 1957. Composer, conductor and critic. Studied at the Amsterdam Conservatoire, and in Berlin with Pfitzner. Teacher of composition, Amsterdam Conservatoire, 1919; director, 1924; director, Royal Conservatoire, The Hague, 1937-40, 1945-9. He has also been active as conductor of madrigal societies. His compositions include orchestral works, chamber music and songs.

Dreyschock [dry'-shock], (1) ALEXANDER: *b.* Zak, Oct. 15, 1818; *d.* Venice, April 1, 1869. Czech pianist and composer, a pupil of Tomášek. He toured Europe as a soloist for many years, and taught at the St. Petersburg Conservatoire, 1862-8.

(2) FELIX: *b.* Leipzig, Dec. 27, 1860; *d.* Berlin, Aug. 1, 1906. Son of (3). Pianist, teacher and composer.

(3) RAIMUND: *b.* Zak, Aug. 30, 1824; *d.* Leipzig, Feb. 6, 1869. Brother of (1). Violinist. Teacher of the violin at the Leipzig Conservatorium and one of the leaders of the Gewandhaus Orchestra.

Dringend [dring'-ĕnt], *G.* Pressing onwards, urgent.

Drohend [droh'-ĕnt], *G.* Threatening.

Drone. The lower pipes of the bagpipe, each of which produces a single persistent note.

Drone Bass. A bass part which imitates the drone of a bagpipe by remaining on the same note, *e.g.* the opening of the finale of Haydn's symphony No. 104 in D major:

Drum. For the various kinds of drum used in the orchestra *v.* BASS DRUM, SIDE DRUM, TABOR, TENOR DRUM, TIMPANI.

Drum Mass. *v.* PAUKENMESSE.

Drum Roll Symphony (*G.* Symphonie mit dem Paukenwirbel). Symphony No. 103 in E♭ major by Haydn (1795), so called because the first movement begins with a timpani roll (*Paukenwirbel*), which also recurs shortly before the end of the movement.

Drysdale, LEARMONT: *b.* Edinburgh, Oct. 3, 1866; *d.* there, June 18, 1909. Scottish composer. Studied at the R.A.M. His compositions, which are better known in Scotland than in England, include operas, cantatas and orchestral pieces. The overture *Tam o' Shanter* (1890) was awarded a prize by the Glasgow Society of Musicians.

Düben [dēēb'-ĕn]. A family of musicians of German origin who settled in Sweden in the 17th cent. The most important are:

(1) ANDREAS (Anders): *b. c.* 1590; *d.* Stockholm, 1662. Son of Andreas D., organist of St. Thomas's, Leipzig. Studied with Sweelinck in Amsterdam, 1614-20. Court organist, Stockholm, 1621; *Kapellmeister*, 1640. His compositions include an 8-part motet, "Pugna triumphalis," for the burial of Gustavus Adolphus.

(2) GUSTAF: Stockholm, 1624; *d.* there, Dec. 19, 1690. Son of (1). Became a member of the court chapel, 1648; succeeded his father as *Kapellmeister*, 1663. In addition to his own compositions, he made a collection of contemporary music which is preserved in the library at Upsala.

Dubois [dēē-bwa], FRANÇOIS CLÉMENT THÉODORE: *b.* Rosnay, Aug. 24, 1837; *d.* Paris, June 11, 1924. Composer and organist. Studied at the Paris Conservatoire; *Prix de Rome*, 1861. Director of the choir at St. Clotilde, 1866, and subsequently at the Madeleine, where he later became organist. Director of the Conservatoire, 1896-1905. His compositions include several operas, church music, orchestral works and chamber music.

Dubourg, MATTHEW: *b.* London, 1703; *d.* there, July 3, 1767. Violinist, a pupil of Geminiani. First appeared in London as a child prodigy. Succeeded Cousser as director of the Viceroy's music in Dublin, 1728. He took part in the first performance of Handel's *Messiah* in Dublin, 1742. His compositions include several odes in honour of the birthdays of members of the Royal Family, written for performance at Dublin.

Ducasse. *v.* ROGER-DUCASSE.

Du Caurroy. *v.* CAURROY.

Dudelsack [dood'-ĕl-zuck], *G.* Bagpipe.

Duet. A composition for two singers or players, with or without accompaniment. Early examples of vocal duets are (a) without accompaniment: Morley's Canzonets for two voices (1595), (b) with accompaniment: several pieces in Monteverdi's 7th and 8th books of madrigals (1619 & 1638). The term "duo" is more generally used for instrumental music, with the exception of the PIANO DUET.

Dufay [dēē-fa-ee], GUILLAUME: *d.* Cambrai, Nov. 27, 1474. Flemish composer. Chorister at Cambrai Cathedral, 1409; singer in the Papal chapel, 1428; canon of Cambrai, 1436. He was the most important composer of his time, a master both of church music and of secular song. Modern editions of church music in *D.T.Ö.*, vii, xi (1), xix (i), xxvii (i), xxxi, xl; *chansons* in Stainer, *Dufay and his Contemporaries* (1898), miscellaneous works in *Das Chorwerk*, nos. 19 & 49. A complete edition of his works, ed. by G. de Van and H. Besseler, is in progress.

C. VAN DEN BORREN: *Guillaume Dufay* (1926).

Dukas [dēē-cuss], PAUL: *b.* Paris, Oct. 1, 1865; *d.* there, May 17, 1935. Composer and critic. Studied at the Paris Conservatoire, and subsequently in charge of the orchestra class there for a short time. He also taught composition at the École Normale de Musique, and contributed criticism to several papers. A severe self-critic, he published comparatively little. He was strongly influenced by Impressionism, but without sacrificing the characteristic clarity of his style. His best-known works are the orchestral scherzo *L'Apprenti Sorcier* (1897), the opera *Ariane et Barbe-Bleue* (Paris, 1907) and the ballet *La Péri* (1912). He also wrote a remarkable piano sonata in E♭ minor. *Ariane et Barbe-Bleue*, a setting of a libretto by Maeterlinck, is one of the outstanding operas of the 20th cent.

G. SAMAZEUILH: *Un Musicien français, Paul Dukas* (2nd ed., 1936).

Duke, VERNON. *v.* DUKELSKY.

Dukelsky [doo-kel'-ski], VLADIMIR: *b.* Parfianovka, Oct. 10, 1903. Composer. Studied in Moscow and Kiev. Left Russia in 1920 and lived subsequently in Turkey, America and France. Now an American citizen and resident in America. His ballet *Zéphyre et Flore*, commissioned by Diaghilev, was produced at Monte Carlo in 1925. He has also composed a piano concerto, 3 symphonies, an oratorio—*The End of St. Petersburg*, and chamber music. Under the pseudonym " Vernon Duke " he has written a quantity of light music for the stage and films.

Dulcian. *v.* DOLCIAN.

Dulcimer (*Fr.* tympanon, *G.* Hackbrett, *I.* cembalo, salterio tedesco). An instrument of Eastern origin which came to Europe in the Middle Ages. Like the psaltery, it consists of strings stretched over a wooden frame, but these, instead of being plucked, are struck with hammers held in the hands. The pianoforte is an adaptation of this principle, the hammers being controlled by a keyboard, with a separate hammer for each note. An enlarged type of dulcimer, called the Pantaleon, was invented by Pantaleon Hebenstreit (1667-1750) and had a considerable vogue in the 18th cent. The dulcimer is still current in Hungary under the name CIMBALOM.

Dulcitone. A keyboard instrument, in which tuning-forks are struck by hammers.

Dulichius [doo-lick'-yŏŏss], PHILIPP: *b.* Chemnitz, Dec. 1562; *d.* Stettin, March 24, 1631. Composer and teacher. His compositions are all for voices. Modern ed. of his *Centuria octonum et septenum vocum harmonias sacras . . . continens* (1607-12) in *D.D.T.*, xxxi & xli.

Dulzian. *v.* DOLCIAN.

Dumka [dŏŏm-ca]. (1) A Slavonic term for a folk-ballad, generally of a sentimental or melancholy character (pl. *dumky*).

(2) Used by Dvořák of an instrumental movement alternating between elegiac melancholy and exuberance. *v.* DUMKY TRIO.

Dumky Trio. Piano trio by Dvořák, Op. 96 (1891), consisting of 6 movements, each in the form of a *dumka*.

Dumont [dĕĕ-mo͡n], (1) HENRY: *b.* Villers l'Évêque, *c.* 1610; *d.* Paris, May 8, 1684. Belgian composer. Organist, St. Paul, Paris, 1639-84; director of the Chapel Royal, Paris, 1665. He was a priest and became canon of Maestricht Cathedral. He published 5 Masses, a large number of motets, *chansons* and instrumental music.

H. QUITTARD: *Un Musicien en France au XVIIe siècle : Henry Dumont.*

(2) LOUISE. *v.* FARRENC.

Dump. An elegy or lament, whether vocal or instrumental. Shakespeare's reference to a " merry dump " (*Romeo and Juliet*, iv, 5) is obviously intended as a paradox. The original meaning of " dump " is a fit of melancholy or depression, and this is still current in the colloquial phrase " to be down in the dumps." The poem by Richard Edwards quoted by Shakespeare in *Romeo and Juliet* is a good example of this primary sense:

Where gripyng griefs the hart would wound
& dolful domps the minde oppresse,
There Musick with her silver sound,
Is wont with spede to give redresse.

It occurs also as a literary term. The words of Weelkes's madrigal in memory of Morley—" Death hath deprived me of my dearest friend " (*E.M.S.*, xiii, no. 26)—were originally entitled " A Dump upon the death of the most noble Henry Earl of Pembroke." An early example of an instrumental dump is the early 16th-cent. " My Lady Carey's Dompe " for harpsichord, built on an alternating drone bass (printed in Davison & Apel, *Historical Anthology of Music*, no. 103).

Dunhill, THOMAS FREDERICK: *b.* London, Feb. 1, 1877; *d.* Scunthorpe, March 13, 1946. Composer and teacher. Studied at the R.C.M., where he was a pupil of Stanford. Assistant music-master at Eton, 1899-1908; teacher at the R.C.M. from 1905. From 1907-19 organized a series of chamber concerts in London, at which works by many English composers were performed. His own works include a symphony, chamber music, songs and operas, of which *Tantivy Towers* (London, 1931), to a libretto by A. P. Herbert, was very successful. He also published the following books: *Chamber Music* (1913), *Sullivan's Comic Operas* (1928) and *Sir Edward Elgar* (1938).

Duni [*I.* doo'-nee, *Fr.* dĕĕ-nee], EGIDIO ROMOALDO: *b.* Matera, Feb. 9, 1709; *d.* Paris, June 11, 1775. Opera composer, a pupil of Durante. An Italian by birth, he settled in Paris, 1757, and became an outstanding composer of *opéra-comique*. His first opera, *Nerone* (Rome, 1735), was a successful essay in *opera seria*. Of his numerous *opéras-comiques* the best known is probably *Les Moissonneurs* (Paris, 1768).

Dunstable, JOHN: *d.* Dec. 24, 1453. One of the most important composers of the early 15th cent., with a considerable reputation on the Continent. In the service of the Duke of Bedford (regent of France, 1422-35). His compositions, found mainly in Continental manuscripts, appear to be almost entirely for the Church: the beautiful setting of " O rosa bella " (Davison & Apel, *Historical Anthology of Music*, no. 61) is attributed to him in only one manuscript. Complete ed. of his works by M. Bukofzer, *Musica Britannica*, viii. He was also a mathematician and wrote treatises on astronomy. The view that he and Leonel Power were the same person is untenable.

M. BUKOFZER : "John Dunstable and the Music of his Time," in *Proceedings of the Musical Association*, lxv (1938-9).
G. REESE : *Music in the Middle Ages* (1940).

Duny. *v.* DUNI.

Duo. Duet.

Duparc [dē-parrk], MARIE EUGÈNE HENRI FOUQUES: *b.* Paris, Jan. 21, 1848; *d.* Mont-de-Marsan, Feb. 12, 1933. Composer, a pupil of César Franck. For reasons of health he abandoned composition after 1885. His reputation rests on a mere handful of songs, which date from his twenties; but these are among the finest products of 20th-cent. lyricism. Among his other works, few in number, is a symphonic poem, *Lénore* (1875).

Duplet. A group of two notes occupying the time normally taken by three, *e.g.*:

Duple Time. Time in which the number of beats in the bar is a multiple of two, *e.g.* 2/4, 4/4, 2/2. (Time in which there are four beats in the bar is also known as " common " or " quadruple " time). If the beats are divisible by two, the time is " simple "; if they are divisible by three, it is " compound," *e.g.*

Simple duple time:

Compound duple time:

v. TIME.

Duplum [doop'-lo͝om], *L.* The part immediately above the tenor in 12th-cent. organum. A third part above these two was called *triplum*. In the 13th-cent. motet the *duplum* came to be known as *motetus*.

Dupont [dē-pon͡], (1) AUGUSTE: *b.* Ensival, Feb. 9, 1827; *d.* Brussels, Dec. 17, 1890. Composer and pianist. Studied at Liége Conservatoire. Taught the piano at Brussels Conservatoire for 30 years. His compositions include 4 piano concertos, piano solos and songs. He also edited a number of classical works.

(2) GABRIEL: *b.* Caen, March 1, 1878; *d.* Vésinet, Aug. 3, 1914. Composer, a pupil of Widor. His first opera, *La Cabrera* (Milan, 1904), shared the prize in the Concorso Sonzogno, 1902; his last, *Antar*, was performed after his death (Paris, 1921). He also wrote orchestral music and piano pieces, but his career was marred by persistent ill-health.

(3) JOSEPH: *b.* Ensival, Jan. 3, 1838; *d.* Brussels, Dec. 21, 1899. Brother of (1). Conductor. Studied at Liége and Brussels Conservatoires; *Prix de Rome*, 1863. Opera conductor at Warsaw, Moscow and Brussels, where he became director of La Monnaie, 1886. He was also conductor of the Concerts Populaires, Brussels. He did much to make Wagner's operas known in Belgium.

Duport [dē-porr], (1) JEAN PIERRE: *b.* Paris, Nov. 27, 1741; *d.* Berlin, Dec. 31, 1818. Principal cellist in the orchestra of Frederick the Great, 1773.

(2) JEAN LOUIS: *b.* Paris, Oct. 4,

1749; *d.* there, Sept. 7, 1819. Brother of (1). Cellist. He held various European appointments and for a time taught at the Paris Conservatoire. He is the founder of the modern technique of cello-playing: his teaching was embodied in his *Essai sur le doigter du violoncelle et la conduite de l'archet.*

Dupré [dē̆-pray], MARCEL: *b.* Rouen, May 3, 1886. Organist and composer, member of a family of musicians. He made his mark as a player when still a boy, and won several prizes at the Paris Conservatoire, including the *Prix de Rome*, 1914. Assistant to Widor at St. Sulpice, 1906; acting organist at Notre Dame, 1916-22; succeeded Widor as organist of St. Sulpice, 1934. Teacher of organ at Paris Conservatoire, 1926. Director, Conservatoire Américain, Fontainebleau, 1947 ; Paris Conservatoire, 1954. He has toured widely as a recitalist and shown remarkable skill in improvisation. In addition to organ works he has composed chamber music, choral works and songs.

Duprez [dē̆-pray], GILBERT: *b.* Paris, Dec. 6, 1806; *d.* there, Sept. 23, 1896. One of the foremost operatic tenors of his time. Studied at the Paris Conservatoire and first appeared at the Odéon, 1825. His reputation dates from 1835, when he sang Edgardo in the first performance of *Lucia di Lammermoor* (Naples, 1835). First appeared at the Paris Opéra, 1837. Teacher of singing, Paris Conservatoire, 1842-50. Founded a school of singing in 1853, and left the stage in 1855. His numerous compositions, which had little success, include 8 operas, an oratorio and other choral works. He published two singing-tutors, also *Souvenirs d'un chanteur* and *Récréations de mon grand âge.*

Dupuis [dē̆-pē̆-ee], (1) ALBERT: *b.* Verviers, March 1, 1877. Composer. Studied at the Schola Cantorum, Paris, under d'Indy and Guilmant; *Prix de Rome*, 1904. Director of the Verviers Conservatoire, 1908. In addition to orchestral works and chamber music he has written several operas, of which *La Passion* (Monte Carlo, 1916) is the most important.

(2) SYLVAIN: *b.* Liège, Oct. 9, 1856; *d.* Bruges, Sept. 28, 1931. Composer and conductor. Studied at Liège Conservatoire; *Prix de Rome*, 1881. Teacher of harmony, Liège Conservatoire, 1886. Founded Société des Nouveaux Concerts, Liège, 1888. Conductor, La Monnaie and Concerts Populaires, Brussels, 1900. Director, Liège Conservatoire, 1911. His compositions include operas, orchestral works, chamber music and a number of male-voice choruses.

Du Puy. *v.* PUY.

Dur [doorr], *G.* " Major," as opposed to " minor " (*moll*). The word derives from the Latin *B durum* (hard B), the name given to the square-shaped B used in medieval times to indicate B♮. *v.* B, MOLL.

Durand [dē̆-rũn]. A French firm of music-publishers, founded in Paris in 1869.

Durante [doo-rahn'-teh], FRANCESCO: *b.* Fratta Maggiore, March 31, 1684; *d.* Naples, Aug. 13, 1755. One of the most important composers of the " Neapolitan " school. Teacher at the Conservatorio di Santa Maria di Loreto, 1742-55 ; Conservatorio di Sant' Onofrio, 1745-55. His works consist principally of church music, but he also wrote 6 harpsichord sonatas—the only compositions to be printed in his lifetime.

Durchkomponiert [dŏŏrr*sh*'-com-poneert'], *G.* " Composed throughout." A term applied to songs in which there is fresh music for each verse, as opposed to strophic songs, where the same music is repeated for each verse. The literal translation " through-composed " is widely used in America but is not English.

Durey [dē̆-ray], LOUIS EDMOND: *b.* Paris, May 27, 1888. Composer, for a few years a member of the group known as " Les Six " (*v.* SIX). He has written large-scale works, including an opera, but his best work is to be found in more intimate music, such as chamber music and songs, which show both individuality and refinement.

Duruflé [dē̆-rē̆-flay], MAURICE: *b.* Louviers, Jan. 11, 1902. Organist and composer. Studied at the Paris Conservatoire, where he won several prizes.

Organist, St. Étienne du Mont, 1930. He is widely known as a brilliant recitalist. His compositions include some very effective organ pieces and chamber music.

Dušek [dōōsh'-eck], (1) FRANTIŠEK XAVER: *b.* Chotěboř, Dec. 8, 1731; *d.* Prague, Feb. 12, 1799. Pianist and composer, a pupil of Wagenseil. He had a considerable reputation as a teacher. He and his wife were close friends of Mozart.

(2) JAN LADISLAV. *v.* DUSSEK.

(3) JOSEPHA: *b.* Prague, March 6, 1754; *d.* there, Jan. 8, 1824. Wife of (1). Soprano, for whom Mozart wrote the concert aria "Bella mia fiamma," K.528 (1787). She also gave the first performance of Beethoven's *scena* "Ah perfido" (1796). Her maiden name was Hambacher.

Dushkin [doosh'-kin], SAMUEL: *b.* Suwaxki, Dec. 13, 1896. Russian violinist, now an American citizen. Pupil of Auer and Kreisler. He has given recitals with Stravinsky, and gave the first performance of the latter's violin concerto in 1931 and *Duo concertant* in 1932 (*v.* I. Stravinsky, *Chronicle of my Life*, pp. 268 *et seq.*).

Dusk of the Gods, The. *v.* GÖTTERDÄMMERUNG.

Dussek [dōōsh'-eck] (originally Dušek), JAN LADISLAV: *b.* Cáslav, Feb. 12, 1760; *d.* St. Germain-en-Laye, March 20, 1812. Pianist and composer, the son of an organist and teacher. He showed great skill as a pianist and organist while still a child. After studying theology at Prague he held organist's posts at Malines and Berg-op-Zoom. He won great success as a pianist in Amsterdam and the Hague, and composed a number of works for the piano. As a soloist he visited Berlin, St. Petersburg, Paris, Milan and London, where he stayed for nearly 12 years. He joined his father-in-law's music-publishing firm, Corri & Co., but financial difficulties compelled him to leave for Hamburg in 1800. He continued to travel as a soloist and was befriended by various patrons, the last of whom was Talleyrand. The beauty of his touch was much praised by his contemporaries. In addition to piano concertos and sonatas he wrote a very considerable amount of chamber music. His piano sonatas, some of which have programmatic titles, foreshadow the characteristics of Romantic piano music, particularly in their use of pathetic chromaticism.

Duval [dēē-vull], FRANÇOIS: *b. c.* 1673; *d.* Versailles, Jan. 27, 1728. Violinist and composer, a member of the orchestra of Louis XIV. The first French composer to publish sonatas for violin and continuo: he wrote 5 books, of which the first appeared in 1704.

Dux [dōōks], *L.* "Leader." The name given by older theorists to the first part to enter in a CANON or FUGUE. The second part to enter, which imitates it, was known as *comes* (companion).

Dux [dōōks], CLAIRE: *b.* Witkowicz, Aug. 2, 1885. Concert and opera soprano. Studied in Berlin and Milan. First appeared at Cologne, 1906. Sang Sophie in the first London production of *Der Rosenkavalier* (1913). Has lived in America since her marriage in 1925. For an appreciation of her outstanding gifts, particularly as a singer of Mozart, *v.* T. Beecham, *A Mingled Chime* (1944), p. 126.

Dvořák [dvorr'-zhahk], ANTONIN: *b.* Nehalozeves, Sept. 8, 1841; *d.* Prague, May 1, 1904. Czech composer, the son of a butcher and innkeeper. Studied at the Organ School, Prague, 1857-9. Became a professional string-player, and played viola in the orchestra of the National Theatre, Prague, 1862-73. During these years he was active as a composer. His patriotic *Hymnus* (op. 30) for choir and orchestra, performed in 1873, was so successful that he left the National Theatre to devote himself to composition and teaching. In 1875 he received a government grant, on the recommendation of Brahms and Hanslick. Brahms continued to show him encouragement and helped him to get his works published. He visited England several times and composed specially for English societies his D minor symphony (1885), the cantata *The Spectre's Bride* (1885) and the oratorio *St. Ludmilla* (1886). Teacher of composition, Prague Conservatoire, 1891 and 1895-1901; director, National Conservatory of Music, New

York, 1892-5; director, Prague Conservatoire, 1901-4.

He was a spontaneous composer: all his music has a natural freshness which sometimes conceals the skill with which it is constructed. The principal influences in his life were the music of Smetana and Brahms, and Czech folksong. None of these influences dominated him; but his appreciation of folksong made it easier for him to welcome the negro idioms with which he became acquainted in America. Like Schubert he was sometimes discursive, but he was more successful in covering up his tracks. His genius for melody did not make him a purely lyrical composer; his second symphony is one of the outstanding works of the later 19th cent. His operas have remained on the whole a local product, better known in Czechoslovakia than abroad.

His principal compositions are:

(a) OPERAS: *Král a Uhlíř* (*King and Collier*, 1874); *Tvrdé Palice* (*The Pigheaded Peasants*, 1874); *Vanda* (1875); *Šelma Sedlák* (*The Peasant a Rogue*, 1877); *Dimitrij* (1882); *Jakobín* (1888, rev. 1897); *Čert a Káča* (*The Devil and Kate*, 1899); *Rusalka* (1900); *Armida* (1904).

(b) CHORAL WORKS: *Hymnus* (1872); *Stabat Mater* (1877); *The Spectre's Bride* (1884); *St. Ludmilla* (1886); Mass in D (1887); Requiem Mass (1890); *Te Deum* (1892).

(c) ORCHESTRA: 9 symphonies, of which the last 7 are published—the last 5 are numbered respectively No. 3 in F, No. 1 in D, No. 2 in D minor, No. 4 in G and No. 5 in E minor (*From the New World*); *Symphonic Variations* (1877); 6 overtures, including *Carnival* (1891); 5 symphonic poems; 3 Slavonic rhapsodies; 2 cello concertos (1865 & 1895); piano concerto (1876); violin concerto (1880).

(d) CHAMBER MUSIC: 4 piano trios (the last is the *Dumky* trio); string trio; 2 piano quartets; 13 string quartets; piano quintet; 2 string quintets; string sextet.

Also many solo songs and duets, piano solos and piano duets.

V. FISCHL (ed.): *Antonín Dvořák* (1942).
R. NEWMARCH: *The Music of Czechoslovakia* (1942).
A. ROBERTSON: *Dvořák* (1945).

Dylan. Opera in three acts by Holbrooke (the second part of the trilogy *The Cauldron of Annwen*). Libretto by Thomas Evelyn Ellis (Lord Howard de Walden). First performed, London, July 4, 1914.

Dynamics. (1) Degrees of loudness or softness in a musical performance. (2) the signs by which these are indicated in the score. Those in ordinary use, with their abbreviations, are: *pianissimo* (*pp*), very soft; *piano* (*p*), soft; *mezzo piano* (*mp*), moderately soft; *mezzo forte* (*mf*), moderately loud; *forte* (*f*), loud; *fortissimo* (*ff*), very loud; *poco forte* (*pf*), moderately loud; *forte piano* (*fp*), loud and immediately soft; *sforzato* and *sforzando* (*sf*, *sfz*), heavily accented; *crescendo* (*cres.*), or $<$), getting louder; *decrescendo* and *diminuendo* (*decresc.* and *dim.*, or $>$), getting softer. For signs used for accentuation *v.* ACCENT.

Indications of dynamics began to appear in the early 17th cent., and were used to a large extent to indicate contrasts, particularly a soft repetition in the form of an echo. A persistent increase or decrease in volume was marked by indicating the several stages, *e.g. forte, piano, pianissimo.* The terms *crescendo* and *diminuendo* began to come into use about the middle of the 18th cent., largely, no doubt, as the result of orchestral practice. Burney, in his *Present State of Music in Germany* (1773), i, p. 94, gives a vivid account of the effect of *crescendo* and *diminuendo* as practised by the Mannheim orchestra. From that time the use of dynamic signs increased, as composers realized more and more the desirability of exactly indicating their intentions if they were not themselves to be in charge of the performance.

R. E. M. HARDING: *Origins of Musical Time and Expression* (1938).

Dyson, GEORGE: *b.* Halifax, May 28, 1883. Composer and teacher. Studied at the R.C.M.; Mendelssohn Scholarship, 1904. Music master, Osborne, 1908; Marlborough, 1911; Rugby, 1914. Director of music, Wellington, 1921; Winchester, 1924. Director, R.C.M., 1937-52. Knighted, 1941. His compositions include a symphony and several choral works, among them *In Honour of the City*, *The Canterbury Pilgrims*, *St. Paul's Voyage to Melita*, *Nebuchadnezzar* and *Quo Vadis*. His critical writings include *The New Music* (1924) and *The Progress of Music* (1932).

Dzerjinsky [dzairr-zheen′-ski], IVAN: *b*. Tambov, Apr. 21, 1909. Russian composer, best known for his opera *Tikhi Don* (*Quiet flows the Don*), based on Sholochov's novel, which was written in 1923-4 and first performed at Leningrad, 1935. He studied at Leningrad Conservatoire, but without acquiring a thorough technical equipment. His music is improvisatory in style and derives what character it has from its imitation of folksong.

G. ABRAHAM : *Eight Soviet Composers* (1943).

E

E. The 3rd note (or mediant) of the scale of C major.

Eagles. *v.* ECCLES.

Eames [aimz], EMMA: *b.* Shanghai, Aug. 13, 1867; *d.* New York, June 13, 1952. American operatic soprano, a pupil of Mathilde Marchesi in Paris. First appeared at the Paris Opéra in *Romeo et Juliette*, 1889. Subsequently appeared at Covent Garden and the New York Metropolitan Opera until her retirement from the stage in 1909.

Ear Training. *v.* AURAL TRAINING.

East (Este), (1) MICHAEL: *d.* 1648. Composer. Organist of Lichfield Cathedral. His compositions include madrigals, music for viols and church music. Modern ed. of madrigals in *E.M.S.*, xxix-xxxi.

(2) THOMAS: *d. c.* 1608. Music-publisher, who issued some of the most important works by late 16th- and early 17th-cent. English composers. Among the many collections which he published were Byrd's *Psalmes, Sonets and Songs* (1588), *Musica Transalpina* (1588 & 1597), *The Triumphes of Oriana* (1601), Byrd's *Gradualia*, pt. i (1605), and madrigals by Morley, Wilbye, Weelkes and Bateson.

Eastman School of Music. Part of the University of Rochester, N.Y. Founded and endowed in 1918 by George Eastman (1854-1932), head of the Eastman Kodak Company. The present director is Howard Hanson.

Easton, FLORENCE: *b.* Middlesbrough, Oct. 24, 1884. Operatic soprano. Studied at the R.C.M. and in Paris. Royal Opera, Berlin, 1907-13; Hamburg Stadttheater, 1914-16; New York Metropolitan, 1917-29. She has also sung at Covent Garden and Sadler's Wells.

Eberl [ay'-berl], ANTON: *b.* Vienna, June 13, 1765; *d.* there, March 11, 1807. Pianist and composer. He travelled widely as a soloist, and from 1796-1800 was *Kapellmeister* at St. Petersburg. His compositions, which were much admired in his day, include 5 operas, symphonies, concertos, chamber music and piano sonatas. He was a close friend of Mozart, and his piano sonata in C minor, Op. 1, and other piano works were originally published under Mozart's name. His symphony in E♭ was performed at the same concert as Beethoven's *Eroica* symphony, Apr. 7, 1805, and was much more successful.

F. EWENS: *Anton Eberl* (1927).

Eberlin [ay'-ber-leen], JOHANN ERNST: *b.* Jettingen, March 27, 1702; *d.* Salzburg, June 21, 1762. Composer and organist. Organist to the court and cathedral, Salzburg, 1729; *Kapellmeister*, 1749. His compositions include a large number of oratorios, Masses and other church music, and keyboard works. Mozart wrote of some of his fugues in 1782:

"They are unfortunately far too trivial to deserve a place beside Handel and Bach. With due respect for his four-part composition I may say that his keyboard fugues are nothing but long-drawn-out voluntaries." (E. Anderson, *The Letters of Mozart and his Family*, p. 1194).

Modern ed. of his oratorio *Der blutschwitzende Jesus* in *D.T.Ö.*, xxviii (1).

Eccard [eck'-arrt], JOHANN: *b.* Mühlhausen (Thuringia), 1553; *d.* Berlin, 1611. Composer, a pupil of Lassus. In the service of Jakob Fugger at Augsburg, 1578; vice-*Kapellmeister*, Königsberg, *c.* 1580; *Kapellmeister*, 1604; *Kapellmeister* to the court of Brandenburg, Berlin, 1608. Most of his compositions are for the Lutheran church and include settings of chorales, but he also published a certain number of secular part-songs. Modern ed. of his *Newe Lieder mit fünff und vier Stimmen* (1589) by R. Eitner (1897); of his *Geistliche Lieder auff den Choral* (2 pts., 1597) by E. von Baussnern (1928); of his *Preussische Festlieder* (2 pts.,

1642 & 1644) by G. W. Teschner (1858).

Eccles (Eagles), (1) HENRY. Violinist. Son of (3). Appointed musician to William III, 1689. Migrated to France *c.* 1715 and published there a volume of violin sonatas (1720), which borrow freely from an earlier set by Giuseppe Valentini.

(2) JOHN: *d.* Kingston-on-Thames, Jan. 12, 1735. Violinist and composer. Son of (3). Appointed musician to William III, 1696; Master of the King's Music, 1700. Won second prize in a competition opened in 1700 for a setting of Congreve's pastoral *The Judgment of Paris.* Wrote music for a large number of plays, including parts i & ii of *Don Quixote* (in association with Purcell, 1694).

(3) SOLOMON. Violinist. In the service of Charles II, James II and William III. Some violin pieces of his were printed in *The Division Violin* (2nd ed. 1695). He is clearly a different person from the Solomon Eccles who was teaching the virginals and viol during the Commonwealth, became a Quaker, published the tract called *A Musick-Lector* (1667: *v.* P. Scholes, *The Puritans and Music*, pp. 52-4), migrated to the West Indies and America and *d.* Feb. 11, 1683.

Échiquier [ay-sheek-yay], *Fr.* *v.* CHEKKER.

Écho et Narcisse. [ay-co ay narr-seece] (Echo and Narcissus). Opera in three acts by Gluck. Libretto by Louis Theodore de Tschudy. First performed, Paris, Sept. 24, 1779.

Echo Organ. A set of pipes placed further away than the main body of the organ and designed to suggest an echo. In modern organs they may be placed a considerable distance away, *e.g.* in the triforium, and be controlled from a separate manual, with several stops.

Écorcheville [ay-corrsh-veel], JULES ARMAND JOSEPH: *b.* Paris, March 17, 1872; *d.* Pertles-lès-Hurlus, Feb. 19, 1915. Historian and editor, a pupil of César Franck and Riemann. Joint founder of the Paris section of the International Musical Society. Published a *Catalogue du fonds de musique ancienne de la Bibliothèque nationale* (1910-14) and various books and articles on the history of music. His edition of *Vingt suites d'orchestra du XVIIe siècle français* (2 vols., 1906) from the library at Cassel has been criticized on the ground that there is no evidence that the manuscript is of French origin.

Écossaise [ay-coss-ez], *Fr.* Short for *danse écossaise,* "Scottish dance." A quick dance in 2/4 time, popular in England and on the Continent in the late 18th and early 19th cent. Examples occur in the works of Beethoven and Schubert, *e.g.*:

SCHUBERT, 11 *Écossaises, No.* 5

There seems to be no evidence that it is of Scottish origin. Not to be confused with the SCHOTTISCHE.

Edinburgh Festival. A summer festival of music and drama, first held in 1947. Part of the policy of the festival is to engage several orchestras of the first rank and also a large number of soloists of international reputation. The Glyndebourne Opera Company has from the first made an important contribution to its success.

Egge [egg'-er], KLAUS : *b.* Granskerad, July 19, 1906. Norwegian composer, a pupil of Valen. From 1932 to 1945 he taught singing in Oslo, and from 1935 to 1938 was editor of the magazine *Tonekunst.* Music critic of *Arbeiderbladet* since 1945. His compositions, which are strongly influenced by folk music, include 2 symphonies, 2 piano concertos, the oratorio *Sveinung Vreim,* chamber music, piano works and songs.

Egk [eck], WERNER: *b.* Auchsesheim (Bavaria), May 17, 1901. Composer. Conductor, Berlin State Opera, 1936-41. Director, Hochschule für Musik, Berlin, 1950-3. His operas include *Die Zaubergeige* (1934), which was very popular, and *Peer Gynt* (1938), based on Ibsen's play. He has also written choral works, including the oratorio *Columbus,* and orchestral music.

Egmont [egg'-mont]. A tragedy by Goethe, dealing with the revolt of the Netherlands against the Spanish domination, for which Beethoven wrote an overture and incidental music (Op. 84) in 1810.

Eichborn [ysh'-borrn], HERMANN LUDWIG: *b.* Breslau, Oct. 30, 1847; *d.* Gries, Apr. 15, 1918. Composer and critic, known chiefly for his researches into the history and manufacture of brass instruments, on which he was himself a performer. His publications include *Die Trompete in alter und neuer Zeit* (1881), *Das alte Klarinblasen auf Trompeten* (1895) and *Die Dämpfung beim Horn* (1897). His compositions include several comic operas, horn solos, piano pieces and songs.

Eichheim [ysh'-hime], HENRY: *b.* Chicago, Jan. 3, 1870; *d.* Montecito, Aug. 22, 1942. Violinist and composer, who devoted himself particularly to the study of Oriental music. A member of the Boston Symphony Orchestra, 1890-1912. His compositions reflect his study of Eastern music.

Eighth-Note. American for "quaver."

Eilen [ile'-ĕn], *G.* "To hurry." *Nicht eilen,* do not hurry.

Ein deutsches Requiem. *v.* DEUTSCHES REQUIEM.

Einem [fon ine'-ĕm], GOTTFRIED VON : *b.* Berne, Jan. 24, 1918. Composer. Son of the German military attaché in Switzerland. On the staff of the Berlin State Opera, 1938 ; Dresden State Opera, 1944. Studied with Boris Blacher in Berlin. Now resident at Salzburg. His compositions include the operas *Dantons Tod* (Salzburg, 1947) and *Der Prozess,* based on Kafka's *The Trial* (Salzburg, 1953), several ballets and orchestral works.

Einleitung [ine'-ly-tŏŏng], *G.* Introduction.

Einstein [ine'-shtine], ALFRED: *b.* Munich, Dec. 30, 1880; *d.* El Cerrito, California, Feb. 13, 1952. Historian and critic. Music critic, *Münchener Post,* 1917; *Berliner Tageblatt,* 1927-33. Editor, *Zeitschrift für Musikwissenschaft,* 1918-33. Editor, Riemann's *Musik-Lexikon,* 9th-11th ed. (1919, 1922, 1929). Left Germany in 1933, and after living in London and Florence settled in America in 1939, where he was professor at Smith College, Northampton, Mass. till 1950. His numerous publications include the third edition of Köchel's catalogue of Mozart's works (1937), books on Gluck, Mozart and Schubert, *Music in the Romantic Era* (1947) and *The Italian Madrigal* (3 vols., 1949). His *Geschichte der Musik* (1917) first appeared in English in 1936 as *A Short History of Music* (new edition with music supplement, 1948). He also edited a number of works, including selected works of Steffani (*D.T.B.*,vi, 2), Gluck's opera *L'innocenza giustificata* (*D.T.Ö.*, xl) and Mozart's string quartets.

Eis [ay'-iss], *G.* E sharp (E♯).

Eisis [ay'-iss-iss], *G.* E double sharp (E×).

Eisteddfod [ace-teth'-vode], *W.* Lit. "assembly" or "session." Applied particularly to a gathering of Welsh bards. Such gatherings were held in very early times. In its modern form the Eisteddfod is a competition festival, not necessarily confined to music. The National Eisteddfod, the most important of these gatherings, is a revival dating from the early 19th cent. An artificial link with the past is maintained by the use of ceremonial and bardic costume.

Eitner [ite'-ner], ROBERT: *b.* Breslau,

Oct. 22, 1832; *d.* Templin, Feb. 2, 1905. Lexicographer and musicologist. Began his career as a music-teacher in Berlin. Founded the Gesellschaft für Musikforschung (Society for Musical Research) in 1868, and edited its journal, *Monatshefte für Musikgeschichte*, 1869-1904, as well as a series of musical and theoretical works of the past entitled *Publikationen älterer praktischer und theoretischer Musikwerke.* His *Bibliographie der Musiksammelwerke des 16. und 17. Jahrhunderts* (1877), though incomplete, is still indispensable. His *Quellen-Lexikon* (10 vols., 1900-4)—a biographical and bibliographical dictionary of musicians up to the middle of the 19th cent.—was a valiant attempt to lay the foundations for a scientific study of musical history. Its bibliographical material is still useful but suffers from the lack of any system in its presentation.

El Amor Brujo. *v.* AMOR BRUJO.

Electronde. An electronic instrument similar to the THEREMIN, but incorporating mechanism designed to interrupt the *glissando* from one note to another and to control amplification. Tone is produced by utilizing the difference between two frequencies. Invented by Martin Taubmann (1929).

Electrone. An electronic organ, first produced in 1939 by the John Compton Organ Co. It is provided with stops and couplers like an ordinary organ, but the sound is produced by amplifying electrically generated vibrations.

Electronic Instruments. There are three principal ways in which electricity is used to produce (as distinct from merely reproducing) musical sounds:

(1) By amplifying existing vibrations, *e.g.* in the Everett Orgatron (1934), which amplifies the vibration of harmonium reeds, and the Neo-Bechstein piano (1931), which amplifies the vibration of strings and also makes possible sustained tone and a crescendo. The same principle has also been applied to string instruments.

(2) By generating frequencies corresponding to the vibrations of notes and converting them into sound, *e.g.* in the Hammond organ (1934), where a system of intensifying or suppressing the individual members of a limited HARMONIC SERIES makes possible the artificial representation of the tone of a large number of different instruments.

(3) By utilizing the difference between two frequencies, *e.g.* in the Theremin (1924), where the difference is controlled by the movement of the hand through the air.

F. W. GALPIN : "The Music of Electricity," in *Proceedings of the Musical Association*, lxiv (1937-8).

E. G. RICHARDSON : "The Production and Analysis of Tone by Electrical Means," *ibid.* lxvi (1939-40).

Elektra [ay-leck'-tra]. Opera in one act by Richard Strauss. Libretto by Hugo von Hofmannsthal (after Sophocles). First performed, Dresden, Jan. 25, 1909. Electra, daughter of Agamemnon, wishes to avenge his death. Her own mother, Clytemnestra, was his murderer. She awaits the coming of her brother Orestes, though Clytemnestra has been told that he is dead. When he returns he kills Clytemnestra and Aegisthus, formerly her lover and now her husband. Electra rejoices that her father's murder is avenged.

Eleventh. The interval of an octave and a fourth, *e.g.*:

For the so-called "chord of the eleventh" *v.* CHORD.

Elgar, EDWARD WILLIAM: *b.* Broadheath, June 2, 1857; *d.* Worcester, Feb. 23, 1934. Composer, the son of a music-dealer and organist in Worcester. He had no formal musical training but learned the organ, violin and bassoon. Intended to become a professional solo violinist and had some lessons in London from Adolphe Pollitzer, but abandoned the idea. Conductor, Worcester Glee Club, 1879; Worcester County Lunatic Asylum, 1879; Worcester Amateur Instrumental Society, 1882. Organist, St. George's Roman Catholic Church, Worcester, 1885. Married Caroline Alice Roberts, 1889, and went to live in London, but finding it impossible to make a career there, settled in Malvern, 1891. First important performance was the concert overture *Froissart* at the Three Choirs Festival, Worcester, 1890. This was followed by various choral works: *The Black Knight* (Worcester, 1893), *Scenes from the Bavarian Highlands* (Worcester, 1896), *The Light of Life* (Worcester, 1896), *King Olaf* (Hanley, 1896), *The Banner of St. George* (London, 1897) and *Caractacus* (Leeds, 1898). His reputation as a composer of the first rank was established by the *Enigma* Variations for orchestra (1899) and the oratorio *The Dream of Gerontius* (Birmingham, 1900). The performance of the latter work, however, was inadequate: it was not until it had been given at Düsseldorf in 1902 that it took its place as an acknowledged masterpiece. The next 20 years (until the death of his wife in 1920) were notable for the composition of two more oratorios, several large-scale orchestral works and some chamber music. After 1920 he wrote little of importance. A third symphony, commissioned by the B.B.C., and an opera, *The Spanish Lady*, survive only in sketches. He was the first professor of music at Birmingham University, 1905-8; Master of the King's Music, 1924. Knighted, 1904; baronet, 1931.

He began his career as a Romantic, and remained one to the end, though the exuberance of his maturity mellowed into the wistful nostalgia of old age. He delighted in colour and showed a mastery of the orchestra unsurpassed by anyone of his time. His generous display of emotion repelled some who felt that English music should be reserved, but to many more the discovery of his rich humanity was like a new awakening. He created for himself a style and an idiom so personal as to win the epithet "Elgarian." His studies of others—in the *Enigma* Variations and in the symphonic poem *Falstaff*—were in reality projections of himself. His second symphony, often regarded as a picture of the Edwardian age, is in fact a revelation of its author. He was not afraid to be popular, and many who never heard his serious works were familiar with his marches. His oratorios are a confession of the faith in which he was brought up. Of these, *The Dream of Gerontius* is unquestionably the finest, because it is a consistent whole. Its successors, in spite of many incidental beauties, suffer a little in coherence from the desire to illustrate the details of a narrative. His principal compositions are:

(a) ORATORIOS: *The Light of Life* (1896); *The Dream of Gerontius* (1900); *The Apostles* (1903); *The Kingdom* (1906).

(b) OTHER CHORAL WORKS: *The Black Knight* (1893); *Scenes from the Bavarian Highlands* (1896); *King Olaf* (1896); *The Banner of St. George* (1897); *Caractacus* (1898); *Coronation Ode* (1902); *The Music Makers* (1912); *The Spirit of England* (1916).

(c) ORCHESTRA: *Froissart* (1890); Serenade for strings (1893); *Enigma* Variations (1899); *Cockaigne* (1901); *In the South* (1904); Introduction and Allegro for strings (1905); *The Wand of Youth* (1907-8); 2 symphonies (1908, 1911); violin concerto (1910); cello concerto (1919); *Falstaff* (1913); *Nursery Suite* (1933).

(d) BRASS BAND: *Severn Suite* (1930; also arranged for orchestra and for organ solo).

(e) CHAMBER MUSIC: Piano quintet (1919); string quartet (1919); violin sonata (1919).

(f) ORGAN: 2 sonatas (1896, 1933; second arranged from the *Severn Suite*).

(g) SONGS: *Sea Pictures*, with orchestra (1899); songs with piano; part-songs.

R. J. BUCKLEY: *Sir Edward Elgar* (1905).
T. F. DUNHILL: *Sir Edward Elgar* (1938).
B. MAINE: *Elgar: his Life and Works* (2 vols., 1933).
D. MCVEAGH: *Edward Elgar: his Life and Music* (1955).
E. NEWMAN: *Elgar* (1922).
(MRS.) R. POWELL: *Edward Elgar: Memories of a Variation* (1937).
W. H. REED: *Elgar as I knew him* (1936). *Elgar* (1939).
P. M. YOUNG: *Elgar O.M.* (1955).

Elijah. Oratorio by Mendelssohn, Op.

70. First performed, Birmingham, Aug. 26, 1946; revised version, London, Apr. 16, 1847.

F. G. EDWARDS: *The History of Mendelssohn's "Elijah"* (1896).

Elkin. A London firm of music-publishers, founded in 1903 by William Wolfe Alexander Elkin and now directed by his son Robert Stiebel Elkin (*b.* London, June 25, 1896).

Ella, JOHN: *b.* Leicester, Dec. 19, 1802; *d.* London, Oct. 2, 1888. Violinist and critic. Studied with Attwood and Fétis. From 1832-48 a member of various orchestras in London. From 1845-1880 directed a series of chamber concerts known as the Musical Union, for which he wrote analytical notes—at that time a novelty. Meyerbeer attended one of these concerts in 1855 and noted with approval the number of ladies who followed the music with the score. Among the works introduced to England by Ella were Schubert's D minor string quartet (1852) and Schumann's piano quartet (1848). He contributed musical criticism to the *Morning Post*, *Musical World* and *Athenaeum.*

Ellinwood, LEONARD: *b.* Thomaston, Feb. 13, 1905. American musicologist. Studied at the Eastman School of Music, Rochester. Taught successively at Mount Hermon School, 1927; University of Rochester, 1934; Michigan State College, 1936-40. On the staff of the Library of Congress, 1940. Ordained deacon, 1948. His special field is medieval music. He has edited *Musica Hermanni Contracti* with English translation (1936) and the complete works of Francesco Landini (1939).

Elman [ell'-mun], MISCHA: *b.* Talnoi, Jan. 20, 1891. Russian violinist. Studied at Odessa, and with Auer at the St. Petersburg Conservatoire. Has toured throughout the world and is now resident in America.

Elmendorff [ell'-mĕn-dorrf], KARL: *b.* Düsseldorf, Jan. 25, 1891. Conductor. Studied at the Cologne Hochshule für Musik. Has been active as an opera conductor at Düsseldorf, Munich, Wiesbaden, Mannheim and Dresden. Bayreuth Festival, 1927; Berlin State Opera, 1938; Cassel, 1948.

Elsner [elce'-ner], JOSEPH XAVER; *b.* Grottkau, June 29, 1769; *d.* Warsaw, Apr. 18, 1854. Composer, German by birth but Polish by residence. Studied medicine at Breslau and Vienna, but also studied the violin and harmony. Decided on music as a career and joined the theatre orchestra at Brünn, 1791. Conductor, Lemberg (Lwów) Theatre, 1792; Warsaw National Theatre, 1799. First director, Warsaw Conservatoire, 1821-30—the result of a society for the encouragement of music which he founded in 1815. His numerous compositions include operas, church music, symphonies, concertos, chamber music and ballets. His pupils included Chopin, who studied at the Conservatoire, 1826-9.

El Sombrero de Tres Picos. *v.* SOMBRERO DE TRES PICOS.

Elwes, GERVASE CARY: *b.* Northampton, Nov. 15, 1866; *d.* nr. Boston, Mass., Jan. 12, 1921. Tenor. Educated at Oratory School, Birmingham, and Christ Church, Oxford. Studied music on the Continent and in London. In the diplomatic service, 1891-5. First professional appearance, Kendal, 1903. He had a great reputation as an interpreter of song—both the classics and the works of modern English composers—and he excelled in the title role of Elgar's oratorio *The Dream of Gerontius.* The Musicians' Benevolent Fund was founded in his memory, 1921.

Embellishments. *v.* ORNAMENTS.

Embouchure. (1) The mouthpiece of a wind instrument.

(2) The correct shaping of the lips necessary to produce accurate intonation and good tone. It is acquired only by persistent practice.

Emmanuel [em-ma-nĕĕ-el], MARIE FRANÇOIS MAURICE: *b.* Bar-sur-Aube, May 2, 1862; *d.* Paris, Dec. 14, 1938. Composer and musicologist. Studied at the Paris Conservatoire and in Brussels. Began his career as a schoolmaster and choirmaster. Taught history of music at the Paris Conservatoire, 1909-36. His compositions include 2 symphonies, 2 operas—*Prométhée enchaîné* (1918) and *Salamine* (1929), and chamber music. His historical studies include *Histoire* *de la langue musicale* (2 vols., 1911), a work of outstanding importance.

Emperor Concerto. A name given in England and America to Beethoven's fifth piano concerto in E♭, Op. 73.

Emperor Quartet (*G.* Kaiserquartett). The name given to Haydn's quartet in C, Op. 76, no. 3, the slow movement of which consists of variations on the EMPEROR'S HYMN.

Emperor's Hymn (*G.* Kaiserlied). The former national anthem of Austria, "Gott erhalte Franz, den Kaiser" (God preserve the Emperor Francis). Words by Leopold Haschka, music by Haydn (1797), who used it as a theme for variations in the slow movement of his string quartet in C, Op. 76, no. 3 (1797). Later sung to the words "Sei gesegnet ohne Ende," by Ottokar Kernstock. In Germany Haydn's music used for "Deutschland, Deutschland über alles," words by Hoffman von Fallersleben (1841); the words now sung in Western Germany begin "Einigkeit und Recht und Freiheit." In England it is used as a hymn-tune, *e.g.* for "Praise the Lord, ye heavens adore him" and "Glorious things of thee are spoken."

Empfindung [em-pfin′-dŏŏng], *G.* "Feeling." *Mit Empfindung*, with feeling. *Empfindungsvoll*, full of feeling.

Enchaînez [ũn-shay-nay], *Fr.* "Link up," *i.e.* go straight on to the next movement or section.

Encina. *v.* ENZINA.

Enclume [ũn-clēēm], *Fr.* Anvil.

Enesco (Enescu) [ay-ness′-coo], GEORGES: *b.* Dorohoiû, Aug. 19, 1881; *d.* Paris, May 4, 1955. Rumanian composer, conductor and violinist. Studied at the Vienna Conservatorium, which he entered at the age of 7, and at the Paris Conservatoire, where he won the *premier prix* for violin-playing, 1899. He was active as a composer, and toured widely as a violinist and a conductor. Yehudi Menuhin was his pupil. His compositions include the opera *Œdipe* (Paris, 1936), 3 symphonies, 2 Rumanian rhapsodies and chamber music. In 1912 he founded a prize for works by young Rumanian composers.

Enfance du Christ, L' [lũn-fũnce dēē creest], (The Childhood of Christ). A sacred trilogy for soloists, chorus and orchestra by Berlioz, Op. 25.

The three parts are: (1) *Le Songe d'Hérode* (Herod's Dream); (2) *La Fuite en Égypte* (The Flight into Egypt); (3) *L'Arrivée à Saïs* (The Arrival at Sais). First performed, Paris, Dec. 10, 1854.

Enfant et les Sortilèges, L' [lũn-fũn ay lay sorr-tee-lezh] (The Child and the Magic Spells). Opera (*fantaisie lyrique*) in two parts by Ravel. Libretto by "Colette" (Sidonie Gabrielle Gauthiers-Villars). First performed, Monte Carlo, March 21, 1925.

Engel [eng′-ĕl], CARL: (1) *b.* Thiedenweise, July 6, 1818; *d.* London, Nov. 17, 1882. Writer on musical instruments. First came to England as a piano-teacher in his 20's, but soon turned his attention to historical research and the collection of musical instruments. His most important works are *The Music of the Most Ancient Nations* (1864), *An Introduction to the Study of National Music* (1866) and *Descriptive Catalogue of the Musical Instruments in the South Kensington Museum* (1874), where many of the instruments in his own collection are now preserved.

(2) *b.* Paris, July 21, 1883; *d.* New York, May 6, 1944. American musicologist, of German origin. Studied at Strasbourg and Munich. Settled in America, 1905, and became an American citizen. Chief of the Music Division, Library of Congress, Washington, 1922-34; Editor, *The Musical Quarterly*, 1929-44. He was active in promoting musical research in the United States and was president of the American Musicological Society, 1937-8. His compositions include chamber music and songs. In addition to articles he published two books, *Alla Breve* (1921) and *Discords Mingled* (1931).

Engführung [eng′-fēē-rŏŏng], *G.* *v.* STRETTO (1).

English Descant. A term introduced by Manfred Bukofzer in his *Geschichte des englischen Diskants und des Fauxbourdons* (1936) to describe a particular type of three-part writing used by English composers in the late 13th and early 14th cent. The two upper parts preserve mainly parallel movement with the melody in the lowest part, or tenor—at intervals respectively of a sixth and a third, *e.g.*

A. HUGHES, *Worcester Medieval Harmony* (*1928*), p. *40*

A similar form of harmonic progression occurs in Continental music in the 15th cent. under the name *fauxbourdon*; but here the melody is not in the tenor but in the soprano. *v.* SIGHT.

English Fingering. A system of fingering piano music (now obsolete) by which the figures 1, 2, 3, 4 represented the four fingers, while the thumb was indicated by a cross. In the so-called Continental fingering, which is now universal, the thumb is represented by the figure 1, and the four fingers by 2, 3, 4, 5.

English Flute. An 18th-cent. name for the RECORDER or beaked flute, as a distinction from the *flauto traverso* (the ordinary orchestral flute), which was known as the German flute. *v.* FLUTE.

English Folk Dance and Song Society. An amalgamation, in 1932, of the Folk-Song Society (founded 1898) and the English Folk Dance Society (founded 1911). Its headquarters are at Cecil Sharp House, 2 Regent's Park Road, London, N.W.1. Its activities include the arranging of lectures, meetings and festivals, and the publication of the *Journal of the English Folk Dance and Song Society*.

English Horn. *v.* COR ANGLAIS.

English Madrigal School, The. An edition by E. H. Fellowes of all the English madrigals published in the reign of Elizabeth and James I, 36 vols. (1913-24).

English Opera Group. An organization founded in 1947 with the object of producing operas with a small instrumental ensemble instead of the usual large and costly orchestra. Benjamin Britten, who founded it in association with Eric Crozier and John Piper, had already written *The Rape of Lucretia* (1946) as an experiment in the use of such resources. Among the works specially written for the group are Britten's *Albert Herring*, *Let's Make an Opera* and *The Turn of the Screw*, and Berkeley's *A Dinner Engagement* and *Ruth*. The Group has also performed revivals of older works, including Blow's *Venus and Adonis* and Purcell's *Dido and Aeneas*. It has no permanent theatre but tours both in England and on the Continent and in 1957 appeared at the Shakespeare Festival at Stratford, Ontario.

English School of Lutenist Song-Writers, The. An edition by E. H. Fellowes of songs for solo voice (or duet) with lute accompanist published by English composers between 1597 and 1622. The 1st series includes the original TABLATURE for the lute, which is omitted in the 2nd series. The alternative versions for four voices found in some of the original song-books are not included. Published, 1920-32.

English Singers, The. An ensemble of six singers formed in 1920 for the purpose of giving authentic performances of English madrigals. Later known as "The New English Singers."

English Suites. The name given to a set of six keyboard suites by J. S. Bach. They are on a larger scale than the FRENCH SUITES. Forkel, Bach's earliest biographer, suggests that they are so called "because the composer wrote them for an Englishman of rank" (*Johann Sebastian Bach*, tr. C. Sanford Terry, p. 128), but there is no evidence to support this. There are clear traces of the influence of a set of six keyboard suites by Charles Dieupart, a French composer who was active in London in the early years of the 18th cent. (*v.* E. Dannreuther, *Musical Ornamentation*, vol.

i, pp. 137-9), but this hardly explains why Bach's suites should be nicknamed "English." The words "fait pour les Anglois" (made for the English), written over the first suite in an early manuscript copy, may provide a clue (*cf.* C. H. H. Parry, *Johann Sebastian Bach*, p. 463).

Engraving. *v.* PRINTING OF MUSIC.

Enharmonic. (1) In Greek music the enharmonic *genus* (*γένος ἐναρμόνιον*) was the oldest of three ways of subdividing a tetrachord, the other two being the diatonic and the chromatic. In its original form it seems to have consisted simply of a major third with a semitone below:

but in quite early times the semitone was divided into two quarter-tones, so that there were four notes in all, instead of three:

(The quarter-tone above E has been represented here by the sign ‡, *i.e.* half a sharp.) The existence of these small intervals, which were in use until Hellenistic times, is evidence of the close association between Greek music and Oriental music.

(2) In modern acoustics the enharmonic *diesis* is the interval between an octave, *i.e.* $\frac{2}{1}$:

and three major thirds, *i.e.* $(\frac{5}{4})^3 = \frac{125}{64}$:

B♯ is therefore flatter than C, and the interval is $2 \div \frac{125}{64} = \frac{128}{125}$ On keyboard instruments, however, B♯ and C are identical, and this has encouraged composers to use harmonic changes which exploit this identity, *e.g.*:

BACH, *St. Matthew Passion*, No. 60

where D♯ becomes E♭. Substitution of this kind is known as an *enharmonic change*. An *enharmonic modulation* is one which makes use of such a change to facilitate the progress from one key to another, *e.g.* instead of writing:

we may treat the B♭ as A♯ and turn the progression in another direction:

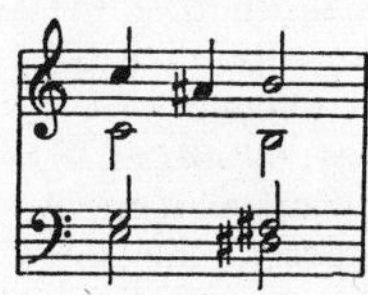

Enigma Variations. "Variations on an original theme for orchestra" by

Elgar, Op. 36. First performed, London, June 19, 1899. The description on the title-page is as quoted above. The word " Enigma " appears only on the first page of the music, underneath the single word " Variations." The page after the title-page bears the words: " Dedicated to my friends pictured within." Each variation is in fact a description of the character or habits of an individual. They are mostly represented by initials or nicknames, which stand for the following:

I. C. A. E.—Caroline Alice Elgar (the composer's wife).
II. H. D. S.-P.—H. D. Steuart-Powell (amateur pianist).
III. R. B. T.—R. B. Townshend (author).
IV. W. M. B.—W. M. Baker (country squire).
V. R. P. A.—R. P. Arnold (son of Matthew Arnold).
VI. Ysobel—Isabel Fitton (amateur viola-player).
VII. Troyte—A. Troyte Griffith (architect).
VIII. W. N.—Winifred Norbury.
IX. Nimrod—A. J. Jaeger (on the staff of Novello's).
X. Dorabella—Dora Penny (now Mrs. Richard Powell).
XI. G. R. S.—G. R. Sinclair (organist, Hereford Cathedral).
XII. B. G. N.—B. G. Nevinson (amateur cellist).
XIII. (***)—Lady Mary Lygon (later Trefusis).
XIV. E. D. U.—" Edu," the name by which Elgar was called by his wife.

Variations X, XIII and XIV are respectively subtitled " Intermezzo," " Romanza " and " Finale."

The subtitle " Enigma " appears, according to the composer, to refer not merely to the initials prefixed to the variations, but also to the fact that both theme and variations are closely associated with another theme which is never heard. The identity of this other theme is not known.

Enna [en′-na], AUGUST: *b.* Nakskov, May 13, 1860; *d.* Copenhagen, Aug. 3, 1939. Danish composer, the son of a shoemaker. His grandfather was Italian, his grandmother German. As a musician he was virtually self-taught. He gained early experience as a violinist and a theatre conductor. Through the interest of Niels Gade he was awarded a travelling scholarship to Germany, 1888-9. He wrote a number of operas, of which *Heksen* (*The Witch*; Copenhagen, 1892) was particularly successful; three of them—*Pigen med Svovlstikkerne* (*The Match Girl*, Copenhagen, 1897), *Prinsessen paa Aerten* (*The Princess on the Pea*, Aarhus, 1900) and *Nattergallen* (*The Nightingale*, Copenhagen, 1912)—were based on stories by Hans Andersen. He also composed several ballets, 2 symphonies and a violin concerto.

Enoch. A London firm of music-publishers, founded in 1869 by Émile Enoch. Bought up by Edwin Ashdown Ltd., 1927, and incorporated with this firm in 1936.

Ensemble [ũn-sũnbl], *Fr.* (1) A group of singers and players, *e.g.* an instrumental ensemble, a vocal ensemble.

(2) In opera, a movement for several singers, with or without chorus.

(3) The artistic co-operation of the individual members of a group. A " good ensemble " means that they are well-matched and the parts well balanced, and that they have been successful in achieving a unified performance.

Entführung aus dem Serail, Die [dee ent-fēē′-rōōng owce dem say-ra′-ill] (The Abduction from the Harem). Comic *Singspiel* (opera with dialogue) by Mozart. Libretto by Christoph Friedrich Bretzner (previously set by Johann André, 1781), adapted by Gottlieb Stephanie. First performed, Vienna, July 16, 1782. Constanze and her maid Blonde are imprisoned in the palace of the Pasha Selim, who wishes to marry Constanze. With the help of Pedrillo, who is in love with Blonde, Belmonte, who loves Constanze, gets into the palace. The attempt to rescue Constanze and Blonde is frustrated by Osmin, guardian of the palace. The Pasha (who has only a speaking part) recognizes Belmonte as the son of an old enemy, but magnanimously sets the four lovers free.

The opera is fully discussed in Mozart's letters (*v.* E. Anderson, *The Letters of Mozart and his Family*, pp. 1123 *et seq.*).

Enthoven [ent'-hoh-vĕn], HENRI ÉMILE *b.* Amsterdam, Oct. 18, 1903 ; *d.* New York, Dec. 26, 1950. Dutch composer, a pupil of Wagenaar and Schreker. Studied law and philosophy at Amsterdam and Utrecht. His compositions include symphonies and other orchestral works, and incidental music for plays. His first symphony was performed when he was 15.

Entr'acte [ũn-truckt], *Fr.* Music played between the acts of a play or opera.

Entrée [ũn-tray], *Fr.* A term used mainly in 17th- and 18th-cent. French music.

(1) An introductory piece in a ballet or opera, for the entry of the characters on the stage.

(2) An independent piece of instrumental music, similar in character to (1).

(3) A section of a ballet or opera, the equivalent of "scene" or even "act."

Enzina (Encina), [del en-thee'-nah] JUAN DEL : *b.* Salamanca, July 12, 1468 ; *d.* León, 1529. Poet and composer, who, though a priest, is known only by secular compositions. Studied at the University of Salamanca. For some time in the service of the first Duke of Alba. Archdeacon of Málaga, 1509; Prior of Leon, 1519. Compositions by him are in the *Cancionero Musical de los siglos xv y xvi*, edited by Asenjo Barbieri (1890) ; also edited by H. Anglès as *El cancionero musical de Palacio*, 3 vols. (1947-53).

Épine, L'. *v.* L'ÉPINE.

Épinette [ay-pee-net], *Fr.* Spinet.

Episode. (1) In a fugue, a passage forming a contrast to the entries of the subject and serving as a link between one entry and the next, often modulating to a related key. The thematic material may be derived from the subject or countersubject, or may be entirely independent. The first episode will normally occur after the EXPOSITION, in which the entries of the subject in the various parts (or "voices") are heard in succession. It is quite possible, however, to have a fugue without any episodes, *e.g.* the fugue in C major in book I of Bach's 48 *Preludes and Fugues*. *v.* FUGUE.

(2) In a rondo, a section separating the entries of the principal theme or section and contrasted with it. *v.* RONDO.

Equale [eh-cwah'-leh], *I.* Old form of *eguale*, "equal." As a noun, a piece for EQUAL VOICES or for instruments of the same kind, *e.g.* the three *equali* for four trombones which Beethoven wrote for All Souls' Day at Linz, 1812.

Equal Temperament. The tuning of keyboard instruments in such a way that all the semitones are equal. This has the effect of putting all the intervals except the octave slightly out of tune. The advantage of the system, which is universally accepted, is that intervals have the same value in all keys. Any other system of tuning favours some keys at the expense of others and makes modulation difficult outside a restricted range.

Equal temperament, or a near approximation to it, was advocated by theorists as early as the 16th cent., and some keyboard compositions of the 17th cent. seem to demand it, if they are to be tolerable to the ear. But it was not until the 18th cent. that the development of modulation and the general use of a wider range of keys made it a practical necessity for all keyboard music (and hence for music played or sung with a keyboard instrument). Bach's collection of preludes and fugues in all the major and minor keys entitled *Das wohltemperirte Clavier* (pt. I, 1722) was clearly designed as a practical demonstration of the advantages of equal temperament. J. K. F. Fischer had given a similar demonstration in his *Ariadne musica neo-organoedum* (*c.* 1700). It was a long time, however, before equal temperament was universally adopted. In England it was not introduced until *c.* 1845. *v.* TEMPERAMENT.

Equal Voices. (1) Voices of the same range, *e.g.* 3 sopranos or 3 basses. (2) Voices of the same kind, *i.e.* male voices as opposed to female voices, and *vice versa*.

Érard [ay-rarr], SÉBASTIEN: *b.* Strasbourg, Apr. 5, 1752; *d.* Passy, Aug. 5, 1831. Founder of a firm of instrument-makers. Of German origin. Came to Paris, 1768, and worked with a harpsichord manufacturer. Patronized by the Duchesse de Villeroi, who provided him with a workshop; here he made the first piano constructed in France, 1777. With his brother Jean-Baptiste established his own business in Paris, and opened a branch in London in 1786. Among the improvements which he introduced into the manufacture of pianos were the double ESCAPEMENT and the CÉLESTE PEDAL. He also perfected the double-action harp, which is still the type in normal use. *v.* HARP, PIANOFORTE.

R. E. M. HARDING: *The Pianoforte: its History traced to the Great Exhibition of* 1851 (1933).

Erbach [airr'-buckh], CHRISTIAN: *b.* Gaualgesheim, *c.* 1570; *d.* Augsburg, 1635. Organist and composer. Private organist to Marx Fugger in Augsburg, *c.* 1597-1614. Organist, St. Moritz, Augsburg, 1602-25; Augsburg Cathedral, 1625-35. City organist and head of the *Stadtpfeifer*, Augsburg, from 1602. His principal compositions are motets. He also wrote secular part-songs and keyboard music (modern ed. of the latter in *D.T.B.*, iv, 2).

Erbe deutscher Musik, Das [duss airr'-ber doytsh'-er moo-zeek'] (The Heritage of German Music). A series of publications of old German music, inaugurated by the National-Socialist government in 1935 and designed to replace the earlier DENKMÄLER DEUTSCHER TONKUNST.

Erdmann [airrd'-mun], EDUARD: *b.* Wenden, March 5, 1896. Pianist and composer. Went to school in Riga. Studied piano and composition in Berlin, 1914-18. Teacher of the piano, Cologne Hochschule, 1925. Well-known for his readiness to perform the works of modern composers. His own works, which are far from simple, include 2 symphonies, a piano concerto, and songs.

Erk [airrk], LUDWIG CHRISTIAN: *b.* Wetzlar, Jan. 6, 1807; *d.* Berlin, Nov. 25, 1883. Conductor and teacher, son of the organist of Wetzlar Cathedral. Played an important part in organizing local musical festivals and in promoting the singing of *Volkslieder*, of which he edited many collections. His valuable library was bought by the government for the Royal Library, Berlin.

Erkel [airr'-kel], FERENCZ: *b.* Gyula (Békés), Nov. 7, 1810; *d.* Budapest, June 15, 1893. Hungarian opera composer. Conductor, National Theatre, Budapest, 1836; later director. His operas, in a strongly marked national vein, were enthusiastically received by his compatriots. His most successful opera was *Hunyady László* (Budapest, 1844), which occupies in Hungary much the same position as Smetana's *The Bartered Bride* in Czechoslovakia. He also composed the music of the Hungarian national anthem, "Ysten áldd meg a Magyart" (1845).

Erlanger [dairr-lũn-zhay], FRÉDÉRIC D': *b.* Paris, May 29, 1868; *d.* London, Apr. 23, 1943. Composer, English by naturalization. His compositions include the operas *Jehan de Saintré* (Aix-les-Bains, 1893), *Inès Mendo* (London, 1897), *Tess* (after Hardy's *Tess of the d'Urbervilles*, Naples, 1906) and *Noël* (Paris, 1910), a violin concerto and chamber music.

Erlebach [airr'-ler-buckh], PHILIPP HEINRICH: *b.* Esens, July 25, 1657; *d.* Rudolstadt, Apr. 17, 1714. Composer. *Kapellmeister* to the court of Rudolstadt. His works include vocal cantatas, instrumental suites and sacred and secular songs. Modern ed. of the collection of songs entitled *Harmonische Freude* (1697, 1710) in *D.D.T.*, xlvi-xlvii.

Ernani [airr-nahn'-ee]. Opera in four acts by Verdi. Libretto by Francesco Maria Piave (based on Victor Hugo's drama of the same title). First performed Venice, March 9, 1844.

Ernst [airrnst], HEINRICH WILHELM: *b.* Brünn, May 6, 1814; *d.* Nice, Oct. 8, 1865. Violinist and composer. Studied at the Vienna Conservatorium. Lived in Paris, 1832-8. Toured widely with great success. His most important work is the *Concerto pathétique* in F♯ minor, Op. 23.

Eroica [eh-ro'-ee-cah], *I.* The popular abbreviation of the title of Beethoven's third symphony in E♭ major, Op. 55 (1804)—*Sinfonia eroica, composta per festeggiare il sovvenire d'un grand' uomo* (Heroic symphony, composed to celebrate the memory of a great man). The title on the original manuscript was *Sinfonia grande Napoleon Bonaparte*, but Beethoven changed it when he heard that Napoleon had become emperor (*v. Beethoven—Impressions of Contemporaries* pp. 51-2). The thematic material on which the last movement is built comes from No. 7 of Beethoven's 12 *Contretänze* (probably written *c.* 1800):

Beethoven also used this theme and bass (1) in the finale of his ballet *Die Geschöpfe des Prometheus* (The men created by Prometheus), Op. 43 (1801), (2) as the basis of 15 variations and fugue for piano solo, Op. 35 (1802), sometimes known illogically as the *Eroica* variations, although they were written before the symphony. It is interesting to compare the opening theme of the first movement of Clementi's piano sonata in G minor, Op. 7, No. 3 (1782):

which in the development section becomes:

Erwartung [airr-vart′-ŏŏng] (Expectation). Opera in one act (four scenes) by Schönberg. Libretto by Marie Pappenheim (described as a *Mimodrama*). First performed, Prague, June 6, 1924.

Erzlaute [airrts′-lout-er], *G.* Archlute.

Es [ess], *G.* E flat (E♭).

Escapement. Mechanism in the piano which enables the hammer to " escape " after the string has been struck, so leaving the string free to vibrate. The *double escapement*, invented by Sébastien Erard, makes it possible to strike the string a second time without waiting for the key to rise to its normal position of rest. *v.* PIANOFORTE.

Eschequier [ay-sheck-yay], *Fr.* *v.* CHEKKER.

Eschig [esh-eeg]. A Paris firm of music-publishers, founded in 1907 by Maximilian Eschig (1872-1927), who was born in Czechoslovakia.

Eses [ess′-ĕss], *G.* E double flat (E♭♭).

Eslava [ess-lah′-vah], MIGUEL HILARIÓN: *b.* Burlada, Oct. 21, 1807; *d.* Madrid, July 23, 1878. Composer and editor, who became a priest in 1832. *Maestro de capilla*, Burgo de Osma, 1828; Seville Cathedral, 1832; court of Queen Isabella, 1844 (also director of the Royal Conservatorio). He wrote a considerable quantity of church music, and also some operas, but is remembered today chiefly by the collection of Spanish church music which he edited under the title *Lira sacro-hispana*, 10 vols. (1869), the contents of which are listed in Grove's *Dictionary*, 5th ed. (1954), ii, p. 970.

Esplá [ess-plah′], OSCAR: *b.* Alicante, Aug. 5, 1886. Composer. Began his career as a civil engineer. Won a prize for composition at Vienna, 1909, with his *Suite Levantina.* His other works, which owe something to his interest in the folk-song of south-eastern Spain, include a number of symphonic poems, chamber music, and the opera *La bella* *durmiente*. Under the Spanish Republic he was director of the National Conservatorio, Madrid, but moved to Brussels with the change of régime.

Esposito [ess-po′-zee-to], MICHELE: *b.* Castellammare, Sept. 29, 1855; *d.* Florence, Nov. 19, 1929. Italian pianist, conductor and composer, who spent most of his life in Dublin. Studied at Naples Conservatorio. In Paris, 1878-82. Teacher of piano, Royal Irish Academy of Music, Dublin, 1882. One of the founders of the Dublin Orchestral Society (1899), which he conducted for many years. His compositions include an "Irish" symphony and the choral cantata *Deirdre* (both prize-winning works), 3 operas, chamber music, songs and piano solos.

Espressivo [ess-press-see′-vo], *I.* Expressive. Often abbreviated *espress.*

Essercizi [ess-air-chee′-tsee], *I.* Lit., "exercises," the title under which 30 of Domenico Scarlatti's harpsichord sonatas were published in 1738.

Estampie [ess-tũn-pee], *Fr.* (*Prov.* estampida). A dance form current in the 13th and 14th cent. It consists of several sections, or *puncta*, each of which has a a first ending (*ouvert*) and a second ending (*clos*). *v.* CLOS, OUVERT.

P. AUBRY : *Estampies et danses royales* (1906).

J. WOLF : "Die Tänze des Mittelalters," in *Archiv für Musikwissenschaft*, i (1918-19).

Este. *v.* EAST.

Esther. Oratorio by Handel. Original libretto attributed to Alexander Pope (after Racine). First performed as a masque, Canons (Edgware), *c.* 1720, and subsequently in London at the house of Bernard Gates, master of the children of the Chapel Royal, Feb. 23, 1732. Revised and enlarged (with additional words by Samuel Humphreys) and performed as an oratorio, London, May 2, 1732 (the original advertisement for this performance announces: "There will be no acting on the Stage, but the house will be fitted up in a decent manner for the audience ").

Estinto [ess-teen′-to], *I.* Lit. "extinct," *i.e.* so soft that the music can hardly be heard.

Etoile du Nord, L' [lay-twull dee norr] (The Star of the North). Opera in three acts by Meyerbeer. Libretto by Augustin Eugène Scribe. First performed, Paris, Feb. 16, 1854.

Eton Choirbook. A manuscript of polyphonic music compiled for the use of the chapel choir of Eton College *c.* 1500, which has been preserved, though in an incomplete form, in the library of the College. It originally contained 92 compositions for four to nine voices (comprising 67 antiphons, 24 Magnificats, and a *St. Matthew* Passion) and a setting of the Apostle's Creed by Robert Wylkynson in the form of a thirteen-part round. Among the 25 composers were Browne, Walter Lambe, Davy, Wylkynson, Cornysh, Fayrfax, Turges, Horwud, Baneaster, Dunstable, Hacumplaynt, Hampton, Hygons, Nesbett, and Sturton. Nearly half the leaves were lost, apparently during the 16th cent., and there remain 43 complete compositions and 21 in various states of incompleteness. Davy's Passion is among the incomplete pieces. In execution and decoration it is the finest English manuscript of polyphonic music which has survived. Modern ed. in *Musica Britannica*, x-xii.

Étouffez [ay - toof - ay], *Fr.* Imperative of *étouffer*, " to damp." An indication to the player of a harp, cymbal, etc. that the sound must be immediately damped (the opposite of *laissez vibrer*). So also *sons étouffés*, " damped notes."

Étranger, L' [lay-trũn-zhay] (The Stranger). Opera in two acts by d'Indy. Libretto by the composer. First performed, Brussels, Jan. 7, 1903.

Ettinger [ett′-ing-er], MAX: *b.* Lwow, Dec. 27, 1874. Composer. Studied in Berlin and at the Munich Conservatorium. Since 1933 resident in Switzerland. He has composed several operas, one of which—*Dolores*—was awarded a share of the Emil Hertzka prize in Vienna, 1936. He has also written choral works (including *Weisheit des Orients*, a setting of words by Omar Khayyám), orchestral works, chamber music and songs.

Étude [ay-teed], *Fr.* "Study," hence a piece of music designed to give practice in some branch of instrumental technique.

There is no intrinsic reason why a piece of this kind should not have artistic merit, as Clementi showed in his *Gradus ad Parnassum* (1817) for piano. The same point was demonstrated even more conclusively by Chopin, whose *études* combine the severest technical discipline with a remarkable invention and a characteristic sensitiveness to the tone of the piano. His example has been followed by other composers, without, however, bringing to an end the composition of *études* of a purely conventional kind, whose only merit is the opportunity they offer for developing the fingers.

Études Symphoniques [ay-tēēd sãn-fon-eek], *Fr.* (Symphonic Studies). Variations for piano by Schumann, Op. 13. Composed, 1834. First published, 1837 ; revised edition, 1852. The full title is : *Études en forme de Variations* (*XII Études symphoniques*). 5 additional variations, not included by Schumann in the original publication, are printed in the supplementary volume to his complete works (1893) and in other modern editions. The theme is by an amateur, Baron von Fricken. The dedication is to William Sterndale Bennett, in whose honour Schumann used in the finale a theme borrowed from Marschner's opera *Der Templer und die Jüdin* (where the words are in praise of England).

Eugene Onegin [yev-geh′-ni on-yeh′-gin]. Opera in three acts by Tchaikovsky, Op. 24. Libretto by the composer and Konstantin Shilovsky (after Pushkin's poem). First performed, Moscow, March 29, 1879. Tatyana, a sensitive young girl, falls in love with Onegin, a cold and selfish man of the world. She declares her passion in a letter, but he will not accept her love. At a ball on her birthday he amuses himself by flirting with her sister Olga and is challenged to a duel by Lensky, who is his friend and in love with Olga. Lensky is killed and Onegin leaves the country. Some years later he returns, to find Tatyana married to the elderly Prince Gremin. He falls in love with her and begs her to go away with him. She admits that she loves him but will not desert her husband. He is left alone, despairing.

Eulenburg [oyl-ĕn-bōōrk]. A Leipzig firm of music-publishers, founded by Ernst Eulenburg (1847-1926) in 1874. In 1892 they took over the series of miniature scores of chamber music published by Albert Payne (also a Leipzig publisher), and by adding orchestral works, oratorios, operas, etc., greatly extended its usefulness. The present headquarters of the firm are in London, with branches in Zürich and New York.

Eunuch Flute. *v.* MIRLITON.

Euphonium. A brass instrument of the saxhorn type, generally with four valves and a compass from

It is a normal instrument in the military band and the brass band, but in the orchestra is used only occasionally, generally for the performance of parts marked " tenor tuba," *e.g.* in Strauss's *Don Quixote* and Holst's *The Planets*. *v.* TUBA.

Euridice, L' [leh-oo-ree-dee′-cheh] (Eurydice). (1) Opera by Caccini. Libretto by Ottavio Rinuccini. Published in 1600, before Peri's opera. First performed, Florence, Dec. 5, 1602. Modern ed. in R. Eitner, *Publikationen älterer praktischer und theoretischer Musikwerke*, x. English translation of the dedication to Giovanni Bardi in O. Strunk, *Source Readings in Music History*, pp. 370-2.

(2) Opera by Peri. The same libretto as (1). First performed, Florence, Oct. 6, 1600. Facsimile ed., 1934; modern ed. by C. Perinello, 1919. English translation of the foreword in Strunk, *op.cit.*, pp. 373-6.

Euryanthe [oy-ryunt′-er]. Opera in three acts by Weber. Libretto by Helmine von Chézy. First performed, Vienna, Oct. 25, 1823. Adolar and Lysiart are both in love with Euryanthe. The treacherous Eglantine betrays to Lysiart a secret of Euryanthe's. Lysiart uses his knowledge of this secret to claim that Euryanthe has been faithless to Adolar. Euryanthe is taken away to the desert by Adolar to be killed, but he spares her life. The king, meeting Euryanthe, discovers Eglantine's treachery. Adolar, confronting the wedding procession of Lysiart and Eglantine, denounces them both. Eglantine, hearing that Euryanthe is reported dead, declares her passion for Adolar and is stabbed by Lysiart. Lysiart is led away to justice, and Adolar is united to Euryanthe.

Evans, EDWIN: *b.* London, Sept. 1, 1874; *d.* there, March 3, 1945. Son of an organist. Music critic, *Pall Mall Gazette*, 1912-23; *Daily Mail*, 1933-45. His particular interests were modern English music and the ballet. President, International Society for Contemporary Music, 1938-45.

Ewer. A London firm of music-publishers, founded in the early 19th cent. by John Ewer. In 1867 the business was acquired by Novello, who published under the name of Novello, Ewer & Co., 1867-88. *v.* NOVELLO.

Expert [ex-pair], HENRY: *b.* Bordeaux, May 12, 1863; *d.* Tourrettes-sur-Loup, Aug. 18, 1952. French musicologist. Studied at the École Niedermeyer, Paris. Librarian, Paris Conservatoire, 1920-33. His principal achievement was the publication of two series of old French music—*Les Maîtres musiciens de la Renaissance française*, 23 vols. (1894-1908) and *Monuments de la musique française au temps de la Renaissance*, 10 vols. (1924-9.) His other publications include *Le Psautier huguenot du XVI*e *siècle* and *Les Maîtres du clavecin des XVII*e *at XVIII*e *siècles*.

Exposition. The statement of the musical material on which a movement is based.

(1) In a FUGUE it consists in introducing the subject in each part (or " voice ") in turn, *i.e.* if the fugue is in three parts, the exposition is complete when all three parts have announced the subject for the first time.

(2) In a movement in SONATA FORM it is more extended and consists in the presentation of the principal thematic material partly in the tonic key and partly in a subsidiary key or keys. In the recapitulation at the end of the movement this material will either appear entirely in the tonic key or will be arranged to end in it.

It was a convention in classical works in sonata form that the exposition should be repeated. This practice is still found in many of Brahms's works in this form. In such cases there is very often a " first ending " which leads back to the beginning, and a "second ending " which leads into the DEVELOPMENT. The omission of such repeats in modern performances is to be condemned on the ground that it violates the composer's expressed intentions.

Expression Marks. Indications provided by the composer as an aid to the accurate interpretation of his text. They are concerned primarily with (1) dynamics—*e.g. forte* (loud), (2) tempo—*e.g. lento* (slow), (3) mood—*e.g. appassionato* (passionate). The vogue of Italian music in the 17th cent. meant that Italian terms came to be used by composers in other countries—for instance, England. The practice was not universal: many French composers preferred to use their own language. But the obvious convenience of having an international language led to the general adoption of Italian for this purpose; and even those composers who have preferred their own language for marks of tempo and mood have been content to use the Italian dynamic signs, either in full or in their commonly accepted abbreviations. The use of German, French and English for marks of tempo and mood makes things easier for composers and interpreters to whom these languages are native; but it complicates the task of performers who lack this natural advantage. On the other hand composers who use Italian sometimes produce curious results, either through misspelling unfamiliar words or through failing to understand exactly what they mean. *v.* DYNAMICS, TEMPO.

R. E. M. HARDING: *Origins of Musical Time and Expression* (1938).

Extemporization. *v.* IMPROVISATION.

Eybler [eye'-bler], JOSEPH, EDLER VON: *b.* Schwechat, Feb. 8, 1765; *d.* Vienna, July 24, 1846. Composer, a pupil of Albrechtsberger and a close friend of Mozart. Vice-*Kapellmeister* to the

Imperial court, Vienna, 1804; *Kapellmeister*, 1824. Ennobled by the Emperor, 1834. Retired from professional life as the result of a stroke, 1833. After Mozart's death in 1791 he began work on the completion of the *Requiem* but did not finish it: the complete work as we have it today is due to Süssmayr. His own works, which were numerous, include 7 Masses and other compositions for the church, symphonies, chamber music, etc.

Ezio [ets'-yo]. Opera in three acts by Handel. Libretto by Pietro Metastasio. First performed, London, Jan. 26, 1732.

F

F. The 4th note (or subdominant) of the scale of C major. As an abbreviation F. = Fellow; *f* = *forte* (loud), *ff* = *fortissimo* (very loud); *fp* = *forte piano* (loud and immediately soft again), *fz* = *forzando* (lit. "forcing," *i.e.* accenting), *mf* = *mezzo forte* (moderately loud), *pf* = *poco forte* (moderately loud), *sf* or *sfz* = *sforzando* (the same as *forzando*). In TONIC SOL-FA **f** = *fah*, the 4th note (or subdominant) of the major scale. The F clef originated as an ornamental form of the letter F and indicates the note a fifth below middle C:

Fa *Fr.* [fa], *I.* [fah]. The note F. Also the fourth note of the Guidonian hexachord ; *v.* SOLMIZATION.

Fabri [fah'-bree], ANNIBALE PIO: *b.* Bologna, 1697; *d.* Lisbon, Aug. 12, 1760. Tenor, a pupil of Pistocchi. Several times president of the Academia Filarmonica, Bologna. Came to England, 1729, and sang in several of Handel's operas with great success. Mrs. Pendarves (later Mrs. Delany) wrote of him:

"Fabri has a tenor voice, sweet, clear and firm, but not strong enough, I doubt, for the stage. He sings like a gentleman, without making faces, and his manner is particularly agreeable. He is the greatest master of music that ever sang upon the stage."

He was subsequently appointed to the Chapel Royal at Lisbon.

Faburden. *v.* FAUXBOURDON.

Façade. A series of poems by Edith Sitwell, recited to the accompaniment of music for flute, clarinet, saxophone, trumpet, cello and percussion by William Walton. First performed, London, June 12, 1923. The music was revised in 1926 and some of the pieces (which were originally designed to match the rhythm of the verse) were issued as a suite for full orchestra. A second suite was published in 1938.

Faccio [fah'-tcho], FRANCO: *b.* Verona, March 8, 1840; *d.* Monza, July 23, 1891. Composer and conductor. Studied at Milan Conservatorio. His first opera, *I profughi Fiamminghi,* was performed at Milan, 1863. He was a close friend of Boito, who wrote the libretto of his opera *Amleto* (Genoa, 1865), and was partly responsible for the collaboration of Boito and Verdi in *Otello.* He became conductor at La Scala, Milan, and directed there the first performance in Europe of Verdi's *Aida* (1872) and the first performance of *Otello* (1887).

Fagott [fug-ot'], *G.* Bassoon.

Fagotto [fah-got'-to], *I.* Bassoon.

Fah. Anglicized form of the Italian *fa* (F). In TONIC SOL-FA the 4th note (or subdominant) of the major scale.

Fairchild, BLAIR: *b.* Belmont, Mass., June 23, 1877; *d.* Paris, Apr. 23, 1933. Composer. Studied at Harvard and in Florence. For a short time in the diplomatic service. Settled in Paris, 1903, and devoted the rest of his life to music. His compositions include the ballet-pantomime *Dame Libellule* (Paris, 1921), symphonic poems, chamber music, choral works and songs.

Fairfax. *v.* FAYRFAX.

Fair Maid of Perth, The. *v.* JOLIE FILLE DE PERTH.

Fair Maid of the Mill, The. *v.* SCHÖNE MÜLLERIN.

Fair Melusina, The. *v.* SCHÖNE MELUSINE.

Fairy Queen, The. Opera with dialogue, adapted from Shakespeare's *A Midsummer Night's Dream.* Music by Purcell. First performed, London, 1692. Modern ed. by J. S. Shedlock (*Purcell Society,* xii).

Fa-la. The name given to a popular type of part-song current in the late 16th and early 17th cent., known also in Italy as *balletto* and in England as ballett.

The name is derived from the use of a refrain composed of the syllables "fa la la." *v.* BALLETT.

Falcon [full-cõn], MARIE CORNÉLIE: *b.* Jan. 28, 1812; *d.* Paris, Feb. 25, 1897. Operatic soprano. Studied at the Paris Conservatoire. First appeared at the Paris Opéra as Alice in *Robert le Diable*, 1832. Lost her voice in 1838 and had to abandon the stage. During her short career she sang leading parts in the first performances of several operas—including Halévy's *La Juive* and Meyerbeer's *Les Huguenots*—and had a great reputation as a singer and actress.

Falla [fahl'-lyah], MANUEL DE: *b.* Cadiz, Nov. 23, 1876; *d.* Alta Gracia, Nov. 14, 1946. Spanish composer and pianist, a pupil of Pedrell and Tragó. He made his reputation with the opera *La Vida Breve*, which was awarded a prize in 1905 but was not performed until 1913 at Nice. From 1907-14 he lived in Paris. Lived in Spain until the Civil War, when he moved to South America. He died in Argentina. He was the outstanding Spanish composer of his time, skilful in the adoption of Andalusian idioms without becoming their slave. His acquaintance with Debussy in Paris inclined him towards impressionism, but in his later works he turned rather towards a neo-classical idiom, which avoids equally impressionism and the more obvious nationalism of his youth. Severely self-critical, he published comparatively little. His orchestration is vivid and precise. His principal works are:

(a) OPERAS: *La vida breve* (1905); *El retablo de Maese Pedro* (1923).

(b) BALLETS: *El amor brujo* (1915); *El sombrero de tres picos* (1919).

(c) ORCHESTRA: *Noches en los jardines de España* (1916) for piano and orchestra; harpsichord concerto (1926).

(d) PIANO: *Fantasia bética* (1919).

J. B. TREND: *Manuel de Falla and Spanish Music* (1930).

Falsa Musica. *v.* MUSICA FICTA.

False Relation. The name given in classical harmony (*i.e.* late 18th and early 19th cent.) to (1) a progression in which a note in one part in the first chord is followed by a chromatic alteration of the same note in another part in the second chord, *e.g.*:

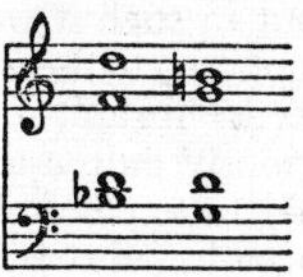

(2) the simultaneous sounding in a single chord of a note and its chromatic alteration, *e.g.*:

"False relations" of both kinds are frequent in late 16th- and early 17th-cent. music, particularly in England, *e.g.*:

BYRD, *Songs of Sundrie Natures*, No. 27

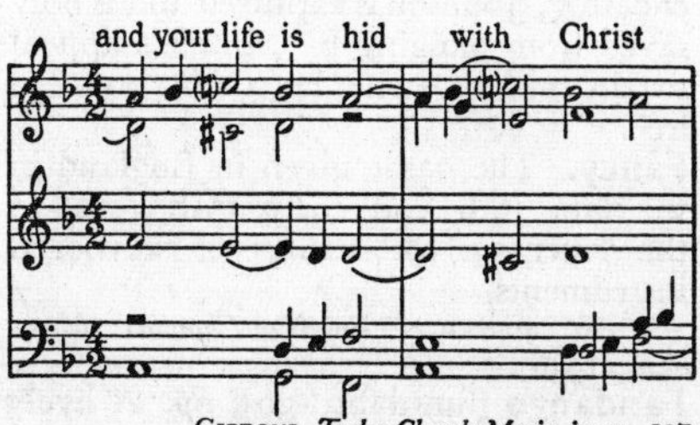

GIBBONS, *Tudor Church Music*, iv, p. 217

Falsetto. An adult male voice, used not in the normal range and with the normal production but in such a way that only the edges, as opposed to the whole mass, of the vocal chords vibrate. If this type of singing is seriously cultivated, the voice becomes a male alto. Falsetto singing is also used occasionally by tenors for notes which lie above their normal range. A good falsetto singer can command a compass up to:

Falso bordone. *v.* FAUXBOURDON.

Falstaff. (1) Comic opera in three acts by Verdi. Libretto by Arrigo Boito (after Shakespeare's *The Merry Wives of Windsor*). First performed, Milan, Feb. 9, 1893. The action of the opera is substantially the same as the play, except that Anne Page, in love with Fenton, becomes Anne (Nannetta) Ford, and some minor characters, such as Shallow and Slender, are eliminated.

(2) Symphonic study for orchestra by Elgar, Op. 68 (after Shakespeare's *King Henry IV*, pts. i & ii). First performed, Leeds, Oct. 1, 1913. For an analysis by the composer see *Musical Times*, Sept. 1913.

Fanciulla del West, La [lah fahn-chool'-lah del west]. Opera in three acts by Puccini. Libretto by Guelfo Civinini and Carlo Zangarini (after David Belasco's play *The Girl of the Golden West*). First performed, New York, Dec. 10, 1910. The scene is laid in California, in the days of the gold rush. Minnie falls in love with an outlaw, Johnson, and hides him in her cabin. When he is found by the sheriff, she plays cards for his life and wins by cheating. Johnson is captured and is only saved from hanging by Minnie's appeal to the miners, who let them both go free.

Fancy. The name given in England in the late 16th and early 17th cent. to the FANTASIA for strings or keyboard instruments.

E. H. MEYER: *English Chamber Music* (1946).

Fandango [fun-dahn'-go], *Sp.* A lively dance in triple time, accompanied by guitar and castanets.

Fantasia [fahn-tah-zee'-ah], *I.* (*Fr.* fantaisie, *G.* Phantasie, Fantasie). In general a piece in which the composer exercises his fancy without following any conventional form. In particular:

(1) In the 16th and 17th cent. frequently used of a composition, either for strings or for a keyboard instrument (*E.* fancy), in which the composer, instead of adopting a dance form or writing variations, lets his imagination play freely in developing his theme contrapuntally. Morley says in his *Plaine and Easie Introduction to Practicall Musicke* (1597): " In this may more art be showne then in any other musicke, because the composer is tide to nothing but that he may adde, deminish, and alter at his pleasure " (p. 181).

(2) A work for keyboard or lute of an improvisatory character, *e.g.* Bach's Chromatic Fantasia.

(3) An extended work, freer in form than the normal sonata, *e.g.* Beethoven's *Sonata quasi una Fantasia* in C♯ minor, Op. 27, No. 2, or Schumann's *Fantaisie*, Op. 17.

(4) A short piece similar to an intermezzo, capriccio, etc.

(5) A work based on an existing theme or themes, *e.g.* Liszt's *Fantaisie sur les motifs favoris de l'opéra "La Sonnambula,"* or Vaughan Williams's *Fantasia on a theme by Thomas Tallis*.

(6) The development section of a movement in sonata form is sometimes known as " free fantasia."

Fantasiestück [fun-tuz-ee'-shtĕĕk], *G.* = FANTASIA (4).

Fantastic Symphony. *v.* SYMPHONIE FANTASTIQUE.

Faramondo [fah-rah-mon'-do]. Opera in three acts by Handel. Libretto by Apostolo Zeno (with alterations). First performed, London, Jan. 18, 1738.

Farandole [fa-rũn-doll], *Fr.* A dance of ancient origin still current in Provence. The dancers—men and women—advance in a long chain, preceded by a player (or players) on the *galoubet* and *tambourin* (pipe and tabor). There is a well-known example in Bizet's music to Daudet's play *L'Arlésienne*, beginning:

The original title is *Danse dei chivau-frus* (Dance of the cardboard horses).

Farewell Sonata. *v.* ADIEUX.

Farewell Symphony (*G.* Abschiedssymphonie). Symphony No. 45 in F♯ minor by Haydn (1772). The finale emphasizes the desire of Prince Esterházy's musicians to obtain leave of absence in order to visit their families. The instruments stop playing in turn, and the players put out their candles and leave the room. At the end only two violins are left.

Farina [fah-ree′-nah], CARLO: *b.* Mantua. Violinist and composer, who flourished in the early 17th cent. He was for a time in the service of the Dresden court, and later had an appointment at Danzig. He was one of the first composers to exploit virtuosity in solo violin music. His "Capriccio stravagante" (1627) includes not only double stops but also *pizzicato, col legno* and harmonics. The following is an extract:

Qui si bate con il legno del archetto sopra le corde

Farinel [fa-ree-nel], MICHEL: *b.* Grenoble, May, 1649. Violinist and composer. One of the earliest of the many composers who wrote chaconnes or variations on the theme known as FOLIES D'ESPAGNE, which for that reason was known in England as "Farinel's Ground."

Farinelli [fah-ree-nell′-lee]: *b.* Naples, Jan. 24, 1705; *d.* Bologna, July 15, 1782. Famous castrato singer, whose real name was Carlo Broschi. A pupil of Porpora, he rapidly acquired a reputation in Southern Italy and made his first appearance in Rome, with enormous success, in his master's opera *Eumene* (1721). Subsequently had some instruction from Bernacchi and appeared in a number of European cities, including London. Visiting Spain in 1737 he was engaged to sing to Philip V and remained there under Philip and his successor, Ferdinand VI, until the accession of Charles III, 1759, when he returned to Italy and settled in Bologna. He told Burney that for ten years he sang the same four songs every night to Philip V; *v.* C. Burney, *The Present State of Music in France and Italy* (1771), pp. 205-17.

Farmer, JOHN. (1) Late 16th- and early 17th-cent. composer, who published a treatise on counterpoint (1591) and a set of madrigals (1599: modern ed. in *E.M.S.*, viii), of which "Fair Phyllis I saw sitting all alone" is well-known. He also contributed to Thomas East's *Whole Booke of Psalmes* (1592).

(2): *b.* Nottingham, Aug. 16, 1836; *d.* Oxford, July 17, 1901. Music master, Harrow, 1862-85, and subsequently organist of Balliol College, Oxford, where he instituted the Sunday evening concerts.

Farnaby, GILES: *d.* London, Nov., 1640. Late 16th- and early 17th-cent. composer. He published an original set of canzonets for four voices (1598: modern ed. in *E.M.S.*, xx). A large number of his keyboard pieces, which show an equally individual imagination, are in the *Fitzwilliam Virginal Book.*

Farrant, RICHARD: *d.* 1581. English composer, principally of church music. Master of the choristers, St. George's, Windsor, and gentleman of the Chapel Royal. His anthems "Call to remembrance" and "Hide not thou thy face" are still sung.

Farrenc [farr-ũnk], (1) JACQUES HIPPOLYTE ARISTIDE: *b.* Marseilles, Apr. 9, 1794; *d.* Paris, Jan. 31, 1865. Flautist, music-publisher and critic.

(2) LOUISE: *b.* Paris, May 31, 1804; *d.* there, Sept. 15, 1875. Wife of (1). Pianist and composer, a pupil of Reicha. Toured with her husband, whom she married in 1821. Taught at the Paris Conservatoire, 1842-73. Best known today by her *Trésor des Pianistes* (1861-72), a valuable collection of keyboard music from the 16th to the 19th cent., which she began in collaboration with her husband. Her maiden name was Dumont.

Fasch [fush], (1) JOHANN FRIEDRICH: *b.* Buttelstedt, Apr. 15, 1688; *d.* Zerbst, Dec. 5, 1758. Studied at St. Thomas's School, Leipzig. *Kapellmeister* to the court at Zerbst, 1722. His numerous compositions include church cantatas, Masses, overtures (suites), concertos and chamber music.

(2) KARL FRIEDRICH CHRISTIAN: *b.* Zerbst, Nov. 18, 1736; *d.* Berlin, Aug. 3, 1800. Son of (1). His first important appointment was as accompanist to Frederick the Great at Potsdam, 1756 (in conjunction with C. P. E. Bach), but the outbreak of the Seven Years War (1756-63) soon brought his duties to an end. He was *Kapellmeister* of the Royal Opera, 1774-6 but for the most part maintained himself by teaching. He founded the Berlin *Singakademie*, 1791, a choral society for the practice of sacred music. He wrote some instrumental works, but his principal compositions were for the church.

Faschingsschwank aus Wien [fush'-ingce-shvunk owce veen], *G.* (Carnival Jest from Vienna). A set of five piano pieces by Schumann, Op. 26 (1839). The title *Faschingsschwank* seems to have been originally designed for the set of pieces published as *Carnaval*, Op. 9, possibly because it includes the letters A S C H on which the latter work is based (*v.* CARNAVAL).

Fastes de la Grande et Ancienne Ménestrandise, Les [lay fust der la grũnd ay ũnce-yen may-ness-trũn-deez] (Annals of the Great and Ancient Order of Minstrelsy). Satirical suite for harpsichord published by François Couperin (le grand) in the second volume of his *Pièces de clavecin* (1717). In the original the vowels in the last word are replaced by crosses: *mxnxstrxndxsx.* The suite refers to a dispute between the organists of Paris and the corporation of minstrels (*Confrérie de Saint-Julien des Ménestriers*), which was settled in 1707. The titles of the pieces are:

1er Acte: *Les notables et jurés mxnxstrxndxurs* (The notable and sworn members of the corporation of minstrels)—*Marche.*

2e Acte: *Les viéleux et les gueux* (The hurdy-gurdy players and the beggars).

3e Acte: *Les jongleurs, sauteurs et saltinbanques, avec les ours et les singes* (The jugglers, tumblers and mountebanks, with the bears and monkeys).

4e Acte: *Les invalides, ou gens estropiés au service de la grande mxnxstrxndxsx* (The invalids, or people crippled in the service of the great minstrelsy).

5e Acte: *Désorde et déroute de toute la troupe, causés par les yvrognes, les singes et les ours* (Disorder and rout of the whole company, caused by the drunkards, monkeys and bears).

Faure [fohrr], JEAN-BAPTISTE: *b.* Moulins, Jan. 15, 1830; *d.* Paris, Nov. 9, 1914. Operatic baritone. Studied at the Paris Conservatoire; also a chorister at the Madeleine. First appeared as an operatic singer, Opéra-Comique, 1852. Principal baritone, Paris Opéra, 1861-76. He also sang in opera in London, Brussels, Berlin and Vienna, and taught singing at the Paris Conservatoire, 1857-60. He published some songs and a treatise on singing (1886).

Fauré [fo-ray], GABRIEL URBAIN: *b.* Pamiers, May 12, 1845; *d.* Paris, Nov. 4, 1924. Composer, organist and teacher, the son of a schoolmaster. Studied at the École Niedermeyer, where he was a pupil of Saint-Saëns. After holding various organist's posts became *maître de chapelle* at the Madeleine in Paris,

1877; organist, 1896. Teacher of composition, Paris Conservatoire, 1896; director, 1905-20. The last 20 years of his life were marred by deafness, which became so acute in the end that he was unable to hear his own music. As a composer he was one of the most original minds of his time. He began as a Romantic, but the idioms of Schumann and Mendelssohn were clarified and refined in his hands till they took on an aspect that was typically French. His harmony, though never revolutionary, is constantly surprising, because of his gift for associating familiar materials in a new way. In this respect he showed an extraordinarily sensitive ear. In his later years his passion for refinement tended to drain away the life-blood of his earlier work, but the zest for experiment remained and one still has the impression that every note was exactly weighed and calculated. He excelled in writing songs, many of which exhibit a magical economy of means. He was not at home with the orchestra, and a good deal of his orchestral music was scored by others. As a teacher he had a great influence on younger men. Among his pupils were Florent Schmitt, Louis Aubert, Nadia Boulanger, Georges Enesco, Roger-Ducasse, Gabriel Grovlez, Charles Koechlin and Maurice Ravel. His principal compositions are:

(a) OPERAS: *Prométhée* (1900); *Pénélope* (1913).

(b) INCIDENTAL MUSIC: *Shylock* (1889); *Pelléas et Mélisande* (1898).

(c) ORCHESTRA: *Pavane* (1887); *Dolly*, suite (1893-6); *Masques et bergamasques*, suite (1920); *Ballade*, piano and orchestra (1881); *Fantaisie*, piano and orchestra (1919).

(d) CHAMBER MUSIC: 2 piano quartets (1879, 1886); 2 piano quintets (1906, 1921); piano trio (1923); string quartet (1924); 2 violin sonatas (1876, 1917); 2 cello sonatas (1918, 1922).

(e) PIANO: 5 impromptus; 13 nocturnes; 13 barcarolles; 9 preludes.

(f) CHURCH MUSIC: Requiem Mass (1887).

(g) SONGS: 3 song-cycles—*La Bonne Chanson* (1891-2), *La Chanson d'Eve* (1907-10), *Le Jardin clos* (1915-18); *Mirages* (4 songs, 1919); *L'Horizon chimérique* (4 songs, 1922); numerous single songs.

P. FAURÉ-FREMIET : *Gabriel Fauré* (1929).
V. JANKÉLÉVITCH : *Gabriel Fauré et ses mélodies* (1938).
C. KOECHLIN : *Fauré* (1927).
N. SUCKLING : *Fauré* (1946).

Faust [*G.* fowst, *Fr.* foast]. Opera in five acts by Gounod. Libretto by Jules Barbier and Michel Carré (after Goethe). First performed, Paris, March 19, 1859. Originally an *opéra-comique* with dialogue; the recitatives were added in 1860. Faust, an elderly scholar, wins from Mephistopheles the gift of youth, in exchange for his own soul. He falls in love with Marguerite, but having ruined her deserts her. Her brother Valentine, returning from the wars, fights a duel with Faust and is killed. Marguerite, having killed her baby, is condemned to death. She refuses to escape with Faust. As she dies, the voices of an angelic choir are heard, while Mephistopheles claims from Faust the promised payment.

For other works on the same subject *v.* DAMNATION DE FAUST, DOKTOR FAUST.

Faust-Ouvertüre, Eine [ine'-er fowst oo-vair-teer'-er], *G.* (A Faust Overture). Orchestral piece by Wagner, based on Goethe (1840).

Faust-Symphonie, Eine [ine'-er fowst zeem-fo-nee'], *G.* (A Faust Symphony). An orchestral work by Liszt in three movements, with chorus in the final movement (based on Goethe). First performed, Weimar, Sept. 5, 1857. The score is dedicated to Berlioz.

Fauvel. *v.* ROMAN DE FAUVEL.

Fauxbourdon [fo-boorr-dõn], *Fr.* (*O. E.* faburden, *I.* falso bordone). Lit. "false bass" (*faux bourdon*). Used in the following senses:

(1) In the 15th cent. to indicate a simple form of three-part harmony in which a plainsong melody in the treble is accompanied by two lower parts, one moving mainly in parallel sixths, the other, to be supplied by the singer, a fourth below the melody, *e.g.* :

DUFAY (in H. Besseler, *Bourdon und Fauxbourdon*, p. 264)

The name presumably refers to the fact that the bass is not the foundation of the harmony, since the plainsong is assigned to the treble. This kind of harmony seems to have originated in England in the late 13th cent. but in a different form—with the melody in the lower part: the name of ENGLISH DESCANT has been given to this form, since it is different from *fauxbourdon* and since the term *fauxbourdon* in any case does not occur before the 15th cent.

(2) Through the use of this kind of harmony for psalm tones the Italian name *falso bordone* came to be applied to a simple four-part harmonization of plainsong, without any polyphonic elaboration.

Be - ne - di - ctus Do - mi - nus

PALESTRINA, *Complete Works*, vol. xxxi, p. 169

(3) In modern English hymnody the name *fauxbourdon* is often given to a counterpoint (or descant) for treble voices superimposed on the melody sung by the congregation.

M. BUKOFZER: *Geschichte des englischen Diskants und des Fauxbourdons* (1936).

H. BESSELER: *Bourdon und Fauxbourdon* (1950).

Favart [fa-varr], (1) CHARLES SIMON: *b.* Paris, Nov. 13, 1710; *d.* Paris, May 18, 1792. A pioneer of the French *opéra-comique*, who wrote the librettos for a large number of works of this kind.

(2) MARIE JUSTINE BENOISTE DURONCERAY: *b.* Avignon, June 15, 1727; *d.* Paris, Apr. 21, 1772. Wife of (1), whom she married in 1745. Singer and dancer. She appeared with great success in a large number of *opéras-comiques*.

Favorite, La [la fa-vo-reet] (The King's Mistress). Opera in four acts by Donizetti (originally in three acts and called *L'Ange de Niside*). Libretto by Alphonse Royer, Gustave Vaëz and Augustin Eugène Scribe. First performed, Paris, Dec. 2, 1840.

Fayrfax, ROBERT: *d.* Oct. 24, 1521. English composer. Organist of St. Albans Abbey. Gentleman of the Chapel Royal. D.Mus., Cambridge, 1502, and Oxford (by incorporation), 1511. He had a great reputation in his lifetime. Most of his music, which shows considerable dignity and a feeling for sonority, is for the church—mainly Masses and motets. Very little is available in modern editions.

Fedra [feh'-drah] (Phaedra). Opera in three acts by Pizzetti. Libretto by Gabriele d'Annunzio (published as a play in 1909). First performed, Milan, March 20, 1915.

Fehrman, MINNY. *v.* BREMA.

Fellerer [fell'-er-er], KARL GUSTAV: *b.* Freising, July 7, 1902. Musicologist who has written extensively on Catholic Church music. Studied at Munich and Berlin. Lecturer, Münster, 1926; professor, Freiburg, 1932; Cologne, 1939. In addition to works in his special field he has also written studies of Puccini and Grieg.

Fellowes, EDMUND HORACE: *b.* London, Nov. 11, 1870; *d.* Windsor, Dec. 20, 1951. English musicologist. Educated at Winchester and Oxford. Precentor, Bristol Cathedral, 1897; Minor Canon,

St. George's, Windsor, 1900. His publications of English music of the past include *The English Madrigal School* (36 vols.), *The English School of Lutenist Songwriters* (1st ser., 15 vols.; 2nd ser., 16 vols.), the complete vocal and instrumental works of Byrd, and a number of compositions published in *Tudor Church Music*. His books include *English Madrigal Verse* (1920), *The English Madrigal Composers* (1921), *William Byrd* (1936), *English Cathedral Music* (1941), *Orlando Gibbons* (rev. ed., 1951).

Fennimore und Gerda [fen-ni-moh'-rer ŏŏnt gairr'-da] (Fennimore and Gerda). Opera in two episodes by Delius. Libretto (in German) by the composer (after Jens Peter Jacobsen's novel *Niels Lyhne*, published in English as *Siren Voices*). First performed, Frankfort, Oct. 21, 1919.

Feo [feh'-o], FRANCESCO : *b*. Naples (?), 1691 ; *d*. there, 1761. Opera composer of the so-called Neapolitan school. In addition to operas he wrote a considerable amount of church music. For a time director of one of the Naples *Conservatori*.

Fermata [fairr-mah'-tah], *I*. Pause, represented by the sign 𝄐.

Ferrabosco [fair-rah-boss'-co], ALFONSO. (1): *b*. Bologna, Jan. 1543; *d*. there, Aug. 12, 1588. Italian composer, who came to England at an early age and entered the service of Queen Elizabeth. Left England in 1578 and received an appointment from the Duke of Savoy, leaving his two children in England. Published 2 volumes of Italian madrigals (1587: modern ed. in *Old English Edition*, vols. xi & xii), several of which appeared with English versions in the 2 volumes of *Musica Transalpina* (1588, 1597). There is evidence that he was employed by Elizabeth as a secret service agent.

(2): *b*. Greenwich; *d*. there, March, 1628. Son (probably illegitimate) of (1). Viol-player and composer, in the service of James I and Charles I. Music-master to Henry, Prince of Wales, and his brother Charles (later Charles I). Wrote music for several of Ben Jonson's masques. His compositions include a book of lute-songs (modern ed. in *E.S.L.S.*) and music for viols (examples in *Musica Britannica*, ix). For further information about the Ferrabosco family see *Musical Antiquary*, July & Oct. 1912, Apr. 1913.

Ferrari [fair-rah'-ree], BENEDETTO: *b*. Reggio, 1597; *d*. Modena, Oct. 22, 1681. Poet and composer. His librettos include *L'Andromeda*, set by Francesco Manelli (Venice, 1637)—the first opera to be given in a public theatre. The music of the operas for which he wrote the music is lost. Among his surviving works are an oratorio *Sansone* (*v*. A. Schering, *Geschichte des Oratoriums*, p. 104) and 3 books of solo cantatas.

Ferrier, KATHLEEN : *b*. Higher Walton, Lancs., Apr. 22, 1912 ; *d*. London, Oct. 8, 1953. Contralto. She studied originally as a pianist and did not have lessons in singing until 1940. She rapidly acquired a reputation as one of the finest singers of her time, and confirmed it by her tours on the Continent and in Canada and the U.S.A. after the war. She appeared as Lucretia in Britten's *The Rape of Lucretia* (Glyndebourne, 1946) and as Orpheus in Gluck's *Orfeo* (Glyndebourne, 1947 ; Covent Garden, 1953) but her principal activity was in the concert room.

Ferroud [ferr-oo], PIERRE OCTAVE: *b*. Chasselay, Jan. 6, 1900; *d*. Debrecen, Aug. 17, 1936. Composer and critic, a pupil of Florent Schmitt. His compositions include the one-act opera *Chirurgie* (Monte Carlo, 1928), ballet music, a symphony, chamber music and songs. He practised for several years as a music-critic and wrote a book on Schmitt (1927). He was killed in a car accident in Hungary.

Fervaal [fair-vahl]. Opera with a prologue and three acts by d'Indy. Libretto by the composer (*action dramatique*). First performed, Brussels, March 12, 1897.

Fes [fess], *G*. F flat (F♭).

Fesch, De. *v*. DEFESCH.

Festa [fest'-ah], COSTANZO: *b*. *c*. 1490; *d*. Rome, Apr. 10, 1545. Composer, a member of the Papal choir in 1517. He composed Masses, motets (modern ed. in *Monumenta Polyphonica Italica*, ii) and madrigals. His madrigal "Quando ritrovo la mia pastorella" is well known to English choral societies as "Down in a flowery vale."

Festing, MICHAEL CHRISTIAN: *d.* London, July 24, 1752. Violinist, a pupil of Geminiani. Conductor, Italian Opera, 1737; Ranelagh Gardens, 1742. His compositions include a number of concertos, sonatas and violin solos. He was one of the founders of the Royal Society of Musicians.

Fétis [fay-teece], FRANÇOIS JOSEPH: *b.* Mons, March 25, 1784; *d.* Brussels, March 26, 1871. Teacher, musicologist and composer. Studied at the Paris Conservatoire, where he became teacher of counterpoint and fugue, 1821, and librarian, 1827. Director, Brussels Conservatoire, 1833. Founded and edited the *Revue Musicale*, 1827-33, and also organized historical concerts in Paris. In addition to a large number of theoretical works he published a *Biographie universelle des musiciens*, 8 vols. (1835-44) and a *Histoire générale de la musique*, 5 vols. (1869-76). His compositions, which include several operas, are of no importance.

Feuermann [foy'-er-mun], EMANUEL: *b.* Kolomea, Nov. 22, 1902; *d.* New York, May 25, 1942. Austrian cellist, a pupil of Klengel. He made his reputation as a soloist at an early age. Teacher of cello, Cologne Conservatorium, 1919-23; Berlin Hochschule für Musik, 1929-33.

Feuersnot [foy'-erce-note] (No Fire in the City). Opera in one act by Richard Strauss. Libretto by Ernst von Wolzogen. First performed, Dresden, Nov. 21, 1901.

Fevin [fer-vaȵ], ANTOINE DE: *d.* Blois, 1512. French composer, of the school of Josquin des Prés. A number of Masses and motets survive. Modern ed. of the Mass *Mente tota* in H. Expert, *Les Maîtres musiciens de la Renaissance française*, v. See also the Mass *Ave Maria* (modern ed., with biography, by J. Delporte, 1934).

Ffrangcon - Davies, (1) DAVID THOMAS: *b.* Bethesda, Dec. 11, 1855; *d.* London, Apr. 13, 1918. Baritone. Studied at the Guildhall School of Music. First public appearance, 1890. He was the original Cedric in Sullivan's opera *Ivanhoe* (London, 1891). Sang frequently at concerts and in oratorio in England, America and on the Continent. Taught singing at the R.A.M., 1903. Retired from public life for reasons of health, 1907. His *Singing of the Future* was first published, with a preface by Elgar, 1906; reissued in an abridged form with short biography by his daughter and correspondence with Elgar, under the title *David Ffrangcon-Davies—his Life and Book*, 1938.

(2) GWEN: *b.* London, Jan. 25, 1896. Singer and actress. She sang the part of Etain in several revivals of Rutland Boughton's *The Immortal Hour*, from 1920 onwards.

Fiato [fee-ah'-to], *I.* "Breath." *Strumenti a fiato*, wind instruments.

Fibich [fib'-ickh], ZDENEK: *b.* Šebořice, Dec. 21, 1850; *d.* Prague, Oct. 10, 1900. Composer. Studied at the Leipzig Conservatorium, where he was a pupil of Moscheles and Jadassohn. Assistant conductor, National Theatre, Prague, 1875-8; choirmaster, Russian Church, Prague, 1878-81. Apart from these posts devoted himself wholly to composition. His compositions, which are Romantic in style and show the influence of Wagner, include 7 operas, a melodrama trilogy—*Hippodamia*, 3 symphonies, several symphonic poems and overtures, chamber music, songs and piano pieces. *Hippodamia* consists of three separate melodramas (*i.e.* spoken drama with continuous orchestral accompaniment).

Ficker [fick'-er], RUDOLF VON: *b.* Munich, June 11, 1886; *d.* Igls (Tyrol), Aug. 2, 1954. Musicologist. Studied in Vienna and Munich. Lecturer, Innsbruck, 1920. Professor, Innsbruck, 1924; Vienna, 1927; Munich, 1930. In addition to editing selections from the Trent Codices for the *Denkmäler der Tonkunst in Österreich*, he published studies of various aspects of medieval and Renaissance music. In particular he was active in promoting performances of medieval music.

Fidelio [fee-dale'-yo]. Opera in two (originally three) acts by Beethoven. Full title: *Fidelio, oder die eheliche Liebe*

(Fidelio, or Wedded Love). Libretto originally by Josef Sonnleithner (after Jean Nicolas Bouilly's *Léonore, ou l'Amour conjugal*); reduced to two acts by Stefan von Breuning (1806), and further revised by Georg Friedrich Treitschke (1814). First performance of original version, Vienna, November 20, 1805; second version, March 29, 1806; final version, May 23, 1814. Florestan is a political prisoner in the hands of Pizarro. His wife, Leonora, disguised as a young man with the name Fidelio, enters the service of the prison gaoler, Rocco, in order to find her husband. Pizarro, learning that the governor, Fernando, is to visit the prison, orders Florestan to be killed. Leonora helps Rocco to dig the grave. When Pizarro arrives, she defies him and reveals herself as Florestan's wife. At that moment a trumpet announces the arrival of Fernando. Florestan and his wife are free.

For the 4 overtures which Beethoven wrote for this opera *v.* LEONORE.

Field, JOHN: *b.* Dublin, July 26, 1782; *d.* Moscow, Jan. 23, 1837. Pianist and composer, the son of a violinist. Apprenticed at an early age to Clementi, whom he accompanied to France, Germany and Russia, his duties being to demonstrate the excellence of the pianos which Clementi sold. Lived in Russia as a teacher and soloist until 1832, when he returned to England and subsequently toured on the Continent. After a long illness in Naples he returned to Russia to die. His reputation as a performer was high. His compositions include 7 piano concertos, 4 sonatas, and a number of other works for the piano, of which the Nocturnes are the most characteristic. The influence of his nocturnes on Chopin's is unmistakable: the common factor is a *cantabile* melody—sometimes simple, sometimes ornamented—with an unobtrusive accompaniment for the left hand.

Fifara [fee'-fah-rah], *I.* A 17th-cent. name for the transverse flute (also spelled *fiffaro*), as opposed to *flauto*, the beaked flute or recorder.

Fife. A small flute, still used, as for centuries past, in the "drum and fife" band. In its modern form it is built a tone lower than the orchestral piccolo and has one or more keys.

Fiffaro [feef-fah-ro], *I.* *v.* FIFARA.

Fifteenth. (1) The interval of two octaves, *e.g.*:

(2) An organ stop pitched two octaves higher than the normal (or 8 ft.) pitch, in other words a 2 ft. stop.

Fifth. The interval reached by ascending four steps in the diatonic scale, *e.g.*:

In the HARMONIC SERIES it is the interval between the 2nd and 3rd notes of the series, and therefore has the ratio $\frac{3}{2}$ A series of 12 fifths, beginning on:

will reach B♯:

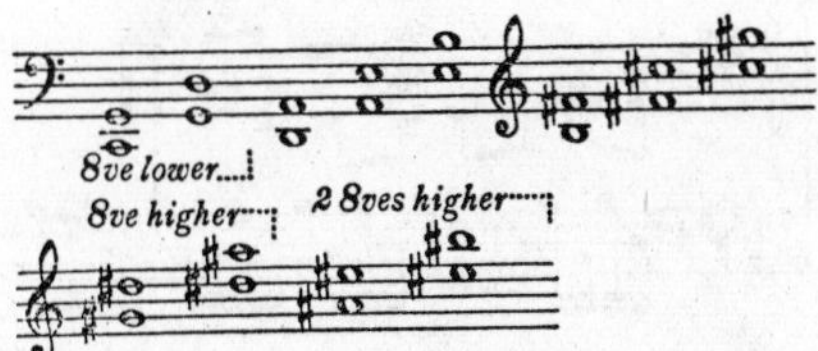

On keyboard instruments this note is the same as C, but if the fifths are accurately tuned there will be a small difference, since 12 fifths: $\left(\frac{3}{2}\right)^{12} = \frac{531441}{4096}$ are larger than 7 octaves: $\left(\frac{2}{1}\right)^{7} = 128$. In other words B♯ by this reckoning is sharper than C, the difference being $\frac{531441}{4096} \div 128$, *i.e.* $\frac{531441}{524288}$

The following terms are in use:

Augmented fifth: a fifth of which the upper note is sharpened or the lower note flattened, *e.g.*:

Diminished fifth: a fifth of which the upper note is flattened or the lower note sharpened, *e.g.*:

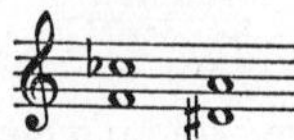

Perfect fifth: the interval defined above, *e.g.*:

v. also CONSECUTIVE INTERVALS.

Fifths Quartet. *v.* QUINTEN-QUARTETT.

Figaro. *v.* NOZZE DI FIGARO.

Figuration. The consistent use of a particular melodic or harmonic figure, *e.g.*:

HANDEL, *Suite No. 5 in E major*

Figured Bass (*Fr.* basse chiffrée, *G.* bezifferter Bass, *I.* basso continuo). Formerly known also as "thorough bass" (a literal translation of *basso continuo*). A bass part (intended primarily for a keyboard instrument) with figures to indicate the harmonies to be played above it; *e.g.* the following figured bass:

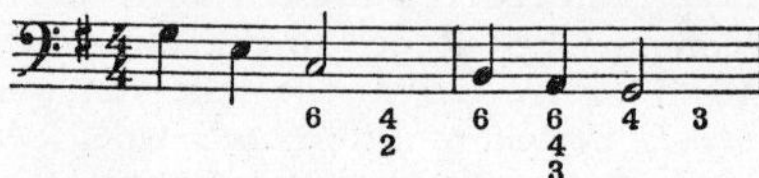

implies these harmonies:

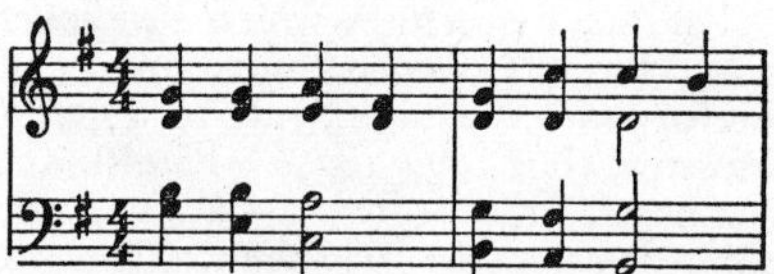

The system originated at the beginning of the 17th cent. and was universally employed until about the middle of the 18th cent., after which it was little used outside church music. It was designed to facilitate (*a*) the accompaniment of one or more solo voices or instruments, *e.g.* in the solo cantata, or the trio sonata for two violins and bass, (*b*) the enrichment of a texture provided by a chorus or an instrumental ensemble or both (*v.* CONTINUO).

Practice was not always consistent, but the following principles were generally observed:

(1) A note without figures implies the fifth and the third above.

(2) The figure 3 by itself implies 5 as well.

(3) The figure 4 by itself implies 5 as well, *e.g.*:

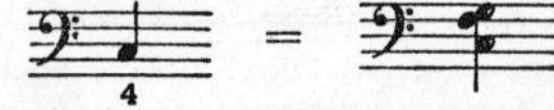

(4) The figure 6 by itself implies 3 as well.

(5) The figure 7 by itself implies 3 as well.

(6) Accidentals are indicated either by the normal signs placed next to the figures, or by the addition of strokes to the figures, *e.g.*:

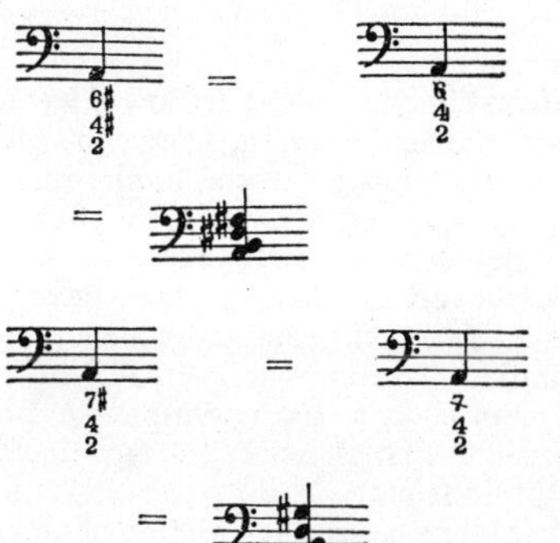

An accidental without any figure refers to the third of the chord, *e.g.*:

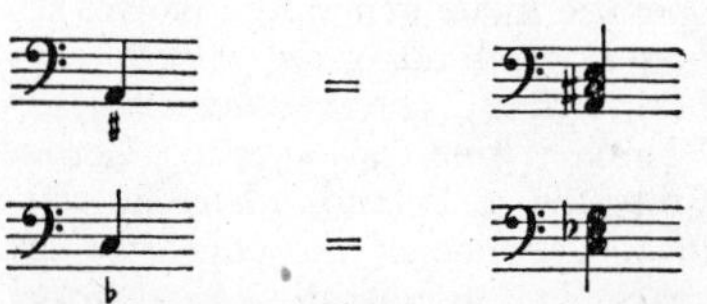

(7) A horizontal stroke indicates that the harmony used above the preceding note is to be continued above a changing bass, *e.g.*:

The stroke, however, is often omitted where it is obvious that notes in the bass are passing notes.

Provided that he uses the correct harmony, the performer is free to dispose the notes of the chord as he likes, *i.e.* close together or widely spaced. It is essential, however, that any melodic line or lines that he is accompanying should not be obscured. The same is true of melodic figuration or imitations of the solo part, which can be very effective provided that they do not monopolize the listener's attention. The practice of playing from figured bass is so little cultivated today that modern editions of old music generally include a fully written out part for the harpsichord, piano or organ. No written part, however, can be a completely adequate substitute for "realization" at the keyboard of the composer's shorthand; and many written parts of this kind do positive harm by neglecting to observe the conventions of the period or by introducing an extravagant amount of original material.

F. T. ARNOLD : *The Art of Accompaniment from a Thorough-Bass* (1931).

Figured Chorale. A setting of a chorale melody for organ, in which a particular figuration is employed throughout, *e.g.*

BACH, *Orgelbüchlein.*

Fille du Régiment, La [la feeyer dĕĕ ray-zhee-mŭn]. Opera in two acts by Donizetti. Libretto by Jules Henri Vernoy de Saint-Georges and Jean François Albert Bayard. First performed, Paris, Feb. 11, 1840.

Film Music. The use of music to accompany films dates from the early part of the 20th cent. Piano music was normal, and continued so in humbler surroundings, but the practice grew of employing other instruments as well, even complete orchestras. With the building of large cinemas, organs were also installed, either to bear the whole burden of accompaniment or to alternate with the orchestra. Piano or organ accompaniment was often improvised. For instrumental ensembles (as well as for pianists and organists) there was available a whole library of short extracts, suitable for every conceivable emotion or situation. The accompaniment to a silent film was a sort of potpourri, in the compilation of which considerable ingenuity was often shown. The practice, however, was inartistic, and dissatisfaction with it led, after the 1914-18 war, to the occasional composition of original music for a complete film, or to the adaptation of existing music—as in the case of the film version of Strauss's *Der Rosenkavalier*, for which the composer made a special arrangement of his own score (1925).

The opportunity for a more complete association of film and music came with the arrival of the sound-film in 1926, but it was only gradually realized that music could be used as an integral part of the film and only gradually that reputable composers were commissioned to provide it. Among English composers who have written film music of this kind are Arnold Bax, Arthur Bliss, William Walton and Vaughan Williams.

Filtz [fillts], ANTON: *b. c.* 1730; *d.* Mannheim, March, 1760. Cellist and composer, a member of the so-called "Mannheim school" of symphony-writers. Became cellist in the Mannheim orchestra, 1754. In addition to symphonies his compositions include concertos and chamber music. Modern ed. of 4 symphonies in *D.T.B.* iii (1) & vii (2); chamber music in *D.T.B.* xvi.

Final. In the church modes the note on which a melody comes to an end, *i.e.* the tonic. In the authentic modes the final is the first degree of the scale, in the plagal modes it is the fourth degree, *e.g.*:

Mode I (*protus authenticus*):

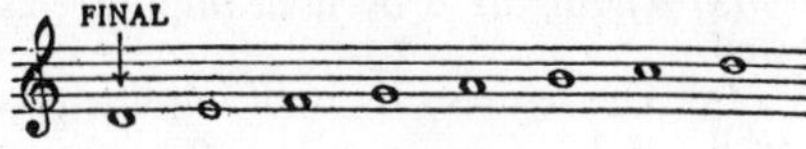

Mode II (*protus plagalis*):

v. MODE.

Finale [fee-nah'-leh], *I.* (now *E.*). (1) The last movement of a work in several movements, *e.g.* a symphony, concerto, string quartet, etc. In the 18th cent. finales were generally brisk and cheerful. Beethoven challenged this convention, and subsequent composers have shown a similar freedom of treatment, *e.g.* Tchaikovsky's sixth symphony has a finale which is marked *Adagio lamentoso* and ends *pppp*.

(2) The concluding section of an act of an opera, often of considerable length and subdivided into smaller sections, with contrasts of tempo and key. An outstanding example is the finale of Act II of Mozart's *Le nozze di Figaro*. An operatic finale generally involves several singers, and often the chorus as well.

Finck [fink], (1) HEINRICH: *b.* 1445; *d.* Vienna, June 9, 1527. Composer. Educated in Poland, where he was also in the service of the court for several years. Subsequently *Kapellmeister* at Stuttgart and Salzburg. His compositions include Masses, motets and secular part-songs; modern ed. of selected works in Eitner, *Publikationen älterer . . . Musikwerke*, viii. Described by his great-nephew as learned and inventive, but hard in style.

(2) HERMANN: *b.* Pirna, March 21, 1527; *d.* Wittenberg, Dec. 28, 1558. Great-nephew of (1). Composer and theorist. Studied at Wittenberg University and appointed organist there, 1557. Best known for his treatise *Practica Musica* (1556), which includes a substantial section on canon. Three of his compositions are in Eitner's volume, mentioned above.

Fine [fee'-neh], *I.* "End." In the *da capo* aria and similar compositions, where the recapitulation of the opening section is not written in full but indicated by a sign to go back to the beginning, the direction "Fine" shows where the piece comes to an end.

Fingal's Cave (*G.* Fingals Höhle). Overture by Mendelssohn, Op. 26 (1832), also known as *The Hebrides* (*G.* Die Hebriden). It was inspired by a visit paid to Scotland. The original version of the work (1830) was entitled *Die einsame Insel* (The Lonely Island).

Finger [fing′-er], GOTTFRIED (Godfrey): *b.* Olmütz (now Olomouc). Moravian composer, active in the late 17th and early 18th cent. Came to England *c.* 1685 and became an instrumentalist in the Catholic chapel of James II. Published instrumental chamber music in London and wrote music for several plays. Having been awarded the fourth prize in a competition for setting Congreve's *Judgment of Paris*, he left England in disgust, saying that "he thought he was to compose musick for men, and not for boys" (*v.* R. North, *Memoirs of Musick*, 1846, pp. 117-20). In the service of Queen Sophia Charlotte of Prussia, 1702, and subsequently of the Elector Palatine.

Finger-Board (*Fr.* touche, *G.* Griffbrett, *I.* tasto). The part of a string instrument on which the fingers of the left hand press down the strings at any chosen point and so shorten their vibrating length and raise the pitch.

Finke [fink′-er], FIDELIO: *b.* Josefsthal, Oct. 22, 1891. Sudeten composer, a pupil of Novák. Studied at the Prague Conservatoire, and taught there, 1915-20. Inspector of German music schools in Czechoslovakia, 1920. Teacher of composition, German Academy of Music, Prague, 1920; director, 1927-45. As a composer he began as a Romantic and developed into a disciple of Schönberg. His compositions include an opera, *Die Jakobsfahrt*, orchestral works, chamber music, choral works and piano pieces.

Finlandia. Orchestral tone-poem by Sibelius, Op. 26. Originally performed in 1899 as the finale of a series of pieces illustrating patriotic "Tableaux from the Past" (other numbers from the same series were published as *Scènes historiques*). Revised, 1900, and performed separately as a concert piece under the title *Suomi* (Finland).

Finot. *v.* PHINOT.

Finta Giardiniera, La [lah feen′-tah jarr-deen-yeh′-rah] (The Girl in Gardener's Disguise). Opera in three acts by Mozart. Libretto by Raniero de' Calzabigi, altered by Marco Coltellini. First performed, Munich, Jan. 13, 1775.

Finzi, GERALD: *b.* London, July 14, 1901; *d.* Oxford, Sept. 27, 1956. English composer, a pupil of Bairstow. Teacher of composition, R.A.M., 1930-1933. His works, which are mainly in the smaller forms, include settings for voice and piano of poems by Thomas Hardy and a cello concerto.

Fiorillo [fee-orr-ill′-lo], FEDERICO: *b.* Brunswick, 1755; *d.* after 1823. Violinist and composer, son of an Italian conductor at Brunswick. Conductor in Riga, 1783; played in Paris, 1785; active in London, 1788-94. A prolific composer for his instrument, he is now remembered only for his 36 *Caprices* or studies, which are still in use.

Fioritura [fee-o-ree-too′-rah], *I.* Lit. "flowering" (plur. *fioriture*), *i.e.* an embellishment or ornamentation, whether improvised or written down.

Fipple Flute. *v.* FLAGEOLET, RECORDER.

Firebird, The. *v.* OISEAU DE FEU.

Fireworks Music. Familiar title for Handel's *Music for the Royal Fireworks*, originally written for wind instruments only and performed in the Green Park, London, April 27, 1749, as an accompaniment to a fireworks display celebrating the Peace of Aix-la-Chapelle. String parts were subsequently added by the composer for concert performances. The movements are: Overture, Bourrée, "La Paix," "La Réjouissance," Menuet I, Menuet II.

First-Movement Form. *v.* SONATA FORM.

Fis [fiss], *G.* F sharp (F♯).

Fisarmonica [fee-zarr-mo′-nee-cah], *I.* Accordion.

Fischer [fish′-er], (1) CARL: *b.* Dec. 7, 1849; *d.* Feb. 14, 1923. Founder of the New York publishing firm which bears his name.

(2) EDWIN: *b.* Basle, Oct. 6, 1886.

Pianist and composer. Studied at the Basle Conservatoire and in Berlin, where he subsequently taught. Has also been active as a conductor, but is best known as a soloist and in particular as an interpreter of the classics.

(3) JOHANN CHRISTIAN: *b.* Freiburg, 1733; *d.* London, Apr. 29, 1800. Oboist. In the service of the Dresden court in 1760. Travelled on the Continent, arriving in England, 1768. Appeared frequently at London concerts, including those organized by J. C. Bach and Abel. Travelled abroad again, 1786-90. Mozart, who heard him in Vienna in 1787 wrote: "He plays like a bad beginner . . His tone is entirely nasal, and his held notes like the tremulant on the organ" (*v.* E. Anderson, *The Letters of Mozart and his Family*, p. 1350). He married the daughter of Gainsborough, who painted his portrait. His compositions, of which Mozart had a poor opinion, were numerous.

(4) JOHANN KASPAR FERDINAND : *d.*. Rastatt, March 27, 1746. Composer. *Kapellmeister* to the Markgraf of Baden. Of his compositions the keyboard works are particularly interesting (modern ed. by E. von Werra). They include harpsichord suites in the French style and *Ariadne musica neo-organoedum* (1715)—a collection of 20 preludes and fugues, each in a different key, and a forerunner of Bach's *Das wohltemperirte Clavier*. His *Journal du printemps*, for orchestra, is printed in *D.D.T.*, x (1), also ed. by E. von Werra.

(5) LUDWIG: *b.* Mainz, Aug. 18, 1745; *d.* Berlin, July 10, 1825. Operatic bass with a phenomenal compass, from

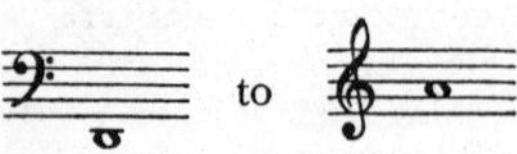

He was the original Osmin in Mozart's *Die Entführung*.

(6) WILHELM: *b.* Vienna, Apr. 19, 1886. Austrian musicologist. Lecturer, Vienna, 1915; professor, Innsbruck, 1928-38 and since 1948; director, Municipal School of Music, Vienna, 1945-8. He has devoted himself particularly to a study of early classical symphonies by Austrian composers and has edited selected works in *D.T.Ö.*, xix (2). He has also contributed the chapters on instrumental music from 1430 to 1880 in Adler's *Handbuch der Musikgeschichte*.

Fischer-Dieskau [fish′-er-deece′-cow], DIETRICH : *b.* Berlin, May 28, 1925. Baritone. Studied at the Berlin Hochschule für Musik. First appeared in Brahms's *Requiem* at Freiburg, 1947. In Germany he has sung frequently in opera, in Berlin and elsewhere, but abroad is best known as a remarkable interpreter of German song.

Fisis [fiss′-iss], *G.* F double sharp (F ×).

Fitelberg [fit′-ĕl-bairrg], (1) GRZEGORZ: *b.* Dinaburg, Oct. 18, 1879 ; *d.* Katowice, June 10, 1953. Polish composer and conductor, son of a bandmaster in the Russian army. Conductor, Warsaw Philharmonic Orchestra, 1908-11 and 1913; Vienna Opera, 1912; in Russia, 1914-21, also conductor of Diaghilev's ballet company; returned to Warsaw, 1921. Lived abroad, 1939-47. One of the founders of the Society of Young Polish Composers, 1905. His compositions include 2 symphonies, symphonic poems, overtures, rhapsodies, violin concerto, chamber music and songs.

(2) JERDY: *b.* Warsaw, May 20, 1903; *d.* New York, Apr. 25, 1951. Son of (1). Composer. Studied in Moscow and Berlin. Settled in France, 1933 ; U.S.A., 1940. He won the Coolidge Prize for chamber music with his fourth string quartet, 1936. His other works include 2 piano concertos, 2 violin concertos, cello concerto and quintet for woodwind and piano.

Fitzwilliam Virginal Book. A manuscript collection of keyboard music (almost entirely English) of the late 16th and early 17th cent., now in the Fitzwilliam Museum, Cambridge. Among the composers represented are Bull, Byrd, Farnaby, Morley, Philips and Tomkins. Modern ed. in 2 vols. by J. A. Fuller-Maitland and W. Barclay Squire.

C. VAN DEN BORREN : *The Sources of Keyboard Music in England* (1913).

E. NAYLOR : *An Elizabethan Virginal Book* (1905).

Five, The. The name sometimes given to the group of Russian nationalist composers of the 19th cent. known in their own country as the KUTCHKA.

Flageolet. A small beaked flute (or recorder), with six holes—four in the front and two at the back, the latter covered by the player's thumbs. It dates from the late 16th cent. and was much in vogue in the 17th cent. There are frequent references in Pepys's diary (*v.* C. Welch, *Six Lectures on the Recorder*, pp. 47-77).

Flageolett-Töne [fluzh-o-lett′-tur′-ner], *G.* Harmonics on string instruments.

Flagstad [flug′-stahd], KIRSTEN: *b.* Hamar, July 12, 1895. Norwegian soprano, daughter of a conductor. Studied in Oslo and Stockholm. First appeared in opera at the age of 18. Sang as Sieglinde in *Die Walküre* at Bayreuth, 1934, and as Isolde at New York, 1935. First sang at Covent Garden, 1936. The purity and strength of her voice make her one of the outstanding singers of our time. Though she excels in opera, particularly in Wagner, she is also a gifted interpreter of solo song and has made excellent records of Grieg's *Haugtussa* cycle.

Flat (*Fr.* bémol, *G.* Be, *I.* bemolle). (1) The sign ♭, indicating that the pitch of the note to which it is prefixed is to be lowered by one semitone. It holds good for the whole of a bar, unless contradicted. If it forms part of the KEY SIGNATURE it holds good, unless contradicted, until there is a new key signature which omits it. The origin of the sign is the "soft" or rounded B (*B molle* or *B rotundum*) used in the Middle Ages to indicate the fourth degree of the hexachord beginning on F:

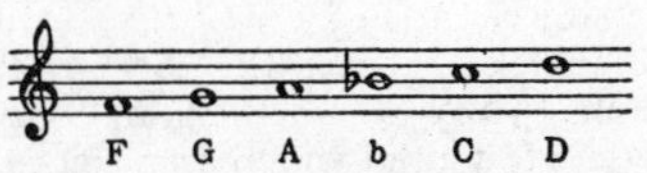

as opposed to the "hard" or square B (*B durum* or *B quadratum*) used to indicate the third degree of the hexachord beginning on G:

The use of the natural sign (♮) to contradict either a ♯ or a ♭ was not normal until the 18th cent. Before that time the ♭ was used to contradict a ♯, as well as to lower the pitch of an uninflected note (*i.e.* one without ♯ or ♭). Two flats side by side (♭♭) are a double flat and lower the pitch of the note to which they are prefixed by two semitones. In *Fr.* and *I.* flattened notes are referred to by the name of the note followed by the word for a flat, as in English: in *G.* the suffix "-s" or "-es" is added to the name of the note, *e.g.* E♭ = *Fr.* si bémol, *G.* Es, *I.* si bemolle. There is one exception to this rule: *G.* B (without any suffix) = B♭ (B♮ is represented by H ; B♭♭ is Bes).

(2) Applied to an interval = minor, *e.g.* flat seventh = minor seventh, flat third = minor third. This use of the word, though not completely obsolete, is old-fashioned.

(3) A "flat key" is now one which has one or more flats in the key signature, *e.g.* F (one flat), B♭ (two flats), E♭ (three flats), etc. It formerly meant a minor key, just as "flat third" meant minor third. *Cf.* the following passage: "They plaid us some flat Tunes . . . with a general applause, it being a thing formerly thought impossible upon an Instrument design'd for a sharp Key" (*Gentleman's Journal*, Jan. 1692).

(4) An instrument or a voice is flat if the notes produced are lower than the normal pitch. A single note can also be flat, as a result of faulty tuning or careless performance.

Flatté [flut-ay], *Fr.* *v.* SLIDE (1).

Flatterzunge [flutt′-er-tsoong-er], *G.* Lit. "flutter tongue." A method of tone production sometimes used on wind instruments. It consists in rolling the tongue as though saying *drrr.* The result, if applied to a single note, is a rapid tremolo. It appears to have been introduced originally by Richard Strauss in *Don Quixote* (1898), where it is prescribed for the flutes and combined with a rapid chromatic scale.

Flautando [flout-ahnd′-o], *I.* "Playing like a flute." A direction to string-players, used in two senses: (1) Playing harmonics; (2) playing gently near the end of the fingerboard.

Flautato [flout-ah′-toh], *I.* = FLAUTANDO.

Flauto [flout′-o], *I.* Flute. *Flauto piccolo*, piccolo. In the time of Bach and Handel (and earlier) *flauto* = *flauto dolce*, *flauto d'èco*, beaked flute or recorder; the transverse flute is indicated by *flauto traverso* or *traversa* alone. In Bach's Brandenburg concertos nos. 2 & 4 require *flauto*, *i.e.* recorder, no. 5 requires *flauto traverso*, *i.e.* flute. *Flauto d'amore*, a transverse flute built a minor third lower than the normal size, now obsolete.

Flautone [flout-o′-neh], *I.* Bass flute.

Flavio, Re de' Longobardi [flahv′-yo reh deh lon-go-barr′-dee] (Flavio, King of the Lombards). Opera in three acts by Handel. Libretto by Nicola Francesco Haym (partly founded on Corneille's *Le Cid* and altered from Stefano Ghigi's earlier Italian libretto). First performed, London, May 25, 1723.

Flebile [fleh′-bee-leh], *I.* Mournful.

Fledermaus, Die [dee flade′-er-mowce] (The Bat). Opera in three acts by Johann Strauss. Libretto by Carl Haffner and Richard Genée (based on Meilhac and Halévy's French vaudeville *Le Réveillon*, which had been taken from *Das Gefängnis*, a German comedy by Roderich Benedix). First performed, Vienna, April 5, 1874. Baron von Eisenstein, who has been committed to prison for eight days, is persuaded by Falke to postpone it in order to go to a ball. After his supposed departure for prison Rosalinde (his wife) is visited by Alfred (the singing teacher). When Frank (the prison governor) comes to take Eisenstein to jail, Alfred (in order not to compromise Rosalinde) pretends that he is Eisenstein and goes to jail. Falke (wishing to have revenge for the ridicule made of him by Eisenstein when he was at a former ball dressed as a bat) has also invited Frank, Adele (Rosalinde's maid) and Rosalinde herself to the ball. The next day they all find themselves at the prison for various reasons: Eisenstein wishes to begin his prison sentence, Rosalinde wants to begin an action for divorce, and Frank is very drunk. Finally Falke appears with all the guests of the ball and declares the whole to be an act of vengeance for the joke played on him by Eisenstein. Thus all the confusion is solved and Eisenstein is left to serve his term in jail.

Fleischer [fly′-sher], OSKAR: *b.* Zörbig, Nov. 2, 1856; *d.* Berlin, Feb. 8, 1933. Musicologist. Studied in Halle and Berlin, where he was a pupil of Spitta Director, Staatliche Musikinstrumentensammlung, Berlin, 1888-1911. Founder, Internationale Musikgesellschaft (1899-1914). His contributions to musicology were mainly concerned with medieval music, particularly notation, his most important work being *Neumenstudien* (3 vols., 1895-1904).

Flem [ler flem], PAUL LE: *b.* Lézardrieux, March 18, 1881. Composer and critic, a pupil of Lavignac, Roussel and d'Indy. His professional activities have included teaching at the Schola Cantorum, acting as chorus master at the Opéra-Comique, directing the choir known as Les Chanteurs de St. Gervais, and writing music criticism for *Comoedia*. His compositions include the opera *Le Rossignol de Saint-Malo*, the "chantefable" *Aucassin et Nicolette* and other works for the stage, a symphony, *Fantaisie* for piano and orchestra, chamber music, choral works, piano pieces and songs.

Flesch [flesh], CARL: *b.* Moson, Oct. 9, 1873; *d.* Lucerne, Nov. 15, 1944. Hungarian violinist, son of a doctor. Studied in Vienna and Paris. First appeared as a soloist in Vienna, 1895. Teacher of the violin, Bucharest Conservatoire, 1897-1902 ; Amsterdam Conservatoire, 1903-8 ; Curtis Institute, Philadelphia, 1924-8 ; Berlin Hochschule, 1929-34. Settled in England, 1934. He toured widely as a soloist, and also gave a series of historical concerts in Berlin. His book on *The Art of Violin-playing* (1923-8) is a standard work.

Fleury [fler-ree], LOUIS FRANÇOIS: *b.* Lyons, May 24, 1878; *d.* Paris, June 10,

1926. Flautist. Studied at the Paris Conservatoire, where he gained the *premier prix*, 1900. Director, Société moderne des instruments à vent, 1905-26. Founded the Société des concerts d'autrefois, 1906. He played frequently in England. He edited a number of works by 17th- and 18th-cent. composers.

Flicorno [flee-corr'-no], *I.* Italian equivalent of the SAXHORN.

Fliegende Holländer, Der [dair fleeg'-ĕn-der holl'-end-er] (The Flying Dutchman). Opera in three acts by Wagner. Libretto by the composer (after Heinrich Heine's *Memoiren des Herrn von Schnabelewopski*). First performed, Dresden, Jan. 2, 1843. The Dutchman, for an act of defiance, has been condemned by Satan to sail the seas for ever, unless he can be redeemed by a woman's love. Allowed to come on shore every seven years, he is entertained by the Norwegian sea-captain, Daland. Senta, Daland's daughter, who already knows the legend, agrees to marry the Dutchman. The latter, overhearing a scene between Senta and her former lover Erik, believes that she has betrayed him and puts out to sea. Senta hurls herself into the sea and by her sacrifice brings him at last redemption.

Flonzaley Quartet. A string quartet founded by an American banker of Swiss origin, Edward de Coppet (1855-1916), in 1902 and maintained by him and his son André. So called from the name of de Coppet's summer residence in Switzerland. The members of the quartet devoted themselves entirely to the study and practice of chamber music; they accepted no individual engagements and took no pupils. The original members were Adolfo Betti, Alfred Pochon, Ugo Ara and Ivan d'Archambeau. Ara was succeeded by Louis Bailly in 1917, and Bailly by Félicien d'Archambeau in 1924. Ivan d'Archambeau was succeeded by Nicholas Moldavan in 1924. The quartet disbanded in 1928.

Floridante, Il [eel flo-ree-dahn'-teh] (Prince Floridantes). Opera in three acts by Handel. Libretto by Paolo Antonio Rolli. First performed, London, Dec. 20, 1721.

Florimo [flo'-ree-mo], FRANCESCO: *b.* San Giorgio Morgeto, Oct. 12, 1800; *d.* Naples, Dec. 18, 1888. Historian and composer. Studied at the Real Collegio di Musica, Naples, where he became librarian in 1826. More important than his compositions are his historical works, which include *Cenno storico sulla scuola musicale di Napoli*, 2 vols. (1869-71), issued in a revised and enlarged edition as *La scuola musicale di Napoli e i suoi Conservatorii*, 4 vols. (1880-4).

Flöte [flur'-ter], *G.* Flute. *Kleine Flöte*, piccolo.

Flotow [flo'-to], FRIEDRICH, Freiherr von: *b.* Teutendorf, Apr. 26, 1812; *d.* Darmstadt, Jan. 24, 1883. Opera-composer, son of a nobleman. Studied in Paris, where he had his first public success with *Le Naufrage de la Méduse*, written in collaboration with Grisar and Pilati, 1839 (subsequently rewritten by Flotow as *Die Matrosen*, Hamburg, 1845). His *Alessandro Stradella* (Hamburg, 1844) established his position in Germany. His most popular work was *Martha* (Vienna, 1847). He was director of the court theatre at Schwerin, 1856-63.

Flue Pipes. In an organ all pipes other than reed pipes, so called because the air passes through a narrow aperture, or flue. The principle is similar to that of the tin whistle. *v.* ORGAN.

Flügel [flĕĕg-'ĕl], *G.* Lit. "wing." Hence a harpsichord or a grand piano, both of which are wing-shaped.

Flügelhorn [flĕĕg'-ĕl-horrn], *G.* (1) A soprano saxhorn in B♭, similar in shape to the bugle, but provided with three pistons. It has the same compass as the B♭ cornet, but a fuller tone. In England it is used only in brass bands, where it is a recognized member of the ensemble.

(2) In general the German equivalent of the SAXHORN family.

Flute (*Fr.* flûte, *G.* Flöte, *I.* flauto).

(1) The beaked flute or English flute (*Fr.* flûte à bec, flûte douce, *G.* Blockflöte, *I.* flauto dolce, flauto d'èco), now known exclusively as the RECORDER.

(2) The transverse or German flute (*Fr.* flûte traversière, flûte allemande, *G.* Querflöte, *I.* flauto traverso), now known simply as the flute. A "woodwind" instrument, generally made

either of wood or silver. One end of the tube is stopped, and sound is produced by blowing across an aperture cut in the side at that end. The compass is normally from

8ve higher

to

though instruments are also made with an extra semitone at the bottom, *i.e.* going down to B♮. The modern flute owes much to the work of Theobald Boehm (1794-1881), who made it possible to pierce the finger-holes in acoustically correct positions and at the same time to provide a convenient means of controlling them with the fingers. In addition to the normal-sized flute there are also (a) the *piccolo* (*Fr.* petite flûte, *G.* kleine Flöte, *I.* flauto piccolo, ottavino), built an octave higher, and (b) the *bass flute*, also known as the *alto flute* (*Fr.* flûte alto, *G.* Altflöte, *I.* flautone), built a fourth lower. The *flûte d'amour* (*G.* Liebesflöte, *I.* flauto d'amore), built a minor third lower, is obsolete. Flutes built a minor third or a semitone above the normal pitch were at one time used in military bands and treated as transposing instruments (*v.* TIERCE FLUTE). Though an instrument of great antiquity the flute did not come into general use in chamber and orchestral music until the early 18th cent. (note that at this period *flauto* by itself means "recorder": the transverse flute is indicated by *flauto traverso* or *traversa*). *v.* also MIRLITON.

A. CARSE : *Musical Wind Instruments* (1939).

Flûte [fleet], *Fr.* Flute. *Flûte à bec*, *flûte douce*, recorder. *Flûte allemande*, *flûte traversière*, transverse flute (the ordinary orchestral flute). *Flûte alto*, bass flute. *Flûte d'amour*, a flute built a minor third below the normal size, now obsolete.

Flûte-eunuque. *v.* MIRLITON.

Flutter Tongue. *v.* FLATTERZUNGE.

Flying Dutchman, The. *v.* FLIEGENDE HOLLÄNDER.

Foerster. *v.* FÖRSTER.

Fogg, ERIC: *b.* Manchester, Feb. 21, 1903; *d.* London, Dec. 19, 1939. Composer, the son of an organist. Chorister at Manchester Cathedral. Won a Cobbett prize in 1919 with a *Dance Phantasy* for piano and string quartet. Joined the staff of the B.B.C. (North Regional), 1924. A prolific composer from his early years, he is remembered chiefly by a bassoon concerto and some songs.

Foli [fo'-lee], ALLAN JAMES: *b.* Cahir, Aug. 7, 1835; *d.* Southport, Oct. 20, 1899. Irish bass, whose real name was Foley. Studied in Naples, and appeared in several Italian theatres. First appeared in London in *Les Huguenots*, 1865. In addition to a large repertory of operatic parts, he also sang frequently in oratorio.

Folía [fo-lee'-ah], *Sp.* (*I.* follia). A Portuguese dance which was the origin of the stylized instrumental form known as FOLIES D'ESPAGNE. As the name implies it was originally of a wild and abandoned character.

Folies d'Espagne [fol-ee dess-pun-yer], *Fr.* A musical form in dance rhythm, current in the 17th cent. and derived from the Portuguese dance known as FOLÍA. As often happens when dance forms become stylized the wild character of the original dance gave place to a stately tempo more in accordance with 17th-cent. conventions. The basic formula was as follows :

The following examples show two different treatments of this formula, the first a simple German working :

J. WOLF, *Handbuch der Notationskunde*, ii, p. 140

the second a more sophisticated version by an Italian composer:

CORELLI, *Op.* 5, *No.* 12

In England the piece acquired the name "Farinel's Ground" from a version by the French composer Michel Farinel. These varied treatments of a basic formula derive from popular practice in improvised dance music. They may be compared with similar treatment of the PASSAMEZZO and the ROMANESCA.

Folk-Song (*Fr.* chanson populaire, *G.* Volkslied, *I.* canto popolare). A term incapable of exact definition. It is generally held to imply a song of no known authorship which has been preserved by oral tradition. Some songs which have been preserved in this way are by known composers, many more exist also in printed song-books, and there are many more still which presuppose an original author. Oral tradition is valuable in that it often appears to preserve forgotten idioms, without being affected by the changing fashions of succeeding centuries. On the other hand it may easily corrupt both words and tune—and often does. The fact that quite a number of folk-songs are modal may be evidence of extreme antiquity; but it may equally be evidence of the fact that medieval peasants imitated the melodic idioms of plainsong which they heard in church (*v.* MODES). The irregular rhythms of melodies which have been collected from singers do not necessarily point to an ancient tradition of rhythmical freedom; it is equally possible (and in many cases practically certain) that they are the result of traditional carelessness in singing a tune which is in regular rhythm—carelessness which is quite understandable with songs which have no accompaniment. The antiquity of any folk-song is a matter that can hardly be proved; it is certainly not possible to assign confidently a date earlier than its first appearance in a manuscript or in print. Survival suggests that it was once popular, even though it may now be remembered only by a mere handful of people or be saved from extinction only by the collector's notebook.

Folk-songs have often been introduced into serious music or been used as themes for variations. It was not, however, until the 19th cent. that the use of them became identified with nationalist sentiment and that composers not only used them but imitated their idioms—in Russia, Bohemia, Norway and elsewhere. The new interest in folk-songs led to systematic attempts to collect them in most European countries. In England the Folk-Song Society was founded in 1898, and extensive collecting was undertaken by Cecil Sharp in the first 20 years of the present century—not only in England, but also in the Appalachian Mountains in America, where many old English songs and ballads had survived in a simple, isolated community of immigrants. There has also been considerable activity in collecting folk-songs in Ireland and in the Hebrides. Among composers who have been specially interested not merely in using and imitating folk-songs, but also in collecting them, may be mentioned Bartók in Hungary and Vaughan Williams in England. For extended bibliographies *v.* Grove's *Dictionary of Music and Musicians,* and *Oxford History of Music,* introd. vol., pp. 229-38.

Follia [fol-lee′-ah], *I.* *v.* FOLÍA.

Forbes, ROBERT JAFFREY: *b.* Stalybridge, May 7, 1878; *d.* May 13, 1958. Pianist and conductor. Studied at Royal Manchester College of Music. Teacher of composition there, 1909; principal, 1929-52. Active for many years as an opera conductor, first with the O'Mara Opera Company and then with the British National Opera Company.

Ford, THOMAS: *d.* London, Nov. 1648. Lutenist and composer. In the service of Henry, Prince of Wales, and subsequently of Charles I. His *Musicke of Sundrie Kindes* (1607)—his only published work—includes what is probably the best-known of all English lute-songs, "Since first I saw your face." Modern ed. of the songs in *Musicke of Sundrie Kindes* in *E.S.L.S.*, 1st ser.

Forellenquintett [fo-rell'-ĕn-cvin-tet'], *G.* *v.* TROUT QUINTET.

Forkel [forr'-kĕl], JOHANN NIKOLAUS: *b.* Meeder, Feb. 22, 1749; *d.* Göttingen, March 20, 1818. Historian, the son of a shoemaker. Studied law and music at Göttingen University; director of music there, 1778 till his death. His numerous publications include *Musikalisch-kritische Bibliothek*, 3 vols. (1778-9), *Allgemeine Geschichte der Musik*, 2 vols. (1788, 1801), *Allgemeine Literatur der Musik* (1792) and—his best-known work—the first biography of Bach, *Über Johann Sebastian Bachs Leben, Kunst und Kunstwerke* (1802). The latter work, though based on incomplete knowledge, is valuable as a pioneer work and stimulating for the enthusiasm shown by the author at a time when Bach's music had been forgotten. Modern ed. of the Bach volume: (a) in the original German: ed. J. Müller-Blattau (1925); (b) in English: trans. and ed. C. S. Terry (1920)—also in H. T. David & A. Mendel, *The Bach Reader* (1945), pp. 295-356.

Forlana [forr-lah'-nah], *I.* (*Fr.* forlane). (1) A lively dance in $\frac{6}{8}$ or $\frac{6}{4}$ time, originating in Friuli in north-eastern Italy. The following examples represent its use by composers of the 18th and 20th cent. respectively:

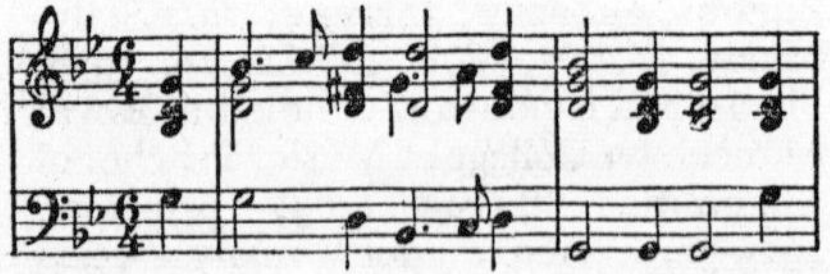

CAMPRA, *Les Festes Vénitiennes* (1710)

RAVEL, *Le Tombeau de Couperin* (1917)

There is also an excellent example in Bach's Suite No. 1 in C major for orchestra.

(2) In the late 16th cent. the name *ballo furlano* is found applied to a dance in $\frac{4}{4}$ time and moderate tempo.

Form. In music, as in the other arts, this means intelligible shape. The basic elements in musical form are (1) repetition, (2) variation, (3) contrast (whether of material, of speed, or of dynamics). Repetition is essential, because the stuff of music is transient and cannot be captured by the ear as a picture can by the eye. Variation is necessary, because unvaried repetition would be intolerable. Contrast is necessary, because even varied repetition of the same material would become monotonous. These three principles operate in the field of (*a*) melody, (*b*) harmony, (*c*) rhythm, (*d*) tone-colour, and can therefore be used simultaneously, *e.g.* a rhythm can remain persistent while the melody is changed, harmony can change while the melody remains the same, melody and harmony can be repeated with a change of tone-colour. A particular form of melodic repetition which is effective in music but has no equivalent in poetry is overlapping repetition or imitation, which is known as CANON if it is exact and also plays an important part in FUGUE. A particular function of harmony is to establish contrasts of KEY.

Among the influences which have helped to shape musical forms are (1) the dance, (2) words, (3) improvisation. Some dances consist of nothing but simple, or slightly varied, repetition. But a very large number fall into contrasted sections and exhibit a simple symmetry. These characteristics naturally appear in the music written for them, and in turn influence music not specifically written for dancing but organized on the same principle. Very characteristic of dances is the practice of varying a repetition by turning an inconclusive ending into a final one; in medieval France the inconclusive ending was called *ouvert* (open), the final one *clos* (closed): for a 14th-cent. example *v.* CLOS. In course of time these melodic conventions were matched by harmonic ones: *e.g.* a cadence which ended on the tonic chord would be final, one which ended on the dominant would be intermediate (*v.* CADENCE). From this contrast developed naturally the division of a piece into two sections, using the same melodic material—the first section ending on a chord other than the tonic (usually the dominant, or in a minor key the relative major), the second bringing the piece to an end in the proper key (*v.* BINARY FORM). Return of the tonic key suggested recapitulation of material from the first section, with the ending altered from the dominant (or relative major) to the tonic. Immediate recapitulation might be too abrupt or too simple: hence the practice of exploring other keys in the second section before returning to the tonic key. The general procedure is then : (*a*) first section beginning in tonic and modulating to dominant, (*b*) second section modulating through related keys to a recapitulation of the material of the first section, but in the tonic key throughout. This procedure is the basis of SONATA FORM, so called because it was used extensively by composers of sonatas (and symphonies, concertos, quartets, etc.) in the late eighteenth century.

The influence of words leads to contrasts of mood in vocal music, and this in turn leads to similar contrasts of mood in instrumental music. If these contrasts are pursued for any length of time they become independent sections. These provide one of the origins of the separate " movements " of sonatas, symphonies, etc., in the 18th and 19th cent.: the other is to be found in the contrasted dance of the SUITE. Such movements are often distinguished not only by contrast of tempo and material but also by contrast of key. The influence of improvisation also results in contrasts, since no performer will wish to persist in the same mood: it also results in a love of decoration, in giving elaborate clothing to a simple idea.

The desire for intelligibility and the infinite variety possible in music has led composers of all periods to use a limited number of basic forms as skeletons for their ideas, just as poets have used the sonnet or the ballad. Among the forms which became standardized in this way were the RONDO, where there is recurrent repetition, and the DA CAPO aria (or song form) which was not only the foundation of 18th-cent. opera and oratorio but proved fruitful in instrumental music as well. The experience of centuries has shown that there is no limit to the possibilities of simple structures of this kind. They are not conventions to which the composer has to submit; on the contrary, they are the servants of his invention.

In addition to the forms mentioned above *v.* CANTO FERMO, CHACONNE, CHORALE, FANTASIA, FUGUE, MADRIGAL, MOTET, OVERTURE, PRELUDE, RICERCAR, SYMPHONIC POEM, TOCCATA. For works in several movements or parts which exhibit the principles of form on a large scale *v.* CANTATA, CONCERTO, MASS, OPERA, ORATORIO, SONATA, SYMPHONY.

Förster [furr'-ster], (1) EMANUEL ALOYS: *b.* Niederstein, Jan. 26, 1748; *d.* Vienna, Nov. 12, 1823. Silesian composer, author of an *Anleitung zum*

Generalbass (1802) His compositions consist mainly of chamber music and keyboard works. Beethoven acknowledged the value of his example in writing string quartets.

(2) JOSEF BOHUSLAV: *b.* Dĕtenice, Dec. 30, 1859; *d.* Stará Boleslav, May 29, 1951. Czech composer, the son of a musician. Studied in Prague, where he was active as organist, choirmaster and critic until 1893, when he went to Hamburg. Taught at Hamburg Conservatorium, 1901; New Conservatorium, Vienna, 1903; Prague Conservatoire, 1918. Director, Prague Conservatoire, 1922-31. His compositions, which are to a very large extent elegiac in mood, include 7 operas, 4 symphonies, 4 symphonic poems, 2 violin concertos, chamber music and choral works.

Forster [forr'-ster], GEORG: *b.* Amberg, *c.* 1514; *d.* Nuremberg, Nov. 14, 1568. A doctor who edited a collection of German songs entitled *Ein Ausszug guter alter und newer teutscher Liedlein* (5 sets, 1539-56), a volume of motets and a volume of psalms. Modern ed. of the second set of secular songs in *Publikationen älterer praktischer und theoretischer Musikwerke*, xxix.

Forte [forr'-teh], *I.* Loud (generally abbreviated *f*). *Forte piano*, loud and immediately soft again (*fp*); *fortissimo*, very loud (*ff*); *mezzo forte*, moderately loud (*mf*); *più forte*, louder (*più f*); *poco forte*, moderately loud (*pf*).

Fortepiano [forr-teh-pyah'-no], *I.* An early name for the PIANOFORTE. For the dynamic indication *forte piano v.* FORTE.

Fortissimo [forr-teece'-see-mo], *I.* Very loud.

Fortner [forrt'-ner], WOLFGANG: *b.* Leipzig, Oct. 12, 1907. Composer. Studied at Leipzig Conservatorium and University. Teacher of composition at Heidelberg since 1931. His compositions include a symphony, concertos for harpsichord, piano, 2 pianos, violin and cello, 3 string quartets and other chamber music, a number of important choral works and music for the stage.

Forty-Eight, The. The name by which Bach's *Das wohltemperirte Clavier* (The Well-Tempered Keyboard) is commonly known. It consists of two parts, each containing 24 preludes and fugues for a keyboard instrument. *v.* WOHLTEMPERIRTE CLAVIER.

Forza [forr'-tzah], *I.* "Force." *Con forza*, emphatically, vigorously.

Forzando [forr-tzahn'-do], *I.* "Forcing," *i.e.* strongly accenting (generally abbreviated *fz*).

Foss, (1) HUBERT JAMES: *b.* Croydon, May 2, 1899; *d.* London, May 27, 1953. Critic and composer. Music editor, Oxford University Press, 1924-41. Founder, Bach Cantata Club, 1926. Editor, *The Heritage of Music* (3 vols., 1927-51). Published *Music in my Time* (1933) and *Ralph Vaughan Williams* (1950), and several songs.

(2) LUKAS: *b.* Berlin, Aug. 15, 1922. American composer, the son of German parents. Studied at the Paris Conservatoire and the Curtis Institute, Philadelphia. His compositions, which have been widely performed in America, include the operas, *The Jumping Frog of Calaveras County* (1950), and *Griffelkin* (1955), a symphony, a piano concerto, and biblical cantatas.

Foster, (1) MURIEL: *b.* Sunderland, Nov. 22, 1877; *d.* London, Dec. 23, 1937. Mezzo-soprano. Studied at the R.C.M. Active principally between 1899 and 1906, when she married. She excelled in works by Elgar. She sang in *The Dream of Gerontius* at Düsseldorf, 1902 and London, 1903 (the first performance there); also in the first performances of *The Apostles* (Birmingham, 1903), *The Kingdom* (Birmingham, 1906) and *The Music Makers* (Birmingham, 1912).

(2) STEPHEN COLLINS: *b.* Pittsburg (Pa.), July 4, 1826; *d.* New York, Jan. 13, 1864. Composer of popular songs which became so widely known that they may legitimately be classed as folk-songs. Many of them are as familiar in England as in America, *e.g.* "The Old Folks at Home" (Swanee Ribber) and "My Old Kentucky Home."

Fourestier [foo-rest-yay], LOUIS FÉLIX ANDRÉ: *b.* Montpellier, May 31, 1892. Composer and conductor. Studied at the Paris Conservatoire. *Prix de Rome*, 1925. His appointments as conductor include Paris, Opéra-Comique, 1927-32, and Paris, Opera, 1938. Teacher of conducting, Paris Conservatoire, 1945.

Four Saints in Three Acts. Opera in four acts (in spite of the title) by Virgil Thomson. Libretto by Gertrude Stein. First performed, Hartford, Conn., Feb. 7, 1934.

Fourth. The interval reached by ascending three steps in the diatonic scale, *e.g.*:

In the HARMONIC SERIES it is the interval between the 3rd and 4th notes of the series, and therefore has the ratio $\frac{4}{3}$.

The following terms are in use:

Augmented fourth: a fourth of which the upper note is sharpened or the lower note flattened, *e.g.*:

Diminished fourth: a fourth of which the upper note is flattened or the lower note sharpened, *e.g.*:

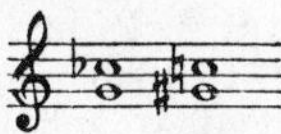

Perfect fourth: the interval defined above, *e.g.*:

Fox Strangways, ARTHUR HENRY: *b.* Norwich, Sept. 14, 1859; *d.* Dinton, May 2, 1948. Critic. Educated at Oxford and the Berlin Hochschule für Musik. Schoolmaster, 1884-1910 (from 1893 to 1901 as director of music, Wellington College). Studied Indian music, 1910-11 and published *The Music of Hindustan* (1914). Assistant music critic, *The Times*, 1911; music critic, *The Observer*, 1925. Founder of the quarterly *Music and Letters*, 1920, and editor, 1920-36. With Maud Karpeles published a life of Cecil Sharp (1934). With Steuart Wilson published translations of Haydn's *The Creation* and many songs by Schubert and Schumann. Also translated Wolf's *Nachgelassene Lieder*. In his retirement he completed translations (unpublished) of all the songs of Brahms, Liszt, Strauss and Wolf. Extracts from his musical criticism were published by Steuart Wilson under the title *Music Observed* (1936).

Foxtrot. A dance of American origin in duple time, which first became popular in 1912. Several variants appeared in course of time, and the word came to lose its limited application to a specific dance. From these variants two main types emerge—one fast, the other slow.

Fra Diavolo, ou L'Hôtellerie de Terracine [fra dya-vo-lo oo loh-tel-l*er*-ree d*er* terr-uss-een] (Fra Diavolo, or the Inn at Terracina). Comic opera in three acts by Auber. Libretto by Augustin Eugène Scribe. First performed, Paris, January 28, 1830. Lord and Lady Allcash, having been robbed on the road from Rome to Naples, reach an inn at Terracina. The innkeeper's daughter Zerlina is in love with Lorenzo, a sergeant, who sets off to find the robbers, while she takes care of the reward offered for the recovery of the jewels. The Marquis di San Marco, who has been pressing his attentions on Lady Allcash, is discovered hiding in a closet after dark and is suspected of improper intentions both by Lord Allcash and by Lorenzo. Lorenzo discovers that at a given signal (the ringing of the chapel bell) the robber chief, Fra Diavolo, intends to kill Lord Allcash and abscond with his money and his wife. He orders the signal to be given. Fra Diavolo, who is none other than the Marquis, falls into the trap and is arrested, while Lorenzo marries Zerlina.

Fra Gherardo [frah geh-rarr'-do]. Opera in three acts by Pizzetti. Libretto by the composer. First performed, Milan, May 16, 1928.

Françaix [frũn-say], JEAN: *b.* Le Mans, May 23, 1912. Composer, a pupil of Nadia Boulanger. His compositions, in a neo-classical style, include a symphony, a comic opera—*Le Diable boiteux*, an oratorio—*L'Apocalypse de St. Jean*, several ballets, *concertino* for piano and orchestra, a piano concerto and chamber music.

Franchetti [frahn-ket'-tee], ALBERTO: *b.* Turin, Sept. 18, 1860; *d.* Villareggio, Aug. 4, 1942. Composer of noble birth, whose operas have had considerable success in Italy and, in some cases, have been performed in other centres as well. Studied in Dresden and Munich, where he was a pupil of Rheinberger. Director, Florence Conservatorio, 1926-8. Among his most successful operas are *Asrael* (Reggio d'Emilia, 1888), *Cristoforo Colombo* (Genoa, 1892) and *Germania* (Milan, 1902). *Giove a Pompei* (Rome, 1921) was written in collaboration with Giordano. He also composed a symphony and other orchestral works.

Franck [frũnk], CÉSAR AUGUSTE: *b.* Liége, Dec. 10, 1822; *d.* Paris, Nov. 8, 1890. Composer and organist. Studied at the Liége and Paris Conservatoires. Returned to Belgium, 1842-4. Lived in Paris from 1844. Choirmaster, St. Clotilde, 1853; organist, 1859. Teacher of the organ, Paris Conservatoire, 1872. His music is Romantic in style and expansive in manner, with a plentiful use of characteristic chromatic harmony. His orchestral and chamber music, though admirably written for the medium, sometimes betrays the influence of the organ in its use of contrasts of colour and in a fondness for repetition and short-breathed phrases. His principal compositions are:

(a) ORATORIOS: *Ruth* (1846), *La Tour de Babel* (1865), *Rédemption* (1872), *Les Béatitudes* (1880), *Rébecca* (1881).

(b) CHURCH MUSIC: Mass for 3 voices; motets; offertories; *Psalm* 150.

(c) OPERAS: *Hulda* (Monte Carlo, 1894); *Ghiselle* (Monte Carlo, 1896).

(d) ORCHESTRA: Symphony in D minor; *Variations symphoniques* for piano and orchestra; symphonic poems: *Les Éolides*, *Le Chasseur maudit*, *Les Djinns* (piano and orchestra), *Psyché* (chorus and orchestra).

(e) CHAMBER MUSIC: string quartet; piano quintet; 4 piano trios; violin sonata.

(f) PIANO: *Prélude, choral et fugue*; *Prélude, aria et final*.

(g) ORGAN: 3 chorales; miscellaneous pieces.

Also songs, miscellaneous piano solos, and pieces for harmonium.

C. VAN DEN BORREN: *L'Oeuvre dramatique de César Franck* (1907).
V. D'INDY: *César Franck* (1906).
L. VALLAS: *César Franck* (1952).

Franck [frunk], (1) JOHANN WOLFGANG: *b. c.* 1641. Composer. *Kapellmeister*, Ansbach, 1673-8. Active as an opera-composer in Hamburg, 1679-86. In London, 1690-5, where he gave concerts in conjunction with Robert King. Modern ed. of his opera *Die drey Töchter Cecrops* (Ansbach, 1679) in *Das Erbe deutscher Musik, Landschaftsdenkmale, Bayern*, ii; modern ed. of his *Geistliche Lieder* (sacred songs, 1681) in *D.D.T.*, xlv. He published a collection of secular songs in London under the title *Remedium Melancholiae* (1690).

W. B. SQUIRE: "J. W. Franck in England" (*Musical Antiquary*, July 1912).

(2) MELCHIOR: *b.* Zittau, *c.* 1573; *d.* Coburg, June 1, 1639. Composer of church music, songs and instrumental works. *Kapellmeister*, Coburg, 1603. Modern ed. of selected instrumental works in *D.D.T.*, xvi.

Franckenstein [frunk'-ĕn-shtine], CLEMENS VON: *b.* Wiestenheid, July 14, 1875; *d.* Hechendorf, Aug. 22, 1942. Composer and conductor, brother of Sir George Franckenstein (formerly Austrian Minister in London). Studied in Vienna, Munich and Frankfort, where he was a pupil of Ivan Knorr. Conductor, Moody-Manners Opera Company, 1902; Wiesbaden and Berlin, 1907; *Intendant*, Munich, 1912-18, 1924-34. He composed several operas, including *Des Kaisers Dichter* on the subject of the Chinese poet Li Tai Po (Hamburg, 1920), a ballet, miscellaneous orchestral works, chamber music, piano solos and songs.

Franco de Colonia [frahn'-co day col-one'-yah] (Franco of Cologne). 13th-cent. theorist, whose treatise *Ars cantus mensurabilis* (printed in Gerbert, *Scriptores*, iii and Coussemaker, *Scriptorum de musica medii aevi nova series*, i ; English translation in O. Strunk, *Source Readings in Music History*, pp. 139-59) systematised the notation of mensural music and did away with many ambiguities, particularly in the interpretation of LIGATURES. For a detailed account of his system see W. Apel, *The Notation of Polyphonic Music*, 900-1600 (1942), chap. v.

Frankel, BENJAMIN : *b.* London, Jan. 31, 1906. Composer. Studied at the Guildhall School of Music. For several years he was active in the field of popular music as violinist, pianist, conductor and arranger of scores. His serious compositions, most of which date from the post-war years, include a violin concerto, 4 string quartets, unaccompanied sonatas for violin and viola, and a considerable amount of film music.

Franz [frunts], ROBERT: *b.* Halle, June 28, 1815; *d.* there, Oct. 24, 1892. Composer. His father, Christoph Franz Knauth, changed his name to Franz in 1847. His musical education was desultory, apart from two years with Friedrich Schneider in Dessau. Organist, Ulrichskirche, Halle, 1841; University director of music, 1859. Deafness and nervous troubles compelled him to retire in 1868. He composed more than 250 songs, as well as church music. His enthusiasm for the works of Bach and Handel led him to write additional accompaniments to Bach's *St. Matthew Passion*, *Magnificat*, and 10 cantatas, Handel's *Messiah* and *L'Allegro*, and other works.

Fraser, MARJORIE KENNEDY. *v.* KENNEDY FRASER.

Frauen-Liebe und Leben [frow'-ĕn-leeb-er ŏŏnt labe'-ĕn], *G.* (Woman's Love and Life). Cycle of 8 songs by Schumann, Op. 42 (1840), depicting the emotional experiences of a woman's life, from falling in love to the death of her husband. Words by Adalbert von Chamisso.

Frauenlob [frow'-ĕn-lope] (Praise of ladies). The name given to Heinrich von Meissen (*d.* Mainz, Nov. 29, 1318), one of the last of the *Minnesinger*. Examples of his melodies are in P. Runge, *Die Sangweisen der Colmarer Handschrift* (1896) and *D.T.Ö.*, xx (2).

Frau ohne Schatten, Die [dee frow ohn'-er shut'-ĕn] (The Woman without a Shadow). Opera in three acts by Richard Strauss. Libretto by Hugo von Hofmannsthal (based on his story with the same title). First performed, Vienna, Oct. 10, 1919.

Freischütz, Der [dair fry'-shēēts] (The Marksman). *Singspiel* (opera with dialogue) in three acts by Weber. Libretto by Friedrich Kind (after a story in Johann August Apel and Friedrich Laun's *Gespensterbuch*, 1811). First performed, Berlin, June 18, 1821. Agathe, daughter of the head forester, is to be the prize in a shooting contest. Max, uncertain of his skill and anxious to win her hand, is persuaded by Caspar to visit the Wolf's Glen, where seven magic bullets are cast under the direction of the evil spirit Samiel. Agathe, warned by a hermit of danger, puts on a bridal wreath made from roses which he has provided. When the contest is held Samiel directs the seventh bullet towards Agathe, but her bridal wreath saves her: his victim is Caspar, whose soul is forfeit to the devil.

French Horn. *v.* HORN.

French Overture. *v.* OVERTURE.

French Sixth. *v.* AUGMENTED SIXTH.

French Suites. The name given to a set of six keyboard suites by J. S. Bach, probably written for his second wife, Anna Magdalena Bach. Forkel, Bach's earliest biographer, says that they were so called "because they are written in the French style" (*Johann Sebastian Bach*, tr. C. Sanford Terry, p. 128). They are on a smaller scale than the ENGLISH SUITES.

Frere, WALTER HOWARD: *b.* Dungate, Nov. 23, 1863; *d.* Mirfield, Apr. 2, 1938. Liturgiologist. Educated at Cambridge and ordained, 1887. Member of the Community of the Resurrection, Mirfield, 1892; superior, 1902-12, 1915-22. Bishop of Truro, 1923-34. His publications include two volumes of facsimiles—*Graduale Sarisburiense* (1894) and *Antiphonale Sarisburiense* (1901-26), a catalogue of liturgical manuscripts in the British Isles—*Bibliotheca Musico-liturgica* (2 vols., 1901-32), an edition of the text (not the music) of *The Winchester Troper* (1894), and the introduction to the historical edition of *Hymns Ancient and Modern* (1909).

Frescobaldi [fress-co-bahl′-dee], GIROLAMO: *b.* Ferrara, 1583; *d.* Rome, March 1, 1643. Organist and composer, a pupil of Luzzaschi. Visited Flanders, 1607-8. Organist, St. Peter's, Rome, 1608-28 (absent for a few months in 1615 at the court of Mantua), 1634-43; organist to the Grand Duke of Tuscany, Florence, 1628-34. One of the outstanding organists of his time. Froberger was his pupil. His keyboard compositions include *ricercari*, *canzoni francesi*, toccatas, capriccios, and a collection entitled *Fiori musicali* (complete ed. in 5 vols. by P. Pidoux). He also published *canzoni* for instrumental ensemble, arias for one or more voices, and a set of madrigals.

L. RONGA : *Gerolamo Frescobaldi* (1930).

Fret (*Fr.* touche, *G.* Bund, *I.* tasto). A thin piece of material fitted to the finger-board of a string instrument to facilitate the stopping of the string. Each fret marks the position of a specific note in the scale, and the effect of stopping on a fret is to produce a quality similar to that of an open note. Frets are used on the viol, lute, guitar and similar instruments, but not on members of the violin family. They were formerly made of pieces of gut tied tightly round the finger-board, but are now generally made of wood or metal fixed permanently in position.

Freund [froynt], MARYA: *b.* Wroclaw, Dec. 12, 1876. Soprano. Originally a violinist, a pupil of Sarasate. First appeared as a singer, 1909. Her reputation depends not only on her singing of the classical repertory but even more on her interpretation of modern music, particularly of Schönberg's *Pierrot Lunaire* and *Das Buch der hängenden Gärten*. Also influential as a teacher in Paris.

Frey [fry], (1) EMIL: *b.* Baden, Apr. 8, 1889; *d.* Zürich, May 20, 1946. Pianist and composer. Studied at the Geneva and Paris Conservatoires, at the latter with Fauré and Widor. Teacher, Imperial Conservatoire, Moscow, 1912-17; Zürich Conservatoire, 1922. He toured as a pianist both in Europe and in South America. His compositions include a Mass, a symphony (with chorus), a setting of Psalm 103, a cello concerto, chamber music, piano and organ pieces and songs.

(2) WALTER: *b.* Basle, Jan. 26, 1898. Pianist. Brother of (1), with whom he has appeared in two-piano recitals. Teacher, Zürich Conservatoire, 1925.

Fricker, (1) HERBERT AUSTIN: *b.* Canterbury, Feb. 12, 1868; *d.* Toronto, Nov. 11, 1943. Conductor and organist. Chorister, Canterbury Cathedral. Held various posts as organist, becoming city organist at Leeds and chorus-master, Leeds Musical Festival. Founder and conductor, Leeds Symphony Orchestra. Organist, Metropolitan Church, Toronto, 1917, and conductor, Mendelssohn Choir. His compositions consist of organ and church music.

(2) PETER RACINE : *b.* London, Sept. 5, 1920. Composer. Studied at the R.C.M. and privately with Mátyás Seiber. He made his mark in 1947 with a wind quintet which won the Alfred Clements prize. As a teacher of composition at the R.C.M. since 1951 and as director of music at Morley College he has had a considerable influence on younger musicians. His compositions, which are highly concentrated and individual in idiom, include 2 symphonies, a violin concerto, a viola concerto, a violin sonata, piano music and songs.

Fried [freet], OSCAR: *b.* Berlin, Aug. 10, 1871. Conductor and composer, a pupil of Humperdinck and Scharwenka. Conductor, Sternsche Gesangverein, Berlin, 1904-10; Berlin Symphony Orchestra, 1925-6; Tiflis Opera, 1934. His principal compositions are choral works and songs.

Friedenstag [freed'-ĕnce-tahk] (Peace Day). Opera in one act by Richard Strauss. Libretto by Joseph Gregor. First performed, Munich, July 24, 1938.

Friedheim [freet'-hime], ARTHUR: *b.* St. Petersburg, Oct. 26, 1859; *d.* New York, Oct. 19, 1932. Pianist, a pupil of Liszt, in the interpretation of whose works he excelled. Lived at various times in Germany, America and England.

Friedländer [freet'-lend-er], MAX: *b.* Brieg, Oct. 12, 1852; *d.* Berlin, May 2, 1934. Baritone. First appeared in London (where he was a pupil of Garcia), 1882. Devoted himself to historical and critical work, editing the songs of Schubert, Schumann and Mendelssohn (Peters), as well as several other collections. His publications include *Das deutsche Lied im 18. Jahrhundert* (3 vols., 1902) and *Brahms' Lieder* (1922; English ed., 1928).

Friedman [freet'-mun], IGNACY: *b.* Podgórze, Feb. 14, 1882; *d.* Sydney, Jan. 26, 1948. Pianist and composer, a pupil of Leschetizky. Edited the piano works of Chopin (Breitkopf & Härtel), Schumann and Liszt (Universal Edition). His compositions are mainly for the piano.

Friska [frish'-ca], *H.* The same as FRISS.

Friss [frish], *H.* *v.* CSÁRDÁS.

Froberger [froh'-bairg-er], JOHANN JAKOB: *b.* Stuttgart, May 19, 1916; *d.* Héricourt, May 7, 1667. Organist and composer, a pupil of Frescobaldi. Court organist, Vienna, 1637 (for 9 months only, after which he went to Rome to study with Frescobaldi), 1641-5, 1653-7 (though he seems to have been in Vienna in 1649). According to Mattheson he visited London in 1662 and was not at first recognized, since he had been robbed on the way and being ignorant of the language could not explain who he was. His later years were spent in the house of Duchess Sibylla of Würtemberg at Héricourt. His keyboard works, consisting of toccatas, fantasias, *canzoni*, capriccios, *ricercari* and suites, were published after his death: modern ed. in *D.T.Ö.*, iv (1), vi (2) & x (2), also issued separately in 2 vols. (ed. G. Adler).

Frog Galliard. The name given to a lute transcription of Dowland's song "Now, oh now I needs must part" (printed in *Musica Britannica*, vi, p. 10).

Frog Quartet (*G.* Froschquartett). The name given to Haydn's string quartet in D major, Op. 50, no. 6. It derives from the principal theme of the finale.

From my Life. *v.* AUS MEINEM LEBEN.

From the New World (*G.* Aus der neuen Welt). The title of Dvořák's symphony No. 5 in E minor, Op. 95, composed in America in 1893 and published in 1894. There is no basis for the popular belief that it borrows or imitates melodies of negro origin.

Frosch [frosh]. *v.* AM FROSCH.

Froschquartett [frosh'-cvarr-tet'], *G.* *v.* FROG QUARTET.

Frottola [frot'-to-lah], *I.* Lit. "little mixture." A type of strophic song of a popular character current in aristocratic circles in late 15th- and early 16th-cent. Italy—a forerunner of the MADRIGAL. It was marked by clearly defined rhythms and simple harmony in three (or more frequently four) parts, intended either for a vocal ensemble or for a solo voice with instrumental accompaniment. Many *frottole* were also issued for solo voice with lute accompaniment. The subject-matter was generally amorous. 11 books of *frottole* were published by Petrucci (1504-14): modern ed. of books i & iv in *Publikationen älterer Musik*, viii.

A. EINSTEIN : *The Italian Madrigal*, 3 vols. (1949).

Frühlingssonate [freel'-ingce-zo-nah'-ter], G. *v.* SPRING SONATA.

Frühlingssymphonie [freel'-ingce-zeem-fo-nee'], G. *v.* SPRING SYMPHONY.

Frumerie [free-mer-ee'], PER GUNNAR FREDRIK DE: *b.* July 20, 1908. Composer and pianist. Studied at the Stockholm Conservatoire, and further in Vienna and Paris. His compositions, at first eclectic in style but later inclined to neo-classicism, include the opera *Singoalla* (Stockholm, 1940), 2 piano concertos, violin concerto, chamber music, piano pieces and songs (including settings of poems by Chinese and Persian authors).

Fuenllana [foo-en-lyahn′-ah], MIGUEL DE: *b.* Navalcarnero, early 16th cent. Blind lutenist and composer. His collection *Orphenica Lyra* (1554) includes original compositions (lute-songs and instrumental pieces) and transcriptions of madrigals and motets by contemporary composers: examples in G. Morphy, *Les Luthistes espagnols du xvie siècle* (1902).

Fuga [foo′-gah]. (1) *L.* In the 15th and 16th cent. = CANON.

(2) *I.* Fugue.

Fugato [foo-gah′-toh], *I.* Lit. "fugued." The name given to a section of a composition which is treated fugally, though the composition as a whole is not a fugue.

Fuge [foog′-er], *G.* Fugue.

Fughetta [foo-get′-tah], *I.* A short fugue.

Fugue (*Fr.* fugue, *I.* fuga, *G.* Fuge). A contrapuntal composition in two or more parts, built on a SUBJECT—a theme (short or long) which is introduced at the beginning in imitation and recurs frequently in the course of the composition. The second entry of the subject (generally a fifth higher or a fourth lower, but sometimes a fourth higher or a fifth lower) is called the ANSWER: it is often slightly modified to preserve the tonality of the piece or to facilitate the third entry of the subject, which will be identical with the first, though in a higher or lower octave. The third entry is often deferred for one or more bars, the intervening space being occupied by a CODETTA. When the answer enters, the subject continues with a counterpoint to it, which if it is used in the rest of the fugue is called the COUNTERSUBJECT. A countersubject is generally so designed that it can be treated in DOUBLE COUNTERPOINT with the subject. The initial entries of the subject are generally as many as the number of parts (or "voices") in the fugue; sometimes, however, there is an additional entry, known rather illogically as a "redundant" entry. When all the parts have made their entries (including a redundant entry, if any), the EXPOSITION of the fugue is complete. The following examples of expositions will serve to illustrate the description given above:

BACH, *48 Preludes & Fugues, Book I, No. 21*

BACH, *48 Preludes & Fugues, Book II, No. 17*

The rest of the fugue consists of further entries of the subject, several of which will be in related keys for the sake of modulation, normally interspersed with contrapuntal EPISODES based on material derived from the subject or countersubject or both, or entirely independent of either. Among the devices which may be used in the presentation of the subject in the course of a fugue are AUGMENTATION (lengthening the note values), DIMINUTION (shortening the note values), INVERSION (presenting it upside down) and STRETTO (two or more entries in close imitation). None of these devices is essential for a fugue, nor are countersubjects (Bach wrote several fugues without them). Bach's 48 *Preludes and Fugues* show an inexhaustible variety of treatment; the first fugue of Book I even dispenses with episodes.

Sometimes one or more countersubjects appear at the beginning of the fugue simultaneously with the subject, in which case the subject and countersubject (or countersubjects) form a unity and the fugue may be said to have a subject in two (or more) parts. Such a fugue is often described as a double (or triple, or quadruple) fugue. The term "double fugue," however, is more properly applied to one in which a second, independent subject appears in the course of the fugue and is subsequently combined with the first subject. A triple fugue is one in which three subjects appear independently and are then combined, a quadruple fugue one in which four subjects are similarly treated.

A fugue may be written for voices (unaccompanied, or doubled by instruments, or with independent instrumental accompaniment), for an instrumental ensemble, or for a keyboard instrument. It may occur as an independent piece, or in association with a prelude, or as a movement in a suite, sonata or symphony or as part of an oratorio, cantata or opera (*e.g.* the finale of Verdi's *Falstaff*). It may also be written so as to form the accompaniment to a CANTO FERMO, *e.g.* a plainsong melody, a hymn-tune, or a theme used for a set of variations.

The origin of the fugue is to be found in the imitative entries introduced in polyphonic vocal music in the late 15th cent. and imitated in the instrumental *ricercar*, and subsequently in the *canzona* and capriccio. As an independent form the fugue may be said to date from the 17th cent.

A. GÉDALGE : *Traité de la fugue* (1901).
C. H. KITSON : *The Elements of Fugal*

Construction (1929). *Studies in Fugue* (1909).
G. OLDROYD : *The Technique and Spirit of Fugue* (1948).
E. PROUT : *Fugal Analysis* (1892).

Full Anthem. An anthem in which the voices (whether the full choir or an ensemble of solo voices) supply all the necessary harmony, without the need for any independent accompaniment, in contrast to the VERSE ANTHEM, where important sections are assigned to one or more solo voices with independent accompaniment. *v.* ANTHEM.

Full Close. Another name for the perfect CADENCE.

Fuller-Maitland, JOHN ALEXANDER: *b.* London, April 7, 1856; *d.* Carnforth, Mar. 30, 1936. Critic and editor. Educated at Cambridge. Music critic, *Pall Mall Gazette*, 1882; *Guardian*, 1884; *The Times*, 1889-1911. Editor of the second edition of Grove's *Dictionary of Music and Musicians* (1904-10). Also edited *English County Songs* (with Lucy Broadwood, 1893), *English Carols of the Fifteenth Century* (with W. S. Rockstro), and *The Fitzwilliam Virginal Book* (with W. B. Squire, 2 vols., 1899), as well as two volumes and part of a third in the Purcell Society's edition. His other publications include *English Music of the XIXth Century* (1902), *The Age of Bach and Handel* (*Oxford History of Music*, vol. iv, 1902), *Brahms* (1911), and *The Consort of Music* (1915). He published his reminiscences under the title *A Door-Keeper of Music* (1929).

Full Score. An orchestral score, in which the parts for the various instruments appear on separate staves arranged in a conventional order on the page. *v.* SCORE.

Fundamental. The first, or lowest, note of the HARMONIC SERIES. On wind instruments it can be produced satisfactorily on the trombone, euphonium and tuba.

Fundamental Bass (*Fr.* basse fondamentale). A term employed by Rameau to indicate the "root" of any chord, or the "roots" of a series of chords. Any two chords composed of the same notes, in whatever vertical order these notes may be arranged are considered to have the same fundamental bass, *e.g.* in the following series of chords:

the fundamental bass would be:

This interpretation is the foundation of the theory of inversions, which is generally accepted in modern textbooks on harmony. Its fallacy lies in the fact that harmony results from the combination of melodic lines, not from a preconceived association of chords. *v.* HARMONY, INVERSION.

Funeral Ode. *v.* TRAUER-ODE.

Fuoco [foo-o′-co], *I.* "Fire." *Con fuoco*, with fire.

Furiant [foor′-i-unt]. A Czech dance, in quick triple time with syncopation. There are several examples in the works of Smetana and Dvořák, *e.g.* :

DVORAK, *Symphony in D*, *Op.* 60.

Furlana [foorr-lah′-nah], *I.* *v.* FORLANA.

Furtwängler [foort′-veng-ler], WILHELM : *b.* Berlin, Jan. 25, 1886 ; *d.* Baden-Baden, Nov. 30, 1954. Conductor and composer, son of the archaeologist Adolf Furtwängler.

Studied in Munich with Rheinberger and Schillings. Acquired experience of conducting in various centres, including Zürich and Strasbourg. Conductor, Lübeck, 1911; Mannheim, 1915; Tonkünstler Orchestra, Vienna, 1919; Berlin State Opera symphony concerts, 1920; Gewandhaus concerts, Leipzig, 1922-8; Berlin Philharmonic Orchestra, 1922-45. He conducted frequently at the Bayreuth and Salzburg festivals, and as guest conductor with numerous orchestras. His compositions include 2 symphonies, a piano concerto, a *Te Deum* and chamber music. He also published books on Brahms and Bruckner and a volume of essays entitled *Gespräche über Musik* (1948).

Future, Music of the. *v.* ZUKUNFTSMUSIK.

Futurism (*I.* futurismo). A movement started by the Italian writer F. T. Marinetti in 1911. The first concert of futurist music was given by him and the composer Luigi Rossolo in Milan in 1914. The programme consisted of "four networks of noises" with the following titles:

1. Awakening of Capital.
2. Meeting of cars and aeroplanes.
3. Dining on the terrace of the Casino.
4. Skirmish in the oasis.

The instruments employed were bumblers, exploders, thunderers, whistlers etc. The concert ended in a violent battle between the performers and the audience (*v.* N. Slonimsky, *Music since 1900*, under Apr. 21, 1914). Futurist music was defined by Marinetti, who appears to have been a passionate admirer of Mussolini, as "a synthetic expression of great economic, erotic, heroic, aviational, mechanical dynamism" (see the manifesto printed in Slonimsky, part III).

Fux [fo͝oks], JOHANN JOSEPH: *b.* Hirtenfeld, 1660; *d.* Vienna, Feb. 14, 1741. Composer and theorist. Court composer, Vienna, 1698; second *Kapellmeister*, St. Stephen's, 1705; *Kapellmeister*, 1712-15; vice-*Kapellmeister* at the court, 1713; *Kapellmeister*, 1715. His compositions include a considerable amount of church music, 10 oratorios, 18 operas and instrumental music. Modern ed. of the opera *Costanza e fortezza*, written to celebrate the coronation of the Emperor Charles VI as King of Bohemia (Prague, 1723), in *D.T.Ö.*, xvii; of selected Masses and motets in *D.T.Ö.*, i (1) and ii (1); of selected *sonate da chiesa* and overtures in *D.T.Ö.*, ix (2); of his *Concentus musico-instrumentalis* (7 partitas for orchestra) in *D.T.Ö.*, xxiii (2); of his keyboard works in *D.T.Ö.*, 85. His treatise on counterpoint, *Gradus ad Parnassum* (1725; modern English ed., 1943) was for long a standard work.

L. VON KÖCHEL : *J. J. Fux* (1872).

G

G, *E.G.* (*Fr. I.* sol). The 5th note (or dominant) of the scale of C major. As an abbreviation *m.g.* = *main gauche* (left hand), G.P. = *Generalpause* (a rest for the complete orchestra).

The G clef, now invariably placed on the second line of the stave, is the treble clef, marking the G above middle C:

Gabrieli [gahb-ryeh'-lee], (1) ANDREA: *b.* Venice, *c.* 1515; *d.* there, 1586. Organist and composer, a pupil of Willaert. Succeeded Merulo as second organist of St. Mark's, Venice. His compositions include madrigals, motets, Masses and a number of instrumental works (see *Instituzioni e monumenti dell'arte musicale italiana*, i). Modern ed. of his organ works by Pierre Pidoux.

(2) GIOVANNI: *b.* Venice, 1555; *d.* there, Aug. 12, 1612. Nephew of (1). Organist and composer, a pupil of his uncle. First organist of St. Mark's, Venice, 1586. Among his pupils was Heinrich Schütz. His numerous compositions include some elaborate motets with orchestral accompaniment, orchestral works which show a lively appreciation of instrumental colour, and organ works. See *Istituzioni e monumenti dell'arte musicale italiana*, vol. ii and L. Torchi, *L'arte musicale in Italia*, ii & iii. For an example of his motets see the Harvard *Historical Anthology of Music*, i, no. 157.

G. S. BEDBROOK : *Keyboard Music from the Middle Ages to the Beginnings of the Baroque* (1949).

C. VON WINTERFELD : *Johannes Gabrieli und sein Zeitalter* (3 vols., 1834).

Gabrielli [gahb-ryell'-lee], CATERINA : *b.* Rome, Nov. 12, 1730 ; *d.* there, Feb. 16, 1796. Soprano, a pupil of Porpora. Sang at Venice, 1754, and in Vienna, 1755-61, where she appeared in operas by Gluck and Traetta. Later visited St. Petersburg and London. A brilliant coloratura who was less well qualified for passages demanding a sustained tone.

Gabrilowitsch [gah-bree-loh'-vitch], OSSIP SALOMONOWITSCH: *b.* St. Petersburg, Feb. 7, 1878; *d.* Detroit, Sept. 14, 1936. Pianist and composer. Studied with Anton Rubinstein, Liadov and Glazounov in St. Petersburg, and with Leschetizky in Vienna. First appeared as a pianist, Berlin, 1896. Conductor, Munich Konzertverein, 1910-14; Detroit Symphony Orchestra, 1918; Philadelphia Symphony Orchestra (with Stokowski), 1928. Married the singer Clara Clemens (daughter of Mark Twain), 1909. His series of concerts illustrating the history of the piano concerto, which were given both in Europe and in America, made a great impression.

C. CLEMENS GABRILOWITSCH : *My Husband Gabrilowitsch* (1938).

Gade [gah'-der], NIELS WILHELM: *b.* Copenhagen, Feb. 22, 1817; *d.* there, Dec. 21, 1890. Composer. Studied in Copenhagen and became a violinist in the Royal Orchestra. Won a prize for composition with his overture *Ossian*, 1840, and went to Leipzig, where he received much encouragement from Mendelssohn. Conductor (partly with Mendelssohn), Leipzig Gewandhaus concerts, 1844-8. On the outbreak of war between Germany and Denmark in 1848, he returned to Copenhagen, where he established himself as organist and conductor. A gentle rather than a forceful composer, he is one of the many who drew their inspiration mainly from the example of Mendelssohn and Schumann, though there are also traces of national colour in his work. His compositions include 8 symphonies, 6 overtures, violin concerto, several cantatas (some of which were performed in England), chamber music, piano solos and songs.

Gadski [gud′-ski], JOHANNA: *b.* Anclam, June 15, 1872; *d.* Berlin, Feb. 23, 1932. Operatic soprano. First appeared in *Der Freischütz*, Berlin, 1889. First appeared in America with Damrosch Opera Company, New York, 1895. Sang the part of Hester Prynne in the first performance of Damrosch's *The Scarlet Letter* (Boston, 1896). Sang subsequently in London and at Bayreuth, but was principally active in America, until her return to Germany in 1917.

Gafori [gah-fo′-ree], FRANCHINO: *b.* Ospitaletto, Jan. 14, 1451; *d.* Milan, June 24, 1522. Theorist and composer, known also by the Latinized form of his name, Franchinus Gafurius. *Maestro di cappella*, Milan Cathedral, 1484. His most important works are *Theorica musicae* (facsimile ed. 1934) and *Practica musicae.* See Hawkins, *A General History of the Science and Practice of Music* (1875 ed.), pp. 277-90.

Gagliano [gah-lyah′-no], (1) MARCO DA: *b.* Gagliano, *c.* 1575; *d.* Florence, Feb. 24, 1642. Composer. *Maestro di cappella*, San Lorenzo, Florence, 1608, and subsequently to the Grand Duke of Tuscany. He published 6 books of madrigals, as well as motets and a Mass, but is best known today as one of the first opera-composers. His *Dafne* (a setting of Rinuccini's libretto) was first performed at Mantua, 1608 (reprinted in part in *Publikationen älterer praktischer und theoreticher Musikwerke*, x.).

(2) A firm of violin-makers active in Naples in the late 17th and 18th cent.

Gagliarda [gah-lyarr′-dah], *I.* Galliard.

Gaillarde [ga-yarrd], *Fr.* Galliard.

Gál [gull], HANS: *b.* Brunn, Aug. 5, 1890. Austrian composer and teacher, a pupil of Mandyczewski. Won a State prize for composition, 1915. Lecturer, Vienna University, 1918; director, Musikhochschule, Mainz, 1929; lecturer, Vienna University, and conductor, 1933; lecturer, Edinburgh University, 1945-56. His compositions include the operas *Der Arzt der Sobeide* (Breslau, 1919), *Die heilage Ente* (Düsseldorf, 1923), *Das Lied der Nacht* (Breslau, 1926) and *Die beiden Klaas*, 2 symphonies, choral and orchestral works, violin concerto and chamber music.

Galant. *v.* STYLE GALANT.

Galanterien [gal-unt-er-ee′-ĕn], *G.* A name given in the 18th cent. to dances in a suite which were added optionally to the regular allemande, courante, sarabande and gigue. Their place was normally after the sarabande and before the gigue. Thus, Bach's six *English Suites* comprise:

I: Prelude, allemande, courante I & II (with two doubles), sarabande, bourrée I & II, gigue.
II: Prelude, allemande, courante, sarabande (with variant), bourrée I & II, gigue.
III: Prelude, allemande, courante, sarabande (with variant), gavotte I & II, gigue.
IV: Prelude, allemande, courante, sarabande, menuet I & II, gigue.
V: Prelude, allemande, courante, sarabande, Passepied I & II, gigue.
VI: Prelude, allemande, courante, sarabande (with double), gavotte I and II, gigue.

Galilei [gah-lee-leh′-ee], VINCENZO: *b.* Santa Maria in Monte, *c.* 1520; *d.* Florence, June, 1591. Lutenist and composer, father of the astronomer, Galileo Galilei. He was prominent among the Florentines who discussed at Count Bardi's house the question of the revival of Greek drama and contributed to the creation of the declamatory song for solo voice which played an important part in the first operas. He published madrigals and lute music (see *Istituzioni e monumenti dell' arte musicale italiana*, iv), two dialogues—*Il Fronimo* (1563), dealing with lute tablature, and *Dialogo della musica antica e della moderna* (1581; 2nd ed., 1602), and *Discorso intorno all' opere di messer Gioseffo Zarlino* (1589). Facsimile ed. of the *Dialogo*, 1934; modern ed. of his *Contrapunti a due voci*, ed. L. Rood, 1947. English translation of part of the *Dialogo* in O. Strunk, *Source Readings in Music History*, pp. 302-22.

Galliard (*Fr.* gaillarde, *I.* gagliarda). A lively dance, generally in triple time, which takes its name from the French *gaillard*, " merry," and is first found in the early 16th cent., *e.g.*:

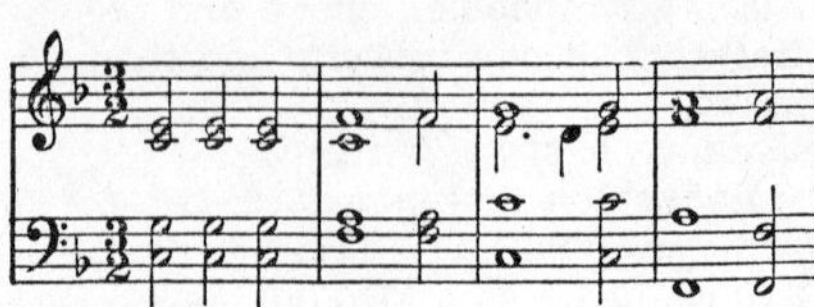

CLAUDE GERVAISE (*Les Maîtres musiciens de la Renaissance française*, xxiii, p. 43).

From the second half of the 16th cent. it was regularly used to provide a contrast to the slow PAVANE, which it followed, and with which it was often thematically connected:

BYRD, *My Lady Nevell's Booke*, nos. 20-1

Galliard, JOHN ERNEST: *b.* Celle, *c.* 1680; *d.* London, 1749. Oboist and composer, of German origin. Came to England in the early 18th cent. as musician to Prince George of Denmark. In addition to numerous compositions he translated into English Pier Francesco Tosi's *Opinioni di cantori antichi e moderni, o sieno osservazioni sopra il canto figurato* (1723) under the title *Observations on the Florid Song* (1742).

Galli-Curci [gahl'-lee-coorr'-chee], AMELITA: *b.* Milan, Nov. 18, 1889. Coloratura soprano. Studied at the Milan Conservatorio but self-taught as a singer. First appeared in *Rigoletto*, Rome, 1909, and subsequently in South America and Spain. First appeared in the United States at Chicago, 1916; sang with the Metropolitan Opera Company, New York, 1920. She has frequently toured as a concert singer.

Gallus. *v.* HANDL.

Galop. A quick dance in 2/4 time, popular in the 19th cent.

Galoubet [ga-loo-bay], *Fr.* A three-hole whistle-flute, held in the player's left hand; with the right hand he beats the tabor (*tambourin*), a small drum suspended from the left arm. Many composers have imitated the effect of this popular music-making. *v.* TAMBOURIN.

Galpin, FRANCIS WILLIAM: *b.* Dorchester, Dec. 25, 1858; *d.* Richmond (Surrey), Dec. 30, 1945. Musicologist and collector of musical instruments. Educated at Trinity College, Cambridge, he was ordained in 1883 and spent some 50 years of his life as a parish priest. His interest in musical instruments, of which he had practical knowledge, ranged from the Sumerians to the latest developments of electronic sound-production. His books include *Old English Instruments of Music* (1910; 3rd ed., 1932), *A Textbook of European Musical Instruments* (1937) and *The Music of the Sumerians, Babylonians and Assyrians* (1937).

Galuppi [gah-loop'-pee], BALDASSARE: *b.* Burano (nr. Venice), Oct. 18, 1706; *d.* Venice, Jan. 3, 1785. Frequently known as *Il Buranello*, from his island birthplace. Composer, a pupil of Lotti in Venice. Between 1728 and 1740 he produced a large number of operas for Venice and Turin. He also produced several operas in London, 1741-3. Second *maestro di cappella*, St. Mark's, Venice, 1748; first *maestro di cappella*, 1762; director, Conservatorio degli Incurabili, 1762. From 1766-8 in St. Petersburg, where he produced several operas; then returned to the directorship of the Conservatorio at Venice. His comic operas are a notable contribution to the history of the form. He also wrote several oratorios, symphonies, concertos and keyboard sonatas. The "Toccata" to which Browning devoted a poem is an imaginary work.

Gamba. Abbreviation for VIOLA DA GAMBA.

Gamme [gum], *Fr.* Scale.

Gamut. (1) In medieval theory the note

a combination of *gamma* (the letter G in Greek) and *ut*, the first note of the HEXACHORD. The Greek capital letter *Γ* (G) was assigned to this note, because it was below the lowest note of the two-octave scale system of the Greeks, to which medieval theorists had assigned the letter A.

(2) The scale beginning on the note *gamma ut*, and hence more generally the range or compass of a voice or instrument.

(3) The key of G, *e.g.* Purcell's "Ground in Gamut" is in the key of G major, his "Overture, Air and Jig in Gamut ♭," in the key of G minor (*v.* FLAT).

Ganassi [ga-nahss'-see], SILVESTRO DI. 16th-cent. Italian theorist, resident in Venice. Author and publisher of a tutor for the recorder, *La Fontegara* (1535; facsimile ed. 1934), and a tutor for the viols, *Regola Rubertina* (1542-3; facsimile ed. by M. Schneider, 1924).

Ganz [gunts], (1) RUDOLPH: *b.* Zürich, Feb. 24, 1877. Swiss pianist, conductor and composer, now a naturalised American. Studied in Zürich, Lausanne and Strasbourg, and subsequently with Busoni in Berlin. First appeared as a soloist in Berlin, 1899. Teacher of piano, Chicago Musical College, 1901-5; vice-president, 1928; president, 1934. Conductor, St. Louis Symphony Orchestra, 1921-7. He has toured widely as a pianist and conductor, and given the first performance of a large number of works by modern composers.

(2) WILHELM: *b.* Mainz, Nov. 6, 1833; *d.* London, Sept. 12, 1914. Pianist, conductor and singing-teacher, resident in England from 1850. He accompanied Jenny Lind and many other famous singers. As a conductor he introduced to England Berlioz's *Symphonie fantastique* and Liszt's *Dante Symphony.* He published *Memories of a Musician* (1913).

Ganze Note [gunts'-er note'-er], *G.* Semibreve.

Ganzton [gunts'-tone], *G.* Whole tone. *v.* TONE (1).

Garcia [garr-thee'-ah], (1) MANUEL DEL POPOLO VICENTE: *b.* Seville, Jan. 27, 1775; *d.* Paris, June 9, 1832. Tenor, composer and conductor. Originally made his reputation in Spain. After his first appearance in Paris, 1808, he became very well known as an opera-singer, and travelled widely, appearing in Italy, England, the United States and Mexico. He also established a school of singing in London. The part of Almaviva in Rossini's *Il barbiere di Siviglia* was written for him. His numerous operas had a considerable success.

(2) MANUEL PATRICIO RODRIGUEZ: *b.* Madrid, March 7, 1805; *d.* London, July 1, 1906. Son of (1). Singing teacher, a pupil of his father. Teacher at the Paris Conservatoire, 1842; R.A.M., London, 1850-95. In addition to inventing the laryngoscope, he published *Mémoire sur la voix humaine* (1840) and *Traité complet de l'art du chant* (1847), both works of outstanding importance. His pupils included Jenny Lind, Mathilde Marchesi, Julius Stockhausen and Charles Santley.

M. STERLING MACKINLAY: *Garcia the Centenarian and his Times* (1908).

(3) MARIA FELICITA: *b.* Paris, March 24, 1808; *d.* Manchester, Sept. 23, 1836. Daughter of (1). *v.* MALIBRAN.

(4) MICHELLE FERDINANDE PAULINE: *b.* Paris, July 18, 1821; *d.* there, May 18, 1910. Daughter of (1). *v.* VIARDOT-GARCIA.

Gardano [garr-dahn'-o]. Venetian music-publishing firm, founded by Antonio Gardano. Their numerous publications of secular and sacred music appeared during the years 1538-1619.

Garden, MARY: *b.* Aberdeen, Feb. 20, 1877. Operatic soprano, resident in America from childhood. Studied in Paris and made her first appearance in Charpentier's *Louise*, 1900, and was chosen by Debussy to sing Mélisande in *Pelléas et Mélisande* (Paris, 1902). First appeared in New York, 1910. Director of the Chicago Opera Company, 1921-2.

Gardiner, (1) HENRY BALFOUR: *b.* London, Nov. 7, 1877; *d.* Salisbury, June 28, 1950. Composer. Educated at Oxford, and also studied music with Ivan Knorr at Frankfort. In addition to a substantial number of compositions, some of which became very popular—*e.g. Shepherd Fennel's Dance* for orchestra (1911) and *News from Whydah* for chorus and orchestra (1912)—he did great service to English music by promoting at his own expense orchestral concerts for the performance of works by contemporary composers, 1912-13.

(2) WILLIAM: *b.* Leicester, March 15, 1770; *d.* there, Nov. 16, 1853. Writer on music. A stocking-manufacturer by profession, he acquired an extensive knowledge of the works of Continental composers, particularly Beethoven, and adapted music by them to sacred words under the title *Sacred Melodies* (6 vols.). His other publications include *The Music of Nature* (1832), *Music and Friends* (1838-53), a collection of reminiscences in three volumes, and *Sights in Italy* (1847), a survey of music and the arts in that country.

Garlande [garr-lũnd], JEAN DE (Johannes de Garlandia). 13th-cent. theorist. Born in the late 12th cent., he studied at Oxford and Paris. Active in the foundation of the University of Toulouse, 1229; in Paris from 1232. Author of *De musica mensurabili positio* (mod. ed. in Coussemaker, i, p. 175). Other works have been conjecturally assigned to a younger writer of the same name, but without documentary authority.

Gasparini [gahss - parr - ee'- nee], FRANCESCO: *b.* Camajore, March 5, 1668 ; *d.* Rome, March 22, 1727. Composer, a pupil of Corelli and Pasquini, and teacher of Marcello. He wrote several oratorios and operas, and also published *L'Armonico pratico al cimbalo* (1708), a treatise on accompaniment from figured bass (see F. T. Arnold, *The Art of Accompaniment from a Thorough-Bass*, pp. 250-5).

Gasparo da Salò [gahss-pah'-ro dah sah-lo']. *v.* SALÒ.

Gassmann [guss'-mun], FLORIAN LEOPOLD: *b.* Brüx, May 3, 1729; *d.* Vienna, Jan. 20, 1774. Sudeten composer. Left home at the age of 12 and studied for two years in Bologna with Martini. After a long period in private service in Venice, he became composer of ballets to the Vienna court and in 1772 court *Kapellmeister*. In 1771 founded the *Tonkünstler-Sozietät* (now the *Haydn-Sozietät*)—a charity for the widows and orphans of musicians. His compositions include symphonies, chamber music, church music (see *D.T.Ö.*, xlv) and operas, of which *La Contessina* (Neustadt, 1770) is printed, with J. A. Hiller's German version, in *D.T.Ö.*, xxi.

Gast [gust], PETER: *b.* Annaberg, Jan. 10, 1854; *d.* there, Aug. 15, 1918. Composer, whose real name was Johann Heinrich Köselitz. Studied at the Leipzig Conservatorium and in Basle, where he became the friend and secretary of Nietzsche, whose letters he subsequently helped to edit. His best-known work is the opera *Die heimliche Ehe* (Danzig, 1891), founded on the libretto of Cimarosa's *Il matrimonio segreto*; it was revived under the title *Der Löwe von Venedig* (Chemnitz, 1933). His other compositions include chamber music, songs and a symphony.

Gastoldi [gust-ol'-dee], GIOVANNI GIACOMO: *b.* Carvaggio, *c.* 1550; *d.* 1622. Composer of church music, madrigals and ballets. *Maestro di cappella*, Mantua, 1582-1609. His most popular work was his *Balletti a 5 voci con li suoi versi per cantare, sonare e ballare* (1591), which was many times reprinted. These gay, cheerful partsongs, with " fa la " refrain, had a considerable influence on other composers, notably in England. Morley's *First Book of Balletts to five voyces* (1595) is a very close imitation of the style. *v.* BALLETT.

Gastoué [guss-too-ay], AMÉDÉE: *b.* Paris, March 13, 1873; *d.* there, June 1, 1943. Writer on music, a pupil of Lavignac and Guilmant. His special subject was Gregorian chant, in which he gave instruction for many years at the Schola Cantorum, Paris. His published works include *Histoire du chant liturgique à Paris* (1904), *Les Origines du chant romain* (1907), *Catalogue des manuscrits de musique byzantine des bibliothèques de France* (1907), *L'Art grégorien* (1911), *Le Graduel et l'antiphonaire romain* (1913), *L'Orgue en France* (1921), *Les Primitifs de la musique française* (1922) and *Catalogue des livres de musique de la Bibliothèque de l'Arsenal à Paris* (with L. de la Laurencie, 1936). He also edited for the Société Française de Musicologie *Le Manuscrit de musique polyphonique du trésor d'Apt* (1937).

Gatti [gaht'-tee], GUIDO MARIA: *b.* Chieti, May 30, 1892. Writer on music. Founded in 1920 the magazine *Il Pianoforte* (known since 1928 as *Rassegna Musicale*). He also organized the first Maggio Musicale in Florence, 1934. He has devoted himself largely to the interests of contemporary composers. In addition to a large number of articles in Italian and foreign periodicals his published works also include *I Lieder di Schumann* (1914), *Figure di musicisti francesi* (1915), *Bizet* (1915), *Musicisti moderni d'Italia e fuori* (1920), *Dizionario musicale* (with A. della Corte, 1925, 2nd ed. 1943), and *Ildebrando Pizzetti* (1934).

Gatty, NICHOLAS COMYN: *b.* Bradfield, Sept. 13, 1874; *d.* London, Nov. 10, 1946. Composer and critic. Educated at Cambridge and the R.C.M., where he was a pupil of Stanford. He was for a time on the staff of Covent Garden Opera House. Music critic, *Pall Mall Gazette*, 1907-14. His numerous compositions include several operas, among them *Greysteel* (1 act, Sheffield, 1906; revised as a full-length opera, London, 1938), *Duke or Devil* (1 act, Manchester, 1909), *The Tempest* (London, 1920) *Prince Ferelon* (London, 1921; previously produced privately, 1919).

Gaubert [go-bair], PHILIPPE · *b* Cahors, July 4, 1879; *d.* Paris, June 10, 1941. Flautist, conductor and composer. Studied at the Paris Conservatoire, where he taught the flute from 1919. Conductor, Société des Concerts du Conservatoire, 1919-38; Paris Opéra, 1920. His compositions include operas, ballets, an oratorio, orchestral works, chamber music and songs.

Gaultier [goat-yay], (1) DENIS: *d.* Paris, 1672. Lutenist and composer. His works include a manuscript collection entitled *La Rhétorique des dieux* (modern ed. in *Publications de la Société française de musicologie*, vi-vii), which consists of dance tunes arranged in groups or suites. This method of arrangement occurs also in the works of the French harpsichord composers. Further evidence of the influence of Gaultier on harpsichord music is the imitation of his technique of broken chords (particularly suitable for the lute and almost equally effective on the harpsichord) and the use of fanciful names for the separate pieces.

(2) JACQUES. 17th-cent. lutenist and composer, a relative of (1). He came to England in 1618 to escape the consequences of having killed a French nobleman, and entered the service of the Marquess (later the Duke) of Buckingham and subsequently of Charles I. Herrick, in his poem "To M. Henry Laws," refers to him as "the rare Gotire"

Gaveau [ga-vo]. A firm of instrument-makers in Paris, founded in 1847 by Joseph Gaveau (*d.* 1903). In addition to making pianos the firm has played a prominent part in the revival of the harpsichord. Étienne Gaveau, son of Joseph, built the Salle Gaveau in Paris, 1907. Another son, Gabriel, established an independent business in 1911.

Gaveaux [ga-vo], PIERRE: *b.* Béziers, Aug. 1761; *d.* Paris, Feb. 5, 1825. Composer. After appearing as a tenor at the Paris Opéra-Comique, 1789, he devoted himself to composition. His numerous operas include *Léonore, ou l'Amour conjugal* (Paris, 1798), a setting of the libretto by J. N. Bouilly which, translated into Italian, was used by Paer for *Leonora ossia l'amore coniugale* (Dresden, 1804), and in German by Beethoven for *Fidelio oder die eheliche Liebe* (Vienna, 1805).

Gaviniès [ga-veen-yay], PIERRE: *b.* Bordeaux, May 11, 1728; *d.* Paris, Sept. 22, 1800. Violinist. First appeared at the Concert Spirituel, 1741, which he directed, 1773-7; later became the first teacher of the violin at the Paris Conservatoire (founded 1795). He had considerable influence as a teacher.

Gavotte [ga-vot], *Fr.* A French dance, the popularity of which dates from its introduction by Lully into ballets and operas in the late 17th cent. It retained its popularity in the 18th cent.: there are several examples in Bach's instrumental suites. It is in fairly quick 4/4 time and generally (though not invariably) starts on the third beat of the bar, *e.g.*:

BACH, *English Suites*, No. 6

Where two gavottes occur together in a suite, the second is often in the form of a MUSETTE.

Gazza Ladra, La [lah gah'-dzah lah'-drah] (The Thievish Magpie). Opera in two acts by Rossini. Libretto by Giovanni Gherardini (after *La Pie voleuse* by Jean Marie Théodore Baudoin d'Aubigny and Louis Charles Caigniez). First performed, Milan, May 31, 1817.

Gazzaniga [gah-dzah-nee'-gah], GIUSEPPE: *b.* Verona, Oct. 1743; *d.* Crema, Feb. 1, 1818. Composer, a pupil of Porpora and Piccinni. Of his numerous operas the one-act *Don Giovanni Tenorio ossia il convitato di pietra* (Venice, 1787) was very successful; the libretto, by Giovanni Bertati, was plainly familiar to da Ponte, librettist of Mozart's *Don Giovanni*, which was performed at Prague later in the same year (*v.* E. J. Dent, *Mozart's Operas*, 2nd ed., pp. 129 foll.).

Gebrauchsmusik [ger-browkhs'-moo-zeek], *G.* Lit. "music for use." A term which arose in Germany in the 1920's to describe music which was intended primarily for practical purposes rather than as a form of self-expression—particularly music suitable for domestic use or for amateur groups. By its nature such music is free from elaboration or technical difficulties and is often so designed that instrumental music, for example, can be performed by any convenient ensemble that is available. Hindemith was prominent among the composers who devoted their attention to this form of practical music-making.

Gédalge [zhay-dulzh], ANDRÉ: *b.* Paris, Dec. 27, 1856; *d.* there, Feb. 5, 1926. Composer and teacher. Teacher of counterpoint and fugue at the Paris Conservatoire, 1905, where he had previously studied (1884-6). His pupils included Ravel, Milhaud, Honegger and Schmitt. His most important educational publication is the *Traité de la fugue* (1901), which is a standard work in France. He also composed a considerable amount of instrumental music and works for the stage.

Gedämpft [ger-dempft'], *G.* Muted.

Gehalten [ger-hult'-ĕn], *G.* Sustained. *Gut gehalten*, well sustained.

Geheimnisvoll [ger-hime'-niss-foll], *G.* Mysterious.

Gehend [gay'-ĕnt], *G.* Lit. "going." *i.e.* moving at a moderate speed—the same as *andante*.

Geige [gy'-ger], *G.* Fiddle, violin. *v.* GIGUE (1).

Geiringer [gy'-ring-er], KARL: *b.* Vienna, Apr. 26, 1899. Writer on music, Austrian by birth, now resident in the United States. Studied in Vienna with Adler, and in Berlin with Johannes Wolf and Sachs. Keeper of the museum and library of the Gesellschaft der Musikfreunde, Vienna, 1930-8. Lived in England, 1938-40. Professor, Boston University, 1941. He was a member of the commission for the *Denkmäler der Tonkunst in Österreich* and edited for it instrumental and vocal compositions by P. Peuerl and I. Posch. His other publications include *Brahms, his Life and Work* (1936; 2nd ed., 1948; orig. German ed., 1934), *Musical Instruments: their History from the Stone Age to the Present Day* (1943), *Haydn: a Creative Life in Music* (1947) and *The Bach Family* (1954).

Geiser [gize'-er], WALTER: *b.* Zofingen,

May 16, 1897. Swiss viola-player, composer and conductor. Studied in Basle and Cologne, and in Berlin with Busoni. Teacher of composition, Basle Conservatoire. His compositions consist mainly of instrumental music and choral works.

Geisslerlieder [gice′-ler-leed-er], *G.* "Flagellants' songs." Songs sung in procession by flagellants in 14th-cent. Germany, a parallel to the *laudi spirituali* in Italy. Modern ed. in P. Runge, *Die Lieder und Melodien der Geissler des Jahres 1349* (1900).

Geistertrio [giced′-er-tree-o], *G.* "Ghost Trio," a nickname given to Beethoven's piano trio in D major, Op. 70, No. 1, on account of the mysterious character of the slow movement.

Geistlich [giced′-li*sh*], *G.* Religious, sacred. *Geistlicher Lieder*, sacred songs.

Gemächlich [ger-me*sh*′-li*sh*], *G.* Comfortable—the equivalent of *comodo.*

Gemessen [ger-mess′-ĕn], *G.* Lit. "measured," hence held back, sustained in tempo.

Geminiani [jeh - meen - yahn′- ee], FRANCESCO: *b.* Lucca, 1679 or 1680; *d.* Dublin, Sept. 17, 1762. Violinist and composer, a pupil of Corelli. He had a great success as a soloist, particularly in England, where he arrived in 1714. He lived in Dublin, 1733-40 and 1759-62; the rest of his life was spent partly in London and partly in Paris. In addition to his numerous compositions (sonatas, trios, concertos and harpsichord solos) he published *Rules for playing in a true Taste on the Violin, German flute, Violoncello and Harpsichord* (1739), *Guida Armonica o Dizionario Armonico* (1742), *A treatise of good taste in the art of musick* (1749), *The art of playing on the Violin* (1751; an earlier anonymous edition appeared in 1731), *The art of accompaniment* (1755), *The art of playing the Guitar* (1760). *The art of playing on the Violin* is important as a record of the established practice of violin-playing at the time and as one of the first published tutors for the instrument. Facsimile ed. of *The art of playing on the Violin* by D. Boyden (1952). For *The art of accompaniment* see F. T. Arnold, *The Art of Accompaniment from a Thorough-Bass,* pp. 438-9, 463-8. For Geminiani's interpretation of ornaments see E. Dannreuther, *Musical Ornamentation*, i, pp. 131-4.

Generalpause [gay-ner-ahl′-pow′-zer], *G.* A rest for the complete orchestra, generally indicated in older scores and parts by the abbreviation G.P. placed above the rest.

Gennrich [gen′-ri*sh*], FRIEDRICH: *b.* Colmar, March 27, 1883. Musicologist, a pupil of Ludwig (at Strasbourg) and Bédier (in Paris). His studies have embraced both the Romance languages and music, and so have qualified him to deal authoritatively with troubadour and trouvère song, which he has dealt with extensively in books and articles. His publications include *Rondeaux, Virelais und Balladen* (2 vols., 1921-7), *Der musikalische Vortrag der altfranzösischen Chansons de geste* (1923), *Die altfranzösische Rotrouenge* (1925), *Formenlehre des mittelalterlichen Liedes* (1932) and a selection of troubadour, trouvère and Minnesinger melodies (1951).

Genoveva [gay-noff-ay′-fa]. Opera in four acts by Schumann. Libretto by Robert Reinick, altered by the composer. First performed, Leipzig, June 25, 1850.

Georges [zhorrzh], ALEXANDRE: *b.* Arras, Feb. 25, 1850; *d.* Paris, Jan. 18, 1938. Composer. Studied at the École Niedermeyer, where he later taught. His compositions include several operas and symphonic poems and the well-known *Chansons de Miarka*—settings of poems from Jean Richepin's *Miarka la fille à l'ours.*

Gerardy [zher-arr-dee], JEAN: *b.* Liége, Dec. 6, 1877; *d.* Spa, July 4, 1929. Cellist. Studied at the Verviers Conservatoire. First appeared with Ysaÿe and Paderewski at Nottingham, 1888. Toured widely in all parts of the world, mainly as a soloist, though he was also heard in piano trios with Kreisler and Hofmann.

Gerber [gairr′-ber], (1) ERNST LUDWIG: *b.* Sondershausen, Sept. 29, 1746; *d.* there, June 30, 1819. Lexicographer, son of the court organist at Sondershausen. After industriously collecting biographical materials, books and music, he published his *Historisch-biographisches*

Lexikon der Tonkünstler (2 vols., 1790-2), followed by his *Neues historisch-biographisches Lexikon der Tonkünstler* (4 vols., 1812-4), a supplement to the preceding work. The two dictionaries were for long standard works. Gerber's library was bought by the Gesellschaft der Musikfreunde in Vienna.

(2) RUDOLF: *b.* Flehingen, Apr. 15, 1899; *d.* May 6, 1957. Musicologist, a pupil of Abert, to whom he became assistant at Berlin University, 1923-8. Professor, Giessen, 1932; Göttingen, 1943. His published works include *Das Passionsrezitativ bei Heinrich Schütz* (1929), *Johannes Brahms* (1938), *Christoph Willibald Gluck* (1941) and a number of contributions to periodicals and collective works. He collaborated in the complete edition of the works of Michael Praetorius and was general editor of a new collected edition of Gluck's works.

Gerbert [gairr'-bert] (**von Hornau**), MARTIN: *b.* Horb, Aug. 12, 1720; *d.* St. Blaise, May 13, 1793. Historian. Entered the Monastery of St. Blaise in the Black Forest, 1737; priest, 1744; prince-abbot, 1764. He travelled extensively in Europe, 1759-65, and published a history of church music under the title *De cantu et musica sacra* (2 vols., 1774). In addition to theological works, liturgical works and an account of his travels in Germany, Italy and France he also published *Scriptores ecclesiastici de musica sacra potissimum* (1784)—a collection of medieval treatises on music, to which Coussemaker's series later formed a supplement. Two facsimile editions of *Scriptores ecclesiastici* have been published—in 1905 and 1931.

Gerhard [zhay-rarr'], ROBERTO: *b.* Valls, Sept. 25, 1896. Catalan composer, son of a Swiss father and a French mother. A pupil of Pedrell and Schönberg. Active as a teacher in Barcelona, 1929-38, where he was music librarian in the Catalan Library. After the Spanish Civil War came to England and settled in Cambridge, 1939. His works include ballets, instrumental music, songs and the opera *The Duenna* (1948).

Gerhardt [gairr'-harrt], ELENA: *b.* Leipzig, Nov. 11, 1883. Concert soprano. She learned much from the conductor Artur Nikisch, who frequently accompanied her. Her reputation was founded on her performance of songs by German composers, notably Schubert, Schumann, Brahms and Wolf.

Gericke [gay'-rick-er], WILHELM: *b.* Graz, Apr. 18, 1845; *d.* Vienna, Oct. 27, 1925. Conductor and composer. Studied at the Vienna Conservatorium. Second conductor, Vienna Court Opera, 1874; Vienna Gesellschaftskonzerte, 1880-4, 1889-95; Boston Symphony Orchestra, 1884-9, 1898-1906.

Gerle [gairrl'-er], HANS: *d.* Nuremberg, 1570. Lute-maker and lutenist. He published *Musica Teusch auf die Instrument der grossen und kleinen Geygen auch Lautten* (1532), an instruction book for viols and lute, which appeared in a revised and enlarged edition in 1546, *Tabulatur auff die Lautten* (1533), and *Ein newes sehr künstlichs Lautenbuch* (1552). The pieces in the first edition of *Musica Teusch* consist almost entirely of transcriptions of German songs and dances; in the revised edition French *chansons* are substituted for the German songs. *Tabulatur auff die Lautten* includes both German and foreign pieces; *Ein newes sehr künstlichs Lautenbuch* includes a substantial number of Italian pieces.

German, EDWARD: *b.* Whitchurch, Feb. 17, 1862; *d.* London, Nov. 11, 1936. Composer, whose name was originally Edward German Jones. Studied organ and violin at the R.A.M., where he won the Charles Lucas medal for composition. After working as an orchestral player (violin), 1887-8, he became conductor at the Globe Theatre, for which he wrote his incidental music to *Richard III*. His music for later productions at other theatres—*Henry VIII* (1892) and *Nell Gwyn* (1900)—won great popularity. In 1901 he completed *The Emerald Isle*, a light opera which had been left unfinished by Sullivan. He had considerable success with the operas *Merrie England* (1902), *A Princess of Kensington* (1903) and *Tom Jones* (1907). His instrumental compositions include 2 symphonies, the symphonic poem *Hamlet*, the *Welsh Rhapsody* and *Theme and Six Diversions*. Though much of his music was popular in character, his craftsmanship was always impeccable. He was knighted in 1928.

W. H. SCOTT: *Sir Edward German—an Intimate Biography* (1932).

German Flute. An 18th-cent. name for the transverse flute (the ordinary orchestral flute), as a distinction from the RECORDER, which was known as the English flute. *v.* FLUTE.

Germani [jairr-mahn'-ee], FERNANDO: *b.* Rome, Apr. 5, 1906. Organist of St. Peter's, Rome, since 1949. He has held teaching appointments both in Italy and in America, and enjoys the reputation of being one of the outstanding performers of the present day.

German Requiem, A. *v.* DEUTSCHES REQUIEM.

German Sixth. *v.* AUGMENTED SIXTH.

Gérold [gay-rollt], THÉODORE: *b.* Strasbourg, Oct. 26, 1866. Historian and musicologist. Originally a student of theology, he also studied history of music, singing and violin. After studying singing further with Stockhausen in Frankfort and French music in Paris, he became assistant to Stockhausen, 1895. Lecturer, Basle University, 1914-8; Strasbourg, 1919-36. He has published a number of important works on the history of music, including *Chansons populaires des XV*e *et XVI*e *siècles* (1913), *Les Psaumes de Clément Marot et leurs mélodies* (1919), *L'Art du chant en France au XVII*e *siècle* (1921), *Le Manuscrit de Bayeux* (1921), *Schubert* (1923), *J. S. Bach* (1925), *Les Pères de l'Église et la musique* (1931), *La Musique au moyen-âge* (1932), *Histoire de la musique des origines à la fin du XIV*e *siècle* (1936). He holds the degrees of Docteur ès Lettres and Docteur en Théologie.

Gershwin, GEORGE: *b.* Brooklyn, Sept. 26, 1898; *d.* Hollywood, July 11, 1937. American composer. Beginning as employee of a music-publishing firm, he began to write songs, and from 1919 onwards a series of musical comedies. He also wrote a series of concert works—*Rhapsody in Blue* for piano and jazz orchestra (1924), piano concerto in F major (1925), *An American in Paris* (1928) and *Second Rhapsody* (1931). His opera *Porgy and Bess* (Boston, 1935) had considerable success. Within a limited field he had an agreeable talent but hardly enough self-discipline to achieve mastery in large-scale composition.

M. ARMITAGE: *George Gershwin—a Biography* (1938).

I. GOLDBERG: *George Gershwin* (1931).

Gervaise [zhair-vez], CLAUDE. 16th-cent. French violinist and composer. His published works consist of dance tunes for instrumental ensemble and *chansons*. Modern ed. of selected dance tunes in H. Expert, *Les Maîtres musiciens de la Renaissance française*, xxiii.

Ges [gess], *G.* G flat (G♭).

Gesangvoll [ger-zung'-foll], *G.* Songful —the same as *cantabile*.

Geschöpfe des Prometheus, Die [dee ger-shurp'-fer dess pro-mate'-oyce]. *v.* PROMETHEUS.

Geschwind [ger-shvint'], *G.* Quick.

Gesellschaft der Musikfreunde [ger-zell'-shuft dair moo-zeek'-froynd-er], *G.* (Society of the Friends of Music). A society in Vienna founded in 1812 by Joseph von Sonnleithner. It was responsible for founding the Vienna Conservatorium, 1817, the Singverein (a choral society), 1859, and a regular series of concerts known as the Gesellschaftskonzerte, 1859. The Society has a valuable museum and library, which includes a number of autograph compositions.

Gesellschaft für Musikforschung [ger-zell'-shuft feer moo-zeek'-forr-shoong], *G.* (Society for Musical Research). (1) An organization founded by F. Commer and R. Eitner in 1868. Is was responsible for the series known at *Publikationen älterer praktischer und theoretischer Musikwerke*, which came to an end in 1905.

(2) A society founded by F. Blume after the 1939-45 war. Its official publication is *Die Musikforschung*, which first appeared in 1948.

Geses [gess'-ess], *G.* G double flat (G♭♭).

Gesius [gaze'-yooss], BARTHOLOMÄUS: *b.* Müncheburg, *c.* 1560; *d.* Frankfort on the Oder, 1613. Composer of church music. Having first studied theology, he became cantor at Frankfort on the Oder, 1592. His publications include volumes of Masses, Magnificats, motets, Lutheran hymns, and a Passion according to St. John (1588).

Gestopft [ger-shtopft], *G.* Stopped. A term used in music for the HORN to indicate that the hand is inserted into the bell. This method was formerly employed to obtain notes not in the natural harmonic series, but is now used only to produce a muffled tone-quality.

Gesualdo [jeh-zoo-ahl′-do], CARLO: *b.* Naples, *c.* 1560; *d.* there, Sept. 8, 1613. Composer. Second son of Fabrizio Gesualdo, Prince of Venosa. He became heir to the title through the early death of his elder brother, and succeeded his father as Prince in 1591. As a young man he developed an interest in music and poetry and became an expert performer on the archlute. He was an intimate friend of Tasso, who addressed three poems to him; he also set several of Tasso's poems to music. He married (1) his cousin Maria d'Avalos, 1586, whom he murdered in 1590 on account of her infidelity; (2) Eleonora d'Este, 1594. He published 6 books of madrigals, 2 books of motets and a volume of *responsoria.* A seventh book of madrigals appeared posthumously in 1626. In his madrigals he went even further than his contemporaries in his desire to give complete expression to the mood of the text, and made considerable use of chromatic harmony and abrupt modulation. Modern ed. of several of the madrigals in L. Torchi, *L'arte musicale in Italia*, iv, and *Raccolta nazionale delle musiche italiane*, vols. 59-62; 8 also ed. by W. Weismann; complete ed. by F. Vatielli. Modern ed. of motets in *Istituzioni e monumenti dell'arte musicale italiana*, v.

A. EINSTEIN : *The Italian Madrigal*, 3 vols. (1949).

C. GRAY & P. HESELTINE : *Carlo Gesualdo, Musician and Murderer* (1926).

Getragen [ger-trahg′-ĕn], *G.* Slow and sustained—the equivalent of *sostenuto.*

Gevaert [gay′- farrt], FRANÇOIS AUGUSTE: *b.* Huysse, July 31, 1828; *d.* Brussels, Dec. 24, 1908. Historian, musicologist and composer. Studied at the Ghent Conservatoire. After serving as an organist while still in his 'teens, he won a composition prize and the *Prix de Rome*, 1847, and travelled in France, Spain and Italy, 1849-52. Several operas were performed with success in Paris, 1853-64. Director of music, Paris Opera, 1867-70; director, Brussels Conservatoire, 1871 till his death. By thorough reorganization he succeeded in raising the reputation of the Conservatoire to a high level. He published a large number of historical and educational works, notably *Traité général d'instrumentation* (1863), revised under the title *Nouveau traité général d'instrumentation* (1885), *Cours méthodique d'orchestration* (2 vols., 1890), *Histoire et théorie de la musique de l'antiquité* (2 vols., 1875-81), *Traité d'harmonie théorique et pratique* (2 vols., 1905-7). Among his editions of old music are *Les Gloires d'Italie* (1868), a collection of vocal solos from the 17th and 18th cent., and *Recueil de chansons du XVe siècle* (1875, in collaboration with Gaston Paris).

Gewandhauskonzerte [ger - vunt′-howce-con-tsairrt′-er], *G.* A series of orchestral concerts at Leipzig, first given privately in 1743. From 1781-1884 they were held in the Gewandhaus (Cloth Hall), from which they took their name. A new concert hall was opened in 1885. Among the conductors of the concerts have been Mendelssohn, Nikisch, Furtwängler, Walter and Abendroth. Chamber concerts were instituted in 1809.

Ghedini [geh-dee′-nee], GIORGIO FEDERICO: *b.* Cuneo, July 11, 1892. Italian composer. Studied at Turin and Bologna. Successively teacher at the conservatoires of Turin, Parma and Milan (since 1942). His compositions include the operas *Maria d'Alessandria* (Bergamo, 1947), *Re Hassan* (Venice, 1939), *La pulce d'oro* (Genoa, 1940), *Le Baccanti* (Milan, 1948) and *Billy Budd* (1 act, Venice, 1949), several orchestral works, chamber music, choral works, piano pieces, songs and film music.

Gherardello [geh-rarr-dell′-lo]. 14th-cent. Florentine composer. For his *caccia* (or canon) " Tosto che l'alba " see the Harvard *Historical Anthology of Music*, i, no. 52.

Ghisi [gee′-zee], FEDERICO: *b.* Shanghai, Feb. 25, 1901. Italian musicologist and composer. Studied at the Turin Conservatorio, and became a lecturer at Florence University, 1937. His published works include *I canti carnascialeschi nelle fonte musicali del XV e XVI secoli* (1937) and *Feste musicali della Firenze Medicea* (1939). His compositions include chamber music and a *Sinfonia italiana*.

Ghost Trio. *v.* GEISTERTRIO.

Giannini [jahn-nee'-nee], (1) DUSOLINA: *b.* Philadelphia, Dec. 19, 1902. American operatic soprano, daughter of an operatic tenor, and a pupil of Marcella Sembrich. First appeared in opera, Hamburg, 1927; subsequently in many European cities. First appeared at the Metropolitan Opera, New York, 1936. She sang the part of Hester at the first performance of her brother's opera *The Scarlet Letter* (Hamburg, 1938).

(2) VITTORIO: *b.* Philadelphia, Oct. 19, 1903. Brother of (1). American composer. Studied in Milan and New York. His compositions include concertos for piano and organ, a symphony *In Memoriam Theodore Roosevelt*, Requiem, *Stabat Mater*, chamber music and the operas *Lucedia* (Munich, 1934), *The Scarlet Letter* (Hamburg, 1938) and *The Taming of the Shrew* (Cincinnati, 1953).

Gianni Schicchi [jahn'-nee skeek'kee]. Comic opera in one act by Puccini. Libretto by Giovacchino Forzano. First performed (together with *Il Tabarro* and *Suor Angelica*), New York, Dec. 14, 1918. The three operas together are known by the collective title *Trittico* (Triptych). Gianni Schicchi, an unscrupulous lawyer, is asked by the relatives of Buoso Donati, a wealthy Florentine, who has just died, to prevent the execution of his will, in which he has left his fortune to the Church. He impersonates the dead man and dictates a new will before witnesses, in which he leaves the relatives virtually nothing and takes the bulk of the property for himself. The relatives are helpless since they have themselves connived at a felony.

Giant Fugue. A nickname for Bach's chorale prelude for organ on "Wir glauben all' an einen Gott, Schöpfer" (We all believe in one God, Creator) from the *Clavierübung*, pt. iii. It appears to be due to the recurrence on the pedals of an imposing figure which properly symbolizes unshakable faith.

Giardini [jarr-dee'-nee], FELICE DE: *b.* Turin, Apr. 12, 1716; *d.* Moscow, June 8, 1796. Violinist. Studied in Milan, where he was a chorister at the cathedral, and Turin. Became a member of the opera orchestra at Rome, and subsequently Naples. Toured as a soloist in Germany, 1748, and England, 1751. Played frequently in England as leader of the orchestra at the Italian Opera (which he also managed for several seasons) and the Three Choirs Festivals. Having failed to establish a company for the performance of comic opera at the Haymarket Theatre, 1790, he emigrated to Russia with his singers. His compositions include operas and a considerable amount of string music.

Gibbons, (1) CHRISTOPHER: *b.* London, 1615; *d.* there, Oct. 20, 1676. Second son of (3) and nephew of (2). Organist and composer. Organist, Winchester Cathedral, 1638; Chapel Royal and Westminster Abbey, 1660. His compositions include fantasias for strings and anthems. He also collaborated with Matthew Locke in the music for Shirley's masque *Cupid and Death* (modern ed. in *Musica Britannica*, ii).

(2) ELLIS: *b.* Cambridge, 1573; *d.* May, 1603. Uncle of (1) and brother of (3). Composer. Two madrigals by him are in *The Triumphes of Oriana* (1601).

(3) ORLANDO: *b.* Oxford, 1583; *d.* Canterbury, June 5, 1625. Younger brother of (2). Composer and organist. Chorister at King's College, Cambridge, from which he matriculated in 1598. Organist, Chapel Royal, 1605-19; Westminster Abbey, 1623-5. Died when attending Charles I on the occasion of the arrival of Henrietta Maria. The works published in his lifetime were *Fantasies of Three parts* for viols (*c.* 1620) and *The First Set of Madrigals and Mottets of 5 Parts* (1612); he also contributed two anthems to William Leighton's *The Teares or Lamentacions of a Sorrowfull Soule* (1614) and six keyboard pieces to *Parthenia* (1611). A large number of anthems, chamber music for strings and keyboard pieces survive in manuscript. Mod. ed. of his

church music in *Tudor Church Music*, iv; madrigals in *E.M.S.*, v.; keyboard works ed. by Margaret Glyn, 5 vols.; chamber music ed. by E. H. Fellowes and E. H. Meyer.

There is in his music a certain reserve, which does not however exclude emotion. His madrigals, the words of which are serious or satirical, have an austerity which is not common among the madrigalists of his time. His church music includes both full anthems and "verse" anthems, *i.e.* works which include sections for one or more solo voices with accompaniment: the accompaniment is in several cases for strings. His instrumental music, of fine quality, forms a substantial and important part of his output.

E. H. FELLOWES: *Orlando Gibbons* (2nd ed., 1951).

E. H. MEYER: *English Chamber Music* (1946).

Gibbs, (1) CECIL ARMSTRONG: *b.* Great Baddow, Aug. 10, 1889. Composer. Educated at Cambridge and the R.C.M., where he later taught composition. Best known for a number of sensitive and imaginative songs, though he has also written large-scale choral works, *e.g. Deborah and Barak* (1937) and the choral symphony *Odysseus* (1938).

(2) JOSEPH: *b.* 1699; *d.* Ipswich, Dec. 12, 1788. Composer, for some time organist at Ipswich. He published a set of sonatas for violin and continuo.

Gieseking [geez'-er-king], WALTER WILHELM: *b.* Lyons, Nov. 5, 1895; *d.* London, Oct. 26, 1956. German pianist and composer. Studied in Hanover. First appeared in public, 1915. He excelled in the works of Debussy. His compositions consist mainly of chamber music and songs.

Giga [jeeg'-ah], *I.* *v.* GIGUE (2).

Gigault [zhee-go], NICOLAS: *b. c.* 1625; *d.* Paris, Aug. 20, 1707. Organist at several Paris churches. He published *Livre de musique dédié à la très-sainte Vierge* (1683—a collection of *noëls* arranged for instruments) and *Livre de musique pour l'orgue* (1685; modern ed. in A. Guilmant, *Archives des maîtres de l'orgue*, iv).

Gigli [jeel'-yee], BENIAMINO: *b.* Recanati, March 20, 1890; *d.* Rome, Nov. 30, 1957. Tenor, one of the outstanding singers of the present century. Studied in Rome. First appeared in *La Gioconda*, Rovigo, 1914. He sang in most of the principal opera-houses of the world—notably La Scala, Milan, and the Metropolitan Opera, New York. He also appeared in films.

Gigout [zhee-goo], EUGÈNE: *b.* Nancy, March 23, 1844; *d.* Paris, Dec. 9, 1925. French organist and composer, a pupil of Niedermeyer and Saint-Saëns. Taught at the École Niedermeyer, 1863-85, 1900-5; Paris Conservatoire, 1911. He toured widely as a soloist and published a large amount of organ music, including 400 short pieces with pedal ad lib., as well as church music.

Gigue [zheeg], *Fr.* (1) Medieval name for a bowed string instrument. Hence possibly the German word *Geige* (fiddle).

(2) A lively dance (*I.* giga). The word appears to be adapted from the English "jig." Examples of the dance are found in English sources, *c.* 1600, *e.g.*:

JOHN BULL (*Fitzwilliam Virginal Book*, vol. ii, p. 157)

but on the Continent not until the middle of the 17th cent. As standardized in the late 17th and early 18th cent. the dance was in 6/8 rhythm, though the music might be noted in a variety of ways, *e.g.* (1) with notes of larger or smaller value, 6/4 or 6/16, (2) with each 6/8 bar divided into two, 3/8, (3) with two 6/8 bars joined together, 12/8, (4) in 2/4 or 4/4 time with the beats subdivided into triplets or their equivalent.

The gigue was the last of the four

Gigue Fugue

regular dances found in the SUITE—allemande, courante, sarabande and gigue. When optional dances (or GALANTERIEN) were added they were generally placed between the sarabande and the gigue. Like the other dances in the suite, the gigue was in binary form, each of the two sections being repeated. There were two main types: (1) generally straightforward in character and simple in texture, *e.g.*:

HANDEL, *Suite No. 7*

(2) more elaborate, with fugal imitation; it was a convention in this type to invert the subject at the beginning of the second section, *e.g.*:

1st section begins:

2nd section begins:

BACH, *Partitas, No. 3*

The gigue in Bach's Partita No. 1 in B♭ (published in the *Clavierübung*, pt. i, 1726) had a curious sequel. It was adapted by Gluck for an aria in the opera *Telemacco* (1765), which was subsequently transferred to *Iphigénie en Tauride* (1779):

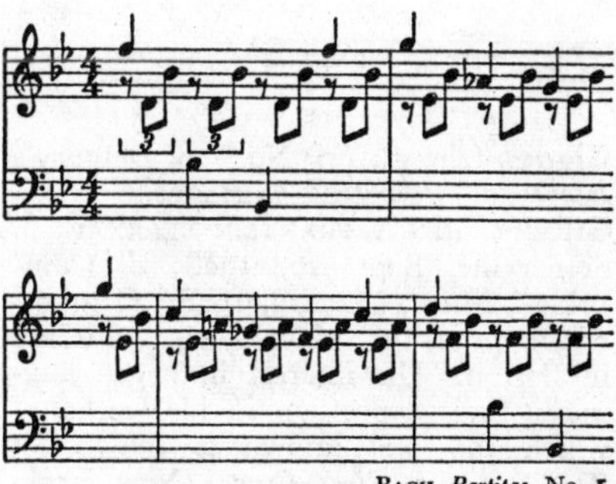

BACH, *Partitas, No. 1*

GLUCK, *Iphigénie en Tauride*

W. DANCKERT: *Geschichte der Gigue* (1924).
J. PULVER: *A Dictionary of Old English Music* (1923).

Gigue Fugue. A nickname given to a fugue in G major for two manuals and pedal in 12/8 time, generally regarded as an early work by Bach (Novello ed. of his organ works, bk. xii, p. 55). The subject is:

Gigues [zheeg], *Fr.* No. 1 of Debussy's *Images* for orchestra. *v.* IMAGES.

Gilbert, HENRY FRANKLIN BELKNAP: *b.* Somerville, Sept. 26, 1928; *d.* Cambridge, Mass., May 19, 1928. Composer, a pupil of MacDowell. Studied in Boston. His interest in negro folk-music finds expression in his works, of which the best known is the ballet *The Dance in Place Congo* (New York, 1918).

Gilly [zhee'-lee], DINH : *b.* Algiers, July 19, 1877 ; *d.* London, May 19, 1940. French operatic baritone. Sang at the Metropolitan Opera, New York, 1909-14, and in London, 1911-14. Prisoner of war, 1914. Subsequently established a singing-school in London.

Gilman, LAWRENCE: *b.* Flushing, N.Y., July 5, 1878; *d.* Franconia, N.H., Sept. 8, 1939. Critic. Wrote for *Harper's Weekly*, 1901-13; *Harper's Magazine*, 1913-5; *North American Review*, 1915-23; *New York Herald-Tribune*, 1923-39. He also wrote a number of programme notes for symphony concerts, 1921-39 and broadcast regularly, 1933-5. His books include *Edward MacDowell* (1905; 2nd ed., 1909), *Stories of Symphonic Music* (1907), *Aspects of Modern Opera* (1908), *Music and the Cultivated Man* (1929), *Wagner's Operas* (1937) and *Toscanini and Great Music* (1938).

Gilson [zheel-so͡n], PAUL: *b.* Brussels, June 15, 1865; *d.* there, Apr. 3, 1942. Composer and critic, a pupil of Gevaert. *Prix de Rome*, 1889. Teacher of harmony, Brussels Conservatoire, 1899; Antwerp Conservatoire, 1904; inspector of schools, 1909. For several years active as a music critic. His compositions include the operas *Prinses Zonneschijn* (Antwerp, 1903), *Zeevolk* (Antwerp, 1904), *Roovers-liefde* (1906), ballets, cantatas (including the *Prix de Rome* cantata *Sinaï*), orchestral music—notably the symphony *La Mer* (1890), 2 saxophone concertos, chamber music, recitations with accompaniment and songs. He also published several works on the theory of music and a volume of memoirs, *Notes de musique et souvenirs* (Brussels, 1942).

Giocoso [jock-o'-zo], *I.* Merry.

Gioioso [jo-ee-o'-zo], *I.* Joyful.

Giordani [jorr-dahn'-ee], (1) GIUSEPPE: *b.* Naples, 1753; *d.* Fermo, Jan. 4, 1798. Composer. His works include numerous operas, oratorios, church music, and instrumental compositions. The well-known aria " Caro mio ben " is attributed to him.

(2) TOMMASO: *b.* Naples, *c.* 1730; *d.* Dublin, Feb., 1806. Composer. Active mainly in London and Dublin, where he produced a number of works for the stage. He also wrote a number of instrumental works.

Giordano [jorr-dahn'-o], UMBERTO: *b.* Foggia, Aug. 27, 1867; *d.* Milan, Nov. 12, 1948. Opera composer. Studied at the Naples Conservatorio. He made his name with the opera *Mala vita* (Rome, 1892), an example of the " veristic " type of opera then popular in Italy. Of his other operas the best known are *Andrea Chénier* (Milan, 1896), *Fedora* (Milan, 1898), and *Madame Sans-Gêne* (New York, 1915).

Giovanelli [jo-vah-nell'-lee], RUGGIERO: *b.* Velletri, *c.* 1560; *d.* Rome, Jan. 7, 1625. Composer. He succeeded Palestrina as *maestro di cappella* of St. Peter's, Rome. In addition to his church music he wrote a considerable number of madrigals, four of which were published with English translations in Morley's *Madrigalls to five voyces: selected out of the best approved Italian Authors* (1598).

Giovanni da Cascia [jo-vahn'-nee dah

cah'-shah]. Early 14th-cent. Italian composer, also known by the Latin name Johannes de Florentia. A prominent member of the group of composers who were active in the composition of secular vocal music at the time. For examples of his work see the Harvard *Historical Anthology of Music*, i, nos. 50-1.

Girl of the Golden West, The. *v.* FANCIULLA DEL WEST.

Gis [giss], *G.* G sharp (G♯).

Gisis [giss'-iss], *G.* G double sharp (G×).

Gittern. Medieval English name for a four-stringed instrument of the guitar family, played with a plectrum. A 14th-cent. example is preserved at Warwick Castle. In Tudor and Stuart times the name seems to have been used rather loosely to refer to more than one kind of instrument, including the Spanish guitar, which became popular in England in the 16th cent. The title of John Playford's *A Booke of new lessons for the Cithren and Gittern* (1652) makes it clear, however, that the gittern was not necessarily identical with the cittern. *v.* CITTERN, GUITAR.

Giulio Cesare in Egitto [jool'-yo cheh'-zah-reh een eh-ject'-to] (Julius Caesar in Egypt). Opera in three acts by Handel. Libretto by Nicola Francesco Haym. First performed, London, March 2, 1724.

Giustiniana [jooss-teen-yahn'-ah], *I.* A popular three-part song current in Italy in the 16th cent. According to Morley (*A Plaine and Easie Introduction to Practicall Musicke*, p. 180) they " are all written in the *Bergamasca* language," *i.e.* in dialect. He adds: " A wanton and rude kinde of musicke it is." *v.* VILLANELLA.

Giusto [jooss'-to], *I.* Proper, reasonable, exact. *A tempo giusto* or *tempo giusto*, (1) in the proper time, at a reasonable speed, (2) in strict time.

Glareanus [gla-reh-ahn'-ōōss], HENRICUS: *b.* Mollis, June 1488; *d.* Freiburg i.B., March 28, 1563. Swiss theorist, who took his name from the canton of Glarus, in which he was born. His real name was Heinrich Loris. He taught mathematics at Basle and philosophy in Paris, returning to Switzerland in 1522. He is chiefly known for his treatise *Dodecachordon* (*q.v.*), published in 1547.

Glasharmonika [glahss'-harr-moh-nee-ca], *G. v.* HARMONICA (1).

Glazounov [gluz'-oo-noff], ALEXANDER CONSTANTINOVICH: *b.* St. Petersburg, Aug. 10, 1865; *d.* Paris, March 21, 1936. Composer, son of a publisher. Studied privately with Rimsky-Korsakov. Teacher, St. Petersburg Conservatoire, 1900; director, 1906. Settled in Paris, 1928. His first symphony was performed in 1882. From that time he continued to compose industriously, and his works rapidly became known outside Russia. Although he was associated with the Russian nationalist composers, most of his music belongs rather to the main stream of European music. Quick to absorb the influence of others, he never developed into a really individual composer. Brilliance, charm and technical skill are the characteristics of his work rather than originality. His principal compositions are:

(a) ORCHESTRA: 8 symphonies; 2 piano concertos; violin concerto; cello concerto; concerto for saxophone, flute and strings; 6 suites (including *Chopiniana* and *The Seasons*); 6 overtures; symphonic poem, *Stenka Rasin*; serenades, fantasias, etc.

(b) CHAMBER MUSIC: 7 string quartets; string quintet; quartet for brass.

(c) CHORAL WORKS: *Memorial Cantata* (Leeds, 1901); *Hymn to Pushkin* (female voices), also works for piano and organ, songs and incidental music.

He also helped Rimsky-Korsakov to complete Borodin's unfinished opera *Prince Igor* and reconstructed the entire overture from memory.

M. D. CALVOCORESSI & G. ABRAHAM: *Masters of Russian Music* (1936).

Glebov [gleh'-boff], IGOR. *v.* ASAFIEV.

Glee (from Anglo-Saxon *glíw* or *gléo*, " entertainment, music "). A simple part-song, generally for male voices. The term first occurs in printed music in Playford's *Select Musicall Ayres and Dialogues* (1652). A popular form of music in England in the 18th and early 19th cent.

Glee Club. (1) A society for singing glees, founded in London in 1787 and dissolved in 1857.

(2) The name was also adopted subsequently by other societies with the same objects. In American universities today it generally means a male-voice choral society: those of Harvard and Yale are particularly famous.

Glière [glyairr], REINHOLD MORITZOVICH: *b.* Kiev, Jan. 11, 1875. Composer, of Belgian origin. Studied at the Moscow Conservatoire. Director, Kiev Conservatoire, 1914; teacher, Moscow Conservatoire, 1920. His compositions include the opera *Shah Senem* (Baku, 1934), which incorporates Azerbaijan melodies, the ballet *Red Poppy*, on the Russian revolution (Moscow, 1927), 3 symphonies, violin concerto, harp concerto, *March of the Red Army*, *Victory Overture*, 4 string quartets and other chamber works, and numerous songs and piano pieces. In his later works he makes use of folk-melodies from the Eastern provinces of the Soviet Republic.

Glinka [gleen′-ca], MICHAEL IVANOVICH: *b.* Novospasskoe, Government of Smolensk, June 1, 1804; *d.* Berlin, Feb. 15, 1857. Composer, son of a wealthy landowner. Educated in St. Petersburg, where he studied music privately. Worked in the Ministry of Communications from 1824 until 1828, when he resigned in order to devote himself to music. Visited several Italian cities and studied in Milan, Vienna and Berlin. He returned to St. Petersburg where he produced his two operas, visited Paris (1844) where he made friends with Berlioz, Spain (1844), Warsaw (1848), France again (1852-54) and died during his last visit to Berlin (1856-57). His first opera, *Zhizn za Tsara* (A Life for the Czar; St. Petersburg, 1836), now known as *Ivan Sussanin* (its original title), is not strikingly Russian in character, though it makes some use of local colour; its strength is in its simplicity—a reaction against the conventions of Italian opera, which were dominant in Russia at the time. It was the second opera, *Russlan y Lyudmila* (Russlan and Ludmila, St. Petersburg, 1842) which first created a characteristically Russian style, including the oriental elements which came to figure so prominently in later Russian music. Glinka also showed in his orchestral fantasia *Kamarinskaya* how folk-song could be used as the basis of instrumental composition.

G. ABRAHAM: *On Russian Music* (n.d.).
M. D. CALVOCORESSI & G. ABRAHAM: *Masters of Russian Music* (1936).

Glissando [gleece-sahnd′-o], *I.* Lit. "sliding" (from *Fr.* "glisser").

(1) On the piano the finger-nail is drawn rapidly over the keys (in either direction), without any articulation of individual notes. On the white keys the procedure is simple and effective; on the black keys it is uncomfortable and less effective, on account of the gaps between the notes. It is also possible for one hand to play a glissando in two (or even three) parts on the white keys. Of the available two-part intervals sixths are the most effective.

(2) On the harp the finger slides rapidly across the strings. The variety of tuning possible makes available quite a number of different scales.

(3) On instruments of the violin family the finger slides rapidly up or down the string. The term is also used, however, to indicate a chromatic scale played with one finger by rapidly sliding from one note to the next, *e.g.*:

STRAUSS, *Till Eulenspiegel*

(4) On the trombone the glissando is played with the slide.

(5) On other wind instruments an imitation of a glissando can be produced by increased lip pressure which raises the pitch of each individual note until the next one is reached.

Glissando is often abbreviated *gliss.* or

indicated by an oblique stroke (straight or wavy) between the highest and lowest notes, *e.g.*:

On the harp it is necessary for the exact notes to be specified, either by writing a specimen octave, *e.g.*:

RIMSKY-KORSAKOV, *Pan Voyevoda*

or by indicating the tuning with letters (*v.* HARP).

Glocke [glock'-er], *G.* (*plur.* Glocken). Bell.

Glockenspiel [glock'-ĕn-shpeel], *G.* (*Fr.* carillon, jeu de clochettes, jeu de timbres, *I.* campanelli). A percussion instrument consisting of a series of steel plates of different sizes, arranged like the keyboard of the piano so as to provide a complete chromatic compass (there are various sizes). The steel plates are struck by wooden hammers held in the player's hands. The instrument was at one time fitted with a keyboard (like the CELESTA) and in this form is required in Handel's *Saul* (1738) and Mozart's *Die Zauberflöte* (1791). The German name has by now become virtually an international term.

Glogauer Liederbuch [glo'-gow-er leed'-er-bŏŏkh], *G.* A 15th-cent. collection of German songs and dances, arranged for vocal or instrumental ensemble. Modern ed. in *Das Erbe deutscher Musik, Reichsdenkmale*, iv & viii.

Gloria [glorr'-ya], *L.* (1) The initial word of " Gloria in excelsis Deo " (Glory to God in the highest), the second part of the Ordinary of the Mass. These opening words were sung by the priest; hence in polyphonic settings of the 15th and 16th cent. the choir regularly begins with the words " et in terra pax " (and on earth peace). This tradition was later abandoned, as it was in the *Credo*.

(2) The *Gloria Patri* (or doxology) sung at the end of a psalm or canticle.

Gloriana. Opera in three acts by Britten. Libretto by William Plomer. First performed, London, June 8, 1953. The story is concerned with the relationship between Elizabeth I and the Earl of Essex.

Gloucester. *v.* THREE CHOIRS FESTIVAL.

Gluck [glŏŏk], CHRISTOPH WILLIBALD: *b.* Erasbach, July 2, 1714; *d.* Vienna, Nov. 15, 1787. Composer. Studied in Prague. Entered the service of Prince Melzi in Vienna, and went with him to Italy. Completed his studies under Sammartini, and from 1741-44 produced a number of operas in the accepted Italian style. Went to London with Prince Lobkowitz and produced there in 1746 two unsuccessful operas and gave concerts on the glass harmonica. Worked with the Mingotti travelling opera company, and in 1750 married and settled in Vienna. Became *Kapellmeister* to the Prince of Sachsen-Hildburghausen, 1752, and at the Court opera, 1754, for which he produced a series of Italian pastorals and French light operas. In *Orfeo* (1762) he created a new style of Italian opera which incorporated the choruses and ballets of French opera and abandoned conventional virtuosity for dramatic truth and a moving simplicity of expression. His adoption of this style was largely due to his librettist, Raniero de' Calzabigi, who in turn derived some of his ideas from the writings of Algarotti.

The principles of their " reform," which sought to " restrict music to its true office of serving poetry by means of expression," were set forth in the prefaces to *Alceste* (1767) and *Paride ed Elena* (1770), and were pursued in the operas which Gluck wrote for Paris—*Iphigénie en Aulide* (1774), *Armide* (1777) and *Iphigénie en Tauride* (1779). In Paris he also produced French versions of *Orfeo* and *Alceste*. The influence of French traditions is strongly marked in the Paris operas, and it was natural that in the controversy which still raged on the rival merits of Italian and French opera he should have been regarded as the champion of the latter. Although he had no immediate imitators, his work had a considerable influence on the operas of

Mozart, Gossec, Cherubini, Beethoven, Spontini and Berlioz. The latter also wrote essays on *Orfeo* and *Alceste*, and Wagner in his Dresden period (1847) produced a revised version of *Iphigénie en Aulide*.

In addition to more than 100 operas, many of which are now lost, Gluck composed 11 symphonies, 7 instrumental trios, a setting of *De profundis* for choir and orchestra, 7 odes by Klopstock for solo voice and keyboard, and a flute concerto. Five volumes of a projected complete edition of his works have appeared, ed. by R. Gerber : *L'Isle de Merlin* (1758), *L'Ivrogne corrigé* (1760), *Écho et Narcisse* (1779), *Paride ed Elena* (1770), *Alceste* (1776). The following are in *D.T.Ö.* : *L'innocenza giustificata* (1755), xliv, *Don Juan* (ballet, 1761), xxx (2), *Orfeo ed Euridice* (original version, 1762), xxi (2) ; in *D.T.B.*, xiv (2) : *Le Nozze d'Ercole e d'Ebe* (1747).

H. BERLIOZ : *Gluck and his Operas* (English ed., 1915).
M. COOPER : *Gluck* (1936).
A. EINSTEIN : *Gluck* (1937).
E. NEWMAN : *Gluck and the Opera* (1895).

Gnecchi [nyeck'-kee], VITTORIO: *b.* Milan, July 17, 1876. Composer, whose opera *Cassandra* (Bologna, 1905) aroused considerable interest in 1909, when the critic Giovanni Tebaldini attempted to prove that Strauss had made use of it in the composition of his *Elektra* (Dresden, 1909). Strauss repudiated any suggestion of plagiarism, and Tebaldini's methods of analysis were vigorously attacked by Romain Rolland.

Gniessin [gnyess'-in], MICHAEL FABIANOVICH: *b.* Rostov, Feb. 4, 1883. Composer, of Jewish origin. Studied at the St. Petersburg Conservatoire, where he was a pupil of Rimsky-Korsakov. Originally influenced by Wagner, he became in his later works inspired by Jewish traditions. His works include two operas on Jewish subjects, dramatic works which exploit a peculiar and individual form of musical declamation, symphonic poems, and a work for chorus and orchestra written to commemorate the revolutions of 1905 and 1917.

Godard [go-dar], BENJAMIN LOUIS PAUL: *b.* Paris, Aug. 18, 1849; *d.* Cannes, Jan. 10, 1895. Composer and violinist. Studied at the Paris Conservatoire from 1863. He was a violin-player in chamber music, founder and conductor of the Concerts Modernes (1885) and winner, with Dubois, of the Prix de la Ville de Paris (1878). He composed several operas, *Le Tasse* for soloists, chorus and orchestra, a symphony, symphonic poems, two violin concertos, a piano concerto, chamber music, incidental music for plays, piano pieces and over 100 songs.

Goddard, ARABELLA: *b.* St. Servan, Jan. 12, 1836; *d.* Boulogne, Apr. 6, 1922. English pianist, who studied with Kalkbrenner in Paris. She first appeared in public in London, 1850. She travelled widely and was much admired in the classics. She married the critic J. W. Davison.

Godfrey, DANIEL (DAN) EYERS: *b.* London, June 20, 1868; *d.* Bournemouth, July 20, 1939. Conductor. Member of a family which supplied several bandmasters to the Army. Studied at the R.C.M. His principal achievement was the creation of a symphony orchestra at Bournemouth in 1893, where he was appointed director of music at the Winter Gardens. Before he retired in 1934 he had introduced several hundred works by English composers. Knighted, 1922.

Godowsky [go-dov'-ski], LEOPOLD: *b.* Vilna, Feb. 13, 1870; *d.* New York, Nov. 21, 1938. Pianist and composer, Polish by birth, American by naturalization. He showed great gifts as a child and first appeared as a soloist in Vilna in 1879. Subsequently studied at the Berlin Hochschule. From 1884 onwards he toured in America and on the Continent. He taught in Philadelphia, Chicago, Berlin and Vienna. From 1914 onwards he lived regularly in the United States. His published works include a number of transcriptions, a series of studies on études by Chopin, and numerous smaller pieces.

God save the Queen. The earliest known version of the National Anthem, a tune in galliard rhythm, appeared in the collection *Thesaurus Musicus* (*c.* 1744) in the following form:

In the second edition (1745) the first four bars are altered to:

Its popularity dates from 1745, when it was sung in London theatres as a loyal demonstration on the occasion of the Rebellion of the Young Pretender. The earliest known arrangement for four voices was made by Arne for Drury Lane Theatre in that year.

In the course of its history alternative verses and alternative words have frequently been written for the tune. It was also adopted in several Continental countries and started the fashion for national anthems all over the world. In the United States it is used for the national song "My country, 'tis of thee" (1831). Among the composers who have written variations on the tune are Beethoven, Cramer, Dussek, Glazounov, Kalkbrenner, Liszt, Paganini and Reger. It has also been introduced into compositions by Beethoven, Brahms, Meyerbeer, Spontini, Verdi and Weber.

P. A. SCHOLES: *God save the Queen* (1954).

Goetz [gerts], HERMANN: *b.* Königsberg, Dec. 7, 1840; *d.* Hottingen, nr. Zürich, Dec. 3, 1876. Composer. Studied at the Stern Conservatorium, Berlin.

Organist, Winterthur, 1863; settled in Zürich, 1867. He composed two operas, a symphony, an overture, a piano concerto, a violin concerto, choral works with orchestra, chamber music, piano pieces, songs and partsongs. His first opera, *Der Widerspänstigen Zähmung* (after Shakespeare's *The Taming of the Shrew*; Mannheim, 1874) had some success in Germany and was given in London (in English) after his death.

Goldberg Variations. The fourth part of Bach's *Clavierübung* (1742), described by him as "an aria with different variations for harpsichord with two manuals, designed for the refreshment of music-lovers." According to Forkel, Bach's first biographer, the variations were written for J. T. Goldberg, a pupil of Bach's, to play to Count Kaiserling, formerly Russian Ambassador at the Court of Saxony, who suffered from insomnia (*v.* H. T. David & A. Mendel, *The Bach Reader*, pp. 338-9). The aria itself is in chaconne rhythm, with a highly ornamented melody. The 30 variations include 9 canons, at different intervals, two of which (at the fourth and at the fifth) are in contrary motion. The last variation is a *quodlibet*, *i.e.* a piece incorporating the melodies of popular songs.

Golden Cockerel, The. *v.* ZOLOTOY PETOUSHOK.

Goldmark [gollt'-mark], (1) CARL: *b.* Keszthely (Hungary), May 18, 1830; *d.* Vienna, Jan. 2, 1915. Composer and teacher. Studied privately and at the Conservatorium in Vienna, where he spent most of his life, as teacher and critic. His compositions include *Die Königin von Saba* (Vienna, 1875) and 5 other operas, the symphony (or symphonic poem) *Die ländliche Hochzeit* (The Rustic Wedding), the overtures *Sakuntala* and *Im Frühling* (In Spring), a symphony, 2 violin concertos, choral works, miscellaneous orchestral works, chamber music, piano pieces and songs. His memoirs were published in 1922.

(2) RUBIN: *b.* New York, Aug. 15, 1872; *d.* there, March 6, 1936. Nephew of (1). Composer and teacher. Studied in Vienna and New York, where he was a pupil of Dvořák. Director, Colorado College Conservatory, 1895-1901; director of composition department, Juilliard Graduate School, New York, 1924. His pupils included Abram Chasins, Aaron Copland and George Gershwin. His compositions are mainly instrumental.

Goldschmidt [gollt'-shmit], (1) HUGO: *b.* Breslau, Sept. 19, 1859; *d.* Wiesbaden, Dec. 26, 1920. Musicologist. Having studied singing with Stockhausen, he interested himself particularly in vocal technique and teaching in the 17th cent. His most important work was his *Studien zu Geschichte der italienischen Oper* (2 vols., 1901-4), with substantial musical examples, including the greater part of Monteverdi's *L'Incoronazione di Poppea*: it is not, however, reliable in detail.

(2) OTTO: *b.* Hamburg, Aug. 21, 1829; *d.* London, Feb. 24, 1907. Conductor and composer. Studied at Leipzig Conservatorium under Mendelssohn. Came to England in 1849 and met Jenny Lind, whom he married in 1852. Vice-principal, R.A.M., 1863. He conducted at festivals in Düsseldorf and Hamburg, and in 1875 founded the Bach Choir in London, which in 1876 gave the first complete performance in England of the B minor Mass under his direction. Choral works by him were performed both at German and English festivals. He also wrote a certain amount of instrumental music, including a piano concerto.

Gombert [gon̂-bair], NICOLAS: *b.* Southern Flanders, *c.* 1500; *d.* probably in Tournai, *c.* 1560. Composer. In the service of the emperor Charles V, 1526-40. Hermann Finck called him in 1556 "he who shows the way to composers." In his polyphonic writing he adopted the method of continuous imitation, which was to become the chief feature of the style of Palestrina, and avoided both homophonic writing and the use of alternating pairs of voices, which were characteristic of Josquin's style. Finck observed that his music was *plena cum concordantiarum tum fugarum* (imitations). He composed more than 160 motets, 10 Masses, 8 Magnificats, and some 60 French *chansons.* The first volume, containing 4 Masses, of a projected complete edition of his works, ed. by J. Schmidt-Görg, was published in 1951. His motet "Super flumina Babilonis" is printed in the Harvard *Historical Anthology*, No. 114, and the second *Agnus Dei* from his Mass *Media vita* in Schering's *History of Music in Examples*, No. 102.

J. SCHMIDT-GÖRG: *Nicolas Gombert—Kapellmeister Karls V* (1938).

Gombosi [gome'-bo-shi], OTTO: *b.* Budapest, Oct. 23, 1902; *d.* Lexington, Mass., Feb. 17, 1955. Musicologist. Studied at the Budapest Academy and in Berlin. Music critic in Budapest, 1926-8. Professor, Washington University (Seattle), 1940; Chicago, 1946; Harvard, 1951. He published a study of Obrecht and edited the hymns and psalms of Thomas Stoltzer (with H. Albrecht), *D.D.T.*, lxv.

Gondoliers, The. Comic opera in two acts by Sullivan. Libretto by William Schwenck Gilbert. First performed, London, Dec. 7, 1889.

Gong. Also known internationally as Tam-tam. A percussion instrument of oriental origin. As used in the orchestra it consists of a piece of circular metal with a rim several inches deep and is hit either by a wooden mallet covered with leather or felt or by a stick similar to that used for the bass drum. If it is played softly, the sound is sinister; a loud stroke produces a menacing and terrifying effect. The pitch of the instrument is indeterminate.

Goossens, EUGENE: *b.* London, May 26, 1893. Conductor and composer, whose father and grandfather were both conductors of the Carl Rosa Opera Company. Studied at Bruges Conservatoire, Liverpool College of Music and R.C.M., London. Violinist in the Queen's Hall Orchestra, 1911-15; assistant conductor to Beecham (until 1920). Founded and conducted his own orchestra (1921) and conducted Russian opera and ballet at Covent Garden. Conductor, Rochester Philharmonic Orchestra (N.Y.), 1923; Cincinnati Symphony Orchestra, 1931. Director, Conservatory of New South Wales and conductor of the Sydney Symphony Orchestra, 1947-56. He has composed two operas—*Judith* (London, 1929) and *Don Juan de Mañara* (London, 1937), a ballet, two symphonies and other orchestral works, an oboe concerto, chamber music, incidental music for plays, French and English songs and piano pieces.

Gopak [gop-ahk′], *R.* *v.* HOPAK.

Gorgia [gorr′-jah], *I.* Lit. "throat." The name given to the improvised embellishments employed by solo singers in the 16th and 17th cent. Examples are given in Caccini's *Nuove musiche* (1602; facsimile ed., 1934).

Goss, JOHN: *b.* Fareham, Dec. 27, 1800; *d.* London, May 10, 1880. Composer and organist. Chorister of the Chapel Royal and a pupil of Attwood, whom he succeeded as organist of St. Paul's Cathedral, 1838. Composer to the Chapel Royal, 1856. Knighted, 1872. He wrote amiable anthems and organ works, and published *An Introduction to Harmony and Thorough-Bass* (1833).

Gossec [goss-eck], FRANÇOIS JOSEPH: *b.* Vergnies (Belgium), Jan. 17, 1734; *d.* Paris, Feb. 16, 1829. Composer. Chorister, Antwerp Cathedral. Came to Paris in 1751 and through the good offices of Rameau became conductor of the concerts organized by La Pouplinière and later director of music to the Prince of Condé. In a large number of compositions, many on a big scale, he showed his sympathy with the ideals of the French Revolution, and was one of the first teachers at the Paris Conservatoire (founded, 1795). His compositions include symphonies, oratorios, and choral works in celebration of the Revolution. Long before Berlioz he experimented with elaborate instrumentation in his *Messe des morts* (Requiem Mass), and in general exercised a stimulating influence on orchestral playing and orchestral composition in Paris.

J. G. PROD'HOMME : *Gossec* (1949).

Gothic Music. In the 18th cent. this would have meant barbarous, primitive music. As used by modern historians it means music in northern Europe contemporary with Gothic architecture—roughly the 13th, 14th and early 15th cent.

Götterdämmerung [gurt-er-dem′-er-ŏŏng] (Twilight of the Gods, *i.e.* the end of the world in German mythology). Opera in three acts (with prologue) by Wagner, the fourth and last part of the cycle *Der Ring des Nibelungen* (*q.v.*). First performed, Bayreuth, August 17, 1876.

Goudimel [goo-dee-mel], CLAUDE: *b.* Besançon, *c.* 1514; *d.* Lyons, Aug. 27, 1572. Composer, first known from his contributions to an anthology of *chansons* published (in 11 volumes) between 1549 and 1554. Originally a Catholic, he turned Protestant and published a number of settings of Huguenot melodies. Modern ed. of 150 psalms in H. Expert, *Les Maîtres musiciens de la Renaissance française*; modern ed. of Masses in Expert, *Monuments de la musique française*, ix.

M. BRENET : *Claude Goudimel* (1898).

W. S. PRATT : *The Music of the French Psalter of* 1562 (1939).

Gounod [goo-no], CHARLES FRANÇOIS: *b.* Paris, June 17, 1818; *d.* Saint-Cloud, Oct. 18, 1893. Composer. Studied at the Paris Conservatoire. *Prix de Rome*, 1839. Visited Austria and Germany and became organist and choirmaster at the Église des Missions Étrangères in Paris. He studied for the priesthood but decided not to be ordained, began composing operas in 1851, was conductor of the Orphéon (united choral societies), 1852-60, and lived in England, 1870-75, where he formed a choir which later became the Royal Choral Society. His work is unequal in quality. *Faust* (Paris, 1859) is so far superior to his other operas that the rumour was at one time spread that it was not his work. Even here the level is not consistently maintained: the enchantment of the garden scene is not always matched by a similar inspiration. Gounod was primarily a lyrical composer, most successful when a light touch was required. When he attempted to be impressive, as in the oratorio *La Rédemption*, he merely became self-conscious: the intended mysticism of this work is wholy artificial. His principal compositions are:

(a) OPERAS: *Sapho* (1851); *La Nonne sanglante* (1854); *Le Médecin malgré lui* (1895); *Faust* (1859); *Philémon et Baucis* (1860); *La Reine de Saba* (1862); *Mireille* (1864); *La Colombe* (1866); *Roméo et Juliette* (1867); *Cinq-Mars* (1877); *Poly-*

eucte (1878); *Le Tribut de Zamora* (1881).

(b) ORATORIOS: *La Rédemption* (1882); *Mors et Vita* (1885).

(c) CANTATAS: *Marie Stuart* (1837): *Gallia* (1871).

(d) CHURCH MUSIC: 9 Masses (including *Messe solennelle*, 1849); 3 Requiems; *Stabat Mater*; *Te Deum*; motets, etc.

(e) ORCHESTRA: 3 symphonies.

P. LANDORMY: *Charles Gounod* (1942).

Gourron [goo-rôn], ALBERT RAYMOND. *v.* ALVAREZ.

Grabu [gra-bēē], LOUIS. French composer of the late 17th cent. who spent some years in London. Composer to Charles II, 1665; master of the king's music, 1666-74. Returned to France, 1679, but was back in England a few years later and composed the music for Dryden's patriotic opera *Albion and Albanius* (1685).

Grace. An ornament, whether vocal or instrumental. *Grace notes*, ornamental notes used to decorate or embellish a melody and normally printed in smaller type.

Grace, HARVEY: *b.* Romsey, Jan. 25, 1874; *d.* Bromley, Feb. 15, 1944. Editor of *The Musical Times*, 1918 till his death. Organist, Chichester Cathedral, 1931-8. Published books on the organ music of Bach, Rheinberger and French composers, a study of Beethoven, a book on choral training, and miscellaneous essays.

Gradevole [grah-deh'-vo-leh], *I.* Pleasing.

Gradual (*L.* graduale). (1) A responsorial chant forming part of the Proper of the Roman Mass and sung between the Epistle and the Gospel. Apparently so called because it was sung from the steps (*L.* gradus) of the ambo (or pulpit). The plainsong melodies, designed for alternations of soloist and chorus, are elaborate.

(2) Originally a book containing graduals and hence, by a natural extension, one containing all the music of the Mass to be sung by the choir.

Gradualia [gra-dōō-ah'-li-a], *L.* The title of two sets of Latin motets by Byrd, published in 1605 and 1607 and designed for liturgical use in the Roman church. A large number of the motets are allocated to particular festivals.

Gradus ad Parnassum [gra'-dōōss ad parr-nass'-ōōm], *L.* Lit. "steps to Parnassus" (home of the Muses).

(1) The title of a treatise on counterpoint by Fux (1725).

(2) The title of a collection of piano studies by Clementi (1817).

(3) *Doctor Gradus ad Parnassum*, a parody of a piano study, is the first piece in Debussy's suite *Children's Corner* (1908).

Graener [grain'-er], PAUL: *b.* Berlin, Jan. 11, 1872; *d.* Salzburg, Nov. 13, 1944. Composer and conductor. Chorister, Berlin Cathedral. Largely self-taught as a composer. After some experience as a conductor in Königsberg and Bremerhaven he settled in London, 1896, where he conducted at the Haymarket Theatre and taught at the R.A.M. Director, Neue Wiener Conservatorium (Vienna), 1908; Mozarteum, Salzburg, 1910-13. Teacher of composition, Leipzig Conservatorium, 1920-5. Director, the Stern Conservatorium, Berlin, 1930. The list of his compositions, romantic in style, is extensive. The most important are:

(a) OPERAS: *Das Narrengericht* (Vienna, 1913); *Don Juans letztes Abenteuer* (Leipzig, 1914); *Theophano* (Munich, 1918; later revived as *Byzanz*); *Schirin und Gertraude* (Dresden, 1920); *Hanneles Himmelfahrt* (Dresden, 1927); *Friedemann Bach* (Schwerin, 1931); *Der Prinz von Homburg* (Berlin, 1935); *Schwanhild* (Cologne, 1941).

(b) ORCHESTRA: Symphony (*Schmied Schmerz*); sinfonietta; *Sinfonia brevis*; piano concerto; cello concerto; violin concerto; suites; variations; overtures.

(c) CHORAL WORKS: *Wiebke Pogwisch*; *Der Retter*; *Marienkantate*.

(d) CHAMBER MUSIC: 4 string quartets; 3 piano trios; violin sonata.

Also several piano pieces and numerous songs.

G. GRÄNER: *Paul Graener* (1922).

Grainger, PERCY ALDRIDGE (originally George Percy): *b.* Brighton (Victoria), July 8, 1882. Pianist and composer. He gave recitals at the age of 10. Studied in Melbourne and Frankfort, and rapidly made a reputation as a recitalist, particularly in England, where he lived from 1900. Having met Grieg in Norway in 1907 he became interested in folk-songs and actively collected them. He settled in the United States in 1914 and became naturalized in 1919. For some years he was head of the music department at Washington Square College, New York University. His arrangements of traditional tunes for a wide variety of resources have won him great popularity. There is in his music, whether original works or transcriptions, no pretentiousness: there is much rhythmical energy and a simple delight in sentiment and jollity. His passion for using colourful English (instead of Italian) for indications of speed and dynamics has caused much amusement but has not created a school.

Granados [grah-nah′-doce], ENRIQUE: *b.* Lérida, July 29, 1867; *d.* at sea, March 24, 1916. Pianist and composer. Studied in Barcelona and Paris, returned to Barcelona (1899), gave many concerts, founded (1900) the Society of Classical Concerts which he conducted, and founded (1901) and directed (until his death) a music school (Academia Granados). He composed 7 operas, 2 symphonic poems, 3 suites and other orchestral works, a choral work with organ and piano accompaniment, chamber music, songs and a collection of *tonadillas*, *Goyescas* (two volumes based on the paintings and tapestries of Goya) and other piano pieces. The music of *Goyescas* was used to form the material of an opera with the same title (New York, 1916). The ship in which he was returning from this performance was torpedoed in the English Channel, 1916.

Gran cassa [grahn cahss′-sah], *I.* Bass drum.

Grand choeur [grũn cur], *Fr.* Full organ.

Grand Duke, The. Comic opera in two acts by Sullivan. Libretto by William Schwenck Gilbert. First performed, London, March 8, 1896.

Grande Messe des Morts [grũnd mess day morr], *F.* A setting of the Requiem Mass by Berlioz, Op. 5 (1837), commissioned by the French Minister of the Interior and performed at a memorial service for French soldiers who had fallen at the siege of Constantine in Algeria. It is scored for an exceptionally large orchestra, including four brass bands.

Grandezza [grahn-deh′-dzah], *I.* Grandeur. *Con grandezza*, with grandeur.

Grandi [grahn′-dee], ALESSANDRO: *d.* Bergamo, 1630. Early 17th-cent. composer of church music, madrigals (with accompaniment) and solo cantatas. Among his appointments were: second *maestro di cappella*, St. Mark's, Venice, 1620; *maestro di cappella*, Santa Maria Maggiore, Bergamo. One of the most important composers of solo cantatas, with considerable influence in his day.

Grandioso [grahnd-yo′-zo], *I.* In an imposing manner.

Grand Opera. The term *grand opéra* (opera on a large scale) grew up in France in the 19th cent. to distinguish serious operas set to music throughout from *opéra-comique*, which had dialogue. Works of this kind, by Meyerbeer and his contemporaries, were often on a lavish scale. Hence "grand opera" came to be used not simply of a form but of the elaborate performances to be heard in a large opera house attended by the aristocracy.

Grand orgue [grũnt orrg], *Fr.* Great organ.

Grand Prix de Rome [grũn pree der rom], *Fr.* *v.* PRIX DE ROME.

Graner Messe [grahn′-er mess′-*er*], *G.* A Mass for soloists, chorus and orchestra by Liszt, composed for the dedication of the cathedral at Esztergom (*G.* Gran) in Hungary, Aug. 31, 1856.

Grassineau, JAMES: *b.* London, *c.* 1715; *d.* Bedford, Apr. 5, 1767. Secretary to Pepusch and author of *A Musical Dictionary . . . of Terms and Characters* (1740), which was to a large extent a translation of Brossard's *Dictionnaire de musique* (1703).

Grassini [grahss-see′-nee], JOSEPHINA: *b.* Varese, Apr. 8, 1773 ; *d.* Milan, Jan. 3, 1850. Operatic contralto. Studied in Milan, where she made her first appearance, 1794. Sang subsequently in various Italian opera houses, in Paris and in London, where she arrived in 1804 and was the rival of Mrs. Billington. Her dramatic as well as her singing ability made a great impression. Sir Charles Bell (1805) said that " she *died* not only without being ridiculous, but with an effect equal to Mrs. Siddons." The title role of Paër's *Didone abbandonata* was written for her.

Graun [grown], (1) JOHANN GOTTLIEB: b. Wahrenbrück, *c.* 1702-3; *d.* Berlin, Oct. 27, 1771. Composer and violinist. Studied under Pisendel and Tartini. *Konzertmeister*, Merseburg, 1726). In the service of Crown Prince Frederick at Rheinsberg, 1732 ; leader of the royal orchestra at Berlin, 1740. He composed about 100 symphonies, 20 violin concertos, church cantatas, string quartets and other chamber music.

(2) KARL HEINRICH: *b.* Wahrenbrück, May 7, 1704; *d.* Berlin, Aug. 8, 1759. Composer and singer. Brother of (1). Treble in the service of the Dresden town council, 1714-20. Tenor (from 1725), assistant conductor (from 1726) and composer at the Brunswick Opera. In the service of the Crown Prince Frederick at Rheinsberg, 1736 ; court *Kapellmeister*, 1740. He composed 30 operas, dramatic cantatas, a Passion-Cantata (*Der Tod Jesu*, 1755) and other church music, piano concertos and trios. Modern ed. of his opera *Montezuma* (1755)—the Italian libretto translated from the French of Frederick the Great —in *D.D.T.*, xv.

Graupner [growp'-ner], CHRISTOPH: *b.* Kirchberg, Jan. 13, 1683; *d.* Darmstadt, May 10, 1760. Composer, a pupil of Kuhnau at St. Thomas's, Leipzig. Harpsichordist at the Hamburg Opera under Keiser, 1706. Vice-*Kapellmeister*, Darmstadt, 1709; *Kapellmeister*, 1712. Elected cantor of St. Thomas's, Leipzig, 1723, but was unable to obtain his dismissal from Darmstadt: the post went instead to Bach. He wrote a few operas, 6 of which were produced at Hamburg, and a vast quantity of church music and instrumental compositions. Selections from the church music in *D.D.T.*, li-lii, a concerto in *D.D.T.*, xxx. Modern ed. of his *Monatliche Klavier-Früchte* (1722 foll.) by Küster (1928).

Grave [grah'-veh], *I.* Solemn, and therefore slow.

Gravicembalo [grah-vee-chem'-bah-lo], *I.* Either a corruption of *clavicembalo* (harpsichord) or a large harpsichord equipped to serve as a solid bass foundation to the harmony.

Grazioso [grahts-yo'-zo], *I.* Graceful.

Great Organ (*Fr.* grand orgue, *G.* Hauptwerk). The principal manual keyboard of an organ, situated below the SWELL ORGAN and above the CHOIR ORGAN. Though it includes a limited number of soft stops its chief function is to provide massive sonority and brilliance.

Grechaninov [greh-chun-een'-off], ALEXANDER TIKHONOVICH: *b.* Moscow, Oct. 25, 1864 ; *d.* New York, Jan. 4, 1956. Composer. Studied under Safonov at the Moscow Conservatoire and under Rimsky-Korsakov at the St. Petersburg Conservatoire. Made a European tour (1922), lived in Paris from 1925 and settled in New York, 1941. He composed operas, five symphonies and other orchestral works, choral works, Catholic church music including Masses and motets, Russian Church music including two complete liturgies, string quartets and other chamber music, incidental music for plays, piano pieces, songs and music for children (including children's operas).

Greek Music. The surviving fragments of ancient Greek music are very few and widely separated in time. There exists a substantial body of theoretical writings of different periods, but the authors of them frequently disagree and it is obvious that both the theory and the practice of Greek music were considerably modified as time went on. We know, however, that the Greeks used modal patterns, though the names of these sometimes changed from one period to another. We know also that they used intervals smaller than a semitone (*v.* ENHARMONIC)—one of the striking evidences of the influence of Asiatic music. So far as our evidence goes they did not employ harmony, though they used the word ἁρμονία, which means properly a fitting together and hence a consistent pattern (in their case of melodic material). We know from Plato that the modes had non-musical associations according to the order in which the intervals occurred: thus one was considered martial, another languorous, and so. The Roman theorist Boethius derived a good deal of his material from Greek writers, but he does not seem to have understood clearly what they wrote; and the medieval theorists who used Boethius as a text-book often added to the confusion by further misunderstandings. Greek names, for example, were assigned to the medieval modes but the medieval nomenclature did not correspond with the Greek. Greek theory may be said to have made two important contributions to medieval and modern theory: (1) it supplied a terminology (words like *tonic*, *diatonic*, *melody*, *harmony*, *diapason* are only a few of the many still in use which were originally employed by Greek theorists; (2) it provided the basis of medieval and modern acoustics by establishing the mathematical basis of musical sounds (here again the medieval writers, though appreciating the principles, sometimes went sadly astray in their calculations). There was also one indirect result of Greek music—the creation of opera at the end of the 16th cent. From the mistaken belief that Greek drama was sung throughout came the attempt to provide a modern equivalent by clothing dialogue with a form of musical declamation which came to be known as RECITATIVE. It is a striking example of the fact that an intellectual error can produce results of high aesthetic value.

v. also CHROMATIC, DIATONIC, DIESIS, ENHARMONIC, MODE.

Greene, (1) HARRY PLUNKETT: *b.* Old Connaught House (Wicklow), June 24, 1865; *d.* London, Aug. 19, 1936. Baritone, who excelled particularly in the interpretation of English songs. Studied in Stuttgart, Florence and London. He also made a few appearances in opera. Published *Interpretation in Song*, a standard work (1912), and a life of Stanford (1935).

(2) MAURICE: *b.* London, 1695; *d.* there, Dec. 1, 1755. Composer and organist. Chorister at St. Paul's Cathedral in London, where he was organist from 1718. Organist and composer to the Chapel Royal, 1727; professor, Cambridge, 1730; master of the King's music, 1735. He inherited an estate in Essex (1750) and began a collection of English church music for publication which was completed by his pupil Boyce. He was an intimate friend of Handel. He composed an opera, oratorios, *Forty Select Anthems* (1743) and other church music, works for organ and for harpsichord, songs, odes for festal occasions, duets, trios, catches and canons.

Greeting, THOMAS. Author of *The Pleasant Companion; or new Lessons and Instructions for the Flagelet* (1673). He was also a member of Charles II's private music, and one of the 24 violins. Among his pupils for the flageolet were Samuel Pepys and his wife. There are several references to him in Pepys's diary.

Gregorian Chant. *v.* PLAINSONG.

Grenon [grer-nõ], NICOLAS. 15th-cent. singer and composer. Examples of his work are in J. Marix, *Les Musiciens de la cour de Bourgogne.*

Gretchaninov. *v.* GRECHANINOV.

Grétry [gray-tree], ANDRÉ ERNEST MODESTE: *b.* Liége, Feb. 11, 1741; *d.* Montmerency, Sept. 24, 1813. Composer. Chorister at St. Denis's Church, Liége. Studied in Rome, 1759-66; taught singing at Geneva, 1767, and produced operas in Paris from 1768. He was made one of the original members of the Institut (1795), an inspector of the new Conservatoire (1795) and a member of the new Légion d'Honneur (1802), and received a pension from Napoleon. He composed many operas (mostly comic), six small symphonies (1758), a Requiem, motets and other church music, two piano quartets with flute, and piano sonatas. The most successful of his operas was *Richard Coeur-de-Lion* (Paris, 1784), an excellent example of the late 18th-cent. *opéra-comique*, which was given all over Europe. Of his literary works the most important is *Mémoires ou essais sur la musique* (3 vols., 1789-97): for an extract in translation *v.* O. Strunk, *Source Readings in Music History*, pp. 711-27.

Grieg [greeg], EDVARD HAGERUP: *b.* Bergen, Norway, June 15, 1843; *d.* there, Sept. 4, 1907. Composer. He began composing at the age of nine and his parents were persuaded by Ole Bull to send him to study in Leipzig (1858), where he entered the Conservatorium but was forced to go home in 1860 to recuperate from a severe illness. He returned to the Conservatorium, from which he graduated in 1862, gave his first concert in Bergen, settled in Copenhagen (1863), where he studied under Niels Gade, and after his return to Norway became an intimate friend of Richard Nordraak, who was working to produce a national Norwegian school of music. He founded (1867) and conducted (until 1880) a musical society in Christiania (now Oslo), married his cousin Nina Hagerup (1867), who sang many of his songs and with whom he later gave concerts, visited Italy (1865 and 1870), and became acquainted with Liszt in Rome. He made several visits to England but spent most of his later life at his country home a few miles from Bergen.

The individual charm of his music lies in the combination of national idioms, which he used constantly, with the romanticism which he had imbibed at Leipzig. He was not, however, content merely to accept the harmonic conventions of German romanticism and evolved for himself a practice of modulation and a use of dissonance, bold for its time, which has no exact parallel in the work of any other contemporary composer. Primarily a lyrical composer, he was most successful in short pieces of a tender or lively character. In longer works, such as the piano concerto, the tendency to repeat short phrases becomes wearisome, and the attempt to create a formal structure in the German tradition results in artificiality. The popularity of his music to *Peer Gynt* is due to the qualities which won success for his other works in the shorter forms. It shows, however, little understanding of the irony and bitter characterization of Ibsen's play.

His principal compositions are:

(a) ORCHESTRA: Overture, *I Höst* (In Autumn, 1866); piano concerto (1868; revised 1907); 2 suites from *Peer Gynt* (1888, 1891); 3 pieces from *Sigurd Jorsalfar* (1892); symphonic dances (1898); suite for strings, *Fra Holbergs Tid* (From Holberg's Time, 1885).

(b) CHAMBER MUSIC: string quartet; 3 violin sonatas; cello sonata.

(c) PIANO: Sonata in E minor; *Lyriske Stykker* (Lyric Pieces, 10 books); *Ballads*; many collections of folk songs and dances.

(c) CHORAL WORKS: *Foran Sydens Kloster* (At a Southern Convent Gate, 1871); *Landkjaenning* (Recognition of Land, 1872; revised, 1881).

(d) INCIDENTAL MUSIC: *Sigurd Jorsalfar* (1872): *Peer Gynt* (1875; revised orchestration, 1886).

Also the melodrama *Bergljot*, numerous songs (including the *Haugtussa* cycle) and part-songs.

G. ABRAHAM (ed.) : *Grieg* (1948).

Griffbrett. *v.* AM GRIFFBRETT.

Griffes, CHARLES TOMLINSON: *b.* Elmira, N.Y., Sept. 17, 1884; *d.* New York, Apr. 8, 1920. Composer. Studied in Berlin. A schoolmaster by profession, he found time to write some striking instrumental and vocal works, including the symphonic poem *The Pleasure Dome of Kubla Khan.*

Grigny [green-yee], NICOLAS DE: *b.* St. Pierre-le-Vieil, Sept. 8, 1672 ; *d.* Rheims, Nov. 30, 1703. Composer and organist of Rheims Cathedral. Bach made a copy of his *Livre d'orgue* (1711 ; modern ed. in A. Guilmant, *Archives des maîtres de l'orgue*, v).

Grisi [gree'-zee], GIULIA: *b.* Milan, July 28, 1811; *d.* Berlin, Nov. 29, 1869. Operatic soprano. She sang Adalgisa in the first performance of Bellini's *Norma* (Milan, 1831). She had an outstanding success in Paris, where she sang in the first performance of Donizetti's *Don Pasquale* (Paris, 1843) and in London. Her second husband was the tenor Giovanni Matteo Mario, with whom she constantly sang in opera.

Grocheo [grock'-ay-o], JOHANNES DE. Theorist active in Paris *c.* 1300. His treatise is especially valuable for its information about the musical forms, sacred and secular, and musical instruments of his time. It has been edited, with a German translation, by E. Rohloff (1943).

Groppo [grop'-po], *I.* *v.* GRUPPO.

Grosse caisse [gross kess], *Fr.* Bass drum.

Grosse Orgelmesse [groce'-er orrg'-ĕl-mess-er] *G.* (Grand Organ Mass). The name given to Haydn's *Missa in honorem Beatissimae Virginis Mariae* in E♭, composed *c.* 1766 (No. 2 in the Haydn Society's edition, No. 12 in Novello's edition). So called on account of the part for organ *obbligato.* *v.* KLEINE ORGELMESSE.

Grosse Trommel [groh'-ser trom'-ĕl], *G.* Bass drum.

Grossi [gross'-see], LODOVICO. *v.* VIADANA.

Ground. (1) = GROUND BASS.

(2) A composition built on a ground bass.

Ground Bass (*I.* basso ostinato). A bass line, whether simple or complex, long or short, which is constantly repeated throughout a vocal or instrumental composition and forms the foundation for varied melodic, harmonic or contrapuntal treatment. Its origin is presumably to be found in the dance. The effect of a ground bass, which was widely cultivated in the 17th and early 18th cent., was to substitute a formal and unifying symmetry for the polyphonic development characteristic of 16th-cent. music. Instrumental improvisation above a ground bass was also common in the 17th cent., particularly in England for the bass viol: *v.* DIVISION (2), DIVISION VIOL. Among the forms related to the use of a ground bass are CHACONNE, FOLÍA, PASSACAGLIA.

Grove, GEORGE: *b.* London, Aug. 13, 1820; *d.* there, May 28, 1900. Writer on music. Originally a civil engineer by profession, he became secretary of the Crystal Palace, 1852-73, and for many years wrote programme notes for the concerts given there. He also devoted himself to biblical studies and helped to establish the Palestine Exploration Fund. With Sullivan he visited Vienna, 1867 and discovered the parts of Schubert's *Rosamunde* music. Edited the *Dictionary of Music and Musicians* which still bears his name (1st ed., 1879-89; 2nd ed., J. A. Fuller-Maitland, 1904-10; 3rd ed., H. C. Colles, 1927-8; 4th ed., H. C. Colles, 1940; 5th ed., E. Blom, 1954). First director, R.C.M., 1882-94. Knighted, 1883. Published *Beethoven and his Nine Symphonies* (1896).

C. L. GRAVES: *The Life and Letters of Sir George Grove, C.B.* (1904).

Grovlez [grov-lay], GABRIEL: *b.* Lille, Apr. 4, 1879; *d.* Paris, Oct. 20, 1944. Conductor and composer. Studied at the Paris Conservatoire and taught piano at the Schola Cantorum. Conductor, Paris Opera, 1914-33. His compositions include symphonic poems, ballets and the comic opera *Le Marquis de Carabas.* He also edited examples of old French keyboard music.

Gruenberg, LOUIS: *b.* Brest-Litovsk, Aug. 3, 1884. Composer and pianist, who has lived in America since early childhood, apart from his musical education in Europe. A pupil of Busoni in Berlin and Vienna. Toured as a pianist, 1912-19. His compositions, which show the influence of negro spirituals and jazz, include the operas *Jack and the Beanstalk* (commissioned by the Juilliard School, 1931) and *Emperor Jones,* based on O'Neill's play (New York, 1933), 5 symphonies, 2 piano concertos, violin concerto, chamber music and songs.

Gruppetto [groop-pet'-to], *I.* Diminutive of *gruppo.*

Gruppo [groop'-po] (also *groppo*), *I.* Lit. "group." A generic term for various ornaments consisting of the association of one or more decorative notes with a melody note, in particular:

(1) A shake or trill employing both the upper and the lower accessory notes, *e.g.*:

is to be played

PRAETORIUS, *Syntagma Musicum*, iii (*1618-19*)

(Note that *trillo* in 17th-cent. usage denoted something quite different—a tremolo or vibrato on a single note.)

(2) A turn (represented also by the diminutive *gruppetto*), *e.g.*:

is to be played

MATTHESON, *Der vollkommene Capellmeister* (*1739*)

Guadagni [goo-ah-dahn′-yee], GAETANO: *b.* Lodi, *c.* 1725; *d.* Padua, 1792. Castrato contralto (and later soprano). He sang in Italy, England, Ireland, France, Portugal, Austria and Germany. In London he sang alto solos in Handel's *Messiah* and *Samson*.

Guadagnini [goo-ah-dahn-yee′-nee]. A family of Italian violin-makers, active throughout the 18th cent.

Guarneri [goo-arr-neh′-ree] (Guarnerius). A family of Italian violin-makers in Cremona, the first of whom was Andrea (*d.* 1698), a pupil (like Stradivari) of Nicola Amati. The most celebrated was Giuseppe (*b.* Oct. 16, 1687; *d.* Oct. 17, 1744), known as Giuseppe del Gesù from the letters IHS (Jesu hominum salvator) which appear after his name on his labels.

Guédron [gay-drõn], PIERRE: *b. c.* 1565; *d.* 1621. Composer, in the service of Henri IV and Louis XIII. He composed ballets for the court and published collections of *airs de cour*. His *Ballet de la délivrance de Renaud* (1617) is printed in H. Prunières, *Le Ballet de cour en France* (1914), pp. 251-65.

Guerre des Bouffons, La [la gairr day boo-fõn] (The War of the Comedians). A violent controversy which arose in Paris as the result of a series of performances of comic opera given there by an Italian company in 1752-4. The subject of the controversy was a familiar theme—the rival merits of French and Italian music; but on this occasion it was pursued with unusual intensity. The arguments for either side were presented in a host of pamphlets: for two examples in translation (by Baron von Grimm and Jean-Jacques Rousseau) *v.* O. Strunk, *Source Readings in Music History*, pp. 619-54.

Guerrero [gair-reh′-ro], (1) FRANCISCO: *b.* Seville, 1527 or 1528; *d.* there, Nov. 8, 1599. Composer. Chorister, Seville Cathedral. After an appointment at Jaén Cathedral was successively director of the choir school and eventually (1574) *maestro di capilla* at Seville Cathedral. He twice visited Rome and also made a pilgrimage to Palestine, of which he published an account. One of the outstanding Spanish composers of church music in the 16th cent.: modern ed. of selected works in F. Pedrell, *Hispaniae schola musica sacra*, ii.

(2) PEDRO. Elder brother of (1), and his first teacher. Examples of his compositions are preserved in printed lute-tablatures and also in manuscript part-books.

R. MITJANA: *Francisco Guerrero: estudio critico-biografico* (1922).

Guglielmi [gool-yel′-mee], PIETRO: *b.* Massa Carrara, Dec. 9, 1728; *d.* Rome, Nov. 19, 1804. Composer. Studied under Durante at the Conservatorio Santa Maria di Loreto, Naples. He composed a large number of operas, winning his first outstanding success with the production of *Il ratto della sposa* at Venice in 1765. He also visited Dresden, Brunswick and London. He became *maestro di cappella* at St. Peter's, Rome, 1793. In addition to some 100 operas he wrote 9 oratorios, motets and chamber music.

Gui [goo′-ee], VITTORIO: *b.* Rome, Sept. 14, 1885. Conductor and composer. Studied at the Liceo di S. Cecilia, Rome. He has conducted at a number of Italian opera-houses (including San Carlo, Naples, and La Scala, Milan), and in England at Covent Garden, Glyndebourne and the Edinburgh Festival. His compositions include the opera *La fata malerba* (Turin, 1927).

Guido d'Arezzo [goo-ee'-do da-reh'-dzo] (Guido Aretinus): *b.* Paris, end of the 10th cent. Theorist and teacher, a Benedictine monk. His name derived from the fact that for some time he was in charge of the choir school at Arezzo in Italy. He simplified the teaching of choirboys by getting them to associate each note of a HEXACHORD with a particular syllable. These syllables—*ut, re, mi, fa, sol, la*—begin the successive lines of the hymn "Ut queant laxis," which was chosen because the initial notes of each line are successively C, D, E, F, G, A. This system, known as SOLMIZATION, created the names for the notes still used in France and Italy, and was the basis of TONIC SOL-FA in the 19th cent. He also extended the principle of using horizontal lines to indicate the pitch of notes, recommending the use of three or four lines for this purpose. This recommendation, once adopted, proved invaluable: the STAFF of four or more lines became indispensable to composers and copyists. Guido's theoretical works are printed in Gerbert, *Scriptores*, ii; new edition of his *Micrologus* by A. M. Amelli (1904); English translation of his *Prologus antiphonarii sui* and *Epistola de ignoto cantu* in O. Strunk, *Source Readings in Music History*, pp. 117-125.

Guildhall School of Music and Drama. Founded in 1880 by the Corporation of the City of London. Principals: Thomas Henry Weist-Hill, 1880; Joseph Barnby, 1892; William Hayman Cummings, 1896; Landon Ronald, 1910; Edric Cundell, 1938.

Guilelmus Monachus [gwill-el'-mooss mon'-a-cooss]. Late 15th-cent. theorist, whose treatise *De praeceptis artis musicae et practicae* contains useful information about the practice of FAUXBOURDON. Modern ed. in Coussemaker's *Scriptores*, iii; corrections in M. Bukofzer, *Geschichte des englischen Diskants*.

Guillaume Tell [gee-yome tell] (William Tell). Opera in four acts by Rossini. Libretto by Victor Joseph Étienne de Jouy and Hippolyte Louis Florent Bis. First performed, Paris, August 3, 1829. The story deals with the rebellion of the Swiss, led by William Tell, against their Governor, Gessler, whose son Arnold also sides with the rebels.

Guilmant [geel-mũn], FÉLIX ALEXANDRE: *b.* Boulogne, March 12, 1837; *d.* Meudon, nr. Paris, March 29, 1911. Organist and composer. He succeeded his father as organist of St. Nicholas, Boulogne, 1857. Studied under Lemmens in Paris and Brussels. Settled in Paris, 1871, where he was organist at the Trinité, 1871-1901. A founder (with Bordes and Vincent d'Indy) of the Schola Cantorum; teacher of the organ there and at the Conservatoire (from 1896). He inaugurated many new organs and toured in England, America and on the Continent. He composed two symphonies for organ and orchestra, sonatas and other works for organ. He also edited 10 vols. of old organ music, under the title *Archives des maîtres de l'orgue* (1898-1910).

Guiraud [gee-ro], ERNEST: *b.* New Orleans, June 23, 1837; *d.* Paris, May 6, 1892. Composer, son of a French composer and music-teacher. Studied at the Paris Conservatoire. *Prix de Rome*, 1859. Teacher, Paris Conservatoire, 1876, till his death. He wrote several operas, of which the most successful was *Piccolino* (Paris, 1876), and composed the recitatives for Bizet's *Carmen* (in place of the spoken dialogue) on the occasion of its production at Vienna in 1875 (the first production outside Paris).

Guitar (*Fr.* guitare, *G.* Guitarre, *I.* chitarra, *Sp.* guitarra). A plucked string instrument, originally brought to Spain by the Moors in the Middle Ages. It differs from the lute in having a flat back. The modern instrument has six strings, tuned:

The earliest known compositions (for a four-stringed instrument) were printed in Fuenllana's *Orphenica lyra* (1554).

Related instruments are the BALALAIKA, BANDURRIA, CITTERN and GITTERN.

Guntram [goŏnt′-rum]. Opera in three acts by Richard Strauss. Libretto by the composer. First performed, Weimar, May 10, 1894.

Gurlitt [goŏr-lit], (1) CORNELIUS: *b.* Altona, Feb. 10, 1820; *d.* there, June 17, 1901. Organist, composer and teacher. A prolific composer of nearly 250 works, including 2 operettas and an opera, he is best known for his teaching pieces for young pianists.

(2) MANFRED: *b.* Berlin, Sept. 6, 1890. Composer and conductor, a pupil of Humperdinck. He has been opera conductor at Essen (1911-12), Augsburg (1912-14) and Bremen (1914-27). Since 1939 he has lived as a teacher and conductor in Tokio. His compositions include the opera *Wozzeck* (Bremen, 1926), a setting of Büchner's play (previously set by Alban Berg, 1922, produced in Berlin, 1925).

(3) WILIBALD: *b.* Dresden, March 1, 1889. Musicologist. Grand-nephew of (1). Studied at Heidelberg and Leipzig. Prisoner of war, 1914-18. Professor, Freiburg, 1920. He has played an important part in the revival of old instruments (including the organ) for the performance of music of the past. He has edited a volume of the complete edition of the works of Praetorius, published a facsimile edition of part II of Praetorius's *Syntagma Musicum*, written a concise but valuable study of Bach (2nd ed., 1949) and made many important contributions to musical periodicals.

Gurney, IVOR BERTIE: *b.* Gloucester, Aug. 28, 1890; *d.* Dartford, Kent, Dec. 26, 1937. Composer and poet. Chorister at Gloucester Cathedral, where he became assistant organist, 1906. Studied at the R.C.M. under Vaughan Williams, Stanford and others and served in the army (from 1915). After he was discharged because of unfitness resulting from being gassed and wounded, he suffered continually from bad health and poverty and was sent to a mental hospital in 1922, where he remained until his death. He composed songs (some to his own poetry), *Ludlow and Teme* (a song-cycle for tenor and string quartet) and two other song-cycles, piano pieces and two works for violin and piano.

Guttoveggio [goot - to - veh′ - djo], JOSEPH. *v.* CRESTON.

Gwendoline [gwŭn-do-leen]. Opera in two acts by Chabrier. Libretto by Catulle Mendès. First performed, Brussels, Apr. 10, 1886.

Gymel (derived from the Latin *cantus gemellus*, "twin song"). A term first occurring in the 15th cent. to denote a characteristically English method of singing in two parts with the same range. Earlier examples make liberal use of parallel thirds. Examples of such music are found as early as the 13th cent. (*v.* M. Bukofzer, in *Music and Letters*, Apr. 1935, pp. 77-84).

Gyrowetz [gee′-ro-vets], ADALBERT: *b.* Budweis, Feb. 19, 1763; *d.* Vienna, March 19, 1850. Composer. Studied law in Prague and music in Vienna (where one of his symphonies was performed by Mozart, 1786), Naples and Milan. He visited Paris where he discovered that several of his symphonies were being performed under Haydn's name, lived in London, 1789-92, and was *Kapellmeister* and *Intendant* of the two court theatres in Vienna, 1804-31. He composed about 30 operas (German and Italian), 40 ballets, 60 symphonies, serenades, overtures and other orchestral works, 19 Masses, cantatas and other choral works, 60 quartets, quintets, trios, 40 piano sonatas and songs. He published his autobiography under the title *Biographie des Adalbert Gyrowetz* (1848; new ed. by A. Einstein in *Lebensläufe deutscher Musiker*, iii-iv, 1915).

H

H [ha], *G.* B natural (B♮). *v.* B.

Haas [hahss], (1) JOSEPH: *b.* Maihingen (Bavaria), March 19, 1879. Composer. Pupil and disciple of Max Reger. Teacher at Munich Academy of Music from 1921, and President there, 1945-49. Has composed operas, oratorios, orchestral works, chamber music, piano pieces, and songs.

(2) ROBERT MARIA: *b.* Prague, Aug. 15, 1886. Historian, composer and conductor. Editor of 7 volumes of the series *D.T.Ö.*, and contributor to Adler's *Handbuch.* Author of a number of books on music of the 17th and 18th cent., including *Die Musik des Barocks* and *Aufführungspraxis der Musik* in Bücken's *Handbuch der Musikwissenschaft.* In 1929 he initiated the publication of the original versions of Bruckner's works and has written (1934) a biography of that composer.

Hába [hah'-ba], ALOIS: *b.* Vyzovice (Moravia), June 21, 1893. Composer and theorist. Since 1921 a protagonist of music written in quarter- and sixth-tones, which he has used in piano music, string quartets, and works for violin and for cello. A quarter-tone piano, clarinets, and trumpets were specially made for the first performance of his quarter-tone opera *Die Mutter* (Munich, 1931).

Habanera [hah-bah-neh'-rah], *Sp.* A Cuban dance adopted in (or reimported into) Spain in the 19th cent. Its characteristic rhythm is

♪♩♩♩♩

One by Sebastian Yradier, "El Arreglito," was adapted by Bizet in *Carmen*, and later examples were written by Chabrier (1885), Ravel (1895) and Debussy.

Habeneck [a-ber-neck], FRANÇOIS ANTOINE: *b.* Mézières, Jan. 22, 1781; *d.* Paris, Feb. 8, 1849. Conductor, violinist and composer. Founded the *Société des Concerts du Conservatoire* in Paris in 1828, and introduced many of the works of Beethoven into France.

A. CARSE : *The Orchestra from Beethoven to Berlioz* (1948).

L. SCHRADE : *Beethoven in France* (1942).

Haberl [hahb'-erl], FRANZ XAVER: *b.* Oberellenbach (Bavaria), Apr. 12, 1840; *d.* Ratisbon, Sept. 5, 1910. Priest, organist and historian of the church music of the 15th, 16th and early 17th cent. In his *Bausteine zur Musikgeschichte* (1885-88) he laid the foundation for later research on Dufay, on the history of the Papal choir, and on the music in the Vatican Library. Edited from vol. x the complete works of Palestrina (finished in 1894).

Hackbrett [huck'-bret], *G. v.* DULCIMER.

Hacomplaynt (Hacomblene), ROBERT: *d.* Sept. 8, 1528. Composer. Educated at Eton (King's Scholar, 1469-72) and King's College, Cambridge. Provost of King's College, 1509-28. His five-part " Salve regina " in the Eton choirbook is printed in *Musica Britannica*, xi.

Hadley, (1) HENRY KIMBALL: *b.* Somerville, Mass., Dec. 20, 1871; *d.* New York, Sept. 6, 1937. Composer and conductor. Studied composition in Boston and Vienna. Conducted the San Francisco Symphony Orchestra from 1911 to 1916. One of the founders of the National Association of American Composers and Conductors, and composer of operas, orchestral and choral works, chamber music, and songs.

(2) PATRICK ARTHUR SHELDON: *b.* Cambridge, March 5, 1899. Composer and teacher. Educated at Winchester, Cambridge, and the R.C.M. Lecturer, Cambridge, 1938; succeeded E. J. Dent as professor, 1946. Most of his compositions are for voices and instruments, and include *The Trees so High* (1931), freely based on the ballad of that name, *La Belle Dame sans Merci* (1935), *My*

Beloved Spake (1938), *The Hills* (1946) and *The Cenci* (1951).

Hadow, WILLIAM HENRY: *b.* Ebrington (Glos.), Dec. 27, 1859; *d.* London, Apr. 8, 1937. Historian, composer, writer on musical criticism and authority on musical and general education. Lectured on music at Oxford from 1890 to 1899. Principal, Armstrong College, Newcastle-on-Tyne, 1909-19; Vice-Chancellor, Sheffield University from 1919-30. Knighted, 1918. His *Studies in Modern Music* (2 vols., 1894-5) contain extended essays on six 19th-cent. composers. General editor of the *Oxford History of Music* and author of the fifth volume, *The Viennese Period* (1904). His position as an administrator and as chairman of the Committee which published the Hadow Report, *The Education of the Adolescent* (1927), gave weight to his claim "that we should admit musical history to the same place in our annals which we now accord to the history of literature" (Rice Institute Lectures, Houston, Texas, 1926; published in *Collected Essays*, 1928).

Haffner [huff′-ner]. The title given to two compositions by Mozart: (1) Serenade in D major (1776, K.250) composed together with a March (K. 249) for the marriage of Elizabeth Haffner at Salzburg on June 22, 1776.

(2) Symphony in D major (1782, K. 385) composed for the Haffner family.

Hahn [ahn], REYNALDO: *b.* Caracas (Venezuela), Aug. 9, 1875; *d.* Paris, Jan. 28, 1947. Composer and conductor. Brought up in Paris, where he studied under Dubois, Lavignac and Massenet at the Conservatoire. His works, beginning with *L'Ile de rêve* (1898) are almost entirely for the stage, and include the operas *La Carmélite* (1902), *La Colombe de Bouddha* (1921), *Le Marchand de Venise* (1935), operettas, ballets, and incidental music. He also composed chamber music, piano pieces, and songs to poems of Verlaine (*Chansons grises*) and Leconte de Lisle (*Études latines*).

Halbe [hulb′-er], *G.* Minim.

Halbton [hulp′-tone], *G.* Semitone.

Halévy [a-lay-vee], JACQUES FRANÇOIS (originally Fromental Elias Lévy): *b.* Paris, May 27, 1799; *d.* Nice, March 17, 1862. Pupil of Berton and Cherubini at the Paris Conservatoire, and winner of the *Prix de Rome* in 1819. Wrote numerous operas, of which only *La Juive* (1835) gained permanent fame. Taught at the Conservatoire, where he became professor of composition, 1840. Among his pupils were Gounod and Bizet, who became his son-in-law.

Half Close. Another name for the imperfect CADENCE.

Half-Note. American for "minim."

Hallé, CHARLES (originally Carl Halle): *b.* Hagen (Westphalia), Apr. 11, 1819; *d.* Manchester, Oct. 25, 1895. Pianist and conductor. Studied with Rinck and Gottfried Weber in Darmstadt (1835) and in Paris with Kalkbrenner (1836). Settled in Manchester in 1848 where he founded the Hallé Orchestra, 1857. Was a prominent figure in English musical life, notably as conductor of the works of Berlioz. Knighted, 1888 and became first Principal of the Royal Manchester College of Music, 1893.

C. E. AND M. HALLÉ: *Life and Letters of Sir Charles Hallé* (1896).

Hallé Concerts. Since the death of Charles Hallé the following have been conductors of the Hallé Orchestra: Frederic Cowen (1896-99), Hans Richter (1899-1911), Michael Balling (1912-14), Hamilton Harty (1920-33), guest conductors until 1939, John Barbirolli (from 1945).

Hallén [hull-ehn′], JOHAN ANDREAS: *b.* Gothenburg, Dec. 22, 1846; *d.* Stockholm, March 11, 1925. Composer, conductor and critic. Studied in Leipzig at the Conservatorium and under Reinecke, in Munich under Rheinberger and in Dresden under Rietz. Conductor, Gothenburg Musical Union, 1872-78 and 1883-84; Stockholm Philharmonic Concerts, 1884-95, and Royal Opera, 1892-97; Malmö Philharmonic Society, 1901-07. Teacher, Stockholm Conservatoire, 1909-19. He composed operas, symphonic poems, suites and other orchestral works, choral works with orchestra, a piano quartet, theatre music and songs. He published a collection of essays on music (1897).

Halling [hull′-ing], *N.* A popular Norwegian dance, moderately fast in tempo and generally in $\frac{2}{4}$ time. The dance is performed by men, with a good deal of dramatic action, including sudden leaps into the air. The music is properly played on the Hardanger fiddle, a violin with four sympathetic strings in addition to the normal four. There are several examples of the dance in Grieg's works.

Hallström [hull′-strurm], IVAR: *b.* Stockholm, June 5, 1826; *d.* there, Apr. 11, 1901. Composer and pianist. Studied music privately and law at Upsala University. He became librarian to Prince Oscar (later King Oscar II) and settled in Stockholm, where he was appointed director of Lindblad's Music School, 1861. He composed operas (one with Prince Gustav, 1847), operettas, ballets, cantatas, piano pieces and songs. His opera *Den Bergtagna* (The Mountain Ghost, 1874) was successful in Sweden.

Halvorsen [hull′-vorr-sĕn], JOHAN: *b.* Drammen (Norway), March 15, 1864; *d.* Oslo, Dec. 4, 1935. Violinist, composer and conductor. Studied in Stockholm at the Conservatoire, in Leipzig, Liége and Berlin and also lived at Bergen, Aberdeen and Helsinki. Conductor, Symphony Concerts, Bergen, 1893; National Theatre, Oslo, 1899. He composed 2 symphonies, a violin concerto, 9 suites and other orchestral works, a coronation cantata for King Haakon, incidental music for plays, 3 suites for violin and piano, choral works, and songs.

Hambacher [hum′-buckh-er], JOSEPHA. *v.* DUŠEK (3).

Hamboys. *v.* HANBOYS.

Hamerik [hum′-er-ick], ASGER: *b.* Copenhagen, Apr. 8, 1843; *d.* Frederiksborg, July 12, 1923. Composer. Brother of Angul Hammerich. His compositions include 7 symphonies, 2 choral trilogies and a *Requiem*, 4 operas, 5 suites for orchestra, cantatas, and chamber music.

Hammerclavier [hum′-er-cluv-eer′], *G.* Lit. " keyboard instrument with hammers." Obsolete German name for the piano. Beethoven used it in the published titles of Op. 101 in A major and Op. 106 in B♭ major; it was also his original intention to use it for Op. 109 in E major (*v.* A. C. Kalischer, *Beethoven's Letters*, trans. J. S. Shedlock, ii, pp. 3-4, 181-2) and Op. 110 in A♭ major. The habit of referring to Op. 106 as "the *Hammerclavier* sonata " is pointless. *Sonate für das Hammerclavier* means simply " piano sonata."

Hammerich [hum′-er-ick], ANGUL: *b.* Copenhagen, Nov. 25, 1848; *d.* there, Apr. 26, 1931. Critic and historian. Brother of Asger Hamerik. From 1896 to 1922 was professor of musical history at the University of Copenhagen. Wrote *Mediaeval Musical Relics of Denmark* (Danish and English, 1912) and *Dansk Musik Historie indtil c.* 1700 (1921).

Hammerschmidt [hum′-er-shmit], ANDREAS: *b.* Brüx (Bohemia), 1611 or 1612; *d.* Zittau, Oct. 29, 1675. Organist and composer. An important figure in the history of Lutheran music. Organist, Freiburg, 1635-39; Zittau from 1639 until his death. In his *Dialogi oder Gespräche zwischen Gott und einer gläubigen Seele*, (*Dialogues between God and a faithful Soul*: 2 parts, Dresden, 1645) he applied the method of dramatic dialogue to settings of Biblical words for 2, 3 or 4 voices with figured bass, in some cases with an introductory *sinfonia* for instruments (modern ed. of Part I in *D.T.Ö.*, viii). His *Musikalische Andachten* (Musical Devotions: 5 parts, 1638-53) contain more than 150 pieces for 1 to 12 voices with figured bass, with or without instruments. A selection was printed in *D.D.T.*, xl, with a list of published works.

Hammerstein [hum′-er-shtine], OSCAR: *b.* Stettin, May 7, 1848; *d.* New York, Aug. 1, 1919. Impresario. Built and managed theatres and opera-houses in New York from 1890. From 1906 to 1910, when his interests were bought by the Metropolitan Opera, his Manhattan Opera House presented many famous singers, and gave first American performances of Debussy's *Pelléas et Mélisande* (1908), and Richard Strauss's *Salome* (1907) and *Elektra* (1910).

Hampel [hump′-el], ANTON JOSEPH : *d.* Dresden, March 30, 1771. Czech horn-player, a member of the Dresden orchestra from 1737. He is said to have invented the practice of using the hand to produce stopped notes on the horn. He wrote a tutor for the horn which was revised by his pupil Giovanni Punto.

Hampton, JOHN: Master of the choristers, Worcester Cathedral, 1484-1522. The Eton College choirbook (*c.* 1500) contains a 5-part setting of "Salve Regina" by him, printed in *Musica Britannica*, xi.

Hanboys, JOHN: 15th-cent. theorist. His treatise *Summa super musicam continuam et discretam* is printed in Coussemaker's *Scriptores*, i, p. 416.

Handel, GEORGE FRIDERIC (originally Händel, Georg Friedrich): *b.* Halle, Feb. 23, 1685; *d.* London, April 14, 1759. Composer. Studied law at Halle and music there under Zachow, and went to Hamburg where he played the violin in Keiser's opera orchestra and had his *Almira* and *Nero* produced in 1705. In Italy, 1706-9, he gained a knowledge of Italian styles in opera, oratorio, serenata, concerto, and chamber music, had a success with his opera *Agrippina* (Venice, 1709), and composed the oratorios *La Resurrezione* and *Trionfo del Tempo*, the serenata *Aci, Galatea e Polifemo*, solo cantatas, and chamber duets. In 1710 he was appointed *Kapellmeister* to the Elector of Hanover, accepted an invitation to write a new opera for London, and in 1711 produced *Rinaldo* there with great success. In 1712 he returned to London on leave of absence from his Hanover post, which he never resumed, and produced *Il Pastor fido* (1712), *Teseo* (1712), *Silla* (1714) and *Amadigi* (1715). He received a life pension from Queen Anne, and wrote for her a Birthday Ode and a *Te Deum* on the Peace of Utrecht (1713). The accession of his former master as George I did not long affect his position adversely, and he was soon in favour with an increased pension, an event which does not appear to have been due to the charms of the *Water Music.*

No Italian operas were given in London 1717-20 and Handel became musical director to the Duke of Chandos, and composed the *Chandos Anthems*, *Acis and Galatea* (1720), and the masque *Haman and Mordecai* (1720), which was revised in 1732 as his first English oratorio, *Esther.* Between 1720 and 1733 he produced 20 new operas at the Royal Academy of Music (King's Theatre, Haymarket) and published fifteen *sonate da camera* (1724), nine trio sonatas (1733), and eight suites for harpsichord (1720). The difficulties of maintaining the Italian opera were complicated by Handel's differences with Bononcini, by the ostentatious rivalry of Faustina and Cuzzoni, and by the great success of *The Beggar's Opera* (1728). After the favourable reception of *Esther* he turned to oratorio for performances in Lent, and wrote *Deborah* (1733), *Athalia* (1733), *Saul* (1739), *Israel in Egypt* (1739), and *Messiah* (Dublin, 1742), besides producing 15 new operas and a revised version of *Il Pastor fido* with an added prologue *Terpsichore* (1734). He composed his last opera, *Deidamia,* in 1741, and between 1743 and 1745 the oratorios *Samson, Joseph,* and *Belshazzar* and the secular choral works *Semele* and *Hercules,* which did not, however, bring him financial success. *Judas Maccabaeus* (1746, to mark the suppression of the rebellion of 1745) was well received, and the last eleven years of his life, during which he wrote six further oratorios and *The Triumph of Time and Truth* (1757), the third version of an oratorio of 1708, brought him acceptance and comparative serenity, though clouded by blindness from 1753.

Handel's writing, though not seldom perfunctory and at times shallow in expression, is at its greatest a brilliant and infallibly effective combination of the Italian traditions of solo and instrumental style, the English choral tradition, and the German contrapuntal style in which he was trained. These qualities are clear in the well-known works, but his remarkable versatility and quickness of response to a really dramatic situation produced many little masterpieces in the course of larger compositions which must be sought to be found, and some of the comparatively neglected oratorios keep this high level of inspiration almost throughout. Likewise the instrumental compositions are, at their best, delightful for their surety of writing and felicity of expression. Handel's borrowings from other composers, though reprehensible from a modern point of view, are in large part due to the 18th-cent. custom of concocting pasticcios, to inadvertence, and possibly to a keen but unconscious memory, rather than to deliberate appropriation.

His principal compositions are:

(a) OPERAS: *Almira* (1705); *Rodrigo* (1707); *Agrippina* (1709); *Rinaldo* (1711); *Il Pastor fido* (1712); *Teseo* (1712); *Silla* (1714); *Amadigi* (1715); *Radamisto* (1720); *Muzio Scevola* (1721); *Floridante* (1721); *Ottone* (1723); *Flavio* (1723); *Giulio Cesare* (1724); *Tamerlano* (1724); *Rodelinda* (1725); *Scipione* (1726); *Alessandro* (1726); *Admeto* (1727); *Riccardo Primo* (1727); *Siroe* (1728); *Tolomeo* (1728); *Lotario* (1729); *Partenope* (1730); *Poro* (1731); *Ezio* (1732); *Sosarme* (1732); *Orlando* (1733); *Arianna* (1734); *Ariodante* (1735); *Alcina* (1735); *Atalanta* (1736); *Arminio* (1737); *Giustino* (1737); *Berenice* (1737); *Faramondo* (1738); *Serse* (1738); *Imeneo* (1740); *Deidamia* (1741).

(b) PASSIONS: *St. John Passion* (1704); *Der für die Sünden der Welt gemarterte und sterbende Jesus* (1716).

(c) ORATORIOS: *La Resurrezione* (1708); *Esther* (1720, 1732); *Deborah* (1733); *Athalia* (1733); *Saul* (1739); *Israel in Egypt* (1739); *Messiah* (1742); *Samson* (1743); *Semele* (1743); *Joseph and his Brethren* (1743); *Belshazzar* (1744); *Hercules* (1744) *Occasional Oratorio* (1746); *Judas Maccabaeus* (1746); *Alexander Balus* (1747); *Joshua* (1747); *Solomon* (1748); *Susanna* (1748); *Theodora* (1749); *Jephtha* (1751); *The Triumph of Time and Truth* (1757).

(d) SECULAR CHORAL WORKS: *Acis and Galatea* (1720); *Alexander's Feast* (1736); *Ode for St. Cecilia's Day* (1739); *L'Allegro, il Penseroso ed il Moderato* (1740).

(e) CHURCH MUSIC: Utrecht *Te Deum* (1713); Chandos *Te Deum* (*c.* 1718); 11 Chandos anthems (1716-19); 3 coronation anthems (1727); funeral anthem for the death of Queen Caroline (1737); Dettingen *Te Deum* (1743).

(f) ORCHESTRA: *Water Music* (1715-17); 6 concertos ("Oboe Concertos," 1729); 12 organ concertos (1738-40); 12 *concerti grossi* (1739); *Fireworks Music* (1749).

(g) CHAMBER MUSIC: Sonatas for flute, recorder, one and two violins, two oboes, with keyboard accompaniment.

(h) HARPSICHORD: 17 suites (1720, 1733).

(i) SONGS: numerous Italian cantatas for one and two voices.

Complete works (with a few omissions) published by the German Handel Society, 96 vols. (1859-1902). A new edition of the complete works (*Hallische Händel-Ausgabe*) under the auspices of the German Handel Society was begun in 1955.

G. ABRAHAM (ed.): *Handel: a Symposium* (1954).
E. J. DENT: *Handel* (1934).
O. E. DEUTSCH: *Handel, a Documentary Biography* (1955).
N. FLOWER: *George Frideric Handel* (1947).
H. LEICHTENTRITT: *Handel* (1924).
E. H. MÜLLER: *The Letters and Writings of George Frideric Handel* (1935).
P. ROBINSON: *Handel and his Orbit* (1908).
R. ROLLAND (trans. A. E. Hull): *Handel* (1916).
W. C. SMITH: *Concerning Handel* (1948).
R. A. STREATFIELD: *Handel* (1910).
S. TAYLOR: *The Indebtedness of Handel to Works by Other Composers* (1906).
P. M. YOUNG: *Handel* (1947). *The Oratorios of Handel* (1949).

Handl [hund'l], JAKOB (*L.* Gallus, Jacobus): *b.* Reifniz (Carniola), July 31, 1550; *d.* Prague, July 18, 1591. Composer. Master of the chapel of the Bishop of Olmütz from 1579; cantor at St. Johann's, Prague, from 1585 until his death. Composed 16 Masses and numerous motets. His *Opus Musicum* (4 vols., 1586-90) containing motets for the liturgical year is reprinted in *D.T.Ö.*, vi, xii (1), xv, xx (1), xxiv, and xxvi. This work ranges from short 4-part pieces to settings for two, three, and four choirs in the Venetian polychoral style, of which he is one of the great masters.

Handlo, ROBERT DE: 14th-cent. English

theorist. His *Regulae cum maximis Magistri Franconis cum additionibus aliorum musicorum,* dated 1326, was reprinted in Coussemaker's *Scriptores* i, p. 383. It consists of the rules of mensural notation by Franco of Cologne, Jean de Garlande and others, with comments and additions by Handlo.

Handschin [hunt'-sheen], JACQUES : *b.* Moscow, Apr. 5, 1886 ; *d.* Basle, Nov. 25, 1955. Swiss musicologist. Studied at Basle and Munich. Organist, St. Petersburg, 1914-19. Returned to Switzerland in 1920. Professor of musical history, University of Basle, 1935. He wrote extensively on medieval music.

Handtrommel [hunt'-trom-ĕl], *G.* Tambourine.

Hans Heiling [hunce hy'-ling]. Opera in three acts, with a prologue, by Marschner. Libretto by Eduard Devrient. First performed, Berlin, May 24, 1833.

Hänsel und Gretel [hen'-zĕl o͝ont grate'-ĕl] (Hänsel and Gretel). Opera in three acts by Humperdinck. Libretto by Adelheid Wette (sister of the composer) from the tale by the Brothers Grimm. First performed, Weimar, Dec. 23, 1893. The two children, Hänsel and Gretel, are sent to pick berries in the woods, where they lose their way. They lie down to rest and are protected by angels during the night but in the morning they are captured by the witch of the forest, who loves to eat children. They succeed in locking her in the oven which had been prepared for them, and her death brings to life all the children who had been turned into ginger-bread figures. The parents of Hänsel and Gretel arrive and the opera closes with the merry dances of the children.

Hanslick [hunce'-lick], EDUARD: *b.* Prague, Sept. 11, 1825; *d.* Baden, near Vienna, Aug. 6, 1904. Critic and writer on the aesthetics of music. Lectured on the aesthetics and history of music at the University of Vienna, 1856-95; professor, 1870. As critic to the *Presse* and *Neue freie Presse* he was one of the most influential writers on the music of his day. In *Vom Musikalisch-Schönen* (1854: 7th ed. of 1885 translated as *The Beautiful in Music,* 1891) he maintained the autonomy of music (" the ideas which a composer expresses are mainly and primarily of a *purely musical* nature "); in his articles he opposed the " New Music " of Liszt and Wagner and praised Schumann and Brahms.

Hanson, HOWARD: *b.* Wahoo, Nebraska, Oct. 28, 1896. Composer and conductor. Of Swedish parentage, educated in the U.S.A. American *Prix de Rome* 1921-24. Director, Eastman School of Music, Rochester, N.Y. since 1924. His opera *Merrymount* was produced at the Metropolitan, New York, on Feb. 10, 1934. He has written 4 symphonies (No. 1, *Nordic*; No. 2, *Romantic*; No. 3, " conceived as a tribute to the epic qualities of the Swedish pioneers in America " ; No. 4, *Requiem*), symphonic poems, works for chorus and orchestra, piano music, chamber music, and songs.

Hardanger Fiddle. *v.* HALLING.

Harding, JAMES: *d.* between Dec. 22, 1625 and Feb. 2, 1626. Composer, and flautist at the English court from 1581 to his death. Instrumental music by him is in two manuscripts in the British Museum and in Füllsack and Hildebrand's collection *Auserlesene Paduanen und Galliarden* (Hamburg, 1607).

Harfe [harrf'-er], *G.* Harp.

Harfenquartett [harrf'-ĕn-cvarr-tet'], *G. v.* HARP QUARTET.

Harmonica. (1) (Musical glasses, glass harmonica, *G.* Glasharmonika). An instrument in which sounds are produced by the application of the moist fingers to drinking glasses (in the earlier form played by Richard Pockrich from 1734 and by Gluck in London in 1746), or to glass bowls (in the form perfected by Benjamin Franklin, *c.* 1761). Its most famous exponents were Marianne Davies (for whom, with her sister Cecilia, Hasse wrote in 1769 an ode for voice and harmonica to words by Metastasio) and Marianne Kirchgessner, the blind player for whom Mozart wrote the *Adagio and Rondo* for harmonica, flute, oboe, viola and cello (K.617) in 1791.

A. HYATT KING : " The Musical Glasses and Glass Harmonica " (*Proceedings of the Royal Musical Association,* 1945-6, pp. 97-120).

(2) (*G.* Mundharmonika). Mouth organ.

Harmonic Bass. *v.* ACOUSTIC BASS.

Harmonic Flute (*Fr.* Flûte harmonique). An organ stop first regularly used by Cavaillé-Col of Paris from 1841. A hole is bored mid-way in an open cylindrical metal pipe, making the predominant pitch the first harmonic, or octave (4 ft. pitch).

Harmonic Minor. *v.* SCALE.

Harmonic Piccolo. An organ stop similar to the HARMONIC FLUTE, but sounding an octave higher (2 ft. pitch).

Harmonics (*Fr.* sons harmoniques, *G.* Flageolett-Töne, *I.* flautato, flautando). Sounds produced on a string instrument or harp by touching the string lightly at one of its nodes, *i.e.*, exact fractional points. They correspond to the upper partials of the string, and have a soft, flute-like quality. A string touched lightly at its half-way point will produce a harmonic an octave higher than the open string. Only the octave harmonic is normally used on the harp. On bowed instruments harmonics played on an open string are called natural, those played on a stopped string are called artificial. The natural harmonics played on the G string of the violin, for example, are:

The black notes indicate at what point the string is touched.

Harmonics are indicated by writing either a small circle over the sound to be produced or a diamond-shaped note corresponding to the point to be touched. An artificial harmonic is played by touching the string a fourth above the point at which it is stopped, and sounds two octaves above the stopped note, *e.g.*:

sounds

The first set of compositions to use harmonics extensively was J. de Mondonville's *Les Sons harmoniques*, op. 4 (1735).

Harmonic Series. The composite series of notes produced by a vibrating substance or air column. If the principal note (or " fundamental ") is:

the first 16 notes of the series will be:

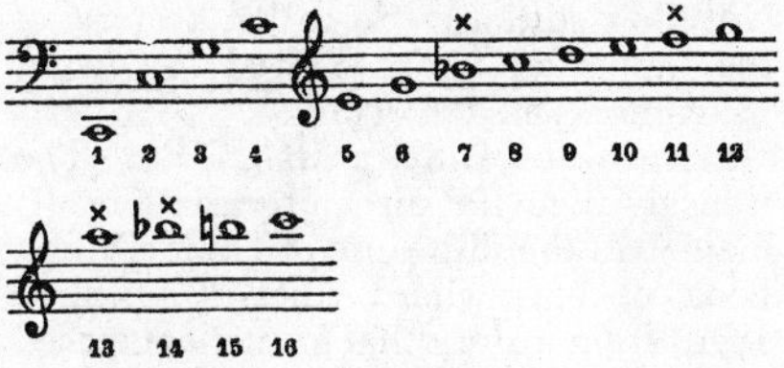

Of these nos. 7, 11, 13 and 14 are not in tune with our normal scale. Nos 2-16 (and upwards) are called " overtones " or " upper partials." The actual sound of the overtones is faint. Their effect in practice is to enrich the sound of the principal note. The individual tone-quality of instruments results from the presence or absence of particular overtones, and from their relative intensity. Thus the clarinet (a cylindrical tube, stopped at one end) produces only the alternate overtones—3, 5, 7 etc. Individual overtones can be isolated from the principal note: this is done on string instruments by touching the string lightly at sectional points (*v.* HARMONICS), and on wind instruments (particularly brass instruments) by overblowing. By this means a brass instrument without valves is able to produce a complete series of notes, the upward limit being determined by the capacity of the lips to increase the tension. The addition of valves makes available several such series and so provides a complete chromatic compass. The same result is achieved on the trombone by the slide, which progressively lengthens the tube and so lowers the pitch of the instrument. *v.* ACOUSTICS, HORN, TROMBONE, TRUMPET, VALVE.

Harmonie [*Fr.* arr-mon-ee, *G.* harr-mo-nee′]. An ensemble of wind instruments.

Harmonie der Welt, Die [dee harr-mo-nee′ dair velt[(The Harmony of the World). Opera in five acts by Hindemith. Libretto by the composer (based on the life of Kepler). First performed, Munich, Aug. 11, 1957.

Harmoniemesse [harr-mo-nee′-mess-*er*], *G.* The name given to Haydn's Mass in B♭, composed in 1802 (No. 12 in the Haydn Society's edition, no. 6 in Novello's edition). So called because of the important part played by wind instruments in the score.

Harmonious Blacksmith, The. The title given to the air and variations (E major) in the fifth suite of Handel's first book of harpsichord suites (published 1720) from a story that he had composed it after listening to a blacksmith at work. The name was first given to the piece *c.* 1822, and the story was concocted during the following years.

Harmonium (*Fr.* orgue expressif). A keyboard instrument in which the sound is produced by free reeds through which air is forced by means of bellows worked by the player's feet. A series of experiments in the first half of the 19th cent. culminated in the work of Alexandre Debain, who in 1840 brought four stops under the control of one keyboard. *v.* AMERICAN ORGAN.

Harmony. (1) Until the 17th cent. the term was used in the general sense of the sound of music. Zarlino used it in the sense of the comprehensive science of music (*Istitutioni harmoniche*, 1558) and Thomas Morley (1597), discussing the sound of music in two parts, says: "But withal you must take this caveat, that you take no note above one minim rest (or three upon the greatest extremity of your point) in two parts, for in that long resting the harmony seemeth bare." In the medieval period chords were viewed as resulting from the addition of intervals to an original part. Although a HOMOPHONIC style of writing was regularly used in the 16th cent., *e.g.* in *frottole*, balletts, and the music of the metrical PSALTERS, the same view persisted. The chromatic "harmony" of such composers as Gesualdo is not based on a theory of harmony in the modern sense, but results from the free alteration of the notes of normal chords, which could go to such extremes as:

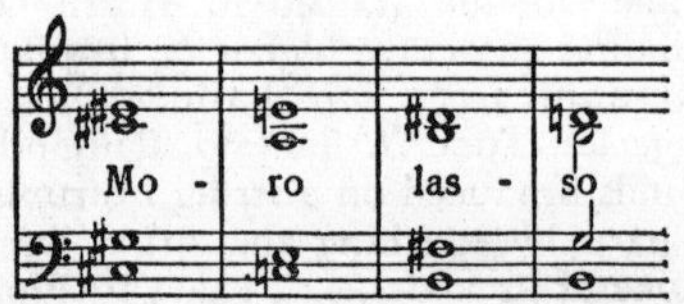

GESUALDO: *Moro lasso.*

(2) In the modern sense harmony means the structure, functions and relationships of chords. It was used by Mersenne (1636) in the sense of the physical and mathematical nature of sound, and this remained its meaning until Rameau founded the modern theory of harmony (1722) by combining the point of view of a rational scientist with that of a practising composer.

The unit of harmony is the CHORD. The smallest element of harmonic "progression," or movement, consists of two chords. A pair of chords which marks off a period or phrase is called a CADENCE. The perfect, imperfect, and plagal cadences show in the simplest form the relation of the dominant and subdominant chords of a KEY to each other and to the tonic chord. The harmonic relationships between the chords of a key are true for every key, since all keys are transpositions of the same two MODES, major and minor. The modern theory of harmony is based on the chords of the major scale. Those of the minor scale, though different in quality, are treated as having the same functions in relation to each other and to the tonic.

The tonic chord, the centre of the harmony of a key, is clearly defined as the tonic when it is preceded by the dominant chord, as in the perfect cadence. The chord which most strongly reinforces that definition by preceding and following a perfect cadence is the subdominant chord, *e.g.*:

These three chords are the primary chords of the key, and since they contain between them all the notes of the scale, they may suffice to harmonise any melody which remains in the key, in the form of spontaneous accompaniment known as "vamping."

Two of the most important parts of Rameau's theory of harmony are (*a*) the theory of INVERSION, in which all chords which do not consist of superimposed thirds (*i.e.* are not in ROOT position) are held to be inverted positions of, and to derive their harmonic function from, chords which do; and (*b*) the theory of the FUNDAMENTAL BASS, in which the successive roots of a series of chords, represented as notes on a staff or, as is now more usual, by Roman numerals, are held, as a consequence of the theory of inversion, to give the clearest picture of the harmonic functions of the chords. In the following phrase the figures (*v.* FIGURED BASS) show the position of a chord ($^{5}_{3}$ is a root position; $^{6}_{3}$ is a first inversion; $^{6}_{5}{}_{3}$ is the first inversion of a seventh chord), the Roman numerals represent the fundamental bass (b denotes first inversion) according to the degrees of the scale, and the notes on the staff are the notes of the fundamental bass:

The progression, or movement, in the example is from the tonic to the dominant. Of the chords within a key, the tonic is a point of rest, the dominant and subdominant play the most important parts in harmonic movement, and the other chords, except the LEADING-NOTE CHORD, have subsidiary functions. The leading-note chord acquires from its bass-note the tendency to "lead" to the tonic. In addition it has two notes in common with the dominant, so that it may precede the tonic in a cadence in the same way as does a dominant, though with less finality. The sense of movement arising from chord-relations within a key is the most important property of harmony. Since key-relations arise from chord-relations, the sense of movement is carried over with enhanced quality into modulation. In a larger context it becomes the sense of movement arising from the key-design of forms as wholes.

Harmonic relations between different keys, and the possibility and functioning of MODULATION, depend on the fact that a chord may exist in several keys and can assume the function appropriate to it in each of those keys. For example

is the dominant in C and the tonic in G, and

is the submediant in C and the supertonic in G. The further fact that the relationships of keys retain the same functions as the relationships of the corresponding chords within the key makes us hear a modulation to the dominant of C:

as merely a more emphasised form of a progression to the dominant in C:

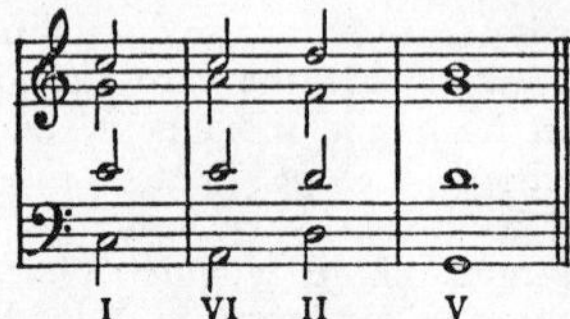

A dominant or a leading-note chord used in this way can not only supply emphasis to a cadence in a short form such as a hymn-tune, but also precede a chord on any degree of the scale, and so enable a simple harmonic progression to become the basis of an extended passage:

In the larger context of forms as a whole such harmonic relationships of keys are the basis of the harmonic design of all 18th- and 19th-cent. forms, however extended the scope of the keys involved, and however numerous the incidental modulations. The key-design of SONATA FORM, which may be represented thus: Tonic ——— Dominant ‖ Free modulations ——— Tonic ‖ is the same, in an enlarged version, as that of the earlier BINARY FORM, and its principle is still valid in, for example, the first movement of Hindemith's second sonata for piano, which has this harmonic plan:

	Exposition	Development	Recapitulation	Coda
Keys:	G F	Modulation	G B C G	G

Another important property of harmony, which is primarily a property of single chords, is the sense of movement caused by the use of discords. The movement from (comparative) discord to (comparative) concord is a movement from tension to relaxation. Since only an octave or a unison is completely consonant, the progression

involves this kind of movement just as does the progression:

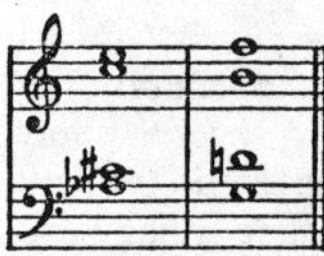

since both are movements towards relative consonance. The principles and effects of the movement from relaxation to tension to relaxation are the same whether the general level of dissonance is relatively low, as in the 18th cent., or high, as in the 20th.

The richness of colour in 19th-cent. harmony, with its increasing complexity of detail, resulted from the extension of the function of chromatic chords (such as the Neapolitan sixth and augmented sixth chord) within a key to their relations to other keys, from the growing chromaticism of melody, which suggested and necessitated new forms of harmonic relations, and from a more continuous use of dissonance to achieve dramatic tension.

E. C. BAIRSTOW : *Counterpoint and Harmony* (1937).
P. C. BUCK : *Unfigured Harmony* (2nd ed. 1920).
M. CARNER : *A Study of Twentieth-Century Harmony*, vol. II (1942).
P. HINDEMITH : *A Concentrated Course in Traditional Harmony*, 2 vols. (1943, 1953).
R. LENORMAND : *A Study of Twentieth-Century Harmony*, vol. I (2nd ed., 1940).
R. O. MORRIS : *Foundations of Practical Harmony and Counterpoint* (1931).
W. PISTON : *Harmony* (1941).
A. SCHOENBERG : *Theory of Harmony* (1948; abridged translation of *Harmonielehre*, 3rd ed., 1921).
M. SHIRLAW : *The Theory of Harmony* (1917).
P. WISHART : *Harmony* (1956).

Harold en Italie [a-rolld ũn nee-ta-lee] (Harold in Italy). Symphony with viola *obbligato* by Berlioz, Op. 16 (1834). The titles of the four movements are:

I. *Harold aux montagnes: scènes de mélancolie, de bonheur et de joie* (Harold in the mountains: scenes of melancholy, happiness and joy).
II. *Marche de pèlerins, chantant la prière du soir* (March of pilgrims, singing the evening prayer).
III. *Sérénade d'un montagnard des Abruzzes à sa maîtresse* (Serenade of a highlander in the Abruzzi to his mistress).
IV. *Orgie de brigands: souvenirs de scènes précédentes* (Brigands' orgy: recollections of earlier scenes).

Harold is represented by the solo viola and by a recurring theme borrowed from Berlioz's *Rob Roy* overture. The use of a solo viola, unusual at this period, is due indirectly to Paganini, who had asked Berlioz to write a piece for this instrument. In spite of the title the work has only a remote connection with Byron's *Childe Harold's Pilgrimage*. Berlioz says that it is in part a recollection of his own wanderings in the Abruzzi and that his intention was that the viola should represent " a sort of poetic dreamer of a similar type to Byron's Childe Harold " (*Mémoires*, chap. xlv, English edition by Ernest Newman, p. 202).

Harp (*Fr.* harpe, *G.* Harfe, *I.* arpa). An instrument which has a long recorded history from the Sumerians and Babylonians to the present day. In the tomb of Rameses III (*c.* 1200 B.C.) are depicted two decorated vertical harps each about 7 ft. high. In the West the harp was played in Ireland in the early Middle Ages, and is frequently mentioned and depicted in Europe in the centuries before the Renaissance. Harpers were attached to royal courts from the 15th cent.

The Bavarians Hochbrucker and Vetter devised about 1720 the first pedal mechanism, enabling the harp to be played in sharp keys as well as diatonically. The modern double action harp with 7 pedals dates from 1820, and is due to Sébastien Érard. Its normal key is C♭, and each pedal raises its strings a semitone when pressed half-way down, and a whole tone when pressed down fully. The compass is from

8ve lower

to

Since then the harp has been used both as a solo instrument and as an occasional member of the symphony orchestra. The harp was used by Monteverdi in *Orfeo* (1607) and by Handel in *Esther* (1720). The last of Handel's *Six Concertos for the Harpsichord or Organ* (Walsh, 1738) is marked *Concerto per la Harpa* in a manuscript in the King's Library at the British Museum. Mozart composed a concerto for flute and harp, K.299, and it has been included in chamber music pieces by Debussy, Ravel, Roussel, Bax, and Hindemith.

H. J. ZINGEL : *Harfe und Harfenspiel* (1932).

Harp-Guitar, HARP-LUTE-GUITAR, HARP-LUTE. Instruments made by E. Light of London, *c.* 1800.

Harp Quartet. The name commonly given to Beethoven's quartet in E flat, Op. 74 (1809), from the *pizzicato* arpeggios in the first movement.

Harpsichord (*Fr.* clavecin; *G.* Flügel, Kielflügel, Klavicimbal; *I.* arpicordo, clavicembalo, gravicembalo, cembalo). A keyboard instrument of horizontal harp- or trapezoid-shape in which the strings are plucked by a quill or leather tongue attached to a jack, an upright piece of wood set in motion by the inner end of the key. References to such an instrument are found in the 14th cent. In the 16th cent. it was made occasionally in an upright form (depicted in Sebastian Virdung's *Musica getutscht*, 1511, as *clavicyterium*), more often in " grand " or " square " (virginal or spinet) form. The leading makers of the 17th cent. were the Ruckers family of Antwerp. In its developed form it had one or two (exceptionally three) keyboards (the second being used either for ease of transposing or for contrast of tone) and up to four stops, for 8 ft. and 4 ft. pitch and for producing special effects such as that of the lute. In the 18th cent. harpsichords were made in London by Tabel, a Fleming, and his pupils Schudi (Tschudi) and Kirkman (Kirchmann), and in Germany by the Silbermann family.

In the Baroque period the harpsichord was used as a solo instrument, in all forms of chamber and ensemble music (except the English viol music of the 17th cent.), and to accompany the voice in opera, cantata and oratorio. As an accompanying instrument its main function was to realise the harmonies indicated by the composer in the form of FIGURED BASS. During the second half of the 18th cent. it was dropped from the orchestra, and its place in solo and chamber music was taken by the piano. In the present century the use of the harpsichord has been revived for the performance of music of the Baroque period, and some modern composers (*e.g.* Poulenc, de Falla) have written concertos for it. Some contemporary makers are Dolmetsch, Goff and Goble in England, Pleyel and Gaveau in Paris, and Chickering and Challis in the U.S.A.

D. BOALCH : *Makers of the Harpsichord and Clavichord*, 1440-1840 (1956).
W. LANDOWSKA : *Music of the Past* (1926).
P. JAMES : *Early Keyboard Instruments* (1930).

Harris, (1) RENATUS : *b.* France, *c.* 1652 ; *d.* Salisbury, Aug. 1724. The most famous member of a family of organ builders. He built a number of cathedral organs and rebuilt the organ in Magdalen College, Oxford, originally built by his grandfather. His sons Renatus and John carried on the family tradition to the middle of the 18th cent.

(2) ROY: *b.* Lincoln Co., Oklahoma, Feb. 12, 1898. Composer. Studied in the U.S.A. and from 1926-28 with Nadia Boulanger in Paris. One of the most prolific of contemporary American composers, he has written 7 symphonies, works for chorus and orchestra and for unaccompanied chorus, chamber music, and a sonata and other pieces for piano. His work is distinguished by its use of American folksong (*Folksong Symphony*, *When Johnny Comes Marching Home* overture, etc.), asymmetrical rhythm, angular melody, and modal and polytonal harmony.

(3) WILLIAM HENRY: *b.* London, March 28, 1883. Organist and composer. Chorister at St. David's Cathedral. Studied at the R.C.M. under Parratt and others. From 1911 assistant organist at Lichfield Cathedral and teacher at the Birmingham and Midland Institute of Music. Organist, New College, Oxford, 1919; Christ Church, Oxford, 1929; St. George's Chapel, Windsor, 1933. Conductor, Oxford Bach Choir, 1926-33. Knighted, 1954. He has composed choral works with orchestra, church music and organ works.

Harrison, JULIUS: *b.* Stourport, March 26, 1885. Composer and conductor. Studied under Bantock in Birmingham. Has conducted the Beecham Opera Company, the British National Opera Company, and the Hastings Municipal Orchestra. Compositions include suites for orchestra, chamber music, piano pieces, a Mass, and songs.

Harsányi [horrsh′-ahn-yi], TIBOR: *b.* Magyarkanizsa, June 27, 1898. Composer. Studied at the Budapest Academy of Music and in 1923 settled in Paris. He has composed 2 operas, ballets, a violin concerto, a symphony, 2 suites and other orchestral works, *Divertimento No.* 1 for two violins and chamber orchestra, *Divertimento No.* 2 for string orchestra and trumpet, chamber music, and piano pieces.

Hart, FRITZ BENNICKE: *b.* Brockley (Kent), Feb. 11, 1874; *d.* Honolulu, July 9, 1949. Composer and conductor. Studied at the R.C.M. and settled in Melbourne, 1912, where he became director of the Conservatoire and conductor of the Symphony Orchestra. He was conductor of the Honolulu Symphony Orchestra from 1931 and taught at Honolulu University, 1937-46. He composed more than 20 operas, works for chorus and orchestra, orchestral works, piano pieces and numerous songs.

Hartmann [harrt′-mun], KARL AMADEUS: *b.* Munich, Aug. 2, 1905. Composer. Studied at the Munich Academy of Music and privately with Scherchen and Anton von Webern. Founded Musica Viva, an organisation for promoting performances of contemporary music, 1945. His compositions, which reflect his admiration for the work of Alban Berg, include 6 symphonies, concertos for various combinations of instruments, 2 string quartets, and the chamber opera *Des Simplicius Simplicissimus Jugend* (1934; performed, Cologne, 1949; revised, 1955).

Harty, HERBERT HAMILTON: *b.* Hillsborough (Ireland), Dec. 4, 1879; *d.* Hove, Feb. 19, 1941. Conductor and composer. Organist in Belfast and Dublin; settled in London in 1900, and in 1920 became conductor of the Hallé Orchestra in Manchester. His compositions include a symphony, a violin concerto and works for voices and orchestra. He also made a modern orchestration of pieces from Handel's *Water Music.* Knighted, 1925.

Harwood, BASIL: *b.* Woodhouse, Olveston (Glos.), Apr. 11, 1859; *d.* London, Apr. 3, 1949. Organist and composer of church music, organ works, and cantatas. Educated at Oxford and Leipzig. Organist, Ely Cathedral, 1887; Christ Church, Oxford, 1892-1909.

Háry János [hah′-ri yahn′-osh]. Ballad opera by Kodály, founded on Hungarian melodies, in five parts with prologue and epilogue. Libretto by Béla Paulini and Zsolt Harsányi, based on a poem by J. Garay. First performed, Budapest, Oct. 16, 1926. From it the composer made a suite for orchestra in 6 sections: *The Tale Begins, Viennese Musical Clock, Song, The Battle and Defeat of Napoleon, Intermezzo, Entrance of the Emperor and his Court.*

Hasse [huss′-er], (1) FAUSTINA BORDONI. *v.* BORDONI.

(2) JOHANN ADOLPH: *b.* Bergedorf (nr. Hamburg), March 25, 1699; *d.* Venice, Dec. 16, 1783. Composer. Tenor at the Hamburg Opera under Keiser, 1718-19, and at Brunswick, 1719-22. Went then to Naples and studied opera composition with Porpora and A. Scarlatti. Thereafter he was at Venice from 1727, at Dresden as *Kapellmeister* from 1734, at Vienna from 1764, and again at Venice from 1773 until his death.

He was in his time the most popular composer of Italian opera in the Neapolitan style. Burney wrote of him (*The Present State of Music in Germany*, ii, 349-50) after his visit to Vienna in 1772, when the work of Metastasio and Hasse was being compared with the new innovations of Calzabigi and Gluck, that he

> "succeeds better perhaps in expressing, with clearness and propriety, whatever is graceful, elegant, and tender, than what is boisterous and violent; whereas Gluck's genius seems more calculated for exciting terror in painting difficult situations, occasioned by complicated misery, and the tempestuous fury of unbridled passions."

Hasse also composed Masses and other church music, oratorios, and instrumental music. Modern ed. of the oratorio *La Conversione di S. Agostino* (1750) in *D.D.T.* xx, and of a concerto for flute and string orchestra in *D.D.T.* xxix-xxx, p. 33.

Hassler [huss'-ler], (1) HANS LEO: *b.* Nuremberg, Oct. 25-26, 1564; *d.* Frankfort, June 8, 1612. Composer and organist. Taught by his father and in 1584-5 by Andrea Gabrieli in Venice. From 1585 was organist to Octavian Fugger in Augsburg, from 1601-04 in Nuremberg, and from 1608 to his death at the Electoral chapel at Dresden. An accomplished master of polyphony and of the Venetian polychoral style, he also wrote secular choral music and compositions for organ. There are available in modern publications: *Cantiones Sacrae* for 4-12 voices in *D.D.T.*, ii; Masses in *D.D.T.*, vii; *Sacri Concentus* for 5-12 voices in *D.D.T.*, xxiv-xxv; Italian canzonets and *Neue teutsche Gesäng* in *D.T.B.*, v (2); Italian madrigals in *D.T.B.*, xi (1); keyboard works in *D.T.B.*, iv (2).

Hassler's song "Mein G'müt ist mir verwirret," published in his *Lustgarten neuer teutschen Gesäng* (1601) was adapted in 1613 to the words of the hymn "Herzlich thut mir verlangen" and subsequently to those used by Bach in his settings in the *St. Matthew Passion*, "O Haupt voll Blut und Wunden"; (O Sacred Head, surrounded). *v.* CHORALE.

(2) JAKOB: *b.* Dec. 17-18, 1569; *d.* Eger, 1622. Organist and composer. Brother of (1) and (3). Composed Italian madrigals and church music. Two organ compositions are printed in *D.D.T.*, iv (2), pp. 127-133.

(3) KASPAR: *b.* Nuremberg, Aug. 17, 1562; *d.* there, Aug. 19, 1618. Organist. Brother of (1) and (2). Edited collections of *Sacrae symphoniae*, including works of the former.

Hatton, JOHN LIPTROTT: *b.* Liverpool, Oct. 12, 1809; *d.* Margate, Sept. 20, 1886. Composer of operas, cantatas, church music, incidental music, and songs, of which "To Anthea" remained popular for some time.

Haubiel, CHARLES: *b.* Delta, Ohio, Jan. 30, 1892. Composer. Piano teacher at the Institute of Musical Art, New York, and subsequently (1923) assistant professor of composition and theory at New York University. Founder of the Composers Press (1935) for the publication of contemporary American music. He has composed a musical satire, incidental music for the stage, symphonic variations and other orchestral works, choral works and chamber music.

Hauer [how'-er], JOSEF MATTHIAS: *b.* Wiener Neustadt, Mar. 19, 1883. Composer and theorist. Developed and expounded in a series of pamphlets a technique of atonal composition based on groups of notes ("tropes") chosen from the twelve notes of the chromatic scale. In this system he has composed an oratorio, orchestral works, chamber music, piano pieces, and songs, mainly to poems of Hölderlin.

Haugtussa [hogue'-tooss-a] (Troll Maiden). A cycle of 8 songs by Grieg, Op. 67 (1896-8). Words from a collection of poems by Arne Garborg. "Haugtussa" is the name given to a girl who had the gift of seeing and hearing the trolls. The titles of the songs are:

1. *Det syng* (The singing).
2. *Veslemöy* (Little maiden).
3. *Blaabaerli* (Bilberry slopes).
4. *Möte* (Meeting).
5. *Elsk* (Love).
6. *Killingdans* (Kidlings' Dance).
7. *Vond Dag* (Evil day).
8. *Ved Gjaetle-Bekken* (By the brook).

Hauk [howk], MINNIE: *b.* New York, Nov. 16, 1852; *d.* Triebschen, Lucerne, Feb. 6, 1929. Operatic soprano. Appeared in the U.S.A., Covent Garden, London (1868), and subsequently in many cities of Europe. After 1881 made three world tours. Famous for her performance as *Carmen*, which she sang in the American *première* at the New York Academy of Music, Oct. 23, 1878. She retired in 1896.

Hauptmann [howpt'-mun], MORITZ: *b.* Dresden, Oct. 13, 1792; *d.* Leipzig, Jan. 3, 1868. Theorist, composer and violinist. Teacher of counterpoint, Leipzig Conservatorium from 1842, where his pupils included Ferdinand David, von Bülow, Joachim, Sullivan, and Cowen. His chief work on theory was translated into English as *The Nature of Harmony and Metre* (1888); and a selection of his letters as *Letters of a Leipzig Cantor* (trans. A. D. Coleridge, 1892). He also composed an opera, chamber music, and choral works.

Hauptwerk [howpt'-vairk]. *G.* Great organ.

Hausegger [howce'-egg-er], SIEGMUND VON: *b.* Graz, Aug. 16, 1872; *d.* Munich, Oct. 10, 1948. Composer and conductor. Studied at the Styrian Musikverein and Graz University. Conducted in Graz (from 1895), Bayreuth, Munich, Frankfort (1903-06), Glasgow, Edinburgh, the Hamburg Philharmonic Concerts (1910-20) and the Munich Konzertverein (1920-36). He was also director of the Munich Academy of Music, 1920-34. He composed 2 operas, symphonic poems, programme symphonies, 3 songs for baritone with orchestra, choral works (some with orchestra) and many songs.

Haussmann [howce'-mun] (Hausmann), VALENTIN. Late 16th-cent. composer and organist at Gerbstädt (Saxony). Wrote secular songs and instrumental dances (a selection is published in *D.D.T.*, xvi) and published works of Marenzio, Vecchi, Gastoldi, and Morley with German texts.

Hautbois [o-bwa], *Fr.* Oboe. The English equivalent from Elizabethan times to the 18th cent. was hautboy (also Hoeboy, Hoboy, etc.).

Haut-dessus [o-dess-ēē], *Fr.* Soprano.

Haute-contre [oat-cōntr], *Fr.* Alto.

Hawkins, JOHN: *b.* London, Mar. 30, 1719; *d.* there, May 21, 1789. Attorney, historian of music, writer, and editor. Member (from 1740) and historian (1770) of the Academy of Ancient Music. Member (from 1752) of the Madrigal Society. Editor of the *Compleat Angler* and the works of Samuel Johnson, and author of lives of Johnson and Walton. Knighted, 1772. His *General History of the Science and Practice of Music* in 5 volumes appeared in 1776, the same year as the first volume of Burney's history. The two were the first, and for many years the only works of their kind in English. Hawkins's *History* was reprinted in 1853 and in 1875 by Novello (London).

P. A. SCHOLES : *The Life and Activities of Sir John Hawkins* (1953).

Haydn [hide'-'n], (1) FRANZ JOSEPH: *b.* Rohrau (Austria), Mar. 31, 1732; *d.* Vienna, May 31, 1809. Composer. Showed early promise of musical ability, and was accepted at eight by Georg Reutter as a choirboy in St. Stephen's, Vienna. In 1749 he left the choir-school and taught, played, acted as assistant to Niccolo Porpora, and received some help from Count Fürnberg, for whom he wrote his first quartets (1755). In 1759 he became musical director to Count Morzin and wrote his first symphony, and in 1761 began his long period of service in the household of the Esterházy family. The greater part of each year was spent at the palace of Esterház, which Prince Nicolaus built in 1766, and there Haydn wrote the greater part of his compositions. His friendship with Mozart began in 1781. In 1784 he wrote 6 symphonies (Nos. 82-87) for the Concerts Spirituels in Paris, and in 1784 *The Seven Words of the Saviour on the Cross* (originally for orchestra; arranged for string quartet, 1787; for voices, 1796) for the Cathedral of Cadiz.

On the death of Prince Nicolaus in 1790 the musical establishment at Esterház was disbanded, but Haydn retained his title and salary, without duties. In 1791 he went to London with a contract from J. P. Salomon to write an opera, 6 new symphonies (Nos. 93-98), and 20 other pieces, and stayed in England for more than a year. There his music was warmly received. He attended the Handel Festival at Westminster Abbey, and became an honorary D.Mus. of Oxford. For his second visit, in 1794-5, he wrote the second set of 6 "Salomon" symphonies (Nos. 99-104). In 1795 Prince Nicolaus II reconstituted the household music, but Haydn's duties were light and he was able to complete the composition of the two great choral works, *The Creation* (1798) and *The Seasons* (1801).

Since there is no complete edition of Haydn's works, he is the only major composer since 1750 of whom it must still be said that his compositions are known as a whole and in detail only to a few specialists. The collected edition begun by Breitkopf and Härtel in 1907 was suspended in 1914. Of a new complete edition published by the Haydn

Society of Boston four volumes, containing symphonies 50-57 and 82-92 and 4 Masses, have appeared. A new German edition is in progress.

Of his work at the Esterházy court Haydn wrote: " There was no one about me to confuse and torment me, and I was compelled to become original." His originality and mastery of technical means are apparent in the symphonies, quartets, and stage works of the years 1761-1780, after a decade in which his work was modelled on that of the Viennese composers Reutter, Monn, and Wagenseil, and, especially in the keyboard works, on C. P. E. Bach. In the next decade (1781-90), partly under the influence of Mozart, his music achieved the maturity of expression and the balance between the harmonic and contrapuntal elements in design and texture which are the marks of the classical style, while retaining its individual traits of energy, warmth, and humour. His unflagging vitality and fertility of imagination enabled him to write in the final period of his life (from 1791) the 12 symphonies which are his best-known works in that form, and, inspired by his English experience of Handel, the two oratorios and 6 great settings of the Mass composed between 1796 and 1802.

His principal compositions are:

(a) ORCHESTRA: 104 symphonies; about 13 keyboard concertos; 3 violin concertos; 1 cello concerto; 2 horn concertos; 1 trumpet concerto; 5 concertos for two *lire organizzate*; *Sinfonia concertante* for violin, cello, oboe, and bassoon with orchestra.

(b) STAGE WORKS: About 18 operas, of which 5 are lost, and 4 marionette operas.

(c) ORATORIOS AND CHURCH MUSIC: 8 oratorios and cantatas; 2 solo cantatas; 12 Masses; 2 settings of the *Te Deum*; 3 of *Salve Regina*; one of *Stabat Mater*.

(d) CHAMBER MUSIC: 84 string quartets, the last unfinished; 31 piano trios; 125 *divertimenti* for baryton, viola, and cello; about 56 string trios; *divertimenti*, *cassations*, and *notturni* for various instruments.

(e) KEYBOARD MUSIC: 52 sonatas, of which 5 have been published with a violin part; 5 sets of variations; a fantasia.

(f) SONGS: 47 songs, 377 arrangements of Scottish and Welsh airs for the Scottish publishers Napier, Thomson, and Whyte.

M. BRENET : *Haydn* (trans. C. L. Leese, 1926).

K. GEIRINGER : *Haydn* (1947).

H. R. C. LANDON : *The Symphonies of Joseph Haydn* (1956).

R. HUGHES : *Haydn* (1950).

J. P. LARSEN : *Die Haydn-Überlieferung* (1939). *Drei Haydn-Kataloge* (1941).

E. F. SCHMID : *Joseph Haydn : ein Buch von Vorfahren und Heimat des Meisters* (1934).

(2) JOHANN MICHAEL: *b.* Rohrau, Sept. 14, 1737; *d.* Salzburg, Aug. 10, 1806. Composer. Brother of (1). Chorister at St. Stephen's, Vienna, 1745-55. Episcopal choirmaster, Grosswardein, 1757. Director of the orchestra of the Archbishop of Salzburg, 1762, and later organist at the Cathedral. Weber, Neukomm and Reicha were among his pupils. He composed 24 Masses, two Requiem Masses, 4 German Masses, and other church music, operas, oratorios and cantatas, 52 symphonies, serenades, divertimenti, 5 concertos, quintets, and other instrumental pieces. 3 Masses have been printed in *D.T.Ö.*, xxii, and an antiphon, an offertory, and 9 graduals in *D.T Ö.*, xxxii (1). In *D.T.Ö.*, xiv (2), are 2 symphonies, a Turkish March, 6 Minuets, and 2 divertimenti for orchestra, a string quartet, and a thematic index of his instrumental works.

H. JANCIK : *Michael Haydn* (1952).

Haydn Variations (Variations on a Theme by Haydn). A set of variations by Brahms on a theme (" St. Anthony Chorale ") taken from a *divertimento* for wind instruments attributed to Haydn. Published in two forms : (1) for orchestra, Op. 56a (1873), (2) for two pianos, Op. 56b (1873).

Haydon, GLEN: *b.* Inman, Kansas, Dec. 9, 1896. Musicologist. Educated at the University of California and the University of Vienna. Since 1934 head of the department of music at the

University of North Carolina. Has published *The Evolution of the Six-four Chord* (1933) and *Introduction to Musicology* (1941).

Hayes, (1) PHILIP: *b.* Oxford, Apr. 1738; *d.* London, Mar. 19, 1797. Organist and composer. Son of (2), whom he succeeded as professor at Oxford and organist of Magdalen College. Composed anthems, an oratorio, a masque, and an ode.

(2) WILLIAM: *b.* Aldgate (Glos.), Dec. 1705; *d.* Oxford, July 27, 1777. Organist and composer. Father of (1). Organist, Worcester Cathedral, 1731; Magdalen College, Oxford, 1734. Professor of music, Oxford, 1741. Composed church music, odes, and glees.

Haym [hime], NICOLA FRANCESCO: *b.* Rome, *c.* 1679; *d.* London, Aug. 11, 1729. Cellist, composer, and librettist. Came to England in 1704, and took part in Italian opera as player and arranger in collaboration with Clayton and Dieupart and from 1713 as librettist for Handel, Ariosti, and Bononcini. Wrote two sets of trio sonatas, a serenata, and church music.

Head Voice. The upper "register" of the voice, as distinct from the lower register ("chest voice").

Heart of Oak. A song in David Garrick's play *Harlequin's Invasion* (1759), set to music by William Boyce. It commemorates the British victories of that year, the *annus mirabilis*.

Heather (Heyther), WILLIAM: *b.* Harmondsworth (Middlesex), *c.* 1563; *d.* July 1627. Gentleman of the Chapel Royal and lay-vicar of Westminster Abbey. In 1627 founded the professorship of music at Oxford which is still called by his name.

Hebenstreit [habe'-ĕn-shtrite], PANTALEON. *v.* DULCIMER.

Hebrides, The. *v.* FINGAL'S CAVE.

Heckelclarina [heck'-ĕl-cla-reen'-a], *G.* Wooden instrument of the saxophone type made by the firm of Heckel of Biebrich. It is in B♭ and has a single reed. Its compass corresponds to that of the soprano saxophone.

Heckelphone. A double reed instrument corresponding to the French baritone oboe, with a range an octave below that of the OBOE. Used for the first time by Strauss in *Salome* (1905).

Heckelphone-Clarinet. Wooden instrument of the saxophone type designed for use in military bands. It has a single reed, and its compass corresponds to that of the alto saxophone.

Hegar [hay'-garr], FRIEDRICH: *b.* Basle, Oct. 11, 1841; *d.* Zürich, June 2, 1927. Conductor, composer, and violinist. Studied at the Leipzig Conservatorium. From 1863 to his death was in Zürich as choral and orchestral conductor, from 1876-1914 director of the School of Music there. His compositions include a violin concerto and other instrumental works, and music for male and mixed chorus and for voices and orchestra.

Heger [hay'-ger], ROBERT: *b.* Strasbourg, Aug. 19, 1886. Conductor and composer. Studied in Zürich and under Max von Schillings in Munich. Has conducted opera in Vienna, Munich, Berlin and London. In 1950 became president of the Munich Academy of Music. Has composed operas, 2 symphonies, a violin concerto, and other instrumental works.

Heidegger [hide'-egg-er], JOHN JAMES: *b.* probably in Switzerland, *c.* 1659; *d.* Sept. 4, 1749. Came to England in 1707, and became manager of the Opera House in the following year. Wrote the libretto of Handel's *Amadigi* (1715) and was his partner at the Haymarket Theatre, 1729-34. Pope refers to his ugliness in the *Dunciad*.

Heifetz [hy'-fets], JASCHA: *b.* Vilna, Feb. 2, 1901. Violinist, a pupil of his father until he entered the Music School at Vilna at the age of five. Subsequently studied with Leopold Auer in St. Petersburg. From 1912 onwards toured as a soloist with remarkable success. He became an American citizen in 1925. Among the works written specially for him are violin concertos by Walton, Gruenberg and Achron.

Heimkehr aus der Fremde, Die [dee hime'-cair owce dair fremd'-er]. One-act operetta by Mendelssohn. First performed privately, Berlin, Dec. 26, 1829. The first public performance was given at Leipzig, Apr. 10, 1851, and the first London performance, translated by H. F. Chorley as *Son and Stranger*, on July 7 of that year.

Heinichen [hine′-ish-ĕn], JOHANN DAVID: *b.* nr. Weissenfels, Apr. 17, 1683; *d.* Dresden, July 15, 1729. Composer and theorist. Pupil of Schelle and Kuhnau in Leipzig, where, after practising law for a short time in Weissenfels, he began the composition of operas. Was in Italy, 1710-16, and produced two operas in Venice. From 1717-20 *Kapellmeister* at Dresden, where he lived until his death. Besides operas he wrote church music and published a treatise on figured bass (first form as *Neu erfundene und gründliche Anweisung*, 1711; second and greatly enlarged form as *Der General-Bass in der Composition*, 1728).

F. T. ARNOLD: *The Art of Accompaniment from a Thorough-Bass* (1931).

Heintz [hynts], WOLFF: *d. c.* 1555. Organist in 1516 at Magdeburg, and from 1523 in Halle. Two 4-part settings of chorales by him were printed in Georg Rhaw's collection of 1544 (modern ed. by J. Wolf in *D.D.T.* xxxiv).

Heinze, BERNARD THOMAS: *b.* Shepparton (Victoria), 1894. Conductor. Studied at Melbourne University, in London at the R.C.M., in Paris under d'Indy and in Berlin, and conducted in various European cities. He returned to Australia in 1923 and was appointed to the staff of Melbourne University. Conductor, University Orchestra, 1924-32; Melbourne Symphony Orchestra, 1933-49. Knighted, 1949. Director, New South Wales Conservatorium, Sydney, 1956.

Heise [hice′-er], PETER ARNOLD: *b.* Copenhagen, Feb. 11, 1830; *d.* Ny Taarbaek, Sept. 12, 1879. Composer. Studied with Gade and at the Leipzig Conservatorium. Wrote operas, incidental music, and songs. His opera *Drot og Marsk* (King and Marshal; Copenhagen, 1878) was successful in Denmark, where it was revived in 1909 and 1922.

Heldenleben, Ein [ine held′-ĕn-labe-ĕn] (*A Hero's Life*). Symphonic poem by Richard Strauss, composed in 1898 and first performed, Mar. 3, 1899. In the section entitled "The Hero's Works of Peace" Strauss quoted themes from his own works.

Helicon. A name given to the tuba when made in the circular form used in marching bands (*Gr.* ἕλιξ = coil, spiral).

Hellendaal [hell′-ĕn-dahl], PIETER: *b.* Rotterdam, 1721; *d.* Cambridge, Apr. 26, 1799. Violinist and composer. Studied the violin with Tartini in Padua. He appeared in London in 1752, and lived in England thereafter, becoming organist of Pembroke College, Cambridge, in 1762 and of St. Peter's College in 1777. Instrumental works, glees, and psalms by him were published in Amsterdam, London and Cambridge between 1744 and 1780.

Heller [hell′-er], STEPHEN: *b.* Pest, May 15, 1813; *d.* Paris, Jan. 14, 1888. Pianist and composer. Studied in Vienna and toured Europe extensively. Composed about 150 pieces for piano.

Hellinck [hell′-ink], LUPUS: *b.* Diocese of Utrecht, *c.* 1495; *d.* Bruges, Jan. 19, 1541. Composer. Belonged to the choir at St. Donatian's, Bruges, in 1511; choirmaster from 1523 until his death. 11 4-part settings of chorales by him were printed in Georg Rhaw's collection of 1544 (modern ed. by J. Wolf in *D.D.T.*, xxxiv). He was for some time confused with Johannes Lupi.

Helmholtz [helm′-hollts], HERMANN LUDWIG FERDINAND VON: *b.* Potsdam, Aug. 31, 1821; *d.* Charlottenburg, Berlin, Sept. 8, 1894. Physiologist and physicist. While professor of physiology at Heidelberg he published in 1862 his *Die Lehre von dem Tonempfindung* (translated by A. J. Ellis as *On the Sensations of Tone as a Physiological Basis for the Theory of Music*, 1875, 2nd ed., 1885). This work is the basis of modern theories of consonance, tone-quality, and resultant tones.

Helmore, THOMAS: *b.* Kidderminster, May 7, 1811; *d.* London, July 6, 1890. Writer on church music. Became Master of the choristers, Chapel Royal, 1846; priest in ordinary, 1847. Edited a number of collections of plainsong melodies, hymns, and carols, including *A Manual of Plainsong.*

Hely-Hutchinson, VICTOR: *b.* Cape

Town, Dec. 26, 1901; *d.* London, Mar. 11, 1947. Pianist, composer and conductor. Educated at Eton and Oxford. Lecturer, Cape Town University, 1922-5. On the staff of the B.B.C., 1926-34. Professor, Birmingham University, 1934-44. Director of Music, B.B.C. from 1944 until his death. Composed a *Carol Symphony*, a symphony for small orchestra, a piano quintet, a string quartet, choral works and songs.

Hemiola (Hemiolia), *Gr.* (ἡμιολία, the ratio of one and a half to one, or $\frac{3}{2}$: *Fr.* hémiole, *G.* Hemiole, *I.* emiolia, *L.* sesquialtera). In medieval and Renaissance theory the proportion of $\frac{3}{2}$ in two senses:

(1) The interval of a perfect fifth, which has the vibration ratio 3 : 2, *e.g.*:

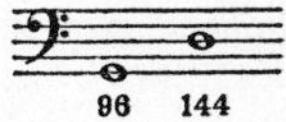

(2) The rhythmic relation of three notes in the time of two, *e.g.* of

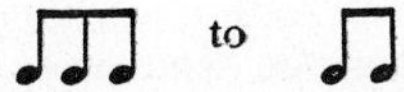

In the Baroque period the idiom was stylised in an instrumental form in the COURANTE, and in a vocal form exemplified in a favourite cadence of Handel (*v.* ACCENT). In the 19th cent. it was exploited most persistently by Chopin, *e.g.*:

CHOPIN, *Étude No.* 27

and by Schumann and Brahms.

Hempson, DENIS: *b.* Craigmore, Co. Londonderry, 1695; *d.* Magilligan, 1807. A blind harper who played throughout Ireland and Scotland. At the gathering of harpers in Belfast in 1792 he was the only one who played with the nails, after the traditional fashion. *v.* E. Bunting, *Ancient Music of Ireland* (1840).

Henderson, WILLIAM JAMES: *b.* Newark (N.J.), Dec. 4, 1855; *d.* New York, June 5, 1937. Critic and writer. Music critic, *New York Times*, 1887 ; *New York Sun*, 1902 until his death. Lecturer, New York College of Music, 1889-95; Institute of Musical Art, from 1904. His writings include *Some Forerunners of Italian Opera* (1907) and *The Early History of Singing* (1921).

Hen, The. *v.* POULE.

Henneberg [hen'-er-bair-yer], CARL ALBERT THEODOR : *b.* Stockholm, March 27, 1901. Composer, son of Richard H. (1853-1925), conductor and composer of German and Swedish origin. Studied at Stockholm Conservatoire and also in Vienna and Paris. His compositions include 5 operas, 5 symphonies, concertos for piano, cello, trumpet and trombone, and 2 string quartets.

Henry IV OF ENGLAND : *b.* Bolingbroke Castle (Lincs.), Apr. 3, 1367 ; *d.* Westminster, March 20, 1413. King of England, 1399-1413. The *Gloria* and *Sanctus* in the OLD HALL MANUSCRIPT under the name " Roy Henry," which are generally attributed to Henry V, are more probably by Henry IV.

Henry V OF ENGLAND: *b.* Monmouth, Aug. 9, 1387; *d.* Bois de Vincennes, Aug. 31, 1422. King of England, 1413-22. Had a " complete chapel full of singers " which went with him to France, and also maintained a large company of minstrels.

Henry VIII [ŏn-ree ĕe-eet]. Opera in four acts by Saint-Saëns. Libretto by Léonie Détroyat and Paul Armand Silvestre. First performed, Paris, Mar. 5, 1883. Reduced to three acts, 1889.

Henry VIII OF ENGLAND: *b.* Greenwich, June 28, 1491; *d.* Westminster, Jan. 28, 1547. King of England, 1509-47. Is said to have played well on the recorder, lute, and virginals, and was a composer, though of no great distinction. His compositions, which have been printed by the Roxburghe Club (ed. Lady Mary Trefusis, 1912), comprise 19 three- and four-part secular songs, 10 three-part instrumental pieces, and an antiphon "Quam pulchra es."

Henschel [hensh'-ĕl], GEORGE (originally Isidor Georg): *b.* Breslau, Feb. 18, 1850; *d.* Aviemore (Inverness), Sept. 10, 1934. Singer, composer, and conductor. Educated in Leipzig and Berlin. First sang in London in 1877. First conductor, Boston Symphony Orchestra, 1881-84. Settled in London, in 1884 as singer and conductor. Conductor, Scottish Orchestra, 1893-95. Retired and was knighted in 1914. His compositions include choral works and songs, 2 operas, and instrumental works. His *Musings and Memories of a Musician* was published in 1918.

Hensel [hen'-zĕl], FANNY CÄCILIA: *b.* Hamburg, Nov. 14, 1805; *d.* Berlin, May 14, 1847. Pianist and composer. Mendelssohn's elder sister. Wrote songs, part-songs, piano pieces, and a piano trio.

Henselt [hen'-zĕlt], ADOLF VON: *b.* Schwabach (Bavaria), May 12, 1814 *d.* Warmbrunn (Silesia), Oct. 10, 1889. Pianist and composer. Studied piano with Hummel in Weimar and theory with Sechter in Vienna. One of the great players of his age. From 1838 lived in St. Petersburg as court pianist. His compositions include a piano concerto, concert studies and other piano works.

Heptachord (*Gr.* ἑπτά, seven). A scale of seven notes, *e.g.* the modern major or minor scale.

Herbeck [hair'-beck], JOHANN FRANZ VON: *b.* Vienna, Dec. 25, 1831; *d.* there, Oct. 28, 1877. Conductor and composer. Conductor, Gesellschaft der Musikfreunde, Vienna, 1859-69 and 1875-77. Court *Kapellmeister*, 1866; conductor, Vienna Opera, 1871. In 1865 he obtained the manuscript of Schubert's *Unfinished Symphony* from Anselm Hüttenbrenner, and conducted its first performance on Dec. 17 of that year. He wrote 4 symphonies and other orchestral works, 2 Masses, 2 string quartets, and choral music.

Herbert, VICTOR: *b.* Dublin, Feb. 1, 1859; *d.* New York, May 26, 1924. Composer, conductor and cellist. Educated in Germany. Went to New York in 1886 and was active as cellist and conductor. Conductor, Pittsburg Symphony Orchestra, 1898-1904. Between 1894 and 1917 he composed a series of some 30 highly successful operettas. Also wrote a cello concerto, a symphonic poem, and other orchestral music.

Herbst [hairrbst], JOHANN ANDREAS: *b.* Nuremberg, 1588; *d.* Frankfort, Jan. 26, 1666. Composer and theorist. Some of his choral compositions were published in 1613 (*Theatrum Amoris*) and 1619 (*Meletemata sacra Davidis*). Was probably the first to disapprove explicitly of "hidden" fifths and octaves, in his *Musica poetica* (1643). Other theoretical works are *Musica practica* (1641) and *Arte prattica e poetica* (1653).

Hercules. Oratorio by Handel. Libretto by Thomas Broughton (after Ovid's *Metamorphoses*, ix, and Sophocles's *Trachiniae*). First performed, London, Jan. 5, 1745.

Heredia [eh-reh'-dee-ah], (1) PEDRO: *d.* Rome, 1648. Spanish composer of Masses and motets. *Maestro di capella*, St. Peter's, Rome, from 1630 until his death.

(2) SEBASTIAN AGUILERA DE: *v.* AGUILERA.

Hereford. *v.* THREE CHOIRS FESTIVAL.

Héritier [lay-reet-yay], JEAN L': *v.* L'HÉRITIER.

Hermannus Contractus: *b.* Saulgau (Swabia), July 18, 1013; *d.* Reichenau, Sept. 24, 1054. Composer and theorist. Trained at St. Gall, and became a monk of Reichenau. His theoretical treatises were printed in Gerbert, *Scriptores*, ii, pp. 124 foll. He composed the antiphon "Alma redemptoris mater," but not the "Salve regina," which was long attributed to him. His treatise *Musica* has been edited with an English translation (1936) by L. Ellinwood.

Hérodiade [ay-rod-yud]. Opera by Massenet. Libretto by Paul Milliet and Henri Grémont (*i.e.* Georges Hartmann), founded on a story by Flaubert. First performed, Brussels, Dec. 19, 1881.

Hérold [ay-rolld], LOUIS JOSEPH FERDINAND: *b.* Paris, Jan. 28, 1791; *d.* there, Jan. 19, 1833. Composer. Studied at the Paris Conservatoire. *Prix de Rome*,

1812. His first opera was produced in Naples in 1815. From 1816 to his death he composed operas and ballets in Paris. Is chiefly remembered by his operas *Zampa* (1831) and *Le Pré aux clercs* (1832), both first performed at the Opéra-Comique.

Hero's Life, A. *v.* HELDENLEBEN.

Herrmann [hairr'-mun], HUGO: *b.* Ravensburg, Apr. 19, 1896. Composer. Educated at Stuttgart and Berlin. Is now choral conductor in Reutlingen and director of the Donaueschingen Festival. Has composed operas, works for chorus and for orchestra, and instrumental music.

Hervé [air-vay]: *b.* Houdain, June 30, 1825; *d.* Paris, Nov. 4, 1892. Composer of operettas, whose real name was Florimond Ronger. Organist in Paris before beginning his career as composer in 1848 and as conductor in 1851. Wrote about 60 works for the stage, of which *L'Oeil crevé* (1867), *Chilpéric* (1868) and *Le Petit Faust* (1869) were the most successful.

Hervelois [airv-lwa]. *v.* CAIX D'HERVELOIS.

Hesdin [ay-dañ], PIERRE. 16th-cent. French composer, a singer in the chapel of Henry II of France, 1547-59. Masses, motets and *chansons* by him were published in collections of the time. A *chanson* was reprinted in 1897 in H. Expert's edition of Attaignant's volume of 1529.

Heseltine, PHILIP ARNOLD : *b.* London, Oct. 30, 1894 ; *d.* there, Dec. 17, 1930. Composer, editor and writer on music. Educated at Eton. Founded and edited *The Sackbut*, 1920. Edited with Philip Wilson 5 volumes of *English Ayres, Elizabethan and Jacobean.* Author of books on Delius (1923), Gesualdo (in collaboration with Cecil Gray, 1926), the English ayre (under the name Peter Warlock, 1926), and Thomas Whythorne (1925). His compositions, all published under the name Warlock, include *Capriol Suite* for orchestra, *The Curlew* for tenor, flute, cor anglais and string quartet and songs.

Hess, MYRA: *b.* London, Feb. 25, 1890. Pianist. Studied at the Guildhall School of Music and the R.A.M. First appeared in 1907 at the Queen's Hall, toured extensively in Europe, the United States and Canada and gave daily lunch-hour concerts at the London National Gallery during the war. She was made a D.B.E. in 1941.

Heterophony (*Gr.* ἑτεροφωνία, difference of sound). The simultaneous playing by two or more performers of differently treated forms of the same melody. The principle may have been used in Greek music, and is the basis of ensemble playing in China, Japan, and Java, *e.g.*:

Heugel [er-zhel]. A firm of music publishers in Paris, founded in 1812 by Jean-Antoine Meissonnier (1783-1857). It takes its name from Jacques Léopold Heugel (1815-83), who became a partner of Meissonnier in 1839, and is still directed by members of the Heugel family.

Heure Espagnole, L' [ler ess-pun-yol] (An Hour in Spain). Opera in one act by Ravel. A setting of the comedy by "Franc-Nohain" (Maurice Legrand). First performed, Paris, May 19, 1911.

Heward, LESLIE HAYS : *b.* Liversedge (Yorks), Dec. 8, 1897 ; *d.* Birmingham, May 3, 1943. Conductor and composer. Organist in Manchester. Composition scholar at the R.C.M. and assistant music master at Eton, 1917. Director of music, Westminster School, 1920. After conducting with the B.N.O.C. went to South Africa in 1924 as director of music of the Broadcasting Corporation and conductor of the Cape Town Orchestra. Returned to England in 1927 and was conductor of the Birmingham Orchestra from 1930 until his death. Compositions include an unfinished opera, works for orchestra, a string quartet, and songs.

E. BLOM (ed.) : *Leslie Heward* (1944).

Hexachord (*Gr.* ἕξ, six; χορδή, string).

A scale of six notes, adopted by Guido d'Arezzo and incorporated in medieval musical theory. There were three hexachords:

(1) *Hexachordum durum* (hard hexachord, requiring *B durum* or *quadratum*, the square B, otherwise B♮): G, A, B♮, C, D, E.

(2) *Hexachordum naturale* (natural hexachord, in which neither B♭ nor B♮ occurred): C, D, E, F, G, A.

(3) *Hexachordum molle* (soft hexachord, requiring *B molle* or *rotundum*, the rounded B, otherwise B♭): F, G, A, B♭, C, D.

(From *durum* is derived the German *dur* (major), from *molle* the German *moll* (minor), and from *B molle* the French *bémol* (flat). The French *bécarre* (natural) is a translation of *B quadratum.*) Each hexachord had the same succession of intervals: two tones, a semitone, and two tones. The range of notes in ordinary use was divided into seven overlapping hexachords:

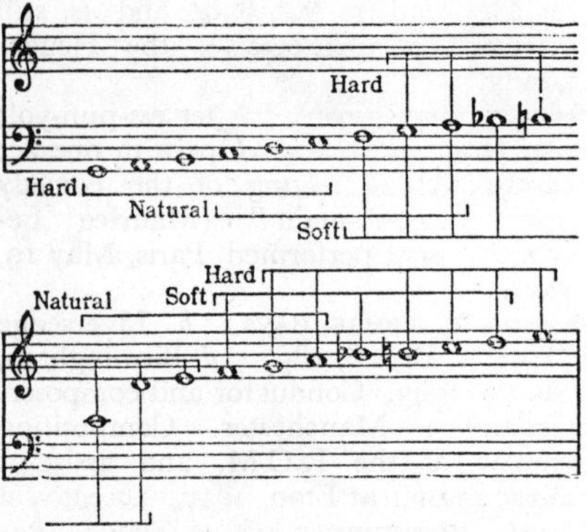

In teaching, the notes of the system could be indicated by their position on the "Guidonian" hand. The application of syllables to the notes of the hexachords was called SOLMIZATION.

In the 16th and 17th cent. many compositions used the hexachord as a *cantus firmus*. The idea was applied to the Mass (*e.g.* Avery Burton), to the madrigal (John Farmer, "Take time while time doth last," *E.M.S.*, viii, p. 59), and especially to instrumental music (examples by Byrd, Bull, and Sweelinck in the *Fitzwilliam Virginal Book*).

Heyden [hide'-ĕn], SEBALD: *b.* Nuremberg, 1499; *d.* there July 9, 1561. Theorist and composer. Cantor at the Spitalkirche, 1519. From 1537 rector of St. Sebaldus school. Wrote a theoretical treatise *Ars canendi* (1537) and composed church music.

Heyther, WILLIAM. *v.* HEATHER.

Hiawatha. Cantata in three sections by Coleridge-Taylor, Op. 30. Words from Longfellow's *Song of Hiawatha.* The three sections are:

(1) *Hiawatha's Wedding-Feast.* First performed, London, Nov. 11, 1898.

(2) *The Death of Minnehaha.* First performed, Hanley, Oct. 26, 1899.

(3) *Hiawatha's Departure.* First performed, London, March 22, 1900, when the complete work was given for the first time.

Hidalgo [ee-dahl'-go], JUAN: *d.* Madrid, 1685. Composer of the earliest Spanish opera to have partly survived, *Celos aun del ayre matan* ("Jealousy, even of air, is fatal"), libretto by Calderon, first performed, Madrid, Dec. 5, 1660. An edition was published by J. Subira in 1933.

Hidden Fifths and Octaves. *v.* SIMILAR MOTION.

Hieronymus de Moravia. *v.* JEROME OF MORAVIA.

Hill, EDWARD BURLINGHAME: *b.* Cambridge, Mass., Sept. 9, 1872. Composer. Educated at Harvard University and under Widor in Paris. From 1908 a member of the Faculty of Music at Harvard. Has composed works for orchestra, ballets, choral music, chamber music, piano pieces, and songs, and published *Modern French Music* (1924).

Hillemacher [eel-mush-ay], (1) PAUL JOSEPH WILHELM: *b.* Paris, Nov. 29, 1852; *d.* there, Aug. 13, 1933; (2) LUCIEN JOSEPH ÉDOUARD: *b.* Paris, June 10, 1860; *d.* there, June 2, 1909. Brothers who collaborated as composers under the name of P. L. Hillemacher. Both were educated at the Conservatoire and both won the *Prix de Rome* (1876, 1880). They composed operas, oratorios, an orchestral suite, songs and instrumental music, and wrote a life of Gounod (1905).

Hiller [hill′-er], (1) FERDINAND: *b.* Frankfort-on-Main, Oct. 24, 1811; *d.* Cologne, May 11, 1885. Pianist, composer and conductor. Studied with Hummel, 1825-27. Gave concerts in Paris, 1828-35, and was soloist in the first Paris performance of Beethoven's fifth concerto. Conductor and composer in Frankfort, Milan, Leipzig, Dresden, Düsseldorf, and finally Cologne from 1850, where he founded the Conservatorium. His compositions include 6 operas, 3 piano concertos, 3 symphonies, and numerous works in other forms. He published a number of books of criticism and commentary on the music and musicians of his time.

(2) JOHANN ADAM: *b.* Wendisch-Ossig, near Görlitz, Dec. 25, 1728; *d.* Leipzig, June 16, 1804. Composer. Studied music in Dresden and law in Leipzig. From 1758 was conductor there of various musical societies which he incorporated into the Gewandhaus Concerts, founded by him in 1781. He conducted the concerts until 1785, and from 1789-1801 was at the Thomasschule, where he succeeded Doles as cantor in 1797. One of the originators of the SINGSPIEL, of which he wrote a series of successful examples for the Leipzig theatre. His first, *Der Teufel ist los* (1766), to a text by C. F. Weisse, was derived from Coffey's *The Devil to Pay*, which was performed in Leipzig in 1750. In these scores Hiller followed English, French, and Italian models in adopting and developing the native *Lied* for stage purposes. His writings include a volume of musical biographies and textbooks on singing and the violin.

Hilton, (1) JOHN: *d.* Cambridge, March, 1608. Organist and composer. Lay-clerk, Lincoln Cathedral, *c.* 1584; organist, Trinity College, Cambridge, 1594. In the manuscript of his seven-part anthem "Call to remembrance" (ed. E. H. Fellowes, 1937) in the Bodleian library he is called "John Hilton, the elder." A five-part madrigal "Fair Oriana, beauty's queen" was included in *The Triumphes of Oriana* (*E.M.S.*, xxxii, p. 49).

(2) JOHN: *b.* 1599; *d.* London, March, 1657. Organist and composer. Possibly a son of the preceding. Parish clerk and organist, St. Margaret's, Westminster, 1628. Composed some church music and fancies for viols. Editor and part-composer of *Catch that catch can* (1652), a collection of catches, rounds and canons which initiated a long period of popularity for the catch in England.

Himmel [him′-ĕl], FRIEDRICH HEINRICH: *b.* Treuenbrietzen (Brandenburg), Nov. 20, 1765; *d.* Berlin, June 8, 1814. Composer. Studied under Naumann at Dresden and in Italy under the patronage of Frederick William II. Court *Kapellmeister*, Berlin, 1795-1806. Produced operas in Venice, Naples, and St. Petersburg. His "Liederspiel" *Frohsinn und Schwärmerei* (1801) and his opera *Fanchon, das Leiermädchen* (1804) were popular in Germany in the first half of the 19th cent. He also composed church music, instrumental music, and songs.

Hindemith [hind′-*er*-mit], PAUL: *b.* Hanau, Nov. 16, 1895. Composer. Studied under Arnold Mendelssohn and Bernhard Sekles at the Hoch Conservatorium in Frankfort. Leader, Frankfort Opera orchestra, 1915-1923. With Licco Amar founded the Amar-Hindemith Quartet, in which he played the viola. He was one of the leading figures in the Donaueschingen Festivals of contemporary music (1921-26), and taught at the Berlin Hochschule from 1927 to 1935. In 1934 a projected performance of his opera *Mathis der Maler* was banned by the Nazi government, and after spending some time in Ankara as musical adviser to the Turkish government, he went to America in 1939 and became professor of theory at Yale in 1942. He is now professor of composition at Zürich University.

One of the most versatile musicians of the day, he has achieved eminence as a composer, theorist, performer, teacher and conductor. The compositions written in the 1920's, which include several operas—*e.g.*, *Mörder*,

Hoffnung der Frauen (Murder, Hope of Women), 1921; *Sancta Susanna*, 1921; *Cardillac*, 1926; *Neues vom Tage* (News of the Day), 1929—on bizarre subjects reflecting the expressionist movement of the period, as well as many instrumental works, (*e.g.*, 6 chamber concertos, 4 string quartets, 2 violin sonatas, a viola sonata, and a cello sonata, solo sonatas for violin, viola, and cello, *Konzertmusik* for wind orchestra and for piano, brass, and two harps, and *Kammermusik* for 5 wind instruments) showed a free and highly resourceful treatment of traditional form and tonality. After 1927, when he observed that "a composer should write to-day only if he knows for what purpose he is writing," he was one of those associated with the idea of *Gebrauchsmusik* ("music for use"), and wrote compositions for player-piano and mechanical organ and pieces intended especially for amateur performance.

From about 1931 his style entered a new phase, marked by increased clarity of tonality and form and greater expressiveness of melody, which came to maturity in the opera *Mathis der Maler* (completed 1935; first performed, Zürich, 1938), the ballets *Nobilissima Visione* (1938) and *The Four Temperaments* (1940), the 3 piano sonatas (1936), the 3 sonatas for organ (1937-40), the violin concerto (1939), and a series of sonatas for solo wind instrument and piano. The new and more comprehensive theory of tonality on which these works were based was expounded in *Unterweisung im Tonsatz* (2 vols., 1937 & 1939; translated into English as *The Craft of Musical Composition*, 1941-2), and further exemplified in a set of preludes and fugues for piano (*Ludus Tonalis*, 1942) which were described as "Studies in Counterpoint, Tonal Organisation and Piano Playing." A composer of wide range and lively imagination and a teacher who sets high standards of practical and theoretical musicianship, he has had an important influence on the music of the past 20 years.

As Charles Eliot Norton professor at Harvard (1949-50) he gave a series of lectures which have been published as *A Composer's World* (1952). He has also published the text-books *A Concentrated Course in Traditional Harmony*, 2 vols., (1943, 1953) and *Elementary Training for Musicians* (1946). His principal compositions since 1931 are:

(a) ORCHESTRA: Concert Music for strings and brass (1930); *Philharmonic Concerto* (variations, 1932); symphony from the opera *Mathis der Maler* (1934); ballet, *Nobilissima Visione* (1938); *Symphonic Dances* (1937); symphony in E♭ (1940); overture, *Cupid and Psyche* (1943); *Symphonic Metamorphosis* on themes by Weber (1943); *Sinfonia serena* (1946); *Hérodiade* (after Mallarmé's poem, 1944) for chamber orchestra; symphony, *Die Harmonie der Welt* (1951), from the opera (1957).

(b) SOLO INSTRUMENTS AND ORCHESTRA: *Der Schwanendreher* for viola and small orchestra (1935); *Trauermusik* for viola and strings (1936); violin concerto (1939); cello concerto (1940); piano concerto (1945); clarinet concerto (1947); horn concerto (1949); *The Four Temperaments* for piano and strings (1944); concerto for trumpet, bassoon and orchestra (1949); concerto for wood-wind, harp and orchestra (1949).

(c) VOICES AND ORCHESTRA: Oratorio, *Das Unaufhörliche* (1931); *Plöner Musiktag* (1932); operas: *Cardillac* (1926; revised 1952), *Neues vom Tage* (1929; revised 1953), *Mathis der Maler* (1934), *Die Harmonie der Welt* (1957); "When lilacs last in the dooryard bloom'd" (Whitman, 1946); *Apparebit repentina dies* for chorus and brass (1947); *In Praise of Music* (revised version of *Frau Musica*, originally composed 1928).

(d) CHAMBER MUSIC: 3 pieces for clarinet, trumpet, violin, double bass and piano; 2 string trios; quartet for clarinet, violin, cello and piano; 6 string quartets; sonatas with piano for violin (4), viola, cello, double bass, flute, oboe, cor anglais, clarinet, bassoon, horn, trumpet, trombone; septet for wind instruments; sonatas for piano duet and for two pianos.

(e) SOLO INSTRUMENTS: 3 sonatas and *Ludus Tonalis* for piano; 3 organ sonatas; harp sonata.

(f) UNACCOMPANIED CHORUS: *Six Chansons*; *Five Songs on Old Texts*.

(g) SONGS : *Das Marienleben* (15 songs, 1922-3 ; revised 1948) ; *Nine English Songs* ; *La Belle dame sans merci*.

Hine, WILLIAM: *b.* Brightwell (Oxon.), 1687; *d.* Gloucester, Aug. 28, 1730. Organist and composer. Chorister and clerk of Magdalen College, Oxford. Organist, Gloucester Cathedral, 1710. Anthems and a voluntary for organ were published posthumously.

Hingston (Hingeston), JOHN : *d.* London, Dec., 1683. Organist and composer. Pupil of Orlando Gibbons. In the service of Charles I, Cromwell and Charles II. Composed fancies with organ accompaniment. He and William Howes signed in 1657 a petition for the founding of a national college of music.

Hipkins, ALFRED JAMES : *b.* London, June 17, 1826 ; *d.* there, June 3, 1903. Pianist and writer on musical instruments. Cultivated an interest in the harpsichord and clavichord, and in problems of tuning and pitch. Published *Musical Instruments, Historic, Rare, and Unique* (1888), with coloured illustrations by William Gibb, and *The Standard of Musical Pitch* (1896).

Hippolyte et Aricie [ee-pol-eet ay a-ree-see]. Opera with a prologue and five acts by Rameau. Libretto by Simon Joseph de Pellegrin. First performed, Paris, Dec. 1, 1733.

Hirsch [hirrsh], PAUL: *b.* Frankfort-on-Main, Feb. 24, 1881; *d.* Cambridge, Nov. 25, 1951. Musical scholar and amateur musician who formed a large and valuable library of music and books on music which was placed in the University Library at Cambridge when he moved to England in 1936. The library was bought for the nation in 1946 and now forms a unit in the music library of the British Museum. Four volumes of the catalogue of the Hirsch library were printed between 1928 and 1947, and a summary catalogue in 1951. Reprints in facsimile of some of the rare earlier works in the library have been edited by Johannes Wolf and others.

His [hiss], *G.* B sharp (B♯).

Hisis [hiss'-iss], *G.* B double sharp (B×).

Histoire du Soldat [eece-twarr dĕĕ sol-da] (The Soldier's Tale). Work by Igor Stravinsky (1918) to be "read, played and danced," based on a text by Charles Ferdinand Ramuz, for reader (optional), clarinet, bassoon, cornet, trombone, violin, double bass and percussion. The movements are *The Soldier's March, Scenes I, II, and III, The Soldier's March, The Royal March, Little Concert, Tango, Waltz, Ragtime, The Devil's Dance, Little Chorale, The Devil's Song, Great Chorale, Triumphal March of the Devil.*

History of Music. Some of the chief works in English are:

GENERAL: C. BURNEY, *General History of Music* (4 vols., 1776-89 ; modern ed. by F. Mercer, 2 vols., 1935). J. HAWKINS, *A General History of Music* (5 vols., 1776; reprinted 1853, 1875). C. H. H. PARRY, *The Evolution of the Art of Music* (1897). *The Oxford History of Music* (7 vols., 1929-34). C. V. STANFORD & C. FORSYTH, *A History of Music* (1916). P. LANDORMY, *A History of Music* (1923). P. A. SCHOLES, *Listener's History of Music*, 3 vols. (1923-29). W. H. HADOW, *Music* (1924). C. GRAY, *The History of Music* (1928). G. DYSON, *The Progress of Music* (1932). K. NEF, *An Outline of the History of Music* (1935). D. N. FERGUSON, *A History of Musical Thought* (1935). T. M. FINNEY, *A History of Music* (1935). A. EINSTEIN, *A Short History of Music* (1938 ; illustrated ed., 1953). H. LEICHTENTRITT, *Music, History, and Ideas* (1938). P. LANG, *Music in Western Civilisation* (1941). C. SACHS, *Our Musical Heritage* (1948 ; published in England as *A Short History of World Music* (1950). *The New Oxford History of Music* : vol. i, *Ancient and Oriental Music*, ed. E. Wellesz (1957) ; vol. ii, *Early Medieval Music*, ed. A. Hughes (1954).

PERIODS: C. SACHS, *The Rise of Music in the Ancient World* (1943). E. WELLESZ, *A*

History of Byzantine Music and Hymnography (1949). H. G. FARMER, *A History of Arabian Music to the 13th Century* (1929). G. REESE, *Music in the Middle Ages* (1940); *Music in the Renaissance* (1954). M. BUKOFZER, *Studies in Mediaeval and Renaissance Music* (1950); *Music in the Baroque Era* (1947). G. ABRAHAM, *A Hundred Years of Music* (1938; new ed. 1949). A. EINSTEIN, *Music in the Romantic Era* (1947). G. DYSON, *The New Music* (1924). C. GRAY, *Contemporary Music* (1924). A. SALAZAR, *Music in Our Time* (1948). H. J. FOSS (ed.), *The Heritage of Music* (studies of particular composers, 1550-1950), 3 vols. (1927, 1934, 1951). N. SLONIMSKY, *Music Since 1900* (1949).

COUNTRIES:

America: F. R. BURTON, *American Primitive Music* (1909). J. T. HOWARD, *Our American Music* (1931). A. COPLAND, *Our New Music* (1941).

China: J. H. LEWIS, *Foundations of Chinese Musical Art* (1936).

Czechoslovakia: R. NEWMARCH, *The Music of Czechoslovakia* (1942).

England: H. DAVEY, *History of English Music* (1921). P. A. SCHOLES, *The Puritans and Music* (1934); *The Mirror of Music, 1844-1944* (2 vols., 1947). R. NETTEL, *Music in the Five Towns, 1840-1914* (1944). E. WALKER, *A History of Music in England*, revised and enlarged by J. A. WESTRUP (1952).

France: G. JEAN-AUBRY, *French Music of Today* (1919). E. B. HILL, *Modern French Music* (1924). M. COOPER, *French Music from the Death of Berlioz to the Death of Fauré* (1951).

Hungary: G. CALDY, *A History of Hungarian Music* (1903).

India: A. H. FOX STRANGWAYS, *Music of Hindostan* (1914). A. B. FYZEE-RAHAMIN, *The Music of India* (1925).

Ireland: W. H. GRATTAN FLOOD, *A History of Irish Music* (1905).

Japan: F. T. PIGGOTT, *The Music of the Japanese* (1909).

Java: J. KUNST, *The Music of Java* (2 vols., 1949).

Jews: A. Z. IDELSOHN, *Jewish Music in its Historical Development* (1929).

Latin America: C. SEEGER, *Music in Latin America* (1942). N. SLONIMSKY, *Music of Latin America* (1945).

Mexico: R. STEVENSON, *Music in Mexico* (1952).

Norway: B. QVAMME, *Norwegian Music and Composers* (1949).

Russia: M. MONTAGUE-NATHAN, *A History of Russian Music* (1914). L. SABANEIEV, *Modern Russian Composers* (1927). G. ABRAHAM, *Studies in Russian Music* (1935); *On Russian Music* (1939); *Eight Soviet Composers* (1943).

Scotland: H. G. FARMER, *History of Scottish Music* (1947).

Spain and Portugal: G. CHASE, *The Music of Spain* (1941). J. B. TREND, *The Music of Spanish History to 1600* (1926).

DICTIONARIES: E. BLOM (ed.), *Grove's Dictionary of Music and Musicians* (9 vols., 1954). W. APEL, *Harvard Dictionary of Music* (1951). A. E. HULL, *Dictionary of Modern Music and Musicians* (1924). P. A. SCHOLES, *The Oxford Companion to Music* (9th ed., 1955). E. BLOM, *Everyman's Dictionary of Music* (2nd ed., 1956). O. THOMPSON & N. SLONIMSKY (ed.), *The International Cyclopedia of Music and Musicians* (1946).

PERIODICALS (wholly or partly in English): *Acta Musicologica* (1931 foll.). *Journal of the American Musicological Society* (1948 foll.). *Journal of the Galpin Society* (for the history of musical instruments) (1948 foll.). *Journal of Renaissance and Baroque Music* (1946-7). *Modern Music* (1924-40). *Monthly Musical Record* (1873 foll.). *Musica Disciplina* (1948 foll.). *Musical Antiquary* (1909-13). *Musical Quarterly* (1915 foll.). *Musical Times* (1844 foll.). *Music and Letters* (1920 foll.). *Music Review* (1940 foll.). *Notes of The Music Library Association* (1944 foll.). *Proceedings of the Royal Musical Association* (1874 foll.).

ANTHOLOGIES: (a) Music: A. SCHERING, *History of Music in Examples* (1931; reprinted, 1950). A. T. DAVISON AND W. APEL, *Historical Anthology of Music* (Vol. i, to 1600, 1946; vol. ii, to *c.* 1780, 1950). J. WOLF, *Music of Earlier Times* (1930; reprinted New York *c.* 1948). C. PARRISH AND J. F. OHL, *Masterpieces of Music before 1750* (1952).

(b) Writings: O. STRUNK, *Source Readings in Music History* (1950).

(c) Pictures: G. KINSKY, *History of Music in Pictures* (1930.)

BIBLIOGRAPHY: W. D. ALLEN, *Philosophies of Music History* (1939; contains a list of histories of music from 1600-1930). E. KROHN, *The History of Music; An Index to a Selected Group of Publications* (1952; an index of the contents of periodicals).

H.M.S. Pinafore. Opera in two acts by Sullivan. Libretto by William Schwenk Gilbert. First performed, London, May 25, 1878.

Hoboe [ho-boh'-er], *G.* Oboe.

Hobrecht, JAKOB. *v.* OBRECHT.

Hochzeit des Camacho, Die [dee hockh'-tsite dess cah-mah'-cho] (Camacho's Wedding). Opera in two acts by Mendelssohn. Libretto by Carl August Ludwig von Lichtenstein (based on an episode from Cervantes's *Don Quixote*). First performed, Berlin, Apr. 29, 1827.

Hocket (*Fr.* hocquet, hoquet; *I.* ochetto; *L.* hoquetus, ochetus). The breaking of a melody into single notes or very short phrases by means of rests, particularly as used by composers and discussed by theorists in the 13th and 14th cent. It is found in parts for instruments (*e.g.* P. Aubry, *Cent Motets du XIIIe siècle*, ii, p. 221) and for voices (*e.g.* in the motets of Machaut, ed. Ludwig). Most often it is used in two parts at a time, so that one sings while the other has a rest. In some cases it may be based on a single melody which is shared by two voices. A *Credo* by Pennard of *c.* 1400 (*The Old Hall Manuscript*, ed. A. Ramsbotham, ii, p. 241) treats this melody:

as a hocket in the final section:

Hofer [hoaf'-er], JOSEPHA. *v.* WEBER (8).

Hoffmann [hoff'-mun], (1) EDUARD. *v.* REMÉNYI.

(2) ERNST THEODOR AMADEUS: *b.* Königsberg, Jan. 24, 1776; *d.* Berlin, June 25, 1822. Author and composer. Changed his third name from Wilhelm in honour of Mozart. Studied music and law, and was a civil servant until 1806. Conducted at the theatre in Bamberg in 1806 and in Leipzig and Dresden from 1813-16, when he re-entered the civil service in Berlin. Composed 11 operas (of which *Undine* (1816) was the most successful), a symphony, piano sonatas, and other works. Published essays on music, collected in *Fantasiestücke in Callot's Manier* (1814) where appears the character Johannes Kreisler who inspired Schumann's *Kreisleriana*. The style of his essays had considerable influence on the musical criticism of the Romantic period, and his stories were used as material for the libretti of a number of operas, including Offenbach's *Tales of Hoffmann* (1881) and Hindemith's *Cardillac* (1926).

Hofhaimer [hoaf'-hime-er], PAUL: *b.* Radstadt, Jan. 25, 1459; *d.* Salzburg, 1537. Organist and composer. Organist, Innsbruck, 1479; Augsburg, 1507; Salzburg, 1519. The leading German organist of his day and the founder of an important school of players and composers. Three- and four-part songs by him have been published in *D.T.Ö.*, xxxvii (2), pp. 31 foll., together with instrumental arrangements of them by later composers.

Hofmann [hoff'-mun], JOSEF CASIMIR:

b. Podgorze (nr. Cracow), Jan. 20, 1876; *d.* Los Angeles, Feb. 16, 1957. Pianist and composer. Played in public at six, toured Europe at nine, and made his first appearance in America in 1887. Studied with Anton Rubinstein, 1892-4, and toured extensively thereafter. From 1926-38 was director of the Curtis Institute of Music at Philadelphia. He composed a number of works for the piano, and a symphony and a "symphonic narrative" for orchestra.

Hogarth, GEORGE: *b.* Carfrae Mill (Berwickshire), 1783; *d.* London, Feb. 12, 1870. Writer on music. Critic, *Morning Chronicle*, 1830; *Daily News*, 1846. Editor of the *Musical Herald.* Published *Musical History, Biography, and Criticism* (1835) and *Memoirs of the Opera* (1851).

Hohoane. An anonymous keyboard piece called *The Irish Hohoane* (Gaelic *ochone*: alas!) is in the *Fitzwilliam Virginal Book*, i, p. 87. *v.* LAMENT.

Holborne, ANTHONY: *d.* 1602. Composer. He is described as "servant to her most Excellent Majestie" on the title-page of his *Cittharn Schoole* (1597), which contains in addition to his pieces six "aers" for three voices by his brother William. The latter are printed in *E.M.S.*, xxxvi (ed. E. H. Fellowes). Anthony also published *Pavans, Galliards, Almains and other short Aeirs* in 1599, and four dances in five parts by him were printed in Füllsack and Hildebrand's *Ausserlesener Paduanen* . . . (Hamburg, 1607). Other compositions are in John Dowland's *Varietie of Lute Lessons* (1610), which refers to him as Gentleman Usher to Queen Elizabeth. Three pieces by him are in *Musica Britannica*, ix.

Holbrooke, JOSEPH: *b.* Croydon, July 5, 1878; *d.* Hampstead, Aug. 5, 1958. Composer, conductor, and pianist. Studied at the R.A.M. Composed symphonic poems for orchestra, including *The Raven* (1900), *Byron* (1906), a setting of Poe's *The Bells* for chorus and orchestra, the operatic trilogy *The Cauldron of Annwen* (*The Children of Don*, 1912, *Dylan*, 1914, and *Bronwen*, 1929), chamber music, songs, and piano pieces. Also published a book on *Contemporary British Composers* (1925).

Holmès [ol-mez] (originally Holmes), AUGUSTA MARY ANNE: *b.* Paris, Dec. 16, 1847, of Irish parents; *d.* there, Jan. 28, 1903. Composer. A pupil of César Franck from 1875. Wrote 4 operas, of which one, *La Montagne noire* (1895) was staged at the Paris Opéra, and a series of symphonic poems or dramatic symphonies including *Irlande* (1882), *Pologne* (1883), and *Au Pays bleu* (1891).

Holmes, JOHN: 16th-17th century composer who was organist of Winchester Cathedral. His five-part madrigal "Thus Bonny-Boots the birthday celebrated" was printed in *The Triumphes of Oriana* (*E.M.S.*, xxxii, p. 77).

Holst (originally von Holst), GUSTAV THEODORE: *b.* Cheltenham, Sept. 21, 1874; *d.* London, May 25, 1934. Composer. Studied at the R.C.M. under Stanford. Played the trombone in the Carl Rosa Opera Orchestra and in the Scottish Orchestra. From 1907 director of music at Morley College and from 1919-24 teacher of composition at the R.C.M. His integrity of ideal and singleness of purpose enabled him to assimilate diverse elements into a style which fused vitality, clarity, and austere mysticism. His early interests were in folk-song (*Somerset Rhapsody*, 1907), and in Sanskrit literature and Hindu scales (*Hymns from the Rig-Veda* for voices and instruments, published 1911, and chamber-opera *Savitri*, composed 1908, produced 1916). The use of five- and seven-beat bars in this period is continued in the next, and is allied with greater harmonic tension (*e.g.*, clashes of unrelated triads) and larger orchestral and choral resources (*The Planets*, completed 1916, and *The Hymn of Jesus* for two choruses, semi-chorus and orchestra, 1917). In the later music Holst pursued his experiments in harmony (*Choral Symphony*, performed 1925; *Egdon Heath* for orchestra, 1927; and the *Choral Fantasia*, 1930), leading to polytonality (*Hammersmith* for orchestra, 1930, *Six Canons for equal voices*, 1932), and showed leanings towards neo-Baroque forms (*Fugal Overture* and *Fugal Concerto*, both completed in 1923) and parody (opera-ballet *The Perfect Fool*, staged in 1923). His principal compositions are:

(a) OPERAS: *Savitri*; *The Perfect Fool*; *At the Boar's Head.*
(b) ORCHESTRA: *Somerset Rhapsody*; *St. Paul's Suite* for strings; *The Planets*; *Fugal Overture*; *Fugal Concerto*; *Egdon Heath*; *Hammersmith.*
(c) CHORAL WORKS: *Hymns from the Rig-Veda*; *The Cloud Messenger*; *The Hymn of Jesus*; *Ode to Death*; Choral Symphony; Choral Fantasia.
(d) SONGS: 9 hymns from the *Rig-Veda*; 12 songs to words by Humbert Wolfe.

I. HOLST: *Gustav Holst* (1938). *The Music of Gustav Holst* (1951).
E. RUBBRA: *Gustav Holst* (1947).

Holzbauer [hollts'-bow-er], IGNAZ: *b.* Vienna, Sept. 17, 1711; *d.* Mannheim, April 7, 1793. Composer. *Kapellmeister* at Holleschau (Moravia), *c.* 1734. Director of music, Vienna court theatre, 1745-7; court *Kapellmeister*, Stuttgart, 1750; Mannheim, 1753, where he directed the orchestra in the period of its greatest fame, and wrote symphonies in the style of Stamitz. A thematic index of his 65 works in this form is given in *D.T.B.* iii (1), p. xliv. Composed 11 Italian operas and one German, *Günther von Schwartzburg* (Mannheim, 1777; modern ed. in *D.D.T.*, viii and ix). A string quintet in two movements is published in *D.T.B.*, xv, p. 61, and a thematic list of his manuscript chamber music in *D.T.B.*, xvi, p. xxxix.

Holzblasinstrumente [hollts'-blahss-in-stroo-men'-ter], *G.* Woodwind instruments.

Home, Sweet Home. A song in the opera *Clari, or the Maid of Milan* (London, 1823); words by John Howard Payne (1791-1852), music by Sir Henry Bishop. Its popularity led to the production of another opera by Bishop with the title *Home, Sweet Home* (London, 1829).

Homme armé, L' [lom arr-may]. The title of a 15th-cent. *chanson* which was more frequently used than any other as a *cantus firmus* for Masses. It was so used from the 15th cent. to the 17th in more than 30 Masses by various composers, including Dufay, Busnois, Caron, Faugues, Regis, Okeghem, de Orto, Basiron, Tinctoris, Vaqueras (these 10 have been published in the series *Monumenta Polyphoniae Liturgicae Sanctae Ecclesiae Romanae*, 1948 foll.), Obrecht, Josquin (2), Brumel, de la Rue, Pipelare, Senfl, Morales, Palestrina, and Carissimi. The tune and its words (first discovered in 1925) were:

A setting of the tune, without words, as a four-part *chanson* by Robert Morton is printed in J. Marix, *Les Musiciens de la cour de Bourgogne au XVe siècle* (1937).

Homophony. Music in which a single melody is supported by chords, whether indicated by FIGURED BASS as in the solo sonata and chorale of the Baroque period, or written out as in the general style of the classical and romantic periods, as distinct from monophony, heterophony and polyphony. Among the earliest examples are the Italian LAUDE and FROTTOLE and the metrical psalm tunes of the 16th cent.; for an example *v.* PSALTER.

Honegger [on-egg-air], ARTHUR: *b.* Le Havre, March 10, 1892; *d.* Paris, Nov. 28, 1955. Swiss composer. Studied in Zürich and at the Paris Conservatoire. With Satie, Milhaud, and Jean Cocteau he formed in 1916 the group *Les Nouveaux Jeunes* which later became *Les Six.* A prolific composer in many forms, he became known chiefly through *Pacific 231* for orchestra (1923), the oratorio *Le Roi David* (completed 1921), and his setting of Claudel's *Jeanne d'Arc au Bûcher* (completed 1935). He also composed operas, ballets, 5 symphonies, chamber music, piano music, and songs.

M. DELANNOY : *Honegger* (1953).

Hongroise [on-grwuz], *Fr. v.* ALL' ONGARESE.

Hook, JAMES: *b.* Norwich, June 3, 1746; *d.* Boulogne, 1827. Composer and organist. Worked at Marylebone Gardens, 1769-73; Vauxhall Gardens, 1774-1820. Wrote music for a number of stage pieces, songs (*e.g.* "The Lass of Richmond Hill," "The Blackbird"), concertos, sonatas, and choral music.

Hooper, EDMUND: *b.* Halberton (Devon), *c.* 1553; *d.* London, July 14, 1621. Organist and composer. Master of the children, Westminster Abbey, 1588; gentleman of the Chapel Royal, 1604; organist, Westminster Abbey, 1606. Two pieces by him were printed in Sir William Leighton's *Teares or Lamentacions of a Sorrowfull Soule* (1614), one in Thomas Myriell's *Tristitiae remedium* (1616), and three of his anthems in Barnard's *Selected Church Music* (1641). The *Fitzwilliam Virginal Book* contains an Almaine and a Coranto (ed. Fuller-Maitland and Barclay Squire, ii, pp. 309 and 312).

Hopak (Gopak) [go-pahk']. A Russian folk-dance in a lively 2-4 time, occasionally used by Russian composers, *e.g.* by Moussorgsky in his unfinished opera *The Fair of Sorochintsy.*

Hopkins, EDWARD JOHN : *b.* London, June 30, 1818 ; *d.* there, Feb. 4, 1901. Organist of the Temple Church, London, 1843-98. Composed church music and wrote *The Organ, its History and Construction* (1855).

Hopkinson, FRANCIS: *b.* Philadelphia, Sept. 21, 1737; *d.* there, May 9, 1791. Statesman and poet, generally regarded as the first American composer. Composed songs, *The Temple of Minerva* (1781) —an "oratorical entertainment" of which the music has not survived, and published *A Collection of Psalm Tunes with a few Anthems* (1770).

Hoquetus, *L.* HOCKET.

Horn (*Fr.* cor, *G.* Horn, *I.* corno). A brass instrument with a conical tube wound into a spiral, ending in a bell, and played with a funnel-shaped mouthpiece. Known in England since the early 18th cent. as the French horn, since it was in France that it was perfected as an orchestral instrument. In its modern form it is built in F (*v.* TRANSPOSING INSTRUMENTS) and equipped with three valves which progressively lower the pitch of the instrument's natural harmonic series and so make available a complete chromatic compass of:

(written a fifth higher in the score).

A particular type of instrument much favoured by players today has a switch which instantaneously turns it into a horn in B♭ *alto.* This facilitates the playing of the high notes. The low notes were formerly written in the bass clef an octave below their written pitch, *i.e.* a fourth below their sounding pitch. The modern practice is to write all the notes —in the bass clef as in the treble—a fifth higher than the sounding pitch. Stopped notes are played by bringing the hand into the bell: the sound produced is a semitone higher than the open note, and the tone is muffled. A similar effect is obtained by inserting a pear-shaped MUTE into the bell, except that the pitch remains unaltered. "Brassy" notes, whether stopped or open, are indicated by the terms *cuivré* (brassed) or *schmetternd* (blaring) and are played with increased lip pressure. The sign + over a note indicates that it is to be stopped; if the note is to be played *forte* it will automatically be brassy, since considerable pressure is necessary to play stopped notes loud.

The valve horn described above (*Fr.* cor à pistons, *G.* Ventilhorn, *I.* corno ventile) came into use towards the middle of the 19th cent.: the earliest parts written for it appear to be in Halévy's opera *La Juive* (1835). It was some time, however, before it was generally adopted. Its predecessor, which survived for several years after this date, was the natural horn without valves. It first came into use at the end of the 17th cent. as an improved form of the earlier hunting horn (*Jagdhorn*). 18th-cent. nomenclature was not always consistent. The following terms (respectively French, German and Italian) were, however, in regular use: *cor de chasse*, *Waldhorn* and *corno da caccia*. *Waldhorn* continued in use in Germany in the 19th cent. to distinguish the natural instrument from the one with valves (*Ventilhorn*). Bach wrote both for *corno* and for *corno da caccia*: attempts have been made (*v.* C. S. Terry, *Bach's Orchestra*, pp. 41-7) to show that he intended two different types of instrument, but the arguments advanced are not wholly convincing. The origin of the horn as a hunting instrument was not merely commemorated by the names *cor de chasse* and *corno da caccia*: it also influenced the practice of composers and the style of music written for it. Among early examples of its use are Carlo Badia's opera *Diana rappacificata* (1700), various concertos by Vivaldi, Bach's first Brandenburg concerto (1721), and Handel's *Water Music* (1715-17) and *Giulio Cesare* (1724), which employs four horns.

In the classical symphony of the later 18th cent. two horns were used as subsidiary instruments, frequently employed to sustain notes of the harmony but occasionally coming into the foreground, *e.g.*:

The characteristic open fifth (a) called, " horn fifth," resulted from the fact that the instrument was virtually restricted to the notes of the harmonic series. It remained an idiom even after the introduction of a third horn by Beethoven in the *Eroica* symphony (1803) and after the invention of valves in 1813. In order to be able to play in more than one key players used a series of " crooks "—additional pieces of tubing of varying lengths—to change the pitch of the instrument. The practice of writing the parts as if the players still used crooks persisted in scores until the end of the 19th cent., long after the valve horn in F had become the standard instrument. The modern practice of writing for the horn as a transposing instrument is a survival of this practice. The only means of playing notes other than those of the harmonic series on the natural horn was by " stopping " with the hand, which altered the pitch of the open notes but at the same time changed the tone-quality.

Concertos for the horn have been composed by Haydn, Mozart, Strauss and Hindemith, and chamber music including the horn by Haydn, Mozart, Beethoven, Schubert, Schumann, Brahms, Hindemith and Wellesz.

The name " horn " is also used, misleadingly, for two wood-wind instruments—the BASSET HORN, which is an alto clarinet, and the English horn or COR ANGLAIS, which is an alto oboe.

A. CARSE: *Musical Wind Instruments* (1939).

F. PIERSIG: *Die Einführung des Hornes in die Kunstmusik* (1927).

Horn, Basset. *v.* BASSET HORN.

Horn, (1) CHARLES EDWARD: *b.* London, June 21, 1786; *d.* Boston, Mass., Oct. 21, 1849. Composer and singer. Son of (2). Sang in and composed operas in London and Dublin, 1809-33. Went to America in 1833 and produced English operas in New York, 4 of his own composition. Was in England again, 1843-47, and then in Boston until his death. Now remembered by his song " Cherry ripe," he also wrote oratorios and glees.

(2) KARL FRIEDRICH: *b.* Nordhausen (Saxony), 1762; *d.* Windsor, Aug. 5, 1830. Composer and organist. Went to London in 1782 and became music master to Queen Charlotte and her daughters, and in 1824 organist of St. George's Chapel, Windsor. Composed some instrumental music and edited, in collaboration with S. Wesley, Bach's *Well-tempered Clavier*.

Horn, English. *v.* COR ANGLAIS.

Hornpipe. (1) A wind instrument with a single reed and a horn attached to each end, played in Celtic countries, and in Wales, where it was called Pibgorn, until the 19th cent.

(2) By the beginning of the 16th cent. applied to a dance in triple time and to its music. Hugh Aston's " Hornpipe " of

that time is an early example of English secular keyboard music (printed in J. Wolf, *Music of Earlier Times*, No. 24).

The following is the first section of a hornpipe from Purcell's *The Married Beau*:

About the middle of the 18th cent. its rhythm changed to 4-4 time and it seems to have acquired an association with sailors.

Horowitz [horr'-ov-its], VLADIMIR : *b.* Kiev, Oct. 1, 1904. Pianist, a pupil of Felix Blumenfeld. Played in Berlin, 1924, and rapidly acquired an international reputation. His career was temporarily interrupted by a severe illness, 1936-9. He married Toscanini's daughter Wanda, 1933.

Horsley, WILLIAM: *b.* London, Nov. 15, 1774; *d.* there, June 12, 1858. Organist and composer. Organist at several churches in London, and one of the founders of the Philharmonic Society. Composed glees, hymn tunes, and piano music, and published *An Explanation of the Major and Minor Scales* (1825).

Horwood, WILLIAM : *d.* probably Lincoln, 1484. Composer. Appointed in 1477 to instruct the choristers of Lincoln Cathedral. The Eton choirbook (*c.* 1500) contains a Magnificat and three antiphons (one now incomplete) by him.

Hothby, JOHN: *d.* Nov. 6, 1487. Theorist. Lectured at Oxford in 1435. Visited Spain, France and Germany, and settled in Florence *c.* 1440. Later he was at Lucca, was recalled to England in 1486, and died there. Some compositions are extant, and 3 theoretical treatises have been reprinted in Coussemaker's *Scriptores*, iii, pp. 328-34.

Hotter [hot'-er], HANS : *b.* Offenbach, Jan. 19, 1909. Baritone, Austrian by naturalization. Studied at the Munich Academy of Music. Began his career as an opera-singer in his twenties. A member of the Munich Opera since 1940. He has also sung at Covent Garden and is well known as a recitalist.

Hotteterre [ot-tairr] (Hotteterre-le-Romain), JACQUES: *b.* Paris; *d.* there, 1760-61. Flautist, author, composer and member of a numerous family of wind instrument makers and players many of whom played in Louis XIV's orchestra. He is sometimes confused with Louis Hotteterre who was royal flute-player at the Court in 1664. He spent part of his early life in Rome. He is believed to have been the first to play the transverse flute in the opera at Paris, *c.* 1697. He wrote *Principes de la Flûte traversière* (1707, and many later editions) and composed flute pieces, sonatas and suites for two flutes and continuo, and a tutor and pieces for the musette.

Howells, HERBERT: *b.* Lydney (Glos.), Oct. 17, 1892. Composer. Studied under Brewer at Gloucester and Stanford at the R.C.M. Teacher of composition, R.C.M. from 1920; director of music, St. Paul's Girls' School from 1936. Professor, London University, 1954. Has written works for orchestra, a concerto and a suite for strings, 2 piano concertos, a *Requiem*, *Hymnus Paradisi*, and *Missa Sabrinensis* for soloists, chorus and orchestra, organ and piano pieces, chamber music and songs.

Howes, FRANK STEWART: *b.* Oxford, April 2, 1891. Music critic and author. Studied at St. John's College, Oxford, and at the R.C.M., where he was appointed lecturer in 1938. He joined the staff of *The Times*, 1925, and became chief music critic, 1943. Editor, English Folk Dance and Song Society *Journal*, 1927. He has written *The Borderland of Music and Psychology* (1926), *William Byrd* (1928), *The Appreciation of Music* (1929), *Beethoven: Orchestral Works* (1933), *A Key to the Art Of Music* (1935), *The*

Music of William Walton (2 vols., 1943) and *The Music of Ralph Vaughan Williams* (1954).

Hubay [hoo'-bah-ee], JENÖ (Huber, Eugen): *b.* Budapest, Sept. 15, 1858; *d.* there, Mar. 12, 1937. Violinist and composer. Studied under Joachim in Berlin. Teacher, Brussels Conservatoire, 1882; Budapest, 1886. Composed operas, orchestral works, and concertos and other pieces for violin. His pupils included Szigeti and Jelly d'Aranyi.

Huber [hoo'-ber], (1) EUGEN. *v.* HUBAY.

(2) HANS: *b.* Eppenberg (nr. Solothurn), June 28, 1852; *d.* Locarno, Dec. 25, 1921. Composer. Studied at the Leipzig Conservatorium. Teacher, Basle Conservatoire, 1889; director, 1896-1918. He wrote 9 symphonies, 5 operas, chamber music, and works for chorus and for piano.

Hucbald : *b. c.* 840 ; *d.* St. Amand (nr. Tournai), probably June 20, 930. Theorist and monk of St. Amand. Wrote *De harmonica institutione* (published in Gerbert, *Scriptores* i, p. 104) but not *Musica enchiriadis* nor certain other treatises formerly thought to be by him.

Hudson, GEORGE: 17th cent. English violinist and composer. Member of the King's orchestra, 1661; composer to the court, with Matthew Locke, 1668. He composed music (with Lawes, Colman and Cooke) for Davenant's *The First Dayes Entertainment at Rutland-House by Declamations and Musick: after the manner of the Ancients* (1656) and (with Colman, Cooke, Lawes and Locke) for Davenant's *Siege of Rhodes* (1656), the first English opera.

Huë [ĕĕ], GEORGES ADOLPHE: *b.* Versailles, May 6, 1858; *d.* Paris, June 7, 1948. Composer. Studied at the Paris Conservatoire. *Prix de Rome*, 1879. He succeeded Saint-Saëns as a member of the Académie des Beaux-Arts in 1922. He composed operas, ballets, a pantomime, a *Romance* for violin and orchestra, symphonic poems and other orchestral works, incidental music for plays, choral works and songs.

Hufnagelschrift [hoof'-nahg-ĕl-shrift], *G.* Lit. "hobnail script." A type of plainsong notation used in Germany in the Middle Ages, so called from the shape of the notes.

Hugh the Drover. Ballad opera in two acts by Vaughan Williams. Libretto by Harold Child. First public performance, London, July 14, 1924. Mary's father (the Constable) has chosen John the Butcher for her husband, but she falls in love with Hugh the Drover who offers to fight with John for the prize of Mary. When John loses the fight he charges Hugh with being in Napoleon's pay as a spy and Hugh is put in the stocks. Mary comes to free him during the night, but being frightened by the sound of people approaching she gets into the stocks with him and is discovered there in the morning. She refuses to leave Hugh, her outraged father and John both disown her, and a fight follows between the supporters of Hugh and those of John, interrupted by the sergeant who has come to arrest the supposed spy. He recognizes Hugh as a loyal servant to the King and demands John for the army, thus leaving Hugh free to take Mary as his bride.

Hugo von Reutlingen [hoog'-o fon royt'-ling-ĕn] (Hugo Spechtshart): *b.* 1285 or 1286; *d.* 1359 or 1360. School cantor in Reutlingen, who in 1332 wrote a treatise entitled *Flores musicae omnis cantus Gregoriani* (published in 1488; reprinted in 1868). His *Chronikon* contained the words and melodies of songs of the flagellants (*Geisslerlieder*) such as were sung during the plague of 1349; modern ed. by P. Runge in *Die Lieder und Melodien der Geissler des Jahres 1349* (1900). *v.* also LAUDA.

Huguenots, Les [lay ĕĕg-no]. Opera in five acts by Meyerbeer. Libretto by Augustin Eugène Scribe. First performed, Paris, Feb. 29, 1836.

Hullah, JOHN PYKE: *b.* Worcester, June 27, 1812; *d.* London, Feb. 21, 1884. Composer and teacher. In 1839-40 he studied in Paris G. L. Wilhelm's method of teaching singing in classes, which he adopted with great success in England. He wrote on the system (*A Grammar of Vocal Music,* 1843) and on other musical topics, and composed 3 operas and many vocal works.

Hume, TOBIAS: *d.* Apr. 16, 1645.

Composer and performer on the *viola da gamba*. He published *Musicall Humors* (1605) which contained some pieces for the lyra viol, and *Captain Hume's Poeticall Musicke* (1607). Seven pieces by him are in *Musica Britannica*, ix.

Humfrey, PELHAM: *b.* 1647; *d.* Windsor, July 14, 1674. Composer. Began to compose when a chorister at the Chapel Royal. Sent to study in France and Italy by Charles II. Gentleman of the Chapel Royal, 1667; master of the choristers, 1672. Wrote anthems, odes, and songs.

Hummel [hŏŏm'-ĕl], JOHAN NEPOMUK: *b.* Pozsony, Nov. 14, 1778; *d.* Weimar, Oct. 17, 1837. Composer and pianist. As a boy he was a pupil of Mozart, gave concerts in Germany, Holland, and England, studied with Clementi in London, and from 1793 with Albrechtsberger and Salieri in Vienna. *Kapellmeister* to Prince Esterházy, 1804-11; Stuttgart, 1816-19; Weimar, until his death. The most important of his many works are the 7 concertos and other compositions for piano. He wrote 9 operas, chamber music, and choral music.

Humoresque. Occasionally used as the title of a piece of music, *e.g.* Schumann's *Humoreske*, Op. 20 and Dvořák's *Humoresque*, Op. 101, both for piano.

Humperdinck [hŏŏmp'-er-dink], ENGELBERT: *b.* Siegburg, Sept. 1, 1854: *d.* Neustrelitz, Sept. 27, 1921. Composer. Studied in Cologne under Hiller, and in Munich under Lachner and Rheinberger. Assisted Wagner at Bayreuth, 1880-81. Taught at Barcelona, 1885-6; Frankfort, 1890-96; Berlin, 1901-20. Composed 6 operas (of which *Hänsel und Gretel* (1893) far exceeded the others in popularity), incidental music, vocal works, and songs.

Huneker, JAMES GIBBONS: *b.* Philadelphia, Jan. 31, 1860; *d.* Brooklyn, N.Y., Feb. 9, 1921. Critic and writer. Studied the piano in Philadelphia, Paris and New York, and taught in New York, 1881-91. Thereafter wrote on music, drama, and art for various newspapers. Published *Mezzotints in Modern Music* (1899) and books on Chopin and Liszt.

Hungarian String Quartet. An ensemble formed in 1935 with the following players: Zoltán Székely, Sándor Végh, Dénes Koromzay and Vilmos Palotai.

Hunnenschlacht [hŏŏn'-ĕn-shluckht], *G.* (Battle of the Huns). Symphonic poem by Liszt (after a painting by Wilhelm von Kaulbach, representing the defeat of the Huns under Attila in 451). First performed, Weimar, Dec. 29, 1857.

Hunt, THOMAS: Composer. A madrigal of his was included in *The Triumphes of Oriana* (1601): modern ed. in *E.M.S.*, xxxii, p. 161. It has some interesting examples of dissonance between the natural and sharp seventh. His 4-part service has been edited by E. H. Fellowes.

Hupf auf [hŏŏpf owf], *G.* Lit. "hopping up." One of the names given to the NACHTANZ.

Hurdy-Gurdy. A medieval stringed instrument in which the tone was produced by the friction of a wooden wheel and the pitch was determined by stopping a string with rods actuated by keys. Instructions for making such an instrument were given by Odo of Cluny in the 10th cent., when it was called *organistrum*. It was still made in the 18th cent., especially in France. The *lira organizzata* for which Haydn wrote 5 concertos and 7 *Notturni* was an 18th-cent. form of the instrument. As a street instrument it was replaced by the street organ, to which the name was transferred.

Huré [ēē-ray], JEAN: *b.* Gien (Loiret), Sept. 17, 1877; *d.* Paris, Jan. 27, 1930. Organist and composer. Appointed to St. Augustin, Paris, 1925. Composed 3 symphonies, Masses, motets, and instrumental music. Published books on music, including *L'Esthétique de l'orgue* (1917) and *Saint-Augustin, musicien* (1924).

Hurlebusch [hŏŏrl'-er-bŏŏsh], KONRAD FRIEDRICH: *b.* Brunswick, 1696; *d.* Amsterdam, Dec. 16, 1765. Organist and composer. Lived in Hamburg, Vienna, Munich, Stockholm, and from 1737 in Amsterdam as organist. Composed operas, cantatas, overtures, and works for harpsichord. A concerto for solo violin accompanied by oboes, bassoon and strings has been published in *D.D.T.*, xxix-xxx, p. 273.

Hurlstone, WILLIAM YEATES: *b.* London,

Jan. 7, 1876; *d.* there, May 30, 1906. Composer and pianist. Studied with Stanford at the R.C.M., where he became teacher of counterpoint, 1905. Works include *Fantasie-Variations on a Swedish Air* for orchestra, much chamber music, piano pieces, songs and part-songs.

Hydraulis (*Gr.* ὕδραυλις water-pipes) An organ described in writings of the 2nd cent. B.C. and used in the Roman circus. The wind pressure was maintained by a water compressor.

Hygons, RICHARD : *d. c.* 1508. Composer. Vicar-choral of Wells Cathedral from 1549 ; one of the organists there in 1461-2 and master of the choristers, 1479-1508. His five-part " Salve regina " in the Eton choirbook is printed in *Musica Britannica*, xi.

Hymn. The Christian hymn is a poem sung to the praise of God. The modern hymn-book is a collection of hymns drawn from various times and places. Among the more important groups are:

(1) Early Eastern Hymns. One of the oldest hymns still in use is the evening hymn " Hail, gladdening Light " (trans. by John Keble), now sung to a tune by John Stainer. The greatest hymn-writer of the Syrian church was St. Ephraim (*c.* 307-373) whose hymns were written to counteract the doctrines of the earlier gnostic hymns of Bardesanes (*d.* 223). Many later Eastern hymns were translated and adapted by J. M. Neale in *Hymns of the Eastern Church* (1862), and are sung to modern tunes.

(2) Latin Hymns. The foundation of Western hymn-writing was laid by St. Ambrose (*d.* 397), and the iambic metre of the few hymns still attributed to him was adopted for the many hymns sung to plainsong tunes in the cycle of Offices in the Western church. In the later Middle Ages the most important development in hymn-writing was the rise of the SEQUENCE. Polyphonic settings of hymns and sequences, either free or based on the plainsong tunes (*e.g.* Dufay's settings in *fauxbourdon*) were written by many composers from the 13th to the 16th cent.

(3) Lutheran Chorales. The earliest collections of Lutheran hymns were edited by Johann Walther in 1524. Some were set to new tunes and others to tunes adapted from plainsong or from secular songs. Their number grew rapidly, especially in the 17th cent., and they were used for polyphonic treatment in a great variety of ways by German composers from Walther to Bach.

(4) English Hymns. The hymns sung in the English church in the 16th and 17th cent. were metrical translations of the psalms (*v.* PSALTER). The history of the modern English and American hymn began with the *Hymns and Spiritual Songs* (1707) of Isaac Watts, whose *Psalms and Hymns* was adopted as the hymnbook of the Congregationalists, and with the Methodist hymns of John Wesley, who published his *Collection of Psalms and Hymns* at Charlestown, Georgia, in 1737. In the 19th cent. new hymns were written by Bishop Heber, Keble, H. F. Lyte and others, and new tunes by Crotch, Elvey, Goss, Dykes, Stainer, Ouseley and others, and in America by Lowell Mason. Among the representative modern collections are *Hymns Ancient and Modern* (1861; revised, 1875; new edition, 1904 ; latest edition, 1950), *The English Hymnal* (1906 ; 2nd ed., 1933), *The Oxford Hymnbook* (1908), *Hymns of Western Europe* (1927), and *Songs of Praise* (1931).

W. H. FRERE : *Hymns Ancient and Modern, Historical Edition* (1909).

M. FROST : *English and Scottish Psalm and Hymn Tunes, 1543-1677* (1953).

J. JULIAN : *Dictionary of Hymnology* (1915).

C. S. TERRY : *The Four-part Chorales of J. S. Bach* (1929).

E. WELLESZ : *History of Byzantine Music and Hymnography* (1949).

Hymn of Praise (*G.* Lobgesang). Symphony-Cantata by Mendelssohn, composed in 1840. The setting of the text for chorus and soloists is preceded by three symphonic movements.

Hypoaeolian, Hypodorian, etc. *v.* AEOLIAN MODE, DORIAN MODE, etc.

I

Iberia [ee-beh′-ree-ah], *Sp.* A set of piano pieces by Albéniz, characterized by the use of the rhythms, harmonies and melodic idioms of Spanish popular music. A selection was arranged for orchestra by Arbós.

Ibéria [ee-bay-rya], *Fr.* No. 2 of Debussy's *Images* for orchestra. *v.* IMAGES.

Ibert [ee-bair], JACQUES FRANÇOIS ANTOINE: *b.* Paris, Aug. 15, 1890. Composer. Studied at the Conservatoire. *Prix de Rome*, 1919. Director of the Académie de France in Rome, 1937; Paris Opéra, 1955. His suite for orchestra *Escales* (1922) is often performed. His works include music for the theatre and films, orchestral and chamber music, and pieces for piano and for organ.

Idomeneo, RE DI CRETA, OSSIA ILIA ED IDAMANTE [ee-do-meh-neh′-o reh di creht′-ah oss-yah eel-yah ed ee-dah-mahn′-teh] (Idomeneus, King of Crete, or Ilia and Idamante). Opera by Mozart in three acts. Libretto by Giovanni Battista Varesco. First performed, Munich, Jan. 29, 1781. Idomeneo on his journey home from the Trojan War vows that if he is delivered safely over the stormy seas he will sacrifice to Poseidon the first living creature he meets after his arrival. When he lands he is greeted by his own son Idamante. Horror-struck, he tells him to fly with Electra (Agamemnon's daughter) and rule in Mycenae. After Poseidon sends a sea-monster to remind Idomeneo of his vow he resolves to kill his son but is saved from the deed when Poseidon's heart is melted by the devotion of Ilia (Idamante's betrothed), who wished to die with him.

Il Barbiere di Siviglia. *v.* BARBIERE DI SIVIGLIA.

Il Tabarro [eel tah-bahrr′-ro]. *v.* TABARRO.

Ilyinsky [eel-yeen′-ski], ALEXANDER ALEXANDROVICH: *b.* Tsarkoe-Selo, Jan. 24, 1859; *d.* Moscow, 1919. Composer. Studied at the Berlin Akademie and from 1885 was professor at the Music School of the Moscow Philharmonic Society. Composed an opera and other stage music, cantatas, orchestral music, chamber music and songs.

Images [ee-muzh]. (1) The collective title of three symphonic poems by Debussy, 1909:

(a) *Gigues.*

(b) *Ibéria* (Spain), in three sections: *Par les rues et par les chemins* (In the Streets and By-ways), *Les Parfums de la nuit* (The Fragrance of the Night) and *Le Matin d'un jour de fête* (The Morning of a Festival Day).

(c) *Rondes de Printemps* (Spring Roundelays).

(2) Also the title of two sets of piano pieces by Debussy (1905 and 1907).

Imitation. The use of the same, or similar, melodic material in different voices successively. If the imitation is exact or governed by a stated rule (canon), *e.g.* of AUGMENTATION or DIMINUTION, it is called CANON. Imitation, as the term is generally used, is less strict and extends over less than a complete phrase, usually over a short figure. It first came into wide use in the church style of the 16th cent., and thence became the basis of the *canzona*, the *ricercar* for instruments, and the English fancy (fantasia), *e.g.*:

BYRD: *Fantasia à 3*

FUGUE results from the systematic organisation of imitation with regard to key relationship. In the Classical and Romantic periods imitation is an occasional device, usually treated with some freedom. *v.* also INVERSION, RETROGRADE MOTION.

Immortal Hour, The. Opera in two acts by Rutland Boughton. Libretto adapted from the works of Fiona Macleod (pen-name of William Sharp). First performed, Glastonbury, Aug. 26, 1914. King Eochaidh, led by Dalua, the shadow-god, meets the fairy Etain and marries her. A year later a fairy prince, Midor, visits the court. Etain is impelled to follow him back to fairyland. Dalua touches Eochaidh, who falls dead.

Imperfect. (1) The INTERVALS of the third and sixth are imperfect consonances.

(2) In mensural NOTATION an imperfect note-value contains two of the next lower note-value, *e.g.* an imperfect breve = 2 semibreves. In the imperfect mode in that notation a long contains two breves; in imperfect time, shown by the sign C, a breve contains two semibreves; in imperfect prolation, shown by the absence of a dot in the circle or semicircle, a semibreve contains two minims. *v.* also PERFECT.

Impresario, L' [leem-preh-zahrr'-yo]. *v.* SCHAUSPIELDIREKTOR, DER.

Impressionism. A term used, by analogy with Impressionist painting, for the musical style of Debussy, Delius, Loeffler and other composers contemporaneous with the Impressionist movement. This style might with more aptness be called "symbolist," for Debussy, with whom it originated, developed his aesthetic ideas in the circle of Mallarmé, who regarded music as the symbolist art *par excellence*, and his music shows rather more evidence of suggestions from the work of the symbolist poets than from that of the impressionist painters. Paul Dukas wrote: "Verlaine, Mallarmé, and Laforgue provided us with new sounds and sonorities. They cast a light on words such as had never been seen before. . . . It was the writers, not the musicians, who exercised the strongest influence on Debussy." Debussy's first important essay in the style was the *Prélude à l'après-midi d'un faune* (1892), originally planned as a prelude, interlude and finale expressive of the imagery of Mallarmé's poem.

Impromptu. A title applied by early Romantic composers, *e.g.* Schubert, Chopin, to a short piece for piano which was thought to have something of the character of an extemporisation, or an air of delicacy and casualness. It was generally, however, perfectly clear in form.

Improperia [im'-prop-err-i-a], *L.* "Reproaches." Part of the Roman liturgy for Good Friday; sung in plainchant, and from the 16th cent. set also in homophonic style for choral singing. Since 1560 they have been sung in the Sistine Chapel to Palestrina's setting.

Improvisation. The improvising or extemporising of music is the art of spontaneous composition, variation or ornamentation. Its chief forms are the improvisation of one or more counterpoints on a given theme or CANTUS FIRMUS, of variations on a given theme or harmonic framework, of ornamentation which embellishes a given melody, and of a part of a movement, *e.g.* a CADENZA, or of a complete movement or set of movements on original or given themes. Since it is the nature of improvisation to be a creation of the moment, not recorded in notation, the style and content of improvisations of the past can only be inferred from the equivalent forms of written composition, from descriptions, and from the few examples given from time to time for instruction and emulation.

It may be assumed that plainsong melodies which existed before the use of NEUMES were improvised by the rearrangement, ornamentation and extension of the melodic idioms of a given MODE. In the medieval period the usual form of improvisation was the addition of a part or parts to a plainsong, often by a simple rule of thumb, as in ORGANUM (parallel fifths and fourths) and in "ENGLISH DESCANT" and FAUXBOURDON (parallel sixths with or without parallel thirds). Elementary composition was taught through improvising a part on a plainsong (*v.* SIGHT). Morley's *Plaine and Easie Introduction* (1597) was a development of this method. The melodies of BASSES DANSES were used in this period in a similar fashion, being treated as "tenors" on which one of the players improvised a running part in triple rhythm (*v.* M. BUKOFZER, *Studies in Medieval and Renaissance Music*, 1950, chap. vi).

With the increased use of instruments in the 16th cent. this form of improvisation was further developed in the extempore playing of variations (in Spanish, *glosas*, as in Ortiz's *Tratado de glosas* of 1553; in English, "divisions," as in Simpson's *Division-Violist* of 1659) on basses which became common property (*e.g.*, PASSAMEZZO, RUGGIERO, ROMANESCA) and on basses which were continuously repeated ("divisions on a GROUND"). At the same time the improvising of more extended polyphonic pieces became a recognised test of the musicianship of a keyboard player, and in the 17th cent. the ability to improvise an accompaniment on a FIGURED BASS became an essential part of a keyboard player's qualifications. When Matthias Weckmann competed for the post of organist in Hamburg in 1654 he was required to improvise on a *cantus firmus* and on its inversion, to improvise a motet on a given bass and a chorale prelude on "An Wasserflüssen Babylon," and to accompany a violin sonata from figured bass. The fame of J. S. Bach in his lifetime rested chiefly on the powers of improvisation which he showed in the well-known instances of the variations on "An Wasserflüssen Babylon" he improvised for Reinken and the fugue he improvised for Frederick the Great on the King's theme which became the basis of the *Musical Offering*. Handel used improvisation freely in playing his organ concertos, and Mozart and Beethoven were renowned for their improvising of cadenzas and of complete movements.

During the Baroque and Classical periods performers customarily embellished the composer's melody, especially in slow movements. Examples of the style in which Corelli is said to have ornamented his own music are printed in the edition of his *sonate da chiesa* by Joachim and Chrysander. The custom of inserting extempore cadenzas in operatic arias was adopted in the classical concerto, and became one of its most characteristic features. In the Romantic period the art of improvisation was cultivated by some pianists (*e.g.* Hummel, Liszt) and organists (*e.g.* S. S. Wesley, Franck, Bruckner). In modern times its display in performance has become the almost exclusive preserve of French organists, notably Marcel Dupré and André Marchal.

M. DUPRÉ: *Cours complet d'Improvisation à l'Orgue* (1937).

E. FERAND: *Die Improvisation in der Musik* (1938).

F. J. SAWYER: *Extemporization*.

Incidental Music. Strictly speaking, music for performance during the action of a play. Commonly used to denote a group of pieces written for a play, including overture and interludes, *e.g.* Beethoven's music for *Egmont* and Grieg's for *Peer Gynt*.

Incognita. Opera in three acts by Wellesz. Libretto by Elizabeth Mackenzie (after Congreve's novel). First performed, Oxford, Dec. 5, 1951.

Incoronazione di Poppea, L' [leen-co-ro-nahts-yo'-neh di pop-peh'-ah] (The Coronation of Poppaea). Opera with a prologue and three acts by Monteverdi. Libretto by Giovanni Francesco Busenello (*opera musicale*). First performed, Venice, autumn of 1642.

Incudine [een-coo'-dee-neh], *I.* = ANCUDINE.

Indy [dan͡-dee], PAUL MARIE THÉODORE VINCENT D': *b.* Paris, March 27, 1851; *d.* there, Dec. 1, 1931. Composer. From 1862-65 studied piano with Diémer and harmony with Lavignac, and after serving in the Franco-Prussian war became a pupil of César Franck in 1872. Franck,

Liszt and Wagner were the most important influences on his musical style, which shows in some works his interest in folksong and in plainsong. In 1894 he joined with Charles Bordes and Guilmant in founding the Schola Cantorum, where he taught composition until his death. He published a *Cours de composition musicale* (vol. i, 1897-8; vol. ii, part 1, 1899-1900; part 2, 1933) and biographies of Beethoven (1906) and César Franck (1911). His compositions include the operas *Fervaal* (Brussels, 1897), *L'Étranger* (Brussels, 1903) and *La Légende de St. Christophe* (Paris, 1920), symphonies, tone-poems (*e.g. Wallenstein*, a trilogy completed in 1882, *Istar*, 1896, and *Jour d'été à la montagne*, 1905), a *Symphonie sur un chant montagnard français* for orchestra and piano (1886), chamber music, piano music, and songs.

M. COOPER : *French Music* (1951).

L. VALLAS : *Vincent d'Indy*, 2 vols. (1946-50).

Inflection. *v.* PSALMODY.

Ingegneri [een-djeh-nyeh'-ree], MARC ANTONIO: *b.* Verona, *c.* 1545; *d.* Cremona, July 1, 1592. Composer. In 1568 became choirmaster at Cremona, where Monteverdi was his pupil. Composed Masses, motets, a set of Responsories for Holy Week which were until 1897 attributed to Palestrina, other church music, and madrigals (modern ed. of book i in *Istituzioni e monumenti dell' arte musicale italiana*, vi).

Inghelbrecht [a͡n-gel-bresht], DÉSIRÉ-ÉMILE: *b.* Paris, Sept. 17, 1880. Composer and conductor. From 1908 was associated with the Pasdeloup concerts as conductor; from 1932 with the Opéra Comique. Has composed symphonic poems, ballet music, chamber music, and piano works, and published *The Composer's World* (1954).

Inglot, WILLIAM: *b.* 1554; *d.* Norwich, Dec. 1621. Composer. Organist, Norwich cathedral, 1608. The *Fitzwilliam Virginal Book* contains two pieces by him: " A Galliard Ground " and " The leaves bee greene " (edition by Fuller-Maitland and Barclay Squire, pp. 375 and 381).

Innig [in'-i*sh*], *G.* " Heartfelt." Used by Beethoven and Schumann to suggest a quietly intense manner of performance.

In Nomine [in noh'-min-ay], *L.* " In the name [of the Lord]." A title used by English composers of the 16th and 17th cent. for an instrumental composition based on a plainsong theme. The origin of the term was an instrumental arrangement (found in the Mulliner Book, *Musica Britannica*, i, p. 30) of that part of the *Benedictus* of Taverner's Mass *Gloria tibi Trinitas* (*Tudor Church Music*, Vol. I, p. 148) which was set to the words " in nomine." Other composers of the time wrote new instrumental pieces on the same *cantus firmus*:

Words in original plainsong Glo-ri-a ti - bi tri-ni- tas

Words in Taverner's Benedictus In no-mi-ne

and the name was applied to the large number of such pieces written by various composers until Purcell.

Instrumentation. *v.* ORCHESTRATION.

Instruments. The instruments used in Western music may for general purposes be divided into five types: (1) *Woodwind*: recorder, transverse flute, and instruments using a single or double reed, even if sometimes made of metal, *e.g.* oboe, clarinet, bassoon, saxophone; (2) *Brass*: trumpet, cornet, bugle, French horn, trombone, and other lip-reed instruments; (3) *Percussion*: drum, cymbal, triangle, etc.; (4) *Keyboard*: harpsichord, virginal, clavichord, pianoforte, organ, celesta; (5) *String*: viol, violin, harp, lute, guitar. For the study and classification of instruments of various times and cultures according to acoustical principles Sachs and von Hornbostel devised in 1914 a system of terminology using five main categories: (1) *Idiophones*: instruments made of naturally sonorous material; (2) *Membranophones*: instruments using a stretched membrane; (3) *Aerophones*: woodwinds, brass, and instruments using a free reed; (4) *Chordophones*: instruments using strings; (5) *Electrophones*: e.g. etherophone and electronic organ.

The history of musical instruments is closely related to the history of musical styles and forms. In the 15th cent. instruments and voices were judiciously mixed to produce contrast of tone-quality and line. In the Renaissance families of instruments of similar qualities were developed, and were used interchangeably with voices of corresponding range. In the Baroque period string instruments were made in great variety, and compositions for instruments alone or in combination with voices were the most important musical forms. In the Classical period definite instruments from each type were combined to form a relatively unvarying orchestra. In the Romantic period the expressive possibilities of these and additional instruments of the same types were explored by the methods subsumed under the term ORCHESTRATION. *v.* also ELECTRONIC INSTRUMENTS, MECHANICAL MUSICAL INSTRUMENTS.

N. BESSARABOFF : *Ancient European Musical Instruments* (1940).
A. BUCHNER : *Musical Instruments through the Ages* (1956).
A. CARSE : *Musical Wind Instruments* (1939).
The Galpin Society Journal (1948 foll.).
F. W. GALPIN : *Old English Instruments of Music* (3rd ed., 1932).
A Textbook of European Musical Instruments (1937).
K. GEIRINGER : *Musical Instruments* (1943).
G. R. HAYES : *Musical Instruments and their Music, 1500-1750*, 2 vols. (1930).
A. J. HIPKINS : *Musical Instruments* (1921).
C. SACHS : *The History of Musical Instruments* (1940).
C. S. TERRY : *Bach's Orchestra* (1932).
R. WRIGHT : *Dictionnaire des instruments de musique* (1941).

Interlude. The term is occasionally used as the title for part of a complete composition, as by Paul Dukas for his *Variations, Interlude, et Finale* on a theme of Rameau (1903). It is applied in the sense of the German *Zwischenspiel* to an instrumental phrase between the lines of a song (Luis Milan, "Durandarte," song with lute, 1536, in Schering, *History of Music in Examples*, No. 96) or of a chorale (Bach, "Gelobet seist du" in Spitta's *Life of Bach*, Eng. ed., iii, p. 400). English organists were formerly in the habit of improvising interludes between the verses of a hymn. In a more general sense an interlude is an intermediate part of incidental music. *v.* ACT TUNE, ENTR'ACTE.

Intermezzo (*Fr.* intermède, *L.* intermedium). A play with music performed between the acts of a drama or opera. There are examples in the 16th cent., and the custom became general in the 17th cent., especially in Italy and France. In the first half of the 18th cent. the comic *intermezzi* of Neapolitan opera began to be performed as separate entertainments. The most famous is Pergolesi's *La serva padrona* which was first performed as two *intermezzi* in the composer's opera *Il prigionier superbo* (1733). It was soon widely performed on its own and gave the impulse to the cultivation of *opera buffa*, and indirectly of the French *opéra-comique*. In the 19th cent. the term was used, e.g. by Schumann (Op. 4) and Brahms (Op. 76, 116, 117, 118, 119), for a short piece for piano.

Interpretation. The activity of the performer in communicating the intentions of the composer, especially those that are not explicitly given by the notation. Since in the 19th cent. notation tended to become more explicit as to tempo, phrasing and dynamics, there would appear to be much less than formerly left to the interpretative ability of the performer or conductor. However, there will always be some parts of the composer's intention, over and above those expressed in the notation, which it must remain the responsibility of the performer to supply by dint of study and insight. Some special problems of certain periods have been made subjects of particular study, such as ornamentation in the 18th cent. and the rendering of continuo parts in the Baroque style. There are peculiar difficulties facing the interpreter of medieval music, both because the notation is very reticent about media of performance and other practical matters, and because tradition supplies no guiding principles. *v.* CONDUCTING.

F. T. ARNOLD : *The Art of Accompaniment from a Thorough-Bass* (1931).
R. T. DART : *The Interpretation of Music* (1954).
A. DOLMETSCH : *The Interpretation of the*

Music of the XVIIth and XVIIIth Centuries (2nd ed., 1946).

Interrupted Cadence. *v.* CADENCE.

Interval. The distance in pitch between two notes, which is expressed in terms of the number of notes of the diatonic scale which they comprise (*e.g.* third, fifth, ninth) and a qualifying word (perfect, imperfect, major, minor, augmented, or diminished). The number is determined by the position of the notes on the staff, the qualifying word by the number of tones and semitones in the interval. Thus

is always a third, while

is a major third, being a distance of two tones, and

is a minor third, being a distance of a tone and a half. Intervals of an octave or less are called simple intervals, those of more than an octave compound intervals. For the purposes of the theory of harmony compound intervals are regarded as the equivalent of the corresponding simple intervals (*e.g.* the tenth as the equivalent of the third) except in the cases of chords of the ninth, and the dominant eleventh and dominant thirteenth chords.

The terms perfect and imperfect are applied only to the octave, fifth and fourth, other intervals being major or minor. The terms diminished and augmented are applied to all intervals. The following table shows the intervals in normal use within and including the octave, reckoned from C, from F♯, and from G♭. The curved bracket indicates intervals which have the same sound, *i.e.* enharmonic intervals. Intervals in square brackets would not normally appear in the form shown, but in the enharmonic equivalent:

Name	Distance in tones	Examples (From C)	(From F♯)	(From G♭)
Unison	0			
Augmented unison	½			
Minor second	½			
Major second	1			
Diminished third	1			
Augmented second	1½			
Minor third	1½			
Major third	2			
Diminished fourth	2			
Perfect fourth	2½			
Augmented fourth	3			
Diminished fifth	3			
Perfect fifth	3½			
Augmented fifth	4			
Minor sixth	4			
Major sixth	4½			
Diminished seventh	4½			
Augmented sixth	5			
Minor seventh	5			
Major seventh	5½			
Octave	6			

In the theory of harmony, octaves, fifths, thirds and sixths, when perfect, major or minor, are counted as consonances; seconds, sevenths and all diminished and augmented intervals are counted as dissonances. An older terminology, based on the mathematical ratios of the intervals arrived at by exact divisions of the single string of the monochord, called the octave, fifth and fourth perfect consonances (having the simple ratios 1 : 2, 2 : 3, 3 : 4) and the third and sixth imperfect consonances (having less simple ratios). In so far as the theory of harmony is based on the triad, *i.e.* on the superimposition of thirds (*v.* CHORD), the fourth is in an anomalous position, being a perfect interval in physical structure and when used melodically, a consonance when used between the upper notes of a chord, *i.e.* as the inversion of a fifth, and a dissonance, *i.e.* requiring resolution, when used between an upper part and the bass, as in the second inversion of a triad. *v.* also ACOUSTICS, INVERSION.

Intonation. (1) The true or false judgement of pitch by a performer is referred to as good or bad intonation.

(2) The opening phrase (sung by the precentor, celebrant, or other person) of a plainsong melody, such as that of the Creed:

used by Bach in the first part of the *Credo* of the *B Minor Mass.*

Intrada [een-trah'-dah] (*Fr.* entrée). A term regularly used by German composers in the 17th cent. for the opening movement of a suite, and occasionally used later, *e.g.* by Mozart for the overture ("Intrade") to *Bastien und Bastienne* (K.50).

Introit. Liturgical music at the beginning of Mass, being the first part of the Proper of the Mass. Originally an antiphon and psalm, it now consists of an antiphon, a verse of a psalm, the *Gloria Patri* and the repeat of the antiphon.

Invention. A title used by Bonporti for violin partitas (*Invenzioni a violino solo*, Bologna, 1712) and by Bach for two-part pieces in contrapuntal style for clavier. The three-part pieces in the same style he called *sinfonie.* They were designed to help "lovers of the clavier . . . not alone to have good *inventiones* but to develop them well."

Inversion. (1) Of an interval. An interval is inverted when the lower note is sounded above the upper note, *e.g.*

inversion:

The number of an interval when inverted is found by subtracting it from nine. The inversion of a fifth is a fourth, of a third a sixth. The qualifying term of a perfect interval is unchanged by inversion, *e.g.* the inversion of a perfect fifth is a perfect fourth. A major interval when inverted becomes minor, a diminished becomes augmented, and vice versa.

(2) Of a melody. A melody is inverted when the intervals through which it proceeds are replaced by their inversions (also called contrary motion, and *per arsin et thesin*). Such an inversion may be inexact, as in Brahms's "How lovely is thy dwelling-place" from the *German Requiem*:

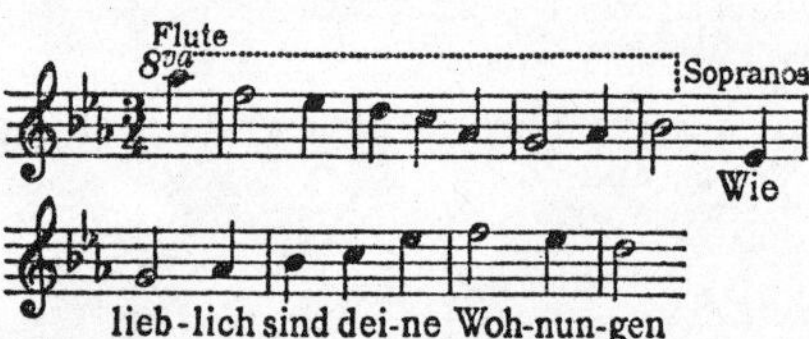

where the inversion follows the statement. In this particular case the second form was probably written first. Where the statement overlaps the inversion we have imitation by contrary motion, also called canon by inversion, as in four of the pieces in Bach's *Musical Offering* and in the Trio in double canon *al rovescio* (this term is used both for inversion and RETROGADE MOTION) in Mozart's Serenade for wind instruments, K.388:

This kind of canon is sometimes called " mirror " canon.

(3) Of a chord. A chord is commonly said to be inverted when its " root " is in an upper part instead of in the bass. A triad, *e.g.* :

has two inversions :

A seventh chord, *e.g.* :

has three inversions :

The theory of inversions, though generally accepted in the teaching of harmony and convenient as a means of describing chords, is however open to the objection that it ignores the functions of chords. A triad in " root position " is at rest. Its " inversions " are not; and the directions in which they are likely to move are not necessarily the same as those that would be taken by the chord in " root position." The theory becomes even more illogical when it is extended to more complex chords, *e.g.* when a diminished seventh chord is analysed as the inversion of a minor ninth with the " root " missing. If the " root " is missing, it is clearly not part of the chord. The theory of inversions is not only illogical: it is also historically unsound, since it ignores the fact that chords other than triads in " root position " derive for the most part from the use of passing notes and appoggiaturas. *v.* CHORD, FIGURED BASS, MODULATION.

(4) Of counterpoint. A piece of counterpoint is inverted when the melody which was originally in the bass is put in one of the upper parts. Counterpoint which is designed so that any one of its parts will make a good bass to the others is called "invertible counterpoint." If it is in two parts, it is in DOUBLE COUNTERPOINT, if in three parts, in TRIPLE COUNTERPOINT.

(5) Of the page. For examples of pieces so made as to be playable upside down, *v.* RETROGRADE MOTION.

Inverted Mordent. Common English term for the ornament introduced about 1750 by C. P. E. Bach and called *Schneller* until *c.* 1800, and *Pralltriller* since. It generally occurs on the upper of two notes in a descending second, and is indicated thus:

and played thus:

Invitation to the Waltz. *v.* AUFFORDERUNG ZUM TANZ.

Iolanthe, or The Peer and the Peri. Comic opera by Sullivan. Libretto by William Schwenk Gilbert. First performed, London and New York, Nov. 25, 1882.

Ionian Mode. (1) In ancient Greek music :

(2) From the 16th cent. onwards applied to :

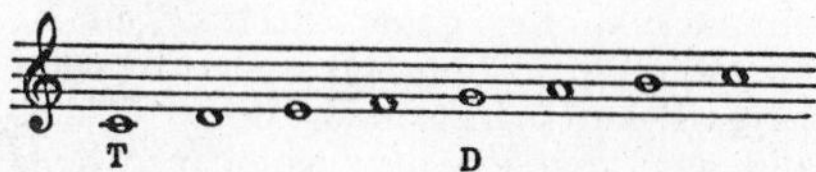

The tonic (or final) and dominant are marked respectively T and D. *v.* GLAREANUS, GREEK MUSIC, MODE.

Iphigénie en Aulide [ee-fee-zhay-nee ũn no-leed] (Iphigenia in Aulis). Opera in three acts by Gluck. Libretto by François Louis Lebland du Roullet. First performed, Paris, Apr. 19, 1774. The goddess Artemis, who has been made angry by Agamemnon, sends winds to prevent the Greek fleet leaving for Troy. Agamemnon offers to sacrifice Iphigenia (his daughter). When she arrives unexpectedly with Clytemnestra (Agamemnon's wife), Calchas (the high priest) declares this to be a sign from the goddess. Clytemnestra claims that Achilles (Iphigenia's bridegroom-to-be) has been unfaithful, but he denies it and is about to lead her to the altar when he is told that Agamemnon is going to sacrifice her. Achilles decides to try to save her from the Greeks by force, but the goddess appears and declares herself appeased and thus Iphigenia is free. Achilles bids farewell to his bride before his departure for Troy.

Iphigénie en Tauride [ee-fee-zhay-nee o͡n to-reed] (Iphigenia in Tauris). Opera in three acts by Gluck. Libretto by Nicholas François Guillard. First performed, Paris, May 18, 1779. After Agamemnon returned from Troy he was slain by Clytemnestra, who was later murdered by her son Orestes. Orestes, pursued by the Furies, consults the oracle of Apollo and is promised safety if he delivers his sister (Iphigenia) from Tauris (where she is a priestess of the temple against her will and longs to see her brother again). Orestes, however, not knowing that his sister is at Tauris interprets the oracle to mean that he is to carry off the statue of Diana. The Scythians capture Orestes and his friend Pylades and bring them as prisoners to the temple where Thoas (king of Scythia) orders that they should be sacrificed to Diana. Iphigenia, although she does not recognise Orestes, declares that she will save him in order that he may take a message to her sister Electra, but he threatens to kill himself if she does not save Pylades instead. When Thoas discovers that Pylades has escaped he is furious and demands that Iphigenia and Orestes shall die together on the altar. Pylades, however, returns with an armed band and stabs Thoas. Diana then tells the Scythians to give her statue to Orestes, promises him her protection and releases Iphigenia so that she may return to Greece with her brother and Pylades.

Ippolitov-Ivanov [eep-po-leet'-off eev-un'-yoff], MICHAEL MICHAELOVICH: *b.* Gatchina (nr. St. Petersburg), Nov. 19, 1859; *d.* Moscow, Jan. 28, 1935. Composer. Studied with Rimsky-Korsakov in St. Petersburg. Taught in the Conservatoire at Tiflis from 1882, in Moscow from 1893. Composed operas, tone-poems and suites for orchestra, cantatas, chamber music, and songs.

Ireland, JOHN: *b.* Bowden (Cheshire), Aug. 13, 1879. Composer. Studied under Stanford at the R.C.M., where he later became teacher of composition. He has written a few orchestral compositions, among them *The Forgotten Rite* (1913) and *Mai-Dun* (1921), a piano concerto (1930), a choral work *These Things shall be* (1937), and a great number of suites and single pieces for piano, song cycles and songs, besides some chamber music.

Irmelin. Opera in three acts by Delius. Libretto by the composer. First performed, Oxford, May 4, 1953.

Isaac [eez'-ahk], HEINRICH (Isaak, Hendryk): *b. c.* 1450; *d.* Florence, 1517. Composer. Was probably a Netherlander from Brabant, although the Italians called him "Arrigo tedesco" (Harry the German). He entered the service of Lorenzo de Medici in Florence in 1480, and of the Emperor Maximilian in 1497. During the remainder of his life he lived at Innsbruck, Constance, Ferrara, and Florence. He composed secular works to German, French, Italian, and Latin texts (modern ed. in *D.T.Ö.*, xiv (1) and xvi) and a number of masses and Motets. His greatest work is the *Choralis Constantinus* (Nüremberg, 1550-55), containing polyphonic settings of the parts of the Proper of the Mass for the whole liturgical year: modern ed. in *D.T.Ö.*, v (1) and xvi (Books 1 and 2) and by the University of Michigan Press, 1950 (Book 3). The melody of "Innsbruch ich muss dich lassen," which Isaac set for four voices, may not be by him. His setting was adapted in 1598 to Johann Hesse's hymn, "O Welt, ich muss dich lassen."

Isle of the Dead, The. *v.* TOTENINSEL.

Isorhythm. A principle of construction used by composers, most often in motets, from *c.* 1300 to *c.* 1450, in which the same rhythmic pattern is applied to successive divisions or to successive repetitions of a melody. In his motet "Veni Sancte Spiritus" (*The Old Hall Manuscript*, ii, p. 66) John Dunstable (*d.* 1453), for example, gives the same rhythm to two phrases of the hymn "Veni Creator Spiritus":

The principle is generally, as here, applied to the tenor, which is usually a plainsong melody. The tenor is normally repeated several times in diminishing note values, governed by the system of proportions, to serve as the basis for the complete composition. The section of tenor quoted above is the last of three such statements. (For a tenor by Dunstable which is repeated in inversion and in retrograde motion, *v.* RETROGRADE MOTION.) As in Dunstable's motet, the parts written above the tenor may also be treated isorhythmically, with more or less strictness. For the purpose of analysis the term *talea* is used for a rhythmic pattern, *color* for a melody. In the example quoted the relation between rhythm and melody may be expressed as *color* = 2 *taleae*; if the same rhythm is applied to successive statements of the same melody (with diminishing note-values in the second and subsequent statements) then *color* = *talea*.

Isouard [ee-zoo-arr], NICOLO: *b.* Malta, Dec. 6, 1775; *d.* Paris, March 23, 1818. Composer. Studied composition in Naples, and under the name Nicolo produced his first opera in Florence in 1795. From 1799 he lived in Paris and produced there 33 operas, some in collaboration with other composers, *e.g.* Méhul, Cherubini, Boïeldieu.

Israel in Egypt. Oratorio by Handel. Words from the Book of Exodus. First performed, London, Apr. 4, 1739.

Istar [eece-tarr], *Fr.* Symphonic variations for orchestra by d'Indy, Op. 42. First performed, Brussels, Jan. 10, 1897.

Istesso tempo, L' [leece-tess'-so tem'-po], *I.* "In the same time," an indication to the performer that the beat is to remain the same, even though the time-signature changes. In Beethoven's piano sonata Op. 111, for example, the theme of the second movement is in 9/16; the second variation, in 6/16, is marked *L'istesso tempo*, and is to be played in the same three in a bar, as is the third variation, in 12/32, also so marked. Also used to refer to a previous beat, as by Beethoven in the third movement of the sonata Op. 110, where he indicates *L'istesso tempo di Arioso.*

Italiana in Algeri, L' [lee-tahl-yahn'-a een ahl-djeh'-ree] (The Italian Girl in Algiers). Comic opera in three acts by Rossini. Libretto by Angelo Anelli. First performed, Venice, May 22, 1813.

Italian Concerto. *Concerto nach Italienischen Gusto* (Concerto in the Italian style). A work in three movements for harpsichord solo by Bach, published in the second part of his *Clavierübung* (1735). It imitates the style of the contemporary Italian concerto with orchestra, reproducing on the keyboard the contrast between soloist and *tutti.*

Italian Serenade (*G.* Italienische Serenade). A single movement by Hugo Wolf which exists in two forms: (1) for string quartet (1887), (2) arranged for small orchestra (1892). The orchestral version was intended by the composer to be the first movement of a longer work.

Italian Sixth. *v.* AUGMENTED SIXTH.

Italian Symphony. Mendelssohn's Symphony No. 4, Op. 90 in A. First performed, London, May 13, 1833, the composer conducting.

Ivanhoe. Opera in three acts by Sullivan. Libretto by Julian Sturgis (after Scott's novel). First performed, London, Jan. 31, 1891.

Ivan Sussanin [ee-vahn' soo-sahn'-een]. The original title (revived in recent years) of Glinka's opera *A Life for the Czar.* *v.* ZHIZN ZA TSARA.

Ivan the Terrible. The name given by Sergei Diaghilev in 1909 to Rimsky-Korsakov's opera *Pskovitianka* (The Maid of Pskov). *v.* PSKOVITIANKA.

Ives, (1) CHARLES EDWARD: *b.* Danbury (Conn.), Oct. 20, 1874; *d.* New York, May, 1954. Composer. Studied under Horatio Parker at Yale, and went into business in New York. Although an amateur he was until the 1920's the most advanced and adventurous composer in America. In 1947 he was awarded a Pulitzer Prize for his third symphony, composed in 1911. He wrote 4 symphonies and other works for orchestra, chamber music and piano works, choral music, and songs.

H. AND S. COWELL: *Charles Ives and his Music* (1955).

(2) SIMON: *b.* Ware, July, 1600; *d.* London, July 1, 1662. Composer. Vicar-choral of St. Paul's and organist of Christ Church, Newgate. In 1633 he collaborated with William Lawes in composing the music for Shirley's masque *The Triumph of Peace.* His surviving compositions include an elegy on the death of William Lawes, catches and rounds, and fancies and an *In nomine* for viols.

J

Jachet of Mantua: *d. c.* 1559. Composer. Masses, motets, and other church music by him appeared in various publications in Italy between 1539 and 1567.

Jack. *v.* HARPSICHORD.

Jackson, WILLIAM: *b.* Exeter, May 29, 1730; *d.* there, July 5, 1803. Composer and organist of Exeter cathedral. Composed church music, odes, and canzonets.

Jacob, GORDON PERCIVAL SEPTIMUS: *b.* London, July 5, 1895. Composer and conductor. Educated under Stanford and Charles Wood at the R.C.M., where he has been teacher of orchestration since 1926. As a composer his main interest is in instrumental music; he has written music for ballet and films, variations for orchestra, concertos for viola, piano, oboe and violin, and chamber music. He has published *Orchestral Technique* (1931) and *The Composer and his Art* (1956).

Jacobi, FREDERICK: *b.* San Francisco, May 4, 1891 ; *d.* New York, Oct. 24, 1952. Composer and conductor. Assistant conductor at the Metropolitan Opera, 1913-1917. Teacher of composition, the Juilliard School, New York, from 1936. His compositions include works for orchestra, concertos for cello, piano and violin, choral works, and chamber music.

Jacobus de Leodio (Jacques de Liége). Author of the treatise *Speculum musicae* (*c.* 1330) in seven books, divided into 518 chapters, in which he shows a strong preference for the music of the 13th cent. over the innovations of the *Ars nova* (*v.* VITRY) of the early 14th cent. His treatise was long attributed to Johannes de Muris (*q.v.*) who took the opposite view. Books 6 and 7 are printed in Coussemaker's *Scriptores*, ii, and an English translation of part of the seventh book in O. Strunk, *Source Readings in Music History* (1950). The first volume of a complete edition by R. Bragard appeared in 1955.

Jacopo da Bologna [yah'-co-po dah bo-lon'-yah]. Italian composer of the mid-14th century. 35 compositions by him have survived. A madrigal for two voices is printed in the *Historical Anthology of Music*, No. 49.

Jacotin [zha-co-tin] (1) (Jacques Godebrie, Jacobus Godefridus) : *d.* March 23, 1529. A singer in Antwerp Cathedral 1479-1528. A *chanson* in Attaingnant's collection of 1529 was reprinted by H. Expert in *Les Maîtres musiciens de la Renaissance française*, v. Another *chanson* was printed in Eitner's *Publikationen älterer praktischer und theoretischer Musikwerke*, xxiii.

(2) (Jacobus Picardus). Musician at the court of Milan, 1473-94. Probably the composer of motets under this name in Petrucci's *Motetti della corona* (1519).

Jacques de Liége. *v.* JACOBUS DE LEODIO.

Jacquet [zha-cay], ÉLISABETH-CLAUDE: *b.* Paris, *c.* 1659; *d.* there, June 27, 1729. Composer and clavecinist. Showed early promise as a player and became a *protégée* of Mme. de Montespan. Married the composer Marin La Guerre in 1687. Her compositions include an opera *Céphale et Procris* and other music for the stage, cantatas, harpsichord pieces, chamber sonatas, and church music.

Jadassohn [yah'-duss-one], SALOMON: *b.* Breslau, Aug. 13, 1831; *d.* Leipzig, Feb. 1, 1902. Theorist and composer. Studied at the Leipzig Conservatorium and under Liszt at Weimar and Hauptmann at Leipzig. Teacher of theoretical subjects at the Leipzig Conservatorium from 1871. Of his many works on harmony, counterpoint and instrumentation the *Harmonielehre* (1883) was published in an English edition in 1893. He composed 4 symphonies and other works for orchestra, chamber music and choral music.

Jagd [yahkt], *G.* " Hunt." *Jagdhorn*, hunting horn. *Jagdquartett*, " Hunt Quartet " (Haydn). *v.* CHASSE, HORN.

Jahn [yahn], OTTO: *b.* Kiel, June 16, 1813; *d.* Göttingen, Sept. 9, 1869. Archaeologist, philologist, and writer on music and art. Was Professor of Archaeology and Philology at Greifswald, 1842-7, director of the Archaeological Museum at Leipzig until 1851, and Professor and Director of the Art Museum at the University of Bonn from 1855. Wrote an important biography of Mozart (1856-9; English translation, 1882), which was subsequently remodelled and rewritten by Abert, and prepared material on the lives of Haydn and Beethoven which he passed on to C. F. Pohl and A. W. Thayer respectively.

Jahreszeiten, Die [dee yahrr′-ĕss-tsite-ĕn], *G.* *v.* SEASONS.

James, PHILIP: *b.* Jersey City (N.J.), May 17, 1890. Composer and conductor. Studied in New York, where he was professor at New York University. Has composed works for orchestra and for chorus, chamber music, and pieces for organ and for piano.

Janáček [yun′-ah-check], LEOŠ: *b.* Hukvaldy (Moravia), July 3, 1854; *d.* Ostrau, Aug. 12, 1928. Composer. Studied in Prague, and later in Leipzig and Vienna. From 1881 directed a School of organ-playing which he founded in Brno. Teacher, Prague Conservatoire, 1920. The worth of his music was not widely recognised until after the performance of the opera *Jenufa* in Vienna in 1918. He composed 9 other operas, orchestral works, a Mass and other choral works, chamber music, piano music, and songs. He published several collections of Moravian folksongs, and a treatise on the theory of harmony.

B. ŠTĚDROŇ (trans. G. Thomsen) : *Leoš Janáček* (1955).

Janequin [zhun-cañ], CLÉMENT: *b. c.* 1485, probably in Châtellerault; *d.* about 1564. Composer. Lived in Bordeaux, Angers, and Paris. A large number of *chansons*, mostly for four voices, were published by Attaingnant during his lifetime. He is best known for the long " pictorial " chansons, such as *Le Chant des Oiseaux*, *La Guerre*, and *La Chasse*, which have been published by Expert in *Les Maîtres musiciens de la Renaissance française*, vii. Five of the shorter chansons have been reprinted in vol. v of the same work, from Attaingnant's publication of 1529. Composed two Masses, a volume of motets, and settings of the *Proverbes de Salomon* and 82 *Psaumes de David*. A bibliography and alphabetical list of his chansons have been published by F. Lesure in *Musica Disciplina*, v.

Janissary Music. In the 18th cent. European military bands adopted some instruments in imitation of those used by the Janissary, the life guards of the Turkish sultan. Among them were the triangle, cymbals, bass drum, and crescent (called in England " Jingling Johnny," in France *chapeau chinois*; a pole with a crescent-shaped top hung with bells and jingles). The sounds of Janissary music were also imitated in opera (*e.g.*, in Mozart's *Die Entführung*) and in instrumental music (*e.g.*, in the Rondo of Mozart's piano sonata in A, K.331, and in the section for tenor solo and male chorus in the last movement of Beethoven's ninth symphony), and the combination of bass drum, cymbals, and triangle, as in Haydn's *Military* Symphony, was called " Turkish music." Michael Haydn's " Turkish March," dated 1795 (*D.T.Ö.*, xiv (2), p. 56), is written for wind band, with *piatelli* (little cymbals) and *tamburo turchese* (bass drum).

Jaques-Dalcroze [zhuck-dull-croze], ÉMILE: *b.* Vienna, July 6, 1865; *d.* Geneva, July 1, 1950. Swiss composer and teacher. Had his musical training in Geneva, Vienna and Paris, and taught theory in Geneva and Hellerau. In 1915 founded the Jaques-Dalcroze Institute in Geneva, where he taught and developed the principles of training through rhythm known as " Eurhythmics." Composed 5 operas, choral works, 2 violin concertos, orchestral works, chamber music, piano pieces, and songs. An English version of his book *Rhythm, Music and Education* was published in 1921.

Jarnach [yahrr′-nuckh], PHILIPP: *b.*

Noisy, July 26, 1892. Composer. Son of a Catalan sculptor. Studied in Paris. Teacher, Zürich, 1918-21; Cologne, from 1927; Hamburg, from 1949. A pupil of Busoni, whose opera *Doktor Faustus* he completed. Composed works for orchestra, chamber music, and piano pieces.

Järnefelt [yairn′-er-felt], ARMAS: *b.* Viipuri, Finland, Aug. 14, 1869; *d.* Stockholm, June 23, 1958. Composer and conductor. After studies in Helsinki, Berlin, and Paris was conductor of the orchestra at Viipuri, 1898-1903, opera and symphony at Helsinki, 1903-07; Royal Opera, Stockholm, until 1932. He directed the Helsinki orchestra from 1932-36, and in 1940 was appointed professor at the University there. His *Praeludium* for orchestra has been widely played. He composed works for orchestra, chorus, piano pieces and songs.

Jazz. The word seems to have originated in Chicago about 1914, being applied to the music of a band which had been formed in New Orleans about 1912. After its arrival in New York and the issuing of the first gramophone records of jazz in 1917, it became popular as a style of dance music played by reed, brass and rhythmic instruments and using improvisation in syncopated rhythms against a regular pulse. Its rhythmic style was inherited from RAGTIME, and its melodic and harmonic style were affected by the minor thirds and sevenths of " blues." In the 1920's it became " sweet," with more normal instrumentation, and in the 1930's " hot," with a revival of improvisation. A later variety, " boogie-woogie," uses a GROUND BASS for the rhythmic background. The style has been used in compositions by Gershwin, Copland, Lambert, Milhaud, Hindemith, Weill, and others.

Jazz Band. An instrumental ensemble which has no fixed constitution. There is inevitably a large percussion section to supply a rhythmic background. This function is shared by plucked string instruments and by the piano, which is also used as a solo instrument. The proportion of strings, woodwind and brass varies considerably. The favoured solo instruments are clarinet, saxophone, trumpet and trombone.

Jean de Garlande. *v.* GARLANDE.

Jeffries, GEORGE: *d.* 1685. Composer. Anthony Wood records that he was steward to Lord Hatton of Kirby, Northamptonshire, and organist to Charles I when the king went to Oxford in 1643. A considerable number of compositions survive in manuscript, including anthems and services, motets, incidental music, and fancies for strings.

Jemnitz [yem′-nits], ALEXANDER (Sándor) : *b.* Budapest, Aug. 9, 1899. Composer and critic. Studied at the Budapest Academy of Music and at Leipzig with Reger. After four years on the staff of the Bremen Opera (1917-21) he studied further with Schönberg (1921-4). Since then he has been active as a critic in Budapest. Apart from a few orchestral works his compositions consist mainly of chamber music, keyboard works and songs. He has devoted himself particularly to the composition of sonatas for solo instruments without accompaniment : 3 for violin, and one each for cello, harp, double bass, trumpet, flute and viola. His other chamber works include 2 string trios, 3 violin sonatas and one cello sonata.

Jenkins, JOHN: *b.* Maidstone, 1592; *d.* Kimberley (Norfolk), Oct. 27, 1678. Composer. Lived in the household of his patrons Sir Hamon L'Estrange, Lord North (1660-66 or 7), and Sir Philip Wodehouse of Kimberley. Anthony Wood called him " the mirrour and wonder of his age for musick " and Roger North, whom he taught, described him as an innovator who " superinduced a more airy sort of composition, wherein he had a fluent and happy fancy." He wrote fancies for strings, an Elegy for voices on the death of William Lawes, songs, and anthems. A selection of his instrumental works was edited by Helen Joy Sleeper in 1950.

Jensen [yen′-zĕn], ADOLF: *b.* Königsberg, Jan. 12, 1837; *d.* Baden-Baden, Jan. 26, 1879. Composer. His grandfather Wilhelm Gottlieb Martin (*d.* 1842) and his brother and pupil Gustav (1843-95) were also composers. Studied with Ehlert and Liszt, taught in Russia in 1856, was in Copenhagen, where he became a friend of Gade, from 1858-60, and taught in Königsberg until 1866 and Berlin until 1868, when he retired on account of ill-health. His numerous songs show the influence of Schumann, whom he greatly admired. Also composed an opera, part-songs, and piano pieces.

Jenufa [yay′-noo-fa]. Opera in three acts by Janáček. Libretto by the composer, based on a story by Gabriela Preissová. First performed, Brno, Jan. 21, 1904. The original Czech title was *Její Pastorkyňa* (Her Foster-Daughter).

Jeppesen [yep′-er-sěn], KNUD: *b.* Copenhagen, Aug. 15, 1892. Musicologist and composer. Studied in Copenhagen and Vienna. From 1934 was director of the Royal Conservatory at Copenhagen and is now professor at the university of Aarhus. Has written numerous studies and articles on the history of music. His *The Style of Palestrina and the Dissonance* (1927) and *Counterpoint* (1939) have been published in English.

Jephtha. (1) Latin oratorio by Carissimi. Text mainly from Judges, xi. Modern ed. by E. Pauer, with English text by John Troutbeck.

(2) Oratorio by Handel. Libretto by Thomas Morell. First performed, London, Feb. 26, 1752.

Jerome of Moravia; 13th-cent. theorist. A Dominican monk in Paris who wrote a *Tractatus de Musica* (published by Coussemaker in *Scriptores*, i, p. 1).

Jeu [zher], *Fr.* Organ stop. *Jeux de fonds,* foundation stops. *Jeux d'anches,* reed stops.

Jeu de clochettes [zher der closh-et], *Fr.* Glockenspiel.

Jeu de timbres [zher der tãnbr], *Fr.* Glockenspiel.

Jeune [ler zhern], CLAUDE LE: *b.* Valenciennes, 1528; *d.* 1600 or 1601. Composer. From 1564, when he published *Dix Pseaumes de David,* he probably lived in Paris under the protection of noblemen of Protestant sympathies. From 1570 he was associated with the *Académie de Poésie et de Musique* of Jean-Antoine de Baïf in the composition of *musique mesurée à l'antique* (*q.v.*). His *chansons* were published in *Livre de mélanges* (1585) and a volume of *Airs* in 1594. A number of works appeared shortly after his death, among them the *Cinquante Pseaumes de David* (1602, 1608), and the *Pseaumes en vers mesurés* (1606). A selection of his works has been republished by Henry Expert in his *Les Maîtres musiciens de la Renaissance française* and *Monuments de la musique française.*

D. P. WALKER and F. LESURE: "Claude le Jeune and Musique mesurée," in *Musica Disciplina.*

Jig. *v.* GIGUE.

Jig Fugue. *v.* GIGUE FUGUE.

Joachim [yoh-ahkh′-im], (1) AMALIE (*née* Schneeweiss): *b.* Marburg, May 10, 1839; *d.* Berlin, Feb. 3, 1898. Contralto. Sang under the name Amalie Weiss until her marriage in 1863 to Joseph Joachim, from whom she separated in 1884. First appeared on the stage at Troppau, 1853. Hanover Opera, 1862-3, 1865-6. From that time devoted herself to concert work. Taught for a time in America and subsequently at the Klindworth-Scharwenka Conservatorium, Berlin. She excelled in the interpretation of Schumann's songs.

(2) JOSEPH: *b.* Kittsee (near Pozsony), June 28, 1831; *d.* Berlin, Aug. 15, 1907. Violinist and composer. Studied in Pest, Vienna, and from 1843 with Mendelssohn and Schumann in Leipzig. Leader under Liszt of the Ducal orchestra at Weimar, 1849-53; director of the new Hochschule für Musik in Berlin, 1869. In the same year he founded the quartet which became famous for its interpretation of Beethoven and Brahms. As a soloist he was most admired for his performances of Bach, Beethoven, Mendelssohn, and Brahms. His compositions include works for violin with orchestra and with piano, overtures, songs, and cadenzas for violin concertos by Mozart, Beethoven, and Brahms.

Johannes Affligemensis. *v.* COTTON.

Johannes de Florentia. *v.* GIOVANNI DA CASCIA.

Johannes de Garlandia. *v.* GARLANDE.

Johannes de Grocheo. *v.* GROCHEO.

Johannes de Limburgia (John of

Limburg). Netherlands composer of the early part of the 15th cent. who probably lived in Italy. The manuscript Q 15 in the Liceo Musicale in Bologna, which came from Piacenza, contains 46 sacred compositions by him.

Johannes de Muris. *v.* MURIS.

John IV of Portugal: *b.* Villa-Viçosa, Mar. 19, 1604; *d.* Lisbon, Nov. 6, 1656. Composer. Having been trained in music, he collected a large library in Lisbon, which was lost in the earthquake of 1755. He composed a Magnificat and several motets, and wrote a *Defensa de la musica moderna*, published in Lisbon in 1649.

Johnson, (1) EDWARD: Composer of the late 16th and early 17th century. Two of his vocal pieces are settings of songs performed at the entertainment for Queen Elizabeth I on her visit to Lord Hertford at Elvetham in Sept., 1591. He contributed a six-part madrigal " Come, blessed byrd " to *The Triumphes of Oriana* (1601; reprinted in *E.M.S.*, xxxii), and the *Fitzwilliam Virginal Book* contains his " Thomson's Medley " (ed. Fuller-Maitland and Barclay Squire, ii, p. 366) and settings by Byrd of a pavan and galliard by him (ii, pp. 436, 440). A pavan by Edward Johnson was printed by Thomas Simpson in the *Taffel Consort*, published at Hamburg in 1621.

(2) JOHN: *d.* probably in 1595. Lutenist and composer. His name appears among the musicians of Sir Thomas Kitson at Hengrave Hall, Suffolk in 1572, as a participant in entertainments given by Leicester at Kenilworth Castle in 1575, and as one of the Queen's musicians from 1581 to his death. Some compositions for lute survive in manuscript.

(3) ROBERT: *b.* Duns, Scotland, probably early in the 16th century. He is said in a manuscript containing his music to have fled to England " before the Reformation . . . for accusation of heresy." Composed music for the Latin and English services, secular songs, and music for strings. Hawkins printed his 4-part " Defyled is my name" in the appendix to his History, and H. B. Collins has edited the motet " Dum transisset Sabbatum."

(4) ROBERT: *d.* London, 1633. Composer and lutenist to James I and Charles I. Son of (2). Composed music for the stage, including two songs from *The Tempest*, and contributed two pieces to Sir William Leighton's *Teares or Lamentacions* of 1614. Instrumental pieces by him were printed in the collections of Brade (Lübeck, 1617) and Simpson (Hamburg, 1621). The *Fitzwilliam Virginal Book* contains several dances by him (ed. Fuller-Maitland and Barclay Squire, i, p. 141, ii, pp. 158-160). Two instrumental pieces are in *Musica Britannica*, ix.

Jolie Fille de Perth, La [la zhol-ee fee-*yer* der pairt]. Opera in four acts by Bizet. Libretto by Jules Henri Vernoy de Saint-Georges and Jules Adenis (based on the novel by Scott). First performed, Paris, Dec. 26, 1867.

Jolivet [zhol-ee-vay], ANDRÉ: *b.* Paris, Aug. 8, 1905. Composer. Studied with Le Flem and Varèse. Associated with Messiaen, Daniel Lesur and Yves Baudrier in the group known as " La Jeune France" (Young France). Musical director of the Comédie-Française since 1945. His compositions include a one-act comic opera, 2 ballets and other stage music, a piano concerto, miscellaneous orchestral works, chamber music, piano works and songs.

Jommelli [yom-mell'-lee], NICCOLO: *b.* Aversa (nr. Naples), Sept. 10, 1714; *d.* Naples, Aug. 25, 1774. Composer. Trained in the Neapolitan operatic tradition he produced his earliest extant opera, *Ricimero*, in Rome in 1740. After producing operas in Bologna, Naples, Venice, and Vienna he served the Duke of Württemburg at Stuttgart as *Kapellmeister*, 1753-1769. In the later operas written for Stuttgart, *Vologeso* (1766) and *Fetonte* (1768), he paid greater attention than did earlier Neapolitan composers to dramatic expression and to instrumentation, and increased the amount of accompanied recitative as compared with *recitativo secco.* Writing to his sister from Naples in June, 1770, Mozart described Jommelli's style as " beautiful, but too clever and too old-fashioned for the theatre." Besides some 70 operas, he wrote church music, including Passion music, Masses, and a Miserere. Modern ed. of the opera *Fetonte* in *D.D.T.*, xxxii-xxxiii.

H. ABERT: *Niccolo Jommelli als Opernkomponist* (1908).

Jones, ROBERT. Composer and lutenist of the late 16th and early 17th century. His six-part madrigal "Fair Oriana, seeming to wink at folly" was included in *The Triumphes of Oriana* (1601; *E.M.S.*, xxxii) and he published a book of madrigals in 1607 (*E.M.S.*, xxxv). His lute songs, which are among the most attractive of the period, were published in five sets: *First Booke*, 1600; *Second Booke*, 1601; *Ultimum Vale*, 1605; *A Musicall Dreame, Or the Fourth Booke*, 1606; *The Muses Gardin for Delights, Or the fift Booke*, 1611. Modern ed. in *E.S.L.S.*, 2nd series. Three pieces by Jones were printed in Leighton's *Teares or Lamentacions* (1614).

Jongen [yong'-ĕn], JOSEPH: *b.* Liège, Dec. 14, 1873; *d.* Sart-lez-Spa (nr. Liège), July 13, 1953. Composer, teacher, organist and pianist. Studied at the Liège Conservatoire, taught there from 1891-98, won the Belgian *Prix de Rome* in 1897 and travelled in Germany, Italy and France. Teacher, Liège Conservatoire, 1903. Lived in England during the war. Teacher, Brussels Conservatoire, 1920; director, 1925-39. He composed an opera, a ballet, *Symphonie concertante* for organ and orchestra, suite for viola and orchestra, *Pièce symphonique* for piano and wind orchestra, concertos for violin, for piano and for cello, a symphony, symphonic poems and other orchestral works, string quartets and other chamber music, pieces for piano, for organ and for harmonium, cantatas, motets, songs and partsongs.

Jongleur [zhõn-gler]. Medieval minstrel and entertainer. *v.* TROUBADOUR.

Jongleur de Notre-Dame, Le [ler zhõn-gler der notr-dum]. Opera in three acts by Massenet. Libretto by Maurice Léna. First performed, Monte Carlo, Feb. 18, 1902.

Jonny spielt auf [yon'-i shpeelt owf]. Opera in two parts (11 scenes) by Křenek. Libretto by the composer. First performed, Leipzig, Feb. 10, 1927.

Joseph [zho-zeff]. Opera in three acts by Méhul. Libretto by Alexandre Duval (after the Bible story). First performed, Paris, Feb. 17, 1807.

Joseph and his Brethren. Oratorio by Handel. Libretto by James Miller. First performed, London, March 2, 1744.

Joshua. Oratorio by Handel. Libretto by Thomas Morell. First performed, London, March 23, 1748.

Josquin des Prés (Desprez) [zhoss-cãn day pray] (*L.* Jodocus Pratensis): *b.* Hainaut, Belgium (or Condé, Flanders), *c.* 1440; *d.* Condé, Aug. 27, 1521. Composer. Singer in Milan Cathedral 1459-72. From 1474 until after 1479 in the service of Duke Galeazzo Maria Sforza of Milan. Member of the Papal Chapel until 1494; choirmaster, Cambrai, 1495-99; from *c.* 1500 in Paris in the service of Louis XII; in 1503 in Ferrara in the chapel of Duke Hercules d'Este, on whose name he wrote the Mass *Hercules dux Ferrarie* (*v.* SOGGETTO). Towards the end of his life he became Provost of Condé. The most celebrated composer of his day, called "*princeps musicorum*" by his pupil Coclico and admired by Luther for his technical mastery, he composed over 30 Masses, more than 50 motets, and some 70 chansons. In his style he developed some of the features which chiefly distinguish the music of the Renaissance from that of the later Middle Ages: use of imitation, the momentary division of the choir into contrasting groups, and a more expressive treatment of words. His music combines a consummate use of artifice with the widest range of expression and feeling. Petrucci included 6 chansons by Josquin in the *Odhecaton* (1501; modern ed. by Helen Hewitt, 1945), and published 3 volumes of his Masses (1502, 1505, 1514). A complete edition of his works by A. Smijers is in the course of publication.

Josten [joss'-tĕn], WERNER: *b.* Elberfeld, Germany, June 12, 1885. Composer and conductor. Studied in Munich, Geneva and Paris and became assistant conductor at the Munich Opera House (1918). He settled in America (1921) and was appointed professor of music at Smith College, Northampton (1923), where he produced first American performances of several early operas. He has composed ballets, two *concerti sacri* for strings and piano, a symphony and other orchestral works, works for tenor solo and orchestra, choral music, songs, chamber music and incidental music for plays.

Jota [ho'-tah]. A Spanish dance from Aragon (*Jota Aragonesa*) in a moderately fast 3/4 time. The best known example is the tune used by Liszt in his *Spanish Rhapsody* for piano and by Glinka in his overture *Jota Aragonesa*:

Jour d'Été à la Montagne [zhoor day-tay a la mōn-tun-y*er*], *Fr.* (Summer Day on the Mountain). Suite of three orchestral pieces by d'Indy, Op. 61. First performed, Paris, Feb. 18, 1905.

Judas Maccabaeus. Oratorio by Handel. Libretto by Thomas Morell. First performed, London, Apr. 1, 1747.

Juive, La [la zhēē-eev]. Opera in five acts by Halévy. Libretto by Augustin Eugène Scribe. First performed, Paris, Feb. 23, 1835.

Julius Caesar. *v.* GIULIO CESARE IN EGITTO.

Jullien [zhēēl-yañ], GILLES: *b.c.* 1650; *d.* Chartres, Sept. 14, 1703. Organist and composer. Organist, Chartres cathedral, 1668. His *Livre d'orgue*, published in Paris in 1690, was reprinted, with an introduction by N. Dufourcq, in 1952.

Juon [yoo'-on], PAUL: *b.* Moscow, March 8, 1872; *d.* Vevey, Aug. 21, 1940. Composer. Studied at the Moscow Conservatoire under Taneiev and Arensky and at the Berlin Hochschule. Teacher of theory at the Baku Conservatoire, 1896-97, professor of composition, Berlin Hochschule, 1906-34, when he moved to Vevey. He composed a symphony, 3 violin concertos, triple concerto for violin, cello and piano with orchestra, a ballet, 3 string quartets and other chamber music, piano solos and duets.

Jupiter Symphony. The name given to Mozart's symphony No. 41 in C major, K. 551 (1788).

Just Intonation. *v.* TEMPERAMENT.

K

K. With a number following refers to the catalogue of Mozart's works compiled by Ludwig von Köchel (third edition by Alfred Einstein, 1937, reprinted with supplement, 1947).

Kabalevsky [ca-ba-leff'-ski], DMITRI BORISOVICH : *b.* St. Petersburg, Dec. 30, 1904. Composer. Studied at Moscow Conservatoire. His compositions include four symphonies (No. 1 in commemoration of the 15th anniversary of the Revolution ; No. 3 with Chorus, a *Requiem* for Lenin ; No. 4 with chorus, entitled *Shchors*, after a Red Army commander), 2 piano concertos, 2 ballets, and the operas *The Master of Clamecy* (1937, after Romain Rolland's *Colas Breugnon*) and *Invincible* (1948), as well as piano music and songs.

G. ABRAHAM : *Eight Soviet Composers* (1943).

Kabasta [cub-ust'-a], OSWALD: *b.* Mistelbach, Dec. 29, 1896; *d.* Kufstein, Feb. 6, 1946. Conductor. Studied in Vienna and Klosterneuburg. Director of music, Graz, 1926; Vienna Radio, 1931. Conductor, *Gesellschaft der Musikfreunde*, Vienna, 1935; Munich Philharmonic Orchestra, 1938.

Kade [cahd'-er], OTTO: *b.* Dresden, May 6, 1819; *d.* Doberan, July 19, 1900. Writer on music. Director of music to the Grand Duke of Mecklenburg-Schwerin, 1860-93. His most important publications were a volume of musical examples, issued as a supplement to Ambros's *Geschichte der Musik*, and *Die ältere Passionskomposition bis zum Jahre 1631* (1892).

Kadosa [cod'-o-shŏ], PÁL : *b.* Léva (now Levice), Sept. 6, 1903. Hungarian pianist and composer. Studied under Kodály and Arnold Székely at the Budapest Academy of Music. Teacher at the Fodor School of Music, Budapest, 1927-43 ; Budapest Academy of Music, from 1945. By his piano recitals and his activity as a composer he has done much to further the cause of contemporary music. His compositions include 2 symphonies, piano concerto, 2 violin concertos, viola concerto, chamber music, piano works and choral works

Kaiserlied [kize'-er-leet], *G.* *v.* EMPEROR'S HYMN.

Kaiserquartett [kize'-er-cvarr-tet'], *G.* *v.* EMPEROR QUARTET.

Kajanus [ky-ah'-nooss], ROBERT: *b.* Helsinki, Dec. 2, 1856; *d.* there, July 6, 1933. Conductor and composer. Studied at the Helsinki Conservatoire and in Leipzig, and also with Svendsen in Paris. Founded the Philharmonic Society Orchestra, Helsinki, 1882. Taught at Helsinki University from 1897. He was a close friend of Sibelius and devoted much of his life to making Finnish music better known abroad. His compositions include several orchestral and choral works.

Kalbeck [cull'-beck], MAX: *b.* Breslau, Jan. 4, 1850; *d.* Vienna, May 4, 1921. Music critic and poet, best known for his four-volume biography of Brahms (1904-14). In addition to his music criticism he was also active as a writer and translator of opera librettos.

Kalinnikov [cull-een'-nee-koff], VASSILY SERGEIVICH: *b.* Voni, Jan. 13, 1866; *d.* Yalta, Jan. 11, 1901. Composer. Studied at the Philharmonic Music School, Moscow. Assistant conductor, Italian Opera, Moscow, 1893-4. For the rest of his life consumption compelled him to abandon an active career. Of his compositions the best-known is the first symphony in G minor, which was not only successful in Russia but was performed in several European cities.

Kalischer [cahl'-ish-er], ALFRED CHRISTLIEB SALOMO LUDWIG: *b.* Thorn, March 4, 1842; *d.* Berlin, Oct. 8, 1909. Poet, critic and teacher, who devoted much of his life to the study of Beethoven. His complete edition of Beethoven's letters (English translation by J. S. Shedlock, 2 vols., 1909) is a standard work.

Kalkbrenner [culk'-bren-er], FRIEDRICH WILHELM MICHAEL : *b.* Nov. 1785 ; *d.* Deuil (Seine-et-Oise), June 10, 1849. Pianist and composer, son of the composer Christian Kalkbrenner. Studied at the Paris Conservatoire. Lived in London, 1814-23, where he was in great demand as a teacher. Joined the firm of Pleyel, piano manufacturers, in Paris, 1824. He had a great reputation as a pianist and was admired by Chopin, who dedicated his E minor piano concerto (Op. 11) to him. His compositions were numerous and many of them purely ephemeral. He is known today only by his *Études*.

Kalliwoda [cull'-i-vo-da], JOHAN WENZESLAUS: *b.* Prague, Feb. 21, 1801; *d.* Carlsruhe, Dec. 3, 1866. Violinist and composer. Studied at the Prague Conservatoire. *Kapellmeister* to Prince von Fürstenburg, Donaueschingen, 1822. His numerous compositions include seven symphonies: No. 5 was admired by Schumann, who dedicated to him his *Intermezzi* (Op. 4).

Kamennyi Gost [cah'-myĕn-ni gosst], (The Stone Guest). Opera in three acts by Dargomijsky, a setting of Pushkin's dramatic poem on the subject of Don Giovanni. First performed, St. Petersburg, Feb. 28, 1872.

Kamieński [cum-yen'-skee], (1) LUCIAN: *b.* Gniezno, Jan. 7, 1885. Polish composer and critic. Studied in Breslau and Berlin. Music critic, *Allgemeine Zeitung*, Königsberg, 1909-19. Assistant director, Poznan Academy of Music, 1920; professor, Poznan University, 1922-39. His compositions, written under the name Dolega-Kamienski, include the comic opera *Damy i Huzary* (Ladies and Hussars, 1932), *Symphonia Paschalis* for chorus and orchestra, and a large number of songs, to German and Polish words. He has also published *Die Oratorien von Joh. Ad. Hasse* (1912).

(2) MATTHIAS : *b.* Sopron, Oct. 13, 1734; *d.* Warsaw, Jan. 25, 1821. The first Polish opera-composer. His *Nędza Uszczęśliwiona* (Misery Contented, Warsaw, 1778) was followed by 7 others (2 unperformed). He also wrote church music and a cantata for the unveiling of the monument to Sobieski.

Kaminski [cum-een'-skee], HEINRICH: *b.* Tiengen, July 4, 1886; *d.* Ried, June 21, 1946. German composer. Studied in Heidelberg and Berlin. Taught composition at Berlin Academy, 1930-2, and directed a series of municipal concerts at Bielefeld, 1930-3. His compositions, serious in character and polyphonic in style, include several large-scale choral works, chamber music, organ works, and the operas *Jürg Jenatsch* (Dresden, 1929) and *Das Spiel vom König Aphelios* (Göttingen, 1950).

Kammermusik [cum'-er-moo-zeek], *G.* Chamber music.

Kammerton [cum'-er-tone], *G.* "Chamber pitch." (1) The pitch of orchestral instruments in the 17th and 18th cent. in Germany. By the early 18th cent. it was substantially lower (by a tone or a minor third or more) han *Chorton* (choir pitch) to which the older organs were tuned. As *Chorton* varied considerably, it is impossible to define the relationship more precisely. A tuning-fork which belonged to Handel gives a pitch which is approximately a semitone flatter than the standard pitch today, and this may be taken as a general pointer to the pitch of *Kammerton* in the middle of the 18th century. The practical advantages of *Kammerton* (particularly for wood-wind instruments) were such that it came to be adopted for the performance of choral works with organ and orchestra. This involved transposing down the organ parts, which was Bach's practice at Leipzig.

C. S. TERRY : *Bach's Orchestra* (1932).

(2) Used exceptionally by Praetorius in his *Syntagma Musicum*, vol. ii (1719) to indicate the highest *Chorton* in general use in North Germany at the time, approximately a minor third higher than our standard pitch today. Though he calls this *Kammerton* he recognizes that it was generally known as *Chorton*. He reserves the name *Chorton* for a pitch a tone lower than this, *i.e.* approximately a semitone higher than our standard pitch today.

(3) In modern German = standard

pitch (*Fr.* diapason normal), according to which the note:

is established, by international agreement, at 440 cycles a second.

v. CHORTON, PITCH.

Kapellmeister [cup-ell'-mice-ter], *G.* (*Fr.* maître de chapelle, *I.* maestro di cappella, *Sp.* maestro de capilla). Lit. "master of the chapel," *i.e.* director of music to a prince, king, bishop or nobleman. The term *Kapellmeistermusik* is used contemptuously by German writers to describe music which is correct but lacking in invention.

Kapp [cup], JULIUS: *b.* Steinbach, Oct. 1, 1883. Opera producer and writer on music. Studied chemistry at Marburg, Berlin and Munich. Founder and editor of the periodical, *Blätter der Staatsoper*, 1921-45. Opera producer at the Berlin State Opera, 1923, and subsequently also at the Berlin-Charlottenburg Municipal Opera. His numerous books include works on Paganini, Berlioz, Meyerbeer, Weber and Schreker, and on the history of the Berlin State Opera. More particularly he has devoted himself to the lives of Liszt and Wagner and has edited their literary works.

Karajan [ca'-ra-yun], HERBERT VON: *b.* Salzburg, Apr. 5, 1908. Conductor, a pupil of Franz Schalk. Conductor, Ulm, 1928; Aix-la-Chapelle, 1934; Berlin State Opera, 1938-45; Vienna Philharmonic Orchestra, 1948. He has also conducted at the Salzburg Festival and in several foreign countries, including England.

Karel [ca'-rel], RUDOLF: *b.* Pilsen, Nov. 9, 1880; *d.* Theresienstadt, March 6, 1945. Composer, a pupil of Dvořák, with whom he studied at the Prague Conservatoire. Interned in Russia, 1914, but appointed to teaching posts at Taganrog and Rostov. Escaped from Russia after the 1917 Revolution and joined the staff of the Prague Conservatoire. Died in a concentration camp. His compositions include several large-scale orchestral works, few of which were published, chamber music, and piano works, and the operas *Ilseino Srdce* (Ilse's Heart, Prague, 1924) and *Smrt Kmotřička* (Godmother Death, Brno, 1933).

Karg-Elert [carrg'-ay'-lert] (originally Karg), SIGFRID: *b.* Oberndorf am Neckar, Nov. 21, 1877; *d.* Leipzig, Apr. 9, 1933. Composer and pianist. Studied at Leipzig Conservatorium, where he was appointed teacher of piano and composition, 1919. His compositions include a large number of songs, chamber music, and piano works, but he is particularly known for his substantial contribution to the organ repertory. His works for the organ, often extremely elaborate and characterized by an over-lush chromaticism, include 66 *Choral-Improvisationen*, 20 preludes and postludes on chorales, 3 *Sinfonische Choräle*, and other pieces of an impressionistic character. His experience as an organist was limited, and he was singularly unsuccessful as a recitalist in the United States.

G. SCEATS: *The Organ Works of Karg-Elert* (1949).

Kastagnetten [cust-un-yet'-ĕn], *G.* Castanets.

Kastner [cust-nair], (1) JEAN GEORGES: *b.* Strasbourg, March 9, 1810; *d.* Paris, Dec. 19, 1867. Composer. Studied in Paris under Reicha. His compositions include 9 operas and a large amount of music of a popular character. He was extremely active as a writer on music: his published works include *Traité général d'instrumentation* (1837, the first work of its kind in France), *Manuel général de musique militaire* (1848), books on harmony and counterpoint, methods for saxophone and timpani, and elementary tutors for a large number of other instruments.

H. LUDWIG: *Johann Georg Kastner*, 3 vols. (1886).

(2) MACARIO SANTIAGO: *b.* London, Oct. 15, 1908. Pianist, harpsichordist and musicologist. Studied in Amsterdam, Leipzig, Berlin and Barcelona. Teacher of harpsichord and clavichord, Lisbon Conservatoire, 1933. He has travelled widely as a recitalist and published editions of old Spanish and

Portuguese keyboard music, as well as *Música Hispánica* (1936), *Contribución al estudio de la música española y portuguesa* (1941) and other historical works.

Kát'a Kabanová [cah'-tya cub'-un-o-vah] Opera in three acts by Janáček. Libretto by Vincenc Červinka (based on Ostrovsky's play *Groza*). First performed, Brno, Oct. 23, 1921.

Kaun [cown], HUGO: *b.* Berlin, March 21, 1863; *d.* there, Apr. 2, 1932. Composer. He was very prolific as a boy, subsequently receiving instruction at the Berlin Academy. In the United States, 1884-1901, where he conducted male-voice choirs at Milwaukee. Member of the Berlin Academy, 1901; teacher of composition at the Klindworth-Scharwenka Conservatorium, 1922. He wrote a number of works for male-voice choirs, and also 3 symphonies, a piano concerto, 4 string quartets, a piano quintet, 2 piano trios and four operas—*Der Pietist*, *Sappho* (Leipzig, 1917), *Der Fremde* (Dresden, 1920), and *Menandra* (Brunswick, Kiel, Osnabrück and Rostock, 1925).

Kazoo. *v.* MIRLITON.

Keilberth [kile'-bairt], JOSEPH : *b.* Carlsruhe, Apr. 19, 1908. Conductor. He acquired experience at the Carlsruhe Opera. Conductor, Deutsche Philharmonie, Prague, 1940 ; Dresden State Opera, 1945 ; Hamburg Philharmonic Orchestra, 1951. He has conducted several times at the Bayreuth Festival.

Keiser [kize'-er], REINHARD: *b.* Teuchern, Jan. 9, 1674; *d.* Hamburg, Sept. 12, 1739. Composer, son of an organist and a pupil at St. Thomas's School, Leipzig. Associated with Johann Kusser in the production of operas in Brunswick and Hamburg, and succeeded him in 1695 as chief composer to the Hamburg opera. For many years active in Hamburg as director of the opera and organizer of orchestral concerts, with famous soloists. Director of music to the King of Denmark, Copenhagen, 1723; cantor of Hamburg Cathedral, 1728. He wrote nearly 120 operas, as well as a great quantity of church music—Passions, oratorios, cantatas, motets—and other vocal and instrumental works. His private life was marked by gross self-indulgence. His music, melodious and expressive, was extremely popular. Handel was employed at the Hamburg opera under Keiser, whose jealousy was so strongly aroused by the success of the younger composer's *Almira* (Hamburg, 1705) that he set the same libretto himself in the following year. The following operas are available in modern editions: *Octavia* (1705), supplement to German Handel Society; *Croesus* (1711), *D.D.T.*, vol. xxxvii-viii (with extracts from *L'inganno fedele*); *Der lächerliche Printz Jodelet* (1726), *Publikationen der Gesellschaft für Musikforschung*, vol. xviii.

Keller [kell'-er], HERMANN: *b.* Stuttgart, Nov. 20, 1885. Organist, editor and teacher, a pupil of Reger and Straube. Municipal organist, Weimar, 1910; organist, St. Mark's, Stuttgart, 1916. He has held teaching posts at Weimar and Stuttgart, and was appointed director of the Würtemberg Hochschule für Musik in 1945. In addition to publishing books on organ music and organ-playing he has also edited several of Bach's keyboard works, Buxtehude's organ works, Frescobaldi's *Fiori musicali*, and miscellaneous organ works by old composers.

Kelley, EDGAR STILLMAN: *b.* Sparta (Wisconsin), Apr. 14, 1857; *d.* New York, Nov. 12, 1944. Composer and critic. Studied in Chicago and Stuttgart. Music critic, *San Francisco Examiner*, 1893-5. Teacher of piano and composition in Berlin, 1902-10; Cincinnati Conservatory, 1910. His compositions include the comic opera *Puritania* (Boston, 1892), 2 symphonies (*Gulliver* and *New England*), incidental music to *Macbeth* and *Ben Hur*, chamber music and songs. Author of *Chopin the Composer* (1913).

Kellner [kell'-ner], JOHANN PETER: *b.* Gräfenroda, Sept. 24, 1705; *d.* there, Apr. 22, 1772. Organist and composer. An admirer of Bach and Handel, whom he knew personally. Better known for the copies he made of Bach's works than for his own compositions, which include keyboard works, a complete set of church cantatas, and an oratorio.

Kelly, MICHAEL : *b.* Dublin, Dec. 25, 1762 ; *d.* Margate, Oct. 9, 1826. Tenor and composer. Studied singing with

Italian masters, and went to Naples, 1779, for further study. Made his first appearance there, 1781, subsequently visiting various Italian cities. At the Court Theatre, Vienna, 1784-7, where he sang Basilo and Curzio in the first performance of Mozart's *Figaro*, 1786. Returned to England, 1787, and from that time sang frequently in opera and concerts. He also wrote the music for more than 60 stage productions. His *Reminiscences* (2 vols., 1826) are valuable, not for the evidence they afford of his own vanity but for their references to his contemporaries, particularly Mozart, whom he knew well and admired.

Kelway, (1) JOSEPH: *d.* 1782. Organist successively of St. Michael's, Cornhill and St. Martin's in the Fields. A pupil of Geminiani, he had a reputation as a harpsichordist and gave lessons to Queen Charlotte. Described by Burney (*A General History of Music*, vol. iv, p. 665) as "at the head of the Scarlatti sect in England."

(2) THOMAS: *d.* Chichester, May 21, 1749. Elder brother of (1). Organist, Chichester Cathedral, 1726. Composed anthems and services.

Kennedy Fraser, MARJORIE: *b.* Perth, Oct. 1, 1857; *d.* Nov. 22, 1930. Singer and collector of Hebridean songs. Daughter of the popular singer David Kennedy, and wife of A. J. Fraser. Her publications include three volumes of *Songs of the Hebrides* (1909-21). She wrote the libretto for Bantock's opera *The Seal Woman* (Birmingham, 1924), which introduces Hebridean melodies.

Kent Bugle. *v.* KEY BUGLE.

Kentner [kent'-ner], LOUIS: *b.* July 19, 1905. Hungarian pianist, now a naturalized British citizen. Studied at the Budapest Academy of Music. His public appearances date from 1920. Settled in England, 1935. He was the soloist in the first performance of Bartók's second piano concerto, 1933, and with Menuhin gave the first performance of Walton's violin sonata, 1949. His compositions include 2 piano sonatinas, 2 string quartets and songs.

Kerle [cairr'-ler], JACOB VAN: *b.* Ypres, 1532; *d.* Prague, Jan. 7, 1591. Organist and composer. He held various church and court appointments in Italy, Germany and Flanders, and from 1582 was in the service of the Emperor Rudolf II in Prague. His work as cathedral organist at Augsburg (1568-75) was of particular importance. His compositions consist of polyphonic church music (Masses, motets, Magnificats, etc.) and include a setting of special prayers (*Preces speciales*) for the Council of Trent in 1562 (modern ed. in *D.T.B.*, xxvi).

Kerll [cairrl], JOHANN CASPAR: *b.* Adorf, Apr. 9, 1627; *d.* Munich, Feb. 13, 1693. Organist and composer. Studied in Vienna and Rome. Vice-*Kapellmeister* to the Bavarian court at Munich, 1656; *Kapellmeister*, 1659-74. Subsequently organist of St. Stephen's and court organist, Vienna. His compositions include several operas, church music, and keyboard works. Modern ed. of 2 Masses, *D.T.Ö.*, xxv (1); Requiem, *D.T.Ö.*, xxx, (1); miscellaneous vocal and instrumental works, *D.T.B.*, ii (2). One of his organ canzonas was adapted by Handel for the chorus "Egypt was glad when they departed" in *Israel in Egypt*.

Kettledrum. *v.* TIMPANI.

Key. (1) On the piano, harpsichord, clavichord, organ, harmonium and similar instruments one of a series of balanced levers operated by the fingers which control the mechanism for producing sound (*Fr.* touche, *G.* Taste, *I.* tasto). *v.* KEYBOARD.

(2) On wood-wind instruments a metal lever operated by the finger which opens or closes one or more sound-holes (*Fr.* clef, *G.* Klappe, *I.* chiave). The purpose of such keys is to bring under control sound-holes which the fingers unaided could not reach or cover.

(3) A term used to indicate the precise tonality of music which uses as its basic material one of the major or minor scales and accepts certain relationships between the notes of the scale and the chords built on them (*Fr.* ton, tonalité, *G.* Tonart, *I.* tonalità). These relationships have not remained constant, but the acceptance of the tonic chord (the triad on the first note of the scale) as the base or centre is fundamental to the conception of key. Keys are of two kinds—*major* and *minor*—

according to whether they are based on the notes of the major or minor scale. In all major keys the relationships between the notes of the scale and the chords built on them are exactly the same, *e.g.*:

The only difference is one of pitch. Similarly with minor keys:

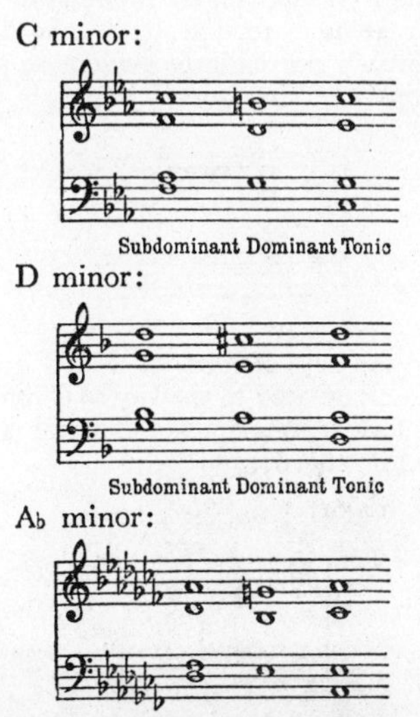

In spite of this identity keys appear to have associations for composers, who frequently use the same key to express a similar mood. The reasons for this have never been satisfactorily established. A contributing factor in orchestral music is undoubtedly the fact that some keys appear brighter than others because they employ the open notes of string instruments: even if the open notes are not actually played they vibrate in sympathy and so contribute resonance. On keyboard instruments, on the other hand, there can be no such difference.

The key of a piece of music is partly indicated to the performer by the KEY SIGNATURE, indicating which notes, if any, are to be consistently sharpened or flattened, unless there is any indication to the contrary, *i.e.* unless the sharps or flats in the key are neutralized by ACCIDENTALS. For the listener, however, the key has to be established by the harmony. In most 18th-cent. works this is done unequivocally by a clear statement of the tonic chord and one or more of the chords most nearly associated with it (particularly the dominant), or by a simple assertion in unison or octaves of the tonic and dominant notes of the scale, *e.g.*:

MOZART, *Overture, "Die Zauberflöte"*

HAYDN, *Symphony No. 104*

In the latter case, however, it is not immediately clear whether the key is major or minor: the third of the tonic chord (in this case F♮) must be heard before the listener can be certain. Later composers often used deliberately ambiguous openings. In the following example:

BEETHOVEN, *Symphony No. 1*

the first two chords suggest to the ear the key of F major: it is not until the end of the passage that the key is clearly heard to be C major.

Structural unity makes it desirable that a piece or movement should end in the key in which it began. To emphasize this unity Beethoven, in particular, often reiterates the tonic chord at the end of a movement. The common exceptions to this principle are: (i) a piece which begins in the minor key may end in the major key with the same tonic (*e.g.* C major instead of C minor), or even *vice versa*; (ii) a movement which is going to lead directly to another movement may end in a key other than the tonic in order to provide a satisfactory transition.

The relationship between keys varies: some are closely related, others distantly. Examples of close relationship are:

(i) Major and minor keys having the same tonic, *e.g.* C major and C minor. The relationship is strengthened by the fact that both keys may have the same dominant chord, through the sharpening of the seventh degree of the minor scale:

C major:

C minor:

C major is said to be the *tonic major* of C minor; C minor is the *tonic minor* of C major.

(ii) Major and minor keys using the same series of notes but with a different tonic, *e.g.* C major and A minor:

C major:

A minor:

C major is said to be the *relative major* of A minor; A minor is the *relative minor* of C major.

(iii) Keys whose tonic chords have a close association, *e.g.* in the key of C major the chords of F major (subdominant) and G major (dominant) are closely related to the tonic chord—a relationship particularly evident in progressions like the following:

Hence the keys of F major and G major are closely related to the key of C major: in the former the chord of C major is the dominant chord:

F major:

in the latter it is the subdominant:

G major:

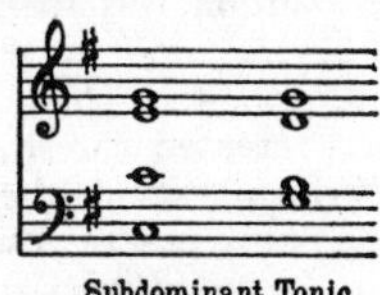

Subdominant Tonic

Relationships between keys facilitate MODULATION from one key to another. Such modulation is normal in any but the simplest and shortest pieces. If the composer announces that he has written a prelude in G minor, he takes it for granted that listeners will not be surprised to find that he has modulated to other keys in the course of the piece. It is, in fact, quite normal to have one or more sections in such a piece which are wholly in keys different from the principal key. The establishment of different key centres for the sake of contrast is the basic principal of what is known as SONATA FORM. In all such divergences the principal key of the piece is thought of as the home base to which the music must return at the end. Key contrast is also used between the several movements of a suite, sonata or symphony; *e.g.* in Brahms's second symphony in D major, the first and last movements are in this key, while the second movement is in B major and the third in G major.

Keyboard (*Fr.* clavier, *G.* Klaviatur, *I.* tastatura). A horizontal series of keys which enable the performer, by means of intervening mechanism, to produce sound on the piano, organ, harpsichord, clavichord and similar instruments. Its origin was the series of sliders on the early medieval ORGAN which were used to admit air to the pipes. A series of levers which could be pressed down was found preferable to the labour of pushing and pulling the sliders, and these were the foundation of the modern keyboard, which dates probably from the 13th century. By the 15th cent. the levers, or keys, had been reduced to manageable size. The earliest keyboards were diatonic (*i.e.* corresponding to the white notes of the modern keyboard), but chromatic notes had certainly been introduced by the early 14th century. The fact that they were an addition to the original keyboard explains why the black notes on the modern keyboard are inserted between the white notes, each black note occupying part of the space properly belonging to the two adjacent white notes.

This arrangement, which enables a large number of notes to lie within the stretch of a normal hand, has certain inconveniences : scales require different fingering, according to the number and position of the black notes involved, and melodic progressions and chords which are comfortable in one key may be awkward if transposed to another. A further inconvenience results from the fact that the keyboard is straight: this means that the notes at either end are further away from the performer than those in the middle, and the angle of approach is different for every note on the keyboard. Attempts have been made to neutralize these inconveniences: they have been defeated, not by argument but by tradition and custom. Keyboard technique is a discipline involving many years' study, since the human hand was not designed by nature to deal with such a mechanism, and it is only natural that systems of technique should be founded on the practice of the past.

In the 14th cent. the keyboard was adopted for instruments with vibrating strings, whether plucked or pressed, resulting in the HARPSICHORD and CLAVICHORD. On the organ the keyboard played by the fingers is known as a manual. For the sake of greater variety and contrast in tone colour organs came to be equipped with two manuals, and this practice was also adopted for the harpsichord. On large organs the number of manuals was increased still further; at the present day four is the largest number normally found, though instruments exist with five or even seven. The piano, having no facilities for contrasts of tone colour, has remained content with a single manual; the Duplex Coupler piano, invented by Emanuel Moór (1863-1931), with an upper manual tuned an octave higher than the lower, has not been generally adopted. A pedal keyboard, to be played by the feet, was in use for the organ by the 15th cent., and was later adopted for the harpsichord and, less frequently, the clavichord. A pedal keyboard has also been added to the piano, to facilitate the practice of organ music at home.

The compass of keyboard instruments, originally small, has gradually increased up to the present day. The standard keyboard of the modern piano has a range from

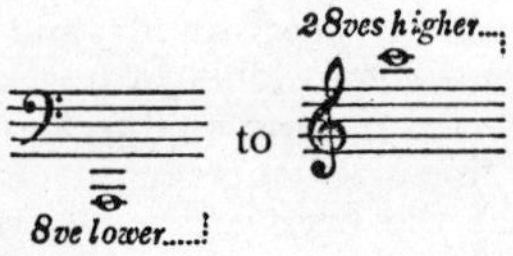

The maximum range of the organ manual keyboard is

and of the pedal keyboard

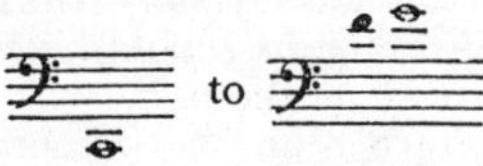

(The black notes indicate the upper limit on less up-to-date instruments). The smaller range of the organ manual keyboard, as compared with the piano, is due to the fact that it is automatically extended by the use of 2 ft., 4 ft. and 16 ft. stops, and by the pedal keyboard. In the 16th and early 17th cent. space was often saved by the use of the so-called SHORT OCTAVE at the lower end of the keyboard. Since sharps and flats were not normally required in this register, the black notes were used to fill up the diatonic octave.

The increasing use of chromaticism in the 16th cent. created problems of tuning, since the black notes had to do double duty, *e.g.* the note E♭ had to serve also as D♯ (for an example see the fantasia on "Ut re mi fa sol la" by John Bull, *Fitzwilliam Virginal Book*, no. 51). One solution was to increase the number of keys, *i.e.* to have separate keys for D♯ and E♭, and so on, but such instruments created fresh problems for the performer and they did not survive. The only practical solution was to retain the existing keyboard and make the tuning of all the semitones equal. This practice came into use in the 18th cent. and is now universal (*v.* EQUAL TEMPERAMENT). It has not been affected by 20th-cent. experiments in constructing keyboards capable of playing quarter-tones.

Reference has been made above to "black" and "white" notes, in accordance with the normal practice today. On many old instruments, however, the white notes of the modern keyboard are black, and the black notes white or ivory. Some modern manufacturers of harpsichords and clavichords have adopted this method, though without any obvious justification other than elegant workmanship.

Keyboard Music. A generic term for all music written for keyboard instruments, applicable particularly to music up to and including the time of Bach and Handel, much of which was not designed specifically for a particular keyboard instrument but could be played equally well on harpsichord, clavichord or organ.

Key Bugle (*Fr.* bugle à clefs, *G.* Klappenhorn, *I.* cornetta a chiavi). A bugle with holes pierced in the tube (like a wood-wind instrument) and controlled by keys, patented by Joseph Halliday, 1810. Also called the Kent bugle (after the Duke of Kent). In the course of the 19th cent. it was superseded by brass instruments with valves—the *Flügelhorn* and the cornet.

Key-Note. The first note of the scale of a key, also known as the tonic. It gives its name to the key, *e.g.* the note E is the key-note of the keys of E major and E minor. *v.* KEY (3).

Key Signature. Sharps or flats placed at the beginning of a composition to indicate the key. Thus the key of A major employs the following scale:

 Key Signature

Since F♯, G♯ and C♯ are normal notes in the key, the key signature for A major is:

The same key signature is used for the relative minor of A major—F♯ minor. Since the seventh degree of the scale in a minor key is frequently sharpened, it has been suggested that the key signature of a minor key should incorporate this sharpening. If this suggestion were adopted, the key signature of F♯ minor would be:

The objections to this suggestion are (i) that a key-signature should indicate a consistent sharpening or flattening, apart from incidental divergences, (ii) that in flat keys there would be illogical or confusing key signatures, *e.g.* the key signature of C minor would be :

(the B remaining ♮) and the key signature of G minor would be:

Modulation and the temporary employment of another key do not necessarily involve a change of key signature. Any alterations that are needed can be indicated by ACCIDENTALS. An extended passage in a new key however, is best given a new key signature, to avoid the persistent use of accidentals. The key signature of a piece is repeated at the beginning of each stave of the composition and remains in force until a new key signature is indicated. It was formerly the practice to use the natural sign (♮) to cancel any sharp or flat that was to be omitted in the new key signature, but this is quite unnecessary (except where the new key is C major or A minor). A double bar preceding the new key signature is normally quite sufficient, *e.g.* :

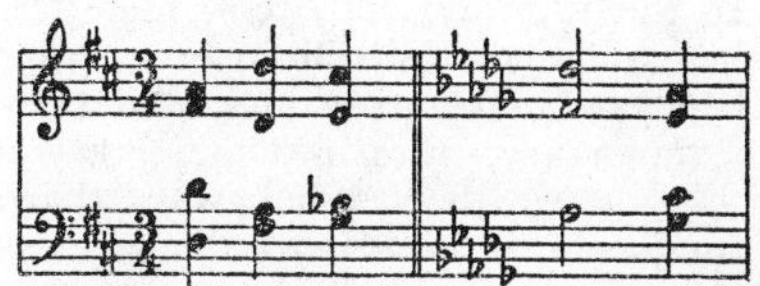

The key signatures of the major keys are:

and of the minor keys:

Keys with one or more sharps in the signature are called *sharp keys*; those with one or more flats are called *flat keys*. In the 17th and 18th cent. these terms had a different significance: a "sharp key" was a major key, and a "flat key" a minor key, since in a major key the third above the key-note was "sharp" (major third), while in a minor key it was "flat" (minor third) (*v.* FLAT).

The following pairs of keys are identical on a keyboard instrument: B major and C♭ major; F♯ major and G♭ major; C♯ major and D♭ major; G♯ minor and A♭ minor; D♯ minor and E♭ minor; A♯ minor and B♭ minor. A further extension of key signatures is theoretically possible, but not practical, as this would involve the use of the double sharp (×) and the double flat (♭♭), *e.g.* the key of G♯ major would require the following key signature:

Beethoven's third symphony (*Eroica*) in E♭ was described at the first performance as in D♯, but this was merely a peculiarity of nomenclature, not a description of the key signature.

A sharp or flat in a key signature is assumed to govern not only the notes occurring on the same line or space but also all notes of the same name, in whichever octave they may occur. Thus the key signature of F major:

indicates that all B's are to be flattened, not merely those directly governed by the ♭ in the signature. This was not always the case; *e.g.* in 15th- and 16th-cent. sources it is quite common to find two B's flattened at the beginning of the line:

Key signatures originated in the practice of transposing plainsong melodies up a fourth: the result of this was that every F in the original melody became B♭ in the transposed version. To save the trouble of marking every B in the melody the rounded B (*B molle* or *B rotundum*), which was the original form of the ♭, was placed at the beginning of the stave to remind the performer to sing B♭ and not B♮ (*v.* FLAT, NATURAL). This labour-saving device was adopted in the secular songs of the troubadours and trouvères and in polyphonic music. In the latter it was reserved for the parts in which it was essential. From the 13th to the early 16th cent. it is quite common to find one or more of the lower parts with a flat in the signature and one or more of the upper parts without any flat. This represents a fundamental difference of tonality between the parts, which may be weakened, however, by the use of the flat as an accidental in the upper part (or parts), and of the natural in the lower. Key signatures with two flats (B♭ and E♭) appear in the 15th cent., but the use of more than two flats, and of sharps, in key signatures did not become general until the 17th cent. This might suggest a rather limited range of tonalities in 16th-cent. music, but accidentals were by this time freely employed (particularly in secular music) and transposition of the written notation could be implied by the clefs used for the voice-parts (*v.* CHIAVETTE). The tradition of limited key signatures was so strong that as late as the early 18th cent. it was normal to omit one of the flats in the signature of flat minor keys, *e.g.* C minor had the signature:

instead of

Khachaturian [kha-cha-too'-ree-un]. ARAM ILYICH: *b.* Tiflis, June 6, 1903. Armenian composer. Studied with M. F. Gniessin in Moscow and at the Moscow Conservatoire. His compositions include 2 symphonies, piano concerto, violin concerto, cello concerto, chamber music, *Song of Stalin* for chorus and orchestra, piano pieces and stage music.

G. ABRAHAM: *Eight Soviet Composers* (1943).

Khovanschina [khov-ahnss'-chee-na]. Opera in five acts by Moussorgsky. Libretto by the composer and Vladimir Vassilievich Stassov. First performed, St. Petersburg, Feb. 21, 1886.

Kidson, FRANK: *b.* Leeds, Nov. 15, 1855; *d.* there, Nov. 7, 1926. Antiquarian, who collected and published a large number of English folksongs and dances. His other publications include *British Music Publishers, Printers and Engravers* (1900) and *The Beggar's Opera, its Predecessors and Successors* (1922).

Kielflügel [keel'-fleeg-ĕl], *G.* Harpsichord.

Kiene [keen'-er], MARIE. *v.* BIGOT DE MOROGUES.

Kienzl [keents'l], WILHELM: *b.* Waizenkirchen, Jan. 17, 1857; *d.* Vienna, Oct. 19, 1941. Composer. Studied in Graz, Prague and Munich. Opera conductor, Amsterdam, Krefeld, Hamburg and Munich. Conductor, Styrian Musikverein, Graz. Music critic in Vienna from 1930. A strong admirer of Wagner, he devoted himself extensively to the composition of operas, of which he wrote 9: the most important are *Der Evangelimann* (Berlin, 1895), which had an enormous success, and *Der Kuhreigen* (Vienna, 1911). He also wrote a large number of songs, chamber music and piano works, and published volumes of collected criticisms and essays, an autobiography entitled *Meine Lebenswanderung* (1926) and studies of Wagner and Richter.

Kiesewetter [keez'-er-vet-er], RAPHAEL GEORG (Edler von Wiesenbrunn): *b.* Holešov, Aug. 29, 1773; *d.* Baden (nr. Vienna), Jan. 1, 1850. Civil servant, who also studied music and particularly the history of music. His publications include works on Greek music, Arab music, Guido d'Arezzo and Palestrina. A. W. Ambros was his nephew.

Kilpinen [kill-peen'-ĕn], YRJÖ: *b.* Helsinki, Feb. 4, 1892. Composer. Studied at the Helsinki Conservatoire, and in Vienna and Berlin. He has written some chamber music and, more recently, orchestral works, but is best known for his very imaginative songs in a romantic idiom, of which there are more than 500. He receives a government grant, as Sibelius did, which enables him to devote himself wholly to composition.

Kindermann [kind'-er-mun], JOHANN ERASMUS: *b.* Nuremberg, March 29, 1616; *d.* there, Apr. 14, 1655. Organist and composer. After spending 2 years in Venice he returned to Nuremberg as organist, first at the Marienkirche, 1636, and then at St. Ägidien, 1640. His published works include sacred and secular songs for one or more voices with instrumental accompaniment, suites for wind instruments, *canzoni* for strings, and preludes, fugues and Magnificats for organ. Modern ed. of selected works in *D.T.B.*, xiii, xxi-iv.

Kinderscenen [kind'-erce-tsain-ĕn], *G.* (Scenes of Childhood). Suite of 13 easy pieces for piano solo by Schumann, Op. 15 (1838). Each piece has a descriptive title. According to the composer " the superscriptions came into existence afterwards and are, indeed, nothing more than delicate directions for the rendering and understanding of the music."

Kindertotenlieder [kind'-er-tote-ĕn-leed-er], *G.* (Dirges for Children). Cycle of 5 songs with orchestral accompaniment by Mahler. Words by Friedrich Rückert.

King Arthur. Opera with a prologue, five acts and an epilogue by Purcell. Libretto by John Dryden. First performed, London, May (?), 1691. The story takes place during the contest between the Britons (under King Arthur) and the Saxon invaders (under Oswald) who had settled in Kent. Arthur, who is betrothed to Emmeline (the blind daughter of the Duke of Cornwall), bids her farewell before making an attack on the enemy. The Saxons employ Osmond (a magician) and his attendant sprites to lead the Britons astray, but Philidel (one of the attendants) is persuaded by Merlin (a British magician) to help the Britons. Emmeline is captured by Oswald but Merlin sends Philidel to her with a magic liquid to restore her sight. Later Osmond imprisons Oswald and makes love to Emmeline, but when his magic spells fail to overcome the approaching Arthur (who is helped to resist them by Philidel) he releases Oswald. Oswald then challenges Arthur but is defeated by him and promises to return to his native land. Emmeline is rescued, Osmond is imprisoned, and Merlin predicts the future greatness of Britain.

Kingdom, The. Oratorio by Elgar, Op. 51, dealing with the activities of the apostles after Christ's ascension. First performed, Birmingham Festival, Oct. 3, 1906. It is the second part of a trilogy which began with *The Apostles* but was never completed.

Kinkeldey [kink′-ĕl-dy], OTTO: *b.* New York, Nov. 27, 1878. Musicologist. Studied at the College of the City of New York, Columbia University and Berlin University. He held various teaching appointments in New York, 1898-1902, and Breslau, 1909-14. Chief of the Music Division, New York Public Library, 1915-23 (apart from war service), 1927-30. Professor, Cornell University, 1923-7, 1930-46 (also librarian). His most important publication is *Orgel und Klavier in der Musik des XVI Jahrhunderts* (1910), which is still a standard work. He also edited Philipp Erlebach's *Harmonische Freude* (1697, 1710) in *D.D.T.*, xlvi-vii. First president, American Musicological Society, 1934-6.

Kinsky [kince′-ki], GEORG LUDWIG: *b.* Marienwerder, Sept. 29, 1882; *d.* Berlin, Apr. 7, 1951. Musicologist. Self-taught as a musician. Curator, William Heyer Museum, Cologne, 1909-27; the collection included instruments and musical autographs, of which he published a catalogue. Teacher, Cologne University, 1921-32. His most widely known, and perhaps his most valuable publication is *Geschichte der Musik in Bildern* (1929; English ed., *A History of Music in Pictures*, 1930), containing illustrations of instruments, title-pages, manuscripts, printed music, musical activities of every kind, and portraits, from the earliest times down to the present day. His other works include *Die Originalausgaben der Werke J. S. Bachs* (1937), *Die Erstausgaben und Handschriften der Sinfonien Beethovens* (1937) and a catalogue of Beethoven's works.

Kipnis [keep′-neece], ALEXANDER: *b.* Jitomir (Ukraine), Feb. 1, 1896. Bass-baritone. Studied in Warsaw (including military band conducting) and Berlin. He has sung in opera at Wiesbaden, Berlin, Chicago, Vienna, Buenos Aires, Bayreuth, Munich, Salzburg, Covent Garden and Glyndebourne. Resident in America since 1934. His interpretations of Wolf's songs have become familiar from the gramophone records made for the Hugo Wolf Society.

Kirbye, GEORGE: *d.* Bury St. Edmunds, Oct. 1634. Composer of a volume of English madrigals (1597; modern ed. in *E.M.S.*, xxiv) which show a sensitive imagination, particularly in the treatment of dissonance. He also contributed to East's *The Whole Booke of Psalmes* (1592) and *The Triumphes of Oriana* (1601). Other works survive incomplete in manuscript.

Kirchenkantate [kirr*sh*′-ĕn-cun-taht′-*er*], *G.* Church cantata. *v.* CANTATA.

Kirchenton [kirr*sh*-ĕn-tone], *G.* Church mode. *v.* MODE.

Kircher [kirr*sh*′-er], ATHANASIUS: *b.* Geisa (nr. Fulda), May 2, 1602; *d.* Rome, Nov. 28, 1680. Jesuit professor of natural science at Würzburg University, who left Germany in 1633 on account of the Thirty Years War and settled first in Avignon and finally in Rome, 1637. His principal work on music is *Musurgia universalis sive ars magna consoni et dissoni* (2 vols., 1650), which is often interesting but thoroughly unreliable, particularly the section on Greek music.

Kirchgessner [kirr*sh*′-gess-ner], MARIANNE: *b.* Waghäusel, 1770; *d.* Schaffhausen, Dec. 9, 1809. A blind musician, who made her reputation as a performer on the glass HARMONICA. Mozart wrote for her a quintet for harmonica, flute, viola, oboe and cello, K.617, and an Adagio for harmonica solo, K.356 (1791).

Kirchner [kirr*sh*′-ner], THEODOR: *b.* Neukirchen (nr. Chemnitz), Dec. 10, 1823; *d.* Hamburg, Sept. 18, 1903. Composer, mainly of works for piano solo or piano duet. Studied in Leipzig and Dresden. Organist, Wintherthur

(Switzerland), 1843-62. Conductor, Zürich, 1862-72. Teacher, Würzburg Musikschule, 1873-5; Dresden Conservatorium, 1883-90. Strongly influenced by Schumann, he excelled in the composition of miniatures.

Kirkman. A firm of harpsichord and piano manufacturers in London, founded by Jacob Kirkman (originally Kirchmann), a German who settled there some time before 1739. They began to make pianos *c.* 1775. The firm was amalgamated with COLLARD in 1896.

Kirkpatrick, RALPH: *b.* Leominster, Mass., June 10, 1911. Harpsichordist. Studied at Harvard and in Paris. In addition to his work as a recitalist he has devoted a good deal of research to the problems of performance and has edited Bach's *Goldberg Variations* and a selection of sonatas by Domenico Scarlatti. His book *Domenico Scarlatti* (1953) is a standard work which includes a substantial amount of new material.

Kirnberger [kirrn'-bairg-er], JOHANN PHILIPP: *b.* Saalfeld, Apr. 1721; *d.* Berlin, July 27, 1783. Composer and teacher, a pupil of Bach in Leipzig, 1739-41. Violinist in the service of Frederick the Great, 1751; *Kapellmeister* to Princess Amalie, 1758. He composed a large number of instrumental and vocal works (keyboard pieces, trio sonatas, orchestral symphonies and suites, motets, songs, etc.) and published a number of technical works, including *Die Kunst des reinen Satzes* (2 vols., 1771) which was several times reprinted. His manuscript copy of Bach's *St. Matthew Passion* preserves the earliest form of that work.

Kistler [kist'-ler], CYRILL: *b.* Gross-Aitingen, March 12, 1848; *d.* Kissingen, Jan. 1, 1907. Opera composer. Originally a schoolmaster, he entered the Munich Conservatorium, where he was a pupil of Rheinberger, in 1876. Taught at the Sondershausen Conservatorium, 1883-5, and subsequently at Kissingen. His first opera, strongly influenced by Wagner, was *Kunhild* (Sondershausen, 1884). His later works include the comic opera *Eulenspiegel* (Würzburg, 1889). He also published technical works, critical essays and a dictionary of composers, which reached a 3rd ed.

Kistner. A Leipzig firm of music-publishers, originally founded by Heinrich Albert Probst in 1823 and taken over by Karl Friedrich Kistner (1797-1844) in 1831. The business was bought by Carl and Richard Linnemann in 1919, and amalgamated with the firm of Siegel in 1923, under the title Fr. Kistner & C. F. W. Siegel.

Kit (*Fr.* pochette, *G.* Taschengeige). A miniature violin, formerly used by dancing-masters and carried in their pockets (hence the French and German names). It was made either in the ordinary shape of a violin (from the late 17th cent.), or long and narrow like a REBEC (the earlier form). It is known to have been in use in the early 16th cent. and may very well be considerably older.

Kitezh [keet'-ezh]. Opera in four acts by Rimsky-Korsakov. Libretto by Vladimir Ivanovich Belsky. First performed, St. Petersburg, Feb. 20, 1907. The translation of the complete title is: *The Legend of the Invisible City of Kitezh and the Maiden Fevronia.*

Kitson, CHARLES HERBERT; *b.* Leyburn, Nov. 13, 1874; *d.* London, May 13, 1944. Organist and teacher. Educated at Cambridge. Organist, Christ Church Cathedral, Dublin, 1913-20. Professor, National University of Ireland, 1916-20; Trinity College, Dublin, 1920-35. He also taught at the R.C.M. Author of several books on counterpoint, harmony, fugue and allied subjects.

Kittel [kit'-ĕl], (1) BRUNO: *b.* Forsthaus Entenbruch, May 26, 1870; *d.* Wassenberg, March 10, 1948. Conductor. Studied in Berlin. Court violinist, 1896-1901. Conductor, Court theatre, 1901-7. Director, Brandenburg Conservatorium, 1901-14; Konservatorium der Reichshaupstadt (previously known as Stern's Conservatorium), 1936-45. Founder and conductor of the Bruno Kittel Choir, 1902.

(2) JOHANN CHRISTIAN: *b.* Erfurt, Feb. 18, 1732; *d.* there, May 18, 1809. Organist and composer, a pupil of Bach in Leipzig. Organist at Langensalza, 1751; Erfurt, 1756. He had a consider-

able reputation as a performer and teacher. His published works include preludes for organ, piano sonatas, *Der angehende praktische Organist* (an instruction book: 3 vols., 1801-8) and *Neues Choralbuch* for Schleswig-Holstein (1803).

Kittl [kit'l], (1) EMMY. *v.* DESTINN.

(2) JOHANN FRIEDRICH: *b.* Worlik, May 8, 1806; *d.* Lissa (Poland), July 20, 1868. Czech composer, a pupil of Tomášek. Director, Prague Conservatoire, 1843. Of his three operas the most successful was *Bianca und Giuseppe oder die Franzozen vor Nizza* (Prague, 1848). The libretto (after Heinrich König's novel *Die hohe Braut*) is by Wagner, who had originally written it in the form of a sketch which he submitted in a French translation (unsuccessfully) to the librettist Augustin Eugène Scribe in Paris. Later he wrote the complete libretto in verse and offered it to Reissiger, who declined it. It was then offered to Kittl.

Kjellström [shell'-strurm], (1) INGRID: *b.* Sept. 9, 1904. Pianist and harpsichordist. Daughter of (2). Studied the harpsichord in Berlin with Ernst Wolf. With her father has toured widely in chamber music, and has also appeared as a soloist.

(2) SVEN : *b.* Luleå, March 30, 1875 ; *d.* Stockholm, Feb. 5, 1951. Violinist. Studied in Stockholm and Paris. Member of the Colonne Orchestra, Paris, 1900-4. Founded the Kjellström Quartet, 1911. Leader of the orchestra, Stockholm Könsertforensingen, 1914-17, 1924-8. Director, Stockholm Conservatoire, 1929-40. He toured widely as a soloist.

Kjerulf [sheh'-roolf], HALFDAN: *b.* Christiania (now Oslo), Sept. 15, 1815; *d.* Grefsen, Aug. 11, 1868. Composer. studied law at Christiania University. Turned to music, 1840, and studied in Christiana and in Leipzig under E. F. E. Richter. Apart from founding a series of subscription concerts in Christiana, 1857, he took little part in public activities. His compositions include songs and part-songs, which have enjoyed considerable popularity in Norway, and piano pieces which have become familiar to most amateur performers.

Klangfarbe [clung'-farrb-*er*], *G.* Tone colour.

Klafsky [cluff'-shki], KATHARINA: *b.* Szt. János (Hungary), Sept. 19, 1855; *d.* Hamburg, Sept. 22, 1896. Operatic soprano, a pupil of Mathilde Marchesi. She began her career as a chorus singer in Vienna and Salzburg, but began to make her name as a soloist in Leipzig, from 1876 onwards. She soon established herself as an outstanding Wagnerian singer, and principal soprano at the Hamburg Opera, 1886-95. She also appeared in St. Petersburg, London and the United States.

Klappenhorn [clup'-ĕn-horrn], *G.* Key bugle.

Klarinette [cla-ree-net'-*er*], *G.* Clarinet.

Klaviatur [cluv-ya-toorr'], *G.* Keyboard.

Klavier [cluv-eer'] *G.* (also *Clavier*)

(1) Keyboard.

(2) Keyboard instrument with strings, *i.e.* clavichord, harpsichord or piano (*v.* CLAVIER, HAMMERKLAVIER).

(3) Specifically, in modern German, the piano.

Kleber [clay'-ber], LEONHARD: *b.* Göppingen, *c.* 1490; *d.* Pforzheim, March 4, 1559. Organist. Studied in Heidelberg. Successively organist at Horb, Esslingen and Pforzheim. Compiler of an early 16th-cent. manuscript collection of organ music in TABLATURE (for examples *v.* H. J. Moser & F. Heitmann, *Frühmeister des deutschen Orgelspiels*).

Kleiber [clibe'-er], ERICH: *b.* Vienna, Aug. 5, 1890 ; *d.* Jan. 27, 1956. Conductor. Studied at Prague Conservatoire and University. Conductor, Darmstadt Court Theatre, 1912-18 ; Barmen-Elberfeld, 1919-21 ; Düsseldorf and Mannheim, 1922-3. Director, Berlin State Opera, 1923-35. He also conducted opera in Buenos Aires, Amsterdam and London, and frequently appeared as a concert conductor in Europe and America. He conducted the first performances of Berg's *Wozzeck* (Berlin, 1925) and Milhaud's *Christophe Colomb* (Berlin, 1930).

Kleine Flöte [cline'-*er* flur'-t*er*], *G.* Piccolo.

Kleine Nachtmusik, Eine [ine'-*er* cline'-*er* nuckht'-moo-zeek], *G.* (A Little Serenade). Serenade for strings in four movements by Mozart, K.525 (1787). According to Mozart's own catalogue there were originally five movements: Allegro, Minuet and Trio, Romance, Minuet and Trio, Finale, but the first Minuet and Trio is now lost.

Kleine Orgelmesse [cline′-*er* orrg′-ĕl-mess-*er*], *G.* (Little Organ Mass). The name given to Haydn's *Missa brevis Sti. Joannis de Deo* in B♭, composed *c.* 1775 (No. 5 in the complete edition, No. 8 in Novello's edition). So called on account of the part for organ *obbligato*. The adjective distinguishes it from the GROSSE ORGELMESSE.

Kleine Trommel [cline′-*er* trom′-ĕl], *G.* Side drum.

Kleinmichel [cline′-mi*sh*-ĕl], RICHARD: *b.* Posen, Dec. 31, 1846; *d.* Charlottenburg, Aug. 18, 1901. Pianist and composer. Studied at the Leipzig Conservatorium. Worked as an opera conductor in Hamburg, Danzig and Magdeburg. He composed 2 operas, 2 symphonies, chamber music and piano works, but is chiefly remembered for his simplified piano scores of Wagner's operas.

Kleinprinzipal [cline′-prints-eep-ull′], *G.* A 4 ft. open diapason stop on the organ.

Klemperer [clemp′-er-er], OTTO: *b.* Breslau, May 15, 1885. Conductor. Studied in Frankfort and Berlin. Conductor, German Opera, Prague, 1907; Hamburg, Stadttheater, 1910; Strasbourg, 1914 (director, 1916); Cologne, 1917 (director, 1923). Director, State Opera, Wiesbaden, 1924; Kroll Opera, Berlin, 1927; Berlin Staatsoper, 1931-3. Compelled to leave Germany he became conductor of the Los Angeles Philharmonic Orchestra, 1933-9. Director, Budapest, 1947. He has also conducted concerts in many of the principal cities in Europe and America. At the Kroll Opera in Berlin he pursued an adventurous policy, introducing works like Schönberg's *Die glückliche Hand*, Stravinsky's *Oedipus Rex* and Hindemith's *Cardillac*. He was also active from 1929 as conductor of the Berlin Philharmonic Choir, which gave the first performance of Hindemith's oratorio *Das Unaufhörliche* in 1931.

Klenau [clain′-ow], PAUL VON: *b.* Copenhagen, Feb. 11, 1883; *d.* there, Aug. 31, 1946. Composer and conductor. Studied at the Berlin Hochschule, and in Munich and Stuttgart. Opera conductor, Freiburg, 1907, 1914; Stuttgart, 1908. Founder and conductor, Philharmonic concerts, Copenhagen, 1920. Conductor, Wiener Singakademie and Konzerthausgesellschaft, Vienna, 1926. As a conductor he devoted particular attention to contemporary composers, and frequently performed works by Delius. His principal compositions are:

(a) OPERAS: *Sulamith* (Munich, 1913); *Kjartan und Gudrun* (Mannheim, 1918; revised as *Gudrun auf Island*, 1924); *Die Lästerschule* (after Sheridan's *The School for Scandal*; Frankfort and Munich, 1927); *Michael Kohlhaas* (Stuttgart, 1933); *Rembrandt van Rijn* (Berlin, 1937); *Elisabeth von England* (Cassel, 1939).

(b) ORCHESTRA: 6 symphonies; *Bank Holiday—Souvenir of Hampstead Heath*; 3 fantasies after Dante's *Inferno*.

(c) VOCAL WORKS: *Die Weise von Liebe und Tod des Cornet Christof Rilke* (baritone, chorus and orchestra); *Ebbe Skammalsen* (ballad for baritone and orchestra); *Gespräche mit dem Tode* (contralto and orchestra).

Also a ballet (*Klein Idas Blumen*), chamber music, piano pieces and songs.

Klengel [cleng′-ĕl], (1) AUGUST ALEXANDER: *b.* Dresden, Jan. 27, 1783; *d.* there, Nov. 22, 1852. Composer, a pupil of Clementi, with whom he visited Russia. Court organist, Dresden, 1816. His compositions include 2 piano concertos and several works for piano. He is chiefly remembered, however, for his *Canons et fugues dans tous les tons majeurs et mineurs*, published in 1854 (after his death) by Moritz Hauptmann.

(2) JULIUS: *b.* Leipzig, Sept. 24, 1859; *d.* there, Oct. 27, 1933. Cellist and composer. Studied privately. Principal cello, Gewandhaus Orchestra, Leipzig, 1881-1924. Teacher, Leipzig Conservatorium, 1881. Toured widely as a soloist. Among his pupils were Guilhermina Suggia and Emanuel Feuermann. His compositions include 3 cello con-

certos and a double concerto for violin and cello.

(3) PAUL: *b.* Leipzig, May 13, 1854; *d.* there, Apr. 24, 1935. Brother of (2). Conductor and composer. Studied at the Leipzig Conservatorium. Conductor, Euterpe Concerts, Leipzig, 1881-6; Stuttgart, 1887-91; Arion and Singakademie, Leipzig, 1892-8; Deutsche Liederkranz, New York, 1898-1902; Arion, Leipzig, 1903-21. Teacher, Leipzig Conservatorium, 1883-6, and from 1907. His compositions include songs and chamber music.

Klindworth [clint'-vorrt], KARL: *b.* Hanover, Sept. 25, 1830; *d.* Stolpe, July 27, 1916. Pianist and conductor, a pupil of Liszt. Lived in London, 1854-68, as pianist and conductor of orchestral concerts. Teacher, Moscow Conservatoire, 1868-84. Subsequently settled in Berlin, where he conducted the Philharmonic Concerts and founded a music school. Made piano scores of Wagner's *Der Ring des Nibelungen* and edited the complete piano works of Chopin. His adopted daughter Winifred married Siegfried Wagner.

Klose [cloze'-er], FRIEDRICH: *b.* Karlsruhe, Nov. 29, 1862; *d.* Ruvigliana (nr. Lugano), Dec. 24, 1942. Composer. Studied in Karlsruhe and Geneva, and in Vienna with Bruckner. Teacher, Basle Conservatoire, 1906; Akademie der Tonkunst, Munich, 1907-19. Lived in Switzerland from 1920. His compositions, which show the influence of Bruckner, include a Mass in D minor, the " dramatic symphony " *Ilsebill*, the oratorio *Der Sonne-Geist*, the symphonic poem *Das Leben ein Traum*, chamber music and songs. Also published a book of reminiscences, *Meine Lehrjahre bei Bruckner* (1927).

Klosé [clo-zay], HYACINTHE ELÉONORE: *b.* Corfu, Oct. 11, 1808; *d.* Paris, Aug. 29, 1880. Clarinettist. Teacher of the clarinet, Paris Conservatoire, 1839-68. He successfully adapted to the clarinet the Boehm system originally designed for the flute. He wrote a number of works for his instrument, as well as instruction books for clarinet and for saxophone.

Klotz. A family of violin-makers active in Mittelwald, in Bavaria, in the 17th and 18th centuries.

Klughardt [clook'-harrt], AUGUST FRIEDRICH MARTIN: *b.* Cöthen, Nov. 30, 1847; *d.* Dessau, Aug. 3, 1902. Conductor and composer. Director of music to the court at Weimar, 1869; Neustrelitz, 1873; Dessau, 1882. His compositions include 4 operas, 3 oratorios—*Die Grablegung Christi*, *Die Zerstörung Jerusalems* and *Judith*—and other choral works, 4 symphonies, 6 overtures, concertos for oboe, violin and cello, and chamber music.

Knab [knup], ARMIN: *b.* Neu-Schleichach, Feb. 19, 1881. Composer. For many years he combined composition with the obligations of a legal career, until he became teacher of composition at the Berlin Hochschule für Musikerziehung, 1934-43. His enthusiasm for National Socialism found expression in a number of unaccompanied choral works. More important are his solo songs, which combine simplicity of structure with extreme sensibility.

Knaben Wunderhorn, Des [dess knahb'-ĕn vo͞ond'-er-horrn], *G.* (The Boy's Magic Horn). A collection of German folk poems, several of which were set by Mahler as solo songs, some with piano accompaniment and some with orchestra.

Knappertsbusch [knup'-erts-bo͞osh], HANS: *b.* Elberfeld, Mar. 12, 1888. Conductor. Studied at Cologne Conservatorium. Conducted opera in Elberfeld, 1913; Leipzig, 1918; Dessau, 1919. Director, Munich Opera, 1922-36; Vienna State Opera, 1938-45. Widely known as a Wagner interpreter, he has conducted in most European countries and at the Salzburg Festivals.

Knarre [knarr'-er], *G.* Rattle.

Knaz Igor [knyahz ee'-gorr] (Prince Igor). Opera with a prologue and four acts by Borodin (completed by Rimsky-Korsakov and Glazounov). Libretto by the composer. First performed, St. Petersburg, Nov. 4, 1890.

Knecht [kne*sh*t], JUSTIN HEINRICH: *b.* Biberach, Sept. 30, 1752; *d.* there, Dec. 1, 1817. Composer and organist. Court *Kapellmeister*, Stuttgart, 1807-9. His numerous compositions include a symphony entitled *Le Portrait musical de la nature*, which successively represents a cheerful woodland scene, the approach of a storm, its full fury and gradual subsidence, and a concluding hymn of thanksgiving. It is possible that this programme suggested to Beethoven the composition of his *Pastoral Symphony*, which has a very similar scheme. He also published a number of theoretical works and instruction books for organ and piano.

Kneisel [knize'-ĕl], FRANZ: *b.* Bucharest, Jan. 26, 1865; *d.* New York, March 26, 1926. Violinist. Studied at Bucharest Conservatorium and Vienna Conservatorium. Leader, Bilse Orchestra, Berlin, 1884; Boston Symphony Orchestra, 1885-1903. Founder and leader, Kneisel String Quartet, 1883-1917. Teacher of violin, Institute of Musical Art, New York, 1905.

Knipper [knip'-er], LEV KONSTANTINOVICH: *b.* Tiflis, Dec. 16, 1898. Composer. He took up music at the age of 24, studying in Berlin, Freiburg and Moscow. His early works show an attempt to follow modern European developments, but in course of time he came to accept the Soviet conception of music which would appeal to the masses, without however satisfying the authorities that his work was ideologically sound. An important influence on his work has been his study of folk-song in the Caucasus and Tajikistan. His compositions include 3 operas, several symphonies (among them the *Far Eastern Symphony*, for orchestra, military band, soloists and male-voice chorus, and *Poem about the Komsomols*, in praise of Communist Youth), orchestral suites on folk melodies, chamber music and songs.

G. ABRAHAM: *Eight Soviet Composers* (1943).

Knorr [knorr], (1) ERNST-LOTHAR VON: *b.* Eitorf (Rhineland), Jan. 2, 1896. Composer and teacher. Studied at the Cologne Conservatorium. After spending three years as a prisoner of war (1915-18) taught in Mannheim, Heidelberg and Berlin. Deputy director, Frankfort Hochschule, 1941; director, Trossingen Hochschule, 1946. His compositions include several cantatas and other choral works, concertos, chamber music and songs.

(2) IWAN: *b.* Mewe, Jan. 3, 1853; *d.* Frankfort, Jan. 22, 1916. Composer and teacher. Studied at the Leipzig Conservatorium. After spending some years in Russia as a teacher, he returned to Germany and became teacher of composition at the Hoch Conservatorium, Frankfort, 1883, and director, 1908. His pupils included several English musicians, among them Cyril Scott, Balfour Gardiner and Roger Quilter. Apart from songs and piano pieces his published compositions are few in number. He was the author of books on harmony and fugue and also wrote a biography of Tchaikovsky.

(3) JULIUS: *b.* Leipzig, Sept. 22, 1807; *d.* there, June 17, 1861. Pianist and teacher. He was a close friend of Schumann and had a considerable reputation as a teacher. He published a number of books of technical exercises.

Koanga. Opera with a prologue, three acts and an epilogue by Delius. Original English libretto by Charles Francis Keary (based on George Washington Cable's novel *The Grandissimes*). First performed (in German), Elberfeld, March 30, 1904.

Koch [cockh], (1) HEINRICH CHRISTOPH: *b.* Rudolstadt, Oct. 10, 1749; *d.* there, March 12, 1816. Critic and theorist, who published a *Musikalisches Lexikon* (2 vols., 1802) and works on harmony and composition.

(2) RICHERT SIGURD VALDEMAR VON: *b.* Ågnö (nr. Stockholm), June 28, 1879; *d.* Stockholm, March 16, 1919. Composer and critic. Studied in Stockholm, Berlin and Dresden. Music critic, *Stockholmstidningen*, 1916-19. He wrote works for orchestra, chamber music, piano pieces and songs.

(3) SIGURD CHRISTIAN ERLAND VON: *b.* Stockholm, Apr. 26, 1910. Son of (2). Composer and conductor. Studied at the Stockholm Conservatoire, and in London, Paris, Dresden and Berlin. Conductor, Stockholm Radio, 1943. His compositions include 3 symphonies, concerto for violin, viola and piano, and chamber music.

Köchel [cursh'-ĕl], LUDWIG ALOIS FRIEDRICH, RITTER VON: *b.* Stein (Lower Austria), Jan. 14, 1800; *d.* Vienna, June 3, 1877. Imperial councillor, who devoted the years of his retirement, from 1852 onwards, to the pursuit of studies in botany, mineralogy and music. His most important publication was the *Chronologisch-thematisches Verzeichnis sämtlicher Tonwerke W. A. Mozarts* (1862; 2nd ed. by P. Waldersee, 1905; 3rd ed. by A. Einstein, 1937, reissued with supplement, 1947), the first attempt to make a systematic list of Mozart's compositions. His numbering, though revised by recent research, is still retained as a means of identification, preceded by the letter K., or by K.V. (Köchel-Verzeichnis).

Kodály [code'-ah-yer], ZOLTÁN: *b.* Kecskemét, Dec. 16, 1882. Composer. Studied at the Budapest Conservatoire, where he taught composition from 1907. Lecturer, Budapest University, 1930. Like Bartók he has been active in collecting and publishing Hungarian folksongs, which have had a decided influence on his work. There is in his music no striking break with tradition. Its dominant characteristics are a passionate sincerity, and a willingness to incorporate elements from folksong. He is, therefore, in some ways a Hungarian counterpart to Vaughan Williams, though there is no actual resemblance between the idioms they employ. His principal compositions are:

(a) BALLAD OPERAS: *Háry János* (Budapest, 1926); *Székely Fonó* (The Spinning Room of the Szekelys; Budapest, 1932); *Czinka Panna* (Budapest, 1948).

(b) CHORAL WORKS: *Psalmus Hungaricus* (1923); *Budavari Te Deum* (1936); *Missa brevis* (1945); miscellaneous works for mixed voices, male voices, and children's choirs.

(c) ORCHESTRA: Suite from *Háry János*; *Dances of Marosszék* (1930); *Dances of Galánta* (1933); *Peacock Variations* (1939); concertos for orchestra (1943), viola (1947) and string quartet (1947).

(d) CHAMBER MUSIC: 2 string quartets (1908, 1917); cello sonata (1910); duo for violin and cello (1914); sonata for cello solo (1917).

Also piano pieces, songs, and arrangements of folk-songs.

Koechlin [kerk-lañ], CHARLES: *b.* Paris, Nov. 27, 1867; *d.* Le Canadel (Var), Dec. 31, 1950. Composer. Studied at the Paris Conservatoire, where he was a pupil of Fauré. His compositions were numerous, but owing to his horror of publicity many of them were for long unknown outside the circle of his friends. They include 3 string quartets, a piano quintet, sonatas for violin, viola, cello, flute, oboe, clarinet, bassoon and horn, many piano pieces and songs, ballets, and a small group of orchestral works. The influence of his refined, austere and disciplined style on his pupils, who include Poulenc, Tailleferre, Désormière and Sauguet, has been very marked. He showed his devotion to his master, Fauré, by orchestrating his suite *Pelléas et Mélisande* and by devoting to him a critical study (1927). His other publications include a *Traité de l'harmonie* (3 vols., 1929-33) and *Traité d'orchestration* (4 vols., 1949 foll.).

Koessler [curce'-ler], HANS: *b.* Waldeck, Jan. 1, 1853; *d.* Ansbach, May 23, 1926. Composer and teacher, a cousin of Reger. Studied in Munich under Rheinberger. Teacher, Dresden Conservatorium, 1877-81; Budapest Conservatorium, 1882-1908, 1920-5. Conductor, Cologne Opera, 1881-2. His compositions include 2 symphonies, a violin concerto, an opera *Der Münzenfranz* (Strasbourg, 1903), several choral works, chamber music and songs. He had a considerable influence on the younger Hungarian composers of his generation.

Köhler [cur'-ler], CHRISTIAN LOUIS HEINRICH: *b.* Brunswick, Sept. 5, 1820; *d.* Königsberg, Feb. 16, 1886. Composer, conductor and teacher. Studied in Brunswick and Vienna. Held various posts as conductor at Marienburg, Elbing and Königsberg. From 1847 lived in Königsberg as teacher and critic. He composed 3 operas and a ballet, but is best known for his numerous piano studies.

Kolisch [co'-lish], RUDOLF: *b.* Klamm

am Semmering, July 20, 1896. Violinist, a pupil of Ševčík, and also of Schreker and Schönberg. Founder of the Kolisch Quartet (1922-39) which rapidly acquired an international reputation, not only for its extensive repertory of modern works, many of which it performed for the first time, but also for its practice (unusual in ensembles) of playing without the music.

Koloratur [co-lo-ra-toorr'), *G.* *v.* COLORATURA.

Königin von Saba, Die [dee cu*rn*'-ig-in fon zah'-bah] (The Queen of Sheba). Opera in four acts by Goldmark. Libretto by Salomon Hermann Mosenthal. First performed, Vienna, March 10, 1875.

Königskinder [cu*rn*'-igs-kind'-er] (Children of the King). Opera in three acts by Humperdinck. Libretto by " Ernst Rosmer " (*i.e.* Elsa Bernstein-Porges). First performed, New York, Dec. 28, 1910. (Originally a play with musical accompaniment; in this form first performed, Munich, Jan. 23, 1897.)

Kontrabass [con'-trub-uss], *G.* Double bass. Also used as a prefix to denote instruments an octave lower than the normal bass members of a family, *e.g.* *Kontrabassposaune*, double bass trombone.

Kontrafagott [con'-truff-ug-ot'], *G.* Double bassoon.

Kontretanz [con'-tre*r*-tunts], *G.* Contredanse.

Konzert [con-tsairrt'], *G.* (1) Concert. (2) Concerto.

Konzertmeister [con-tsairrt'-mice-ter], *G.* The principal first violin in an orchestra (*E.* Leader of the orchestra, *A.* concert-master).

Konzertstück [con-tsairrt'-shtĕĕk], *G.* (*I.* concertino). A work for one or more solo instruments with orchestra, less formal in structure and often shorter than an ordinary concerto, *e.g.* Weber's *Concertstück* for piano and orchestra (Op. 79).

Kornauth [corrn'-owt], EGON: *b.* Olmütz, May 14, 1891. Composer. Studied in Vienna. Répétiteur, Vienna Opera, 1916. Teacher, Hochschule für Musik, Vienna, 1940; Salzburg Mozarteum, 1945 (deputy director, 1947). He has also toured as an accompanist, and conducted in Sumatra (1926-7). His compositions include suites and other orchestral works, sonatas for violin (2), viola, cello, clarinet, and other chamber works for strings and wind, numerous songs, and piano pieces.

Kornett [corr-net'], *G.* The modern cornet. (The German for the obsolete cornett is *Zink*).

Korngold [corrn'-gollt], (1) ERICH WOLFGANG: *b.* Brno, May 29, 1897; *d.* 1957. Composer. Son of (2). Studied in Vienna and showed extraordinary precocity as a child. His music to the pantomime *Der Schneeman* (The Snow Man), composed in 1908, was orchestrated by Zemlinsky and performed at the Vienna Opera, 1910. His *Schauspiel-Ouvertüre*, performed in Leipzig, 1911, prompted an American critic to remark: " If Master Korngold could make such a noise at fourteen, what will he not do when he is twenty-eight ? The thought is appalling." A prolific composer of chamber music, he also wrote the following operas: *Violanta* (one act, Munich, 1916), *Der Ring des Polycrates* (one act, Munich, 1916), *Die tote Stadt* (Hamburg and Cologne, 1920—his most successful opera), and *Das Wunder der Heliane* (Hamburg, 1927). He was for a short time conductor in Hamburg and also taught in Vienna. In 1938 he migrated to Hollywood, where his natural facility assured him a successful career as a composer of film music. Among the films to which he contributed were *Anthony Adverse*, *Adventures of Robin Hood*, *Elizabeth and Essex*, *The Constant Nymph* and *Of Human Bondage*.

(2) JULIUS: *b.* Brno, Dec. 24, 1860: *d.* Hollywood, Sept. 25, 1945. For many years music critic of the *Neue Freie Presse*, Vienna. Published two volumes of collected criticisms (1920, 1922).

Kósa [coh'-sho*t*], GEORG (György) : *b.* Budapest, Apr. 24, 1897. Pianist and composer. Studied under Bartók and Dohnányi at the Budapest Academy of Music, and taught the piano there from 1927. In addition to solo recitals he has also been active as an accompanist. His compositions include 6 operas, several ballets, 3 oratorios and other choral works, 6 symphonies, 4 string quartets and other chamber works, piano music and songs.

Köselitz [cur′-zer-lits], JOHANN HEINRICH. *v.* GAST.

Kosleck [coss′-leck], JULIUS: *b.* Neugrad, Dec. 1, 1825; *d.* Berlin, Nov. 5, 1905. Trumpeter. Originally an army bandsman, he became a member of the court orchestra in Berlin and taught the trumpet and trombone at the Hochschule für Musik. In 1871 he discovered a medieval trumpet which he reconstructed so as to be able to play the high trumpet parts in the works of Bach and Handel. In 1884, at a Bach festival at Eisenach, he introduced a modern trumpet in A, with two valves, on which he performed with considerable success, his tone in particular being much admired. In the following year he played in England, and a similar instrument was used by English players until in 1894 the Belgian firm of Mahillon produced a trumpet in high D, which is now the instrument normally used for playing works by Bach and Handel.

W. F. H. BLANDFORD: 'The "Bach Trumpet"' (*Monthly Musical Record*, March-April and May, 1935).

Kotter [cot′-ter], HANS: *b.* Strasbourg, *c.* 1485; *d.* Berne, 1541. Organist, a pupil of Paul Hofhaimer. Organist at Freiburg (Switzerland), 1514-30. His collection of organ pieces in TABLATURE is an important source for the early history of organ music: examples in W. Apel, *Musik aus früher Zeit*, i. and H. J. Moser and F. Heitmann, *Frühmeister des deutschen Orgelspiels*.

Kotzeluch, LEOPOLD ANTON. *v.* KOŽELUCH.

Koussevitsky [cooce-er-vit′-ski], SERGEI ALEXANDROVICH: *b.* Tver (nr. Moscow), June 26, 1874; *d.* Boston (Mass.), June 4, 1951. Conductor. Studied at the Philharmonic Music School, Moscow. Began his career as a double-bass player and rapidly became known as a virtuoso. In 1909 he founded an orchestra which toured in Russia and also a firm for publishing modern Russian music. Conductor, Russian State Orchestra (formerly Court Orchestra, St. Petersburg), 1917; Koussevitsky concerts, Paris, 1921; Boston Symphony Orchestra, 1924. He conducted a very large number of first performances of important works by Stravinsky, Prokofiev, Ravel and others.

H. LEICHTENTRITT: *Serge Koussevitsky* (1946).

Kovařovic [co-varr′-zho-vits], KAREL: *b.* Prague, Dec. 9, 1862; *d.* there, Dec. 6, 1920. Conductor and composer. Studied at the Prague Conservatoire, and subsequently with Fibich. After early experience as a harpist in the National Opera, as an accompanist and as conductor in Plzeň (Pilsen) and Brno he became conductor of the National Opera in Prague, 1900, where he raised the standard of performance to a high level. His compositions include 5 operas—*Ženichové* (The Bridegrooms, 1884), *Cesta oknem* (The Way through the Window, 1886), *Noc Šimona a Judy* (The Night of St. Simon and St. Jude, 1892), *Psohlavci* (Dog Heads, 1898), and *Na starém Bělidle* (At the Old Bleaching Ground, 1901), 7 ballets, 2 melodramas, a symphonic poem, a piano concerto and chamber music.

Koven, HENRY LOUIS REGINALD DE: *b.* Middletown (Conn.), Apr. 3, 1859; *d.* Chicago, Jan. 16, 1920. Composer. Studied at Oxford and on the Continent. Very successful as a composer of operettas—particularly *Robin Hood* (Chicago, 1890)—but less so with his serious operas *The Canterbury Pilgrims* (New York, 1917) and *Rip van Winkle* (Chicago, 1920). Also very prolific as a song composer.

Koželuch [co′-zhel-ōōkh] (Kotzeluch), LEOPOLD ANTON: *b.* Welwarn, Dec. 9, 1752; *d.* Vienna, May 7, 1818. Composer. Taught in Vienna from 1778 and succeeded Mozart as composer to the imperial court, 1792. He composed several operas, an oratorio, symphonies, piano concertos (including one for 2 pianos), cello concertos, 2 clarinet concertos, 2 basset horn concertos, chamber music and piano works.

Kraft [cruft], ANTON: *b.* Rokitzan (nr. Plzeň), Dec. 30, 1752; *d.* Vienna, Aug. 28, 1820. Cellist and composer. Member of the Esterházy Orchestra (under Haydn), 1778-90. Subsequently in the service of Prince Grassalkovich, 1790, and Prince Lobkowitz, 1795, till his death. There is no justification for ascribing Haydn's cello concerto to him (*v.* K. Geiringer, *Haydn*, pp. 257-8).

Kräftig [creft'-i*sh*], *G.* Vigorously.

Krakowiak [cruck-ove'-yuck] (*Fr.* cracovienne). A Polish dance (so called after the town of Cracow) in a lively 2/4 time with syncopated accents. Chopin wrote a *Rondo à la Krakowiak*, Op. 14 (1828), for piano and orchestra.

Kramer, ARTHUR WALTER: *b.* New York, Sept. 23, 1890. Composer and critic. On the staff of *Musical America*, 1910-22; editor, 1929-36. Managing director, Galaxy Music Corporation (music publishers). His compositions are numerous, for a wide variety of vocal and instrumental resources.

Kraus [crowce], JOSEPH MARTIN; *b.* Miltenberg, June 20, 1756; *d.* Stockholm, Dec. 15, 1792. Composer and conductor, a pupil of Abt Vogler. Having studied philosophy and law at Mainz, Erfurt and Göttingen, he migrated to Sweden, where he became conductor at the Stockholm Opera, 1778. He travelled extensively in Germany, Italy, France and England, and became court *Kapellmeister* in Stockholm, 1788. His compositions include 4 operas, symphonies, overtures, chamber music and vocal works (sacred and secular). He attacked Forkel in the anonymous essay *Etwas von und über Musik* (1777). His autobiography (in Swedish), together with 50 letters, was published in 1833.

Krauss [crowce], (1) CLEMENS: *b.* Vienna, March 31, 1893; *d.* Mexico City, May 16, 1954. Conductor. Great-nephew of (2). Chorister, Imperial Chapel, Vienna. Studied at the Vienna Conservatorium. Chorus master, Brno, 1912. Opera conductor, Riga, 1913; Nuremberg, 1915; Stettin, 1916; Graz, 1921 (also conductor of symphony concerts); Vienna, 1922. Director, Frankfort Opera, 1924; Vienna Staatsoper, 1929; Berlin Staatsoper, 1934; Munich, 1938-45. Conducted the first performances of Richard Strauss's *Arabella* (Dresden, 1933) and *Friedenstag* (Munich, 1938). Married the soprano Viorica Ursuleac.

(2) MARIA GABRIELLE: *b.* Vienna, March 24, 1842; *d.* Paris, Jan. 6, 1906. Operatic soprano. Studied at the Vienna Conservatorium. First appeared in opera, Vienna, 1859. After some years at the Vienna Opera appeared also in Paris, Naples, Milan and St. Petersburg. Among the first performances in Paris in which she sang the principal soprano role were Mermet's *Jeanne d'Arc* (1876), Gounod's *Polyeucte* (1878), *Le Tribut de Zamora* (1881) and the enlarged version of *Sapho* (1884), and Saint-Saëns's *Henry VIII* (1883).

Krebs [crapes], (1) JOHANN LUDWIG: *b.* Buttelstedt (nr. Weimar), Oct. 10, 1713; *d.* Altenburg, Jan. 1780. Composer and organist, a pupil of Bach at the Thomasschule, Leipzig. Organist, Zwickau, 1737; Zeitz, 1744; Altenburg, 1756. His compositions include *Klavierübungen* for organ (modern ed. by K. Soldan), trio sonatas for flute, violin and continuo, flute sonatas, a harpsichord concerto and preludes for harpsichord. Modern ed. of his organ trios by H. Keller.

(2) KARL AUGUST: *b.* Nuremberg, Jan. 16, 1804; *d.* Dresden, May 16, 1880. Composer and conductor. Studied under Seyfried in Vienna. Conductor, Vienna Opera, 1826; Hamburg Opera, 1827. Court *Kapellmeister*, Dresden, 1850-72. He wrote several operas, of which *Agnes Bernauer* (Hamburg, 1833) was the most successful (revived in a new version as *Agnes der Engel von Augsburg*, Dresden, 1858), as well as church music, songs and piano works.

(3) MARIE: *b.* Dresden, Dec. 5, 1851; *d.* there, June 27, 1900. Pianist. Daughter of (2). Studied with her father and made her first public appearance at Meissen in 1862. Toured as a soloist in Europe and America for many years until her marriage, when she retired.

Krehbiel, HENRY EDWARD: *b.* Ann Arbor (Mich.), March 10, 1854; *d.* New York, March 20, 1923. Music critic, *Cincinnati Gazette*, 1874; *New York Tribune*, 1880. His published works include the revised edition of Thayer's *Life of Beethoven* (3 vols., 1921), *Studies in the Wagnerian Drama* (1891), *How to Listen to Music* (1897), *Music and Manners in the Classical Period* (1898), *Chapters of Opera*

(1908, with two further volumes in 1917 and 1919) and *Afro-American Folk-Songs* (1914).

Krein [crine], (1) ALEXANDER ABRAMOVICH: *b.* Nijni-Novgorod, Oct. 20, 1883. Composer. Studied at the Moscow Conservatoire (where he became a teacher in 1912) and the Philharmonic School of Music. His compositions are strongly influenced by Jewish music. They include the opera *Zagmuth*, a symphony, the ballet *Laurencia*, the trilogy *The Soviet Shock Brigade* for chorus and orchestra (words from Marx, Lenin and Stalin) and the cantata *Kaddish* for tenor, chorus and orchestra.

(2) GRIGORY ABRAMOVICH: *b.* Nijni-Novgorod, Apr. 15, 1880. Brother of (1). Composer. Studied in Moscow and Leipzig, where he was a pupil of Reger. His compositions include a violin concerto, 2 piano concertos, 3 symphonic episodes entitled *Lenin*, and chamber music.

(3) JULIAN GRIGORIEVICH: *b.* Moscow, March 5, 1913. Son of (2). Studied at the École Normale, Paris, where he was a pupil of Dukas. He was already active as a composer while still a boy. His compositions include a cello concerto, *Lyrical Poem* for piano and orchestra, *Ballad* and *Destruction* for orchestra, and *Spring Symphony*.

Kreisler [crice'-ler], FRITZ: *b.* Vienna, Feb. 2, 1875. Violinist and composer. Entered the Vienna Conservatorium at the age of 7. Studied also at the Paris Conservatoire. After a successful tour of the United States in 1889 he temporarily abandoned music, studying medicine and art and becoming an army officer. He returned to the concert platform in 1899 and thereafter acquired a world-wide reputation by the brilliance and suavity of his playing. He gave the first performance of Elgar's violin concerto in 1910. He has lived in America since 1940. His compositions include 3 operettas, a string quartet, and a series of violin pieces published under the names of 17th- and 18th-cent. composers.

Kreisleriana [crice-ler-i-ahn'-a], *G.* A suite of 8 piano pieces by Schumann, Op. 16 (1838). The name derives from the eccentric "Kapellmeister Johannes Kreisler," the name under which E. T. A. Hoffmann contributed articles to the Leipzig *Allgemeine Musikalische Zeitung*, subsequently republished, with additions, in *Fantasiestücke in Callots Manier* (2 vols., 1814). Schumann's work was dedicated to Chopin. A revised edition appeared in 1850.

Křenek [crzhen'-eck], ERNST: *b.* Vienna, Aug. 23, 1900. Composer, of Czech origin. Studied with Schreker in Vienna and Berlin. Conductor and stage director, Cassel, 1925-7; Wiesbaden, 1927-8. From 1928-37 lived in Vienna, apart from concert tours as a pianist. Migrated to the United States, 1938, and has since taught at various colleges and universities. Now living in Los Angeles. Married (1) Anna Mahler (daughter of the composer), (2) Berta Hermann. His compositions show several varieties of style. In the 1920's he became interested in jazz idioms, which he employed with remarkable success in the opera *Jonny spielt auf* (Jonny strikes up; Leipzig, 1927). In the 1930's he seriously adopted the twelve-note method of composition employed by Schönberg. At heart he is probably a romantic, as the song-cycle *Reisebuch aus den österreichischen Alpen* (Travel Book from the Austrian Alps) would suggest. His principal compositions are :

(a) OPERAS : *Zwingburg* (Berlin, 1924) ; *Der Sprung über den Schatten* (Frankfort, 1924) ; *Orpheus und Eurydike* (Cassel, 1926); *Jonny spielt auf* (Leipzig, 1927); *Schwergewicht* (*Die Ehre der Nation*, Wiesbaden, 1928): *Der Diktator* (Wiesbaden, 1928); *Das geheime Königreich* (Wiesbaden, 1928); *Leben des Orest* (Leipzig, 1930); *Karl V* (Prague, 1938); *Tarquin* (Vienna, 1950) ; *Dark Waters* (Darmstadt, 1954).

(b) CHORAL WORKS: *Die Jahreszeiten* (4 unaccompanied choruses); 4 choruses to words by Goethe; 3 choruses to words by Keller; *Kantate von der Vergänglichkeit des Irdischen* ; *Lamentatio Jeremiae* ; *Cantata for Wartime*.

(c) BALLETS: *Mammon*; *Der vertauschte Cupido* ; *Eight Column Line.*

(d) ORCHESTRA: 5 symphonies; 2 *concerti grossi*; *Kleine Symphonie*; 4 piano concertos; violin concerto; *concertino* for flute, violin, harpsichord and strings ; *Potpourri* ; *Theme and* 13 *variations* ; *Brazilian Sinfonietta* for strings.

(e) CHAMBER MUSIC: *Symphonic Music* (9 solo instruments) ; 7 string quartets ; 2 violin sonatas ; viola sonata ; unaccompanied sonatas for violin (2) and viola ; unaccompanied suite for cello.

(f) PIANO: 6 sonatas; 5 sonatinas; 2 suites.

(g) SONG CYCLES: *Reisebuch aus den österreichischen Alpen*; *Fiedellieder*; *Durch die Nacht*; *Gesänge des späten Jahres.*

He has also produced a modernized version of Monteverdi's opera *L'Incoronazione di Poppea* and a book on Johannes Okeghem.

Kretzschmar [cretch'-mar], AUGUST FERDINAND HERMANN: *b.* Olbernhau, Jan. 19, 1848; *d.* Nikolassee (nr. Berlin), May 12, 1924. Conductor and writer on music. Studied in Dresden and Leipzig. For several years active as a conductor in Leipzig, Metz and Rostock. Director of music and lecturer in musical history, Leipzig University, 1887; lecturer, Leipzig Conservatorium, 1898; professor, Berlin, 1907. Director, Königliches Institut für Kirchenmusik, Berlin, 1907; Hochschule, 1909-20. His publications include *Führer durch den Konzertsaal* (1887-90)—a series of analytical programme notes, *Geschichte des neuen deutschen Liedes* (1912), *Geschichte der Oper* (1919) and *Einführung in die Musikgeschichte* (1920). His collected essays were published in 1911 (2 vols.). He also edited *D.D.T.*, viii-ix and xlii.

Kreutzer [croyts'-er], (1) KONRADIN: *b.* Messkirch, Nov. 22, 1780; *d.* Riga, Dec. 14, 1849. Composer. Began to study law at Freiburg, but turned to music and studied in Vienna with Albrechtsberger from 1804. Court *Kapellmeister*, Stuttgart, 1812; Donaueschingen, 1817. Conductor Vienna Kärntnertor Theatre, 1822-7, 1829-32, 1837-40; Josefstadt Theatre, 1833-7; Cologne, 1840-6; Vienna Opera, 1846-9. He wrote 30 operas, of which *Das Nachtlager von Granada* (Vienna, 1834) was remarkably successful in Germany and Austria and was also performed in several other countries, including France, Belgium, Holland, England and the United States. His other compositions include an oratorio, 3 piano concertos, chamber music, songs, and male-voice choruses.

(2) RODOLPHE: *b.* Versailles, Nov. 16, 1766; *d.* Geneva, Jan. 6, 1831. Violinist and composer, who served Louis XVI, Napoleon and Louis XVIII. For many years active as an opera-composer in Paris, including the Revolution. Teacher of the violin at the Paris Conservatoire from its foundation in 1795 till 1825. Conductor, Paris Opéra 1816-24. He toured successfully as a soloist in Italy, Germany, Austria (where he met Beethoven) and Holland. His compositions include (in addition to 40 operas) 19 violin concertos, 2 concertos for 2 violins, a concerto for violin and cello, 15 string quartets, 15 string trios, several violin sonatas, and other chamber works. His 40 *Études ou caprices* for solo violin has remained a standard work.

Kreutzer Sonata. Sonata for violin and piano in A major by Beethoven, Op. 47 (1802-3). Described by the composer as *scritta in uno stilo molto concertante quasi come d'un concerto* (written in a highly concerted style, almost as it were a concerto). Composed for the mulatt violinist George Augustus Polgreen Bridgetower, and first performed by him with Beethoven, May 17, 1803. Published in 1805 with a dedication to the French violinist Rodolphe Kreutzer The finale was originally intended fo an earlier sonata in A major, Op. 3 no. 1.

Kreuz [croyts], *G.* Sharp (lit., " cross," so called because this was an earlier form of the sign).

Křička [crzhitch'-ca], JAROSLAV: *b.* Kelč, Aug. 27, 1882. Composer. Studied at the Prague Conservatoire. Teacher of composition, School of Music, Ekaterinoslav (Russia), 1906-9; Prague Conservatoire, 1918 (director, 1942). Also active in Prague as a choral conductor. His compositions, some of which show the influence of his stay in Russia, include the operas *Hypolita* (after Maurice Hewlett; Prague, 1917) and *Bílý pán* (The Gentleman in White: after Oscar Wilde's *The Canterville Ghost*), several choral works, a symphony and other orchestral works, chamber music and song cycles.

Krieger [creeg'-er], (1) ADAM: *b.* Driesen (Neumark), Jan. 7, 1634; *d.* Dresden, June 30, 1666. Organist and composer, a pupil of Scheidt. Organist, St. Nicolas, Leipzig, 1655; court organist, Dresden, 1657. Published a collection of songs (to his own words) for 1, 2 and 3 voices with continuo and *ritornelli* for 2 violins and continuo (1657). A second collection, for 1, 2, 3 and 5 voices with five-part *ritornelli* for strings, appeared posthumously (1667; enlarged edition, 1676). No copy of the first collection (*Arien*) survives, but the text has been reconstructed from manuscript sources by H. Osthoff, *Adam Krieger* (1929). Modern ed. of the second collection (*Neue Arien*) in *D.D.T.*, xix.

(2) JOHANN: *b.* Nuremberg, Dec. 28, 1651; *d.* Zittau, July 18, 1735. Brother of (3). Composer. Court organist, Bayreuth, 1672-7. Court *Kapellmeister*, Greiz and Eisenberg, 1678. Director of music, Zittau, 1681. Published *Neue musicalische Ergetzlichkeit* (1684, in three parts: *Geistliche Andachten*, *Politische Tugendlieder*, and *Theatralische Sachen*), *Sechs musicalische Partien* (1697, suites for harpsichord) and *Anmuthige Clavierübung* (1699, preludes and fugues, etc., for organ, much admired by Handel). Modern ed. of harpsichord and organ works in *D.T.B.*, xviii. Motets and Masses survive in manuscript.

(3) JOHANN PHILIPP: *b.* Nuremberg, Feb. 25, 1649; *d.* Weissenfels, Feb. 7, 1725. Brother of (2). Composer. Studied in Copenhagen and later (1673) in Venice with Rosenmüller and in Rome with Pasquini. Chamber organist, Bayreuth, 1670-2. Court organist and vice-*Kapellmeister*, Halle, 1677; court *Kapellmeister*, Weissenfels, 1680. He wrote a large number of operas (some 50 for Weissenfels), trio sonatas, sonatas for violin, viola da gamba and continuo, *Lustige Feldmusik* for wind instruments, and *Musikalischer Seelenfriede* (sacred songs). Selections from his church music in *D.D.T.*, liii-liv; some organ pieces in *D.T.B.*, xviii.

Krips [crips], JOSEF : *b.* Vienna, Apr. 8, 1902. Conductor. Studied at the Vienna Academy of Music. Conductor, Vienna Volksoper, 1921 ; Dortmund, 1925 ; Carlsruhe, 1926 ; Vienna State Opera, 1933-8, 1945-50 ; London Symphony Orchestra, 1950.

Krohn [crone], ILMARI HENRIK REINHOLD: *b.* Helsinki, Nov. 8, 1867. Musicologist and composer. Studied in Helsinki and at the Leipzig Conservatorium. Lecturer in musicology, Helsinki University, 1900; professor, 1918-35. He has published a collection of some 7000 Finnish folksongs and theoretical works. His compositions include the opera *Tuhotulva* (Deluge; Helsinki, 1928), 2 oratorios, church cantatas, choruses, songs, &c. He has also edited a series of volumes of liturgical melodies (psalms, introits, &c.) for the Finnish church.

Krönungskonzert [cru*r*n'-ŏŏngss-contsairrt], *G. v.* CORONATION CONCERTO.

Krönungsmesse [cru*r*n'-ŏŏngss-messer], *G. v.* CORONATION MASS.

Kroyer [croy'-er], THEODOR: *b.* Munich, Sept. 9, 1873; *d.* Cologne, Jan. 12, 1945. Musicologist. Originally studied theology, but turned to music and studied in Munich with Sandberger and Rheinberger. Music critic, *Münchener Allgemeine Zeitung*, 1897-1910. Lecturer, Munich University, 1902; professor, 1907. Professor, Heidelberg, 1920; Leipzig, 1925; Cologne, 1932-8. Founder of the series *Publikationen älterer Musik* (1926-41). Editor of *D.T.B.*, iii (2) and x (1) (works by Senfl and Aichinger). Author of *Die Anfänge der Chromatik im italienischen Madrigal* (1902), *Josef Rheinberger* (1906), *Walter Courvoisier* (1928) and many contributions to periodicals, congress proceedings, etc. His compositions, which include 2 symphonies, chamber music, piano works and songs, remain unpublished.

Krummhorn [crŏŏm'-horrn], *G.* (*Fr.* cromorne, *I.* storto, cornamuto torto).

A double reed instrument, current in the Middle Ages and at the Renaissance. Its tube was curved at the end, rather like a hockey stick, and the reed was enclosed in a sort of capsule, through which the player directed his breath without having direct contact with the reed. The instrument was made in several sizes.

Kubelík [co͝ob′-er-leek], (1) JAN: *b.* Michle (nr. Prague), July 5, 1880; *d.* Prague, Dec. 5, 1940. Violinist. Studied at the Prague Conservatoire, where he was a pupil of Ševčík. He rapidly made his name as a soloist and toured widely in Europe and America. He became a naturalised Hungarian in 1903. Composed 3 violin concertos.

(2) JERONYM RAFAEL: *b.* Bychor, June 29, 1914. Son of (1). Conductor and composer. Studied at the Prague Conservatoire. Conductor, Czech Philharmonic Orchestra, 1936-9 ; Chicago Symphony Orchestra, 1950 ; Covent Garden Opera, 1955-8. His compositions include 2 symphonies, a piano concerto, a fantasia for violin and orchestra, and chamber music.

Kücken [ke͞eck′-ĕn], FRIEDRICH WILHELM: *b.* Bleckede (nr. Lüneburg), Nov. 16, 1810; *d.* Schwerin, Apr. 3, 1882. Composer. Studied at Schwerin and became a member of the court orchestra there. Studied further in Berlin (1832), Vienna (1841) and Paris (1843). *Kapellmeister*, Stuttgart, 1851-61. A prolific composer, he wrote a considerable number of violin and cello sonatas and choral works, but his reputation rested chiefly on his songs, which were very popular in their day. His operas *Die Flucht nach der Schweiz* (Berlin, 1839) and *Der Prätendent* (Stuttgart, 1847) were also very successful.

Kufferath [co͝of′-er-ut], (1) HUBERT FERDINAND: *b.* Mülheim (Ruhr), June 10, 1818; *d.* Brussels, June 23, 1896. Violinist, pianist, and composer. Brother of (2) and (3), father of (4). Studied with David and Mendelssohn in Leipzig. Conductor, Männergesangsverein, Cologne, 1841. Settled in Brussels, 1844; teacher, Brussels Conservatoire, 1872. Among his pupils were de Bériot, de Greef and Tinel. He organized a series of chamber concerts in Brussels. His compositions include a symphony, chamber music, piano solos and songs.

(2) JOHANN HERMANN: *b.* Mülheim, May 12, 1797; *d.* Wiesbaden, July 28, 1864. Violinist. Brother of (1) and (3), uncle of (4). A pupil of Spohr. Director of music, Bielefeld, 1823; Utrecht, 1830-62. His compositions include choral works and overtures for orchestra. Also published a manual on singing for schools.

(3) LOUIS: *b.* Mülheim, Nov. 10, 1811: *d.* Brussels, March 2, 1882. Pianist. Brother of (1) and (2), uncle of (4). Director, Music School, Leeuwarden, 1836-50. His compositions include choral works, canons, piano solos and songs.

(4) MAURICE: *b.* Brussels, Jan. 8, 1852: *d.* there, Dec. 8, 1919. Son of (1), nephew of (2) and (3). Trained as a cellist, and studied law at the university. Foreign editor, *Indépendance Belge*, 1873-1900. Also editor and eventually proprietor, *Le Guide Musical*. Director, Théâtre de la Monnaie, Brussels, 1900. Published essays on Wagner's operas, a biography of Vieuxtemps, *L'Art de diriger l'orchestre*, and other works, and translated several operas, including Beethoven's *Fidelio* and Mozart's *Die Entführung aus dem Serail*, and other vocal works.

Kuhnau [coo′-now], JOHANN: *b.* Geising (Saxony), Apr. 6, 1660; *d.* Leipzig, June 5, 1722. Organist and composer. Chorister, Kreuzschule, Dresden. Studied law in Leipzig, where he became organist of St. Thomas's, 1684. University director of music and cantor of St. Thomas's, (Bach's immediate predecessor), 1701. His compositions include church cantatas (modern ed. of 4 in *D.D.T.*, lxviii-lix) and the following keyboard works (modern ed. in *D.D.T.*, iv): *Neue Clavier Übung* (2 vols., each containing 7 suites, 1689 & 1692), *Frische Clavier-Früchte oder sieben Sonaten von guter Invention* (1696), and *Musicalische Vorstellung einiger biblischer Historien in 6 Sonaten, auff dem Claviere zu spielen* (1700). He also published literary works on music. His keyboard compositions have an important place in the music of the 18th cent.:

in particular, the *Biblische Historien* are interesting as early examples of programme music.

Kühnel [cēēn′-ĕl], AUGUST: *b.* Delmenhorst, Aug. 3, 1645. Viola da gamba player. Active as a soloist in Germany and France. He also gave concerts in London in 1685. *Kapellmeister*, Cassel, 1695. Published *Sonate o Partite ad una o due Viole da gamba con il basso continuo* (1698); modern ed. of selected works by A. Einstein, F. Bennat and C. Döbereiner.

Kulenkampff [cōōl′-ĕn-cumpf], GEORGE: *b.* Bremen, Jan. 23, 1898; *d.* Zürich, Oct. 5, 1948. Violinist, a pupil of Willy Hess at the Berlin Hochschule. Leader, Bremen Philharmonic Orchestra, 1916-19. Teacher, Berlin Hochschule, 1923-6. Well-known as a soloist. Lived in Switzerland from 1943.

Kunst der Fuge, Die [dee kōōnst dair foo′-ger], *G. v.* ART OF FUGUE.

Kunzen [cōōnts′-ĕn], FRIEDRICH LUDWIG ÄMILIUS: *b.* Lübeck, Sept. 24, 1761; *d.* Copenhagen, Jan. 28, 1817. Composer. Studied law at Kiel University. Having decided to follow a musical career, he settled in Copenhagen, where his first opera, *Holger Danske* (founded on Wieland's *Oberon*) was performed, 1789. Edited (with Reichardt) the *Musikalische Wochenblatt* and *Musikalische Monatschrift* in Berlin, 1791-2. Opera conductor, Frankfort, 1792; Prague, 1794; Copenhagen, 1795. His compositions include oratorios, operas, cantatas, overtures, sonatas and songs: many of his vocal works are settings of Danish texts. Of his operas the most successful were *Die Weinlese* (Frankfort, 1793) and *Hemmeligheden* (Copenhagen, 1796).

Kurth [cōōrrt], ERNST: *b.* Vienna, Sept. 1, 1886; *d.* Berne, Aug. 2, 1946. Musicologist. Studied at Vienna University. After spending a few years as a theatre conductor and schoolmaster he became lecturer at Berne University, 1912, and professor, 1920. His most important publication is *Grundlagen des linearen Kontrapunkts* (1917), a study of Bach's polyphony. He also published *Romantische Harmonik und ihre Krise in Wagners Tristan* (1920), a study of Bruckner (2 vols., 1925) and *Musikpsychologie* (1931). He was editor of the series *Berner Veröffentlichungen zur Musikforschung*.

Kusser [cōōss′-er] (Cousser), JOHANN SIGMUND: *b.* Pressburg (now Bratislava), Feb. 13, 1660; *d.* Dublin, 1727. Composer, who spent his formative years (1674-82) in Paris, where he was a close friend of Lully. Subsequently court *Kapellmeister*, Brunswick. Director Hamburg Opera, 1694-5. Conductor, Stuttgart Opera, 1698-1704. Came to England and settled in Dublin, where he was appointed master of the King's band and master of the choristers, Christ Church Cathedral, 1710. He published a number of orchestral suites expressly modelled on the French style (4 sets, 1682 & 1700). He also wrote several operas for Brunswick, Hamburg and Stuttgart; modern ed. of the surviving arias of *Erindo* (Hamburg, 1693) in *Das Erbe deutscher Musik, Landschaftsdenkmale, Schleswig-Holstein*, iii. The compositions of his Irish period include a *serenata teatrale* in honour of Queen Anne and a birthday serenade for George I (1724).

Kussevitsky [cooss-er-vit′-ski], SERGEI ALEXANDROVICH. *v.* KOUSSEVITSKY.

Kutchka [cooch′-ca]. Lit. "handful." The name given in Russia to a group of five musicians who were active in the 19th cent. in proclaiming the virtues of a national style based on folk music, and in practising (in varying degrees) what they preached. The leader of the group (known outside Russia as the Five) was Balakirev. The other original members were Borodin, Cui, Moussorgsky and Rimsky-Korsakov.

Kylisma. *v.* QUILISMA.

Kyrie [kirr′-i-ay]. Short for "Kyrie eleison" (*Gr.* κύριε ἐλέησον), "Lord, have mercy." The first part of the Ordinary of the Mass, consisting of three sections: "Kyrie eleison," "Christe eleison," and "Kyrie eleison"—the only part of the Mass in which Greek words survive. The text of each petition is sung three times. Three types of musical setting are found in Gregorian chant: (*a*) with the repetitions in each section sung to the same music, and the third section

("Kyrie eleison") sung to the same music as the first; (*b*) with the repetitions in each section sung to the same music, but different music for sections 1 and 3; (*c*) with independent music for each section, as in (*b*), but with the music of each section cast in the basic form *A B A*. These three types may be expressed diagrammatically as: (*a*) *A A A, B B B, A A A*; (*b*) *A A A, B B B, C C C*; (*c*) *A B A, C D C, E F E* (the third part of the third section being slightly amplified—a feature which also occurs in several examples of the second type). The following *Kyrie* from Mass VIII (known as the *Missa de angelis*) is an example of type (*b*), in which the three sections, though independent, may also be regarded as variants of a single melody:

The custom arose of interpolating into the more elaborate settings additional words, which were sung syllabically to the notes of the melody, or to a portion of it (for an example see *Historical Anthology*, no. 15). A *Kyrie* treated in this way was known as a "farced *Kyrie*" (*Kyrie cum farsura*, lit. "*Kyrie* with stuffing") or a "troped *Kyrie*." The initial words of these interpolations were used as titles for the *Kyries* to which they were added, and these titles survived after the use of tropes was abolished by the Council of Trent in the 16th century.

Polyphonic settings of the *Kyrie* (whether plain or troped) appeared as early as the 13th century. The *Kyrie* naturally had its place in the complete polyphonic settings of the Mass which came into use on the Continent in the 15th century. In England, however, it was the practice of pre-Reformation composers to omit it from their Masses.

After the Reformation the first Prayer-Book of Edward VI (1549) translated the nine-fold *Kyrie* into English as:

Lord, have mercy upon us (3 times)
Christ, have mercy upon us (3 times)
Lord, have mercy upon us (3 times).

The Second Prayer-Book of 1552 introduced the practice of the recitation of the ten commandments by the Priest. After the first nine the people had the petition:

Lord, have mercy upon us, and incline our hearts to keep this law.

After the tenth:

Lord, have mercy upon us, and write all these thy laws in our hearts, we beseech thee.

In this extended form the petition was set polyphonically by English composers: examples will be found in Byrd's "Short Service" and "Great Service" (*T.C.M.*, ii, pp. 72, 81, 175).

L

L. In TONIC SOL-FA = *lah*, the 6th note (or submediant) of the major scale.

La, *Fr. I.* (1) The note A. Also the sixth note of the Guidonian hexachord. *v.* SOLMIZATION.

(2) For French and Italian titles beginning thus see the second word of the title.

Labarre [la-barr], THÉODORE: *b.* Paris March 5, 1805; *d.* there, March 9, 1870. Harpist and composer. Wrote operas, ballets, and compositions and a *Méthode* for harp.

L'Abbé. *v.* ABBÉ.

Labey [la-bay], MARCEL: *b.* Le Vésinet (Seine-et-Oise), Aug. 6, 1875. Composer, conductor and teacher. Studied with Lenormand and d'Indy, on whose style he has modelled his compositions. Has written an opera, orchestral works and chamber music.

Lablache [la-blush], LUIGI: *b.* Naples, Dec. 6, 1794 (of a French father and an Irish mother); *d.* there, Jan. 23, 1858. Bass singer. Trained in the Conservatorio at Naples, he made his début at the San Carlino theatre there in 1812, and thereafter sang with great success all over Europe. He made his first appearance in London in 1830, and in Paris in the same year. Leporello was one of his most famous roles. He was a torch bearer at the burial of Beethoven, and in 1836-7 was Queen Victoria's singing-master.

Labuński [lah-boonss'-ki], (1) FELIX RODERICK: *b.* Ksawerynowo (Poland), Dec. 27, 1892. Composer. Studied in Warsaw and with Nadia Boulanger and Paul Dukas in Paris, and settled in the U.S.A. in 1936. Has composed orchestral works, chamber music, songs, and piano pieces.

(2) WIKTOR: *b.* St. Petersburg, Apr. 14, 1895. Polish pianist, composer, and conductor. Studied at St. Petersburg, and settled in America in 1928. Has composed works for piano and orchestra and for piano solo.

Lach [luckh], ROBERT: *b.* Vienna, Jan. 29, 1874. Historian and composer. From 1911 to 1920 was music librarian at the Vienna State Library, became a lecturer at the University in 1915, and succeeded Adler as professor, 1927-39. Has published a number of studies in musical history, and composed a considerable amount of music in various forms.

Lachmann [luckh'-mun], ROBERT: *b.* Berlin, Nov. 28, 1892; *d.* Jerusalem, May 8, 1939. Collaborated with A. H. Fox Strangways in studies in Eastern music, and worked under Johannes Wolf and Carl Stumpf in Berlin. From 1927 he was attached to the music department of the Prussian State Library, and from 1934 to the Hebrew University at Jerusalem as lecturer. His writings include the section on non-European music in Bücken's *Handbuch der Musikwissenschaft*.

Lachner [luckh'-ner], FRANZ: *b.* Rain (Bavaria), Apr. 2, 1803; *d.* Munich, Jan. 20, 1890. Composer and conductor. Studied in Munich and with the Abbé Stadler in Vienna, where he became *Kapellmeister* at the Kärntnertor Theatre in 1826, and was a friend of Schubert. He conducted at Mannheim from 1834 and at Munich from 1836 until 1865. His numerous compositions in many forms, including eight suites for orchestra, are now forgotten.

Lacombe [la-cõnb], (1) LOUIS TROUILLON: *b.* Bourges, Nov. 26, 1818; *d.* St. Vaast-la-Hougue, Sept. 30, 1884. Pianist and composer. Studied in Paris under Zimmerman and Vienna under Czerny. Composed operas, dramatic symphonies, chamber music and piano pieces. His *Philosophie et Musique* was published in 1895.

(2) PAUL: *b.* Carcassonne, July 11, 1837;

d. there, June 5, 1927. Late romantic composer of early romantic tendencies. Wrote a considerable amount of orchestral music, chamber music and songs.

Ladmirault [lud-mee-ro], PAUL ÉMILE: *b.* Nantes, Dec. 8, 1877; *d.* Camoël, Oct. 30, 1944. Composer. Studied at the Paris Conservatoire under Fauré and Gédalge. Composed a ballet, 2 operas, programmatic works for orchestra, chamber music, piano music, and songs.

Lady Macbeth of Mzensk (Lady Macbeth Mtsenskago Uyezda). Opera in four acts by Shostakovich. Libretto by A. Preiss and the composer (after a novel by Nikolai Leskov). First performed, Moscow, Jan. 22, 1934. Condemned in *Pravda*, Jan. 28, 1936, as a " leftist mess instead of human music."

Lafage (La Fage) [la fuzh], JUSTE ADRIEN LENOIR DE: *b.* Paris, March 28, 1801; *d.* Charenton, March 8, 1862. Historian and writer on music. Studied in Paris and under Baini in Rome. Did much pioneer research into the history and theory of plainsong, and published among other works a *Cours complet de plainchant* (2 vols., 1855-6) and *Essais de dipthérographie musicale* (2 vols., 1864). He composed some vocal and instrumental music.

L'Africaine. *v.* AFRICAINE.

Lage [lah'-ger], *G.* (1) Position, *e.g.* on a stringed instrument or of a chord (*v.* INVERSION).

(2) The range of instruments or voices.

La Guerre [la gairr]. *v.* JACQUET, ÉLISABETH-CLAUDE.

Lah. Anglicized form of the Italian *la* (A). In TONIC SOL-FA the 6th note (or submediant) of the major scale.

La Hale (Halle), ADAM DE. *v.* ADAM.

Lai [lay], *F.* A type of trouvère song closely related in form to the SEQUENCE, consisting of sections of irregular length, each with melodic repetition. A single stanza of the poem could comprise one or more sections. Machaut's 18 *lais*, of which 16 are monodic, were more regular in form than those of the 13th cent.; each stanza falls, with few exceptions, into two parts, each sung to the same melody. In the *Leich*, the equivalent form adopted by the *Minnesinger* in the 14th cent., complete regularity in the setting of each pair of stanzas to one melody is observed, as in the sequence. Examples of trouvère *lais* are printed in A. Jeanroy, L. Brandin, and P. Aubry, *Lais et descorts français* (1901).

Laissez vibrer [lace-ay vee-bray], *Fr.* " Let it vibrate." An indication to the player of a harp, cymbal, etc. that the sound must not be damped (the opposite of *étouffez*).

Lajtha [loy'-tŏ], LÁSZLÓ: *b.* Budapest, June 30, 1892. Composer. Became in 1913 a member of the folklore division of the Hungarian National Museum, where he carried out researches in Hungarian folk music, and in 1938 teacher at the Budapest Conservatory. Has composed a ballet, chamber music, piano works, and songs.

Lakmé [luck-may]. Opera in three acts by Delibes. Libretto by Edmond Gondinet and Philippe Gille (based on Gondinet's poem *Le Mariage de Loti*). First performed, Paris, Apr. 14, 1883.

Lalande [la-lũnd], MICHEL RICHARD DE; *b.* Paris, Dec. 15, 1657; *d.* Versailles, June 18, 1726. The most significant French composer of church music of his time. In 1683 he became one of the superintendents, and later sole superintendent, of the music of Louis XIV's chapel, for which he wrote 42 motets for chorus and instruments. A complete copy is in the Fitzwilliam Museum at Cambridge. He also composed three *Leçons de Ténèbres* for solo voice, cantatas, ballets and chamber music.

La Laurencie. *v.* LAURENCIE.

Lalla-Roukh [lull-a rook]. Opera in two acts by Félicien David. Libretto by Hippolyte Lucas and Michel Carré (based on Moore's poem). First performed, Paris, May 12, 1862.

L'Allegro. *v.* ALLEGRO, IL PENSEROSO.

Lalo [la-lo], VICTOR ANTOINE ÉDOUARD: *b.* Lille, Jan. 27, 1823; *d.* Paris, April 22, 1892. French composer of Spanish origin. Studied at Lille and at the Paris Conservatoire under Habeneck and Crèvecoeur. His most successful work is the *Symphonie espagnole* for violin and orchestra, first played by Sarasate in Paris in 1875. His opera *Le Roi d'Ys* (Paris, 1888) and ballet *Namouna* have also kept a place in the repertory. His other compositions include 2 operas and a pantomime, 3 concertos, works for violin and orchestra, chamber music and songs.

Laloy [la-lwa], LOUIS: *b.* Grey (Saône), Feb. 18, 1874; *d.* Dôle, March 3, 1944. Historian and critic. Studied at the Schola Cantorum and the University of Paris. Founded in 1905 the *Mercure Musical*, which became in 1907 the Bulletin of the International Music Society. From 1915 was general secretary of the Paris Opéra. Published books on Greek and Chinese music, and on Rameau and Debussy.

Lambe. (1) English composer of the early 15th century. His only surviving composition is a three-part *Sanctus* in the Old Hall manuscript (ed. A. Ramsbotham and H. B. Collins, iii, p. 9).

(2) WALTER: *b.* Salisbury, 1451. Composer. Elected King's Scholar at Eton on July 8, 1467 (at the age of fifteen), and was later a member of the choir of St. George's, Windsor, where he was Master of the Choristers, with William Edmonds, in 1479-80. One of the most accomplished composers of his generation. Compositions that have survived complete comprise six antiphons and a Magnificat printed in *Musica Britannica*, x-xii.

Lambert, CONSTANT: *b.* London, Aug. 23, 1905; *d.* there, Aug. 21, 1951. Composer, conductor, and critic. While he was still a student at the R.C.M. Diaghilev commissioned from him the music for the ballet *Romeo and Juliet*, produced at Monte Carlo in 1926. The great success of his setting for chorus, solo piano, and orchestra without woodwind of Sacheverell Sitwell's *Rio Grande* (1929), which makes effective use of jazz idioms, was not repeated by his later works, which did not achieve a consistent style. They include *Music for Orchestra* (1931), the masque *Summer's Last Will and Testament* (1936), the ballet *Horoscope* (1938), a piano concerto, a piano sonata, and songs. He conducted the Sadler's Wells ballet from 1937, was music critic for the *Sunday Referee*, and published a book *Music Ho!* (1934), containing witty and penetrating observations on contemporary music.

Lament. There are examples of early medieval laments (*L.* planctus) with music which may date from the seventh century. A transcription of a lament on the death of Charlemagne (814) is printed in Naumann's *History of Music*, (English ed., 1880), vol. i, p. 199. A *Planctus Mariae Virginis* in the form of a sequence by Godefrid of Breteuil (*d.* 1196) is printed in F. Gennrich, *Grundriss einer Formenlehre des mittelalterlichen Liedes* (1932), p. 143. The troubadour Gaucelm Faidit wrote a lament (*planh*) on the death (1199) of Richard Lion-Heart (J. Beck, *La Musique des troubadours*, 1910, p. 92).

In Irish and Scottish folk music the lament is a type of song or piece for bagpipes. Examples will be found in Bunting's *Ancient Music of Ireland* (1840) and in the standard collections of Irish and Scottish folk music.

The earliest and one of the most famous of the laments in seventeenth-century opera is Monteverdi's "Lamento d'Arianna," the only surviving fragment of the opera *Arianna* (1608). Later examples in opera and oratorio were conventionally written on a falling chromatic GROUND BASS, as is the lament of Dido in Purcell's *Dido and Aeneas* (1689).

There are three laments for harpsichord by J. J. Froberger, which have been published in *D.T.Ö.*, x (2). They are a Lamentation on the death of the Emperor Ferdinand III (1657), a *Plainte* in the form of an Allemande composed in London "to purge Melancoly," and a *Tombeau* on the death of M. Blancrocher. Ravel copied the idea of the 17th-cent. *tombeau* in his *Tombeau de Couperin* (for piano 1914-17; transcribed for orchestra, 1919). *v.* also TOMBEAU.

Lamentations. At Matins (*Tenebrae*) on Thursday, Friday, and Saturday of Holy Week the first three lessons, from the Lamentations of Jeremiah, are sung to a chant, including their initial Hebrew letters (*Aleph*, *Beth*, etc.). The first polyphonic setting is that of Okeghem (1474); Palestrina's setting (1588) has continued to be sung ever since in the

Sistine Chapel. Settings by three English composers of the 16th cent., Tallis, Byrd, and White, have been published in *Tudor Church Music*, vi, ix, & v.

L'Amico Fritz. *v.* AMICO FRITZ.

Lamond, FREDERIC: *b.* Glasgow, Jan. 28, 1868; *d.* Stirling, Feb. 21, 1948. Pianist. Studied in Frankfort, and under von Bülow and Liszt. From 1885 gave recitals in many countries and became known for his fine playing of Beethoven. He taught in Berlin from 1904 and at The Hague for several years after 1917. He composed a symphony and some chamber music and piano pieces.

E. NEWMAN & IRENE TRIESCH-LAMOND: *The Memoirs of Frederic Lamond* (1949).

L'Amore dei Tre Re. *v.* AMORE DEI TRE RE.

L'Amour des Trois Oranges. *v.* AMOUR.

Lamoureux [la-moo-rer], CHARLES: *b.* Bordeaux, Sept. 28, 1834; *d.* Paris, Dec. 21, 1899. Violinist and conductor. Studied at the Paris Conservatoire. Conductor, Opéra-Comique, 1876-7; Opéra, 1877-9. In 1881 he founded the Concerts Lamoureux, at which he conducted extracts from Wagner's operas and compositions by the younger French composers of the day.

Lampe [lump'-er], JOHN FREDERICK: *b.* Saxony, 1703; *d.* Edinburgh, July 25, 1751. Composer. Arrived in England about 1725 as bassoonist in the opera orchestra, and lived in London. Went to Dublin in 1748 and to Edinburgh in 1750. Composed music for plays and burlesque operas, including *Pyramus and Thisbe, a mock opera, the words taken from Shakespeare* (1745), songs, and tunes for Charles Wesley's hymns. He published a thorough-bass method in 1737 and *The Art of Music* in 1740.

Lampugnani [lahm-poon-yahn'-ee], GIOVANNI BATTISTA: *b.* Milan, 1706; *d.* there 1781. Composer. Lived in London from 1743 as opera composer and conductor. His opera *Semiramide* (Rome, 1741), songs from other operas, and two sets of trio sonatas were published in England by Walsh.

Landi [lahn'-dee], STEFANO: *b.* Rome, *c.* 1590; *d.* there, *c.* 1655. Composer. *Maestro di cappella* in Padua from about 1619 and a member of the Papal chapel from 1629. Composed madrigals, monodies, church music and instrumental canzonas. Of special importance in the history of opera is his *Sant' Alessio* (Rome, 1632), on a sacred subject with comic scenes and dance songs. Extracts are printed in Torchi, *L'arte musicale in Italia*, v and in H. Goldschmidt, *Studien zur Geschichte der italienischen Oper*, i, which also contains examples from his *La morte d'Orfeo* (Rome, 1619).

Landini [lahn-dee'-nee], FRANCESCO: *b.* Fiesole, 1325; *d.* Florence, Sept. 2, 1397. The most famous Italian composer of his age. Became blind in childhood. His surviving compositions number 154, of which all but 13 are *ballate*. Most of them are contained in a 15th-cent. manuscript which belonged to the organist Antonio Squarcialupi (*d.* 1475) and which depicts him with his *organetto*. He was celebrated for his playing on this and other instruments. His complete works, with an introduction, are published in L. Ellinwood, *The Works of Francesco Landini* (1939).

Landini Cadence, Landini Sixth. A cadential formula, called after the composer Francesco Landini, in which the cadence note is preceded by notes a second and a third below it, *i.e.*, by the seventh and sixth degrees of its scale. It appears in Landini's contemporaries, and was widely used by French and English composers of the 15th century.

DUNSTABLE, *Veni sancti Spiritus*.

Ländler [lent'-ler], *G.* An Austrian dance having the rhythm and character of a slow WALTZ. There are examples by Mozart, Beethoven, Schubert, and Lanner.

Landormy [lũn-dorr-mee], PAUL CHARLES RENÉ: *b.* Issy-les-Moulineaux (Seine), Jan. 3, 1869; *d.* Paris, Nov. 17, 1943. Critic and historian. Was a teacher of philosophy until 1892, when he went to Paris to study musical subjects. From 1918 was music critic for

La Victoire and also wrote for *Le Temps*. His books include biographies of Brahms, Bizet, Gluck, Schubert and Gounod, and various studies in 19th-cent. music. His *Histoire de la Musique* was published in 1910, and an English translation, with a supplementary chapter on American music, by F. H. Martens in 1923.

Landowska [lahn-dov'-ska], WANDA: *b.* Warsaw, July 5, 1877. Harpsichordist and pianist. Studied in Warsaw and Berlin. In 1919 she opened a school and centre for concerts at Saint-Leu-la-Forêt, near Paris, and since 1940 has lived in New York. By her playing, teaching, and writing she has played an important part in the revival of the harpsichord and its music. She has published two books, *Bach et ses interprètes* (1906) and *La Musique ancienne* (1908), and many articles. Manuel de Falla and Francis Poulenc have composed harpsichord concertos specially for her.

Lang, PAUL HENRY: *b.* Budapest, Aug. 28, 1901. Musical historian. In 1943 became Professor of Musicology at Columbia University, New York, and in 1945 editor of the *Musical Quarterly*. Has published *Music in Western Civilisation* (1943).

Lange [lung'-er], (1) ALOYSIA. *v.* WEBER (1).

(2) HIERONYMUS GREGOR: *b.* Havelberg, *c.* 1540; *d.* Breslau, May 1, 1587. Composer. Cantor at Frankfort-on-the-Oder from 1574-84. Wrote Latin and German motets and German songs. A selection of motets for 4 to 8 voices from his *Cantiones sacrae* (1580) was printed in *Publikationen der Gesellschaft für Musikforschung*, xxv. His "Vae misero mihi" (p. 6) is remarkable for its chromaticism.

Lange-Müller [lung'-er-meel'-er], PETER ERASMUS: *b.* Frederiksborg, Dec. 1, 1850; *d.* Copenhagen, Feb. 25, 1926. Composer. Studied at the Royal Conservatoire in Copenhagen, and composed operas, two symphonies, choral works, songs, and chamber music.

Langhans [lung'-hunce], FRIEDRICH WILHELM: *b.* Hamburg, Sept. 21, 1832; *d.* Berlin, June 9, 1892. Violinist and historian. Studied at Berlin and Leipzig. Was leader of the Düsseldorf orchestra from 1857-60, and from 1874 taught musical history in Berlin. Published several books on the history of music. His *Die Musikgeschichte in 12 Vorträgen* (1879) was translated into English by J. H. Cornell as *The History of Music in 12 Lectures* (1896).

Langlais [lũn-glay], JEAN: *b.* La Fontenelle (Ille-et-Vilaine), Feb. 15, 1907. Blind organist and composer. A pupil of Dupré and Dukas at the Paris Conservatoire, where he won the *premier prix* for organ in 1930. Organist, St. Clotilde, Paris, since 1953. In addition to organ music his compositions include orchestral works (among them a piano concerto and a concerto for organ or harpsichord), choral works, chamber music and songs.

Langsam [lung'-zum], *G.* Slow.

Laniere. A family of English musicians of French descent in the 16th and 17th centuries. The most famous member, Nicholas, was baptized in London in Sept. 10, 1588 and died there in Feb., 1666. He may have been the first to write recitative in England when in 1617 Ben Jonson's *Lovers made Men* "was sung (after the Italian manner) *Stylo recitativo*, by Master Nicholas Lanier; who ordered and made both the Scene, and the Musicke." He wrote music for other masques, besides a cantata, songs, and dialogues. In 1625 he was sent to Italy to buy pictures for Charles I, and in the following year became Master of the King's Music. During the Commonwealth he was in the Netherlands, and returned at the Restoration and resumed his positions at Court. A self-portrait is in the School of Music at Oxford.

Lanner [lun'-er], JOSEPH FRANZ KARL: *b.* Vienna, Apr. 12, 1801; *d.* Oberdöbling, (nr. Vienna), Apr. 14, 1843. The first composer on a large scale of Viennese dance music in the 19th century. Published 208 waltzes, *Ländler*, polkas, etc.

Lantins [lũn-tãn], (1) ARNOLD DE. Born in the province of Liège, he became a singer in the Papal chapel in 1431. Of his 13 sacred compositions, which include a complete Mass, four have been published by Charles van den Borren in *Polyphonia Sacra* (1938). The same editor has published the 14 surviving three-part *chan-*

sons in *Pièces polyphoniques profanes de provenance liègeoise* (1950).

(2) HUGH DE. Composer of the first half of the 15th cent., born in the province of Liège. His compositions show that he spent some time in Italy. Charles van den Borren has edited 4 of his 12 liturgical compositions in *Polyphonia Sacra* (1932), and four Italian *canzoni* and 14 French *chansons* in *Pièces polyphoniques profanes de provenance liègeoise* (1950). The latter make, for their time, remarkably constant use of imitation.

L'Apprenti Sorcier. *v.* APPRENTI SORCIER.

L'Après-Midi d'un Faune. *v.* PRÉLUDE À L'APRÈS-MIDI D'UN FAUNE.

Lara, ISIDORE DE (Cohen): *b.* London, Aug. 9, 1858; *d.* Paris, Sept. 2, 1935. Singer and composer. Studied in Milan and Paris. Composed songs, and a number of operas in an easy lyric style which were produced at Covent Garden and abroad.

Largamente [larr-gah-men'-teh], *I.* Broadly.

Largando [larr-gahnd'-o]. *v.* ALLARGANDO.

Large. The longest note (*L.* maxima) in the medieval system of MENSURAL NOTATION. It had virtually disappeared from practical use by the beginning of the 16th century.

Larghetto [larr-get'-to], *I.* Slow and broad, but less so than *largo.*

Largo [larr'-go], *I.* Slow and broad.

Larigot [la-ree-go], *Fr.* An organ stop. Its pipes are open cylindrical metal pipes which sound at the 19th, *i.e* two octaves and a fifth above normal (8 ft.) pitch.

L'Arlésienne. *v.* ARLÉSIENNE.

Larsson [larrsh'-on], LARS-ERIK: *b.* Åkarp, Sweden, May 15, 1908. Composer. Studied in Stockholm, in Vienna under Alban Berg, and in Leipzig. In 1929-30 he was chorus master at the Stockholm Opera and since 1937 has been conductor in the State Radio. Has composed 3 symphonies, 3 overtures and other orchestral music, chamber music, choral works, film music and songs.

La Rue, PIERRE DE. *v.* RUE.

Lassú [losh'-oo], *H.* *v.* CSÁRDÁS.

Lassus [lahss'-ooss], ROLAND DE (Orlando di Lasso): *b.* Mons, 1532; *d.* Munich, June 14, 1594. Composer. The most famous contemporary of Palestrina, remarkable for the wide range of his forms and the versatility of his expression. He was taken to Italy as a boy, and in 1553-4 was choirmaster at St. John Lateran in Rome. In 1554 he travelled with Giulio Cesare Brancaccio to England and then to Anvers. In 1556 he became a member of the chapel of the Duke of Bavaria at Munich, which he directed from 1560 until his death.

Among his very numerous compositions are Masses, motets, Magnificats, Passions, psalms, Italian madrigals and *villanelles,* French *chansons,* and German choral *Lieder* and chorale-motets. His style encompasses every resource of 16th-cent. choral technique. Of the projected 60 volumes of the complete edition of his works 22 have been published.

C. VAN DEN BORREN : *Orlande de Lassus* (4th ed., 1943).

La Tombelle [la tõn-bell], FERNAND DE (Antoine Louis Joseph Gueyrand Fernand Fouant): *b.* Paris, Aug. 3, 1854 ; *d.* Château de Fayrac (Dordogne), Aug. 13, 1928. Organist and composer. Studied under Guilmant and Dubois at the Paris Conservatoire and under Saint-Saëns, won various prizes for composition and toured as an organist. He was assistant organist (to Dubois) at the Madeleine in Paris (1885-98), gave organ concerts at the Trocadero with Guilmant (from 1878) and was appointed professor at the Schola Cantorum. He composed two operettas, incidental music for plays, ballets, a symphonic poem, orchestral suites, oratorios, cantatas, a Mass, motets, works for orgen and for harmonium, chamber music and songs.

L'Attaque du Moulin. *v.* ATTAQUE DU MOULIN.

Lauda [lowd'-ah], *I.* *Laude* were songs of popular devotion in Italy which probably date from the time of St. Francis (1182-1226). The 14th-cent. examples which survive with their melodies, numbering about 150, are associated with the flagellants of Northern Italy, who sang *laude spirituali* in their processions (*v.* also HUGO VON REUTLINGEN). In later centuries the singing of *laude* was fostered by local fraternities of *Laudisti.* Throughout the 16th cent. polyphonic *laude* in the style of the simpler secular forms were published, and the addition of the dramatic element to their performance in the oratory of Filippo Neri in Florence after 1560 provided one of the points of departure for the ORATORIO. Examples of monophonic *laude* are published in F. Liuzzi, *La Lauda* (2 vols., 1934), of polyphonic in K. Jeppesen, *Die mehrstimmige italienische Lauda* (1935).

Launis [low′-neece], ARMAS: *b.* Hämeenlinna, Finland, Apr. 22, 1884. Composer and musicologist. Studied at Helsinki and Berlin. Has composed operas, orchestral works and piano music, and published books on traditional Finnish music.

Laurencie [lo-rŭn-see], COMTE MARIE BERTRAND LIONEL JULES DE LA: *b.* Nantes, July 24, 1861; *d.* Paris, Nov. 21, 1933. Historian. Studied music and law in Paris and musical subjects at the Paris Conservatoire. Began his musical writings with a study of *Parsifal* in 1888-94, and after 1898 devoted himself entirely to musical history. Lecturer, *École des hautes études sociales,* 1906. Editor, *Encyclopédie de la Musique,* 1916. Founded the *Société française de Musicologie,* 1917. His writings include books on Lully and Rameau, and on the history of French opera and instrumental music.

Laute [lowt′-er], *G.* Lute.

Lautenclavicymbel [lowt′-ĕn-cluv-ee-tseĕm′-bĕl], *G.* Lute-harpsichord, *i.e.* harpsichord with gut strings instead of metal strings. The instrument existed in the sixteenth century, and Bach had one made in 1740.

Lavallée [la-vull-ay], CALIXA: *b.* Verchères (Quebec), Dec. 28, 1842; *d.* Boston, Jan. 21, 1891. Pianist and composer. Studied at the Paris Conservatoire, and settled in Boston as a teacher. He is best known as the composer of the Canadian national anthem *O Canada.*

Lavignac [la-veen-yuck], ALEXANDRE JEAN ALBERT: *b.* Paris, Jan. 21, 1846; *d.* there, May 28, 1916. Theorist and writer. Studied theory and organ at the Conservatoire, and became teacher of solfège in 1875 and of harmony in 1891. Founded and edited the *Encyclopédie de la Musique,* which was continued after his death by Laurencie. Wrote on theoretical subjects and on the operas of Wagner. His *Voyage artistique à Bayreuth* (1895) was translated into English by Esther Singleton as *The Music Dramas of Richard Wagner* (1898).

Lavoix [la-vwa], HENRI MARIE FRANÇOIS: *b.* Paris, Apr. 26, 1846; *d.* there Dec. 27, 1897. Writer on music. Educated at the Sorbonne, and studied music privately. Became librarian of the Bibliothèque Nationale in 1865. Wrote a history of music and books on music in medieval iconography and other subjects.

Lawes, (1) HENRY: *b.* Dinton (Wilts.), Jan. 5, 1596; *d.* London, Oct. 21, 1662. Composer. Became a member of the Chapel Royal in 1626; resumed his position there at the Restoration in 1660 and wrote a coronation anthem for Charles II. Milton and Herrick wrote poems in praise of his music and performance. His compositions include songs, music for masques, including Milton's *Comus* (1634), part of the music for Davenant's *The Siege of Rhodes* (1656), psalm tunes, and anthems.

(2) WILLIAM: *b.* Salisbury, Apr., 1602; *d.* Chester, 1645. Brother of (1). Composer. Was a pupil of Coprario, and became one of the musicians of Charles I after his accession in 1625. He joined the Royalist army in the Civil War, and was killed at the siege of Chester. He was an accomplished composer of instrumental fancies, two of which are printed in E. H. Meyer, *English Chamber Music* (1946), and wrote anthems, psalms, songs, and catches.

Lazzari [lah-tsah′-ree], SYLVIO: *b.* Bozen (Tyrol), Dec. 30, 1857; *d.* Paris, June 18, 1944. Composer. Studied at Innsbruck, Munich, and at the Paris Conservatoire under Franck and Guiraud. Became a naturalised Frenchman. Has composed operas, symphonic poems, a symphony, chamber music, piano music, and songs.

Leader. (1) The principal first violin

of an orchestra (*A.* concert-master, *Fr.* chef d'attaque, *G.* Konzertmeister).

(2) The first violin of a string quartet.

(3) *A.* Conductor.

Leading-Note (*Fr.* note sensible, *G.* Leitton): The seventh degree of the scale (*e.g.* B in the scale of C), so-called because of its tendency to rise to ("lead to") the tonic. It is a semitone below the tonic in the major and in both forms of the minor scale. In the medieval modes this was true only of the modes with the finals F and C, whereas in the modes with the finals D, G and A the seventh degree was a whole tone below the final. It is generally held that in these modes the singers were accustomed to sharpening the leading note in certain contexts before it became usual to mark such sharpening in manuscript and prints. Editors of music written before 1600 have usually supplied such accidentals, but the evidence is not at all clear, and the practice probably varied according to period and place. In any event, the term implies that the rise of a semitone tends to support the tonic as the key-note, and is thus essentially bound up with post-Renaissance theories of harmony and tonality. The fall of a semitone to the tonic has a similar function of supporting the tonic in chromatic harmony, as in Hindemith's theory of tonality, in which both D♭ and B in the key of C, for example, are leading-notes.

Leading-Note Chord. The chord on the leading note contains a diminished fifth, and is therefore a discord, which is usually resolved on the tonic chord, *e.g.*, in the key of C:

It is much more often used in the first inversion than in the root position:

The second inversion normally occurs only in three-part writing:

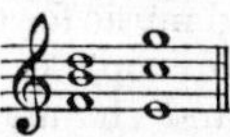

v. CHORD, HARMONY, INVERSION.

Le Bègue. *v.* BÈGUE.

Lebhaft [labe'-huft], *G.* Lively.

Lechner [le*sh*'-ner], LEONHARD: *b.* Etschtal (Austrian Tyrol), *c.* 1553; *d.* Stuttgart, Sept. 9, 1606. Composer. Was a choirboy under Lassus in Munich, a teacher in Nuremberg from 1575, *Kapellmeister* at Hechingen from 1584 and at Stuttgart from 1595 to his death. One of the most important and capable German composers of his time, he wrote Masses, motets, Magnificats, a St. John Passion, sacred and secular songs to German words, and edited works of Lassus. His little 3-part song *Gut Singer und ein Organist* (from the *Teutschen Villanelle,* 1590) is printed in Wolf's *Music of Earlier Times,* No. 42.

Leclair [le*r*-clair], JEAN-MARIE: *b.* Lyons, May 10, 1697; *d.* Paris, Oct. 22, 1764. Composer and violinist. In 1722 was a dancing-master in Turin where he studied the violin under Somis. From 1729 he lived in Paris. Was the first to adapt the French instrumental style to the concerto form of Vivaldi. In his chamber music he shows both a progressive technique and a mature command of expression in writing for the violin. Besides concertos and solo and trio sonatas he composed an opera and ballets.

Lecocq [le*r*-cock], ALEXANDRE CHARLES: *b.* Paris, June 3, 1832; *d.* there, Oct. 24, 1918. Composer. Studied at the Paris Conservatoire, where Halévy was one of his teachers. His first successful operetta was *Fleur de Thé,* and with *La Fille de Madame Angot* (1872) and *Giroflé-Girofla* (1874) his position was established. He wrote a series of operettas until 1911, and in 1877 edited a vocal score of Rameau's *Castor et Pollux.*

Ledger Lines. *v.* LEGER LINES.

Lefébure-Wély [le*r*-fay-bēer-vay-lee], LOUIS JAMES ALFRED: *b.* Paris, Nov. 13, 1817; *d.* there, Dec. 31, 1869. Organist and composer. Studied at the Conservatoire, and was organist at the Madeleine from 1847-58 and at St. Sulpice from 1863. Composed music for the organ and harmonium, an opera, symphonies, church music, and chamber music.

Lefebvre [ler-fevr], CHARLES ÉDOUARD: *b.* Paris, June 19, 1843; *d.* Aix-les-Bains, Sept. 8, 1917. Composer. Studied at the Conservatoire and was awarded the *Prix de Rome* in 1870. In 1895 became professor in charge of the ensemble class at the Conservatoire. Composed operas, a symphony and other orchestral music, church music and chamber music.

Le Flem, PAUL. *v.* FLEM.

Legatissimo [leh-gah-tee'-see-mo], *I.* As smooth as possible.

Legato [leh-gah'-toh], *I.* Smooth.

Legatura [leh-gah-too'-rah], *I.* Slur.

Légature [lay-ga-teer], *Fr.* Slur.

Legend of St. Elizabeth, The. Oratorio with a prologue and four scenes by Liszt. Text by Otto Roquette. First performed, in Hungarian, Budapest, Aug. 15, 1865. Subsequently produced as an opera, for the first time at the Weimar Court Theatre, Oct. 23, 1881.

Legend of the Invisible City of Kitezh, The. Opera in four acts by Rimsky-Korsakov. Libretto by Vladimir Ivanovich Belsky. First performed, St. Petersburg, Feb. 20, 1907.

Legend of the Czar Saltan, The. Opera with a prologue and four acts by Rimsky-Korsakov. Libretto by Vladimir Ivanovich Belsky (on a tale by Pushkin). First performed, Moscow, Nov. 3, 1900.

Legends. The title given to a set of four symphonic poems by Sibelius (Op. 22) which are based on the Finnish national epic *Kalevala.* They are entitled:

No. 1 *Lemminkäinen and the Maidens* (1895 ; final form, 1900).

No. 2 *Lemminkäinen in Tuonela* (1895 ; final form, 1900).

No. 3 *The Swan of Tuonela* (1893, as prelude to the unfinished opera *The Building of the Boat* ; final form, 1900).

No. 4 *Lemminkäinen's Homecoming* (1895 ; final form, 1900).

Leger Lines. Short lines above or below the staff, used to indicate the pitch of notes which lie outside it.

Légèrement [lay-zhairr-mũn], *Fr.* Lightly.

Leggero [leh-djeh'-ro], *I.* = LEGGIERO.

Leggiero [leh-djeh'-ro], *I.* Light.

Legno [lehn'-yo], *I.* Wood. *Col legno,* lit. " with the wood," *i.e.* a direction to string players to bounce the stick of the bow on the strings instead of playing with the hair (*v.* BOW, BOWING). *Organo di legno,* a 17th-cent. term for a chamber organ with flue pipes, as opposed to the *regale* (*E.* regal), which had only reed pipes. *Stromenti di legno,* woodwind instruments.

Legrenzi [leh-gren'-tsee], GIOVANNI: baptised Clusone (nr. Bergamo), Aug. 12, 1626 ; *d.* Venice, May 26, 1690. Composer. Director of the *Conservatario dei Mendicanti* at Venice, and from 1685 was choirmaster at St. Mark's. His work has an important place in the history both of opera and of instrumental music in the 17th cent. In the arias of his 17 operas he makes some use of a short *da capo* form. Was an early practitioner of the TRIO SONATA, and also wrote oratorios, cantatas, ensemble sonatas and church music. Bach wrote a fugue for organ on a theme by Legrenzi (*B.G.* xxxviii, p. 94). An ensemble sonata is printed in Apel and Davison's *Historical Anthology,* Vol. II, No. 220, and an aria in Schering's *History of Music in Examples,* No. 231.

Lehár [leh'-harr], FRANZ: *b.* Komárom (Hungary), April 30, 1870; *d.* Bad Ischl, Oct. 24, 1948. Composer. Studied at the Prague Conservatoire. After conducting military bands in various cities he settled in Vienna in 1902, and became famous as a composer of operettas, of which the most successful was *Die lustige Witwe* (The Merry Widow, Vienna, 1905).

Lehmann [leh'-mun], (1) LILLI: *b.* Würzburg, Nov. 24, 1848; *d.* Berlin, May 17, 1929. Soprano at the Berlin Opera from 1870, at the Metropolitan, New York, 1885-9; returned to Germany in 1889. First appeared in London in 1880. Was associated with the Mozart Festivals in Salzburg from 1905. Her performances in Wagner and Mozart were especially notable. Her books *Meine Gesangkunst* and *Mein Weg* were translated into English as *How to Sing* (1903) and *My Path through Life* (1914).

(2) LOTTE: *b.* Perleberg, July 2, 1885. Soprano. Studied in Berlin and made her début in Hamburg in 1910. Sang in the first production of Strauss's *Ariadne* (Vienna, 1912) and *Die Frau ohne Schatten* (Vienna, 1919). Joined the Metropolitan Opera, New York, in 1933, and has lived in America since 1938. Has published *Wings of Song* (1938), *More than Singing* (1945), *My Many Lives* (1948), and a novel *Eternal Flight* (1938).

Leich [ly*sh*], *G. v.* LAI.

Leichtentritt [ly*sh*′-tĕn-tritt], HUGO: *b.* Pleschen (nr. Posen), Jan. 1, 1874; *d.* Cambridge (Mass.), Nov. 13, 1951. Musicologist and composer. Studied at Harvard University (1891-94), in Paris (1894) and in Berlin at the Hochschule für Musik (1895-98) and the University. He was appointed teacher at the Klindworth-Scharwenka Conservatoire, critic for the Berlin *Vossische Zeitung* and lecturer on music at Harvard (1933). He retired in 1941. He edited several volumes of the *Denkmäler deutscher Tonkunst* and other collections, and wrote a history of the motet (1908), *Musikalische Formenlehre* (1911; published in English as *Musical Form*, 1952), *Music, History and Ideas* (1938) and *Serge Koussevitzky* (1946). He composed operas, a symphony and other orchestral works, a piano concerto, a cycle for women's chorus and orchestra, chamber music, variations and études for piano, and many songs.

Leider [lide′-er], FRIEDA: *b.* Berlin, Apr. 18, 1888. Operatic soprano, who excelled in performances of Wagner's works. She sang for many years at the Berlin State Opera, as well as at Covent Garden, the Vienna State Opera and other European opera houses.

Leier [ly′-er], *G.* Hurdy-gurdy (*Drehleier*). Also, in a general sense, *lyra* (lyre). The instrument which figures in Schubert's song *Der Leiermann* is a hurdy-gurdy.

Leifs [lifes], JÓN: *b.* Sólheimar (Iceland), May 1, 1899. Composer and conductor. Studied in Leipzig and conducted in various German cities. He was conductor of the Leipzig Volksakademie (1923-24) and of the Hamburg Philharmonic during a tour of the northland, and was appointed state music and radio director at Reykjavik (1935). He has arranged Icelandic folksongs and dances and composed an overture, *Iceland*, and other orchestral works, an organ concerto, choral works, songs and piano pieces.

Leigh, WALTER: *b.* London, June 22, 1905; *d.* Libya, June 12, 1942. Composer. Studied at Cambridge under Dent and at the Berlin Hochschule für Musik under Hindemith. Musical director, Festival Theatre, Cambridge, 1931-2. Killed while serving as a British soldier in Libya. He composed two comic operas, a pantomime, two revues, incidental music for plays and for films, an overture, orchestral works for amateurs, a concertino for harpsichord and strings, chamber music and songs.

Leighton, WILLIAM: *d.* before 1617. Composer, publisher and poet. He was one of the Gentlemen Pensioners of the court under Elizabeth I and James I, and published in 1614 (during a period of imprisonment for debt) a collection of fifty-three metrical psalms and hymns, entitled *Teares or Lamentacions of a Sorrowfull Soule.* Eight were set by himself and the remainder by contemporary composers, including Byrd, Bull, Dowland, Gibbons, Peerson, Weelkes, Wilbye and "Timolphus Thopul" (=Th. Lupo). Seventeen of the pieces are "consort songs," a treble viol and lute playing with the cantus part, recorder and cittern with the altus, bandora with the tenor, and bass viol with the bassus. The others are for four and five parts without accompaniment.

Leitmotiv [lite′-mo-teef], *G.* "Leading theme." Term used in 1887 by H. von Wolzogen in a discussion of Wagner's *Götterdämmerung* for the numerous recurring themes symbolising characters, objects, and ideas which Wagner used in the *Ring*. Two reasons in particular contributed to the extensive use of "leading themes" in the *Ring* cycle: the fact that the thematic substance of the music is contained in the orchestral part, and the large scale of the drama.

Recurring themes had been used in earlier operas, *e.g.* in Mozart's *Don Giovanni* and *Così fan tutte*, Grétry's *Richard Coeur-de-Lion* and Weber's *Der Freischütz*, and the idea of the recurrence and transformation of themes had been developed in orchestral music by Berlioz, Schumann, and Liszt. From Wagner's later operas the principle was adopted by a number of opera composers, notably by Richard Strauss.

Leitton [lite'-tone], *G.* Leading-note.

Le Jeune, CLAUDE. *v.* JEUNE.

Lekeu [ler-ker], GUILLAUME: *b.* Heusy (nr. Verviers), Jan. 20, 1870; *d.* Angers, Jan. 21, 1894. Composer. Studied in Paris (from 1888) under César Franck and d'Indy, and won the second prize in the Belgian *Prix de Rome* competition of 1891. He composed orchestral works, *Chant Lyrique* for chorus and orchestra, *Introduction* and *Adagio* for brass, chamber music, *Trois Poèmes* for voice and piano, and piano pieces.

Le Maistre [ler metr] (Le Maître), MATTHIEU: *d.* Dresden, 1577. Dutch composer. He was appointed court *Kapellmeister* at Dresden in 1554 and retired in 1567. He composed Magnificats (1577), five-part motets (1570), Latin and German sacred music (1563, 1574), German secular songs and Quodlibets.

Lemminkäinen. *v.* LEGENDS.

Léner Quartet. A string quartet of Hungarian players, founded in 1918 by Jenö Léner (*d.* 1948). The other members of the original ensemble were Joseph Smilovits (second violin), Sandor Roth (viola) and Imre Hartman (cello).

L'Enfance du Christ. *v.* ENFANCE DU CHRIST.

Lenormand [ler-norr-mũn], RENÉ: *b.* Elboeuf, Aug. 5, 1846; *d.* Paris, Dec. 3, 1932. Composer. Studied in Paris from 1868 and was founder and director of *Le Lied en Tous Pays* society. He composed many songs, an opera, a mimed drama, a cantata, orchestral works, a piano concerto, chamber music and piano pieces. His *Study of Modern Harmony* (1912) has been published in an English translation (1915) by H. Antcliffe.

Lento [lent'-o], *I.* Slow.

Lenz [lents], WILHELM VON: *b.* Riga, June 1, 1809; *d.* St. Petersburg, Jan. 31, 1883. Musical historian. He was Russian councillor at St. Petersburg and wrote two books on Beethoven (1852 and 1855-60), a book on contemporary piano-playing (1872) and a collection of essays on Liszt, Chopin and other musicians. In his first book on Beethoven, *Beethoven et ses trois styles*, he analysed Beethoven's development according to the three periods first suggested by Fétis and generally adopted after Lenz's time.

Leo [leh'-o], LEONARDO (Lionardo Oronzo Salvatore de Leo): *b.* S. Vito degli Schiavi, Aug. 5, 1694; *d.* Naples, Oct. 31, 1744. Composer. Studied at the Conservatorio della Pietà dei Turchini in Naples (1703-15), where he became second master (1715) and first master (1741). He was appointed organist (1717) and first organist (1725) of the Royal Chapel and teacher at the Conservatorio di S. Onofrio (1725). His pupils included Pergolesi, Piccinni and Jommelli. He composed many operas, oratorios, Masses, motets, psalms and other church music, 6 concertos for cello with two violins and continuo, a concerto for four violins, and pieces for organ and for harpsichord. The most successful of his serious operas was *Demofoonte* (Naples, 1733), of his comic operas *Amor vuol sofferenza* (Naples, 1739).

Leoncavallo [leh-on-cah-vahl'-lo], RUGGIERO: *b.* Naples, March 8, 1858; *d.* Montecatini (nr. Florence), Aug. 9, 1919. Composer. Studied at Naples Conservatorio, visited Bologna, became a café pianist and travelled in England, France, Holland, Germany and Egypt. He returned to Italy and in 1892 his first performed and most successful opera, *Pagliacci*, was produced in Milan. In 1906 he toured America with an opera company. He composed operas to librettos by himself, including *La Bohème*, produced fifteen months after Puccini's opera with the same title, a ballet and a symphonic poem.

Leoni [leh-o'-nee], (1) FRANCO: *b.* Milan, Oct. 24, 1865; *d.* Dover, Nov. 11, 1938. Composer. He lived in London from 1892-1914 when he returned to Milan. His operas *Ib and Little Christina* (1901) and *L'Oracolo* (1905), the latter his most successful work, were produced at Covent Garden. He also composed three oratorios and some songs.

(2) LEONE: *b.* 16th cent.; *d.* Vicenza, early 17th century. Italian composer. He was choirmaster of Vicenza Cathedral from *c.* 1588. He composed Masses, motets (some for double choir), Magnificats, psalms, *Sacrae cantiones* (1608) and other church music, 5 books of madrigals (1588-1602), a book of sacred madrigals (1596) and concertos in the style of Giovanni Gabrieli for four voices and six instruments (1615).

Leoninus (Léonin). Late 12th-cent. composer at Notre Dame, Paris, where he was succeeded by Perotin. The 13th-cent. theorist Anonymus IV describes him as *optimus organista* (a very excellent composer of *organa*) and as the composer of a *Magnus Liber Organi de Gradali et Antiphonario pro servitio divino multiplicando* (a great book of *organum* music on melodies from the Gradual and Antiphoner, designed to augment and enrich divine service). Transcription of the *Magnus Liber* from the so-called St. Andrews manuscript (Wolfenbüttel 677, facsimile in *An Old St. Andrews Music Book*, ed. J. H. Baxter, 1931) in W. G. Waite, *The Rhythm of Twelfth-Century Polyphony* (1954).

Leonore [lay-o-noh'-rer]. The title of three overtures written by Beethoven for his opera *Fidelio*, first produced at Vienna in 1805. The name is that of the heroine, who disguises herself as a man in order to rescue her husband Florestan from prison. The history of the three overtures is as follows:

Leonore No. 1 : never used (now thought to have been the original overture, though Thayer maintained that it was written for a performance at Prague in 1807 which never took place, *v.* A. W. Thayer, *The Life of Ludwig van Beethoven*, vol. iii, pp. 24-5).

Leonore No. 2 : played at the first performance in 1805.

Leonore No. 3 : replaced *Leonore No.* 2 when a revised version of the opera was produced in 1806.

For the third and final version of the opera, produced in 1814, Beethoven wrote a fourth overture, called *Fidelio*. *Leonore No.* 2 and *Leonore No.* 3 are closely related. *Leonore No.* 1 and the *Fidelio* overture are independent works. The reason for discarding *Leonore No.* 3 was that its powerfully dramatic character and preoccupation with the heroic climax of the opera made it unsuitable as an introduction to the homely comedy of the opening scene. It survives in the concert room, its proper home.

D. F. TOVEY : *Essays in Musical Analysis*, vol. iv (1936), pp. 28-43.

Leopold I: *b.* Vienna, June 9, 1640; *d.* there, May 5, 1705. Emperor and composer. He composed music for the opera *Apollo deluso* (1669) by Sances and for many operas by his court musician Antonio Draghi, Masses, offices and ballet suites.

L'Épine [lay-peen], FRANÇOISE MARGUERITE DE (Francesca Margherita de) : *d.* London, Aug. 1746. Soprano. She arrived in England in the early years of the 18th cent. and appeared in association with the composer Jakob Greber, earning in consequence the contemptuous nickname "Greber's Peg." She rapidly acquired a reputation and sang frequently in operas and other dramatic representations between 1703 and 1716. Some time after her retirement from the stage she married J. C. Pepusch.

E. L. MORE : "Some notes on the life of Françoise Marguerite de L'Épine" in *Music and Letters*, Oct., 1947.

Leroux [ler-roo], XAVIER HENRY NAPOLÉON: *b.* Velletri (Italy), Oct. 11, 1863; *d.* Paris, Feb. 2, 1919. Composer. Studied under Massenet at the Paris Conservatoire, where he won the *Prix de Rome* (1885) and was teacher of harmony from 1896 until his death. He composed operas, incidental music for plays, an overture, cantatas, a Mass with orchestra, motets and numerous songs. His most successful opera was *Le Chemineau* (Paris, 1907).

Le Roy, ADRIEN. *v.* ROY.

Les Adieux. *v.* ADIEUX.

Leschetizky [lesh-et-it'-shki], THEODOR: *b.* Lańcut (Poland), June 22, 1830; *d.* Dresden, Nov. 14, 1915. Teacher, pianist and composer. Studied under Czerny, began teaching at a young age and made concert tours from 1842-48 and in 1852. He taught at St. Petersburg Conservatoire (1852-78), gave concerts in England, Holland and Germany and settled in Vienna. His pupils included Paderewski and Schnabel. He composed many piano pieces and an opera.

A. HULLAH: *Theodor Leschetizky* (1906).

Les Six. *v.* SIX.

Lesson. Title for a piece of music used in England in the seventeenth and eighteenth centuries. It was used by Morley as a title for ensemble music (*First Booke of Consort Lessons*, 1611), but later was usually applied only to pieces for harpsichord or other solo instrument which would now be called suites (*e.g.*, Purcell's posthumous *A Choice Collection of Lessons for the Harpsichord or Spinet*, 1696) or sonatas (*e.g.* Thomas Roseingrave's edition of *Forty-two Suites of Lessons for the Harpsichord by Domenico Scarlatti*) or studies (*e.g.*, the various collections of *Select Lessons* for flute, solo violin, and bass viol published by John Walsh).

Lesueur [ler-sēē-er], JEAN FRANÇOIS: *b.* Drucat-Plessiel (nr. Abbeville), Feb. 15, 1760; *d.* Paris, Oct. 6, 1837. Composer. He was a chorister at Abbeville and from 1779 held church appointments at Séez, Paris, Dijon, Le Mans and Tours. He returned to Paris (1784) and was appointed music director at Notre Dame (1786), where he introduced a full orchestra during the Mass, causing a controversy which finally forced him to resign (1788). He was professor at the École de la Garde Nationale (from 1793) and inspector (1795-1802) and professor of composition (1818 until his death) at the Conservatoire. He was also Paisiello's successor as *maître de chapelle* to Napoleon (from 1804) and held the post under Louis XVIII. His pupils included Berlioz and Gounod. He composed operas, oratorios, cantatas, a *Te Deum* and Mass for Napoleon's coronation, about thirty Masses, psalms, motets and other church music and wrote an essay on Paisiello. His *La Caverne* (1793) was one of the earliest examples of the type called "bandit" opera, fashionable at the time. His *Le Triomphe de Trajan* (1807) was written, with Persuis, to celebrate Napoleon's return from Prussia. He anticipated his pupil Berlioz in using a large orchestra, and in giving the audience a programme for his orchestral compositions.

Lesur [ler-sēēr], DANIEL (Daniel-Lesur): *b.* Paris, Nov. 19, 1908. Composer and organist. He became organist of the Benedictine Abbey in Paris and professor of counterpoint at the Schola Cantorum (from 1938) and with Jolivet, Baudrier and Messiaen formed the group called *La Jeune France*. He has composed an orchestral suite, Passacaille for piano and orchestra, a string quartet, three songs for voice and string quartet and other songs, a piano suite and organ works.

Leveridge, RICHARD: *b.* London, *c.* 1670; *d.* there, March 22, 1758. Composer and singer. He appeared in London operas, plays, masques, etc., from *c.* 1695-1751. He composed incidental music for plays, a masque, songs and a "new Entertainment of Vocal and Instrumental Musick (after the manner of an Opera)" called *Britain's Happiness* (1704).

Levi [lay'-vee], HERMANN: *b.* Giessen, Nov. 7, 1839; *d.* Munich, May 13, 1900. Conductor. Studied in Mannheim and at the Leipzig Conservatorium. He conducted at Saarbrücken (1859), Rotterdam (1861) and Karlsruhe (1864), where he became a friend of Brahms. Conductor, Munich Court Theatre, 1872-96. Conducted the first performance of Wagner's *Parsifal* at Bayreuth in 1882. He composed a piano concerto and songs.

Lévy [lay-vee], ROLAND ALEXIS MANUEL. *v.* ROLAND-MANUEL.

Ley, HENRY GEORGE: *b.* Chagford, Dec. 30, 1887. Organist and composer. Studied at the R.C.M. under Parratt and at Keble College, Oxford. Organist, Christ Church, Oxford, 1909; also Choragus of the University and organ teacher at the R.C.M. Director of music, Eton College, 1926-45. He has composed orchestral variations on a Handel theme, chamber music, church music, works for organ and songs.

L'Héritier [lay-reet-yay], JEAN. French composer of the first half of the 16th cent. Pupil of Josquin. Motets and a Mass by him were published in contemporary collections.

L'Heure Espagnole. *v.* HEURE ESPAGNOLE.

L'Homme Armé [lom arr-may]. *v.* HOMME ARMÉ.

Liadov [lyah'-doff], ANATOL CONSTANTINOVICH: *b.* St. Petersburg, May 11, 1855; *d.* Novgorod, Aug. 28, 1914. Composer, teacher and conductor. Studied at St. Petersburg Conservatoire under Rimsky-Korsakov until 1877 and from 1878 taught at the Conservatoire and at the Imperial Chapel. He was commissioned by the Imperial Geographical Society to study and collect Russian folksongs. He composed symphonic poems, two scherzos and other orchestral works, choral works, variations, mazurkas and other piano pieces, songs and settings of folksongs.

Liapounov [lyah'-poo-noff], SERGEI MIKHAILOVICH: *b.* Yaroslav, Nov. 30, 1859; *d.* Paris, Nov. 8, 1924. Composer. Studied at the Moscow Conservatoire (1878-83) under Tchaikovsky and Taneiev. Assistant director, Imperial Choir, St. Petersburg, 1884-1902; teacher, St. Petersburg Conservatoire, 1910-18. He was commissioned (with Liadov and Balakirev) by the Imperial Geographical Society to study and collect Russian folksongs, went to Paris during the revolution and appeared as pianist and conductor in Germany and Austria. He composed two symphonies, a symphonic poem and other orchestral works, two concertos and a *Rhapsody* for piano and orchestra, settings of folksongs, mazurkas and numerous other piano pieces.

Libretto [lee-bret'-to], *I.* Lit. " booklet." The text of an opera or oratorio. The ideas and work of a librettist have at times had an important influence on the style and character of opera, *e.g.* those of Rinuccini on the early Florentine operas, of Metastasio on 18th-cent. opera, of Calzabigi on the later operas of Gluck, of Scribe on French grand opera of the 1830's, and of Hofmannsthal on the later operas of Richard Strauss. Wagner is the most famous composer-librettist; other composers who have written some or all of their own libretti are Berlioz, Busoni, Rimsky-Korsakov, Delius, Holst, Hindemith and Tippett.

Lichfield (Lichfild), HENRY: 16th-17th century. English composer who was probably in the service of Lord and later Lady Cheney (Cheyney) at Toddington House near Luton. He published a book of five-part madrigals " apt for both Viols and Voyces " (1613; modern ed. in *E.M.S.*, xvii).

Liebenthaler [leeb'-ĕn-tahl-er], MARIE. *v.* WILT.

Liebe der Danae, Die [dee leeb-*er* dair dun'-a-ay] (The Love of Danae). Opera in three acts by Richard Strauss. Libretto by Joseph Gregor. Dress rehearsal, Salzburg, Aug. 16, 1944; performance postponed. First public performance, Salzburg, Aug. 14, 1952.

Liebesflöte [leeb'-ĕss-flu*r*-te*r*], *G.* A flute built a minor third below the normal size, now obsolete.

Liebesgeige [leeb'-ĕss-gy-ge*r*], *G.* Viola d'amore.

Liebeslieder [leeb'-ĕss-leed-er], *G.* (Songs of Love). A set of 18 waltzes for vocal quartet and piano duet by Brahms, Op. 52 (also published for piano duet only as Op. 52a). Words from Georg Friedrich Daumer's *Polydora.* A second set of 15 was issued under the title *Neue Liebeslieder,* Op. 65. Brahms also made a version of 9 of the *Liebeslieder* for voices and small orchestra, with the addition of a tenth waltz which was later revised for incorporation in the *Neue Liebeslieder.*

Liebesoboe [leeb'-ĕss-o-boh'-e*r*], *G.* Oboe d' amore.

Liebesverbot, Das [duss leeb'-ĕss-fair-boat'] (The Love Ban). Opera in two acts by Wagner. Libretto by the composer (based on Shakespeare's *Measure for Measure*). First performed, Magdeburg, March 29, 1836.

Lieblich [leep'-li*sh*]. *G.* " Sweet." Applied to a family of sweet-toned stops on the organ which have stopped pipes, *e.g.* to the Lieblichflöte, Lieblich Gedeckt (*gedeckt* or *gedackt* = " stopped "), and Lieblich Bourdon.

Lied [leet]. *G.* " Song." The term has come to be particularly applied to the German Romantic songs of Schubert, Schumann, Brahms, Wolf and others but has also been used since the Middle Ages in the more general sense.

Lieder aus "Des Knaben Wunderhorn" [leed′-er owce dess knahb′-ĕn vŏŏn′-der-horrn], *G.* (Songs from "The Boy's Magic Horn"). A set of 12 songs by Mahler (1888), the words taken from an anthology of German folk poetry.

Lieder eines fahrenden Gesellen [leed′-er ine′-ĕss fah′-rend-ĕn ger-zell′-ĕn], *G.* (Songs of a Wayfaring Fellow). A set of four songs with orchestral accompaniment by Mahler (1883). Words by the composer.

Liederkreis [leed′-er-crice]. *G.* Song cycle.

Lieder ohne Worte [leed′-er ohn′-er vorr′-ter] *G.* (Songs without Words). The title given by Mendelssohn to eight books of six short piano pieces which he composed between 1830 and 1845. He also wrote one *Lied ohne Worte* in D major for cello and piano (Op. 109, 1845).

Liederspiel [leed-′er-shpeel], *G.* "Song play." (1) The German equivalent of ballad opera and of the French *vaudeville*, in which the songs are folk-songs or in folk-song style. It was originated by J. F. Reichart, whose *Lieb' und Treue*, first performed in Berlin in 1800, was the first example.

(2) Also applied to a song-cycle of which the text involves some element of action, *e.g.*, to Schumann's *Spanisches Liederspiel*, Op. 74, for quartet and piano, and Brahms's *Liebeslieder* Waltzes, Op. 52, for quartet and piano duet, and *Zigeunerlieder*, Op. 103, for quartet and piano.

Lied von der Erde, Das [duss leet fon dair aird′-er], *G.* (The Song of the Earth). The title of a composition for contralto, tenor and orchestra by Mahler (1908), with words from a German translation of six 8th-cent. Chinese poems (in Hans Bethge's anthology, *Die Chinesische Flöte*): 1. *Das Trinklied vom Jammer der Erde* (The Drinking Song of Earthly Woe), 2. *Der Einsame in Herbst* (The Solitary Soul in Autumn), 3. *Von der Jugend* (Of Youth), 4. *Von der Schönheit* (Of Beauty), 5. *Der Trunkene im Frühling* (The Drunkard in Spring), 6. *Der Abschied* (The Farewell). Mahler called the work a "symphony" but it is not numbered as such.

Life for the Czar, A. *v.* ZHIZN ZA TSARA.

Ligature. Form used for the writing of a group of notes in plainsong notation after *c.* 1150, in the modal notation of polyphony of *c.* 1200 (*v.* RHYTHMIC MODES) and in the mensural notation (*q.v.*) of *c.* 1250 to *c.* 1600. In mensural notation ligatures were used for writing successions of longs and breves, and their rhythm was interpreted according to the principles of PERFECTION and PROPRIETY, and in the single form in which semibreves appeared, by the principle of opposite propriety. In vocal performance a ligature was sung to one syllable. Because they were derived originally from the NEUMES of plainsong notation, their forms differed in descending and ascending. Ligatures of two notes had the following meanings:

Descending	Ascending		Rhythm
	or	With propriety and perfection	Breve-Long
	or	Without propriety and with perfection	Long-Long
		With propriety and without perfection	Breve-Breve
		Without propriety and without perfection	Long-Breve
or	or	With opposite propriety (used only at the beginning of a ligature or separately)	Semibreve-Semibreve

In ligatures of more than two notes, all but the first and last, whose values were determined by the two-note forms, were breves unless shown as long or large, and except in the case of a ligature beginning with two semibreves in opposite propriety, *e.g.*:

= Semibreve-semibreve-breve-breve-long-breve-long

Like single notes, notes in a ligature could be dotted, to increase their value by one-half, or coloured (red in black notation, black in white notation) to decrease their value by one-third:

= dotted semibreve - dotted semibreve

Lightstone, PAULINE. *v.* DONALDA.

Liliencron [leel′-yĕn-crone], ROCHUS, FREIHERR VON: *b.* Plön (Holstein), Dec. 8, 1820; *d.* Coblenz, March 5, 1912.

Musicologist, theologian and philologist. Studied at Kiel and Berlin Universities and at Copenhagen. Professor of old Norse literature, Kiel, 1850; of German literature, Jena, 1852. Privy Councillor to the Duke of Meiningen, 1855-68; editor of the Munich *Allgemeine deutsche Biographie* (from 1868) and honorary provost of the Johanniskloster at Schleswig (from 1876). He wrote books on medieval German songs, Lutheran liturgical music, and Danish music.

Lilliburlero. The words of a topical satire, beginning "Ho! broder Teague, dost hear de decree, Lilliburlero, bullen a la", on Irish Roman Catholics and on the appointment of General Talbot as Lord Lieutenant of Ireland in 1687 were set to a tune called "Quick Step" in *The Delightful Companion* (2nd ed. 1686):

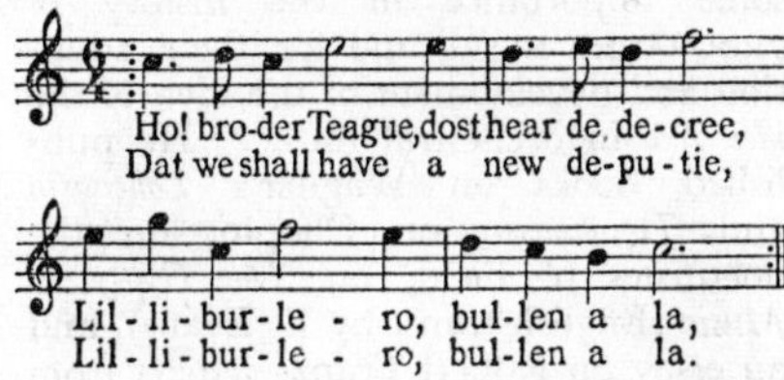

and became the most popular political ballad of the day. It appeared as "A New Irish Tune" in the second part of *Musick's Hand-Maid . . . for the Virginal and Spinet* (1689) in a setting by Purcell, who also used it as the bass of the Jig in the *Gordian Knot unty'd* (1691; *Purcell Society*, xx, p. 32).

Lily of Killarney, The. Opera in three acts by Benedict. Libretto by John Oxenford and Dion Boucicault (founded on Boucicault's *Colleen Bawn*). First performed, London, Jan. 11, 1862.

Limburgia, JOHANNES DE. *v.* JOHANNES DE LIMBURGIA.

Limma (*Gr.* λεῖμμα). Lit. "remainder." *v.* DIESIS (1).

Lind [lind], JENNY: *b.* Stockholm, Oct. 6, 1820; *d.* Malvern, Nov. 2, 1887. Soprano singer who was called "The Swedish Nightingale." She made her début as Agatha in Weber's *Der Freischütz*, Stockholm, 1838. Member of the Royal Swedish Academy of Music, 1840. Studied in Paris under M. García (1841-42), sang in various German cities and moved to London in 1847. She toured extensively, visited the United States (1850-52) and was appointed singing teacher at the R.C.M., 1883. She sang the soprano part which had been written for her in Meyerbeer's *Feldlager in Schlesien* (1844) and the role of Amalia in the first performance of Verdi's *I Masnadieri* (1847). Made her last operatic appearance in 1849 but continued to sing in oratorios and concerts until 1870. She married Otto Goldschmidt.

Linda di Chamounix [leend'-ah dee shah-moo-nee'] (Linda of Chamonix). Opera in three acts by Donizetti. Libretto by Gaetano Rossi. First performed, Vienna, May 19, 1842.

Liniensystem [leen'-yen-zeece-tame], *G.* Staff, stave. Commonly abbreviated to *System*.

Linley, THOMAS : *b.* Badminton (Gloucester), Jan. 17, 1733 ; *d.* London, Nov. 19, 1795. Composer and singing teacher. Studied in Bath and London and lived in Bath, where he taught singing and produced concerts. He was appointed manager of the oratorios (with Stanley from 1774 and with Arnold from 1786) at the London Drury Lane Theatre, where he became part owner (succeeding Garrick) and music director in 1776. He composed an opera, incidental music (with his son Thomas) for *The Duenna* by Sheridan (his son-in-law) and many other stage works, cantatas, six elegies for three voices and piano, part-songs and ballads. His children were all musicians and included Thomas (1756-78) a violinist, composer and friend of Mozart, and Elizabeth Ann (1754-92) a singer and wife of Sheridan.

Lira [lee'-rah], *I.* A bowed instrument in use between *c.* 1580 and *c.* 1650 in two sizes, the *lira da braccio* played on the arm and the *lira da gamba* (or *lirone*) played between the knees. Both had two drone (*i.e.* always played as open) strings; in addition, the *lira da braccio* had five strings and the *lira da gamba* from nine to fourteen strings in fourths, fifths and octaves in various ways, *e.g.*:

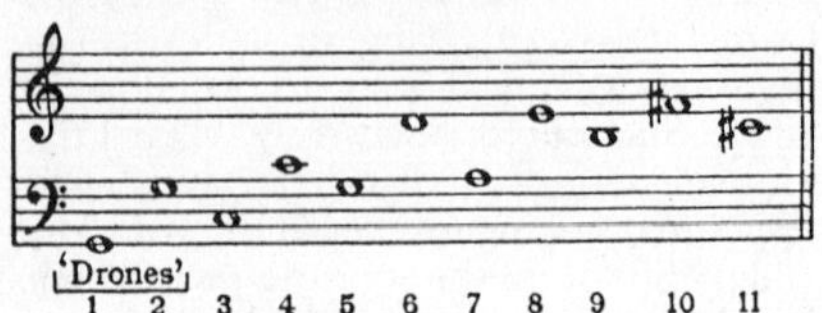

given by Cerreto (1601), and always played in chords. The *lira organizzata* for which Haydn wrote five concertos and seven *Notturni* was an 18th-cent. form of the HURDY-GURDY.

Lisley, JOHN: 16th-17th cent. English composer who contributed a six-part madrigal to *The Triumphes of Oriana* (1601). Nothing more is known of his life or works.

Listenius [list-ain′-yoŏss], MAGISTER NIKOLAUS: *b.* Hamburg, *c.* 1500. Studied in Wittenberg (1529) and was in Salzwedel (1535), perhaps as a cantor. He wrote an elementary treatise *Rudimenta musices* which was published at Wittemberg in 1533, was revised as *Musica* in 1536, and appeared in many editions until 1583. Facsimile ed. by G. Schünemann (1927).

L'istesso tempo [leece-tess′-so temp′-o]. *I.* The same tempo. *v.* ISTESSO TEMPO.

Liszt [list], FRANZ: *b.* Raiding (Hungary), Oct. 22, 1811; *d.* Bayreuth, July 31, 1886. Composer and pianist. Gave his first concert in 1820, and from 1821 studied under Czerny and Salieri in Vienna, where he met Beethoven and Schubert. From 1823 to 1835 he lived in Paris, became famous as a pianist, and absorbed the many musical influences of the city, including those of Chopin, Berlioz, and Paganini. In 1835 he eloped with the Countess d'Agoult, and their daughter Cosima (*v.* WAGNER, 2) was born at Como in 1837. During the years in Paris he wrote many compositions for piano, including the first two parts of the *Années de Pèlerinage* and studies based on the caprices of Paganini. From 1838 to 1847 he gave concerts in all parts of Europe, and was acknowledged as the greatest virtuoso of the day. From 1848-61 he was director of music at the court at Weimar, where he composed the symphonic poems and Hungarian Rhapsodies, and introduced music of his contemporaries, including Wagner's *Lohengrin* (1850). From 1861 to 1869 he lived in Rome, composed his two oratorios and other works and took minor orders. From 1869 to his death he lived in Rome, Budapest, and Weimar, and in his later years received as pupils many musicians who later became famous, among them Busoni, Siloti, Rosenthal, Lamond, Sauer and Weingartner.

One of the most stimulating musical personalities of the 19th cent., Liszt was the first of the great piano recitalists, and in sheer virtuosity is probably still unmatched. His symphonies, symphonic poems (a title he invented), and concertos, though weakened by an over-rhetorical style and a comparative poverty of thematic invention, have some importance in the history of PROGRAMME MUSIC, and for their adoption and development of the idea of the *idée fixe* in orchestral music. He published books on Wagner's *Lohengrin* and *Tannhäuser*, on Chopin, on the nocturnes of Field, on *The Gypsy in Music* (English trans. by E. Evans), and an essay on Robert Franz. Apart from the many transcriptions of orchestral works, operas, songs, and other compositions, his more important works are:

(a) ORCHESTRA: *Faust* Symphony (1853-61), *Dante* Symphony (1856), twelve symphonic poems, piano concertos in E♭ (1857) and A (1863).

(b) PIANO: *Années de Pèlerinage*: *Suisse* (1852), *Italie* (1848), *Troisième année* (posthumously collected, 1890); twelve *Études d'Exécution Transcendante* (final form, 1854); three *Études de Concert* (1849); *Deux Études de Concert*: *Waldesrauchen*, *Gnomenreigen* (1849-63); *Deux Légendes* (1866); twenty Hungarian Rhapsodies (1851-86).

(c) CHORAL WORKS: Two oratorios: *The Legend of St. Elizabeth* (1862), *Christus* (1866); *Psalm XIII* (1863); Hungarian Coronation Mass (1867).

(d) SONGS: Fifty-five songs (collected edition, 1860).

(e) ORGAN: Fugue on the name BACH (1857); Fantasia and fugue on the chorale *Ad nos ad salutarem undam* from Meyerbeer's *Le Prophète*.

A selection from the letters of Liszt was published in two volumes in 1894, and the letters of Liszt and von Bülow in 1896, both translated by C. Bache.

W. BECKETT: *Liszt* (1956).
F. CORDER: *Franz Liszt* (1933).
E. NEWMAN: *The Man Liszt* (1934).
H. SEARLE: *The Music of Liszt* (1954).
S. SITWELL: *Franz Liszt* (1934).
W. WALLACE: *Liszt, Wagner, and the Princess* (1927).

Litany. A series of invocations to God, the Blessed Virgin, and the Saints sung by the priest and responded to by the people with *Kyrie eleison* ("Lord, have mercy") or a similar response, both to a simple plainsong formula. Polyphonic settings of one such litany, the *Litaniae Lauretanae* ("Litanies of Loreto") were written by Palestrina, Lassus, and Mozart (K.109 for choir, strings, and organ; K.195 for choir, orchestra, and organ). Mozart also set the *Litaniae de venerabili altaris sacramento* (K.243 for choir, orchestra, and organ).

At the command of Henry VIII Archbishop Cranmer made and adapted to the plainsong an English version of the Litany which was printed in 1544. There is evidence that a five-part setting was printed in the same year. Cranmer's Litany (facsimile ed. in J. E. Hunt, *Cranmer's First Litany, 1544 and Merbecke's Book of Common Prayer Noted 1550*, (1939)) became, with few changes, the Litany of the English Prayer Book, and its music was the basis of settings in four and five parts composed by Tallis.

Liturgical Drama. *v.* TROPE.

Lituus [lit'-oo-ŏŏss], (1) Hooked trumpet used by the Roman army. It was a long tube of bronze curved upwards at the end to form the bell.

(2) Given by Praetorius (1619) as a name for the KRUMMHORN.

(3) The two instruments marked *lituus* by Bach in Cantata No. 118 appear to be horns (*Waldhörner*) in high B♭ (*v.* C. S. Terry, *Bach's Orchestra*, p. 47).

Liuto [lee-oo'-to]. *I.* LUTE.

Liuzzi [lee-oo'-dzee], FERNANDO: *b.* Sinigallia, Dec. 19, 1884; *d.* Florence, Oct. 6, 1940. Musicologist and composer. Studied in Bologna and in Munich under Reger and Mottl and became an operatic conductor. Teacher of composition, Parma Conservatorio, 1910-17, and later in Florence; professor of musical history, University of Rome (from 1927). He went to the United States in 1939. He composed a chamber opera for puppets, three oratorios, an orchestral work, five sets of songs, organ pieces and works for piano and violin, published two volumes of monophonic *laude* in *La Lauda* (1934), *Estetica della Musica* (1924) and numerous articles.

Lloyd, JOHN: *d.* Apr. 3, 1523. Composer. Gentleman of the English Chapel Royal from 1511 or earlier. His five-part Mass *O quam suavis*, which is remarkable for the "canons" or riddles used for the notation of the tenor, has been edited by H. B. Collins (1927). The composer's name is hidden in the enigmatic inscription "Hoc fecit Johannes maris," *i.e.* "This is the work of John of the Sea" (Lloyd = flood).

Lobgesang [lope'-ger-zung], *G. v.* HYMN OF PRAISE.

Locatelli [lo-cah-tell'-lee], PIETRO: *b.* Bergamo, Sept. 3, 1695; *d.* Amsterdam, April 1, 1764. Violinist and composer. Studied in Rome under Corelli, toured extensively and settled in Amsterdam where he produced concerts. He composed twelve *concerti grossi* (1721), flute sonatas (1732), twelve violin concertos with twenty-four caprices to serve as cadenzas (1733), concertos and caprices for four-part strings, trio sonatas, and solo sonatas.

Locke, MATTHEW: *b.* Exeter, *c.* 1630; *d.* London, Aug. 1677. Composer. Chorister at Exeter Cathedral under E. Gibbons. Settled in London *c.* 1650. Composer in ordinary to Charles II, 1660; later organist to Queen Catherine. He composed music for Shirley's masque *Cupid and Death* (with Christopher Gibbons, 1653; edited by E. J. Dent in *Musica Britannica*, ii), for Davenant's *The Siege of Rhodes* (with Colman, Cooke, Hudson and Lawes, 1656) and for Shadwell's *Psyche* (with instrumental pieces by G. B. Draghi, 1675)—the earliest surviving English opera, written in imitation of a *comédie-ballet* with the same title by Molière and Lully (1671). Locke's music for *Psyche* was published together with his instrumental incidental music to *The Tempest* as *The English Opera* (1675). He also composed incidental music for other plays, consorts (suites) for viols, music for Charles II's coronation, a *Kyrie*, a *Credo*, anthems, and songs. His *Melothesia* (1673) is the earliest extant printed English treatise on playing from figured bass.

Lockwood, NORMAND: *b.* New York, March 19, 1906. Composer. He won the American *Prix de Rome* (1929), studied under Boulanger and Respighi, was appointed associate professor of theory and composition at Oberlin College (1933) and later taught at Columbia University. He has composed choral works (some with orchestra), a chamber opera *The Scarecrow*, string quartets and other chamber music and piano pieces.

Loco [lo′-co], *I.* "Place," *i.e.* in the normal place. Used (1) to contradict a previous indication *8va* or *all'ottava*, by indicating that the music is to be played at the normal pitch, not an octave higher or lower; (2) also in string music to indicate that a passage is to be played in the normal position, after some previous indication to the contrary.

Locrian Mode. (1) In ancient Greek music:

(2) In modern usage applied to:

This mode was called Hyperaeolian by Glareanus in his *Dodecachordon* (1547) and its plagal form (F to F, with B as final) Hyperphrygian. He points out, however, that it is of no practical use, since the interval between the first and fifth notes is not a perfect fifth, as in all the other modes, but a diminished fifth. For this reason it had virtually only a theoretical existence. *v.* GREEK MUSIC, MODE.

Loder, EDWARD JAMES: *b.* Bath, 1813; *d.* London, April 5, 1865. Composer and conductor. He was the son of a music publisher, studied in Frankfort under Ferdinand Ries and was conductor at the Princess's Theatre in London and later at a theatre in Manchester, but due to a brain disease was forced to retire in 1856. The new English Opera House (Lyceum Theatre) opened with his first opera, *Nourjahad*, in 1834. He composed *The Night Dancers* (1846) and other operas and stage works, a cantata, string quartets, and sacred and secular songs.

Loeffler, CHARLES MARTIN: *b.* Mulhouse (Alsace), Jan. 30, 1861; *d.* Medfield (Mass.), May 19, 1935. Composer. Studied under Joachim in Berlin and Massart and Ernest Guiraud in Paris. Played in orchestras in Europe, in New York (1881-2) and in the Boston Symphony Orchestra (1882-1903). His compositions, written in a delicate and evocative style resembling in some respects that of Debussy, include *La Mort de Tintagiles* for orchestra and viola d'amore (1905), *A Pagan Poem* for orchestra (1905-6), *The Canticle of the Sun* for solo voice and orchestra (1925), *Five Irish Fantasies* for voice and orchestra (1922), choral works, chamber music, and songs.

Loeillet [lur-yay], JEAN-BAPTISTE: *b.* Ghent, Nov. 18, 1680; *d.* London, July 19, 1730. Composer, flautist and oboist. He lived in Paris from 1702 and in London from 1705, where he became a member of the King's Theatre orchestra. In one of his publications he calls himself chamber musician to the elector of Bavaria and concert-master to Duke Ferdinand. Composed sonatas for one to three flutes and a set for flute, oboe or violin, and gave concerts in 1710 at which some of Corelli's works received their first London performance. He also composed sonatas for flute, oboe or violin and flute trios and published a set of six lessons for harpsichord.

Loewe [lur-ver], (1) (Loew), JOHANN JAKOB: *b.* Vienna, 1628; *d.* Lüneburg, early in Sept., 1703. Composer and organist. He studied under Heinrich

Schütz at Dresden (1652), was *Kapellmeister* at Wolfenbüttel (from 1655), went to Zeitz (1663) and was organist of St. Nicholas's Church at Lüneburg (from 1682). He composed two operas, ballets, instrumental suites (with introductory movements called *Synfonia*), and songs for solo voice.

(2) JOHANN KARL GOTTFRIED: *b.* Löbejün (nr. Halle), Nov. 30, 1796; *d.* Kiel, April 20, 1869. Composer, conductor, pianist and singer. He was a chorister at Cöthen (1807-09), studied in Halle and later taught at the Singakademie there. He settled in Stettin where he was appointed professor at the Gymnasium, municipal music director, and organist of St. Jacob's (1821). He travelled extensively, visiting Vienna (1844), London (1847), Scandinavia (1851) and France (1857), and retired to Kiel in 1866. He composed five operas (one produced), oratorios, a cantata, a ballad *Die Walpurgisnacht* for soloists, chorus and orchestra, string quartets and other chamber music, numerous solo songs, part-songs, piano solos and duets, and orchestral works (unpublished). He is most notable as a composer of the dramatic type of *Lied* known as "ballad," of which he wrote about 150.

Loewenberg [lur-vĕn-bairg], ALFRED: *b.* Berlin, May 14, 1902; *d.* London, Dec. 29, 1949. Musicologist. He studied at Jena University, left Germany in 1934 and settled in London. His *Annals of Opera* (1943 ; rev. ed., 1955) is a valuable chronological tabulation of first and subsequent performances of operas from 1597 to 1940.

Logier, JOHANN BERNHARD: *b.* Cassel, Feb. 9, 1777; *d.* Dublin, July 27, 1846. Inventor of the Chiroplast (mechanism to train hands for piano-playing), a flautist, piano teacher, bandmaster and organist. He came to England when he was ten and later settled in Dublin (1809) where he opened a music shop (1811). He patented the Chiroplast (1814), gave lectures on its use and lived in Berlin for three years. He wrote a *Thoroughbass* (which was the first musical textbook used by Wagner) and books on his piano-teaching system, and composed a piano concerto, trios, ode on the 50th year of George III's reign (1809), and piano sonatas.

Logroscino [lo-grosh-een'-o] (Lo Groscino), NICOLA: *b.* Bitonto, baptized Oct. 22, 1698; *d.* Palermo, after 1765. Composer. Studied at the Conservatorio di Loreto in Naples (1714-27), was an organist in Conza, later lived in Naples and from 1747 was teacher of counterpoint at the Conservatorio in Palermo. He composed more than 25 operas, of which only three have survived, two settings of the *Stabat Mater*, psalms and other church music.

Lohengrin [loh'-ĕn-grin]. Opera in three acts by Wagner. Libretto by the composer. First performed, Weimar, Aug. 28, 1850. Elsa, sister of Gottfried, Duke of Brabant, is accused by Count Telramund of having murdered her brother. An unknown champion appears in a boat drawn by a swan. He agrees to espouse Elsa's cause on condition that she does not ask his name. He defeats Telramund in combat and marries Elsa. Her curiosity having been aroused by Ortrud, Telramund's wife, she asks her husband's name, but he refuses to tell her. Telramund rushes in to attack him, but is instantly killed. The next morning before the king the knight reveals that his name is Lohengrin: he is the son of Parsifal and a knight of the Holy Grail. In answer to his prayers the swan disappears and is replaced by the young Duke Gottfried. Lohengrin departs in the boat, now drawn by the dove of the Holy Grail, and Elsa falls dead.

Lombardi alla Prima Crociata, I [ee lom-barr'-dee ahl'-la pree'-ma crotchah'-tah] (The Lombards on the First Crusade). Opera in four acts by Verdi. Libretto by Temistocle Solera. First performed, Milan, Feb. 11, 1843.

Lombardic Rhythm. *v.* SCOTCH SNAP.

London Philharmonic Orchestra. Founded by Sir Thomas Beecham in 1932. Until the 1939-45 war it played regularly for the concerts of the Royal Philharmonic Society, for the Courtauld-Sargent concerts and for the summer season of opera at Covent Garden. On the outbreak of war the orchestra became a self-governing body, engaging its own conductors. This policy continued until 1949. There have thus been only two permanent conductors: Sir Thomas Beecham, 1932-9; Sir Adrian Boult, since 1949.

London Symphony. (1) Haydn's Symphony No. 104 in D (1795) the twelfth of the "Salomon" symphonies written for performance in London.

(2) Vaughan Williams's second symphony (composed 1914, revised 1920), which incorporates sounds of London life such as street cries and the chimes of Big Ben.

London Symphony Orchestra. Founded in 1904 by a group of players who resigned from the Queen's Hall Orchestra because they refused to accept Wood's ruling that deputies should not be employed. From its inception it has managed its own affairs, engaging conductors either for single concerts or for whole seasons. It was for many years the only orchestra, and is still the principal orchestra, engaged for the Three Choirs Festival.

Long (*L.* longa). In modal notation and mensural notation the note written ꟷ (later ꟷ) which had the value of three breves if perfect and of two breves if imperfect. A perfect large (*L.* maxima) contained three longs and an imperfect large two longs.

Loosemore, HENRY: *d.* Cambridge, 1670. English composer and organist. Chorister at Cambridge, where he was organist of King's College Chapel from 1627 until his death. He composed a service, anthems, two Latin litanies and a fantasia for three viols and organ. His son George, who was organist of Trinity College (1660-82), composed anthems.

Lopatnikov [lop-aht'-nee-coff], NICOLAI LVOVICH: *b.* Reval, March 16, 1903. Composer and pianist. He studied at the St. Petersburg Conservatoire (1914-17), went to Helsinki (1920), studied in Heidelberg, lived in Berlin (from 1929) and returned to Finland where he received advice from Sibelius. He visited London (1934) and settled in the United States (1939), where he taught at the Carnegie Institute in Pittsburg. He has composed an opera, two symphonies and other orchestral works, two piano concertos, a violin concerto, string quartets and other chamber music and piano pieces.

Lorenzani [lo-ren-tsahn'-ee], PAOLO: *b.* Rome, 1640; *d.* there, Oct. 28, 1713. Composer. Studied in Rome under Benevoli, was choirmaster at Messina Cathedral (from 1675) and went to France (1678), where he was *maître de musique* to the Queen (1679-83) and afterwards *maître de chapelle* at the Theatine monastery in Paris. In 1694 he returned to Rome as choirmaster at St. Peter's. He composed operas, Magnificats, cantatas, motets, Italian and French airs, and serenades. His *Nicandro e Fileno* (Fontainebleau, 1681) was the only Italian opera given in France between 1662 (Cavalli's *Ercole amante*) and 1729.

Loris [lo'-reece], HEINRICH. *v.* GLAREANUS.

Lortzing [lorrt'-tsing], GUSTAV ALBERT: *b.* Berlin, Oct. 23, 1801; *d.* there, Jan. 21, 1851. Composer, singer, conductor and librettist. He was the son of wandering actors, learnt to play the piano, violin and cello and was a member of a travelling opera company. He was first tenor at the Stadt Theater in Leipzig (1833-43), conductor for short periods at the Leipzig theatre (1844) and at the Theater an der Wien in Vienna (1848) and from 1850 conductor of the Friedrich-Wilhelmstadt Theater in Berlin. He composed operas to his own libretti, incidental music for plays, two oratorios, partsongs and songs. His most important opera, *Czaar und Zimmermann* (1837), is still performed; others which had some success were *Die beiden Schützen* (1837), *Hans Sachs* (1840; the subject anticipated Wagner's *Die Meistersinger*), *Der Wildschütz* (1842), *Undine* (1845), *Der Waffenschmied* (1846), and *Die vornehmen Dilettanten* (1851). His *Regina* was first produced in 1899.

Lossius [loss'-yoss] LUCAS: *b.* Fack (nr. Münden-on-the-Weser), Oct. 18, 1508; *d.* Lüneburg, July 8, 1582. Rector of St. John's School in Lüneburg from 1533 until his death. He published the theoretical treatise *Erotemata musicae practicae* (1563) and *Psalmodia sacra veteris ecclesiae* (1553), a collection of Latin texts and their plainsong melodies for use in the Lutheran liturgy.

Lotti [lot′-tee], ANTONIO: *b.* Venice, *c.* 1667; *d.* there, Jan. 5, 1740. Composer. Studied under Legrenzi in Venice where he produced his first opera in 1683, and was at St. Mark's Cathedral as chorister (1687), deputy organist (1690), second organist (1692), first organist (1704) and choirmaster (1736). He visited Dresden (1717-19) with his own opera company from Venice, and produced there his *Giove in Argo* (1717) and his last opera *Teofane* (1719). He composed operas, oratorios, a Requiem, Misereres, Masses, motets and other church music, cantatas and madrigals.

Louis Ferdinand of Prussia, PRINCE: *b.* Friedrichsfelde (nr. Berlin), Nov. 18. 1772; *d.* in battle at Saalfeld, Oct. 10, 1806. Nephew of Frederick the Great, amateur composer and pianist. He was a friend of Beethoven (who praised his playing and dedicated to him the C minor piano concerto) and of Dussek (who was in his service teaching him piano and composition). He composed two Rondos for piano and orchestra, piano trios, piano quartets and quintets and other chamber music, and piano pieces.

Louise [loo-eez]. Opera in four acts by Gustave Charpentier. Libretto by the composer. First performed, Paris, Feb. 2, 1900. Louise, a dressmaker's employee, is in love with Julien, an artist, in spite of the opposition of her parents. She goes to live with her lover in Montmartre. She responds to her mother's appeal to go home and see her father, who is seriously ill, but she refuses to stay with her parents and rejoins her lover.

Loure [loor]. Type of bagpipe used in Normandy in the 16th century. Hence, probably (1) a dance adopted into the ballet, *e.g.* in Lully's *Alceste* (1677), and the instrumental suite, *e.g.* the sixth movement of Bach's fifth French Suite, which begins :

and (2) the French term *louré* for legato bowing with emphasis on each note, indicated thus:

Lourié [loorr-yay], ARTHUR VINCENT: *b.* St. Petersburg, May 14, 1892. Composer. Studied at St. Petersburg Conservatoire, was appointed director of the music department of the Ministry of Education (1918), left Russia (1922), lived in France, where he met Stravinsky, and settled in the United States (1941). He has composed *Feast During the Plague*, a symphonic suite with chorus and soloist (1945, originally a short opera, 1933), ballets, *Symphonie dialectique* (1930) and other orchestral works, church music, a cantata and other choral works, chamber music, song-cycles and piano pieces.

Love for the Three Oranges, The. *v.* AMOUR DES TROIS ORANGES.

Love of the Three Kings, The. *v.* AMORE DEI TRE RE.

Love, the Magician. *v.* AMOR BRUJO.

Lowe, EDWARD: *b.* Salisbury, *c.* 1610; *d.* Oxford, July 11, 1682. Organist and composer. He became a chorister at Salisbury Cathedral, organist of Christ Church, Oxford (*c.* 1630) and the Chapel Royal (1660), and professor of music at Oxford (1662). He published *A Short Direction for the performance of Cathedrall Service* (1661) and composed anthems.

Lualdi [loo-ahl′-dee], ADRIANO: *b.* Larino, March 22, 1887. Composer and critic. Studied in Venice under Wolf-Ferrari and was critic for the *Secolo* in Milan (1923-27) and for the *Giornale d'Italia* in Rome (from 1936). He was appointed music representative to the Italian National Parliament (1927) and director of the Conservatorio of S. Pietro e Maiella in Naples, and travelled in Italy, Europe, South America and Russia. He was one of the founders of the International Music Festivals in Venice (1932). He has composed operas, a ballet, a symphonic poem and other orchestral works, works for solo voice and orchestra, chamber music, a Passacaglia for organ, partsongs and songs.

Lübeck [lee'-beck], VINCENT: *b.* probably at Padingbüttel (Hanover), Sept., 1654; *d.* Hamburg, Feb. 9, 1740. Organist and composer. A pupil of Buxtehude, he was organist in Stade from 1673 and at St. Nicholas Church in Hamburg from 1702 until his death. He composed cantatas, chorale preludes and other organ works.

Lubin [lee-ban], GERMAINE LÉONTINE ANGÉLIQUE: *b.* Paris, Feb. 1, 1890. Soprano. Studied at the Paris Conservatoire. Sang at the Opéra-Comique, 1912-14; Opéra, from 1914. An excellent Wagnerian singer, she appeared as Kundry in *Parsifal* at Bayreuth in 1938. She had a wide repertory of classical and modern works and appeared at several European opera houses, including those in London, Berlin, Vienna and Prague.

Lucas, CHARLES: *b.* Salisbury, July 28, 1808; *d.* March 30, 1869. Conductor, composer, cellist and organist. He was a chorister at Salisbury Cathedral and studied at the Royal Academy of Music where he was conductor from 1832 and Principal (succeeding Potter) from 1859-66. He became a member of Queen Adelaide's private orchestra (1830) and cellist at the opera (1832) and was active as a music publisher (1856-65). He composed an opera, three symphonies, overtures, a cello concerto, string quartets, anthems and songs.

Lucas, LEIGHTON: *b.* London, Jan. 5, 1903. Composer and conductor. Studied music by himself while employed as a ballet dancer and began conducting at the age of nineteen. He has composed works for orchestra, for chorus and orchestra, a *Sonatina concertante* for saxophone and orchestra, ballets, masques, a string quartet and songs.

Lucia di Lammermoor [loo-chee'-ah dee lahm-mer-moor'] (Lucy of Lammermoor). Opera in three acts by Donizetti. Libretto by Salvatore Cammarano (based on Scott's novel *The Bride of Lammermoor*). First performed, Naples, Sept. 26, 1835.

Lucio Silla [loo-chee'-o seel'-lah] (Lucius Sulla). Opera in three acts by Mozart. Libretto by Giovanni de Gamerra (altered by Metastasio). First performed, Milan, Dec. 26, 1772.

Lucrezia Borgia [loo-crehts'-yah borr'-jah]. Opera with a prologue and two acts by Donizetti. Libretto by Felice Romani (after Hugo). First performed, Milan, Dec. 26, 1833.

Ludford, NICHOLAS. Early 16th-cent. English composer. His earliest compositions date from *c.* 1520, and he was a member of St. Stephen's Chapel, Westminster, at its dissolution in 1547-8. He composed Masses, a Magnificat, and antiphons.

Ludwig [loot'-vi*sh*], FRIEDRICH: *b.* Potsdam, May 8, 1872; *d.* Göttingen, Oct. 3, 1930. Musicologist. Studied at Marburg and Strasbourg Universities, travelled from 1899 and lived in Potsdam. Lecturer, Strasbourg, 1905; professor, 1911, and later Rector at Göttingen. His publications dealing with his researches in the music of the 13th and 14th cent. laid the foundation for many later writings. He edited the complete works of Machaut (4 vols, 1926-43).

Luening, OTTO: *b.* Milwaukee (Wis.), June 15, 1900. Composer, conductor and flautist. He studied in Munich at the State Music Academy (1914-17), in Zürich at the Conservatorium and the University and under Busoni, and was a founder of the American Opera in Chicago (1920). Was attached to the Eastman Music School and the Opera in Rochester (1925-28) and won a Guggenheim Fellowship (1930). He has also taught at the University of Arizona, Bennington College in Vermont, and Columbia University. He has composed an opera, a symphony, symphonic poems and other orchestral works, choral works, string quartets and other chamber music, songs and pieces for piano and organ.

Lugg, (1) JOHN. Composer and organist. Was a vicar-choral at Exeter Cathedral in 1634 and sometime organist of St. Peter's in Exeter. He composed services (some of which may be by Robert Lugg), anthems, organ pieces, and a "Jigg" for harpsichord. An anthem "It is a good thing" was published in Myriell's *Tristitiae remedium* (1616) and a canon in Hilton's *Catch that catch can* (2nd ed.,

1658). Three voluntaries for "double organ" (*i.e.* organ with two manuals) were published in 1956 (ed. Susi Jeans and John Steele).

(2) ROBERT: Early 17th-cent. English organist and composer; may have been a relation of John. He received an Oxford B.Mus. (1638), was appointed organist of St. John's College, became a Roman Catholic and went abroad. He composed a service and three anthems. Other compositions by "Lugg" may be by him or by John Lugg.

Luisa Miller [loo-ee'-zah mill'-ler]. Opera in three acts by Verdi. Libretto by Salvatore Cammarano (based on Schiller's drama *Kabale und Liebe*). First performed, Naples, Dec. 8, 1849.

Lully [lēēl-lee] (originally Lulli, Giambattista), JEAN-BAPTISTE: *b.* Florence, Nov. 28, 1632; *d.* Paris, March 22, 1687. Composer. Came to Paris as a kitchen-boy in 1646, and at fourteen entered the service of Louis XIV as a player in the royal string orchestra (*Les Vingt-quatre Violons du Roi*), becoming its leader in 1652. Formed and directed a smaller group, *Les Petits Violons*, which became famous for the perfection of its ensemble, and became court composer and music-master to the royal family. From 1664 he composed music for the comedy-ballets of Molière, including *Le Mariage forcé* (1664), *L'Amour médecin* (1665), *Le Sicilien* (1667), *Monsieur de Pourceaugnac* (1669), *Les Amants magnifiques* (1670), and *Le Bourgeois Gentilhomme* (1670), in which he appeared as actor and dancer. By 1673 he had intrigued Perrin and Cambert out of their patent to establish opera in Paris, and became, with the collaboration of the poet Quinault, the founder of French opera, then called *tragédie lyrique*. The chief characteristics of French opera which he established were: (1) the overture in the form of a slow section in dotted rhythm followed by a fugal quick section; (2) extensive use of the ballet; (3) the important place given to choruses; and (4) the development of a rhetorical style of recitative closely related to the rhythms of the language. His arias, save in a few cases, are of minor importance. Besides operas and comedy-ballets, Lully composed music for court ballets and *divertissements*, some church music, and two instrumental suites. He died of an injury to his foot caused by the staff with which he was conducting. Nine volumes of his complete works, edited by H. Prunières, have been published (1930-38). Vocal scores of many of the operas have been published in the series *Chefs d'oeuvre classiques de l'opéra français*.

Operas: *Cadmus et Hermione* (1673), *Alceste* (1674), *Thésée* (1675), *Atys* (1676), *Isis* (1677), *Psyché* (1678), *Bellérophon* (1679), *Proserpine* (1680), *Persée* (1682), *Phaëton* (1683), *Amadis de Gaule* (1684), *Roland* (1685), *Armide et Renaud* (1686), *Acis et Galatée* (1686), *Achille et Polyxène* (with Colasse, 1687).

Lulu [loo'-loo]. Opera in three acts by Berg. Libretto by the composer (from Wedekind's plays *Erdgeist* and *Die Büchse der Pandora*). First performed, Zürich, June 2, 1937.

Lupi [loo'-pee], JOHANNES (Jennet le Leu): *b.* perhaps at Liège, *c.* 1500; *d.* Cambrai, Dec. 20, 1539. He studied at Louvain (1522-27) and became choir-master at the Cathedral in Cambrai. He composed motets and *chansons* published by Attaingnant and others. Ten *chansons* have been published in a modern edition by H. Albrecht (1931).

Lupo. The name of a family of musicians of Italian origin who were active at the English court between 1540 and 1640. They included Ambrose (*d.* 1594), Thomas I (*d.* 1628), Thomas II (*d.* before 1660) and Theophilus (*d.* before 1660). Compositions under the name Thomas Lupo include pieces in Leighton's *Teares or Lamentacions* of 1614 (one by "Timolphus Thopul", who may be Thomas or Theophilus or both), 25 three-part Fantasies, 13 in four parts, 28 in five parts, 13 in six parts, and a *Miserere* for strings in five parts. Modern ed. of 8 fantasias in *Musica Britannica*, ix.

Lupus Hellinck. *v.* HELLINCK.

Lur. A primitive horn of bronze found in Denmark and Sweden.

H. C. BROHOLM: *The Lures of the Bronze Age* (1949).

Luscinius (Nachtgall, Nachtigall), OTTO-

MAR (Othmar): *b.* Strasbourg, 1487; *d.* 1537. Organist, theorist, theologian and composer. He studied under Hofhaimer, became organist at Strasbourg (1517), cathedral preacher at Augsburg (1523) and at Basle (1526), and later lived at Freiburg-im-Breisgau. He published two treatises, *Musicae Institutiones* (1515) and *Musurgia seu praxis musicae* (1536), and composed pieces for organ.

Lusingando [loo-zeen-gahn′-do]. *I.* Lit. " flattering." Hence, in a tender manner.

Lusitano [loo-zee-tahn′-o], VICENTE: *b.* Olivença, early 16th cent.; *d.* after 1553. Portuguese composer and theorist. He settled in Rome *c.* 1550 and had a controversy on music with Vicentino. He published a treatise *Introdutione facilissima et novissima de canto fermo* (1553) and a book of motets (1551).

Lustigen Weiber von Windsor, Die [dee lo͝oss′-tig-ĕn vibe′-er fon vint′-zorr]. Opera in three acts by Nicolai. Libretto by S. H. Mosenthal (from Shakespeare's *The Merry Wives of Windsor*). First performed, Berlin, March 9, 1849.

Lute (*Arab.* al'ud, *Sp.* laúd, *Port.* alaude, *L.* testudo, *Fr.* luth, *G.* Laute, *I.* liuto).

Plucked instrument with a pear-shaped body, fretted finger-board, and peg-box bent back, which was one of the most popular instruments for solo-playing and song accompaniment in the 16th and early 17th century. It had eleven strings in six courses, *i.e.* five pairs in double courses at the octave and a single string, tuned thus:

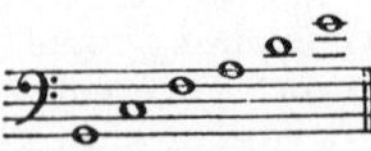

About the middle of the 17th cent. the French lutenist Denis Gaultier introduced a new tuning:

which was generally adopted. Lute music was written in the various forms of lute TABLATURE. The music for lute solo consisted of dance pieces, variations, preludes, ricercars, and arrangements of sacred and secular choral music and of folk and popular songs. The instrument for which such music and song-accompaniments were written in Spain was the *vihuela da mano* which, having a flat back, was actually a member of the guitar family, but was in other respects equivalent to the lute. Large quantities of lute music, both printed and manuscript, exist, dating from Petrucci's first collection of 1507 to the middle of the 18th century. Among the more important are the compositions of Luis Milan (*El Maestro*, 1535; modern ed. by L. Schrade, 1927), Francesco da Milano (four publications between 1536 and 1563), Adrien le Roy (three publications between 1551 and 1562 and a treatise, 1557, which was published in English translations in 1568 and 1574), the English school of lutenist song composers (including Dowland, Ford, Pilkington, Campian, Jones, Danyel and others; modern editions by E. H. Fellowes), Denis Gaultier (*Pièces de luth*, 1669; *Rhétorique des Dieux* in manuscript; facsimile edition by A. Tessier, 1932), and Esaias Reusner (*Deliciae testitudinis*, 1667; *Neue Lautenfrüchte*, 1676). The second part of Thomas Mace's *Musick's Monument* (1676) contained a detailed discussion of the lute, its playing, and its music. Two volumes of lute music from the sixteenth century to 1720 have been printed in *D.T.Ö.*, xviii (2) and xxv (2). J. S. Bach wrote some pieces for lute and wrote a part for it in the accompaniment to the arioso " Consider, O my soul " in the *St. John* Passion. Among Haydn's works are a *Cassazione* for lute, violin, and cello, and a quartet for lute, violin, viola, and cello. The chief varieties of the lute used in the same period were the ARCHLUTE, THEORBO, CHITARRONE, MANDOLA and MANDOLINE.

Lute-Harpsichord. *v.* LAUTENCLAVICYMBEL.

Luther [loot′-er], MARTIN: *b.* Eisleben, Nov. 10, 1483; *d.* there, Feb. 18, 1546. The reformer's love for music and his views on its importance in the liturgy, in the school, and in the home, had important results in the history of music in Germany. He considered that music should have "the next place to theology and the highest honour," and laid the foundations of the reformed liturgy in his Latin Mass (*Formula missae et communionis pro ecclesia Wittenbergensi*, 1523) and German Mass (1526; facsimile edition by J. Wolf, 1934). He wrote of Josquin: "He is master of the notes, which must do as he wills; other composers must do as the notes wish," and of his joy in singing polyphony: "Is it not singular and admirable that one can sing a simple tune or tenor (as the musicians call it) while three or five other voices envelop this simple tune with exultation, playing and leaping around and embellishing it wonderfully through craftsmanship as if they were leading a celestial dance?" In his preface to the first collection of four-part chorales, Johann Walther's Songbook of 1524, he wrote that he was "not of the opinion that all the arts shall be crushed to earth and perish through the Gospel, as some bigoted persons pretend, but would willingly see them all, and especially music, servants of Him who gave and created them" (trans. in O. Strunk, *Source Readings in Music History*, 1950, p. 341). The thoroughness with which music was taught in the Lutheran schools may be seen in the theory-books of Rhaw, Listenius, Henry Faber, and others. Luther composed a motet "Non moriar sed vivam" for Joachim Greff's play *Lazarus*, and may have written the music of the *Sanctus* in his German Mass and of the chorales "Ein feste Burg" and "Mit Fried und Freud."

W. E. BUSZIN: "Luther on Music," in *The Musical Quarterly*, xxxii.

P. NETTL: *Luther and Music* (1948).

Lutyens, ELISABETH: *b.* London, July 9, 1906. Composer. She studied at the Royal College of Music and at the Paris Conservatoire. She has composed 2 ballets, a viola concerto, chamber concertos, an overture and other orchestral works, songs for tenor and string quartet, string quartets and other chamber music, piano pieces and English and French songs.

Luython [loy'-ton], KAREL: *b.* Antwerp; *d.* Prague, 1620. Composer. From *c.* 1576 he was court organist in Prague to the Emperor Maximilian II and his successor Rudolf II. He published a volume of madrigals (1582), of motets (1603), of Lamentations (1604), and of Masses (1609), and built a harpsichord with separate keys for C♯ and D♭, D♯ and E♭, F♯ and G♭, G♯ and A♭, E♯, and B♯ to overcome the inadequacy of the MEANTONE SYSTEM to provide a practical tuning for these notes.

Luzzaschi [loo-dzusk'-ee], LUZZASCO: *b.* 1545; *d.* Ferrara, Sept. 11, 1607. Composer, organist and harpsichordist. He was court organist at Ferrara from *c.* 1576 and his organ pupils included Frescobaldi. Of his seven books of madrigals published between *c.* 1575 and 1604 the first and sixth have not survived. He dedicated the fourth book (1594) to Gesualdo, and the style of his later madrigals, especially those in the posthumous collection *Seconda scelta delli madrigali* (1613), resembles that of Gesualdo in its texture, though not in the extent of its chromaticism. In 1601 he published a collection of madrigals for one, two and three sopranos *per cantare et sonare*; an example with a highly ornamented solo part and keyboard accompaniment is printed in Schering's *History of Music in Examples*, No. 166, and one for three sopranos and accompaniment in the third volume of Einstein's *The Italian Madrigal* (1949), which also reprints two madrigals from the 1594 and 1613 sets. Two ricercars and a toccata for organ from Diruta's *Il Transilvano* are reprinted in Torchi's *L'arte musicale in Italia*, vol. iv. Luzzaschi also published a volume of motets in 1598.

Lydian Mode. (1) In ancient Greek music:

(2) From the Middle Ages onwards applied to:

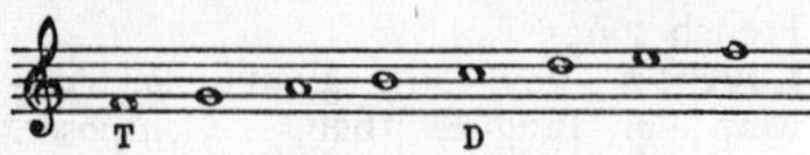

The tonic (or final) and dominant are marked respectively T and D. This mode is often found with flattened B, which makes it identical with the modern major scale. *v.* GREEK MUSIC, MODE.

Lyra. Alternative name for the medieval REBEC, which was continued in the Italian LIRA of the 16th-17th century.

Lyraflügel [lĕĕr′-a-flĕĕg-ĕl], *G.* Type of upright piano, in the form of a Greek lyre, made in Germany between *c.* 1825 and *c.* 1850.

Lyra Viol. Bowed instrument used in England in the 17th century. Being intermediate in size between the bass viol for playing divisions (which was smaller than the bass viol for playing in consort) and the tenor viol, it was also called the *viola bastarda.* Its tuning was called " lyra-way " (also " harp-way ") tuning, and its music, which made use of chords, was written in TABLATURE. One of its regular tunings was :

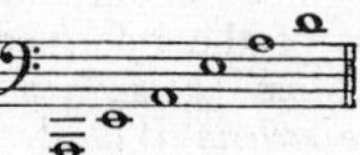

In his *Musick's Recreation on the Viol, Lyra-way* (1661) Playford observes that Daniel Farrant, Alphonso Ferrabosco and Giovanni Coprario were the first composers to write for the instrument, and that Daniel Farrant had invented a lyra viol with wire sympathetic strings under the playing strings.

Lyre (*Gr.* λύρα). An ancient Greek instrument which was a simpler form of cithara, having a body made of a tortoise shell or wood, and two horns or wooden arms joined by a cross bar; it had the same number of strings, varying from 3 to 12, as the cithara.

M

M. As an abbreviation M.=*medius*, the middle voice (in polyphonic music). M.M.=Maelzel's metronome (*v.* METRONOME). M.-S.=mezzo-soprano. *m.d.* =*mano destra* or *main droite*, right hand (in keyboard music); *mf*=*mezzo forte*, moderately loud; *m.g.*=*main gauche*, left hand; *mp*=*mezzo piano*, moderately soft; *m.s.*=*mano sinistra*, left hand; *m.v.*=*mezza voce*, with a moderate volume of tone. In TONIC SOL-FA **m** = *me*, the 3rd note (or mediant) of the major scale.

Macbeth. (1) Incidental music by Locke for Davenant's version (1672) of Shakespeare's play.

(2) Opera in four acts by Verdi. Libretto by Francesco Maria Piave (after Shakespeare). First performed, Florence, March 14, 1847.

(3) Symphonic poem by Richard Strauss (Op. 23) based on Shakespeare's play. First performed, Weimar, Oct. 13, 1890.

(4) Opera with a prologue and three acts by Bloch. Libretto by Edmond Fleg (after Shakespeare). First performed, Paris, Nov. 30, 1910.

MacCunn, HAMISH: *b.* Greenock, March 22, 1868; *d.* London, Aug. 2, 1916. Composer and conductor. Studied under Parry at the R.C.M., and became conductor to the Carl Rosa Opera company and later at the Savoy Theatre. Composed operas, cantatas and orchestral works with a Scottish flavour, besides songs, part-songs and piano pieces.

Macdowell, EDWARD ALEXANDER: *b.* New York, Dec. 18, 1861; *d.* there, Jan. 23, 1908. Composer. Studied piano in New York and Paris and composition in Frankfort under Joachim Raff. Liszt encouraged him in composition, in which he was engaged in Europe before returning permanently to America in 1888. In 1896 he became head of the newly-founded Department of Music at Columbia University, New York. He resigned in 1904 and became mentally ill in the following year. His most characteristic compositions are those for piano, which include 4 sonatas and a large number of smaller pieces. For orchestra he wrote symphonic poems and 2 suites, of which the second uses melodies of the North American Indians, and also composed two piano concertos, songs and part-songs.

L. GILMAN: *Edward Macdowell* (1905).

Mace, THOMAS: *b.* Cambridge, *c.* 1613; *d. c.* 1709. Writer and instrumentalist, chiefly known for his *Musick's Monument; or A Remembrancer of the best Practical Musick, both Divine and Civil, that has ever been known to have been in the world* (1676), which deals with the lute, viol and musical affairs in general. An anthem "I heard a voice" has survived in manuscript.

Macfarren, (1) GEORGE ALEXANDER: *b.* London, March 2, 1813; *d.* there, Oct. 31, 1887. Composer and teacher. Educated at the R.A.M., where he became teacher in 1834 and principal in 1876. His compositions include operas, oratorios, cantatas, orchestral works, chamber music and songs. He published text-books on harmony and a volume of *Addresses and Lectures* (1888). Professor, Cambridge, 1875. Knighted, 1883.

(2) WALTER CECIL: *b.* London, Aug. 28, 1826; *d.* there, Sept. 2, 1905. Brother of (1). Composer and conductor. Teacher of piano, R.A.M., 1846-1903. His works include a symphony and overtures for orchestra, piano compositions, church music, songs and part-songs.

Machaut (Machault) [ma-sho], GUILLAUME DE: *b.* Champagne, *c.* 1300; *d.* Rheims, 1377. Poet and composer. Ordained and became secretary to John, Duke of Luxembourg and King of Bohemia, with whom he travelled. Later served Charles V of France and became canon of Rheims. The dominant French composer of the 14th cent., he composed the first known setting of the Ordinary of the Mass by a single composer (*Messe Notre Dame*). In his *Remède de Fortune* he explained the seven forms of lyric poetry and wrote a composition to illustrate each one. Of his 23 motets all but three are isorhythmic. His secular compositions form the first great repertory of the polyphonic *chanson*, and comprise *ballades*, *rondeaux*, and *virelais*. He also composed monophonic *lais* and *virelais*. The edition of his musical works by Friedrich Ludwig comprises two volumes (1926, 1929) containing respectively the *ballades*, *rondeau* and *virelais*, and the motets, a volume of commentary (1928) and a volume containing the Mass and the *lais* (1943 ; reprinted, 1954). Another edition by Leo Schrade is in *Polyphonic Music of the Fourteenth Century*, ii-iii. There are several modern editions of the Mass.

A. MACHABEY : *Guillaume de Machault*, 2 vols. (1955).

G. REESE : *Music in the Middle Ages* (1940), chap. xii.

Mackenzie, ALEXANDER CAMPBELL: *b.* Edinburgh, Aug. 22, 1847; *d.* London, April 28, 1935. Composer and teacher. Educated in Germany and at the R.A.M., where he was appointed principal in 1888. His compositions consist chiefly of cantatas and operas, works for violin, songs, and suites and overtures for orchestra. Knighted, 1895.

A. C. MACKENZIE : *A Musician's Narrative* (1927).

Macmillan, ERNEST CAMPBELL: *b.* Mimico, Ont., Aug. 18, 1893. Conductor and composer. Educated in Toronto, Edinburgh and Paris. Principal, Toronto Conservatory of Music (now the Royal Conservatory) and Dean of the Faculty of Music at Toronto University, 1926-53. Conductor, Toronto Symphony Orchestra, 1931; Mendelssohn Choir, 1944. Knighted, 1935. His compositions include a choral ode *England*, orchestral works, chamber music, songs and folk-song settings.

Maconchy, ELIZABETH : *b.* Broxbourne (Herts.), March 19, 1907. Composer. Studied at the R.C.M. under Vaughan Williams. Her compositions, in which she has developed an individual treatment of contemporary idioms within the traditional forms, include orchestral works, ballet music, concertos for piano, viola and clarinet, and chamber music.

Macpherson, STEWART: *b.* Liverpool, March 29, 1865; *d.* London, March 27, 1941. Teacher and writer. Educated at R.A.M., where he taught harmony from 1887. Wrote a number of textbooks on harmony, counterpoint, form and musical history, and composed a symphony and other orchestral works, a Mass, songs and piano pieces.

Macque [der muck], JEAN DE : *b.* Valenciennes, *c.* 1551 ; *d.* Naples, Sept. 1614. A pupil of Philip de Monte, he was in Rome from 1576 to 1582 and in Naples from 1586 until after 1610. He composed some motets and published a number of books of madrigals, of which two appeared with English words in Nicholas Yonge's *Musica Transalpina* (1588) and in Morley's collection of Italian madrigals (1598).

Madama Butterfly. Opera originally in two acts, later in three acts, by Puccini. Libretto by Giuseppe Giacosa and Luigi Illica. First performed, Milan, Feb. 17, 1904. Pinkerton (a United States navy officer) while stationed in Japan marries Cio-Cio-San, who renounces the faith of her ancestors to show her trust in him and thus can never return to her own people. After he leaves for America she bears his son and is befriended by Sharpless (the American consul). Pinkerton later returns with his American wife, who wishes to adopt the child. Cio-Cio-San, having asked them to come back in a short time for the child, blindfolds him and kills herself.

Madrigal. The name may connote a poem in the mother tongue (*matricale*) or a pastoral poem (*mandriale*). Musical settings first appeared in the 14th cent. in Italy, in two or three parts, by *e.g.* Jacopo da Bologna, Giovanni da Cascia and Francesco Landini. Examples are printed in the *Historical Anthology* (Nos. 49, 50, 54) and in Schering's *History of Music in Examples* (No. 22). Each of the two or three verses of the poem has three lines in iambic pentameters, sung to the same music, and there is a final *ritornello* of two lines, sung to different music. The madrigal poem of the 16th cent. was a free form, and the musical style of the earliest published collection entitled *Madrigali* (1533) was derived from the *frottola*. The work of Verdelot, Festa and Arcadelt in this style was followed by that of Willaert and his pupil Cipriano de Rore, who widened the scope of the madrigal in the expression of the words and the use of technical resources. The "classic" Italian madrigal of the second half of the century was written in imitative polyphony, usually in five parts, and made a moderate use of word-painting and word-symbolism (A. Gabrieli, Palestrina, Lasso, Philippe de Monte). The mannered style of the late madrigal (Marenzio, Gesualdo, Monteverdi) used less restrained forms of word-painting, chromaticism, and dramatic effects of melodic line and choral texture. The transition from the imitative madrigal to the madrigal for solo, duet or trio accompanied by continuo, which resulted from the pursuit of dramatic expression, can be traced in the seven books published by Monteverdi from 1587 to 1619.

Italian madrigals were sung in England before 1588, when Byrd's *Psalmes, Sonets, and Songs of Sadnes and Pietie* appeared and Nicholas Yonge published *Musica Transalpina, Madrigales translated* from the Italian. About forty publications of or containing madrigals by some thirty composers appeared between 1589 and 1627 (modern ed. in *E.M.S.*, ed. E. H. Fellowes). Morley's collection of 1594 was the first to use the term madrigal in the title. In style the English madrigal is "an artistic compromise, of astonishing perfection and success," combining the polyphonic style of the classic Italian madrigal with the homophonic style of the *frottola*. This style remains virtually constant, and only slightly affected by the mannered style of the late Italian madrigal, throughout the work of its greatest masters, Morley, Wilbye, Weelkes, Bennet, Bateson and Gibbons.

A. EINSTEIN: *The Italian Madrigal* (3 vols., 1949).

E. H. FELLOWES: *English Madrigal Composers* (1921).

C. KENNEDY SCOTT: *Madrigal Singing* (1931).

Maelzel (Mälzel), [mell'-tsĕl], JOHANN NEPOMUK: *b.* Ratisbon, Aug. 15, 1772: *d.* at sea, July 21, 1838. Inventor and constructor of mechanical musical instruments. He constructed a Panharmonicon, or mechanical orchestra, a mechanical trumpeter, a chronometer about which Beethoven wrote a canon *Ta, ta, ta, lieber Mälzel* which is musically related to the Allegretto of the eighth symphony, and perfected the metronome which still bears his name, and which Beethoven was the first composer to use to indicate the tempi of his compositions. Maelzel spent the later part of his life in the United States.

Maestoso [mah-ess-to'-zo], *I.* Majestic, dignified.

Maestro de capilla [mah-ess'-tro deh cah-peel'-lyah], *Sp.* = *I.* maestro di cappella.

Maestro di cappella [mah-ess'-tro dee cahp-pell'-lah], *I.* (*Fr.* maître de chapelle, *G.* Kapellmeister, *Sp.* maestro de capilla). Lit. "master of the chapel," *i.e.* director of music to a prince, king, bishop or nobleman.

Mage [dĕe muzh], PIERRE DU. 18th-cent. organist and composer. A pupil of Louis Marchand, he published his *Livre d'Orgue* in 1708 (modern ed. by A. Guilmant in *Archives des maîtres de l'orgue*, vol. iii).

Maggini [mah-djee'-nee], GIOVANNI PAOLO: *b.* Brescia, 1581; *d.* there, *c.* 1630. Celebrated violin-maker. He was an apprentice to Gasparo da Salò in 1602, and later improved on Salò's designs and methods in several respects.

M. L. HUGGINS: *Gio. Paolo Maggini* (1892).

Maggiore [mah-djoh'-reh], *I.* Major mode.

Magic Flute, The. *v.* ZAUBERFLÖTE.

Magnificat. Canticle of the Virgin sung at Vespers in the Roman rite and at Evensong in the English rite. In plainsong it is sung antiphonally to one of its eight tones. Polyphonic settings first appeared as early as the 14th cent. and many were written for the Latin and

Lutheran liturgies thereafter. Most often the even-numbered verses were set, for voices or organ, the other verses being sung in plainsong, which was commonly used as the basis of the polyphony. Bach set the Magnificat in the form of an elaborate cantata. In its English translation the Magnificat has been set as part of the Evening Service by English composers from the Reformation to the present.

Mahagonny. *v.* AUFSTIEG UND FALL.

Mahillon [ma-ee-yo͡n], CHARLES VICTOR: *b.* Brussels, March, 10, 1841; *d.* St. Jean, Cap Ferrat, June 17, 1924. Writer on musical instruments. In 1865 he entered the wind-instrument firm founded by his father and in 1876 became curator of the museum of the Brussels Conservatoire. He published a catalogue of the museum and *Les Éléments d'acoustique musicale et instrumentale* (1874).

Mahler [mahl′-er], GUSTAV: *b.* Kališt (Bohemia), July 7, 1860; *d.* Vienna, May 18, 1911. Composer and conductor. Studied at the Vienna Conservatorium. Conducted opera in various places until his appointment as director of the Budapest Opera, 1888. Conductor, Hamburg Opera, 1891; director, Vienna Opera, 1897; conductor, Metropolitan Opera, New York, 1907; New York Philharmonic Orchestra, 1908. His period at the Vienna Opera was one of the most brilliant in its history. His compositions combine a late Romantic style in thematic material and harmony with an individual treatment of form and orchestration. Of his 9 symphonies (a tenth was left unfinished) the second (*Resurrection,* 1894), third (1895), fourth (*Ode to Heavenly Joy,* 1900), and eighth (*Symphony of a Thousand,* 1907) have parts for voices. Apart from the symphonies he published only songs and song-cycles, including *Lieder eines fahrenden Gesellen* (1884), *Kindertotenlieder* (1902), and *Das Lied von der Erde* for solo voices and orchestra (1908).

G. ENGEL: *Gustav Mahler* (1933).

A. MAHLER: *Gustav Mahler* (Eng. trans.; 1946).

D. NEWLIN: *Bruckner, Mahler, Schönberg* (1947).

H. F. REDLICH: *Mahler and Bruckner* (1956).

B. WALTER: *Gustav Mahler* (Eng. trans., 1937).

Maid of Pskov, The. *v.* PSKOVITIANKA.

Maiskaya Noch [ma-i-ska′-ya nockh] (A Night in May). Opera in three acts by Rimsky-Korsakov. Libretto by the composer (based on a story by Gogol). First performed, St. Petersburg, Jan. 21, 1880.

Maistre [ler metr], MATTHEUS LE. *v.* LE MAISTRE.

Maître de chapelle [metr der sha-pell], *Fr.* (*G.* Kapellmeister, *I.* maestro di cappella, *Sp.* maestro de capilla). Lit. "master of the chapel," *i.e.* director of music to a prince, king, bishop or nobleman.

Major. Greater. The term is used in referring to an interval, a chord, a mode, and to PROLATION in mensural notation. *v.* CHORD, INTERVAL, SCALE.

Majorano [mah-yo-rahn′-o], GAETANO. *v.* CAFFARELLI.

Malagueña [mah-lah-gay′-nya], *Sp.* Andalusian folk-dance. The music is said to be improvised in parallel chords on a repeated bass of the pattern AGFE with a G♯ (major third) in the last chord. However, the examples with words printed in Subirá's *Antología Musical de Cantos Populares Españoles* (1930) follow that formula rather freely, *e.g.*:

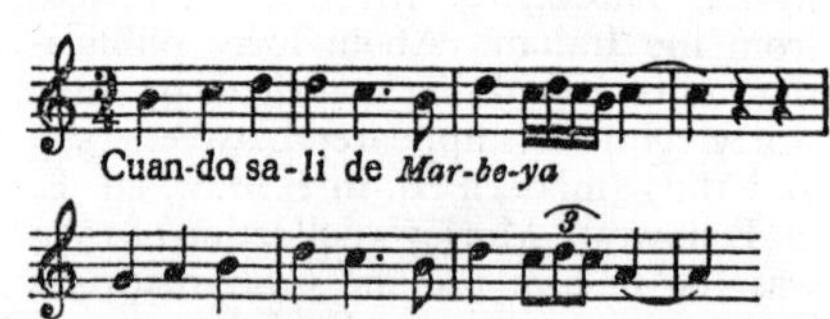

Malcolm, ALEXANDER: *b.* Edinburgh, 1687; *d.* after 1721. Author of the first important treatise on the theory of music to be printed in Scotland: *A Treatise of Musick, Speculative, Practical and Historical* (Edinburgh, 1721).

Maldeghem [fun mull′-dĕg-ĕm], ROBERT JULLIEN VAN: *b.* Deuterghem (Flanders), 1810; *d.* Ixilles (nr. Brussels), Nov. 13, 1893. Organist, and editor of a pioneer collection of *chansons* and motets by composers of the early 16th cent., *Trésor musical* (1865-93). A revised list of its contents is given in G. Reese, "Maldeghem and his buried Treasure," in *Notes of the Music Library Association*, vi, p. 75.

Maldere [fun mull′-der-er], PIERRE VAN: *b.* Brussels, Oct. 16, 1729; *d.* there, Nov. 3, 1768. Violinist and composer. Became first violinist in the Royal Chapel in Brussels, visited Dublin, Austria, Paris, and perhaps Italy, and after 1758 produced his operas in Brussels. He also composed chamber music, and his symphonies played a part in the early history of the form.

Maleingreau [ma-lan͡-gro], PAUL DE: *b.* Trélon-en-Thiérache, Nov. 23, 1887. Organist and composer. Educated at the Brussels Conservatoire, where he became teacher of harmony. His interest in liturgical studies has given a special character to most of his compositions for organ, *e.g.* *Opus sacrum*, *Préludes à l'introit*, *Symphonie de Nöel*, *Symphonie de la Passion*. He has also written several works for piano.

Malherbe [mull-airb], CHARLES THÉODORE: *b.* Paris, April 21, 1853; *d.* Cormeilles, Oct. 5, 1911. Writer and composer. Studied law and composition. Curator of archives, Paris Opera, 1898. His publications include *L'œuvre dramatique de R. Wagner* (1886), *Précis de l'histoire de l'Opéra-Comique* (1887), and a biography of Auber (1911).

Malibran [ma-lee-brun͡], MARIA FELICITA: *b.* Paris, March 24, 1808; *d.* Manchester, Sept. 23, 1836. Operatic singer, who combined a natural contralto with a soprano range. Taught by her father Manuel Garcia and by Hérold in Paris. First appeared in opera, London, 1825. Sang with great success in London, Paris, New York and Italy. Her marriage with Malibran was annulled in 1836 and she married the violinist Charles de Bériot.

Malinconia [mah-leen-co-nee′-ah], *I.* Melancholy (noun). The adjective is *malinconico*.

Malipiero [mah-lee-pyeh′-ro], GIAN FRANCESCO: *b.* Venice, March 18, 1882. Composer. Studied under Enrico Bossi in Bologna. Taught composition at the Parma Conservatorio, 1921-1923. Director, Liceo Benedetto Marcello, Venice, 1939. Has edited the complete works of Monteverdi and music by Frescobaldi and Stradella, and as a composer is representative of the neo-Baroque in modern Italian music. His first work to gain general notice was *Pause del Silenzio* (1917), consisting of 7 "impressions" for orchestra portraying states of mind. His first string quartet, called *Rispetti e Strambotti*, was awarded the Coolidge Prize in 1920. Among the orchestral works are 9 symphonies, and he has written operas and other stage works, oratorios, chamber music, piano music and songs. He has published a book on *The Orchestra* (Italian and English), and essays on Monteverdi (1930) and Stravinsky (1945).

Ma Mère l'Oye [ma mair lwa], *Fr.* (Mother Goose). A suite of five children's pieces for piano duet by Ravel (1908; published, 1910) based on fairy-tales by Perrault and entitled:

1. *Pavane de la Belle au Bois Dormant* (Pavan of the Sleeping Beauty).
2. *Petit Poucet* (Tom Thumb).
3. *Laideronette Impératrice des Pagodes* (Little Ugly, Empress of the Pagodas).
4. *Les entretiens de la Belle et de la Bête* (Colloquy between Beauty and the Beast).
5. *Le Jardin Féerique* (The Fairy Garden).

Ravel scored the work for orchestra (1912) and it was produced as a ballet.

Manchicourt [der mun͡-shee-coor], PIERRE DE: *b.* Béthune, *c.* 1510; *d.* Madrid, Oct. 5, 1564. Composer. *Maître de chapelle* at Tournai, 1539; *maestro de capilla* in the royal chapel, Madrid, 1560. His motets were published by Attaingnant (1539) and by Phalèse at Louvain (1554), and a collection of 29 *chansons* by Susato at Antwerp in 1545.

Mancinelli [mahn-chee-nell′-lee], LUIGI: *b.* Orvieto, Feb. 5, 1848; *d.* Rome, Feb. 2, 1921. Conductor and composer. Studied the cello in Florence, and from 1874 was conductor in Rome, Bologna, London, New York (Metropolitan Opera, 1894-1903) and

Buenos Aires (Teatro Colon, 1906-12). Composed several operas, choral works, overtures for orchestra, and church music.

Mancini [mahn-chee'-nee], FRANCESCO: *b.* Naples, 1679; *d.* there, June 11, 1739. Composer. Educated at Naples. His opera *L'Idaspe fedele*, produced in London in 1710, was one of the few Italian operas given there before the arrival of Handel (Addison in *The Spectator*, March 15, 1711).

Mancinus. *v.* MENCKEN.

Mandola [mahn-do'-lah], *I.* (mandora, mandore), **Mandoline.** Instruments of the lute family. The mandola was played in the 16th cent., and had a curved peg-box and double strings. The mandoline, of smaller size, has been in use since the early 18th cent. Handel wrote for it in *Alexander Balus* (1748), Mozart in the serenade " Deh vieni " in *Don Giovanni* (1787), Verdi in *Otello* (1887), Mahler in his seventh symphony (1908), and Schönberg in his *Serenade*, Op. 24 (1924).

Mandyczewski [mund-i-chef'-ski], EUSEBIUS : *b.* Czernowitz, Aug. 18, 1857; *d.* Vienna, July 13, 1929. Historian and editor. Educated in Vienna. Keeper of the archives of the Gesellschaft der Musikfreunde, 1887; teacher, Vienna Conservatorium, 1897. Edited the complete works of Schubert and began the unfinished edition of the works of Haydn published by Breitkopf and Härtel.

Manfred. (1) Incidental music to Byron's poem by Schumann, Op. 115 (1848-9). It consists of an overture, melodramas, solos and choruses.

(2) Symphony by Tchaikovsky, Op. 58 (1885), based on the same poem.

Manicorde [ma-nee-corrd], *Fr.* 16th-cent. term for the clavichord.

Manieren [mun-eer'-ĕn], *G.* 18th-cent. term for musical ornaments or grace notes.

Mannheim [mun'-hime]. A town in Western Germany, famous in the mid-18th cent. for its orchestra. The reputation of this ensemble was due to its excellent discipline, the individual skill of its players and a lively style of performance which included boldly contrasted dynamics and a calculated use of *crescendo* and *diminuendo*. A number of composers wrote symphonies for this orchestra, among them Johann Stamitz, Franz Xaver Richter, Ignaz Holzbauer and Christian Cannabich. The fame of the orchestra ensured that the composers also became well-known and so helped to extend the demand for this type of composition, in which the main elements were pregnant themes, bold contrasts and the minimum of contrapuntal elaboration. *v.* SYMPHONY.

Manns, AUGUST FRIEDRICH : *b.* Stolzenburg (nr. Stettin), March 12, 1825; *d.* London, March 1, 1907. Conductor. Played in and conducted military bands in Germany until 1854, when he came to England. Became conductor of the Crystal Palace band in 1855, and conducted the Crystal Palace Saturday Concerts until 1901. Knighted, 1903.

H. S. WYNDHAM : *August Manns and the Saturday Concerts* (1909).

Manon [ma-nõn]. Opera in five acts by Massenet. Libretto by Henri Meilhac and Philippe Gille (founded on Prévost's novel). First performed, Paris, Jan. 19, 1884.

Manon Lescaut [ma-nõn less-co]. (1) Opera in three acts by Auber. Libretto by Augustine Eugène Scribe (founded on Prévost's novel). First performed, Paris, Feb. 23, 1856.

(2) Opera in four acts by Puccini. Libretto by Marco Praga, Domenico Oliva and Luigi Illica (after Prévost's novel). First performed, Turin, Feb. 1, 1893.

Manual (*L.* manus, " hand "). A keyboard; in particular one of the keyboards of an organ or harpsichord. A small organ may have only one manual; larger instruments have two or more, each of which controls its own set of pipes. The manuals normally found on English organs are: Solo, Swell, Great, Choir in this order, beginning from the top. A three-manual organ will have Swell, Great and Choir; a two-manual organ, Swell and Great. By using a COUPLER it is possible to play on the pipes of two manuals simultaneously. *v.* CHOIR ORGAN, GREAT ORGAN, ORGAN, SOLO ORGAN, SWELL ORGAN.

Manuel, Roland- [rol-ũn-ma-nēē-el]. *v.* ROLAND-MANUEL.

Man without a Country, The. Opera in two acts by Walter Damrosch. Libretto by Arthur Guiterman (based on a story by Edward Everett Hale). First performed, New York, May 12, 1937.

Manziarly [mũnz-yarr-lee], MARCELLE DE: *b.* Oct. 5, 1899. Composer of French-Russian extraction. Studied with Nadia Boulanger, and has written orchestral works, chamber music and a concerto for piano and orchestra.

Maometto II [mah-o-met′-to seh-con′-do]. Opera in two acts by Rossini. Libretto by Cesare della Valle, Duke of Ventignano. First performed, Naples, Dec. 3, 1820. The music was subsequently adapted to a new French libretto in three acts by Louis Alexandre Soumet and Giuseppe Luigi Balochi (with additional numbers) and performed as *Le Siège de Corinthe*, Paris, Oct. 9, 1826.

Marais [ma-ray], MARIN: *b.* Paris, March 31, 1656; *d.* there, Aug. 15, 1728. Composer and viola da gamba player. Studied the gamba with Hottemann and composition with Lully, and was from 1685 to 1727 solo gambist to Louis XIV. He played on a gamba with 7 strings instead of the usual 6, and published 5 books of pieces for his instrument, besides other chamber music. Among his programmatic pieces is a curiosity describing an operation for the removal of gallstones. He also composed operas and some church music.

Marazzoli [mah-rah-tso′-lee], MARCO: *d.* Rome, Jan. 24, 1662. Singer in the papal chapel in Rome *c.* 1637 and composer. In collaboration with Virgilio Mazzochi he wrote the music of the first comic opera, *Chi soffre, speri* (Rome, 1639). He also composed the music for the second act of another comic opera, *Dal male il bene* (Rome, 1653), the music of the first and third acts being by Abbatini.

Marbeck (Merbecke), JOHN: *b. c.* 1510; *d.* Windsor, *c.* 1585. English singer, organist and composer. Chorister and later organist of St. George's Chapel, Windsor. He was arrested as a Protestant heretic in 1543 and narrowly escaped burning. In 1550 he issued his well-known *Booke of Common Praier noted* (facsimile ed. with commentary by J. Eric Hunt, 1939) and, having escaped persecution under Mary, produced in the following reign several vigorously Protestant theological books. His *Booke of Common Praier noted* was the first setting to music of the English liturgy as authorized by the 1549 Act of Uniformity. A Mass, two motets (one lacking the tenor part) and a carol have been published in *T.C.M.*, x.

Marcato [marr-cah′-toh], *I.* Marked, emphatic.

Marcello [marr-chell′-lo], (1) ALESSANDRO: *b.* Venice, *c.* 1684; *d.* there, *c.* 1750. Composer and philosopher. Brother of (2). Published cantatas, solo sonatas and concertos.

(2) BENEDETTO: *b.* Venice, Aug. 1, 1686; *d.* Brescia, July 24, 1739. Composer. Educated in the law, and combined its profession with those of composer, librettist, and writer on music. His most famous composition is *Estro poetico-armonico* (8 vols., Venice, 1724-27), consisting of settings of fifty paraphrases of psalms by G. A. Giustiniani. He also composed cantatas, oratorios, concertos and sonatas. His *Il teatro alla moda* (English translation by R. G. Pauly in *Musical Quarterly*, 1948) is a satirical commentary on early 18th-cent. opera. He wrote the libretto for Ruggeri's *Arato in Sparta* in 1709.

March (*Fr.* marche, *G.* Marsch, *I.* marcia). Music for a procession or parade must necessarily be in duple time (2/4 or 6/8 for a quick march) or in quadruple time (common time for a regular march and a slow common time for a funeral march). In form a modern march (Schubert, Sousa, Elgar, Walton) consists of a main section alternating with one or more trios. Marches to accompany a stage procession appear in the operas of *e.g.* Lully, Handel, Mozart, Meyerbeer, Verdi, and Wagner, and in incidental music, *e.g.* Mendelssohn's *Wedding March*. In the form of instrumental music not intended to accompany action marches are found *e.g.* in English virginal music of the 16th cent., in suites in the Baroque period, and in

Beethoven's piano sonata, Op. 101. Examples of funeral marches are in Beethoven's sonata, Op. 26, and third symphony, and in Chopin's B♭ minor sonata.

Marchal [marr-shull], ANDRÉ : *b.* Paris, Feb. 6, 1894. Blind organist. Studied at the Paris Conservatoire, where he won several prizes. Organist, St. Germain-des-Prés, 1915 ; St. Eustache, since 1945. He has toured widely as a recitalist in Europe, America and Australia and enjoys a reputation as a master of improvisation.

Marchand [marr-shūn͡], LOUIS: *b.* Lyons, Feb. 2, 1669; *d.* Paris, Feb. 17, 1732. Organist and composer. Lived in Paris from about 1698. Court organist, Versailles; organist, Royal Chapel, 1708-14. Exiled in 1717, he went to Dresden. At a concert there Bach and Marchand improvised variations on the same theme; Marchand avoided a further contest and returned to Paris. He composed organ music and an opera, and published two books of harpsichord pieces. Two volumes of his organ music have been edited by A. Guilmant in *Archives des maîtres de l'orgue*, iii & v.

Märchen von der schönen Melusine [mair*sh*'-ĕn fon dair shurn'-ĕn may-loo-zeen'-er], *G.* (Legend of the Fair Melusina). *v.* SCHÖNE MELUSINE.

Marchetto [marr-ket'-to] (Marchettus of Padua). Early 14th-cent. theorist. He expounded the use of imperfect as well as perfect time and the Italian method of notation of the various divisions of the breve and semibreve. His two treatises, *Lucidarium in arte musicae planae* and *Pomerium artis musicae mensurabilis* (1318) were published in Gerbert's *Scriptores*, iii, pp. 64 and 123, and a shorter form of the *Pomerium* in Coussemaker's *Scriptores*, iii, p.1. An English translation of part of the *Pomerium* is printed in O. Strunk's *Source Readings in Music History* (1950).

Marcia [marr'-chah], *I.* March. *Tempo di marcia*, march time.

Marenzio [mah-rents'-yo], LUCA: *b.* Coccaglio (nr. Brescia), 1553; *d.* Rome, Aug. 22, 1599. Composer. In the service of the Cardinal d'Este, 1578-87; of the Polish court, 1596-98; and finally of the Papal chapel. One of the greatest composers of madrigals, and perhaps the most resourceful in expression and technical command. His style, of which ten examples were included in *Musica Transalpina* (1588), had a strong influence on madrigal composition in England, Morley recommended him as a model of "good air and fine invention," and Peacham (1622) goes further: "For delicious Aire and sweet Invention in Madrigals, Luca Marenzio excelleth all other whatsoever." He published sixteen books of madrigals and one book of *Madrigali spirituali*, besides other volumes of sacred and secular music. Two volumes of madrigals have been edited by Alfred Einstein, and single examples are printed in the *Historical Anthology* (No. 155) and Schering's *History of Music in Examples* (No. 165).

Maria Theresia. The name given to Haydn's Symphony No. 48 in C major (1772), performed in 1773 on the occasion of a visit of the Empress to Prince Esterházy.

Mariazellermesse [ma-rya-tsell'-er-mess-*er*] (Mariazell Mass). The title of a Mass in C major by Haydn, composed in 1782 (No. 6 in the new complete edition, no. 15 in Novello's edition). So called after a shrine of Our Lady at Mariazell in the Styrian Alps and commissioned as a votive offering by a government official, Anton Liebe von Kreutzner. Also known as *Missa Cellensis*.

Marimba. A type of xylophone used in Africa and South America. It consists of wooden bars suspended in a frame, with a gourd or wooden box below each bar to act as resonator.

Marine Trumpet. *v.* TROMBA MARINA.

Marini [mah-ree'-nee], BIAGIO: *b.* Brescia, *c.* 1597; *d.* Venice, March 20 1665. Composer and violinist. He was a player in St. Mark's, Venice from 1615-18. Marini and Farina, whose pupil he may have been, were the earliest composers of sonatas for solo violin and continuo. Two examples are printed in Schering's *History of Music in Examples* (Nos. 182 and 183), and one in the *Historical Anthology* (No. 199).

Mario [mah'-ryo], GIOVANNI MATTEO: *b.*

Cagliari, Oct. 17, 1810; *d.* Rome, Dec. 11, 1883. Tenor. His early years were spent in preparing for a military career, and he became an officer in the Piedmontese Guard. An excellent amateur singer, he was persuaded in Paris to embark on an operatic career and made his first appearance there in 1838 in *Robert le diable.* For nearly 30 years he sang regularly in opera in Paris and London, and also visited St. Petersburg. He married the soprano Giula Grisi.

Maritana. Opera in three acts by Vincent Wallace. Libretto by Edward Fitzball (based on the French play *Don César de Bazan* by Adolphe Philippe d'Ennery and Philippe François Pinel Dumanoir). First performed, London, Nov. 15, 1845.

Markevitch [mahrr'-ker-vitch], IGOR: *b.* Kiev, July 27, 1912. Composer. His earliest compositions date from 1926 when he went to Paris to study under Nadia Boulanger. His ballet suite for orchestra, *Rebus,* dedicated to the memory of Diaghilev, who had encouraged his work, was played in Paris in 1931. He has composed other orchestral works, cantatas, a Partita for piano and orchestra, and chamber music.

Marpurg [marr'-pŏŏrk], FRIEDRICH WILHELM: *b.* nr. Seehausen (Brandenburg), Nov. 21, 1718; *d.* Berlin, May 22, 1795. Theorist and writer on music. In Paris in 1746 he became acquainted with Rameau's theory of harmony, on which he based his *Handbuch bey dem Generalbasse* (1755-62). Later he lived in Berlin, Hamburg and from 1763 again in Berlin. Among his other writings are treatises on keyboard playing, on fugue, and on musical history. He composed sonatas and other keyboard pieces, organ works, and songs.

Marriage of Figaro, The. *v.* NOZZE DI FIGARO.

Marsch [marrsh], *G.* March.

Marschner [marrsh'-ner], HEINRICH AUGUST: *b.* Zittau, Aug. 16, 1795; *d.* Hanover, Dec. 14, 1861. Composer. Studied in Leipzig under Schicht. Directed the Dresden Opera from 1824. *Kapellmeister,* Leipzig, 1827; Hanover, 1831 till his retirement in 1859. The most successful composer of German Romantic opera between Weber and Wagner. His *Heinrich IV und Aubigne* was produced by Weber at Dresden in 1820. *Der Templer und die Jüdin* (Leipzig, 1829) was based on Scott's *Ivanhoe.* His most representative opera, *Hans Heiling* (Berlin, 1833), has kept its place in the repertory of German opera houses. He also composed songs and choral music.

Marseillaise, La [la marr-say-yez] *Fr.* French national hymn. The words and music were written by Rouget de Lisle on the night of Apr. 24, 1792. It acquired the name because it was sung in Paris by troops from Marseilles on their entry into the city in July of that year. It was used by Salieri in the opera *Palmira* (1795) and by Schumann in his *Faschingsschwank aus Wien* for piano and the song "Die beiden Grenadiere" (The Two Grenadiers).

Marson, GEORGE: *b.* Worcester, *c.* 1573; *d.* Canterbury, Feb. 3, 1632. Composer. Organist at Canterbury from about 1599 until his death. His five-part madrigal "The nymphs and shepherds danced lavoltas" was published in *The Triumphes of Oriana* (*E.M.S.,* xxxii). He also composed church music.

Martelé [marr-ter-lay], *Fr.* *v.* MARTELLATO.

Martellato [marr-tel-lah'-toh), *I.* (*Fr.* martelé). Lit. "hammered." A term used in string-playing, indicating heavy, detached up-and-down strokes, played with the point of the bow, without taking the bow from the string, and in piano-playing, indicating a forceful, detached touch.

Martenot, Les Ondes [laze ond marr-ter-no]. *v.* ONDES MARTENOT.

Martha. Opera in four acts by Flotow. Libretto by W. Friedrich (*i.e.* Friedrich Wilhelm Riese). First performed, Vienna, Nov. 25, 1847. (An operatic version of a ballet-pantomime *Lady Henriette ou La Servante de Greenwich,* music by Flotow, Burgmüller and Deldevez: first performed, Paris, Feb. 21, 1844).

Martin [marr-tan], (1) FRANK: *b.* Geneva, Sept. 15, 1890. Composer. Studied at his birthplace under Joseph Lauber. Has been widely recognised as a composer of originality and power.

His compositions include incidental music for *Oedipus Rex* and *Oedipus at Colonus*, cantatas, a Mass, and chamber music. For orchestra he has written a symphony, a *Petite symphonie concertante* for two string orchestras, harp, harpsichord and piano, a piano concerto, a violin concerto, a harpsichord concerto and other works.

(2) GEORGES. *v.* WITKOWSKI.

Martini [marr-tee′-nee], GIOVANNI BATTISTA (Giambattista): *b.* Bologna, Apr. 24, 1706; *d.* there, Oct. 4, 1784. Theorist, historian and composer, the most renowned musical *savant* of his day. Studied the harpsichord, violin and counterpoint. Ordained in 1722 (hence called " Padre "), and became *maestro di cappella* at S. Francesco, Bologna, 1725. He corresponded with a wide circle of professional and amateur musicians, and gave advice on technical points to many celebrated composers, among them Mozart and J. C. Bach. His most important works are the unfinished history (*Storia della musica*, 3 vols., 1757-81) and a treatise on counterpoint (*Esemplare . . . di contrappunto*, 2 vols., 1774-5). His compositions include church music, oratorios and keyboard sonatas.

Martinů [marr′-tin-oo], BOHUSLAV: *b.* Polička (Bohemia), Dec. 8, 1890. Composer. Studied under Suk in Prague and Roussel in Paris. In 1933 his string sextet gained the Coolidge Prize. A prolific composer, his works include operas, ballets, 4 symphonies, symphonic poems, 2 piano concertos, concertos for violin and cello, and chamber music. He now lives in the United States.

M. ŠAFRÁNEK : *Bohuslav Martinů* (1944).

Martin y Soler [marr-teen′ ee so-lairr′] VINCENTE: *b.* Valencia, June 18, 1754; *d.* St. Petersburg, Jan, 30, 1806. Composer. Chorister at Valencia and organist at Alicante. Produced his first Italian opera at Florence in 1781. A melody from his most successful opera *Una cosa rara*, written to a libretto by da Ponte and produced in Vienna in 1786, was used by Mozart in the banquet music in the finale of the second act of *Don Giovanni* (1787). He produced two operas in St. Petersburg (the second with Pashkeievich) to libretti by the Empress Catharine II (1789, 1791) and two in London to Italian texts by da Ponte (1795).

Martyre de Saint Sébastien, Le [ler marr-teer der sa͡n say-bust-ya͡n], *Fr.* (The Martyrdom of St. Sebastian). A mystery play by Gabriele d'Annunzio for which Debussy wrote incidental music for solo voices, chorus and orchestra (1911).

Marx [marrks], (1) ADOLPH BERNHARD: *b.* Halle, May 15, 1795; *d.* Berlin, May 17, 1866. Theorist and writer on music. Studied law, and then music in Berlin under Turck and Zelter. First professor of music, Berlin University, 1820. In 1850 founded, with Kullak and Stern, the school of music which afterwards became the Stern Conservatorium. His writings include a treatise on composition (*Lehre von der musikalischen Composition*, 4 vols., 1837-47), books on Beethoven (1859) and Gluck (2 vols., 1863) and on the performance of Beethoven's piano sonatas (1863 ; English translation, 1895). He composed an opera and oratorios.

(2) JOSEPH: *b.* Graz, May 11, 1882. Composer. Studied in Vienna. Teacher at the Academy of Music there, 1914; director, 1924. His compositions, in a late Romantic style, include symphonic poems, choral works with orchestra, chamber music and songs.

Marxsen [marrks′-ĕn], EDUARD: *b.* Nienstädten (nr. Altona), July 23, 1806; *d.* Altona, Nov. 18, 1887. Composer. Studied at Hamburg and Vienna, and later became a teacher in Hamburg, where Brahms was one of his pupils.

Marziale [marr-tsyahl′-eh], *I.* Martial, warlike.

Masaniello [mah-sahn-yell′-lo]. *v.* MUETTE DE PORTICI.

Mascagni [muss-cahn′-yee], PIETRO: *b.* Leghorn, Dec. 7, 1863; *d.* Rome, August 2, 1945. After studies in Leghorn and at the Milan Conservatorio under Ponchielli he travelled as an opera conductor and taught music at Cerignola in Apulia. His one-act opera *Cavalleria rusticana* gained first prize in a competition in 1889 and brought him world-wide fame. None of his later compositions has equalled its success.

Masked Ball, A. *v.* BALLO IN MASCHERA.

Mason (1) DANIEL GREGORY : *b.* Brookline (Mass.), Nov. 20, 1873 ; *d.* Greenwich (Conn.), Dec. 4, 1953. Composer and writer on music. Son of (3). Studied at Harvard, and later under Arthur Whiting in New York and d'Indy in Paris. Taught at Columbia University from 1919; MacDowell professor, 1929. He composed 3 symphonies and other orchestral works, choral music, chamber music, songs and piano pieces. His books include : *From Grieg to Brahms* (1902), *The Romantic Composers* (1906), *The Chamber Music of Brahms* (1932) and *The Quartets of Beethoven* (1947).

(2) LOWELL : *b.* Medfield (Mass.), Jan. 24, 1792 ; *d.* Orange (N.J.), Aug. 11, 1872. Organist and teacher. Grandfather of (1). Compiled a collection of psalm tunes which was published in Boston in 1822 under the auspices of the Handel and Haydn Society. One of the pioneers in musical education in schools in New England, where his work left a lasting impression. One of the founders of the Boston Academy of Music in 1832.

(3) WILLIAM : *b.* Boston, Jan. 24, 1829; *d.* New York, July 14, 1908. Pianist. Son of (2). His account of his studies in Leipzig under Moscheles and Moritz Hauptmann and in Weimar under Liszt is contained in his *Memories of a Musical Life* (1902).

Masque. The English masque (mask, maske) inherited the tradition of the choirboy plays with music of the first half of the 16th cent., and by the early 17th cent. had become an elaborate court entertainment combining poetry and dancing with vocal and instrumental music, and with scenery, machinery and costume. Among the writers of pre-Commonwealth masques were Ben Jonson, Beaumont, Campion, Dekker, and Shirley, among the composers Campion, Robert Johnson, the younger Ferrabosco, Laniere (who " ordered and made both the scene and the music " of Jonson's *Lovers made Men* in 1617), and the brothers Lawes. Inigo Jones designed the scenery and machines of some of Jonson's masques. The most extravagant and expensive masque of the period was Shirley's *The Triumph of Peace* (1633) for which some music of William Lawes has survived. Henry Lawes wrote the music for Milton's *Comus,* produced at Ludlow Castle in 1634. The masque came closer to the opera with the increasing use of recitative instead of spoken dialogue, as in the fifth entry of Shirley's *Cupid and Death* (1653), with music by Matthew Locke and Christopher Gibbons (modern ed. by E. J. Dent in *Musica Britannica,* ii). After the Restoration the masque was still popular, its artistic importance much less, if we except Blow's *Venus and Adonis* (ed. A. Lewis, 1949), actually a miniature opera, and the masque which forms part of Purcell's incidental music to *Dioclesian.* The 18th-cent. masques of Arne, Hayes, and others were light and elegant entertainments.

E. J. DENT : *Foundations of English Opera* (1928).

P. REYHER : *Les Masques Anglais* (1909).

Mass. In the musical sense, a setting of the Ordinary, or invariable parts (*Kyrie, Gloria, Credo, Sanctus* with *Benedictus, Agnus Dei*) of the Mass. From the 11th to the 13th cent. the original plainsong melodies were used as a basis for polyphonic settings of some parts of the Ordinary, particularly the *Kyrie, Sanctus,* and *Agnus Dei.* The practice of setting single movements, and later also pairs of movements (*e.g. Gloria-Credo, Sanctus-Agnus*) was continued in the 14th and 15th cent. Settings of the Ordinary as a musical whole, such as Machaut's *Messe Notre Dame,* were uncommon in the 14th cent. but became usual after *c.* 1430. The most frequent methods of establishing musical unity were (1) the use of a *cantus firmus,* taken either from plainsong, *e.g.* Leonel Power's *Alma redemptoris* Mass and Dufay's *Caput* Mass, or from secular song, *e.g.* Dufay's *Se la face ay pale* Mass, and the *L'Homme armé* Masses by Dufay, Okeghem, Obrecht and others ; (2) the use of a common opening for each movement. Besides this scheme the 16th-cent. settings in imitative polyphony more commonly derived their material from a motet or *chanson* (*v.* PARODY MASS), or were independent compositions (*sine nomine*). From the 15th to the 17th cent. the Mass was often performed in plainsong alternating with organ : there exist a number of ORGAN MASSES written for this purpose.

Lutheran composers in the 17th cent. wrote Masses for combinations of voices and instruments: the final stage of this tradition is seen in Bach's *Mass in B minor*. The Masses of the classical and romantic periods reflect the dominant styles of those periods in other forms. Beethoven's *Missa solennis*, like Bach's *Mass in B minor*, ignores the practical requirements of liturgical performance to attain its grandeur of conception. In the present century there have been some notable examples of settings of the Mass, *e.g.* those by Vaughan Williams, Rubbra and Stravinsky. For the individual items of the Mass (*Kyrie*, *Gloria*, etc.) see under these headings.

P. WAGNER : *Geschichte der Messe* (1914).

Massenet [muss-nay], JULES ÉMILE FRÉDÉRIC: *b.* Montaud (nr. Saint-Étienne), May 12, 1842; *d.* Paris, August 13, 1912. Studied composition under Thomas at the Paris Conservatoire, where he was teacher of composition from 1878-96. One of the favourite opera composers of his period. His most successful works were *Le Roi de Lahore* (1877), *Manon*(1884), *Werther* (1892) and *Le Jongleur de Notre-Dame* (1902). Composed other operas, serious and comic, oratorios, orchestral works, concertos, and songs.

Mässig [mess'-*ish*], *G.* Moderate.

Mass of Life, A. A setting of passages from Nietzsche's *Also sprach Zarathustra* for soli, chorus and orchestra by Delius (1905). First complete performance, London, June 7, 1909.

Masson [muss-on͡], PAUL MARIE : *b.* Sète, Sept. 19, 1882 ; *d.* Paris, Jan. 27, 1954. Musical historian. Studied history of music with Rolland at the École Normale Supérieure, Paris, and composition at the Schola Cantorum with d'Indy and Koechlin. Lecturer, Institut Français, Florence, 1910. Director, Institut Français, Naples, 1919. Professor, Sorbonne, 1931-52. His publications include *Chants de carnaval florentins* (1913), *Berlioz* (1923) and *L'Opéra de Rameau* (1930).

Mastersinger. *v.* MEISTERSINGER.

Mastersingers of Nuremberg, The. *v.* MEISTERSINGER VON NÜRNBERG.

Mathieu [mut-yer], ÉMILE LOUIS VICTOR: *b.* Lille, Oct. 16, 1844; *d.* Ghent, Aug. 22, 1932. Composer. Studied at the Brussels Conservatoire. Director, Academy of Music, Louvain, 1881; Conservatoire Royale, Ghent, 1896-1924. Composed operas, choral works and songs.

Mathis der Maler [mut-eece' dair mahl'-er] (Matt the Painter). Opera in seven scenes by Hindemith. Libretto by the composer. First performed, Zürich, May 28, 1938. The story is based on the life of the 16th-cent. painter Matthias Grünewald and deals with the conflict between a creative artist's duty to himself and his obligations to society. A "symphony" in three movements with the same title, consisting of the overture and other music from the opera, was first performed in 1934.

Matin, Le [ler ma-tan͡], **Le Midi** [ler mee-dee], **Le Soir et la Tempête** [ler swarr ay la tun͡-pet], *Fr.* (Morning, Midday, Evening and Storm). The titles of three symphonies by Haydn (No. 6 in D major, No. 7 in C major, and No. 8 in G major), composed, *c.* 1761.

Matrimonio Segreto, Il [eel mah-tree-mone'-yo seh-greh'-to] (The Secret Wedding). Comic opera in two acts by Cimarosa. Libretto by Giovanni Bertati (based on *The Clandestine Marriage* by George Colman and David Garrick). First performed, Vienna, Feb. 7, 1792.

Matteis [maht-teh'-eece], NICOLA: 17th-cent. Italian violinist who came to London in 1672. His playing is praised in Evelyn's *Diary* under the date of Nov. 19, 1674. He published three books of ayres for violin (between 1685-88) and a book entitled *The False Consonances of Musick*. In 1696 he published a collection of songs in two books and composed an Ode on St. Cecilia's Day for the annual celebration in

London. Burney studied French and the violin under his son, Nicholas Matteis.

Matthay, TOBIAS: *b.* London, Feb. 19, 1858; *d.* High Marley (Haslemere), Dec. 15, 1945. Pianist, teacher and composer. Studied at the R.A.M., where he won the Sterndale Bennett scholarship and continued piano with Macfarren and composition with Bennett, Prout and Sullivan. Appointed teacher of piano, 1880, and later founded his own piano school. He became one of the leading teachers of Europe; his pupils included Harriet Cohen, Myra Hess and Ray Lev. He is well known for his books on piano technique, which include *The Act of Touch* (1926) and *The First Principles of Pianoforte Playing* (1905).

Mattheson [mut′-er-zone], JOHANN: *b.* Hamburg, Sept. 28, 1681; *d.* there, Apr. 17, 1764. Composer, theorist and organist. He was versatile in many fields. From 1690 he sang in the Hamburg opera and in 1699 he produced his first opera, *Die Pleyaden.* In 1703 he fought a duel with Handel and later they became friends. In 1704 he made his last appearance in Handel's *Nero* and then retired from the stage. He later became tutor-secretary to the English envoy and ambassador. In 1715 he was appointed canon and cantor of Hamburg Cathedral, where he took an active part in the development of the church cantata. Among his compositions are 8 operas, 24 oratorios and cantatas, a Passion and 12 sonatas for flute and violin. His books include *Der musikalische Patriot* (1728), *Grundlage einer Ehrenpforte* (1740; modern ed. by M. Schneider, 1910), *Der vollkommene Kapellmeister* (1739; facsimile ed. 1954), and *Kleine General-Bass-Schule* (1735).

F. T. ARNOLD: *The Art of Accompaniment from a Thorough-Bass* (1931).

B. C. CANNON: *Johann Mattheson* (1947).

Mauduit [mo-dē̆e-ee], JACQUES: *b.* Paris, Sept. 16, 1557; *d.* there, Aug. 21, 1627. Composer. Associated with Antoine de Baïf's Academy in the setting of poetry to music on the basis of the classical metres (*musique mesurée à l'antique, q.v.*). His volume of *Chansonnettes mesurées de Jean-Antoine de Baïf mises en musique à quatre parties* (Paris, 1586) has been reprinted by H. Expert in *Les Maîtres musiciens de la Renaissance française*, x.

Maurel [mo-rel], VICTOR: *b.* Marseilles, June 17, 1848; *d.* New York, Oct. 22, 1923. Baritone. Studied at the Paris Conservatoire. First appeared at the Paris Opéra in *Les Huguenots* in 1867. He sang frequently in Italy and regularly in London from 1873-9 (including Wagnerian roles). He sang Iago at the first performance of Verdi's *Otello* (Milan, 1887) and the title role in the same composer's *Falstaff* (Milan, 1893). He repeated his success in both works in performances in Paris, London and New York, where he eventually settled as a teacher in 1909. He published four books on singing and an autobiography, and was also active as a painter and stage designer.

Má Vlast [mah vlust], *Cz.* (My Fatherland). A cycle of six symphonic poems by Smetana (1874-79):

1. *Vyšehrad* (The citadel of Prague).
2. *Vltava* (The Moldau River).
3. *Šárka* (Leader of the Bohemian Amazons).
4. *Z Českych Luhův a Hájův* (From Bohemia's Fields and Groves).
5. *Tábor* (Stronghold of the blind leader of the Hussites).
6. *Blaník* (Mountain in southern Bohemia).

Maxima, *L.* The note of the greatest time value in the medieval system of MENSURAL NOTATION, written ꟷ|. It was called a "large" in England.

Maynard, JOHN: 16th-17th cent. lutenist and composer. In 1611 he published *The XII wonders of the world, Set and composed for the Violl de Gambo, the Lute and the Voyce to sing the Verse, all three jointly and none severall,* which contains 12 songs describing character-types and 12 pavans and galliards for the lute, and refers to the composer as "Lutenist at the most famous Schoole of St. Julian's in Hartfordshire."

May Night. *v.* MAISKAYA NOCH.

Mayr [mire], JOHANN SIMON: *b.* Mendorf (Bavaria), June 14, 1763; *d.* Bergamo,

Dec. 2, 1845. Composer. Studied under Bertoni in Venice, and in 1805 became teacher of composition at the Institute of Music in Bergamo, where Donizetti was one of his pupils. After 1794 he composed about 70 operas, in which he anticipated some of the effects of Rossini and Meyerbeer. Also wrote oratorios and a book on Haydn (1809).

Mazeppa. (1) Opera in three acts by Tchaikovsky. Libretto by "Viktor Petrovich Burenin" (*i.e.* Count Alexei Zhasminov), after Pushkin's *Poltava.* First performed, Moscow, Feb. 15, 1884.

(2) Symphonic poem by Liszt, originally written as a piano study in *Études d'exécution transcendante* (1852).

Mazurka [ma-zoor′-ca]. A Polish folk-dance in a moderate to fast triple time with the second or third beat often strongly accented. First adapted as a stylised piece for piano by Chopin, who wrote 52 mazurkas, and later used by other composers, *e.g.* Tchaikovsky and Szymanowski. Its most characteristic rhythm is

CHOPIN, *Mazurkas*, Op. 33, No. 2

Mazzocchi [maht-tsock′-ee], (1) DOMENICO: *b.* Veia (nr. Civita Castellana, Nov. 8, 1592; *d.* Rome, Jan. 20, 1665. Composer. His book of madrigals of 1638 contained madrigals in both the old and new (continuo) styles, and used signs for *crescendo* and *diminuendo* for the first time. He composed the opera *La Catena d'Adone* (Rome, 1626; extracts in H. Goldschmidt, *Studien zur Geschichte der italienischen Oper im 17. Jahrhundert,* i), motets, and monodic *laude.* His monody *Planctus matris Euryali* was quoted by Kircher (*Musurgia universalis,* 1650) as an example of the mixture of diatonic, chromatic and enharmonic genera. It is printed in Schering's *History of Music in Examples,* No. 197.

(2) VIRGILIO: *b.* Veia (nr. Civita Castellana), July 22, 1597; *d.* there, Oct. 3, 1646. Composer. Brother of (1). *Maestro di cappella* at St. John Lateran, 1628; St. Peter's, 1629. Composed with Marazzoli the earliest comic opera, *Chi soffre, speri* (Rome, 1639; extracts in H. Goldschmidt, *Studien zur Geschichte der italienischen Oper im 17. Jahrhundert,* i), and wrote choral music and monodic *laude.*

McCormack, JOHN: *b.* Athlone, June 14, 1884; *d.* Dublin, Sept. 16, 1945. Tenor. Studied in Italy. First appeared in opera in *Cavalleria rusticana* at Covent Garden, 1907. He sang with the Boston Opera Company, 1910-11, and the Chicago Opera Company, 1912-14, and became an American citizen in 1917. He excelled in Mozart and Verdi, and was also widely known as a concert singer. In England his reputation with the general public was based largely on his interpretation of popular ballads.

McEwen, JOHN BLACKWOOD: *b.* Hawick, Apr. 13, 1868; *d.* London, June 14, 1948. Composer and teacher. Educated in Glasgow and at the R.A.M. Teacher of harmony, R.A.M., 1898; principal, 1924-36. He wrote books on musical subjects, including *Tempo Rubato* (1928), and composed 5 symphonies and other orchestral works, chamber music, cantatas, and piano music. Knighted, 1931.

Me. Anglicized form of the Italian *mi* (E). In TONIC SOL-FA the 3rd note (or mediant) of the major scale.

Meane (Mene). A term used in England in the 15th and early 16th cent. for the voice between the treble and tenor (*L. medius*) in a choral composition. In the method of extemporising a part above a plainsong used at that time (*v.* SIGHT) the meane sight was a fifth above the tenor. Also used *c.* 1550 for the middle part of a three-part keyboard piece.

Meantone Tuning. A system of tuning keyboard instruments described by *e.g.* Schlick (1511) and Salinas (1577), which was in general use from the beginning of the 16th cent. until the adoption of EQUAL TEMPERAMENT. The major third arrived at in the Pythagorean tuning (*v.* TEMPERAMENT) by superimposing four "just" fifths (64 : 81) is larger than a "just" major third (4 : 5, *i.e.* 64 : 80). A fifth smaller than a just fifth by one-fourth of this difference was adopted as the basis of meantone tuning. It was an adequate system for the normal chords of modal harmony and for keys which did not involve the use of more than two sharps or flats. If chords containing G♯, D♯, or A♯ as major thirds were to be played, some further compromise in tuning was necessary, or an instrument with more than the normal number of keys to the octave was used.

J. BARBOUR: *Tuning and Temperament* (1951).

Measure. (1) In general = RHYTHM, TIME. (2) In America = BAR.

Mechanical Musical Instruments. The principal of the revolving cylinder with protruding pins was applied in the 15th and 16th cent. to the carillon, and to keyboard instruments. The addition of a clockwork mechanism made it possible to apply it to a number of contrivances, such as musical clocks, mechanical organs and orchestras, and musical boxes, which were very popular in the 18th cent. Mozart wrote three pieces for a mechanical organ (K.594, 608, 616) of which the first two are major compositions. Beethoven's *Wellington's Victory* or *The Battle of Vittoria* (1813) was originally written for Maelzel's "Panharmonicon," a mechanical orchestra. *v.* also PIANOLA.

J. E. T. CLARK: *Musical Boxes* (1948).

Medesimo tempo [meh-deh'-zee-mo temp'-o], *I.* In the same tempo.

Mediant. The third degree of the diatonic scale, *e.g.* E in the scale of C.

Medtner [met'-ner], NIKOLAI KARLOVICH: *b.* Moscow, Jan. 5, 1880; *d.* London, Nov. 13, 1951. Composer and pianist. Studied in Moscow under Arensky, Taneiev and Safonov. Teacher of piano, Moscow Conservatoire, 1909-10, 1918-21. From that time he lived successively in Berlin, France, and England. His most important compositions, which are in a traditional style, are for piano, and include 2 concertos, a sonata-trilogy, *Fairy Tales* and *Dithyrambs.* He also composed a *Sonata-Vocalise* for voice without words and piano, violin sonatas, and songs.

R. HOLT: *Medtner and his Music* (1948).

Meeresstille und glückliche Fahrt [may'-rĕss-shtill-*er* ŏŏnt glĕĕk'-li*sh-er* fahrrt], *G.* (Calm Sea and Prosperous Voyage). (1) A cantata by Beethoven, Op. 112 (1815) for chorus and orchestra, to words from a poem with the same title by Goethe.

(2) An overture by Mendelssohn, Op. 27 (1828), based on Goethe's poem.

Mefistofele [meh-fee-sto'-feh-leh]. (Mephistofeles). Opera with a prologue, four acts and an epilogue by Boïto. Libretto by the composer (after Goethe's *Faust*). First performed, Milan, March 5, 1868.

Megli [mehl'-yee] (Melio, Melli), DOMENICO. 16th-17th cent. composer. One of the earliest composers of monodic solos and dialogues, published between 1602 and 1609. His first book probably came out about two months before Caccini's *Le nuove musiche.* A monody with lute was included in Robert Dowland's *Musicall Banquet* (1610).

Mehrstimmigkeit [mehr'-shtim-i*sh*-kite], *G.* Polyphony.

Méhul [may-ĕĕl], ÉTIENNE HENRI NICOLAS: *b.* Givet (nr. Mézières), June 22, 1763; *d.* Paris, Oct. 18, 1817. Composer. An organist from the age of ten, he studied and taught in Paris from 1778. Encouraged by Gluck, he wrote several operas, of which the first to be staged was *Euphrosine et Coradin* (1790). His later operas developed the style of Grétry, and he became one of the most prominent composers of the period of the Revolution. The most mature of his works are *Uthal* (1806), which has no violins in the orchestra, and *Joseph* (1807).

Meibom [my'-bom] (Meibomius), MARCUS: *b.* Tönning (Schleswig-Holstein), 1626; *d.* Utrecht, 1711. Philologist. He printed in 1652 the texts, with Latin translations and commentary, of treatises on music by Aristoxenus, Aristeides Quintilianus, Nichomachus, Cleonides, Gaudentius, Alypius and Baccheius the Elder. Some were re-edited by Karl von Jan in *Musici Scriptores Graeci* (1895).

Meissen [mice'-ĕn], HEINRICH VON. *v.* FRAUENLOB.

Meistersinger [mice'-ter-zing-er], *G.* "Mastersinger." A member of the highest grade in the guilds for the cultivation of poetry and music in German cities in the 15th and 16th centuries. The guilds succeeded to the tradition of the MINNESINGER, and held song-schools in which compositions were marked and prizes given. The lowest grade was that of scholar. One who had mastered the rules was a "school-friend," one who could sing five or six "tones" a singer; one who wrote poems to existing tones a poet, and one who invented a tone a master. Songs which had been composed by Mastersingers were named, *e.g.* "The Frog-tone" by Heinrich Frauenlob, "The Extra-short Evening red tone" by Georg Hagers, and became part of the repertory of the guild. Each verse or *Bar* of a song consisted of two *Stollen* and an *Abgesang*, in the form *AAB*. The song-school in Wagner's *Die Meistersinger* is founded on an account of the Mastersingers printed by J. G. Wagenseil in 1697; Hans Sachs was the most renowned mastersinger of the 16th cent., and all but one of the names of the mastersingers in the opera (Fritz Zorn was changed to Balthasar Zorn) were listed by Wagenseil as distinguished masters of Nuremberg.

H. THOMPSON: *Wagner and Wagenseil* (1927).

Meistersinger von Nürnberg, Die [dee mice'-ter-zing-er fon neern'-bairk] (The Mastersingers of Nuremberg). Opera in three acts by Wagner. Libretto by the composer. First performed, Munich, June 21, 1868. Walther von Stolzing (a knight) sees Eva Pogner (the daughter of a rich goldsmith) in a church and falls in love with her. He discovers that her father has promised her hand to the winner of the singing contest on St. John's day and applies to the Mastersingers to take part in the competition. Beckmesser (the marker and a rival for Eva's hand) attempts to discredit Walther by noisily noting one error after another during his singing. At night Eva agrees to fly away secretly with Walther but they are forced to take shelter when Hans Sachs (the cobbler at whose house Walther had been staying) opens a window and throws a light on the street. Beckmesser, who comes on to serenade Eva, is constantly interrupted by Hans Sachs, who marks his errors by loudly hammering a nail into a shoe. Walther dreams of a prize song and sings it to Sachs who writes it down; but it is later stolen by Beckmesser, who is greeted with laughter when he tries to sing it at the contest. He claims that it was written by Sachs, but Sachs denies this and asks Walther to sing. Walther then sings his song successfully, is asked to become a member of the guild and receives the hand of Eva.

Mel [dell mell], RINALDO DEL: *b.* Malines, 16th-cent. Flemish composer. In the service of the King of Portugal, of Archdeacon Carolo Valigano in Rome from 1580, of the Duke of Bavaria from *c.* 1588, and of Cardinal Paleotto, Archbishop of Bologna, from 1591. He published between 1581 and 1595 6 books of motets and 15 books of madrigals.

Melba, NELLIE (originally Helen Mitchell): *b.* Burnley (nr. Melbourne), May 19, 1859; *d.* Sydney, Feb. 23, 1931. Operatic soprano. Came to Europe in 1886, studied in Paris under Madame Marchesi. Made her début in Brussels in the following year. One of the greatest singers of her day in lyric and coloratura roles in opera. The name part in Saint-Saëns's *Hélène* (Monte Carlo 1904) was written for her. She published *Melodies and Memories* (London, 1925), and retired in 1926.

P. COLSON: *Melba* (1931).
A. MURPHY: *Nellie Melba* (1909).

Melisma (*Gr. μέλισμα*, song). A unit of melody which is sung to one syllable, more especially in plainsong.

Mellers, WILFRID HOWARD: *b.* Leamington, Apr. 26, 1914. Musical historian and composer. Studied at Cambridge. Lecturer, Extramural Department, Birmingham University. He has composed an opera (*The Tragicall History of Christopher Marlowe*), a symphony, a string trio and other chamber music, piano pieces and songs, and has published *Music and Society* (1946), *Studies in Contemporary Music* (1948) and *François Couperin* (1950).

Mélodie [may-lod-ee], *Fr.* (1) In general, melody. (2) In particular, a song with piano accompaniment (*G.* Lied).

Melodrama. Spoken words with musical accompaniment, either as a complete work (also called monodrama or duodrama) or as part of an opera. Complete plays in this style were written by J. J. Rousseau (*Pigmalion*, 1762) and Georg Benda (*Ariadne auf Naxos*, 1775; *Medea*, 1778). "Melodramatic" scenes in opera were used by Cherubini in *Les Deux Journées* (1800), Beethoven in the grave-digging scene in *Fidelio* (1805), and Weber in *Der Freischütz* (1820). Modern works in this form include Fibich's trilogy *Hippodamia* (1889-91).

Melody. A succession of single musical sounds. The factors which determine the character and effect of a melody are its MODE, its RHYTHM, and its design in relation to pitch, which may for convenience be referred to as its "contour." The only one of these factors which has in the past been the subject of more or less clear and consistent theories is mode. Since the melodies of any given period are composed by the manipulation of a set of idioms comprised within a system of modes, and only for special expressive purposes come to their final end on a note other than the final or key-note, their mode or key is always determinable. The differences of effect which result from differences of mode may be illustrated by a comparison of a melody in the eighth ecclesiastical mode:

with one in the modern minor mode:

MOZART, *Symphony in G minor*, K. 550.

and one in the Hindu Rāg (mode) called Bhairau:

The rhythmic character of a melody is communicated by the composer primarily in the comparatively inflexible symbols of notation, but is also given to the listener to a very important degree by the indeterminable effects of rubato, of slight delay and of slight anticipation which a good performer applies where they are stylistically appropriate. The most obvious varieties of effect in rhythm may be exemplified in the gentle accumulation of movement of:

PALESTRINA, *Tribulationes civitatum.*

in the exuberant onrush of:

R. STRUASS, *Don Juan.*

and in the placid gait of:

BEETHOVEN, *Piano sonata, Op. 90.*

Melodic contour is the subject of a section of Hindemith's *Craft of Musical Composition* (vol. ii) in which he plots on a graph the higher and lower points of a melodic line, and the extent to which the idioms of the melody group themselves around notes which tend to become momentary key-notes. The possible range of melody depends on the voice or instrument for which it is written: hence the range of a plainsong melody seldom exceeds a tenth, while the pitch range of an organ is greater than that of any other instrument. The examples from Palestrina and Strauss above show the extremes of effect resulting from melodic contour. *v.* also METRE, RHYTHM, SEQUENCE.

Melusine [may-loo-zeen'-*er*]. *v.* SCHÖNE MELUSINE.

Mencken [menk'-ĕn] (*L.* Mancinus), THOMAS : *b.* Schwerin (Mecklenburg), 1550; *d.* there, 1611-12. From 1587 to 1604 *Kapellmeister* at Wolfenbüttel, being succeeded by Michael Praetorius. Composed a setting of the Passion (1608), motets, and madrigals.

Mendelssohn [mend'-ĕlss-zone] (properly Mendelssohn-Bartholdy), (1) FANNY CÄCILIA. Sister of (2). *v.* HENSEL.

(2) JAKOB LUDWIG FELIX : *b.* Hamburg, Feb. 3, 1809 ; *d.* Leipzig, Nov. 4, 1847. Composer. As a boy he showed remarkable gifts as a composer, conductor and pianist. Studied composition with Zelter in Berlin in 1817. From 1829 he travelled in England, Scotland, Italy and France, and in 1833 was appointed musical director at Düsseldorf. In 1835 he became conductor of the Gewandhaus concerts in Leipzig, and in 1842 founded, with Schumann and others, the Leipzig Conservatorium. His earliest mature works, the overtures *A Midsummer Night's Dream* (1826) and *The Hebrides* (1830-32), showed superb craftsmanship and an individual melodic style and marked an important stage in the history of the programmatic or pictorial concert overture. In later compositions his range was greatly extended (symphonies, concertos, oratorios, choral music, chamber music, piano works, organ sonatas, songs), but there was little development in technique or expression. He crowned a series of visits to England with the first performance of *Elijah* at Birmingham in 1846, and his music set the canons of mid-Victorian musical taste. His performance of the *St. Matthew Passion* in Leipzig in 1829 gave a strong impulse to the revival of Bach's music, and his conducting of the Gewandhaus Orchestra initiated its great reputation and set new standards in orchestral performance.

His principal compositions are:

(a) ORCHESTRA: 5 symphonies (No. 2, *Lobgesang*, symphony-cantata, 1840 ; No. 3, *Scotch*, 1842 ; No. 4, *Italian*, 1833 ; No. 5, *Reformation*, 1830) ; overtures : *A Midsummer Night's Dream* (1826); *Die Hebriden* (The Hebrides, 1830-2; also known as *Fingals Höhle*, Fingal's Cave), *Meeresstille und glückliche Fahrt* (Calm Sea and Prosperous Voyage, 1828), *Märchen von der schönen Melusine* (The Legend of the Fair Melusina, 1833), *Ruy Blas* (1839); piano concertos: G minor (1831), D minor (1837); violin concerto (1844).

(b) CHORAL WORKS: Oratorios: *St. Paul* (1834-6), *Elijah* (1846-7), *Christus* (unfinished, 1847); symphony-cantata, *Lobgesang* (Hymn of Praise, 1840; also known as symphony No. 2); 9 psalms; 9 motets.

(c) STAGE MUSIC: Operas: *Die Hochzeit des Camacho* (The Wedding of Camacho, 1825), *Die Heimkehr aus der Fremde* (Son and Stranger, 1829), *Lorelei* (unfinished, 1847); incidental music: *Antigone* (1841), *Die erste Walpurgisnacht* (The First Witches' Sabbath, 1831, 1842), *A Midsummer Night's Dream* (1843), *Athalie* (1843-5), *Oedipus at Colonus* (1845).

(d) CHAMBER MUSIC: 6 string quartets; 3 piano quartets (1822-25); 2 string quintets (1831, 1845); string sextet (1824); string octet (1825); 2 trios (D minor, 1839; C minor, 1845); violin sonata; 2 cello sonatas (1838, 1843).

(e) PIANO: *Capriccio* in F♯ minor (1825); *Rondo capriccioso* in E minor; 6 preludes and fugues (1832-7); 8 books of *Lieder ohne Worte* (Songs without words).

(f) ORGAN: 3 preludes and fugues (1833-37); 6 sonatas (1839-44).

(g) SONGS AND PART-SONGS: 10 sets of songs with piano; 11 sets of part-songs.

T. ARMSTRONG: *Mendelssohn's "Elijah"* (1931).
R. B. GOTCH: *Mendelssohn and his Friends in Kensington* (1934).
S. KAUFMAN: *Mendelssohn* (1934).
P. RADCLIFFE: *Mendelssohn* (1954).
G. SELDEN-GOTH (ed.): *Mendelssohn's Letters* (1946).

Mene. *v.* MEANE.

Mengelberg [meng'-ĕl-bairkh], JOSEF WILLEM: *b.* Utrecht, March 28, 1871; *d.* Remos (nr. Schuls), March 21, 1951. Conductor. Studied at the Cologne Conservatorium. Music director, Lucerne, 1892. Conductor, Concertgebouw Orchestra, Amsterdam, 1895-1941; Toonkunst Choir, 1898; Museumgesellschaft, 1907-20; Frankfort Cäcilienverein, 1908. From 1911-14 he was a regular conductor of the London Symphony Orchestra and the Royal Philharmonic Society. Also conducted in Italy, France, Russia and the United States, where he was conductor of the New York Philharmonic for nine seasons. He made many tours with the Concertgebouw, and conducted festivals of music by Mahler, Strauss, and French composers.

Meno mosso [meh'-no moss'-so], *I.* With less movement, *i.e.* less quickly. *Meno* by itself is used in the same sense.

Menotti [meh-not'-tee], GIAN CARLO: *b.* Cadigliano (nr. Milan), July 7, 1911. Composer. Studied at the Curtis Institute of Music, Philadelphia, with Scalero. His comic opera *Amelia goes to the Ball*, to his own libretto, was produced at the Curtis Institute and in New York in 1937 and again in New York by the Metropolitan Opera House in 1938. His works include the operas *The Island God, The Old Maid and the Thief, The Medium, The Telephone, The Consul, Amahl and the Night Visitors* and *The Saint of Bleecker Street.* He has also composed ballets and a piano concerto.

Mensural Music (*L.* musica mensurata). A medieval term for music with definite relative note-values, as distinct from plainsong (*musica plana*).

Mensural Notation. A system of notation formulated by Franco of Cologne in his *Ars cantus mensurabilis* (*c.* 1260) and used, with various additions, refinements and modifications, until the gradual adoption of metrical rhythm with bar-lines during the 17th century. In the course of the 15th cent. black notes began to be written as white, and red as black (*v.* NOTATION). In white notation the notes and corresponding rests were:

Their relations were governed by a time-signature at the beginning of a part, and by signs of PROPORTION and the use of black (imperfect, *i.e.* duple subdivision) notes instead of white (perfect, *i.e.* triple subdivision) in the course of a part. The relation of the long to the breve was called mode (or "mood") and was normally imperfect; of the breve to the semi-breve, time; of the semibreve to the minim, prolation. The time signatures were:

⊙ perfect time and perfect prolation; O perfect time and imperfect prolation; ⊂· imperfect time and perfect prolation; C imperfect time and imperfect prolation. Under ⊙ a breve=3 semibreves=9 minims; under O a breve=3 semibreves=6 minims; under ⊂· a breve=2 semibreves=6 minims; and under C a breve=2 semibreves=4 minims.

A dot was used both to add to a note half its value, making an imperfect note perfect (*punctus additionis*) and to mark off a group of three notes (*punctus divisionis*). A perfect note followed by one of the next lower value became imperfect by position, whether marked off by a *punctus divisionis* or not. Thus a breve followed by a minim followed by a *punctus divisionis* was sung within the value of a perfect breve (*i.e.* two perfect or three imperfect semibreves). The *punctus additionis* was also used with notes written in LIGATURE. The principle of alteration, adopted in the pre-mensural system of the RHYTHMIC MODES, whereby the second of two breves preceding a long was doubled in length, was extended in mensural notation to semibreves preceding a breve and minims preceding a semibreve.

These general principles may be seen in the opening of the *cantus* part of Dufay's four-part *chanson* "Ma belle dame souverainne." The signature ⊂·, though not indicated, is understood:

which, transcribed in its original note-values, would read:

or, as is more usual, in one-quarter of the original values (crotchet=semibreve):

Menuet [mer-nĕĕ-ay], *Fr.*, **Menuett** [mane-oo-et′], *G.* Minuet. The form *menuetto*, frequently used by German composers, is a corruption of the Italian *minuetto*.

Menuhin [men-yoo′-in], YEHUDI. *b.* New York, Apr. 22, 1916. Violinist. Began violin lessons at a young age with Sigmund Anker and later with Louis Persinger. At seven he made his first public appearance at a San Francisco Symphony Young People's concert. Studied in Europe with Adolph Busch and Georges Enesco. He gave a Carnegie Hall recital in 1927 and from 1928-29 he played on the Pacific Coast. He then returned to Europe and made his London début. He has given sonata recitals with his sister, Hephzibah, who is a pianist.

Mercadante [mair-cah-dahn′-teh], GUISEPPE SAVERIO RAFFAELE: *bapt.* Altamura (nr. Bari), Sept. 17, 1795; *d.* Naples, Dec. 17, 1870. Composer. Studied at Collegio di San Sebastiano, Naples, under Zingarelli. From 1827-29 he visited Spain and in 1833 became *maestro di cappella* at Novara Cathedral. In 1839 he was music director of Lanciano Cathedral and in 1840 he was appointed director of Naples Conservatorio. He lost an eye while at Novara and became totally blind in 1862. He wrote almost 60 operas, of which *Elisa e Claudio* (1821) and *Il Giuramento* (his chief work, 1837) were the most successful, 21 Masses and other church music, four funeral symphonies, instrumental pieces, and songs.

Mer hahn en neue Oberkeet. [mair hahn en noy'-*er* o'-ber-cate]. *v.* PEASANT CANTATA.

Merbecke, JOHN. *v.* MARBECK.

Mer, La [la mair], *Fr.* (The Sea). Suite of three orchestral pieces by Debussy (1905): (1) *De l'aube a midi sur la mer* (From dawn to mid-day on the sea); (2) *Jeux de vagues* (Waves' frolic); (3) *Dialogue du vent et de la mer* (Dialogue of the wind and the sea). The original titles of Nos. 1 and 2 were *Mer belle aux Îles Sanguinaires* and *Le vent fait danser la mer.*

Merlo [mair'-lo], ALESSANDRO (Alessandro Romano or Alessandro della Viola): *b.* Rome, *c.* 1530. Singer, violinist and composer, a pupil of Willaert and Rore. He was a bass-tenor with a range of three octaves. In 1594 he became a singer in the Papal Chapel. His compositions include *canzoni*, madrigals, a book of *villanelle,* and a book of motets.

Merry Mount. Opera in three acts by Howard Hanson. Libretto by Richard Stokes (after Hawthorne's story, *The Maypole of Merry Mount*). First performed, New York, Feb. 10, 1934. Previously performed in concert form at Ann Arbor (Mich.), May 20, 1933.

Merry Wives of Windsor, The. *v.* LUSTIGEN WEIBER VON WINDSOR.

Mersenne [mair-sen] (Mersennus), MARIN: *b.* Oizé (Sarthe), Sept. 8, 1588; *d.* Paris, Sept. 1, 1648. Theorist. Member of the Franciscan order from 1613. He taught philosophy at Nevers and later studied mathematics and music in Paris, where he made the acquaintance of Descartes and the elder Pascal. He corresponded with scholars in England, Holland and Italy and visited Italy three times. His works include *Harmonie Universelle* (1636) and *De la Nature des Sons* (1635).

Merula [meh'-roo-la], TARQUINIO. Composer. Held appointments alternately at Bergamo and Cremona, except in 1624 when he was court organist at Warsaw. He also held a court appointment at Florence sometime before 1680. His compositions include canzonas, madrigals, motets, and sonatas for solo violin and continuo. The canzona "La Strada" (1637) has been reprinted in Schering's *History of Music in Examples* (No. 184), and the canzona "La Vesconta" (1639) in the *Historical Anthology* (No. 210).

Merulo [meh'-roo-lo], CLAUDIO (Claudio da Correggio or Merlotti): *b.* Correggio, Apr. 8, 1533; *d.* Parma, May 4, 1604. Organist and composer. Organist, Brescia, 1556; second organist, St. Mark's, Venice, 1557; first organist, 1566. Became a publisher in 1566 and from 1578-81 wrote madrigals and motets. Later organist in the ducal chapel, Parma. His compositions include 2 books of *Sacrae Cantiones* (1578), madrigals, 4 Masses, and organ pieces. In 1574 he produced an opera in madrigal style, *La Tragedia.* His organ toccatas (examples in Schering's *History of Music in Examples,* No. 149, in the *Historical Anthology,* No. 153, and in Torchi's *L'arte musicale in Italia,* iii) are the most developed works in this form in the 16th cent.

Messa di voce [mess'-sah dee vo'-cheh], *I.* "Placing of the voice." Used to indicate a *crescendo* and *diminuendo* on a long note in singing.

Messager [mess-uzh-ay], ANDRÉ CHARLES PROSPER: *b.* Montluçon, Dec. 30, 1853; *d.* Paris, Feb. 24, 1929. Composer and conductor. Studied at the École Niedermeyer in Paris under Gigout and later under Saint-Saëns. His three-act operetta *La Béarnaise* was produced in Paris (1885) and London (1886). Became conductor at the Opéra-Comique in 1898, and from 1901-07 artistic director of the Royal Opera, Covent Garden. After touring the U.S.A. he conducted again at the Opéra-Comique. His works include light operas, ballets, a symphony (1875), piano works and songs.

Messa per i Defunti [mess′-sah pair ee deh-foon′-tee], *I.* Requiem Mass.

Messe des Morts [mess day morr], *Fr.* Requiem Mass.

Messiaen [mess-yũn], OLIVIER EUGÈNE PROSPER CHARLES: *b.* Avignon, Dec. 10, 1908. Composer and organist; son of the poetess Cécile Sauvage. Studied at the Paris Conservatoire under Dukas (composition) and Dupré (organ). Organist, La Trinité, Paris; teacher at the École Normale de Musique and at the Schola Cantorum. In 1936 with Baudrier, Lesur and Jolivet he formed the group known as *La Jeune France.* In 1941 he became teacher of harmony at the Conservatoire. His compositions, which include symphonic poems, vocal, piano and organ works, exploit complex rhythmic patterns, oriental modes and, in orchestral works, effects suggested by oriental instruments. He has written a treatise on his methods of composition.

Messiah. Oratorio by Handel. Words from the Bible. First performed, Dublin, Apr. 13, 1742.

Mesto [mest′-o], *I.* Sad.

Mesure [mer-zëer], *Fr.* (1) Bar. (2) Time. *Battre la mesure*, to beat time.

Metastasio [meh-tah-stahz′-yo] (originally Trapassi), PIETRO ANTONIO DOMENICO BONAVENTURA: *b.* Rome, Jan. 13, 1698; *d.* Vienna, April 12, 1782. Poet and librettist. Court poet at Vienna, succeeding Apostolo Zeno, from 1730 till his death. He inherited from Zeno the three-act plan of the opera libretto, and stabilised it as an alternation of recitatives with arias in a consistent order and form. His libretti remained the basis of the form of classical opera from A. Scarlatti to Mozart's *La clemenza di Tito* (1791), and many were set over and over again. The form and style of his libretti for serious opera held complete sway until questioned by the ideas of Calzabigi and Gluck.

Metre. The scheme of regularly recurring accents, indicated by a time-signature, which underlies the particular rhythm of a melody or harmonic progression. The time-signatures in mensural notation (13th-16th cent.) did not imply metrical accents in performance. Music in which the rhythm was directly related to the metre of poetry was written in the early 16th cent. by Tritonius (*q.v.*) and in the late 16th century by the members of the French Academy of de Baïf (*v.* MUSIQUE MESURÉE À L'ANTIQUE). Bar-lines to show metrical schemes were used in the lute and keyboard music of the 16th cent., and first came into general use in the early 17th century. Since then the rhythmic design of melodies and harmonies has been contained in and related to the underlying metrical scheme of each composition, which is indicated by its TIME-SIGNATURE. A new metrical scheme may replace or be imposed upon the original one, either momentarily, as in HEMIOLA, and in this passage from the scherzo of Beethoven's *Eroica* symphony :

or for a complete section, as in the last movement of Schumann's piano concerto:

Two or more metrical schemes are occasionally combined in one piece, as in Brahms's Intermezzo, Op. 76, No. 6, in which 2/4, 6/8 and 3/4 are combined in various ways throughout:

More frequent and more extended use of combined metres has been made by contemporary composers, both in succession, *e.g.* in Stravinsky's *Rite of Spring*, and in Constant Lambert's piano concerto:

and in combination, as in the second movement of Hindemith's third sonata for piano:

An interesting example of the use of combined metres as the rhythmic scheme of a movement is the *Scherzo polimetrico* of Rubbra's second string quartet (1951).

Metrical Psalter. *v.* PSALTER.

Metronome. A device which produces regular beats. The model in general use was invented by Maelzel in 1816 and adopted in the following year by Beethoven to indicate the tempo of his compositions. ♩=M.M.. (*i.e.*, Maelzel Metronome) 60, for example, indicates 60 crotchet beats per minute.

R. E. M. HARDING : *Origins of Musical Time and Expression* (1938).

Meyerbeer [my'-er-bair], GIACOMO (originally Jakob Liebmann Beer): *b.* Berlin, Sept. 5, 1791; *d.* Paris, May 2, 1864. Composer. Studied with Clementi, Zelter and Vogler and wrote his first opera in 1813. In 1816 he went to Venice, and in Italy wrote operas in the style of Rossini. After 1830 he became the dominant composer in the most brilliant period of French grand opera in Paris under Scribe, who wrote his libretti. In this elaborate and spectacular style he found his métier in such works as *Robert le Diable* (1831), *Les Huguenots* (1836) and *Le Prophète* (1849). The style of Wagner's *Rienzi* (1842) owes much to Meyerbeer.

Mezzo [meh'-dzo], *I.* Half. *Mezzo forte*, moderately loud (abbreviated *mf*); *mezzo piano*, moderately soft (abbreviated *mp*).

Mezzo-soprano, the voice between a soprano and a contralto in range. *Mezza voce*, with a moderate volume of tone.

Mi [mee], *Fr. I.* The note E. Also the third note of the Guidonian hexachord. *v.* SOLMIZATION.

Miaskovsky [mya-skoff′-ski], NIKOLAI YAKOVLEVICH : *b.* Novogeorgievsk, Apr. 20, 1881 ; *d.* Moscow, Aug. 9, 1950. Composer. Trained for a military career but studied music with Glière in Moscow and in 1906 entered the St. Petersburg Conservatoire as a pupil of Rimsky-Korsakov and Liadov. Teacher of composition, Moscow Conservatoire, 1921. In 1948 was one of the composers denounced by the Central Committee of the Communist Party as inculcators of inharmonious music in the educational institutions of the Soviet Union. His compositions include 27 symphonies, 9 string quartets, piano works and songs.

Michael [mi*sh*′-a-ell], (1) ROGIER: *b.* Mons, *c.* 1550; *d.* Dresden, *c.* 1619. Singer and composer. Tenor in the Electoral Chapel, Dresden, 1575; *Kapellmeister*, 1587. He was succeeded by Heinrich Schütz in 1619. His compositions are introits in motet style, four-part chorales, and other church music.

(2) TOBIAS: *b.* Dresden, June 13, 1592; *d.* Leipzig, June 26, 1657. Composer. Son of (1). *Kapellmeister*, Sondershausen, 1619; cantor, St. Thomas's, Leipzig, 1631. His works include the *Musikalischer Seelenlust* (1634-7), which is a collection of sacred concertos, and other church music.

Micheli [mee-keh′-lee], ROMANO: *b.* Rome, *c.* 1575; *d.* there, *c.* 1659. Composer. Studied under Soriano. Was made *maestro di cappella*, Church of Concordia, Modena, 1616; San Luigi de' Francesi, Rome, 1625. His compositions include psalms, motets, canons and madrigals.

Microtones. Intervals which are fractions of a semitone. Such intervals have always been a part of the theory and practice of tuning (*v.* TEMPERAMENT), but only in modern times have they been introduced by some composers into notation and performance. Alois Hába has written a string quartet in a system of sixth-tones, and the Mexican composer Julián Carrillo has written some works in a system which divides the octave into 96 parts.

Midi, Le [ler mee-dee], *Fr. v.* MATIN.

Midsummer Night's Dream, A. The title of an overture by Mendelssohn, Op. 21 (1826), who also composed incidental music to Shakespeare's play of that name for solo, chorus and orchestra, Op. 61 (first performed, 1843).

Mignon [mee-nyo͞n]. Opera in three acts by Thomas. Libretto by Jules Barbier and Michel Carré (after Goethe's *Wilhelm Meister*). First performed, Paris, Nov. 17, 1866.

Migot [mee-go], GEORGES ELBERT: *b.* Paris, Feb. 27, 1891. Composer, painter and writer on aesthetics. Studied at the Paris Conservatoire under Widor. His works include *Essais pour une esthétique générale* (1919), chamber music, suite for piano and orchestra, ballets, songs and piano works.

Mihalovici [mee-cah-loh′-veech-ee], MARCEL : *b.* Bucharest, Oct. 22, 1898. Composer. Studied under d'Indy in Paris. His compositions include an opera (*L'Intransigeant Pluton*), several ballets, a Fantasia for orchestra, *Symphonie du temps présent* (1943), and chamber music.

Mikado, The. Comic opera in two acts by Sullivan. Libretto by William Schwenk Gilbert. First performed, London, March 14, 1885.

Mikrokosmos. A collection of more than 150 short piano pieces by Bartók, intended as a complete course of instruction in technique and also illustrating a rich variety of invention.

Milan [mee-lahn′], LUIS: *b.* perhaps in Valencia, *c.* 1500; *d.* there, after 1561. Composer and player of the *vihuela*. His *Libro de música de vihuela de mano, intitulado El Maestro* (1536; modern ed. by L. Schrade, 1927) contained the earliest collection of accompanied solo songs of the Renaissance period, together with fantasias and pavanes for the *vihuela*. He also published *El Cortesano* (1561), an account of life and music at the court of Germaine de Foix at Valencia. The song "Durandarte" from *El Maestro* is printed in Schering's *History of Music in Examples*, No. 96, and a fantasia in the *Historical Anthology*, No. 121.

J. B. TREND: *Luis Milan and the Vihuelistas* (1925).

Milford, ROBIN HUMPHREY: *b.* Oxford, Jan. 22, 1903. Composer. Educated at Rugby where he studied music under A. H. Peppin. Later studied composition under Holst, Vaughan Williams and R. O. Morris. His compositions include two oratorios (*A Prophet in the Land* and *The Pilgrim's Progress*), orchestral works, a violin concerto, and songs.

Milhaud [mee-yo], DARIUS: *b.* Aix-en-Provence, Sept. 4, 1892. Composer. Studied in Paris under Gédalge and Widor and became a member of the group called "Les Six." Since 1940 he has taught composition at Mills College, California. He is a prolific composer with a fine craftsmanship and a lively sense of wit. His compositions include operas and ballets, several symphonies, concertos, much other orchestral music, chamber music and piano pieces. He has written two autobiographical books: *L'Écran des musiciens* (1930) and *Notes sans musique* (1949). The latter has been published in an English translation (1952).

Military Band. The instruments included in a military band comprise both wood-wind and brass instruments, as distinct from a BRASS BAND, which has brass instruments only. The instruments in a military band vary considerably in different countries. An English band usually consists of the following: 2 flutes and piccolo, 2 clarinets in E♭, 2 oboes, 4 clarinets in B♭, alto saxophone, tenor saxophone, 2 bassoons, 4 horns in F or E♭, 2 cornets in B♭, 2 trumpets in B♭, 2 tenor trombones and bass trombone, euphonium, tubas in E♭ and B♭, timpani, side drum, bass drum, and other percussion instruments. The number of players to a part will depend on the size of the band, *e.g.* there may be as many as 16 B♭ clarinet players, divided as follows: 6 solo clarinets, 4 firsts, 3 seconds, 3 thirds.

H. E. ADKIN: *Treatise on the Military Band*, 3 vols. (1931).

Military Music. In the 15th and 16th cent. composers occasionally imitated the sounds of trumpets and drums to symbolise an amorous assault or depict a battle, as in Dufay's *chanson* "Donnez l'assaut," Jannequin's *chanson* "La Guerre" (1529), and Alessandro Striggio's madrigal "Non rumor di tamburi" (1571). Similar effects, suggested by the words of psalms, are found in the motets of Byrd and of Lutheran composers in the 17th cent. (*v.* BATTLE MUSIC). Military bands arose in France under Louis XIV, in Germany under Frederick the Great, and in England later in the 18th cent. The late 18th-cent. fashion for things Turkish (*v.* JANISSARY MUSIC) suggested the imitations of Turkish military music in the Turkish March in Mozart's piano sonata in A, and in some passages in his *Die Entführung* and in the finale of Beethoven's ninth symphony. During the 19th cent. military bands containing all the usual wind and percussion instruments were established in most countries.

H. G. FARMER: *Military Music and its Story* (1912).

Military Symphony. Haydn's symphony No. 100 in G major (1794), the eighth of the "Salomon" symphonies written for performance in London. It derives its name from the fact that a bugle call is introduced into the second movement, which also has parts for triangle, bass drum and cymbals (instruments which were not a normal part of the 18th-cent. orchestra).

Milleran [mee-ler-rũn], RENÉ: 17th-18th cent. A grammarian, and amateur lutenist. Pupil of Mouton. He compiled a manuscript of lute music entitled *Livre de lut de M. Milleran, interprète du Roy . . . Recueil des plus belles pièces de lut des meilleurs maîtres sur les 14 modes de la musique, savoir sept en bémol et sept en bécarre* which is in the Conservatoire Library, Paris.

Milton, JOHN: *b.* Stanton St. John (nr. Oxford), *c.* 1563; *d.* London, March, 1647. Father of the poet. In 1600 he became a member of the Scriveners' Company. His musical abilities are alluded to in his son's poem "Ad Patrem." His compositions include a madrigal in *The Triumphes of Oriana* (modern edition in *E.M.S.*, xxxii), 4 pieces in Leighton's *Teares or Lamentacions* (1614), 2 psalms in Ravenscroft's *Psalter* (1621) and 5 fancies for viols, one of which is printed in *Musica Britannica*, ix.

E. BRENNECKE : *John Milton the Elder and his Music* (1938).

Minacciando [mee-nah-tchahn'-do], **Minaccevole** [mee-nah-tcheh'-vo-leh], *I.* In a menacing fashion.

Minim (*A.* half-note, *Fr.* blanche, *G.* Halbe, *I.* minima). From the Latin *minima* [*nota*], smallest [note]. Introduced in the early 14th cent. as a subdivision of the semi-breve, and then the shortest note value in mensural notation. In modern notation it is one half of a semibreve (whole-note) and is represented by the sign 𝅗𝅥. The minim rest is 𝄼. *v.* CROTCHET.

Minnesinger [min'-er-zing-er], *G.* (*Minne*=chivalrous love, *Fr.* amour courtois). A German poet and musician of the period of chivalry, corresponding to the troubadour and trouvère of Provence and France. The chief form of their songs, the *Bar* form consisting of two *Stollen* and an *Abgesang*, was adopted from the troubadours. The period of the *Minnesinger* lasted from *c.* 1150 to 1450, when their traditions were taken over by the guilds of MEISTERSINGER; it includes the names of Walther von der Vogelweide (*d. c.* 1230), Neidhart von Reuenthal (*d. c.* 1240), Heinrich Frauenlob (*d.* 1318), and Oswald von Wolkenstein (*d.* 1445). Wagner's opera *Tannhäuser* is founded on an actual "contest of singers" (*Sängerkrieg*) held at Wartburg by the Landgrave Hermann of Thuringia in 1207, in which the *Minnesinger* Tannhäuser and Wolfram von Eschenbach took part. Wolkenstein composed. besides monophonic songs, songs in two, three, and four parts. Songs by Reuenthal have been published in *D.T.Ö.*, xxxvii (1), by Frauenlob in *D.T.Ö.*, xx (2), and by Wolkenstein in *D.T.Ö.*, ix (1).

Minor. Lesser. The term is used in referring to an INTERVAL, a CHORD, a MODE, or a PROLATION.

Minore [mee-noh'-reh], *I.* Minor mode.

Minuet (*Fr.* menuet, *G.* Menuett, *I.* minuetto). A French dance in 3/4 time at a moderate pace. It was first introduced in a stylised form by Lully about 1650, and thereafter appeared in many instrumental suites and ballets during the baroque period. It remained to be one of the regular movements in the classical sonata and symphony, always in ternary form (Minuet-Trio-Minuet). In Beethoven, by taking on a much quicker tempo and a boisterously playful style, it was transformed into the SCHERZO.

Miracle, The. The name popularly given to Haydn's symphony No. 96 in D major (1791). It derives its name from the story that at the first performance a chandelier fell from the ceiling and missed the audience by a miracle. In actual fact this accident occurred at the first performance of Haydn's symphony No. 102 in B♭ major (1794) ; see H. C. Robbins Landon, *The Symphonies of Joseph Haydn*, pp. 534-5.

Miracle Play. *v.* TROPE.

Mireille [mee-ray-yer]. Opera in five acts by Gounod. Libretto by Michel Carré (founded on a poem by Mistral). First performed, Paris, March 19, 1864.

Mirliton [meer-lee-tōn], *Fr.* A wind instrument consisting of a pipe with one end closed by thin parchment or skin and a hole in the side into which the performer sings. The tone produced is similar to the bleating of a sheep. An instrument of this type was known in the 17th cent. under the name *flûte-eunuque* (eunuch flute) and is described by Mersenne in his *Harmonie universelle* (1636). At the present day it is merely a toy, known in England and America as the "kazoo." The passage for brass instruments in the *Danse des mirlitons* in Tchaikovsky's ballet *Casse-Noisette* appears to be intended as a grotesque imitation of the sound of this instrument.

Missa [miss'-a], *L.* Mass. Presumably

derived from the concluding words of the Mass: "Ite, missa est" (Go, [the congregation] is dismissed). *Missa brevis*, a short Mass. *Missa Cellensis*, *v.* MARIAZELLERMESSE. *Missa in angustiis*, *v.* NELSONMESSE. *Missa in tempore belli*, *v.* PAUKENMESSE. *Missa pro defunctis*, Requiem Mass. *Missa sine nomine*, a Mass which is not founded on any pre-existing melody (or *canto fermo*) and hence has no title. *Missa solennis*, High Mass. *Missa supra voces musicales*, a Mass which uses as a *canto fermo* the notes of the HEXACHORD.

Other titles fall into the following categories: (1) Those which indicate the plainsong on which the Mass is built, or the motet from which it borrows material; (2) those which indicate a particular saint's day or festival for which the Mass is intended; (3) those which indicate the mode in which the Mass is written, *e.g.* *Missa quarti toni*, a Mass in the fourth (Hypophrygian) mode. *v.* MASS.

Mitchell, HELEN. *v.* MELBA.

Mit dem Hornsignal [mit dem horrn'-zig-nahl'], *G.* *v.* AUF DEM ANSTAND.

Mitropoulos [mee-trop'-oo-loss], DIMITRI: *b.* Athens, March 1, 1896. Conductor and pianist. Studied in Athens under Gilson and Busoni. Assistant conductor, Berlin State Opera, 1920; conductor, Paris Symphony Orchestra, 1932. Later director of the Athens Conservatoire and conductor of the Athens Symphony Orchestra. Conductor, Minneapolis Symphony Orchestra, 1937; New York Symphony Orchestra, 1950. He has composed an opera, orchestral works, violin sonata, piano sonata and piano pieces.

Mixolydian Mode. (1) In ancient Greek music:

(2) From the Middle Ages onwards applied to:

The tonic (or final) and dominant are marked respectively T and D. The sharpening of the seventh note of this mode makes it identical with the modern major scale. *v.* GREEK MUSIC, MODE.

Mixture. Organ stop which produces three or four sounds higher than the pitch corresponding to the key which is depressed. A three-rank mixture sounds the fifteenth, nineteenth, and twenty-second, which are the fourth, sixth, and eighth notes of the harmonic series, above the foundation note. *v.* ORGAN.

Mock Trumpet. *v.* TRUMPET (3).

Mocquereau [mock-ro], DOM ANDRÉ: *b.* Tessoualle (nr. Cholet), June 6, 1849, *d.* Solesmes, Jan. 18, 1930. Benedictine monk. Pupil of Dom Joseph Pothier, whose work for the restoration of Gregorian chant he continued. In 1890 he founded *Paléographie Musicale*, a series in which facsimiles of important manuscripts of plainsong have since been published. He trained the choir of the Abbey of Solesmes according to his principles of rhythmic interpretation, and published treatises, notably *Rhythmique grégorienne* (1908), in which they were expounded.

Mode (*Fr.* ton, *G.* Tonart, *I.* tuono). A set of notes which form the material of melodic idioms used in composition. Medieval theorists commonly illustrated the characteristics of modes by giving the NEUMA of the mode and quoting from plainsong melodies; this had a practical value in classifying the antiphons of plainsong and the psalm-tones and endings which were used with them. For the purposes of theoretical discussion the notes of a mode may be arranged in scalewise order. The medieval (also called ecclesiastical) modes may thus be represented by scales of white notes on the modern keyboard. They bear names derived from the Greek musical system, though neither this concept of mode nor the application of the names corresponds to Greek theory:

Early numbering	Later numbering	Name	Compass	Final	Dominant
Protus (authentic)	I	Dorian	D-D	D	A
„ (plagal)	II	Hypodorian	A-A	D	F
Deuterus (authentic)	III	Phrygian	E-E	E	C
„ (plagal)	IV	Hypophrygian	B-B	E	A
Tritus (authentic)	V	Lydian	F-F	F	C
„ (plagal)	VI	Hypolydian	C-C	F	A
Tetrardus (authentic)	VII	Mixolydian	G-G	G	D
„ (plagal)	VIII	Hypomixolydian	D-D	G	C

The *final* of the mode is the note on which its melodies end; for the meaning of *dominant v.* PSALMODY. The distinction between authentic and plagal is in the range of the melody; they have the same final, or note of ending. Modes on A and C (Aeolian and Ionian) were first theoretically recognized in the *Dodecachordon* (system of 12 modes) of Glareanus in 1547. He also gave the name Hyperaeolian to the mode on B, and Hyperphrygian to its plagal form, but rejected both as impractical on account of the diminished fifth between B and F. These modes are now generally known as Locrian and Hypolocrian. Glareanus's additions to the medieval modal system are therefore as follows :

Numbering	Name	Compass	Final	Dominant
IX	Aeolian	A-A	A	E
X	Hypoaeolian	E-E	A	C
XI	Ionian	C-C	C	G
XII	Hypoionian	G-G	C	E

Until the end of the 16th cent. the medieval modal theory and the medieval interval theory were the bases of polyphonic composition. By the end of the 17th cent. the exclusive use of the two modern modes, major and minor (*v.* SCALE) was established. The first of these was, melodically, of great antiquity, though it was not officially recognized by medieval theorists. It occurs frequently in plainsong melodies and in the secular songs of the Middle Ages, in the form of the F mode with flattened B. The intervals are thus identical with those of Glareanus's Ionian mode. The practice of sharpening the seventh in the Mixolydian mode resulted in a similar identity. The minor mode was a conflation of the Dorian and Aeolian modes, with the seventh sharpened as required.

Modal idioms, generally derived from folksong, reappeared in the 19th cent. (*e.g.* the Lydian mode in Chopin's *Rondeau à la Mazurka*, Op. 5), and are an element of some importance in the style of Debussy, Ravel, Sibelius and Vaughan Williams, among others. For the use of the term in the rhythmic sense, *v.* RHYTHMIC MODES.

Modes, Rhythmic. *v.* RHYTHMIC MODES.

Moderato [mo-deh-rah'-toh], *I.* At a moderate speed.

Modulation. A change of key. The establishment of a new key is effected by a perfect cadence in that key, *e.g.*:

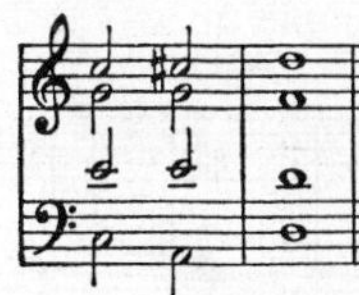

In this modulation from C to D minor, three of the notes (A, E, G) in the second chord, the dominant seventh of D, belong to both keys, and the other note moves chromatically from C to C♯.

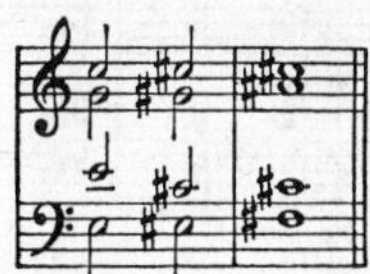

In modulating from C to F♯, there are no notes common to the first two chords, and three of the notes move chromatically. Modulations which involve chromatic movement in one or more of the parts are sometimes called "direct" modulations.

Modulation is most commonly effected by passing through a chord, called a "pivot" chord, in which two or more of the notes belong to both of the keys concerned, on the way to the dominant of the new key. In this modulation from C to E minor:

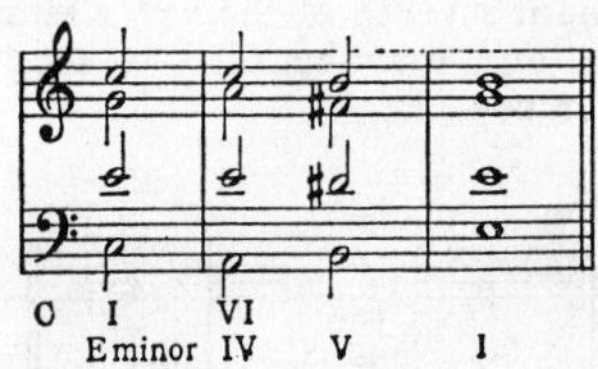

the second chord acts as a pivot chord, being the sub-mediant chord (VI) in C, and the sub-dominant chord (IV) in E minor. Such pivot chords exist, and may be similarly used for modulation, between every major key and the key of its supertonic minor, mediant minor, subdominant, dominant, relative minor and leading-note minor, *e.g.* between C and D minor, E minor, F, G, A minor, and B minor.

Chords of which the root and fifth are common to the two keys concerned are equally effective as pivot chords, *e.g.*:

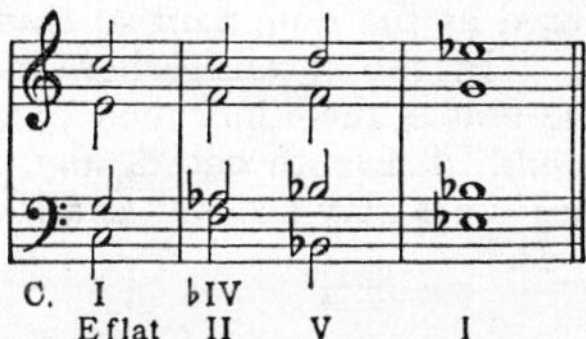

where the second chord is the subdominant of C with the third flattened and also the supertonic of E flat. Chords in which the root and fifth are common exist between every two major keys, except those of which the key-notes are a tritone apart. Modulation which takes its departure from a minor key may be effected along similar lines.

Modulation may also be effected by using as the intermediate step (1) chords which, since they divide the octave into equal parts, are inherently capable of assuming as many key-contexts as they have notes (*e.g.*, the augmented triad and the diminished seventh chord), and (2) chromatic chords which have by historical usage established themselves within the key (*e.g.*, the Neapolitan sixth and augmented sixth chords). In the mediant chord of the minor mode with sharpened fifth, which is an augmented triad, any one of the three notes may be used as a dominant.

In

for example, G♯ in the mediant chord of A minor is used as the dominant to lead to C♯ minor, and in

C is used as the dominant to lead to F minor. In the seventh chord on the leading-note of the minor mode, which is a diminished seventh chord, any one of the four notes may be used as a leading-note. In

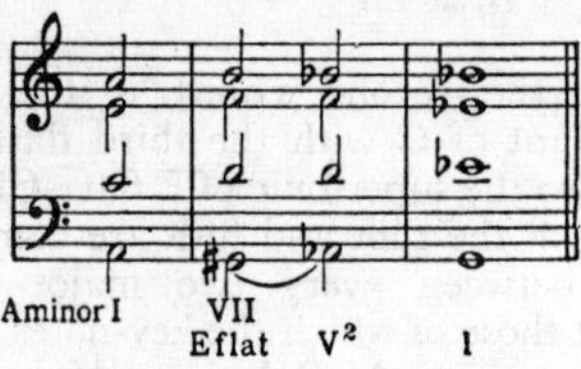

for example, D is used as the leading note in modulating to E♭, in

F (E♯) as the leading-note to modulate to F♯ minor, and in

B as the leading-note to modulate to C. In modulations in this group the chord through which the modulation is made is, in fact, a pivot chord, since it belongs to both keys, and an enharmonic change, shown in the examples by a tie, is always expressed or implied.

The Neapolitan sixth chord, the root of which is a semi-tone above the tonic (*e.g.* D♭ in C), can effect a modulation either up or down a semitone from the key, for example from C to B minor:

or from C to D♭:

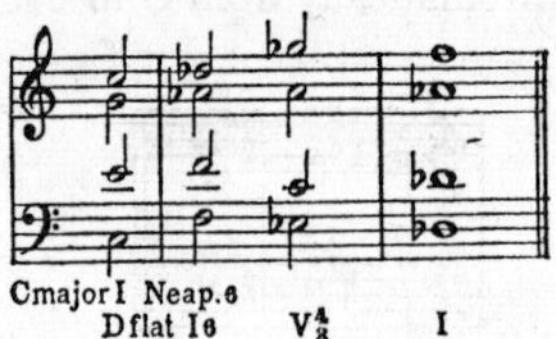

The augmented sixth chord, which in its most usual form ("German" sixth chord) is based on the flattened sub-mediant of the key, *e.g.*

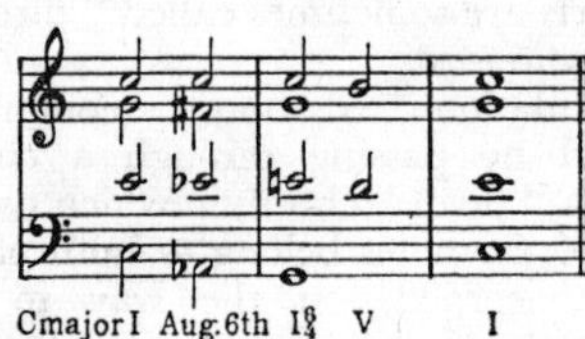

in C, is identical in sound with the dominant seventh of the key a semitone above, and may be used to modulate to that key:

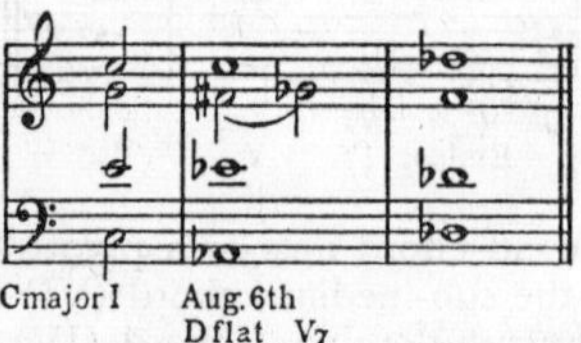

An enharmonic change is always involved.

If a modulation is repeated from the new key as a starting point, *i.e.* transposed into that key, the result is a modulating or " real " sequence. A special case of such a sequence is the canon *per tonos* in Bach's *Musikalisches Opfer*, which modulates up a tone with each repetition of the theme until it arrives at the original key an octave higher.

Such formulae as are given in these examples may be the basis of modulations which are momentary (sometimes called " transitions ") and are soon followed by a return to the original key, or are modulations (or " transitions ") on the way to a further modulation, or are part of a large tonal design. The question of their terminology is unimportant, so long as they are heard and understood in relation to the time-scale of the complete composition, be it hymn-tune, symphony, or opera. The technique and art of modulation is fundamental to the artistic use of the effects of tonality, to the control of tonal design, and thus to the art of composition. *v.* also HARMONY.

Moeran, ERNEST JOHN: *b.* London, Dec. 31, 1894; *d.* Kenmare, Ireland, Dec. 1, 1950. Composer of Irish descent. Educated at Uppingham. Began composing at the age of seventeen and entered the R.C.M. in 1913. In 1924 his first orchestral *Rhapsody* was performed in Manchester and the second at the Norwich Festival. After a period of retirement for further study he composed a sonata for two unaccompanied violins (1930) and a second piano trio (1931). Some of his works show the influence of Delius, Vaughan Williams and Bernard van Dieren. His compositions include a symphony (1937), violin concerto (1942), cello concerto (1945), many songs, choral works, church music, and chamber music.

Moeschinger [mursh-ing-er], ALBERT: *b.* Basle, Jan. 10, 1897. Composer. Studied in Berne, Leipzig and Munich. Teacher of theory and piano in Berne until his retirement in 1943. Though he has written a large number of outstanding chamber works (including 4 string quartets), he has also been prolific in other fields and has composed 3 symphonies, 3 piano concertos, an opera (*Die sieben Raben*), works for piano and organ, choral music and songs.

Moiseiwitsch [mo-i-say'-i-vitch], BENNO: *b.* Odessa, Feb. 22, 1890. English pianist of Russian origin, a pupil of Leschetizky in Vienna. First appeared in England in 1908. Naturalized, 1937. A player with a large repertory, he has appeared as a recitalist in every continent in the world.

Moll [moll], *G.* " Minor," as opposed to " major " (*dur*). The word derives from the Latin *B molle* (soft B), the name given to the rounded B used in medieval times to indicate B♭, and hence adopted as the symbol for flattening. *v.* B, DUR.

Molteni [mol-teh'-nee], BENEDETTA EMILIA. *v.* AGRICOLA (2).

Molto [moll'-to], *I.* Very. *Allegro molto,* very fast.

Mompou [mom-po'-oo], FEDERICO: *b.* Barcelona, April 16, 1893. Composer and pianist. Studied at the Barcelona Conservatoire and from 1911 in Paris under Philipp and Lacroix (piano) and Samuel Rousseau (harmony). From 1914-21 he lived in Barcelona and since 1921 has lived in Paris. He has developed an individual style of composition which he calls *primitivista* and which has no bar-divisions, key-signatures or cadences. His compositions are chiefly piano music and songs.

Mondonville [mo͡n-do͡n-veel], JEAN JOSEPH CASSANÉA DE: *b.* Narbonne, Dec. 25, 1711; *d.* Belleville (nr. Paris), Oct. 8, 1772. Violinist and composer. Went to Paris *c.* 1733, became director of the Royal Chapel in 1744, and of the Concerts Spirituels in 1755. He composed operas, including *Titon et l' Aurore* (1753), 3 oratorios, and motets. His violin sonatas *Les sons harmoniques* (*c.* 1738) made the first extended use of harmonics.

Moniuszko [mo-nyoosh'-co], STANISLAW: *b.* Ubiel (Minsk), May 5, 1819; *d.* Warsaw, June 4, 1872. Composer and conductor. Studied under Freyer in Warsaw from 1827-30 and under Rungenhagen in Berlin from 1837-39.

Organist, St. John's Church, Wilno, 1840-58. Later conductor at the Warsaw Opera and teacher at the Conservatoire. His opera *Halka*, the first Polish opera on a national theme (1847), was given more than a thousand performances in Warsaw alone. He composed 17 other operas including *Straszny Dwór* (The Haunted Manor) and *Flis* (The Raftsman). He also composed songs, choral works, incidental music for plays, church music and a symphonic poem, *Bajka* (The Fairy Tale).

Monn [mon], GEORG MATTHIAS: *b.* Austria, 1717; *d.* Vienna, Oct. 3, 1750. Organist and composer. Organist, Karlskirche, Vienna. His compositions, which are sometimes confused with works by a younger composer (Johann Matthias Monn or Mann), include symphonies, quartets and trio sonatas. He is one of the composers whose symphonies were being played in Vienna when Haydn was growing up. Of the 4 symphonies published in *D.T.Ö.*, xv (2), two are in four movements, including a minuet. Other symphonies and 2 concertos have been published in *D.T.Ö.*, xix (2).

Monochord. An instrument consisting of a single string stretched over a wooden resonator and used, especially in the Middle Ages, to demonstrate the relation between musical intervals and the division of the string.

Monodrama. (1) A dramatic work involving only one character, *e.g.* Schönberg's one-act opera *Erwartung* (1909).

(2) In particular a work for speaking voice with instrumental accompaniment. *v.* MELODRAMA.

Monody. Solo song with accompaniment. Solo songs with lute, for example in Luis Milan's collection of 1535, and arrangements of madrigals for solo voice and lute, were common in the 16th century. The term is particularly applied to the Italian monody (for solo voice and continuo) in the new style, exploiting the dramatic and expressive possibilities of the solo singer, written in the early 17th cent. This style appeared in solo monodies, *e.g.* Caccini's *Le nuove musiche* (1602) and in opera. For a summary, *v.* N. Fortune, "Italian Secular Monody from 1600 to 1635," in *The Musical Quarterly*, xxxix, p. 171.

Monophony (*Gr.* μόνος, alone; φωνή, sound). Music which consists of melody only, without independent or supporting accompaniment, as in plainsong, folk song, troubadour and trouvère *chansons* and in most non-European music.

Monotone. The recitation of words on a single note.

Monsigny [mo͂n-see-nyee], PIERRE ALEXANDRE: *b.* Fauquembergue (nr. St. Omer), Oct. 17, 1729; *d.* Paris, Jan. 14, 1817. Composer. He studied the violin in his youth and went to Paris in 1749. On hearing Pergolesi's *La serva padrona* he was inspired with a desire to compose a comic opera and after only five months study wrote his first stage work, *Les Aveux indiscrets*, which was produced at the Théâtre de la Foire. In 1777 he stopped composing although he was then at the height of his success. He lost his fortune during the Revolution but in 1798 he was granted a pension by the Opéra-Comique. His most important operas were *Rose et Colas* (1764), *Le Déserteur* (his most famous work, 1769), and *La belle Arsène* (1773).

Montalant [mo͂n-ta-lu͂n], LAURE CYNTHIE. *v.* DAMOREAU.

Monte [deh mon′-teh], PHILIPPE DE: *b.* nr. Mechlin, 1521; *d.* Prague, July 4, 1603. Flemish composer, who spent his early years in Italy. Became a member of the chapel of Philip II of Spain, *c.* 1555, and with him visited England. He returned to Italy shortly after this and eventually succeeded Jakob Vaet as *Kapellmeister* to the Emperor Maximilian II in 1568. He continued to hold this office under Maximilian's successor, Rudolf II. With Palestrina, Lassus and Victoria he is one of the great masters of 16th-cent. polyphony and one of the most prolific. He published 36 books of secular madrigals and 5 books of *madrigali spirituali*. He also composed French *chansons*, Masses (24 of which are published in modern editions) and an enormous number of motets. A complete edition of his works, ed. by C. van den Borren and J. van Nuffel, is in progress.

G. VAN DOORSLAER : *La Vie et les œuvres de Philippe de Monte* (1921).

Montéclair [mo͞n-tay-clair], MICHEL PINOLET DE : *bapt.* Andelot (Haute-Marne), Dec. 4, 1667 ; *d.* St. Denis (nr. Paris), Sept. 27, 1737. Composer and teacher. Chorister in the cathedral of Langres. He went to Italy in the service of the Prince de Vaudémont, and later settled in Paris, becoming in 1707 a double-bass player in the Opéra orchestra. He also became a distinguished teacher of the violin. He composed operas, cantatas, chamber music and church music, and published textbooks, among them *Méthode pour apprendre la musique* (1700) and *Méthode pour apprendre à jouer le Violon* (1712). The latter is one of the earliest on its subject.

Montemezzi [mon-teh-meh′-dzee], ITALO : *b.* Vigasio (nr. Verona), Aug. 4, 1875 ; *d.* there, May 15, 1952. Composer. He was sent to a technical school to study engineering but later decided to study music. After being rejected twice he was admitted to the Milan Conservatorio and obtained a diploma in composition in 1900. His first opera, *Giovanni Gallurese,* was produced at Turin in 1905 and at the Metropolitan Opera House, New York, in 1925. His best-known opera is *L'Amore dei Tre Re*, a setting of Sem Benelli's drama. He also composed a symphonic poem, *Paolo e Virginia,* and an elegy for cello and piano.

Monteux [mo͞n-ter], PIERRE: *b.* Paris, Apr. 4, 1875. Conductor. Studied at the Paris Conservatoire and won first prize for violin in 1896. He founded the Société des Concerts Populaires (1914). In 1912 he became conductor of Diaghilev's Ballet Russe, with which he went to New York in 1916. From 1917-19 he conducted at the Metropolitan Opera House, from 1919-24 the Boston Symphony Orchestra, and from 1929-38 the Orchestre Symphonique de Paris. Conductor, San Francisco Symphony Orchestra, 1936-54. He is one of the most enterprising and accomplished conductors of his time.

Monteverdi [mon-teh-vairr′-dee] (Monteverde), CLAUDIO GIOVANNI ANTONIO : *bapt.* Cremona, May 15, 1567 ; *d.* Venice, Nov. 29, 1643. Composer, the eldest son of a doctor. Studied with Ingegneri in Cremona. His first published work was a collection of *Cantiunculae sacrae* (1582). Violist in the service of the Duke of Mantua, *c.* 1590 ; *maestro di cappella, c.* 1602-12 (when he was dismissed). *Maestro di cappella,* St. Mark's, Venice, 1613. Ordained priest, 1632. His church music includes 3 Masses (the earliest of which is founded on Gombert's motet " In illo tempore "), Vespers, Magnificats and numerous motets. His secular vocal music includes 9 books of madrigals (the last posthumous), a book of *canzonette* and 2 books of *Scherzi musicali.* His stage music includes at least 12 operas (of which only three survive complete) and ballets.

His madrigals show an increasing tendency to break away from tradition by the use of new forms of dissonance for the sake of pathetic expression and by the writing of melodic lines akin to the declamatory style of recitative. The fifth book (1605) was published with a *basso continuo* part, which is obligatory for the last six pieces in the collection. In the sixth book (1614) there are also six pieces which require a harpsichord accompaniment. In the seventh book (1619) none of the pieces are madrigals in the traditional sense : most of them are solos, duets and trios with accompaniment. The eighth book (1638), divided into *madrigali guerrieri* (warlike madrigals) and *madrigali amorosi* (amorous madrigals), is on similar lines. The seventh and eighth books also include shorter stage works. The church music may be divided into two contrasted groups, one of which accepts the traditional polyphonic style while the other adopts the new baroque methods of brilliant and expressive writing for solo voices and chorus, together with an effective use of instrumental resources.

The earliest of the three surviving operas, *Orfeo*, was performed at Mantua in 1607. It is clearly modelled to some extent on the earlier *Euridice* by Peri and also includes a substantial amount of choral writing in the style of the madrigal and motet ; but it is also a landmark in the history of opera on account of its remarkable understanding of the contribution that music can make to dramatic representation. Of the music of *Arianna* (Mantua, 1608) only the heroine's lament survives—an expressive piece of extended recitative which had a great vogue in the 17th cent. The two Venetian operas—*Il ritorno d'Ulisse in patria* (1641) and *L'incoronazione di Poppea* (1642)—are no less expressive in their declamation but incorporate also a rich variety of symmetrical songs and duets.

A complete edition of Monteverdi's works has been published by Malipiero.

A. ABERT : *Claudio Monteverdi und das musikalische Drama* (1954).
G. F. MALIPIERO : *Claudio Monteverdi* (1930, including all the composer's letters).
H. PRUNIÈRES : *Claudio Monteverdi* (1924 ; Eng. trans. 1926).
H. F. REDLICH : *Claudio Monteverdi : Life and Works* (1952).
L. SCHRADE : *Monteverdi : Creator of Modern Music* (1950).

Montre [mõtr], *Fr.* One of the names for an 8 ft. open diapason stop on the organ.

Mood. English 16th-17th cent. term, used, *e.g.* by Morley in his *Plaine and Easie Introduction* (1597), for the note relationships (mode, time, prolation) of MENSURAL NOTATION.

Moonlight Sonata. A name given (though not by the composer) to Beethoven's *Sonata quasi una fantasia* in C♯ minor for piano, Op. 27, no. 2 (1801). Its origin seems to be due to H. F. L. Rellstab (1799-1860), who thought that the first movement suggested moonlight on Lake Lucerne.

Moór [mohr], EMANUEL: *b.* Kecskemet (Hungary), Feb. 19, 1863; *d.* Vevey, Oct. 21, 1931. Composer and pianist. Studied in Budapest and Vienna and from 1885-87 toured Europe and the U.S.A. as conductor and pianist. Several of his operas have been produced in Germany. He invented the Duplex Coupler piano, with two manuals which can be coupled to simplify the playing of octaves. His compositions include operas, 8 symphonies, piano, cello and violin concertos, violin and cello sonatas, many piano pieces and songs.

Moore, (1) DOUGLAS STUART: *b.* Cutchogue (N.Y.), Aug. 10, 1893. Composer and teacher. Graduated from Yale in 1915. Studied composition with Parker, Bloch and d'Indy. Received a Guggenheim Fellowship, the Pulitzer Scholarship and the Eastman School Publication award. Associate professor, Columbia University, 1926; now professor. Has published *Listening to Music* (1931) and *From Madrigal to Modern Music* (1942). His compositions include an opera *The Devil and Daniel Webster*, with text by Stephen Vincent Benét (1938), an operetta *The Headless Horseman* with text by Benét (1937), orchestral works, choral works, and chamber music.

(2) THOMAS: *b.* Dublin, May 28, 1779; *d.* Devizes, Feb. 25, 1852. Poet and musician. Studied at Trinity College, Dublin, and was musically largely self-taught. From about 1802 he published songs for which he composed the music as well as the words. In 1807-08 he published the first set of *Irish Melodies*, for which he wrote the poems and Sir John Stevenson edited traditional folk melodies, many from the collections of Edward Bunting. In 1816 he published the first number of *Sacred Songs* and from 1818-28 six sets of a *Selection of Popular National Airs.* He produced an opera *M.P., or The Blue Stocking* with text by himself and music by himself and Charles Edward Horn. His songs became very popular, and he had a singular gift for writing new poems which very aptly caught the spirit of traditional tunes.

Morales [mo-rah'-less], CRISTÓBAL: *b.* Seville, *c.* 1500 ; *d.* Sept. or Oct., 1553. The first important Spanish composer of polyphonic church music. Studied under the Seville Cathedral choirmaster, Fernández de Castilleja. *Maestro de capilla*, Avila, 1526. Later went to Rome, where he was ordained a priest and in 1535 became singer in the Papal chapel. *Maestro de capilla*, Toledo, 1545-7; was in the service of the Duke of Arcos at Marchena, 1550; *maestro de capilla*, Málaga, 1551. He published two books of Masses, Magnificats and motets. His compositions also include Lamentations, a motet for the peace conference at Nice (1538) and a few madrigals. His motet "Emendemus in melius" is printed in the *Historical Anthology*, No. 128. A complete edition of his works by H. Anglès is in course of publication.

Mordent (*Fr.* pincé, *I.* mordente). Ornament played by alternating rapidly once or twice the written note with the note below it. The speed and number of alternations depend on the length of the written note, having regard to the tempo in which it occurs. It is indicated thus:

and performed thus:

v. also INVERTED MORDENT.

Moreau [morr-o], JEAN BAPTISTE: *b.* Angers, 1656: *d.* Paris, Aug. 24, 1733. Church musician and composer. Chorister at Angers Cathedral; *maître de chapelle*, Langres Cathedral, and later at Dijon. In Paris from *c.* 1686, he wrote incidental music for Racine's *Esther* (1688) and *Athalie* (1691), and also for plays by Abbé Boyer and Duché. He set to music a large number of poems by Laînez. He taught singing and composition, and his pupils included Montéclair and Clérambault.

Morendo [mo-rend'-o], *I.* "Dying." Used to indicate a *diminuendo* at an intermediate or final cadence.

Moresca [mo-ress'-cah], *I.* A dance of the 15th and 16th cent., most often a sword dance in which a fight between Christians and Mohammedans was represented. The English Morris Dance is related to it. It appeared as a dance in Venetian operas and Viennese operas in the 17th cent. It was originally in triple time, more often in march rhythm in the ballets of opera, as in this example from a ballet suite by J. H. Schmeltzer (from E. Wellesz, *Die Ballettsuiten von J. H. und A. A. Schmeltzer*, 1914):

Morhange [morr-ũnzh], CHARLES HENRI VALENTIN. *v.* ALKAN.

Morigi [mo-ree'-djee], ANGELO: *b.* Rimini, 1725; *d.* Parma, Jan. 22, 1801. Violinist, composer and teacher. He studied violin under Tartini and theory and harmony under Valotti. He was appointed first violin of the Prince of Parma's orchestra and later director of his court-music. His pupils included Bonifazio Asioli, who published Morigi's *Trattato di contrappunto fugato*. He wrote chamber music and *concerti grossi*.

Morin [morr-ãn], JEAN BAPTISTE: *b.* Orléans, *c.* 1677; *d.* Paris, 1745. Musician to the Duke of Orléans and one of the first French composers of cantatas. He also wrote motets and songs.

Morlacchi [morr-lahk'-kee], FRANCESCO: *b.* Perugia, June 14, 1784; *d.* Innsbruck, Oct. 28, 1841. Composer and conductor. Studied under his father, Caruso and Mazetti in Perugia; later under Zingarelli at Loreto and finally under Mattei at Bologna. He was commissioned to write a cantata for the coronation of Napoleon as King of Italy, 1805. In 1807 his first *opera buffa*, *Il ritratto*, was produced at Verona. Conductor of the Dresden Opera from 1810 until his death, being succeeded there by Wagner. His works include operas, 10 Masses, oratorios and cantatas.

Morley, THOMAS: *b.* 1557; *d. c.* 1602. Composer and theorist, pupil of Byrd. Organist, St. Paul's Cathedral, 1591; gentleman of the Chapel Royal, 1592. He was granted a monopoly of music printing in 1598, and assigned it to East in 1600. He published canzonets, madrigals, balletts, consort lessons for 6 instruments, and ayres, and edited *The Triumphes of Oriana* (reprinted in *E.M.S.*, xxxii). His *Plaine and Easie Introduction to Practicall Musicke* (1597; modern ed. by R. A. Harman, 1952) was the first comprehensive treatise on composition printed in England. He introduced the ballett, modelled on the *balletti* of Gastoldi, into England. E. H. Fellowes has edited the canzonets, balletts, and madrigals in *E.M.S.*, i-iv, and the *First Book of Ayres* (1600) in *E.S.L.S.*, xvi.

Morning Heroes. Symphony by Arthur Bliss (1930) for orator, chorus and orchestra. Words selected from Homer, Li-Tai-Po, Whitman, Robert Nichols and Wilfred Owen.

Mornington, GARRETT COLLEY WELLESLEY, EARL OF : *b.* Dangan (Ireland), July 19, 1735 ; *d.* London, May 22, 1781. Violinist, organist and composer, largely self-taught. In 1757 he founded the Academy of Music in Dublin and in 1764 was elected the first professor of music at Dublin University. A complete collection of his glees and madrigals was published in 1846, edited by Sir H. R. Bishop. He was the father of the Duke of Wellington.

Morris, REGINALD OWEN: *b.* York, March 3, 1886; *d.* London, Dec. 14, 1948. Teacher, composer and theorist. Educated at Harrow, New College, Oxford, and the R.C.M., where he was appointed teacher of counterpoint and composition in 1920. From 1926-28 he taught at the Curtis Institute of Music in Philadelphia and then rejoined the R.C.M. His publications include: *Contrapuntal Technique in the 16th Century* (1922), *Foundations of Practical Harmony and Counterpoint* (1925), and *The Structure of Music* (1935). He composed a symphony in D major (1935), a violin concerto, chamber music and songs.

Mortaro [morr-tah′-ro], ANTONIO. Composer. He entered the Minorite monastery at Brescia in 1595 and in 1598 was in the Franciscan monastery at Milan. From 1602 was organist at Novara Cathedral and from 1606-8 was again at Brescia. His compositions are written in the elaborate polychoral style of which Giovanni Gabrieli was the greatest exponent.

Moscaglia [moss-cahl′-yah], GIOVANNI BATTISTA. Late 16th-cent. madrigal composer, and an associate of Luca Marenzio in Rome. In 1585 he published a book of settings of his own madrigal poems by himself and other Roman composers, including Marenzio. He published other books of madrigals and a volume of villanellas *alla Napolitana.*

Moscheles [mosh′-er-lĕss], IGNAZ: *b.* Prague, May 30, 1794; *d.* Leipzig, March 10, 1870. Pianist, teacher and composer. Studied under Dionys Weber at the Prague Conservatorium, and later in Vienna under Albrechtsberger and Salieri. In 1814 he arranged the piano score of *Fidelio* under Beethoven's supervision. He toured throughout Europe for 10 years and in 1824 gave piano lessons to Mendelssohn in Paris. After 1826 he settled in London playing, composing and teaching. In 1846 he became teacher of piano at the new Leipzig Conservatorium founded by Mendelssohn. His compositions include 8 piano concertos, many piano sonatas and studies, and chamber music. His memoirs (English trans. by A. D. Coleridge, 1873) give an interesting picture of the musical life of his day.

Mosè in Egitto [moh-zeh′ een eh-jeet′-to] (Moses in Egypt). Opera in three acts by Rossini. Libretto by Andrea Leone Tottola. First performed, Naples, March 5, 1818. Enlarged French four-act version by Giuseppe Luigi Balochi and Victor Joseph Étienne de Jouy: first performed, Paris, March 26, 1872.

Moser [moh′-zer], HANS JOACHIM: *b.* Berlin, May 25, 1889. Historian, composer and singer. Studied under his father, Andreas Moser, and in Berlin, Marburg and Leipzig. Active as a singer in Berlin before the 1914-18 War. Professor, Halle, 1922; Heidelberg, 1925; Berlin, 1927-34; Jena, 1947. Director, Akademie für Kirchen- und Schulmusik, Berlin, 1927-33; Städtisches Konservatorium, Berlin, 1950. His publications, which are numerous, include *Geschichte der deutschen Musik* (3 vols., 1920-4), *Tönende Volksaltertümer* (1935), *J. S. Bach* (1935), *Heinrich Schütz* (1936), *Das deutsche Lied seit Mozart* (2 vols., 1937), *G. F. Händel* (1941), *Chr. W. Gluck* (1941), *C. M. von Weber* (1941). The fourth edition of his *Musik Lexikon* (2 vols.) was published in 1955. He is editor of a new complete edition of the works of Weber (in progress). He has also written a large number of vocal and instrumental works, and several novels.

Moses und Aron [moh′-zess oŏont ah′-ron] (Moses and Aaron). Unfinished opera in two acts by Schönberg. Libretto by the composer. First performed, Zürich, June 6, 1957.

Mosonyi [mo′-so-nyi], MIHÁLY (originally Michael Brand): *b.* Frauenkirchen (Austria), Sept. 1815; *d.* Pest, Oct. 31, 1870. Hungarian double-bass player, composer and critic. As a composer he was largely self-taught. Beginning as a composer in the German tradition, he became more and more aware of the Hungarian heritage of folk music and was honoured after his death as a pioneer in the development of a national style. His compositions include 3 operas, 2 symphonies, 6 string quartets, church music, piano music and songs.

Mosso [moss′-so], *I.* Lit. "moved," *i.e.* lively. *Più mosso*, faster; *meno mosso*, slower. Also used as a warning against dragging, *e.g. Andante mosso*, not too slow.

Mossolov [moss′-ol-off], ALEXANDER VASSILIEVICH: *b.* Kiev, Aug. 10, 1900. Pianist and composer, a pupil of Glière and Prokofiev. Several of his compositions have been influenced by his studies of the folk music of Turkmenia and other central Asian republics. His works include 3 operas, 4 symphonies and 2 piano concertos. His symphonic poem *The Steel Foundry* (or *Music of the Machines*) enjoyed at one time a wide, though hardly justified, popularity.

Mosto [moss′-to], GIOVANNI BATTISTA. 16th-cent. composer, a native of Udine. Studied under Merulo and from 1580-89 was *maestro di cappella* of Padua Cathedral. With Merulo he published an anthology (*Il primo fiore della ghirlanda musicale*, Venice, 1577) which contained the first published madrigal by Marenzio. He also published 4 books of madrigals and a second anthology (1579).

Moszkowski [mosh-kov′-ski], MORITZ: *b.* Breslau, Aug. 23, 1854; *d.* Paris, March 4, 1925. Pianist and composer of Polish origin. Studied in Dresden and Berlin, where he subsequently taught the piano. Though he wrote a number of large-scale works (*e.g.* piano concerto, violin concerto), his reputation rested mainly on his lighter works, particularly his *Spanische Tänze* (Spanish Dances) for piano duet. The ballet music from his opera *Boabdil* (Berlin, 1892) became a standard item in the orchestral repertory.

Motet. The term first arose in the early 13th cent. by the addition of words (*Fr.* mot) to the hitherto vocalised upper part of a two-part *clausula*. The motet became an independent composition, and flourished throughout the 13th century. It was most frequently in three parts. The lowest part, the tenor, was the basis; it was taken from plainsong, and was disposed in a regularly recurring rhythmic pattern. The other parts, called *duplum* and *triplum*, had different words, sacred or secular. In the latter case, they sometimes quoted the words and music of a well-known REFRAIN, *e.g.*:

The isorhythmic motet of the period from 1300 to 1450 (Machaut, Dunstable, Dufay) represented an expansion of this principle. The tenor was still the basis, and was disposed in two or more sections, each with the same rhythm in successively diminished note values. For an example using inversion, retrograde motion, and diminution *v.* RETROGRADE MOTION.

Motets of this time could be secular, sacred, or written to mark a notable occasion. From *c.* 1450 to 1600 the term denoted a setting for unaccompanied voices of a sacred Latin text, all the parts having the same words. The use of a tenor taken from plainsong continued in some cases until after 1500, but after *c.* 1530 the imitative style with original themes was generally adopted.

In the following centuries a motet was a setting of a sacred text in the current style of the period, for solo voices and/or choir, with or without instrumental accompaniment. In the *Psalmen Davids* (1619) Schütz used the term for two pieces written for voices and instruments without distinction of style between their parts. A *Motetto concertato* written *c.* 1663 by Matthias Weckmann has all the appearance of a cantata. Bach's motets are for unaccompanied double chorus, for five-part chorus, and for four-part chorus with organ continuo. Schubert and Mendelssohn wrote both accompanied and unaccompanied motets; those of Brahms are unaccompanied and in polyphonic styel.

H. LEICHTENTRITT: *Geschichte der Motette* (1908).

Mother Goose Suite. *v.* MA MÈRE L'OYE.

Motif, Motive. *v.* SUBJECT.

Mottl [mott'l], FELIX: *b.* Unter-St. Veit (nr. Vienna), Aug. 24, 1856; *d.* Munich, July 2, 1911. Conductor and composer. Studied at the Vienna Conservatorium under Hellmesberger, Dessoff and Bruckner. In 1876 he was a stage conductor for Wagner at Bayreuth, and was Court *Kapellmeister* at the Karlsruhe Opera and conductor of the Philharmonic until 1892. He produced many important modern works including the complete operas of Berlioz and Wagner. He was chief conductor at Bayreuth in 1886, director of the Munich Opera (1903), co-director of the Berlin Royal Academy and director of Court Opera in 1907. He also conducted in London and New York. He composed 3 operas, a string quartet and songs.

Motu Proprio [moh'-too prop'-ryoh], *L.* Instruction on sacred music given by Pope Pius X (November 22, 1903), in which Gregorian melodies "which the most recent studies [*i.e.*, those of the monks of Solesmes] have so happily restored to their integrity and purity" were affirmed to be its supreme models, and requiring the classic polyphony of the Roman school, especially of Palestrina, to be used in ecclesiastical functions. For an English translation of the text *v.* N. Slonimsky, *Music since 1900* (3rd ed., 1949), pp. 629-35.

Mount of Olives, The. *v.* CHRISTUS AM ÖLBERGE.

Mourning Waltz. *v.* TRAUERWALZER.

Moussorgsky [moo-sorrg'-ski], MODEST PETROVICH: *b.* Karevo (Pskov), March 21, 1839; *d.* St. Petersburg, March 28, 1881. Composer. Studied under Anton Henke at St. Petersburg. In 1852 he entered the Cadet School of the Guards; in 1857 he met Balakirev, who gave him lessons, and in the following year he resigned his commission. In 1863 he became a government clerk. His greatest work, and the only large work he completed, was the opera *Boris Godounov* composed in 1868-9. Its style, like that of his songs, is highly original, penetrating and direct. He left other operas incomplete, and wrote piano pieces, including *Pictures from an Exhibition* (1874), and orchestral works, among them the tone poem *Night on the Bare Mountain.*

V. BELAIEV: *Musorgsky's* "Boris Godounov" (1928).

M. D. CALVOCORESSI: *Mussorgsky* (1946); *Modest Mussorgsky—his Life and Works* (1956).

J. LEYDA and S. BERTENSON: *The Mussorgsky Reader* (1947).

Mouton [moo-tõ͡n], JEAN: *b.* nr. Metz, *c.* 1470; *d.* Saint-Quentin, Oct. 30, 1522. Composer. A pupil of Josquin des Prés, teacher of Willaert and musician to Louis XII and François I. Canon of Thérouanne and later of Saint-Quentin. His compositions include Masses, motets, psalms and *chansons.* A four-part canon, "Salve mater," is printed in Schering's *History of Music in Examples*, No. 66, and the Mass *Alma redemptoris* in *Les Maîtres musiciens de la Renaissance française* (ed. H. Expert), ix.

Mouvement [moov-mũ͡n], *Fr.* (1) Time,

speed. *Au mouvement*, in time (*I.* a tempo). *Premier* (or 1er) *mouvement*, at the original speed (*I. tempo primo*). *v.* TEMPO.

(2) Movement (of a sonata, symphony, etc.).

Movement (*Fr.* mouvement, *G.* Satz, *I.* movimento, tempo). A section, self-contained but not necessarily wholly independent, of an extended instrumental composition such as a symphony, sonata, string quartet, suite, etc. The movements of the 17th-cent. trio sonata grew out of the contrasts of mood, metre and tempo to be found in the 16th-cent. *capriccio*, *canzona* and *ricercar* (which in turn developed from the contrasts of mood to be found in the madrigal and the motet). The structure of the trio sonata was also influenced by the suite, consisting of a series of contrasted dances—a development of the 16th-cent. practice of pairing a slow dance with a quick one (*v.* PAVANE, GALLIARD). The 18th-cent. symphony normally consisted of three or four movements. The three-movement symphony consisted of two quick movements with a slow movement in between (hence the term "slow movement" generally means a middle movement). If there were four movements, a minuet was generally included before or after the slow movement. Beethoven, in his fifth symphony, combined the scherzo (successor of the minuet) and the finale into a single movement. Later composers have gone further in relating movements together, *e.g.* Schumann in his fourth symphony, and Sibelius in his seventh symphony, where the various movements are linked into a continuous whole. *v.* SONATA, SONATA FORM, SYMPHONY.

Movimento [mo-vee-men'-to], *I.* (1) Speed. *Lo stesso movimento*, at the same speed.

(2) Movement (of a sonata, symphony, etc.).

Mozart [mo'-tsarrt], (1) CONSTANZE. *v.* WEBER (5).

(2) JOHANN GEORG LEOPOLD; *b.* Augsburg, Nov. 14, 1719; *d.* Salzburg, May 28, 1787. Violinist and composer. Studied at Salzburg University and later became court composer and vice-*Kapellmeister* of the Archbishop's orchestra. In 1747 he married Anna Maria Pertl. He taught and arranged tours for his children, Maria Anna and Wolfgang Amadeus. He wrote compositions in many forms. His *Versuch einer gründlichen Violinschule* (1756), one of the most important sources of information on the musical practices of his time, has been published, with an introduction, in an English translation by Editha Knocker (1948).

E. ANDERSON : *Letters of Mozart and his Family* (1938).

(3) WOLFGANG AMADEUS (christened Joannes Chrysostomus Wolfgangus Theophilus): *b.* Salzburg, Jan. 27, 1756; *d.* Vienna, Dec. 5, 1791. Composer. Son of (2). Showed early signs of musical talent and began to compose at 5. At 6 he played in Munich and Vienna, and in 1763 entered on a long tour with his father and sister Maria Anna ("Nannerl"), who as a player was also a prodigy, in Germany, Belgium, Paris, London (1764-5) and Holland. By the time of his return to Salzburg in Nov. 1766, he had composed his first three symphonies and some 30 other works, and arranged several piano concertos from sonatas of J. C. Bach. In 1768 he wrote his first stage works, and in 1769-71 accompanied his father to Italy, where he took lessons from Martini, copied Allegri's *Miserere* from memory, and showed enough knowledge of counterpoint to be elected a member of the Philharmonic Society of Bologna. His father's efforts to secure him a court position at Vienna failed, and he remained at Salzburg, composing prolifically, until his abrupt severance from the Archbishop's household in 1781. In the meantime he had the valuable experience of a tour which included Mannheim, Paris and Munich. After his dismissal he stayed in Vienna, taught and gave concerts, and married Constanze Weber; the minor appointment of chamber musician to the court (1787) merely involved him in the composition of quantities of dances. In 1789 he visited and played in Dresden, Leipzig (where he discussed Bach's music with Bach's successor Doles) and Berlin, and in the following year was disappointed

in his hope of being made *Kapellmeister* by the new Emperor Leopold II. Financial worries continued to the premature end of his life, which seemed to be foreshadowed in a strange way by the appearance in July 1791 of a mysterious stranger who was actually the steward of a nobleman who needed a composition in order to announce himself as a composer, and who commissioned from Mozart a *Requiem* for this anonymous patron. Mozart died before the work was finished and it was completed by his pupil Süssmayr.

Music flowed from Mozart unceasingly. He was in the habit of composing complete movements in his mind in all their detail before writing them down, as in the case of the overture to *Don Giovanni*, written two nights before the performance. With his innate liveliness of imagination went the ability to seize immediately on the essence of another composer's style and to possess it as part of his own. He was influenced all his life by the music of others, including J. C. Bach, C. P. E. Bach, Handel, Haydn, Johann Stamitz, and Gluck, yet he is the composer above all others to whose style the word " influence " is least appropriate. The endowments of surety of technique, infallible command of design, and keen dramatic sense made him the supreme master of the classical style in all the forms of the period.

Mozart's works were catalogued by Ludwig Köchel (1862) and are referred to by their numbers in Köchel (" K." numbers). The most recent edition of Köchel's catalogue is that by A. Einstein (1937). His principal compositions are:

(a) OPERAS: *Bastien und Bastienne* (K.50, 1788); *Mitridate* (K.87, 1770); *Lucio Silla* (K.135; 1772), *Il Re pastore* (K.208, 1775); *Idomeneo* (K.366, 1781); *Die Entführung aus dem Serail* (K.384, 1782); *Der Schauspieldirektor* (K.486, 1786); *Le nozze di Figaro* (K.492, 1786); *Don Giovanni* (K.527, 1787); *Così fan tutte* (K.588, 1790); *Die Zauberflöte* (K.620, 1791); *La clemenza di Tito* (K.621, 1791).

(b) ORCHESTRA: 41 symphonies which have acquired numbers, including *Paris* (No. 31, K.297, 1778), *Haffner* (No. 35, K.385, 1782), *Linz* (No. 36, K.425, 1783), *Prague* (No. 38, K.504, 1786), E♭ (No. 39, K.543, 1788), G minor (No. 40, K.550, 1788), *Jupiter* (No. 41, K. 551, 1788), and about 8 other symphonies. Numerous *divertimenti*, serenades, marches, etc., including *Eine kleine Nachtmusik* for strings (K.525, 1787).

(c) CONCERTOS: 21 for piano; one for two pianos; one for three pianos; 5 violin concertos; 2 for flute; one for clarinet; 4 for horn; one for flute and harp; *Sinfonia concertante* for violin and viola (K.364, 1779); *Sinfonia concertante* for oboe, clarinet, horn, and bassoon (K. App. 9,1778); 14 sonatas for organ and strings; 3 sonatas for organ and orchestra.

(d) CHAMBER MUSIC: 5 string quintets; 23 string quartets; *Adagio and Fugue* in C minor (K.546, 1788) for string quartet; 2 piano quartets; 7 piano trios; trio for clarinet, viola and piano (K.498, 1786); clarinet quintet; horn quintet; quintet for piano and wind; 2 flute quartets; oboe quartet; 37 violin sonatas (two unfinished).

(e) PIANO: 17 sonatas; 2 Fantasias; 15 sets of variations; sonata for two pianos (K.448, 1781); 6 sonatas for piano duet (one unpublished); *Adagio and Allegro* in F minor (K.594, 1790) and *Fantasia* in F minor (K.608, 1791) for piano duet (both originally for a mechanical organ).

(f) CHURCH MUSIC: 18 Masses; 4 litanies; *Requiem* (K.626, 1791).

H. ABERT : *W. A. Mozart* (enlarged ed. of Jahn), 2 vols. (7th ed., 1955-6).

E. ANDERSON : *The Letters of Mozart and his Family*, 3 vols. (1938).

E. BLOM : *Mozart* (1935).

E. J. DENT : *Mozart's Operas* (2nd ed., 1947).

A. E. F. DICKINSON : *Mozart's Last Three Symphonies* (1927).

T. DUNHILL: *Mozart's String Quartets* (1927).
A. EINSTEIN: *Mozart* (1945).
C. M. GIRDLESTONE: *Mozart and his Piano Concertos* (1948).
A. HUTCHINGS: *A Companion to Mozart's Piano Concertos* (1948).
O. JAHN: *The Life of Mozart*, trans. by P. D. Townsend, 3 vols. (1891).
A. H. KING: *Mozart in Retrospect* (1956).
H. C. R. LANDON AND D. MITCHELL: *The Mozart Companion* (1956).
T. DE WYZEWA & G. DE SAINT-FOIX: *W. A. Mozart: sa vie musicale et son oeuvre*, 5 vols. (1912-46).

Mudd, THOMAS: *b. c.* 1560. Organist and composer. Studied at Cambridge and was a fellow of Pembroke until 1590. Organist, Peterborough Cathedral, 1631. His anthems are confused with those of John Mudd who was organist of Peterborough Cathedral from 1584. A set of 9 dances in manuscript in the British Museum is by Thomas.

Muette de Portici, La [la mee-et der porr-tee-see] (The Dumb Girl of Portici). Opera in five acts by Auber (known in Italian as *Masaniello*). Libretto by Augustin Eugène Scribe and Germain Delavigne. First performed, Paris, Feb. 29, 1828.

Muffat [moof'-ut], (1) GEORG: *b.* Schlettstadt, *c.* 1645; *d.* Passau, Feb. 23, 1740. Composer and organist. Studied for six years with Lully in Paris. He was organist of Strasbourg Cathedral and *c.* 1678 became organist to the Bishop of Salzburg. Organist, 1690, and *Kapellmeister*, 1695, to the Bishop of Passau. He published many organ works, including *Apparatus musico-organisticus* (1690). His *Florilegium* (1695-6), consisting of orchestral suites (*ouvertures*) in the style of Lully has been reprinted in *D.T.Ö.*, i & ii, some of the sonatas from *Armonico tributo* (1682) and his *Auserlesene Instrumental-Musik* (1701) in *D.T.Ö.*, xi (2). The prefaces to three of his publications have been published in an English translation by O. Strunk in *Source Readings in Music History* (1950). The preface to the *Auserlesene Instrumental-Musik* tells us that he met Corelli and heard his concertos in Rome about 1682, and gives some interesting observations on the performance of concertos.

(2) GOTTLIEB (Theophil): *b.* Passau, April, 1690; *d.* Vienna, Dec. 10, 1770. Organist and composer. Son of (1). A pupil of Fux, and from 1717 court organist in Vienna. Organ and harpsichord works by him have been published in *D.T.O.*, xxix (2) and iii (3).

Mulliner, THOMAS. Organist. In the only contemporary record of his life he was entered in 1563 as *modulator organorum* at Corpus Christi College, Oxford. He compiled *c.* 1545 - *c.* 1570 a manuscript containing keyboard compositions and arrangements by Redford, Blitheman, Allwood, Shepherd, Tallis, Johnson and others, to which were added before 1587 some pieces for the cittern and gittern. Modern ed. in *Musica Britannica*, i.

D. STEVENS: *The Mulliner Book* (1952).

Munch [meensh], CHARLES: *b.* Strasbourg, Sept. 26, 1891. Violinist and conductor. Studied the violin at Strasbourg and in Berlin. Leader, Gewandhaus Orchestra, Leipzig, 1926. His career as a conductor began in Paris in 1933. Conductor, Société des Concerts du Conservatoire, 1938-45; Boston Symphony Orchestra, 1948.

Mundharmonika [moont'-harr-moh'-nee-ca], *G.* Mouth organ.

Mundy, (1) JOHN: *d.* Windsor, 1630. Organist and composer. Educated by his father, William Mundy. Gentleman of the Chapel Royal, organist of Eton College and afterwards John Marbeck's successor at St. George's Chapel, Windsor. He published *Songs and Psalms* (1594), a collection of madrigals and airs (modern ed. in *E.M.S.*, xxxv), and contributed a madrigal to *The Triumphes of Oriana*, xxxii). Several of his keyboard compositions are in the *Fitzwilliam Virginal Book*.

(2) WILLIAM: *d. c.* 1591. Composer. Father of (1). Chorister at Westminster Abbey, vicar-choral of St. Paul's Cathedral, and a gentleman of the Chapel Royal for nearly 30 years under Elizabeth. His compositions include services, anthems and motets.

Muris [deh moo'-reece], JOHANNES (Jean) DE: *b.* before 1300; *d. c.* 1351. Theorist, mathematician, and philosopher. A friend of Philippe de Vitry, he supported the style and principles of notation of the *ars nova*. The *Speculum musicae* of Jacobus of Liège, formerly attributed to de Muris, takes the opposite view. His writings have been reprinted in Gerbert's *Scriptores*, iii and in Coussemaker's *Scriptores*, iii. An English translation of his *Ars novae musicae* is in O. Strunk, *Source Readings in Music History* (1950).

Murrill, HERBERT HENRY JOHN: *b.* London, May 11, 1909; *d.* there, July 25, 1952. Composer. Studied at the R.A.M. and at Worcester College, Oxford. Teacher of composition, R.A.M., 1933. Joined the music staff of the B.B.C. in 1936, and later became B.B.C. Head of Music. His compositions include 2 concertos for cello and orchestra, *Man in Cage* (a jazz opera, 1929), and incidental music for films, ballets and plays.

Musette [mēē-zet], *Fr.* Bagpipe. It became popular in the pastoral entertainments fashionable in the French court in the early 18th century. From it is derived the musical style of suite movements called by the same name.

Musica Britannica. A collection of British music published by the Royal Musical Association with the support of the Arts Council of Great Britain. The following volumes have appeared:

I. *The Mulliner Book*, ed. D. Stevens (1951).
II. M. LOCKE AND C. GIBBONS: *Cupid and Death*, ed. E. J. Dent (1951).
III. T. A. ARNE: *Comus*, ed. J. Herbage (1951).
IV. *Mediaeval Carols*, ed. J. Stevens (1952).
V. T. TOMKINS: *Keyboard Music*, ed. S. D. Tuttle (1955).
VI. J. DOWLAND: *Ayres for Four Voices*, transcribed by E. H. Fellowes, ed. R. T. Dart and N. Fortune (1953).
VII. J. BLOW: *Coronation Anthems and Anthems with Strings*, ed. A. Lewis and H. W. Shaw (1953).
VIII. J. DUNSTABLE: *Complete Works*, ed. M. F. Bukofzer (1953).
IX. *Jacobean Consort Music*, ed. R. T. Dart and W. Coates (1955).
X-XI. *The Eton Choirbook*, i & ii, ed. F. Ll. Harrison (1956, 1959).
XIII. WILLIAM BOYCE: *Overtures*, ed. G. Finzi (1957).
XV. *Music of Scotland, 1500-1700*, ed. K. Elliott (1957).

Musica da camera [moo'-zee-cah dah cah'-meh-rah], *I.* Chamber music.

Musica falsa [moo'-si-ca fahl'-sa], **Musica ficta** [moo'-si-ca fick'-ta], *L.* The former term was used by theorists in the early Middle Ages in discussing the use of accidentals which lay outside the Guidonian hexachord system. Later medieval theorists applied the latter term to transpositions of the hexachord whereby (in addition to B♭), E♭, A♭, and D♭ became necessary. In modern times this term is also used in referring to the accidentals which, it is presumed, singers in the 15th and early 16th cent. supplied to provide a B♭ for the mode on F and leading notes for the modes on D, G and A. In modern editions these are indicated above the staff. No convincing basis for the presumption has been proposed, and there is no general agreement about the extent of its application.

Musical Box. *v.* MECHANICAL MUSICAL INSTRUMENTS.

Musical Criticism. *v.* CRITICISM.

Musical Glasses. *v.* HARMONICA.

Musical Joke, A. *v.* MUSIKALISCHER SPASS.

Musical Offering. *v.* MUSIKALISCHES OPFER.

Musica mensurata [moo'-si-ca men-soo-rah'-ta], *L.* *v.* MENSURAL MUSIC.

Musica plana [moo'-si-ca plah'-na], *L.* Medieval term for plainsong.

Musica reservata [moo'-si-ca ress-air-vah'-ta], *L.* A term used in the latter part of the 16th cent. to indicate music suitable for connoisseurs and private occasions, and more particularly music which gave vivid and faithful expression to the spirit of the words. The first known reference to it is in the work of Adrianus Petit Coclicus, author of a *Compendium musices* (1552) and a collection of psalm settings entitled *Musica reservata*.

E. LOWINSKY: *Secret Chromatic Art in the Netherlands Motet* (1946).

Musica Transalpina [moo'-si-ca trahnss-ahl-pee'-na], *L.* Title of the first printed collection of Italian madrigals with English words, published by Nicholas Yonge in 1588, shortly after Byrd's *Psalmes, Sonets and Songs.* It contained 55 madrigals by Italian composers and 2 by Byrd, and was the first of a series of anthologies of Italian madrigals published in England in the latter part of the 16th century. Yonge published a second collection with the same title in 1597.

Music Makers, The. Ode for contralto solo, chorus and orchestra by Elgar, Op. 69. Words by Arthur O'Shaughnessy. First performed, Birmingham, Oct. 1, 1912. The music includes quotations from the following works by the composer: *The Dream of Gerontius*, *Sea Pictures*, *Enigma* Variations, violin concerto, 1st and 2nd symphonies. Fragments of "Rule Britannia" and the "Marseillaise" are also introduced.

Music Printing. *v.* PRINTING OF MUSIC.

Musicology (*Fr.* musicologie, *G.* Musikwissenschaft). The systematic study of musical composition and its history. The term *musikalische Wissenschaft* (musical science), implying the application of scientific methods to the investigation of the nature and history of music, was first used in 1863 by Friedrich Chrysander, and was adopted in the title of the periodical *Vierteljahrschrift für Musikwissenschaft* (1885). In its first volume Guido Adler divided the subject of musicology into a *historical* part (comprising musical palaeography, the grouping of musical forms, the norms of composition in practice and theory, and musical instruments) and a *systematic* part (including canons of harmony, rhythm, and melody, musical aesthetics, musical pedagogics, and musical ethnography), and enumerated the general and particular studies auxiliary to each part (*e.g.* liturgiology, history of the dance, acoustics). As both the value and the limitations of a "scientific" approach to the explanation of the historical development of musical styles have become apparent, the term has more recently been applied to the study of musical history, and in particular to the transcribing and editing of manuscripts and early prints, and the discovery and interpretation of new knowledge about composers, institutions, instruments, forms, and methods of performance. Besides compositions, modern editions extend to the treatises of theorists, textbooks on performance, dictionaries, and the writings of critics. The central object of musicology remains the search for fuller understanding of the art of the composer as it concerns the performer, the listener and the historian.

G. HAYDON: *Introduction to Musicology* (1941).

Musikalischer Spass, Ein [ine moo-zee-cah′-lish-er shpahss], *G.* (A Musical Joke). A miniature symphony in F by Mozart, K.522 (1787), for 2 horns and strings. There are four movements. The work is a caricature of the work of any third-rate composer of the period. It imitates remorselessly all the most threadbare conventions—melodic, harmonic and rhythmic—and provides each movement with a form as rigid as a strait-jacket. For good measure the slow movement includes a pretentious cadenza for solo violin. The alternative title *Dorfmusikanten-Sextett* (sextet for village musicians), which it has inherited from a 19th-cent. publisher, has neither authority nor justification. The work is not chamber music, and it is not incompetent performers who are parodied but incompetent composers.

Musikalisches Opfer [moo-zi-cah′-lish-ĕss ope′-fer], *G.* (Musical Offering). A set of pieces, including two *ricercari* (fugues), several canons and a sonata for flute, violin and harpsichord, written by Bach (1747) on a theme by Frederick the Great (*B.G.*, xxxi, 2). It originated in an improvisation which Bach was invited to give when he visited Potsdam. The work was printed and dedicated to Frederick the Great (*v.* H. T. David & A. Mendel, *The Bach Reader*, p. 179.) The initial letters of the inscription "Regis Iussu Cantio Et Reliqua Canonica Arte Resoluta" (a theme and other things worked out in canon by the king's command) make the word *ricercar*. Bach's delight in acrostics, evident from this inscription, finds expression also in the directions given for solving the canons. There are practical modern editions by Ludwig Landshoff and H. T. David.

Musique concrète [mēē-zeek cōn-cret], *Fr.* A type of music which has been made possible by recent developments in tape-recording. The sounds are produced not by voices and instruments but by electronic means and are combined in any way suggested by the fancy or the ingenuity of the composer. Music of this kind has been found effective as a background to dramatic action on the stage but is not yet universally accepted as a form of art.

P. SCHAEFFER (ed.): *Vers une musique expérimentale* (1957).

Musique de chambre [mĕĕ-zeek der shŭnbr], *Fr.* Chamber music.

Musique de table [mĕĕ-zeek der tubl], *Fr.* *v.* TABLE (3).

Musique mesurée à l'antique [mĕĕ-zeek mer-zĕĕ-ray a lŭn-teek], *Fr.* Music in which the rhythm was rigidly governed by the metre of the poetry which it set, practised by the composers and poets of the *Académie de Poésie et de Musique* founded by de Baïf and de Courville in Paris in 1570. Costeley, Mauduit, Claude le Jeune and Caurroy were the chief composers concerned. A long syllable in the metre was always set to a minim or its equivalent and a short syllable to a crotchet or its equivalent, and all the parts moved in syllabic homophony. Le Jeune's *Pseaumes en vers mesurées* (1606) have been reprinted by H. Expert in *Les Maîtres musiciens de la Renaissance française*, xx-xxii, and Mauduit's *Chansonettes mesurees de Jean-Antoine de Baïf* (1586) in the same series, x.

F. A. YATES: *The French Academies of the Sixteenth Century* (1947).

Mussorgsky. *v.* MOUSSORGSKY.

Muta [moo'-tah], *I.* Imperative of *mutare* (to change). A direction to the performer found in parts for wind instruments and timpani, indicating either a change of instrument (*e.g.* flute to piccolo, oboe to cor anglais, B♭ clarinet to A clarinet), or a change of crook (*e.g.* horn in F to horn in E), or a change of tuning (for timpani). *Muta in flauto grande* (in a piccolo part) = change from piccolo to flute. *Muta in mi* (in a horn part) = change to horn in E. *Mutano* (3rd person plur. of the present indicative) also occurs where more than one instrument is concerned.

Mutano [moo'-tah-no], *I.* "They change." *v.* MUTA.

Mutation. The change from the syllables of one HEXACHORD to those of another in SOLMIZATION. In singing the scale the change was usually made by substituting *re* for *sol* or *la* in ascending and *la* for *re* or *mi* in descending, *ut* being used for the lowest note only, *e.g.* (from N. Listenius, *Musica*, 1549):

Morley's examples in his *Plaine and Easie Introduction* dispense with *ut* and *re*, *e.g.*:

The use of *fa* on E♭ is an example of MUSICA FICTA, by which hexachords on notes other than C, G and F had gradually been brought into use.

Mutation Stops. Organ stops which produce a sound other than the pitch corresponding to the key which is depressed or to its octaves. Quint stops (*e.g.*, the twelfth, $2\frac{2}{3}$ ft.) sound the twelfth (the third note of the HARMONIC SERIES), and Tierce stops (*e.g.*, Tierce, Larigot $1\frac{3}{5}$ ft.) the seventeenth (the fifth note of the harmonic series), above the foundation note or one of its octaves. *v.* MIXTURE, ORGAN.

Mute (*Fr.* sourdine, *G.* Dämpfer, *I.* sordino). A device for softening the tone of a musical instrument. Stringed instruments are muted by placing the mute across the strings at the bridge. The muting of brass instruments, which involves a more noticeable change of tone-quality, is done by inserting into the bell a pear-shaped piece of wood or metal. The indication is *con sordino*. The piano is muted by means of a soft pedal, which moves the hammers either towards the strings, so that their length of travel is shortened, or parallel to the strings so that they strike only one or two strings. The indication is *una corda*. Drums may be muted by the use either of a cloth or of sponge-headed drumsticks. Mahler writes for drums *con sordino* in the third movement of his first symphony.

My Fatherland. *v.* MÁ VLAST.

Mystery Play. *v.* TROPE.

N

Nabokov [na-baw′-coff], NICOLAS: *b.* St. Petersburg, Apr. 17, 1903. Composer. Studied in Berlin and Stuttgart. During the 1920's he worked with Diaghilev's ballet and later settled in the United States. His compositions include ballets, orchestral and choral works, a piano concerto, flute concerto, a string quartet and 2 piano sonatas. A book of reminiscences, *Old Friends and New Music*, was published in 1951.

Nabucodonosor [nah-boo-co-do-no′-zorr]. Opera in four acts by Verdi (generally known as *Nabucco*). Libretto by Temistocle Solera. First performed, Milan, March 9, 1842.

Nacaire [na-cair], *Fr.* (*E.* naker). Medieval name for a small kettledrum. Derived from the Arabic *naqqára*, small kettledrums used in pairs, which were brought into Europe *c.* 1300.

Nachschlag [nahkh′-shlahk], *G.* (*E.* springer, acute; *Fr.* accent, aspiration, plainte). An ornament in German music of the 17th and 18th centuries. In its most usual form it was played as a short passing note between two notes a third apart (the French called this *couler les tierces*), as in this example from the opening of Bach's choral prelude "Allein Gott in der Höh' sei Ehr'":

Notation

Played

In another form the *Nachschlag* is an equivalent to the English SPRINGER.

In later music the term denotes the two notes which end a trill:

Notation

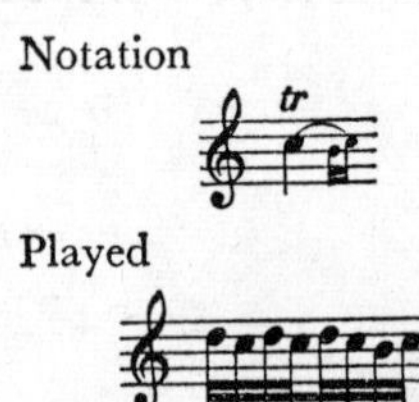

Played

Nachtanz [nahkh′-tunts], *G.* Lit. "following dance." A dance in quick triple time which follows a dance in duple time in German instrumental music of the 16th and 17th centuries. It was also called *Proportz* (*i.e.*, in *proportio tripla*), *Hupf auff* (hopping up) as in Hans Neusiedler's *Hoftanz* for lute printed in the *Historical Anthology* (No. 105), and *tripla*, as in the suites in J. H. Schein's *Banchetto musicale* of 1617 (modern ed. by A. H. Prufer, 1901). Dances most often paired in this way were the PAVANE and GALLIARD in the 16th cent. and the ALLEMANDE and COURANTE in the 17th. The second dance of the pair was commonly a rhythmically altered form of the first, as in Posch's *Musikalische Tafelfreudt* of 1621, reprinted in *D.T.Ö.*, XXV (2). The allemande-courante sequence was incorporated into the SUITE.

Nagel [nahg′-ĕl], WILLIBALD: *b.* Mulheim-on-Ruhr, Jan. 12, 1863; *d.* Stuttgart, Oct. 17, 1929. Studied in Berlin under Spitta and Bellermann. He taught music history at Zürich and from 1893-6 lived in London doing research in early English music. He afterwards lived in Darmstadt, Stuttgart, and Zürich. Published the results of his researches in a history of English music (2 vols., 1891, 1897) and also wrote on the piano sonatas of Beethoven.

Nagelclavier [nahg′-ĕl-cluv-eer], *G.* Nail piano. *v.* under NAIL VIOLIN.

Nagelgeige (nahg′-ĕl-gy-ger), *G.* Nail violin.

Nail Violin (*G.* Nagelgeige). An

instrument devised by Johann Wilde in St. Petersburg in 1740. It consisted of a semicircular resonator of wood into which were driven U-shaped nails of graduated lengths. The sound was produced by a bow. In 1791 Träger of Bernburg extended the idea to the nail piano (*Nagelclavier*) in which the sound was produced by the friction of a wheel.

Naker. English medieval name for a small kettledrum. *v.* NACAIRE.

Nanino [nah-nee'-no], GIOVANNI MARIA: *b.* Tivoli, *c.* 1545; *d.* Rome, March 11, 1607. Composer. Chorister at Vallerano. Studied in Rome under Palestrina, whom he succeeded at S. Maria Maggiore. *Maestro di cappella*, S. Luigi de' Francesi, 1575; singer in the Papal Chapel, 1577; *maestro di cappella*, Sistine Chapel, 1604. Assisted by his brother, Giovanni Bernardino, who was also a composer, and Palestrina he established a school of composition in Rome. In general, his madrigals, motets, and other church music are in the style of his teacher, though somewhat less conservative. A four-part motet, "Hic est beatissimus Evangelista," is printed in the *Historical Anthology*, No. 152.

Nardini [narr-dee'-nee], PIETRO: *b.* Leghorn, Apr. 12, 1722; *d.* Florence, May 7, 1793. Violinist and composer. Studied at Leghorn and later at Padua under Tartini. He was appointed solo violinist at the ducal court of Würtemberg at Stuttgart and in 1771 musical director at the court in Florence. His violin-playing was praised by Leopold Mozart. His compositions include 6 violin concertos, sonatas, string quartets, and keyboard sonatas.

Nares, JAMES: *bapt.* Stanwell (Middlesex), Apr. 19, 1715; *d.* London, Feb. 10, 1783. Organist and composer. Studied with Pepusch as a chorister at the Chapel Royal in London. He became deputy organist at St. George's Chapel, Windsor, and in 1734 was appointed organist of York Minster. From 1756 he was Greene's successor at the Chapel Royal and from 1757-80 master of the children. Composed church music, harpsichord lessons (a Sonata in D, which has been edited by H. G. Ley, is one of his best works), glees and catches, and wrote treatises on singing and keyboard playing.

Narvaez [deh narr-vah'-eth], LUIS DE; 16th-cent. Spanish lutenist and composer. His book of lute music of 1538 (*Los seys libros del Delphín de música*) contains some of the earliest examples of variation form (modern ed. by E. M. Torner). An example is printed in the *Historical Anthology* (No. 122). He also composed motets.

National Music. In addition to those traits of national character in music which can be described only in the most general terms, the more concrete differences of practice in composition and performance, of musical forms and their social functions, and of idioms in folk music have always had their effects on the course of musical history. In the 15th cent. Tinctoris remarked on the conservatism of the English, who in contrast to the French persisted in using the same way of composing, "which is a sign of a very poor talent"; and the Italian theorist Guilielmus explained to his fellow countrymen how some of the English methods (*regulae contrapuncti Anglicorum*) worked. The English madrigal and ballet were at first imitations of the "kinds of songs which the Italians make." Both J. H. Schein in his *Opella Nova* (1618) and Heinrich Schütz in his *Psalms* (1619) mentioned the Italian composers to whom they owed their knowledge of the new styles they introduced to Lutheran music, Schein to Viadana and Schütz to Giovanni Gabrieli. Italian opera and Italian instrumental music led the way in the 17th cent., as Dryden observed:

> The wise *Italians* first invented show;
> Thence, into *France* the noble Pageant past;
> 'Tis *England's* Credit to be cozen'd last.
> (Prologue to *Albion and Albanius*).

Both Purcell (Preface to *Sonatas of Three Parts*, 1683) and Couperin (Preface to *Les Goûts réunis*, 1724) acknowledged Italian influence. Couperin essayed the union of French and Italian styles (*Les Goûts réunis* and *Les Nations*, 1726), while J. S. Bach and Georg Muffat united both with traditions of North and South Germany. The differences between the French and Italian styles in opera were the issues in the *guerre des bouffons*. The object of the nationalist movement in the music of the Romantic period was to accentuate these differences rather than to absorb them, and folk music and folk stories were the obvious means of doing so. Glinka wrote from Berlin in 1833 about the opera (*A Life for the Czar*) which was taking shape in his mind; " In every way it will be absolutely national—and not only the subject but the music." In the past hundred years every country has had its national music and its folksong revival, but since 1910 national differences have once more been absorbed and overridden in the cosmopolitan styles of Schönberg, Stravinsky, Walton, Bartók and Hindemith.

R. VAUGHAN WILLIAMS : *National Music* (1934).

Natural. A note which is neither sharp nor flat is natural. The sign ♮ is used to indicate it for a note which is sharp or flat in the key-signature or had an accidental earlier in the same bar. *v.* also B.

Natural Horn, Natural Trumpet. A horn or trumpet which is not provided with any method, such as valves, of altering the length of the tube, and can therefore sound no other notes than those of the HARMONIC SERIES above its fundamental, except as stopped notes. The natural instruments were used until early in the 19th cent. *v.* HORN, STOP (4), TRUMPET, VALVE.

Naufrageurs, Les [lay no-fra-zher]. *v.* WRECKERS.

Naumann [now'-mun], (1) EMIL; *b.* Berlin, Sept. 8, 1827; *d.* Dresden, June 23, 1888. Musical historian. Studied at the Leipzig Conservatorium and at Bonn University. In 1856 he was appointed Court director of church music in Berlin, in 1873 lecturer at the Conservatorium in Dresden, and in 1880 succeeded W. Rust as organist of St. Thomas's, Leipzig. His books include a *History of Music* (1880-85) which was translated into English in 1886.

(2) JOHANN GOTTLIEB; *b.* Blasewitz (nr. Dresden), Apr. 17, 1741; *d.* Dresden, Oct. 13, 1801. Composer. Travelled to Padua, where he had lessons from Tartini and met Hasse. He went to Naples in 1761 and later studied counterpoint under Padre Martini at Bologna. He produced his first opera in Venice and in 1764 became court composer of church music in Dresden. From 1765-68 he lived in Italy and in 1776 became *Kapellmeister* at Dresden. He composed some 26 operas, oratorios, church music, chamber music and songs.

Naylor, EDWARD WOODALL: *b.* Scarborough, Feb. 9, 1867; *d.* Cambridge, May 7, 1934. Writer and composer. Studied at the R.C.M. from 1888-92 and at Cambridge. Organist, St. Michael's, Chester Square, London, 1889; St. Mary's, Kilburn, 1896-7. He then became organist and in 1908 lecturer at Emmanuel College, Cambridge. His compositions include an opera *The Angelus* (1909), which won the Ricordi prize for an English work, services and other church music, songs and part-songs. He wrote *Shakespeare and Music* (1896, revised 1931), and *An Elizabethan Virginal Book* (1905), a discussion of the Fitzwilliam Virginal Book.

Neapolitan Sixth. The name given to a 6/3 chord with a minor sixth and minor third on the fourth degree of the scale, *e.g.* in the key of A minor:

It derives from the following cadential progression:

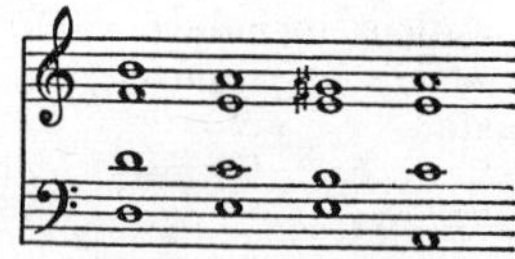

If the B in the first chord is flattened, the chord becomes a Neapolitan sixth:

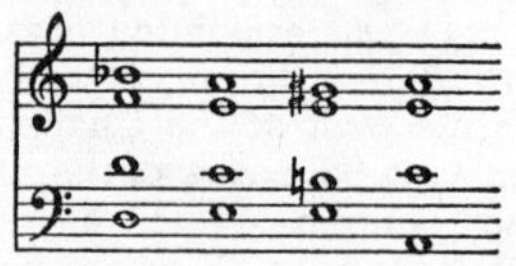

The progression can be made more concise by eliminating the second chord:

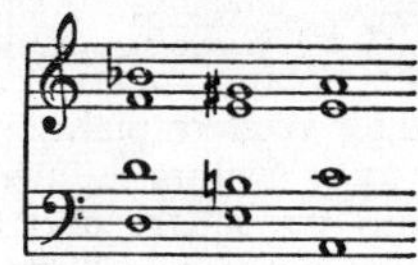

Though the chord occurs more frequently in minor keys, it was also used in a similar way in major keys. Its name seems to be due to the use made of it, for pathetic effect, by opera-composers at Naples in the 17th century. It retained its pathetic associations in the work of later composers, *e.g.*:

SULLIVAN, *H.M.S. Pinafore*

Neefe [nafe'-*er*], CHRISTIAN GOTTLOB: *b.* Chemnitz, Feb. 5, 1748; *d.* Dessau, Jan. 26, 1798. Conductor and composer. Studied under Hiller and succeeded him as conductor of a travelling opera company in 1776. Conducted the Grossman-Hellmuth Society at Bonn in 1779 and became organist at the Court of the Elector in 1781. Beethoven became his pupil at the age of 11. In 1796-7 he conducted the Dessau opera. He wrote 8 *Singspiele*, and his *Adelheit von Veltheim* (1780), produced two years before Mozart's *Entführung*, was one of the earliest German operas on a Turkish subject. He also composed songs and piano sonatas.

Neel, LOUIS BOYD : *b.* London, July 19, 1905. Conductor. Educated at Cambridge and studied medicine in London. Founded the Boyd Neel Orchestra (originally consisting only of strings), 1932. In the course of the next twenty years the orchestra established a reputation and toured frequently abroad. Neel was appointed Dean of the Faculty of Music, Toronto University, in 1953, and was succeeded as director of the orchestra by Thurston Dart.

Nelsonmesse [nell'-son-mess'-*er*], *G.* The name given to Haydn's Mass in D minor, composed in 1798 (No. 9 in the new complete edition, no. 3 in Novello's edition). The dramatic entry of trumpets and timpani in the *Benedictus* is said to commemorate Nelson's victory at the Battle of the Nile. Also known as the *Missa de angustiis*, and in England as the *Imperial Mass*.

Nenna [nen'-nah], POMPONIO: *b.* Bari (nr. Naples), *c.* 1560; *d.* before 1618. Italian composer. Probably the teacher of Gesualdo. He published his first book of madrigals in 1582, and 8 books thereafter.

Neri [neh'-ree], MASSIMILIANO: 17th-cent. organist and composer. First organist at St. Mark's, Venice, 1644; court organist to the Elector of Cologne, 1664. His compositions include a book of motets (1664), *Sonate e canzone in chiesa et in camera* (1644) and sonatas for 3 to 12 instruments (1651). He continued the tradition of the ensemble *canzona* of Giovanni Gabrieli and was also a practitioner of the new style of the sonata.

Nettl [net'l], PAUL: *b.* Hohenelbe, Jan. 10, 1889. Musical historian. Studied in Prague. Lecturer, German University, Prague, 1920. Director, Prague German Radio, 1931. In 1938 he went to the United States and later became professor of music history at the University of Indiana. His publications include *The Story of Dance Music* (1947), *The Book of Musical Documents* (1948), *The Other Casanova* (1950), *Forgotten Composers* (1951) and *Beethoven Encyclopedia* (1956).

Neue Liebeslieder [noy'-*er* leeb'-ěssleed-er], *G.* (New Songs of Love). A set of 14 waltzes with an epilogue (*Zum Schluss*) for vocal quartet and piano by Brahms, Op. 65—a sequel to the earlier set entitled *Liebeslieder*, Op. 65. Words of the waltzes by Georg Friedrich Daumer; words of the epilogue by Goethe.

Neues vom Tage [noy'-ĕss fom tahg'-er] (News of the Day). Opera in three parts by Hindemith. Libretto by Marcellus Schiffer. First performed, Berlin, June 8, 1929. Revised version, 1953.

Neukomm [noy'-com], SIGISMUND, CHEVALIER VON: *b.* Salzburg, July 10, 1778; *d.* Paris, Apr. 3, 1858. Composer. Chorister at Salzburg Cathedral. Studied under Michael Haydn, and under Joseph Haydn in Vienna. He went to Sweden and Russia in 1806 and became *Kapellmeister* of the German theatre in St. Petersburg. In 1809 he settled in Paris and made the acquaintance of Grétry, Cherubini and Cuvier. In 1812 he succeeded Dussek as pianist to Talleyrand. He accompanied the Duke of Luxembourg to Rio de Janeiro in 1816 and stayed there as *maître de chapelle* to Dom Pedro until the revolution of 1821. He accompanied Talleyrand on several of his tours. He went to London and met Mendelssohn at the home of Moscheles. The last years of his life he lived alternately in Paris and London. His compositions include operas, over 200 songs, piano and organ pieces, choral and chamber music, oratorios, Masses and a requiem for Louis XVI (1815).

Neuma [new'-ma] (a misspelling of *Gr.* πνεῦμα, breath). A phrase of melody used by medieval theorists to illustrate the characteristics and range of a MODE. The following is the neuma of the first mode in the Salisbury rite (W. H. Frere, *The Use of Sarum*, ii, Appendix p. lxvii):

A neuma was occasionally used as the tenor in a 13th-cent. MOTET, *e.g.* the neuma given above is the tenor of the motet "Salve virgo Ave lux" (Y. Rokseth, *Polyphonies du XIIIe siècle*, ii, p. 131).

Neume (*Gr.* νεῦμα, sign). An individual sign in the notation used for Eastern chant, and for Western plainsong. By the end of the 12th century the neumes had evolved into the square and diamond-shaped forms of note which are still used in the printing of plainsong. *v.* NOTATION.

Neusiedler [noy'-zeed-ler], (1) HANS: *b.* Pressburg (now Bratislava), 1508-9; *d.* Nuremberg, Feb. 2, 1563. Lutenist and composer. Lived in Nuremberg from *c.* 1530 and published collections of lute music in German tablature in 1536, 1540 and 1544. Some compositions have been published in *D.T.Ö.*, xviii (2), and a very curious "bitonal" *Jew's Dance* in the *Historical Anthology*, No. 105.

(2) MELCHIOR: *b.* Pressburg, 1507; *d.* Nuremberg, 1590. Brother of (1). Lutenist and composer. Lived in Augsburg from 1552-61, in Italy for some time after 1565, and in Innsbruck from 1580. Published two collections of lute music in Italian tablature at Venice in 1566, a *Deutsch Lautenbuch* in 1574, and lute versions of 6 motets by Josquin des Prés in 1587. Some compositions have been published in *D.T.Ö.*, xviii (2).

Newman, ERNEST: *b.* Liverpool, Nov. 30, 1868. Music critic and writer on music. Studied at Liverpool College and University and later went into business in Liverpool. In 1903 he was appointed to the staff of the Midland Institute, Birmingham. Music critic, *Manchester Guardian*, 1905; *Birmingham Post*, 1906; *Observer*, 1919; *Sunday Times*, 1920-58. He was guest critic on the New York *Evening Post*, 1924-5. His publications include *Gluck and the Opera* (1895), *Hugo Wolf* (1907), *A Musical Critic's Holiday* (1925), *Opera Nights* (1943), *More Opera Nights* (1955) and *The Life of Richard Wagner* (4 vols., 1933-47).

Newmarch, ROSA HARRIET (*née* Jeaffreson): *b.* Leamington, Dec. 18, 1857; *d.* Worthing, Apr. 9, 1940. Writer on music. In 1897 she went to Russia, studied at the Imperial Public Library under Vladimir Stassov and came into contact with most of the composers of the day. She wrote many articles and lectures on Russian music and art, and from 1908-27 wrote programme notes for the Queen's Hall concerts. Her publications include *Tchaikovsky* (1900), *The Concert-goer's Diary* (1931) and *The Music of Czechoslovakia* (1942).

New World Symphony. *v.* FROM THE NEW WORLD.

New York Philharmonic-Symphony Orchestra. Founded by U. C. Hill in 1842 as the Philharmonic Society of New York. The oldest symphony orchestra in America. The New York Symphony Society (founded 1878 and conducted until 1885 by Leopold Damrosch, then by his son Walter) was absorbed in 1928. Permanent conductors have been: A. Seidl, 1892-8; E. Paur, 1898-1902; Safanov, 1906-09; Mahler, 1909-11; Stransky, 1911-20; Mengelberg, 1921-30; Toscanini, 1930-1936; Barbirolli, 1937-40; Rodzinsky, 1943-47; Bruno Walter, 1947-9; Dmitri Mitropoulos, 1950; Bernstein, 1958.

Niccolò [neek-co-lo']. *v.* ISOUARD.

Nichelmann [ni*sh*'-ĕl-mun], CHRISTOPHE: *b.* Treuenbrietzen (Brandenburg), Aug. 13, 1717; *d.* Berlin, July 20, 1762. Composer. Studied under J. S. Bach at Leipzig and later visited Hamburg, where he made the acquaintance of Mattheson and Telemann. Studied counterpoint under Quantz in Berlin and in 1744 was appointed second cembalist under C. P. E. Bach at the Court of Frederick the Great. His works include a treatise on melody (1755), harpsichord concertos and sonatas.

Nicholson (1) RICHARD: *d.* 1639. Organist and composer. Organist and choirmaster, Magdalen College, Oxford, 1595. In 1627 became the first professor of music at Oxford under Dr. William Heather's foundation. His compositions include anthems, a motet, madrigals, and a five-part pavan for viols. His five-part madrigal "Sing shepherds all" was published in *The Triumphes of Oriana* (modern ed. in *E.M.S.*, xxxii).

(2) SYDNEY: *b.* London, Feb. 9, 1875; *d.* Ashford (Kent), May 30, 1947. Organist and teacher. Educated at Rugby and New College, Oxford, and later studied at the R.C.M. under Parratt and Stanford, and at Frankfort-on-Main under Knorr. Organist, Carlisle Cathedral, 1904; Manchester Cathedral, 1908; Westminster Abbey, 1918-27. He then founded the School of English Church Music, which became the Royal School of Church Music in 1945, and directed it until his death. Knighted, 1938. His works include a history of English church choirs—*Quires and Places where they Sing* (1932), church music, and three light operas.

Nicolai [neek'-o-ly], (1) CARL OTTO EHRENFRIED: *b.* Königsberg, June 9, 1810; *d.* Berlin, May 11, 1849. Composer and conductor. Studied in Berlin under Zelter and Klein. Organist of the chapel of the Prussian Embassy at Rome in 1833, and studied there under Baini. In 1837-8 he was *Kapellmeister* of the Kärntnertor Theatre in Vienna, returned to Rome in 1838 and composed a series of operas, and from 1841-47 was first *Kapellmeister* of the court opera at Vienna. He founded the Vienna Philharmonic concerts in 1842. In 1847 he became director of the Court Opera in Berlin. His most famous work, the lively comic opera *Die lustigen Weiber von Windsor* (The Merry Wives of Windsor), was first produced there two months before his death. He also wrote 2 symphonies, chamber music, and some church music.

(2) PHILIPP: *b.* Mengeringhausen, Aug. 10, 1556; *d.* Hamburg, Oct. 26, 1608. Lutheran pastor, poet and amateur musician. Published his *Freudenspiegel des ewigen Lebens* (Frankfort, 1599) containing the melodies of two chorales which were frequently used by Lutheran composers down to J. S. Bach. They are known in English collections as "Sleepers, wake" and "How brightly shines the morning star."

Niecks [neeks], FRIEDRICH: *b.* Düsseldorf, Feb. 3, 1845; *d.* Edinburgh, June 24, 1924. Violinist and musical historian. Studied under his father and later under Langhans, Grunewald, Auer and Tausch. At thirteen he made his début as a violinist in Düsseldorf. In 1868 A. C. Mackenzie invited him to be violinist in his string quartet in Edinburgh. He was appointed Reid

Professor of Music at Edinburgh University in 1891. His books include *Frederick Chopin* (1888), *A History of Programme Music* (1907) and a biography of Schumann which was published posthumously in 1925.

Niedt [neet], FRIEDRICH ERHARD : *b.* Jena, May 31, 1674 ; *d.* Copenhagen, *c.* 1717. A notary-public of Jena. He published a *Musicalische Handleitung*, of which the first part (Hamburg, 1700) gives rules for playing from figured bass, contained in a story which has interesting particulars on the teaching practices of German organists. Bach borrowed from it in compiling rules and examples for use in teaching. The second part appeared in 1706, and the third, edited by Mattheson, posthumously in 1717.

F. T. ARNOLD : *The Art of Accompaniment from a Thorough-Bass* (1931).

Nielsen [neelce'-ĕn], (1) CARL AUGUST: *b.* Odense, June 9, 1865; *d.* Copenhagen, Oct. 2, 1931. Composer and conductor. Studied at the Copenhagen Conservatoire under Gade. Member of the Royal Orchestra, 1891; conductor, 1908-14. Director of the Conservatoire and conductor of the Musical Society, 1915-27. He also conducted in Scandinavia, Germany, Finland and London. His compositions include 2 operas, 6 symphonies, 3 concertos, 4 string quartets, cantatas, songs and piano pieces. The most important Danish composer of his time, he was a symphonist of an independent spirit who evolved a " modern " technique without renouncing tonal principles. Two volumes of his writings have been published in English translations: *My Childhood* (1953) and *Living Music* (1953).

R. SIMPSON : *Carl Nielsen* (1952).

(2) RICCARDO: *b.* Bologna, March 3, 1908. Composer. Studied at the Liceo Musicale of Bologna, at Salzburg and under Carlo Gatti in Milan. His compositions include *Sinfonia concertante* for piano and orchestra (1932), psalms for male voices and orchestra, chamber music, piano works and songs.

Niemann [nee'-mun], WALTER: *b.* Hamburg, Oct. 10, 1876. Composer and writer on music. Studied under his father and Humperdinck and at Leipzig under Riemann, Kretzschmar and Reinecke. Teacher, Hamburg Conservatorium, 1906-7; music critic, Leipzig *Neueste Nachrichten*, 1907-17. He has composed many piano pieces, works for string orchestra and chamber music, and published many books of musical biography and history.

Night in May, A. *v.* MAISKAYA NOCH.

Night on the Bare Mountain. Moussorgsky seems originally to have planned this composition as part of the music to Mengden's play *The Witch.* Later he turned it into a fantasia for orchestra (1886-7), used it in the third act of the opera *Mlada* (1872), and when he died left it as part of his unfinished opera *Sorochintsi Fair* (1875). Rimsky-Korsakov re-orchestrated the music and directed its first performance in St. Petersburg, 1886. There is a verbal description attached to the score:

> " Subterranean sounds of unearthly voices. Appearance of the spirits of darkness followed by that of the God Chernobog. Chernobog's glorification and the Black Mass. The Revels. At the height of the orgies is heard from afar the bell of a little church, which causes the spirits to disperse. Dawn."

Nights in the Gardens of Spain. *v.* NOCHES EN LOS JARDINES DE ESPAÑA.

Nikisch [nick'-ish], ARTHUR: *b.* Szent Miklos (Hungary), Oct. 12, 1855; *d.* Leipzig, Jan. 23, 1922. Conductor. Studied at the Vienna Conservatorium under Dessoff and Hellmesberger. Violinist in the Vienna Hofkapelle; second, and later (1882) first conductor of the Opera in Leipzig. Conductor, Boston Symphony Orchestra, 1889-93; Royal Opera, Budapest until 1895; Leipzig Gewandhaus and Berlin Philharmonic Orchestra (with which he made many tours) until his death. Director, Leipzig Conservatorium, 1902-07; Stadttheater, 1905-06. Toured the United States with the London Symphony Orchestra in 1912. One of the greatest conductors of his time, notably of Bruckner and Tchaikovsky.

Nin-Culmell [neen-cool-mell'], JOAQUÍN MARÍA: *b.* Berlin, Sept. 5, 1908. Pianist and composer. Son of Nin y Castellano. Studied in New York, in

Paris under Paul Braud and Dukas and in Granada under Manuel de Falla. His compositions include a sonata and a concerto for piano, a quintet for piano and strings, and songs. Now professor at the University of California.

Ninth. The interval of an octave and a second, *e.g.*:

For the so-called " chord of the ninth" *v.* CHORD.

Nin y Castellano [neen ee cust-el-lyah′-no], JOAQUÍN: *b.* Havana (Cuba), Sept. 29, 1879. Pianist and composer. Father of Nin-Culmell. Studied piano under Carlos Vidiella in Barcelona and in Paris under Moszkowski and at the Schola Cantorum, where he became teacher of piano in 1906. He lived for short periods in Berlin, Cuba, Brussels and Paris and in 1939 returned to Havana. He has edited collections of Spanish music and has composed piano pieces, works for violin and piano, a ballet and songs for voice and orchestra.

Nivers [nee-vair], GUILLAUME GABRIEL: *b.* nr. Malun, 1617; *d.* Paris, Dec. 1714. Composer and theorist, a pupil of Chambonnières. Organist of St. Sulpice, also organist to the King and music-master to the Queen. His *Méthode facile pour apprendre à chanter* (1666) established the use in France of *solfège* as opposed to SOLMIZATION, and the use of *si* for the leading-note of the scale. He also published a *Traité de la composition* (1667) and other treatises.

Nobilmente [no-beel-men′-teh], *I.* Nobly. A term often used by Elgar. It refers to the method of performance and not, as has sometimes been mistakenly supposed, to the composer's estimate of his music.

Noble, THOMAS TERTIUS: *b.* Bath, May 5, 1867; *d.* Rockport (Mass.), May 4, 1953. Organist and composer. Studied under Parratt, Bridge and Stanford at the R.C.M. Organist, Ely Cathedral, 1892; York Minster, 1898; St. Thomas's, Fifth Avenue, New York, 1912 (where he founded a choir school). He composed organ works, anthems and other church music.

Noces, Les [lay noss], *Fr.* (The Wedding). Ballet with music by Stravinsky for chorus, soloists, 4 pianos and 17 percussion instruments. First performed in Paris, June 13, 1923.

Noches en los Jardines de España [no′-chace en loss harr-deen′-ess deh ess-pah′-nyah] *Sp.* (Nights in the Gardens of Spain). Three " symphonic impressions " for piano and orchestra by Falla, composed 1909-15. Their titles are: *En el Generalife, Danza lejana* (Distant Dance), *En los jardines de la Sierra de Córdoba.*

Nocturne. Night-song. A name given by John Field, from whom Chopin adopted it, to piano pieces which had a *cantabile* melody, often elaborately ornamented, over an arpeggiated or chordal accompaniment.

Nocturnes [nock-tēērn], *Fr.* A set of three pieces for orchestra by Debussy, composed between 1893 and 1899. Their titles are: *Nuages, Fêtes* and *Sirènes.*

Noël [no-ell], *Fr.* A Christmas carol or song. Many collections of *noëls* have been published in vocal form since the 16th cent., and as arrangements and variations for organ since the 17th century. An example by N. A. Le Bègue from his *Troisième Livre d'Orgue* (*c.* 1690) is printed in the *Historical Anthology* (No. 231). A modern example is Marcel Dupré's *Variations sur un Noël.*

Noire [nwahrr], *Fr.* Crotchet (lit. " black note ").

Nola [dah no′-lah], GIOVANNI DOMENICO DEL GIOVANE DA: *b.* Nola; *d.* Naples, 1592. *Maestro di cappella,* Church of the Annunziata, Naples, 1563-88. His compositions, which were published between 1541-64, include motets, madrigals, and villanellas *alla Napolitana,* of which he was one of the earliest composers.

Nonet. A piece for nine solo instruments, *e.g.* Schubert's *Eine kleine Trauermusik,* for two clarinets, two bassoons and double bassoon, two horns, and two trombones (1812).

Nonnengeige [non′-ĕn-gy-ger], *G.* Lit., " nun's fiddle." One of the alternative names for the TROMBA MARINA.

Norcombe (Norcome), DANIEL : *b. c.* 1576 ; *d.* before 1626. Composer and violinist. At the Danish court, 1599, but fled from Copenhagen, travelling through Germany and Hungary to Venice. Later appointed a minor canon at St. George's Chapel, Windsor. The madrigal "With angel's face and brightness" in *The Triumphes of Oriana* (1601, modern ed. in *E.M.S.*, xxxii) is probably by him, while the pieces for viol in Simpson's *The Division Violist*, 1659) are probably by a relation with the same name.

Nordoff, PAUL : *b.* Philadelphia, June 4, 1909. Composer. Studied at the Philadelphia Conservatory and at the Juilliard School, New York, under Olga Samaroff and Goldmark. He was awarded Guggenheim fellowships in 1933 and in 1935. In 1938 he was appointed head of the composition department of the Philadelphia Conservatory of Music. He has composed an opera, piano concertos, chamber music and a *Secular Mass* for chorus and orchestra.

Norlind [noorr'-lind], JOHAN HENRIK TOBIAS : *b.* Hvellinge (Sweden), May 6, 1879 ; *d.* Stockholm, Aug. 13, 1947. Musical historian. Studied at the Leipzig Conservatorium under Bose and Jadassohn, in Munich under Thuille and Sandberger, and in Paris, London and Berlin. Professor, Lund, 1909. Director, Museum of Music History, 1918. He was the author of many books on music history and a Swedish dictionary of music.

Norma [norr'-mah]. Opera in two acts by Bellini. Libretto by Felice Romani. First performed, Milan, Dec. 26, 1831.

North, ROGER : *b.* Tostock (Suffolk), Sept. 3, 1653; *d.* Rougham, March 1, 1734. Lawyer and amateur musician. Attorney-General to James II. His *Memoires of Musick* (ed. by E. Rimbault, 1846) and *Musicall Gramarian* (ed. by Hilda Andrews, 1926) contain an interesting account of the music of his time and of the immediate past. His brother Francis, Lord Guilford, published *A Philosophical Essay on Music* (1677).

Nota cambiata [no'-tah cahm-byah'-ta], *I. v.* CAMBIATA.

Notation. The recording of music in writing must deal with the two chief elements in musical sound, pitch and rhythm. From the early Middle Ages letters were used to designate notes (*v.* ODO), as at present. By the 6th-7th cent. signs (neumes) over the words of plainsong were in use, both in the Eastern and Western churches. They had a common origin in the Greek prosodic signs, of which there were three which affected pitch—*oxeia* / (rise in pitch), *bareia* \ (fall in pitch), and *perispomene* ∧ (rise and fall). In evolving these signs into groups representing two or more notes, Eastern (*v.* BYZANTINE MUSIC) and Western notation followed different paths. In their early stages both were mnemonic notations, inexact as to pitch, and serving to remind singers of music they had already memorised.

The first step towards a more exact notation of pitch was the use of a red line, drawn through the neumes, to represent the pitch of F, the next the addition of a yellow or green line for C. In the preface to his Antiphoner of *c.* 1025 Guido of Arezzo pointed out that the writing of neumes on three, four or more lines, marked at the beginning with letters of the monochord, made it possible for singers to read the music for themselves. By the 13th cent. the four-line staff was accepted for plainsong and monophonic chansons, and the five-line staff for polyphonic music. There have been only occasional or periodic exceptions, such as the six- or seven-line staff in English keyboard music in the 16th century. Theoretically, any one of the three or more CLEFS may be placed on any line of the staff. The variety of positions in use until the 17th cent. has been progressively reduced in practice to one position each for the G and F clefs, and two for the C clef.

ACCIDENTALS are a device for changing the pitch of a line or space by a semitone, or two successive semitones. Their use has developed from the ♭ as a clef in plainsong to the KEY SIGNATURES of the complete key-system of the 18th century. The complications which arise from the notation of music in a completely chromatic (or even microtonal) system on a staff devised for diatonic music have given rise to some attempts to "reform" the notation of pitch, without practical result.

For the writing of music for stringed instruments on which chords and arpeggios were normally played, and of organ music in polyphonic style, various forms of TABLATURE notation were used in the 16th and 17th centuries. The advantage of tablature lies in its closer relation to the actual fingering of the stringed instrument, and to the style of organ music, as well as in its greater compactness.

The notation of rhythm has had a more varied history. The rhythm of neumes was not shown in their notation, but was established by their relation to the words, and by tradition and usage. Some manuscripts shortly before the 10th cent. had letters above the neumes (*e.g.* x=*expectare*, to wait; c=*celeriter*, quickly) which affected the rhythm, and *ad hoc* rhythmic signs were an important part of Byzantine notation. In the first period of mensurable music (*c.* 1150-*c.* 1250) the note-forms which had been evolved from the neumes were used in rhythmic patterns involving the relation: long=3 breves. The long ꟷ and breve ■ were used both singly and in combinations, called LIGATURES, which had developed from compound neumes, and the arrangement and order of the ligatures indicated a particular rhythmic mode (*v.* RHYTHMIC MODES), which was maintained more or less throughout the part.

By the middle of the 13th cent. the rhythm of the upper parts in a MOTET had become more varied than modal notation could intelligibly comprise, and a notation more adequate to the newer motets was formulated by Franco of Cologne. His *Ars cantus mensurabilis* (*c.* 1260), which was the basis of all subsequent developments in the notation of rhythm, was based on the four note-values: duplex long ▬, long, breve, and semibreve ◆, and their corresponding rests, and laid the foundation of the system of MENSURAL NOTATION.

The differences in the 14th cent. between French notation as outlined by Philippe de Vitry (*Ars nova, c.* 1320) and Italian notation as expounded by Marchetto of Padua (*Pomerium,* 1318) were mainly concerned with the method of writing groups of semibreves and minims (*semibreves minimae*). Both recognised duple (imperfect) time as having equal standing with triple (perfect), and both used time signatures to indicate the relations of note-values in a composition. By the end of the century the French signatures were generally accepted, and one (C) is still in use. To represent more complex rhythms the use of red for imperfect notes was introduced, and the degree of complication possible with the combination of colour and signs of PROPORTION reached its highest point *c.* 1400 (see the facsimiles in W. Apel, *French Secular Music of the Late Fourteenth Century*, 1950, and in *The Old Hall Manuscript*, iii, 1938, where there are black, red and blue notes).

In the course of the 15th cent. the writing of notes changed, so that black became white and red became black. This was a change of convenience, largely due to writing on paper instead of parchment, and not a change of system. The gradual change during the course of the 16th and 17th cent. from the concept of measured rhythm to that of metrical rhythm caused more than the usual number of anomalies and of differences of local practice in the notation of rhythm. This change involved the introduction of BAR lines, of TIME SIGNATURES, of TEMPO marks, of the TIE, and of the grouping of notes smaller than the crotchet (called in England "the new tied-note"). By the middle of the 18th cent. all these devices had settled down into their modern usages.

The chief accessories to modern notation are the various marks of expression, which multiplied enormously during the 19th century. They may affect rhythm (*e.g. accelerando, rallentando*), intensity (*e.g. piano, forte, crescendo, diminuendo*), phrasing (*e.g.* the slur, the *staccato* dot), accentuation (*e.g. sforzando, marcato*), touch (*e.g. martellato*), or a mental attitude to be conveyed (*e.g. innig, nobilmente*).

W. APEL: *The Notation of Polyphonic Music*, 900-1600 (4th ed., 1949).

F. ROTHSCHILD : *The Lost Tradition in Music* (1953).
G. M. SUÑOL : *Introduction à la paléographie musicale grégorienne* (1935).
E. WELLESZ : *History of Byzantine Music and Hymnography* (1949).
J. WOLF : *Handbuch der Notationskunde*, 2 vols. (1913-19).

Notes égales [nots ay-gull], *Fr.* (equal notes). An indication found in French music of the 17th and early 18th cent. Its purpose is to warn the player that where there is a group of short notes of the same value (*e.g.* a group of quavers) he is to make all the notes of the group equal, as written, and not to follow the conventions of the period by making them alternately long and short. A series of dots, one over each note of a group, is sometimes used to convey the same warning. In such cases the modern performer needs a further warning that the dots do not mean *staccato*. *v.* DOT (2.iv), NOTES INÉGALES.

Note sensible [not sũn-seebl], *Fr.* Leading note.

Notes inégales [not see-nay-gull], *Fr.* (unequal notes). In French music of the 17th and early 18th cent. it was the custom to vary the monotony of a succession of short notes (*e.g.* quavers) of the same value by making them unequal in length. Normally no instruction to this effect was given by the composer : the practice was taken for granted. The commonest treatment was to lengthen the odd-numbered notes and shorten the even-numbered notes in compensation. *v.* DOT (2.IV), NOTES ÉGALES.

Notker (called BALBULUS, *i.e.* the stammerer) : *b.* Elgg (Switzerland), *c.* 840; *d.* St. Gall, Apr. 6, 912. The most famous member of the Music School of St. Gall, who wrote poems to the melodies of the Alleluia of the Mass to form sequences, and the poems, and probably the music, of new sequences. From his time until the Council of Trent in the 16th cent. the SEQUENCE was the most widely cultivated form of liturgical poetry.

Notre Dame [notr dum], *Fr.* (Our Lady). The cathedral church of Paris, the construction of which began in 1163. During the late 12th and early 13th cent. it was an important centre for church music and particularly for the development of the contrapuntal form known as *organum*. The two leading composers associated with Notre Dame at this period were Léonin and Perotin. Because of its reputation as a musical centre the term " Notre Dame school " is generally applied to all the polyphonic music of this period which appears to be of French or Anglo-French origin. *v.* LEONINUS, ORGANUM, PEROTINUS.

Nottebohm [not′-ter-bome], MARTIN GUSTAV : *b.* Lüdenscheid (Westphalia), Nov. 12, 1817; *d.* Graz, Oct. 29, 1882. Musical historian. Studied in Berlin under Berger and Dehn, and in Leipzig, where he became a friend of Mendelssohn and Schumann. From 1845 lived in Vienna. Edited Beethoven's sketch-books, and compiled thematic catalogues of Beethoven's and Schubert's works.

Notturno [not-toorr′-no], *I.* " Night song." (1) A title given by 18th-cent. composers to music for evening entertainment, *e.g.* Mozart's *Notturno*, K.286, for four small orchestras, each composed of string quartet and two horns, and Haydn's 8 *Notturni* for 9 instruments, written in 1790 for the King of Naples.

(2) = NOCTURNE.

Novák [no′-vahk], VÍTĚZSLAV : *b.* Kamenitz, Dec. 5, 1870; *d.* Skuteč, July 18, 1949. Composer and teacher. Studied at the Prague Conservatoire under Jiránek (piano) and Dvořák (composition) and taught there, 1909-20. Teacher at the State Conservatoire and subsequently director. He composed operas, symphonic poems, chamber music, choral works, piano pieces and songs.

Novello, VINCENT : *b.* London, Sept. 6, 1781; *d.* Nice, Aug. 9, 1861. Publisher, editor, organist and composer. Organist of the chapel at the Portuguese Embassy from 1797-1822. Founded the music publishing firm of Novello in London, 1811. Edited many collections of music including anthems by Boyce, Croft, and Greene, Masses by Mozart, Haydn and Beethoven, and Purcell's church music. Composed Masses, motets, cantatas and other church music.

Nozze di Figaro, Le [leh not′-tseh dee

fee′-gah-ro] (The Marriage of Figaro). Opera in four acts by Mozart. Libretto by Lorenzo da Ponte (based on Beaumarchais's comedy *La folle journée ou Le Mariage de Figaro*). First performed, Vienna, May 11, 1786. Figaro, valet to Count Almaviva, is going to marry Susanna, the Countess's maid. The plot is concerned with his successful frustration of the Count's designs on his bride. In the process he discovers a father, Dr. Bartolo, and a mother, Marcellina. The situation is complicated by the behaviour of the page Cherubino, who is ready to fall in love with any woman he meets and imagines himself in love with the Countess. The Countess also has her problems. Weary of her husband's infidelities, she impersonates Susanna and meets him in the garden. When all the misunderstandings have been sorted out, Figaro wins his bride and the Countess shows herself ready to forgive her husband.

Nuove Musiche, Le [leh noo-o′-veh moo′-zee-keh], I. A collection of monodies published in 1602 by Giulio Caccini. In the foreword (English trans. in O. Strunk, *Source Readings in Music History*, p. 377) he discusses the new style of singing, his own part in developing it, and the use of such ornaments as the *trillo* and the *gruppo*.

Nut. (1) The part of a bow which is held by the player of a stringed instrument. It incorporates a screw device by which the tension of the hairs can be adjusted.

(2) A strip of ebony at the peg-box end of the finger-board of a stringed instrument which keeps the strings raised slightly above the level of the finger-board.

Nutcracker Suite. *v.* CASSE-NOISETTE.

O

Obbligato [ob-blee-gah′-toh], *I.* Lit., "essential." A part, usually instrumental, which cannot be dispensed with in performance, as distinct from a part which is *ad libitum.* Used especially in the baroque period. Muffat pointed out that the concertos in his *Auserlesene... Instrumental-Musik* (1701), which were modelled on those of Corelli, could be played by the solo instruments of the *concertino* alone; hence these were *obbligato* instruments. The term came to be applied particularly in this sense, as in Vivaldi's *L'Estro Armonico*, for example, where the first concerto is *con* 4 *violini obbligati.* In some music in the 19th cent. the term was applied, in the opposite sense, to an additional part which is optional.

Oberon. Opera in three acts by Weber. Libretto by James Robinson Planché (founded on William Sotheby's translation of Wieland's *Oberon*). First performed, London, Apr. 12, 1826.

Oberwerk [oh′-ber-vairk], *G.* Swell organ.

Oblique Motion. The motion of two parts of which one remains on the same note while the other moves:

Oboe [in England generally pronounced o′bo] (*Fr.* hautbois, "high wood", whence *O.E.* hautboy, *G.* Oboe, Hoboe, *I.* oboe). A woodwind instrument with a conical bore and a double reed. Its range is from

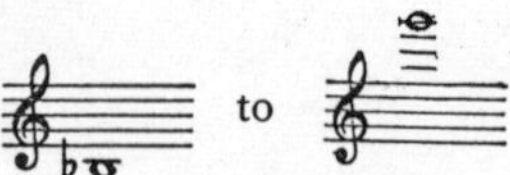

The natural scale is D, and the music is written at the actual pitch. Medieval instruments of the double-reed type were made in a variety of sizes under the general name "shawm." In Germany the small sizes were called *Schalmey* and the large *Pommer* (*Fr.* bombarde). The modern form and name came into use in the second half of the 17th cent. in the orchestra of the French opera (the earliest instance is Cambert's *Pomone*, 1671). In the 18th cent. the oboes, which by then had two or three keys, were the predominant high woodwind instruments in the orchestra. In the late baroque period the oboe was used frequently as a solo instrument in chamber music, concertos and cantatas. The pairing of two solo oboes in the orchestra was adopted in the late classical symphony. In the 19th cent. the instrument acquired a number of mechanical improvements. For other members of the family *v.* COR ANGLAIS, HECKELPHONE, OBOE DA CACCIA, OBOE D'AMORE.

A. CARSE: *Musical Wind Instruments* (1939).

Oboe da caccia [o′-bo-eh da cah-tchah], *I.* (*Fr.* taille, *O.E.* tenor hautboy). Lit. "hunting oboe." An instrument developed from the alto *Pommer* (*v.* OBOE), with a range a fifth below the oboe. It appears to have come into use at the end of the 17th cent. In a modified form it acquired the name COR ANGLAIS (*Fr.*) or *corno inglese* (*I.*) about the middle of the 18th cent.

Oboe d'amore [o′-bo-eh dah-moh′-reh], *I.* (*Fr.* hautbois d'amour, *G.* Liebesoboe). An instrument of a slightly larger size than the regular oboe, having a range down to

and a pear-shaped bell. It originated in Germany about 1720, and was used by Bach in many of his cantatas and other choral works. It was revived by Richard Strauss in the *Symphonia domestica* (1903).

Obrecht [o'-breckht] (Hobrecht), JACOB: *b*. Bergen-op-Zoom, Nov. 22, 1450; *d*. Ferrara, 1505. Composer. *Maître de chapelle*, Bergen-op-Zoom, 1479. At Cambrai Cathedral, 1484-5. Appointed succentor at St. Donatian, Bruges, and spent some time at Ferrara before 1488. Succeeded Barbireau at Notre Dame, Antwerp, 1492. At Bergen-op-Zoom, 1496-8, and in Italy again in 1504. One of the leading composers of his period. As compared with Okeghem's works in the same forms, his 24 Masses (a much larger number than any of his contemporaries) and 22 motets show their slightly later style in their more frequent use of sequence in the melodies, of imitation between the parts and of definite cadences. He also composed *chansons* to Dutch, French and Italian words. A complete edition of his works has been edited by Johannes Wolf (1912-21). It is not certain that the setting of the *St. Matthew Passion* published in vol. xxviii is actually by Obrecht; it may be by Longueval. A new edition of Obrecht's works by Albert Smijers is in progress.

O'Carolan, TURLOUGH: *b*. nr. Nobber (Co. Meath), 1670; *d*. nr. Kilronan, March 25, 1738. Harper and composer, blinded by smallpox in his youth. Many of his airs were well-known in the 18th cent. and appear in the Bunting and Petrie collections, while some were set to new words by Thomas Moore. Shield adapted one as "The Arethusa." An edition of his 220 tunes by Donal O'Sullivan has recently been published.

Occasional Oratorio. Oratorio by Handel, composed in 1746 to celebrate the suppression of the Jacobite rebellion. Text compiled from various sources. First performed, London, Feb. 14, 1746.

Ochetto [o-ket'-to], *I*. Hocket.

Ochsenmenuette, Die [dee ockhs'-ĕn-mane-oo-et'-ter], *G*. (The Ox Minuet). The title of a *Singspiel* by Seyfried (Vienna, 1823), with music arranged from compositions by Haydn. It is based on two earlier French works (*Le Menuet du Boeuf, ou Une Leçon de Haydn*, 1805 and *Haydn, ou Le Menuet du Boeuf*, 1812), which also used music by Haydn "Ox Minuet" is sometimes mistakenly believed to be the title of one of Haydn's minuets.

Ockeghem. *v*. OKEGHEM.

Octave. (1) The INTERVAL between the first and eighth notes of the diatonic SCALE, *e.g.*:

Notes which are an octave apart are called by the same letter name, have the simplest possible vibration ratio 1 : 2 (*v*. ACOUSTICS), and have the effect of mutual duplication and reinforcement.

(2) A 4 ft. diapason stop on the organ, also known as "principal."

(3) *Octave coupler*. A mechanical device on the organ which automatically doubles in the octave above any note which is played. A *sub-octave coupler* similarly doubles in the octave below.

Octet. A piece for eight solo instruments, *e.g.*, Beethoven's Octet in E♭, Op. 103, for two oboes, two clarinets, two horns, and two bassoons, Schubert's in F, Op. 166 and Wellesz's Op. 67, for two violins, viola, cello, double bass, clarinet, bassoon, and horn. Mendelssohn's octet in E♭, Op. 20, is for a double string quartet of four violins, two violas, and two cellos.

Ode (*Gr*. ᾠδή, song). (1) A form of strophic poetry. Odes of Horace were set in the first half of the 16th cent. for solo voice and lute in note-values corresponding to their metrical feet. An example by Petrus Tritonius from his *Melopoiae sive harmoniae tetracenticae* (Augsburg, 1507) is printed in Schering's *History of Music in Examples*, No. 73.

(2) A vocal composition in honour of some person or occasion, *e.g.* in the 17th cent. Purcell's Welcome Songs and Birthday Odes and his three Odes for St. Cecilia's Day. In musical form these works are cantatas, as are the odes of John Blow and Handel's *St. Cecilia's Day* and *Alexander's Feast*. Following this tradition, later odes, *e.g.*, Parry's setting of A. C. Benson's *Ode to Music* (1901) and Holst's of Whitman's *Ode to Death* (1919)

are usually written for chorus, with or without soloists, and orchestra.

Odhecaton (*Gr.* ᾠδή, song, and ἑκατόν, hundred). The *Harmonice musices Odhecaton A*, published in Venice by Petrucci in 1501, was the first printed collection of polyphonic music. It contained 99 chansons written in the latter part of the 15th cent. by Agricola, Compère, Busnois, Isaak, Josquin, Okeghem, Obrecht, and other composers. Modern ed. by Helen Hewitt (1945). Two further collections (labelled *B* and *C*) were published in 1502 and 1503.

Odington, WALTER DE (Walter of Evesham): *d.* after 1330. Benedictine monk, musical theorist, and astronomer who spent some time at the monastery at Evesham and also at Oxford. His treatise *De Speculatione Musicae* (*c.* 1300; printed in Coussemaker's *Scriptores*, i, p. 182) is one of the most informative of the period.

Odo (Otto) OF CLUNY: *b.* 879; *d.* Tours, Nov. 18, 942. Pupil of Rémy d'Auxerre. Canon of St. Martin's, Tours, monk at Beaune, 909; abbot of Cluny, 927. His *Dialogus de Musica*, *c.* 935 (printed in Gerbert's *Scriptores*, i, p. 251; translation in O. Strunk, *Source Readings in Music History*, p. 103) contains a discussion of the MONOCHORD which is the earliest to give a complete set of letters for the notes of the scale from *Γ*:

to *aa*:

Oedipus auf Kolonos [urd'-ee-po͝oss owf col-oh'-noss], *G.* (Oedipus at Colonos). Tragedy by Sophocles for which Mendelssohn wrote incidental music for male chorus and orchestra, Op. 93. First performed, Potsdam, Nov. 1, 1845.

Oedipus Rex [eed'-ip-o͝oss recks]. "Opera-oratorio" in two acts by Stravinsky. Libretto (originally French) by Jean Cocteau (after Sophocles), translated into Latin by Jean Daniélou. First performed, Paris, May 30, 1927.

Offenbach [off'-ĕn-buckh], JACQUES: *b.* Deutz (nr. Cologne), June 20, 1819; *d.* Paris, Oct. 4, 1880. Composer. Studied at the Paris Conservatoire, and in 1849 became conductor at the Théâtre Français. From 1855-61 he was manager of the Bouffes Parisiens, and from 1873-5 of the Théâtre de la Gaîté. Of his 90 operettas the sparkling and satirical *Orphée aux Enfers* (1858), *La Belle Hélène* (1864) and *La Vie Parisienne* (1866) achieved very great popularity. His best work, *Tales of Hoffmann*, was not produced until 1881. He published in 1877 *Notes d'un musicien en voyage*—an account of his visit to America in the previous year.

S. SITWELL: *La Vie Parisienne*: *A Tribute to Offenbach* (1937).

Offertorium [off-air-to'-ri-o͝om], *L.* (*Fr.* offertoire). Offertory. Part of the Proper of the Mass, sung after the Credo while the priest is preparing and offering the oblation of bread and wine. It was originally a psalm with an antiphon but now consists simply of an antiphon. Polyphonic settings of the offertory were composed during the 15th and 16th cent., and in the 17th cent. instrumental *offertoria* were written for performance at this point in the service, *e.g.* Frescobaldi's organ ricercars *dopo il Credo* in the *Fiori Musicali* (1635).

Oiseau de Feu, L' [lwa-zo der fer] (The Firebird). Ballet with music by Stravinsky. First performed, Paris, June 25, 1910.

Okeghem [ock'-eg-em] (Ockeghem, Ockenheim), JOHANNES (Jan): *b.* Flanders, *c.* 1430; *d.* Tours, *c.* 1495. Composer. Chorister at Antwerp Cathedral, 1443-4; in the chapel of the Duke of Bourbon, 1446-8. He joined the chapel of the King of France in Paris in 1453 and was in the royal service until his death. In 1459, he became Treasurer of St. Martin's Abbey in Tours, and in 1465 the king's *maître de chapelle*. He composed some 16 Masses, motets, and *chansons*. He was the first in the long succession of famous Flemish composers. The characteristics of his style are continuity of flow, achieved by long overlapping phrases and infrequent use of cadences, and independence of the parts, which implies, of course, absence of imitation. Two volumes, containing 16 Masses, of the projected complete edition of his works have been edited (1927-1948) by D. Plamenac; two *chansons* were printed in Petrucci's *Odhecaton* (1501; modern edition by H. Hewitt, 1945).

E. KŘENEK: *Johannes Ockeghem* (1953).

Okeover (Okar, Oker), JOHN. Organist and composer. Studied at Oxford. Organist, Wells Cathedral, 1619-39, 1660-2; Gloucester Cathedral, 1640-44. He composed anthems and 3- and 5-part fancies for viols. A fancy and a pavan are printed in *Musica Britannica*, ix.

Oktave [ock-tahv'-er], *G.* (1) Octave. (2) A 4 ft. open diapason stop on the organ.

Old Hall Manuscript. A collection of polyphonic music sung in the Royal Household chapel in the first half of the 15th cent., which was acquired by John Stafford Smith (1750-1836) and was given by his descendants to the library of St. Edmund's College, Old Hall, near Ware. Its compilation was begun probably during the reign of Henry IV (1399-1413); if so, the two compositions by "Roy Henry" are by him and not, as has been thought, by Henry V (1413-22). It contains 148 pieces, comprising settings of the movements of the Ordinary of the Mass (excepting the *Kyrie*), isorhythmic motets, and antiphons, by 24 composers (many of the pieces are anonymous) including Byttering, Chirbury, Cooke, Damett, Dunstable, Forest, Oliver, Power, Pycard, Sturgeon, and Typp. The greater part of the music has been published in *The Old Hall Manuscript* (ed. A. Ramsbotham, completed by H. B. Collins and Dom Anselm Hughes, 1930-8).

M. BUKOFZER: *Studies in Medieval and Renaissance Music* (1950), chap. ii.

F. LI. HARRISON: *Music in Medieval Britain* (1958), chap. v.

Old Hundredth. The hymn-tune known by this name first appeared in the Genevan Psalter of 1551, set to Psalm 134, in this form:

It was adopted in Thomas Sternhold's "Anglo-Genevan" Psalter *Four Score and Seven Psalmes of David in English Mitre* (1561), where it was set to Psalm 100 and also to a metrical version of the Lord's Prayer. It was known as the "Hundredth" in the Psalters of the old version, and became the "Old Hundredth" after the publication of Tate and Brady's new version of the Psalter in 1696.

Oliphant, THOMAS: *b.* Condie (Perthshire), Dec. 25, 1799; *d.* March 9, 1873. Honorary secretary of the Madrigal Society, 1830, and later president. He wrote English words to many Italian madrigals, published *A Brief Account of the Madrigal Society* (1835), *A Short Account of Madrigals* (1836) and *La musa madrigalesca,* a collection of madrigal verse (1837).

Olsen [ool'-sĕn], OLE: *b.* Hammerfest, July 4, 1850; *d.* Oslo, Nov. 10, 1927. Composer. Studied in Leipzig under E. F. Richter, Oscar Paul and Reinecke from 1870-74 and then settled in Christiania (now Oslo), where he conducted and wrote music criticism. Composed 4 operas to his own libretti, symphonic poems, cantatas, a symphony and an oratorio. His suite for Rolfsen's children's play *Svein Uræd* is still popular in Norway.

Ondeggiando [on-deh-djahnd'-o], *I. v.* ONDULÉ.

Ondes Martenot, Les [laze o͡nd marr-ter-no]. Electronic instrument invented (patented 1922) by Maurice Martenot. The pitch is infinitely variable, and some variety of tone-colour is possible. The instrument has been written for by Olivier Messiaen, notably in his orchestral suite *Turangalila.*

Ondulé [o͡n-dee-lay], *Fr.* (*I.* ondeggiando). "Undulating." An effect, indicated by the sign ∿∿, used in violin playing in the baroque period either on a single note or on several notes in ARPEGGIO, and produced by an undulating motion of the bow.

Ongarese. *v.* ALL' ONGARESE.

On Hearing the First Cuckoo in Spring. Piece for orchestra by Delius (1912). It introduces the Norwegian folk-song "I Ola dalom" (In Ola valley), for which see Grieg's 19 *Norwegian Folk Tunes*, Op. 66.

Onslow, ANDRÉ GEORGES LOUIS : *b.* Clermont-Ferrand, July 27, 1784; *d.* there, Oct. 3, 1853. Composer. Studied the piano under Dussek and Cramer in London and composition under Reicha in Paris. He was elected a member of the London Philharmonic Society in 1832 and in 1842 succeeded Cherubini as member of the *Académie Française.* He composed a great deal of chamber music, various works for piano, comic operas and symphonies.

Op. Abbreviation for *L.* opus, "work." Now used by composers to indicate the order in which their works have been composed, *e.g.* Op. 60. In the 17th and early 18th cent. opus numbers were used only occasionally, generally to draw attention to the importance of a collection of pieces, *e.g.* a set of sonatas or concertos. Some composers (or their publishers) have used opus numbers erratically, so that they do not always accurately indicate the order of composition. This is true of Beethoven. In the case of Schubert the opus numbers are virtually meaningless.

Open Diapason. *v.* DIAPASON.

Open Fifth. A common chord without a third is said to have an open fifth. In medieval polyphony it was usual to end a composition on a unison, octave or open fifth, in the 16th cent. on a chord with an open fifth or with a major third (*v.* also ACOUSTICS). The open fifth was one of the idioms in the writing for two horns in the 18th-cent. orchestra: for an example *v.* HORN.

Open Notes. On a brass or woodwind instrument, the notes which correspond to the notes of the HARMONIC SERIES.

Open Strings. On stringed instruments, the strings, and the notes which they sound, when not stopped by the finger. The sign o above a note indicates that it is to be played on an open string (for a further use of the same sign *v.* HARMONICS).

Opera. A dramatic work in which the whole, or the greater part, of the text is sung with instrumental accompaniment. The word "opera," now in universal use (*Fr.* opéra, *G.* Oper, *I.* opera, *Sp.* ópera), was originally a colloquial abbreviation of the Italian *opera in musica* (a musical work). The early Italian operas of the 17th cent. were described as *favola in musica* (a story in music), *dramma per musica* (a play for music) or some similar term. In 17th-cent. France serious opera was entitled *tragédie mise en musique* (a tragedy set to music).

The association of music with drama is as old as civilization. In Western Europe music was an essential part of the liturgical drama of the Middle Ages, which was therefore in a sense the ancestor of the oratorio, and it also figured prominently in the many dramatic entertainments presented at Italian courts in the 16th cent. However, though opera owed much to these entertainments, which were marked by a love of spectacle and a lively interest in classical mythology, it was essentially a new form. The cult of the antique which was a feature of Renaissance humanism induced a group of artists, musicians and scholars in Florence to attempt a revival of Greek drama, which they falsely supposed to have been sung throughout. The first product of this movement was Rinuccini's *Dafne*, performed privately in 1597, with music by Peri and Jacopo Corsi. Apart from a few fragments by Corsi the music of this work has not survived. A suitable musical formula for setting the text of a dramatic work was found in the new type of declamatory song, which began to be practised in the late 16th cent. as a reaction against the madrigal, where the clear enunciation of words often suffered from the complexities of independent part-writing. The purpose of declamatory song, which came to be known as *recitativo* (from *recitare*, to recite), was to translate the accents of speech into music and to allow the individual singer the greatest freedom of interpretation. For this reason the accompaniment, assigned primarily to a keyboard instrument or to the lute, was treated as a subordinate harmonic background. *Dafne* was followed in 1600 by *Euridice* (libretto by Rinuccini, music mainly by Peri), which was performed at Florence to celebrate the wedding of Henry IV of France and Maria de Medici.

The most important opera on the Florentine model was Monteverdi's *Orfeo* (Mantua, 1607), which also included a substantial amount of choral writing. Choruses were also employed extensively at Rome, where the first secular opera to be performed was Landi's *La morte d'Orfeo*. The erection of a magnificent theatre by the Barberini family in 1632 also encouraged the development of opera as a spectacle, with splendid scenery and elaborate machines. In 1637 the first public opera house was opened at Venice, followed by several others. Opera was no longer an entertainment for invited guests but appealed to a wider audience. For economic reasons the chorus was neglected in favour of solo singing, and the orchestra consisted normally of strings and harpsichord. Already in Rome there had been a tendency to relieve the monotony of continuous recitative by incorporating arias (or songs), and this tendency was continued in the Venetian operas, which also frequently introduced duets. Castrato singers, who had become familiar in opera in Rome, now acquired an even greater vogue, which continued down to the end of the 18th cent. The subject-matter of opera was also broadened. Monteverdi's last opera, *L'incoronazione di Poppea* (Venice, 1642) was the first to deal with a historical theme, as distinct from mythology ; it also introduced comic characters as a relief from the serious tone of the rest of the work. Comic characters had already made their appearance at Rome before this, and a complete comic opera, *Chi soffre, speri*, by Mazzochi and Marazzoli, had been performed there in 1639. The staple elements of comic opera (or *opera buffa*, as it came to be known) were rapid recitative, patter songs, and scenes parodying serious opera. Comic opera also contributed the concerted finale for an ensemble of singers, which was not normally used in serious opera before the late 18th cent., presumably because it would have been undignified for princely characters to have to struggle to make themselves heard.

In the course of the 17th cent. Italian opera also became known abroad, *e.g.* in Vienna, where the court became a centre for lavish productions, in Brussels and in Warsaw. It was also introduced to Paris in 1645, but the hostility which it aroused, both aesthetic and political, led the French to produce their own operas, which owed much to the traditions of the spoken drama and to the ballet. The earliest French opera dates from 1655, but its success as a national form was due to the Italian-born Lully, whose first opera, *Cadmus et Hermione*, was performed in 1673. Lully was already at this time an experienced composer of ballets, *pastorales* and *comédies-ballets*—the last a form which combined the spoken drama and ballet. Ballet continued to be an integral part of French opera right down to the 19th cent. In England, where the masque (a form of ballet with dialogue) was popular at court and in private societies in the early 17th cent., an attempt at establishing opera was made by Davenant, whose *Siege of Rhodes*, with music by several composers, was performed in London in 1656. Restoration society, however, rejected opera on the Italian model and preferred a type similar to the French *comédie-ballet*, *i.e.* an association of music and spoken dialogue. Purcell's *King Arthur* (text by Dryden, 1691) is a work of this kind. His *Dido and Aeneas* (1689), a miniature opera on the Italian model, was written not for the public theatre but for a girls' school at Chelsea.

The traditions of Italian opera were continued by Stradella (*d.* 1682) and Alessandro Scarlatti (1659-1725). In the work of Scarlatti the aria acquired absolute supremacy : recitative became virtually a series of conventional formulas used for essential conversation or simple reflection, except where the dramatic situation justified an outburst with orchestral accompaniment (*recitativo stromentato*). The standard type of aria was in *da capo* form, which may be represented by the formula *A B A*, the repetition of the first section offering the singer opportunities for improvised ornamentation. In general ornamentation was freely used to embroider a simple vocal line, particularly in slow arias which offered ample scope for such treatment. The overture also developed into a standard form—two quick movements separated by one in slower tempo. French composers, on the other hand, preferred a slow introduction followed by a quick movement in fugal style.

In Germany Schütz had set a translation of Rinuccini's *Dafne* as early as 1627, but German opera did not become fully established until the opening of the first public opera house at Hamburg in 1678, though Italian opera flourished in the work of Steffani (1654-1728) at Munich, Hanover and Düsseldorf. It was at Hamburg that Handel won his first operatic experience, which he developed further by a visit to Italy. The great majority of his Italian operas, however, were written between 1711 and 1741 for London, where he took advantage of the nobility's newly awakened enthusiasm for the form.

In the course of the 18th cent. there was a growing dissatisfaction with the rigidity of operatic conventions. It was felt that vocal virtuosity was exploited at the expense of dramatic expression and that an overture should be an integral part of the work and not merely an instrumental introduction to which nobody listened seriously. These views found expression in the work of several writers, notably Francesco Algarotti in his *Saggio sopra l'opera in musica* (1755). The operas of Jommelli and Traetta show that they were aware of these problems, but it was above all Gluck who demonstrated in his later works, particularly in *Alceste* (Vienna, 1767), *Iphigénie en Aulide* (Paris, 1774) and *Iphigénie en Tauride* (Paris, 1779), that a simple, sincere and direct form of expression could be more truly dramatic than the emphasis on fine singing which counted for so much in earlier 18th-cent. works. Rameau, whose operatic activity in Paris covered the years 1733-64, had already shown what an important contribution the orchestra could make to dramatic intensity. Gluck's imagination went further: he realized that the instruments could speak, as if they were themselves witnesses of the drama. This conception of instrumental writing was to have a powerful effect on the development of the symphony.

Comic opera (*opera buffa*) did not become firmly established in Italy until the early years of the 18th cent. It aimed above all at being " natural," in contrast to the artificiality of *opera seria*. Hence when Pergolesi's *La serva padrona* (originally a comic *intermezzo*) was re-introduced to Paris in 1752 it was seized upon by the critics of French opera, particularly Rousseau, as a stick with which to attack all that was stilted and conventional in the French tradition. The violent controversy which ensued was known as the *guerre des bouffons* (war of the comedians). Hostility was still active when Gluck, who was accepted as the champion of French opera, came to Paris in 1773. The *guerre des bouffons* had the important effect of stimulating the composition of French *opéras-comiques*, for which there was a modest precedent in the comedies interspersed with popular songs which had been performed at the Paris fairs from the early years of the 18th cent. *Opéra-comique*, unlike *opera buffa*, employed spoken dialogue in place of recitative. In the course of time romantic and pathetic elements were introduced into *opera buffa* (as in Mozart's *Don Giovanni*, 1787) and into *opéra-comique*—so much so that in the 19th cent. *opéra-comique* came to mean simply opera with dialogue, as opposed to *grand opéra*, which was set to music throughout and produced on a lavish scale.

In England comic opera also employed dialogue. It had its forerunners in the Restoration parodies of plays with music, but as an independent form its history began with Gay's *Beggar's Opera*

(1728), in which the songs were set to popular tunes, either traditional or by well-known composers like Purcell and Handel. *The Beggar's Opera* was followed by a host of works of a similar kind, known as "ballad operas." The term was still retained when later in the century it became the custom to have the songs specially written by living composers, *e.g.* Arne, Dibdin and Shield. The popularity of opera with dialogue and the example of French *opéra-comique* led to the Romantic opera of the early 19th cent., *e.g.* Balfe's *The Bohemian Girl* (1843) and Wallace's *Maritana* (1845). Ballad opera also had an influence in Germany, where a translation of an English work was performed in 1743. This started the fashion for a German counterpart to *opéra-comique*, for which the German name was *Singspiel*. Mozart's *Die Entführung* (1782), which incorporates many of the elements of Italian opera, was an elaborate response to the Emperor Joseph II's desire to found a National *Singspiel* in Vienna—an institution which lasted only a few years. Mozart's *Die Zauberflöte* (1791), written for a popular theatre in Vienna, is technically a *Singspiel*, but is unique in its combination of pantomime and Masonic symbolism.

Mozart's principal activity was in the field of Italian opera—a form which he learned to master by writing operas in Italy while still in his 'teens. His first mature work in this form was *Idomeneo* (Munich, 1781), which owes much to the influence of Gluck. In Vienna, however, circumstances compelled him to devote himself to *opera buffa*, of which he wrote three outstanding examples—*Le nozze di Figaro* (1786), *Don Giovanni* (1787) and *Così fan tutte* (1789). The one exception, *La clemenza di Tito* (1791), was an *opera seria* commissioned to celebrate the coronation of Leopold II as King of Bohemia in Prague.

In France the horrors of the Revolution led to the composition of *opéras-comiques* dealing with dramatic rescues, *e.g.* Cherubini's *Les deux journées* (Paris, 1800), known in England as *The Water-Carrier*. Beethoven, who admired Cherubini, chose a story from the Revolution for his only opera *Fidelio* (Vienna, 1805), which also has spoken dialogue. *Fidelio*, however, had no successors. The impact of Romantic literature on German composers led to the composition of works which combined supernatural elements with homely, rustic sentiment—*e.g.* Weber's *Der Freischütz* (1821) and Marschner's *Hans Heiling* (1833)—and a Romantic interpretation of the pageantry and intrigue of the Middle Ages, *e.g.* Weber's *Euryanthe* (1823), in which dialogue was abandoned. Contemporary with this movement in Germany was the development of the so-called *grand opéra* in Paris—a form which gave scope for the representation of reaction against tyranny, *e.g.* Rossini's *Guillaume Tell* (1829), and spectacular scenes on a large scale. The outstanding practitioner of this type of opera was Meyerbeer, of German-Jewish origin, whose *Les Huguenots* (1836) is a vivid picture of the conflict between Catholics and Protestants in 16th-cent. France. Berlioz's *Les Troyens* (1856-9) accepts this tradition but transmutes it into a wholly individual approach and an intellectual awareness of the dignity of Virgil's epic. Many of the conventions of *opéra-comique* came to be incorporated in *grand opéra*, *e.g.* choruses of soldiers, conspirators, etc., and the building of an organ in the Paris Opéra made possible the inclusion of church scenes.

In Germany Wagner was familiar with the traditions of *grand opéra* and also of Romantic German opera. The former is represented in his work by *Rienzi* (1842), the latter by *Der fliegende Holländer* (1843), *Tannhäuser* (1845) and *Lohengrin* (1850)—the dates are those of performance. A growing reaction against tradition, however, led him to expound a new theory of opera, arguing that the form should be a union of all the arts, with dignified (*i.e.* legendary) subject-matter, verse forms which would stimulate by the use of alliteration, and a continuous running commentary (explaining the action by the repeated introduction of significant themes) in the orchestra. This theory was put into practice in the tetralogy *Der Ring des Nibelungen*, the composition of which occupied him, with intervals, from 1853 to 1874. Wagner's principles, however, were to some extent relaxed in *Tristan und Isolde* (first performed, 1865) and *Die Meistersinger von Nürnberg* (first performed, 1868) ; the latter work includes not only set songs but also elaborate ensembles—a form of dramatic expression which is specifically condemned in his theoretical works.

In Italy in the 19th cent. the traditions of the past were maintained in the work of Rossini (1792-1868), Donizetti (1797-1848) and Bellini (1801-35). Of these three composers Rossini was the most original and the most influential. He assigned to the orchestra more importance than was customary in Italian opera, broke with the convention of recitative accompanied merely by a keyboard instrument, and put an end to the practice of improvised ornamentation for singers. His *Il barbiere di Siviglia* (Rome, 1816) brought new life into the traditional form of *opera buffa* and won the admiration of Beethoven. Verdi, whose first opera, *Oberto, Conte di S. Bonifacio*, was performed in 1839, inherited the traditions established by his predecessors. But in the course of the years his art grew steadily in stature. He proved himself to be a superbly equipped musician, with a new mastery of orchestral technique and a remarkable instinct for dramatic effect. The culmination of his development is to be found in *Aida* (Cairo, 1871—a spectacular work in the tradition of French *grand opéra*), *Otello* (Milan, 1887) and *Falstaff* (Milan, 1893)—the last two a brilliant recreation of Shakespearian drama in Italian terms.

Simultaneously the growth of nationalism was having stimulating effects in other countries, notably Russia and Czechoslovakia (then a part of the Austro-Hungarian Empire). The foundations of Russian opera, hitherto dependent on Italy, were laid by Glinka in 1836. Among his successors in this field were Moussorgsky, whose *Boris Godounov* (1868) is the most original and the most characteristically Russian work of this period, Borodin and Rimsky-Korsakov. Tchaikovsky, happier in ballet than in opera, was more inclined to model his lyrical style on Western European music. In Czechoslovakia Smetana, though attacked by critics as "Wagnerian," won a striking and enduring popular success with *Prodaná Nevěsta* (Prague, 1866), known in England as *The Bartered Bride*.

20th-cent. opera has pursued no consistent path. In Germany Richard Strauss, using an orchestra even larger than Wagner's, found that a combination of bourgeois sentiment and wild extravagance could be utilized equally for tragedy—*e.g. Salome* (1905), *Elektra* (1909)—and for romantic comedy, *e.g. Der Rosenkavalier* (1911). In France Debussy utilized the technique of impressionism to clothe with a tenuous musical fabric Maeterlinck's fantastic drama *Pelléas et Mélisande* (1902). The work has influenced many other composers but has had no imitators. In Italy a movement for exploiting realism (*verismo*), already foreshadowed by Bizet's *Carmen* (Paris, 1875), had been inaugurated by Mascagni's *Cavalleria rusticana* (1890) and Leoncavallo's *Pagliacci* (1892). This type of treatment was accepted by Puccini but handled with far more imagination and with a more sensitive awareness of the stage, and in *Madama Butterfly* (1904) and *Turandot* (1926) coloured by a skilful suggestion of an oriental atmosphere. Realism is also a characteristic of Berg's *Wozzeck* (1925), but it is associated with an interpretation of character reminiscent of pyschoanalysis, and the musical idiom, based on the twelve-note system of composition, far removed from Puccini's frankly is sentimental melody and harmony. In England Britten's *Peter Grimes* (1945) also presented a psychological study of a personality at odds with society, but without abandoning traditional tonality. Some of his later works have employed a small chamber orchestra—a practice which has also been used by some continental composers, for aesthetic or economic reasons or both. His *The Rape of Lucretia* (1946), based on a play by Obey, employs a "chorus" of two singers, who stand outside the action, as in Greek tragedy, and comment on it. Symbolism is a not uncommon element in modern opera, no doubt as a reaction against realism; it has also influenced opera production. A further reaction against the continuity of Wagnerian opera has led to a return to the 18th-cent. system of using recitative to link arias, duets, etc., *e.g.* in Stravinsky's *The Rake's Progress* (1951). *v. also* BALLAD OPERA, LIBRETTO, OPERETTA, ORATORIO, OVERTURE, SINGSPIEL, ZARZUELA.

A. ABERT: *Claudio Monteverdi und das musikalische Drama* (1954).
E. J. DENT: *Foundations of English Opera* (1928). *Mozart's Operas* (2nd ed., 1947). *Opera* (1940).
H. GOLDSCHMIDT: *Studien zur Geschichte der italienischen Oper im 17. Jahrhundert*, 2 vols. (1901-4).
D. J. GROUT: *A Short History of Opera*, 2 vols. (1947).
A. LOEWENBERG: *Annals of Opera*, 1597-1940, 2 vols. (2nd ed., 1955).
E. NEWMAN: *Wagner Nights* (1949).
H. PRUNIÈRES: *L'Opéra italien en France avant Lulli* (1913).
E. WELLESZ: *Essays on Opera* (1950).
S. T. WORSTHORNE: *Venetian Opera in the Seventeenth Century* (1954).

Operetta. Originally a diminutive of "opera," the term came to be used in the 19th cent. for a type of opera with dialogue which employed music of a popular character and used for its subject-matter a judicious mixture of romantic sentiment, comedy and parody of serious opera. The outstanding composers of this type in the 19th cent. were Offenbach in Paris, Johann Strauss in Vienna and Sullivan in London. The waltz became an indispensable element in Viennese operetta and hence found its way also into the work of composers in other countries. In the 20th cent. operetta became known as "musical comedy," acquiring often a more spectacular mode of production but not losing its essential character. The term "musical comedy" has in recent years become abbreviated to "musical," used as a noun.

Ophicleide (*Gr.* ὄφις, snake; κλείς, key). Lit. "keyed serpent." A bass brass instrument with holes pierced in the tube and covered by keys, like the KEY BUGLE. Patented by Halary (*i.e.* Jean-Hilaire Asté) in Paris in 1821. Parts for it occur in Spohr's opera *Olympia* (1819), Mendelssohn's overture to *A Midsummer Night's Dream* (1826), and Verdi's *Requiem* (1874). Berlioz's *La Damnation de Faust* (1846) requires two ophicleides. In the course of the 19th cent. it came to be generally superseded by the TUBA, on which parts originally written for it are now played. It was normally built in C or B♭, and had a compass of about three octaves. An alto ophicleide, built a fourth higher, existed for a short time in the early 19th century.

Opieński [o-pyen'-ski], HENRYK: *b.* Cracow, Jan. 13, 1870; *d.* Morges (Switzerland), Jan. 22, 1942. Composer and conductor. Studied under Zelenski and Paderewski, in Paris at the Schola Cantorum under Vincent d'Indy, in Berlin under H. Urban and in Leipzig under Riemann and Nikisch. He taught music history at the Warsaw Conservatoire from 1908-12, founded and directed the *Motet et Madrigal* choir in Lausanne in 1918, and directed the State Conservatoire in Poznan from 1920-26. He composed operas, choral works, symphonic poems and songs, and published books on Polish music and an edition of Chopin's letters (English translation, 1932).

Opus. *v.* OP.

Oratorio. A setting of a text on a sacred or epic theme for chorus, soloists and orchestra, for performance in a church or concert hall. The name arose from the Oratory of the church in Vallicella where St. Philip Neri instituted, in the second half of the 16th cent., the performance of sacred plays with music. Emilio Cavalieri's *Rappresentazione di anima e di corpo* (Representation of the Soul and Body, 1600), sometimes described as the first oratorio, is closely related in style to the early Florentine operas, and was staged. The first important composer of oratorios proper was Carissimi, who adopted the forms of opera with a more extensive use of the chorus, a practice which has always tended to distinguish the form of oratorio from that of opera. The later history of Italian oratorio runs parallel to that of Italian opera: its composers (*e.g.* Draghi, A. Scarlatti, Caldara) were primarily opera composers, and opera librettists (*e.g.* Zeno and Metastasio) wrote many of the texts.

In Germany Schütz's *Historia der fröhlichen und siegreichen Auferstehung* (Story of the Joyful and Triumphant Resurrection, 1623) was the first work in a new style which was later developed by Lutheran composers in their settings of the PASSION. The words of the Evangelist (the *testo* of Italian oratorio) are set in imitation plainsong, accompanied by four viols. In his Passions there is a similar musical declamation, but without any accompaniment. In *Die sieben Worte* (The Seven Words, 1645) and the *Weihnachtsoratorium* (Christmas Oratorio, 1664) the narration is in accompanied recitative. J. S. Bach used the term *Oratorium* for the set of six cantatas for the season Christmas to Epiphany (*Christmas Oratorio*), for the Easter cantata *Kommt, eilet und lauftet*, and for the Ascensiontide cantata *Lobet Gott in seinen Reichen*. The two oratorios of C. P. E. Bach—*Die Israeliten in der Wüste* (The Israelites in the Wilderness, 1775) and *Auferstehung und Himmelfahrt Jesu* (The Resurrection and Ascension of Jesus, 1787)—are among his finest and most mature works, and in some of their movements approach the full realization of the classical style in oratorio which was achieved in Haydn's *Creation* (1797). The only oratorios by German composers in the Romantic period which have had more than an occasional performance are those of Mendelssohn, although Spohr, Liszt and Max Bruch each wrote more than one work in the form.

Apart from *Messiah* and *Israel in Egypt* (which uses a double choir) Handel's oratorios differ little in style (the choruses excepted) from his operas. It is through those two works that he has exercised his continuous influence on English oratorio until the present century. Mendelssohn's influence, which was also very strong, complemented rather than excluded that of Handel, but no English composer between Arne and Parry was able to equal the largeness of Handel or rise above the suavity of Mendelssohn. Since Parry began his series of oratorios with *Judith* in 1888, the oratorio has been one of the chief forms of the English choral renascence, especially in the work of Elgar (*The Dream of Gerontius*), Vaughan Williams (*Sancta Civitas*) and William Walton (*Belshazzar's Feast*).

In France the oratorio has been cultivated only sporadically. In the second half of the 17th cent. M. A. Charpentier composed a series of *Histoires sacrées* which were more than mere imitations of his teacher Carissimi. Berlioz's *L' Enfance du Christ* contains some of his most beautiful music, but the later examples by Franck, Saint-Saëns and d'Indy have not emulated its simplicity of style. Arthur Honegger's dramatic psalm *Le Roi David* (1921) and Kodály's *Psalmus Hungaricus* (1923) are two of the more successful modern essays in the oratorio tradition.

A. SCHERING: *Geschichte des Oratoriums* (1911).

Orchésographie [orr-cay-sog-ra-fee], *Fr.* A treatise on the dance, in the form of a dialogue, by Thoinot Arbeau (an anagram of his real name, Jehan Tabourot), published in 1589. It has a musical interest in that it is the earliest surviving book on the dance which prints the tunes, of which there are some 50. An English translation has been published by C. W. Beaumont (1925).

Orchestra (*Gr.* ὀρχήστρα, place for dancing). The name arose from the position of the orchestra in the opera house, which is the same as that of the semicircle for the dancers and instrumentalists in the ancient Greek theatre, between the audience and the stage. The orchestra as a definite group of instruments grew up in the opera houses of the 17th century. Groups (consorts) of instruments, such as strings, recorders, or trumpets, had earlier played together, and occasionally several consorts had been joined. Monteverdi used wind, string and continuo instruments for the performance of *Orfeo* in 1607, but the regular opera orchestra of the baroque period consisted of strings, usually with oboes and bassoons, and other instruments were added for solo *obbligati*. The same principle held in the concerto, the chorus instruments being strings and the solo group variable, either strings or wind or both. The standardization of the orchestra took place in the classical period, with the regular use of wind, brass and timpani, and the division into four groups; strings, woodwind (1 or 2 flutes, 2 oboes, 2 bassoons), brass (2 horns, 2 trumpets) and two kettledrums. Clarinets were added later in the course of the 18th century. On this basis the orchestra was expanded in the 19th cent. to include triple and eventually quadruple woodwind, a complete brass section, harp, and auxiliary percussion. Trombones had been used for special scenes in 18th-cent. opera. Beethoven added them in the fifth symphony and wrote for four horns in the ninth. The composition of the late Romantic orchestra may be seen in the score of Strauss's *Ein Heldenleben* (1899):

Woodwind—
- Piccolo
- 3 Flutes
- 3 Oboes
- English Horn (also playing 4th Oboe)
- E♭ Clarinet
- 2 B♭ Clarinets
- Bass Clarinet
- 3 Bassoons
- Double Bassoon

Brass—
- 8 Horns
- 5 Trumpets
- 3 Trombones
- B♭ Tenor Tuba
- Bass Tuba

Percussion—
- Kettledrums (mechanical)
- Bass Drum
- Cymbals
- Small Side-drum
- Tenor Drum

Strings—
- 16 First Violins
- 16 Second Violins
- 12 Violas
- 12 Cellos
- 8 Double Basses
- 2 Harps

Mahler used an equally large orchestra; the turn towards a less massive orchestra came about 1910, and many later composers have written for double woodwind, or for an even smaller chamber orchestra.

P. BEKKER: *The Story of the Orchestra* (1936).
A. CARSE: *The Orchestra in the Eighteenth Century* (1940). *The Orchestra from Beethoven to Berlioz* (1948).
F. HOWES: *Full Orchestra* (1942).
R. NETTEL: *The Orchestra in England* (1948).
C. S. TERRY: *Bach's Orchestra* (1932).

Orchestration. The art of writing for the orchestra is concerned with the tone colour, technical capacity, and effective range of instruments, with their use in combination, and with the setting out of an orchestral SCORE. Though single instruments of contrasting colour played together in 15th-cent. *chansons*, and consorts of instruments were sometimes combined in the 16th cent., the basic elements of such an art did not appear until the early 17th century. Between 1600 and 1620 Giovanni Gabrieli indicated specific instruments in his *Sacrae Symphoniae*, Monteverdi used instruments in accordance with the dramatic situation in *Orfeo*, and Praetorius wrote the first comprehensive account of instruments in the *Syntagma Musicum* (1617). The choice of a particular instrument to express a text or a dramatic situation in the baroque period appeared mainly in the essentially chamber-music combinations used in the opera, cantata and Passion; larger combinations were arrived at by superimposition, as with Bach's trumpets and drums, or by doubling.

Contrasts of tone colour and weight were essential elements in the late baroque concerto, but they first became allied to a standardized orchestra in the early classical symphonies of the Mannheim and Viennese composers. In the classical style of Haydn, Mozart and Beethoven the woodwind, though often used to play a leading melody, are in general subordinated to the strings, who alone can play rapid figuration. The brass provide support for climaxes, though the horns, more versatile than the trumpets, are also used for soft accompaniment and for idiomatic melody. In Beethoven, the section for three horns in the scherzo of the *Eroica* symphony and the variation for solo horn in the finale of the ninth symphony are signs of a new direction, as is Weber's writing for horns in the overture to *Der Freischütz*.

The rise of the Romantic idea of orchestration as the art of dramatic expression in music is due largely to Berlioz, both as a composer and as the writer of the first modern textbook of orchestration. Wagner, Strauss (who produced a new edition of Berlioz's treatise) and Mahler developed his methods. The orchestration of Rimsky-Korsakov, who also wrote a treatise, took a new turn, though continuing to develop its individual characteristics, after the performance of Wagner's *Der Ring des Nibelungen* in St. Petersburg in 1889. A more selective and delicate treatment of the orchestra is characteristic of the impressionistic orchestration of Debussy and Ravel. In general the tendency of modern orchestration is to be linear rather than massive, and to exploit the rhythmic and melodic possibilities of all instruments equally, without any overt poetic or symbolic intention.

H. BERLIOZ: *Grand Traité d'Instrumentation et d'Orchestration* (1844; English trans. by M. C. Clarke, 1858).
A. CARSE: *The History of Orchestration* (1925).
C. FORSYTH: *Orchestration* (2nd ed., 1935).
G. JACOB: *Orchestral Technique* (2nd ed. 1940).
W. PISTON: *Orchestration* (1955).
N. RIMSKY-KORSAKOV: *Principles of Orchestration*, 2 vols. (1922).
E. WELLESZ: *Die neue Instrumentation*, 2 vols. (1928-9).
C. M. WIDOR: *The Technique of the Modern Orchestra*, trans. E. Suddard (1906).

Ordinary. The parts of the Ordinary of the Mass, *i.e.* those with invariable texts, as distinct from the Proper (those with texts which are proper to their day or season), are the *Kyrie*, *Gloria*, *Credo*, *Sanctus* and *Benedictus*, and *Agnus Dei*.

Ordre [orrdr], *Fr.* Name given by François Couperin to a group of pieces, more usually called SUITE, for harpsichord.

Orfeo, L' [lorr-feh'-o] (The Story of Orpheus). Opera by Monteverdi consisting of a prologue and five acts. Libretto by Alessandro Striggio. First produced, Mantua, 1607. The plot of this opera is similar to that of *Orfeo ed Euridice* by Gluck but does not have the same happy ending.

Orfeo ed Euridice [orr-feh'-o ed eh-oo-ree-dee'-cheh] (Orpheus and Eurydice). Opera in three acts by Gluck. Libretto by Raniero de' Calzabigi. First performed, Vienna, Oct. 5, 1762. The first performance of the revised version *Orphée* (translated by Pierre Louis Moline) was given in Paris, Aug. 2, 1774. Orpheus, mourning the death of Eurydice, is told by Amor that Zeus has taken pity on him and that he may descend into Hades to search for her. He is warned however that if he looks at her before they have left the shores of the Styx death will reclaim her for ever. He charms the Furies with his singing and succeeds in gaining an entrance to Hades. He reaches the Elysian Fields, where the happy ones bring Eurydice to him. Without looking at her he takes her by the hand and leads her away. She implores him for one look of love; finally unable to resist any longer he turns around and she immediately disappears. Orpheus in despair declares that he will die also and follow her, but Amor, believing he has suffered enough, decides to restore Eurydice to life.

Orff [orrf], CARL: *b.* Munich, July 10, 1895. Studied in Munich and conducted opera in Munich, Mannheim and Darmstadt. Taught at the Dorothee Günter School in Munich, 1925-36, and at the Academy of Music there since 1950. His compositions comprise stage works of three types: cantatas with optional action and dance (*e.g. Carmina Burana*, 1937; *Trionfo di Afrodite*, 1953), operas (*e.g. Der Mond*, 1945), and plays with music (*e.g. Die Bernauerin*, 1947; *Antigonae*, 1949).

K. WÖRNER: "Egk and Orff," in *The Music Review*, xiv.

Organ (*Fr.* orgue, or *plur.* orgues, *G.* Orgel, *I.* organo). The mechanism of the organ comprises: (1) A supply of wind under constant pressure, by hand pump, water pump, or electric blower; (2) one or more MANUALS and a PEDAL BOARD, connected with the pipes by means of trackers, electro-pneumatic devices, or electric contacts and wires; (3) pipes, of flue type, and also, in all but the smallest instruments, of reed type; (4) stops, to admit wind to each register or set of pipes; (5) couplers, to join the actions of manuals to each other, and to that of the pedal.

Flue pipes are of the whistle (*i.e.* recorder) type, and may be open or stopped; stopping lowers the pitch an octave. Reed pipes have a beating reed and a cylindrical or conical resonator. Since organ specifications (*i.e.* number and character of stops) vary widely, the choice of stops (*v.* REGISTRATION), apart from general indications, is usually left to the player. Flue stops are of three classes: diapason, flute, and string; reeds are classified as chorus reeds and solo reeds. The range of pitch within which a stop sounds is indicated by reference to the length, which is approximately 8 ft., of an unstopped pipe which sounds the C below the bass stave. Since this is the lowest note of the keyboard, it is taken as a convenient standard of measurement. An 8 ft. stop sounds at a pitch corresponding to the key which is depressed, a 4 ft. stop an octave higher, a 2 ft. stop two octaves higher, and 16 ft. and 32 ft. stops an octave and two octaves lower. A MIXTURE stop has three or four sets (ranks) of pipes which sound the octave, fifteenth, double octave, etc., above the normal pitch of the key; MUTATION STOPS sound at the twelfth or seventeenth, or their octaves.

The tonal design of each of the three MANUALS, Great, Choir, and Swell, is complete in itself; the Great includes the most powerful stops, the Swell the softest. In large organs the Pedal stops will also have their own tonal design, and the Solo manual will have stops of more individual character. Large instruments may also have an ECHO ORGAN. Designers and makers use a great variety of names for stops, but the following may be regarded as basic: Diapasons of 16, 8, 4 and 2 ft. and a mutation stop on the Great and Swell: one or more flute stops on each manual; a flue stop of string quality (gamba) on the Choir, Swell and Solo; chorus reeds (*e.g.* Trumpet, Clarion) on the Great and Solo; solo reeds (*e.g.* Clarinet, Oboe) on the Choir, Swell and Solo; diapasons and flute stops of 16, 8 and 4 ft., and on large organs a reed of 16 ft. and a double diapason of 32 ft., on the Pedal Organ. The effect of a 32 ft. stop is sometimes simulated, with indifferent results, by combining an open diapason pipe with a stopped pipe a fifth above to produce a difference tone (*v.* ACOUSTICS).

The Swell is always enclosed in a box, and usually also the Choir and Solo; this enables a *crescendo*, controlled by a pedal, to be made by opening one side of the box.

The organ is one of the most ancient instruments still in use. It was known to the Greeks and Romans as *hydraulis*. In 757 the Byzantine Emperor Constantinus Copronymus sent an organ as a gift to Pippin. There are accounts of organs in Christian churches all through the Middle Ages, but the earliest surviving manuscript collections of organ music date from the 15th century. The smaller medieval organs were called, according to size, POSITIVE or PORTATIVE. The greatest period of organ music began with Merulo and ended with Bach. In the course of the 19th cent. the action was completely changed by the use of electricity, and organs increased steadily in size. Organs with as many as seven manuals have been built; the organ in the Royal Festival Hall, London, has four manuals controlling five manual departments, and 102 stops. The most recent tendency in organ designing is towards the revival of the tone qualities of the late baroque organ, either in smaller instruments or as part of the scheme of a larger organ.

G. A. AUDSLEY: *The Art of Organ Building*, 2 vols. (1905).
E. M. SKINNER: *The Modern Organ* (1917).
W. L. SUMNER: *The Organ* (1951).
C. F. ABDY WILLIAMS: *The Story of the Organ* (1903).

Organ, Electronic. An instrument, of which the Hammond organ and the Compton Electrone are examples, with manuals and pedals in which the tone is produced and amplified electrically. By means of controls which select and regulate the intensity of a certain number of overtones the player is able to produce some variety of tone colour. *v.* ACOUSTICS, ELECTRONIC INSTRUMENTS.

Organetto [orr-gah-net'-to], *I.* Small PORTATIVE organ of the Middle Ages.

Organistrum [orr-ga-niss'-troom], *L.* Hurdy-gurdy.

Organ Mass. (1) From the 15th cent. it was customary to perform the music of the Ordinary of the Mass by singers and organ in alternating phrases. The singers sang the plainsong and the organist played a polyphonic elaboration of it. In England this was referred to as "keeping the Mass with organs." An example of an Organ Mass (1542/3) by Girolamo Cavazzoni is printed in the *Historical Anthology*, No. 117. Scheidt composed a complete Organ Mass for the Lutheran rite in Part III of his *Tablatura nova* (1624).

(2) The name has also been given to two Masses by Haydn with orchestral accompaniment which include a part for organ *obbligato*. *v.* GROSSE ORGELMESSE, KLEINE ORGELMESSE.

Organo di coro [orr'-gah-no dee coh'-ro], *I.* Choir organ.

Organo di legno [orr'-gah-no dee lehn'-yo], *I.* Lit., "wooden organ." A term used in the 16th and 17th cent. for a small organ with flue pipes, as opposed to the REGAL, which was a reed organ.

Organ Point. *v.* PEDAL POINT.

Organum [orr'-ga-noom], *L.* (*Gr.* ὄργανον, instrument). (1) Organ. *Pro organo pleno*, for full organ, *i.e.* for an instrument of substantial size and adequate resources.

(2) A name (probably of popular origin) for a method of composition used in the several stages of medieval polyphony. The first stage was expounded *c.* 900 in *Musica Enchiriadis*. The *Scholia Enchiriadis* (English translation in O. Strunk, *Source Readings in Music History*, p. 126), of about the same time, gives these examples:

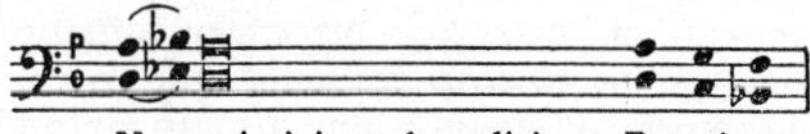

P is the plainsong and O the added part, which follows the plainsong in parallel fifths or fourths, and in the latter case uses thirds and ends on a unison. If either or both of the parts were doubled at the octave above the result was called "composite" *organum*.

In the next stage (11th-12th cent.) the added part moves in perfect intervals (octaves, fifths and fourths) above the plainsong. This is the earliest form of true polyphony:

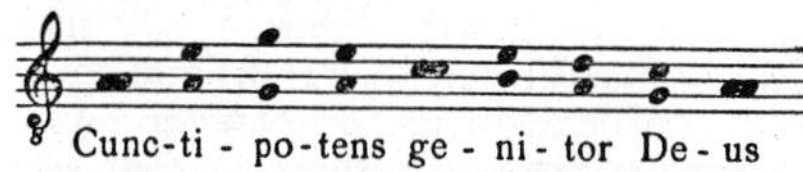

In compositions of the middle of the 12th cent. the added part is much more florid, and the plainsong must have been sung quite slowly:

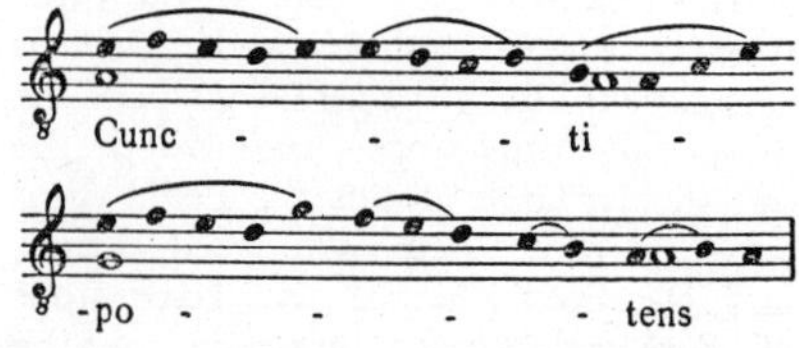

Léonin, the composer attached to Notre Dame, Paris, in the second half of the 12th cent., wrote long liturgical compositions partly in plainsong, partly in florid *organum*, and partly in measured descant:

Such measured sections were called *clausulae.* The addition of words to the upper parts of *clausulae* gave rise to the motet of the following century. The tenor of the last example is the same as that of the motet "*Mout me fugriés / In omni fratre / In seculum,*" of which the opening is quoted under MOTET.

Orgelbüchlein [orrg'-ĕl-bēēsh-line], *G.* "Little organ book." A collection of 46 short chorale preludes, composed by Bach between 1708 and 1717, "in which a beginner at the organ is given instruction in developing a chorale in many different ways, and at the same time in acquiring facility in the study of the pedal, since in the chorales contained therein the pedal is treated as wholly *obbligato.*" It was originally intended to include 164 preludes, dealing with the church's year and with the principal articles of the Christian faith, but was never completed. The best modern edition is by Ivor Atkins, which retains the original order and also prints the chorales on which the preludes are based.

H. GRACE : *The Organ Works of Bach* (1922).

S. DE B. TAYLOR : *The Chorale Preludes of J. S. Bach* (1942).

Orgelmesse [orrg'-ĕl-mess-er], *G.* (Organ Mass). (1) The name given to two Masses by Haydn which include a part for organ *obbligato.* *v.* GROSSE ORGELMESSE, KLEINE ORGELMESSE.

(2) *v.* ORGAN MASS (1).

Orgelpunkt [orrg'-ĕl-pŏŏnkt], *G.* Pedal point.

Orgelwalze [orrg'-ĕl-vults-er], *G.* Mechanical organ. *v.* MECHANICAL MUSICAL INSTRUMENTS.

Orgue [orrg], *Fr.* Organ. The plur. *orgues* is also common.

Orgue expressif [orrg ex-press-eef], *Fr.* Harmonium.

Orlando [orr-lahnd'-o]. Opera in three acts by Handel. Libretto by Grazio Braccioli. First performed, London, Feb. 7, 1733.

Ormandy, EUGENE : *b.* Budapest, Nov. 18, 1899. Conductor, now an American citizen. He studied the violin at the Budapest Royal Academy of Music from an early age and appeared frequently as a child prodigy. He settled in America after a visit in 1921 and began his career as a conductor by directing a cinema orchestra in New York. Conductor, Minneapolis Symphony Orchestra, 1931; Philadelphia Orchestra, 1938.

Ornaments (*Fr.* agréments, *G.* Manieren, *I.* abbellimenti). In some periods ornaments (graces) have been an important feature of melodic style, whether added extemporaneously by singers and players, or indicated by the composer in the form of signs, or incorporated in the notation. In the keyboard and lute pieces of the 16th cent., some of which were elaborations of choral pieces, conventions of ornamentation arose, and to some extent, as in English virginal music, signs were used to indicate them. In the 17th and 18th cent. the principal types for which signs were used, varying somewhat in different countries, were: TRILL, MORDENT, APPOGGIATURA, ARPEGGIO, TURN, SPRINGER or NACHSCHLAG. In later periods most ornaments have been written out by the composer.

P. ALDRICH : *Ornamentation in J. S. Bach's Organ Works* (1951).

E. DANNREUTHER: *Musical Ornamentation* (1893).

A. DOLMETSCH : *The Interpretation of the Music of the Seventeenth and Eighteenth Centuries* (1946).

W. EMERY : *Bach's Ornaments* (1953).

Ornithoparchus, ANDREAS: *b.* Meiningen, *c.* 1485; *d.* Munster, 1535. Theorist. His *Musicae activae micrologus* (1516) was translated into English by John Dowland(1606).

Orphée [orr-fay] (Orpheus). Title of the revised (French) version of Gluck's opera ORFEO ED EURIDICE.

Orpheus Britannicus. A collection of songs by Purcell (1659-95), published in two volumes in 1698 and 1702. A second edition, enlarged, appeared in 1706 and 1711.

Orr, ROBIN : *b.* Brechin, June 2, 1909. Composer. Studied at the R.C.M. and at Cambridge, and under Casella in Siena and Nadia Boulanger in Paris. Organist, St. John's College, Cambridge, 1938. Professor, Glasgow, 1956. His compositions include an *Italian Overture* for orchestra, a *Divertimento* for chamber orchestra, choral music, chamber music, piano pieces, and songs.

Ortigue [dorr-teeg], JOSEPH LOUIS D': *b.* Cavaillon, May 22, 1802; *d.* Paris, Nov. 20, 1866. Writer on church music. In 1829 he moved to Paris where he wrote for many periodicals, succeeding Berlioz as critic of the *Journal des Débats*. With A. L. Niedermeyer he founded *La Maîtrise*, a review of sacred music. His most important work was the *Dictionnaire liturgique, historique, et théorique de Plain-chant et de Musique religieuse*, published in 1854.

Ortiz [orr-teeth'], DIEGO: *b.* Toledo, *c.* 1510. Composer. Court *maestro di cappella* in Naples from 1553. Wrote a treatise (*Tratado de glosas . . . en la música de Violones*, 1553) on the extemporising of variations (*glosas*, *diferencias*) on the viola da gamba in the style originated by Luis de Narvaez for the lute. A volume of his church music was published in 1565.

Orto [orr'-to], MARBRIANO DE: *d.* 1529. Flemish singer and composer. Singer in the Papal Chapel at Rome, 1484-94; became singer and chaplain at the court of Philip of Burgundy, 1505. His "Ave Maria" and a *chanson* were printed in Petrucci's *Odhecaton* (1501; modern ed. by H. Hewitt, 1945), and Masses and motets in later publications of Petrucci.

Osiander [oze-i-und'-er], LUCAS: *b.* Nuremberg, Dec. 16, 1534; *d.* Stuttgart, Sept. 7, 1604. Musician and theologian. His *Fünfzig geistliche Lieder und Psalmen* of 1586 was the first collection of chorales in which the tune was put in the treble; Lutheran composers had previously followed the old tradition of putting it in the tenor. His setting of "Komm, heiliger Geist" is published in Schering's *History of Music in Examples*, No. 143.

Ossia [oss'-yah], *I.* "Or." Used to indicate an alternative, usually simplified, to a passage in a composition.

Ostinato [oss-tee-nah'-toh], *I.* Abbreviation for *basso ostinato* (lit. "obstinate bass"), *i.e.* a figure repeated in the bass throughout a composition, while the upper parts change. *v.* GROUND BASS.

Otello [o-tell'-lo] (Othello). Opera in four acts by Verdi. Libretto by Arrigo Boito (from Shakespeare). First performed, Milan, Feb. 5, 1887.

Othmayr [oat'-mire], CASPAR: *b.* Amberg (Upper Palatinate), March 12, 1515; *d.* Nuremberg, Feb. 7, 1553. Studied at Heidelberg University under Lemlin and in 1545 was Rector of the school at Heilbronn, near Ansbach. In 1548 he became Provost in Ansbach. He wrote settings of German songs, and composed motets and settings of Lutheran hymns. His *Symbola* (1547), a collection of five-part pieces each in honour of a notable person of his time, have been printed in a modern edition (1941) by Hans Albrecht.

Ottava [ot-tah'-vah], *I.* "Octave." Often abbreviated 8*va*. *All'ottava* or 8*va*, an octave higher or lower (generally the former); *ottava alta* or *ottava sopra*, an octave higher; *ottava bassa* or *ottava sotto*, an octave lower; *coll'ottava* or *con ottava*, doubled at the octave above or below. The indications are written above the notes when they refer to the higher octave, below when they refer to the lower. A dotted line indicates how long the indication is valid. When the term 8*va* (or its equivalents) ceases to be valid, it is often contradicted by *loco*, "[in the normal] place."

Ottavino [ot-tah-vee'-no], *I.* Piccolo.

Ottobi [ot-to'-bee], GIOVANNI. *v.* HOTHBY.

Ottone [ot-to'-neh], *I.* Brass. *Strumenti d'ottone* (or *ottoni* alone), brass instruments.

Ottone, Re di Germania [ot-to'-neh reh dee jair-mahn-yah] (Otho, King of Germany). Opera in three acts by Handel. Libretto by Nicola Francesco

Haym. First performed, London, Jan. 23, 1723.

Ours, L' [loorss], *Fr.* (The Bear). The title given to Haydn's symphony No. 82 in C major (1786), which was one of the six commissioned by the Concert de la Loge Olympique in Paris and called the "Paris Symphonies."

Ouseley, FREDERICK ARTHUR GORE: *b.* London, Aug. 12, 1825; *d.* Hereford, Apr. 6, 1889. Composer and historian of music. Son of the diplomat and oriental scholar Sir Gore Ouseley, Bart., whom he succeeded as second baronet, 1844. Educated at Oxford, where he became professor in 1855. Ordained, 1849. Founder of St. Michael's College, Tenbury, 1854, and later warden. He composed services, anthems, and organ works and edited the sacred music of Orlando Gibbons. His valuable collection of manuscripts, books and scores is now in St. Michael's, Tenbury. A catalogue of the manuscripts by E. H. Fellowes was published in 1934.

F. T. HAVERGAL: *Memorial of Sir Frederick A. G. Ouseley* (1889).

Ouvert [oo-vair], *Fr.* (*L.* apertum, *I.* verto). "Open." A medieval term used in dance music, and in vocal pieces similar in structure, to indicate an intermediate cadence at the end of a repeated section when it is performed the first time, in contrast to a final cadence (*Fr.* clos, *L.* clausum, *I.* chiuso) used when it is performed the second time. *Ouvert* and *clos* thus correspond to what is now called "1st time" (or "1st ending") and "2nd time." For a 14th-cent. example *v.* CLOS.

Ouverture [oo-vair-tēer], *Fr.* Overture.

Overtones. *v.* HARMONIC SERIES.

Overture. There is no difference in musical form between an opera overture, an overture which is part of the incidental music to a play, *e.g.* Beethoven's *Egmont*, and an overture which is an independent piece (concert overture), *e.g.* Brahms's *Tragic Overture.* The first established form was the French overture of Lully, which consisted of a slow section in a pompous dotted rhythm followed by a fast section in imitative style, as in his overture to *Thésée* (1675):

In some cases the Allegro ended with a short section in similar style to the opening. Blow's *Venus and Adonis*, Purcell's *Dido and Aeneas* (1689), Handel's *Rinaldo* (1711) and *Messiah* (1742) have overtures in the French style. The instrumental overtures of German composers such as Muffat, Telemann, and Bach are French overtures followed by dance movements, and are now generally called SUITES.

The Italian opera overture (*sinfonia avanti l'opera*) in three movements, Allegro-Adagio-Allegro, was established by A. Scarlatti after 1680, and its later history merged with that of the symphony. The opera overture of the classical period was a single movement, usually in sonata form. Gluck's idea that it should prepare the audience for the nature of the action (dedication of *Alceste*, 1769) was adopted in many later overtures, *e.g.* Mozart's *Don Giovanni* and Beethoven's *Leonore No.* 2 and *No.* 3, by using musical themes from the opera, and was carried a stage further in such overtures as Weber's *Der Freischütz* and Wagner's *Tannhäuser.* Similarly, since Beethoven, overtures to incidental music generally use themes from the following scenes, a process which was carried out in reverse in Mendelssohn's *Midsummer Night's Dream* music. Following Wagner's *Lohengrin* (1847), operas and incidental music frequently open with a PRELUDE. The programmatic concert overture of the early Romantic period (*e.g.* Mendelssohn's *Hebrides*) was the ancestor of the symphonic poem ; the form has continued as the equivalent of the first movement of a symphony, either as a work originally for a special occasion, *e.g.* Brahms's *Academic Festival Overture*. or as a tone-picture, *e.g.* Rimsky-Korsakov's *Russian Easter Overture* and Walton's *Portsmouth Point*.

H. BOTSTIBER : *Geschichte der Ouvertüre* (1913).

Oxford Symphony. The title given to Haydn's symphony No. 92 in G major (1788), after it was performed at a concert in Oxford (July, 1791) during his visit there to receive an honorary D.Mus.

Ox Minuet, The. *v.* OCHSENMENUETTE.

P

P. As an abbreviation P.=pedal, *positif* (in French organ music). Pf.= pianoforte. Pk.=*Pauken*, timpani. *p*= *piano*, soft, *poco*, a little; *pf*=*poco forte*, moderately loud; *pp*=*pianissimo*, very soft; *mp*=*mezzo piano*, moderately soft.

Pachelbel [puckh′-ĕl-bel], (1) JOHANN: *b.* Nuremberg, Aug. 1653; *d.* there, March 6, 1706. Organist and composer. Studied under Heinrich Schwemmer and in Vienna under Kerll from 1674. Organist at the court, Eisenach (where he became a friend of J. S. Bach's father), 1677; Erfurt, 1678; Stuttgart, 1690; Gotha, 1692; St. Sebaldus, Nuremberg, 1695. As a composer of suites for harpsichord and chorale preludes in fughetta style for organ he was one of the important precursors of J. S. Bach. His harpsichord works are printed in *D.T.B.*, ii (1), organ works in *D.T.B.*, iv (1), and his 94 organ verses for the eight tones of the Magnificat in the form of short fugues in *D.T.Ö.*, viii (2).

(2) WILHELM HIERONYMUS: *b.* Erfurt, 1685; *d.* Nuremberg, 1764. Composer. Son of (1). Organist, St. Jacobi, Nuremberg, 1706; St. Sebaldus, 1725. Organ works by him are in *D.T.B.*, ii (1) and iv (1).

Pachmann [pahkh′-mun], VLADIMIR DE: *b.* Odessa, July 27, 1848; *d.* Rome, Jan. 6, 1933. Pianist. Studied with his father in Odessa and at the Vienna Conservatorium. After making his first public appearance in Russia in 1869 he devoted himself to ten years further study (interrupted by a brief emergence on the concert platform) before he finally embarked on the career of a travelling virtuoso. He excelled in the performance of Chopin, whose works he played with a remarkable delicacy. His habit of making remarks to an audience (or to himself) during a performance endeared him to some listeners and infuriated others.

Pacific 231. An orchestral work by Honegger (1923) describing the "visual impression and physical enjoyment" produced by a railway engine.

Pacini [pah-chee′-nee], GIOVANNI: *b.* Catania, Feb. 17, 1796; *d.* Pescia, Dec. 6, 1867. Composer. Studied under his father, under Marchesi in Bologna and under Furlanetto in Venice. He produced his first opera at Milan in 1813. Appointed *Kapellmeister* to the Empress Marie Louise and in 1834 founded a school of music in Viareggio. He composed more than 70 stage works, besides Masses, oratorios, and cantatas.

Pacius [pah′-tsi-ŏŏss], FREDRIK: *b.* Hamburg, March 19, 1809; *d.* Helsinki, Jan. 8, 1891. German (naturalized Finnish) composer and violinist. Studied under Spohr and Hauptmann in Cassel. Violinist in the court orchestra at Stockholm, 1828. Violin teacher at Helsinki University, 1834; professor, 1860. His *Kung Carls Jakt*, generally referred to as the first Finnish opera, was sung in Swedish on its first production in Helsinki in 1852, and was revived in a Finnish translation in 1905.

Paderewski [pud-er-ev′-ski], IGNACY JAN: *b.* Kuryłówka, Nov. 18, 1860; *d.* New York, June 29, 1941. Pianist and composer. Studied in Warsaw, Berlin, and in Vienna under Leschetizky. The most renowned pianist of modern times. From 1915 he worked and spoke in the cause of Polish independence, and in 1919 became Prime Minister of his country. He resumed his concert tours in 1922. He composed many piano works including a concerto, an opera, a symphony, and songs.

Padilla [pah-deel′-lyah], JUAN DE: *b.* *c.* 1610; *d.* Toledo, Dec. 1673. Spanish composer. *Maestro de capilla*, Puebla Cathedral (Mexico), 1649; convent of San Pablo, Zamora (Spain), 1660; Zamora Cathedral, 1661; Toledo Cathedral, 1663. A large number of church compositions, including 5

Masses, are in manuscript at Puebla; others are preserved at Valladolid (Spain). Several of his works are for double choir. One of the most important composers in the history of music in Mexico.

Paer [pah'-air], FERDINANDO: *b.* Parma, June 1, 1771; *d.* Paris, May 3, 1839. Composer of 43 operas, which were produced at Parma, Venice, Vienna (1799-1801), Dresden (1802-7), and Paris (from 1809) where he brought out in 1821 his most successful work, the *opéra-comique Le Maître de Chapelle*, which has been frequently revived. Conductor, Opéra-Comique, Paris; Théâtre des Italiens, 1812, succeeding Spontini; royal chamber music, 1832. He also composed 2 oratorios, cantatas, church music, and some instrumental music.

Paesiello. *v.* PAISIELLO.

Paganini [pah-gah-nee'-nee], NICCOLÒ: *b.* Genoa, Oct. 27, 1782; *d.* Nice, May 27, 1840. Violinist and composer. Studied at Genoa and Parma, and made his first concert tour at thirteen. From 1805-13 he was music director at the court of the Princess of Lucca, and in 1828 began a tour which took him to Vienna, Germany, Paris (1831) and the British Isles. Berlioz wrote *Harold en Italie* (1834) in response to Paganini's request for a viola solo. The greatest of all violinists in technical accomplishment, and a performer of extraordinary fascination. He allowed only a few of his compositions to be published during his lifetime, among them the 24 *Caprices*, Op. 1. Some of the new technical developments in these pieces were adapted to the piano in the studies of Liszt and Schumann, and used for piano variations by Brahms and Rachmaninov. Sonatas for violin and guitar and for violin, viola, guitar and cello were also printed during his lifetime. Compositions published after his death include 2 concertos, 9 sets of variations, and other pieces for violin.

J. PULVER: *Paganini: the Romantic Virtuoso* (1936).

H. SPIVACKE: *Paganiniana* (1945).

Pagliacci [pahl-yah'-chee] (Clowns). Opera with a prologue and two acts by Leoncavallo. Libretto by the composer. First performed, Milan, May 21, 1892. Tonio explains in the prologue that actors are but human. The comedians erect their booth and parade in their costumes before the villagers. After the angelus is heard Nedda (the wife of Canio) and Tonio are left alone but she, annoyed by his attentions, strikes him with a whip. He leaves her swearing revenge. Silvio (a young peasant) tries to persuade Nedda to fly away with him that night. Tonio, who has been listening to their conversation, fetches Canio and brings him to the scene. Silvio escapes unrecognized, and Nedda will not reveal the name of her lover. During the play Canio stumbles through his part and finally demands again to know her lover's name. When she answers lightly he becomes enraged and stabs her with a knife. Silvio who leaps on to the stage to try to protect her is recognized by Canio, who quickly plunges the knife into his heart. Everybody stands irresolute with horror. Canio turns to the audience and announces: "The comedy is ended."

Paine, JOHN KNOWLES: *b.* Portland (Maine), Jan. 9, 1839; *d.* Cambridge, (Mass.), Apr. 25, 1906. Composer. Studied in Portland under Hermann Kotzschmar and in Berlin under Haupt, Wiepricht and Teschner. Instructor in music, Harvard, 1862; assistant professor, 1873; professor (the first in an American University), 1875. He composed 2 symphonies, symphonic poems, cantatas and other choral works, chamber music, piano and organ works and incidental music for plays.

Paisiello [pah-eez-yell'-lo] (Paesiello), GIOVANNI: *b.* Taranto, May 8, 1740; *d.* Naples, June 5, 1816. Composer. Studied with Durante in Naples, and began as a composer of church music, but from 1763 found his true *métier* in *opera buffa*, of which he is one of the greatest masters. Court conductor to Catherine II and director of the Italian opera in St. Petersburg, 1776. Court conductor, Naples, 1784; director of the music in the chapel of Napoleon Bonaparte, Paris, 1802-3. His *Il barbiere di Siviglia* (1782) was the most famous setting of the text before

Rossini's. Beethoven wrote a set of variations for piano on his aria "Nel cor più" from *La Molinara* (1788). Of his more than 100 operas, 7 have been published. He also composed symphonies, piano concertos, and chamber music.

Paix [pah'-icks], JACOB: *b.* Augsburg, 1550; *d.* Hilpoltstein, *c.* 1618. Organist, Launingen, 1575-1601; court organist, Neuburg, until 1617. He published organ transcriptions of motets in tablature, Masses, and a collection of motets (1589) by various composers.

Paladilhe [pa-la-deel], ÉMILE: *b.* Montpellier, June 3, 1844; *d.* Paris, Jan. 8, 1926. Composer. Studied at the Paris Conservatoire under Halévy. *Prix de Rome*, 1860. He composed operas, a symphony, 2 Masses and songs.

Paléographie Musicale [pa-lay-og-ra-fee mē̆-zee-cull], *Fr.* A series of facsimiles, with commentaries, of important manuscripts of plainsong which has been published by the Benedictines of SOLESMES since 1889. 16 volumes have been completed.

Palester [pa-lest'-er], ROMAN: *b.* Śniatyn (Ukraine), Dec. 28, 1907. Polish composer, now resident in Paris. Studied at Lwow and Warsaw. He first became known outside Poland through the performance of his works at festivals of the International Society for Contemporary Music. His compositions include 3 symphonies, violin concerto, saxophone concertino, chamber music, choral works, an opera and a ballet, as well as music for the theatre, films and radio.

Palestrina [pah-less-tree'-nah], GIOVANNI PIERLUIGI DA (Johannes Praenestinus): *b.* Palestrina (nr. Rome), *c.* 1525; *d.* Rome, Feb. 2, 1594. Composer. Chorister at Santa Maria Maggiore in Rome, 1537; organist and choirmaster, Palestrina Cathedral, 1544. In 1551 was summoned to be choirmaster of the Cappella Giulia by Pope Julius III, who in 1555 made him a member of the Papal Choir. With two others, he was dismissed in the same year, apparently because he was married, but nevertheless was appointed musical director at St. John Lateran in succession to Lassus. He resigned in 1560, and from 1561 was choirmaster at Santa Maria Maggiore, from 1567 in the service of Cardinal Ippolito d'Este, and from 1571 director of the Capella Giulia, succeeding Animuccia. On the death of his wife in 1580 he decided to become a priest and received the tonsure, but three months later married a wealthy widow.

Since the writing of Fux's *Gradus* in 1725 Palestrina's style has been regarded as the exemplar of the greatest age of counterpoint, and since Baini's monograph of 1828 as the purest model of devotional polyphony (*v.* MOTU PROPRIO). While his style is noteworthy for its serenity of expression, artistic discipline and thorough consistency (*v.* K. JEPPESEN, *The Style of Palestrina*, 2nd ed., 1946), it is by no means representative of 16th-cent. contrapuntal style as a whole. Nor is there any historical basis for Baini's story that his *Missa Papae Marcelli* influenced decisions of the Council of Trent. The reforms instituted by Pius IV and Pius V forbade the singing of Masses whose counterpoint was so elaborate as to obscure the words, and which contained words foreign to the liturgy of the Mass. Palestrina's later works were in conformity with those decrees, and his position caused him to be entrusted with a "reformed" version of the plainsong of the mass, published in the "Medicean" Gradual of 1614, which has been replaced in this century by the Solesmes versions of the medieval chant.

Palestrina's most typical style is a diatonic and modal imitative polyphony, beautifully balanced in rhythm, in melody, and in the use of dissonance. In compositions in six or more parts it leans more often towards the originally Venetian and more homophonic style of antiphonal writing for divided choir, as in the *Stabat Mater*. About three-quarters of his Masses, for four to eight voices, are PARODY masses; a few are based on a plainsong *cantus firmus*, *e.g.* *Ecce sacerdos magnus*, or on a secular song, *e.g.*, *L'homme armé*. His church music includes motets in four to eight and in twelve parts, Lamentations, Magnificats, Litanies and Psalms; his other works are sacred madrigals (in Italian) and secular madrigals.

A complete edition of the works of Palestrina in 33 volumes was published by Breitkopf & Härtel (1862-1903). A new complete edition in 34 volumes, edited by R. Casimiri and L. Bianchi, is in process of publication (22 volumes to 1957).

H. COATES : *Palestrina* (1938).

Z. K. PYNE : *Palestrina ; his Life and Times* (1922).

Palestrina [pa-less-tree′-na]. Opera in three acts by Pfitzner. Libretto by the composer. First performed, Munich, June 12, 1917.

Palindrome (*Gr.* *παλίνδρομος*, running backwards). A sentence which reads the same backwards as forwards. Hence, a piece of music of which the second half is the first half in RETROGRADE MOTION, *e.g.* the " crab " canon in Bach's *Musikalisches Opfer.*

Pallavicini [pahl-lah-vee-chee′-nee] (Pallavicino), CARLO: *b.* Salò, 1630; *d.* Dresden, Jan. 26, 1688. Composer. He lived in Venice and also (from 1667) in Dresden, where he was appointed court *Kapellmeister.* He contributed greatly to the development of the aria in Venetian opera. The most mature of his 21 operas is *Gerusalemme liberata* (Dresden, 1687; modern ed. in *D.D.T.*, lv).

Pallavicino [pahl-lah-vee-chee′-no], (1) BENEDETTO : *b.* Cremona ; *d.* Mantua, May 6, 1601. Composer. At the court of Mantua from 1581. In 1596 he succeeded Giaches de Wert as *maestro di cappella* to the Duke of Mantua. Monteverdi was his successor in this post. He published 10 books of madrigals between 1579 and 1612. A five-part madrigal " Dolcemente dormiva " is printed by Torchi in *L'arte musicale in Italia,* ii.

(2) CARLO. *v.* PALLAVICINI.

Palmgren [pullm′-grehn], SELIM: *b.* Pori (Björneborg), Feb. 16, 1878 ; *d.* Helsinki, Dec. 13, 1951. Pianist, conductor and composer. Studied at Helsinki Conservatoire from 1895-99 and later in Germany and Italy. Conductor in Turku (Åbo), 1909 ; teacher of piano and composition at the Eastman School, Rochester (N.Y.), 1923. Music critic in Helsinki, 1930. Teacher of piano, Sibelius Academy, 1939. He composed piano concertos, choral works and songs, operas and orchestral works, and piano pieces.

Palotta [pah-lot′-tah], MATTEO: *b.* Palermo, 1680; *d.* Vienna, March 28, 1758. Composer. Studied in Naples, was ordained priest, and in 1733 was appointed one of the court composers to the Emperor Charles VI in Vienna. He wrote a treatise on Gregorian chant and composed Masses, motets and other church music.

Pålson-Wettergren [pawl′-son-vet′-er-grehn], GERTRUD (*née* Pålson) : *b.* Eslöv (Sweden), Feb. 17, 1897. Mezzo-soprano. Studied at the Stockholm Conservatoire and made her first appearance as Cherubino in *Le nozze di Figaro* at Stockholm, 1922. In addition to her appearances in Scandinavian centres she has sung frequently in America and was a guest artist at Covent Garden in 1936 and 1939. Her large repertory of operatic parts include Carmen, Amneris in *Aida,* Brangäne in *Tristan und Isolde,* Ortrud in *Lohengrin,* Princess Eboli in *Don Carlos,* and Herodias in *Salome.* She has also appeared in *La Fille de Madame Angot* (Lecocq) and other operettas.

Pammelia. Title of Thomas Ravenscroft's collection (1609) of anonymous canons, rounds, and catches, the first such collection to be published in England. A continuation, *Deuteromelia,* was published in the same year.

Pandora (pandore, bandora, bandore). A plucked string instrument of the CITTERN family, invented in England *c.* 1560. Its characteristic feature was its shape : the sides were scalloped so as to form three lobes—a small one at the top, a larger one in the middle, and a still broader one at the base. There is a part for the pandora in Morley's *First Booke of Consort Lessons* (1599) and also in Sir William Leighton's *Teares or Lamentacions of a Sorrowfull Soule* (1614). The name is presumably derived from the PANDURA, but is not to be confused with it.

Pandura [pan-doo′-ra], *Gr.* (*πανδοῦρα*). An Oriental name (supposedly of Sumerian origin) applied by the Greeks to the three-stringed lute, for which the vernacular term was *trichordon* (τρίχορδον *i.e.* an instrument with three strings). Not to be confused with the PANDORA.

Pannain [pahn-nah'-een], GUIDO: *b.* Naples, Nov. 17, 1891. Writer on music and composer. Studied at Naples Conservatorio, where he was later appointed teacher of music history, and at the University. With Andrea della Corte he has written a history of music and has published books on music of the past and present, one of which has been translated into English under the title *Modern Composers* (1933).

Pantaleon. *v.* DULCIMER.

Panufnik [pa-noof'-nyeek], ANDRZEJ: *b.* Warsaw, Sept. 24, 1914. Conductor and composer, son of a Polish father and an English mother. Studied at the Warsaw Conservatoire and with Weingartner in Vienna. Conductor, Cracow Philharmonic Orchestra, 1945; Warsaw Philharmonic Orchestra, 1946; City of Birmingham Symphony Orchestra, 1957. His compositions, mainly for orchestra, include 2 overtures and a *Sinfonia rustica*.

Papandopulo [pup-un-daw'-poo-lo], BORIS: *b.* Zagreb, Feb. 25, 1906. Composer, conductor and music critic. Studied in Zagreb and Vienna. Conductor of the Kolo and Filipović choirs and of the orchestra of the Zagreb Music Institute; teacher at the Music School in Split, 1935-8; director, Sarajevo Opera, 1949. He has composed choral works, chamber music, 2 operas, 2 piano concertos, piano works and songs.

Papillons [pa-pee-yon͞], *Fr.* (Butterflies). A set of short piano pieces by Schumann, Op. 2 (published, 1832). The composer claimed that his inspiration derived from a scene describing a masked ball in Jean Paul's novel *Die Flegeljahre*, though some of the material is in fact derived from a set of eight Polonaises for piano duet, composed in 1828 but not published till 1933.

Paradies [pah-rah-deece'] (Paradisi), PIETRO DOMENICO: *b.* Naples, 1707; *d.* Venice, Aug. 25, 1791. Composer. Studied under Porpora and in 1747 went to London, where he taught the harpsichord and singing. He composed harpsichord sonatas and operas.

Paradise and the Peri. (1) *Das Paradies und die Peri*, a composition for soli, chorus and orchestra by Schumann, Op. 50 (1843) with words from a German translation of a poem in Thomas Moore's *Lalla Rookh*.

(2) Fantasia-Overture by Sterndale Bennett, Op. 42 (1862), based on the poem by Thomas Moore.

Paradisi. *v.* PARADIES.

Parallel Intervals. *v.* CONSECUTIVE INTERVALS.

Parallel Motion. The movement of two or more parts by the same INTERVAL, whether the interval is major or minor, perfect or imperfect. *v.* CONSECUTIVE INTERVALS.

Paray [pa-ray], PAUL M. A. CHARLES: *b.* Le Tréport, May 24, 1886. Conductor and composer. Studied at the Paris Conservatoire. *Prix de Rome*, 1911. Conductor, Concerts Pasdeloup, 1923; Municipal Orchestra, Monte Carlo, 1928; Concerts Colonne, 1933. He has composed chamber music, an oratorio and a Mass, a symphony and a symphonic poem, and songs.

Pardessus de viole [parr-dess-ee͞ de vyoll], *Fr.* Descant viol made in the 18th century. It was tuned a fourth higher than the treble viol (*Dessus de viole*).

Paride e Elena [pah'-ree-deh eh ehleh'-nah] (Paris and Helen). Opera in five acts by Gluck. Libretto by Raniero de' Calzabigi. First performed, Vienna, Nov. 3, 1770.

Paris Symphonies. A set of six symphonies by Haydn commissioned by the Concert de la Loge Olympique in Paris:

No. 82 in C major, *L'Ours* (The Bear), 1786.
No. 83 in G minor, *La Poule* (The Hen), 1785.
No. 84 in E♭ major, 1786.
No. 85 in B♭ major, *La Reine* (*de France*) (The Queen of France), *c.* 1786.
No. 86 in D major, 1786.
No. 87 in A major, 1785.

Paris Symphony. The title given to Mozart's symphony No. 31 in D major,

K.297 (1778), which was composed in Paris and performed at a *Concert spirituel*. After the first performance he wrote a new slow movement.

Parker, HORATIO WILLIAM: *b.* Auburndale (Mass.), Sept. 15, 1863; *d.* Cedarhurst (N.Y.), Dec. 18, 1919. Organist and composer. Studied under Chadwick in Boston and Rheinberger in Munich. Teacher, National Conservatory, New York (of which Dvořák was the director). Professor, Yale, 1894. He composed oratorios (including *Hora Novissima*, frequently performed in America and in England) cantatas and choral works, 2 operas, overtures and other orchestral works, piano and organ pieces, and songs.

Parlando [parr-lahnd'-o], *I.* "Speaking." A style of singing approximating to speech, usually very rapid.

Parody Mass (*L.* missa parodia). A term used for a polyphonic Mass composed by using the existing music, in more or less complete sections, of a motet or *chanson*, a procedure adopted by many composers from Okeghem to Palestrina. Nicholas Gombert's Mass *Je suis déshéritée*, for example, begins thus:

The *chanson* by Pierre Cadéac on which it was based begins:

Parratt, WALTER: *b.* Huddersfield, Feb. 10, 1841; *d.* Windsor, March 27, 1924. Organist and composer. Organist, Magdalen College, Oxford, 1872; St. George's Chapel, Windsor, 1882-1924. Teacher, R.C.M., 1883-1923. Professor, Oxford, 1908-18. Knighted, 1892. He composed incidental music for plays, anthems and organ pieces.

D. TOVEY AND G. PARRATT: *Walter Parratt* (1941).

Parry, CHARLES HUBERT HASTINGS: *b.* Bournemouth, Feb. 27, 1848; *d.* Rustington, Oct. 7, 1918. Composer and musical historian. Educated at Eton and Oxford. After further studies with Sterndale Bennett, Macfarren, Henry Hugo Pierson and Dannreuther, his piano concerto in F♯ minor and *Prometheus Unbound* for chorus were performed in 1880. A series of choral works, including *Ode on St. Cecilia's Day* (1889), *L'Allegro ed il Penseroso* (1890), *Job* (1892), *The Lotus-Eaters* (1892), *Ode to Music* (1901), *The Pied Piper of Hamelin* (1905) and *Songs of Farewell* (1916-18), and his work as Director of the R.C.M. from 1894 made him the leader, with Stanford, of the English musical renaissance. Knighted 1898; baronet, 1903. Professor, Oxford, 1900-8. His chief writings are *Studies of Great Composers* (1886), *The Evolution of the Art of Music* (1896), *The Seventeenth*

Century (vol. iii of *The Oxford History of Music*, 1902), *J. S. Bach* (1909), and *Style in Musical Art* (1911).

J. A. FULLER-MAITLAND : *The Music of Parry and Stanford* (1934).

C. L. GRAVES : *Hubert Parry*, 2 vols. (1926).

Parsifal [parr′-see-full]. Opera in three acts by Wagner. Libretto by the composer. First performed, Bayreuth, July 26, 1882. Amfortas, ruler of the Knights of the Holy Grail, having yielded to the charms of Kundry, has been wounded by the spear which pierced the side of Christ. Klingsor, an evil magician, possesses the spear. Only one who is completely guileless and simple can recapture the spear and with it heal Amfortas's wound. Parsifal, a forest lad, has in ignorance killed a swan and is brought to the castle of the knights where Gurnemanz, an old knight, hopes to find in him the deliverer from sin. He is, however, so simple and ignorant that he fails to understand the celebration of the Eucharist which he is allowed to witness, and is dismissed. Having found his way into Klingsor's magic garden, he resists the enchantment offered him by Kundry and captures the spear from Klingsor. Years later he returns as a knight to the castle, where he finds Kundry, now a penitent in the service of the Grail. He heals Amfortas's wound, and uncovers the Grail. As the knights kneel before their new ruler, Kundry dies.

Parsley, OSBERT : *b. c.* 1511 ; *d.* Norwich, 1585. Singer at Norwich Cathedral for fifty years. He composed church music, which has been printed in *Tudor Church Music*, x.

Parsons, ROBERT : *b.* Exeter; *d.* Newark-on-Trent, Jan. 25, 1570. Gentleman of the Chapel Royal, 1563. He composed services, anthems, motets, madrigals and pieces for viols. A five-part *In nomine* by him was arranged for virginals by Byrd (ed. E. H. Fellowes, *The Works of Byrd*, xx).

Part-Book. When large CHOIRBOOKS began to go out of use in the early 16th cent. it became usual to write and print the parts (*e.g. cantus, altus, tenor, bassus*) of a choral work, and later of pieces for instruments, in separate part-books. In some cases it has unfortunately resulted that sets of early manuscript or printed part-books have been dispersed, and one or more of the set has been lost. Since *c.* 1600 SCORE form has been used for orchestral, chamber and choral works, while the various parts of an orchestral or chamber piece, and occasionally the voice parts of a choral work, are published or written separately for performance.

Parthenia (*Gr.* παρθενία, maidenhood). The title, which continues thus: *or The Maydenhead of the first musicke that ever was printed for the Virginalls*, of a collection of 21 pieces by Byrd, Bull, and Gibbons, published in 1612 or early in 1613. It was probably the first book of music engraved in England. A facsimile was published in 1942. *Parthenia In-violata*, containing 20 anonymous duets for virginals and bass viol, was published about 1614.

Partials. Overtones of the HARMONIC SERIES.

Partial Signature. A term used to denote a situation common in music between *c.* 1350 and *c.* 1520 in which the key signatures of some parts, usually higher parts, have fewer flats than those of others, usually the lower parts. The theoretical implications of the practice have not been fully explained. From it arose the frequent occurrences of FALSE RELATION, *e.g.*:

DAVY, *Stabat Mater* (c.1500)

which was a persistent idiom in English music until Purcell.

Partita [parr-tee′-tah], *I.* "Division." The term originally meant variation, and was first used in the early 17th cent., *e.g.* in Frescobaldi's *Toccate e Partite d'Intavolatura di Cembalo* of 1615. It is not clear why German composers at the end of the century began to use it in the sense of SUITE, as Bach did in the 6 partitas for harpsichord (*Clavierübung*, pt. 1), in the Suite (*Ouverture*) in the French style (*Clavierübung*, pt. 2), and in the three partitas for solo violin.

Partition [parr-teece-yon͡], *Fr.* Score. *Partition d'orchestre*, full score. *Partition chant et piano*, vocal score.

Partitur [parr-teet-oorr′], *G.* Full score.

Partitura [parr-tee-too′-rah], *I.* Score. *Partitura d'orchestra*, full score.

Partsong. A term used, especially in the 19th-cent., for a short unaccompanied piece for choir in HOMOPHONIC style, as distinct from the polyphonic style of the 16th-cent. MADRIGAL.

Part-writing (*G.* Stimmführung, hence "voice leading," used in America). The writing of the parts of a polyphonic composition in such a way as to produce a good melodic line in each part, which is the chief end of the study of COUNTERPOINT.

Paspy. English 17th-cent. equivalent of PASSEPIED.

Pasquali [puss-cwah′-lee], NICOLÒ: *d.* Edinburgh, Oct. 13, 1757. Italian violinist and composer. Lived in Edinburgh from *c.* 1740, in Dublin from 1748-52, and then returned to Edinburgh. He composed songs, overtures, and solo and trio sonatas. He wrote *Thoroughbass Made Easy* (1757) and *The Art of Fingering the Harpsichord*, published about three years after his death.

Pasquini [puss-cwee′-nee], BERNARDO: *b.* Massa di Valdinievole (Tuscany), Dec. 7, 1637; *d.* Rome, Nov. 21, 1710. Composer, pupil of Vittori and Cesti. Organist, Santa Maria Maggiore, Rome, and harpsichordist of the opera orchestra, in which Corelli was first violinist. His pupils included Durante, Georg Muffat, Gasparini and Domenico Scarlatti. He composed keyboard music, operas, oratorios, and cantatas. Three keyboard pieces are printed in Torchi, *L'arte musicale in Italia*, iii.

Passacaglia [pahss-sah-cahl′-yah], *I.* (*Fr.* passecaille; both possibly from *Sp.* pasacalle, "street song.") A dance introduced into keyboard music early in the 17th century. Composers made no effective distinction between the passacaglia and the CHACONNE; both were normally in triple time, were composed in regular phrases of two, four, or eight bars, and had a FULL CLOSE at the end of each phrase. (For a passacaglia in duple time see Handel's harpsichord suite No. 7.) French composers wrote the passacaglia in RONDO form (*passecaille en rondeau*) by alternating it with a series of different phrases. In the *Passacaille* in F. Couperin's eighth *ordre* for clavecin the theme:

is repeated after each of eight different *couplets*. German composers usually composed the passacaglia in variation form, over a regular GROUND BASS, as in the passacaglias for organ by Buxtehude:

and Bach. Modern examples, *e.g.* the finale of Hindemith's fourth string quartet, are invariably in this form.

Passamezzo [pahss-sah-meh'-dzo], *I.* "Half step." A dance in duple time and in fairly quick tempo, which was popular in the second half of the 16th century. The melody (a) is thus given by Nicholaus Ammerbach in his *Orgel oder Instrument Tablatur* (1571):

The bass, of which (b) is the simplest form, was later used as a basis for variations, *e.g.*, the Passamezzo pavanes and galliards by Byrd and Philips in the *Fitzwilliam Virginal Book* and Scheidt's *Passamezzo* Variations in Part I of the *Tabulatura Nova* (1624). Philips's *Galiarda Passamezzo* begins thus:

The word appears in other English virginal books as "passinge mesures" and "passa measures." New tunes were composed on this or slightly varied forms of the *passamezzo* bass, *e.g. Greensleeves, Quodling's Delight*, used for a set of variations by Giles Farnaby (*Fitzwilliam Virginal Book*, ii, p. 19) and Campion's "Fain would I wed" in his *Fourth Booke of Ayres* (*c.* 1617). The bass known as *passamezzo nuovo* or *moderno*:

was used in the same fashion, as in the variations for five instruments called *Passameza* in Valentin Haussmann's *Neue Intrade* of 1604, printed in *D.D.T.*, xvi, p. 141.

Passecaille [puss-ca-y*er*], *Fr.* Passacaglia.

Passepied [puss-pyay], *Fr.* A French dance, said to have come from Brittany, which was introduced into the French ballet *c.* 1650 and thence into the SUITE, as in Bach's fifth *English Suite.* It is in quick triple time. The *passepied* in Couperin's second *ordre* for clavecin begins thus:

English composers wrote the word as "paspy."

Passing Note (*Fr.* note de passage, *G.* Durchgangsnote). A note taken scalewise between two notes consonant with the prevailing harmony, which may itself be dissonant with that harmony, *e.g.*:

where both the C and A are passing notes. The principal may be extended to two or more notes taken scalewise, as in the penultimate bar of Chopin's Nocturne, Op. 48. No. 2:

Passion. From about the 12th cent. the plainsong to which the gospel accounts of the Passion were recited on Palm Sunday and the following days was divided between three singers who recited the parts of Christ (*bassa voce,* in a low range), the Evangelist (*media voce,* in middle range), and the crowd or *turba* (*alta voce,* in a high range). In the 15th cent. part-singing began to be used for the words of the *turba*, the other parts being still sung in plainsong; three of the earliest settings of this kind are English, two by unknown composers (*c.* 1450), the other by Richard Davy (*c.* 1500). Another method, that of setting the whole text in polyphony, sometimes using the plainsong as a CANTUS FIRMUS in the tenor, arose about the beginning of the 16th century. During the next century and a half Passions, in one or other of these ways, were written by many composers, among them Lassus, Victoria, Scandello, Byrd, Gallus, Lechner and Schütz. A number of settings of the Passion composed between *c.* 1500 and 1631 are printed in whole or in part in O. Kade's *Die ältere Passionskomposition* (1893).

The new features in settings of the Passion by Lutheran composers after 1640 were the use of recitative, and the introduction of contemplative poems in the form of chorales and arias. The *St. John* (1723) and *St. Matthew* (1729) Passions by Bach are the final flowering of this development. Thomas Selle used recitative in his *St. John* Passion of 1643, Johann Sebastiani included chorales for solo voice in his *St. Matthew* Passion, composed in 1663, and Johann Theile's *St. Matthew* Passion of 1673 has arias with instrumental ritornelli. C. P. E. Bach composed two Passions in Hamburg (1787 and 1788), but in later times there have been no important works in this form.

Passione, La [lah pahss-yo′-neh] *I.* (The Passion). Symphony No. 49 in F minor by Haydn (1768), which was probably composed for performance in Holy Week.

Pasticcio [puss-teech′-yo], *I.* Lit. "pie." A work that has been put together by taking items from the works of various composers, as was often the case with 18th-cent. operas. For example, J. C. Bach's first appearance before an English audience was with the comic opera *Il Tutore e la Pupilla,* a *pasticcio* "selected from various celebrated authors" (*i.e.* composers) and "performed under the direction of Mr. John Bach, a Saxon Master of Music," who also composed the overture. A *pasticcio* may be the result of voluntary collaboration, as with the opera *Muzio Scevola* (1721), of which Mattei, Bononcini and Handel each composed one act.

Pastoral. (1) Alternative name for the madrigal, as in F. Pilkington's two sets of *Madrigals and Pastorals* (1614 and 1624).

(2) Any work dealing with, or representing, country life, *e.g.* Bliss's *Lie strewn the white flocks* for mezzo-soprano, chorus, flute, timpani and strings.

Pastorale [puss-to-rah′-leh], *I.* An instrumental movement, usually in 6/8 or 12/8 time, with long bass notes, giving a drone effect similar to that of the MUSETTE. One of the earliest examples in this style is a *Capriccio pastorale* in Frescobaldi's *Toccate d'Intavolatura di Cimbalo et Organo* of 1614/15. Later instances are the optional last movement of Corelli's *Concerto Grosso No.* 8:

the pastoral symphonies in Handel's *Messiah* and Bach's *Christmas Oratorio*, and Bach's *Pastorale* for organ.

Pastoral Sonata. (1) The name given to Beethoven's piano sonata in D major, Op. 28, by the Hamburg publisher August Cranz (1789-1870).

(2) Rheinberger's third organ sonata in G major, Op. 88.

Pastoral Symphony. (1) Beethoven's sixth symphony in F major, Op. 68 (1808), entitled *Sinfonia pastorale.* The titles of the five movements are:

I. *Erwachen heiterer Empfindungen bei der Ankunft auf dem Lande* (Awakening of happy feelings on arriving in the country).
II. *Scene am Bach* (Scene by the brook).
III. *Lustiges Zusammensein der Landleute* (Merry gathering of peasants), interrupted by
IV. *Gewitter. Sturm* (Thunderstorm), leading to
V. *Hirtengesang. Frohe und dankbare Gefühle nach dem Sturm* (Shepherds' song. Cheerful and thankful feelings after the storm).

The second movement introduces the characteristic calls of the nightingale (flute), quail (oboe) and cuckoo (clarinet). In the programme of the first performance, Dec. 22, 1808, the work was described as " Pastoral Symphonie: mehr Ausdruck der Empfindung als Malerei " (Pastoral symphony: an expression of emotion rather than tone-painting). Beethoven may have got the idea of a work on this subject from J. H. Knecht's symphony *Le Portrait Musical de la Nature* (*c.* 1785), which has a similar programme.

(2) Vaughan Williams's third symphony (1924).

(3) The name given to an instrumental piece in *siciliano* rhythm in Handel's *Messiah* (1742). It occurs immediately before the recitative beginning " There were shepherds abiding in the field " and was called " Pifa " by the composer.

(4) Also applied to an instrumental piece in the same rhythm at the beginning of Part II of Bach's *Christmas Oratorio* (1734). *v.* PASTORALE.

Pastor Fido, Il [eel pust′-orr fee′-do] (The Faithful Shepherd). Opera in three acts by Handel. Libretto by Giacomo Rossi (from Guarini's pastoral play). First performed, London, Dec. 3, 1712.

Pathetic Sonata. Beethoven's piano sonata in C minor, Op. 13, published in 1799 with the title *Grande sonate pathétique.* The plan of the first movement, with its alternation of slow and quick sections, is similar to that of the first movement of a sonata in F minor dating from 1783, when Beethoven was 12 years old. It is also possible that he was influenced by Dussek's sonata in C minor (*c.* 1793), the slow movement of which is marked *patetico.*

Pathetic Symphony. Tchaikovsky's sixth symphony in B minor, Op. 74 (1893). The title was suggested by the composer's brother Modeste after the first performance.

Patience. Comic opera in two acts by Sullivan. Libretto by William Schwenk

Gilbert. First performed, London, Apr. 25, 1881.

Patrick, NATHANIEL: *d.* Worcester, March 1595. Organist and master of the choristers at Worcester Cathedral from *c.* 1590. He composed services and madrigals.

Patti [paht′-tee], ADELINA (Adela Juana Maria): *b.* Madrid, Feb. 10, 1843; *d.* Craig-y-Nos Castle (Wales), Sept. 27, 1919. Italian operatic soprano. Studied under Maurice Strakosch and in 1859 made her opera début in New York as Lucia. Sang in England, Europe, North and South America and in 1914 made her last public appearance. She was the most famous soprano of her time, excelling both in opera and in oratorio.

Patzak [putt′-suck], JULIUS: *b.* Vienna, Apr. 9, 1898. Tenor. He was originally active as a conductor but turned to singing in his 20's and sang at the Munich Opera from 1928-45. Since 1946 he has been a member of the Vienna State Opera. He has appeared at many European theatres and has also sung in oratorio and given song recitals.

Pauer [pow′-er], ERNST: *b.* Vienna, Dec. 21, 1826; *d.* Jugenheim (nr. Darmstadt), May 9, 1905. Pianist and teacher. Studied under Mozart's son Wolfgang Amadeus and Franz Lachner. Settled in London in 1851, and taught at the R.A.M., 1859-64, and the R.C.M. from 1883. Returned to Germany in 1896. He gave several series of historical programmes of piano music and lectured on music. He edited collections of keyboard music, published several books, and composed chamber music, operas, a symphony, and works for the piano.

Pauken [powk′-ĕn], *G.* Timpani.

Paukenmesse [powk′-ĕn-mess′-er], *G.* The name given to Haydn's Mass in C major, composed in 1796 and entitled *Missa in tempore belli* (Mass in time of war).

Paukenschlag [powk′-ĕn-shlahk], **Symphonie mit dem,** *G. v.* SURPRISE SYMPHONY.

Paukenwirbel [powk′-ĕn-virr′-bĕl], **Symphonie mit dem,** *G. v.* DRUM ROLL SYMPHONY.

Paulus [powl′-ŏŏss]. *v.* ST. PAUL.

Paumann [pow′-mun] CONRAD: *b.* Nuremberg, *c.* 1410; *d.* Munich, Jan. 24, 1473. Organist and composer. Blind from birth, he was organist at St. Sebaldus in Nuremberg from 1446, and court organist at Munich from 1467. His gravestone in the Frauenkirche in Munich shows him playing a portative organ. His *Fundamentum organisandi* (=Foundations of Composition) of 1452 is one of the earliest manuscripts of keyboard tablature. It contains exercises in composing in organ style and arrangements of German songs. A facsimile of the *Lochamer Liederbuch,* which contains the *Fundamentum,* was published by K. Ameln in 1925. Paumann's organ setting of " Mit ganczem Willen " from this manuscript is printed in the *Historical Anthology,* No. 81.

Paumgartner [powm′-gart-ner], BERNHARD: *b.* Vienna, Nov. 14, 1887. Composer, conductor and musicologist. Director, Salzburg Mozarteum, 1917-38 and since 1945. He has taken a prominent part in the organization of the Salzburg festivals and founded the Salzburg Mozart Orchestra, which he conducts. His studies have been devoted principally to the 18th cent.: he has published a biography of Mozart and also edited (with O. E. Deutsch) Leopold Mozart's letters to his daughter. His most important compositions are for the stage and include operas, ballets and incidental music for the open-air production of Goethe's *Faust* at Salzburg.

Paur [powr], EMIL: *b.* Czernowitz (Bukovina), Aug. 29, 1855; *d.* Mistek (Moravia), June 7, 1932. Conductor. Studied at the Vienna Conservatorium. After holding posts as conductor at Cassel, Königsberg, Mannheim, and Leipzig, he was appointed conductor of the Boston Symphony Orchestra (succeeding Nikisch), 1893; New York Philharmonic Orchestra (succeeding Anton Seidl), 1898; Pittsburgh Orchestra, 1903; Berlin Royal Opera, 1912. He composed a symphony, chamber music and piano pieces.

Pausa [pow′-zah], *I.* A rest.

Pause. (1) *E.* (*Fr.* point d'orgue, *G.* Fermate, *I.* fermata). A wait of indefinite length on a note or rest, indicated by the sign 𝄐.

(2) *Fr.* [poze], *G.* [powz'-er] (*I.* pausa). A rest (in particular, in French, a semibreve rest). *Generalpause* [gay-ner-ahl'-powz'-er], *G.*, abbreviated *G.P.*, a rest for the complete orchestra, generally of a whole bar (or even several bars in a quick tempo).

Pavane. A Spanish dance in slow duple time which was introduced into instrumental music early in the 16th century. The name may derive from *pavo*, peacock, or from *paduana*, a dance from Padua. After *c.* 1550 it was usually followed by a GALLIARD (*q.v.* for an example of both), which often used the same theme. In the numerous pavanes (usually written "pavana," also "pavian," "pavin," etc.) in the English virginal books each of the two sections is followed by a variation. In suites by German composers in the first half of the 17th cent., *e.g.* Schein's *Banchetto musicale* of 1617, the pavane (*paduana*) and galliard (*gagliarda*) are the first two movements.

Paz [pahth], JUAN CARLOS: *b.* Buenos Aires, Aug. 5, 1897. Composer. Studied under Roberto Nery (piano) and Constantino Gaito (harmony). Founded in 1938 "Nueva Música," a society for the performance of contemporary music. He has composed a Passacaglia for orchestra (twelve-tonal) and other orchestral works, variations for 11 wind instruments and other chamber music, and piano works.

Pearl Fishers, The. *v.* PÊCHEURS DE PERLES.

Pearsall, ROBERT LUCAS: *b.* Clifton, March 14, 1795; *d.* Wartensee, Aug. 5, 1856. Composer. Spent most of his life from 1825 in Germany, at Mainz, at Carlsruhe, and at Wartensee on Lake Constance. Composed many sacred works (nearly all still in manuscript), partsongs, and madrigals. The latter, though imitations of the Elizabethan and Jacobean madrigal, stand out from the English choral music of their time by their distinction and craftsmanship.

Peasant Cantata (*Mer hahn en neue Oberkeet,* We have a new magistracy). Secular cantata No. 10 (cantata No. 212) by J. S. Bach (1742) for solo voices, chorus and orchestra, with words in Saxon dialect.

Pêcheurs de Perles, Les [lay pesh-er der pairl] (The Pearl Fishers). Opera in three acts by Bizet. Libretto by Eugène Cormon and Michel Carré. First performed, Paris, Sept. 30, 1863.

Pedal. (1) Part of the mechanism of an instrument, controlled by the feet. *v.* HARP, HARPSICHORD, ORGAN, PEDAL BOARD, PIANOFORTE.

(2) A sustained note which persists through changes of harmony. *v.* PEDAL POINT.

(3) The fundamental (or first note of the HARMONIC SERIES) on a brass instrument. A few of these notes can be produced with a slack lip on the trombone, the tuba and the B♭ section of the double horn. On the trumpet they have no practical value.

Pedal Board. Pedals were added to the organ in the 14th cent. in the Netherlands, probably from the carillon, and in Germany. They were in use in Italy from the 15th cent. The first definite reference to pedals on an English organ is at St. Paul's Cathedral in 1720-21; many English organs did not have pedals until more than a century later. The modern organ has a concave and radiating pedal-board with a compass of two octaves and a fifth above:

For the application of pedals to the harpsichord and piano *v.* PEDAL HARPSICHORD, PEDAL PIANO.

Pedal Clarinet. Another name for the CONTRABASS CLARINET.

Pedale [peh-dahl'-eh], *I.* (1) Pedal (of an organ, piano, etc.).

(2) Pedal point.

Pedalflügel [pay-dahl'-flĕĕg-ĕl], *G.* Pedal piano.

Pedal Harpsichord. Bach owned a *Pedal-Klavizimbel* which was a harpsichord with pedal board for practising organ music. It is not to be assumed that he intended his trio-sonatas for two manuals and pedal for this instrument rather than for the organ.

Pédalier [pay-dull-yay], *Fr.* Pedal board.

Pedal Notes. *v.* PEDAL (3).

Pedal Piano (*Fr.* pédalier pianoforte, *G.* Pedalflügel). The piano with pedal board made sporadic appearances in the 19th century. Besides Schumann (*Studies for the Pedal Piano*, Op. 56 and 58, 1845), Alkan and Gounod composed for the instrument.

Pedal Point (*Fr.* point d'orgue, *G.* Orgelpunkt, *I.* pedale). A note, most commonly in the bass, which is held while harmonic progressions, with which it may be discordant, continue above it. Generally known simply as "pedal." A pedal on the tonic frequently comes at the end of a piece, as at the close of Bach's fugue in C minor from the first book of the *Wohltemperirte Clavier*:

A dominant pedal often precedes the re-establishment of the tonic, after a series of modulations, as at the end of the DEVELOPMENT in sonata form.

Drones, which occur in primitive music and in some branches of Eastern chant, are a form of pedal point. Its earliest forms in Western polyphonic music are the third stage of ORGANUM (from which the alternative term "organ point," *punctus organicus*, may arise), and the *clausulae* of Perotin (*q.v.* for an example).

Pedrell [peh-drell-yer], (1) CARLOS: *b.* Minas (Uruguay), Oct. 16, 1878; *d.* Montrouge (nr. Paris), March 9, 1941. Composer. Nephew of (2). Studied at Montevideo, at Barcelona under his uncle from 1898-1900, and at the Schola Cantorium, Paris, under Vincent d'Indy. In 1906 he settled in Buenos Aires, where he became inspector of school music, lecturer and founder of the Sociedad Nacional de Música. He later moved to Paris. He composed operas, orchestral works and songs.

(2) FELIPE: *b.* Tortosa, Feb. 19, 1841; *d.* Barcelona, Aug. 19, 1922. Composer and musicologist. Although he studied music at home and was a chorister at Tortosa Cathedral he was largely self-taught. Appointed teacher of music history and aesthetics at the Madrid Conservatorio and later settled in Barcelona. His pupils included Albéniz, Granados and Manuel de Falla. He edited the complete works of Victoria, and composed operas, symphonic poems and other orchestral works, chamber music, cantatas, and songs. His most important work was the publication of the results of his researches in collections of Spanish church music, organ music, music for the stage before the 19th cent., and folksong.

Peer Gynt [pair geent]. A play by Ibsen for which Grieg composed incidental music (first performed, 1876) which he arranged as two orchestral suites:

Peer Gynt Suite No. 1 (Op. 46):
(1) *Morning Mood*; (2) *The Death of Aase*; (3) *Anitra's Dance*; (4) *In the Hall of the Mountain King*.

Peer Gynt Suite No. 2 (Op. 55):
(1) *Abduction of the Bride and Ingrid's Lament*; (2) *Arabian Dance*; (3) *Peer Gynt's Home-coming*; (4) *Solvejg's Song*.

(2) Opera in three acts by Egk. Libretto by the composer (after Ibsen's play). First performed, Berlin, Nov. 24, 1938.

Peerson, MARTIN: *b.* March (Cambridgeshire), *c.* 1572; *d.* London, Dec. 1650. Composer, organist and master of the choristers at St. Paul's Cathedral. He published *Private Musicke or the First Booke of Ayres and Dialogues* (1620), and *Mottects or Grave Chamber Musique* (1630) with an organ part. Some of his compositions are in the *Fitzwilliam Virginal Book* and in Leighton's *Teares or Lamentacions* (1614). He also wrote music for viols (modern ed. of 2 pieces in *Musica Britannica*, ix).

Peeters [pate′-erce], FLOR : *b.* Tielen (nr. Turnhout), July 4, 1903. Belgian organist and composer, a pupil of Dupré and Tournemire. Organist, St. Rombout, Mechlin, 1925. Teacher of organ, Ghent Conservatoire, 1931. Director, Antwerp Conservatoire, 1952. He has travelled widely as a soloist, including visits to America and South Africa. In addition to a large number of organ works (including a concerto with orchestra) he has composed church music and piano works.

Pelléas et Mélisande [pell-ay-uss ay may-lee-sũnd]. Opera in five acts by Debussy, a setting of the play by Maurice Maeterlinck (with slight alterations). First performed, Paris, Apr. 30, 1902. Mélisande is discovered weeping by Golaud, who had lost his way while hunting in a forest. She tells him that she has thrown her crown into the well but will not explain who she is. Golaud, having married her, writes a letter to Pelléas (his half-brother), asking him to tell his mother (Geneviève) and grandfather (Arkel, the king of Allemonde), who had wanted him to marry the Princess Ursula. Pelléas and Mélisande are attracted to each other and Golaud becomes extremely jealous, even using his child by a former marriage to spy on them. Finally he discovers them by a fountain, where they have met for a last farewell, and slays Pelléas with his sword. Mélisande bears a child and lies dying. Golaud begs her forgiveness, which she grants but confesses that she loved Pelléas. A distant bell tolls and she dies.

Pellegrini [pell-leh-gree′-nee], VINCENZO: *b.* Pesaro. Canon at Pesaro *c.* 1603 and from 1611-31 *maestro di cappella* at Milan Cathedral. He composed Masses, canzonets for organ (1599), secular canzonets for voices, and 3- and 4-part instrumental pieces.

Pénélope [pay-nay-lop]. Opera in three acts by Fauré. Libretto by René Fauchois. First performed, Monte Carlo, March 4, 1913.

Penitential Psalms. Psalms of a penitential character, *i.e.*, Nos. 6, 32 (31), 38 (37), 51 (50), 102 (101), 130 (129), and 143 (142). The numbers in brackets are those of the Roman Bible. They were set complete by Lassus (*Psalmi penitentiales*, 1565).

Penna [pen′-nah], LORENZO: *b.* Bologna, 1613; *d.* Imola, Oct. 20, 1693. *Maestro di cappella* of S. Ilario, Casale Monferrato, 1656. Entered the Carmelite order at Mantua *c.* 1669, and became *maestro di cappella* of the Carmelite church at Parma and at Imola Cathedral. Composed Masses, psalms and other church music, and "French Correntes" in 4 parts (1673). The third part of his *Li Primi Albori Musicali* (1672) is one of the important treatments in the 17th cent. of the rules for playing the organ from figured bass, with examples of the use of the trill (*v.* F. T. Arnold, *The Art of Accompaniment from a Thorough-Bass*, pp. 133-54).

Pentatonic Scale. A scale which has five notes to the octave, *e.g.*:

This, the most usual form, can also be played by striking the black keys of the piano from C♯ upwards. It is used in the traditional music of China and Japan, and also elsewhere in the Far East, and in Africa. The pentatonic scale (*slendro*) of the music of Java and Bali consists of five equal divisions of the octave, and cannot be reproduced on the piano. Some Irish and Scottish folksongs are in a pentatonic scale:

Gala Water (Scottish)

and modern composers have occasionally used it for its "oriental" effect, *e.g.* Debussy in *Pagodes* in the suite *Estampes* (1903) for piano, and Ravel in *Laidero-*

nette Impératrice des Pagodes from the suite *Ma Mère l'oye* (1908) for piano duet:

Pepping [pep′-ing], ERNST : *b.* Duisburg, Sept. 12, 1901. Composer. Studied at the Berlin Hochschule für Musik. Professor of composition, Kirchenmusik-Schule, Spandau (nr. Berlin), 1947. His compositions include 3 symphonies, 4 piano sonatas, chamber music, songs and organ works, but his major activity has been in the field of Protestant church music (Masses, motets, choral works for the Church's year, chorale settings, etc.).

Pepusch [pay′-pŏŏsh], JOHANN CHRISTOPH: *b.* Berlin, 1667; *d.* London, July 20, 1752. Composer and theorist. From fourteen he was in the service of the Prussian court, in 1698 went to Holland and in 1700 settled in London, where he was appointed violinist in the Drury Lane orchestra, and in 1710 was one of the founders of the Academy of Ancient Music. From 1712-18 he was organist and composer to the Duke of Chandos, being succeeded by Handel, from 1713 music director of Lincoln's Inn Fields Theatre and from 1737-52 organist of the Charterhouse. He composed music for masques, odes, cantatas, motets, and instrumental music, and selected and arranged the tunes for John Gay's *Beggar's Opera* (1728). He published *A Treatise on Harmony* (1730; reprinted, with the addition of musical examples, 1731).

Percussion Instruments (*Fr.* instruments à percussion, *G.* Schlaginstrumente, *I.* strumenti a percossa). Instruments on which the sound is produced by striking or shaking. Their function is chiefly rhythmic, though some set up regular vibrations and thus produce sounds of definite pitch, *e.g.* TIMPANI, BELLS, GLOCKENSPIEL, XYLOPHONE and CELESTA. Others, *e.g.* SIDE DRUM, TENOR DRUM, BASS DRUM, TRIANGLE, CYMBALS, GONG, TAMBOURINE, WIND MACHINE, RATTLE, produce sounds of indefinite pitch.

K. GEIRINGER : *Musical Instruments* (1943).
C. SACHS : *The History of Musical Instruments* (1940).

Perez [peh′-reth], DAVIDE (David Peres): *b.* Naples, 1711; *d.* Lisbon, after 1780. Spanish composer. Studied at Naples. Court *maestro di cappella*, Palermo, 1740-48; Lisbon, 1752-80. From 1755 director of the Lisbon opera. He composed operas which were produced in Palermo, Naples, Rome, Lisbon and London (*Ezio*, 1755), and oratorios.

Perfect. (1) The INTERVALS of the octave, fifth and fourth are called perfect consonances.

(2) A perfect note-value in MENSURAL NOTATION contains three of the next lower note-value, *e.g.*, a perfect breve= 3 semibreves. In the perfect mode in that notation a long contains three breves; in perfect time, shown by the sign O, a breve contains three semibreves; in perfect prolation, shown by a dot in the circle or semicircle, a semibreve contains three minims. A perfect note-value is made imperfect by being written in red or white in black notation, or black in white notation. An imperfect note-value, which contains two of the next lower value, is made perfect by a dot (*punctus perfectionis* or *additionis*) following it.

(3) In a combination (LIGATURE) of two notes in mensural notation the normal ("proper" and "perfect") sequence was considered to be that which had the shorter note (*brevis*) followed by the longer (*longa*); the term "perfection" referred to the latter note, so that a ligature of two or more notes ending with a long, *e.g.* ▫▫ (= B L) was defined as a ligature "with perfection" (*cum perfectione*), and a ligature ending with a breve, *e.g.*, ▫▫ (= B B) was *sine perfectione*.

Perfect Fool, The. Opera in one act by Holst. Libretto by the composer. First performed, London, May 14, 1923.

Pergolesi [pair-go-leh′-zee], GIOVANNI BATTISTA: *b.* Jesi (nr. Ancona), Jan. 4,

1710; *d.* Pozzuoli (nr. Naples), March 16, 1736. Composer. Studied at Naples under Durante, Feo, and others. His comic intemezzo *La serva padrona* was first performed between the acts of his serious opera *Il prigioner superbo* in 1733, and with his other intermezzo *Il maestro di musica* became the prototype of the later form of the *opera buffa*. Its 1752 production at the Opéra in Paris made it the centre of the *Guerre des Bouffons*. His renown as a composer of church music, of which he wrote much, has rested mainly on his *Stabat mater*. In his trio sonatas he cultivated the melodious style of allegro movement later adopted by J. C. Bach, and made some contribution to the development of sonata form. A complete edition of his works, edited by F. Caffarelli, has been published in Italy (1939-43).

Peri [peh′-ree], JACOPO: *b.* Rome, Aug. 20, 1561; *d.* Florence, Aug. 12, 1633. Composer and singer. Studied under Cristoforo Malvezzi in Lucca. As a member of the *camerata* of Count Giovanni Bardi he composed the music, which has not survived, of the first opera *La Dafne*, to a text by Rinuccini, performed in the palace of Jacopo Corsi in Florence during the Carnival of 1597. His *Euridice*, also to a text by Rinuccini, which was performed in Florence in 1600, is the first opera of which the music is extant. Part of the music was by Caccini, whose complete setting of the same text was produced in Florence in 1602. Peri's score was published in 1601 and in a facsimile edition in 1934; extracts will be found in Schering's *History of Music in Examples*, No. 171 and in the *Historical Anthology*, No. 182.

Periodicals. *v.* HISTORY OF MUSIC.

Perosi [peh-ro′-zee], LORENZO: *b.* Tortona, Dec. 20, 1872 ; *d.* Rome, Oct. 12, 1956. Composer and church musician. Studied at Milan Conservatorio and at Haberl's School of Church Music in Ratisbon. *Maestro di cappella*, St. Mark's, Venice, 1895 ; Sistine Chapel, 1898. Perpetual master of the Pontifical Chapel, 1905 ; member of the Italian Academy, 1930. He was ordained in 1896. His works include oratorios, Masses, cantatas, motets and other church choral works, organ pieces, symphonic poems, suites for orchestra and chamber music.

Perotinus (Perotin), called *Magnus Magister*. Composer (called *optimus discantor* by the 13th-cent. English theorist Anonymus IV) at Notre Dame, Paris, succeeding Léonin, from *c.* 1183. He was renowned as a composer of *clausulae*. In these, as in the MOTETS of the following century, the rhythm was measured, according to the RHYTHMIC MODES (*v.* NOTATION), in all the voices. The style of his three *quadrupla* (*clausulae* in four parts), based on notes of great length in the tenor, may be seen in the opening of *Viderunt*:

Two three-part settings of *Alleluia* melodies are printed in Y. Rokseth, *Polyphonies du XIIIe siècle* (1936), pp. 16, 31.

Persée [pair-say] (Perseus). Opera with a prologue and five acts by Lully. Libretto by Philippe Quinault. First performed, Paris, Apr. 18, 1682.

Perséphone [pair-say-fon]. Melodrama in three parts by Stravinsky (1933) for orchestra, chorus, a tenor and a speaking voice. Poem by André Gide. First performed, Paris, Apr. 30, 1934.

Pes [pace], *L.* "Foot." A term used in

English 13th-14th cent. music for the tenor of a MOTET (as in Worcester manuscripts; *v.* A. HUGHES, *Worcester Mediaeval Harmony*, 1928) and for the lowest part or parts of a ROTA, as in the manuscript of *Sumer is icumen in*.

Pesante [peh-zahn'-teh], *I.* Heavy, *i.e.* ponderous and solid.

Pescetti [peh-shet'-tee], GIOVANNI BATTISTA: *b.* Venice, *c.* 1704; *d.* there, 1766. Composer. Studied under Lotti in Venice, where he produced his first opera in 1725. Director of Covent Garden, 1739; King's Theatre, London, 1740. Second organist, St. Mark's, Venice, 1762. He composed operas, an oratorio, church music and harpsichord sonatas.

Peter Grimes. Opera by Britten. Libretto by Montagu Slater (from part of Crabbe's poem *The Borough*). First performed, London, June 7, 1945. Grimes is a fisherman in a town on the east coast of England. Imaginative and wayward, he fails to come to terms with his neighbours. Accused of having murdered a boy in his employment, he is acquitted; but the townsfolk still suspect him, and when another boy dies in his service (again by accident) they pursue him. In the thick fog he evades them, puts out to sea in his boat and sinks it.

Peter Ibbetson. Opera in three acts by Deems Taylor. Libretto by the composer and Constance Collier (from the novel by du Maurier). First performed, New York, Feb. 7, 1931.

Peters [pate'-erce]. A firm of publishers founded in 1814 by C. F. Peters, who bought the business of Kühnel and Hoffmeister. Dr. H. Hinrichsen became head of the firm in 1900. Publishing is now carried on under the original name in London and New York by Max and Walter Hinrichsen.

Peterson-Berger [peh'-ter-shon-bairr'-yer], OLOF WILHELM: *b.* Ullånger (Sweden), Feb. 27, 1867; *d.* Östersund, Dec. 3, 1942. Composer, music critic and poet. Studied at the Stockholm Conservatoire and in Dresden, where he taught at the Musikschule from 1892-94. In Stockholm he was music critic from 1896 and director of the Royal Opera, 1908-11. He composed operas (some with librettos by himself), 5 symphonies, festival cantatas, violin sonatas, songs and piano pieces, and also wrote books and critical essays on music.

Petit Chaperon Rouge, Le [ler per-tee sha-per-rõn roozh] (Little Red Riding Hood). Opera in three acts by Boieldieu. Libretto by Emmanuel Guillaume Marguérite Théaulon de Lambert. First performed, Paris, June 30, 1818.

Petite flûte [per-teet fleet], *Fr.* Piccolo.

Petits Riens, Les [lay per-tee ryañ] (The Little Nothings). Ballet with music by Mozart, K. App. 10, and choreography by Jean Noverre. First performed, Paris, June 11, 1778.

Petrassi [peh-trahss'-see], GOFFREDO: *b.* Zagarolo (nr. Rome), July 16, 1904. Composer. Studied under di Donato and Bustini at the S. Cecilia Conservatorio in Rome, where he later became teacher. Has composed works for orchestra, 2 piano concertos, chamber music, ballets, Magnificat for voice and orchestra, and songs.

G. M. GATTI: "Modern Italian Composers, I: Goffredo Petrassi," in *Monthly Musical Record*, Jan. 1937.

Petri [pate'-ree], EGON: *b.* Hanover, March 23, 1881. Pianist. Son of the Dutch violinist Henri Petri (1856-1914), who settled in Germany in 1877. He studied the violin from an early age and was a member of his father's quartet from 1899-1901, but having decided to be a pianist, studied with Busoni, of whose works he has given authentic interpretations. He was also joint editor, with Busoni, of Bach's keyboard works. For many years he was widely known as a soloist. During the years 1905-11 he taught successively at the Royal Manchester College of Music (1905-11), the Basle Conservatoire, the Berlin Hochschule für Musik (1921-6), and at Zakopane (in southern Poland). He migrated to the United States in 1939. Resident pianist, Cornell University, 1940; Mills College, Oakland (Cal.), 1947.

Petroushka [pet-roosh'-ca]. Ballet with music by Stravinsky (first performed, 1911) from which he arranged an orchestral suite (first performed,

1914). The ballet is based on the story of three puppets.

Petrucci [peh-troo'-tchee], OTTAVIANO DEI: *b.* Fossombrone, June 18, 1466; *d.* Venice, May 7, 1539. Music printer. Published the first printed collection of part-music, the *Harmonice Musices Odhecaton A*, in 1501. He printed in all 59 volumes of music, sacred and secular, between that date and 1520. A bibliography of his publications has been published by C. Sartori, *Bibliografia delle opere musicali stampata da Ottaviano Petrucci* (1948).

Peuerl [poy'-erl] (Peurl, Bäurl, Beurlin or Bäwerl), PAUL: *b. c.* 1570; *d.* 1625. Composer and organist. Organist at Horn in 1601 and at Steyr from 1609 until his death. His *Newe Padouan, Intrada, Däntz, und Galliarda* (1611) contains the earliest known examples of the variation SUITE. Pieces from this and his other publications, *Weltspiegel* (1613), which contains secular part-songs, and *Gantz Neue Padouanen* (1625) are printed in *D.T.Ö.*, xxxvi (2).

Pfitzner [pfits'-ner], HANS: *b.* Moscow, May 5, 1869; *d.* Salzburg, May 22, 1949. Composer, the son of German parents. He was brought up in Frankfort, where he studied at Hoch's Conservatorium. Teacher at Coblenz Conservatorium, 1892-3. On the staff of Mainz Opera, 1894-5; second conductor, 1896. Teacher of composition and conducting, Stern's Conservatorium, Berlin, 1897 and first conductor at the Theater des Westens, 1903. Conductor, Kaim Orchestra, Munich, 1907. Director, Strasbourg Conservatorium, 1908; Strasbourg Opera, 1908-16. Conductor, Munich subscription concerts, 1919-20. Director of the master class in composition, Berlin Akademie der Künste, 1920-9. Professor, Munich Akademie der Tonkunst, 1930-3. During the immediate post-war years he lived in an institution for old people in Munich until he finally retired to Salzburg.

Pfitzner was active as a composer from his student days to the end of his life. He was a Romantic in an age when Romanticism was turning to extravagance. From these tendencies he held aloof. His writing for the orchestra has none of the glitter of Strauss's works; he was in fact closer to the traditions established by Schumann and Brahms. An idealist with a passionate belief in his own integrity, he fought vigorously against what he held to be corrupting influences in modern music. He was in a sense a visionary who lived in a world of his own creations. In his best-known work, the opera *Palestrina* (Munich, 1917), he strives to identify himself with a composer whom he does not seem to have fully understood. Though his music is often said by German writers to express the very spirit of the German race, he was by no means universally appreciated even in his own country. Elsewhere his reputation has been tenuous.

His principal compositions are:

(a) OPERAS: *Der arme Heinrich* (1895); *Die Rose vom Liebesgarten* (1901); *Christelflein* (1906; revised, 1917); *Palestrina* (1917); *Das Herz* (1931).

(b) CHORAL WORKS: *Von deutscher Seele*, cantata for soli, chorus, organ and orchestra (1921; revised, 1937); *Das dunkle Reich*, choral fantasia (1929); *Fons salutifer* (1942).

(c) ORCHESTRA: 2 symphonies; piano concerto; violin concerto; 2 cello concertos.

(d) CHAMBER MUSIC: 3 string quartets; piano quartet; sextet for clarinet, violin, viola, cello, double bass and piano; violin sonata; cello sonata.

(e) SONGS: 100 solo songs, published in 23 sets.

Phaéton [fa-ay-tõn]. Opera with prologue and five acts by Lully. Libretto by Philippe Quinault. First performed, Versailles, Jan. 9, 1683.

Phantasie [fun-tuz-ee'], *G.* Fantasia.

Phantasy. A title used for a number of chamber music compositions written between 1906 and 1930 for the competitions instituted by W. W. Cobbett. The first of the series of prizes was won by W. Y. Hurlstone's Phantasy string quartet in A minor and later prizes by compositions of Frank Bridge, John Ireland and Vaughan Williams.

Philadelphia Orchestra. Founded 1900 by Fritz Scheel, who was its conductor until 1907. Later conductors: Karl Pohlig, 1907-12; Leopold Stokowski, 1912-38; Eugene Ormandy, 1938.

Philémon et Baucis [fee-lay-mon͡ ay bo-seece]. Opera in three acts by Gounod. Libretto by Jules Barbier and Michel Carré. First performed, Paris, Feb. 18, 1860.

Philidor [fee-lee-dorr], FRANÇOIS ANDRÉ DANICAN: *b.* Dreux, Sept. 7, 1726; *d.* London, Aug. 24, 1795. Composer, chess-player and member of a family of musicians whose original name was Danican. Studied music under Campra, played chess in Holland, Germany and England and in 1754 returned to Paris, where he produced his first *opéra-comique* in 1759. He composed operas, motets and a Requiem for Rameau (1766). The Library of St. Michael's College, Tenbury (catalogue by E. H. Fellowes, 1934) contains a collection of manuscript scores of operas, ballets, motets, and instrumental music by French composers of the 17th and early 18th cent. written by Philidor's father, André Philidor *l'aîné*, which formerly formed part of the French Royal Library. His half-brother Anne Philidor (*b.* Paris, Apr. 11, 1681; *d.* there, Oct. 8, 1728) founded the *Concert spirituel* in Paris in 1725.

Philips, PETER: *b. c.* 1560; *d.* Brussels, *c.* 1635. Composer and organist. In the Netherlands by 1591, when he edited a collection of madrigals published in Antwerp. A Roman Catholic, he was appointed organist to the Archduke Albert, and *c.* 1611 at the Chapel Royal in Brussels. He took orders, and was appointed to a canonry at Soignies in 1610. Between 1596 and 1603 he published 3 books of madrigals, from 1612 to 1628 7 books of motets and other sacred music. In style he is closer to his continental than to his English contemporaries; his *Gemmulae Sacrae . . . cum Basso Continuo ad Organum* (1613) seems to be the earliest use of a continuo part by an English composer. Peacham observed that " he affecteth altogether the *Italian* veine." 19 keyboard pieces, the earliest dated 1580, are in the *Fitzwilliam Virginal Book.* Among them are keyboard arrangements of vocal pieces by Marenzio, Lassus, Striggio and Caccini. 3 pieces for viols are printed in *Musica Britannica*, ix.

Philosopher, The (*G.* Der Philosoph). Haydn's symphony No. 22 in E♭ major (1764).

Phinot [fee-no] (Finot), DOMINICUS. 16th-cent. French musician who composed 2 books of motets (Lyons, 1547-48), 2 books of *chansons* (Lyons, 1548), a book of Psalms and Magnificats (Venice, 1555) and other church music.

Phoebus and Pan. *v.* STREIT ZWISCHEN PHÖBUS UND PAN.

Phrase. A unit of melody, of indeterminate length. In the classical period it is most frequently of four bars, and since it usually ends with some form of cadence, is a unit of harmonic progression as well as of melody:

If a smaller unit, such as that marked (*a*), comes under discussion, as when it is used separately in a later context:

it is more conveniently referred to as a MOTIVE. Though it is not necessary to use the term with complete consistency, shorter or longer units may be called phrases if they form a unit in both melodic design and underlying harmony.

The art of " phrasing " concerns not

only the articulation of complete phrases, but the articulation of their details. The chief marks by which phrasing is indicated are the slur and the *staccato* dot. The player of an instrument will observe these by means of short rests, for example:

is played:

Phrygian Cadence. The Phrygian mode was the only mode in which the interval between the final and note above it was a semitone. Hence the harmonization of a cadence in this mode presented a peculiar problem to composers of polyphonic music. The seventh note of the scale (D) could not be sharpened because that would have created an augmented sixth, and to have sharpened the note above the final would have destroyed the character of the mode. The following, therefore, came to be adopted as the standard harmonization of the cadence (with a TIERCE DE PICARDIE, or major third) in the final chord:

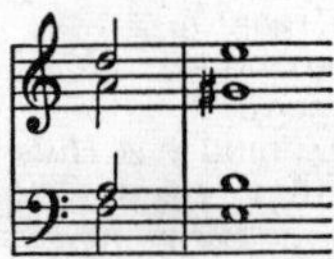

When the modal system settled down into major and minor in the 17th cent. this cadence survived in use, but with a changed implication, the final chord now suggesting dominant harmony in a minor key. The cadence was therefore no longer final and was regularly used in the 17th and early 18th cent. as a transition from one movement to another. This became so much a convention that the new movement did not necessarily accept the concluding chord of the previous movement as a dominant but began instead in a related key. This practice was particularly common where the first and third movements of a sonata or concerto were in a major key and the middle movement in a minor key. Thus in Bach's fourth Brandenburg concerto in G major the slow movement, which is in E minor, ends with a Phrygian cadence on the chord of B major, and this leads to the opening of the last movement in G major. In the third concerto, also in G major, there is no middle movement at all. The two movements in G major are simply separated by the two chords which constitute a Phrygian cadence in E minor (*i.e.* $^{6}_{3}$ on C and major triad on B).

Phrygian Mode. (1) In ancient Greek music:

(2) From the Middle Ages onwards applied to:

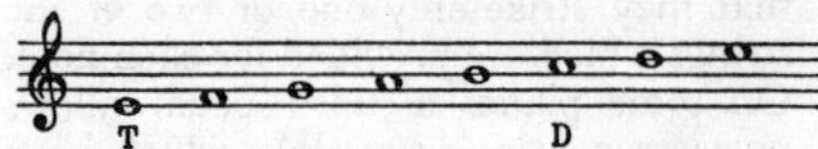

The tonic (or final) and dominant are marked respectively T and D. The dominant was originally B (a fifth above the tonic, as in the other modes) but was changed to C as early as the 11th cent., since B was regarded as an ambiguous note: its relation to F was dissonant and it was the one note which was not common to all three hexachords. The change, however, though accepted by theorists, was not always observed in practice. *v.* GREEK MUSIC, HEXACHORD, MODE.

Piacevole [pee-ah-cheh′-vo-leh], *I.* In an agreeable, pleasant manner.

Piangendo [pee-ahn-jend′-o], *I.* "Crying," *i.e.* in a plaintive manner.

Pianissimo [pee-ah-neece′-see-mo], *I.* Very soft. Abbreviated *pp.*

Piano. [pee-ahn′-o]. (1) *I.* Soft. Abbreviated *p.*

(2) *E.Fr.* Abbreviation of PIANOFORTE.

Piano Duet. A term which normally implies two players at one instrument. A work for two pianos is generally described as such. The earliest known work for two performers at one keyboard is a 16th-cent. piece by Nicholas Carlton "for two to play on one Virginal or Organ" (*v. Musical Quarterly*, Oct. 1943). Burney published 8 sonatas for piano (or harpsichord) duet in 1777-8. Among the composers who wrote original piano duets were Mozart, Beethoven, Schubert and Brahms.

Pianoforte (Piano). The mechanism of the piano comprises a keyboard, action, hammers, dampers, strings, and pedals. The keyboard of the modern piano has a compass of seven octaves when the highest note is A, or seven octaves and a minor third when the highest note is C. A damper stops the vibration of the strings when the key returns to its normal position. The right (or sustaining) pedal suspends the action of the dampers, allowing the strings to vibrate freely; the left (or soft) pedal mutes the sound by moving the hammers either towards the strings so that their length of travel is shortened or parallel to the strings so that they strike only one or two of the strings which are provided for each note. On some pianos a third pedal allows notes to continue sounding which have been played before the pedal is depressed, while any other notes remain unaffected.

The piano and its name originated in instruments made in Florence about 1710 by Bartolommeo Cristofori, who called them *gravicembali col pian e forte*, *i.e.* harpsichords which can produce *piano* and *forte* by touch. The most important makers in the 18th cent. were Silbermann and Stein in Germany, Kirkman, Zumpe and Broadwood in England; the main developments were the escapement, which allowed the hammer to return for the repetition of a note though the key was still down, the pedal (patented by Broadwood in 1783), and the return to Cristofori's "grand" shape in addition to the square. The piano was played as a solo instrument for the first time in England by J. C. Bach in 1768. Mozart praised Stein's pianos in a letter to his father in 1777.

The chief developments in the nineteenth century were the extension of the compass (the Broadwood presented to Beethoven in 1817 had six octaves from C_1 to c^{1111}), the increase in sonority, the devising of a double escapement which allowed quicker repetition (patented by Érard of Paris in 1821), and the adoption of the upright shape.

The earliest known publication of music for the piano is a set of sonatas for *cembalo di piano e forte* by Lodovico Giustini (1732). The first English music to mention pianoforte in the title was John Burton's (1730-85) *Ten Sonatas for the Harpsichord, Organ, or Pianoforte*, published by the composer in 1766. Clementi published piano sonatas in 1773, and all but the first set of C. P. E. Bach's sets of sonatas (*für Kenner und Liebhaber*) of 1779-87 are for the "Fortepiano." The chief landmarks in the later developments of the technique of piano-playing are the studies of Clementi (*Gradus ad Parnassum*, 1817), Hummel (*Ausführliche Anweisung zum Pianoforte-spiel*, 1828), Czerny, Cramer, Schumann (*VI Études de concert pour le pianoforte, composées d'après les Caprices de Paganini*, 1832), Chopin (*Études*, 1837), Liszt (*Études d'exécution transcendante*, final form, 1854; also inspired by Paganini), and the teaching and methods of Tausig, Leschetitzky, Breithaupt, Scharwenka and Matthay.

M. BREE : *The Groundwork of the Leschetitzky Method* (1905).

R. M. BREITHAUPT : *Natural Piano-Technique* (1909).

R. E. M. HARDING : *A History of the Pianoforte to 1851* (1933).

P. JAMES : *Early Keyboard Instruments* (1930).

T. A. MATTHAY : *The Act of Touch* (1924).

Pianola (Player-Piano). A piano played mechanically by means of rolls pierced with openings corresponding to the duration and pitch of the notes, thus allowing air under pressure to act on a device which moves the hammers. It was widely used from the late 19th cent. until the rise of the gramophone and wireless.

Piano Quartet. Usually applied only to quartets for piano, violin, viola and cello, of which there are examples by Mozart, Beethoven, Mendelssohn, Schumann, Brahms, Dvořák, Strauss and Fauré. Quartets for keyboard and other instruments, *e.g.* those by J. C. Bach for violin, flute, oboe and keyboard (with cello), have only occasionally been written since the 18th cent. (*e.g.* Hindemith's quartet for clarinet, violin, cello and piano, 1939).

Piano Quintet. The combination of piano with string quartet. Compositions in this medium have been written by Schumann, Brahms, Dvořák, Fauré, Elgar, Shostakovich, Roy Harris and others. Mozart (K.452) and Beethoven (Op. 16) wrote quintets for piano, oboe, clarinet, horn, and bassoon. Schubert's *Trout* quintet is for piano, violin, viola, cello and double bass.

Piatti [pee-aht′-tee], *I.* Cymbals.

Piatti [pee-aht′-tee], ALFREDO CARLO: *b.* Bergamo, Jan. 8, 1822; *d.* Crocetta di Nozzo (nr. Bergamo), July 18, 1901. Cellist. Studied under his great-uncle Zanetti and under Merighi in Milan, where he made his first public appearance in 1837. He gave concerts in Munich (with Liszt, 1843), Paris, the British Isles, Italy and Russia. First cellist at the Italian Opera, London, 1846-9. The leading solo cellist of the 19th cent. He composed cello concertos, songs with cello accompaniment, and sonatas and other works for cello.

Pibgorn. *v.* HORNPIPE.

Pibroch (*Gaelic,* piobaireachd, " pipe-tune "). The most important category of bag-pipe music. It consists of variations on a theme (*urlar*), played with an increase of tempo in each variation, and with many grace-notes.

Picardy Third. *v.* TIERCE DE PICARDIE.

Picchi [peek′-kee], GIOVANNI: 17th-cent. Italian organist and composer. Organist at the church Della Casa Grande in Venice *c.* 1620. He composed a book of harpsichord music (1620), canzonas and sonatas for instruments, and church music. There is a toccata by him in the *Fitzwilliam Virginal Book.*

Piccinni [pee-tcheen′-nee], NICCOLA: *b.* Bari, Jan. 16, 1728; *d.* Passy (Paris), May 7, 1800. Composer. Studied in Naples under Leo and Durante, and from 1755 produced there and in Rome a number of successful operas, serious and comic. In 1776 he went to Paris, was tutor in singing to Marie Antoinette, and produced Italian operas, and after 1778 operas to French texts. The management of the Opera took advantage of the feud between his supporters and those of Gluck by commissioning a setting of *Iphigénie en Tauride* from both composers. Piccinni's, produced in 1781, was not unsuccessful, being given more than 30 performances. He went to Naples during the Revolution, and returned to Paris in 1798. In all he wrote some 120 operas. His comic opera *La buona figliuola* (Rome, 1760), to a libretto by Goldoni (after Samuel Richardon's novel *Pamela, or Virtue Rewarded*), enjoyed an extraordinary popularity (modern ed. in *I classici musicali italiani,* vii). Vocal scores of *Roland* (1778) and *Didon* (1783) are in *Chefs d'oeuvre de l'opéra français.*

Piccolo (*Fr.* petite flûte, *G.* kleine Flöte, Pickelflöte, *I.* flauto piccolo, ottavino). An abbreviation of *flauto piccolo,* " little flute." A small flute, with the natural scale of D and a range of about three octaves, written:

and sounding an octave higher. It was not a regular member of the orchestra before the middle of the 19th century. Among its earlier appearances are Gluck's *Iphigénie en Tauride* (1779), Beethoven's fifth and sixth symphonies (1807-8) and Weber's *Der Freischütz* (1821).

Pick-Mangiagalli [peek-mahn-djah-gahl′-lee], RICCARDO: *b.* Strakonice (Bohemia), July 10, 1882; *d.* Milan,

July 8, 1949. Italian composer and pianist. Studied at Prague, Vienna and at the Milan Conservatorio, where he became director in 1936. He composed ballets, operas, orchestral works, chamber music, piano pieces and songs.

Pictures at an Exhibition. A set of piano pieces by Moussorgsky (1874), composed in memory of the painter and architect Victor Alexandrovich Hartmann and based on some of his works. In addition to the following there are also a prelude and interludes (each entitled *Promenade*):

No. 1 : *Gnomus* (a limping dwarf).
No. 2 : *Il Vecchio Castello* (" A Medieval Castle ").
No. 3 : *Tuileries* (Children playing and quarrelling).
No. 4 : *Bydlo* (a Polish ox-cart on enormous wheels).
No. 5 : *Ballet of the Chickens in their Shells.*
No. 6 : *Samuel Goldenberg et Schmuyle* (two Polish Jews, rich and poor).
No. 7 : *Limoges* (" The Market ").
No. 8 : *Catacombae.*
No. 9 : *The Hut on Fowl's Legs.*
No. 10 : *The Great Gates of Kiev.*

Orchestral arrangements have been made by Ravel, Henry Wood and Walter Goehr.

Pieno [pee-eh'-no], *I.* Full. *Organo pieno,* full organ. *A voce piena,* with full voice.

Pierné [pyair-nay], (1) HENRI CONSTANT GABRIEL : *b.* Metz, Aug. 16, 1863 ; *d.* Ploujean (Finistère), July 17, 1937. Composer and conductor. Studied at the Paris Conservatoire under Franck and Massenet. *Prix de Rome,* 1882. Organist, Sainte-Clotilde, Paris, 1890-98. Assistant conductor, Concerts Colonne, 1903 ; first conductor, 1910-32. He composed operas, ballets, pantomimes, oratorios, suites and other works for orchestra, chamber music, incidental music for plays, piano pieces and songs.

(2) PAUL: *b.* Metz, June 30, 1874. Composer. Cousin of (1). Studied at the Paris Conservatoire. Has composed symphonic poems, 2 symphonies, operas, chamber music, a Mass, and songs.

Pierrot Lunaire [pyair-ro lēē-nair]. Melodrama in the form of a song-cycle by Schönberg, Op. 21 (1912), for a singing-speaking voice and chamber orchestra. Poems by Albert Giraud (German translation by Otto Erich Hartleben).

Pierson, HEINRICH HUGO (originally Henry Hugh Pearson) : *b.* Oxford, April 12, 1815 ; *d.* Leipzig, Jan. 28, 1873. English composer who lived most of his life in Germany. Studied at Cambridge and from 1839 under Rinck, Tomášek and Reissiger in Germany, where he met Mendelssohn and Schumann. Reid professor, Edinburgh, 1844. In 1846 returned to the continent, and lived in Vienna, Hamburg and Leipzig. He composed operas, oratorios, overtures, music to the second part of Goethe's *Faust* (1854), church music, songs and partsongs. The most interesting of the mid-Victorian composers, he failed to find appreciation in England, but was highly regarded in Germany.

Pietoso [pee-eh-to'-zo], *I.* Compassionate, sympathetic.

Pifa [pee'-fah]. Handel's name for the " Pastoral Symphony " in *Messiah,* indicating that it is intended to represent the sound of music played on *pifferi* by shepherds.

Piffero [peef'-feh-ro], *I.* Italian small flute, or shepherd's pipe, of the 18th century.

Pijper [pipe'-er], WILLEM: *b.* Zeist, Sept. 8, 1894; *d.* Leidschendam, March 19, 1947. Composer and pianist. Studied under Johan Wagenaar in Utrecht, where he was music critic from 1918-23. Teacher of composition, Amsterdam Conservatoire, 1925; director, Rotterdam Conservatoire, 1930. He composed 3 symphonies, string quartets and other chamber music, concertos for piano, cello and violin, choral works, incidental music for plays, piano pieces and songs, and wrote essays on music and musicians.

Pikovaya Dama [pick'-ov-a-ya dah'-ma] (The Queen of Spades). Opera in three acts by Tchaikovsky (often known by its German title, *Pique-Dame*). Libretto by Modeste Tchaikovsky (based on Pushkin's novel). First performed, St. Petersburg, Dec. 19, 1890.

Pilgrims from Mecca, The. *v.* RENCONTRE IMPRÉVUE.

Pilgrim's Progress, The. Opera in four acts, with a prologue and epilogue, by Vaughan Williams. Libretto by the composer (after Bunyan's allegory). First performed, London, Apr. 26, 1951. The greater part of the earlier one-act opera *The Shepherds of the Delectable Mountains* (1922) is incorporated in this work as Act IV, sc. 2.

Pilkington, FRANCIS: *d.* Chester, 1638. Composer. Chorister (1602), minor canon, and precentor (1623) of Chester Cathedral. He composed ayres, two sets of *Madrigals and Pastorals* (1614, 1624), sacred partsongs (in Leighton's *Teares or Lamentacions,* 1614) and pieces for viols and for lute. The madrigals have been reprinted in *E.M.S.*, xxv and xxvi, and the *First Booke of Songs or Ayres* (1605) in *E.S.L.S.*, 2nd series.

Pinafore, H.M.S. *v.* H.M.S. PINAFORE.

Pincé [pa͡n-say], *Fr.* Mordent.

Pincherle [pa͡n-shairl], MARC: *b.* Constantine (Algeria), June 13, 1888. Musicologist. Studied under Rolland, Laloy and Pirro and became teacher at the École Normale in Paris. He has written books on the history of the violin, on Corelli (1934), and on Vivaldi (2 vols., 1948; the second volume contains a thematic catalogue of Vivaldi's works).

Piozzi [pee-ot'-tsee], GABRIEL: *b.* Brescia, June 8, 1740; *d.* Dymerchion (Denbighshire), March, 1809. Settled in Bath as a music teacher *c.* 1780. He composed violin sonatas, string quartets, canzonets, vocal duets, and songs. In 1784 he married Mrs. Thrale, to the displeasure of Johnson and the Burneys (*v.* P. A. Scholes, *The Great Dr. Burney,* 1948).

Pique-Dame [peek'-dahm-er]. *v.* PIKOVAYA DAMA.

Pirates of Penzance, The. Comic opera in two acts by Sullivan. Libretto by William Schwenck Gilbert. First performed, Paignton, Dec. 30, 1897.

Pirro [peer-ro], ANDRÉ: *b.* Saint-Didier, Feb. 12, 1869; *d.* Paris, Nov. 11, 1943. Musicologist. Studied law, letters, and organ under Franck and Widor at the Paris Conservatoire. Director and teacher at the Schola Cantorum on its foundation in 1896; lecturer, École des Hautes Études Sociales, 1904; succeeded Romain Rolland as professor of musical history at the Sorbonne, 1912. He was the leading French musicologist of his time. Among his many writings are books on Bach, Buxtehude and Schütz, and a history of music in the 15th and 16th centuries.

Pisendel [peez'-ĕnd-ĕl], JOHANN GEORG: *b.* Kadolzburg (Bavaria), Dec. 26, 1687; *d.* Dresden, Nov. 25, 1755. Violinist and composer. He studied as a choirboy under Torelli and Pistocchi, from 1709 at Leipzig University and later under Vivaldi in Venice and Montanari in Rome. Violinist, Dresden court chapel, 1712. From 1714 travelled with the Prince of Saxony to Paris, Berlin, Italy and Vienna, and was leader of the Dresden court orchestra from 1730. He composed a symphony, 2 *concerti grossi,* 8 violin concertos and other works for violin. A violin concerto in D is published in *D.D.T.*, xxix-xxx, p. 1.

Pistocchi [peece-tock'-kee], FRANCESCO ANTONIO MAMILIANO: *b.* Palermo, 1659; *d.* Bologna, May 13, 1726. Composer, conductor and singer. His *Cappricci puerili* for keyboard and other instruments was published at Bologna when he was eight years old. He was a chorister at San Petronio in 1670, first appeared as an opera singer at Ferrara in 1675. Court singer, Parma, 1687; *Kapellmeister* to the Margrave of Ansbach, 1696. He retired from the operatic stage *c.* 1705 and founded an important school of singing in Bologna. He composed operas, oratorios, cantatas and other church music, vocal duets, trios and arias.

Piston [peece-to͡n], *Fr.* Short for *cornet à pistons,* the modern cornet.

Piston, WALTER: *b.* Rockland (Maine), Ian. 20, 1894. Composer. Studied at Harvard University from 1914-24 and under Nadia Boulanger in Paris. He has taught composition at Harvard since 1932. He has composed 6 symphonies and other orchestral works, 3 string quartets, sonatas and other chamber music, and a ballet—*The Incredible Flautist.* He has also published *Principles of Harmonic Analysis* (1933), *Harmony* (1941), *Counterpoint* (1947) and *Orchestration* (1955).

Pitch. The relative height or depth of a sound, determined by the rate of vibration of the medium (*v.* ACOUSTICS).

During the 17th cent. three standards of pitch were in common use: the pitch for chamber music was either about a semitone lower than our international pitch or identical with it, while that for organ and choir music and for town band music about a tone higher. Instrumental music of the 18th cent. used the first of these and consequently sounded about a semitone lower than it does today. The standard of pitch rose steadily until a French Commission of 1859 recommended the fixing of *diapason normal* at A

=435 vibrations a second at a temperature of 59°F., or 439 vibrations at 68°F. (*i.e.* the average temperature of a concert hall, hence called "Concert Pitch"). This was adopted as international pitch at a conference in Vienna in 1889. In 1939 it was amended to an absolute frequency (*i.e.* independent of temperature) of 440 cycles per second. *v.* CHORTON, KAMMERTON.

Pitch-Pipe. A small pipe with a graduated stopper by which it can be made to sound any note of the scale. It is used for giving the pitch to a choir which is about to sing without accompaniment.

Più [pee-oo'], *I.* "More." *Più allegro, più mosso,* faster; *più forte,* louder. *Più andante* is an ambiguous direction: if *andante* is taken in its literal meaning of "moving," it means "a little faster"; if it is regarded as meaning moderately slow, *più andante* will mean "slower." *Più* by itself=*più mosso. Il più*=the most: *il più piano possibile,* as soft as possible.

Piuttosto [pee-oot-toss'-to], *I.* Rather. *Andante piuttosto allegro,* rather fast than slow, *i.e.* not too much on the slow side. *v.* also TOSTO.

Pizzetti [pee-tset'-tee], ILDEBRANDO: *b.* Parma, Sept. 20, 1880. Composer and writer on music. Studied at the Parma Conservatorio. Teacher of harmony and counterpoint, Instituto Musicale, Florence, 1908; director, 1917. Director of the Verdi Conservatorio, Milan, 1924. Teacher of composition, Accademia di S. Cecilia, Rome, 1936. He is primarily a composer for the stage and for the voice. The libretti of his operas, which he calls "dramas," are on tragic or religious subjects, and have been written either wholly or partly by himself for the works composed since 1921. They include *Debora e Jaele* (Milan, 1922), *Fra Gherardo* (Milan, 1928), *Lo Straniero* (Rome, 1930), *Orsèolo* (Florence, 1935), *Vanna Lupa* (Florence, 1949), *Higenia* (Florence, 1951) and *Cagliostro* (Milan, 1954). His choral style is polyphonic, and his songs are for the most part in a serious vein. He has composed some orchestral music, a cello concerto, chamber music and piano music, and has published books on Bellini, on Paganini, on contemporary composers, and on dramatic music.

G. M. GATTI: *Ildebrando Pizzetti* (1934; English trans., 1951).

Pizzicato [pee-tsee-cah'-toh], *I.* Plucked. Used, generally in the abbreviated form *pizz.,* to indicate plucking of the string by the finger on a bowed instrument. Early examples of printed directions to play *pizzicato* occur in Tobias Hume's *Ayres . . . for the Viole de Gambo* (1605) and Monteverdi's *Il Combattimento di Tancredi e Clorinda* (1638; composed in 1624). Paganini introduced *pizzicato* for the left hand, with and without another note bowed.

Plagal Cadence. A cadence which has the harmony of the subdominant preceding that of the tonic:

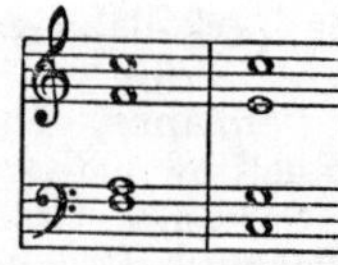

Its most familiar use is for the Amen at end of a hymn or prayer. *v.* CADENCE.

Plagal Mode. *v.* MODE.

Plainsong (*L.* cantus planus). The term "plainsong" is most commonly used for Western, *i.e.* Gregorian, chant. The liturgical melodies of other Western rites, *e.g.* Gallican, Ambrosian, Mozarabic, as well as those of Eastern rites, *e.g.* Byzantine, Syrian, are usually referred to simply as "chant." The term was first used about the 13th cent., when it became desirable to distinguish plainsong from measured song (*cantus mensuratus*). The most important forms used in plainsong are RESPOND, ANTIPHON, HYMN, SEQUENCE and Psalm (*v.* PSALMODY). The NOTATION of the earliest plainsong of which there is record was in neumes; after *c.* 1200 it was written on a four-line staff in note-forms derived from neumes.

P. WAGNER: *Einführung in die gregorianischen Melodien*, 3 vols. (latest ed., 1911-21; English trans. of vol. i, 1910).

Plainsong and Mediaeval Music Society. Formed in 1888 with the object of cataloguing and publishing the sources for plainsong and medieval music in England and promoting performances of it. The most important publications of the society are:

Graduale Sarisburiense (1894)—facsimile.

Bibliotheca Musico-Liturgica (1894-1932)—catalogue.

Early English Harmony (1897)—facsimiles.

Antiphonale Sarisburiense (1901-25)—facsimile.

Piae Cantiones (1910)—a reprint of a Swedish publication of 1582.

Missa "O quam suavis" (1927)—transcription.

Worcester Mediaeval Harmony (1928)—transcriptions.

The Old Hall Manuscript (1933-8)—transcriptions.

Anglo-French Sequelae (1934)—transcriptions.

Plainte [plañt], *Fr.* An ornament used in French music of the 17th and 18th centuries, equivalent to the German NACHSCHLAG.

Planets, The. Suite for orchestra, organ and (in the last movement) female chorus by Holst, Op. 32 (1915), in seven movements entitled: (1) *Mars, the Bringer of War*; (2) *Venus, the Bringer of Peace*; (3) *Mercury, the Winged Messenger*; (4) *Jupiter, the Bringer of Jollity*; (5) *Saturn, the Bringer of Old Age*; (6) *Uranus, the Magician*; (7) *Neptune, the Mystic.*

Player-Piano. *v.* PIANOLA.

Playford, JOHN: *b.* Norwich, 1623; *d.* London, Nov. 1686. The first regular music-publisher in England and the most active in the 17th century. His first publication was a collection of folk-tunes entitled *The English Dancing Master* (1651) which he later reprinted in many editions. Among his other publications were *A Musicall Banquet* (1651), Hilton's *Catch that Catch can* (1652), *Introduction to the Skill of Musick* (1654 and many later editions, written by himself), *Cantica sacra* (1674), *The Whole Book of Psalms* (1677; twenty editions to 1757), and *Choice Ayres* (5 books, 1676-84). His son, Henry Playford, continued his business.

Plein jeu [plañ zher], *Fr.* Full organ.

Pleyel [*G.* ply'-ĕl, *Fr.* play-yel], IGNAZ JOSEPH: *b.* Ruppertsthal (nr. Vienna), June 1, 1757; *d.* nr. Paris, Nov. 14, 1831. Piano manufacturer and composer. Studied under Wanhal and Haydn. *Kapellmeister* to Count Erdödy (who granted him leave to study in Rome), 1777. Vice-*Kapellmeister*, Strasbourg Cathedral, 1783; *Kapellmeister*, 1789. In 1792 he conducted in London several concerts in rivalry to those organized by Salomon for Haydn. Went to Paris in 1795, established himself as a music-dealer, and founded the piano factory which still bears his name, 1807. His compositions include 29 symphonies, concertos for piano and violin, string quintets and quartets, piano sonatas and songs.

Plectrum. A piece of horn, ivory, wood or other suitable substance used for playing such instruments as the psaltery (which may be considered a prototype of the harpsichord, but was also played with the fingers), mandoline and zither.

Plica [plick'-a], *Med. L.* (from the classical *plicare*, to fold). Lit. "plait." An ornament in early medieval notation, indicated by a vertical stroke attached to the note. The ornament was a passing note, and the descriptions of the theorists seem to suggest that it was sung with an effect resembling a TREMOLO. By the middle of the 13th cent. the notation of the *plica* was more or less systematised. If the stroke went up, the *plica* was above the note to which it was attached; if it went down, the *plica* was below. Thus the sign for a breve with a descending *plica* was:

If the next note was a third below the first, this example was sung:

If the succeeding note was the same as the first, the *plica* would descend a second in the same way (or rise, in the case of an ascending *plica*). Where the interval between the two principal notes was other than a third, the pitch of the *plica* had to be decided by the context. The sign for a breve with an ascending *plica* was:

for a long with an ascending *plica*:

for a long with a descending *plica*:

The value of a perfect long (*v.* PERFECT) with a *plica* was divided as follows: two-thirds of the normal value to the principal note, one-third to the *plica*. An imperfect long with a *plica* was divided into two equal halves, one half to the principal note and one to the *plica*. It would appear, therefore, that it was the method of performance which properly differentiated the *plica* from other forms of notation. On the other hand copyists seem often to have used it simply as a conveniently rapid way of writing two notes with a single symbol. In modern transcriptions it is generally represented by a note of smaller size. See further W. Apel, *The Notation of Polyphonic Music, 900-1600*, pp. 234-8, 298.

Plunket Greene, HARRY. *v.* GREENE (1).

Pneuma. *v.* NEUMA.

Pochette [posh-et], *Fr.* Lit. "little pocket." A miniature violin formerly used by dancing-masters. *v.* KIT.

Pochettino [po-keh-tee′-no], *I.* Very little, *i.e.* very slightly.

Poco [po′-co], *I.* Little, *i.e.* slightly, rather. *Poco più lento*, rather slower. *Poco diminuendo*, getting slightly softer. *Poco a poco*, little by little, gradually.

Poème de l'Extase, Le [ler po-em der lecks-tuz] *Fr.* (Poem of Ecstasy). Tone poem for orchestra by Scriabin, Op. 54 (1908).

Poème symphonique [po-em sa͡n-fon-eek], *Fr.* Symphonic poem.

Poglietti [poll-yet′-tee], ALESSANDRO: *d.* Vienna, July 1683. Composer. Organist at the court chapel in Vienna from 1661 until he was killed during the Turkish siege. He composed *ricercari* for organ. suites for harpsichord and church music, Two suites published in *D.T.Ö.*, xiii (2), contain some picturesque items. The second is a musical depiction of the Hungarian rebellion of 1671, with appropriate sub-titles. The first, written for the twenty-second birthday of the third wife of the Emperor Leopold I, contains a German air (*Aria Allemagna*) with 22 variations, some of which illustrate the style of regional dances, *e.g.* Bohemian *Dudlsackh*, Dutch *Flagolett*, Bavarian *Schalmay*. This movement is printed in part in the *Historical Anthology*, No. 236.

Pohjola's Daughter. Symphonic fantasia by Sibelius, Op. 49 (1906), one of a group of orchestral works based on the *Kalevala*.

Pohl [pole], (1) CARL FERDINAND: *b.* Darmstad, Sept. 6, 1819; *d.* Vienna, Apr. 28, 1887. Musicologist and organist. Studied under Sechter in Vienna, where he was a church organist, 1849-55. Lived in London, 1863-6, doing research on Mozart and Haydn. Librarian, Gesellschaft der Musikfreunde, Vienna, 1866 till his death. His publications include *Zur Geschichte der Glasharmonika* (1862), *Mozart und Haydn in London* (2 vols., 1867), *Joseph Haydn* (2 vols., 1875-82—the standard biography, completed by Hugo Botstiber,

1927), and *Die Gesellschaft der Musikfreunde und ihr Konservatorium* (1871).

(2) RICHARD: *b.* Leipzig, Sept. 12, 1826; *d.* Baden-Baden, Dec. 17, 1896. Music critic. Studied at Göttingen and Leipzig. Lived in Dresden, 1852; Weimar (where he was a friend of Liszt), 1854; Baden-Baden, 1864. He wrote a three-volume work on Richard Wagner, studies of Liszt and Berlioz and contributions to various periodicals, and composed choral works, songs and chamber music. He also translated Berlioz's literary works into German.

Point. A 16th-cent. English term for the theme used in a passage in imitative counterpoint. Thus Morley in *A Plaine and Easie Introduction to Practicall Musicke* (1597) says that in writing a fantasy (*i.e.* fancy) " a musician taketh a point at his pleasure and wresteth and turneth it as he list."

Point d'orgue [pwa͡n dorrg], *Fr.* (1) Pedal point.

(2) Pause.

(3) Cadenza (since the place for it, in a concerto or similar work, is indicated by a pause).

Pointé [pwa͡n-tay], *Fr.* A term used by French composers of the late 17th and early 18th cent. to indicate that a succession of short notes (*e.g.* quavers) of apparently equal value should actually be played with a marked inequality, the odd-numbered notes being lengthened and the even-numbered ones being proportionately shortened. If there were already dotted notes in the music (*e.g.* dotted quaver followed by semiquaver), the dotted note was to be prolonged and the note after it shortened still further. *v.* DOT (2), NOTES INÉGALES.

Pointing. *v.* ANGLICAN CHANT.

Poisoned Kiss, The. Comic opera in three acts by Vaughan Williams. Libretto by Evelyn Sharp. First performed, Cambridge, May 12, 1936.

Polacca [po-lahk'-cah], *I.* Polonaise.

Polka. A dance in moderately quick 2/4 time, said to have originated in Bohemia about 1830. After 1835 it spread to other European countries and to America, and became immensely popular. It was used by Smetana in his string quartet *From my Life* and in *The Bartered Bride*:

and by Dvořák.

Polly. Ballad opera with text by John Gay. It was published 1729 but was not allowed to be acted until 1777, when it was performed with alterations in the text by George Colman the elder and six new songs by Samuel Arnold. A modern adaptation by Clifford Bax, with the music arranged and newly composed by Frederic Austin, was first performed in London, Dec. 30, 1922.

Polo [po'-lo], *Sp.* An Andalusian folk dance in a moderately fast 3/8 time, frequently syncopated, and with periodic ornamental phrases on a syllable such as " Ay! " Bizet adapted a *polo* by Manuel Garcia in the prelude to the fourth act of *Carmen.*

Polonaise [pol-on-ez], *Fr.* (*I.* polacca). A Polish dance in moderately fast 3/4 time. Its chief characteristics are its stately rhythm in a persistent pattern:

or (J.S. Bach, W. F. Bach)

(Beethoven, Chopin)

and its use of a feminine ending :

W.F. BACH: *Polonaise No.* 6

It is found in the works of J. S. Bach (*e.g.* in the first Brandenburg Concerto and the second Suite for Orchestra), W. F. Bach, Mozart (in the piano sonata K.284), Beethoven, Weber and Schubert. Chopin's polonaises, which may be martial or funereal in expression and in a ternary or free form, *e.g.* the *Polonaise-Fantasie*, Op. 61, represent the Romantic concept of its style.

Polyphony (*Gr.* πολυφωνία, multiplication of sounds; *G.* Mehrstimmigkeit). The style of music in the writing of which the composer pays particular attention to the melodic value of each part, as distinct from HOMOPHONY, the style consisting of melody with chordal accompaniment. The most important polyphonic forms are MOTET, ROTA or ROUND, polyphonic MASS, CANON, polyphonic CHANSON, CANZONA, RICERCAR, and FUGUE. True polyphony was first written in the second stage (11th-12th century) of ORGANUM. Medieval polyphony was written by the method of successive composition, *i.e.* by the addition of a complete part or parts to the first complete part (*v.* MOTET, CANTUS FIRMUS). The imitative polyphony of the 16th-cent. choral music and of the *canzona* and *ricercar* was composed by disposing the same theme in each of the parts successively. The tonal or harmonic polyphony of the 18th-cent. fugue was composed in a similar fashion, but normally used a single theme (subject) throughout, and was organised according to the principles of TONALITY. In modern compositions the employment of polyphonic forms and devices may follow the principles of chromatic tonality, as in Hindemith's *Ludus Tonalis* (1942), or of atonality, as in Schönberg's *Pierrot Lunaire* (1912).

Polytonality. The use of two or more keys simultaneously, generally by superimposing chords, arpeggios, or melodies each of which unequivocally defines a different KEY (tonality). Before the present century deliberate examples, such as in Hans Neusiedler's *Jew's Dance* (*Historical Anthology*, No. 105) and Mozart's *Ein musikalischer Spass* (A Musical Joke), were rare. Pietro Raimondi (1786-1853) composed as a scientific curiosity (*Opera Scientifica* fugues for four and for six four-part choirs, each in a different key, which could be performed separately or simultaneously. Among modern composers, Stravinsky, Bartók and Milhaud have used polytonality quite frequently, *e.g.*:

BARTOK, *Bagatelle Op.6, No.1*

v. BITONALITY.

Pommer [pom′-mer], *G.* (*Fr.* bombarde). One of the larger members of the shawn family of instruments. *v.* OBOE.

Pomo d'Oro, Il [eel po′-mo doh′-ro] (The Golden Apple). Opera with a prologue and five acts by Cesti. Libretto by Francesco Sbarra. First performed, Vienna, 1667. The prologue and acts I, II and IV (all that survive) are printed in *D.T.Ö.*, iii (2) and iv (2).

Pomone [pom-on]. Opera with a prologue and five acts by Cambert. Libretto by Pierre Perrin. First performed, Paris, March 3, 1671.

Pomposo [pom-po′-zo], *I.* In a pompous manner.

Ponce [pon′-theh], MANUEL: *b.* Fresnillo, Dec. 8, 1882; *d.* Mexico, Apr. 24, 1948. Composer. Studied at the National Conservatorio in Mexico City, the Stern Conservatorium in Berlin under Martin Krause (piano), and in Bologna under Bossi (composition). In 1906 he returned to Mexico where he was teacher at the National Conservatorio and conductor of the National Symphony Orchestra. From 1915-18 he taught at Havana (Cuba), in 1926 studied composition in Paris under Dukas and in 1933 returned again to Mexico. He composed orchestral works, concertos, chamber music, piano works and songs, and collected and arranged Mexican folksongs.

Ponchielli [ponk-yell′-lee], AMILCARE : *b.* Paderno Fasolaro (nr. Cremona), Aug. 31, 1834; *d.* Milan, Jan. 16, 1886. Composer. Studied at the Milan Conservatorio. Organist in Cremona; *maestro di cappella,* Bergamo Cathedral, 1881; teacher of composition, Milan Conservatorio, 1883. He composed operas, ballets, cantatas, a Hymn to Garibaldi (1882) and church music. Of his 9 operas only *Gioconda* (Milan, 1876) has been widely performed. It is still popular in Italy.

Ponte, LORENZO DA [dah pon′-teh] (Emmanuele Conegliano): *b.* Ceneda (nr. Venice), March 10, 1749; *d.* New York, Aug. 17, 1838. Poet and librettist, of Jewish parents. Educated for the church, became a priest in 1773, and was appointed a teacher in the seminary in Trieste (1774). He became poet to the Court Opera in Vienna (1784), where he met Mozart and wrote librettos for *Le nozze di Figaro, Don Giovanni* and *Così fan tutte.* He lived in London as teacher of Italian and poet to the Italian Opera, in Holland and in New York (from 1805, to escape his London creditors) as a businessman, and later as a teacher of Italian at Columbia College. He wrote an autobiography (4 vols., 1823-27; English edition in one volume, 1929).

A. FITZLYON : *The Libertine Librettist* (1955).

Ponticello [pon-tee-chel′-lo], *I.* (*Fr.* chevalet, *G.* Steg). Bridge of a string instrument (lit. " little bridge "). *Sul ponticello* (or *ponticello* alone), on the bridge, *i.e.* play near the bridge, thus producing a glassy, brittle tone.

Poot [poat], MARCEL : *b.* Vilvoorde (Brabant), May 7, 1901. Composer, son of the director of the Royal Flemish Theatre, Brussels. Studied at the Brussels Conservatoire, the Royal Flemish Conservatoire, Antwerp, and the École Normale de Musique, Paris. Among his teachers were Gilson and Dukas. For many years he taught music in schools and also at the Brussels Conservatoire, of which he has been director since 1949. He was also active as a music critic until the latter appointment. His compositions include 3 operas, 2 ballets, 2 oratorios, 2 symphonies and other orchestral works, and a string quartet.

Popov [pop′-off], GABRIEL NIKOLAIEVICH : *b.* Novocherkasso, Sept. 25, 1904. Composer. Studied at Rostov and from 1922 at the Leningrad Conservatoire under Steinberg. He has composed operas, a symphony and two suites for orchestra, film and chamber music, and piano works.

Popper [pop′-per], DAVID : *b.* Prague, Dec. 9, 1843; *d.* Baden (nr. Vienna), Aug. 7, 1913. Cellist. Studied at the Prague Conservatoire under Goltermann and made his first tour in 1863. First cellist, Vienna Court Opera, and member of the Hubay Quartet, 1868-73; teacher, National Academy of Music, Budapest, 1896. He toured in Germany, Holland, Switzerland and England. He composed concertos and many other works for cello.

Porgy and Bess. Opera in three acts by George Gershwin. Libretto by Du Bose Heyward and Ira Gershwin. First performed, Boston, Sept. 30, 1935.

Porpora [porr′-po-rah], NICOLA ANTONIO : *b.* Naples, Aug. 19, 1686; *d.* there, Feb. 1767. Composer and singing teacher. Studied in Naples, where he became music director to the Portuguese Ambassador. Produced his first opera in 1708, established a school of singing, became singing teacher at the Conservatorio di San Onofrio in 1715 and at the Conservatorio della Pietà in Venice in 1725. He then visited Vienna, Dresden (as conductor of the Court Opera and rival to Hasse), London (from 1729 as rival conductor to Handel), in 1745 returned to Vienna (where he taught Haydn) and in 1747 to Dresden as teacher of the Electoral Princess and conductor with Hasse. In 1760 he settled in Naples as *maestro di cappella* of the Cathedral and director of the Conservatorio di San Onofrio. He composed 53 operas, oratorios, Masses, solo cantatas and other church music, violin sonatas and other chamber music, and pieces for harpsichord.

Porta [porr′-tah], COSTANZO : *b.* Cremona, *c.* 1530; *d.* Padua, May 26, 1601. Composer and Franciscan monk. Studied under Willaert in Venice.

Maestro di cappella, Osimo Cathedral, 1552; S. Antonio, Padua, 1564; Ravenna Cathedral, 1567; Loreto Cathedral, 1575. Later returned to Padua. He taught Viadana and Diruta. Composed motets, Masses, hymns and other church music, and madrigals. 2 motets and 2 madrigals are printed in Torchi, *L'arte musicale in Italia*, i.

Portamento [porr-tah-men′-to], *I.* (*Fr.* port de voix). Lit. "carrying." An effect used in singing, obtained by carrying the sound in a continuous glide from one note to the next. A similar effect on the trombone is generally referred to as GLISSANDO:

The examples are from Alban Berg's *Wozzeck* (1914-21). The upward *portamento* (a) is rare; (b) is a *portamento* which is partly defined as to pitch.

Portative (*I.* organetto). A medieval portable organ. It is shown frequently in miniatures and paintings from the 12th to the 16th centuries, *e.g.* in Memling's shrine of St. Ursula in the Hospital of St. John in Bruges.

Portato [porr-tah′-toh], *I.* Mezzo staccato. *v.* STACCATO.

Port de voix [porr der vwa], *Fr.* (1) A 17th-18th cent. term for the APPOGGIATURA.

(2) Portamento.

Portée [porr-tay], *Fr.* Staff, stave.

Porter, (1) QUINCY: *b.* New Haven (Conn.), Feb. 7, 1897. Composer. Studied at Yale under Horatio Parker and David Stanley Smith, in Paris under d'Indy, and later in America under Bloch. He taught theory at Cleveland Institute of Music from 1922, in 1928 went to Paris for two years as a Guggenheim Fellow, was professor of music and conductor at Vassar College from 1932 and was appointed Dean of the Faculty of New England Conservatory, Boston in 1938. In 1946 he became professor of theory at the Yale School of Music. He has composed a symphony and other orchestral works, a viola concerto, string quartets and other chamber music, and incidental music for plays.

(2) WALTER: *b. c.* 1595; *d.* London, Nov. 1659. Composer. Studied under Monteverdi. Gentleman of the Chapel Royal, 1617; master of the choristers, Westminster Abbey, 1639. After the suppression of the choral service in 1644 came under the patronage of Sir Edward Spencer. Published *Madrigales and Ayres . . . with Toccatas, Sinfonias and Rittornelles to them after the manner of Consort Musique* (1632; with a continuo part), and *Mottets of Two Voyces . . . with the Continued Bass or Score* (1657). Was one of the earliest English composers to publish a continuo part, and to use the *trillo* in the manner of the Italian monodists.

G. E. P. ARKWRIGHT: "An English Pupil of Monteverdi," in *The Musical Antiquary*, iv.

C. W. HUGHES: "Porter, Pupil of Monteverdi," in *The Musical Quarterly*, July, 1934.

Posaune [po-zown′-er], *G.* Trombone.

Posch [posh], ISAAK: *d.* before 1623. Organist at Laibach. He published two books of instrumental dances between 1618 and 1621. His *Musicalische Tafelfreudt* of 1621 (modern ed. in *D.T.Ö.*, xxxvi, 2) contains a number of Paduana-Gagliarda pairs, each pair being thematically related, followed by a number of Intrada-Couranta pairs, similarly related. A set of sacred concertos for one to four voices with continuo was published in 1623 under the title *Harmonia concertans*.

Positif [poz-ee-teef], *Fr.* Choir organ.

Position. (1) On a stringed instrument, the placing of the left hand on the string in relation to the open note of the string. Thus in the first position on the G string the first finger plays A, in the second position it plays B, and so on. The thumb is used in the higher positions on the cello.

(2) The placing of the slide of the TROMBONE.

(3) The disposition of a chord in relation to its ROOT. Root position, first inversion, second inversion, etc., of a chord are all said to be positions of that chord, in that they consist of the same notes, though differently arranged.

Positive. A medieval chamber organ, frequently depicted in paintings and illustrations, *e.g.* in the Van Eyck altarpiece *The Adoration of the Lamb* at Ghent and on the title-page of Gafori's *Theorica musicae* (1492).

Possenti [poss-sen′-tee], PELLEGRINO: Early 17th century Italian composer who published two books of madrigals (1623, 1625), and was one of the earliest composers of sonatas for two, three, and four instruments with continuo (*Concentus armonici*, 1628).

Postlude. A piece played on the organ at the end of a service.

Pothier [pot-yay], DOM JOSEPH: *b.* Bouzemont (nr. St. Dié), Dec. 7, 1835; *d.* Conques (Belgium), Dec. 8, 1923. Entered the Benedictine Order at the Abbey of Solesmes in 1859 and in 1898 became abbot of St. Wandrille monastery which was later moved to Belgium. He continued the study of plainsong begun by his teacher Dom Guéranger, published many works on that subject, and initiated the series *Paléographie musicale* for publishing facsimiles of manuscripts of the 9th-16th cent.

Pot-pourri [po-poo-ree], *Fr.* A stew containing various kinds of meat, or a mixture of dried flowers kept in a jar. Hence a succession of familiar tunes fashioned, with links, into a continuous composition.

Potter, PHILIP CIPRIANI HAMBLEY: *b.* London, Oct. 2, 1792; *d.* there, Sept. 28, 1871. Pianist, composer and conductor. Studied under Attwood, Callcott, Crotch, Woelfl, and (after his appearance with the London Philharmonic Society in 1816) under Aloys Förster in Vienna, where he met Beethoven. After a tour in Italy he returned to London. Teacher of piano, R.A.M., 1822; principal, 1832-59. Conductor, Madrigal Society, 1855-70. His published works include sonatas and other piano pieces, a sextet for strings and piano and other chamber music ; he also composed 9 symphonies, 4 overtures, piano concertos, and a cantata.

Pougin [poo-zhan͡], FRANÇOIS AUGUSTE ARTHUR: *b.* Châteauroux, Aug. 6, 1834; *d.* Paris, Aug. 8, 1921. Writer on music. Studied at the Paris Conservatoire under Alard and Henri Reber, and played the violin and conducted in various Paris theatres, 1856-63. He wrote for several musical periodicals, edited *Le Ménestrel* from 1885, and published many biographies of composers.

Poule, La [la pool], *Fr.* (The Hen). The title given to Haydn's symphony No. 83 in G minor (1785), one of the 6 symphonies commissioned by the Concert de la Loge Olympique in Paris and called the "Paris Symphonies."

Poulenc [poo-lan͡k], FRANCIS: *b.* Paris, Jan. 7, 1899. Composer and pianist. Studied under Ricardo Viñes and Koechlin. Member of the group of French composers known as *Les Six.* He has composed ballets, chamber music, a concerto for two pianos and many piano pieces, a concerto for harpsichord, songs, choral works and a cantata. His style combines classical clarity with an irrepressible talent for satire and caricature.

Pouplinière [la poo-pleen-yairr], ALEXANDRE JEAN JOSEPH LE RICHE DE LA: *b.* Chinon, July 29, 1693 ; *d.* there, Dec. 5, 1762. Amateur and patron of music. Studied under Rameau, who lived in his house for a number of years and conducted his private orchestra. He was the patron of the concerts conducted by Johann Stamitz in Paris in 1754-5, and on the advice of Stamitz added clarinets, horns and harp to his orchestra for the first time in France.

G. CUCUEL : *La Pouplinière et la musique de chambre au XVIIIe siècle* (1913).

Poussez [poo-say], *Fr.* Lit. "push ahead," *i.e.* quicken the tempo.

Power, LEONEL : *d.* Canterbury, June 5, 1445. Composer, the most important contemporary of Dunstable. Like Dunstable, he may have been abroad, since many of his compositions survive in continental manuscripts. His music, with that of Dunstable and other English composers, had a considerable influence on the style of continental composers. His *Alma redemptoris* Mass (modern ed. by L. Feininger) is the earliest complete Mass on a *cantus firmus.* Those of his compositions contained in the Old Hall manuscript have been published (*The Old Hall Manuscript*, ed. A. Ramsbotham, 3 vols., 1930-38) and those in the Trent manuscripts in *D.T.Ö.*, vii, xxvii (1), and xxxi. He wrote an elementary treatise on descant, which has been printed in M. F. Bukofzer, *Geschichte des englischen Diskants* (1936).

Praetorius [pray-to'-ri-ŏŏss], (1) HIERONYMUS : *b.* Hamburg, Aug. 10, 1560 ; *d.* there, Jan. 27, 1629. Organist and composer. Studied with his father (organist of St. James's, Hamburg) and in Cologne. Cantor, Erfurt, 1580. Assistant organist, St. James's, Hamburg, 1582 ; organist (in succession to his father), 1586. His compositions, exclusively for the church and written for as many as 20 voices, were at first published in separate volumes and then reissued in a collected edition in 5 volumes entitled *Opus musicum novum et perfectum.* The contents include Masses, Magnificats, and motets with Latin and German texts. 16 numbers are printed in *D.D.T.*, xxiii.

(2) MICHAEL : *b.* Kreuzburg (Thuringia), Feb. 15, 1571 ; *d.* Wolfenbüttel, Feb. 15, 1621. Composer and theorist, one of the most versatile and prolific musicians of his time. Among the posts which he held were those of *Kapellmeister* and secretary to the Duke of Brunswick and *Kapellmeister* to the Saxon court. He was one of the foremost composers in Germany to practise the elaborate style of writing for several choirs which was cultivated in Venice. His works for the church include settings of both Latin and German words. Among them are settings of the Magnificat (*Megalynodia Sionia*), Kyries, Glorias, etc. (*Missodia Sionia*) and many settings of Lutheran chorales ranging from simple harmonizations to elaborate contrapuntal treatment. His *Polyhymnia Caduceatrix et Panegyrica* consists of choral works with independent instrumental accompaniment. A few organ settings were printed in *Musae Sioniae*, pt. vii and *Hymnodia Sionia.* The dances for instrumental ensemble in *Terpsichore* include several by French composers. Praetorius's principal publications were :

Musae Sioniae, 9 pts. (1605-10)
Musarum Sioniarum Motectae et Psalmi Latini (1607).
Missodia Sionia (1611).
Hymnodia Sionia (1611).
Eulogodia Sionia (1611).
Megalynodia Sionia (1611).
Terpsichore (1612).
Urania (1613).
Polyhymnia Caduceatrix et Panegyrica (1619).
Polyhymnia Exercitatrix (1620).
Puericinium (1621).

Modern ed. in 20 volumes under the general editorship of F. Blume (1928-42). Organ works also published separately, ed. K. Matthei.

In addition to his musical compositions Praetorius also published *Syntagma Musicum* in 3 vols. (1615-20). The first volume deals with the origins and history of liturgical music and also with the secular music of the ancient world. The second volume, sub-titled *Organographia* (facsimile ed., 1929), gives a detailed account of instruments and their function and includes a valuable series of illustrations, drawn to scale. The third volume (modern ed. by E. Bernouilli, 1916) deals with notation and the various forms of secular music current in the early 17th cent. and adds an important section on methods of performance and principles of choir-training. The second and third volumes together shed light on a great many details of 17th-cent. music and performance which would otherwise remain obscure. The treatment is systematic and the approach scholarly.

Prague Symphony. The title given to Mozart's symphony No. 38 in D major, K.504 (1786), after its first performance in Prague, 1787.

Pralltriller [prull'-trill-er], *G.* An ornament used in instrumental music in the 18th century. C. P. E. Bach, in his *Versuch über die wahre Art, das Klavier zu spielen* (1753-62), calls it "Der halbe (*i.e.* half) oder Prall-Triller" and gives this example:

He points out that it occurs only on the lower of two notes in a descending second played legato, that it must be played very fast and with a "snap," and that it is doubtful therefore that it can be properly executed on the pianoforte. When it is marked over a pause note preceded by an appoggiatura, the latter is held, and the *Pralltriller* is played immediately before the end of the note:

Since *c.* 1800 the name has been applied to the ornament formerly called *Schneller*, and commonly called INVERTED MORDENT. *v.* also TRILL.

Pré aux Clercs, Le [ler pray o clair]. Opera in three acts by Hérold. Libretto by François Antoine Eugène de Planard. First performed, Paris, Dec. 15, 1832.

Precentor (*L.* praecentor, cantor). The official charged with the supervision of music in a cathedral, college chapel or monastery.

Prelude (*L.* praeludium). An introductory movement; also, in Chopin and later composers, a short piano piece in one movement. The preludes written for organ, lute, and virginals in the 15th and 16th centuries were free pieces in an extemporary style. In Italy such pieces for lute were called *tastar* ("touching") and in Spain *tañer*. Some of the SUITE preludes of the baroque period continued this style, *e.g.* those of Louis Couperin, which he wrote down without giving the rhythm, a practice which continued to the time of Rameau, as in:

from his first book of clavecin pieces (1706), and in the prelude to Handel's first Suite for harpsichord. In others a more regular and extended form was adopted, *e.g.* the cyclic form of the preludes in Bach's *English Suites*, and of some of his organ preludes. The preludes of the *Wohltemperirte Clavier* are, with one or two exceptions, short pieces based on a single musical idea, as in the prelude in D minor in the first book:

The 24 Preludes of Chopin, while Romantic in style and piano technique, have in common with those of Bach's *Forty-eight* the use of a single theme and of the complete cycle of keys, and later sets of preludes, though not always using a complete key sequence, have followed the same plan, *e.g.* Scriabin's 12 Preludes, Op. 11, Debussy's two sets of 12 Preludes, and Shostakovich's 24 Preludes, Op. 34.

Since about 1840 many composers have written a short orchestral piece as a prelude to, and usually taking its music from, an opera, as in Wagner's *Lohengrin* and *Tristan und Isolde* and Verdi's *La Traviata*, rather than a full-length OVERTURE. *v.* also CHORALE PRELUDE.

Prélude à l'Après-Midi d'un Faune [pray-leed a la-pray-mee-dee dŭrn fone], *Fr.* (Prelude to a faun's afternoon). Orchestral piece by Debussy (1894), designed to illustrate a poem by Mallarmé—one of his earliest essays in impressionism.

Près de la table [pray der la tubl], *Fr.* " Near the sounding-board." An indication found in harp music, resulting in metallic sounds similar to those of the banjo.

Prestant [press-tūn], *Fr.* A 4 ft. open diapason stop on the organ (*E.* principal).

Presto [press'-to], *I.* The original meaning was " lively, brisk," but it came to be used to indicate the fastest speed in normal use. The superlative, *prestissimo*, can only mean the fastest speed of which the performer or performers are capable.

Prick-Song. A term derived from " pricking," in the sense of writing musical notes, used in England in the first half of the 16th cent. to distinguish polyphonic music from plainsong, and later extended to include all music except plainsong, whether written or printed.

Prima [pree'-mah], *I.* " First of all, formerly." *Come prima*, as at first, *i.e.* resume the original tempo of a piece or movement.

Prima donna [pree'-mah don'-nah], *I.* " First lady." The singer of the most important female part in an opera. The corresponding term in the 18th cent. for the singer of the most important *castrato* or tenor role was *primo uomo.*

Primavera [pree-mah-veh'-rah], GIOVANNI LEONARDO: *b.* Barletta (nr. Naples), 16th cent. *Maestro di cappella* to the Spanish Governor of Milan, 1573. He composed madrigals and *canzone napoletane* for 3 voices, published between 1565-84. Palestrina composed a PARODY MASS on his madrigal " Nasce la gioia mia."

Prima vista, A [ah pree'-mah veece'-tah], *I.* At first sight.

Prima volta [pree'-mah voll'-tah], *I.* " First time," *i.e.* a first ending when a repeat is indicated. It is usually shown by |1 , and the second ending (*seconda volta*) by |2 . *v.* CLOS, OUVERT.

Primo [pree'-mo], *I.* " First." (1) The upper part of a piano duet, the lower part being termed *secondo* (second). In most editions of piano duets the *primo* part is printed on the right-hand page and the *secondo* on the left-hand page. This is in many ways the most convenient arrangement for the performers. Some publishers, however, prefer to print the two parts together, in score, which enables each player to see what the other is doing but imposes an inconvenient angle of vision.

(2) The first of two or more players or singers, or of two or more groups of performers. *Violino primo*, the first violin in a string quartet, or the whole body of first violins in an orchestra. *Flauto* (*oboe, clarinetto*, etc.) *primo*, first flute (oboe, clarinet, etc.). In an orchestral score the parts for two wind instruments of the same kind are generally printed on the same stave. Hence when only one is playing, *primo* (abbreviated *Imo*, or simply I) indicates that the first player is intended.

(3) *Tempo primo* (abbreviated *tempo Imo* or *tempo I*). " The original speed." An indication that the speed of the opening of a movement or piece is to be resumed after one or more sections in a slower or faster tempo.

Primo uomo [pree'-mo oo-o'-mo], *I.* " First man." *v.* PRIMA DONNA.

Prince Igor. *v.* KNAZ IGOR.

Princess Ida. Comic opera in two acts by Sullivan. Libretto by William Schwenk Gilbert (" a respectful operatic perversion of Tennyson's *Princess* "). First performed, London, Jan. 1, 1884.

Principal (*G.* Prinzipal, *I.* principale). On organs in Germany and Italy the 8 ft. open diapason ; in England the 4 ft. diapason. *v.* ORGAN.

Printing of Music. Plainsong books with music were printed in Rome (1476), Venice and Würzburg in the second half of the 15th cent., the notes being printed in black and the staves separately in red. Ottaviano dei Petrucci of Venice published the *Harmonice Musices Odhecaton*, the first book of printed part-music, in 1501, and some 50 collections thereafter. Pierre Attaingnant began printing in Paris in 1528, and a book of *XX Songes* in three and four parts was published in London in 1530. Engraving of music was practised in Italy in the second half of the

16th cent., and *Parthenia*, engraved in 1612 or early 1613, was "the first musicke that ever was printed for the Virginalls." Early in the 18th cent. John Walsh introduced the use of special punches for engraving music, a system which is still in use and has almost entirely superseded the use of type. At the end of the century lithography was invented, and Weber himself lithographed his Variations for Piano, Op. 2, in 1800. In recent years photo-lithography has been used to publish scores from the composer's, or a copyist's, manuscript.

W. GAMBLE : *Music Engraving and Printing* (1923).

C. HUMPHRIES AND W. C. SMITH : *Music Publishing in the British Isles* (1954).

O. KINKELDEY : *Music and Music Printing in Incunabula* (1932).

R. R. STEELE : *The Earliest English Music Printing* (1903).

Printz [prints], WOLFGANG KASPAR: *b.* Waldthurn (Upper Palatinate), Oct. 10, 1641; *d.* Sorau, Oct. 13, 1717. Studied theology, and was appointed cantor at Promnitz, at Triebel, and in 1665 at Sorau. His *Historische Beschreibung der edlen Sing- und Klingkunst . . . von Anfang der Welt bis auf unserer Zeit* (Dresden, 1690) was the first history of music written in German.

Prinzipal [prints-ee-pahl'], *G.* Open diapason, an 8 ft. organ stop. The English " principal " is a 4 ft. stop.

Prise de Troie, La [la preez der trwa]. *v.* TROYENS.

Prix de Rome [pree der rom], *Fr.* A prize given by the French Government for excellence in each of the following fields : painting, sculpture, engraving, architecture and music. The prizes are awarded by the Académie des Beaux-Arts on the results of examinations. The winners are required to reside for three years at the Villa Medici (headquarters of the Académie de France) in Rome, and to submit for inspection the work completed during their period of residence. The prize for music was first awarded in 1803. It has on occasion been divided. Among the composers who have won it are Hérold (1812), Halévy (1819), Berlioz (1830), Thomas (1832), Gounod (1839), Bizet (1857), Guiraud (1859), Paladilhe (1860), Dubois (1861), Bourgault-Ducoudray (1862), Massenet (1863), Lenepveu (1865), Wormser (1875), P. Hillemacher (1876), Huë (1879), L. Hillemacher (1880), Pierné (1882), Debussy (1884), Charpentier (1887), Büsser (1893), Rabaud (1894), Schmitt (1900), Caplet (1901), Paray (1911), L. Boulanger (1913), Delvincourt (1913), Dupré (1914), Ibert (1919), Fourestier (1925), Barraine (1929).

Prodaná Nevěsta [pro'-da-nah nev'-yast-a] (The Bartered Bride). Comic opera in three acts by Smetana. Libretto by Karel Sabini. First performed, Prague, May 30, 1866. Jeník is in love with Mařenka, whose parents, however, want her to marry the stupid, stammering Vašek (son of the wealthy Mícha). He agrees with the marriage-broker Kecal to give up Mařenka in return for a money payment, on condition that Mařenka shall marry only Mícha's son. As Jeník himself turns out to be a son of Mícha by an earlier marriage he gets the best of the bargain.

Prod'homme [prod-om], JACQUES-GABRIEL: *b.* Paris, Nov. 28, 1871. Musicologist. Studied in Germany and from 1879-1900 lived in Munich where he founded and edited a periodical; then returned to Paris where he became curator of the Musée de l' Opéra and librarian of the Conservatoire. He has written books on Mozart, Beethoven, Berlioz, Wagner and other composers, and on the history of opera.

Programme Music. Music in which sound is used to depict the concrete elements of, and whose form is governed by, a story or image, as distinct from ABSOLUTE MUSIC. A few pictorial passages may be found in plainsong, in 16th-cent. Masses and motets, in English virginal music, and in French harpsichord music of the 17th cent., and many in the madrigals of the 16th cent., and in the operas, oratorios and cantatas of the 17th and 18th cent. In all of these they are incidental factors in compositions which have an orthodox musical design. Only in rare instances, such as some of the Italian *caccie* of the 14th cent., the bird and battle *chansons* of Janequin, the battle piece for virginals by Byrd, and the *Biblical Sonatas* of Johann Kuhnau, are both the form and the themes directly related to a programme.

Beethoven affirmed that his *Pastoral Symphony* was " an expression of emotion rather than tone-painting "; nevertheless the fourth movement, like all storm scenes in music, is programme music. Berlioz, on the other hand, introduced the written programme of his *Symphonie Fantastique* in terms which show that he regarded the symphony as an instrumental drama " deprived of the resource of words." There is an even stronger contrast of attitude between Mendelssohn, who kept the pictorial elements in his concert overtures well within the limits of the traditional form, and Liszt, whose SYMPHONIC POEMS were in form and expression so closely related to their subject that he thought it desirable to provide a programme or preface " to guard the listener against a wrong poetical interpretation." The difference between the tone-poet, as Liszt preferred to call the composer of programme music, and the " mere musician " was that, in his view, the former " reproduces his impression and the adventures of his soul in order to communicate them, while the latter manipulates, groups and connects the tones according to certain established rules, and, thus playfully conquering difficulties, attains at best to novel, bold, unusual and complex combinations " (English version of the essay on *Berlioz and his Harold Symphony* of 1855 printed in O. Strunk's *Source Readings in Music History*, 1950).

In the series of symphonic poems which culminated in *Ein Heldenleben* (1898) and the *Symphonia domestica* (1903) Richard Strauss brought the pictorial possibilities of orchestral music with an accompanying programme to their final point. The idea that all music is by its nature an expression of such a " programme," avowed or implied, had been vigorously attacked many years earlier by Hanslick in his *Vom Musikalisch-Schönen* (1854). The question is no longer a burning one, but Hanslick's view, though put in an extreme form, is much closer to the generally accepted view in this century: that any judgment of the value of a programme to music must ultimately be a judgment of the musical qualities of the result.

F. NIECKS : *Programme Music* (1907).

Prokofiev [prock-off'-yeff], SERGEI: *b.* Sontsovka, in the Ekaterinoslav district, Apr. 23, 1891; *d.* Moscow, March 4, 1953. Composer. He showed creative talent at an early age, studied with Glière, and wrote a complete opera score at the age of twelve. At the Petrograd Conservatoire he studied under Rimsky-Korsakov, Liadov and Tcherepnin. In 1918 he went to America, and in 1921 conducted the first performance of his opera *The Love for Three Oranges* in Chicago. In 1922 he went to Paris and wrote ballets for Diaghilev's company. He returned to Russia in 1934. In 1948 his music was criticised in a resolution of the Central Committee of the Communist Party. In his reply he affirmed his intention of using " lucid melody and, as far as possible, a simple harmonic language " in a new opera. The work was however described by Khrennikov as " modernistic and anti-melodic." The resolution and Prokofiev's letter are printed in N. Slonimsky, *Music since 1900* (1949). Prokofiev was awarded a Stalin Prize in 1951.

His earlier music, *e.g.* the *Scythian Suite* (1914), the *Classical Symphony* (1916-17), and the third piano concerto, was remarkable for its rhythmic impulse and individual harmonic style. These qualities complemented by more lyrical feeling, came to maturity in the works written in Paris, which include three symphonies and the fourth and fifth piano concertos. The lyrical quality became more apparent in such later works as the second violin concerto (1935) and *Peter and the Wolf* (1936), though the satirical element is strong in his music for the film *Lieutenant Kije* (1934). The eight piano sonatas contain some of his best and most characteristic music. His principal compositions are:

(a) STAGE WORKS: Operas: *Magdalen* (1913); *The Gambler* (1927); *The Love for Three Oranges* (1919);

The Flaming Angel (1925); *Simeon Kotko* (1939); *Betrothal in the Monastery* (1941); *War and Peace* (1942); 6 ballets.

(b) ORCHESTRA: 7 symphonies; sinfonietta; overtures; symphonic suites; film music; 5 piano concertos; 2 violin concertos; cello concerto.

(c) CHAMBER WORKS: Quintet for wind and strings; string quintet; 2 string quartets.

(d) PIANO: 9 sonatas; 2 sonatinas; suites; studies.

Also choral cantatas and songs.

G. ABRAHAM: *Eight Soviet Composers* (1943).

I. W. NESTYEV: *Serge Prokofiev* (1946).

Prolation. In mensural NOTATION prolation is the relation of the semibreve to the minim, and is either perfect or imperfect. In perfect prolation, shown by a dot in the circle or semicircle which indicates the time (*tempus, i.e.* the relation of the breve to the semibreve), thus: ⊙, ⋐, the semibreve has three minims. In imperfect prolation, shown by the absence of a dot, the semibreve has two minims. *v.* MENSURAL NOTATION.

Promenade Concerts. In 1838 a series of concerts called "Promenade Concerts à la Musard" was given in London. The idea was imported from Paris, where Musard, a composer of popular quadrilles, had conducted promenade concerts from 1833. Occasional series of promenade concerts were organised during the nineteenth century, conducted by Musard, Jullien, Balfe and others. The present Promenade Concerts, held in the summer, were instituted in 1895 by Robert Newman; the character of the programmes, which always include a number of new works, was the creation of Sir Henry Wood, who conducted the concerts from their beginning until his death in 1944. In 1927 the responsibility for the organisation of the concerts was assumed by the B.B.C.

Prometheus. (1) *Die Geschöpfe des Prometheus* (The Creatures of Prometheus). Ballet with music by Beethoven, Op. 43 (1800). It consists of an overture and 18 numbers. The finale contains the theme, used about the same time for a *contredanse*, which he subsequently used for the Variations and fugue in E♭, Op. 35, for piano, and for the variations in the finale of the EROICA SYMPHONY.

(2) *Prometheus: the Poem of Fire.* Tone-poem for orchestra by Scriabin, Op. 60 (1819). The score calls for a *tastiera per luce*, a keyboard instrument which projects colours on a screen.

Proper. The parts of the Proper of the MASS, *i.e.*, those with texts and music which are proper to their day or season, as distinct from the Ordinary (the parts with invariable texts), are the Introit, Gradual, Alleluia (Tract in penitential seasons), Offertory, and Communion.

Prophète, Le [ler prof-et] (The Prophet). Opera in five acts by Meyerbeer. Libretto by Augustin Eugène Scribe. First performed, Paris, Apr. 16, 1849.

Proportion. The rhythmic system of all part-music is based on proportion. Our present TIME-SIGNATURES are derived from signs of proportion which were used in mensural NOTATION to show the relation between a new note-value and an immediately preceding one. This relation could be one of AUGMENTATION, or more frequently, of DIMINUTION, and was shown by a fraction or ratio, as in this example by Richard Davy (*c.* 1500):

(called *Sesquialtera* proportion or HEMIOLA) where the proportion 3 : 2 is the equivalent of the modern triplet. In his *Plaine and Easie Introduction* (ed. R. A. Harman, 1952) Morley gives a table of the usual proportions, copied from Gafori, for the benefit of those who "would be curious in Proportions," and a song "Christ's Cross be my speed" for practice in performing them. Some signs were still used in the 17th cent. in the proportional rather than the time-signature sense, as in the following:

in which 3/1 means that three semibreves following are to be sung in the time of one preceding. In more modern notation:

Proporz [pro-porrts′]. *v.* NACHTANZ.

Propriety (*L.* proprietas). In a combination (LIGATURE) of two notes in mensural NOTATION the normal ("proper" and "perfect") sequence was considered to be that which had the shorter note (*brevis*) followed by the longer (*longa*). The term propriety referred to the first note, so that a ligature of two or more notes beginning with a breve, *e.g.* (= B L), was defined as a ligature "with propriety" (*cum proprietate*), and a ligature beginning with a long, *e.g.*, (= L B), was *sine proprietate*. A ligature beginning with two semibreves, shown by upward stem, *e.g.*, (= S S B) was defined as a ligature "with opposite propriety" (*cum opposita proprietate*).

Prosa [proce′-a], *L.* *v.* SEQUENCE (2).

Proske [pross-ker], KARL: *b.* Grobnig (Silesia), Feb. 11, 1794; *d.* Ratisbon, Dec. 20, 1861. Editor of church music. Practised medicine until 1823 and then studied theology at Ratisbon where he was ordained in 1826 and became canon and *Kapellmeister* of the Cathedral in 1830. He visited Italy, collected and published choral church music of the 16th and 17th cent. in *Musica divina* (4 vols., 1853-62) and *Selectus novus missarum* (1855-59), which contributed greatly to the revival of the music of Palestrina and his contemporaries. His valuable library is now in the Episcopal Library at Ratisbon.

Prout, EBENEZER: *b.* Oundle (Northants.), March 1, 1835; *d.* London, Dec. 5, 1909. Composer, theorist and teacher. Lived in London as organist. Teacher, R.A.M., 1879, Guildhall School of Music, 1884. Choral conductor, music critic, and editor. Professor, Dublin, 1894-1909. He wrote *Harmony, its Theory and Practice* (1889) and other text-books which had very wide use, and a biography of Mozart (1903), and composed 4 symphonies, cantatas and other church music, and chamber music.

Provenzale [pro-ven-tsahl′-eh], FRANCESCO: *b.* Naples, *c.* 1627; *d.* there, Sept. 1704. Composer. He lived in Naples as teacher at the Conservatorio S. Maria di Loreto, 1663, and director there, 1673-1701. *Maestro di cappella*, S. Gennaro, 1686-99. He composed operas, cantatas, oratorios, motets and other church music, and was the first of a line of Neapolitan opera composers who assumed the leadership in the development of opera in the late baroque period. His aria on an *ostinato* bass "Lasciatemi morir" is published in the *Historical Anthology*, No. 222.

Prunières [preēn-yairr], HENRY: *b.* Paris, May 24, 1886; *d.* Nanterre (nr. Paris), Apr. 11, 1942. Musicologist. Studied under Romain Rolland at the Sorbonne, founded and became editor of *Revue Musicale* (1920) and edited the works of Lully. His writings include books on opera in the 17th cent., and on Lully, Monteverdi and Cavalli. His *Monteverdi* (1924) and *New History of Music* (1945) have been published in English.

Prussian Quartets. A set of three string quartets by Mozart, composed in 1789-90 for King Frederick William of

Prussia, who was an amateur cellist. His original intention was to write six. The three quartets are: No. 1 in D major, K.575; No. 2 in B♭ major, K.589; No. 3 in F major, K.590. All three works have a prominent part for the cello.

Psalmody. The oldest part of Christian liturgical music. The verses of a complete psalm are normally sung in alternation by the two sides of the choir to an ANGLICAN CHANT, or to one of the eight psalm tones of plainsong, *e.g.*:

The example is the first tone; I is the opening (*initium*), D the dominant or reciting note (*tenor*), M the half-verse ending (*mediatio*), and T the verse-ending (*terminatio*). Originally an ANTIPHON, which varied with the church calendar, was sung after each verse, later before and after the psalm only. The psalm-tone is chosen to agree with the MODE of the antiphon. Each psalm-tone has a series of verse-endings, called "differences," to agree with the opening notes of the antiphon.

A verse of a psalm is sung in more elaborate plainsong as part of a RESPOND. *v.* also TONUS PEREGRINUS, TRACT.

Psalter, Metrical. In the 16th cent. the Reformed churches in the Netherlands, England, Scotland and Switzerland decided to replace the singing of psalms to plainsong by the singing of metrical translations of the psalms to tunes suitable for congregational use. The tunes were set in imitative style, as in Goudimel's *Les CL pseaumes de David* of 1564 (published from the 1580 edition by H. Expert in *Les Maîtres musiciens de la Renaissance française*, iv, 1896), or more frequently in HOMOPHONIC style with the tune in the tenor or treble:

The example, from the first of Tallis's eight tunes for Archbishop Parker's Psalter of 1567/8, has the tune in the tenor. The psalter of Sternhold and Hopkins was published (with four-part music) by Day in 1563, and later English psalters by East (1592), Ravenscroft (1621) and Playford (1677). The first complete form of the Genevan Psalter was published in 1562, with music composed and arranged by Louis Bourgeois, and the Scottish Psalter, which adopted a number of the French tunes, in 1564-5. The first Netherlands psalter, the *Souterliedekens* of 1540, used secular tunes; it was replaced by the French Psalter in 1566. Some tunes contained in the psalters of the 16th and 17th centuries were included in later hymn-books, and are still in use.

M. FROST: *English and Scottish Psalm and Hymn Tunes, 1543-1677* (1953).

W. S. PRATT: *The Music of the French Psalter of 1562* (1939).

R. R. TERRY: *Calvin's First Psalter* (1932). *The Scottish Psalter of 1635* (1935).

Psaltery (*Fr.* psalterion, *I.* salterio). A medieval instrument of the zither type with plucked strings, of similar shape to the DULCIMER, the strings of which were struck. It usually had the shape of a symmetrical trapezoid; a half-psaltery had a wing shape, which was kept when it was developed into the harpsichord by the addition of a keyboard.

Pskovitianka [pscov'-it-yunk-a] (The Maid of Pskov). Opera in four acts by

Rimsky-Korsakov (christened *Ivan the Terrible* by Diaghilev, 1909). Libretto by the composer (after a play by Lev Alexandrovich Mei). First performed, St. Petersburg, Jan. 13, 1873. Revived with a new prologue, Moscow, Dec. 27, 1898.

Puccini [poo-tchee′-nee], GIACOMO ANTONIO DOMENICO MICHELE SECONDO MARIA: *b.* Lucca, Dec. 22, 1858; *d.* Brussels, Nov. 29, 1924. Opera composer. Of a musical family, he studied in Lucca and at the Milan Conservatorio. He entered his first opera *Le Villi* (1884) for a competition which was won by Mascagni's *Cavalleria rusticana,* and had a moderate success with *Manon Lescaut* in 1893. *La Bohème* was first performed, with Toscanini conducting, in 1896, *Tosca* in 1900, *Madama Butterfly,* which was initially a failure, in 1904. The success of these three was not equalled by *La Fanciulla del West* (*The Girl of the Golden West*), produced in New York in 1910, nor by *Il Trittico,* the triptych of one-act operas (*Il Tabarro, Suor Angelica, Gianni Schicchi*) on which he worked during the 1914-18 war, although the latter contains some of his best music. The final duet of *Turandot,* left unfinished at his death, was completed by Alfano. Gifted with a vivid sense of the stage and a natural melodic talent, Puccini developed with them an impressive resource in harmony and orchestration which have made his operas among the most successful of modern times.

M. CARNER: *Puccini: a Critical Biography* (1958).
DANTE DEL FIORENTINO: *Immortal Bohemian: An Intimate Memoir of Giacomo Puccini* (1952).
G. R. MAREK: *Puccini* (1952).
R. SPECHT: *Puccini* (1933).

Pugnani [poo-nyahn′-ee], GAETANO: *b.* Turin, Nov. 27, 1731; *d.* there, July 15, 1798. Violinist and teacher. Studied under Somis and Tartini. Became leader of the court orchestra in Turin, travelled as a violinist from 1754-70, spending some time in London as leader of the Italian Opera orchestra, and then returned to Turin where he was leader, conductor and teacher. His pupils included Viotti, Bruni and Conforti. He composed operas, ballets, cantatas, violin concertos and sonatas, quintets, quartets and other chamber music.

Pugno [pe͞e-nyo], STÉPHANE RAOUL: *b.* Paris, June 23, 1852; *d.* Moscow, Jan. 3, 1914. Pianist and composer. Studied at the Paris Conservatoire, where he later taught harmony (1892-6) and piano (1896-1901). It was not until 1893 that he became known as a pianist. He rapidly acquired an international reputation, not only as a soloist but also as Ysaÿe's partner in sonatas for violin and piano. As a composer he was active at a much earlier age. His oratorio *La Résurrection de Lazare* was performed in Paris in 1879. From that time until the end of the 19th cent. he produced a number of *opéras-comiques,* ballets and other stage works. His other compositions include a piano sonata.

Pujol [poo′-holl], JUAN PABLO: *b.* Barcelona, 1573; *d.* there, 1626. Composer. *Maestro de capilla,* Tarragona, 1593; Saragossa, 1595; Barcelona, from 1612 until his death. Ordained priest, 1600. He composed Masses and other church music and secular songs. Two volumes of his church music have been published by H. Anglès (1926, 1932).

Pulcinella [pool-chee-nell′-lah]. Ballet with music by Stravinsky (after Pergolesi), composed in 1919 and later arranged as a Suite for small orchestra, No. 1 (1921) with four movements entitled: (1) *March,* (2) *Waltz,* (3) *Polka,* (4) *Galop.*

Punctum [po͞onk′-to͞om] or **Punctus** [po͞onk′-to͞oss], *L.* "Point."

(1) A note, as in *contrapunctus,* counterpoint.

(2) In mensural NOTATION a point after a note (*punctus additionis*) adds one half of its value, a point placed between two notes or beside the stem of a note (*punctus divisionis*) marks off a group of three notes in PERFECT time or perfect PROLATION. *v.* MENSURAL NOTATION.

(3) Each of the repeated sections in the ESTAMPIE, a medieval dance, was called a *punctus.*

(4) The theorist Anonymus IV uses *punctum* as an alternative for *clausula* (*clausulae sive puncta*) in discussing the compositions of Perotin.

Punta d'arco [poon'-tah darr'-co]. *v.* A PUNTA D'ARCO.

Purcell, (1) DANIEL : *b. c.* 1663 ; *d.* London, 1717. Organist and composer. Brother of (2). Chorister of the Chapel Royal. Organist, Magdalen College, Oxford, 1688-95 ; St. Andrew's, Holborn, 1713-17. In 1700 he won the third prize for a setting of Congreve's *The Judgment of Paris.* In 1695 he completed his brother's music for *The Indian Queen* by writing a masque for the fifth act. From that time until *c.* 1707 he was active as a composer for the theatre. He also set several odes for St. Cecilia's day and an ode in honour of Princess Anne's birthday (1700). His published works include the music in *The Indian Queen* (in *Deliciae Musicae*, ii, 1, 1696), *The Judgment of Paris*, sacred and secular songs in various collections, 6 cantatas for solo voice, flute sonatas, violin sonatas and *The Psalms set full for the Organ or Harpsicord.* Some anthems survive in manuscript.

(2) HENRY : *b.* 1659 ; *d.* London, Nov. 21, 1695. Organist and composer, son of a Gentleman of the Chapel Royal. Chorister of the Chapel Royal, *c.* 1668-1673. Composer for the violins, 1677. Organist, Westminster Abbey, 1679 ; Chapel Royal, 1682. Keeper of the king's instruments, 1683. The most original and most gifted English composer of his time, he was active in every field—theatre music, church music, court odes, secular and sacred songs, odes for various occasions and instrumental music. His early work shows a certain attachment to the past combined with an awareness of newer harmonic resources. As he developed he came to accept the conventions of baroque music—its clear-cut outlines, its brilliance and its inclination to pathetic expression—without ever sacrificing his own personality. His theatre music includes 6 operas, only one of which (*Dido and Aeneas*) is set to continuous music ; the others all contain a substantial amount of dialogue. His church music includes both full anthems in traditional style and up-to-date verse anthems with solos for counter-tenor, tenor and bass. His odes are rich in contrasts between solo voices, chorus and orchestra. As a writer of solo songs he has never been surpassed, either for imagination, technical adroitness or skill in catching the accents of English words. The most remarkable of his instrumental works are the fantasias for viols composed in 1680, which handle a traditional form in a curiously individual way. His trio sonatas are the most striking evidence of his capacity for mastering the Italian style, for which he had a confessed admiration. His contributions to the 12th edition of Playford's *Introduction to the Skill of Music* (1694) show more than a conventional interest in technical procedures.

His principal compositions are :

(a) STAGE MUSIC : *Dido and Aeneas* (1689) ; *Dioclesian* (1690) ; *King Arthur* (1691) ; *The Fairy Queen* (1692) ; *The Indian Queen* (1695); *The Tempest* (1695) ; music for more than 40 plays.

(b) ODES : 17 odes for the king and other members of the royal family ; 4 odes for St. Cecilia's day ; 3 odes for other occasions.

(c) SONGS AND CANTATAS : 9 cantatas for two or more voices with instruments ; 41 secular duets ; more than 100 secular songs ; sacred songs, duets, trios and quartets ; numerous catches.

(d) CHURCH MUSIC : 12 complete full anthems ; more than 40 verse anthems ; 3 services.

(e) CHAMBER MUSIC : Fantasias in 3, 4 and 5 parts ; 2 In Nomines; 12 *Sonatas of III Parts* (1683) ; 10 *Sonatas of IV Parts* (1697).

(f) KEYBOARD WORKS : Various pieces printed in *Musick's Hand-Maid*, ii (1689) and *A Choice Collection of Lessons* (1696) ; others in manuscript.

The first volume of a complete edition, under the auspices of the Purcell Society, was published in 1878 ; the last is due to appear in 1959.

D. ARUNDELL : *Henry Purcell* (1927).

H. C. COLLES : *Voice and Verse : a Study in English Song* (1928).

E. J. DENT : *Foundations of English Opera* (1928).

A. K. HOLLAND : *Henry Purcell : the English Musical Tradition* (1932).
J. A. WESTRUP : *Purcell* (1937).

Puritani di Scozia, I [ee poo-ree-tahn′-ee dee scots′-yah] (The Puritans of Scotland). Opera in three parts by Bellini. Libretto by Carlo Pepoli (founded on a play by François Ancelot and Xavier Boniface Saintine, *Têtes Rondes et Cavaliers*). First performed, Paris, Jan. 25, 1835.

Puy [dēē pēē-ee], JEAN BAPTISTE ÉDOUARD LOUIS CAMILLE DU : *b.* Corcelles (Neuchâtel), *c.* 1770 ; *d.* Stockholm, Apr. 3, 1822. Violinist, baritone, conductor and composer. Studied in Paris. Settled in Stockholm, 1793, where he played in the court orchestra and also sang at the opera. Having incurred the displeasure of Gustaf Adolf in 1799, he was compelled to leave Sweden and moved to Copenhagen. Here he was active as a composer and singer until 1809, when he was exiled on account of a love affair with the wife of Prince Christian Frederik. After a temporary residence in Paris he returned to Stockholm in 1812 and became conductor to the court. He sang the title role in Mozart's *Don Giovanni* at the first performance in Copenhagen (1807) and again at the first performance in Stockholm (1813). He also appeared as Figaro in the first performance of Mozart's *Le nozze di Figaro* in Stockholm (1821). His compositions include ballets and other works for the stage, a flute concerto, dances and choral works.

Q

Q. As an abbreviation Q. = *quintus, quinto,* or *quinta pars,* the fifth part in a 16th-cent. composition for five or more voices or instruments. *v.* QUINTUS.

Quadratum. *v.* B.

Quadrille. A fashionable French dance in the early 19th cent., introduced into England in 1815 and Germany in 1821. Danced by two or four couples, it had five parts (*Le Pantalon, L'Été, La Poule, La Trénise, La Pastourelle*) in 6/8 and 2/4 time alternately. Its name is said to have originated with the introduction of *contredanses* performed by an even number of couples (*Quadrille de contredanse*) in the fifth act of Rousseau's *Fêtes de Polymnie* in 1745.

Quadrivium [cwa-driv'-i-oom], *L.* The division of the seven liberal arts, which formed the course of studies in the medieval university, in which music was included. It comprised the four mathematical arts of arithmetic, geometry, music, and astronomy. The other division, the *trivium,* consisted of the rhetorical arts of grammar, dialectics, and rhetoric. The material of the musical part was chiefly the study of the proportions of intervals as contained in Boethius's *De Musica.* In England it was replaced during the 16th cent. by DEGREES IN MUSIC.

Quadruple croche [cwa-dreepl crosh], *Fr.* Hemidemisemiquaver.

Quadruple Stop. A chord of four notes played on a bowed string instrument by using four adjacent strings.

Quadruplet. A group of 4 notes which is to be performed in the time of 3, *e.g.*:

Quadruplum [cwa'-droop-loom], *L.* The fourth part above the tenor, counting the tenor itself as the first part, of the ORGANUM and CLAUSULA of the period *c.* 1200. Hence applied also to the whole composition, *e.g.* those of Perotin.

Quagliati [cwahl-yah'-tee], PAOLO: *b.* Chioggia, *c.* 1555; *d.* Rome, Nov. 16, 1628. Organist at Santa Maria Maggiore, Rome, from 1606. A composer whose work stands between the old and the new styles of the early 17th century. His pageant with monodic and polyphonic music, *Carro di fedeltà d'amore,* was performed in Rome in 1606. His four-part madrigals of 1608 could be sung either as monodies or as madrigals with continuo. His *Sfera armoniosa* (1623) contains duets with obbligato instrumental solos. A toccata for keyboard has been printed in Torchi's *L'arte musicale in Italia,* ii.

Quantz [cvunts], JOHANN JOACHIM: *b.* Oberscheden (Hanover), Jan. 30, 1697; *d.* Potsdam, July 12, 1773. Flautist and composer. As a young boy he learned to play several instruments, was appointed assistant to the Town Musician of Radeburg in 1714, later in Pirna, and in 1716 member of the Dresden orchestra. He studied counterpoint under Fux and Zelenka in Vienna, from 1718 played in Dresden and Warsaw as oboist to the King of Poland, studied the flute under Buffardin in Paris and in 1724 counterpoint under Gasparini in Rome, visited Paris and London and then returned to Dresden. From 1728 he taught the flute to the Crown Prince Frederick, who after he became King of Prussia in 1741 appointed him as chamber musician and court composer. He composed about 300 flute concertos, sonatas and about 200 other works for flute. His *Versuch einer Anweisung die Flöte traversiere zu spielen* (1752) is more than a treatise on flute-playing; it has a place beside the treatises of C. P. E.

Bach and Leopold Mozart as an important source of information on the performance of 18th-cent. music (facsimile ed., 1953).

Quarter-Note. American for "crotchet."

Quarter-Tone. Half a semitone, which is the smallest interval normally used in Western music. Quarter-tones had a place in the enharmonic tetrachord of Greek music, and were discussed in that connection by some medieval and Renaissance theorists, *e.g.* Guido and Vicentino. They have been used by some modern composers as an occasional effect or as a complete system. Alois Hába has written a number of compositions using a complete quarter-tone scale for strings, for quarter-tone piano, and for quarter-tone harmonium, as well as in a complete opera (*Die Mutter*, 1931). The notes are indicated by modified forms of the usual signs for accidentals. Ernest Bloch has used occasional quarter-tones, marked with an x, in the string parts of his piano quintet (1923-4).

The quarter-tone piano for which Hába wrote was devised by A. Förster in Prague in 1923, and has two manuals, of which one is tuned a quarter-tone higher than the other. A patent for a quarter-tone piano had earlier been taken out by G. A. Behrens-Senegalden in Berlin (1892). *v.* ENHARMONIC, MICROTONES.

Quartet (*Fr.* quatuor, *G.* Quartett, *I.* quartetto). A composition, vocal or instrumental, for four performers. Since the mid-18th cent. its most frequent forms are the STRING QUARTET, PIANO QUARTET, quartets for mixed instruments, *e.g.* Mozart's quartet, K.370, for oboe and strings, and the solo vocal quartets of opera, oratorio, glee and partsong. Mozart composed a *Sinfonia concertante* for wind quartet and orchestra (1778) and Rossini wrote six quartets for flute, clarinet, horn and bassoon.

Quartettsatz [cvarr-tet'-zuts], *G.* (quartet movement). A single Allegro movement in C minor for string quartet by Schubert (1820). It was clearly intended to be the first movement of a complete quartet, since it is followed in the autograph manuscript by 41 bars of an Andante in A♭ (printed in the *Revisionsbericht* to the complete edition, pp. 78-82).

Quartfagott [cvarrt'-fug-ot'], *G.* An instrument listed by Praetorius (1619), who calls it *Doppel Fagott* (*Quart*), having a compass a fourth below the regular bassoon (*Chorist Fagott*) of the time. Some bassoons of this size were made in the late 18th and early 19th cent., but were not in common use.

Quartgeige [cvarrt'-gy'-ger], *G.* A violin tuned a fourth higher than the usual pitch. *v.* VIOLINO PICCOLO.

Quartposaune [cvarrt'-po-zown'-er], *G.* TROMBONE in F, a fourth below the regular B♭ size, used in the 16th and 17th cent., and in Germany until the early 19th century. The *Quintposaune* had a compass a fifth below that of the regular trombone.

Quasi [cwah'-zee], *I.* "As if," "nearly," *e.g.*, in the tempo mark *Andante quasi allegretto*, or in the expression mark *quasi niente*, "almost nothing," *i.e.* as softly as possible.

Quatreble. A term used in the 15th and early 16th cent. as the equivalent of the Latin *quadruplex*, for the highest voice in a choir, being the fourth part above the tenor (counting the tenor itself as the first part, as with the *quadruplum*, *q.v.*, of *c.* 1200). The parts between quatreble and tenor were the meane and the treble. In the method of extemporising a part above a plainsong used at that time (*v.* SIGHT) the quatreble sight was a twelfth above the tenor.

Quattro Rusteghi, I [ee cwaht'-tro rooce-teh'-gee]. *v.* VIER GROBIANE.

Quatuor [cwa-tēe-orr]. *Fr.* Quartet.

Quaver (*A.* eighth-note, *Fr.* croche, *G.* Achtel, *I.* croma). The note

♪ grouped ♫

which is half the length of a crotchet (quarter-note) and an eighth of the length of a semibreve (whole-note). The word meant originally a shake or trill and hence was applied in the 16th cent. to the short notes of which a shake is composed.

Queen of Cornwall, The. Opera in two acts by Boughton, a setting of Thomas Hardy's play, with some alterations. First performed, London, Aug. 4, 1924.

Queen of France, The. *v.* REINE (DE FRANCE).

Queen of Sheba, The. *v.* KÖNIGIN VON SABA.

Queen of Spades, The. *v.* PIKOVAYA DAMA.

Quercu [day cwair′-coo], SIMON DE (VAN EIJCKEN): *b.* Brabant. Late 15th-cent. Flemish theorist, and cantor at the court of Milan. He went to Vienna, where he was still living in 1513. He published a treatise on elementary theory, *Opusculum musices* (1509), and a volume of motets (1513).

Querflöte [cvair′-flurt′-er], *G.* "Cross" or "transverse flute," *i.e.* the modern flute as distinct from the RECORDER or *Blockflöte.*

Querstand [cvair′-shtunt], *G.* False relation.

Quiet Flows the Don. *v.* TIKHI DON.

Quilisma. A NEUME used in the notation of plainsong, written thus ⁓. It usually came between two notes a third apart, and was probably sung with a trill or tremolo in the same way as the later PLICA. It occurs in Byzantine chant as the *kylisma* (*κύλισμα*), where it indicated a "rolling and rotating of the voice."

Quilter, ROGER: *b.* Brighton, Nov. 1, 1877; *d.* London, Sept. 21, 1953. Composer. Educated at Eton and later studied composition under Iwan Knorr at Frankfort. He composed many songs, small orchestral works, incidental music for plays, and pieces for piano and for violin.

Quinet [kee-nay], FERNAND: *b.* Charleroi, Jan. 29, 1898. Belgian composer and cellist. Studied at the Brussels Conservatoire, where he won the *Prix de Rome* in 1921. He was a member of the Pro Arte String Quartet and became director of the Charleroi Conservatoire. He has composed string quartets and other chamber music and songs.

Quintatön [cvint′-a-turn], *G.* An organ STOP of the stopped flue type in which the twelfth, *i.e.* the third note of the HARMONIC SERIES, is present as well as the fundamental. The smaller size is called Quintadena.

Quinte [cãnt], *Fr.* A term used in France in the 17th and early 18th cent. for the fifth part (*L. quinta pars*) in a five-part instrumental piece and applied specifically to the viola.

Quinten-Quartett [cvint′-ĕn-cvarr-tet′], *G.* The name given in Germany to Haydn's string quartet in D minor, Op. 76, No. 2, composed in 1797-8. Its principal theme begins with two falling fifths, thus:

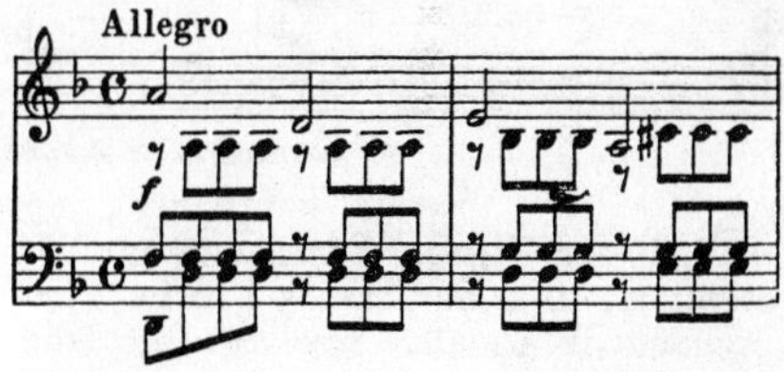

Quintet (*Fr.* quintette, quintuor, *G.* Quintett, *I.* quintetto). A composition, vocal or instrumental, for 5 performers. A string quintet is usually for 2 violins, 2 violas and cello, as in those of Mozart, Beethoven, Mendelssohn, Brahms, and the *Fantasy Quintet* by Vaughan Williams; Boccherini and Schubert (Op. 163 in C) have written quintets for 2 violins, viola and 2 cellos. The combination of piano with string quartet is called a PIANO QUINTET. Similarly a work for clarinet and string quartet is known as a clarinet quintet, *e.g.* Mozart's K.581 and Brahms's Op. 115. Mozart's horn quintet, K.407, is for violin, 2 violas, horn and cello. The term is usually applied to vocal pieces only in opera, *e.g.* the quintet in the third act of Wagner's *Die Meistersinger.*

Quintfagott [cvint′-fug-ot′], *G.* *v.* TENOROON.

Quinticlave [cãn-tee-cluv], *Fr.* *v.* OPHICLEIDE.

Quinto [cween′-to], *I.* *v.* QUINTUS.

Quinton [cãn-tõn], *Fr.* A violin with

five strings used in France in the 18th century. Its tuning was:

Quintposaune [cvint′-po-zown′-*er*], *G.* *v.* QUARTPOSAUNE.

Quintuor [kĕē-ān-tĕē-orr], *Fr.* Quintet.

Quintuplet. A group of 5 notes which is to be performed, in equal lengths, in the time of 4, *e.g.*:

Quintuple Time. Five beats, usually crotchets, in a bar, *i.e.* 5/4 time. In practice it usually resolves into the alternation, regular or irregular, of 3/4 and 2/4, occasionally into 4/4 plus 1/4. It was quite uncommon before the 20th century. There are earlier examples in Act 2, Scene xi of Handel's *Orlando* (1732), where occasional bars of 5/8 express mental confusion, in the third movement of Chopin's sonata in C minor, Op. 4 and the second movement of Tchaikovsky's sixth (*Pathétique*) symphony (a complete movement in both cases), and in the recurring interludes in Moussorgsky's *Pictures at an Exhibition*:

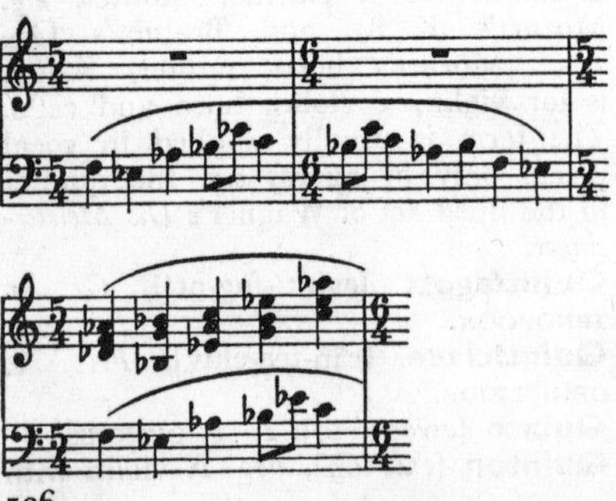

Quintus [cwin′-tŏŏss], *L.* (*I.* quinto). The fifth part (also *quinta pars*) in a 16th-cent. composition for five or more voices or instruments. The term does not imply any specific range: it could be used for any part other than the highest (*cantus superius*) or lowest (*bassus*).

Quittard [kee-tarr], HENRI CHARLES ÉTIENNE: *b.* Clermont-Ferrand, May 13, 1864; *d.* Paris, July 21, 1919. Musicologist and music critic for *Le Matin* and *Le Figaro*. Studied in Paris under César Franck, became lecturer at the École des Hautes Études Sociales and from 1912 until his death curator of archives at the Opéra. Wrote a few books and many articles for periodicals, and edited the harpsichord works of Louis Couperin.

Quodlibet [cwod′-lib-et], *L.* "What you will." (1) A composition, extemporised or written down, in which two or more well-known tunes are sung or played simultaneously. It was practised in the 16th and 17th cent., especially by German composers, and was a favourite amusement in family gatherings of the Bach households. A *quodlibet* of *c.* 1460, in which the melody of Dunstable's "O rosa bella" is accompanied by snatches of a number of German songs, is printed in the *Historical Anthology*, No. 82. Other examples are in the German songs of Ludwig Senfl, *e.g.*:

A well-known instance is the last of Bach's *Goldberg Variations*, in which he combines two popular songs thus:

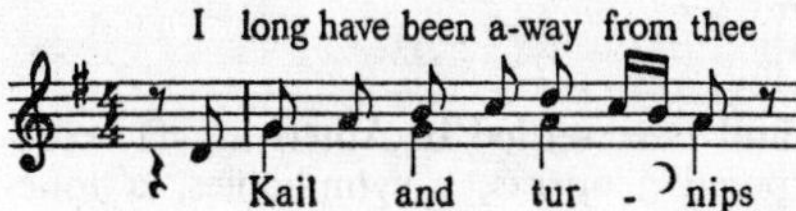

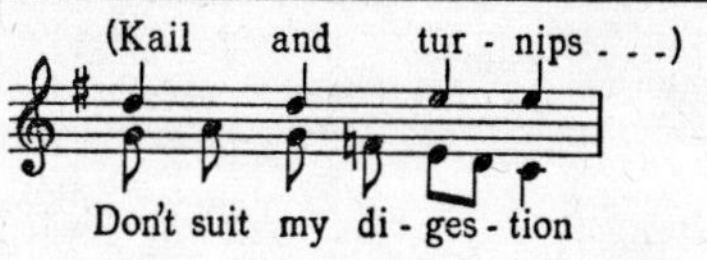

(2) The term is also used for a succession of pieces or songs spontaneously strung together.

R

R. In TONIC SOL-FA **r**=ray, the 2nd note (or supertonic) of the major scale. ℟ (abbreviation of *L.* responsorium) =Respond.

Rabaud [ra-bo], HENRI BENJAMIN: *b.* Paris, Nov. 10, 1873; *d.* there, Sept. 11, 1949. Composer. Studied under Massenet and Gédalge at the Paris Conservatoire, where he won the *Prix de Rome* (1894) and later taught harmony. Conductor, Paris Opéra, 1908; Boston Symphony Orchestra, 1918-19. Succeeded Fauré as director of the Paris Conservatoire, 1920-40. He composed operas, 2 symphonies and other orchestral works, chamber music, an oratorio and songs. His opera *Marouf, savetier du Caire* (Paris, 1914) has been very successful in France and has also been performed in other European countries and in North and South America.

Rachlew [ruck'-leff], ANDERS: *b.* Drammen, Aug. 26, 1882. Norwegian pianist, teacher and conductor. Completed his musical studies in Germany and gave concerts in Norway and Denmark. Active as a choral and orchestral conductor in Denmark since 1920. Conductor, Southern Swedish Philharmonic Society, Malmö, 1943. He has composed pieces for piano and for violin, choral works and songs.

Rachmaninov [ruckh-mah'-nee-noff], SERGEI: *b.* Oneg (Novgorod), Apr. 1, 1873; *d.* Beverly Hills (Cal.), March 28, 1943. Composer and pianist. Studied in St. Petersburg and at the Moscow Conservatoire under Zverev and Arensky. His early compositions were influenced by his warm admiration for Tchaikovsky, and the fame of the prelude in C♯ minor brought him an invitation to conduct in London in 1898. He lived in Dresden for several years, gave concerts in America in 1909-10, and then returned to Moscow, where he conducted the Philharmonic concerts from 1911-13. He left Russia in 1917, and later settled in America. He composed 3 operas, 2 symphonies, a tone-poem *The Isle of the Dead* (1907) and other works for orchestra, 4 concertos and a Rhapsody on a theme by Paganini (the same as that used by Brahms for his Variations) for piano and orchestra, piano music, choral works, chamber music, and songs.

S. BERTENSSON & J. LEYDA: *Sergei Rachmaninov* (1956).

Racket (Ranket). A woodwind instrument in use from the late 16th to the early 18th cent. The body was solid; in it were pierced a number of vertical channels, parallel to each other and connected alternately at the top and the bottom so as to form a continuous tube. Holes pierced in the side made available a limited scale. The instrument was played with a double reed, which at first was partly enclosed in a kind of cup and later was inserted into a crook similar to that used for the bassoon. The tone was subdued—rather like a man blowing through a comb, according to Praetorius (1619). In consequence of its shape it was popularly known in France as *cervelas* (saveloy) and in Germany as *Wurstfagott* (sausage bassoon).

Radamisto (rah-dah-meece'-to] (Rhadamistus). Opera in three acts by Handel. Libretto by Nicola Francesco Haym. First performed, London, May 5, 1720.

Raddoppiamento [rahd-dop-yah-men'-to], *I.* "Doubling," usually to indicate the doubling of the bass at the octave below.

Radiciotti [rah-dee-chot'-tee], GIUSEPPE: *b.* Jesi le Marche, Jan. 25, 1858; *d.* Tivoli, Apr. 4, 1931. Music historian and critic. Studied under his uncle G. Faini, later lived in Rome and in 1881 became teacher of music history at the Liceo in Tivoli. He wrote a book on Pergolesi (1910), a biography of Rossini (1927-29) and other works on the history of Italian music.

Radio. *v.* BROADCASTING.

Radziwill [raht'-tsiv-ill], PRINCE ANTONI HENRYK: *b.* Wilno, June 13, 1775; *d.* Berlin, Apr. 7, 1833. Amateur cellist, singer and composer. Governor of Posen, and a friend of Beethoven and Chopin. He composed incidental music to Goethe's *Faust* (published 1835), vocal duets, part songs, and songs with guitar and cello. Beethoven dedicated to him his *Namensfeier* (Name-day) overture, Op. 115.

Raff [ruff], JOSEPH JOACHIM: *b.* Lachen (Switzerland), May 27, 1822; *d.* Frankfort, June 25, 1882. Composer, teacher and music critic. As a schoolmaster he taught himself piano, violin and composition, and later became a friend of Liszt and Mendelssohn. He lived in Cologne, Stuttgart, Weimar from 1850, Wiesbaden from 1856 as a piano teacher, and in Frankfort from 1877 until his death as director of the Hoch Conservatorium. He composed operas, 11 symphonies, concertos, overtures and other orchestral works, choral works, chamber music, incidental music for plays, songs and piano pieces, none of which proved to have any lasting qualities.

Ragtime. A style of dance music popular from the late 19th cent. until the arrival of Blues and JAZZ about 1910-15. It used such rhythms as

and various kinds of syncopation against a regular rhythmic background in 2/4 or 4/4 time. Stravinsky composed *Ragtime* for 11 instruments on Nov. 11, 1918, and *Piano Rag-Music* in 1920.

Raimondi [rah-ee-mond'-ee], PIETRO: *b.* Rome, Dec. 20, 1786; *d.* there, Oct. 30, 1853. Composer and conductor. Studied at the Naples Conservatorio, and from 1807 produced operas at Genoa, Rome, Milan, Naples and in Sicily. Director, Royal Theatre, Naples, 1824; teacher of composition, Palermo Conservatorio, 1832; *maestro di cappella*, St. Peter's, Rome, 1852. He composed 62 operas, 21 ballets, 8 oratorios, Masses, Requiems, psalms and other church music. He was famed as a deviser of multiple counterpoint, and wrote 3 opera-oratorios—*Potiphar*, *Joseph* and *Jacob*—which were staged separately and then simultaneously in Rome on Aug. 8, 1852.

C. GRAY: "Pietro Raimondi," in *The Music Review*, i (1940), p. 25.

Raindrop Prelude. The name given to Chopin's prelude in D♭ major for piano, Op. 28, No. 15 (1839), which is supposed to have been suggested by dripping rain.

Rainier, PRIAULX: *b.* Howick (Natal), Feb. 3, 1903. Composer. Studied at the South African College of Music, Cape Town, and the R.A.M., where she has taught since 1942. Her compositions include a *Sinfonia da camera* for strings, 2 string quartets, a viola sonata, and songs (including settings of Donne for unaccompanied voice).

Raison [rez-õn], ANDRÉ: 17th-18th century. Organist of Sainte-Geneviève and of the Jacobin Church in Paris. He composed 2 books of organ works (1687-88, 1714; modern ed. of the first book in A. Guilmant, *Archives des maîtres de l'orgue*, ii). Bach used the theme of a Passacaglia in G minor from the first book as the first four bars of his Passacaglia in C minor for organ.

Raitio [ry'-tee-o], VÄINÖ: *b.* Sortavala (Finland), Apr. 15, 1891; *d.* Helsinki, Sept. 10, 1945. Composer. Studied composition at Helsinki Conservatoire, in Moscow under Ilyinski, in Berlin and in Paris. Teacher of composition in Viipuri from 1926-32; he settled at Helsinki in 1938. He composed operas, symphonic poems and a symphony, concertos, chamber music and songs.

Rake's Progress, The. Opera in three acts by Stravinsky. Libretto by Wystan Hugh Auden and Chester Kallman. First performed, Venice, Sept. 11, 1951.

Rákóczy [rah'-co-tsi] **March.** The title of the Hungarian national tune which is called after Prince Ferencz Rákóczi (leader of the revolt against Austria, 1703-11). It has been used by Berlioz (the Hungarian March in *Damnation of Faust*), Liszt (the 15th Hungarian Rhapsody for piano and *Rákóczy March* for orchestra), and other composers.

Rallentando [rahl-len-tahnd'-o], *I.*

Becoming gradually slower. Often abbreviated *rall.*

Rameau [ra-mo], JEAN PHILIPPE: *bapt.* Dijon, Sept. 25, 1683; *d.* Paris, Sept. 12, 1764. Composer and theorist. The first part of his life was spent as an organist in Clermont-Ferrand (1702-6), Paris, Lyons, and from 1722 again at Clermont. In 1706 he published his first book of *Pièces de clavecin,* modelled on those of Couperin, and in 1722 his *Traité de l'Harmonie reduite à ses Principes naturels,* in which he laid the foundation of the modern theory of harmony by setting forth the principles of key-centre, of fundamental bass, and of the roots and inversions of chords. He settled in Paris in 1732 and began with *Hippo'y'e et Aricie* (1733) a new and distinguished career as the most important composer of French opera since Lully. His chief stage works were the operas *Castor et Pollux* (1737) and *Dardanus* (1739), the opera-ballets *Les Indes galantes* (1735) and *Les Fêtes d'Hébé* (1739), and the ballet-bouffon *Platée* (1745). The revival of *Platée* in 1754 sealed the fate of the Italian *intermezzo* in Paris. Rameau published in 1741 a book of *Pièces de clavecin en concerts* which contained trio-sonatas, and in 1750 a *Démonstration du principe de l'harmonie.* His complete works were edited by Saint-Saëns (1895-1924).

C. GIRDLESTONE: *Jean-Philippe Rameau* (1957).
L. LALOY: *Rameau* (1908).
L. DE LA LAURENCIE: *Rameau* (1908).
P.-M. MASSON: *L'Opéra de Rameau* (2nd ed., 1943).
G. MIGOT: *J. P. Rameau et le génie de la musique française* (1930).

Ramin [rah'-min], GÜNTHER: *b.* Karlsruhe, Oct. 15, 1898; *d.* Leipzig, Feb. 27, 1956. Organist, harpsichordist and composer. Studied in Leipzig at the Thomasschule and from 1914 at the Conservatorium under Teichmüller and Straube, whom he succeeded as organist of the Thomaskirche in 1918. Organ teacher at the Conservatorium and organist of the Gewandhaus concerts, 1920; teacher at the Berlin Hochschule in 1931; cantor of the Thomaskirche, Leipzig, 1939. He composed organ works and church music.

Ramis (Ramos) **de Pareja** [rah'-meece deh pah-reh'-hah], BARTOLOMÉ: *b.* Baeza, *c.* 1440; *d.* Rome, 1521(?). Spanish theorist and composer. Taught in Salamanca, lived in Bologna from 1480-82 and was in Rome in 1491. In his *Musica practica* of 1482 (English trans. in O. Strunk, *Source Readings in Music History,* p. 201) he set forth a simpler method of dividing a string than the Pythagorean tuning given by Boethius and taught throughout the Middle Ages. This system was disputed by Gafori and developed by Zarlino.

Randall, WILLIAM: *d.* 1780. He succeeded to the Walsh music-publishing business in 1766 and published in 1768, with his partner, Abell, the first complete edition of Handel's *Messiah* and in 1771 a reissue of Morley's *Plaine and Easie Introduction.*

Randegger, ALBERTO: *b.* Trieste, Apr. 13, 1832; *d.* London, Dec. 18, 1911. Singing teacher, conductor, and composer. Conducted operas in various Italian cities until 1854 when he went to England and was appointed singing teacher at the R.A.M. (1868) and at the R.C.M., conducted the Carl Rosa Company (1879-95), at Drury Lane and Covent Garden (1887-98) and at the Norwich Festivals (1881-1905). He composed operas, a dramatic cantata, Masses and other church music, works for solo voice and orchestra, choral music and songs, and wrote a *Primer of Singing.*

Ranelagh Gardens. Gardens on the bank of the Thames in London in which a Rotunda was built for concerts and to which it was fashionable to resort for entertainment for some years after its opening in 1742. Arne and other English composers wrote music and arranged concerts for Ranelagh; Mozart played the harpsichord and organ there, at the age of eight. The gardens were closed in 1803.

M. SANDS: *Invitation to Ranelagh* (1946).

Rangström [rung'-strurm], ANDERS JOHAN TURE: *b.* Stockholm, Nov. 30, 1884; *d.* there, May 11, 1947. Composer and critic. Studied in Stockholm under Lindgren, in Berlin, and in Munich under Pfitzner; worked as music critic in Stockholm from 1907-21, conducted the Gothenburg Symphony Orchestra from 1922-25 and was attached to the Stockholm Royal Opera from 1930-36. He composed numerous songs, operas, symphonic poems and symphonies, suites and other works for orchestra, cantatas, choral works with orchestra, incidental music for plays, chamber music and piano pieces.

Rank. The set of pipes belonging to one stop on the organ. The word is most often used in connection with MUTATION STOPS; thus a Mixture is referred to as 3-rank or 4-rank according to the number of pipes which sound for each note. *v.* ORGAN.

Ranket. *v.* RACKET.

Rankl [runk'l], KARL: *b.* Gaden bei Mödling, Oct. 1, 1898. Conductor and composer. Studied composition under Schönberg and Webern. Conductor, Stadttheater, Reichenberg, 1925; Königsberg Opera House and radio, 1927; Berlin State Opera, 1928; Wiesbaden, 1931. Director, Graz Opera, 1933; German Theatre, Prague, 1937; Covent Garden Opera, London, 1946-51; conductor, Scottish National Orchestra, 1952-7. Elizabethan Trust Opera Company (Australia), 1957. He has composed an opera (*Deirdre*), a symphony for orchestra and three (S.S.A.) voices (1934), a string quartet, choral works and songs.

Ranz des Vaches [rũnts day vush], *Fr.* (*G.* Kuhreigen). A melody sung or played on the Alpine horn by Swiss shepherds. It exists in a number of forms. Common idioms are:

in which the F is about a quarter of a tone higher than normal. It has been used by composers in various versions, *e.g.* by Rossini in the overture to *William Tell*:

A. HYATT KING: "Mountains, Music and Musicians," in *Musical Quarterly*, xxxi (1945).

Rape of Lucretia, The. Opera in two acts by Benjamin Britten. Libretto by Ronald Duncan (after André Obey's play *Le Viol de Lucrèce*). First performed, Glyndebourne (Sussex), July 12, 1946.

Rappresentativo, Stile [stee'-leh rahp-preh-zen-tah-tee'-vo]. *v.* STILE (3).

Rappresentazione di Anima e di Corpo [rahp-preh-zen-tahts-yo'-neh dee ah'-nee-mah eh dee corr'-po] (Representation of Soul and Body). A morality play set to music by Emilio de' Cavalieri and staged in Rome, Feb. 1600. Often described as " the first oratorio."

Rapsodie Espagnole [rup-sod-ee ess-pun-yoll], *Fr.* (Spanish Rhapsody). An orchestral composition by Ravel (1907) in four movements : *Prélude à la Nuit*, *Malagueña*, *Habanera* and *Feria*.

Raselius [ruz-ay'-li-ooss] (Rasel), ANDREAS: *b.* Hahnbach (Upper Palatinate), *c.* 1563 ; *d.* Heidelberg, Jan. 6, 1602. Composer. Studied at the Lutheran University in Heidelberg. Cantor and teacher at the Gymnasium, Ratisbon, 1584 ; court *Kapellmeister* to Friedrich IV in Heidelberg, 1600 until his death. In *D.T.B.*, xxix-xxx there have been published 9 Latin motets from the *Dodecachordum vivum*, a manuscript collection of 1589, 53 German motets from *Teutscher Sprüche* (1594) and 22 German motets from *Neue Teutscher Sprüche* (1595). He also wrote a theoretical treatise, *Hexachordum seu quaestiones musicae practicae* (1589).

Rasiermesserquartett [ruz-eer'-messer-cvarr-tet'], *G.* *v.* RAZOR QUARTET.

Rasoumovsky [ra-soo-moff'-ski], COUNT (from 1815 PRINCE) ANDREAS KYRILLOVICH: *b.* Ukraine, Nov. 2, 1752 ; *d.* Sept. 23, 1836. Patron of music and amateur musician. In Vienna as Russian ambassador from 1792. From 1808 played the violin in his own string quartet (leader Schuppanzigh, violist Weiss, and cellist Lincke), which played new quartets by Beethoven. The latter dedicated 3 quartets, Op. 59 (1806) to Rasoumovsky, and the fifth and sixth symphonies (published in 1809) to him and Prince Lobkowitz jointly. In 1816 he pensioned the members of his quartet, but they continued to play with Sina, and later Holz, as second violinist.

Rasoumovsky Quartets. Three string quartets by Beethoven, Op. 59 (1806)—No. 1 in F major, No. 2 in E minor, No. 3 in C major—dedicated to Count Andreas Kyrillovich Rasoumovsky (*q.v.*). The finale of No. 1 has a tune marked *thème russe* ; so has the third movement of No. 2 (in this case the tune which Moussorgsky used in the coronation scene of *Boris Godounov*). It has been suggested that the slow movement of No. 3 is also based on a Russian folksong, though there is no indication of this in the score.

Rathaus [raht'-howce], KAROL: *b.* Tarnopol (Galicia), Sept. 16, 1895. Studied composition under Schreker in Vienna and Berlin where he was teacher at the Hochschule from 1925-34. Later lived in Paris, London and the U.S.A., where he became attached to Queen's College, Flushing (N.Y.), in 1940. He has composed symphonies, suites and other orchestral works, an opera, ballets, string quartets and other chamber music, choral works, incidental music for plays, songs, and pieces for piano and organ.

Ratsche [rahtsh'-er], *G.* Rattle.

Rattle (*Fr.* crécelle, *G.* Knarre, Ratsche). A percussion instrument in which the sound is produced by the striking of a flexible piece of wood or metal against a revolving cog-wheel. It makes occasional appearances in the orchestra, *e.g.*, in Richard Strauss's *Till Eulenspiegel.*

Rauzzini [rah-oot-tsee'-nee], VENANZIO: *b.* Camerino, Dec. 19, 1746 ; *d.* Bath, April 8, 1810. Singer and composer. Sang in opera in Rome, Munich and other cities, and settled in England in 1774. Of some 10 operas which he produced in Munich and London the most successful was *Piramo e Tisbe* (London, 1775). In 1780 he settled in Bath, where he remained until his death.

Ravanello [rah-vah-nell'-lo], ORESTE: *b.* Venice, Aug. 25, 1871 ; *d.* Padua, July 1, 1938. Organist and composer. Organist, St. Mark's, Venice, 1893 ; choirmaster, S. Antonio, Padua, 1898. Organ teacher in Venice, 1902; director, Istituto Musicale, Padua, 1914. He composed Masses, cantatas, motets and other church music, works for orchestra, chamber music, songs and pieces for organ and for piano, and wrote a method for the organ and a treatise on the rhythm of Gregorian chant.

Ravel [ra-vel], MAURICE: *b.* Ciboure, March 7, 1875 ; *d.* Paris, Dec. 28, 1937. Composer. Studied at the Paris Conservatoire under Fauré and Gédalge. His first mature works—*Jeux d'eau* for piano and the string quartet—showed the virtuosity of means and compact clarity of form which were characteristic of his style. Like Debussy, he was strongly influenced by Chabrier and Satie, but his interest in French harpsichord music, in the orchestration of Rimsky-Korsakov, and in the piano writing of Liszt led his development away from impressionism to a precise and often wittily ironic style based on traditional harmonies and forms. The source of his inspiration, however, was more often poetic than abstract, and only two of his orchestral works, *Rapsodie espagnole* and *La Valse*, were not originally written for the theatre or as piano pieces. Of his ballet scores the most successful was *Daphnis et Chloé.* The later works, such as the sonata for violin and cello, the opera-ballet *L'Enfant et les sortilèges*, the 2 piano concertos, and *Don Quichotte à Dulcinée* for baritone and chamber orchestra, tended towards more economy of means without losing in deftness of expression and versatility of technique. His principal compositions are :

(a) BALLETS : *Daphnis et Chloé* (1912); *Ma Mère l'Oye* (from the suite for piano duet, 1915).

(b) OPERAS : *L'Heure espagnole* (1907); *L'Enfant et les sortilèges* (1925).

(c) ORCHESTRA : *Rapsodie espagnole*

(1907); *La Valse* (1920); *Bolero* (1928); concerto for piano (left hand alone) and orchestra (1931); concerto for piano and orchestra (1931).

(d) CHAMBER MUSIC: string quartet (1903); *Introduction and Allegro* for harp, string quartet, flute, clarinet (1906); piano trio (1915); cello sonata (1922); violin sonata (1927).

(e) PIANO: *Jeux d'eau* (1901); *Miroirs* (1905); *Sonatine* (1905); *Gaspard de la Nuit* (1908); *Ma Mère l'Oye* (piano duet, 1908); *Valses nobles et sentimentales* (1911); *Le Tombeau de Couperin* (1917).

(f) SONGS: *Shéhérazade* (1903; the accompaniment was later orchestrated); *Histoires naturelles* (1906); *Deux Mélodies hébraïques* (1914); *Ronsard à son âme* (1924); *Chansons madécasses* (for voice, flute, cello, piano, 1926); *Don Quichotte à Dulcinée* (baritone and chamber orchestra, 1932).

V. JANKELÉVITCH: *Maurice Ravel* (1939).
ROLAND-MANUEL: *Maurice Ravel*, trans. C. Jolly (1947).
F. H. SHERA: *Debussy and Ravel* (1925).

Ravenscroft, THOMAS: *b. c.* 1590; *d. c.* 1633. Composer and editor. Chorister at St. Paul's Cathedral. Studied at Cambridge and was music master at Christ's Hospital from 1618-22. He published *Pammelia*, a collection of rounds and catches (1609), *Deuteromelia*, settings of poems and rounds (1609), *Melismata*, containing madrigals and rounds (1611), a Psalter (1621, with 48 settings by himself), and composed anthems and instrumental works. His *Briefe Discourse of the true (but neglected) use of Charact'ring the Degrees . . . in Measurable Musicke* (1614) drew some of its material from Morley's *Plaine and Easie Introduction*, and included songs by various composers for "Hunting, Hawking, Dauncing, Drinking, and Enamouring."

Rawsthorne, ALAN: *b.* Haslingden, (Lancashire), May 2, 1905. Composer. Studied at the Royal Manchester College of Music and later under Egon Petri, was appointed teacher at Dartington Hall and in 1935 settled in London. He has composed *Symphonic Studies* (1938) and other works for orchestra, concertos for clarinet, piano (1942 and 1951) and violin (1947), chamber music and songs. He is a versatile composer who has developed an individual style and an ability to write both succinctly and expressively in the larger forms.

Ray. Anglicized form of the Italian *re* (D). In TONIC SOL-FA the 2nd note (or supertonic) of the major scale.

Razor Quartet (*G.* Rasiermesser-quartett). The name given to Haydn's string quartet in F minor and major, Op. 55, No. 2 (published in 1789). The story is that when Haydn told John Bland (a London music publisher who happened to visit him while he was shaving) that he would give his "best quartet for a good razor" Bland presented him with his own set of razors and Haydn later produced the promised quartet. However, the set of quartets to which this belongs was not published by Bland but by Longman and Broderip.

Re [ray]. (1) The 2nd note of the hexachord. *v.* SOLMIZATION.

(2) *I.* (*Fr.* ré). The note D.

Read, GARDNER: *b.* Evanston, Illinois, Jan. 2, 1913. Composer. Studied at the Northwestern University School of Music and at the Eastman School in Rochester. He has composed symphonies and other orchestral works, chamber music, works for solo voice and instruments and pieces for piano and for organ.

Reading, (1) JOHN: *d.* Winchester, 1692. Organist. Junior vicar-choral (1667) and master of the choristers (1670) of Lincoln Cathedral. Organist from 1675 of Winchester Cathedral and from 1681 of Winchester College, for which he composed Latin Graces and the Winchester School song, *Dulce domum.*

(2) JOHN: *b.* Winchester, 1677; *d.* London, Sept. 2, 1764. Organist. Son of (1). Chorister of the Chapel Royal. Organist of Dulwich College, 1696-8; junior vicar-choral (1702), master (1703) and instructor (1704) of the choristers at Lincoln Cathedral; after 1707 organist of several London churches. He published

a book of *New Songs* (*after the Italian manner*) and a book of anthems.

Reading Rota. *v.* SUMER IS ICUMEN IN.

Real Answer. *v.* FUGUE.

Realization. The act of completing the harmony of a 17th- or 18th-cent. work by providing a keyboard accompaniment based on the indications afforded by the FIGURED BASS.

Rebec. A small bowed instrument of an elongated pear-shape, adopted from the Arabian *rebâb*, used in Europe from the 16th cent. As described by Agricola in *Musica instrumentalis deudsch* (1528) the treble size had three strings tuned as are the three lower strings of the violin; it is one of the instruments from which the violin was developed in the course of the 16th cent. In a form with four strings of which the lowest was:

it survived into the 17th and 18th cent. as the KIT (or *pochette*) used by dancing masters.

Reber [ray-bair], NAPOLÉON HENRI: *b.* Mülhausen, Oct. 21, 1807; *d.* Paris, Nov. 24, 1880. Composer. Studied under Lesueur at the Paris Conservatoire, where he became teacher of harmony, 1851, and succeeded Halévy as teacher of composition, 1862. He composed chamber music, operas, a ballet, 4 symphonies, a cantata, church music, songs and choral works, pieces for piano solo and duet, and wrote a textbook on harmony (1862).

Rebikov [ray′-bick-off], VLADIMIR: *b.* Krasnoyarsk (Siberia), May 31, 1866; *d.* Yalta (Crimea), Dec. 1, 1920. Composer. Studied at the Moscow Conservatoire and in Berlin and Vienna. Lived in Odessa and Kishinev, where he founded music societies, taught in Berlin and Vienna, and in 1901 settled in Moscow. He composed operas, ballets, suites and other works for orchestra, church music, vocal works and pieces for piano. In his time he was considered an advanced composer on account of his occasional use of the whole-tone scale and of parallel fifths.

Recapitulation. *v.* SONATA FORM.

Récit [ray-see], *Fr.* (1) Recitative. (2) Swell organ.

Recital. A public programme of solo or chamber music. The term was probably used for the first time in the announcement of Liszt's concert at the Hanover Square Rooms, London, on June 9, 1840, which read: " M. Liszt will give Recitals on the Pianoforte of the following pieces."

Recitative (*Fr.* récit, récitatif, *G.* Rezitativ, Sprechgesang, *I.* recitativo). A style of singing which is more closely related in pitch and rhythm to dramatic speech than to song. It originated *c.* 1590 in the works of the Florentine composers, *e.g.* Jacopo Peri, and was adopted also in operas, oratorios, cantatas and some forms of church music during the first half of the 17th cent. With few exceptions, it was accompanied by a harpsichord, organ or other CONTINUO instrument, with or without a string bass, *e.g.* in the Prologue to Monteverdi's *Orfeo* :

The principle of recitative had long

been used in the less ornate forms of plainsong, and its relation to plainsong can be observed in the work of Schütz, who wrote it both in the free rhythm of the chant, unaccompanied in the Passions, accompanied by four viols in the *Resurrection History*, and in the usual style, accompanied by the continuo, in the *Christmas Oratorio*.

In England Nicholas Laniere wrote recitative in his music for Ben Jonson's *Lovers made Men* in 1617. Purcell's recitative shows a finer application of the style to the characteristics of the language than that of any composer before the present century, *e.g.* :

from *Dido and Aeneas*. Similarly, Lully developed special idioms in his treatment of recitative in French opera, where the language imposed a distinctive style.

In the 18th cent. the accepted style of recitative, that of Italian opera, sung in the quick free rhythm of stage dialogue, the composer's notation merely indicating approximate note-values, was called *recitativo secco*. Recitative in a more expressive style accompanied by the orchestra, as in Bach's setting of the words of Christ in the *St. Matthew Passion*, was called *recitativo stromentato* or *accompagnato*. The style of recitative was at times transferred to instruments, as in the second movement, marked *Recitativo*, of Haydn's symphony No. 7 (*Le Midi*), in one of the variations, marked *Recitativo, senza rigor di tempo*, in the fourth movement of Michael Haydn's Divertimento in B♭, in Beethoven's piano sonatas Op. 31, No. 2 and Op. 110, and in the introduction to the finale of his ninth symphony.

In Wagner's later operas neither recitative nor aria was used in the distinct and formal manner of previous operas; both styles were absorbed into the vocal line and used freely as the dramatic situation required. Opera since Wagner has tended to use the style of recitative to an even greater extent, to the exclusion of all but the shortest passages in aria style. At the same time the orchestral part, as in Wagner, has assumed the function of providing thematic continuity and development. Stravinsky has used recitative in the earlier sense, accompanied by harpsichord or piano, in *The Rake's Progress* (1951).

J. A. WESTRUP : "The Nature of Recitative" (*Proceedings of the British Academy*, xlii, p. 27).

Recitativo [reh-chee-tah-tee′-vo], *I.* Recitative. *Recitativo secco*, recitative accompanied only by continuo and largely made up of conventional formulas. *Recitativo stromentato* (or *accompagnato*), dramatic or expressive recitative accompanied by the orchestra. *v.* RECITATIVE.

Reciting Note (*L.* repercussio, tuba). The note on which the intermediate words of each verse of a psalm are sung in plainsong. It is the dominant of the MODE in which the psalm-tone is written. *v.* PSALMODY.

Recorder (*Fr.* flûte douce, flûte à bec, *G.* Blockflöte, *I.* flauto dolce). A straight, or end-blown flute, as distinct from the transverse or side-blown flute, which was used from the Middle Ages until the 18th cent. and has been revived in modern times. In the 16th cent. recorders were made in sets, or consorts, and the most usual sizes were the descant (in Germany, soprano or treble), treble (in Germany, alto), tenor and bass, of which the lowest notes were normally:

Praetorius, in the *Syntagma musicum* (1619), lists also a *Kleines Flötlein*, a fourth or fifth above the descant, a bass with

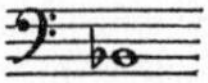

as its lowest note, and a double bass a fourth lower than the bass. When Bach writes for the recorder, as in the accompaniment to the aria known as " Sheep may safely graze " in the secular cantata *Was mir behagt*, or in Brandenburg Concertos Nos. 2 and 4, he designates it as *flauto* ; where the transverse flute is intended he calls it *traverso*. He occasionally uses one of the smaller sizes of descant recorder, calling it *flauto piccolo*, as in the opening chorus of Cantata No. 96 (*Herr Christ, der ein'ge Gottessohn*), where it has an important part to play, in unison with a *violino piccolo*. The recorder has a sweet and gentle tone—hence the French name *flûte douce* ; its English name seems to be derived from the verb " record," to practise a song or tune—a term used particularly of birds. There are a number of modern instruction-books for the instrument.

A. CARSE: " Fingering the Recorder," in *The Music Review*, i (1940), p. 96.
C. WELCH: *Six Lectures on the Recorder* (1911).

Recte et retro, Per [pair reck'-tay et ray'-tro], *L.* Retrograde motion (*q.v.*).

Redford, JOHN: *d.* 1547. English organist, composer and dramatist. Organist and master of the choristers, St. Paul's Cathedral, from *c.* 1530. Judging from the organ pieces by him in the " Mulliner " manuscript (*Musica Britannica*, i) he was one of the most important English composers of keyboard music before the Reformation. Apart from a few short " points " all the pieces are based on plainsong themes. The anthem " Rejoice in the Lord," which appears in the " Mulliner " manuscript without words and without a composer's name, is not by him. He was concerned with the production of plays, probably acted (as many were throughout the 16th cent.) by the St. Paul's choristers. One play by him, *Wyt and Science* (printed by the Shakespeare Society, 1848), has survived.

C. PFATTEICHER: *John Redford, Organist and Almoner of St. Paul's Cathedral* (1934).

Reed (*Fr.* anche, *G.* Zunge, *I.* ancia). The vibrating element in many musical instruments. A single beating reed, *i.e.* one which vibrates against the material of the instrument, is used in the reed stops of the organ (metal reed) and in the clarinet and saxophone (cane reed). Double beating reeds, *i.e.*, two reeds of cane which vibrate against each other, are used in the instruments of the shawm family, *e.g.* oboe, English horn and bassoon. Free, as distinct from beating, reeds—*i.e.* reeds of metal which vibrate freely in a slot—are used in the harmonium and concertina. The pitch of a metal reed, being determined by its length and thickness, is fixed ; that of a cane reed is variable, being determined by the length of the pipe to which it is attached.

Reed, WILLIAM HENRY: *b.* Frome (Somerset), July 29, 1876; *d.* Dumfries, July 2, 1942. Violinist and composer. Studied at the R.A.M. Became a member of the London Symphony Orchestra when it was founded in 1904; leader, 1912. Teacher, R.C.M. He composed 2 tone-poems for orchestra, string quartets and other chamber music, a violin concerto and pieces for violin, songs and part-songs, and wrote two books on the life and work of Elgar.

Reel. A dance, probably of Celtic origin, practised in northern countries of Europe, in which the dancers stand face to face and perform figures of eight. The music is usually in a quick 4/4 time and in regular 4-bar phrases. The Scottish Strathspey is related to the reel, but is danced in a slower tempo. The rhythms :

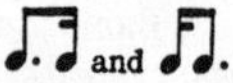

and

occur constantly in its music.

Reese, GUSTAVE: *b.* New York, Nov. 29, 1899. Musicologist. Studied at New York University, where he was lecturer from 1927-37. Associate editor (1933) and editor (1944-45) of *The Musical Quarterly*, and one of the founders of the American Musicological Society (1934).

Professor of musicology at New York University, 1945. His *Music in the Middle Ages* (1940) and *Music of the Renaissance* (1954) are the most comprehensive works on their respective periods.

Reformation Symphony (*G.* Reformationssinfonie). The title given to Mendelssohn's symphony No. 5 in D major, Op. 107 (1830), which was composed for the tercentenary of the Augsburg Conference but not performed there. It uses the chorale " Ein feste Burg " in the last movement.

Refrain. Recurring lines in a poem, which are usually set to the same music, as in the monophonic and polyphonic settings of such forms as the BALLADE, RONDEAU and VIRELAI from the 12th to the 15th century. In trouvère *chansons* the melody and words of well-known refrains were sometimes quoted in new songs, as in the *chanson avec des refrains,* in which, paradoxically, each refrain was different, since it consisted of a quotation. Similarly, refrains were frequently quoted in the upper parts of 13th-cent. MOTETS. A motet which quotes the first part of a refrain at the beginning and the second part at the end is called a *motet enté.* The prototypes of the refrain are the plainsong RESPOND and the original use of the ANTIPHON between the verses of a psalm ; its related forms are the burden of the CAROL and the recurring section of the instrumental RONDO.

Regal. A portable reed organ used in the 16th and 17th centuries. It had beating reeds, and unlike the portable organ with flue pipes, was capable of *crescendo* and *diminuendo.* The Bible-regal could be folded up and packed into the bellows. When flue stops and reed stops were combined in the same instrument, the word was used both for the instrument and for a reed stop. The regal was commonly used in the music of plays and mysteries; the office of keeper of the King's Regals existed in England until the 18th century. Monteverdi specified the regal to accompany the recitative of Charon in the third act of *Orfeo* (1607).

Reger [rague'-er], MAX: *b.* Brand (Bavaria), March 19, 1873; *d.* Leipzig, May 11, 1916. Composer and pianist. Organist, Weiden Cathedral, 1886-89. Studied under Hugo Riemann in Sondershausen and Wiesbaden. Teacher, Wiesbaden Conservatorium, 1895-6; Munich Academy of Music, 1905-06; director of music, Leipzig University, 1907-08; teacher of composition, Leipzig Conservatorium from 1907 until his death. Conductor, Meiningen Court Orchestra, 1911-14. After 1915 lived in Jena. He gave concerts in Germany, Switzerland, Russia, Holland and England.

Through Riemann's influence he early became attached to the music of Bach and Brahms, and acquired a mastery of counterpoint as well as of the complete resources of late Romantic harmony. In his instrumental music he avoided using any kind of programme, building up large structures on the basis of classical and pre-classical forms to a degree of harmonic complexity that at its best is splendidly massive but too often tends to become turgid and cumbersome. He did not live to develop the discipline over his prodigious gifts which began to appear in his later works. His organ music, which includes chorale preludes, preludes and fugues, passacaglias, and many shorter pieces, has an important place in the literature of the instrument, especially in Germany. His opus numbers run to 147 and comprise, besides orchestral and organ works, chamber music, choral works, concertos, 2 large works for 2 pianos, piano pieces in many forms, and songs. He also wrote a textbook on modulation.

A. LINDNER: *Max Reger* (1923).

Regino (of Prüm): *d.* Treves, 915. Abbot of the Benedictine monastery at Prüm (nr. Treves), 892 ; St. Maximin in Treves, *c.* 899. His *De harmonica institutione,* which discusses music as one of the seven liberal arts, is published in Gerbert's *Scriptores,* i, p. 230, and his *Tonarius,* one of the earliest examples of the classification of plainsong melodies according to MODE, in Coussemaker's *Scriptores,* ii, p. 1.

Regis [ray'-giss], JOHANNES : *b.c.* 1430 ; *d.* Soignies, *c.* 1485. Composer. Master of the choristers, Notre Dame, Antwerp, 1463; later secretary to Dufay. He went to Mons in 1474, and in 1481 was at Soignies, where he became canon. His surviving works, which comprise Masses, motets and *chansons*, have been published by C. W. H. Lindenburg (2 vols., 1956).

Régisseur [ray-zhee-ser], *Fr.* A term used in France and Germany for the person in charge of the artistic and technical parts of the production of opera.

Register. (1) A set of pipes, which may consist of one or more RANKS, controlled by a single stop on an organ.

(2) A division in the compass of a singer's voice, *e.g.* head register, chest register.

Registration. The art of choosing and combining stops in organ playing. Indications given by the composer may include changes of manual, a particular type of solo stop, or the relative weight of sound. Indications of any kind are infrequent before the 19th cent., though Scheidt gave general directions and suggested some specific stops for the registration of the chorales, Magnificats, and hymns in his *Tabulatura nova* (1624), and French composers in the baroque period commonly gave some information about registration, either in the title, as in Couperin's *Fugue sur les jeux d'anches* and *Dialogue sur la Trompette et le Cromhorne* in the *Kyrie* of his first Organ Mass, or in the course of the piece. Details of Bach's registration of a few of his organ pieces have been recorded, but his own markings are rare, and concern changes of manual, as in the "Dorian" toccata, or a particular stop, as in the second prelude in the *Orgelbüchlein*. In the 19th cent. the practices of registration tended to approach those of orchestration; more recently they have been reconsidered in connection with the revival of the tonal design of the Baroque organ.

G. A. AUDSLEY: *Organ Stops and their Artistic Registration* (1921).
W. L. SUMNER: *The Organ* (1952).

Regnart [reckh'-nahrt], (1) FRANÇOIS: 16th-cent. Flemish composer. Studied at the Cathedral of Tournai and the University of Douai. He composed motets which were published by Augustin Regnart in 1590 in a collection of 39 motets by the brothers François, Jacques, Paschaise and Charles. A volume of *chansons, Poésies de P. Ronsard et autres poètes* (1575), has been published by Henri Expert in *Les Maîtres musiciens de la Renaissance française*, xv.

(2) JACQUES: *b.* Netherlands, *c.* 1540; *d.* Prague, Oct. 16, 1599. Composer. Brother of (1). Tenor in the Imperial Chapel at Vienna and Prague from 1564, and deputy choirmaster from 1576. He held a similar post in Innsbruck from 1582 to 1595, and again in Prague from 1595 to his death. Some of his motets appeared in his brother Augustin's publication of 1590 (*v.* F. REGNART); others and his 29 Masses were published after his death. A volume of five-part German songs was printed in 1580, and 3 volumes of three-part songs to German words after the style of the Neapolitan or Italian villanellas between 1576 and 1579. The latter were published in *Publikationen der Gesellschaft für Musikforschung*, xix (1895), and two pieces from this volume were reprinted in Schering's *History of Music in Examples*, No. 139.

Reicha [*G.* rysh'-a, *Fr.* resh-a], ANTON: *b.* Prague, Feb. 26, 1770; *d.* Paris, May 28, 1836. Theorist and composer. Studied at Wallerstein under his uncle Joseph Reicha and went in 1788 to Bonn, where he became flautist in the Electoral Orchestra and a friend of Beethoven. He lived in Hamburg from 1794, Paris from 1799 and Vienna from 1802 to 1808, when he returned to Paris and became teacher of composition at the Conservatoire in 1818. His pupils included Berlioz, Liszt, Gounod and César Franck. He composed operas, 2 symphonies and other orchestral works, 24 quintets for wood-wind and horn, 20 string quartets, 24 horn trios and other chamber music, duets for flutes and for violins, violin and piano sonatas and pieces for piano, and wrote treatises on harmony, melody and composition.

M. EMMANUEL: *Antonin Reicha* (1937).

Reid (originally Robertson), JOHN: *b.* Straloch (Perthshire), Feb. 13, 1721; *d.* London, Feb. 6, 1807. Army general who left his fortune to Edinburgh University where he had studied, mainly for the foundation of a chair of music and an annual Reid concert to be given on the anniversary of his birth. Among those who have held the Reid professorship are Henry Bishop, Frederick Niecks, and Donald Tovey, who organised and conducted the Reid orchestral concerts for which his *Essays in Musical Analysis* were written.

Reinach [ren-uck], THÉODORE: *b.* St. Germain-en-Laye, July 3, 1860; *d.* Paris, Oct. 28, 1928. Archaeologist and historian. Taught at the École du Louvre. Wrote a book on Greek music (Paris, 1926), and the librettos of Emmanuel's *Salamine* (Paris, 1929) and Roussel's *La Naissance de la lyre* (Paris, 1925).

Reinagle, ALEXANDER: *b.* Portsmouth, 1756; *d.* Baltimore, Sept. 21, 1809. Pianist, composer and conductor. Studied in Scotland under Raynor Taylor, settled in the United States and from 1786 gave concerts and taught in New York and in Philadelphia, where, in 1793, in partnership with Thomas Wignell he built a theatre for which he directed the music. He composed incidental music for plays, songs, quartets and a concerto for "the Improved Pianoforte with Additional Keys."

Reinecke [rine'-ĕck-er], CARL HEINRICH CARSTEN: *b.* Altona, June 23, 1824; *d.* Leipzig, March 10, 1910. Pianist, violinist, composer and conductor. Court pianist in Copenhagen, 1846-48; teacher at the Cologne Conservatorium, 1851; music director in Barmen, 1854; Breslau University, 1859-60; conductor of the Gewandhaus Orchestra and teacher at the Leipzig Conservatorium, 1860. He composed operas, canons and fairy tale cantatas for female voices, an oratorio, two Masses and other choral works, symphonies, overtures, 4 piano concertos, cadenzas for piano concertos and other pieces for piano, chamber music, numerous songs and duets, and wrote books on musical subjects and 2 vols. of memoirs.

Reine de Chypre, La [la ren der sheepr] (The Queen of Cyprus). Opera in five acts by Halévy. Libretto by Jules Henri Vernoy de Saint-Georges. First performed, Paris, July 22, 1841.

Reine (de France), La [la ren der frûnce] (The Queen of France). The name given to Haydn's symphony No. 85 in B♭ major (*c.* 1786), one of the 6 symphonies commissioned by the Concert de la Loge Olympique in Paris and called the "Paris Symphonies."

Reine de Saba, La [la ren der sa-ba] (The Queen of Sheba). Opera in four acts by Gounod. Libretto by Jules Barbier and Michel Carré. First performed, Paris, Feb. 28, 1862.

Reinken (Reincken) [rine'-kĕn], JAN ADAMS: *b.* Wilshausen (Alsace), Apr. 27, 1623; *d.* Hamburg, Nov. 24, 1722. Organist and composer. Studied under Scheidemann in 1654 and 1657, and in 1663 succeeded him as organist of St. Catherine's in Hamburg, where J. S. Bach made several visits to hear him play. His chorale preludes for organ are in the extended fantasia style practised by North German organists of the period; in 1720, at the age of 97, on hearing Bach extemporise in that style on "Am Wasserflüssen Babylons," he said: "I thought this art was dead, but I see that it lives still in you." His *Hortus musicus* (1687), a set of pieces for 2 violins, gamba and continuo, each consisting of a sonata followed by several dance movements, has been reprinted (1886) in the publications of the Society for Netherlands Music History, xiii, and his 18 variations on "Schweiget mir vom Weibernehmen" in vol. xiv of the same series and in part in Schering's *History of Music in Examples*, No. 207. Bach transcribed two sonatas and a fugue from the *Hortus musicus* for harpsichord (*B.G.* xlii, pp. 29, 42 and 50).

Reissiger [rice'-ig-er], KARL GOTTLIEB: *b.* Belzig (nr. Wittenberg), Jan. 31, 1798; *d.* Dresden, Nov. 7, 1859. Composer and conductor. Studied at the Thomasschule in Leipzig, in Vienna and in Munich. Succeeded Marschner as director of the Dresden opera, and from 1856-59 was director of the Dresden Conservatorium. He composed operas, an oratorio, Masses, motets and other church music, a symphony, 27 piano trios and other chamber music, many works for piano, and songs.

Relative Major, Relative Minor. Terms used to indicate the relation between two keys, one major and the other minor, which have the same key-signature, *e.g.* A minor is the relative minor of C major, and C major is the relative major of A minor.

Reményi [rem′-ay-nyi], EDUARD: *b.* Miskolcz (Hungary), July 17, 1830; *d.* San Francisco, May 15, 1898. Violinist, whose real name was Hoffmann. Studied at the Vienna Conservatorium. Forced to flee to America after the 1848 Revolution. He toured Germany with Brahms (1852-53) and made friends with Liszt in Weimar, was appointed violinist to Queen Victoria (1854) and at the Austrian Court (1860). He gave many concerts and made a world tour in 1887. He composed a violin concerto and other works for violin.

Renaissance Music. The period covered by the variety of musical styles which may for the sake of convenience, and by analogy with the histories of literature and art, be termed the Renaissance is *c.* 1475 (one year after the death of Dufay and the beginning of Josquin's professional career) to *c.* 1600 (the year of Peri's *Euridice*). Since there were no examples of ancient Greek music to imitate, the classical "revival" was confined to experiments in the relating of poetic metres to musical rhythm, as in the odes of Tritonius and in *musique mesurée à l'antique* (*q.v.*), in what was conceived to be the modern equivalent of Greek tragedy, as in the operas of the Florentine Camerata, and in the theory and practice of chromatic and enharmonic intervals, as in the writings of Zarlino and Vicentino and in Luython's chromatic harpsichord.

The most important changes which took place in the early decades of the period were from polyphony based on a *cantus firmus* to freer and more flexible polyphony, from writing for a mixture of voices and instruments to purely choral writing, and from the courtly to the popular forms of secular music. By *c.* 1540 imitation had become the established method of polyphonic writing, whether on original or derived themes (*v.* PARODY MASS) or around a *cantus firmus*, instruments were beginning to be disposed and written for in families ("consorts") and to be written about (*v.* SCHLICK, VIRDUNG), and new forms of secular vocal music (*v.* MADRIGAL) and of instrumental music, both sacred and secular, were being developed.

The chief characteristic of imitative polyphony is the direct relation of the themes to the words, which, in the secular forms, was carried further into details of word-painting and word-symbolism. In conformity with the more expressive treatment of words the melodic style of Renaissance music was less florid than that of the 15th cent., the rhythms were simpler and more controlled, and the use of dissonance was more clearly regulated.

The beginning of the baroque period was marked by criticism of the polyphonic style, *e.g.* by Galilei, and by the appearance of monody, which, though founded on a Renaissance concept of the nature of Greek music and allied to the lute-songs of the 16th cent., became one of the chief embodiments of the baroque style. Other 16th-cent. styles which were maintained and developed in the early baroque period were the divided-choir style (*v.* CORI SPEZZATI), the styles of the keyboard toccata, fantasia and variations, of the homophonic dance-piece, and of the English fantasia for viols.

Rencontre Imprévue, La [la rũn-cõntr ãn-pray-vẽe] (The Unforeseen Encounter). Comic opera in three acts by Gluck. Libretto by L. H. Dancourt (from an earlier French *vaudeville* by Alain René Lesage and d'Orneval). First performed, Vienna, Jan. 7, 1764. The German version—*Die unvermuthete Zusammenkunft oder Die Pilgrimme von Mecca*, now generally known simply as *Die Pilger von Mekka* (The Pilgrims from Mecca)—was first performed at Frankfort, Apr. 16, 1771.

Re Pastore, Il [eel reh pust-oh′-reh] (The King as Shepherd). (1) Opera in three acts by Gluck. Libretto by Pietro Metastasio. First performed, Vienna, Dec. 27, 1756.

(2) Opera in two acts by Mozart, a setting of the same libretto. First performed, Salzburg, Apr. 23, 1775.

Repeat. A repeat from the beginning of a composition is indicated by :||. The repeat of a section is indicated by ||: at the beginning and :|| at the end of the section. A repeat of a first section after a middle section has been performed, as in the aria and in the Minuet and Trio, is marked *Da capo* (from the beginning) ; a repeat from the sign·$· in such a case is marked *Dal segno* (from the sign). *v.* also OUVERT.

Repercussio [rep-air-cōōss'-i-o], *L.* *v.* RECITING NOTE.

Répétiteur [ray-pay-tee-ter], *Fr.* A coach, generally in an opera house, who teaches singers their parts.

Répétition [ray-pay-teece-yon̄], *Fr.* Rehearsal. *Répétition générale*, dress rehearsal.

Reports. A term used in England and Scotland in the 17th cent. for entries in IMITATION, especially in connection with psalm-tunes, as in the title of the Scottish Psalter of 1635 : *The Psalmes of David in Prose and Meeter. With their whole Tunes in four or more parts, and some Psalmes in Reports.* The tune in reports for Psalm 120 in this collection, reprinted in M. Frost's *English and Scottish Psalm and Hymn Tunes* (1953, p. 290) contains one imitative entry in the alto ; it also contains some parallel fifths and other curiosities.

Reprise [rer-preez], *Fr.* (1) REPEAT. In C. P. E. Bach's Sonatas *mit veränderten Reprisen* (with varied *reprises*) of 1760 the repeat of the exposition is varied.

(2) Recapitulation. *v.* SONATA FORM.

(3) The recurrence of the first section as the latter part of the second section of a binary form, as commonly in the classical Minuet.

Requiem (*Fr.* messe des morts, *G.* Totenmesse, *I.* messa per i defunti). Accusative case of *L.* requies, " rest." (1) A Mass for the dead (*L.* missa pro defunctis) in the Roman Catholic church, so called from the opening words of the introit, " Requiem aeternam dona eis, Domine " (Lord, grant them eternal rest). It consists normally of the following sections : (1) *Introit* : " Requiem aeternam " (Grant them eternal rest) ; (2) *Kyrie* (Lord, have mercy upon us) ; (3) *Sequence*: " Dies irae " (Day of wrath) ; (4) *Offertorium* : "Domine Jesu" (Lord Jesus Christ, King of glory) ; (5) *Sanctus* (Holy, holy, holy) ; (6) *Benedictus* (Blessed is he that cometh) ; (7) *Agnus Dei* (O Lamb of God); (8) *Communion* : " Lux aeterna " (Light eternal shine on them). To these may be added at the end the *Responsorium* : " Libera me, Domine " (Deliver me, O Lord). It will be noticed that the *Gloria* and *Credo* of the ordinary Mass are not included.

The three great continental masters of the 16th cent.—Palestrina, Lassus and Victoria—all wrote Requiem Masses. Later settings, with solos and orchestral accompaniment, include those by Mozart, Berlioz (*Grande Messe des Morts*), Dvořák, Verdi and Fauré.

H. C. COLLES: *Verdi's Requiem—Notes on the Words for English Singers* (1943).

(2) Brahms gave the name *Ein deutsches Requiem* to a setting for soloists, chorus and orchestra of passages chosen from the German Bible, Op. 45 (1868). It is a sacred cantata, not a Mass. *v.* DEUTSCHES REQUIEM.

Reservata, Musica [moo'-sick-a ray-sair-vah'-ta], *L.* *v.* MUSICA RESERVATA.

Resolution. The following of a dissonant interval, whether alone or as part of a discord, by a less dissonant or consonant interval. For example the dissonant *appoggiatura* of the seventh in :

is resolved on an octave, a consonance ; the dissonant *appoggiatura* of the augmented unison in :

is resolved on a less dissonant major second. The regular resolution of a diminished fifth is a major or minor third, *e.g.*:

that of an augmented fourth is a major or minor sixth, *e.g.*:

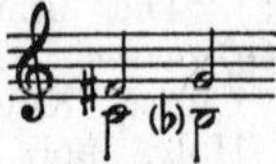

v. DISSONANCE, HARMONY, SUSPENSION.

Resonance. The creation by a vibrating body of vibrations in another body. It occurs in the form of (1) *sympathetic vibrations* in such cases as those of two tuning forks of the same pitch, (2) of a sung note acting on the free strings of a piano, (3) of a stopped string on a violin acting on an open string of the same pitch, and (4) of the overtones of a vibrating string on the piano acting on the corresponding higher strings when the sustaining pedal is held down. In a wind instrument played with a reed, the column of air which determines the pitch causes the reed to vibrate in its period. Resonance occurs in the form of *forced vibrations* in the sounding board of the piano and the belly of the violin, which do not naturally vibrate in the same period as the notes of the strings. *v.* ACOUSTICS.

Respighi [ress-pee'-gee] OTTORINO: *b.* Bologna, July 9, 1879; *d.* Rome, Apr. 18, 1936. Composer. Studied at the Liceo Musicale in Bologna. Became leading viola in the opera orchestra at St. Petersburg and there studied composition and orchestration with Rimsky-Korsakov. Teacher of composition, Liceo Musicale, St. Cecilia Academy, Rome, 1913; director of the Conservatorio Regio, Rome, 1923; teacher of composition there from 1925 to his death. He was a composer of considerable talent who lacked a decided musical personality. His compositions include operas, of which *La Fiamma* (Rome, 1934) was the most successful, tone-poems and other works for orchestra, concertos, chamber music and songs.

R. DE RENSIS: *Ottorino Respighi* (1935).

Respond, Responsory (*L.* responsorium). A plainsong chant sung by a chorus which alternates with one or more verses sung by a soloist. This method of performance, which is used *e.g.* for the Responds between the lessons at Matins and for the Gradual and Alleluia in the Mass, is called "responsorial psalmody." In the 12th and 13th cent. it was customary, as in the ORGANUM of Léonin, to set the solo parts in polyphony for two or more soloists, leaving the other sections to be sung by the choir in plainsong as before. Instances of this practice recur until the 16th cent. An example by Tallis, a four-part setting of the solo parts of "Audivi vocem," the eighth respond at Matins on All Saints Day in the Sarum rite, is printed with the plainsong sung by the choir in the *Historical Anthology*, No. 127. The editors include the plainsong of the *Gloria patri*, which, however, was not sung with the eighth respond and should be omitted.

Rest (*Fr.* pause, *G.* Pause, *I.* pausa). A silence. *v.* NOTATION.

Resultant Tone. *v.* COMBINATION TONE.

Reszke [derr-esh'-kĕ], (1) ÉDOUARD DE: *b.* Warsaw, Dec. 23, 1853; *d.* Garnek (Poland), May 25, 1917. Operatic bass. Brother of (2), with whom (among others) he studied. First appeared in *Aida* in Paris, 1876, and subsequently sang there frequently at the Opéra. He had an equal success in Italy, Belgium, England and the United States. His repertory, which was considerable, included not only the standard French and Italian works of the time but also Wagner's *Der Ring des Nibelungen*, *Tristan und Isolde* and *Die Meistersinger*.

(2) JEAN DE (Jan Mieczysław): *b.* Warsaw, Jan. 14, 1850; *d.* Nice, Apr. 3, 1925. Operatic tenor (originally a baritone). First appeared in Donizetti's *La Favorite* in Venice, 1874, and subsequently in London (1874) and Paris (1876). His first appearance as a tenor was in Madrid in 1879. In addition to regular appearances at the Paris Opéra and Covent Garden he also sang in Belgium, Poland, Russia and the United States. Like his brother he sang Wagner (Lohengrin, Walther, Siegfried and Tristan) as well as the standard French and Italian works.

(3) JOSEPHINE DE: *b.* Warsaw, June 4, 1855; *d.* there, Feb. 22, 1891. Operatic soprano. Sister of (1) and (2). Studied at St. Petersburg Conservatoire and first appeared at the Paris Opéra in 1875.

Her successful career ended with her marriage in 1884.

Retablo de Maese Pedro, El [ell reh-tahb'-lo deh mah-eh'-seh peh'-dro] (Master Peter's Puppet Show). Opera in one act by Falla. Libretto from a chapter of Cervantes' *Don Quixote*. First performed, Seville, March 23, 1923.

Reti [reh'-tee], RUDOLPH : *b.* Uzice (Yugoslavia), Nov. 27, 1885; *d.* Feb. 7, 1957. Critic and composer, who became an American citizen. Studied in Vienna, where he was music critic of *Das Echo*, 1930-8. One of the founders of the International Society for Contemporary Music, 1922. His compositions include an opera, a piano concerto and a violin sonata. He also published *The Thematic Process in Music* (1950) and *Tonality, Atonality, Pantonality* (1958).

Retrograde Motion (*I.* al rovescio, *L.* cancrizans, per recte et retro). The use of retrograde, *i.e.* backwards, motion has been applied in composition both to melodies, as a contrapuntal device, and to entire textures, as a formal device. Examples of the former are found in the tenors of 15th-cent. motets, as in that of Dunstable's three-part setting of *Veni Sancte Spiritus* (*D.T.Ö.*, vii, p. 201), which is first sung thus :

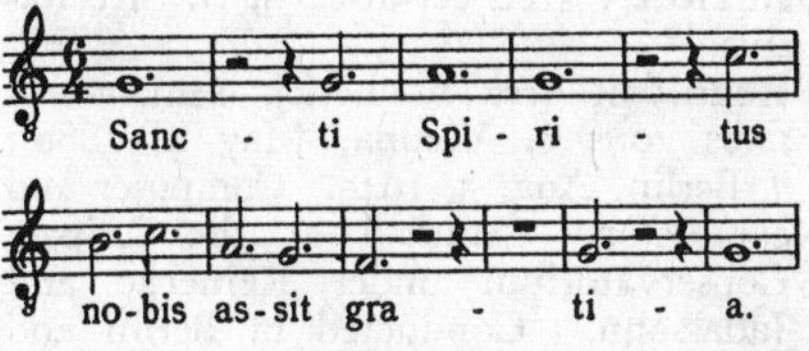

then in its inversion, thus :

and finally in retrograde motion a fifth lower in notes of two-thirds of the original value:

Later examples occur in Bach's *Musikalisches Opfer*, in the fugue in the last movement of Beethoven's "Hammerklavier" sonata, Op. 106, and in modern compositions written in the twelve-note technique by Schönberg and others. Among examples of the second type are Machaut's *rondeau* "Ma fin est mon commencement," Byrd's 8-part motet "Diliges Dominum" (*Works*, ed. Fellowes, vol. i), the two-part crab canon in Bach's *Musikalisches Opfer*, the minuet of Haydn's fourth violin sonata, and the fugue in F in Hindemith's *Ludus Tonalis*.

A special kind of retrograde motion, combined with inversion, is produced when the music is performed with the page turned upside down. The Prelude and Postlude of Hindemith's *Ludus Tonalis* are related in this fashion.

In the following example by Johann Schobert (printed, with others, in *D.D.T.*, xxxix) the second half of the Minuet will be found by turning the first half upside down :

Return of Lemminkäinen, The. *v.* LEGENDS.

Reubke [royp'-ker], JULIUS: *b.* Hausneindorf, March 23, 1834 ; *d.* Pillnitz,

June 3, 1858. Pianist and composer. Studied under Liszt at Weimar. He is known only for his programme-sonata for organ *The Ninety-fourth Psalm*, published posthumously, as were some piano pieces and songs.

Reusner [roice′-ner], ESAJAS: *b.* Löwenberg (Silesia), Apr. 29, 1636; *d.* Berlin, May 1, 1679. Lutenist. Studied under a French lutenist at the court of the Polish Princess Radziwill. Court lutenist at Liegnitz and Berg (1655) and in Berlin (1674). He composed 3 books of dance suites for the lute and published several books of lute arrangements. A Courante, Sarabande, and Gigue from his *Deliciae testudinis* (1667) are printed in Schering's *History of Music in Examples*, No. 216.

Reutlingen, Hugo von [hoog′-o fon royt′-ling-ĕn]. *v.* HUGO VON REUTLINGEN.

Reutter [royt′-er], (1) GEORG: *b.* Vienna, 1656; *d.* there, Aug. 29, 1738. Composer. Theorbo player (1697) and organist (1700) of the court chapel, Vienna. *Kapellmeister* of St. Stephen's, 1715. Five of the 6 *capriccii* for organ printed in *D.T.Ö.*, xiii (2), as by him are said by H. J. Moser to be compositions by Nikolaus Strungk.

(2) HERMANN: *b.* Stuttgart, June 17, 1900. Composer and pianist. Studied in Munich. Teacher of composition in the High School for Music in Würtemberg, 1932; director, High School for Music, Frankfort, 1936; teacher in Stuttgart, 1945. He has composed operas, oratorios and other choral works, a ballet, chamber music, piano works and songs.

(3) JOHANN ADAM KARL GEORG: *bapt.* Vienna, Apr. 6, 1708; *d.* there, March 11, 1772. Composer. Son of (1). Court composer at Vienna, 1731. Succeeded his father as *Kapellmeister* of St. Stephen's in 1738; court *Kapellmeister*, 1747. Ennobled (thus becoming von Reutter) in 1740. He was *Kapellmeister* at St. Stephen's when Haydn was a choirboy there, but took little interest in Haydn's efforts at composition and expelled him from the choir-school in 1749. Haydn must have been familiar in his youth with Reutter's symphonies, one of which, in four movements with a minuet, is printed in *D.T.O.*, xv (2).

Revueltas [reh-voo-ell′-tuss], SILVESTRE: *b.* Santiago Papasquiaro, Dec. 31, 1899; *d.* Mexico City, Oct. 5, 1940. Composer, violinist and pianist. Studied in the U.S.A. and was violinist at Mexico City from 1920. He gave recitals of contemporary music with Chávez as pianist, assisted him in conducting the Mexico Symphony Orchestra and became professor at the Conservatoire. Composed music for many films, orchestral works, chamber music, ballets and songs.

Reyer [ray-yair], ERNEST (Louis Ernest Étienne Rey): *b.* Marseilles, Dec. 1, 1823; *d.* Lavendou, Hyères, Jan. 15, 1909. Composer and critic. Studied in Marseilles. In 1839 was sent to Algiers to work in the civil service but continued to compose. In 1848 he settled in Paris where he met Gautier, Flaubert and Méry, who provided texts for his compositions, and in 1871 succeeded d'Ortigue as music critic for the *Journal des Débats*. He succeeded Berlioz as librarian of the Conservatoire. His compositions include operas, of which *Sigurd* (Brussels, 1884) and *Salammbô* (Brussels, 1890) were the most notable, a ballet-pantomime, a Mass, the dramatic cantata *Victoire* and other choral works, piano works and songs.

Rezitativ [rets-eet-ut-eef′], *G.* Recitative.

Rezniček [rez′-ni-check], EMIL NIKOLAUS VON: *b.* Vienna, May 4, 1860; *d.* Berlin, Aug. 5, 1945. Composer and conductor. Studied at the Leipzig Conservatorium under Reinecke and Jadassohn. Conducted in Berlin and elsewhere, and at the court in Mannheim from 1896-99. Settled in 1902 at Berlin where he founded chamber concerts, taught at the Klindworth-Scharwenka Conservatorium from 1906 and at the Hochschule from 1920. He was director of the Warsaw Opera and Philharmonic from 1907-09. Composed operas, a Requiem, a Mass and other choral works, 4 symphonies and other orchestral works, 3 string quartets, works for organ and for piano, and songs.

Rhapsody (*Gr.* ῥαψῳδία, an epic poem, or an extract suitable for recitation).

A title given by composers in the 19th and early 20th cent. to instrumental compositions of a heroic, national, or rhetorical character, *e.g.* Liszt's *Hungarian Rhapsodies* and Brahms's 2 Rhapsodies, Op. 79 for piano, Lalo's *Norwegian Rhapsody* (1881) for orchestra, and Bartók's 2 Rhapsodies for violin and orchestra. Brahms's *Rhapsodie*, Op. 53, for alto solo, male choir and orchestra is an exception both in style and medium.

Rhau (Rhaw) [row], GEORG: *b.* Eisfeld (Franconia), 1488; *d.* Wittenberg, Aug. 6, 1548. Publisher and composer. Studied from 1508 in Erfurt and from 1512 in Wittenberg. Teacher, Leipzig University and cantor at the Thomasschule, 1518. Settled in Wittenberg, where he founded a printing business in 1525. He published many of the early collections of Lutheran church music, including *Newe deudsche geistliche Gesenge* (1544), which contains polyphonic settings of chorales by various composers. In 1542 he published a volume of polyphonic settings of Latin hymns for the Lutheran liturgy by Heinrich Finck, Thomas Stoltzer, Ludwig Senfl and others (modern ed. in *E.D.M.*, xxi and xxv). His handbook of elementary theory, *Enchiridion utriusque musicae practicae*, was published in a facsimile ed. in 1951.

Rheinberger [rine'-bairg-er], JOSEPH GABRIEL: *b.* Vaduz (Liechtenstein), March 17, 1839; *d.* Munich, Nov. 25, 1901. Organist and composer. Appointed an organist at the age of seven, he studied at the Munich Royal Conservatorium, where he taught from 1859-65 and from 1867 until his death. Organist at St. Michael's, 1860-66; conductor of the Munich Choral Society, 1864-77; attached to the Court Opera, 1865-67; from 1877 director of court church music. He composed several operas, 2 symphonies, overtures and other orchestral works, Requiems, 14 Masses, motets and other church music, secular choral works, incidental music for plays, chamber music, 2 organ concertos, 20 sonatas and other works for organ, piano pieces and songs.

H. GRACE: *The Organ Works of Rheinberger* (1925).

Rheingold, Das [duss rine'-gollt] (The Rhine Gold). Opera in one act by Wagner, the first part of the cycle *Der Ring des Nibelungen* (*q.v.*). First performed, Munich, Sept. 22, 1869.

Rheinische Sinfonie [rine'-ish-er zinfo-nee'], *G.* *v.* RHENISH SYMPHONY.

Rhené-Baton [rer-nay-ba-tõn] (René Baton): *b.* Courseulles-sur-Mer, Sept. 5, 1879; *d.* Le Mans, Sept. 23, 1940. Conductor and composer. Studied at the Paris Conservatoire under Gédalge, worked at the Opéra-Comique and from 1918-32 was conductor of the Concerts Pasdeloup. He composed a lyric drama, a ballet, orchestral works, piano pieces and songs.

Rhenish Symphony (*G.* rheinische Sinfonie). The name given to Schumann's symphony No. 3 in E♭ major, Op. 97 (1850), which was intended to convey the impressions he received during a visit to Cologne.

Rhine Gold, The. *v.* RHEINGOLD.

Rhythm. The organisation of music in respect to time. Rhythm may be (1) free, as in some types of Oriental music; (2) flexible, as in plainsong, where each note is regarded as having approximately the same length; (3) measured, either in rhythmic modes (*v.* MENSURAL NOTATION) as in the 11th-12th cent., or in a complete system of duple and triple note-values, as in the 13th to the 16th cent.; or (4) metrical, *i.e.* accentual, as from the 16th cent. to the present. Within each of these systems the rhythmic character of a phrase, period, section or movement of a composition is a fundamental element in its style, and the chief criterion for distinctions of style, *e.g.* between the plainsong hymn, psalm and antiphon, between the 13th-cent. motet and *conductus*, between the isorhythmic motet and non-isorhythmic *chanson* in the 14th and 15th cent., between the motet and madrigal in the 16th, between the movements of a suite in the baroque period, and between the movements and themes of a movement in the modern symphony and sonata. The effect of good polyphonic writing is caused by apt combinations of rhythm as much as by melodic independence, as in the measured rhythm of:

from a *Credo* by Leonel Power, or the metrical rhythm of :

from the fugue in C♯ minor in the first book of Bach's *Forty-eight*.

The effect of the metrical rhythm of homophonic writing arises from both the melodic and the harmonic rhythm, as well as from the relation between them, since they may be contrasted, as in the opening of John Blow's anthem, "How doth the city sit solitary" :

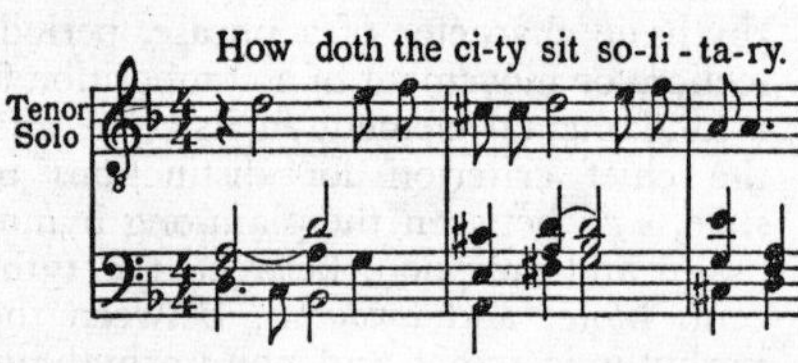

or combined, as in the Allegretto of Beethoven's seventh symphony :

In the present century composers have extended the possibilities of metrical rhythm by the use of different metres in succession and in combination, of more complex melodic rhythms, and of more varied relations between melodic and harmonic rhythm by syncopation and other methods. *v.* ACCENT, BAR, METRE, SYNCOPATION, TIME-SIGNATURE.

C. SACHS: *Rhythm and Tempo* (1953).

Rhythmic Modes. The term mode had a rhythmic meaning in the NOTATION of *c.* 1150 to *c.* 1250, and denoted a rhythmic pattern used more or less consistently in each part of a polyphonic composition. These patterns were arrangements of the long and the breve, which were used in the following combinations : Mode I : long-breve ; Mode II : breve-long ; Mode III : long-breve-breve ; Mode IV: breve-breve-long ; Mode V ; successive longs ; Mode VI : successive breves. Since the relation of long to breve was considered to be always perfect, *i.e.* long=3 breves, the principles of imperfection, whereby a long followed by a breve became imperfect (2 breves), and alteration, whereby a breve preceding a long was doubled (*brevis altera*), were applied in the first four modes, in order to keep them within perfect (triple) units. The equivalent patterns in modern notation, *i.e.*, reduced to one-sixteenth of the original values, would be :

Mode I : ♩♪♩♪ etc.,

Mode II : ♪♩♪♩ etc. ;

Mode III : ♩.♪♩ etc. ;

Mode IV : ♪♩♩. etc. ;

Mode V : ♩.♩. etc. ;

Mode VI : ♪♪♪ ♪♪♪ etc. ;

Music composed in the rhythmic modes was written in ligatures (*q.v.*) and the form of the opening ligatures showed in what mode the part was to be interpreted. In practice it was not possible to use ligatures throughout, for example in the case of repeated notes, which cannot be written in ligature. The term mode continued to be used for the relation of the long to the breve in the period of MENSURAL NOTATION.

Rhythmicon. An electrical instrument invented by Leon Theremin and Henry Cowell. It is designed to produce different rhythms simultaneously.

Riccardo I, Re d'Inghilterra [reek-carr′-do pree′-mo reh deen-geel-tair′-rah] (Richard I, King of England). Opera in three acts by Handel. Libretto by Paolo Antonio Rolli. First performed, London, Nov. 22, 1727.

Ricci [ree′-tchee], LUIGI: *b.* Naples, July 8, 1805; *d.* Prague, Dec. 1859. Composer. Studied under Zingarelli at Naples Conservatorio where he became teacher in 1819. Later went to Trieste as conductor of the Opera and director of music at the Cathedral. He composed about 30 operas, some with his brother Federico (1809-1877), who was also an opera composer. Their most successful collaboration was in the comic opera *Crispino e la Comare* (Venice, 1850).

Riccio [ree′-tcho], ANTONIO TEODORO: *b.* Brescia, *c.* 1540; *d.* Ansbach, 1603/4. Choirmaster in Brescia. Appointed *Kapellmeister* to Georg Friedrich at Ansbach, 1564, and in 1579 moved with him to Königsberg. Composed Masses, motets and Magnificats, madrigals and *Canzoni alla napolitana.*

Ricercar [ree-chair-carr′], *I.* (from *ricercare*, to seek out). A term used in the general sense of essay or study as the title of certain compositions in the 16th and 17th cent. The earliest ricercars for organ in Marcantonio Cavazzoni's *Recerchari, motetti, canzoni* (1523), were in free style, but the later examples by G. Cavazzoni (1542), A. Gabrieli, Frescobaldi, and Lutheran composers up to Bach are in imitative polyphonic style. A ricercar is based on one or a succession of themes of a rather abstract character, is usually in 4/2 time throughout, and is not clearly distinguishable in style from a contrapuntal FANTASIA, the term which German composers preferred for pieces in this style until late in the seventeenth century. Froberger used both titles, without effective distinction, for pieces in contrapuntal style in 2/2 time, with or without changes of metre. Themes with solmization titles were frequently used, as in Frescobaldi's *Recercar sopra Mi, Re, Fa, Mi* in his first book of *Capricci, Canzon franzese e Recercari* (1626). The same collection contains a *Recercar obligo di non uscir di grado, i.e.* without using stepwise motion, in which no part uses the interval of a second. It begins:

Later ricercars on one theme are fugues, which is the sense in which Bach uses the term in his *Musikalisches Opfer.*

Contrapuntal ricercars were written for instrumental ensembles in the 16th cent. by Willaert, Annibale, Padovano and others, and studies termed ricercar for string instruments by Diego Ortiz and in the 17th cent. by D. Gabrielli. The two-part ricercars by Metallo (1605; 12 editions to 1685) are *per sonare et cantare* ("to play and sing"), while those of Giovanni Gentile (1642) are for singers.

The earliest ricercars for lute, in Petrucci's publications, were in free style. Later examples, *e.g.*, those of V. Galilei (ed. F. Fano in *Istituzioni e Monumenti*, iv, pp. 8-11), were in pseudo-contrapuntal or in homophonic style.

Richafort [ree-sha-forr], JEAN. Early 16th-cent. Flemish composer. Studied under Josquin des Prés and from

1543-47 was choirmaster of St. Gilles at Bruges. He composed a Requiem, Masses, motets and *chansons*. The *chanson* " Sur tous regrets " was printed in vol. ii of Ott's *Liederbuch* of 1544 (reprinted in *Publikationen der Gesellschaft für Musikforschung*, ii) and the motet " Christus resurgens," on which Willaert wrote a Mass, was printed by Glareanus in the *Dodecachordon* (1547) as an example of the Ionian mode, and reprinted in P. Bohn's translation of the *Dodecachordon* (1899), p. 243.

Richard Cœur-de-Lion [ree-sharr curd-lyo͞n]. Opera in three acts by Grétry. Libretto by Jean Michel Sedaine. First performed, Paris, Oct. 21, 1784.

Richardson (originally Heybourne), FERDINANDO: *b. c.* 1558; *d.* Tottenham (Middlesex), June 4, 1618. Composer and poet. Studied under Tallis and was groom of the Privy Chamber from 1587-1611. Two pavanes and two galliards, each with a variation, were included in the *Fitzwilliam Virginal Book*.

Richter [*rish'*-ter], (1) ERNST FRIEDRICH EDUARD: *b.* Gross-schönau (nr. Zittau), Oct. 24, 1808; *d.* Leipzig, Apr. 9, 1879. Theorist and organist. Studied in Leipzig, where he taught at the Conservatorium (1843), conducted at the Singakademie (1843-47), was organist of the Peterskirche (1851), of Neukirche and Nicolaikirche (1862) and cantor of the Thomasschule (1868). Three of his books were translated into English by Franklin Taylor: *Harmony* (1864), *Simple and Double Counterpoint* (1874) and *Fugue* (1878). He composed a cantata, oratorio, Masses, motets and other church music, chamber music, organ pieces and songs.

(2) FRANZ XAVER: *b.* Holleschau (Moravia), Dec. 1, 1709; *d.* Strasbourg, Sept. 12, 1789. Composer. Choirmaster of the abbey at Kempten, Swabia, from 1740, singer and violinist at Mannheim Electoral Court from 1747 and choirmaster of Strasbourg Cathedral from 1769 until his death. He composed 69 symphonies, 6 harpsichord concertos with string orchestra, 12 trio sonatas for 2 violins and continuo and other chamber music, 28 Masses, 2 Requiems, motets and other church music, and wrote a textbook on harmony. He was one of the group of composers connected with the Mannheim orchestra whose work contributed much to the early history of the symphony. A symphony has been published in *D.T.B.*, vii (2), a trio in *D.T.B.*, xvi, and 6 quartets in *D.T.B.*, xv.

(3) HANS: *b.* Raab (Hungary), Apr. 4, 1843; *d.* Bayreuth, Dec. 5, 1916. Conductor. Chorister in Vienna, where he studied at the Conservatorium (1860-65) and was horn player in the Kärntnertor Theatre Orchestra (1862-66). Chorus master, Munich Court Opera, 1868-69. Conductor, Budapest National Opera (1871-75). Conductor, Court Opera and Philharmonic Concerts, Vienna, 1875; Hallé Orchestra in Manchester, 1900-11. He conducted at the Bayreuth Festivals and the Birmingham triennial festivals, and from 1879 gave an annual series of Richter concerts in London. He worked with Wagner preparing for publication the score of *Die Meistersinger* (1866-67) and of *Der Ring* (1870-71), of which he conducted the first performance in 1876 at Bayreuth. One of the great conductors of his age, he did much to improve the standards of conducting and of orchestral playing, and to further the knowledge of Wagner's works both in Vienna and in England. He conducted the first English performances of *Die Meistersinger* and of *Tristan und Isolde* in 1882 and 1884.

Riders to the Sea. Opera in one act by Vaughan Williams, a setting of John Millington Synge's play. First performed at the R.C.M., London, Dec. 1, 1937. First public performance, Cambridge, Nov. 22, 1938.

Riegger, WALLINGFORD: *b.* Albany (Georgia), April 29, 1885. Composer. Studied at the Institute of Musical Art in New York under Goetschius and at the Berlin Hochschule. Conducted at the opera in Würzburg and Königsberg (1915-16) and the Berlin Bluethner Orchestra (1916-17). Taught at Drake University, 1918-22; Institute of Musical Art, 1924-25; Ithaca Conservatory, 1926-28. He has lived for many years in New York. Composed numerous works for modern dancers, including

Martha Graham, Charles Weidman and Doris Humphrey, symphonies and other orchestral works, and chamber music.

Riemann [ree′-mun], KARL WILHELM JULIUS HUGO: *b.* Grossmehlra (nr. Sondershausen), July 18, 1849; *d.* Leipzig, July 10, 1919. Musicologist and theorist. Studied at the Leipzig Conservatorium and at Göttingen (1873). Lecturer, Leipzig University, 1878. Taught in Bromberg (1880), at the Hamburg Conservatorium (1881-90) and at the Wiesbaden Conservatorium (1880-95). Returned to Leipzig University where he was made professor in 1905, director of the Institute of Musical Science in 1908 and of the State Institute of Musicology in 1914. He wrote many books and articles on musical history and theory, edited collections of music and composed chamber music, choral works, songs and piano pieces. A number of his textbooks have been translated into English, among them *The Nature of Harmony* (1882), *Textbook of Counterpoint* (1888), *Musical Instruments* (1888), *Harmony Simplified* (1893), *Score-reading* (1903), as well as his *Dictionary of Music* (1882, English trans., 1893). The most recent edition of the Dictionary (*Musik-Lexikon*) has been revised by W. Gurlitt (1959).

Rienzi, der Letzte der Tribunen [ree-en′-tsee dair lets′-ter dair tree-boon′-ĕn] (Rienzi, the Last of the Tribunes). Opera in five acts by Wagner. Libretto by the composer (founded on Bulwer Lytton's novel). First performed, Dresden, Oct. 20, 1842. (Original title *Cola Rienzi, der Letzte der Tribunen*).

Ries [reece], FERDINAND: *bapt.* Bonn. Nov. 29, 1784; *d.* Frankfort, Jan, 13, 1838. Pianist, composer and conductor. Studied under Beethoven in Vienna, toured as a pianist, and lived in London as pianist and teacher, 1813-24. Municipal music director, Aix-la-Chapelle, 1834-36. Director of the St. Cecilia Society in Frankfort from 1836 until his death. He also conducted at the Lower Rhine Festivals, 1825-37. He published a biographical work on Beethoven with Wegeler (1838) and composed 3 operas, 2 oratorios, 6 symphonies, overtures, piano concertos, string quartets and other chamber music, and many works for piano.

Rieti [ree-eh′-tee], VITTORIO: *b.* Alexandria, Jan. 28, 1898. Italian composer. Studied in Milan and under Respighi in Rome. Settled in New York in 1939. He has composed ballets, an opera, a symphony, concertos for piano, for violin, for harpsichord and for wind quintet with orchestra, chamber music and piano pieces.

Rietsch [reech], HEINRICH: *b.* Falkenau, Sept. 22, 1860; *d.* Prague, Dec. 12, 1927. Musicologist and composer. Studied under Hanslick, Adler, Mandyczewski and Robert Fuchs in Vienna, where he was appointed lecturer at the University in 1895. In 1900 became professor at the German University in Prague, where he founded the Institute of Musicology of which he was director from 1909. Joint editor of a collection of Minnesinger music (1896) and editor of Georg Muffat's *Florilegium* (*D.T.Ö.*, i and ii) and Fux's *Concentus musico-instrumentalis* (*D.T.Ö.*, xxiii, 2). His compositions include an opera, orchestral works, choral works, chamber music, piano pieces and songs.

Rietz [reets], JULIUS: *b.* Berlin, Dec. 28, 1812; *d.* Dresden, Sept. 12, 1877. Cellist, conductor and composer. Studied under B. Romberg and Zelter. Member of the Berlin Königstadt Theatre Orchestra from 1828; assistant conductor to Mendelssohn at the Düsseldorf Opera from 1834; succeeded him in 1835; municipal music director there, 1836-47. In Leipzig conductor of the Opera and Singakademie, 1847-54, director of Gewandhaus Concerts, and teacher of composition at the Conservatorium, 1848-60. In Dresden from 1860 as Court conductor and director of the Conservatorium. He composed 4 operas, incidental music for plays, symphonies, overtures, choral works with orchestra, concertos, Masses, motets and other church music, chamber music and songs, and edited the operas of Mozart and the complete works of Mendelssohn.

Rigaudon [ree-go-dŏn], *Fr.* A Provençal dance in lively 2/2 time which was adopted into the suite and into the ballet of French opera in the late 17th cent.

There is a "rigadoon" for harpsichord by Purcell in the second part of Playford's *Musick's Handmaid.* The *rigaudon* in Couperin's second *ordre* for harpsichord begins thus:

Rigo [ree′-go], *I.* Staff, stave.

Rigoletto [ree-go-let′-to]. Opera in three acts by Verdi. Libretto by Francesco Maria Piave (based on Victor Hugo's *Le Roi s'amuse*). First performed, Venice, March 11, 1851. Rigoletto (the humpbacked jester of the Duke of Mantua) mocks the court noblemen and advises the duke to get rid of them. The noblemen in turn resolve to take vengeance on him, and Count Monterone (whose daughter the duke has dishonoured) curses both the jester and the duke. Meanwhile the duke disguised as a student has been courting Gilda (Rigoletto's daughter). The noblemen, believing Gilda to be the mistress of Rigoletto, abduct her, telling him that they are abducting the Countess Ceprano (one of the duke's favourites), so that unawares he assists them with their plans. Rigoletto later finds Gilda with the duke at the palace and admitting that she is his daughter he takes her away, cursing his master. Gilda is taken by her father to spy on the duke, who is at the house of Sparafucile (a professional assassin) in conversation with Maddalena (Sparafucile's sister). Rigoletto pays Sparafucile to kill his guest. When Maddalena begs her brother not to do the deed, he promises that he will spare the duke if he can find another to take the duke's place by midnight. Gilda overhearing this conversation enters the house disguised as a man. When the jester returns with the money he is given a body tied in a bag and is about to throw it into the river when he hears in the distance the voice of the duke singing. He quickly opens the bag and discovers his dying daughter, who declares that she is happy to die for her lover. In horror Rigoletto realises that the curse of Count Monterone is fulfilled.

Riisager [reece′-ahg-er], KNUDÅGE: *b.* Port Kunda (Estonia), March 6, 1897. Composer, the son of Danish parents. Educated at Copenhagen University, where he took a degree in political economy. Studied music there and in Paris with Roussel and Le Flem. Wilhelm Hansen prize for composition, 1925. His compositions include 4 symphonies, sinfonietta for wind instruments, 9 overtures and other orchestral works, trumpet concerto, ballet music, choral works, 5 string quartets and other chamber music, piano pieces and songs.

Rimbault, EDWARD FRANCIS: *b.* London, June 13, 1816; *d.* there, Sept. 26, 1876. Musical historian and organist. Organist of the Swiss Church in Soho, one of the founders and later secretary of the Musical Antiquarian Society and of the Percy Society, and editor of the Motet Society publications. He gave lectures in England and Scotland. He edited many collections of early English music, wrote books on music history, and composed an operetta, a cantata and songs.

Rimsky-Korsakov [rim′-ski-corr′-sacoff], NICOLAS ANDREIEVICH: *b.* Tikhvin, March 18, 1844; *d.* Lubensk, June 21, 1908. Composer. At 12 he entered the Corps of Naval Cadets at St. Petersburg, and five years later met Balakirev, Cui and Moussorgsky, and began the serious study of music under Balakirev. Sailed to London and New York as a petty officer in 1862, returning in 1865, and in 1871 was appointed professor of composition at St. Petersburg Conservatoire. In 1874 became director of the New Free School of Music in St. Petersburg and soon became the leader of a new group of composers including Liadov, Glazounov and Arensky. After the performance of Wagner's *Ring* in St. Petersburg in

1888 he began to write for a larger orchestra and to develop the ideas on orchestration which were published in *Principles of Orchestration* (English trans. by E. Agate, 1912). In 1902 he met Stravinsky, who became his pupil. He showed sympathy with the cause of the revolution of 1905 and was dismissed from the Conservatoire, but was later reinstated. The element of satire on government in his last work, the opera *The Golden Cockerel* (1907), caused its performance to be forbidden until 1910.

Like the other members of the group led by Balakirev, Rimsky-Korsakov was strongly influenced by national ideas in his early work. His later development acquired a solid foundation through concentrated work on technical matters after 1871, through his work on the collection of folk songs, published as Op. 24, and through the experience of editing Glinka's operas. After 1887-8 when he wrote his most mature orchestral pieces, *Spanish Capriccio*, *Scheherazade*, and the *Russian Easter* overture, he re-orchestrated many of his earlier works, but gave his main creative effort to the composition of the operas—*Mlada*, 1890; *Christmas Eve*, 1895; *Sadko*, 1896; *Czar Saltan*, 1898; *Kitezh*, 1904; and *The Golden Cockerel*—which are his greatest achievement. His clear and brilliant orchestration had a marked effect on Stravinsky, and through Stravinsky on the orchestral writing of many contemporary composers. His memoirs were published in English in 1924 as *My Musical Life*.

G. ABRAHAM: *On Russian Music* (1939). *Rimsky-Korsakov* (1945). *Studies in Russian Music* (1935).

M. MONTAGU-NATHAN: *Rimsky-Korsakov* (1916).

Rinaldo [ree-nahl′-do]. Opera in three acts by Handel. Libretto by Giacomo Rossi (from a sketch, after Tasso, by Aaron Hill). First performed, London, March 7, 1711.

Rinck [rink], JOHANN CHRISTIAN HEINRICH: *b.* Elgersburg (Thuringia), Feb. 18, 1770; *d.* Darmstadt, Aug. 7, 1846. Organist and composer. Studied under Kittel, a pupil of Bach, at Erfurt from 1786-89. Municipal organist, Giessen, 1790; Darmstadt, 1805, and also professor, court organist from 1813 and ducal chamber musician from 1817. He composed organ works, motets, a Mass and other church music, and chamber music.

Rinforzando [reen-forr-tsahnd′-o], *I.* "Reinforcing." Generally abbreviated *rinf.*, *rfz.*, or *rf.* Used (1) as the equivalent of *sforzando* for a sudden accent; (2) as the equivalent of the French *en dehors*, to indicate that a particular phrase is to be made prominent; (3) to indicate a sudden and quick *crescendo*.

Ring des Nibelungen, Der [dair ring dess nee′-bĕl-ŏŏng-ĕn] (The Ring of the Nibelung). Cycle of four operas by Wagner, described by him as "Ein Bühnenfestspiel fur drei Tage und einen Vorabend" (a festival drama for three days and a preliminary evening) and dedicated to Ludwig II, King of Bavaria. Libretto by the composer. The four operas are: (1) *Das Rheingold* (The Rhine Gold), first performed, Munich, Sept. 22, 1869; (2) *Die Walküre* (The Valkyrie,) first performed, Munich, June 26, 1870; (3) *Siegfried*, first performed, Bayreuth, Aug. 16, 1876; (4) *Götterdämmerung* (Twilight of the Gods), first performed, Bayreuth, Aug. 17 1876. First performance of the complete cycle, Bayreuth, Aug. 13-17, 1876.

(1) *Das Rheingold.* The Rhine gold is stolen from the Rhine maidens by the dwarf Alberich, who makes from it the ring that gives mastery of the world. The gods, led by Wotan, steal both gold and ring, to pay for the building of Valhalla by the giants. The curse placed on the ring by Alberich operates immediately. The giants Fasolt and Fafner quarrel, and Fasolt is slain.

(2) *Die Walküre.* Wotan has children by the earth goddess Erda (the Valkyries) and also others by a human mother (Siegmund and Sieglinde). He hopes that his human progeny will recover the ring, now guarded by Fafner in the shape of a dragon. The human children are under the same curse. Brünnhilde, one of the Valkyries, disobeys Wotan by protecting Siegmund against Hunding, Sieglinde's husband, and is punished by losing her godhead. She is surrounded by

fire, which only a fearless hero can penetrate.

(3) *Siegfried.* Siegfried, child of the incestuous union of Siegmund and Sieglinde, has been brought up in the forest by Alberich's brother, the dwarf Mime. He forges a sword from the fragments of his father's weapon, broken by Hunding's attack, kills Fafner, possesses the ring and the magic helm, and wins Brünnhilde.

(4) *Götterdämmerung.* Hagen, son of Alberich, plots to recover the ring. Siegfried is drugged with a potion, captures Brünnhilde for Gunther, Hagen's half-brother, and marries Gunther's sister Gutrune. Brünnhilde, with Hagen and Gunther, plots Siegfried's destruction. Siegfried is killed, and so is Gunther, from whom Hagen demands the ring. Brünnhilde, now aware of the truth, builds a funeral pyre and rides into it. The Rhine overwhelms the stage. The ring, vainly pursued by Hagen, returns to the Rhine maidens, and Valhalla is seen in flames. The curse is complete.

Ripieno [reep-yeh′-no], *I.* Lit. "full." As a technical term used, particularly in the *concerto grosso* of the baroque period, for the full body of the orchestra, as distinct from the soloist or group of soloists (*concertino*). *Senza ripieni* indicates that the first desks only of the accompanying orchestra are to play.

Ripresa [ree-preh′-zah], *I.* "Repeat". (1) The REFRAIN in the Italian BALLATA of the 14th cent.

(2) A dance movement for lute in the form of a variation in the 16th cent.

(3) In later music any REPEAT or recapitulation. *v.* SONATA FORM.

Risoluto [ree-so-loo′-toh], *I.* In a resolute manner.

Risposta [reece-posst′-ah], *I.* (1) The answer in a FUGUE or IMITATION. (2) The *comes* in a CANON.

Risvegliato [reece-vehl-yah′-toh], *I.* In an animated (or re-animated) manner.

Ritardando [ree-tarr-dahnd′-o], *I.* Becoming gradually slower—the equivalent of *rallentando.* Commonly abbreviated *rit.*

Ritenuto [ree-ten-oo′-toh], *I.* Held back in tempo, *i.e.* slower, though sometimes used as the equivalent of *ritardando.*

Rite of Spring, The. *v.* SACRE DU PRINTEMPS.

Ritornello [ree-torr-nell′-lo], *I.* "Return." (1) The last section of an Italian MADRIGAL of the 14th cent., which is thus a conclusion, not a return.

(2) An instrumental piece in early opera. In Monteverdi's *Orfeo,* for example, the *ritornello* of four bars before the Prologue returns four times with the first bar omitted during the Prologue, and is played complete between the Prologue and the first act.

(3) The orchestral prelude, interludes, and postlude in an aria of the 17th and 18th cent., and the recurrences of the *tutti* theme in the main movements of a *concerto grosso* of the baroque period. In both cases the intermediate *ritornelli* are in nearly-related keys, and the final *ritornello* is in the tonic.

(4) An interlude for instrumental ensemble played after each verse of German songs in the 17th cent., as in Adam Krieger's *Neue Arien* of 1676 (modern ed. in *D.D.T.*, xix).

Ritorno d'Ulisse in Patria, Il [eel ree-torr′-no doo-leece′-seh in pahtr′-yah] (The Return of Ulysses to his Fatherland). Opera with a prologue and three acts by Monteverdi. Libretto by Giacomo Badoaro. First performed, Venice, Feb. 1641.

Ritter [rit′-er], ALEXANDER: *b.* Narva (Russia), June 27, 1833; *d.* Munich, Apr. 12, 1896. Composer. Went to Germany as a boy and later became a strong admirer of Wagner. Studied at the Leipzig Conservatorium. Married Wagner's niece, Franziska Wagner, in 1854 and moved to Weimar. From 1856-58 he conducted at the Stettin Opera, and in 1863 settled in Würzburg where he ran a music shop. As a violinist in the Meiningen Court Orchestra (1882-86) he met Richard Strauss and imbued him with enthusiasm for the "modern" style of Liszt and Wagner. In 1886 he moved to Munich. He composed 2 operas, 6 symphonic poems, a string quartet, piano pieces and songs.

Roberday [rob-air-day], FRANÇOIS: *d.*

Paris, *c.* 1695. Attached to the courts of Queen Anne of Austria and Queen Marie-Thérèse, one of the teachers of Lully and organist at the Church of the Petits-pères in Paris. He published *Fugues et caprices* for organ (1660), reprinted in A. Guilmant, *Archives des maîtres de l'orgue*, iii.

Robert le Diable [rob-air ler dyubl] (Robert the Devil). Opera in five acts by Meyerbeer. Libretto by Augustin Eugène Scribe. First performed, Paris, Nov. 21, 1831.

Robinson, JOSEPH: *b.* Dublin, Aug. 20, 1816 ; *d.* there, Aug. 23, 1898. Singer and conductor. Studied under his father, Francis. Chorister in the Dublin Cathedrals. Member of the Philharmonic Orchestra, founder and conductor of the Ancient Concert Society, conductor of the University Choral Society (1837-47), teacher at the Irish Academy of Music (1856-76) and conductor of the Dublin Music Society (1876-88). He composed anthems, songs and partsongs.

Rochlitz [rockh'-lits], JOHANN FRIEDRICH: *b.* Leipzig, Feb. 12, 1769 ; *d.* there, Dec. 16, 1842. Music critic and poet. Studied at the Thomasschule in Leipzig. Founded the *Allgemeine musikalische Zeitung* in 1798, edited it until 1818, and wrote articles for it until 1835. He wrote oratorio texts, translated operas, edited a collection of vocal music from Dufay to Michael Haydn and composed a Mass, hymns and partsongs.

Rockstro (originally Rackstraw), WILLIAM SMITH: *b.* North Cheam (Surrey), Jan. 5, 1823 ; *d.* London, July 2, 1895. Writer on music and composer. Studied under Sterndale Bennett and at the Leipzig Conservatorium, where he was a friend of Mendelssohn. Organist in Babbacombe, 1876. Lecturer at the R.A.M. and R.C.M., 1891. He wrote biographies of Handel (1883), Mendelssohn (1884), and Jenny Lind, two histories of music (1879, 1886) and textbooks on harmony and counterpoint. He composed an oratorio, a ballet, madrigals, piano pieces and songs.

Rococo. *v.* STYLE GALANT.

Rodelinda [ro-deh-leen'-dah]. Opera in three acts by Handel. Libretto by Antonio Salvi (altered by Nicola Francesco Haym). First performed, London, Feb. 24, 1725.

Rode [rod], JACQUES PIERRE JOSEPH: *b.* Bordeaux, Feb. 16, 1774; *d.* nr. Damazon, Nov. 25, 1830. Violinist and composer. Studied under Viotti in Paris. Teacher of violin at the Paris Conservatoire, 1795. Court violinist in St. Petersburg under Boieldieu, 1803. From 1808 was in Paris, Vienna (1813), Berlin (1814), and later retired to Bordeaux. He was a fine player in his early years, but his powers had declined when he played Beethoven's sonata in G, Op. 96, for the composer in Vienna. Besides studies and caprices for violin he wrote 13 concertos for the instrument, quartets, duets for violins, and other short pieces.

Roger-Ducasse [rozh-ay-dĕĕ-cuss], JEAN JULES AIMABLE : *b.* Bordeaux, Apr. 18, 1873 ; *d.* July 20, 1954. Composer. Studied under Fauré at the Paris Conservatoire, where he won the second *Prix de Rome* in 1902, and under de Bériot, Pessard and Gédalge. Inspector of singing in the Paris schools, 1909 ; succeeded Dukas as teacher of composition at the Conservatoire, 1935. He composed an opera and a mimed drama, orchestral works, choral works with orchestra, motets and other vocal works, chamber music, songs and piano pieces.

Rogers, (1) BENJAMIN: *b.* Windsor June 2, 1614 ; *d.* Oxford, June 19, 1698. Organist and composer. Organist, Christ Church, Dublin, 1639 ; lay clerk, St. George's, Windsor, 1641 ; organist, Eton College, 1660 ; again at St. George's, 1662, and choirmaster and organist of Magdalen College in Oxford, 1664. He composed organ pieces, fancies for viols and organ, services, anthems and other church music. His " Te Deum Patrem colimus " is still sung from the top of Magdalen College tower on the morning of May 1.

(2) BERNARD: *b.* New York, Feb. 4, 1893. Composer. Studied at the Institute of Musical Art in New York and under Ernest Bloch in Cleveland. On the staff of *Musical America* and in 1938 was appointed teacher of composition at the Eastman School of Music in Rochester. He received a Pulitzer Scholarship and a Guggenheim Fellow-

ship. He has composed 2 operas, 4 symphonies and other orchestral works, an oratorio, cantatas, chamber music and songs.

Rohrflöte [rohrr′-flurt′-er], *G.* (*Fr.* flûte à cheminée). " Chimney flute." An organ stop of the flue type. The pipe is stopped at one end, but the stopper is pierced by a hole, in which is inserted a metal tube or chimney.

Rohrwerk [rohrr′-vairk], *G.* The reed stops on an organ.

Roi de Lahore, Le [ler rwa der la-orr] (The King of Lahore). Opera in five acts by Massenet. Libretto by Louis Gallet. First performed, Paris, Apr. 27, 1877.

Roi d'Ys, Le [ler rwa deece] (The King of Ys). Opera in three acts by Lalo. Libretto by Edouard Blau. First performed, Paris, May 7, 1888.

Roi l'a Dit, Le [ler rwa la dee] (The King has said it). Opera in three acts by Delibes. Libretto by Edmond Gondinet. First performed, Paris, May 24, 1873.

Roi Malgré Lui, Le [ler rwa mull-gray lee-ee] (The Involuntary King). Opera in three acts by Chabrier. Libretto by Emile de Najac and Paul Burani (based on a comedy by François Ancelot). First performed, Paris, May 18, 1887.

Roland [rol-ũn]. Opera by Lully with a prologue and five acts. Libretto by Philippe Quinault. First performed, Versailles, Jan. 8, 1685.

Roland-Manuel [rol-ũn-ma-nee-el] (originally Lévy, Roland Alexis Manuel) : *b.* Paris, March 22, 1891. Composer and writer on music. Studied under Roussel and Ravel. Has composed operas, chamber music (including a *Suite dans le goût espagnol* for oboe, bassoon, trumpet and harpsichord), orchestral works and film music. Has also written musical criticism, a book on Falla (1930) and three works on Ravel: *Maurice Ravel et son oeuvre* (1914), *Maurice Ravel et son oeuvre dramatique* (1928) and *Maurice Ravel* (1938 ; Eng. ed., 1947).

Rolland [rol-ũn], ROMAIN : *b.* Clamecy, Jan. 29, 1866 ; *d.* Vézelay, Dec. 30, 1944. Writer and musical historian. President of the musical division of the École des Hautes-Études Sociales, 1901. Lectured on musical history at the Sorbonne, from 1903 till 1913, when he retired to Switzerland. He returned to France in 1938. He wrote a valuable work on the opera of the 17th cent. (*Histoire de l'opéra en Europe avant Lulli et Scarlatti*, 1895), biographies of Handel and Beethoven, and shorter studies of other composers. Among the works which have been translated into English are *Beethoven* (1917), *Beethoven the Creator* (1929), *Goethe and Beethoven* (1931), *Musicians of Former Days* (1933) and *Musicians of To-day* (1933). The subject of his novel *Jean-Christophe* (1904-12) is a musician.

Rolle [rol′-er], JOHANN HEINRICH : *b.* Quedlinburg, Dec. 23, 1718 ; *d.* Magdeburg, Dec. 29, 1785. Composer. Organist of St. Peter's, Magdeburg, 1732-6 ; law student at Leipzig University, 1734-40 ; violist in the court orchestra of Frederick the Great, 1741-6. Organist of St. John's, Magdeburg, 1746 ; succeeded his father, Christian Friedrich, as municipal music director, 1752. He composed 20 oratorios, sets of cantatas, 5 Passions, motets and organ works.

Rolltrommel [rol′-trom-ĕl], *G.* *v.* TENOR DRUM.

Roman [roo′-mun], JOHAN HELMICH : *b.* Stockholm, Oct. 26, 1694 ; *d.* Haraldsmåla, near Kalmar, Oct. 19, 1758. Composer. Studied under Ariosti and Pepusch in London and was in the service of the Duke of Newcastle. Returned to Stockholm (1720) where he was appointed *Kapellmeister* (1729). Visited Italy, France and England (1735-37), became a member of the Swedish Academy in 1740 and retired in 1745. He composed a Mass, motets and psalms, 21 symphonies, overtures, concertos, sonatas for violin and for flute and vocal works.

Romance (*G.* Romanze, *I.* romanza). A title used occasionally for a piece of instrumental or vocal music. Examples are the second movement of Mozart's piano concerto in D minor, K.466, Beethoven's two Romances for violin and orchestra, Op. 40 and Op. 50, Schumann's three Romances, Op. 94, for oboe and piano, the second movement of his fourth symphony, and his four sets of

Romanzen und Balladen for mixed voices, Brahms's Fifteen Romances from Tieck's *Magelone* for voice and piano, Op. 33, and Fauré's Romance for violin and orchestra, Op. 28.

Roman de Fauvel [rom-ũñ der fo-vel]. A poem written in 1310-14 by Gervais de Bus, in which he attacked abuses prevalent in the Church at the time. The letters of the word *Fauvel* represent the first letters of *Flaterie, Avarice, Vilaniè, Variété, Envie* and *Lacheté.* The manuscript of the poem, now in the Bibliothèque Nationale, Paris (facsimile ed. by P. Aubry, 1907), contains a number of musical pieces written in by Chaillou de Pesstain in 1316, consisting of motets, monophonic pieces and plainsong pieces. The motets are printed in *Polyphonic Music of the Fourteenth Century*, i, ed. L. Schrade (1956).

Romanesca [ro-mah-ness'-ca], *Sp.* The earliest settings of this song ("O guardame las vacas") occur in Spanish lute-books about 1540, *e.g.* in Alonso Mudarra's *Tres libros de música en cifra para vihuela* (1546; modern edition by E. Pujol, 1949). A version used in a set of variations by A. de Valderravano in 1547 is printed in the *Historical Anthology*, No. 124. The simplest form of its bass:

became known as the *romanesca* bass, and was used as a basis for variations in the same fashion as was the PASSAMEZZO bass. Frescobaldi wrote a set of variations on it (*Partite sopra l'aria della Romanesca*) in the *Toccate d'Involatura* of 1614, and his *Arie Musicali per Cantarsi* of 1630 contains an *Aria di romanesca* which begins thus:

Romantic Music. The Romantic era in music may be dated *c.* 1820 (Weber's *Der Freischütz* was produced in 1821; Schubert scored the *Unfinished* Symphony in 1822 and wrote *Die schöne Mullerin* in 1823) to *c.* 1920 (Schönberg arrived at the principles of "twelve-note composition" in 1921; Stravinsky composed *Histoire du Soldat* in 1918). In the broadest terms, the change from the Classical age to the Romantic may be described as a change of emphasis from the universal to the individual (Rousseau: "I am different from all men I have seen"); from the conservative to the liberal (Hugo : [Romanticism is] "Liberalism in literature"); from the abstract to the poetic (Schumann : "Romanticism is not a question of figures and forms, but of the composer's being a poet or not"). In such a period music, because its symbols are more remote than those of the other arts, is considered the ideal of the arts (E. T. A. Hoffman : "Music is the most Romantic of all the arts"; Schopenhauer : "Music is the direct manifestation of the original nature of the world, of the will"), music and poetry are more intimately allied (Baudelaire: "La poésie touche à la musique par une prosodie dont les racines plongent plus avant dans l'âme humaine que ne l'indique aucune théorie classique"; Mallarmé : "La musique rejoint le vers pour former, depuis Wagner, la poésie"), and a union of the arts becomes the highest form of art. There is a clear relation between these ideas and the chief forms which were developed in the 19th cent., the *Lied*, the poetic piano-piece, the symphonic poem, and the music-drama.

Within the broad unifying ideas of Romantic music there developed such apparent contradictions as those between the musician's remoteness from society, in that he regarded himself as essentially different from his fellows and was no longer, with them, a member of a patron's household, and his closeness to it, expressed in his use of folksong and national idioms and in the development of virtuosos and of public concerts: between the "modernist" and more conservative elements in the movement itself, which led to the controversy between the supporters of the "New Music" and those of Brahms; and between the cultivation of the smaller and more intimate forms and the creation of the largest and most spectacular. The attitude of the Romantic musician to the past, which is chiefly, as in most periods, a rejection of the immediate past, may take the form of valuing it for its remoteness (*e.g.* the use of exotic and medieval subjects for operas), adopting its methods (*e.g.* Brahms's use of fugue and variations), and investigating and publishing its productions (*e.g.* the editions of the Tudor composers, and of Palestrina, Schütz, Purcell, Bach, Handel).

The changes in style and in technical matters which took place during the Romantic period can be most clearly seen in (1) harmony, which went through a very rapid development of chromaticism (valuable to the Romantic composer because of its ambiguity, sense of remoteness, and tension) to its extreme forms in *Tristan* and in the writing of Strauss and Schönberg between 1900 and 1910; (2) the orchestra, which grew rapidly from the time of Berlioz's new conception of its possibilities of dramatic and poetic expression to the monster orchestras of 1900-1910 in Strauss's *Ein Heldenleben*, Schönberg's *Gurrelieder* and Mahler's eighth symphony; and (3) the technique of instruments, which from the invention of the valve mechanism in 1813 kept pace with the development of chromatic harmony and the growth of the orchestra, and in the extension of the capacities of the piano and organ provided solo players with media of greatly increased power and range. Of less importance were the changes in melodic style, which tended to become more lyrical in the small forms and more rhetorical in the large, in rhythmic style, which in some composers tended to become more diffused by the use of conflicting metres and of rubato, and in form, in which the Romantic composers aimed at a greater continuity of texture, a more "organic" unfolding and development of themes, and a closer relation to the programme in a symphonic poem or to the dramatic conflict in a music-drama.

In the two decades 1890-1910 a new conflict in the working out of the Romantic ideal in music appeared between the two forms of the association of music and poetry, one represented by the extreme realism of Strauss's later tone-poems and the other by the Impressionist (or symbolist) style developed by Debussy under the influence of Mallarmé and his circle. *v.* IMPRESSIONISM.

Romberg [rom'-bairk], (1) ANDREAS JAKOB: *b.* Vechta (nr. Münster), Apr. 27, 1767; *d.* Gotha, Nov. 10, 1821. Violinist and composer at 9. He played at the Concert Spirituel in Paris at the age of 17, toured with his cousin Bernhard from 1784-96 and played with him in the Electoral Court Orchestra in Bonn from 1790-93. He settled in Hamburg in 1801 until appointed court conductor in Gotha in 1815. He composed operas, choral works, symphonies, numerous violin concertos, string quartets and other chamber music, part-songs and pieces for violin.

(2) BERNHARD: *b.* Dinklage (Oldenburg), Nov. 12, 1767; *d.* Hamburg, Aug. 13, 1841. Cellist and composer. Toured with his cousin Andreas from 1784-96 and played with him in the Electoral Court Orchestra in Bonn from 1790-93, taught at the Paris Conservatoire from 1800-03, was first cellist (1805-06) and conductor (1815-19) of the Berlin Court Orchestra, and in 1819 retired to Hamburg. He also gave concerts in England, France, Spain, Austria, Sweden and Russia. He composed operas, 10 cello concertos and other works for cello, incidental music for plays and chamber music.

Romeo and Juliet. (1) Orchestral piece by Tchaikovsky, originally (1869) described as "overture." Twice revised, in 1870 and 1880, and after the second revision called "overture-fantasia."

(2) Opera in four acts by John Edmund Barkworth, a setting of Shakespeare's text. First performed, Middlesbrough, July 1, 1916.

v. also ROMÉO ET JULIETTE, ROMEO UND JULIA AUF DEM DORFE.

Roméo et Juliette [rom-ay-o ay zhēēl-yet] (Romeo and Juliet). (1) Dramatic symphony in 7 movements for soloists, chorus and orchestra by Berlioz, Op. 17 (1839), described as "after Shakespeare's tragedy." A complete performance is unusual. The best known movement is No. 4, the *Queen Mab* scherzo. The work is dedicated to Paganini, who had given Berlioz 20,000 francs.

(2) Opera in five acts by Gounod. Libretto by Jules Barbier and Michel Carré (after Shakespeare). First performed, Paris, Apr. 27, 1867.

Romeo und Julia auf dem Dorfe [rom-ay'-o o͝ont yool'-i-a owf dem dorrf'-*er*] (A Village Romeo and Juliet). Opera by Delius, with a prologue and 3 acts. Libretto by the composer (based on a story by Gottfried Keller). First performed, Berlin, Feb. 21, 1907. The lands of Manz and Marti (two farmers) are separated by a narrow strip of ground which has been allowed to run wild by the Dark Fiddler (the bastard son of its former owner). The farmers' children (Sali, the son of Manz, and Vrenchen, the daughter of Marti) use this strip of wild land as their playground until the farmers, each having encroached on the plot, finally have a violent quarrel over it and separate, taking their children with them. While their fathers are involved in a long and expensive law action Sali and Vrenchen meet secretly on their beloved playground. But one day they are discovered together by Marti, who tries to drag his daughter from her lover's arms and is later sent to a lunatic asylum. Sali comes to visit the destitute Vrenchen on the last night she may spend in her old home and they both dream that they are being married in a church. The next day they go to a fair, but being disturbed by the malicious tongues of local gossipers they walk to an inn, where they meet the Dark Fiddler and his vagabond friends, who invite them to join their company and live with them in the mountains. They refuse, feeling that this would not be the ideal life they both long for. Hearing a boatman's song they decide that they will also drift down the river and "drift away for ever." They find a barge filled with hay moored to the river-bank, which Sali proclaims is their marriage-bed. After drifting a little way down the river he pulls the plug from the bottom of the boat and throws it into the river. In the far distance is heard the voice of the boatman: "Heigho, travellers we a-passing by."

Ronde [ro͡nd], *Fr.* Semibreve.

Rondeau [ro͡n-do], *Fr.* A form of medieval French poetry, practised by the trouvères and by poets of the 14th and 15th cent., which has a recurring refrain. Musical settings by the trouvères were monophonic. Polyphonic *rondeaux* were composed by Adam de la Hale, by Machaut to his own poems, and by Grenon, Binchois, Dufay and many other composers in the 15th cent. The music of a *rondeau* is composed of two sections, which serve both for the refrain and the verses. The simplest type with six lines, *e.g.* :

has this form : *aAabAB*, capital letters indicating the refrain which is underlined in the example. In the more elaborate type (used in polyphonic *rondeaux*) the complete refrain was sung at the beginning as well as at the end, giving the form *ABaAabAB* ; the first section of the refrain, and of each verse, had either two or three lines, and the second section two lines. Examples of the four-line rondeau (*rondeau quatrain*) by Binchois (*De plus en plus*) and of the five-line rondeau (*rondeau cinquaine*) by Arnold de Lantins (*Puisque je voy*) are printed in the *Historical Anthology*, Nos. 69 and 71.

(2) A form of French instrumental music in the baroque period, *e.g.*, the *Rondeau* and the *Passacaille en rondeau* in François Couperin's eighth *ordre* for harpsichord, in which the opening section recurs after each of two (as in the former) or more (as in the latter) different sections, called *couplets*.

Rondel (*L.* rondellus). *v.* ROUND.

Rondes de Printemps [ro͡nd der pra͡n-tu͡n], *Fr.* *v.* IMAGES.

Rondine, La [lah ron′-dee-neh] (The Swallow). Opera in two acts by Puccini. Libretto by Giuseppe Adami (adapted from a German libretto by Alfred Maria Willner and Heinrich Reichert). First performed, Monte Carlo, March 27, 1917.

Rondo. A form of instrumental music with a recurring section. It may occur as a single piece, *e.g.* Mozart's Rondo for piano in A minor, K. 511, or more often as the last movement of a sonata, symphony or concerto. The chief varieties of the form are : (a) The simple rondo, in which the opening section alternates with a number of different sections, or "episodes," in the form *ABACADA* . . . , as in the third movement of Bach's violin concerto in E ; (b) The symmetrical rondo, in which the first episode, initially in the dominant key, returns at a later stage in the tonic, as in the last movement of Beethoven's piano sonata in E♭, Op. 7, in the form *A B* (in the dominant) *A C* (in the relative minor) *A B* (in the tonic) *A*; or the last movement of Mozart's piano sonata in B♭, K.281, in the form *A B* (dominant) *A C* (relative minor) *A D* (subdominant) *A B* (tonic) *A*. In this variety, as in the "sonata-rondo," there are commonly transitions between the sections and a coda, and the recurring section is varied and shortened, though always in the tonic key : (c) the sonata-rondo, having three sections, corresponding to the exposition, development and recapitulation of a sonata movement, and two episodes, of which the first returns in the dominant and the second is actually a development. Instances are frequent in Beethoven, *e.g.* the last movement of the piano sonata in G, Op. 31, No. 1, in the form *A B* (dominant) *A C* (development) *A B* (tonic) *A*. A variety of (b) and (c) is the short-circuited rondo, in which the third appearance of *A* is omitted, so that the form is *A B A C B A*. Examples are frequent in Mozart, Schubert and Brahms, *e.g.*, the finale of Mozart's string quintet in G minor, K.516.

Ronger [ro͡n-zhay], FLORIMOND. *v.* HERVÉ.

Röntgen [rurnt′-gĕn], JULIUS : *b.* Leipzig, May 9, 1855 ; *d.* Utrecht, Sept. 13, 1932. Composer. Son of Engelbert Röntgen, Dutch violinist who was leader of the Leipzig Gewandhaus Orchestra from 1873. He studied at the Leipzig Conservatorium and from 1878 taught at the Amsterdam Music School. In 1885 he was one of the founders of the new Amsterdam Conservatoire, which he directed from 1918-24. He was a friend of Brahms and Grieg and edited Brahms's correspondence with Theodor Engelmann (1918). His compositions include 2 operas, a symphony, concertos for piano and violin, chamber music, and arrangements of Dutch folksongs. Donald Tovey called him "one of the greatest musical scholars within the orbit of Brahms", and wrote analyses of his symphony, triple concerto for violin, viola and cello (*Essays in Musical Analysis*, vol. ii) and *Old Netherland Suite* for orchestra (*ibid.*, vol. iv).

Root. A term used by 19th-cent. theorists to indicate the "fundamental" or "generating" note of a chord. According to this theory the chords:

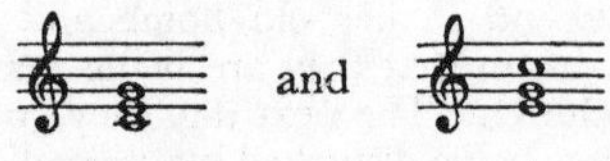

have the same "root" C ; the former is

said to be in root position, *i.e.* having the " root " in the lowest part, and the latter the first INVERSION. Likewise

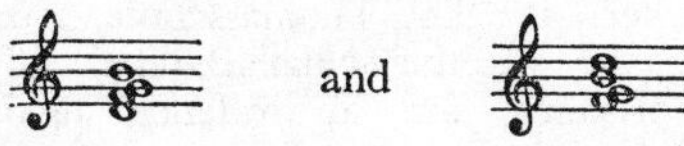

are respectively the second and third " inversions " of the dominant seventh chord :

of which the " root " is G. *v.* HARMONY, INVERSION.

Rootham, CYRIL BRADLEY: *b.* Bristol, Oct. 5, 1875 ; *d.* Cambridge, March 18, 1938. Organist and composer. Studied under Parratt and Stanford at the R.C.M., and at St. John's College, Cambridge, where he became organist in 1901. Conductor, Cambridge University Musical Society, 1912 ; university lecturer, 1913. He composed an opera—*The Two Sisters* (Cambridge, 1922), choral works with orchestra, 2 symphonies (the second completed by Patrick Hadley) and other orchestral works, chamber music, songs and part-songs, pieces for violin, flute, piano and organ.

Ropartz [ro-parrts], JOSEPH GUY MARIE: *b.* Guingamp (Côtes-du-Nord), June 15, 1864 ; *d.* Nov. 22, 1955. Composer. Studied under Dubois and Massenet at the Paris Conservatoire and under César Franck. Director, Nancy Conservatoire, 1894 ; Strasbourg Conservatoire, 1919-29. Later retired to Brittany. He composed 5 symphonies and other orchestral works, 2 operas, chamber music, Masses, motets and other church music, choral works, incidental music for plays, works for piano and for organ, and songs.

Roquet [rock-ay], ANTOINE ERNEST. *v.* THOINAN.

Rore [deh ro'-reh], CIPRIANO DE: *b.* Antwerp or Malines, 1516 ; *d.* Parma, 1565. Composer. Studied under Willaert in Venice, went to Ferrara *c.* 1547, where he was appointed court *maestro di cappella c.* 1549. Was in Flanders 1558-61, then at Parma, succeeded Willaert as *maestro di cappella* of St. Mark's in 1563, but in 1564 returned to the court at Parma; He published 5 books of five-part and 3 books of four-part madrigals, motets, Masses, a St. John Passion (1557) and other church music, and a volume of three-part fantasies and ricercari (with Willaert, 1549). The greatest madrigal writer of his time, he established the five-part madrigal in imitative polyphony as the norm, and after 1550 added to his style the expressive chromaticism and harmonic experiments which were developed by later composers, such as Marenzio and Gesualdo. Five madrigals are printed in the third volume of A. Einstein's *The Italian Madrigal* (1949), and single examples in the *Historical Anthology,* No. 131, and in Schering's *History of Music in Examples,* No. 106.

Rosamunde, Fürstin von Cypern [ro-zum-ōōnd'-er fēērst'-in fon tsēēp'-ern] (Rosamund, Princess of Cyprus). Play in four acts by Helmina von Chézy, produced, with incidental music by Schubert, at the Theater-an-der-Wien, Vienna, Dec. 20, 1823. The overture played at that performance had been written for *Alfonso und Estrella.* The overture now known as *Rosamunde* was originally the overture to *Die Zauberharfe* (*The Magic Harp*) produced in 1820, and was published in a piano duet arrangement under the title *Ouvertüre zum Drama Rosamunde* about 1827.

Roseingrave, (1) DANIEL: *d.* Dublin, May, 1727. Organist and composer. Chorister of the Chapel Royal. Organist, Gloucester Cathedral, 1679 ; Winchester, 1682 ; Salisbury, 1692 ; St. Patrick's and Christ Church, Dublin, 1698. He composed services, anthems and other church music.

(2) RALPH: *b.* Salisbury, *c.* 1695 ; *d.* Dublin, 1747. Organist and composer. Son of (1). Studied under his father, whom he succeeded as vicar-choral (1719) and organist (1726) of St. Patrick's Cathedral, Dublin, and as organist of Christ Church Cathedral (1727). He composed services and anthems.

(3) THOMAS : *b.* Winchester, 1690 ; *d.*

Dunleary (nr. Dublin), June 23, 1766. Organist and composer. Son of (1), brother of (2). Studied under his father and at Trinity College, Dublin, travelled to Italy in 1710 and became a friend of Domenico Scarlatti. He settled in London, was appointed organist of St. George's, Hanover Square, in 1725 and later returned to Dublin. He composed an opera, 6 Italian cantatas, services and other church music, *Fifteen Voluntarys and Fugues* for organ or harpsichord, lessons for harpsichord or spinet, pieces for German flute with continuo, additional songs for Scarlatti's opera *Narciso*, which he produced in London (1720). and edited a collection of sonatas by Scarlatti.

Rosenkavalier, Der (dair ro′-zĕn-cuv-ull-eer′] (The Knight of the Rose). Opera in three acts by Richard Strauss. Libretto by Hugo von Hofmannsthal. First performed, Dresden, Jan. 26, 1911. The Princess von Werdenberg is entertaining her lover Octavian (a youth of seventeen) in the absence of her husband (a Field-Marshal), when Baron von Lerchenau (a cousin of the Princess) is announced and Octavian is forced to disguise himself hastily as a chamber maid. The Baron, who is seeking a messenger to be the bearer of a silver rose (his betrothal token) to Sophie (daughter of a wealthy noble), is charmed by the supposed chambermaid. After his departure the Princess, who is cynical about her growing age, delivers the rose to Octavian in order that he may take it to Sophie. When Octavian visits Sophie to bring her the rose he falls in love with her, but her father is determined that she shall marry the Baron. Octavian later returns to his maid's disguise to keep an appointment which he had made with the Baron to meet him at a country tavern. Here the Baron is made very much an object of ridicule. He calls for the police, who in turn demand an explanation of his presence there with a young woman. Sophie now receives her outraged father's permission not to marry the Baron. The Princess, now resigned to the loss of Octavian, induces him to give his blessing to the young pair.

Rosenmüller [ro′-zĕn-me͞el-er], JOHANN: *b.* Ölsnitz (Vogtland), *c.* 1620; buried Wolfenbüttel, Sept. 12, 1684. Composer. Studied at Leipzig University. Assistant master at the Thomasschule, 1642; organist at the Nikolaikirche, 1651. Imprisoned for an offence against morals in 1655, but later escaped and went to Hamburg and to Venice until 1674, when he returned to Germany as court conductor at Wolfenbüttel. He composed sonatas and dance suites for instruments, Masses, Latin and German motets with instruments and continuo, cantatas, psalms and other church music. He was one of the most important composers of Lutheran church music between Schütz and Buxtehude. His setting of the *Lamentations* for solo voice and continuo is printed in the *Historical Anthology*, No. 218, and 11 suites from his *Sonate da camera a* 5, first printed in Venice in 1667, in *D.D.T.*, xviii.

Rosseter, PHILIP: *b. c.* 1568; *d.* London, May 5, 1623. Composer of songs to the lute. The second portion, consisting of twenty-one songs, in *A Booke of Ayres* published in 1601 is by Rosseter, the first part being by his friend Campian; modern ed. by E. H. Fellowes in *E.S.L.S.* 1st ser. He published in 1609 a set of consort lessons "made by sundrie excellent Authors and set to sixe severall instruments."

Rossi [ross′-see], (1) LAURO: *b.* Macerata, Feb. 19, 1812; *d.* Cremona, May 5, 1885. Composer and conductor. Studied in Naples and produced operas from the age of 18. Conductor, Teatro Valle, Rome, 1832. Went to Milan in 1834, to Mexico in 1835 and later to Havana, New Orleans and Madras. Returned to Italy in 1844. Director, Milan Conservatorio, 1850; Naples Conservatorio, 1870. Retired to Cremona in 1880. He composed 29 operas, cantatas, an oratorio and a Mass, six fugues for string quartet, and songs, and wrote a textbook on harmony.

(2) LUIGI: *b.* Torre Maggiore, *c.* 1598; *d.* Rome, Feb. 19, 1653. A prolific composer of cantatas in monodic style, of which about 250 have survived. His arias are generally in binary form, but

occasionally, as in the solo cantata "Io lo vedo," printed in the *Historical Anthology* (No. 203), there is a short *da capo*. His longer cantatas show a clear distinction between recitative, aria and arioso. The opera *Palazzo d'Atlante incantato* was staged in the Barberini Palace in Rome in 1642, and *Orfeo*, the first Italian opera commissioned for performance in Paris though not the first to be played there, was produced at the Palais Royal in 1647. Extracts from *Orfeo* are printed in H. Goldschmidt, *Studien zur Geschichte der italienischen Oper im* 17. *Jahrhundert*, pp. 295-311.

(3) MICHEL ANGELO. Early 17th-cent. Italian organist and composer. Studied under Frescobaldi in Rome. He composed operas and a book of *Toccate e Correnti* (2nd ed., 1657) for organ or harpischord. Extracts from his opera *Erminia sul Giordano*, staged in the Barberini Palace, Rome, in 1633, are printed in H. Goldschmidt's, *Studien zur Geschichte der italienischen Oper im* 17. *Jahrhundert*, pp. 258-272; 10 toccatas from the publication of 1657 and 10 *correnti* for harpischord in L. Torchi's *L'arte musicale in Italia*, vol. iii. The toccata in A printed as Bach's in *B.G.*, xlii, p. 250, and as Purcell's in *Purcell Society*, vi, p. 42, is probably by M. A. Rossi.

(4) SALOMONE. 16th-17th cent. Jewish composer, who was at the court of Mantua from 1587 to 1628. He published 5 books of five-part madrigals between 1600 and 1622. The second book (1602) was probably the earliest book of madrigals to be published with a continuo part (*basso continuo per sonare in Concerto*). In 1628 he published a set of *Madrigaletti a due*. That he was one of the modernists of his time is also shown by his early use of the medium of the trio sonata in his 2 volumes of *Sinfonie e gagliarde a* 3-5 (1607-8). He published 2 further volumes of instrumental music, and in 1620 a volume of church music.

Rossignol [ross-een-yol] (Nightingale). Opera in three acts by Stravinsky. Libretto (in Russian) by the composer and Stepan Nikolaevich Mitusov (based on Hans Andersen's tale). First performed, Paris, May 26, 1914. Produced as a ballet, *Le Chant du Rossignol*, with choreography by Massine, Paris, Feb. 2, 1920.

Rossini [ross-see'-nee], GIOACCHINO ANTONIO: *b.* Pesaro, Feb. 29, 1792; *d.* Paris, Nov. 13, 1868. Composer. Studied at the Liceo Musicale in Bologna, and produced his first comic opera, *La cambiale di matrimonio*, in 1810, and *Tancredi*, his first *opera seria*, in 1813, both in Venice. Under the title *Almaviva* his *Il barbiere di Siviglia* had an unfortunate first night at Rome in 1816, but later became his greatest triumph. Between 1816 and 1824, when he became director of the Théâtre Italien in Paris, *Otello* and *Mosé in Egitto* were produced in Naples, *La Cenerentola* in Rome, and *Semiramide* in Venice; in Paris were staged *Moïse* (a revised version of *Mosé in Egitto*), *Le Comte Ory*, and *Guillaume Tell*, apart from *Il barbiere di Siviglia* his most renowned work. As a result of the revolution of 1830 his contract with the government to write 5 operas in the following 10 years was broken; his claim to an annuity was, however, granted in 1835. He had composed 40 operas in 15 years, and during the remainder of his life wrote only the *Stabat mater* (1842), the *Petite Messe solennelle* (1864) and some short pieces. After living in Italy from 1836 to 1855, Rossini settled in Paris, where his house was famous as a meeting place and he as a wit. Besides opera, he composed cantatas, songs and piano pieces (*Péchés de vieillesse*, 1857-68), and 6 wood-wind quartets.

LORD DERWENT: *Rossini and some Forgotten Nightingales* (1934).

F. TOYE: *Rossini; a study in Tragicomedy* (1934).

F. BONAVIA: *Rossini* (1941).

G. RADICIOTTI: *Gioacchino Rossini* (3 vols. 1927-9).

Rota *v.* ROUND.

Rotta. A medieval instrument with plucked strings, also known as *chrotta*. *v.* CRWTH.

Rouget de Lisle [roo-zhade-leel], CLAUDE JOSEPH: *b.* Lons-le-Saulnier, May 10, 1760; *d.* Choisy-le-Roi (nr. Paris), June 26, 1836. Royalist soldier, poet, violinist, and composer. He settled in Strasbourg in 1791, wrote the words and music of the *Marseillaise* in 1792 and was imprisoned during the Revolution. He also wrote hymns, romances with violin obbligato, *Chants français* with piano and libretti for operas.

Round. A composition in three or more parts in which the parts enter in succession with the same music and words, sing as many phrases as there are parts, and return to the first phrase. The phrases are of equal length, and are so written as to make harmony. The round and the CATCH, a variety of round, were much sung on convivial occasions in England in the 17th and 18th cent. The form goes back to the medieval *rota* (lit. " wheel "), of which the most famous example is " Sumer is icumen in " (*q. v.*). The *rondellus*, which was discussed by Walter Odington *c.* 1300, is composed in the same fashion, but the singers begin together. The following is the beginning of a 13th-cent. English *rondellus*:

Rousseau [roo-so], JEAN-JACQUES: *b.* Geneva, June 28, 1712; *d.* Ermenonville (nr. Paris), July 2, 1778. Apart from the observations on music and musical education in the writings of Rousseau, his direct interventions into the musical life of his time are not without interest. His own education in music was slight, and his opera-ballet *Les Muses galantes*, privately produced in 1747, was a failure. His one-act *intermède, Le Devin du village*, was an immediate and lasting success, as were both the French and German versions of Favart's parody *Les Amours de Bastien et Bastienne* (the latter set by Mozart). Paradoxically, however, Rousseau took the side of Italian opera in the *guerre des bouffons*, declaring in his *Lettre sur la musique française* that " the French have no music, and never will have any." Rousseau composed two pieces for the melodrama *Pigmalion* (Lyons, 1770), the rest of the music being by Coignet; some music for an opera *Daphnis et Chloé* and a volume of songs with the title *Consolations des misères de ma vie* were published after his death. In 1743 he proposed a new system of musical notation by numbers in a *Dissertation sur la musique moderne.* His articles on music in Diderot's *Encyclopédie* were severely criticised by Rameau, but his *Dictionnaire de musique* (1767) has valuable information on the musical terminology and ideas of the period. He wrote two pamphlets in support of Gluck, one being a commentary on *Alceste*, written at the request of the composer, in the form of a letter to Burney.

A. R. OLIVER: *The Encyclopedists as Critics of Music* (1947).
A. POUGIN: *Jean-Jacques Rousseau musicien* (1901).
J. TIERSOT: *Jean-Jacques Rousseau* (1912).

Roussel [roo-sel], ALBERT: *b.* Tourcoing, April 5, 1869; *d.* Royan, Aug. 23, 1937. Composer. Marine officer in Indo-China from 1887 to 1894, then studied under Gigout and Vincent d'Indy at the Schola Cantorum, where he was appointed teacher of counterpoint in 1902. Visited Cochin China and India and served in the war of 1914-18. He composed operas, ballets, 4 symphonies and other orchestral works, chamber music, songs and piano pieces. Taking its departure from the late Romantic style of Franck and d'Indy, as in his first symphony (*Le Poème de la forêt*) of 1908, his music developed through a period of Impressionism in such works as *Évocations* (1912) to the mature and impressive writing of the *Eightieth Psalm* for chorus and orchestra (1928) and the third symphony (1930).

N. DEMUTH: *Albert Roussel* (1947).
A. HOÉRÉE: *Albert Roussel* (1937).
L. VUILLEMIN: *Albert Roussel et son oeuvre* (1924).

Rovescio, Al [ahl ro-vess'-sho], *I.* "In reverse." (1) Melodic INVERSION. (2) RETROGRADE MOTION.

Rowley, ALEC: *b.* London, March 13, 1892; *d.* Shepperton, Jan. 12, 1958. Composer, pianist and organist. Studied at the R.A.M. under Corder and Richards. Teacher and examiner, Trinity College of Music, 1920. He composed 2 piano concertos, a suite and other works for orchestra, a ballet (Carnegie award, 1927), cantatas and other choral works, chamber music, numerous pieces for organ, piano and violin, and songs.

Roy [ler rwa], ADRIEN LE. 16th-cent. French lutenist, composer, and music printer in partnership with Robert Ballard. He wrote an instruction book for the lute (1557) and for the guitar (1578), and published a collection of *Airs de cour* for the lute (1571), and 20 books of *chansons* between 1551 and 1568. His lute-book of 1557 exists only in the English translations printed in 1568 and 1574.

Royal Philharmonic Orchestra. Founded by Sir Thomas Beecham in 1946. It takes its name from the Royal Philharmonic Society, for whose concerts it regularly plays. Its other activities include independent concerts in London, the provinces and abroad, and playing for opera at Glyndebourne (Sussex).

Royal Philharmonic Society. A society for the encouragement of orchestral and instrumental music founded in London in 1813. The title "Royal" was granted on its centenary. The first series of concerts in 1813 were conducted at the piano by Clementi, and Salomon was the leader. Spohr conducted with a baton on his first visit to the society in 1820, and the term "conductor" was used thereafter instead of "at the pianoforte." Many works were introduced to England at concerts of the society; among new works commissioned by it were Beethoven's ninth symphony (1825), Mendelssohn's *Italian* symphony (1833), Dvořák's *Husitzka* overture (1884), Saint-Saëns's symphony in C minor (1886), and Stanford's symphony in D minor (1911-12).

R. ELKIN: *Royal Philharmonic* (1946).
M. B. FOSTER: *History of the Philharmonic Society of London* (1912).
T. RUSSELL: *Philharmonic Decade* (1945).

Rubato [roo-bah'-toh], *I.* Lit. "robbed." Controlled flexibility of tempo by which notes are deprived of part of their length by slight quickening of the tempo, or given more than their strict length by slight slowing. Such "expressive" variation of tempo may have been practised by solo performers in the 16th and 17th cent.; J. J. Froberger's lament (*Tombeau*) on the death of M. Blancrocher (*D.T.Ö.*, x (2), p. 114), for example, was marked by the composer to be played very slowly, and "without observing any beat." The use of *rubato* is referred to in the 18th-cent. writings of C. P. E. Bach, Leopold Mozart and others. There are contemporary accounts of Chopin's style of *rubato*, and it is commonly applied to the performance of both solo and orchestral music of the 19th cent. In so far as *rubato*, which is at its best when least obtrusive and least susceptible to analysis, can be defined, it may affect: (*a*) an ornamental group of notes in a melody over a standing harmony; or (*b*) a phrase of melody, while the accompaniment keeps a strict rhythm; this is said to have been characteristic of Chopin's *rubato*, and Leopold Mozart observed that "when a true virtuoso who is worthy of the title is to be accompanied, then one must not allow oneself to be beguiled by the postponing or anticipating of the notes which he knows how to shape so adroitly and touchingly, into hesitating or hurrying, but must continue to play throughout in the same manner," (translation by Editha Knocker); or (*c*) the melody and harmony of a phrase, period, or section of a composition.

J. B. MCEWEN: *Tempo Rubato or Time-variation in Musical Performance* (1928).

Rubbra, CHARLES EDMUND : *b.* Northampton, May 23, 1901. Composer and pianist. Studied at Reading University and the R.C.M. Lecturer, Oxford, 1947. Hon. D.Mus., Durham, 1949. The chief influence in his work is that of the music of the 16th cent. This influence results in acute awareness of melody and in the use of every kind of contrapuntal elaboration. He has, on the whole, been less successful in vocal music than in instrumental works, where his instinct for thematic development has had more scope. His orchestration, which at first was almost excessively austere, has shown a greater interest in colour in his later works. His compositions include 7 symphonies, concertos for viola and piano, *Festival Overture*, 3 Masses, motets, madrigals, 2 string quartets, piano trio, 2 violin sonatas, cello sonata, and songs.

Rubinstein [roo'-bin-shtine], (1) ANTON GREGORYEVICH: *b.* Vekhvotinets (Podolia), Nov. 28, 1829; *d.* Peterhof, Nov. 20, 1894. Composer and pianist. Toured as a pianist from 1840 to 1843, studied with Dehn in Berlin 1844-46, and after other tours settled in 1858 in St. Petersburg, where he founded the Conservatoire and was its director from 1862-7 and again from 1887-90. As a composer and teacher he represented the traditional Western and anti-national ideas in Russian music. He adopted the methods of Liszt in such works as the three *Musical Portraits* (*Faust, Ivan the Terrible, Don Quixote*) for orchestra, but his numerous compositions had not enough individual qualities to take any lasting place in musical history. His autobiography was translated into English by A. Delano (1890).

(2) NICHOLAS: *b.* Moscow, June 14, 1835; *d.* Paris, March 23, 1881. Pianist, conductor and composer. Brother of (1). Studied under Kullak (piano) and Dehn (composition) in Berlin from 1844-46, and settled in Moscow, where he founded the Russian Musical Society in 1860 and the Conservatoire in 1866. His pupils included Sauer, Siloti and Taneiev. He introduced the early works of Tchaikovsky, who dedicated to him the piano trio in A minor, Op. 50.

Ruckers [rēēk'-erce], HANS: *b. c.* 1550; *d.* soon after 1623. The first member of a family of harpischord makers who lived in Antwerp, and whose instruments were famous for their quality and tone. They were made from *c.* 1580 to *c.* 1670, and many were still in use late in the 18th cent. After Hans the chief members of the family were his sons Hans the younger, also called Jean (*b.* 1578), and Andries (*b.* 1579), and the latter's son Andries the younger (*b.* 1607).

Rückpositif [rēēk'-po-zee-teef'], *G. v.* CHAIR ORGAN.

Ruddigore (originally *Ruddygore*). Comic opera in two acts by Sullivan. Libretto by William Schwenk Gilbert. First performed, London, Jan. 22, 1887.

Rue [der la rēē], PIERRE DE LA (Petrus Platensis): *b.* Picardy, *c.* 1460; *d.* Courtrai, Nov. 20, 1518. Composer. A disciple of Okeghem, he was in the service of Maximilian from 1492, of Philip of Burgundy in Brussels from 1496 to 1506, and subsequently of Margaret of Austria, Regent of the Netherlands. He held a canonry at Courtrai, and retired there in 1516. Some of his Masses were published by Petrucci and other early printers, and some motets and *chansons* in various collections between 1501 and 1560. There are few modern editions. The Mass *Ave Maria* was published by H. Expert in *Maîtres musiciens de la Renaissance française*, *Kyries* I and II from the *L'Homme armé* Mass in the *Historical Anthology of Music*, No. 92, and the *Kyrie* from the Mass *De Sancto Antonio* in Schering's *History of Music in Examples*, No. 65.

Ruffo [roof'-fo], VINCENZO: *b.* Verona, *c.* 1520; *d.* Sacile (nr. Udine), Feb. 9, 1587. Composer. *Maestro di cappella*, Verona Cathedral, 1554; Milan Cathedral, 1563; Pistoia, 1574. In 1580 he became *maestro di cappella* at Sacile.

Though he was a church musician, his madrigals, of which he published 9 books, are more numerous than his sacred works. Without reaching great depth of expression, the madrigals have considerable variety of style, at times approaching the later *canzonetta* in lightness of touch. He also published 3 books of Masses, 3 of motets, Magnificats (1578) and five-part Psalms (1574) written " in conformity with the decree of the Council of Trent." Three madrigals are printed in A. Einstein, *The Italian Madrigal*, vol. iii, and 3 sacred and 2 secular pieces in L. Torchi, *L'arte musicale in Italia*, vol. i.

Rugby. A symphonic movement by Honegger (1928) which describes the game.

Ruggiero [roo-djeh′-ro], *I.* The bass of a 16th-cent. song, probably a setting of lines from Ariosto's *Orlando furioso*, which was used as the basis for variations and for new melodies in the same way as were the PASSAMEZZO and the ROMANESCA:

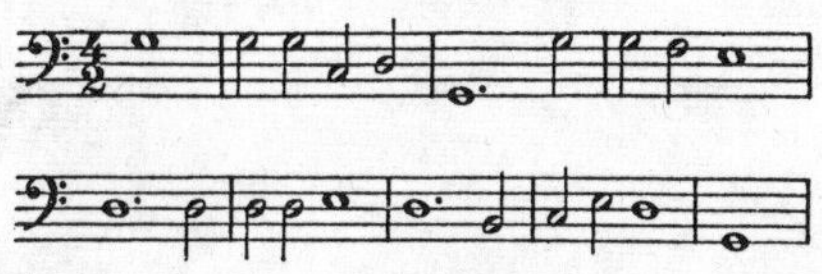

Frescobaldi, for example, published in his *Toccate d'Intavolatura* . . . (1614) a set of 12 variations on it, and a set of 6 variations on the tune of *Fra Jacopino*:

combined with it, which begins:

In addition, his *Primo Libro di Capricci* (1624) contains a *Capriccio sopra l'Aria di Ruggiero* which uses the phrases of the bass as points of imitation:

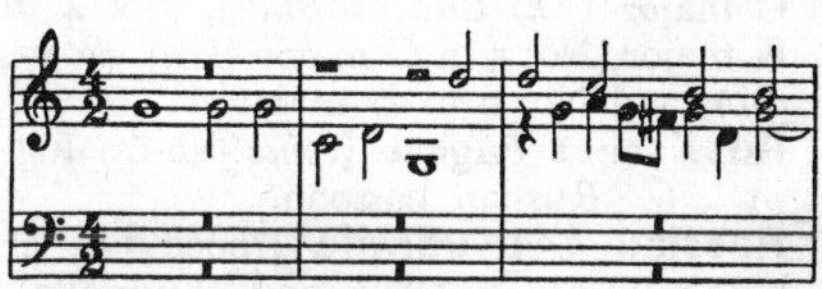

Rührtrommel [rēer′-trom-ĕl], *G. v.* TENOR DRUM.

Ruinen von Athen, Die [dee roo-een′-ĕn fon ut-ane′] (The Ruins of Athens). A play by August Friedrich Ferdinand von Kotzebue for which Beethoven composed incidental music, Op. 113, first produced in 1812, comprising an overture and 8 pieces for chorus and orchestra.

Rule Britannia. A song in the masque *Alfred* (1740), with music by Thomas Arne, generally sung today in a garbled version. There is a modern edition of the original score by Adam Carse. Beethoven wrote a set of variations for piano on the tune (1804) and also introduced it into the orchestral piece *Wellington's Sieg oder die Schlacht bei Vittoria* (Wellington's Victory or the Battle of Vittoria), Op. 91 (1813).

Rule of the Octave. A simple formula for harmonising a bass rising and descending stepwise through an octave, used in teaching harmony in the 18th cent.

Russian Bassoon (*Fr.* basson russe, *G.* russisches Fagott). A variety of the BASS HORN, a late 18th-cent. instrument consisting of a serpent made in the shape of a bassoon.

Russian Quartets. The title given to a set of six string quartets by Haydn, Op. 33 (1781) which was dedicated to the Grand Duke of Russia. The set, which was also called *Gli Scherzi* (as Haydn gave the name of *scherzo* to the minuet movements) or *Jungfernquartette* (according to the title page of an old edition), includes: No. 1 in B minor, No. 2 in E♭ major (*The Joke*), No. 3 in C major (*The Bird* or *Birds*), No. 4 in B♭ major, No. 5 in G major (*How do you do?*), and No. 6 in D major.

Russisches Fagott [rŏŏss'-ish-ĕss fug-ot'], *G.* Russian bassoon.

Russlan i Lyudmila [rooce'-lun ee lude-mill'-a] (Russlan and Ludmilla). Opera in five acts by Glinka. Libretto by Valeryan Fedorovich Shirkov and Konstantin Alexandrovich Bakhturin (founded on Pushkin's poem). First performed, St. Petersburg, Dec. 9, 1842.

Rust [rŏŏst], WILHELM: *b.* Dessau, Aug. 15, 1822; *d.* Leipzig, May 2, 1892. Pianist, violinist and composer. Studied under Friedrich Schneider, and settled in Berlin as teacher. Director of the Bach Society, 1862, teacher at the Stern Conservatorium, 1870. Went to Leipzig where he became organist (1878) and cantor (1880) at St. Thomas's Church and teacher at the Conservatorium. He edited 18 volumes of the *Bach Gesellschaft* and the piano sonatas of his grandfather, Friedrich Wilhelm Rust (with additions of his own), and composed vocal works and pieces for piano.

Ruy Blas [*Sp.* roo'-ee blahss, *Fr.* rēē-ee bla]. A play by Victor Hugo for which Mendelssohn composed an overture (C minor, Op. 95) and a two-part song (*Lied aus Ruy Blas*, Op. 77, No. 3) for a production at Leipzig in 1839.

S

S. As an abbreviation S.=*superius* (the highest part in 16th-cent. vocal and instrumental compositions), soprano. *D.S.*=*dal segno* (*v.* REPEAT); *m.s.* (in keyboard music)=*mano sinistra*, left hand. In TONIC SOL-FA **s**=*soh*, the 5th note (or dominant) of the major scale.

Sabaneiev [sa-ba-nay'-yef], LEONID LEONIDOVICH: *b.* Moscow, Nov. 19, 1881. Music critic and writer. Studied under Taneiev at the Moscow Conservatoire, and after the Revolution was attached to the State Institute for Musical Science, and in 1924 left Russia. He has written *Modern Russian Composers* (1927), *Music for the Films* (1935), books on Wagner, Medtner and Scriabin, and a history of Russian music. He has also composed songs and piano pieces.

Sabata [sah'-bah-tah], VICTOR DE: *b.* Trieste, April 10, 1892. Composer and conductor. Studied at the Milan Conservatorio under Orefice from 1902-10 and later was appointed conductor at La Scala. He has also conducted in Europe and America. He has composed operas, a ballet, symphonic poems and a suite for orchestra, and chamber music.

Sacchini [sahk-kee'-nee], ANTONIO MARIA GASPARO: *b.* Florence, June 14, 1730; *d.* Paris, Oct. 8, 1786. Studied in Naples under Durante, lived in Rome (1762-69), Venice, Munich, Stuttgart, London (1772-82) and Paris, where he was under the patronage of Marie Antoinette and produced his best opera, *Oedipe à Colone* (1786). He composed about 60 operas, 2 symphonies, an intermezzo, oratorios, Masses, motets and other church music, chamber music, and sonatas for harpsichord and for violin.

Sacher [zuckh'-er], PAUL: *b.* Basle, April 28, 1906. Studied at the Basle Conservatorium under R. Moser and Weingartner and at the University under Karl Nef. He founded the Basle Chamber Orchestra in 1926, the Chamber Choir in 1928 and the Schola Cantorum Basiliensis in 1933. He was appointed president of the Swiss section of the I.S.C.M. in 1935 and conductor at the Collegium Musicum in Zürich in 1941. He has conducted many first performances of music by contemporary composers.

Sachs [zuckhs], (1) CURT: *b.* Berlin, 6/29/1881; *d.* 2/6/1959. Musicologist. Studied at Berlin and under Fleischer, Kretzschmar and Wolf. In Berlin he was appointed professor of musicology at the University, teacher at the Hochschule and at the Academy for Church and School Music and curator of the State Collection of ancient instruments (1919). In 1938 he became professor of musicology at New York University. He has published in English *The Rise of Music in the Ancient World* (1943), *History of Musical Instruments* (1943), *The Commonwealth of Art* (1946), and *Our Musical Heritage* (1948; published in England as *A Short History of World Music*, 1950).

(2) HANS: *b.* Nuremberg, Nov. 5, 1494; *d.* there, Jan. 19, 1576. Shoemaker, poet and composer. The most famous personality amongst the Mastersingers of the 16th cent. He is the hero of operas by Lortzing, Gyrowetz and Wagner (*Die Meistersinger*). Two of his songs are published in anthologies, one in Schering's *History of Music in Examples*, No. 78, and one in the *Historical Anthology*, No. 24.

Sackbut (from *Med. Fr.* saquierboter, "to pull and push"). 16th-17th cent. English name for the TROMBONE.

Sackpfeife [zuck'-pfy-fer], *G.* Bagpipe.

Sacre du Printemps, Le [ler suckr dēē pran͡-tun͡] (The Rite of Spring). Ballet with music by Stravinsky (completed in 1913). First performed, Paris, May 28, 1913.

Sadko [sahd'-co]. Opera by Rimsky-

Korsakov in seven scenes (to be divided into 3 or 5 acts). Libretto by the composer and Vladimir Ivanovich Belsky. First performed, Moscow, Jan. 7, 1898.

Saga, En [en sah′-ga], (A Tale). A symphonic poem by Sibelius (Op. 9, 1892; revised, 1901) which has only the general programme indicated by the title.

Sagittarius, HENRICUS. *v.* SCHÜTZ.

St. Anne. The name of a hymn-tune, probably by Croft, first published in 1708. It begins:

Hence Bach's Fugue in E♭ at the end of the *Clavierübung*, Part III, which has the same theme, is sometimes called the *St. Anne* fugue.

St. John Passion. *v.* PASSION.

St. Matthew Passion. *v.* PASSION.

St. Paul (*G.* Paulus). Oratorio by Mendelssohn (Op. 36), completed in 1836. First performed, Düsseldorf, May 22, 1836.

Saint-Saëns [sa͡n-su͡nce], CHARLES CAMILLE: *b.* Paris, Oct. 9, 1835; *d.* Algiers, Dec. 16, 1921. Composer and pianist. Gave his first concert at the age of ten, and from 1848 studied organ under Benoist and composition under Halévy at the Conservatoire. Organist at the Madeleine, 1857. The influence of Liszt, whom he met in 1852, turned him towards a "cyclic" design in his symphonies and concertos—the third symphony is based on a single theme—and towards the symphonic poem (*Le Rouet d'Omphale*, 1871; *Phaëton*, 1873; *Danse macabre*, 1874; *La Jeunesse d'Hercule*, 1877), but had no effect on the rather shallow elegance of his style or the natural lucidity of his form. His first opera, *Le Timbre d'argent*, composed in 1864-5, was produced in 1877, and the first performance of *Samson et Dalila*, which was refused by the Paris Opéra until 1892, was given (in German) by Liszt at Weimar in the same year. It is his most lasting work. He was an extremely prolific composer (his opus numbers run to 169 and his compositions to the last year of his life), but his music suffers from superficiality and lack of adventurousness, which have caused it to fade very rapidly. He edited the works of Rameau, and wrote essays on music and on philosophy, and some plays and poems. Two volumes of his essays have been translated into English: *Musical Memories* (1921) and *Outspoken Essays* (1922).

A. DANDELOT: *La Vie et l'oeuvre de Saint-Saëns* (1930).
A. HERVEY: *Saint-Saëns* (1921).
L. WATSON: *Camille Saint-Saëns* (1923).

Saite [zite′-er], *G.* String.

Saiteninstrument [zite′-ĕn-in-stroo-ment], *G.* String instrument.

Salazar [sah-lah-thahrr′], ADOLFO: *b.* Madrid, March 6, 1890. Musicologist and composer. Studied under Pérez Casas and Manuel de Falla. Editor, *Revista Musical Hispano-Americana*, 1914-18. Founder of the Sociedad Nacional de Música, 1915. Music critic, *El Sol* (Madrid), 1918-36. In 1938 he moved to Mexico where he gave lectures on musical history at various universities. He has written books on musical history, contributed to periodicals and composed a symphonic poem and other orchestral works, chamber music, and piano pieces. His *Music in Our Time: Trends of Music since the Romantic Era* has been published in an English translation (1948).

Salicional (*L.* salix, "willow"). Soft open metal organ stop of 8 ft. or 16 ft. pitch.

Salieri [sahl-yeh′-ree], ANTONIO: *b.* Legnago, nr. Verona, Aug. 18, 1750; *d.* Vienna, May 7, 1825. Composer, conductor and teacher. Studied at the San Marco singing school in Venice and under Gassmann, who took him to Vienna (1766), conducted at the Court Opera as Gassmann's deputy (1770) and succeeded him as chamber composer and conductor of the Italian Opera (1774). The story of his intrigues against Mozart was inflated into the fable that he poisoned Mozart, used in a dramatic poem by Pushkin (1830), which became the libretto of Rimsky-Korsakov's opera *Mozart and Salieri*

(1898). He produced operas in several Italian cities (1778-79) and one in Paris, *Les Danaïdes* (1784), announced as written in collaboration with Gluck, then his teacher, but actually entirely by Salieri. Succeeded Bonno as court music director in Vienna (1788), conducted the Tonkünstler Society until 1818 and in 1824 retired from court service. He was a teacher of Beethoven, Schubert and Liszt. He composed about 40 operas, 4 oratorios, cantatas, Masses, a Passion, a Requiem, motets and other church music, a symphony, concertos for organ, for two pianos, and for flute and oboe, odes, canons and other vocal works.

Salinas [sah-lee'-nuss], FRANCISCO DE: *b.* Burgos, March 1, 1513; *d.* Salamanca, Jan. 13, 1590. Musical theorist and organist who was blind from the age of ten. He went to Italy in 1538 and lived in Rome and in Naples until 1561 as organist to the Spanish Viceroy, returned to Spain and became organist of León in 1563 and from 1567-87 was professor at the University of Salamanca. In his theoretical treatise *De musica libri septem* (1577) he expounded the theories of Zarlino and quoted a number of Spanish folk-songs of the time.

J. B. TREND: "Salinas," in *Music and Letters* (1927), p. 13.

Salò [dah sah-lo'], (originally DI BERTOLOTTI), GASPARO DA: *b.* Salò, 1540; *d.* Brescia, April 14, 1609. Violin-maker and grandson of the lute-maker, Santino di Bertolotti. He was one of the first to use the form of the violin instead of the viol.

Salome [*G.* zull'-o-may]. Opera in one act by Richard Strauss, a setting of Oscar Wilde's drama, translated into German by H. Lachmann. First performed, Dresden, Dec. 9, 1905. The Tetrarch, Herod, has imprisoned Jokanaan (John the Baptist) in a cistern as punishment for his words against Herod's marriage to his brother's wife (Herodias). Salome (daughter of Herodias) hearing the voice of the prophet becomes fascinated by him and demands to be allowed to see him. Narraboth (the captain of the guard, who loves Salome) against strict orders gives in to her and Jokanaan is brought forth. He denounces Herodias and begs Salome to turn to a virtuous life; when she pleads for a kiss from his lips he returns to his prison. Narraboth, in fear of what he has done, kills himself. When Herod arrives he is angered by the sight of blood. Herodias demands that the prophet be given to the Jews for punishment but Herod replies that he is holy and must not be injured. Herod, disturbed by the prophet's voice and by two Nazarenes who announce that the Messiah has already come, asks Salome to dance for him. She finally consents after he swears an oath to grant anything she demands. She dances the dance of the seven veils and then asks for the head of Jokanaan as her reward. Herod begs her to ask for anything else but when she refuses he reluctantly orders the execution of the prophet. Salome is presented with his head, addresses words of love to it and kisses the mouth. Herodias is triumphant but Herod is revolted by the scene and, unable to bear it any longer, commands his soldiers to kill Salome.

Salomon [zull'-o-mone], JOHANN PETER: *b.* Bonn, baptized Feb. 2, 1745; *d.* London, Nov. 28, 1815. Violinist and composer. Studied in Bonn, where he became a member of the Electoral orchestra in 1758. After a concert tour in 1765 he was appointed orchestra leader and composer to Prince Heinrich of Prussia in Rheinsberg. In 1781 he visited Paris and then settled in London where he played symphonies by Haydn and Mozart in his concerts (1786). He arranged Haydn's visits to England (1791-92 and 1794-95); hence the 12 symphonies written for those visits are known as the "Salomon" symphonies. He gave Haydn the text which Lidley had adapted from *Paradise Lost*, and which became, in a translation by van Swieten, the text of *The Creation*.

Saltando [sahl-tahnd'-o], *I.* (*Fr.* sautillé). Lit. "leaping." In string-playing indicates that the bow is to be allowed to bounce lightly on the string.

Saltarello [sahl-tah-rell'-lo], *I.* (from *saltare*, to jump). An Italian dance in quick tempo, most often in 6/8 time with a jumping effect in the rhythm, as in the first theme of the last movement of Mendelssohn's *Italian* symphony:

A 14th-cent. example is printed in Schering's *History of Music in Examples*, No. 28. It occurs in the 16th and early 17th cent. as the second dance (*v.* NACHTANZ) of a pair of which the first is a passamezzo. Peter Philips follows the seven variations of his *Galiarda Passamezzo* (of which the opening is quoted under PASSAMEZZO) with a *Saltarella* which begins thus:

Salterio [sahl-teh′-ryo], *I.* Psaltery. *Salterio tedesco*, dulcimer.

Salve Regina, *L.* "Hail Queen." An antiphon to the Blessed Virgin Mary sung at the end of Compline, the last service of the day, in the Latin liturgy. It has long been attributed to Hermannus Contractus, but is most probably by Aymar, Bishop of Puy (*d.* 1098), who may or may not have written the music. The Sarum form began thus:

Settings of the words are very numerous from early in the 15th cent. to Haydn, who wrote 4. Those in polyphonic style sometimes made use of the plainsong melody, as in this example by Walter Lambe, *c.* 1490:

Salzedo [sull-zay′-do], CARLOS: *b.* Arcachon, Apr. 6, 1885. Harpist and composer. Studied at the Paris Conservatoire, toured America and Europe, and settled in New York where he was appointed first harpist at the Metropolitan Opera (1909) and teacher at the Juilliard School. He also became head of the harp department at the Curtis Institute in Philadelphia, and with Varèse founded the International Composer's Guild (1921). He has composed a work for harp and orchestra, a concerto for harp and 7 wind instruments and other works for harp and groups of instruments, and pieces for harp solo and for harp ensemble. He has published *Modern Study of the Harp* (1921).

Samazeuilh [sa-ma-zer-*yer*], GUSTAVE MARIE VICTOR FERNAND: *b.* Bordeaux, June 2, 1877. Composer and music critic. Studied under Chausson and at the Schola Cantorum under d'Indy and Dukas. He was appointed music critic for *La République Française*, and has contributed to various French periodicals and published two books on contemporary music. He has also composed orchestral works, chamber music, pieces for piano, for organ, for violin and for guitar, a ballet and songs.

Saminsky [sah-min'-sky], LAZARE: *b.* Odessa, Russia, Nov. 8, 1882. Composer and writer on music. Studied at the Moscow Conservatoire and the Petrograd Conservatoire, visited London and Paris and in 1920 settled in America, where he became director of music at the Temple Emanu-El, New York. He has conducted in Europe, South America and Canada and was one of the founders of the League of Composers (1923). He has composed opera ballets, a chamber opera, 5 symphonies (one with chorus), symphonic poems, a Requiem, chamber music, choral works, songs and piano pieces, and has written *Music of Our Day* (1923) and *Music of the Ghetto and the Bible* (1934).

Sammartini [sahm-marr-tee'-nee] (San Martini), (1) GIOVANNI BATTISTA: *b.* Milan, 1698; *d.* there, Jan. 15, 1775. Composer and organist. Studied in Milan, where from 1725 he held several posts as organist and was also *maestro di cappella* at various churches and at the Convent of Santa Maria Maddalena (1730-70). He taught Gluck from 1737-41. He composed 2 operas, serenatas, more than 23 symphonies, overtures, many Masses, motets and other church music, *concerti grossi*, trio sonatas and other chamber music, violin concertos and other works for violin. He was the most important Italian composer of symphonies of his day.

(2) GIUSEPPE: *b.* Milan, *c.* 1693; *d.* London, *c.* 1750. Oboe-player and composer. Brother of (1). Settled in London (*c.* 1727) where he became oboe-player at the Opera, gave concerts with Arrigoni in 1732 and later was appointed musical director of chamber concerts for the Prince of Wales. He composed 12 *concerti grossi*, overtures, concertos for violin and for harpischord, an oratorio, trio sonatas and other chamber music, violin sonatas and flute solos and duets.

Sammons, ALBERT EDWARD: *b.* London, Feb. 23, 1886; *d.* Southdean (Sussex), Aug. 24, 1957. Violinist, mainly self-taught. Leader for five years of the orchestra founded by Sir Thomas Beecham in 1908. Leader of the London String Quartet from its foundation in 1908 till 1917. As a soloist he excelled in the Elgar and Delius concertos. His compositions include a Phantasy Quartet for strings and violin solos.

Sampson, RICHARD: *b. c.* 1470; *d.* Eccleshall, Sept. 25, 1554. Dean of the Chapel Royal; Bishop of Chichester, 1536; of Lichfield and Coventry, 1543. Two motets by him are extant.

Samson. Oratorio by Handel. Text by Newburgh Hamilton, based on Milton (*Samson Agonistes*, *Hymn on the Nativity* and *At a Solemn Musick*). First performed, London, Feb. 18, 1743.

Samson et Dalila [sũn-sõn ay da-lee-la] (Samson and Delilah). Opera in three acts by Saint-Saëns. Libretto by Ferdinand Lemaire. German version by Richard Pohl, *Samson und Delila.* First performed, Weimar, Dec. 2, 1877.

Sances [sahn'-chess], GIOVANNI FELICE: *b.* Rome, *c.* 1600; *d.* Vienna, Nov. 24, 1679. Tenor, 1636, assistant *Kapellmeister*, 1649, *Kapellmeister*, 1669 at the Vienna Court Chapel. He composed operas (one with Emperor Leopold I), 4 oratorios, and monodies and duets with continuo.

Sancta Civitas (The Holy City). Oratorio by Vaughan Williams for solo voices, chorus and orchestra. Text from the Bible and other sources. First performed, Oxford, May 7, 1926.

Sanctus [sahnk'-tooss], *L.* "Holy, holy." One of the parts of the Ordinary of the MASS and of the Communion SERVICE.

Sandberger [zunt′-bairg-er], ADOLF: *b.* Würzburg, Dec. 19, 1864; *d.* Munich, Jan. 14, 1943. Musicologist and composer. Studied in Berlin and Munich, where he was curator of the music department of the State Library from 1889 and lecturer (1894) and professor (1900) at the University. He composed 2 operas (one unfinished), a symphonic poem and other works for orchestra, choral works, 2 string quartets and other chamber music, violin sonata, songs and piano pieces, wrote books and essays on musical history and was one of the editors of the complete works of Lassus and of *D.T.B.*

San Martini. *v.* SAMMARTINI.

Santini [sahn-tee′-nee], ABBÉ FORTUNATO: *b.* Rome, Jan. 5, 1778; *d.* there, 1862. Studied music under Jannaconi, was ordained in 1801 and devoted his life to collecting, copying and scoring early church music. He became friends with Mendelssohn and introduced much German music into Italy. His library is now at the University Library in Münster, Westphalia. He composed a Requiem for 8 voices, Masses, motets and other church music.

Santoliquido [sahn′-to-lee′-cwee-do], FRANCESCO: *b.* S. Giorgio a Cremano, nr. Naples, Aug. 6, 1883. Composer and poet. Studied at the Liceo S. Cecilia in Rome, conducted in Nuremberg (1909) and Milan (1910), lived in an Arab village in Tunisia from 1911, and after 1921 settled in Rome and made yearly visits to Tunisia. He has composed operas, a symphony, symphonic impressions and other orchestral works, a Mass, a cantata, piano pieces and songs. Much of his work reflects his interest in Oriental life.

Sarabande [sa-ra-bũnd], *Fr.* A dance in slow 3/2 or 3/4 time which was one of the four dances (Allemande, Courante, Sarabande, Gigue) regularly included in the SUITE between *c.* 1650 and *c.* 1750. In Bach and Handel it often has a predominating rhythm:

as in Handel's harpsichord suite No. 11:

It seems to have been originally introduced from the East into Spain, where it was ordered to be suppressed in the 16th cent. because of its lascivious character. Gibbons's *Sarabrande* with variations is an innocuous tune in folksong style in moderately quick 6/8 time. Later in the century it frequently appears as a slow and rather pensive movement, as in Blow's *Sarabrande for the Graces* in *Venus and Adonis* (*c.* 1682):

Sarasate [sah-rah-sah′-teh] (Sarasate y Navascues), PABLO MARTIN MELITON: *b.* Pamplona, March 10, 1844; *d.* Biarritz, Sept. 20, 1908. Violinist. Studied at the Paris Conservatoire. He rapidly made a reputation as a soloist and toured widely, both in Europe and in America. Among the works written for him were Lalo's first violin concerto and Bruch's second violin concerto. He wrote a number of works for the violin, as well as transcriptions of Spanish dances.

Sargent, HAROLD MALCOLM WATTS: *b.* Stamford, Apr. 29, 1895. Conductor. He became assistant to Dr. Keeton of Peterborough Cathedral in 1911, and organist of Melton Mowbray parish church in 1914. Honorary D.Mus. Oxford, 1942. He has conducted the British National Opera Company, the D'Oyle Carte Opera (1926), Robert Mayer's children's concerts, the Courtauld-Sargent concerts (from 1929), the Royal Choral Society at the Albert Hall (from 1928), the Leeds Festivals and the B.B.C. orchestra (1951-7). Knighted 1947.

Sarro [sahrr'-ro] (Sarri), DOMENICO: *b.* Trani, Naples, 1678; *d.* Naples, 1744. Composer. Studied under Provenzale at the Conservatorio de' Turchini in Naples, where he became assistant *maestro di cappella* in 1712 and later *maestro di cappella* of the court chapel. He composed about 50 operas, oratorios, cantatas, Masses and other church music, a concerto for strings and flute, serenades and arias. Metastasio's fame began with Sarro's *Didone abbandonata* (1724), which was the first setting of his first libretto.

Sarrusophone. A family of double reed instruments made of metal, devised by a French bandmaster named Sarrus and patented in 1856. The complete family consists of 9 instruments from a contrabass in low B♭ to a sopranino in high E♭. They were intended to replace the oboes and bassoons in military bands, but have done so only in France. In French orchestras the contrabass sarrusophone in C has been used instead of the double bassoon.

Sarti [sarr'-tee], GIUSEPPE: *bapt.* Faenza, Dec. 1, 1729; *d.* Berlin, July 28, 1802. Composer and conductor. Studied under Martini in Bologna. Organist, Faenza Cathedral, 1748; opera conductor under Mingotti, 1752; director of Italian opera (1753) and court conductor (1755) in Copenhagen. He visited Italy from 1765-68 and returned to Copenhagen as court composer (1768) and court Opera conductor (1770). Director, Ospedaletto Conservatorio, Venice, 1775; *maestro di cappella,* Milan Cathedral, 1779; court conductor to Catherine II of Russia, 1784; director of a music school in the Ukraine, 1787, and of the new conservatoire in St. Petersburg, 1793. He invented a machine for counting sound vibrations and used an A of 436 vibrations in his orchestra. He was a teacher of Cherubini. He composed operas to Italian, Danish and Russian texts, an oratorio, Requiem, Te Deum, Masses, motets and other church music, choral works, two concerti, and harpsichord sonatas. Mozart used the aria "Come un agnello" from his opera *Fra due litiganti* (1782) in the banquet music in the finale of the second act of *Don Giovanni* (1787) and wrote variations on it for piano solo, K.460.

Sarum Rite. The liturgy, with its plainsong, of the cathedral church of Salisbury, which was the most widely used rite in England until the Reformation. Its origins are traced back to the work of St. Osmund (*d.* 1099), and its earliest surviving complete form is contained in a manuscript *Consuetudinarium* of *c.* 1210.

W. H. FRERE: *The Use of Sarum* (2 vols., 1898, 1901). *The Sarum Gradual,* facsimile edition (1894). *The Sarum Antiphonary,* facsimile edition (1901-24).

Satie [sa-tee], ERIK ALFRED LESLIE: *b.* Honfleur, May 17, 1866; *d.* Paris, July 1, 1925. Composer. Studied at the Paris Conservatoire from 1879 and at the Schola Cantorum under d'Indy and Roussel from 1905-08. He became friends with Debussy in 1890 and had some influence on his style. He composed 3 ballets (including *Parade,* produced by Satie, Cocteau, Picasso and Diaghilev in Paris, 1917), operettas, a symphonic drama *Socrate, Messe des pauvres* for voice and organ, four sets of songs and many piano pieces. The ironically humorous character of his style, which is strongly in contrast with the impressionism of his period, is indicated in the satirical titles of his piano pieces, *e.g. Pièces froides, Pièces en forme de poire, Choses vues à droite et à gauche (sans lunettes), Aperçus désagréables, Croquis et agaceries d'un gros bonhomme en bois.*

R. MYERS: *Erik Satie* (1948).
P.-D. TEMPLIER : *Erik Satie* (1932).

Satz [zuts], *G.* (1) A movement of a sonata, symphony, suite, etc., *e.g.*, *erster Satz,* " first movement." Schubert's *Quartettsatz* is a string quartet in a single movement intended by the composer to be the first movement of an extended work.

(2) Composition (in full, *Tonsatz,* " musical composition ").

(3) Style in composition, *e.g. freier Satz,* " free style."

Saudades [sah-oo-dahd′-ess], *Port.* (plur. of *saudade,* " nostalgia," " wistful yearning "). (1) The title of a set of three songs by Warlock (1917), comprising: " Along the Stream " (Li Po, trans. L. Cranmer-Byng,) " Take, O take those lips away " (Shakespeare) and " Heracleitus " (Callimachus, trans. W. Cory).

(2) *Saudades do Brasil.* Two volumes of piano pieces by Milhaud (1920-1).

Saul. Oratorio by Handel. Text by Charles Jennens. First performed, London, Jan. 16, 1739.

Sautillé [so-tee-yay), *Fr.*=SALTANDO.

Sauveur [so-ver], JOSEPH: *b.* La Flèche, March 24, 1653; *d.* Paris, July 9, 1716. Though a deaf-mute from birth he studied and wrote about the science of sounds, which he was the first to call " acoustics." He was elected a member of the Académie in 1696.

Sāvitri [sah′-vee-tree]. Opera in one act by Holst. Libretto by the composer (*An Episode from the Mahabharata*). First performed, London, Nov. 5, 1916.

Saxhorn. A family of brass instruments standardized by Adolphe Sax and patented by him in 1845, originally oval in shape with a wide conical bore similar to that of the bugle. The complete family consisted of 6 or 7 instruments from a contrabass in E♭ to a soprano in high E♭. The present terminology for such instruments varies greatly ; in France they are called saxhorn, elsewhere flügelhorn, tenor horn, baritone, euphonium, and tuba according to size and local custom.

A. CARSE : *Musical Wind Instruments* (1939).

Saxophone. A family of instruments devised by Adolphe Sax and patented by him in 1846. It has the mouthpiece and single reed of a clarinet, the conical bore of an oboe, and is made of metal. The complete family has 7 sizes : sopranino in high E♭, soprano in B♭, alto in E♭, tenor in B♭, baritone in E♭, bass in B♭, and contrabass in E♭. The larger sizes have an upturned bell. It is used in military bands and in jazz bands, and occasionally appears in orchestral scores. French composers, *e.g.* Thomas, Bizet, Saint-Saëns, d'Indy, have written for the saxophone not infrequently : Debussy wrote a *Rapsodie* for saxophone and orchestra (1903-5) and Milhaud used it in the ballet *La Création du monde* (1923). Richard Strauss included a quartet of saxophones in the orchestra of the *Symphonia domestica* (1903).

A. CARSE : *Musical Wind Instruments* (1939).

Scacchi [scahk′-kee], MARCO: *b.* Rome, late 16th cent. ; *d.* Galese (nr. Rome), before 1685. Composer. Studied under Anerio. He was composer at the Polish Court in Warsaw from 1623-48, when he returned to Italy. He composed an opera, an oratorio, Masses, motets and madrigals. He published in two books (1643, 1644) a critical examination of the style of the Psalms of Paul Siefert of Danzig, and proposed a division of styles into those appropriate to the church, to the chamber, and to the theatre.

Scala di Seta, La [lah scah′-lah dee seh′-tah] (The Silken Ladder). Opera in one act by Rossini. Libretto by Gaetano Rossi (based on a French libretto by François Antoine Eugène de Planard). First performed, Venice, May 9, 1812.

Scale (*Fr.* gamme, *G.* Tonleiter, *I.* scala). The melodic material of music arranged in ascending or descending order for theoretical purposes, for vocal or instrumental exercise, or in the course of a composition. In composition scales are used in a great variety of ways, *e.g.* in transitional passage work, in ornamentation (*v.* PASSING NOTE), and as the whole or part of a theme, as in:

from the third movement of Mozart's piano concerto in A, K.488.

A scale consists of a certain number of divisions of a fourth (TETRACHORD) or of an OCTAVE. The manner of such division is a MODE, though scale is commonly used in the sense of mode in referring to a PENTATONIC SCALE, a major or minor scale, a CHROMATIC scale, and a WHOLE-TONE scale. The medieval HEXACHORD was a six-note scale in which the order of intervals was TTSTT, where T = tone and S = semitone.

The modern DIATONIC scale has two modes: major (TTSTTTS):

and minor (TSTTSTT):

The latter has only a theoretical existence; in practice it has two forms, both of which involve an element of chromaticism in the treatment of the LEADING NOTE. They are the harmonic minor scale:

and the melodic minor scale, in which the ascending and descending forms differ:

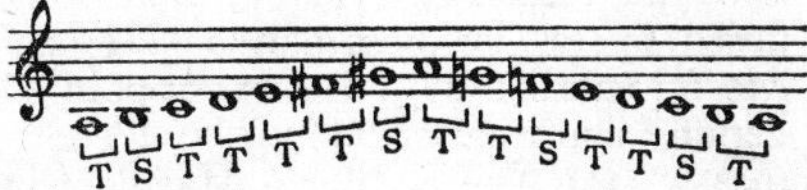

In the system of EQUAL TEMPERAMENT each of the two modes may begin on any of the twelve notes from C upwards to B by using sharps or flats, usually shown by a KEY-SIGNATURE, thus giving rise to the twelve scales in the major mode and twelve in the minor mode, on which music has been based since the early eighteenth century. The notes of the scale are designated in both modes and in all positions by names which express their function in relation to their KEY, *viz.*, tonic, supertonic, mediant, subdominant, dominant, submediant, leading note. *v.* also QUARTER-TONE.

Scandello [scahn-dell'-lo] (Scandelli), ANTONIO: *b.* Bergamo, 1517; *d.* Dresden, Jan. 18, 1580. Composer and cornett-player. He was cornett-player in Bergamo (1541) and in Trent (1547), at the Dresden Court from *c.* 1553, assistant *Kapellmeister* to Le Maistre from 1566 and *Kapellmeister* from 1568 until his death. He composed Masses, motets, a Passion and other church music, two books of *Canzoni napolitane* (1566, 1577), and sacred and secular choral songs to German words. His *St. John Passion* (*c.* 1560; printed in O. Kade, *Die ältere Passionskomposition*, 1893), was intermediate in method between those with plainsong narrative and polyphonic choruses and those which were set in polyphony throughout. He used Johann Walther's monophonic music for the Evangelist, and wrote in five parts for the people (*Turba*), four for Christ, and two or three for other persons. His "Vorria che tu cantass' una canzon" from the first book of *Canzoni* (1566) is printed in Schering's *History of Music in Examples*, No. 132.

Scarlatti [scarr-laht'-tee], (1) ALESSANDRO: *b.* Palermo, May 2, 1660; *d.* Naples, Oct. 24, 1725. Composer.

Studied at Rome, where he became conductor at the private theatre of Queen Christina of Sweden, 1680-84. He was court conductor at Naples, 1684-1702, lived at Florence, 1702-03, and composed operas for Ferdinando (III) de' Medici (until 1707). He was appointed deputy choirmaster (1703) and choirmaster (1707) of S. Maria Maggiore in Rome and music director to Cardinal Pietro Ottoboni. He returned to Naples (1709) as musical director to the Austrian Viceroy and was later director of the Conservatorio S. Onofrio. His pupils included Logroscino, Durante and Hasse. He was the greatest and most prolific of the composers of Italian opera in a period when its forms were assuming their most lasting characteristics. In his mature works are found the fully-developed *da capo* aria with instrumental accompaniment and *ritornelli*, the rapid style and special cadence formulas of *secco* recitative and the use of accompanied recitative for more intense dramatic effects. In his later operas he used the three-movement form which became the distinguishing mark of the Italian overture. Besides 115 operas, by his own count, he composed 150 oratorios, some 600 cantatas with continuo and sixty-one with instrumental accompaniment, Masses, a Passion, motets and other church music, concertos, chamber music, and pieces for harpsichord. The cantatas contain music in a more intimate and a more deeply expressive style than was appropriate to that of the operas. The first two acts of an early opera, *La Rosaura* (*c.* 1690), were printed in Eitner's *Publikationen*, XIV, a duet from *Gl' inganni felici* (Naples, 1699) and a scene in recitative from *La Griselda* (Rome, 1721) in Schering's *History of Music in Examples*, Nos. 258-9, and the overture (*sinfonia avanti l'opera*) to *La Griselda* in the *Historical Anthology*, No. 259. Schering also prints the solo cantata *Lascia, deh lascia* (No. 260), and the *Historical Anthology* the solo cantata *Mitilde, mio tesor* and a concerto in F from the *Six Concertos* published in London *c.* 1750. There are also modern editions of the opera *Mitridate Eupatore* (1707) and the comic opera *Il trionfo dell' onore* (1718).

E. J. DENT: *Alessandro Scarlatti, his Life and Works* (1905).

(2) GIUSEPPE DOMENICO: *b.* Naples, Oct. 26, 1685; *d.* Madrid, July 23, 1757. Composer and harpsichordist. Son of (1). Studied under his father, Gasparini and Pasquini. In 1705 he went to Florence with the singer Nicolino and is said to have had in 1709 a contest with Handel in Rome which was arranged by Cardinal Ottoboni. He was attached to the court of the Polish Queen Maria Casimira from 1709 and wrote 8 operas for her private theatre in Rome where he was also musical director of St. Peter's, 1715-19. He was in the service of the King of Portugal in Lisbon, *c.* 1721-25, lived in Italy, 1725-29, and was at the Madrid Court, 1729-57. The greatest Italian writer for the harpsichord of his time, he composed about 600 pieces in one movement, now generally called sonatas, though some printed in his lifetime were called *Essercizi*. Within the binary form in which most of them are written there is inexhaustible variety in the character of the themes and continuous flexibility in their texture and treatment. Among the most original and characteristic technical devices which appear in them are wide skips, crossing of hands, rapidly repeated notes, and repeated dissonant chords which suggest, and were presumably suggested by, the strumming of the guitar. The complete edition in 10 volumes by A. Longo (1906 foll.) contains 545 pieces. Scarlatti's other compositions, besides operas, include concertos, cantatas, Masses, a *Stabat Mater* and two *Salve regina*'s.

R. KIRKPATRICK: *Domenico Scarlatti* (1953).
S. SITWELL: *A Background for Domenico Scarlatti* (1935).

Scena [sheh'-nah], *I.* "Scene." (1) Stage (of a theatre). *Sulla scena*, on the stage (as opposed to "in the orchestra").

(2) A dramatic scene in an opera, including one or more arias.

(3) A concert piece for solo voice with accompaniment, similar in character to an operatic *scene*.

(4) Spohr's violin concerto No. 8 in A

minor is described as "in modo d'una scena cantante" (in the style of a vocal *scena*).

Schalmei [shull-my'], *G.* Shawm. *v.* OBOE.

Scharwenka [sharr-veng'-ca], (1) FRANZ XAVER: *b.* Samter (Posen) Jan. 6, 1850; *d.* Berlin, Dec. 8, 1924. Pianist, composer, and teacher. Studied at the Kullak Academy in Berlin where he taught from 1868-73, gave chamber concerts, conducted, founded a conservatoire in 1881 (joined with the Klindworth Conservatorium, 1893) and with Walter Petzet a new Master School in 1914. He toured extensively as a pianist in Europe and in America, where he lived from 1891-98 and founded a conservatoire in New York. He composed an opera, a symphony, 4 piano concertos, piano trios, church music, songs, sonatas and other piano pieces, edited the piano works of Schumann and wrote (with A. Spanuth) *Methodik des Klavierspiels* (1908).

(2) LUDWIG PHILIPP: *b.* Samter (Posen), Feb. 16, 1847; *d.* Bad Nauheim, July 16, 1917. Composer and teacher. Brother of (1). Studied at the Kullak Academy in Berlin where he taught from 1870. He worked at his brother's conservatoire as composition teacher from 1881 and was director in 1892 and co-director from 1893, when it was joined with the Klindworth Conservatorium. He composed an opera, 2 symphonies, symphonic poems and other works for orchestra, works for solo voices, chorus and orchestra, a violin concerto and other pieces for violin, chamber music, sonatas and other piano pieces, partsongs and songs.

Schauspieldirektor, Der [dair show'-shpeel-dee-reck-torr] (The Impresario). Comedy with music by Mozart. Text by Gottlieb Stephanie. First performed at a garden-party given by the Emperor Joseph II at Schönbrunn, Vienna, Feb. 7, 1786.

Scheherazade (Shahrazad). Symphonic suite by Rimsky-Korsakov, Op. 35 (1888), based on sections from the *Arabian Nights*. The movements originally had titles, which were later omitted. *v.* also SHÉHÉRAZADE.

Scheibe [shibe'-er], JOHANN ADOLPH: *b.* Leipzig, May 3, 1708; *d.* Copenhagen, April 22, 1776. Composer and writer. Taught at Hamburg from 1736, was conductor to the Margrave of Brandenburg-Kulmbach from 1740, of Court Opera in Copenhagen from 1745, and director of a music school in Sonderburg (Holstein), from 1758. He published a periodical entitled *Der critische Musicus* (1737-40) in which he wrote against Italian operatic conventions and also against the style of J. S. Bach (though he withdrew the latter attack in the second edition of his paper, 1745). He composed an opera, cantatas, 2 oratorios, Masses and many other church works, 150 flute concertos, 30 violin concertos, 70 quartet-symphonies, incidental music for plays, trios, flute sonatas and songs. He published books on the origins of music, on intervals, on recitative, and the first volume of a projected work on composition.

Scheidemann [shide'-er-mun], HEINRICH: *b.* Hamburg, *c.* 1596; *d.* there, early in 1663. Organist and composer. Studied under his father, Hans, and Sweelinck in Amsterdam. He succeeded his father as organist of St. Catherine's, Hamburg, in 1625 and was in turn succeeded by his pupil J. A. Reinken. His organ music is of some historical importance. Of two organ preludes by him printed in the *Historical Anthology* (No. 195), the second is a brief prelude and fugue, an early example of that form. He wrote 10 chorale melodies for Rist's fifth book of chorales (1651), and published a volume of sacred dialogues (1658).

Scheidt [shite], SAMUEL: *b.* Halle, *bapt.* Nov. 4, 1587; *d.* there, March 24, 1654. Organist and composer. He was appointed organist of the Moritzkirche in Halle, studied under Sweelinck in Amsterdam and returned to Halle, where he became court organist in 1609 and archiepiscopal *Kapellmeister* in 1619. He published *Cantiones sacrae* (1620) for 8 voices, *Paduana, Galliarda . . .* for 4 and 5 instruments with continuo (1621), *Concerti sacri* (1621-22) for 2-12 voices with instruments, *Tabulatura nova* for organ (3 vols., 1624), *Ludi musici* (2 vols.,

1621-2) containing dance pieces for instruments, *Newe geistliche Concerte* (4 vols., 1631-40 ; vols. v and vi are lost) for two and three voices with continuo, *Liebliche Kraftblümlein* (1635) for two voices and instruments, 70 *Symphonien auf Concerten-Manier* (1644) for three voices and continuo, and a *Tabulaturbuch* (1650) containing 100 harmonised chorales for organs. The *Tabulatura nova*, so called because the music was written in score with five lines for each part, and not in TABLATURE as was the German custom, nor on two staves of six lines, as was usual in England and Holland, marked the beginning of a new era in German organ music. The first and second volumes contain variations on sacred and secular melodies, fantasies, and a few dance movements, the third volume a complete set of liturgical organ music for the Lutheran Mass and Vespers. The work is reprinted in *D.D.T.*, i. 7 vols. of a projected complete edition of Scheidt's works have appeared, edited by G. Harms and C. Mahrenholz ; they contain (I) the *Tabulaturbuch* (printed by Gorlitz, 1650), (II-III) the *Paduana, Galliarda . . . Canzonetto* of 1621, (IV) the *Cantiones Sacrae* of 1620, (V) various keyboard compositions and (VI-VII) the *Tabulatura nova* of 1624.

Schein [shine], JOHANN HERMANN: *b.* Grünhain (Saxony), Jan. 20, 1586 ; *d.* Leipzig, Nov. 19, 1630. Composer. Choirboy in the Dresden court chapel, studied at the University of Leipzig (1607), from 1613 was a teacher in the household of von Wolffersdorf in Weissenfels, from 1615 at the Weimar court chapel, and from 1616 cantor at St. Thomas's, Leipzig, succeeding Seth Calvisius. Schütz wrote a lament on his death (complete ed., xii, p. 25). He was the first Lutheran composer to adapt the Italian monodic style to the treatment of the chorale melodies. His first publication, *Cymbalum Sionium* (1615), was in the Venetian polychoral style which Hassler and Praetorius had used before him. The two parts of his *Opella nova* (1618-1626) contained settings of chorales for 3, 4 and 5 voices with continuo. His *Venuskränzlein* (1609) contained five-part choral songs and some instrumental dances and canzonas, his *Musica boscareccia* (1621) songs in villanella style for 3 voices and continuo, and his *Diletti pastorali* (1624) five-part choral pieces in madrigal style with continuo. The instrumental suites of his *Banchetto musicale* are among the earliest in which some or all of the movements use the same theme (" variation-suite "). The works referred to have been reprinted in the 7 volumes which have appeared of the complete edition, ed. by A. Prüfer.

Schelle [shell'-er], JOHANN: *b.* Geising (nr. Meissen), Sept. 6, 1648 ; *d.* Leipzig, March 10, 1701. He sang under Schütz in Dresden from 1655-57, lived in Wolfenbüttel until 1664, studied under S. Knüpfer in Leipzig, was appointed cantor in 1670 at Eilenburg and in 1676 at St. Thomas's Church, Leipzig. He composed cantatas and motets to German words, and Latin motets, Magnificats, and a Mass. 4 of his cantatas are printed in *D.D.T.*, lviii-lix, which also contains a list of his compositions.

Schellen [shell'-ĕn], *G.* Jingles, sleigh bells.

Schellentrommel [shell'-ĕn-trom'-ĕl], *G.* Tambourine.

Schelomo (Solomon). Rhapsody for cello and orchestra by Bloch (1915).

Schemelli [shem-ell'-ee], GEORG CHRISTIAN: *b.* Herzberg, 1676 or 1680 ; *d.* Zeitz, March 5, 1762. Studied in Leipzig under Schelle at the Thomasschule (1695-1700) and in Wittenberg. He later became cantor at the castle of Zeitz. In 1736 he published a collection of songs entitled *Musicalisches Gesangbuch* edited, and some composed, by J. S. Bach.

Schenk [shenk], (1) (Schenck), JOHANN: Late 17th cent. Viola da gamba player at the electoral court in Düsseldorf (*c.* 1690); later lived in Amsterdam. He composed suites and sonatas for gamba, chamber sonatas for 2 violins, gamba and bass, sonatas for violin and continuo, an opera, and a setting of the *Song of Solomon* for voice and continuo. His *Scherzi musicali*, a book of suites for viola da gamba and continuo published in Amsterdam as Op. 6, is reprinted as vol. xxviii (1907) of the publications of the Society for Netherlands Music History, a fugue from that volume in Schering's *History of Music in Examples*, No. 245, and *Le Nymphe del Rheno*, Op.8, for two gambas as vol. xliv of *E.D.M.*

(2) JOHANN: *b.* Wiener-Neustadt, Nov. 30, 1753; *d.* Vienna, Dec. 29, 1836. Composer and teacher. He studied under Wagenseil in Vienna (1774) and was appointed musical director to Prince Carl von Auersperg in 1794. He taught Beethoven (1793), when he was also studying with Haydn, and became friends with Mozart and Schubert. He composed *Singspiele*, Masses, cantatas, symphonies, concertos, string quartets and songs. His most popular *Singspiel*, *Der Dorfbarbier* (1796), is printed in *D.T.Ö.*, lxvi.

Schenker [shenk′-er], HEINRICH: *b.* Wisniowczyki (Galicia), June 19, 1868; *d.* Vienna, Jan. 22, 1935. Theorist and teacher. Studied under Bruckner in Vienna, where he settled and taught music privately. He is best known for the methods of analysis of form, harmony and tonality in the music of the 18th and 19th cent. which he taught and discussed in his writings.

A. KATZ: *Challenge to Musical Tradition* (1945).

F. SALZER: *Structural Hearing*, 2 vols. (1952).

Scherchen [shair*sh*′-ĕn], HERMANN: *b.* Berlin, June 21, 1891. Conductor. Conducted in Riga in 1914, and from 1918 lived in Berlin, where he founded a periodical *Melos* and lectured on modern music. From 1921 he conducted at Leipzig and from 1923 at Frankfort and at festivals of contemporary music. He left Germany in 1932 and has since held courses and conducted in various cities, showing a special interest in the performance of new compositions. His *Handbook of Conducting* has been published in English (1923).

Scherer [shair′-er], SEBASTIAN ANTON: *bapt.* Ulm, Oct. 4, 1631; *d.* there, Aug. 26, 1712. Composer. Deputy organist to Tobias Eberlin at the cathedral of Ulm in 1653; director of the Collegium Musicum there in 1662; organist of the cathedral in 1671. He became organist of St. Thomas's in Strasbourg in 1684 and returned to the cathedral at Ulm in the following year. He published a volume of Masses, psalms and motets in 1657, a volume of *Tabulatura in cymbalo et organo* containing Intonations in the eight modes, with a second part (*Partitura*) containing Toccatas in the eight modes in 1664 (both parts edited by Guilmant, 1907), and a set of 14 trio sonatas in 1680.

Schering [shair′-ing], ARNOLD: *b.* Breslau, Apr. 2, 1877; *d.* Berlin, March 7, 1941. Musicologist. Studied at the Berlin Hochschule and under Kretzschmar at Leipzig University, where he became lecturer, 1907, and professor, 1915-20. Teacher, Leipzig Conservatorium, 1909-23. Professor, Halle, 1920; Berlin, 1928. Editor, *Bach-Jahrbuch*, 1904. In 1908 he discovered the parts of Schütz's *Christmas Oratorio*, which he edited as vol. xvii of the complete edition of Schütz's works. His numerous writings include a history of the concerto and of the oratorio and a *History of Music in Examples* (Leipzig, 1931; reprinted, New York, 1950).

Scherzando [scairrts-ahnd′-o], *I.* Playfully, in a lighthearted fashion.

Scherzi, Gli [l'yee scairrts′-ee], *I.* *v.* RUSSIAN QUARTETS.

Scherzo [scairrts′-o], *I.* Lit. "joke." The term was occasionally used for both vocal and instrumental compositions before 1750, as in Monteverdi's *Scherzi musicali* (1607), Antonio Brunelli's *Scherzi, Arie, Canzonette, e Madrigali* (1616) for voices and instruments, Johann Schenk's *Scherzi musicali* (*c.* 1700), consisting of 14 suites for gamba and continuo, Steffani's *Scherzi* for solo voice with two violins and continuo and the Scherzo in Bach's third partita for harpsichord. The scherzo (and trio) after 1750 is almost always in quick triple time, and is generally a movement in a sonata, symphony, etc., where it takes the place of the minuet. Haydn wrote a scherzo and trio in each of the 6 quartets of his Op. 33 without making any effective distinction between their style and that of his minuets. The minuet in Beethoven's first symphony is marked *Allegro molto e vivace* with a metronome mark of

108 bars to the minute, so that it is actually a scherzo, and all the later symphonies except the eighth, which has a classical minuet, have a scherzo and trio. With Beethoven the style of the scherzo becomes boisterous as in :

BEETHOVEN, *Symphony No.9*

or on occasion eerie, as in the fifth symphony. Brahms wrote no scherzos in his symphonies, though his first orchestral work, the Serenade Op. 11, includes a scherzo marked *Allegro non troppo*. There is an *Allegro appassionato* in his B♭ piano concerto, Op. 83, in quick 3/4 time (76 bars to the minute) which is more akin to the wayward style of his Scherzo for piano, Op. 4 and to the 4 Scherzos by Chopin than to that of Beethoven's scherzos. Other composers since the mid-19th cent., *e.g.* Bruckner, Sibelius, Walton, Wellesz, have, however, written symphonic scherzos in the Beethoven tradition.

Schicksalslied [shicks'-ullce-leet], (Song of Destiny). A composition for chorus and orchestra by Brahms, Op. 54 (1871), with words from a poem in Hölderlin's *Hyperion.*

Schikaneder [shee-cun-ay'-der], JOHANN EMANUEL : *b.* Straubing, Sept. 1, 1751 ; *d.* Vienna, Sept. 21, 1812. Librettist, singer and theatre manager. He was singer, actor and later manager for a group of travelling players and in 1784 settled in Vienna, where he was manager of several theatres and from 1801 of the Theater an der Wien. He wrote, with J. G. Metzler (*i.e.* K. L. Giesecke), the libretto for Mozart's *Die Zauberflöte* and also produced it and played the role of Papageno.

E. VON KOMORZYNSKI : *Emanuel Schikaneder* (1951).

Schildt [shilt], MELCHIOR: *b.* Hanover, 1593; *d.* there, May 28, 1667. Organist and composer. He studied under Sweelinck in Amsterdam (1609) and was appointed organist at Wolfenbüttel (1623), at the Copenhagen Court (1626) and of the Market Church in Hanover (1629). His published compositions include 2 sets of harpischord variations, 2 preludes and 2 chorales for organ.

Schillings [shill'-ingce], MAX VON: *b.* Duren (Rhineland), Apr. 19, 1868; *d.* Berlin, July 23, 1933. Composer and conductor. Studied in Bonn and in Munich and was appointed assistant stage conductor (1892) and chorus master (1902) at the Bayreuth Festivals. In 1908 he settled in Stuttgart and worked at the Court Opera where he became music director in 1911. He was director of the Berlin State Opera from 1919-25 and in 1932 became President of the Prussian Academy of Arts. Of his 4 operas, written in Wagnerian style, the last, *Mona Lisa* (Stuttgart, 1915), was one of the most successful German operas of its time. He also composed 4 melodramas, incidental music, symphonic poems, a violin concerto, chamber music, choral works, piano pieces, and songs.

Schindler [shint'-ler], ANTON: *b.* Meedl (nr. Neustadt), June 13, 1794; *d.* Bockenheim (nr. Frankfort), Jan. 16, 1864. Violinist and conductor. Friend and biographer of Beethoven. Studied in Vienna where he was appointed leader and conductor at Josephstädter Theater (1822) and Kärntnertor Theater (1825). He became choirmaster of Münster Cathedral (1831), city music director in Aix-la-Chapelle (1835) and settled in Frankfort (1848). He met Beethoven in 1814, became his secretary in 1816, lived in his house from 1822-24 and returned in Dec. 1826 to care for him until his death. He wrote a biography of Beethoven (1840) and left a number of autographs and papers.

Schirmer. A firm of publishers founded in New York in 1861 by Gustav Schirmer and B. Beer. Since 1866, when Schirmer assumed sole control, the business has been carried on under its present name.

Schlag [shlahk], *G.* Beat.

Schlaginstrumente [shlahk'-in-stroo-ment-er], *G.* Percussion instruments.

Schleifer [shlife'-er], *G.* A SLIDE or slur, *i.e.* an appoggiatura consisting of two grace notes.

Schleppen [shlep'-ĕn], *G.* "To drag." *Nicht schleppen*, do not drag.

Schlick [shlick], ARNOLT: *b.* 15th cent.; *d.* after 1527. Blind organist and composer. He played in Germany and Holland, was in Strasbourg in 1492 and Worms in 1495. He became organist at the court in Heidelberg sometime before 1496. His book on organs and methods of constructing them, *Spiegel der Orgelmacher und Organisten* (1511), of which the only surviving copy is in the Hirsch library (now in the British Museum), has been reprinted by Eitner (1869) and by P. Smets (1937). Two organ settings, one of "Salve regina" and one of "Maria zart," from the *Tabulaturen etlicher Lobgesang und Lidlein* (1512; mod. ed. by G. Harms, 1924), are printed in the *Historical Anthology*, Nos. 100, 101.

Schlöger [shlurg'-er], MATTHÄUS: *b.* 1722; *d.* Vienna, June 30, 1766. A composer of instrumental music in the early classical period; he was court cembalist at Vienna. His surviving compositions are 2 symphonies and a Partita for 2 violins and bass in four movements with minuet, which is printed in *D.T.Ö.*, xv (2).

Schlüssel [shlēēce'-ĕl], *G.* Clef.

Schmelzer [shmelts'-er], JOHANN HEINRICH: *b.* Vienna, *c.* 1623; *d.* there, Feb. or March, 1680. He was at the court in Vienna as chamber musician (1649), assistant *Kapellmeister* (1671) and *Kapellmeister* (1679). He published three volumes of chamber music and composed a number of ballets for the Viennese court opera. One of his ballets has been printed in *D.T.Ö.*, xxviii, and his *Nuptial Mass* in *D.T.Ö.*, xxv (1). His son Andreas Anton (1653-1701) also composed music for ballets.

Schmetternd [shmet'-ernt], *G.* (*Fr.* cuivré). "Blaring." An indication to horn-players to play with a harsh, brassy tone.

Schmid [shmit] (Schmidt), BERNHARD: *b.* Strasbourg, 1520; *d.* there, probably 1592. Organist in Strasbourg at St. Thomas's, 1560-64, and at the Cathedral, 1564-92. He published in 1577 2 books in tablature for keyboard instruments containing arrangements of sacred and secular pieces, including dances, by various composers. His son, Bernhard (*b.* 1548) succeeded him as organist at St. Thomas's in 1564 and at the Cathedral in 1592. He published a tablature book with similar contents in 1606.

Schmidt [shmit], (1) BERNHARD (Bernard Smith): *b.* Germany, *c.* 1630; *d.* London, 1708. Organ builder, known in England as "Father Smith." Settled in England (1660) with two nephews, Christian and Gerard, as his assistants. He built his first English organ at the Chapel Royal in London and was appointed Organ-maker in Ordinary to the King and later court organ-builder to Queen Anne. In 1676 he became organist at St. Margaret's Church, Westminster, where he had built the organ (1675).

A. FREEMAN : *Father Smith* (1926).

(2) FRANZ : *b.* Pressburg (now Bratislava), Dec. 22, 1874 ; *d.* Perchtoldsdorf (nr. Vienna), Feb. 11, 1939. Cellist, organist, pianist and composer. Studied at the Vienna Conservatorium. Cellist in the Vienna Court Opera orchestra, 1896-1910. Teacher of the piano, Vienna Music Academy, 1910 ; director, 1925-37. His compositions include two operas—*Notre Dame* (Vienna, 1914) and *Fredegundis* (Berlin, 1922), the oratorio *Das Buch mit sieben Siegeln* (The Book of the Seven Seals), 4 symphonies, orchestral variations on a Hungarian Hussar song, 2 piano concertos (originally for left hand only), 2 string quartets and other chamber music, and several works for organ.

Schmitt [shmeet], FLORENT: *b.* Blamont, Sept. 28, 1870; *d.* Neuilly-sur-Seine, Aug. 17, 1958. Composer. Studied at Nancy from 1887 and under Lavignac, Massenet and Fauré at the Paris Conservatoire from 1889. He won the *Prix de Rome* in 1900. Director, Lyons Conservatoire from 1922-24, when he settled in St. Cloud, nr. Paris. He wrote many articles on music criticism for periodicals, and composed ballets, orchestral works, choral works with orchestra, including a setting of the 47th Psalm (1904), pieces for piano, for piano duet, and for 2 pianos, chamber music, and songs.

Schnabel [shnahb'-ĕl], ARTUR: *b.* Lipnik (Austrian Poland), April 17, 1882; *d.* Axenstein (Switzerland), Aug. 15, 1951. Pianist, teacher and composer. He made his debut as a pianist at the age of eight, studied under Leschetizky in Vienna (1888-97) and settled in Berlin where he was teacher at the Hochschule (1925-33). He toured extensively in Europe and America, and later settled in New York. He composed in his later years a symphony, an orchestral Rhapsody, and other works. As a pianist he was most renowned for his playing of Beethoven and Schubert. He published *Music and the Line of Most Resistance* (1942).

Schnabelflöte [shnahb'-ĕl-flurt-er], *G.* "Beaked flute." Obsolete name for the RECORDER.

Schneeweiss [shnay'-vice], AMALIE. *v.* JOACHIM (1).

Schnell [shnell], *G.* Quick.

Schneller [shnell'-er], *G.* An ornament used in the 18th cent. It was indicated thus:

and performed thus:

Since *c.* 1800 it has been called *Pralltriller* or INVERTED MORDENT.

Schobert [shobe'-ert], JOHANN: *b. c.* 1720; *d.* Paris, Aug. 28, 1767. Composer. He taught in Strasbourg and became organist at Versailles. In 1760 he settled in Paris as chamber cembalist to the Prince of Conti. A selection of his compositions, comprising 5 sonatas for harpsichord and violin, 2 trios, 2 quartets for harpsichord, two violins and cello, and 2 harpsichord concertos is published in *D.D.T.*, xxxix, which also contains a thematic catalogue of his compositions. The keyboard instrument is designated as *clavecin* or *cembalo*; in the chamber music Schobert's style is quite pianistic, and the violin part in the sonatas is either subsidiary or optional, as was customary in the early part of the classical period. His keyboard style had some influence on Mozart; the second movement of Mozart's concerto K. 39 (1767) is an arrangement of a movement from a sonata by Schobert.

Schoeck [shurk], OTHMAR: *b.* Brunnen (Switzerland), Sept. 1, 1886; *d.* Zürich, 1957. Composer and conductor. Studied at the Zürich Conservatorium, and at Leipzig with Reger. He was for many years active as a choral and orchestral conductor in Zürich. His compositions include 5 operas and other stage works, several choral works, concertos for violin, cello and horn, chamber music and nearly 400 songs.

Scholes, PERCY ALFRED: *b.* Leeds, July 24, 1877; *d.* Switzerland, July 31, 1958. Music critic, author and lexicographer. He founded and edited the *Music Student* (1908) and *Music and Youth*, was appointed music critic for the London *Evening Standard* (1913) and *Observer*, music consultant to the B.B.C. (1923), an editor of *Radio Times* (1925) and extension lecturer for Oxford, Cambridge and London Universities. He settled in Montreux, Switzerland until 1939, and after living in Oxford for several years returned to Switzerland in 1957. His books include *The Listener's History of Music* (3 vols., 1923-8), *The Puritans and Music* (1934), *Music, the Child and the Masterpiece* (1935), *The Oxford Companion to Music* (1938; 9th ed., 1955), *The Mirror of Music, 1844-1944* (2 vols., 1947), *The Great Dr. Burney* (2 vols., 1948), *The Concise Oxford Dictionary of Music* (1952), and *Sir John Hawkins* (1953).

Schönberg [shurn'-bairk], ARNOLD: *b.* Vienna, Sept. 13, 1874; *d.* Los Angeles, July 13, 1951. Composer. Largely self-taught, he made some study of counterpoint under Alexander von Zemlinsky, composed *Verklärte Nacht* (" Transfigured Night ") in 1899 and in 1900 began work on the *Gurrelieder*, which was not completed until 1911. He taught at the Stern Conservatorium in Berlin from 1901-3, then in Vienna, from 1911-18 in Berlin, 1918-25 in Vienna; was appointed to the staff of the Prussian Academy of Arts, Berlin, in 1925, and in 1933 moved to America, and settled in California. From the early works, which showed a complete command of late Romantic style, he turned about 1907, under a self-confessed " inner compulsion," to a period of experimentation in such pieces as the Three Piano Pieces, Op. 11 (1909), the 15 songs from Stefan George's *The Book of the Hanging Gardens*, Op. 15 (1907-9), the Five Pieces for Orchestra, Op. 16 (1909), the monodrama *Erwartung*, (" Expectation "), Op. 17 (1909), the drama with music *Die glückliche Hand* (The Lucky Hand), Op. 18 (1913), and the 21 songs from Albert Giraud's *Pierrot lunaire* for *Sprechgesang* and instruments, Op. 21 (1912). The technique towards which these works, which aroused bitter opposition and controversy, had been moving was formulated about 1921 in the principle of " composition with twelve notes " (*v.* TWELVE-NOTE COMPOSITION), essentially a return to polyphony, which the composer regarded as an ascent to " higher and better order." The working of this order is exemplified particularly in the compositions written between 1921 and 1933, which include the Five Pieces, Op. 23, and Suite, Op. 25, for piano, the *Serenade* for 7 instruments and bass-baritone, Op. 24, and the quintet for wind instruments, Op. 26, the third string quartet, Op. 30, and the Variations for Orchestra, Op. 31.

In many of the compositions written in America Schönberg returned to more traditional principles of form and tonality—he had, in fact, always regarded "atonality" as a misnomer—and the string suite in G major (1935) was the first work since the second quartet (1907) to have a key-signature; the second to do so was the Theme and Variations for Band, Op. 43 (1943), which was arranged for orchestra as Op. 43b in the following year. The most notable works of this last period were the violin concerto, Op. 36 (1936), the fourth string quartet, Op. 37 (1936), the *Ode to Napoleon*, a setting of Byron's poem for piano, strings, and narrator, Op. 41 (1943), the piano concerto, Op. 42 (1943), the string trio, Op. 45 (1946), and *A Survivor from Warsaw*, for narrator, male chorus, and orchestra, Op. 46 (1947). The opera *Moses und Aron* was left unfinished at his death.

His most distinguished pupils were Alban Berg, Anton von Webern, and Egon Wellesz. His *Harmonielehre* (1911; English trans. by D. Adams, 1948) is one of the most important modern treatises on harmony. He also published a book of essays, *Style and Idea* (1949), and *Models for Beginners in Composition* (1942). Between 1907 and 1910 he painted a considerable number of pictures.

D. NEWLIN : *Bruckner, Mahler, Schönberg* (1947).

E. WELLESZ : *Arnold Schönberg* (1925).

Schöne Melusine, Die [dee shurn'-*er* may-loo-zeen'-*er*] (The Fair Melusina). Overture by Mendelssohn, Op. 32 (1833), composed after the opera *Melusina* (by Kreutzer to a libretto by Grillparzer) was performed in Berlin.

Schöne Müllerin, Die [dee shurn'-*ner* mĕel'-er-in], (The Fair Maid of the Mill). A cycle of 20 songs by Schubert (1823). Words selected from the *Müllerlieder* of Wilhelm Müller, who also wrote *Die Winterreise*; modern English version by A. H. Fox Strangways and Steuart Wilson. The titles of the songs are:

1. *Das Wandern* (Wandering).
2. *Wohin* ? (Whither ?).
3. *Halt* ! (Stop !).
4. *Danksagung an den Bach* (Giving thanks to the brook).
5. *Am Feierabend* (Evening rest).
6. *Der Neugierige* (The inquisitive one).
7. *Ungeduld* (Impatience).
8. *Morgengruss* (Morning greeting).
9. *Des Müllers Blumen* (The miller's flowers).

10. *Thränenregen* (Shower of tears).
11. *Mein* (Mine).
12. *Pause* (Break).
13. *Mit dem grünen Lautenbande* (With the green lute-ribbon).
14. *Der Jäger* (The hunter).
15. *Eifersucht und Stolz* (Jealousy and pride).
16. *Die liebe Farbe* (The favourite colour).
17. *Die böse Farbe* (The hateful colour).
18. *Trockne Blumen* (Dead flowers).
19. *Der Müller und der Bach* (The miller and the brook).
20. *Des Baches Wiegenlied* (The brook's cradle-song).

School for Fathers. The title of an English version by E. J. Dent of Wolf-Ferrari's opera *I quattro rusteghi*, which was first performed in German as *Die vier Grobiane* (Munich, 1906).

School for Lovers, The. An English version of the alternative title of Mozart's opera *Così fan tutte, o sia La scuola degli amanti*.

Schoolmaster, The *G.* (Der Schulmeister). The title given to Haydn's symphony No. 55 in E♭ (1774).

Schop [shop] (Schopp), JOHANN: *d.* Hamburg, *c.* 1665. Composer, violinist, lutenist and trombonist. Studied under Brade in Hamburg. He was court musician at Wolfenbüttel and at Copenhagen and in 1621 settled in Hamburg, where he became director of the city music and organist of St. James. He composed sacred concertos (1643-44), sacred songs (1654) and instrumental music, of which little has survived, and was one of the musical editors of Rist's collections of sacred and secular songs.

Schöpfung, Die [dee shur*p*'-fōōng], *G. v.* CREATION.

Schöpfungsmesse [shur*p*'-fōōngss-mess-e*r*], *G. v.* CREATION MASS.

Schottische [shot'-ish-e*r*], *G.* Lit. "Scottish," known in England as "German polka." A round dance similar to and slower than the polka danced in the 19th cent. It is not to be identified with the ÉCOSSAISE.

Schreker [shreck'-er], FRANZ: *b.* Monaco, March 23, 1878; *d.* Berlin, March 21, 1934. Composer. Studied under Fuchs in Vienna, where he founded and conducted the Philharmonic Chorus (1911) and was teacher of composition at the Royal Academy. He was director of the Berlin Hochschule from 1920-32. He wrote the librettos for his operas, of which *Der Schatzgräber* ("The Digger for Treasure"), produced at Frankfort in 1920, was the most successful. He also composed orchestral works, works for chorus and orchestra, and songs.

Schröder-Devrient [shru*r*d'-er-de*r*-freent'], WILHELMINE: *b.* Hamburg, Dec. 6, 1804; *d.* Coburg, Jan. 26, 1860. Soprano, daughter of the baritone Friedrich Schröder and the actress Antoinette Sophie Burger. Studied in Vienna, where she made her début as Pamina in *Die Zauberflöte* at the Hofburg Theater (1821) and sang the role of Leonore in *Fidelio* (1822). From 1823-47 she was at the Court Opera in Dresden and made appearances in other cities including Paris, London and Berlin. The performances of Wagner's early operas owed much to her great dramatic and musical ability. She was Adriano in the first performance of *Rienzi*, Senta in *Der fliegende Holländer* (in which her performance averted a fiasco), and Venus in *Tannhaüser*. She was the wife of the baritone Eduard Devrient.

Schröter [shru*r*t'-er], (1) CHRISTOPH GOTTLIEB: *b.* Hohenstein (Saxony), Aug. 10, 1699; *d.* Nordhausen, 1782. Theorist and writer on music. Chorister with Graun at Dresden. Became Lotti's amanuensis, devised a hammer action for keyboard instruments in 1721, travelled to Holland and England, and from 1724-26 was at the University of Jena. Organist, Minden, 1726; Nordhausen, 1732. He published a treatise on figured bass based on the theory of Rameau (*Deutliche Anweisung zum General-Bass*, completed 1754; published 1772) and pamphlets on systems of temperament.

F. J. ARNOLD: *The Art of Accompaniment from a Thorough-Bass* (1931).

(2) JOHANN SAMUEL: *b.* Warsaw, *c.* 1750; *d.* Pimlico, nr. London, Nov. 2, 1788. Pianist and composer. Travelled with his father, the oboist J. F. Schröter,

and his sister, the celebrated singer Corona Schröter, through Holland to London, where they appeared at a J. C. Bach-Abel concert in 1772. In 1782 he succeeded J. C. Bach as music-master to the Queen. He composed chamber music and a considerable number of concertos and sonatas for the piano which were published in London, Amsterdam, Paris and elsewhere.

(3) LEONHART: *b.* Torgau, *c.* 1532; *d.* Magdeburg, *c.* 1601. Composer. Cantor, Saalfeld, 1561; Magdeburg, 1576-95. Published a number of collections of music for the Lutheran service, including settings of Latin and German hymns, psalms, an 8-part German Te Deum, and a Latin Te Deum.

Schubart [shoo'-bart], CHRISTIAN FRIEDRICH DANIEL: *b.* Sontheim (Swabia), March 24, 1739; *d.* Stuttgart, Oct. 10, 1791. Musician, poet and editor. Organist at Geislingen and music-teacher at Ludwigsburg. Later lived in Mannheim, Munich and Augsburg, where he founded his *Deutsche Chronik* (1774). He moved with his paper to Ulm and was imprisoned at Hohenasperg from 1777-87, when he became director of the Stuttgart Court Opera. He wrote the words of three songs by Schubert, an autobiography (1791-3) and a book on musical aesthetics (published in 1806), and composed songs and piano pieces.

Schubert [shoo'-bert], FRANZ PETER: *b.* Lichtental (nr. Vienna), Jan. 31, 1797; *d.* Vienna, Nov. 19, 1828. Composer. From 1805 he learnt the violin from his father, piano from his brother Ignaz, and piano, organ and counterpoint from Michael Holzer, and in 1808 was admitted as a chorister at the Imperial Chapel and a pupil at the Imperial Seminary (Konvikt). Composed his first song, *Hagar's Lament*, at 14, three quartets at 15, his first symphony and quartets Nos. 4-6 at 16; in 1814 completed his first opera, a Mass, 2 quartets, and many songs, including *Gretchen am Spinnrade*, and in 1815, with a prodigious rapidity which continued unabated to the end of his life, 4 *Singspiele*, 2 symphonies, the first piano sonata, and about 145 songs, including *Heidenröslein* and *Der Erlkönig*. He taught in his father's school from 1814-16 and was piano teacher in 1818 in the household of Count Johann Esterházy; from 1819 he lived and composed in Vienna, made very unremunerative bargains with his publishers, and was often acutely short of money.

At the centre of his art are the songs, the sheer number of which testifies to his immediate and spontaneous response to the spirit and feeling of early Romantic poetry. They are duets for singer and pianist, who are partners on equal terms, and in the range of their musical resources form a compendium, as well as a foundation, of the whole vocabulary of Romantic musical speech. Up to 1823 he made strenuous but unsuccessful efforts to achieve a practicable opera, as distinct from *Singspiel*; and the choral works of the last years show a breadth and consistency of choral style which he did not live to develop. It was in the *Unfinished* (1822) and "Great" C major (1828) symphonies, the chamber music, notably the A minor (1824), D minor (*Tod und das Mädchen*, 1824-26) and G major (1826) quartets, the piano trios in B♭ (1826) and E♭ (1827), the piano quintet (*Forelle*, 1819), the string quintet in C (1828) and the octet (1824), and the piano sonatas and duets that his lyrical melodic style is most perfectly allied to largeness of conception and form and to a consummate sense of key-design and harmonic detail.

The chronological thematic catalogue of Schubert's works by O. E. Deutsch lists 998 works. The main divisions, arranged according to their publication in the complete edition (1884-97) are: I. 8 symphonies; II. 10 overtures and other orchestral works; III. 3 octets; IV. 1 string quintet; V. 15 string quartets; VI. 1 string trio; VII. 3 piano trios, 1 piano quartet, 1 piano quintet; VIII. 8 works for piano and one instrument; IX. 32 works for piano duet; X. 15 piano sonatas; XI. 16 other works for piano; XII. 31 dances for piano; XIII. 7 Masses; XIV. 22 sacred works; XV. 15 stage works; XVI. 46 works for male choir; XVII. 19 works for mixed choir; XVIII. 6 works for female choir; XIX. 36 vocal trios and duets; XX. 567

songs with piano and 36 other solo vocal pieces; XXI. Supplement of 31 instrumental pieces and 13 vocal pieces.

G. ABRAHAM (ed.) : *Schubert : a Symposium* (1946).

A. BRENT-SMITH : *Schubert : Quartet in D minor and Octet* (1927). *Schubert : the Symphonies (C major and B minor)* (1926).

R. CAPELL : *Schubert's Songs* (1928).

O. E. DEUTSCH : *Schubert : a Documentary Biography* (1946). *Schubert : Thematic Catalogue* (1951).

A. EINSTEIN : *Schubert* (1951).

N. FLOWER : *Franz Schubert* (1928).

A. HUTCHINGS : *Schubert* (1945).

K. KOBALD : *Franz Schubert and his Time* (1928).

Schulmeister, Der [dair shool'-micever], *G. v.* SCHOOLMASTER.

Schulz [shoolts], JOHANN ABRAHAM PETER: *b.* Lüneburg, March 31, 1747; *d.* Schwedt, June 10, 1800. Conductor, author and composer. Studied under Kirnberger in Berlin, travelled in Germany, France and Italy (1768), taught in Poland and returned to Berlin in 1773, where he did some work for Kirnberger and Sulzer's encyclopedia of the fine arts, and conducted at the French theatre (1776-78). Conductor at the theatre of Prince Heinrich of Prussia in Rheinsberg, 1780; at the Danish court in Copenhagen, 1787-95, when he returned to Germany. His songs with piano in folk-song style, of which he published 3 books (1782-1790), were the first of their kind, and some are still well known in Germany. He composed 5 operas to French texts, including *Le Barbier de Séville* (1786) and *Aline, Reine de Golconde* (1787), which afterwards became popular in a Danish adaptation, and 3 operas to Danish texts.

Schuman, WILLIAM HOWARD: *b.* New York, Aug. 4, 1910. Composer. Studied at Columbia University and at the Mozarteum Academy in Salzburg. Teacher, Sarah Lawrence College, 1938; president, Juilliard Music School, New York, 1945. He has composed 6 symphonies, an *American Festival* overture, and other orchestral works, a piano concerto and a violin concerto, ballets, 4 string quartets and other chamber music, and choral works.

Schumann [shoo'-mun], (1) CLARA JOSEPHINE (*née* Wieck): *b.* Leipzig, Sept. 13, 1819; *d.* Frankfort, May 20, 1896. Pianist. Daughter of Friedrich Wieck, who taught her and Robert Schumann. Gave her first recital in 1830 at Leipzig, subsequently appeared in other German towns, and in Paris and Vienna. After considerable opposition from her father she married Robert Schumann, 1840. After her husband's death in 1856 she played frequently in England. Teacher at the Hoch Conservatorium, Frankfort, 1878-92. One of the outstanding interpreters of her time, particularly of her husband's music, she was also influential as a teacher. Her compositions include a piano concerto, a piano trio, piano solos and songs. Themes from some of her works were used by Schumann in his own compositions.

B. LITZMANN: *Clara Schumann—an Artist's Life*, 2 vols. (1913). *Letters of Clara Schumann and Johannes Brahms, 1853-96* 2 vols. (1927).

F. MAY : *The Girlhood of Clara Schumann* (1912).

(2) ROBERT: *b.* Zwickau, June 8, 1810; *d.* Endenich (nr. Bonn), July 29, 1856. Composer. With the encouragement of his father, an editor, writer and bookseller who died when he was 16, he developed in his boyhood both musical and literary interests, which were concentrated in his late teens in a burning admiration for the extravagantly romantic sentiment of Jean Paul Richter. As a law student at Leipzig in 1829 he studied piano and harmony with Friedrich Wieck, and at the end of the following year gave up his university studies for music, and composed his Op. 1, the Variations on the Name *Abegg* (that of a person, giving the theme A B♭ E G G). He studied counterpoint with Heinrich Dorn in 1831. In 1832 an injury to his right hand, caused by a contrivance of his own for developing finger technique, ruled out the possibility of a career as a pianist. In 1833 he founded the *Neue Zeitschrift für Musik* (first issue, April 3, 1834), and in 1840 married Clara Wieck, daughter of his former teacher, who became the most

renowned interpreter of his piano music. All his compositions up to 1839 were for piano; in 1840 he composed 15 sets of songs, including the cycles *Myrten*, *Frauen-Liebe und Leben* and *Dichterliebe*, comprising some 120 songs; in 1841 wrote the first symphony, the first movement of the piano concerto (then called *Phantasie* in A minor), and began the D minor symphony (later No. 4); and in 1842 wrote the 3 string quartets, the piano quartet, and the piano quintet. On the founding of the Leipzig Conservatorium in 1843 he was appointed teacher of composition, but moved in 1844 to Dresden, and in 1850 to Düsseldorf as conductor. From 1843 his work had been disturbed by periodic crises of mental exhaustion; in 1854 he threw himself into the Rhine, and was taken to a private asylum at Endenich.

His piano music embodies many of the traits which became the idioms of the piano style of the Romantic period, such as the impetuous waywardness of rhythm expressed in syncopations and in combinations of different metres, and the new effects of tonal distance resulting from sudden changes of harmony and of sonority and fusion from the use of the pedal. The subjective and literary element in his music takes the forms of deriving themes from names (*e.g.* from Abegg in the Variations, Op. 1, from Asch, the birthplace of his beloved of 1834, Ernestine von Fricken, in *Carnaval*, from Bach in the Six Fugues, Op. 60) and of relating musical styles to personalities (*e.g.* to the two aspects of his own personality, symbolised as *Eusebius* and *Florestan*, and to Chopin, Paganini and Clara Wieck—*Chiarina*—in *Carnaval*, to his imaginary society of anti-philistines, the *Davidsbund*, in the *Davidsbündlertänze* and *Carnaval*, and to a character in E. T. A. Hoffmann's *Fantasiestücke in Callot's Manier* in *Kreisleriana*, rather than of dramatic musical narrative, as with Berlioz.

His quick and intuitive insight into Romantic poetry shows itself in the varied forms and intimate expression of his songs, although he occasionally upsets the perfect balance which Schubert had achieved between singer and pianist in favour of the piano. Apart from the first symphony, which was inspired by a poem of Adolf Böttger and has some thematic cross-references in the first three movements, the third (*Rhenish*) symphony, written after a visit to Cologne in 1850 and 3 concert overtures, the orchestral and chamber music is without programmatic titles. The D minor symphony, published in its revised form as No. 4 in 1851, is a remarkable example of thematic transformation, being based almost entirely on two motives; others are the first movements of the piano concerto and of the second quartet. The ineptitude which at times mars his scoring for orchestra is due to his lack of orchestral training and experience, and his inherently " pianistic " way of thinking. His only opera *Genoveva* (Leipzig, 1850) did not achieve a real success, and his other dramatic works and choral works, although containing some of the finest of his later music, are rarely performed. In his writings Schumann deprecated the prevalent taste of the 1830's for superficial salon music and was enthusiastic about Bach and Beethoven and the new music of his more significant contemporaries; his first article saluted the genius of Chopin, his last the promise of Brahms. His articles on *Music and Musicians* were published in English in two volumes in 1877, and a selection in one volume in 1947. His principal compositions are:

(a) PIANO SOLO : 3 sonatas; 3 " sonatas for the Young " ; a *Fantasie* in three movements; 12 studies on Caprices by Paganini; Variations on *Abegg*; Impromptus on a Theme by Clara Wieck; 12 Studies in the form of Variations (*Études symphoniques*); 3 Romances; 4 Fugues and 7 " Little Fugues " (*Clavierstücke in Fughettenform*); 4 Marches; sets of pieces with the titles *Papillons*, *Intermezzi*, *Davidsbündlertänze*, *Carnaval*, *Fantasiestücke* (two), *Kinderscenen* (Scenes from Childhood); *Kreisleriana*, *Novelletten*, *Nachtstücke* (Nightpieces), *Faschingsschwank aus Wien* (Carnival Jest from Vienna), *Clavierstücke*, *Album für die Jugend* (Album for the Young), *Waldscenen* (Woodland Scenes), *Bunte Blätter* (Motley Leaves), *Albumblätter*, *Gesänge der Frühe* (Songs of the Early Morning); Toccata; Allegro in B minor; *Arabeske*; *Blumenstücke* (Flower-Pieces); *Humoreske*.

(b) PIANO DUET: 8 Polonaises; 6 Impromptus (*Bilder aus Osten*); 12 pieces for "small and big children"; 9 dances (*Ball-Scenen*); 6 Easy Dances (*Kinderball*).

(c) TWO PIANOS: Andante and Variations; 8 Polonaises.

(d) PEDAL-PIANO: 6 studies and 4 sketches.

(e) ORGAN OR PEDAL-PIANO: 6 Fugues on the name of Bach.

(f) ORCHESTRA: 4 symphonies; Overture, Scherzo and Finale; overtures to Schiller's *Braut von Messina* (Bride of Messina), Shakespeare's *Julius Caesar*; Goethe's *Hermann und Dorothea*; concerto in A minor; Introduction and Allegro Appassionato in G, and *Concert Allegro* in D for piano and orchestra; violin concerto; *Phantasie* for violin and orchestra; cello concerto; and *Concertstücke* for four horns and orchestra.

(g) CHAMBER MUSIC: 3 quartets; 3 trios; 4 *Fantasiestücke* for trio; piano quartet; piano quintet; *Märchenerzählungen* for piano, clarinet (or violin) and viola; 2 violin sonatas; *Märchenbilder* for viola and piano; 5 pieces "in folksong style" for cello and piano; 3 Romances for oboe and piano; *Fantasiestücke* for clarinet and piano; Adagio and Allegro for horn and piano.

(h) VOCAL WORKS: 33 sets or cycles and 14 single songs with piano; 3 ballads for declamation to piano; 4 sets of vocal duets, one of vocal trios, and 4 of vocal quartets with piano; 7 sets of part-songs for mixed voices, 4 for male voices and 2 for female voices; 15 choral works with orchestra.

(i) STAGE WORKS: *Genoveva* (opera); incidental music to Byron's *Manfred* (intended for performance in a version adapted by Schumann).

G. ABRAHAM (ed.): *Schumann: a Symposium* (1952).

V. BASCH: *Schumann* (1932).

H. BEDFORD: *Schumann* (1933).

J. A. FULLER-MAITLAND: *Schumann's Concerted Chamber Music* (1929). *Schumann's Pianoforte Works* (1927).

G. JANSEN: *The Life of Robert Schumann told in his Letters*, trans. M. Herbert (1890).

F. NIECKS: *Robert Schumann* (1925).

C. SCHUMANN: *Robert Schumanns Jugendbriefe* (1885; Eng. trans. 1888).

E. SCHUMANN: *Memoirs*, trans. M. Bush (1930).

K. STORCK: *The Letters of Robert Schumann*, trans. H. Bryant (1907).

Schuppanzigh [shŏŏp'-un-tsi*sh*], IGNAZ: *b.* Vienna, 1776; *d.* there, March 2, 1830. Violinist; a friend and a teacher of Beethoven. Lived in Vienna, where he was a member of Prince Lichnowsky's quartet (1794-95), conductor of the Augarten concerts (1798-99) and founder and leader of the Rasoumovsky Quartet (1808), which toured in Germany, Russia and Poland (1815-24) and gave first performances of quartets by Beethoven and Schubert. He was a member of the Vienna court orchestra from 1824 and conductor of the court opera from 1828.

Schürmann [shēēr'-mun], GEORG CASPAR: *b.* Hanover, *c.* 1672; *d.* Wolfenbüttel, Feb. 25, 1751. Composer and singer. In Hamburg as a singer at the Opera from 1693, and in the service of the Duke of Brunswick at Wolfenbüttel from 1697. He visited Italy, was in the service of the Duke of Meiningen from 1703-06, and returned to Wolfenbüttel in 1707 as court opera conductor. After Keiser (*d.* 1739) he was the most important composer for the German stage in the baroque period, and wrote some 40 operas. His *Ludovicus Pius* (Brunswick, 1726), in which he used some music by Campra, Destouches and Graun, is printed in Eitner's *Publikationen*, xvii.

Schütz [shēēts], HEINRICH (*L.* Henricus Sagittarius): *b.* Köstritz (Saxony), Oct. 8, 1585; *d.* Dresden, Nov. 6, 1672. Composer. Chorister at the Court Chapel in Cassel from 1599, studied law at Marburg University from 1607 and later music under G. Gabrieli in Venice, where he lived from 1609 to 1612. Court organist, Cassel, 1613; *Kapellmeister* to the Electoral Court in Dresden, 1617. Visited Venice again in 1628-29. He worked in Copenhagen from 1633-35, in 1637 and from 1642-45, and then remained in Dresden until his death. The greatest German composer of his century, his first published compositions were Italian madrigals (1611). In a series of compositions written for the Lutheran church (*Psalms of David*, 1619; *Resurrection Story*, 1623;

Cantiones Sacrae, 1625; *Symphoniae Sacrae*, 3 vols., 1629, 1647, 1650; *Kleine geistliche Konzerte*, 2 vols., 1636, 1639) he adopted the elaborate polychoral style of Gabrieli, the continuo madrigal style and some elements of the opera style of Monteverdi, and the *concertante* style for voices and instruments of his Italian contemporaries. In the preface to the German motets in the *Musicalia ad Chorum Sacrum* (1648), which are for 5, 6, and 7 voices with continuo, he deprecated the tendency of younger German composers to write in the Italian style without a thorough grounding in counterpoint. In the *Twelve Sacred Songs* (1657) and the *Christmas Oratorio* he achieved a perfect balance between the Italian style and the Lutheran polyphonic tradition, and in the three Passions (St. Matthew, St. Luke, St. John, 1665-66) he refined his style even further by composing the words of the Evangelist in unaccompanied chant modelled on that of the earliest Lutheran Passions. He made much less use of chorale melodies than did Lutheran composers before him and after him. His complete works have been edited, mainly by Philipp Spitta, in 18 vols. (1885-1927).

H. J. MOSER: *Heinrich Schütz, Leben und Werk* (1936).

A. PIRRO: *Schütz* (1924).

Schwanda the Bagpiper. *v.* ŠVANDA DUDÁK.

Schwanengesang [shvahn'-ĕn-ger-zung] (Swansong). A cycle of 14 songs by Schubert, composed in 1828 and published after his death. The title was supplied by the publisher. The words of the songs are by Ludwig Rellstab (7), Heinrich Heine (6) and Gabriel Seidl (1): modern English version by A. H. Fox Strangways and Steuart Wilson. The titles of the songs are:

1. *Liebesbotschaft* (Love's message).
2. *Krieger's Ahnung* (Warrior's foreboding).
3. *Frühlingssehnsucht* (Spring longing).
4. *Ständchen* (Serenade).
5. *Aufenthalt* (Resting place).
6. *In der Ferne* (In the distance).
7. *Abschied* (Farewell).
8. *Der Atlas* (Atlas).
9. *Ihr Bild* (Her picture).
10. *Das Fischermädchen* (The fisher girl).
11. *Die Stadt* (The town).
12. *Am Meer* (By the sea).
13. *Der Doppelgänger* (The spectral self).
14. *Die Taubenpost* (Pigeon post).

Schweitzer [shvites'-er], (1) ALBERT: *b.* Kaysersberg (Upper Alsace), Jan. 14, 1875. Theologian, medical missionary, organist and musical historian. Studied at Strasbourg, Paris and Berlin Universities, and organ under Eugen Münch, Ernst Münch and Widor. Organist of the Strasbourg Bach concerts from 1896 and of the Paris Bach Society concerts from 1906. He became a medical missionary in the French Congo but has made visits to Europe to give lectures and organ recitals. In his book on J. S. Bach (English trans. by E. Newman, 1911) he expounded his view of Bach as a "poet-musician" who conceived his musical ideas as expressions of various kinds of emotion suggested by his texts. While his ideas have been contested and may not be valid in all their details, their general soundness has become apparent as Bach's methods have come to be seen as a particular example of the established theory of his period concerning the nature of musical expression. Schweitzer's discussion of the relation of the music of the cantatas to their texts and of Bach's treatment of the melodies of the chorales to their words contributed much to a deeper understanding of Bach's sacred music. His autobiography has been published in an English translation as *My Life and Thought* (1933).

G. SEAVER: *Albert Schweitzer, the Man and his Mind* (1947).

(2) ANTON: *b.* Coburg, *bapt.* June 6, 1735; *d.* Gotha, Nov. 23, 1787. Conductor and composer. Studied in Bayreuth and in Italy, 1764-66. Court conductor and composer, Hildburghausen, 1766; conductor of Seyler's opera troupe, 1769. From 1772 he lived in Weimar, where he was music director at the court theatre, and from 1774 in Gotha, where he was court conductor from 1780. He composed a number of successful *Singspiele*, including *Die*

Dorfgala (1772). His *Alceste* (Weimar, 1773), to a libretto by C. M. Wieland, was written as the first step towards the creation of serious German opera, and was followed by Holzbauer's *Günther von Schwartzburg* (Mannheim, 1777) and in 1780 by Schweitzer's *Rosamund* (Mannheim), also with a libretto by Wieland. His setting of J. J. Rousseau's *Pigmalion* (1772) was the first important MELODRAMA written by a German composer.

Schwindend [shvind′-ĕnt], *G.* Dying away.

Sciolto [sholl′-to], I. Free and easy.

Scipione [sheep-yo′-neh] (Scipio). Opera in three acts by Handel. Libretto by Paolo Antonio Rolli (based on Zeno's *Scipione nelle Spagne*). First performed, London, March 23, 1726.

Scordatura [scorr-dah-too′-rah], *I.* Lit. "mistuning." Unusual tuning of a stringed instrument, generally to accommodate the chords it can play to the requirements of a particular composition. Tuning up may also be adopted to brighten the tone-colour, tuning down to increase the range downwards, and either of them to facilitate playing in certain keys. In lute-playing it was customary to depart often from the basic tuning, and the particular tuning was shown at the beginning of the piece. This procedure was adopted in the 17th and 18th cent., when *scordatura* was used on the violin and occasionally on the cello, as in Bach's fifth suite for cello solo. The music was written as if the tuning were normal, and the player used the normal fingering, so that a passage written:

which is the opening of the sixth (*Lamento*) of Heinrich Biber's 16 "mystery" sonatas for violin and continuo of *c.* 1675, would sound thus:

There are examples of *scordatura* in the music of Vivaldi and Tartini; an example for viola d'amore may be seen in a sonata by Carl Stamitz, published in *D.T.B.*, xvi, p. 113. Paganini tuned up the G string as much as a major third to brighten its quality. Saint-Saëns in his *Danse macabre* and Mahler in the scherzo of his fourth symphony have used *scordatura* for a special effect.

Score (*Fr.* partition, *G.* Partitur, *I.* partitura). Music written down in such a way that the parts for different performers appear vertically above one another is said to be written in score. Score form was used for writing down the earliest polyphony, but was replaced by CHOIRBOOK form in the 13th cent. In England, however, score form was still used for simpler church music and for carols until late in the 15th cent. PART-BOOKS were normal in the 16th cent. Since *c.* 1600 the modern method of writing in score with bar-lines has been used.

A "full" orchestral score comprises all the parts of an orchestral composition, or of an opera or a work for chorus and orchestra; a "short" score (piano score, piano reduction) is a reduction of the essential parts of an orchestral or choral work to two staves; a vocal score contains the separate vocal parts of an opera or other composition for voices and orchestra together with a reduction of the orchestral part to two staves for use with piano or organ.

A modern full score is set down in the following fashion:

Woodwind (for details see ORCHESTRA).
Brass (for details see ORCHESTRA).
Percussion.
Harp and keyboard instruments.
Solo instrument(s) in a concerto.
Voices.
First and second violins.
Violas.
Cellos and double basses.

(The older method was to place the voices between the violas and the cellos.)

As a part of musical education, score-reading means playing on the piano the essentials of a full score or all the parts of a choral piece, *e.g.* Mass or motet, written in score. It involves reading the various clefs and restoring to their true pitch the sounds of transposing instruments.

H. GÁL : *Directions for Score-reading* (1924).
R. O. MORRIS and H. FERGUSON : *Preparatory Exercises in Score-reading* (1931).

Scotch Snap. A name for the rhythm

which is one of the idioms of Scottish folk music. J. J. Quantz discussed it as a fashion of the Lombardic violinists, *i.e.* Vivaldi and Tartini, and it is more commonly called " Lombardic " rhythm on the Continent.

Scotch Symphony. Mendelssohn's third symphony in A minor, Op. 56 (completed in 1842), which he began during a visit to Scotland in 1830.

Scott, CYRIL MEIR: *b.* Oxton (Cheshire), Sept. 27, 1879. Composer and poet. Studied in Frankfort at the Hoch Conservatorium under Uzielli and Iwan Knorr, lived from 1898 in Liverpool and later in London. He has been interested in spiritualism and Oriental philosophy and has written *The Philosophy of Modernism in its Connection with Music* (1926), *The Influence of Music on History and Morals* (1929) and *Music: its Secret Influence throughout the Ages* (1933). He has composed a great deal of piano music, including a concerto (1915), a sonata (1909) and 5 *Poems* (1912), orchestral works, choral works, including a setting of Crashaw's *Nativity Hymn* (1914), a violin concerto, chamber music and songs. His opera *The Alchemist* was performed at Essen (in a German translation) in 1925.

Scottish Symphony. *v.* SCOTCH SYMPHONY.

Scriabin [scree-ah'-been], ALEXANDER NIKOLAIEVICH: *b.* Moscow, Jan. 6, 1872; *d.* there, Apr. 27, 1915. Composer and pianist. Studied piano under Safonov and composition under Taneiev and Arensky at the Moscow Conservatoire. Belaiev published his compositions and in 1896 sent him on a tour giving concerts of his own works in Berlin, Paris, Brussels, Amsterdam and The Hague. He was piano teacher at the Moscow Conservatoire from 1898-1903, lived in Switzerland until 1905 and in Brussels from 1908-10. His early works (2 symphonies, piano concerto, 3 sonatas, 7 sets of preludes, and other works for piano) had little relation to the Russian music of their time (1890-1903) but were written under the influence of Chopin, Liszt and Wagner, coupled with a subtle sense of harmony. In succeeding compositions (*The Divine Poem* and *Poem of Ecstasy* for orchestra, 7 further sonatas, 8 further sets of preludes, 6 *Poèmes*, *Vers la flamme* and other piano works) he embarked on experiments with esoteric harmonies, which were connected in his mind with his ideas on theosophy. As a basis for his harmonies he devised a chord in which the 8th to the 14th notes of the HARMONIC SERIES were disposed in fourths, thus:

In his latest works (*Prometheus* and an unfinished *Mystery*) he was moving towards his conception of a synthesis of the arts. The score of *Prometheus* includes a " colour organ," invented by Rimington; the only performance with colours simultaneously thrown on a screen was given in New York in 1914.

A. E. HULL : *A Russian Tone-Poet* (1922).
A. J. SWAN : *Scriabin* (1923).

Scriptores. *v.* COUSSEMAKER, GERBERT, MEIBOM.

Sea, The. *v.* MER.

Sea-Drift. A setting of a poem by Walt Whitman for baritone solo, chorus and orchestra by Delius (1903).

Seasons, The (*G.* Die Jahreszeiten) Secular oratorio by Haydn. Words translated and adapted from James

Thomson's poem by Baron van Swieten. The English text in current use is a translation of van Swieten's original German. First performed, Vienna, Apr. 24, 1801. There are four parts: *Spring* (*Der Frühling*), *Summer* (*Der Sommer*), *Autumn* (*Der Herbst*) and *Winter* (*Der Winter*).

Sebastiani [zay-buss-ti-ahn'-ee], JOHANN : *b*. Weimar, Sept. 30, 1622; *d*. Königsberg, 1683. Composer. Lived in Königsberg from 1650, where he was cantor of the Cathedral church from 1661, choirmaster of the Electoral church from 1663, and retired in 1679. His *St. Matthew Passion* (composed 1663, published 1672; modern edition in *D.D.T.*, xvii), which includes chorales for solo voice accompanied by 4 *viole da gamba*, illustrates one of the steps in the development of the Lutheran Passion between the 16th cent. and J. S. Bach. He also published 2 volumes of sacred and secular songs, *Parnassblumen* (1672, 1675).

Sechzehntel [ze*sh*'-tsane-tĕl], *G*. Semiquaver.

Second. The INTERVAL of a semitone (minor second), tone (major second), or tone and a half (augmented second) when the two notes concerned have adjacent letter names. For example,

is a minor second,

a major second, and

an augmented second. *v*. also TONE, SEMITONE, INTERVAL.

Seconda volta [seh-con'-dah voll'-tah], *I*. "Second time," *i.e.* the second ending when a repeat has been indicated. *v*. VOLTA (2).

Secondo [seh-con'-do], *I*. "Second." (1) The lower part of a piano duet, the upper part being termed *primo* (first). (2) The second of two or more players or singers, or of two or more groups of performers. *Violino secondo*, the second violin in a string quartet, or the whole body of second violins in an orchestra. *v*. PRIMO.

Segno, Dal [dahl sehn'-yo], *I*. From the sign, *i.e.*, repeat from the sign ·$·. *v*. REPEAT.

Segreto di Susanna, Il [eel seh-greh'-to dee soo-zahn'-nah] (Susanna's Secret). Opera in one act by Wolf-Ferrari. Libretto by Enrico Golisciani. First performed in the German version by Max Kalbeck (*Susannens Geheimnis*), Munich, Dec. 4, 1909.

Segue [seh'-goo-eh], *I*. "Follows." Used as a direction (1) to proceed to the following movement without a break, and (2) to continue a formula which has been indicated, such as arpeggiating of chords or doubling in octaves.

Seguidilla [seh-gee-deel'-lyah], *Sp*. A Spanish dance in 3/8 or 3/4 time in the style of, and faster than, the Bolero, with *coplas* sung by the players. Carmen's "Séguidille" in the first act of Bizet's opera is modelled on the *seguidilla*:

Seiber [shibe'-er], MÁTYÁS GYÖRGY : *b*. Budapest, May 4, 1905. Composer, cellist and conductor. Studied at the Budapest Academy of Music, where he was a pupil of Kodály. Taught at the Hoch Conservatorium, Frankfort, 1928-

33 ; Morley College, London, from 1942. Settled in London, 1939, and is now a British citizen. Founder (1945) and conductor of the Dorian Singers. His interests range from 16th-cent. music to jazz and twelve-note music. His compositions include several choral works (among them the cantata *Ulysses*, a setting of extracts from James Joyce's book), stage music, 3 string quartets and other chamber works, piano music and songs.

Seidl [zide'l], ANTON: *b.* Budapest, May 7, 1850; *d.* New York, March 28, 1898. Conductor. Studied at the Leipzig Conservatorium from 1870-72, when he went to Bayreuth as Wagner's assistant and made the first copy of the score of *Der Ring des Nibelungen.* He was conductor of the Leipzig Opera (1879-82) and toured Germany, Holland, England and other countries as conductor of A. Neumann's "Nibelungen" opera company. He was appointed conductor of the Bremen Opera in 1883, of German opera at the Metropolitan Opera in New York in 1885, and of the New York Philharmonic Orchestra in 1891. He conducted the first performances in America of *Tristan und Isolde* (1886), of the complete *Ring* (1889), and of Dvořák's symphony *From the New World* (1893).

Seiffert [zife'-ert], MAX: *b.* Beeskow a.d. Spree, Feb. 9, 1868; *d.* Slesvig, Apr. 13, 1948. Musicologist. Studied under Spitta in Berlin. Professor, Berlin, 1907. Taught at the Berlin Hochschule für Musik and the Hochschule für Kirchen- und Schulmusik. Director, Staatliches Institut für Musikforschung, 1936-42. His numerous publications include *Geschichte der Klaviermusik* (1899). He edited the complete works of Sweelinck and several volumes of *D.D.T.* and *D.T.B.*, and completed Chrysander's edition of *Messiah.* He was also responsible for practical editions of a large number of works by Bach, Handel and other 18th-cent. composers, and edited a series of editions of old music entitled *Organum.* Editor, *Sammelbände der Internationalen Musikgesellschaft*, 1904-14; *Archiv für Musikwissenschaft*, 1918-28.

Sekles [zeck'-lĕss], BERNHARD: *b.* Frankfort, June 20, 1872 ; *d.* there, Dec. 15, 1934. Composer. Studied at the Hoch Conservatorium in Frankfort and conducted in Heidelberg (1893-94) and in Mayence (1894-95). Teacher, Hoch Conservatorium, 1896 ; co-director, 1916 ; director, 1923-33. He composed 2 operas, a symphony, Passacaglia and Fugue for organ and orchestra, a symphonic poem and other orchestral works, choral works, a Serenade for 11 instruments and other chamber music, songs and piano pieces.

Selle [zell'-er], THOMAS: *b.* Zörbig, March 23, 1599 ; *d.* Hamburg, July 2, 1663. Composer. Rector and cantor at various churches, and in 1641 cantor at the Johanneum and musical director at the five principal churches in Hamburg. He published several sets of solo songs with continuo, of sacred concertos, and of secular choral pieces, and contributed melodies to Johann Rist's collections of chorale texts. He was one of the first composers who introduced settings of other words into the Passion ; his *St. John Passion* of 1643 contained choruses to words from Isaiah and Psalm 22.

Semele. Secular oratorio by Handel. Text after an opera libretto by William Congreve. First performed, London, Feb. 10, 1744.

Semibreve (*A.* whole-note, *Fr.* ronde, *G.* ganze Note, *I.* semibreve). "Half a breve". The longest note-value normally used in modern notation, written o. In the 13th cent. it was the shortest note, and the breve could be divided into from 2 to 9 semibreves. In the 15th cent. it became the normal beat (*tactus*), and in the 18th cent. became the theoretical term of reference for all time-signatures and for all other note-values

Semicroma [seh-mee-cro'-mah], *I.* Semiquaver.

Semiminima [seh-mee-mee'-nee-mah], *I.* "Half a minim," *i.e.* a crotchet.

Semiquaver (*A.* sixteenth-note, *Fr.* double croche, *G.* Sechzehntel, *I.* semicroma). The note

♬ grouped ♬

which is half the length of a quaver (eighth-note) and a sixteenth of the length of a semibreve (whole-note).

Semiramide [seh-mee-rah′-mee-deh] (Semiramis). Opera in two acts by Rossini. Libretto by Gaetano Rossi (based on Voltaire's tragedy). First performed, Venice, Feb. 3, 1823.

Semitone. Half a tone—the smallest interval in normal use in Western music. It can be written either as an augmented unison :

or as a minor second :

according to context. In EQUAL TEMPERAMENT there are 12 equal semitones in an octave, and the vibration ratio of a semitone is $1 : \sqrt[12]{2}$.

Semplice [sem′-plee-cheh], *I.* In a simple manner.

Sempre [sem′-preh], *I.* "Always, still," as in *sempre piano*, still softly.

Senaillé [ser-na-yay], JEAN BAPTISTE: *b.* Paris, Nov. 23, 1687; *d.* there, Oct. 8, 1730. Violinist. Studied under Baptiste Anet, and under Vitali in Modena, where he became attached to the ducal court; from 1720 he was a member of the royal string orchestra in Paris. He introduced Italian violin technique into France, and was one of the first French composers of solo sonatas for violin, of which he published 5 books between 1710 and 1727.

Senfl [zenf'l] (Senffl, Sänftli, Senfel), LUDWIG: *b.* Zürich, between 1488 and 1490; *d.* Munich, early in 1543. Composer. Studied under Isaac and in 1517 was his successor as court *Kapellmeister* at Vienna. In 1520 he was in Augsburg, and in 1523 became director of the court chapel at Munich. Although attached to a Roman Catholic court he corresponded with Luther and composed polyphonic choral settings of Lutheran chorales, of which 11 were published in Rhau's collection of 1544 (modern ed. in *D.D.T.*, xxxiv). In 1530-31 he completed an unfinished sequence in Isaac's *Choralis Constantinus* and supervised the copying of the whole work. He was a prolific and versatile composer. The range of his choral compositions extends from settings of German secular songs, printed in such collections as those of Georg Forster (1540; partly reprinted in *Publikationen der Gesellschaft für Musikforschung*, xxix) and Johann Ott (1544; reprinted in the same series, i-iii) to settings of Latin hymns in Georg Rhau's collection of 1542 (reprinted in *Das Erbe deutscher Musik*, xxi and xxv), Magnificats in the 8 tones and motets (8 Magnificats and 12 motets were printed in *D.T.B.*, iii, 2), and Masses. Five volumes of a complete edition of his works have appeared between 1937 and 1949; Vol. I contains seven Masses, Vols. II, IV and V German songs for 4 to 6 voices, and Vol. III 14 motets.

Sennet (Synnet, Cynet, Signet). A direction in Elizabethan plays that instrumental music is to be played. It is probably a corruption of *sonata* as TUCKET is of *toccata*.

Senza [sen′-tsah], *I.* "Without," as in *senza rall.*, without slowing down; *senza sordino,* without the mute.

Septet (*Fr.* septuor, *I.* settimino). A composition, usually instrumental, for 7 performers. Beethoven wrote a septet (Op. 20) for violin, viola, horn, clarinet, bassoon, cello and double bass, and there are later examples by Saint-Saëns (piano, strings and trumpet, Op. 65), d'Indy (suite for trumpet, two flutes, and string quartet, Op. 24), and Ravel (Introduction and Allegro for harp, string quartet, flute and clarinet, 1906).

Septuor [sep-tēē-orr], *Fr.* Septet.

Sequence. (1) Repetition of the same melodic pattern at a different pitch, *e.g.* :

from the fugue in B♭ in the first book of Bach's *Forty-eight.* The repetition may be ornamented, as in the subject of the same fugue :

Sequential melody, if it is based on more than one chord, is usually accompanied by sequential harmony. If such a sequence is an exact transposition, involving modulation, it is called a " real " or modulating sequence, if not, " tonal " or diatonic.

(2) A form of Latin liturgical poetry (*sequentia*) which was very widely used in the Middle Ages, especially in France and England. It was sometimes called *prosa.* Only 5 sequences now remain in the Roman liturgy : *Dies irae* (Requiem Mass), *Lauda Sion Salvatorem* (Corpus Christi), *Stabat Mater* (Feast of the Seven Sorrows of the Blessed Virgin Mary), *Veni Sancte Spiritus* (Whitsunday), and *Victimae paschali laudes* (Easter). In form the sequence consists of a series of pairs of lines, each pair being sung to the same melody, thus :

1. Sta - bat Ma - ter__ do - lo - ro - sa
2. Cu - jus a - ni - mam ge - men - tem,

Jux - ta cru - cem__ la - cri - mo - sa,
Con - tris - ta - tam__ et do - len - tem,

Dum pen - de - bat Fi - li - us.
Per trans - i - vit gla - di - us.

3. O quam tris - tis__ et af - flic - ta *etc.*
4. Quae mae - re - bat__ et do - le - bat *etc.*

The text of the *Stabat Mater* has been frequently set by composers from the late 15th cent. to modern times.

The sequence probably originated in northern France by the adoption of methods used in Byzantine hymns, as a musical and verbal extension of the Alleluia of the Mass. The first important writer of sequences, Notker Balbulus of St. Gall (*d.* 912) describes it as the writing of words (*i.e.* " tropes ") to the long melodies (called *jubilus*) sung to the last syllable of the Alleluia. The sequence soon became a separate form of rhymed poetry with paired lines, sung after the Alleluia on festivals and important Saints' days. All but four were excluded from the liturgy in the reforms of the Council of Trent; a fifth, the *Stabat Mater,* was admitted to the Roman Missal in 1727. *v.* also DIES IRAE, STABAT MATER, TROPE.

Seraglio, Il [eel seh-rahl′-yo]. *v.* ENTFÜHRUNG.

Serenade. (1) A set of movements for chamber orchestra or for wind instruments, similar in style to the cassation and divertimento, composed for evening entertainment in the 18th century. Mozart's serenades usually have two minuets and a varying number of sonata movements. Beethoven wrote a Serenade for string trio, Op. 8 (afterwards revised as Op. 41 for flute or violin and piano) and a Serenade for flute, violin, and viola, Op. 25 (arranged as a Notturno, Op. 42, for piano and viola). Brahms's first works for orchestra were two serenades, Op. 11 for orchestra with four horns and Op. 16 for small orchestra without violins. Schönberg wrote a Serenade (Op. 24, 1924) in 7 movements, for clarinet, bass clarinet, mandoline, guitar, violin, viola, cello, with a bass voice in the fourth movement.

(2) A song of amorous devotion, *e.g.* Don Giovanni's " Deh vieni alla finestra " in Mozart's opera, and Schubert's *Ständchen.*

Serenata [seh-reh-nah′-tah], *I.* (1) A title used in the early 18th cent. for a secular cantata or short opera composed to do homage to a patron. Bach used the term for his cantata *Durchlaucht'ster Leopold* (B.G. xxxiv, p. 1) written for the birthday of Prince Leopold of Anhalt-Cöthen in 1717, and Handel for his *Aci, Galatea e Polifemo* (Naples, 1709) and his masque *Acis and Galatea*, composed at Cannons in 1720.

(2) Serenade.

Sermisy [sair-mee-zee], CLAUDE DE (Claudin): *b. c.* 1490; *d.* 1562. Composer. He was at the Sainte-Chapelle in Paris from 1508-14 and in 1515 was appointed a singer at the King's chapel, where he later became master of the choristers. With François I he visited Bologna, where the French choir competed with the Papal choir (1515). They also sang with the choir of Henry VIII at the Field of the Cloth of Gold in 1520 and at Boulogne in 1532. His compositions, which were numerous and included Masses, motets, a Passion and *chansons*, were published in Paris, Nuremberg, Rome, and Venice. Attaingnant's collection of 31 *chansons* of 1629, which contained 11 *chansons* by him, has been reprinted in H. Expert's *Les Maîtres musiciens de la Renaissance française*, v (1897).

Serov [syehr'-off], ALEXANDER NIKOLAIEVICH: *b.* St. Petersburg, Jan. 23, 1820; *d.* there, Feb. 1, 1871. Composer and music critic. He studied law and music and began work as a critic in 1851 when he wrote articles for the Russian *Contemporary*. He visited Germany in 1858 and became a supporter of Wagner. He was university lecturer at St. Petersburg (1859-64) and at Moscow (1865). In 1867 he married Valentina Semenovna Bergmann who was also a composer and music critic. His operas *Judith* (1863), *Rogneda* (1865), and *Vrazhya Sila* (The Power of Evil, 1871) were very successful in Russia. He composed a few orchestral works, choral works, and piano pieces.

Serpent (*Fr. G.* Serpent, *I.* serpentone). An obsolete wind instrument, the name of which was suggested by the shape, and which was the bass of the cornett (*G.* Zink) family. It was made of wood covered with leather, and though in the opinion of Cecil Forsyth it "presented the appearance of a dishevelled drain-pipe which was suffering internally" it pursued a versatile career for some 300 years. As the *serpent d'église* it was used in France from the 16th cent. to support the singing of plainsong. It was adopted by English church bands in the 19th cent. Handel wrote for it, as bass to a large wind group, in the *Fireworks* music. Having changed its name to the *serpent droit* it appeared in the scores of Rossini (*Le Siège de Corinthe*), Mendelssohn (*St. Paul*), Wagner (*Rienzi*), and Verdi (*Les Vêpres Siciliennes*). *v.* BASS HORN, RUSSIAN BASSOON.

Serpent droit [sair-pun͡ drwa], *Fr. v.* BASS HORN, SERPENT.

Serpentone [sair-pen-to'-neh], *I.* Serpent.

Serse [sair'-seh] (Xerxes). Opera in three acts by Handel. Libretto adapted from an earlier text by Niccolò Minato. First performed, London, Apr. 26, 1738.

Serva Padrona, La [lah sair'-vah pah-dro'-nah] (The Maid as Mistress). Opera in two parts by Pergolesi. Libretto by Gennaro Antonio Federico. First performed as two *intermezzi* in the composer's opera *Il prigionier superbo*, Naples, Aug. 28, 1733. It was soon widely performed on its own and gave the impulse to the cultivation of *opera buffa*, and indirectly of the French *opéra-comique* (first performance in Paris, 1746). Serpina (Uberto's maid) wants to marry her bachelor master and so devises a plan to arouse his jealousy. She persuades Vespone (Uberto's servant) to dress as a sailor who has come to plead for her hand. Uberto, fearing that the supposed sailor will take his maid away from him, marries her himself and thus the maid becomes the mistress.

Service. The musical setting of the canticles at Morning and Evening Prayer and of the congregational part of the Communion service in the Anglican liturgy. In the Morning Service are the *Te Deum* and *Benedictus* (or *Jubilate*); in the Evening Service the *Magnificat* (or *Cantate domino*) and *Nunc dimittis* (or *Deus misereatur*); in the Communion Service the *Kyrie*, *Sanctus* and *Gloria in excelsis*, and also, in modern times, the *Benedictus* and *Agnus Dei*. A full service includes settings of all these parts, which are sung in English, although they have retained their Latin names.

16th-cent. composers were accustomed to distinguish between a "short" service, set in simple style, and a "great" service, set in a more elaborate polyphonic style or in antiphonal style for the two sides of the choir, *Decani* and *Cantoris*, in alternation and combination. Among the best examples of the early period are the services of Tallis, Byrd and Tomkins. Byrd's Second Service "with verses to the organs" initiated a style of service corresponding to that of the Verse Anthem, but after Tomkins and Gibbons the composition of services became rather perfunctory, and those of post-Restoration composers are much inferior to their best anthems, with the exception of Purcell's *Te Deum* and *Jubilate* in D and his full service in B♭. The services of S. S. Wesley and Walmisley suggest higher artistic aims than those of their 18th-cent. predecessors, but few services of the past hundred years, with the possible exception of those of C. V. Stanford, have succeeded in fulfilling them or in rising above the general level of the church music of the period.

Sesquialtera, *L.* Short for *pars sesquialtera*, a quantity one and a half times as much. In the theory of PROPORTIONS, which had its musical application in the rhythmic practice and in the theory of intervals of medieval and Renaissance music, the prefix *sesqui-* denoted a proportion in which one term was greater than the other by one, *e.g.* 3 : 2 (*sesquialtera*), 4 : 3 (*sesquitertia*), etc. In connection with rhythm and interval *sesquialtera* was commonly called HEMIOLA, *q.v.* The organ stop *sesquialtera* is a MUTATION stop normally having two ranks of $2\frac{2}{3}$ ft. and $1\frac{3}{5}$ ft. giving the intervals of the 12th and the 17th from the fundamental.

Sessions, ROGER: *b.* Brooklyn, N.Y., Dec. 28, 1896. Composer. Studied at Harvard University, under Horatio Parker at Yale University, and under Ernest Bloch in Cleveland and New York. Teacher, Smith College, 1917; head of the theory department at Cleveland Institute of Music, 1921. From 1925-33 he lived in Florence, Rome and Berlin. He taught at Boston University, at Princeton University from 1937, at the University of California from 1945, and again at Princeton from 1953. His compositions include 3 symphonies and other orchestral works, a violin concerto, piano pieces, organ works and songs. Published *The Musical Experience of Composer, Performer, Listener* (1950); *Harmonic Practice* (1951); *& Reflections on Musical Life in the United States.*

Sestetto [sess-tet′-to], *I.* Sextet.

Settimino [set-tee-mee′-no], *I.* Septet.

Ševčik [shev′-chick], OTTOKAR: *b.* Horazdowitz (Bohemia), March 22, 1852; *d.* Písek, Jan. 18, 1934. Violinist and teacher. Studied at the Prague Conservatoire under Sitt and Bennewitz. Leader of the Mozarteum Orchestra, Salzburg, 1870; Vienna Comic Opera, 1873. Teacher, Imperial Russian Music School, Kiev, 1875; Prague Conservatoire, 1892; the Vienna Academy of Music, 1909; Prague from 1919. He also taught in London, visited the United States (1922-31) and later settled in Písek. His many pupils included Kubelik, Zimbalist, Erica Morini and Marie Hall. He wrote a violin method (4 vols., 1883) and other studies for the violin.

Seventh. The interval comprised by the first and last of any series of seven notes in a diatonic scale, *e.g.*:

A major seventh:

is a semitone less than an octave, a minor seventh:

is a tone less than an octave, and a diminished seventh:

is a tone and a half less than an octave. Since the seventh is a dissonance, a chord containing a seventh required resolution in traditional harmony. The most important chords containing sevenths are the DOMINANT seventh chord and the DIMINISHED SEVENTH chord. *v.* CHORD, INTERVAL.

Seven Words of the Redeemer on the Cross, The (Die Sieben Worte des Erlösers am Kreuze). (1) An orchestral work by Haydn (1785) commissioned by the Cathedral of Cadiz and composed in seven slow movements which the composer later arranged (1) as a set of seven string quartets (Op. 51, 1787) and (2) as a choral work (1796).

(2) For an oratorio by Schütz with a similar title *v.* SIEBEN WORTE.

Séverac [save-ruck], JOSEPH MARIE DÉODAT DE: *b.* St. Félix de Caraman, July 20, 1873; *d.* Céret, March 24, 1921. Composer. Studied at the Toulouse Conservatoire and from 1897-1907 under Magnard and d'Indy at the Schola Cantorum in Paris. He composed an opera (*Le Coeur du moulin*, Paris, 1909) and other stage works, symphonic poems, chamber music, a sonata and other pieces for piano, a suite for organ, and songs.

Sextet (*Fr.* sextette, sextuor, *I.* sestetto). A composition, instrumental or vocal, for 6 performers. The instruments normally in a string sextet are 2 violins, 2 violas, and 2 cellos, as in Brahms's 2 string sextets, Op. 18 and 36, and Schönberg's *Verklärte Nacht* (1899). Haydn wrote an *Echo* for 4 violins and 2 cellos, and Eugene Goossens a string sextet, Op. 35 for 3 violins, viola and 2 cellos. Beethoven's wind sextet, Op. 71, is for 2 clarinets, 2 horns and 2 bassoons, and his Op. 81b is for 2 violins, viola, cello and 2 horns. In vocal music the term is usually applied only to operatic ensembles.

Sextolet. A group of 6 notes to be performed in the time of 4 of the same kind in the prevailing metre, thus :

It is most often the equivalent of two successive triplets, and is therefore more properly written with that grouping :

Where it is not so grouped and is not accompanied by another rhythm, it should be played evenly, without a subsidiary accent, as in :

CHOPIN, *Nocturne Op.* 48, *No.* 2

Sextuor [sex-tēē-orr], *Fr.* Sextet.

Seyfried [zy'-freet], IGNAZ XAVER, RITTER VON: *b.* Vienna, Aug. 15, 1776; *d.* there, Aug. 27, 1841. Composer, conductor and teacher. Studied piano under Mozart and Kozeluch and composition under Albrechtsberger, Haydn and P. Winter. From 1797-1828 he was conductor at Schikaneder's theatre, which became the Theater-an-der-Wien in 1801. He edited the theoretical works of Albrechtsberger and Preindl and published a work on *Beethoven's Studies in Figured Bass, Counterpoint, and Composition* (1832). His compositions include over 100 stage works, church music, orchestral and chamber music, and piano sonatas.

Sforzando [sforr-tsahnd'-o], *I.* Lit. "forcing," *i.e.* giving a strong accent on a single note or chord. Usually abbreviated *sfz* or *sf*.

Sforzato [sforr-tsah'-toh), *I.* Lit. "forced." *v.* SFORZANDO.

Sgambati [sgahm-bah'-tee], GIOVANNI: *b.* Rome, May 28, 1841; *d.* there, Dec. 14, 1914. Pianist, conductor and composer. He appeared as pianist and as conductor from the age of 6. Studied under Liszt in Rome, where he lived from 1860 and conducted concerts, mainly of German music, from 1866. He visited Germany (1869), London (1882, 1891), Paris (1884), Cologne (1887) and Russia (1903). He was pianist and director of Queen Margherita's quintet and a founder of, and teacher at, the Liceo Musicale from 1877. His compositions include 2 symphonies, an *Epitalamio sinfonico* (1887) and 2 overtures for orchestra, a *Requiem* for chorus and orchestra, chamber music, pieces for piano and for violin and piano, and songs.

Shahrazad. *v.* SCHEHERAZADE.

Shake. Old English term for TRILL.

Shamus O'Brien. Opera in two acts by Stanford. Libretto by George H. Jessop (founded on the poem by Joseph Sheridan Le Fanu). First performed, London, March 2, 1896.

Shanty. A work-song sung by sailors in the days of sailing ships. Shanties usually have a decided rhythm, and are in the form of solo verses and chorus. Collections of shanties have been published by J. Bradford and A. Fagge (1904), Cecil Sharp (1914), H. Kemp (1922), W. B. Whall (1912) and R. R. Terry (2 vols., 1921 and 1926).

Shaporin [sha-po′-reen], YOURI ALEXANDROVICH: *b.* Glukhov (Ukraine), Nov. 8, 1889. Composer. Studied law at the University of St. Petersburg and music at the Conservatoire from 1913 to 1917 under Sokolov, Steinberg and Tcherepnin. He worked in the theatre as conductor and composer and composed a great deal of incidental music for plays, besides piano sonatas and songs. His 3 major works are a symphony for orchestra, brass band and chorus, completed in 1932, in which he attempts "to show the development of the fate of a human being in a great historical upheaval," a setting for chorus, soloists and orchestra of Blok's poem *On the Field of Kulikovo* (1939), and an oratorio *The Battle on Russian Soil* (1944). Parts of an opera *The Decembrists* were privately performed in Moscow in 1938; the work was completed in 1941.

G. ABRAHAM: *Eight Soviet Composers* (1943).

Sharp (*Fr.* dièse, *G.* Kreuz, *I.* diesis). The sign ♯ which raises by a semitone the pitch of the line or space on which it stands.

Sharp, CECIL JAMES: *b.* London, Nov. 22, 1859; *d.* there, June 23, 1924. Collector of English folk-music. Educated at Cambridge and from 1889-92 lived in Australia, where he was organist of Adelaide Cathedral and founded a school of music. He was director of Hampstead Conservatoire in London from 1896-1905 and in 1911 founded the English Folk-Dance Society and became director of the School of Folk-song and Dance, Stratford-on-Avon. He also collected folk-music in the Appalachian Mountains in America. His collections, which laid the foundation of the English folk-song and folk-dance revival, include *Folk-songs from Somerset* (1904-19), *Country Dance Tunes* (1909 ff.), *The Morris Book* (1907-13), *The Sword Dances of Northern England* (1911), *English Folk-chanteys* (1914) and *English Folk-songs from the Southern Appalachians* (1917; new ed. by Maud Karpeles, 2 vols., 1932). His collaborators in these volumes were C. L. Marson, G. S. K. Butterworth, H. MacIlwaine and Maud Karpeles. He also published *English Folk-song; some Conclusions* (1907).

A. H. FOX STRANGWAYS & M. KARPELES: *Cecil Sharp* (2nd ed., 1955).

Shawm (*Fr.* chalumeau, *G.* Schalmei, *I.* cialamello). Earlier name for the family of wind instruments played with a double reed. *v.* OBOE.

Shebalin [sheb-ah′-leen], VISSARION YAKOVLEVICH: *b.* Omsk, June 11, 1902. Composer. Studied at the Omsk School of Music and at the Moscow Conservatoire, where he was a pupil of Miaskovsky and subsequently became teacher and director (till 1948). In 1948 he was cited by the Communist Party as one of the "inculcators of inharmonious music in the educational institutions." His compositions include an opera (*The Embassy Bridegroom*), 4 symphonies (the third, *Lenin*, with chorus), cantatas, overtures, *concertino* for horn and small orchestra, *concertino* for violin and strings, violin concerto, cello concerto, 6 string quartets, violin sonata, 2 sonatas and 3 sonatinas for piano, and songs.

G. ABRAHAM: *Eight Soviet Composers* (1943).

Sheep may safely graze. An English translation of "Schafe können sicher weiden," an aria for soprano with two recorders and figured bass from Bach's earliest secular cantata *Was mir behagt* (1716), composed to celebrate the birthday of Duke Christian of Sachsen-Weissenfels. The cantata, the words of which are by Salomo Franck, is in praise of hunting. The text of this aria compares the sense of security felt by a people governed by a wise ruler to that of sheep in the care of a reliable shepherd.

Shéhérazade [shay-ay-ra-zud], *Fr.* A set of three songs (*Asie, La Flûte enchantée* and *L'Indifférent*) by Ravel (1903) for voice and orchestra (originally piano accompaniment) with words from poems by Tristan Klingsor. The work is based on an unpublished overture (1898) with the same title. *v.* also SCHEHERAZADE.

Shepherds of the Delectable Mountains, The. Opera in one act by Vaughan Williams. Libretto from Bunyan's *The Pilgrim's Progress.* First performed, London, July 11, 1922. The greater part of this work was later incorporated in the opera *The Pilgrim's Progress* (London, 1951).

Sheppard (Shepherd, Shepheard, Shepperd), JOHN: 16th-cent. English composer. Chorister at St. Paul's Cathedral. Organist and choirmaster, Magdalen College, Oxford, 1542-43 and 1545-47. Also a member of Queen Mary's Chapel. He composed church music to both Latin and English words, little of which has been published in modern editions. Burney printed the "Esurientes" section from a Magnificat, Hawkins a three-part anthem "Stev'n first after Christ," and his *French Mass* has been edited by H. B. Collins. He composed a Mass on the song "The Western Wynde," which was also used in Masses by Taverner and Tye.

Shield, WILLIAM: *b.* Whickham (Co. Durham), March 5, 1748; *d.* Brightling, Jan. 25, 1829. Composer. He was apprenticed to a boat-builder and studied under Avison in Newcastle, where he became leader of the subscription concerts. He was appointed leader of the Scarborough theatre orchestra, first viola of the London Opera (1773-91), and composer to Covent Garden from 1782-91. In 1791 he met Haydn in London and visited France and Italy. He returned to Covent Garden as composer (1792-7) and in 1817 became Master of the King's Music. He "composed and selected" the music for many stage works, of which the opera *Rosina* (1782) was one of the most successful, and published collections of songs, ballads, rounds and glees, a set of 6 string trios, a set of duets for violins, and two theoretical works: *An Introduction to Harmony* (1800) and *Rudiments of Thorough Bass* (*c.* 1815). The song, "The Arethusa," generally attributed to Shield, was adapted from a country dance tune, "The Princess Royal," first published in 1730.

Shift. (1) Change of POSITION of the left hand in playing a stringed instrument.

(2) Change of position of the slide of a TROMBONE.

Short Octave. The lowest notes on keyboard instruments in the 16th and 17th cent. were often arranged so as to provide within the compass of a sixth (short octave) the bass notes normally required, leaving out those which did not occur on account of the restricted range of keys used in the music. In one such arrangement the lowest keys appeared to be from E to C, but the notes they actually played ran thus:

As a further result, left-hand chords occasionally appear in the music which seem to involve the stretch of a tenth, but actually do not. The chord:

for example, in the last bar of a piece by Peter Philips in *The Fitzwilliam Virginal Book* (modern ed. by Fuller-Maitland and Squire, i, p. 287) was played as if the notes were:

Short Score. A reduction of all the essential parts of an orchestral or choral score to two staves. *v.* SCORE.

Shostakovich [shoss-ta-co′-vitch], DMITRI: *b.* St. Petersburg, Sept. 25, 1906. Composer. Studied composition under Steinberg and piano under Nikolaiev at St. Petersburg Conservatoire. He wrote a Scherzo for orchestra at 13, and his first symphony was performed in Leningrad in 1926. The works of the next few years alternated between the political, as in the second symphony (1927), dedicated to the October Revolution of 1917, and the third (*May the First*) symphony (1930), and the satirical, as in the opera *The Nose* (1927-8), and the ballet *The Golden Age* (1930). Unfortunately for Shostakovich, official disfavour fell on the more extreme forms of social caricature in music, and the blow fell on his opera *Lady Macbeth of Mzensk* in 1936, although it had for two years been performed in Russia and elsewhere. It was criticised as " the negation of the very principles of opera," and as a " thoroughly non-political concoction." The fourth symphony was withdrawn (1936) in rehearsal, and the fifth (1937), in more serious vein and in traditional form without a programme, was described by the composer as " a Soviet artist's practical reply to just criticism " which depicted " the re-education of the human mind . . . under the influence of the new ideals." The seventh symphony was composed during the siege of Leningrad in 1941, and depicts peace, struggle and victory. In acknowledging renewed criticism of his music by the Central Committee of the Communist Party in 1948 Shostakovich admitted that his " artistic reconstruction " had not been complete, and undertook to bring his work closer to " folk art." Besides his 11 symphonies and the operas, his notable works are the piano concerto (1933), 24 preludes for piano (1932-33), 24 preludes and fugues for piano (1951), a cello sonata (1934), a piano quintet (1940) and 3 string quartets (1938, 1944, 1947).

S. MARTINOV : *Dmitri Shostakovich* (1947).
V. I. SEROV : *Dmitri Shostakovich* (1943).

Shudi [shoo′-di], BURKAT (Burkhardt Tschudi): *b.* Schwanden, Glarus (Switzerland), March 13, 1702; *d.* London, Aug. 19, 1773. Harpsichord maker. He became apprentice to Tabel, a London harpsichord maker, in 1718 and founded his own business in 1742. His son-in-law, John Broadwood, succeeded him and was in turn succeeded by his own sons. He patented a " Venetian swell " for the harpsichord in 1769.

Si [see], *Fr. I.* The note B.

Sibelius [see-bay′-lee-ooss], JEAN: *b.* Hämeenlinna (Tavastehus), Finland, Dec. 8, 1865; *d.* Träskända (nr. Helsinki), Sept. 22, 1957. Composer. Studied at Helsinki Conservatoire under Wegelius, in Berlin under Albert Becker, and in Vienna under Robert Fuchs and Carl Goldmark. The works of 1890-1900 expressed the aspirations of Finland towards a national musical culture, and included the tone-poems *En Saga* (1892) and *Finlandia* (1899) and 4 *Legends* (*Lemminkäinen and the Maidens*, 1895; *Lemminkäinen in Tuonela*, 1895; *The Swan of Tuonela*, 1893; *The Return of Lemminkäinen*, 1895) based on the Finnish epic, the Kalevala. These works showed an individual approach to the treatment of the orchestra and of thematic material which was further developed in the 7 symphonies (1899-1924). In the exposition of the first movement of the second symphony a number of short motives are presented, in the development they are built into long phrases, and in the recapitulation they are combined and compressed. The fourth symphony is concise in form and is mainly based on the melodic and harmonic relation of the tritone. In the seventh symphony the normal scheme is compressed into one movement, the final section being a partial recapitulation of the first section. Other notable works of Sibelius are the symphonic poems *Pohjola's Daughter* (1906), *Night-*

ride and Sunrise (1909), *The Bard* (1913), *The Oceanides* (written for his visit to America in 1914), *Tapiola* (1925), the incidental music to Shakespeare's *The Tempest* (1926), the violin concerto (1903-5), and the string quartet *Voces intimae* (1909). He also composed a great many pieces for violin and piano, cello and piano, voice and piano, piano solo, and chorus.

G. ABRAHAM (ed.) : *Sibelius : a Symposium* (1947).
K. EKMAN : *Jean Sibelius* (1936).
C. GRAY : *Sibelius* (1934). *Sibelius : the Symphonies* (1935).
I. HANNIKAINEN : *Sibelius and the Development of Finnish Music* (1948).
R. NEWMARCH : *Jean Sibelius* (1905).
B. DE TÖRNE : *Sibelius : a Close-up* (1937).

Siciliano [see-cheel-yahn'-o] (Siciliana), *I.* A type of Sicilian dance used in the baroque period in instrumental music and in arias, written in a moderately slow 6/8 or 12/8 time. In style and in its frequent use of the rhythm

it is similar to the PASTORALE. For example, the second movement of J. S. Bach's Sonata in E♭ for flute and harpsichord (*B.G.*, ix, p. 22) is a *siciliano* which begins thus:

Sicilian Vespers, The. *v.* VÊPRES SICILIENNES.

Side Drum (*Fr.* tambour militaire, *G.* kleine Trommel, *I.* tamburo militare). The smallest of the orchestral drums, also called "snare drum" because it has pieces of catgut (snares) stretched across the lower head. Besides the roll (" Daddy-Mammy "), which is played with alternating double strokes, its special strokes are:

the " open flam "

the " closed flam "

and the " drag "

For some extended passages of writing for the side drum see the score of Strauss's *Ein Heldenleben*, from No. 45 to No. 75.

Sieben Worte, Die [dee zeeb'-ĕn vorrt'-*er*] (The Seven Words).

(1) *Die sieben Worte unsers lieben Erlösers und Seligmachers Jesu Christi* (The Seven Words of our beloved Redeemer and Saviour Jesus Christ). Short oratorio by Schütz (1645). Text compiled from the four gospels.

(2) *Die sieben Worte des Erlösers am Kreuze* (The Seven Words of the Redeemer on the Cross). A work by Haydn which exists in three forms. *v.* SEVEN WORDS.

Siefert [zee'-fert], PAUL: *b.* Danzig, 1586; *d.* there, May 6, 1666. Composer and organist. Studied under Sweelinck at Amsterdam, was attached to the chapel of Sigismund III in Warsaw and in 1623 was appointed organist of St. Mary's in Danzig. The style of his *Psalmen Davids* of 1640 was criticised by Marco Scacchi in his *Cribrum musicum* (1643), to which Siefert replied in his *Anticribratio* (1645), which called forth Scacchi's *Judicium Cribri musici.* He also composed fantasies for organ, and a second volume of Psalms was published in 1651.

Siège de Corinthe, Le [ler syezh der corr-ãnt]. *v.* MAOMETTO II.

Siege of Rhodes, The. Opera (" Representation by the Art of Prospective in Scenes, And the Story sung in Recitative Music") in five entries. Libretto by William Davenant. First performed, London, Sept. 1656. The libretto was published in the same year and gave the names of the composers as follows: first and fifth entries by Henry Lawes, second and third entries by Henry Cooke and fourth entry by Matthew Locke. The first English opera. The music is lost.

Siegfried [zeek'-freet]. Opera in three acts by Wagner, the third part of the cycle *Der Ring des Nibelungen* (*q.v.*). First performed, Bayreuth, Aug. 16, 1876.

Siegfried Idyll. A work for small orchestra by Wagner (1870), in which he used themes from the opera *Siegfried*. It was also called *Triebschener Idyll*, as it had been performed on the staircase of the Wagner villa in Triebschen on Cosima's birthday.

Sight. A system used in England in the 15th and 16th cent. for teaching choristers to descant, *i.e.* to extemporise a simple part to go with a plainsong melody. The singer imagined his notes to be on the same staff as the plainsong (tenor) but sang them at a pitch suitable to the compass of his voice. Thus, to a treble descanter, who sang an octave above his " sight " pitch, a third below the plainsong in " sight " actually sounded a sixth above the plainsong, *e.g.*

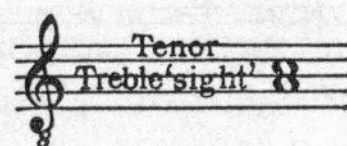

in sight was

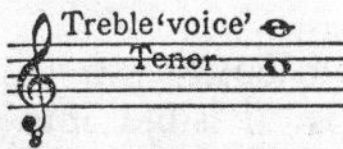

in " voice," that is, in sound. The method was applied only to singing in two parts, and used only consonant intervals. There is no evidence in the short treatises on the subject, which are the earliest theoretical works in English, dating from *c.* 1450, that it was applied to singing in three parts in parallel thirds and sixths. Singing in two parts in parallel sixths was separately treated (under the name FAUXBOURDON) in one of the treatises. *v.* DESCANT.

Signature. *v.* KEY-SIGNATURE, TIME-SIGNATURE.

Sigurd [see-gēer]. Opera in four acts by Reyer. Libretto by Camille du Locle and Alfred Blau (based on the Nibelung saga). First performed, Brussels, Jan. 7, 1884.

Si j'étais Roi [see zhay-tay rwa] (If I were King). Opera in three acts by Adam. Libretto by Adolphe Philippe d'Ennery and Jules Brésil. First performed, Paris, Sept. 4, 1852.

Silbermann [zilb'-er-mun], GOTTFRIED: *b.* Kleinbobritzsch (Saxcny), Jan. 14, 1683; *d.* Dresden, Aug. 4, 1753. The most celebrated member of a family of organ builders and harpsichord makers. He was apprenticed to a bookbinder, from 1703 lived with his brother, Andreas, in Strasbourg and in 1707 returned to Frauenstein where he built his first organ. He settled in Freiberg in 1709 and built the cathedral organ there in 1714. He built forty-seven organs in Saxony and died while building the organ at the Dresden court. He made clavichords and harpsichords and was the first German to make pianos. C. P. E. Bach wrote a piece entitled *Farewell to my Silbermann Clavichord* in 1781. His nephews Johann Daniel (who finished his Dresden organ) and Johann Andreas built organs, and Johann Heinrich made harpsichords and pianos.

Silva [deh seel'-vah], (Silvanus, Sylvanus), ANDREAS DE: 16th-cent. Flemish composer and singer. Singer in the Papal Chapel, 1519-20, attached to the Mantuan Court from 1522. He composed Masses, motets, and madrigals. A madrigal "Che sentisti donna pensier" was printed in Ott's collection of 1544 (modern ed. in *Publikationen der Gesellschaft für Musikforschung*, iii). Palestrina's six-part Mass *Illumina oculos meos* is based on a motet by de Silva.

Similar Motion. The movement of two or more parts in the same direction, *e.g.*,

When the parts move by the same interval, parallel or CONSECUTIVE INTERVALS result. When two parts rise to a fifth, *e.g.*,

or to an octave, *e.g.*,

the effect is referred to as "hidden" fifths or octaves, and is usually avoided between the outer parts in contrapuntal writing, unless the higher part moves by step, *e.g.*,

Simile [see′-mee-leh], *I.* Lit. "like, similar." Used as a direction to continue a formula which has been indicated, such as arpeggiating of chords.

Simone Boccanegra [see-mo′-neh bock-cah-neh′-grah]. Opera with a prologue and three acts by Verdi. Libretto by Francesco Maria Piave (based on a Spanish drama by Antonio García Gutiérrez). First performed, Venice, Mar. 12, 1857. The story takes place in Genoa during the 14th cent. Paolo and Pietro are plotting to place Boccanegra (a popular corsair) on the Doge's throne. When Boccanegra goes to visit his mistress, Maria, he is confronted by her father (Fiesco) who demands that he should relinquish the daughter born of their love affair. Boccanegra confesses that the child has been lost and when he manages to gain entrance to Fiesco's palace he discovers that Maria is dead. As he leaves the palace he is greeted by a cheering crowd who announce that he is the Doge of Genoa. Boccanegra discovers his lost daughter (Amelia Grimaldi) living with an old man who is known as Andrea (in reality Fiesco, who does not know that she is his grandaughter). She is in love with Gabriele Adorno who has entered into a conspiracy with Andrea to overthrow the Doge. Paolo kidnaps Amelia in order to be revenged against her father who has refused to consent to his marriage with her. Andrea and Gabriele accuse Boccanegra of being the kidnapper and when Gabriele attacks Boccanegra Amelia comes between them and saves her father. Paolo, still desiring revenge on Boccanegra, plays on the jealous feelings of Gabriele who does not know the true relationship between Boccanegra and his beloved Amelia. Again Amelia saves her father when he attempts to murder him, and when they explain to him that they are father and daughter he begs for pardon. Paolo as the leader of an uprising against the Doge is condemned to death, but in the meantime Boccanegra has drunk some wine which was poisoned by him. As he is dying he tells Fiesco that Amelia is the lost child, gives his consent and blessing to her marriage with Gabriele, and names Gabriele as his successor as Doge.

Simple Time. Time in which each beat in the bar is divisible into two, *e.g.*:

as opposed to COMPOUND TIME, in which each beat is divisible into three, *e.g.*:

Simpson (1) (Sympson), CHRISTOPHER: *b.* Yorkshire, *c.* 1610; *d.* Turnstile, early in the summer of 1669. Viol player, composer, teacher and theorist. He joined the royalist army under the Duke of Newcastle in 1643 and later was under the patronage of Sir Robert Bolles. He wrote *The Division-Violist* (1659), *A Compendium of Practical Musick* (1667) and annotations on Campian's *Art of Discant* (1655). In the *Division-Violist* he expounded the two methods of playing variations (" divisions ") on a GROUND which were practised in England: the ornamenting of the bass (" Breaking of the Ground ") and the playing of variations above it (" Descanting upon it "). He composed fantasias for strings, among them a set entitled *Months and Seasons* for violin, 2 bass viols, and continuo.

(2) THOMAS. 16th-17th cent. English viol player and composer. He went to Germany, where he played in the orchestra of the Elector Palatine (1610), and also served Christian IV at Copenhagen (1618-25). Compositions by him for four and five-part string ensemble were published in continental collections of the early 17th cent. and in his own publications; *Opusculum Neuwer Pavanen, Galliarden, Couranten und Volten* . . . (Frankfort, 1610), *Pavanen, Volten und Galliarden* (Frankfort, 1611), *Opus Newer Paduanen, Galliarden, Intraden, Canzonen, Ricercaren, Fantasien, Balletten, Allmanden, Couranten, Volten und Passamezen* (Hamburg, 1617), and *Taffel Consort* . . . *mit* 4 *Stimmen, neben einem General-Bass* (Hamburg, 1621), which included compositions by other English composers, such as Dowland, Farmer, Bateman, Edward and Robert Johnson, and Philips.

Sinding [sind′-ing], CHRISTIAN: *b.* Kongsberg (Norway), Jan. 11, 1856; *d.* Oslo, Dec. 3, 1941. Composer. Studied under L. M. Londeman, at the Leipzig Conservatorium under Reinecke and others, and in Berlin, Dresden and Munich. He settled in Oslo in 1882 and lived there and in Berlin from 1909. He was given an annual allowance (from 1890) and life pension (from 1915) by the Norwegian government. He taught at the Eastman School in Rochester, N.Y., 1921-22. His compositions include an opera (*Der heilige Berg*, Dessau, 1914), 3 symphonies, a violin concerto and a piano concerto, a piano quintet, a string quartet, and other chamber music, sonatas and other pieces for violin and piano, a sonata and numerous other pieces for piano, choruses and songs.

Sinfonia [seen-fo-nee′-ah], *I.* (1) Symphony. (2) Overture.

Sinfonia Antartica [seen-fo-nee′-ah ahn - tarr′ - tee - cah], *I.* (Antarctic Symphony). Vaughan Williams's seventh symphony, based on the music written for the film *Scott of the Antarctic.* First performed, Manchester, Jan. 14, 1953.

Sinfonia concertante [seen-fo-nee′-ah con-chair-tahn′-teh], *I.* An orchestral work, normally in several movements, in which there are parts for solo instruments, generally two or more, but sometimes only one, *e.g.* Walton's *Sinfonia concertante* for piano and orchestra.

Sinfonia Domestica [seen-fo-nee′-ah do-mess′-tee-cah], *I.* *v.* SYMPHONIA DOMESTICA.

Sinfonie [zin-fo-nee′], *G.* Symphony. An alternative spelling is *Symphonie.*

Sinfonietta [seen-fone-yet′-tah], *I.* A short, small-scale symphony.

Sinfonische Dichtung [zin-fone′-ish-er dish′-tŏŏng], *G.* Symphonic poem.

Singspiel [zing′-shpeel], *G.* German comic opera with spoken dialogue. The earliest examples were written in imitation of English ballad operas, and were in fact settings of translations of ballad opera libretti. The text of Johann Standfuss's *Der Teufel ist los* (Leipzig, 1752, also set by J. A. Hiller, 1766) was translated from Coffey's *The Devil to Pay* (1728) and that of his *Der lustige Schuster* (Lübeck, 1759) from Coffey's *The Merry Cobbler* (1735). The music of Haydn's *Singspiel, Der krumme Teufel,* which was produced with some success in Vienna in 1752, has been lost (1752 was also the year of J. J. Rousseau's *Le Devin du Village*). A special company for the performing of *Singspiele* was established in Vienna by the Emperor Joseph II in 1778, and it was for this

National *Singspiel* that Mozart's *Die Entführung* was commissioned. The history of the *Singspiel* merges with that of German romantic opera in the early 19th cent.; one of the latest examples is Schubert's *Die Zwillingsbrüder* (1819). Others which have been published in modern editions are Umlauff's *Die Bergknappen*, of 1778 (*D.T.Ö.*, xviii, 1) and Johann Schenk's *Der Dorfbarbier*, 1796 (*D.T.Ö.*, xxxiv). Later the term *Singspiel* came to be used in Germany as the equivalent of musical comedy.

Sink-a-Pace. *v.* CINQUE-PACE.

Sir John in Love. Opera in four acts by Vaughan Williams. Libretto from Shakespeare's *The Merry Wives of Windsor*. First performed, London, Mar. 21, 1929.

Siroe, Re di Persia [see-ro-eh′ reh dee pairce′-yah] (Siroes, King of Persia). Opera in three acts by Handel. Libretto adapted from Metastasio, altered by Nicola Francesco Haym. First performed, London, Feb. 28, 1728.

Sistema [seece-teh′-mah], *I.* Staff.

Six, Les [lay seece], *Fr.* "The six." The name given by Henri Collet in 1920 to a group of six young French composers who were influenced by Erik Satie's emphasis on simplicity and by the artistic ideals of Jean Cocteau. Their association was inaugurated by the joint publication of an album of six pieces. The name *Les Six* was imitated from the title "The Five" given to the group of Russian composers consisting of Balakirev, Cui, Borodin, Moussorgsky and Rimsky-Korsakov. The members of the French group, who soon ceased to be six, were Darius Milhaud, Louis Durey, Georges Auric, Arthur Honegger, Francis Poulenc and Germaine Tailleferre.

Six-Four Chord. A chord containing a sixth and a fourth from its bass note. It is the second INVERSION of the chord based on the note which is the fourth from its bass, *e.g.*

is the second inversion of

Since it contains a fourth from the bass its use in traditional harmony is usually restricted to those progressions which correspond to the treatment of the fourth in two-part counterpoint. They are (1) the appoggiatura or "cadential" six-four *e.g.*:

(2) the passing six-four, *e.g.*:

and (3) the auxiliary six-four, *e.g.*:

v. CHORD, INVERSION.

Sixte ajoutée [seext a-zhoo-tay], *Fr.* *v.* ADDED SIXTH.

Sixteenth-Note. American for "semiquaver."

Sixth. The interval comprised by the first and last of any six notes in a diatonic scale, *e.g.*

A sixth may be minor, as

major, as

or augmented, as

The sixth, like the third, of which it is the INVERSION, is an imperfect consonance. The term "sixth chord" is sometimes used in referring to the SIX-THREE chord. *v.* AUGMENTED SIXTH, CHORD, INTERVAL.

Sixth, Added. *v.* ADDED SIXTH.

Six-Three Chord. A chord containing a sixth and a third from its bass note. It is the first INVERSION of the chord based on the note which is the sixth from its bass, *e.g.*

is the first inversion of

The chord has an interesting early history, in which it is generally associated with the affection of the English, not fully shared by other nations in the Middle Ages, for the sweetness of imperfect consonances. A 13th-cent. English treatment of part of the *Te Deum* shows how wholeheartedly it was beloved :

Perhaps in imitation of this English practice, it became the working chord of FAUXBOURDON in the 15th cent. It is, in fact, the only position of the common chord, which, in traditional harmony, can be used in continuous parallels, as by Beethoven in the fourth movement of his piano sonata, Op. 3, No. 2 :

v. CHORD, INVERSION.

Skazka o Tsare Saltane [scahz′-ca ŏ tsahrr′-yĕ sull-tahn′-yĕ] (The Legend of Czar Saltan). Opera with a prologue and four acts by Rimsky-Korsakov. Libretto by Vladimir Ivanovich Belsky. First performed, Moscow, Nov. 3, 1900.

Skryabin. *v.* SCRIABIN.

Slentando [slen-tahnd′-o], *I.* Becoming gradually slower.

Slide (*Fr.* coulé, flatté, *G.* Schleifer). (1) An ornament used in the music of the 17th and early 18th cent., also called "elevation" or "wholefall," consisting of two grace notes moving up by step to the principal note. It was indicated thus:

by Playford and

or

by Marpurg, and played

and

Purcell, who calls it a " slur," gives

played

and Chambonnières gives

played

Later composers have usually written out the grace notes, as do most editors of Bach, *e.g.* in the *St. Matthew Passion*:

(2) Movement of the left hand on the violin which effects a quick change of POSITION, at the same time producing a slight *portamento*. Paganini extended the use of the slide to the rapid playing of chromatic scale passages.

(3) A device which alters the length of the air column in the TROMBONE and slide TRUMPET.

Slide Trumpet. *v.* TRUMPET.

Slur (*Fr.* légature, *G.* Bindungszeichen, *I.* legatura). (1) A curved line over or under a group of notes which indicates that they are to be played or sung *legato*, or, on a stringed instrument, in one bow. If the slur is combined with staccato marks, it indicates *mezzo staccato.*

(2) Purcell used the term as the equivalent of SLIDE.

Smert, RICHARD: English composer of carols (some with John Truelove or Trouluffe), who may be identical with one of that name who was vicar-choral of Exeter Cathedral from 1428- *c.*1465 and rector of Plymtree, near Exeter, from 1435 to 1477. The carols which bear his name are published in *Mediaeval Carols* (*Musica Britannica,* iv. ed. John Stevens, 1952).

Smetana [smet′-a-na], BEDŘICH : *b.* Litomyschl (Bohemia), March 2, 1824; *d.* Prague, May 12, 1884. Composer. Studied composition in Prague under Proksch, where until 1856 he taught and wrote his first compositions, and lived as a conductor and teacher in Gothenburg in Sweden from 1857-59 and in the winter of 1860-61. He visited Liszt in Weimar, and between 1858 and 1861 wrote 3 symphonic poems for orchestra, *Richard III*, *Wallenstein's Camp* and *Hakon Jarl.* Settling in Prague in 1863, he wrote his most famous opera, *The Bartered Bride*, in 1866, and three other operas on national subjects by 1874, in which year he suddenly became stone deaf. Nevertheless, he composed in the following years his best instrumental works, *Má vlast* ("My Country"), a set of 6 musical landscapes, and the first string quartet, *From my Life*, in four movements with an autobiographical programme. Though he very seldom used actual folksongs in his music (his only folksong settings are the *Czech Dances* for piano of 1878), his Czech operas are thoroughly national in subject and feeling. He also composed a trio, a second string quartet, piano pieces, choruses and songs. His operas are : *Braniboři v Čechách* (The Brandenburgers in Bohemia), 1866; *Prodaná nevěsta* (The Bartered Bride), 1866 ; *Dalibor*, 1868 ; *Libuše*, composed in 1871-2, produced in 1881 ; *Dvě* *vdovy* (Two Widows), 1874; *Hubička* (The Kiss), 1876; *Tajemství* (The Secret), 1878; *Čertova stěna* (The Devil's Wall), 1882; and an unfinished work, *Viola*.

F. BARTOŠ (ed.): *Bedřich Smetana: Letters and Reminiscences* (1955).
W. RITTER: *Smetana* (1907).
J. TIERSOT: *Smetana* (1926).
Z. NEJEDLY: *Frederick Smetana* (1924).

Smith, (1) BERNARD ("Father Smith"). *v.* SCHMIDT (1).

(2) DAVID STANLEY: *b.* Toledo (Ohio), July 6, 1877; *d.* New Haven (Conn.), Dec. 17, 1949. Teacher, composer and conductor. Studied at Yale University and Music School under Horatio Parker, at Munich under Thuille and at Paris under d'Indy. He was appointed professor at the Yale Music School, and succeeded Horatio Parker as dean (1920) and also as conductor of the New Haven Orchestra (1919). He composed an opera, 4 symphonies and other orchestral works, chamber music, anthems and choral works.

(3) JOHN STAFFORD: *b.* Gloucester, 1750; *d.* London, Sept. 21, 1836. Organist, composer and editor. Studied under Boyce. Gentleman of the Chapel Royal, 1784; lay-vicar, Westminster Abbey, 1785; organist (1802) and master of the children (1805) at the Chapel Royal. He collected and published early English music, including *A Collection of English Songs* (1779) and *Musica Antiqua* (1812), and worked with Hawkins on his *History of Music.* He composed glees (5 books), catches, canons, madrigals, anthems, part-songs and songs. The tune of his "Anacreon in Heaven" was adopted for "The Star-Spangled Banner."

Smorzando [smorr-tsahnd'-o], *I.* Dying away.

Smyth, ETHEL MARY: *b.* London, Apr. 23, 1858; *d.* Woking (Surrey) May 8, 1944. Composer and author. Studied in Leipzig at the Conservatorium and under Herzogenberg. Was a leader of the women's suffrage movement. She composed the following operas: *Fantasio* (1898), *Der Wald* (1902), *The Wreckers* (first produced as *Strandrecht*, Leipzig, 1906), *The Boatswain's Mate* (1916), *Fête galante* (1923) and *Entente cordiale* (1926). She also wrote a Mass, *The Prison* (1930) and other choral works with orchestra, orchestral works, chamber music, pieces for piano and for organ, a concerto for violin, horn and orchestra, and songs. She published a series of autobiographical books: *Impressions that Remained* (2 vols., 1919), *Streaks of Life* (1921), *Beecham and Pharaoh* (1925), *A Final Burning of Boats* (1928), *Female Pipings in Eden* (1932), *As Time Went On* (1936), and *What Happened Next* (1940). Created D.B.E., 1920.

Snare Drum. *v.* SIDE DRUM.

Snegourochka [snyeg-oo-rotch'-ca] (The Snow Maiden). Opera by Rimsky-Korsakov with a prologue and four acts. Libretto by the composer (based on a play by Alexander Nikolaievich Ostrovsky). First performed, St. Petersburg, Feb. 10, 1882.

Snow Maiden, The. *v.* SNEGOUROCHKA.

Soave [so-ah'-veh]. *I.* In a smooth and gentle manner.

Söderman [sur'-der-mun], AUGUST JOHAN: *b.* Stockholm, July 17, 1832; *d.* there Feb. 10, 1876. Composer and conductor. Studied under Richter and Hauptmann in Leipzig. Chorus master (1860) and a conductor (1862) at the Royal Opera in Stockholm. He composed operettas, a Mass, incidental music for plays, vocal settings of Bellman's poems, many ballades and other vocal works.

Soggetto [so-djet'-to], *I.* "Subject, theme." (1) The subject of a fugue or other contrapuntal piece which is short and of an abstract or stock type, *e.g.* that of the fugue in E major in the second book of Bach's *Forty-eight*:

It is thus distinguished from an *andamento*, a longer subject of a more individual character, and from an *attacco*, which is a POINT of imitation.

(2) The term *soggetto cavato* ("carved-out" or derived subject) was used by 16th-cent. theorists for a theme derived from words by using the SOLMIZATION

syllables corresponding to their vowels. Thus the theme

on which Josquin composed a Mass in honour of his patron, Duke Hercules of Ferrara, was derived from the words

re ut re ut re fa mi re
Her-cu-les dux Fer-ra-ri-e.

Soh. Anglicized form of the Italian *sol* (G). In TONIC SOL-FA the 5th note (or dominant) of the major scale.

Soir et la Tempête, Le [ler swahr ay la tũn-pet]. *v.* MATIN.

Sol (1) The 5th note of the hexachord. *v.* SOLMIZATION.

(2) *Fr. I.* [soll]. The note G.

Soldier's Tale, The. *v.* HISTOIRE DU SOLDAT.

Soler [so-lerr'], PADRE ANTONIO: *b.* Olot (nr. Gerona), Dec. 3, 1729; *d.* Monastery of the Escorial, Dec. 20, 1783. Composer and monk. Studied at the Escalonía of Montserrat, appointed choirmaster at Lérida Cathedral, and entered the Monastery of the Escorial (1753), where he was organist. He composed a Requiem and other church music, sonatas for harpsichord, incidental music for plays, 6 quintets for strings and keyboard, and other chamber music, and wrote a theoretical treatise, *Llave de la Modulación* (1762). His harpsichord sonatas show the influence of Domenico Scarlatti, who spent much time in Madrid between 1729 and 1754. Modern ed. of 6 quintets by R. Gerhard (1933).

Solesmes [sol-em]. The Benedictine monastery of Solesmes, near Le Mans, has been since the abbacy of Dom Guéranger (*d.* 1875) the chief centre of the study of plainsong. Under Dom Guéranger's successors Dom Pothier and Dom Mocquereau the work of restoring plainsong melodies to their earliest written form (9th-10th cent.) was begun, and since 1904 the Solesmes editions of liturgical chant have been the official Vatican editions. In preparing their editions the monks studied all the available early manuscripts, some of which have been published in facsimile in the series *Paléographie Musicale*, and evolved a new theory concerning the treatment of rhythm in the performance of plainsong. In this theory each note of the melody is given approximately the same length, and the first of a group of notes is given an *ictus*, which is a "rhythmic step" of varying strength "felt and intimated by tone of voice rather than expressed by any material emphasis." Though the rhythmic theories and methods of performance of Solesmes have not been everywhere accepted, the research which has been carried out there is universally recognised as the most valuable of all modern studies in the history of medieval plainsong. The results of these studies, which are now under the direction of Dom Gajard, are still being published both in the *Paléographie Musicale* and in the periodical *Revue Grégorienne*. A short summary of the rules for the interpretation of plainsong according to Solesmes principles will be found in the edition with English rubrics of the *Liber Usualis* (1950).

Sol-fa. *v.* TONIC SOL-FA.

Solfeggio [sol-feh'-djo], *I.* (*Fr.* solfège). The study of ear-training through the singing of exercises to the syllables of sol-fa, the modern form of SOLMIZATION. Many volumes of *solfeggi* have been published in Italy and France since the 18th cent. In their more advanced forms such exercises are sung to vowels, and are then more properly called *vocalises* (*vocalizzi*), as in the collection *Repertoire moderne de vocalises-études* by Fauré, Dukas, d'Indy, Ravel and other composers. In Italy the term *solfeggi* is still used for exercises and studies for singers, whether sung to sol-fa syllables or vocalized. In France the term *solfège* is applied to a course in ear-training and general musicianship. C. P. E. Bach used the term "Solfeggio" for a short keyboard piece, *e.g.* in his *Clavierstücke verscheidener Art* (1765).

Solmization. The use of syllables to designate the notes of the hexachord. Those adopted by Guido d'Arezzo were used in medieval theory as a system of reference and as a means of ear-training.

He derived them from a plainsong hymn to St. John the Baptist, in which the first syllable of each line was sung to a note of the hexachord in rising succession:

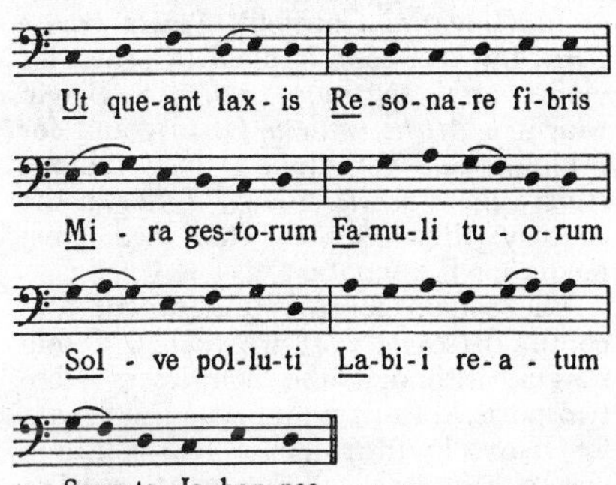

and applied them to the hexachords:

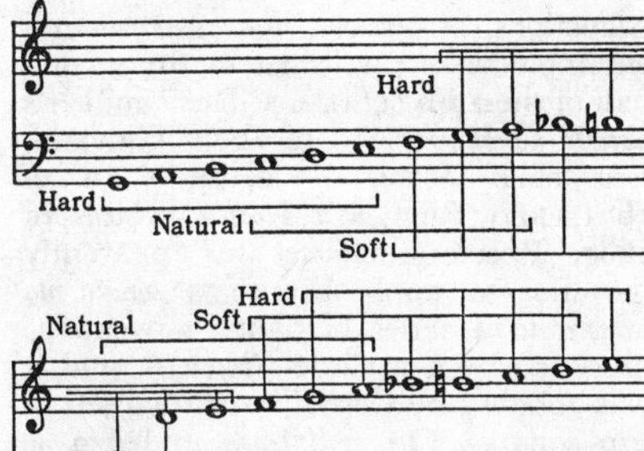

In teaching and discussion the notes were referred to by combining their appropriate syllables. The lowest note was called *Gamma ut* or *Gamut*, a term later applied to the whole system. The designations of the other notes may be found by reading the syllables upwards:

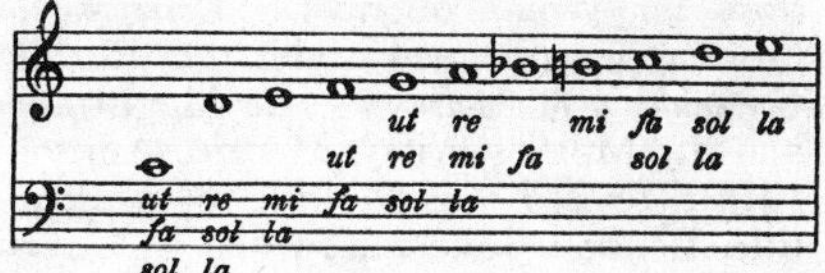

Middle C, for example, is C sol fa ut, the D next above it is D la sol re. Hortensio declared his love for Bianca (*Taming of the Shrew*, iii, 1) through the notes of the first hexachord. In singing, the change of syllable when changing from one hexachord to another was called MUTATION.

In the 16th and 17th cent. a composition which used the hexachord as a *cantus firmus* was usually called "Ut Re Mi Fa Sol La." There are examples of keyboard pieces of this kind by Byrd, Bull and Sweelinck in the *Fitzwilliam Virginal Book*. The syllables were also used to indicate the theme of a piece by its title, as in Byrd's fantasia on "Ut Mi Re" (*Fitzwilliam Virginal Book*, I, 401), and to derive a theme from words (*soggetto cavato*), as in Josquin's Mass *Hercules dux Ferrariae* (*v.* SOGGETTO).

Solomon. Secular oratorio by Handel. Text attributed (without sufficient authority) to Thomas Morell. First performed, London, Mar. 17, 1749.

Solo Organ. The manual on an organ which includes stops intended for solo, rather than combined, use. It is found on organs of four or more manuals and is placed above the Swell. Its stops are enclosed in a swell-box. It normally contains a set of loud reeds, and such other stops as Viola da Gamba, Concert Flute, Clarinet, Orchestral Oboe and French Horn. More recently sets of mutation stops have also been included, as in the Solo division of the organ in the Royal Festival Hall, London, which has a Rauschquint sounding the 12th and 15th, a Tertian sounding the 17th and 19th, and a six-rank Mixture. *v.* ORGAN.

Sombrero de Tres Picos, El [el sombreh'-ro deh trace pee'-coce] (The Three-Cornered Hat). Ballet by Falla, based on Pedro de Alarcón's story with the same title (which also provided the story for Wolf's opera *Der Corregidor*). Originally performed under the title *El Corregidor y la Molinera* (The Magistrate and the Miller's Wife), Madrid, Apr. 7, 1917; revised version with the present title, London, June 22, 1919.

Somervell, ARTHUR: *b.* Windermere, June 5, 1863; *d.* London, May 2, 1937. Composer. Studied at Cambridge under Stanford, at the Berlin Hochschule under Kiel, and under Parry at the R.C.M., where he taught from 1894 to 1901. He was inspector of school music from 1901 to 1928. He composed a symphony and other orchestral works, works for piano and orchestra and for cello and orchestra, two Masses, an oratorio, cantatas, five children's operettas, a clarinet quintet, part-songs and song cycles (of which the best known is *Maud*), pieces for violin and for piano, and edited *Songs of Four Nations*, a collection of folksongs of the British Isles. Knighted, 1929.

Somis [so'-meece], GIOVANNI BATTISTA: *b.* Turin, Dec. 25, 1686; *d.* Turin, Aug. 14, 1763. Violinist and composer. Studied under Corelli in Rome and Vivaldi in Venice, was appointed violinist in the Turin Court Orchestra, played at the Concert Spirituel in Paris in 1733 and became director of the court music at Turin. His pupils included Leclair, Giardini and Pugnani. He composed 2 violin concertos, solo sonatas, trio sonatas, and other chamber music. A solo sonata in D minor (*c.* 1725), printed in the appendix of musical examples in A. Einstein's *Short History of Music* (1948), has an abbreviated recapitulation in each of the Allegro movements, which are in binary form.

Sommernachtstraum [zom'-er-nuckhts-trowm]. *v.* MIDSUMMER NIGHT'S DREAM.

Son and Stranger. *v.* HEIMKEHR AUS DER FREMDE.

Sonata. The term is derived from the Italian *suonare*, to sound, *i.e.* to play on (originally) non-keyed instruments. The year 1750 may be taken as a rough dividing line in its history. Before that date it was a composition for a single instrument, *e.g.* harpsichord or clavichord (after *c.* 1700), violin, or for one or more solo instruments accompanied by continuo. Since that date, it denotes a composition in several movements for a keyboard instrument, or for a solo instrument and pianoforte. At the beginning of its history it was used as the equivalent of canzona (*canzon da sonar*), as in Giovanni Gabrieli's *Sonata Pian e Forte*, but was soon applied to pieces for violin and continuo, *e.g.* in Biagio Marini's *Affetti musicali* (1617), and for 2 violins and continuo, as in Salomone Rossi's *Varie Sonate* (1623). Later in the century these became the two chief media for the sonata.

The sonata for solo instrument and continuo (*sonata a 2*) was called a solo sonata, although the composer wrote two parts, solo part and bass; a sonata for two solo instruments and continuo (*sonata a 3*) was called a TRIO SONATA because the composer wrote three parts, although four players usually took part in its performance. In addition, many collections of sonatas for instrumental ensemble were published in the second half of the 17th cent., *e.g.* Rosenmüller's *Sonate da camera a* 5 of 1677, Giovanni Legrenzi's *Sonate a* 2, 3, 5, 6 of 1671, and Reinken's *Hortus musicus* of 1687. Rosenmüller's set was apparently the first to apply the term *sonata da camera* to a series of dance movements preceded by a prelude (*sinfonia*), and it was adopted by Corelli in his two sets of trio sonatas, Op. 2 (1685) and Op. 4 (1694). Corelli also adopted the term *sonata da chiesa* for his trio sonatas of 1683 and 1689, which have four movements in the order slow-fast-slow-fast. This scheme had appeared in the earliest published sonatas written by an English composer, William Young's collection published at Innsbruck in 1653, and is the general basis of Purcell's sonatas of three and four parts (1683, 1697), though in these, as in many sonatas before 1750, the actual number of movements varies considerably. While movements of a dance type, *e.g.* sarabande, gavotte, gigue, often appear (though not so entitled) in a *sonata da chiesa*, its historical connection with the canzona is clear in the frequent use of imitative style in the Allegro movements. Both Bach and Handel used the four-movement scheme consistently for solo sonatas and trio sonatas.

Sonatas for an unaccompanied stringed instrument were comparatively rare. The most notable examples before Bach's set of three sonatas and three partitas (he does not use the term *sonata da camera*) for solo violin are those of J. J. Walther and Heinrich Biber. As a term for keyboard works sonata was hardly known before D. Scarlatti's one-movement pieces (also called *Essercizi* or Lessons). The earliest appear to be the single sonata in Johann Kuhnau's *Clavierübung*, Part II (1692), the seven " suonaten " in his *Frisch Clavierfrüchte* (1696) and his *Biblical Sonatas* of 1700.

The modern convention which restricts the use of the term sonata to instrumental solos and duets is not based on a distinction of form except as to number of movements, but of medium. The three-movement form (I. Allegro in SONATA FORM ; II. Slow movement ; III. Allegro in sonata or Rondo form) of the classical and romantic duet-sonata is shared by the corresponding movements of the TRIO, STRING QUARTET, quintet, sextet, etc., as well as by the SYMPHONY. The early keyboard and violin sonatas of Mozart are keyboard sonatas with an optional violin part, and have three movements, Allegro-Adagio-Minuet. All of J. C. Bach's pieces in this medium are described as Sonatas for Harpsichord or Pianoforte, accompanied by Violin (or German flute). Haydn wrote practically no duets, and it was in Mozart's mature violin sonatas that a true duet style was developed. His three-movement scheme, Allegro-Adagio-Allegro, was continued by Beethoven, who included a Scherzo in his violin sonata, Op. 24 (1801) and in his cello sonata, Op. 69 (1809), but not always thereafter, and three movements became the normal number for duet sonatas. As with Mozart, the second or third movement could be in the form of Theme and Variations. While the composers of the Romantic and modern periods have effected some changes in the style of the sonata, the classical basis of its form has remained relatively stable until the present. Among the noteworthy examples of sonatas for a wind instrument and piano are the two clarinet sonatas of Brahms, Op. 120, and the series of sonatas for flute, oboe, English horn, clarinet, bassoon, horn, trumpet and trombone by Hindemith.

The modern keyboard sonata takes its departure from the works of C. P. E. Bach for clavichord and harpsichord, and after 1780 for piano. Three movements are normal in the piano sonatas of Haydn, Mozart and Clementi, four in the earlier sonatas of Beethoven. The remarkable development of Beethoven's pianoforte style after the two sonatas *quasi una fantasia*, Op. 27, affected both the number and form of the movements, and two of the later sonatas, Op. 90 and 111, have two movements only (though this is not unknown in Haydn and Clementi). Liszt's essay towards a more fluid form in the Sonata in B minor (1854) had little effect on the later history of the form which includes the 3 early sonatas by Brahms, 2 by Stravinsky, 8 by Prokofiev and 3 by Hindemith.

Mozart used the term in an earlier sense in his 14 sonatas for organ and strings and 3 for organ and orchestra, all in one movement, written for Salzburg Cathedral between 1767 and 1780. The later history of the sonata for organ solo was begun by Mendelssohn's 6 sonatas (1839-44) and continued in the sonatas of Rheinberger and Guilmant, in the so-called " symphonies " of Widor and Vierne, and in the sonatas of Reger, Elgar and Hindemith.

Sonata Form. A term for the design most often used since *c.* 1750 for the first movement, and on occasions for the slow movement and finale, of a symphony, sonata, TRIO, quartet, etc., and for an OVERTURE. The procedures denoted by the names of its three sections—Exposition (*i.e.* presentation), DEVELOPMENT (*i.e.* discursive treatment), and Recapitulation (*i.e.* return)—were present in earlier music, and both these and the basis of its scheme of TONALITY were developed from its immediate ancestor, the BINARY FORM of the late baroque period. Its special characteristics are the definite distinction between the part which these procedures play in the design, and the complete co-ordination of thematic character, thematic treatment, and tonality in making that design clear, logical, and symmetrical. Its basic plan in the late 18th cent. is:

	(Introduction) Exposition		Development	Recapitulation	(Coda)
	1st group	2nd group		1st group	2nd group
TONALITY	(In major mode) Tonic	Dominant	Varying	Tonic	Tonic
	(In minor mode) Tonic	Relative major	Varying	Tonic	Tonic major
THEMATIC CHARACTER	Leading theme is direct and concise.	Leading theme is *cantabile.*	Varying	As Exposition	
THEMATIC TREATMENT	Complete and successive presentation.		Discursive, *e.g.* by dismemberment, transposition, contrapuntal treatment, combination.	Re-presentation	

The introduction may be unrelated to the exposition, as is usual before Beethoven, or related, as in the first movement of Beethoven's piano sonata, Op. 81a (*Les Adieux*) and in the first and fourth movements of Brahms's first symphony. It is frequently dispensed with. The leading theme of the first group and that of the second group are commonly called "first subject" and "second subject." The first group frequently contains one theme only, the second group seldom less than two, and in Beethoven's longer movements as many as six, as in the first movement of the *Eroica* symphony. The latter part of the first group in the Exposition has normally the function of making a transition to a related key ; hence, the corresponding part of the first group in the Recapitulation differs from it, not having that function. The Recapitulation may differ from the Exposition in details, *e.g.* in orchestration and in the use of new accompaniments to themes. The latter part of the development has the function of preparing for the return of the tonic. The coda, which in the classical sonata was usually a short addendum by way of "rounding-off," was extended by Beethoven in many cases to the length of the other sections, and treated as a second Development.

The interest which this design has had for composers over a period of 200 years arises from its capacity for expansion and contraction, its scope for inter-relations between the sections and for varieties of treatment of the Development and Coda, and its cheerful submission to those departures from its inherent principles, such as the appearance of the same thematic material in the first and second groups, the use of new themes in the Development, and the return of a theme in the Recapitulation in a key other than the tonic, which depend for their effect on the strength and clarity of the basic scheme. Since a calculated plan of tonality is essential to its working, its development in the late Romantic and modern periods has chiefly been in the direction of greater flexibility in the proportions and relations of the sections, *e.g.* by the use of discursive treatment in the Exposition and Recapitulation and by abbreviating the Recapitulation, and by extending the range of key-relations used in all the sections. The object in many cases has been to give a form which was originally sectional and symmetrical the effect of continuous and organic growth.

W. H. HADOW : *Sonata Form* (1896).

Sonate Pathétique [son-ut pa-tay-teek], *Fr.* V. PATHETIC SONATA.

Sonatina. A short sonata, usually elementary in its technical requirements, *e.g.* Clementi's sonatinas and Beethoven's Op. 79, but not always so, *e.g.* Ravel's *Sonatine* and Busoni's 6 sonatinas.

Song. Solo song as a form of musical expression is of indeterminate antiquity. The earliest recorded examples in Western Europe, however, date from the 10th cent. These songs are in Latin, which continued in use as a popular medium for lyrical expression down to the end of the 13th cent. The relatively few melodies which are decipherable show a simple symmetrical structure similar to that found in folksong. This symmetry is characteristic also of the vernacular songs of the TROUBADOURS in Provence (11th-13th cent.), the trouvères in northern France (12th-13th cent.) and the MINNESINGER in Germany and Austria (12th-14th cent.), the Spanish *cantigas* in honour of the Virgin (13th cent. ; *v.* ALFONSO EL SABIO) and the Italian *laudi spirituali* (13th cent.). Neither in form nor in tonality is there any valid distinction between secular and religious songs : melodies are found both in the church modes and in the major key. Common to all these songs is the absence of any written accompaniment.

Though the traditions of this type of song died hard in Germany and were in fact continued in the 15th and 16th cent. by the MEISTERSINGER, elsewhere the 14th cent. saw a considerable change. Songs (and also duets) of a highly sophisticated character, with accompaniment for one or more instruments, were composed in France and Italy by men like Machaut and Landini. The simple structure of the earlier songs has now been largely replaced by a greater subtlety of rhythm and form. Elaborate ornamentation, particularly in the late 14th cent., is often found in these songs, and also an intimate relationship between two voices or between voice and accompaniment (*e.g.* imitation, canon). With the temporary decline of Italian music in the 15th cent. the French song (or *chanson*) became the dominant form of secular vocal music, so much so that we find many examples recorded in Italian and German sources. At the same time German composers were developing a characteristic type of song with the melody in an inner part.

Both at this period and in the 16th cent. there were no hard and fast conditions for performance. Words could be, and often were, applied to the accompanying instrumental parts, so that it is often impossible to make a clear-cut distinction between solo songs and part-songs. On the other hand there are numerous examples where the melodic shape of the accompanying parts makes them unsuitable, though not impossible, for vocal performance. This easy-going attitude towards the medium persists in the 16th cent.—in the Italian *frottole* of the early part of the century, in the French *airs de cour*, and in many of the songs of the English lutenists of the late 16th and early 17th cent. Many 16th-cent. madrigals (as well as church motets) were arranged for performance by solo and lute, which by this time was the accompanying instrument most in favour. The old tradition of solo song accompanied by an instrumental ensemble survives in English music of the late 16th cent., *e.g.* in Byrd's *Psalms, Sonets, & Songs of sadness and pietie* (1588), most of which were originally written for this medium. The lute-song, as opposed to transcriptions of madrigals, had its origin in Spain with the publication of Milan's *El maestro* in 1535.

A significant development in Italy in the late 16th cent. was the cultivation of a new form of declamatory song, soon known as RECITATIVE, by Caccini, Peri and others. Here the accompaniment was designed for figured bass and was made completely subordinate to the voice. Accurate declamation, intense expression and ornamentation were among the characteristics of this type of song, as well as the striking effect of original harmonic progressions. It proved to be the ideal medium for the new opera, created about the same time, but it did not kill the instinct for rhythmical song-writing, which also found encouragement in the popularity of court dances. Both in opera and in the chamber CANTATA the ARIA became in the course of the 17th cent. an indispensable element. Similar developments took place in England, France and Germany, though with differences resulting from the nature of the language. The distinction between songs from operas and songs for concert use is a narrow one at this period, though it is often true that songs published for domestic use have a greater simplicity.

The domination of opera continued through the 18th cent., relieved however by the popular style of the songs in the English BALLAD OPERA, which were imitated in Germany and became a staple element in the SINGSPIEL. But songs of this kind, whether designed for the stage or for private music-making, received little attention from serious composers. The songs with keyboard accompaniment written by Haydn and Mozart form a very minor part of their output. Nor did Beethoven, in spite of having written the earliest known song cycle (*An die ferne Geliebte*, 1817), contribute very much to the form. It was Schubert who showed how the traditional simplicity of German popular song could be combined with a Romantic awareness of the text and how an imaginative accompaniment could serve to illuminate the words. Indeed many of his songs are even more subtle than this generalization would suggest ; at his best he shows an extraordinary capacity for translating the mood of a poem into sound.

Schubert's example had a powerful influence on Romantic composers of the 19th cent., notably Schumann and Brahms. Schumann's songs often seem designed for a single performer, and the accompaniment not infrequently suggests a piano solo, to which a voice part has been added (a characteristic which has a parallel in his chamber music with piano). Brahms's accompaniments are generally on more traditional lines, and the vocal melodies in many cases show the influence of the traditions of popular song. The songs of Wolf, on the other hand, are strongly influenced by Wagner. The accompaniments are often orchestral in character, and the vocal line avoids symmetry in favour of precise accentuation of the words. The influence of Wolf is apparent in Strauss's songs ; Mahler, on the other hand, follows more closely in the footsteps of Brahms.

In France the language, which lacks a tonic accent, resulted in a refinement which finds its most remarkable expression in the songs of Fauré. England, which in Purcell had had one of the most remarkable song-writers of the 17th cent., made little serious contribution to the form after his death until the end of the 19th cent. The folk-song revival has proved both a stimulus and a snare to English composers of the 20th cent. Its influence was for the most part resisted by Warlock, who drew his inspiration rather from Elizabethan and Jacobean composers, and has had no effect on Britten. Russian song found a purely national expression in the picturesque and often very dramatic songs of Moussorgsky. In Norway Grieg was in his element as a song-writer, often combining the melodic idioms of folk-song with a peculiarly individual harmony.

The tendency among the more advanced composers of the 20th cent. has been to ignore the tradition that a vocal line should be singable. Some composers, *e.g.* Schönberg, have gone further and substituted for pure singing a form of declamation known as *Sprechgesang*, which is half-way between speech and song. The complete abandonment of anything like a vocal *cantilena* has not been without its effect on instrumental composition.

Song Cycle (*G.* Liederkreis). A set of songs to words by a single poet. In most cases a song cycle is intended to be performed complete, but single songs from Schubert's and Schumann's cycles are commonly sung separately. The first use of the term was in Beethoven's *An die ferne Geliebte* (To the distant Beloved), to poems by A. Jeitteles. Other examples are Schubert's *Die schöne Müllerin* (The Fair Maid of the Mill) (W. Müller) and *Winterreise* (Winter Journey) (Müller), Schumann's *Dichterliebe* (Poet's Love) (Heine) and *Frauen-Liebe und Leben* (Woman's Love and Life) (Chamisso), Brahms's *Magelone* (Tieck), Debussy's *Chansons de Bilitis* (Pierre Louÿs), and Vaughan Williams's *Mystical Songs* (George Herbert) and *On Wenlock Edge* (Housman).

Songe d'une Nuit d'Été, Le [ler sõnzh dēēn nēē-ee day-tay] (A Summer Night's Dream). Opera in three acts by Thomas. Libretto by Joseph Bernard Rosier and Adolphe de Leuven (based on an episode in Shakespeare's life). First performed, Paris, Apr. 20, 1850.

Song of Destiny. *v.* SCHICKSALSLIED.

Song of the Earth, The. *v.* LIED VON DER ERDE.

Song of Triumph. *v.* TRIUMPHLIED.

Songs Without Words. *v.* LIEDER OHNE WORTE.

Sonnambula, La [lah son-nahm'-boo-lah] (The Girl who Walked in her Sleep). Opera in two acts by Bellini. Libretto by Felice Romani. First performed, Milan, Jan. 12, 1831.

Sonnenquartetten [zon'-ĕn-cvarr-tet'-ĕn], *G.* *v.* SUN QUARTETS.

Sonore [son-orr], *Fr.* Sonorous, with full tone—an indication frequently applied to individual parts in an orchestral score. English composers appear to use the word in the mistaken belief that it is Italian. The Italian word, however, is *sonoro*.

Sons bouchés [sõn boosh-ay], *Fr.* (*G.* gestopft). Stopped notes on the horn, produced by inserting the hand into the bell. If they are played quietly the sound is remote and mysterious; if loud, it is harsh.

Sons étouffés [sõnz ay-toof-ay], *Fr.* "Damped sounds," *e.g.* on a harp, indicating that the sound must be immediately damped (the opposite of *laissez vibrer*).

Sons harmoniques [sõn arr-mon-eek], *Fr.* Harmonics.

Sons près de la table [sõn pray der la tubl], *Fr.* *v.* PRÈS DE LA TABLE.

Sopra [so'-prah], *I.* "Above." In piano music used to indicate that one hand has to pass above the other.

Soprano. The female voice of the highest register; also occasionally applied to instruments, *e.g.* soprano saxophone. In England the corresponding term for a boy singer was "quatreble" in the 15th cent., "treble" later.

Sorabji, KAIKHOSRU SHAPURJI: *b.* Chingford (Essex), Aug. 14, 1895. Composer and pianist, son of a Parsee father and a Spanish mother. Played the piano in his own compositions from 1920 in London, Paris and Vienna. He has composed 2 symphonies for orchestra with chorus, piano and organ, 5 piano concertos, symphonic variations for piano and orchestra, piano quintets, piano sonatas, an elaborate work entitled *Opus Clavicembalisticum* and other piano works, organ symphonies, 5 Michelangelo sonnets for baritone and chamber orchestra, and songs, and has written a book of critical essays, *Around Music* (1932).

Sorcerer, The. Comic opera in two acts by Sullivan. Libretto by William Schwenk Gilbert. First performed, London, Nov. 17, 1877.

Sordina [sorr-dee'-nah], *I.* = SORDINO.

Sordino [sorr-dee'-no], *I.* (1) Mute (of a string or wind instrument). *Con sordino*, with the mute; *senza sordino*, without the mute.

(2) Damper (in the piano). The indication *senza sordini* in the first movement of Beethoven's piano sonata in C♯ minor, Op. 27, No. 2, means that the dampers are to be raised, *i.e.* the strings are to be left free to vibrate. This was originally done by means of stops (similar to those used on the harpsichord). When later on a pedal was introduced to perform the same function the abbreviation *Ped.* came to replace the indication *senza sordini*.

(3) Also applied in the late 18th and 19th cent. to a strip of leather (later

felt) used to mute the strings of a piano and controlled by a pedal. For an example of its use see the slow movement of Schubert's piano sonata in A minor, Op. 143. *v.* also CORDA.

Sordun [zorr-doon'], *G.* (*I.* sordone). An instrument of the bassoon family, current in the late 16th and early 17th cent. It had a cylindrical bore and was played with a double reed. As the name suggests, the sound was muffled. It was made in several sizes.

Sore. *v.* AGRICOLA (3).

Soriano [sorr-yahn'-o] (Suriano, Surianus, Suriani), FRANCESCO: *b.* Soriano, 1549; *d.* Rome, after 1621. Singer and composer. Chorister at St. John Lateran in Rome (1564) and pupil of G. B. Nanini and Palestrina. *Maestro di cappella* at St. Ludovico dei Francesi (1581), attached to the court in Mantua (1583-86), in Rome *maestro di cappella* at Santa Maria Maggiore (1587), at St. John Lateran (1599) and at St. Peter's (1603). He composed Masses, motets, psalms, 110 canons on *Ave maris stella*, Magnificats, a Passion and other church music, madrigals and *villanelle*.

Sorochinskaya Yarmarka [sorr-ŏ-chince-cah'-ya yarr'-marr-ca] (Sorochintsi Fair). Opera in three acts by Moussorgsky. Libretto by the composer (based on an episode from Gogol's *Evenings on a Farm near Dekanka*). It was left incomplete by the composer, and without orchestration. Among the versions which have been performed are those by Cui (Petrograd, 1917), Tcherepnin (Monte Carlo, 1923) and Shebalin (Leningrad, 1931).

Sosarme, Re di Media [so-zarr'-meh reh di mehd'-yah] (Sosarmes, King of Media). Opera in three acts by Handel. Libretto adapted from *Alfonso Primo* by Matteo Noris. First performed, London, Feb. 26, 1732.

Sospiro [soss-pee'-ro], *I.* Crochet rest (lit. " sigh ").

Sostenuto [soss-teh-noo'-toh], *I.* " Sustained." A direction to sustain the tone, which is usually equivalent to slowing the tempo.

Sotto [sot'-to], *I.* " Under." (1) In piano music used to indicate that one hand has to pass under the other. (2) *Sotto voce*, in an undertone, quietly.

Soupir [soo-peer], *Fr.* Crotchet rest (lit. " sigh "). A quaver rest is *demi-soupir*, a semiquaver rest *quart de soupir*, a demisemiquaver rest *huitième de soupir*, and a hemidemisemiquaver rest *seizième de soupir*.

Sourdine [soor-deen], *Fr.* (1) Mute (of a string or wind instrument). (2) Damper (in the piano). (3) A device for muting the strings of the piano. *v.* SORDINO.

Sousa, JOHN PHILIP: *b.* Washington (D.C.), Nov. 6, 1854; *d.* Reading (Pa.), March 6, 1932. Bandmaster and composer. Leader of the United States Marine Corps Band, 1880. In 1892 he organized his own band which later made European tours and a world tour (1910-11). He composed many marches, light operas, orchestral suites, and songs, wrote an autobiography, *Marching Along* (1928), and edited *National Patriotic and Typical Airs* (1890).

Souterliedekens [sowt'-er-leed'-er-kenz], *Fl.* (Psalter Songs). The title of a Flemish PSALTER which contained the earliest metrical translations of the Psalms, with their melodies (which were folk-songs), first published in Antwerp in 1540. Clemens non Papa made three-part settings of the tunes, with the melodies in the tenor, which were published in 4 volumes by Susato in 1556-57.

Sowerby, LEO: *b.* Grand Rapids (Mich.), May 1, 1895. Composer and pianist. Studied at the American Conservatory in Chicago, served as a bandmaster in the American army (1917), was appointed teacher at the American Conservatory and organist at St. James's Church, Chicago, and received the first fellowship at the American Academy in Rome (1922). He has composed symphonies and other orchestral works, concertos for piano, for cello and for organ, choral works, chamber music, works for organ and for piano, and songs.

Spadaro. *v.* SPATARO.

Spanisches Liederbuch [shpahn'-ish-ĕss leed'-er-bookh] (Spanish Song-Book). A set of 44 songs by Hugo Wolf (1889-90), to words from a collection of

Spanish poems translated into German by Emanuel Geibel and Paul Heyse.

Spanish Rhapsody. *v.* RAPSODIE ESPAGNOLE.

Spataro [spah-tah'-ro] (Spadaro, Spadarius), GIOVANNI: *b.* Bologna, *c.* 1458; *d.* there, Jan. 17, 1541. Musical theorist. *Maestro di cappella* of San Petronio from 1512 until his death. He defended the system of tuning of the monochord advocated by Ramis de Pareja against the criticisms of Burzio (*Musices opusculum*, 1487) and Gafori (*Apologia*, 1520). A Mass by him has survived.

Speaker-Key. A key on a reed instrument, *e.g.* oboe or clarinet, which opens a hole at such a point as to facilitate the playing of notes which are sounded by overblowing at the octave, twelfth or fifteenth.

Spezzato [speh-dzah'-toh], *I.* "Divided", as in *cori spezzati, q.v.*

Spianato [spyah-nah'-toh], *I.* "Even," *i.e.* in an even, unvaried manner.

Spiccato [speek-cah'-toh], *I.* Lit. "clearly articulated." Used in string-playing for a light staccato played with the middle of the bow and a loose wrist.

Spinet (*Fr.* épinette, *I.* spinetta; from *L.* spina, "a thorn," referring to the quill which plucked the string.) A term which replaced the word "virginals" in the course of the 17th cent. in England for a small, one-manual harpsichord. In the 16th cent. the Italian spinet was made in a pentagonal shape; the Flemish spinet, like the virginals, was rectangular. The octave or 4-ft. spinet was triangular, with the strings at an angle of 45 degrees to the keyboard, and English makers adopted an enlarged version of this shape for the 8-ft. or normal pitch spinet towards the end of the 17th cent. Pepys bought an "espinette" from Haward for £5 in 1668, noting that he had had in mind a small harpsichord, "but this takes up less room." *v.* HARPSICHORD.

Spirito [spee'-ree-to], *I.* Spirit. *Con spirito*, with spirit, lively.

Spiritoso [spee-ree-to'-zo], *I.* In a spirited manner.

Spiritual. Religious song of the North American negro. Its melodic style is simple, with occasional use of modes or of a pentatonic scale, its rhythms are frequently syncopated, and its harmonies are similar to, and possibly modelled on, those of the mission hymns of white communities. As the first indigenous music of the North American continent to come to notice, the spirituals attracted much attention in the late 19th cent. through the travels of choirs from educational institutions for negroes.

G. P. JACKSON: *White and Negro Spirituals* (1943).

H. E. KREHBIEL: *Afro-American Folk Songs* (1914).

Spitta [shpit'-ta], JULIUS AUGUST PHILIPP: *b.* Wechold (Hanover), Dec. 27, 1841; *d.* Berlin, Apr. 13, 1894. Musicologist. Studied at Göttingen, taught at Reval, Sondershausen and Leipzig, where he was a founder of the Bachverein. Was appointed secretary to the Academy of Arts and professor of musical history at the University in Berlin (1875), where he also taught and was a director, from 1882, of the Hochschule für Musik. His *Life of Bach* (in German, 2 vols., 1873, 1880; English trans., 3 vols., 1884-5) was the first comprehensive work on the life and music of Bach, the Lutheran tradition which he inherited, and the Italian and other influences on his music. Published other writings on musical history, and edited the complete works of Schütz, the organ works of Buxtehude, and a selection of pieces by Frederick the Great.

Spohr [shpohr], LUDWIG (Louis): *b.* Brunswick, Apr. 5, 1784; *d.* Cassel, Oct. 22, 1859. Violinist, composer, conductor and teacher. Studied in Brunswick under Franz Eck, with whom he went on a tour of Russia (1802). He played with Meyerbeer in Berlin (1804), became orchestra leader to the Duke of Gotha (1805), toured with his wife (the harpist Dorette Scheidler) and met Weber in Stuttgart (1807). He was leader of the orchestra at the new Theater-an-der-Wien in Vienna from 1812-16, conductor at the Frankfort Opera from 1817-20 and in 1822, on the recommendation of Weber, was appointed *Kapellmeister* to the Elector of

Hesse-Cassel. He gave concerts in Switzerland, Italy, Holland, London and Paris, and conducted music festivals at Frankenhausen (1810-11, the first one in Germany), Aix-la-Chapelle (1840) and Bonn. He conducted Wagner's *Der fliegende Holländer* in Cassel in 1843 and *Tannhäuser* in 1853. He was a violinist of great ability, a capable conductor, and a prolific composer. His 9 symphonies (three with titles : No. 4, *The Consecration of Sound* ; No. 6, *The Historic*, illustrating the musical style of four periods, dated 1720, 1780, 1810 and 1840 ; No. 7, *The Worldly and Divine in Man's Life*, for double orchestra) and 15 violin concertos were highly regarded in their time. The most successful of his 10 operas were *Faust* (1816), *Zemire und Azor* (1819) and *Jessonda* (1823), the last his chief work in this form. His chamber music includes 36 quartets and 2 double quartets, trios, 15 duets for 2 violins and other compositions, and he also wrote choral music, piano pieces, and pieces for harp. His autobiography was published in an English translation in 1865 and reprinted in 1874.

Spontini [spon-tee′-nee], GASPARO LUIGI PACIFICO: *b.* Majolati (nr. Jesi), Nov. 14, 1774; *d.* there, Jan. 24, 1851. Composer. Studied in Naples at the Conservatorio della Pietà de' Turchini and, after his first opera had been produced in Rome (1796), under Piccinni. In 1798 he went to Palermo as music director to the Neapolitan court. He settled in Paris in 1803 and became composer to the Empress Josephine and director of the Italian Opera (1810-12). He was appointed director of music to the Prussian Court in Berlin (1820) but was dismissed (1841) after the death of Friedrich Wilhelm III. He visited Paris and Dresden (1844), returned to Italy in 1848 and founded a music school at Jesi. His most famous and most successful operas, *La Vestale* (1807) and *Fernand Cortez* (1809), were written for Paris, and were the first to reflect the taste of the Napoleonic era for operas with sumptuous production and plots with historical and political significance. *Nurmahal* (Berlin, 1822) and *Agnes von Hohenstaufen* (Berlin, 1829) were less successful.

C. BOUVET : *Spontini* (1930).

Sprechgesang [shpre*sh*′-ger-zung], *G.* Lit. "spoken song." (1) Recitative.

(2) A form of speech used, in association with instrumental accompaniment, by some modern composers. The speaker's part is not sung but the approximate pitch of the voice is indicated by musical notation. Examples are to be found in Schönberg's song-cycle *Pierrot lunaire* and Berg's opera *Wozzeck*.

Sprechstimme [shpre*sh*′-shtim-er], *G.* Lit. "speaking part." *v.* MELODRAMA, SPRECHGESANG (2).

Springer. An ornament used in 17th-cent. English music. It is equivalent to one of the forms of the German NACHSCHLAG. According to Christopher Simpson in *The Division Violist* it "concludes the Sound of a Note more acute, by clapping down another Finger just at the expiring of it."

Notation:

Played:

Spring Sonata (*G.* Frühlingssonate). The title given to Beethoven's violin and piano sonata in F major, Op. 24 (1801).

Spring Symphony. (1) (*G.* Frühlingssymphonie). The original title of Schumann's symphony No. 1 in B♭ major, Op. 38 (1841). He wrote in a letter to Spohr :

> "It was inspired, if I may say so, by the spirit of spring which seems to possess us all anew every year, irrespective of age. The music is not intended to describe or paint anything definite, but I believe the season did much to shape the particular form it took."

The four movements were to have been called *Frühlingsbeginn* (Spring's Coming), *Abend* (Evening), *Frohe Gespielen* (Merry Playmates) and *Voller Frühling* (Full Spring).

(2) A work in four main sections for soloists, chorus and orchestra by Britten,

Op. 44. The authors of the texts are (in alphabetical order) Auden, Barnefield, Beaumont and Fletcher, Blake, Clare, Herrick, Milton, Nashe, Peele, Spenser, Vaughan, and Anon. First performed, Amsterdam, July 9, 1949.

Squarcialupi [scwarr-chah-loo′-pee], ANTONIO : *b.* Florence, March 27, 1416 ; *d.* there, July 6, 1480. Organist. Lived in Siena (1450) and at the Florentine court (1467) as organist of Santa Maria. He is known chiefly through a fine manuscript of which he was the first owner, commonly called the Squarcialupi manuscript, now in the Laurentian Library in Florence, which is the largest surviving collection of the 14th cent. It contains music by 12 composers, including 145 pieces by Francesco Landini. Modern ed. by J. Wolf.

Squire, WILLIAM BARCLAY : *b.* London, Oct. 16, 1855 ; *d.* there, Jan. 13, 1927. Music librarian and editor. Educated at Cambridge. Practised as a solicitor, 1883-5. Joined the staff of the British Museum and became superintendent of printed music, retiring in 1920. Music critic, *Saturday Review*, 1890-4 ; *Westminster Gazette*, 1893 ; *Globe*, 1894-1901; *Pilot*, 1900-4. Editor, *Catalogue of Printed Music 1487-1800*, now *in the British Museum*, a catalogue of music in Westminster Abbey chapter library, *Catalogue of the King's Music Library*, vols. i and iii, *Catalogue of the Printed Music in the Royal College of Music*. Joint editor, with J. A. Fuller-Maitland, of the *Fitzwilliam Virginal Book*. Also edited Purcell's harpsichord music, and works by Byrd and Palestrina, as well as an anthology of madrigals. He wrote the libretto of Stanford's opera *The Veiled Prophet*.

Stabat Mater [stah′-but mah′-ter], *L.* " The Mother was standing." The initial words of a sequence probably written by Jacopone da Todi. The opening is quoted under SEQUENCE. The earliest polyphonic settings (*c.* 1500) were by English composers (John Browne, William Cornyshe, Richard Davy) and by Josquin des Prés. Later settings occur in all periods ; among the most notable are those of Palestrina, Caldara, Pergolesi, Haydn, Schubert, Rossini, Verdi, Dvořák and Stanford.

Staccato [stahk-cah′-toh], *I.* " Detached." It may be indicated either by a pointed dash (▼), which was the standard notation in the baroque period, or by a dot over each note to be detached. The dash indicates that the note is to be as short as possible, the dot that it is to be short. In *mezzo-staccato*, also called *portato*, indicated by a combination of slur and dots, the notes are to be slightly detached. *v.* DOT.

Staden [shtahd′-ĕn], JOHANN: *b.* Nuremberg, 1581 ; *d.* there, buried Nov. 15, 1634. Composer and organist. Organist to the Margrave of Kulmbach and Bayreuth, 1603-16 ; later in Nuremberg at the Lorenzkirche and Sebalduskirche, 1618. He composed 6 books of church music, including motets and sacred concertos for voices and instruments, solo songs with continuo for organ, lute or theorbo, *Hausmusik* (4 parts, 1623-28) containing pieces in three and four parts for voices or instruments, secular songs, dances and other instrumental pieces. A selection of his works is printed in *D.T.B.*, vii (1) and viii (1).

Stadler [shtahd′-ler] (1) ANTON: *b.* 1753 ; *d.* Vienna, June 15, 1812. Austrian clarinettist, whose virtuosity and beauty of tone encouraged the composition of several works by Mozart including the trio in E♭ for clarinet, viola and piano, K.498, the clarinet quintet, K.581, and the clarinet concerto, K.622. The obbligatos for clarinet and for basset horn in *La clemenza di Tito* (1791) were also written for him ; the low notes in the clarinet obbligato were specially designed for Stadler's instrument, which had a compass extending a major third below the normal.

(2) MAXIMILIAN : *b.* Melk (Lower Austria), Aug. 7, 1748 ; *d.* Vienna, Nov. 8, 1833. Composer and organist. Studied at the Jesuit College in Vienna, entered the Benedictine order at the monastery of Melk in 1772, appointed abbot of Lilienfeld in 1786 and of Kremsmunster in 1798, later settled in Vienna where he made friends with

Haydn and Mozart, and worked as a parish priest from 1803-15, when he returned to Vienna. He completed Mozart's piano sonata in A, K.402, and his trio in D, K.442 and wrote two pamphlets in defence of his Requiem. He composed an oratorio, two Requiems, Masses, psalms and other church music, a cantata, sonatas and fugues for piano and for organ and songs.

Stadtpfeifer [shtut'-pfife-er], *G.* A performer on a wind instrument, employed by a municipality, the equivalent of the *E.* WAIT. Several members of Bach's family belonged to this profession. For a description of the *Stadtpfeifer* in Leipzig in the 18th cent. *v.* C. S. Terry, *Bach's Orchestra*, p. 14 foll.

Staff (or Stave) (*Fr.* portée, *G.* Liniensystem, System, *I.* rigo, sistema). The set of lines, each representing a pitch (as do the spaces between them), on which music is written. Five lines are now used fcr all music except plainsong, which is written on four lines. LEGER LINES are used for notes above and below the staff, and a CLEF indicates the pitch of one of the lines and hence the particular pitch-position of a staff.

One or two lines, coloured red for F and yellow for C, were used in NEUME notation shortly before the 11th cent. Guido d' Arezzo's proposal (*c.* 1000) that four lines be used was adopted for plainsong, and five lines became usual for polyphonic music after 1200. Six or more lines were used for the writing of keyboard music in the 16th and 17th cent.

Music for the harp, piano, harpsichord, clavichord and celesta is normally written on two staves, joined together by a BRACE. Organ music normally uses three, except when there is no pedal part. For the combination of several staves required for an ensemble of voices or instruments or both *v.* SCORE.

Stainer, JOHN: *b.* London, June 6, 1840; *d.* Verona, March 31, 1901. Organist and composer. Chorister at St. Paul's Cathedral from 1847-56, when he became organist at St. Michael's College, Tenbury. He studied at Oxford from 1860, and was organist at Magdalen College and later to the University. Organist, St. Paul's Cathedral, 1872; principal of the National Training School for Musicians, 1881; professor, Oxford, 1889. One of the founders of the Musical Association (1874) and president of the College of Organists. Knighted, 1888. He edited (with W. A. Barrett) a *Dictionary of Musical Terms*, (with his children, J. F. R. and C. Stainer) *Dufay and his Contemporaries* (1898) and *Early Bodleian Music* (1901), and composed cantatas, anthems, services and other church music.

Stamitz [shtahm'-its], (1) CARL: *b.* Mannheim, May 7, 1745; *d.* Jena, buried Nov. 11, 1801. Violinist and composer. Son of (2). Second violinist in the Mannheim orchestra from 1762-70 when he went to Strasbourg, Paris and London (1778) as a viola and viola d'amore player. Returned to Germany in 1785, and lived in Cassel, St. Petersburg, and in Jena from 1794 as music director to the University. He composed 70 symphonies (some with two *concertante* violin parts), a symphony for two orchestras, concertos for piano, for viola, and for viola d'amore, string quartets, trio sonatas and other chamber music, and two operas. Two of his symphonies were published in *D.T.B.*, viii (2), and a string trio, an orchestral quartet, and a sonata for viola d'amore and bass in *D.T.B.*, xvi.

(2) JOHANN WENZL ANTON: *b.* Deutsch-Brod (Bohemia), June 19, 1717; *d.* Mannheim, buried March 30, 1757. Composer and violinist. Solo violinist at the coronation of Emperor Karl VII (1742). Invited to the electoral court of Mannheim, where he became leading violinist and chamber music director, 1745. He composed 50 symphonies, 100 orchestral trios, harpsichord, violin and oboe concertos, violin sonatas and other chamber music. The most important of the group of composers attached to the Mannheim orchestra who developed some of the chief traits in the style of the symphony, such as marked contrast between *forte* and *piano*, the *crescendo* for full orchestra, contrast of style between themes, the dropping of the continuo, and the fuller use of wind instruments. An orchestral trio and 4

symphonies are printed in *D.T.B.*, iii (1), 3 symphonies in *D.T.B.*, vii (2), a trio sonata and a solo sonata in *D.T.B.*, vii (2), and a trio sonata and a solo sonata in *D.T.B.*, xvi.

Ständchen [shtentsh'-ĕn], *G.* Serenade.

Stanford, CHARLES VILLIERS: *b.* Dublin, Sept. 30, 1852; *d.* London, March 29, 1924. Composer. Studied in Dublin, and in 1870 became choral scholar at Queen's College, Cambridge, and in 1873 organist of Trinity College. Teacher of composition, R.C.M., from its opening in 1883; professor, Cambridge, 1887 to his death. Knighted, 1901. One of the leaders of the English musical renaissance, he was an imaginative and versatile composer. Some of his music is coloured by Irish folk-song, particularly the opera *Shamus O'Brien* (1896), the choral ballad *Phaudrig Crohoore* (1896), and the *Irish Rhapsodies* and third symphony (*Irish,* 1887), and there are continental influences in the opera *The Veiled Prophet of Khorassan* (1881), in the Requiem (1897), and in the chamber music. Nevertheless, his style, though varied, is individual, and his technique eminently skilful; his choral works, songs and part-songs are among the finest of their period. He published, with C. Forsyth, a *History of Music* (1916), a treatise on *Musical Composition* (1911), and three volumes of essays and memoirs: *Studies and Memories* (1908), *Pages from an Unwritten Diary* (1914) and *Interludes* (1922).

J. A. FULLER-MAITLAND: *The Music of Parry and Stanford* (1934).

H. P. GREENE: *Charles Villiers Stanford* (1935).

Stanley, JOHN: *b.* London, Jan. 17, 1713; *d.* there, May 19, 1786. Composer and organist who was blind from the age of two. Studied under Maurice Greene and later at Oxford. From 1726 organist of several London churches. Conducted oratorio performances, formerly conducted by Handel, from 1760 with J. C. Smith and from 1774 with T. Linley, and in 1779 succeeded Boyce as Master of the King's Music. He composed cantatas and songs for solo voice and instruments, oratorios, 6 concertos for strings, a dramatic pastoral. pieces for German flute, violin or harpsichord, and organ voluntaries.

G. FINZI: "John Stanley (1713-1786)" in *Proceedings of the Royal Musical Association*, lxxvii (1950-1).

Stantipes. *v.* ESTAMPIE.

Starzer [shtarrts'-er], JOSEPH: *b.* 1726; *d.* Vienna, Apr. 22, 1787. From 1760-70 he was in St. Petersburg as leader of the orchestra and composer of ballets, then in Vienna as leader of the court orchestra. His compositions include symphonies, a violin concerto, *divertimenti*, and an oratorio. Two *divertimenti* for string quartet are printed in *D.T.Ö.*, xv (2).

Stave. *v.* STAFF.

Steffani [stef'-fah-nee], AGOSTINO: *b.* Castelfranco, July 25, 1654; *d.* Frankfort, Feb. 12, 1728. Composer and diplomat. He lived as a boy in Padua, studied while at the Munich electoral court (from 1667) under Kerll and at Rome under Bernabei (1672-74). He returned to the Munich court as organist from 1675 and chamber music director from 1681 and visited Paris (1678-79), where he studied the music of Lully. Ordained priest, 1680; Abbot of Lepsing, 1682. In 1688 he went to Hanover where he became court music director and held several diplomatic posts, and from 1703 was in the service of the Elector Palatine at Düsseldorf. During a visit to Italy (1708-09) he met Handel, for whom he obtained the post of *Kapellmeister* at the Hanoverian Court. He lived at Padua from 1722-25. His most noteworthy compositions were operas and chamber duets with continuo. In the 6 operas performed at Munich, 8 at Hanover, and 2 at Düsseldorf he combined features of the Italian, French and German styles in a manner afterwards developed by Handel, and his chamber duets also served Handel as models. His opera *Alarico* (Munich, 1687) is published in *D.T.B.*, xi (2), and extracts from 13 other operas in *D.T.B.*, xii (2); *D.T.B.*, vi (2) contains 16 chamber duets, 2 *Scherzi* for voice, 2 violins, and continuo, and 2 cantatas to Latin words for three voices and continuo. His six-part *Stabat Mater* with accompaniment for strings and organ was published in London in 1935. 8 songs with woodwind and continuo are in *Smith College Archives*, xi.

Steg [shtake], *G.* (*Fr.* chevalet, *I.* ponticello). Bridge (of a string instrument). *Am Steg*, on the bridge, *i.e.* play near the bridge, thus producing a glassy, brittle tone.

Steibelt [shtibe-ĕlt], DANIEL: *b.* Berlin, Oct. 22, 1765; *d.* St. Petersburg, Oct. 2, 1823. Pianist and composer. Studied harpsichord and composition under Kirnberger until *c.* 1784, lived in Paris as pianist, teacher and composer, and in London from 1796-98, toured Germany and Austria (1799) and played in contest with Beethoven. Spent the next few years moving between Paris and London to avoid his creditors, and settled in St. Petersburg (1808), where he became *Kapellmeister* to the Emperor Alexander (1810) and director of the French Opera. He composed operas, ballets, overtures, piano concertos, many sonatas for violin and for harp and piano, incidental music, and études and other pieces for piano.

Steinbach [shtine′-buckh], FRITZ: *b.* Grünsfeld (Baden), June 17, 1855; *d.* Munich, Aug. 13, 1916. Conductor. Studied at the Leipzig Conservatorium. Second *Kapellmeister*, Mainz, 1880; court *Kapellmeister*, Meinigen, 1886; municipal *Kapellmeister* and director of the Conservatorium, Cologne, 1902-14. His performances with the Meinigen orchestra, particularly of Brahms's works, gave him a European reputation.

Steinberg [stine′-bairk], MAXIMILIAN OSSEIEVICH: *b.* Vilna, July 4, 1883; *d.* Leningrad, Dec. 6, 1946. Composer. Studied at St. Petersburg University and Conservatoire and under Liadov, Glazounov and Rimsky-Korsakov, whose daughter he married in 1908. Teacher, St. Petersburg (Leningrad) Conservatoire, 1908; director, 1934. His pupils included Shostakovich and Shaporin. He composed 4 symphonies and other orchestral works, ballets, an oratorio and other choral works (some with orchestra), piano concertos and sonatas, string quartets, songs, song cycles and folk-song arrangements.

Steinway. A New York firm of piano manufacturers, founded in 1853 by Henry Engelhard Steinway (originally Steinweg), who was previously established in Brunswick. The London branch of the firm in Wigmore Street, opened in 1875, included the Steinway Hall, an excellent small concert hall which became the Grotrian Hall in 1925 and was closed in 1938, when it passed into the possession of Messrs. Selfridge. Steinway Hall in New York played an important part in the musical life of the city from 1866 to 1925.

Stenhammar [stehn′-hum-arr], KARL WILHELM EUGEN: *b.* Stockholm, Feb. 7, 1871; *d.* there, Nov. 20, 1927. Composer, conductor and pianist. Son of the composer Per Ulrik Stenhammar (1829-75). He began to compose while still a boy, and pursued his studies in Stockholm and Berlin. He spent several years touring as a pianist and also conducted in Stockholm, 1897-1901. Conductor, Gothenburg Symphony Orchestra, 1908-21; Stockholm Opera, 1925. His compositions include the operas *Tirfing* (Stockholm, 1898) and *Das Fest auf Solhaug* (Stuttgart, 1899; in Swedish as *Gillet på Solhaug*, Stockholm, 1902), the choral works *Snöfrid*, *Prinsessan och svennen* (Princess and Page), *Ett folk* (including the popular chorus "Sverige"), *Folket i Nifelhem*, *Vårnatt* and *Hemmarsch*, incidental music to several plays, 2 symphonies, 2 piano concertos and other orchestral works, chamber music, piano works and songs.

Stentando [sten-tahn′-do], *I.* "Labouring," *i.e.* holding back each note in a passage. Hence equivalent to *molto ritenuto*. Often abbreviated *stent.*

Sterndale Bennett, WILLIAM. *v.* BENNETT.

Stile [stee′-leh], *I.* Style. In particular:

(1) *Stile antico*: the contrapuntal style of the 16th cent. as practised by Italian composers and formulated by Italian theorists in the 17th and early 18th cent. Its principles were expounded by J. J. Fux in his *Gradus ad Parnassum* (1725) and thereafter became the rules of "strict" COUNTERPOINT.

(2) *Stile* (*genere*) *concitato*: a style fitted to express anger or agitation. The term was first used by Monteverdi in

his preface to *Madrigali guerrieri et amorosi* (1638). He points out that there should be three types of music—*concitato*, *molle* and *temperato*—to correspond to the three principal passions—anger, temperance and humility—and avers, not quite correctly, that earlier composers had not written in a *genere concitato*.

(3) *Stile rappresentativo*: the style of dramatic RECITATIVE practised in the earliest operas and in shorter works such as Monteverdi's *Combattimento di Tancredi e Clorinda*, composed in 1624.

(4) *Stile moderno* (*concertato*) : the "modern" style of the early 17th cent., in which (a) the continuo, with or without other instruments with independent parts, was used to accompany a voice or voices, as distinct from the older practice of doubling or replacing voices by instruments, or (b) the parts in an instrumental composition were written for specific instruments and accompanied by continuo, as in Merula's *Canzoni, overo Sonate concertate per chiesa e camera* (1637).

Stimme [shtim'-er], *G.* (1) Voice.

(2) A separate part, vocal or instrumental, in a composition. Hence *Stimmbuch*, part-book ; *Stimmführung*, part-writing.

Stockhausen [shtock'-howz-ĕn], JULIUS: *b.* Paris, July 22, 1826 ; *d.* Frankfort, Sept. 22, 1906. Baritone, singing-teacher and conductor. Son of the harpist Franz Stockhausen and the singer Margarete Stockhausen (*née* Schmuck). Studied at the Paris Conservatoire and with Manuel Garcia. He rapidly made his name as a *Lieder* singer and for a short time sang at the Opéra-Comique, Paris. Director, Philharmonic Concerts and Singakademie, Hamburg, 1862-7 ; Stern Gesangverein, Berlin, 1874-8. Teacher, Hoch Conservatorium, Frankfort, 1878-9. He excelled in the songs of Schubert, Schumann and Brahms, who dedicated to him his *Romanzen* from Tieck's *Magelone*.

Stokowski [stock-ov'-ski], LEOPOLD ANTON STANISLAW : *b.* London, April 18, 1882. Conductor. Studied at the R.C.M. under Stanford, and also in Germany and at the Paris Conservatoire. Organist of St. James's Piccadilly, 1900 ; St. Bartholomew's, New York, 1905. Conductor, Cincinnati Orchestra, 1909-12 ; Philadelphia Orchestra, 1913-36 ; City Symphony Orchestra, New York, 1942-45; New York Philharmonic, 1946, and with Mitropoulos, in 1949-50. He organized the All-American Youth Orchestra in 1939. He has made orchestral transcriptions of many works by J. S. Bach and has appeared in films.

Stollen [shtoll'-en], *G.* The first portion of a stanza of a MINNESINGER or MEISTERSINGER song commonly consisted of two *Stollen* (lit. "props"), the music of the first being repeated for the second. *v.* BAR (3).

Stoltzer [shtollts'-er], THOMAS. *b.* Schweidnitz (Silesia), *c.* 1475 ; *d.* Ofen, Aug. 29, 1526. Composer. *Kapellmeister* to King Louis of Hungary and Bohemia. He composed Masses, Latin motets, psalms and hymns, German psalms and secular songs. Some Masses and motets have been published in *Das Erbe deutscher Musik*, xxii, and his Latin hymns and psalms in *D.D.T.*, lxv ; some Latin hymns were also contained in Rhaw's *Sacrorum Hymnorum Liber Primus* (modern ed. in *Das Erbe deutscher Musik*, xxi). 12 German part-songs are printed in *D.T.Ö.*, xxxvii (2) and others were included in Georg Forster's collection of 1539, reprinted in *Das Erbe deutscher Musik*, xx.

Stölzel [shturlts'-ĕl], GOTTFRIED HEINRICH: *b.* Grünstädtl (Saxony), Jan. 13, 1690 ; *d.* Gotha, Nov. 27, 1749. Composer. Studied in Schneeberg under Umlauf and in Leipzig under Hofmann and at the University, taught in Breslau (1710-12), visited Italy (1713), lived in Prague, Bayreuth and Gera, and in 1719 was appointed *Kapellmeister* to the Duke at Gotha. He composed 22 operas, 14 oratorios, Masses, 8 sets of cantatas and motets for the church year, chamber cantatas with piano, concertos and trio sonatas, and wrote 2 theoretical treatises. A *concerto grosso* for 2 groups of trumpets, wind and strings is printed in *D.D.T.*, xxix-xxx. He was the composer of the song "Bist du bei mir," generally attributed to J. S. Bach on the basis of a copy made by his second wife, Anna Magdalena.

Stone Guest, The. *v.* KAMENNY GOST.

Stop. (1) On an organ, the handle or draw-stop which controls the admission of wind to a particular register, or set of pipes. The term is also applied to the register itself. On a harpsichord, stops were formerly used to produce variations of tone or pitch; their function is now generally performed by pedals.

(2) A stopped pipe on an organ is one in which the upper end is closed. The effect of stopping is to lower the pitch by an octave.

(3) A string is said to be stopped when its playing length is shortened by the finger. The term "double stopping" is applied to the playing of two notes simultaneously on a stringed instrument even though this may involve the use of an OPEN STRING.

(4) A stopped note on the horn is produced by inserting the hand into the bell and so modifying the pitch of an open note. *v.* HORN.

Storace, STEPHEN: *b.* London, Jan. 4, 1763; *d.* there, March 19, 1796. Composer. Studied at the S. Onofrio Conservatorio in Naples, made the acquaintance of Mozart in Vienna, where he produced his first opera in 1785, and returned to England in 1787 with his sister Nancy (Anna Selina), who was the original Susanna in Mozart's *Le nozze di Figaro.* He composed operas, a ballet, chamber music, harpsichord sonatas and songs. The most successful operas for which he "selected, adapted, and composed" the music were *The Haunted Tower* (1789), *No Song, no Supper* (1790), *The Pirates* (1792) and *The Cherokee* (1794).

Storto [storr'-to], *I.* Krummhorn.

Story of the Lovely Melusina, The. *v.* SCHÖNE MELUSINE.

Stradella [strah-dell'-lah], ALESSANDRO: *b.* Monfestino, 1642; *d.* Genoa, Feb. 25, 1682. Composer, violinist and singer. Taught singing at Venice and later visited Turin and Rome. The story told by the Abbé Bourdelot (*Histoire de la musique,* 1715) of his attempted murder following his elopement with the mistress of a Venetian nobleman is the basis of Flotow's opera *Alessandro Stradella* (1844). He composed 6 oratorios, sacred and secular cantatas, operas, serenatas, concertos for strings, and trio sonatas. He considered his oratorio *S. Giovanni Battista* (1676) to be his best work. Modern ed. of the opera *La forza dell' amor paterno* (1678) by Alberto Gentili. An aria with instrumental *ritornelli* at the beginning and end, *Tra cruci funeste,* from the opera *Il Corispero* (*c.* 1665) is printed in the *Historical Anthology,* No. 241. His work is important both in the history of vocal forms and in the early history of the concerto; in his *Sinfonie a più stromenti* of *c.* 1680 he separated the solo instruments from the *concerto grosso.* It is not certain that the *serenata* used by Handel in the chorus "He spake the word, and there came all manner of flies" in *Israel in Egypt* and printed by Chrysander as the third supplement to his complete edition of Handel is actually by Stradella.

R. GIASOTTO: *La Musica a Genova* (1951).
H. HESS: *Die Opern Alessandro Stradellas* (1906).

Stradivari [strah-dee-vah'-ree] (Stradivarius), ANTONIO: *b.* Cremona, 1644; *d.* there, Dec. 18, 1737. Violin maker. Apprenticed to Nicolo Amati and founded his own workshop at Cremona. He began to use his own labels *c.* 1667 and made his best instruments between 1700 and 1720. He was assisted by two of his sons, Francesco and Omobono, who carried on their father's work after his death. Among his other pupils were Guadagnini and Gagliano. Although later makers have carried on the methods he evolved, none has surpassed his instruments in craftsmanship and quality of tone.

W., A. F. & A. HILL: *Antonio Stradivari, his Life and Work* (1909).
E. N. DORING: *How many Strads?* (1945).

Strambotto [strahm-bot'-to], *I.* (1) A form of Italian poetry of the 15th and 16th centuries. It has a verse of 8 lines with the rhyme scheme *abababcc,* or less frequently *abababab.* The musical settings published in the fourth of Petrucci's collections of *frottole* (1505) have music for the first pair of lines, which is to be repeated for the other three pairs. Two examples from that collection are printed in the third volume of Einstein's *The Italian Madrigal* (1949).

(2) Malipiero used the term in his *Rispetti e Strambotti* for string quartet, in which he wished to evoke " the character of old Italian poetry." The work is in the form of 20 instrumental " stanzas " each preceded by a recurring " ritornello."

Strandrecht [shtrunt'-re*sh*t]. *v.* WRECKERS.

Strangways, ARTHUR HENRY FOX. *v.* FOX STRANGWAYS.

Strathspey. Scottish dance. *v.* REEL.

Straube [shtrowb'-*er*], KARL: *b.* Berlin, Jan. 6, 1873 ; *d.* Leipzig, Apr. 27, 1950. Organist and conductor, son of a German father and an English mother. Studied in Berlin, and soon became widely known as a virtuoso on the organ. Organist, Wesel Cathedral, 1897 ; St. Thomas's, Leipzig, 1902. Cantor, St. Thomas's, 1918. Teacher of organ, Leipzig Conservatorium, 1907 ; professor, 1908. Conductor, Leipzig Bach Society, 1903 ; Gewandhaus Choir (incorporating the Bach Society), 1919. As an organist he excelled in the performance of Reger's works, many of which were written as a tribute to his skill. As a conductor, he was responsible for the performance of a vast amount of music of all periods and all countries, including the complete cycle of Bach's cantatas. His collections *Alte Orgelmeister* (1904), 45 *Choralvorspiele alter Meister* (1907) and *Alte Meister des Orgelspiels* (2 vols., 1929) are indispensable to organists.

Strauss [shtrowce], (1) CHRISTOPH : *b.* Vienna, *c.* 1580 ; *d.* there, June 1631. Composer. In the service of the imperial court from 1594, as conductor from 1617-19. Organist, St. Michael's, Vienna, 1601 ; later *Kapellmeister*, St. Stephen's Cathedral. He published a collection of 36 motets in 5-10 parts (1613) and a set of 16 Masses in 8-20 parts with continuo (1631). Modern ed. of a Requiem Mass in *D.T.O.*, xxx (1).

(2) JOHANN: *b.* Vienna, Oct. 25, 1825 ; *d.* there, June 3, 1899. Composer, violinist, conductor and son of Johann (1804-1849), who was also a famous composer of waltzes. Studied composition under Drechsler and founded his own orchestra in 1844, joined it with his father's orchestra in 1849 and toured Austria, Poland and Germany. He directed summer Park Concerts in St. Petersburg (1855-65), conducted court balls (from 1863) and visited Paris, London, Italy and America. He composed 16 operettas, a ballet, waltzes, polkas, galops and other dances. The most successful of his operettas were *Die Fledermaus* (The Bat, 1874) and *Der Zigeunerbaron* (The Gipsy Baron, 1885). His brother Josef (1827-70) also composed waltzes.

(3) RICHARD: *b.* Munich, June 11, 1864 ; *d.* Garmisch (Upper Bavaria), Sept. 8, 1949. Composer. Wrote his earliest compositions, including a *Festival March* for orchestra, Op. 1, before he was ten. In 1885 became assistant conductor to von Bülow at Meiningen, and later in the same year conductor. Under the influence of Alexander Ritter, a member of the orchestra, he turned from the style of Brahms to that of Liszt and Wagner, and began with *Aus Italien* (1887) the series of tone-poems which brought him fame and caused much controversy on the merits of PROGRAMME MUSIC. Assistant conductor, Munich Opera, 1886; Weimar Court Opera, 1889. Returned in 1894 to Munich, where he became chief conductor two years later. From 1898 he was conductor and from 1908 one of the directors of the Berlin Opera, and from 1919-24 conductor with Schalk of the Vienna Opera. Thereafter he lived in Garmisch, and from 1945 in Switzerland.

He composed his first opera, *Guntram*, in 1892-3. *Feuersnot* was produced in 1901, *Salome* in 1905, both at Dresden. In 1905 he began a fruitful collaboration with Hugo von Hofmannsthal, who wrote the libretti of 6 of his operas and (with Harry Kessler) the scenario of the ballet *The Legend of Joseph*, produced by Diaghilev in 1914.

A composer with a fertile imagination, brilliant musical and dramatic gifts, and a supreme mastery of orchestral technique, he pursued the late Romantic style to its utmost limits in the tone-poems and stage works up to *Elektra* (1909). In *Der Rosenkavalier* (completed in Sept. 1909), at the time when Schönberg was writing his first atonal compositions, he abandoned, through the influence of von Hofmannsthal, the Wagnerian style of opera, and returned to a lyrical Romanticism of a warm and vital character, which he continued in *Ariadne auf Naxos* (1912), *Intermezzo* (1925), *Arabella* (1933) and *Die Liebe der Danae* (completed in 1940), and which he brought to its most serene form in the instrumental works of his last years, such as the oboe concerto and the *Metamorphosen* for 23 solo strings of 1945. Of his many songs the few which are frequently sung are in the direct tradition of the 19th-cent. *Lied.* His principal compositions are :

(a) OPERAS: *Guntram* (Weimar, 1894); *Feuersnot* (Dresden, 1901); *Salome* (Dresden, 1905); *Elektra* (Dresden, 1909); *Der Rosenkavalier* (Dresden, 1911); *Ariadne auf Naxos* (Stuttgart, 1912; revised version, Vienna, 1916); *Die Frau ohne Schatten* (Vienna, 1919); *Intermezzo* (Dresden, 1924); *Die ägyptische Helena* (Dresden, 1928); *Arabella* (Dresden, 1933); *Die schweigsame Frau* (Dresden, 1935); *Friedenstag* (Munich, 1938); *Daphne* (Dresden, 1938); *Capriccio* (Munich, 1942); *Die Liebe der Danae* (Salzburg, 1952).

(b) BALLETS: *Josephslegende* (Paris. 1914); *Schlagobers* (Vienna, 1924).

(c) ORCHESTRA: Tone-poems: *Aus Italien* (1887), *Macbeth* (1887), *Don Juan* (1888), *Tod und Verklärung* (1889), *Till Eulenspiegel* (1895), *Also sprach Zarathustra* (1896), *Don Quixote* (1897), *Ein Heldenleben* (1898), *Symphonia domestica* (1903), *Eine Alpensinfonie* (1915); symphony in F minor (1884); violin concerto (1883); 2 horn concertos (1884, 1942); oboe concerto (1945); duet-concertino for clarinet and bassoon (1948); *Metamorphosen* for 23 solo strings (1945); suite from *Le Bourgeois gentilhomme* (1919).

(d) CHAMBER MUSIC: string quartet (1881); cello sonata (1883); piano quartet (1884); violin sonata (1887).

(e) SONGS: 4 sets with orchestra (1897-1921); 26 sets with piano (1882-1929).

(f) PIANO: sonata in B minor (1881); 2 sets of short pieces (1881, 1883).

Also editions of Gluck's *Iphigénie en Tauride* (1894), Mozart's *Idomeneo* (1930), Berlioz's *Instrumentation* (1905).

T. ARMSTRONG : *Strauss's Tone-Poems* (1931).

E. BLOM : *Strauss—The Rose Cavalier* (1930 ; an analysis of the opera).

Correspondence of Strauss and von Hofmannsthal (trans. Paul England, 1928 ; complete edition in German, 1952).

E. KRAUSE : *Richard Strauss—Gestalt und Werk* (1955).

E. NEWMAN : *Richard Strauss* (1908).

W. SCHUH (ed.) : *Richard Strauss : Briefe an die Eltern,* 1882-1906 (1954). *Richard Strauss : Recollections and Reflections* (1953). *Richard Strauss—Stefan Zweig : Briefwechsel* (1957).

W. SCHUH & F. TRENNER (ed.): *Hans von Bülow and Richard Strauss : Correspondence* (1955).

Stravinsky [stra-vince'-ki], IGOR: *b.* Oranienbaum (nr. St. Petersburg), June 17, 1882. Composer. He studied with Rimsky-Korsakov in 1907, and his first symphony, Op. 1, was performed in the following year. Diaghilev commissioned him to arrange two pieces by Chopin for the ballet *Les Sylphides,* and this led to his first success with *The Fire Bird,* produced in Paris by Diaghilev in 1910, which showed him an apt pupil of Rimsky-Korsakov. He moved rapidly to a more advanced style in *Petroushka* and in *The Rite of Spring,* one of the epoch-marking works of modern times, which was received with riotous protests at its first performance in Paris. During the war of 1914-18 his style entered a new phase marked by economy of medium in *The Soldier's Tale* for narrator and 7 instruments and *Ragtime* for 11 instruments, and by economy of texture and the clarity of baroque and classical forms in the octet for wind instruments, the concerto for piano and wind instruments, the ballet suite *Apollon Musagète,* and the oratorio *Oedipus Rex* and cantata *Symphony of Psalms,* both to Latin words.

Concern with style and its further refinement and his view of the composer (elaborated in *Poetics of Music*, first given as lectures at Harvard in 1939-40) as an artisan with an appetite for "putting in order musical elements" gave to the major works of the next decade—the concerto for 2 pianos without orchestra, the *Dumbarton Oaks* concerto for 16 instruments, and the symphony in C—the character of essays in musical patterns reduced to the essentials of rhythmic motion, form and tonality. In more recent works, such as the symphony in three movements, the concerto for strings, the Ballet *Orpheus*, the *Mass*, and the opera *The Rake's Progress*, this attitude to the nature of composition has been brought to bear on forms of a wider range, and on material in a variety of styles. One of the most gifted musicians of his age, and a composer of fertile imagination and impeccable craftsmanship, Stravinsky has exercised a strong influence on many of his younger contemporaries, especially in France and the United States. He made his last visit to Russia in 1914, became a French citizen in 1934, and settled in the United States in 1941. He has published an autobiography, *Chronicles of my Life* (1936) and a volume of essays, *Poetics of Music* (1947). His principal compositions are:

(a) STAGE WORKS—Ballets: *The Fire Bird* (1910), *Petroushka* (1911), *The Rite of Spring* (1913), *Les Noces* (with chorus, 1923), *Histoire du Soldat* (with speaking voice, 1918), *Pulcinella* (after Pergolesi, 1920), *Apollon Musagète* (1928), *Le Baiser de la Fée* (1928), *Jeu de Cartes* (1937), *Orpheus* (1948), *Agon* (1957). Operas: *Rossignol* (1914), *Mavra* (1922), *The Rake's Progress* (1951); Opera-oratorio: *Oedipus Rex* (1927); Melodrama: *Perséphone* (1933).

(b) ORCHESTRA: *Fireworks* (1908); *Symphonies of Wind Instruments* (1920); *Dumbarton Oaks* concerto (1938); symphony in C (1940); *Danses Concertantes* (1942); symphony in three movements (1945); concerto for string orchestra (1946); concerto for piano and wind (1924); *Capriccio* for piano and orchestra (1929); violin concerto (1931).

(c) CHORAL WORKS: *Symphony of Psalms* (1930); *Mass* (1948); *Canticum sacrum* (1956).

(d) OTHER WORKS: *Berceuses du chat* (4 songs for female voice and 3 clarinets, 1916); octet for wind (1923); concerto for 2 pianos (1935); sonata for two pianos (1944); septet for clarinet, bassoon, horn, violin, viola, cello and piano (1954); *In memoriam Dylan Thomas* (tenor, string quartet and 4 trombones (1954).

M. ARMITAGE: *Igor Stravinsky* (1936).
V. BELAIEV: *Igor Stravinsky's "Les Noces"* (1928).
E. EVANS: *Stravinsky: The Fire-Bird and Petroushka* (1933).
E. W. WHITE: *Stravinsky's Sacrifice to Apollo* (1930).

Streit zwischen Phöbus und Pan, Der [dair shtrite tsvish′-ĕn ferb′-o͝oss o͝ont pahn] (The Dispute between Phoebus and Pan). Secular cantata (*dramma per musica*) by J. S. Bach (1731). Text by "Picander," *i.e.* Christian Friedrich Henrici. The subject is a musical contest. The work contains an aria for Midas (probably representing Bach's critic J. A. Scheibe) which parodies the dull style of the lesser professionals of the time.

Strepitoso [streh-pee-to′-zo], *I.* Noisy.

Stretto [stret′-to], *I.* "Close, narrow". (1) The bringing in of entries of the subject in a fugue "closer," *i.e.* after shorter intervals of time, than those at which they originally came (*G.* Engführung). The objects of *stretto* are to show the contrapuntal possibilities of the subject and to increase the cumulative effect of successive sets, or of a final set, of entries. For example, in the exposition of the fugue in E♭ in the second book of Bach's *Forty-Eight* the answer comes at the seventh bar:

In bars 30-31 the answer comes at one bar's distance:

(2) The word is also used of a quickening of tempo towards the end of a piece.

Striggio [stree′-djo], ALESSANDRO: *b.* Mantua, *c.* 1535; *d.* possibly Sept. 22, 1587 in Mantua. Composer and player of the *lira da gamba*. A nobleman, he was attached to the court of Cosimo de' Medici in Florence from *c.* 1560 and later went to Mantua. He visited France, Flanders and England in 1567. One of the earliest composers of *intermezzi*, his *Psiche ed Amore* was performed in 1565. He published 7 books of madrigals and a set of programme madrigals, "The Chatter of Women at their Washing" (1567). Five of his madrigals are printed in Torchi's *L'arte musicale in Italia*, i, and his "naturalistic" madrigal "The Game of Cards" in the third volume of Einstein's *The Italian Madrigal*. There is a keyboard transcription of his madrigal "Chi fara fede al cielo" by Peter Philips in the Fitzwilliam Virginal Book (ed. Fuller-Maitland and Barclay Squire, i, p. 312). His son Alessandro, a player of the *lira* and a librettist, wrote the libretto of Monteverdi's *Orfeo* (1607).

Stringendo [streen-jend′-o], *I.* "Tightening," *i.e.* accelerating the tempo.

String Quartet. The medium (and music for the medium) of two violins, viola and cello. A string quartet is, in effect, a SONATA in three or four movements for those instruments. Its history begins between 1750 and 1760 with the early quartets of Haydn, which were probably written for outdoor performance—hence the absence of a continuo part. The 12 quartets of his Op. 1 and 2 are in the style of *divertimenti*, and have 5 movements, including 2 minuets. From Op. 3 (*c.* 1765) onwards Haydn adopted the four-movement form, and with Op. 9 (1769) he began the development of style, form and texture in quartet writing which continued to the end of his life. Mozart dedicated to Haydn the first 6 of his 10 mature quartets. The concept of the possibilities of the medium at which Beethoven arrived in his last three quartets put them for nearly a century outside the main stream of the history both of the string quartet and of sonata form. In their linear style, and in their treatment of thematic development and tonality, they are closer to the quartets written in the past 30 years than to those of the nineteenth century. Between Schubert and Brahms the quartet, an apt medium for lyrical expression but not for rhetoric, had a patchy history. With Debussy's quartet of 1893 it entered a new phase, which has included the remarkable series of 6 quartets by Bartók and some of the most characteristic compositions of Ravel, Schönberg, Hindemith, Walton and Wellesz.

String Quintet. *v.* QUINTET.

Strogers, NICHOLAS: 16th-17th cent. English organist and composer. His compositions include services, anthems, motets, *In Nomines* for strings, and pieces for virginals, and for lute. There is a Fantasia by him in the *Fitzwilliam Virginal Book*.

Stromentato [stro-men-tah′-toh], *I.* Played by instruments. In particular, *recitativo stromentato*, recitative accompanied by the orchestra instead of simply by a keyboard instrument. *v.* RECITATIVE.

Stromento [stro-men′-to], *I.* Instrument. *v.* STRUMENTO.

Strumento [stroo-men′-to], *I.* Instrument. *Strumenti a corde*, string instruments; *strumenti a fiato*, wind instruments; *strumenti a percossa* (or *percussione*), percussion instruments. *Strumenti d'arco*, bowed string instruments; *strumenti di legno*, woodwind instruments; *strumenti d'ottone*, brass instruments.

Strungk [shtrŏŏnk], NIKOLAUS ADAM: *b.* Brunswick, *bapt.* Nov. 15, 1640; *d.* Dresden, Sept. 23, 1700. Composer, violinist and organist. At twelve he was assistant organist to his father, the composer Delphin Strungk, at the

Magnuskirche in Brunswick. He studied at Helmstadt University and became first violinist in the Celle orchestra (1661). He was in Hanover (1665), music director in Hamburg (1678), and returned to Hanover (1682) as chamber composer to the Elector Ernst August, whom he accompanied on a visit to Italy where he received praise from Corelli for his violin playing. He also visited Vienna, where he played for Leopold I. He was appointed chamber organist and assistant *Kapellmeister* (1688) and *Kapellmeister* (1692) of the Dresden Court. He composed about 8 operas for Hamburg between 1678 and 1693, when he opened the Leipzig opera, which he founded, with a performance of his *Alceste*. Five of the 6 *Cappricci* for organ printed in *D.T.Ö.*, xiii (2), as by G. Reutter are said by H. J. Moser to be compositions by Strungk.

Stück [shtee̯k], *G.* Piece, composition; *e.g.* Schumann's *Fantaisiestücke* for piano.

Study. *v.* ÉTUDE.

Sturgeon, NICHOLAS: *d.* 1454. Composer. He received an annuity from Henry V in 1419. Canon of Windsor, 1441; prebendary of Kentish Town in St. Paul's, 1452. He probably had a part in the writing of the Old Hall manuscript, which contains 3 *Glorias*, 2 *Credos* (one incomplete), a *Sanctus*, an incomplete *Benedictus*, and an isorhythmic motet by him.

Style. The tracing of the history of musical styles and of the changes in social, technical and aesthetic ideas which accompany and interact with changes in musical style is the chief object of the study of musical history. The style of a composition is its manner of treating form, melody, rhythm, counterpoint, harmony and tone-colour; it is closely related to and limited by its medium, but not entirely dependent on it, since features of the style appropriate to one medium may be transferred to another. The analysis of compositions written in a particular period, in a particular genre and by a particular composer provides the material for the history of the style of that period, genre or composer. Musical historians have adopted from historians of painting and sculpture terms for the main periods in the history of style, the use of which is obviously justified by their convenience (Gothic, 1150-1475; Renaissance, 1475-1600; Baroque, 1600-1750; Rococo or Galant, 1730-1770; Classical, 1750-1820; Romantic, 1820-1890; Impressionist, 1890-1910; Expressionist, 1910-1930), although their implications in terms of musical styles may not have been fully investigated. The history of the style of a genre (more commonly called "form" in this context, *e.g.* Opera, Concerto, etc.) includes changes in its form as well as in its other technical elements. Among the genres which have been studied in this way are Mass, Motet, Italian Madrigal, Opera, Concerto, Symphony and Suite, and Oratorio. The progress of a composer's style assumes a pattern which may be determined by a variety of circumstances, such as his response to outside influences, as in Schütz, his writing in different genres, as in Rameau and Schumann, or an inner development in clearly defined phases, as in Beethoven. *v.* also NATIONAL MUSIC, STILE.

Style galant [steel ga-lũn], *Fr.* (*G.* galanter Stil). A term adopted by German writers on music in the 18th cent. (*e.g.* Mattheson) for the homophonic and rather elaborately ornamented style of French and Italian music, *e.g.* that of F. Couperin and D. Scarlatti, as opposed to the contrapuntal style (*gearbeiteter Stil*) of the main German tradition. It is thus the equivalent in music of the Rococo style in painting. This style appears in J. S. Bach's music in the variable dances in the suite, which he refers to as "Menuetten und anderen Galanterien" in the title of the first part of the *Clavierübung*. Its adoption by such contemporaries of Bach as Telemann and Mattheson led to its becoming an important factor in the marked change of style between Bach and his sons C. P. E. and J. C. Bach, from whom it passed into the early work of Haydn and Mozart. In 1752 J. J. Quantz suggested that a style acceptable to many people might well arise from a mixture of the musical tastes of the three nations, an ideal which was in fact realised some 20 years later in the emergence of the classical style. The period of the *galant* style may be dated *c.* 1730 - *c.* 1770, overlapping the late baroque and the early classical styles.

Subdominant. The fourth degree of the diatonic scale, *e.g.* F in the scale of C. The subdominant triad is one of the three "primary" or principal triads—tonic, dominant and subdominant—in a key. The chord of the subdominant followed by the tonic chord forms a plagal CADENCE. The addition of a sixth to the subdominant chord forms the chord of the ADDED SIXTH.

Subito [soo′-bee-to], *I.* Suddenly. *Piano subito,* suddenly soft.

Subject. A theme which is used as the basis, or one of the bases, of a musical form, as are the *soggetto cavato* in a Mass (*v.* SOGGETTO), the subjects or "points" in a fancy or ricercar, the subject in a fugue, and the first and second subjects (or groups of subjects) in a movement in sonata form. The term "motive" or *motif* is applied to a part of a subject in a movement in sonata form which is later used in a development section, or to a concise theme which is later used to construct a subject, or becomes a recurring motive (*v.* LEITMOTIV) in an opera.

Submediant. The sixth degree of the diatonic scale, *e.g.* A in the scale of C major.

Succentor. The official in charge of the music, under the supervision of the precentor, in a cathedral, college chapel or monastery.

Suggia [soo′-djah], GUILHERMINA : *b.* Oporto, June 27, 1888 ; *d.* there, July 31, 1950. Cellist, of mixed Portuguese and Italian origin. She appeared in public while still a child. Studied with Klengel in Leipzig (1904), where she became a member of the Gewandhaus Orchestra, and subsequently with Casals, whom she married in 1906. After a temporary retirement of six years she reappeared as a soloist. She lived for many years in England. The well-known portrait by Augustus John gives a vivid impression of the magnetism which she exercised on an audience.

Suite. Before *c.* 1750 a composition consisting of a group of movements which are dance-types and are in the same key ; after that date a composition consisting of any group of instrumental movements, frequently drawn from the incidental music to a play or from a ballet. The prototypes of the baroque suite were the pairs (*v.* NACHTANZ) or groups of dance pieces in the keyboard and lute music of the 16th cent. Early in the 17th cent. some German composers published instrumental dances in sets of four or more, as in Peuerl's *Neue Padouan, Intrada, Däntz und Galliarda* (1611) and Schein's *Banchetto musicale* (1617). Some or all of the dances of a set were related thematically, forming what is known as a "variation suite." Later in the century Froberger's keyboard suites had the order Allemande-Courante-Sarabande, with or without a Gigue after the Allemande or Courante, while ballet-suites, such as those written for operas in Vienna by J. H. and A. A. Schmelzer, varied in the number and type of the dances according to the nature of the ballet. When Froberger's suites were published in 1693 they were disposed in the order Allemande-Courante-Sarabande-Gigue, which was adopted by Bach and Handel. In addition, Bach's suites and partitas contain one or more dances of French type (*Galanterien*), *e.g.* bourrée, gavotte, minuet, passepied, after the Sarabande, or occasionally, in the partitas, after the Courante. The English Suites and Partitas of Bach also contain a prelude, which may be in quite an extended form.

Each of François Couperin's Suites for harpsichord (which he called *Ordres*) consists of a considerable number of movements which have the title either of a dance or of a descriptive idea, *e.g. Les Abeilles, L'Enchanteresse.* A second type of French suite, modelled on the overture and set of dances which came at the beginning of the opera and opera-ballet of Lully was adopted by German composers, *e.g.* Georg Muffat, Telemann (*Musique de Table*) and Bach, and called *Ouverture.* As in Bach's four

Overtures, now generally called Orchestral Suites, the dances are French, and vary in number and type.

The Italian term *sonata da camera* seems to have been first applied to the suite by Rosenmüller, who gave his *sonate* the order Sinfonia-Allemanda-Correnta-Ballo-Sarabanda. Corelli's trio-sonatas *da camera* have a short prelude followed by Allemanda, Corrente or Sarabanda, and Giga or Gavotta.

There were dance movements in the *divertimenti* of the mid-18th cent., and the minuet became one of the movements of the sonata, but the use of the term " suite " was not resumed until late in the 19th century. It was not used for incidental music by Beethoven or Mendelssohn, but has been applied since Bizet's *L'Arlésienne* (1872) to a suite of incidental music such as Grieg's *Peer Gynt* and Prokofiev's *Lieutenant Kije*, to a suite abstracted from an opera such as Kodaly's *Háry János*, to a ballet-suite such as Ravel's *Daphnis et Chloé* and Stravinsky's *Petroushka*, and in some instances to a suite of instrumental music such as Sibelius's *Suite champêtre* for strings.

Suite Bergamasque [sēē-eet bair-ga-musk], *Fr.* Suite for piano solo by Debussy, published in 1905. The four movements are *Prélude*, *Menuet*, *Clair de lune*, and *Passepied*. *v.* BERGAMASCA.

Suivez [sēē-ee-vay], *Fr.* " Follow."
(1) Begin the next movement or section without a break (*I.* attacca).
(2) The accompaniment is to follow any modifications of tempo made by the soloist (*I.* colla parte).

Suk [sŏŏk], JOSEF: *b.* Křečovice, Jan. 4, 1874; *d.* Benešov, May 29, 1935. Composer, violinist and viola player. Studied at the Prague Conservatoire and under his future father-in-law Dvořák. Second violinist of the Bohemian String Quartet, 1892. Teacher of composition (1922) and director (1930), Prague Conservatoire. He composed 2 symphonies, symphonic poems, overtures and other orchestral works, a Mass, chamber music, part-songs and many pieces for piano.

Sulla scena [sool'-lah sheh'-nah], *I.* On the stage.

Sulla tastiera [sool'-lah tust-yeh'-rah], *I.* SUL TASTO.

Sullivan, ARTHUR SEYMOUR: *b.* London, May 13, 1842; *d.* there, Nov. 22, 1900. Composer, organist and conductor. Chorister at the Chapel Royal. Studied at the R.A.M. under Sterndale Bennett and Goss and at the Leipzig Conservatorium. Organist, St. Michael's, Chester Square, 1861 ; teacher of composition, R.A.M., 1866 ; principal, National Training School of Music, 1876-81. In 1867 he went with Sir George Grove to Vienna where they discovered some important Schubert manuscripts. Knighted, 1883. His light operas written to libretti by W. S. Gilbert were highly successful in many parts of the world. He also composed a grand opera, *Ivanhoe*, with libretto after Scott by Julian Sturgis (London, 1891), 2 ballets, oratorios, cantatas (including *The Golden Legend*), a symphony, overtures, incidental music for plays, anthems, hymns and other church music, songs and piano pieces.

In the operettas he combined tunefulness with neat craftsmanship and a brilliant flair for parody. The more important are:

Cox and Box (1867 ; libretto by F. C. Burnand ; all others except the *Rose of Persia* are by W. S. Gilbert) ; *Thespis*, or *The Gods Grown Old* (1871) ; *Trial by Jury* (1875) ; *The Sorcerer* (1877) ; *H.M.S. Pinafore* (1878); *The Pirates of Penzance* (1879) ; *Patience* (1881) ; *Iolanthe* (1882) ; *Princess Ida* (1884) ; *The Mikado* (1885) ; *Ruddigore* (1887) ; *The Yeomen of the Guard* (1888) ; *The Gondoliers* (1889) ; *Utopia, Limited* (1893) ; *The Grand Duke* (1896) ; *The Rose of Persia* (1899 ; libretto by B. Hood).

T F. DUNHILL : *Sullivan's Comic Operas* (1928).
C. L. PURDY : *Gilbert and Sullivan* (1946).
H. SULLIVAN & N. FLOWER : *Sir Arthur Sullivan* (1927).

Sul ponticello [sool pon-tee-chell'-lo], *I.* On the bridge. *v.* PONTICELLO.

Sul tasto [sool tust'-o], *I.* (*Fr.* sur la touche, *G.* am Griffbrett). On the fingerboard (of a string instrument), *i.e.* play near, or actually above, the fingerboard, thus producing a rather colourless tone.

Sumer is icumen in. A *rota* (or round)

found in a manuscript written at Reading Abbey *c.* 1240. In the manuscript it also has Latin words, beginning "Perspice christicola," and directions for performance. The melody, which begins:

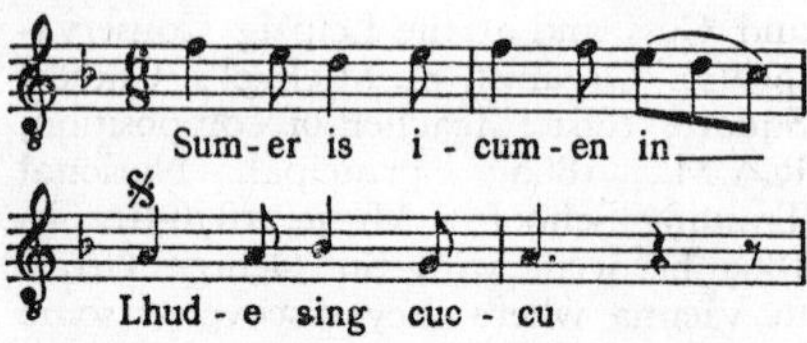

is sung by four voices. One begins alone, and each of the others begins when the previous voice has reached the sign ·$·. At the same time two lower voices repeat continuously the following:

which is called *pes* (*q.v.*). The result, after all the parts have entered, is:

It is the earliest extant piece in six parts.

Summation Tone. A very faint note resulting from the sum of the frequencies of two notes sounded simultaneously. *v.* ACOUSTICS, COMBINATION TONE.

Sun Quartets (*G.* Sonnenquartetten). The name given to Haydn's six string quartets, Op. 20, composed in 1772. It derives from the title-page of an old edition.

Suor Angelica [soo-ohrr' ahn-jeh'-lee-cah] (Sister Angelica). Opera in one act by Puccini. Libretto by Giovacchino Forzano. The second of three one-act operas forming *Il trittico* (The Triptych), the others being *Il tabarro* and *Gianni Schicchi.* First performed, New York, Dec. 14, 1918. Sister Angelica has entered a convent after giving birth to an illegitimate child. She learns from her aunt, who comes to visit her, that the child is dead. In despair she commits suicide. As she prays for forgiveness a vision appears of the Virgin surrounded by angels, with the child before her.

Superius [soo-perr'-i-o͝os], *L.* The highest part (also *cantus*) in a 16th-cent. composition for voices or instruments.

Supertonic. The second degree of the diatonic scale, *e.g.* D in the scale of C.

Suppé [so͝op'-ay], FRANZ VON (Francesco Ezechiele Ermenegildo Cavaliere Suppe-Demelli): *b.* Spalato (Dalmatia), Apr. 18, 1819; *d.* Vienna, May 21, 1895. Composer and conductor. Studied at the University of Padua and at the Vienna Conservatorium under Sechter and Seyfried. Conducted at theatres in Vienna, Pressburg and Baden, at the Theater-an-der-Wien, and from 1865 at the Leopoldstadt Theater in Vienna. He composed 31 operettas, farces, ballets, incidental music for plays, a Mass, a Requiem, a symphony, quartets and songs.

Sur la touche [sēer la toosh], *Fr.* (*G.* am Griffbrett, *I.* sul tasto). On the fingerboard (of a string instrument), *i.e.* play near, or actually above, the fingerboard, thus producing a rather colourless tone.

Suriano [soor-yahn'-o], FRANCESCO. *v.* SORIANO.

Surprise Symphony (*G.* Symphonie mit dem Paukenschlag). Symphony No. 94 in G major by Haydn (1791), so called from the abrupt fortissimo for full orchestra which interrupts the quiet opening of the slow movement. *Paukenschlag* = stroke on the timpani.

Susanna. Oratorio by Handel. Text anonymous. First performed, London, Feb. 10, 1749.

Susannens Geheimnis [zoo-zun'-ĕnce ger-hime'-niss]. *v.* SEGRETO DI SUSANNA.

Susato [sēe-zah'-to], TYLMAN (Tielmann, Thielemann): *b.* at or nr. Cologne, end of 15th cent.; *d.* Antwerp, before 1564. Music printer and composer. He settled in Antwerp as music copyist and transcriber, began printing in 1543 and was a city musician until 1549. He published many collections (containing some compositions of his own) of *chansons*, madrigals, motets, Masses and instrumental pieces. A collection of Dutch part-songs which he published in 1551 has been reprinted as vol. xxix (1908) of the publications of the Society for Netherlands Music History. A rondo and saltarello for 4 instruments is printed in Schering's *History of Music in Examples*, No. 119.

Suspension. The sustaining of one of the notes of a consonant interval while the other note moves so that it becomes dissonant, this dissonance then being resolved, usually by the movement of the dissonant note one step downwards :

The three steps in the process are : (1) preparation by a consonance on a relatively weak beat ; (2) suspension on a dissonance on a relatively strong beat ; (3) resolution on a consonance on a relatively weak beat. A suspension is a delayed movement in a part, and is therefore as much a rhythmic as a harmonic effect. Hence, it is essential that the point of dissonance should coincide with a metrical accent. Its principle is extended to suspension of two notes :

or of a chord :

A suspended leading note resolves upwards, as the B does in the second example. A suspension may be "prepared" on a common discord, *e.g.* a dominant seventh, as in the third example.

Süssmayr [zēēce′-mire], FRANZ XAVER : *b.* Steyer (Upper Austria) 1766 ; *d.* Vienna, Sept. 16, 1803. Composer. Studied in Vienna under Salieri and Mozart. *Kapellmeister*, National Theatre, 1792; second *Kapellmeister*, Court Theatre, 1794. He wrote the recitatives for Mozart's *La clemenza di Tito* (1791) and completed his unfinished *Requiem.* He also composed operas, 2 ballets, Masses and other church music, cantatas, a clarinet concerto, serenades and other instrumental pieces.

Sustaining Pedal. *v.* PIANO.

Sutermeister [zoot′-er-mice-ter], HEINRICH : *b.* Feuerthalen (Switzerland), Aug. 12, 1910. Composer. Studied at the Munich Academy of Music. Apart from a short period as an opera *répétiteur* at Berne, he has devoted himself wholly to composition. His earlier works show the influence of Orff, with whom he studied in Munich, in their emphasis on simplicity and clear outlines. His compositions include 6 operas, of which the earliest, *Romeo und Julia* (Dresden, 1940), has been performed in England, choral works, a piano concerto, and divertimento for string orchestra.

Švanda Dudák [shvund′-a dŏŏd′-ahk] (Schwanda the Bagpiper). Comic opera in two acts by Weinberger. Libretto by Miloš Karěs. First performed, Prague, Apr. 27, 1927. The brigand Babinsky, in love with Schwanda's wife Dorota, persuades him to visit the court of Queen Ice-Heart. Here he is so successful that the Queen wishes to marry him, but the arrival of Dorota makes it clear that he is married already, and the Queen orders his execution. The execution is prevented by a trick of Babinsky's, and Schwanda, having been given back his pipes, sets everyone dancing. Unfortunately, having uttered a curse, he is taken off to Hell. Dorota will have nothing to do with Babinsky, who is compelled to bring Schwanda back to earth by playing cards for him with the Devil.

Svendsen [svence′-ĕn], JOHAN SEVERIN : *b.* Oslo, Sept. 30, 1840 ; *d.* Copenhagen, June 14, 1911. Composer, violinist and conductor. Studied at the Leipzig Conservatorium under Hauptmann, David Richter and Reinecke. Played in Musard's orchestra in Paris, 1868-9 ; conducted the Euterpe Concerts in Leipzig, 1870, the Music Association Concerts in Oslo with Grieg, 1872-83, and at the court in Copenhagen, 1883-1908. He also travelled extensively, visiting London, Rome, Munich and other cities. He composed 2 symphonies and other orchestral works, concertos for violin and for cello, chamber music, a Wedding Cantata and songs. He made orchestral arrangements of various compositions and of Scandinavian folksongs.

Swan of Tuonela, The. *v.* LEGENDS.

Swansong. *v.* SCHWANENGESANG.

Sweelinck [svay′-link], JAN PIETERSZOON : *b.* Deventer or Amsterdam, 1562 ; *d.* Amsterdam, Oct. 16, 1621. Organist, harpsichordist, composer and teacher. Studied under Zarlino in Venice and succeeded his father as organist of the Old Church, Amsterdam, 1580. Published 4 books of metrical psalms for 4 to 8 voices (1604-23), *Cantiones sacrae* for five parts and continuo (1619) and *Rimes françoises et italiennes* (1612). His complete works have been edited by Max Seiffert (10 vols., 1895-1903 ; second ed. of vol. i, 1943), and include a theoretical treatise, *Rules for Composition.* He was acquainted with the music of the English virginalists (four of his compositions are in the Fitzwilliam Virginal Book), and developed their style in his variations on psalm tunes and on secular songs, and in his fantasias, which he constructed on a single subject, anticipating the form of the fugue. His toccatas and " echo " fantasias are in the Venetian tradition. He handed on these styles to his German pupils, of whom Scheidt and Scheidemann were the most eminent.

Swell Organ (*Fr.* recit, *G.* Oberwerk). The idea of producing an effect of *crescendo* and *diminuendo* by enclosing the source of sound in a box of which one side could be opened and closed by a Venetian shutter arrangement controlled by a pedal was first applied to the harpsichord by Schudi, who patented it in 1769. In 1712 Jordan had made an organ with a swell which acted by the raising of one shutter. When Shudi's patent expired his device was generally adopted for one of the manuals of the organ. The manual so enclosed is called the Swell Organ, and is placed immediately above the GREAT ORGAN. In most modern organs the CHOIR ORGAN and the SOLO ORGAN are similarly enclosed. *v.* ORGAN.

Swieten [fun sveet′-ĕn], GOTTFRIED, BARON VAN : *b.* Leyden, 1734 ; *d.* Vienna, Mar. 29, 1803. Amateur musician and diplomat. Ambassador at the Court of Frederick II of Prussia (1771), returned to Vienna (1776), where he was director of the Royal Library (from which he ordered works used only for the " fantasy and pedantry " of scholars to be removed), and founded the Musikalische Gesellschaft. He was a patron of Mozart, who wrote accompaniments to Handel oratorios for his concerts, Haydn, for whom he translated the *Creation* and the *Seasons* into German, C. P. E. Bach, from whom he commissioned 6 string quartets, and Beethoven, who dedicated to him his first symphony.

Sylvanus. *v.* SILVA.

Sympathetic Vibrations. Vibrations created in a body by the action of the vibrations of another body. They occur, for example, when a note sung to the free strings of the piano, *i.e.* with the sustaining pedal down, causes the strings of corresponding pitch to vibrate, and when a vibrating tuning fork acts on another of the same pitch. Sympathetic vibrations are one means by which RESONANCE is produced. Free strings, called " sympathetic " strings and disposed under the playing strings, were used on some obsolete instruments such as the viola d'amore and the baryton, and sounded " sympathetically " with the corresponding notes of the bowed strings. In these cases the overtones of sounding strings also cause sympathetic vibrations in the corresponding free strings, which happens likewise in the case of open strings on a string instrument and free strings on a piano.

Symphonia [sim-fo′-ni-a], *L.* (from *Gr.* συμφωνία, simultaneous sound).

(1) In ancient Greek theory (*a*) unison, (*b*) a consonant interval.

(2) According to Isidorus (*c.* 600 A.D.) the popular name for a kind of drum, the two ends of which produced notes of different pitches.

(3) A 14th-cent. name for the HURDY-GURDY, earlier known as *organistrum.*

(4) In the 16th and early 17th cent. apparently an alternative name for the virginals (Praetorius, *Syntagma musicum,* 1619).

(5) Symphony.

Symphonia Domestica [sim-fo′-ni-a dom-ess′-ti-ca], *L.* (Domestic Symphony). An orchestral work by Richard Strauss, Op. 53, in four linked movements, representing the domestic life of father, mother and child. The dedication reads: "Meiner lieben Frau und unserm Jungen gewidmet." First performed, New York, Mar. 21, 1904.

Symphonic Poem (*Fr.* poème symphonique, *G.* symphonische Dichtung, Tondichtung). The term was applied by Liszt to an orchestral piece in which the composer "reproduces his impressions and the adventures of his soul in order to communicate them." Specific clues to the source of the impressions and the nature of the adventures are given to the listener by a title and sub-titles, and if they are somewhat complex a "programme" is also provided. The symphonic poem is PROGRAMME MUSIC, since the form becomes a function of the programme. Its immediate ancestors were the concert overture, such as Mendelssohn's *Midsummer Night's Dream,* and the symphony with a programme, such as Berlioz's *Symphonie fantastique.* Liszt wrote his symphonic poems in one movement, and abandoning sonata form, used a more flexible treatment of Berlioz's *idée fixe.* His thematic material is restricted to a small number of motives, which he subjects to such rhythmic transformations as may enable them to depict the impressions and adventures of the programme. A method of this kind is likely to be used for a narrative or dramatic kind of programme and one closer to an orthodox form for the more general kind of programme.

After Liszt, symphonic poems (or "tone pictures" or "fantasies") were written by composers of various countries, *e.g.* Borodin, Smetana, Franck, Dukas, Sibelius, Delius and Elgar; the most famous are the nine (including the *Symphonia domestica*) by Richard Strauss, who used the term tone-poem (*Tondichtung*), and brought the genre to its highest point of circumstantial and realistic depiction. The "Fantasy Overtures" of Tchaikovsky are dramatic concert overtures rather than symphonic poems. The form was an ideal one for the impressionistic style; Debussy's five chief orchestral works are symphonic poems in one or more movements. Since 1910 it has been much less cultivated.

Symphonie, *Fr.* [sa͡n-fon-ee], *G.* [zēēm-fo-nee′] (also *Sinfonie*). Symphony.

Symphonie Cévenole [sa͡n-fon-ee save-noll], *Fr. v.* SYMPHONIE SUR UN CHANT MONTAGNARD FRANÇAIS.

Symphonie concertante [sa͡n-fon-ee co͡n-sair-tu͡nt], *Fr.* An orchestral work, normally in several movements, in which there are parts for solo instruments (generally two or more), *e.g.* Mozart's *Symphonie concertante* for violin, viola and orchestra (K.364), which is virtually a double concerto.

Symphonie Espagnole [sa͡n-fon-ee ess-pun-yoll], *Fr.* (Spanish Symphony). A composition for violin and orchestra by Edouard Lalo (first performed, 1875).

Symphonie Fantastique [sa͡n-fon-ee fu͡n-tuss-teek], *Fr.* (Fantastic Symphony). An orchestral work in five movements by Berlioz, Op. 14 (1830), also entitled *Épisode de la vie d'un artiste* (Episode in an artist's life). The titles of the movements are:

I. *Rêveries—Passions* (Daydreams—Passions).
II. *Un bal* (A ball).
III. *Scène aux champs* (Scene in the country).
IV. *Marche au supplice* (March to execution).
V. *Songe d'une nuit de Sabbat* (Dream of a witches' Sabbath).

Berlioz issued a detailed programme for the work, according to which a young and exceptionally sensitive musician (*i.e.* Berlioz himself), unable to drive from his mind the image of his beloved (*i.e.* Harriet Smithson), attempts to poison himself with opium. In his delirium he imagines that he has killed his loved one and is led to execution. Finally he dreams that he is present at the witches' sabbath, which includes a parody of the *Dies irae*. His beloved is represented by an *idée fixe*, beginning :

which recurs throughout the work in various forms. In spite of its programme the *Symphonie fantastique* is heavily indebted to earlier works by Berlioz, *e.g.* the *idée fixe* is borrowed from the cantata *Herminie*, which he submitted unsuccessfully for the *Prix de Rome* in 1828, and the *Marche au supplice* comes from the unfinished opera *Les Francs-Juges*. Only the first movement (apart from the *idée fixe*) is certainly new.

T. S. WOTTON: *Berlioz : Four Works* (1929)

Symphonie Funèbre et Triomphale [sa͞n-fon-ee fe͞e-nebr ay tree-o͞n-full], *Fr.* (Funeral and Triumphal Symphony). A symphony by Berlioz, Op. 15 (1840), for military band, string orchestra and chorus, which was commissioned by the French Government and performed at the 10th anniversary of the 1830 Revolution.

Symphonie mit dem Paukenschlag [ze͞em-fo-nee′ mit dem powk′-ĕn-shlahk], *G. v.* SURPRISE SYMPHONY.

Symphonie mit dem Paukenwirbel [ze͞em-fo-nee′ mit dem powk′-ĕn-veerr′-bĕl], *G. v.* DRUM ROLL SYMPHONY.

Symphonie Pathétique [sa͞n-fon-ee pa-tay-teek], *Fr. v.* PATHETIC SYMPHONY.

Symphonie sur un Chant Montagnard Français [sa͞n-fon-ee se͞er un shu͞n mo͞n-ta-nyarr fru͞n-say], *Fr.* (Symphony on a French mountain song). A symphony for orchestra and piano by d'Indy, Op. 25 (1886), also known as *Symphonie cévenole* because it uses a theme from the region of the Cevennes mountains.

Symphonie zu Dante's 'Divina Commedia,' Eine [ine′-*er* ze͞em-fo-nee′ tsoo dahn′-tace dee-vee′-nah com-meh′-dyah], *G. v.* DANTE SYMPHONY.

Symphonische Dichtung [ze͞em-fone′-ish-*er* di*sh*′-to͞ong], *G.* Symphonic poem.

Symphony (*Fr.* symphonie, *G.* Sinfonie, Symphonie, *I.* sinfonia). In the period of the modern use of the term SONATA, *i.e.* since *c.* 1750, a symphony is a sonata for orchestra. Previously the word was used in a variety of ways, usually for instrumental music, but occasionally, as in the *Sacrae symphoniae* of G. Gabrieli and Schütz, for music for instruments and voices. It was applied to instrumental movements in an opera, as in Monteverdi's *Orfeo*, to the prelude to an instrumental suite, as in Rosenmüller's *Sonate da camera*, to the prelude of a cantata, as in Bach's Cantata No. 156 (*Ich steh' mit einem Fuss im Grabe*), to the Italian opera overture (*sinfonia avanti l'opera*), to the introduction to a song, and, exceptionally, by Bach to his three-part Inventions.

The modern symphony emerged as an independent piece, modelled on the Italian overture, between 1730 and 1750. A minuet was added to the three movements of the Italian overture in some of the symphonies of the Viennese composers Georg Monn and Georg Wagenseil, and in those of the composers attached to the Mannheim orchestra, *e.g.* F. X. Richter and Johann Stamitz. All Stamitz's symphonies have four movements. Some of Haydn's first 30 or so symphonies (the first was written in 1759) have three movements, either having no minuet or ending with a minuet, and some have resemblances to the *concerto grosso* in their use of solo instruments. In the four-movement form which became normal after *c.* 1765 the symphony drew the elements of its style from the overture, *concerto grosso* and suite, and from the aria and finale of opera. In the symphonies written after 1780, which include the 12 Salomon symphonies (Nos. 93-104) composed for London, Haydn absorbed some of the grace and delicacy of Mozart, but kept his characteristic waywardness, humour and spontaneity in such features as the varying of recapitulations and the unpredictable course of his Rondo finales. Mozart's first three symphonies were played when he was eight years old at the J. C. Bach-Abel concerts in London in 1765, the year in which J. C. Bach published his first set of 6 symphonies. Besides J. C. Bach's symphonies, those of the Mannheim and Viennese composers, including Haydn, influenced his development, which was crowned by the consummate balance of expression and design of the last three symphonies of 1788.

In writing to his publishers in 1803 about the *Prometheus* Variations for piano, Op. 35, Beethoven observed that he had "done nothing in the same manner before." The first symphony in the "new manner" was the *Eroica*, the ancestor of all Romantic symphonies, and, with the ninth symphony, the largest conception of the form before Mahler. While in the *Eroica* form is expanded and expression deepened, the only radical departure from tradition is the variation form of the last movement, which may be compared in that respect with the last movement of Brahms's fourth symphony. Wagner saw in Beethoven's ninth symphony the inevitable destiny of dramatic instrumental music to throw off its limitations and use the human voice ; nevertheless, its only direct successors before Mahler were Mendelssohn's symphony-cantata *Lobgesang* (*Hymn of Praise*), not one of his best works, in which the cantata overbalances the symphony and fails to achieve unity with it, and Liszt's *Dante* symphony. The choral endings in his *Faust* symphony and in Berlioz's *Symphonie funèbre et triomphale* are optional. The tendency towards a programme in Beethoven's sixth symphony was pursued by Berlioz in the *Symphonie fantastique* and in the "Dramatic Symphony" *Roméo et Juliette* for orchestra and voices, and was diverted into a new form by Liszt in the SYMPHONIC POEM.

Schubert's 8 symphonies encompassed three styles, the classical, the lyrical (in the *Unfinished*) and the "grand" (in No. 7 in C). The main tradition goes in a thinning line through Mendelssohn and Schumann to its marked revival in the 4 symphonies of Brahms (1875-85), the 9 of Bruckner (1866-94), the 2 of Borodin (1862-76), the 6 of Tchaikovsky (1868-93), the 9 of Dvořák (1880-93), the 9 of Mahler (1888-1909), and the 7 of Sibelius (1898-1924). That its methods were not unaffected by the use of thematic transformation, first applied to a symphony in a comprehensive way by Schumann in his D minor symphony and developed in the symphonic poem, is clear in the first movement of Brahms's first symphony, in Tchaikovsky's fourth and in those of Franck and Saint-Saëns. Mahler treated the traditional number and disposition of movements quite flexibly, Sibelius less so ; Mahler tended towards expansion, Sibelius to contraction and concentration. Mahler used voices in four of his symphonies, and his all-embracing view of its possibilities culminated in the eighth symphony ("Symphony of a Thousand") for large orchestra, eight soloists, two mixed choirs and children's choir. The first part is a setting of the hymn "Veni creator spiritus," the second, comprising Adagio, Scherzo and Finale, of the closing scene of the second part of Goethe's *Faust*. The tendency to contraction is noticeable in the fourth and sixth symphonies of Sibelius, and his seventh is in one movement.

In general, contemporary composers tend to cast their symphonies in three or four movements, but the advantage of a title to the listener and to the memory of the public is sometimes not overlooked. Notable works composed since 1914 are the symphonies of Vaughan Williams (9), Prokofiev (7), Shostakovich (11), Hindemith (2), Stravinsky (2—the *Symphony of Psalms* is a cantata), Honegger (5), Wellesz (5), Walton (1), Bartók (1—called *Concerto*), Roy Harris (5) and Walter Piston (3).

Symphony of a Thousand. The name

sometimes given to Mahler's 8th symphony in E♭ major (completed in 1906) because of the large number of performers it requires. The work is in two parts entitled :

(1) *Veni creator spiritus* (based on the 9th-cent. hymn) for two choruses.
(2) *Concluding scene from Faust*—symphonic poem with chorus.

Symphony on a French Mountain Song. *v.* SYMPHONIE SUR UN CHANT MONTAGNARD FRANÇAIS.

Sympson, CHRISTOPHER. *v.* SIMPSON (1).

Syncopation (*Gr.*συγκοπή, a cutting short). A rhythm having stresses which do not agree with the normal metrical stresses is said to be syncopated. It occurs in various ways, *e.g.* (1) by rhythmic anticipation :

BEETHOVEN, *Piano Sonata Op.31, No.1*

(2) by rhythmic suspension, as in the rhythm

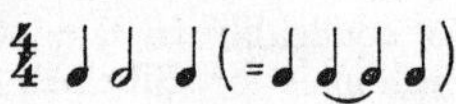

and in

SCHUMANN, *Fast zu ernst, Op.15 (Kinderscenen) No.10*

(3) by an indicated stress on an unaccented beat or on a subdivision of the beat :

MOZART, *Piano Sonata K.309*

(4) by having a rest on the beat and sound on a subdivision of the beat :

SCHUMANN, *Phantasie Op.17*

If, as in these examples, a regularly syncopated rhythm is continued for more than a bar, it has the effect of a displaced metre superimposed on the basic metre.

Syncopation is a characteristic idiom of Negro spirituals, ragtime and jazz. Rhythms made up of different metres in succession, which are not infrequent in modern music, *e.g.*

CONSTANT LAMBERT, *Piano Concerto*

have an effect similar to, but not identical with, that of syncopation, since there is not a continuous basic metre. *v.* ACCENT, BAR, METRE, RHYTHM.

System [zeece-tame'], *G.* Staff (abbreviation of *Liniensystem*).

Szell [sell], GEORG: *b.* Budapest, June 7, 1897. Pianist, composer and conductor. Studied in Vienna and Leipzig. After considerable success as a pianist and composer while still a boy he decided to devote himself to conducting. He has held the following posts : Strasbourg Opera, 1917 ; German Theatre, Prague, 1919-21, 1929-37 ; Darmstadt, 1921 ; Düsseldorf, 1922 ; Berlin Staatsoper, 1924-9 ; Scottish Orchestra, Glasgow, 1937 ; Residence Orchestra, The Hague, (with Frits Schuurman), 1938 ; Cleveland (Ohio), 1946.

Szigeti [sig′-et-i], JOSEPH : *b.* Budapest, Sept. 5, 1892. Violinist, a pupil of Hubay. Made his first appearance as a soloist in Berlin, 1905. Lived in England, 1906-13. Taught at the Geneva Conservatoire, 1917-24. Gave the first performance of Busoni's violin concerto, 1912. He has travelled extensively as a soloist in Europe, America and Asia. He has published his reminiscences under the title *With Strings Attached* (1949).

Szymanowski [shee-mun-ov′-ski], KAROL : *b.* Timoshovka (Ukraine), Oct. 6, 1882; *d.* Lausanne, Mar. 28, 1937. Composer. Member of a family of musicians. Studied under Noskowski at the Warsaw Conservatoire, settled in Berlin in 1905, and from 1908 lived in Russia. He lost his estates in the revolution of 1917, but escaped to Warsaw where he was appointed director of the State Conservatoire in 1926. He composed 2 operas, ballets, 3 symphonies (one with men's chorus and tenor solo), works for solo voices, chorus and orchestra, 2 violin concertos, *Symphonie concertante* for piano and orchestra, works for violin and piano and other chamber music, many piano pieces and songs.

T

T. As an abbreviation T. = tenor, tonic. *t.c.* = TUTTE LE CORDE or TRE CORDE. In 17th-cent. music *t.* = trill (or shake): the modern sign for a TRILL is *tr*. In continuo parts *t.s.* = *tasto solo* (lit. " only the key "), *i.e.* the player is to play only the written bass notes without filling up chords above them. In TONIC SOL-FA **t** = *te*, the 7th note (or leading note) of the major scale.

Tabarro, Il [eel tah-bahr′-ro] (The Cloak). Opera in one act by Puccini. Libretto by Giuseppe Adami (after Didier Gold's *Houppelande*). The first of three one-act operas forming *Il trittico* (The Triptych), the others being *Suor Angelica* and *Gianni Schicchi*. First performed, New York, Dec. 14, 1918. Michele, a barge-owner, jealous of his wife's association with the young stevedore Luigi, strangles him and hides the body in his cloak. When his wife comes to him he throws open the cloak and reveals the corpse.

Tablature (*G.* Tablatur, *I.* intavolatura). A type of notation used in the 16th and 17th cent. for writing music for lute, *vihuela* and organ, in which the pitch of the notes is indicated by letters or numbers.

(1) In the two chief varieties of lute and *vihuela* tablature, the Italian-Spanish and the French, lines represented the strings of the instrument, and letters or numbers the frets at which the strings were to be stopped. The rhythm was indicated above the tablature by signs corresponding to the usual note forms, and each sign held good until another appeared. In Italian tablature and in Spanish (except in Luis Milan's *El Maestro*, 1535), *e.g.*:

ALONSO MUDARRA, *Fantasia* (1546)

the highest line represented the lowest string in the tuning:

the figure 0 indicated an open string and the figures 1 to 9 the frets, which marked off semitones. In staff notation the passage would read:

In French lute tablature (and in Milan's *El Maestro*) the highest line or space represented the highest string, the letter a indicated an open string and the letters b, c, d, etc. the frets. A few English tablatures followed the Italian method, but most, including those of the lutenist song composers, were written in the French way, *e.g.*:

transcribed:

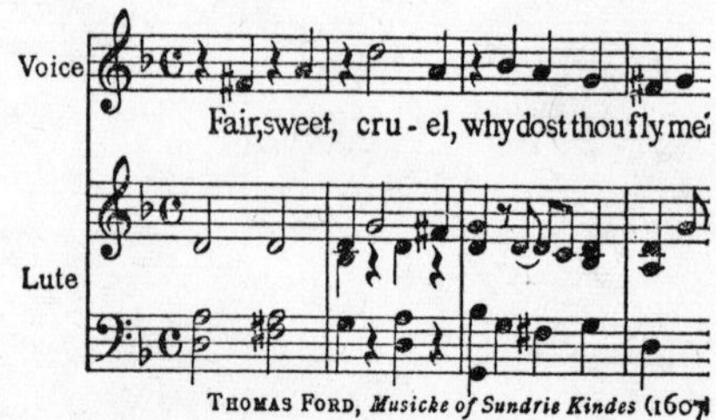

THOMAS FORD, *Musicke of Sundrie Kindes* (1607)

In German lute notation a separate

number or letter was used to represent the position of each fret with respect to each string. These symbols were written in rows corresponding to the positions of the strings, without, however, using horizontal lines to represent the strings.

The modern notation for the guitar and similar instruments is a tablature in the form of a diagram of the strings and frets on which dots indicate the positions of the fingers.

(2) The principle of tablature for organ (or other keyed instruments) is the representation of the notes of each part of a composition by letters or numbers. In German organ tablature from *c.* 1450 to *c.* 1550 the highest part was written in staff notation, the lower parts in letters, which had their normal meaning. After *c.* 1550 letters were used for all the parts, the rhythm being indicated above each part. Bach was familiar with this notation, and used it (*e.g.*) to fit the last four bars of the chorale prelude *Der Tag, der ist so freudenreich* in the *Orgelbüchlein* in a space that was too small to write them in staff notation. Scheidt's *Tabulatura nova* of 1624 was "new" to German organists in that it was printed with a separate five-line staff for each part, using the normal note-forms. It was not, therefore, properly called a tablature but was the equivalent of the Italian *partitura* ("score"). Frescobaldi published some of his organ works in this way, *e.g.* his first keyboard publication the *Fantasie a quattro* (1608), and his *Fiori musicali . . . in partitura a quattro* (1635). Scheidt pointed out that any organist who wished could easily copy from this notation into the German tablature. Italian organ notation (*e.g.* in Frescobaldi's *Toccate . . . d'intavolatura*, 1614) sometimes used two staves, the upper with six lines and the lower with eight, and normal note-forms. This was a tablature only in the sense that it disposed the notes for each hand on a separate staff, the method best suited to the style of the music. For his organ music published in 1664 S. A. Scherer used this Italian method, engraved by himself, for the first part (entitled *Tabulatura*) and Scheidt's "new tablature" for the second part (entitled *Partitura*).

In Spanish organ tablature a horizontal line was used to represent each part, and the numbers 1 to 7 on each line to represent the notes of the scale from F up to E, *e.g.*:

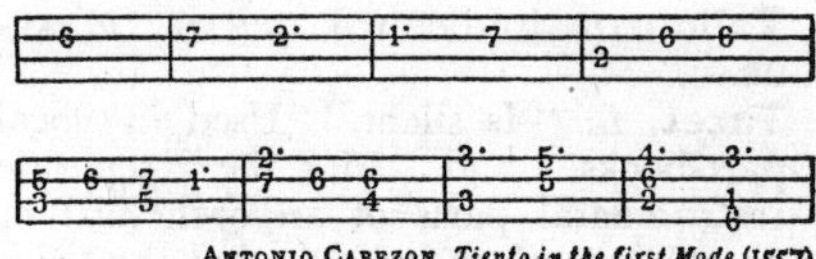

ANTONIO CABEZON, *Tiento in the first Mode* (1557)

in staff notation:

(3) Tablature which relates fingering to the notes of the scale has been used to a limited extent for woodwind instruments, generally for teaching purposes.

W. APEL: *The Notation of Polyphonic Music* (4th ed., 1949).

E. HALFPENNY: "The French Hautboy," in *Galpin Society Journal*, vi, p. 23.

Table [tubl], *Fr.* (1) The belly, or upper part of the soundbox of a string instrument. (2) The sounding-board of a harp, rising diagonally from the foot of the vertical pillar to the upper end of the neck. *Près de la table*, play near the sounding-board, thus producing a metallic sound, similar to that of the banjo. (3) *Musique de table*, music for a banquet (*G.* Tafelmusik).

Table Entertainment. A performance given by a single person seated at a table. It originated in England in the latter part of the 18th cent. The performance consisted of songs, stories, recitations, sketches, impersonations, etc.

A prominent figure in this type of entertainment was Dibdin, who also wrote his own songs.

Tabor. A small drum played with one stick and used in England with a small recorder with three finger holes (hence pipe and tabor) to accompany dancing. *v.* also TAMBOURIN.

Tabourot [ta-boo-ro], JEHAN. *v.* ARBEAU.

Tacet, *L.* " Is silent." Used in vocal part-books and in the separate instrumental parts of an orchestral or chamber work to indicate that the voice or instrument does not play in a particular movement or section of a movement.

Tactus [tuck'-tŏŏss], *L.* (from *tangere*, to touch, beat). A term used for "beat" by theorists of the 15th and 16th cent. It was a measure of the time-length of the note which was the unit of the composition, and was given by the leader to the singers as a regular downward stroke of the finger, hand or arm—a method which was used in England at least until the late 17th cent. The semibreve was the normal *tactus* in the 15th cent. ; in the course of the 16th cent. the minim became the normal, but the semibreve continued to be the theoretical basis of signs of proportion. With the introduction of bar-lines the semibreve became the unit of a bar and the measuring *tactus* was replaced by the metrical beat.

Tafelmusik [tahf'-ĕl-moo-zeek], *G.* *v.* TABLE (3).

Taille [ta-y*er*]. *Fr.* A term used in the 17th and 18th cent. (1) The tenor or middle part of a composition. (2) The tenor member of a family of instruments, *e.g. taille de violon* = viola. *Taille* by itself was often used to indicate (a) viola, (b) *oboe da caccia.*

Tailleferre [ta-y*er*-fair], GERMAINE : *b.* Pau St. Maur (nr. Paris), Apr. 19, 1892. Composer ; one of the group known as *Les Six*. Studied harmony and counterpoint at the Paris Conservatoire and settled in the United States in 1942. She has composed a piano concerto, a Ballade for piano and orchestra, a ballet, *Pastorale* for small orchestra, a quartet and other chamber music, and songs.

Takt [tuckt], *G.* (1) Bar, (2) beat, (3) time.

Taktstrich [tuckt'-shtri*sh*], *G.* Barline.

Talea. *v.* ISORHYTHM.

Tales of Hoffmann. *v.* CONTES D'HOFFMANN.

Tallis, THOMAS : *b. c.* 1505 ; *d.* Greenwich, Nov. 23, 1585. Composer and organist. Organist of Waltham Abbey before 1540, gentleman of the Chapel Royal from *c.* 1545 until his death, and organist of the Chapel with William Byrd. In 1575 he and Byrd were granted by Queen Elizabeth the sole right to print music and music paper in England. Their first publication was *Cantiones Sacrae* (1575) containing 17 motets by Tallis and 17 by Byrd. Tallis composed 2 Magnificats, 2 Masses, Lamentations for 5 voices, Latin motets (including *Spem in alium* for 8 choirs of 5 parts each), services, psalms, anthems and other church music, 2 *In Nomines* for strings and one for lute, secular vocal works and pieces for keyboard. Such works as the forty-part motet and the seven-part canon " Miserere nostri " (*Cantiones Sacrae*, No. 34) are both technically skilful and artistically satisfying. The deeper aspects of his style are more evident in the Mass *Salve intemerata* (based on the antiphon with that title), in the *Lamentations* and in the motets of the *Cantiones Sacrae*, works which place him among the greatest of the composers of the mid-16th cent. Two pieces on the plainsong " Felix namque " are in the *Fitzwilliam Virginal Book* and 18 keyboard pieces and arrangements in the *Mulliner Book* (modern ed. in *Musica Britannica*, i). Complete keyboard works ed. by D. Stevens (1953). His Latin church music has been published in *Tudor Church Music*, vi (1928). He composed 9 tunes for Archbishop Parker's Psalter of 1567-8 (*v.* PSALTER).

Talon [ta-lo͡n], *Fr.* The nut of a bow. *v.* AU TALON.

Tambour [tu͡n-boor], *Fr.* Drum. *Tambour militaire*, side drum ; *tambour de basque*, tambourine.

Tambourin [tu͡n-boo-ra͡n], *Fr.* (1) A long, narrow drum, played with one stick when used, especially in Provence (*tambourin de Provence*), with a small, one-handed recorder (*flûtet, galoubet*) to accompany dancing.

(2) The *tambourin du Béarn* (*I.* altobasso) was a zither with gut strings sounding only the tonic and dominant, and was used similarly with a small recorder to accompany dancing. The term *tambourin* was applied to a dance so accompanied which was introduced by Rameau into his opera-ballet *Les Fêtes d'Hébé* (1739) and into his *Pièces de clavecin* :

Tambourine (*Fr.* tambour de basque, *G.* Tamburin, baskische Trommel, Schellentrommel, *I.* tamburino). A small drum with a single parchment head surrounded by a wooden hoop into which pairs of metal plates, called "jingles," are inserted at intervals. In its medieval form it sometimes had a snare (*Fr.* timbre). The modern name was adopted in the late 18th cent. when it was introduced into military bands in imitation of the Turkish JANISSARY music. In the orchestra it is played by striking with the knuckles, by shaking, or by rubbing with the thumb.

Tamburo [tahm-boo′-ro], *I.* Drum. *Tamburo militare*, side-drum ; *tamburo rullante*, tenor drum.

Tamerlano [tah-mair-lah′-no] (Tamburlaine). Opera in three acts by Handel. Libretto by Agostino Piovene, adapted by Nicola Francesco Haym. First performed, London, Nov. 11, 1724.

Taming of the Shrew, The. *v.* WIDERSPÄNSTIGEN ZÄHMUNG.

Tampon [tũn-põn], *Fr.* A two-headed drumstick held in the middle and used with an alternating motion of the wrist to produce a roll on the bass drum.

Tam-Tam. *v.* GONG.

Tancredi [tahn-creh′-dee] (Tancred). Opera in two acts by Rossini. Libretto by Gaetano Rossi (*melodramma eroica*, based on Tasso's *Gerusalemme liberata* and Voltaire's tragedy *Tancrède*). First performed, Venice, Feb. 6, 1813.

Taneiev [ta-nay′-yeff], SERGEI IVANOVICH : *b.* Government of Vladimir, Nov. 25, 1856 ; *d.* Moscow, June 19, 1915. Composer and pianist. Studied at the Moscow Conservatoire under Tchaikovsky and Nicholas Rubinstein. Appeared as a pianist in Moscow (1875), toured Russia with Leopold Auer (1867) and visited Paris (1877-78). He was teacher, Moscow Conservatoire, 1880-1906 ; director, 1885-89. He wrote a treatise on counterpoint and composed 4 symphonies, an overture, 6 string quartets and other chamber music, an operatic trilogy, choral works and songs.

Tañer [tahn-yair′], *Sp.* *v.* TASTAR.

Tangent. *v.* CLAVICHORD.

Tanglewood. *v.* BERKSHIRE FESTIVAL.

Tango. A dance in a moderately slow 2/4 time with syncopated rhythms which originated in Argentina about the beginning of this century and appeared in Europe and America about 1910. There are a few examples in instrumental suites by contemporary composers.

Tannhäuser und der Sängerkrieg auf Wartburg (tun′-hoise-er ŏŏnt dair zeng′-er-creek owf varrt′-bŏŏrrk] (Tannhäuser and the Tournament of Song at Wartburg). Opera in three acts by Wagner. Libretto by the composer. First performed, Dresden, Oct. 19, 1845. Tannhäuser, a minstrel knight, weary of the monotony of a year spent with Venus, decides to return to his earthly friends. At the tournament of song held in the Wartburg he competes for the prize, the hand of the landgrave's niece Elisabeth, but shocks the whole assembly by singing the praises of Venus. In remorse he joins a band of pilgrims and journeys to Rome. Denied absolution by the Pope, he decides, in spite of the remonstrances of his fellow-minstrel Wolfram, to return to Venus. At the last moment, however, he learns that he has been saved by the prayers of Elisabeth, whose funeral procession now appears. As he too dies, the chorus sing of the miracle of God's forgiveness.

Tansman [tunce′-mun], ALEXANDER: *b.* Lódz, Poland, June 12, 1897. Composer and pianist. Studied composition in Warsaw, lived in Paris from 1920 and toured in Austria, Germany, Switzerland, England, Japan and the United States, where he settled in 1941. He returned to Paris in 1946. His compositions include operas, 2 ballets, 7 symphonies and other orchestral works, 2 concertos and a *concertino* for piano and orchestra, string quartets and other chamber music, songs, piano pieces and music for films.

Tans'ur (originally Tanzer), WILLIAM: *b.* Dunchurch (Warwickshire), Nov. 6, 1706; *d.* St. Neot's, Oct. 7, 1783. Composer, teacher and organist. He was organist at Barnes in Surrey, at Ewell (1739), at Stamford in Lincolnshire and St. Neot's. He published books of metrical psalms containing some composed by himself and some with words by himself, and *A New Musical Grammar* (1746-56), later published as *The Elements of Musick Display'd* (1772), which was widely used, and reprinted as late as 1829.

Tanto [tahnt′-o], *I.* "So much." It has been used as the equivalent of *troppo, e.g. allegro non tanto,* not too fast.

Tapiola. Symphonic poem by Sibelius, Op. 112 (1925). Tapio is the name of the God of the Forests in Finnish mythology. The score is prefaced by the following quatrain:

> Wide-spread they stand, the Northland's dusky forests,
> Ancient, mysterious, brooding savage dreams;
> Within them dwells the Forest's mighty God,
> And wood-sprites in the gloom weave magic secrets.

Tapissier [ta-peece-yay], JEAN. Early 15th-cent. composer mentioned in Martin le Franc's poem *Champion des Dames* (*c.* 1440) as one of the three composers famous in Paris immediately before the rise of Dufay and Binchois:

> "Tapissier Carmen Cesaris
> N'a pas longtemps si bien chanterrent
> Qu'ilz esbahirent tout Paris
> Et tous ceulx qui les frequenterrent . . ."

A *Credo* and a *Sanctus* in three parts and a four-part motet, "Eya dulcis/Vale placens" (printed in J. Stainer, *Dufay and his Contemporaries,* p. 187) by him have survived: all three are printed in *Early Fifteenth-Century Music,* ed. G. Reaney, i (*Corpus Mensurabilis Musicae,* xi, 1).

Tarantella [tah-rahn-tell′-lah], *I.* (*Fr.* tarantelle). In its 19th-cent. form a dance in very quick 6/8 time of which there are examples by, among others, Weber, Chopin and Liszt:

CHOPIN, *Tarentelle, Op.* 43

An instance by a contemporary composer is the third movement of Rawsthorne's first piano concerto (1945).

There are many accounts from the 15th to the 18th cent. of the legendary virtue of the *tarantella,* which derived its name from Taranto in Italy, as the only cure for the effects of the bite of the *tarantula* spider.

C. ENGEL: *Musical Myths and Facts,* vol. ii (1876).

Tardo [tarr′-do], *I.* Slow. *Tardando,* becoming slower.

Tárogató [tah′-ro-got-oh]. A woodwind instrument of Oriental origin, intermittently popular in Hungary from the Middle Ages onwards. The bore is conical. In its original form it had a double-reed mouthpiece and hence was a member of the shawm family. In the late 19th cent. it was fitted with a clarinet mouthpiece and is therefore now akin to the saxophone. It has been used at Bayreuth and elsewhere to play the shepherd's tune which announces the arrival of the ship in Act III of *Tristan und Isolde* (scored by Wagner for cor anglais, but with a note to say that he would prefer some kind of wooden trumpet).

Tartini [tarr-tee′-nee], GIUSEPPE : *b.* Pirano (Istria), Apr. 8, 1692 ; *d.* Padua, Feb. 26, 1770. Violinist, composer, teacher and theorist. Studied at Capo d'Istria and at the University of Padua (from 1709), which he was forced to leave after marrying a pupil in 1713. He played as an orchestral violinist in the provinces (1713-16), stayed at the Franciscan Monastery at Assisi, and went to Ancona for further study. He was first violinist at the Basilica di Sant' Antonia in Padua (from 1721) and conductor of Count Kinsky's orchestra in Prague (1723-26). He visited Vienna, and in 1728 established a school of violin-playing in Padua where his pupils included Graun, Nardini and Pugnani. He discovered COMBINATION TONES and advised his pupils to use the "third sound," as it was then called, to ensure true intonation in double-stopping. He wrote many treatises on violin-playing and on problems in acoustics, and composed over 100 violin concertos, symphonies, numerous solo sonatas and trio sonatas, and some church music. *v.* TRILLO DEL DIAVOLO.

A. CAPRI : *Giuseppe Tartini* (1945).

Taschengeige [tush′-ĕn-gy-ger], *G.* Lit. "pocket fiddle." A miniature violin formerly used by dancing-masters. *v.* KIT.

Tastar [tust-ahrr′], *I.* (*Sp.* tañer). "Touching." A 16th-cent. term for a prelude in extemporary style for lute, *e.g.* the *Tastar de corde* followed by a *ricercar* by Joanambrosio Dalza, printed in the *Historical Anthology*, No. 99a.

Tastatura [tust-ah-too′-rah], *I.* Keyboard.

Taste [tust′-er], *G.* Key of a keyboard instrument.

Tastiera [tust-yeh′-rah], *I.* (*Fr.* touche, *G.* Griffbrett). Fingerboard of a string instrument. *Sulla tastiera*, on the fingerboard, *i.e.* play near, or actually above, the fingerboard, thus producing a rather colourless tone.

Tasto [tust′-o], *I.* (1) Key of a keyboard instrument. *Tasto solo* (in figured bass), play only the bass notes without adding harmonies above them.

(2) Fret (on a viol, lute, etc.).

(3) Fingerboard of a string instrument (*Fr.* touche, *G.* Griffbrett). *Sul tasto*, on the fingerboard, *i.e.* play near, or actually above, the fingerboard, thus producing a rather colourless tone.

Tausig [towz′-ish], CARL : *b.* Warsaw, Nov. 4, 1841 ; *d.* Leipzig, July 17, 1871. Pianist and composer. One of the greatest piano virtuosos of his day, he studied under his father (Aloys Tausig) and Thalberg, and from 1855-59 under Liszt at Weimar. He made his début in Berlin at a concert conducted by von Bülow (1858), toured Germany (1859-60) and later lived in Dresden. He gave orchestral concerts of modern music in Vienna (1862) and settled in Berlin (1865), where he founded a school of advanced piano-playing. He composed symphonic poems, a piano concerto and studies and transcriptions for piano.

Taverner, JOHN : *b. c.* 1495 ; *d.* Boston (Lincolnshire), Oct. 25, 1545. Composer. Master of the choristers at Cardinal College (later Christ Church), Oxford, 1526-30. He was accused of heresy and imprisoned for a time in 1528, worked as an agent of Thomas Cromwell in the suppression of monasteries and settled in Boston, where he was elected a member (1537) and a steward (1541) of the Guild of Corpus Christi. He composed 8 Masses, 3 Magnificats, motets, and other church music, which has been published in *Tudor Church Music*, i (1923) and iii (1924).

He was one of the last and one of the greatest composers to write Masses, Magnificats and antiphons to the Virgin in the elaborate style practised by English composers in the first decades of the 16th cent. Compared with his immediate predecessors, he makes greater use of imitation, a technique which became general in the work of Tye and Tallis. His Masses show an interesting variety of method. Three —*Corona spinea*, *Gloria tibi Trinitas*, and *O Michael*—are large works on a *cantus firmus* in the older style ; *The Western Wynde* is a set of variations on the secular tune, a unique example of this way of designing a Mass on an adopted melody ; three—*Playne song*, *Sine nomine* and *Small Devotion*—are in a "familiar" (*i.e.* chordal) style, making use of divided choir technique (*v.* CORI SPEZZATI) to some extent ; and one, *Mater Christi*, is a parody Mass, being based in part on Taverner's antiphon of that name. The "In nomine" section of the *Benedictus* of his Mass *Gloria tibi Trinitas* was the starting-point of the history of the English IN NOMINE. Four of the pieces printed in *Tudor Church Music*, iii as by Taverner are actually by other composers (Fayrfax, Aston and Tallis; for details *v.* F. Ll. Harrison, *Music in Medieval Britain* (1958), p. 334).

Taylor, JOSEPH DEEMS: *b.* New York, Dec. 22, 1885. Composer, critic and writer on music. Studied at New York University. Music critic, *New York World*, 1921-25 ; editor of *Musical America*, 1927-29; musical adviser to the Columbia Broadcasting System from 1940. He has written *Of Men and Music* (1938), made translations of French, Russian, German and Italian songs, and composed operas (*The King's Henchman*, 1927 ; *Peter Ibbetson*, 1931), a ballet, symphonic poems, suites and other orchestral works, cantatas and other choral works and incidental music for plays.

Tchaikovsky [cha-i-coff'-ski], PETER ILYICH: *b.* Votkinsk, May 7, 1840 ; *d.* St. Petersburg, Nov. 6, 1893. After a brief period as a student of law and clerk in the Ministry of Justice, he studied composition under Anton Rubinstein at St. Petersburg Conservatoire, and in 1866 became a teacher in the new Moscow Conservatoire just established by Nicholas Rubinstein. His first 3 symphonies (*Winter Dreams*, 1868; "Little Russian," 1873 ; "Polish," 1875) showed him to be a composer interested in the possibilities of folk-song as material, but not to the extent of being a fanatical nationalist like the St. Petersburg group of "The Five," whom he regarded, with the exception of Rimsky-Korsakov, as talented but rather presumptuous amateurs. They, for their part, regarded him as a somewhat dull eclectic. His marriage to Antonina Milyukov in 1877 was after a few months treated as null and void by mutual consent. From 1877 he was provided with an income by an admirer and patroness, Nadezhda von Meck, with whom he corresponded but never talked, and entered on the most successful period of his career, which included the last 3 symphonies, his most effective operas—*Eugene Onegin* and *The Queen of Spades*, the violin concerto, the ballets *Sleeping Beauty* and *Casse-Noisette*, and the piano trio in A minor. He toured Europe (1888) and visited America (1891) as a conductor. He died of cholera contracted from a drink of tainted water nine days after the first performance of his sixth (later called "Pathetic") symphony.

Tchaikovsky recognised one of his serious weaknesses as a composer when he observed : "I cannot complain of lack of inventive power, but I have always suffered from want of skill in the management of form." Save in a few instances, such as the *Romeo and Juliet* overture and the first and third movements of the sixth symphony, his treatment of form is quite unsubtle and leads him to depend too much on sequence as a means to continuity. His most characteristic types of expression are warm and open-hearted melody and the idioms of a delicate and fanciful, if somewhat conventional, ballet music, but he is capable of achieving moments of intense dramatic expression. His principal compositions are :

(a) STAGE WORKS : 11 operas, including *Vakula the Smith* (1876 ; revived as *The Little Shoes*, 1887 ; published as *Les Caprices d'Oxane*), *Eugene Onegin* (1879), *Joan of Arc* (1881), *Mazeppa* (1884), *The Enchantress* (1887), *The Queen of Spades* (1890), *Iolanthe* (1892); 3 ballets—*Swan Lake* (1876), *Sleeping Beauty* (1889), *Casse-Noisette* (1891-2); incidental music for *Snow-maiden* (1873) and *Hamlet* (1891).

(b) ORCHESTRA : 6 symphonies (No. 4, 1877 ; No. 5, 1888 ; No. 6, 1893) ; *Manfred* symphony (1885); overture-fantasia *Romeo and Juliet* (1869 ; final revision, 1880) ; fantasias: *The Tempest* (1873) and *Francesca da Rimini* (1876) ; overtures: *The Storm* (1864) and *The Year 1812* (1880) ; 3 suites (1879, 1883, 1884) ; symphonic poem *Faet*

(1868); symphonic ballad *The Voevoda* (1891); *Capriccio Italien* (1880); serenade in C for string orchestra.

(c) ORCHESTRA AND SOLO INSTRUMENT: 3 piano concertos (B♭ minor, 1875; G 1880, revised 1893; E♭, in one movement, 1893); concert-fantasia for piano and orchestra (1884); violin concerto (1878); *Variations on a Rococo Theme* for cello and orchestra (1876).

(d) CHAMBER MUSIC: 3 string quartets (D, 1871; F, 1874; E♭ minor, 1876); piano trio in A minor (1882); string sextet *Souvenir de Florence* (begun 1887; revised 1892); *Souvenir d'un lieu cher* for violin and piano.

(e) PIANO: sonata in C♯ minor (1865); *The Seasons* (1876); sonata in G (1878); *Children's Album* (1878); *Dumka* (1886).

(f) SONGS: 9 sets of 6 songs (1869, 1872, 1874, 1875, 1878, 1884, 1887, 1893); 7 songs (1880); 16 songs for children (1881-3); 12 songs (1886); 6 French songs (1888); 6 duets (1880).

Also church music, cantatas, and other choral works; translations of Gevaert's *Traité d'Instrumentation* (1865) and J. C. Lobe's *Musical Catechism* (1869); *Guide to the Practical Study of Harmony* (1871); *Short Manual of Harmony, adapted to the study of religious music in Russia* (1874); *Autobiographical Descriptions of a Journey abroad in* 1888.

G. ABRAHAM: *On Russian Music* (1939). (ed.): *Tchaikovsky: a Symposium* (1945).
E. BLOM: *Tchaikovsky: Orchestral Works* (1927).
C. D. BOWEN and B. VON MECK: *Beloved Friend* (1937).
E. EVANS: *Tchaikovsky* (1935).
W. LAKOND: *The Diaries of Tchaikovsky* (1945).
R. NEWMARCH: *Tchaikovsky, his Life and Works* (1900).
H. WEINSTOCK: *Tchaikovsky* (1943).

Tcherepnin [cherr-ep'-nin], (1) ALEXANDER: *b.* St. Petersburg, Jan. 20, 1899. Composer and pianist. Son of (2). Studied at the St. Petersburg Conservatoire under his father, visited Tiflis and lived in Paris (from 1921), where he studied at the Conservatoire. He toured extensively as a pianist, lived in China and Japan (1935-37), where he published collections of modern oriental music, and later settled in New York. He has composed operas, 8 ballets, 2 symphonies, overtures, piano concertos, cantatas, chamber music, many piano pieces and incidental music for plays.

(2) NICOLAI: *b.* St. Petersburg, May 14, 1873; *d.* Issy-les-Moulineaux (nr. Paris), June 26, 1945. Composer, pianist and conductor. Studied under Rimsky-Korsakov at the St. Petersburg Conservatoire. Conductor, Belaiev Symphony Concerts, 1901, and later of the opera at the Maryinsky Theatre. He was conductor for the Diaghilev Ballets in Paris and other cities from 1909-14 and returned to St. Petersburg from 1914-18, when he became director of the Conservatoire at Tiflis. He settled in Paris in 1921. He composed operas, ballets, 2 symphonies, symphonic poems and other orchestral works, a piano concerto, 2 Masses, piano pieces and songs, and completed Moussorgsky's *Sorochintsi Fair*.

Te. An English substitution for the Italian *si* (B), used in TONIC SOL-FA for the 7th note (or leading note) of the major scale.

Tedesca [teh-dess'-cah], *I.* Short for *danza tedesca*, "German dance." *v.* ALLA TEDESCA, ALLEMANDE, DEUTSCHER TANZ.

Te Deum [tay day'-ŏŏm, *E.* tee dee'-um], *L.* The opening words of "Te Deum laudamus" (We praise thee, God), a Christian hymn attributed to Nicetas (*b. c.* 340), Bishop of Remesiana in Dacia. It is sung at Matins on festivals, on occasions of thanksgiving, and (in the English translation) at Morning Prayer in the Anglican service. The plainsong begins thus:

Among the choral settings written in the 16th cent. are those of Hugh Aston, John Taverner, Felice Anerio and Jacob Handl. There are organ settings for *alternatim* performance by John Redford, William Blitheman and Nicolas Gigault. Aston and Palestrina composed

Masses on its plainsong. John Marbeck's adaptation of the plainsong to the English translation was printed in his *Booke of Common Praier noted* (1550; facsimile edition by J. E. Hunt, 1939). The Lutheran form of the melody, for alternating choirs or for choir alternating with the congregation, set to Martin Luther's translation ("Herr Gott, dich loben wir"), was reprinted in von Winterfeld's *Martin Luthers geistliche Lieder* (1840). Organ settings, presumably intended to accompany this version, were composed by Scheidt (in four parts; *Complete Works*, vol i) and Bach (five parts, *B.G.*, xl, p. 66).

Settings in festive style for voices and instruments have been written by Purcell (St. Cecilia's Day, 1694), Blow (1695), Handel (Peace of Utrecht, 1712 and Battle of Dettingen, 1743), Berlioz (Paris Exhibition of 1855), Bruckner (1884), Dvořák (1892), Verdi (1898), Stanford (Leeds Festival, 1898), Parry (coronation of George V, 1911), Vaughan Williams (coronation of George VI, 1936) and Walton (coronation of Elizabeth II, 1953). *v.* also SERVICE.

Telemann [tay'-ler-mun], (1) GEORG MICHAEL: *b.* Plön (Holstein), Apr. 20, 1748; *d.* Riga, March 4, 1831. Composer and writer. Grandson of (2). Published in 1773 an introduction to figured bass (*Unterricht im Generalbass-Spielen*) and composed trio sonatas, solo sonatas (published by Walsh), organ preludes, and church music. He became cantor at Riga about 1775.

(2) GEORG PHILIPP: *b.* Magdeburg, March 14, 1681; *d.* Hamburg, June 25, 1767. Composer. Educated in Magdeburg and Hildesheim, studied law at Leipzig University (where he founded a student *Collegium musicum*) but taught himself music and wrote compositions for the Thomaskirche and operas for the Leipzig Theatre. Organist of the Neukirche and *Kapellmeister* to Prince Promnitz at Sorau, 1704; *Konzertmeister* (1708) and later *Kapellmeister* at Eisenach (where he made friends with J. S. Bach); *Kapellmeister* of the Katharinenkirche (1712) and later city music director at Frankfort; *Kapellmeister* to the Prince of Bayreuth and at the Barfüsserkirche. From 1721 until his death he was cantor of the Johanneum and music director at Hamburg. He visited Paris in 1737 and made several visits to Berlin.

The most prolific composer in an age of prodigious production, he wrote 12 cycles of cantatas for the church year, 44 Passions, oratorios, and much other church music, 40 operas, 600 French overtures (*i.e.* suites for orchestra), concertos, a great deal of chamber music in various forms, fantasies for harpsichord, and short fugues for organ. He also published *Singe-, Spiel- und Generalbass-Übungen* ("Exercises in Singing, Playing, and Figured Bass"), engraved by himself (1733-1735). Among the modern editions of his works are: oratorio, *The Day of Judgement*, and cantata, *Ino*, in *D.D.T.*, xxviii; 24 odes for solo voices and continuo in *D.D.T.*, lvii; *Musique de Table* (three chamber suites, Hamburg, 1733) in *D.D.T.*, lxi/lxii; violin concerto in F in *D.D.T.*, xxix; 12 *Methodische Sonaten* Hamburg (1728, 1732) for transverse flute and continuo, ed. Max Seiffert (1951, the first vol. of a collected ed.); opera, *Pimpinone*, in *E.D.M.*, vi.

Tema [teh'-mah], *I.* Theme. *Tema con variazioni*, theme and variations.

Temperament (*G.* Temperatur). A system of tuning. In a theoretically perfect system the intervals would agree with those found by the successive fractional division of a string; the ratio of the octave would be 1 : 2, that of the fifth 2 : 3, of the fourth 3 : 4, of the major third 4 : 5, and so on. Such a scale would have two sizes of whole tone, a greater, with the ratio 8 : 9, and a lesser, with the ratio 9 : 10; its semitones would be 15 : 16. It is possible, in the system called "just intonation," to construct a scale on C, for example, in which these ratios would hold, except that the fifth D-A would be 27 : 40 instead of 2 : 3. It is also possible, as Pythagoras (*b.* 582 B.C.) showed, to construct, by calculating successive fifths (2 : 3) above F (called "Pythagorean" tuning), a scale on C in which all the whole tones have the ratio 8 : 9 and both semitones

243 : 256. While just intonation, being possible in only one scale at a time, has no practical value, the Pythagorean system was the basis of the diatonic modes of plainsong. It was, however, inadequate when used to determine chromatic notes such as D♯-E♭ and G♯-A♭ which differ considerably when calculated by fifths, but must be treated as identical on an instrument, such as the organ, with fixed pitches and a limited keyboard.

After *c.* 1500 the system of MEANTONE TEMPERAMENT was generally adopted for keyboard instruments, though some successful experiments were made with keyboards which provided separate keys for the nominally enharmonic chromatic notes, such as Karel Luython's harpsichord with 18 keys to the octave which was highly praised by Praetorius. With the use in composition of the complete cycle of major and minor keys, as in Bach's *Wohltemperirte Clavier*, the system of EQUAL TEMPERAMENT began to be adopted, but was not universally accepted before *c.* 1850. *v.* DIESIS, FIFTH.

Tempest, The. (1) *The Tempest, or the Enchanted Island*, opera with dialogue by Purcell (1695), the text adapted from Shakespeare by Thomas Shadwell.

(2) Opera in three acts by Gatty. Libretto by Reginald Gatty (after Shakespeare). First performed, London, Apr. 17, 1920.

(3) Operas by foreign composers based on the same play include Reichardt's *Die Geisterinsel* and Zumsteeg's setting of the same libretto (both 1798), Halévy's *La tempesta* (1850), Fibich's *Bouře* (1895) and Lattuada's *La tempesta* (1922).

(4) Among 17th-cent. composers in England who wrote music for the play were Banister, Humfrey, Reggio, Draghi and Locke.

(5) Incidental music for the play by Sibelius, Op. 109 (1926).

(6) Symphonic fantasy by Tchaikovsky, Op. 18 (1873), based on the play.

Tempo [tem′-po], *I.* (1) "Time." The pace of a composition as determined by the speed of the beat to which it is performed. Until *c.* 1600 the beat (*v.* TACTUS) in any composition in a particular style (*e.g.*, motet, madrigal) was more or less uniform, and differences of pace were conveyed by the conventions of the notation. Towards the end of the 17th cent. the modern tempo indications, such as *largo*, *adagio*, *allegro*, *presto*, were adopted in Italy and gradually came into general use. They indicate in a general way the tempo of the beat, which is given by the lower figure of the TIME SIGNATURE. Within certain limits the tempo which they suggested remained a matter of convention based on the style of the music, on local custom, and on individual choice until the invention of the METRONOME. Even with both tempo and metronome marks the practice of performers and conductors is by no means uniform, and choice of tempo is generally regarded as an element in interpretation, dependent to some extent on acoustical and other conditions of performance.

F. ROTHSCHILD: *The Lost Tradition in Music: Rhythm and Tempo in J. S. Bach's Time* (1953).

C. SACHS: *Rhythm and Tempo* (1953).

(2) Movement (of a sonata, symphony, etc.) : *il secondo tempo*, the second movement.

Temps [tœ̃], *Fr.* Beat. *Temps fort*, strong beat ; *temps faible*, weak beat.

Teneramente [teh-neh-rah-men′-teh], *I.* Tenderly.

Tenor (from *L.* tenere, "to hold"). (1) In psalmody, the note of recitation, also known as the dominant. *v.* RECITING NOTE.

(2) In sacred polyphonic music (*e.g.* organum, motet, Mass) until *c.* 1450, the lowest part, which was most often derived from plainsong, and on which the composition was based. In a polyphonic *chanson* of the same period the part which formed, with the highest part (*cantus*), the two-part frame-work of the composition. It was as melodious as the *cantus* part, and could be used as the tenor of a Mass, *e.g.* Dufay's Mass *Se la face ay pale*. *v.* also CANTUS FIRMUS.

(3) In music after *c.* 1450, when a bass part began to be used, the part above the bass in a four-part vocal composition (S.A.T.B.). Hence applied to the adult

male voice intermediate between the bass and the alto.

(4) Prefixed to the name of an instrument it indicates a size intermediate between the alto (or treble) member of the family and the bass, *e.g.* tenor saxophone, tenor trombone. *v.* also TENOR HAUTBOY.

(5) English term for the viola (short for tenor violin), now obsolete.

(6) The tenor clef is the C clef on the fourth line:

used in the 16th and 17th cent. for the tenor voice and instruments of equivalent range, now usual only for the tenor trombone and the upper notes of the bassoon, cello and double bass. The tenor voice is now written, except in short score, in the G (treble) clef read an octave lower:

Tenor Drum (*Fr.* caisse roulante, *G.* Rolltrommel, Rührtrommel, *I.* tamburo rullante). A drum intermediate in size between a bass drum and a side drum, without snares. Used in military bands, seldom in the orchestra.

Tenor Hautboy. Old English name for the COR ANGLAIS.

Tenorhorn [ten-orr'-horrn], *G.* A brass instrument of the SAXHORN family, the equivalent of the English BARITONE.

Tenoroon. (1) A name commonly applied to an instrument of the double-reed family with a range a fifth higher than the bassoon (*Fr.* bassoon quinte, *G.* Quintfagott, Tenorfagott, *I.* fagottino). According to Praetorius (1619) the English called it a "single curtall," the bassoon being a "double curtall."

(2) Also applied to the "alto fagotto," an instrument with a single-reed mouthpiece, which was made *c.* 1830 and was a precursor of the saxophone.

Tenor Saxophone, *v.* SAXOPHONE.

Tenor Trombone. *v.* TROMBONE.

Tenor Tuba. (1) A small tuba, the equivalent of the normal English EUPHONIUM. *v.* also TUBA (1).

(2) The smallest of the "Wagner tubas." *v.* TUBA (2).

Tenor Viol. *v.* VIOL.

Tenth. The interval of an octave plus a third, *e.g*;

In the theory of harmony and in figured bass it is treated as the equivalent of the third.

Tento. *v.* TIENTO.

Tenuto [teh-noo'-toh], *I.* "Held." Used for a single note or chord to enjoin its being held for its full value in a context in which the performer might be inclined to play it *staccato*. Generally abbreviated *ten.*

Ternary Form. A form, represented by the formula *ABA*, in which a first section is restated, with or without modifications or embellishments, after a middle section of different content. Where the restatement is without change it is often indicated by *dal capo al fine* at the end of the middle section, as in the *da capo* aria and the minuet or scherzo with trio; where it is to be abbreviated, by *dal segno al fine*, or as in plainsong responds of the office by an asterisk or by quoting the word with which the restatement begins. Most of the short piano pieces of the Romantic period (Nocturne, Impromptu, Intermezzo, Rhapsody, etc.) are in ternary form. SONATA FORM, having evolved from an earlier binary form, is a special case of ternary form in which the middle section is a development, the recapitulation involves a partial change of key, and the coda may be as long as each of the other sections.

Terradellas [terr-rah-dell'-lyahss] (Terradeglias), DOMINGO MIGUEL BERNABÉ (Domenico): *bapt.* Barcelona, Feb. 13, 1713; *d.* Rome, May 20, 1751. Composer. Studied at a Catalan monastery and under Durante at the Conservatorio Sant' Onofrio in Naples. He lived in London from 1746-47, visited Paris and returned to Rome, where he became *maestro di cappella* at S. Giacomo. He composed operas, of which *Artaserse*, the most important, was produced at Venice in 1744, and *Bellerofonte* in London in 1747, on which Burney remarked that " crescendo is used in this opera, seemingly for the first time ; and new effects are frequently produced by pianos and fortes." He also composed some church music.

Terry, (1) CHARLES SANFORD : *b.* Newport Pagnell (Buckinghamshire), Oct. 24, 1864 ; *d.* Aberdeen, Nov. 5, 1936. Historian. Studied at St. Paul's Choir School and King's College School, lectured at Newcastle and at Cambridge and founded the first Prize Festival in Scotland at Aberdeen (1900), where he was appointed professor of history at the University in 1903. He published an English translation of Forkel's *Life of J. S. Bach* (1920), *J. S. Bach, Cantata Texts* (1925), *J. S. Bach* (1928, revised 1933), *Johann Christian Bach* (1929), *The Origin of the Family of Bach Musicians* (1929), *Bach : The Historical Approach* (1930), *Bach's Orchestra* (1932), *The Music of Bach* (1933), essays on the B minor Mass, the Cantatas and Oratorios, the Passions, and on the Magnificat, Lutheran Masses, and Motets (all in *The Musical Pilgrim* series), and an edition of the *Coffee Cantata*.

(2) RICHARD RUNCIMAN : *b.* Ellington (Northumberland), Jan. 3, 1865 ; *d.* London, Apr. 18, 1938. Organist, composer and editor. Music master, Elstow School, 1890. Organist and choirmaster, St. John's Cathedral, Antigua (West Indies), 1892 ; Downside Abbey (Somerset), 1896 ; Westminster Cathedral, 1901-24. Knighted, 1922. Editor of *Music News*, 1924-25. He gave many performances of early English church music, and edited Tudor motets and the *Westminster Hymnal* (1912). He published *Catholic Church Music* (1907, revised as *The Music of the Roman Rite*, 1931), and other books on church music, and a collection of sea shanties (*Shanty Book*, 1921, 1926), and composed 5 Masses, a Requiem and motets.

Tertis, LIONEL : *b.* West Hartlepool, Dec. 29, 1876. Viola player and teacher. Studied at Leipzig and the R.A.M. and settled in London. He toured in Europe and America and retired from the concert platform in 1936. Several contemporary composers, including Bax, Bliss and Cyril Scott, have written music for him. He published *Beauty of Tone in String Playing* (1938).

Terzetto [tair-tset′-to], *I.* (*G.* Terzett). A vocal trio. Very rarely applied to a piece for three instruments.

Terzina [tair-tsee′-nah], *I.* Triplet.

Teschner [tesh′-ner], MELCHIOR : *b.* Fraustadt, 1584 ; *d.* Oberpritschen, Dec. 1, 1635. Cantor at Fraustadt, 1609 ; pastor at Oberpritschen, 1614. Composer of the hymn " Valet will ich dir geben " (first published, 1614), which is sung in England to the words " All glory, laud and honour " (*E.H.*, No. 622).

Teseo [teh′-zeh-o] (Theseus). Opera in five acts by Handel. Libretto by Nicola Francesco Haym. First performed, London, Jan. 21, 1713.

Tessarini [tess-sah-ree′-nee], CARLO : *b.* Rimini, 1690 ; *d.* after 1762. Violinist and composer, probably a pupil of Vivaldi. He was violinist in Venice at St. Mark's (from 1729) and at SS. Giovanni e Paolo, and in Brünn for Cardinal Wolfgang Hannibal (before 1738). He was orchestra leader at Urbino (1742) and played at Amsterdam (1762). He composed violin sonatas, trio sonatas, violin duets, *concertini* and *concerti grossi* for strings. His *Grammatica di musica* (1741) was published in French and English translations.

Tessier [tess-yay], CHARLES (Carles) : *b.* Pézénas (Hérault), *c.* 1550. Composer and lutenist. He was chamber musician to Henry IV and visited England. Composed a book of *Chansons et airs de cour* for four to five voices (London, 1597) dedicated to Lady Penelope Riche (Stella in Sir Philip Sidney's sonnets), *Airs et villanelles* for three to five voices (Paris, 1604) and a setting of a song from Sidney's *Astrophel and Stella*.

Tessitura [tess-ee-too′-rah], *I.* " Texture." The general compass of a particular voice or of a vocal or instrumental part in a particular piece, used especially when that compass does not coincide with the total range of the voice or instrument.

Testo [tess′-to], *I.* Lit. "text." The narrator in early ORATORIO.

Testudo [tess-too′-do], *L.* Lit. "tortoise, tortoise-shell." Hence (1) in the Graeco-Roman world a lyre; (2) in the 16th and 17th cent. a lute.

Tetrachord (*Gr.* τετράχορδον, lit. "that which has four strings"). A segment of the scale of ancient Greek music, consisting of four notes descending through a perfect fourth in the order tone-tone-semitone, *e.g.* *A-G-F-E.* This, the diatonic tetrachord, was the basis of the complete diatonic scale. The chromatic tetrachord had two steps of a semitone above the lowest note, the enharmonic tetrachord two steps of a quarter-tone above the lowest note. *v.* CHROMATIC, ENHARMONIC.

Tetrazzini [teh-trah-tsee′-nee], LUISA: *b.* Florence, June 29, 1871; *d.* Milan, Apr. 28, 1940. Operatic soprano. Studied at the Liceo Musicale in Florence, where she first appeared in 1890 as Inez in *L'Africaine.* She sang in various Italian theatres, settled in Buenos Aires and was a member of a company in the Argentine (from 1898) and in Mexico City (from 1905). She gave many performances in European and American cities and in London at Covent Garden (from 1907), in New York at the Manhattan Opera (1908-10) and the Metropolitan (1910), and in Chicago at the Chicago Opera (1913-14). She sang in Italy for charity during the war and later taught singing in Milan. She published *My Life of Song* (1921) and *How to Sing* (1925).

Teutsch [toytsh], *G.* *v.* DEUTSCHER TANZ.

Thaïs [ta-eece]. Opera in three acts by Massenet. Libretto by Louis Gallet (based on Anatole France's novel). First performed, Paris, March 16, 1894.

Thalben Ball, GEORGE. *v.* BALL.

Thalberg [tahl′-bairk], SIGISMOND: *b.* Geneva, 1812; *d.* Posilipo, Apr. 27, 1871. Austrian pianist and composer. Natural son of Prince Moritz Dietrichstein and Baroness von Wetzlar. Studied in Vienna under Sechter and Hummel, made his début as pianist in 1826 and published his first works in 1828. He toured in Germany (1830), was chamber pianist to the Austrian Emperor (1834), and played in Paris (1835), where he was a rival to Liszt. He also gave concerts in London, Belgium, Holland, Russia, Spain, Brazil and the United States. He composed 2 operas, a piano concerto, a sonata, studies and many other piano pieces, transcriptions for piano and songs.

Thayer, ALEXANDER WHEELOCK: *b.* South Natick (Mass.), Oct. 22, 1817; *d.* Trieste, July 15, 1897. Studied at Harvard University, where he worked in the library for several years. He made visits to Berlin, Bonn, Prague, Vienna and other cities, collecting material for a life of Beethoven, wrote for the *New York Tribune* (1852) and was appointed United States Consul at Trieste (1865), where he lived until his death. He contributed to Dwight's *Journal of Music* and many other American publications. His life of Beethoven, which is the standard biographical work on the composer, was published in German (Vol. I, 1866, Vol. II, 1872, Vol. III, 1879; the projected fourth volume was not completed). The English edition in 3 vols., translated and completed by H. E. Krehbiel, was published in 1921. Thayer also published a chronological index of Beethoven's compositions (1865).

The. For English titles beginning thus see the second word of the title.

Theile [tile′-er], JOHANN: *b.* Naumburg (Saxony), July 29, 1646; *d.* there, June 21, 1724. Composer. Studied at Magdeburg, Halle, Leipzig University (where he played the *viola da gamba*) and at Weissenfels under Heinrich Schütz. He taught at Stettin and Lübeck, and was appointed *Kapellmeister* of the ducal court at Gottorp (1673) but was forced to flee in 1675 from the Danish troops to Hamburg, where he wrote operas for the new opera house from 1678. *Kapellmeister*, Wolfenbüttel, 1685; Merseburg, 1689. Later settled at Naumburg. He composed Masses, Magnificats, a Passion, cantatas and other church music, and instrumental pieces for two to five parts (1686), with movements in double counterpoint. He was notable as a composer of works in strict contrapuntal style, of the biblical opera *Adam and Eve* (the music is lost), with which the first German opera house, the *Theater am Gansemarkt* in Hamburg, was opened, and of a *St. Matthew Passion* (Lübeck, 1673) which was one of the earliest to include contemplative arias with continuo accompaniment and instrumental ritornelli. The Passion is published in *D.D.T.*, xvii, and a song, "*Durchkläre dich, du Silbernacht*," with instrumental accompaniment in Schering's *History of Music in Examples*, No. 210.

Theme. A musical entity which is the chief idea, or one of the chief ideas, in a composition. It is used especially of an idea in an instrumental work which is used as the basis for discussion, development or variation, as are the themes in a sonata of the baroque period and in SONATA FORM, and a theme used for a series of VARIATIONS. *v.* also MOTIF.

Theodora. Oratorio by Handel. Text by Thomas Morell. First performed, London, Mar. 16, 1750.

Theorbo (*Fr.* théorbe, *G.* Theorbe, *I.* tiorba). A small bass lute or ARCHLUTE used in the 17th cent. as a continuo instrument in ensembles, and less frequently to accompany monodies. Besides the stopped strings it had a number of unstopped bass strings running from a separate peg-box. A tuning for a *liuto attiorbato* given by C. Saracini in 1614 was :

In his *Musick's Monument* (1676) Thomas Mace gives this tuning :

There is a late use of the theorbo in Handel's *Esther* (1732) for the accompaniment to "Breathe soft, ye winds."

Theory of Music. According to the period in which they were written, works on the theory of music may deal with one or more of the following aspects of the subject: acoustics, notation, melody, rhythm, harmony, counterpoint, composition, form, and musical aesthetics. References to the writings of the following theorists will be found under their respective entries : St. Augustine, Boethius, Regino, Hucbald, Guido, Hermannus Contractus, Jerome of Moravia, Franco of Cologne, Jean de Garlande, Odington, de Vitry, Marchettus of Padua, Jacobus of Liège, Johannes de Muris, Tunsted, Handlo, Power, Hothby, Guilelmus Monachus, Tinctoris, Ramis de Pareja, Gafori, Aaron, Heyden, Listenius, Glareanus, Vicentino, Zarlino, Zacconi, Galilei, Morley, Coprario, Praetorius, Herbst, Sweelinck, Mersenne, Doni, Kircher, Mattheson, Heinichen, Rameau, Pepusch, Marpurg, Soler, Morigi, Martini, Tartini, Kirnberger, Cherubini, Albrechtsberger, Vogler, Marx, Day, Hauptmann, Helmholtz, Jadassohn, Riemann, Richter, Ziehn, Schenker, Prout, d'Indy, Morris, Schönberg, Jeppesen, Piston, Hindemith. In addition, references to works on figured bass, which have both a practical and theoretical aspect, will be found under Locke, Penna, Niedt, Agazzari, Keller, Gasparini, Lampe, G. P. and G. M. Telemann, Pasquali, C. P. E. Bach, Geminiani, C. G. Schröter, and Türk.

Theremin. An electronic instrument invented by the Russian physicist Leo Theremin (*b.* 1896) and first demonstrated by him in 1920. The notes are produced by variations in the frequency of an oscillating electric circuit, controlled by movement of the player's hand in the air towards, or away from, an antenna. It is a purely melodic instrument.

Theresienmesse [tay-raze'-i-ĕn-mess-*er*] (Theresa Mass). Mass in B♭ major by Haydn, composed in 1799 (Haydn Society, No. 10 ; Novello's ed., No. 16). No satisfactory explanation of the name has been advanced.

Thesis. *v.* ARSIS.

Thibaud [tee-bo], JACQUES: *b.* Bordeaux, Sept. 27, 1880; *d.* (in an air crash in the Alps), Sept. 2, 1953. Violinist. Studied at the Paris Conservatoire. For a short time a member of the Colonne Orchestra, but rapidly made his name as a virtuoso. He toured widely as a soloist, and in association with Alfred Cortot (piano) and Pau Casals (cello).

Third. The interval comprised by two notes written on adjacent lines or spaces, *e.g.*:

A major third has two whole tones, a minor third a tone and a semitone, and a diminished third a whole tone:

The mode of a triad is determined by its third, as is the mode of a scale, since the sixth and seventh degrees are treated as variable in the harmonic minor and melodic minor scales. The diminished third is most often used as the inversion of the AUGMENTED SIXTH. *v.* also IMPERFECT INTERVAL.

Thirteenth. The interval of an octave and a sixth, *e.g.*:

For the so-called "chord of the thirteenth" *v.* CHORD.

Thirty-Second Note. American for "demisemiquaver."

Thoinan [twa nũn], ERNEST (*nom de plume* of Antoine Ernest Roquet): *b.* Nantes, Jan. 23, 1827; *d.* Paris, *c.* end of May, 1894. Musical scholar who lived in Paris from 1844 as a businessman. He collected works on music and became a contributor to *La France musicale*, *L'Art musical* and other periodicals. He published many of his essays in pamphlet form.

Thomas, (1) ARTHUR GORING: *b.* Ratton Park (Sussex), Nov. 21, 1850; *d.* London, March 20, 1892. Composer. Educated for the Civil Service but later studied music in Paris under Émile Durand (from 1873), in London at the R.A.M. under Sullivan and Prout (from 1877) and in Berlin under Bruch. He was commissioned by the Carl Rosa Opera to write *Esmeralda*, which was first performed in 1883. He composed other operas (including *Nadeshda*, 1883), 4 concert-scenas, cantatas and other choral works, an orchestral *Suite de Ballet*, and many songs (chiefly to French words).

(2) THEODORE: *b.* Essens (Hanover), Oct. 11, 1835; *d.* Chicago, Jan. 4, 1905. Conductor and violinist who was almost entirely self-taught. His family moved to New York in 1845, where he played the violin for dances and other occasions. He made a concert tour while still in his 'teens, became a member of the New York Philharmonic Orchestra (1854) and of the Mason-Thomas Quintet (1855), and orchestra leader and later conductor at the New York Academy of Music. He founded his own orchestra (1862) and with it made many tours in America. Conductor, Brooklyn Philharmonic Orchestra, 1866; New York Philharmonic Orchestra, 1877; Chicago Symphony Orchestra, 1891 until his death. He gave many first performances in America of modern music and wrote *A Musical Autobiography* (edited by G. P. Upton, 1905).

Thomas [tom-a], CHARLES LOUIS AMBROISE: *b.* Metz, Aug. 5, 1811; *d.* Paris, Feb. 12, 1896. Composer. Studied at the Paris Conservatoire, where he won the *Prix de Rome* (1832), and under Kalkbrenner (piano) and Lesueur (composition). After three years in Italy he returned to Paris, where he wrote many operas for the Opéra-Comique and was appointed teacher of composition (1852) and director (1871) at the Conservatoire. He composed operas, ballets, a *Fantasia* for piano and orchestra, cantatas, 2 Masses, motets, chamber music, part-songs, songs and piano pieces. His most successful operas were *Mignon* (1866), which reached its 500th performance in 1878, and *Hamlet* (1868), which seems to have been the first opera in which a saxophone was used in the orchestra.

Thompson, RANDALL: *b.* New York, Apr. 21, 1899. Composer. Studied at Harvard University and under Ernest Bloch. Fellow of the American Academy at Rome, 1922-25; assistant professor of music, Wellesley College, 1927-29; Guggenheim Fellowship, 1929 and 1930; taught at the Juilliard School in New York, 1931-32. Professor, University of California, Berkeley, 1937; director, Curtis Institute, Philadelphia, 1938-40. Professor, Princeton, 1946; Harvard, 1948. He has composed a one-act opera, 3 symphonies, *Jazz Poem* for piano and orchestra and other orchestral works, choral works, chamber music, incidental music for the theatre, piano pieces and songs. After a study of music in American universities he published *College Music* (1935).

Thomson, VIRGIL: *b.* Kansas City, Nov. 25, 1896. Composer and music critic. Studied at Harvard University and under Nadia Boulanger. He received several fellowships, was an instructor at Harvard (1920-25) and lived in Paris (1925-32), where he came under the influence of Eric Satie, *Les Six*, Cocteau, and Stravinsky. He became organist at King's Chapel in Boston and music critic for various American publications and for the *New York Herald Tribune* (from 1940). He has written *The State of Music* (1939), *The Musical Scene* (1945) and *The Art of Judging Music* (1948) and has composed 2 operas—*Four Saints in Three Acts*, 1934, and *The Mother of us All*, 1947 (both to texts by Gertrude Stein)—2 symphonies and other orchestral works, a ballet, choral works, chamber music, music for plays and for films, pieces for piano and for organ, and songs (many to French words).

Thorne, JOHN: *d.* York, Dec. 7, 1573. Composer. He was probably organist of York Minster from 1550 until his death and was mentioned as a "practicioner" of music in Morley's *Plaine and Easie Introduction* (1597). His motet "Stella coeli" was printed in Hawkins's *History of Music* (1875 ed., p. 360).

Thorough-Bass. *v.* FIGURED BASS.

Three Choirs Festival. An annual festival, founded in 1724, given by the combined choirs of the cathedrals of Gloucester, Worcester and Hereford, and held in each cathedral in turn. It opens with a service on the first Sunday in September, and performances take place from the following Tuesday to Saturday. The scope of the programmes, which in the 18th cent. consisted largely of choral works by Handel, was enlarged during S. S. Wesley's tenure at Hereford (1832-42), and later in the century the festival played an important part in the English choral renaissance by giving performances of works by Parry and Elgar. The custom of including new works by English composers has continued.

D. LYSONS: *History of the Origin and Progress of the Meetings of the Three Choirs of Gloucester, Worcester and Hereford* (1st ed., 1812; 4th ed., with various supplements, 1931).

Three-Cornered Hat, The. *v.* SOMBRERO DE TRES PICOS.

Through-Composed. A literal American translation of *G.* DURCHKOMPONIERT. It is not English.

Thuille [too-eel'-er], LUDWIG: *b.* Bozen, Nov. 30, 1861; *d.* Munich, Feb. 5, 1907. Composer. Chorister at the Benedictine Abbey at Kremsmünster. Studied under Pembaur at the Innsbruck School of Music and under Rheinberger at the Munich Conservatorium. Teacher of piano and theory, Munich Conservatorium, 1883. He was a friend of Richard Strauss and of Alexander Ritter. His compositions include 4 operas (one unfinished), an overture and other orchestral works, works for female and for male choirs, chamber music, songs and piano pieces. His *Harmonielehre* (Textbook of Harmony, 1907), written in collaboration with Rudolf Louis, was widely used in Germany.

Thus spoke Zarathustra. *v.* ALSO SPRACH ZARATHUSTRA.

Tibia [tee'-bi-a], *L.* A pipe. (1) The Greek *aulos*. (2) An organ stop, usually with some further qualifications, *e.g. tibia clausa*, a flue stop of large scale.

Tie (*Fr.* liaison, *G.* Bindung, *I.* legatura). A curved line, also called a bind, joining two notes of the same pitch into a continuous sound.

Tiefland [teef′-lunt] (Lowland). Opera with a prologue and three acts by d'Albert. Libretto by " Rudolf Lothar " (*i.e.* Rudolf Spitzer), founded on the play *Terra baixa* by the Catalan author Angel Guimerá. First performed, Prague, Nov. 15, 1903.

Tiento [tee-en′-to], *Sp.* (*Port.* tento). Lit. " touch." A term for *ricercar* used in the 16th cent., *e.g.* by Cabezón in his *Obras de música* of 1578.

Tierce [tyairce], *Fr.* (1) Third, *e.g. tierce de Picardie*.

(2) An organ stop of $1\frac{3}{5}$ ft., sounding two octaves and a third above the note corresponding to the key played. *v.* MUTATION STOPS.

Tierce de Picardie [tyairce der pee-carr-dee], *Fr.* Lit. " Picardy third." A major third used in the final chord of a composition in the minor mode. Before the 16th cent. a final chord almost invariably had no third; in the 16th cent. it became usual to have a major third in the last chord, whatever the mode. The earliest recorded use of the term is in J. J. Rousseau's Dictionary of 1764.

Tierce Flute. The 18th-cent. name for a flute built a minor third higher than the normal form, also known as " third flute." Since it was treated as a transposing instrument it was therefore properly a flute in E♭; but since its natural scale was F major (the natural scale of the ordinary flute being D major) it was misleadingly described as " flute in F." The so-called " flute in E♭ " which was used in military bands until comparatively recent times was properly a flute in D♭, since its pitch was a semitone above that of the ordinary flute.

Tiersot [tyair-so], JEAN BAPTISTE ELISÉE JULIEN: *b.* Bourg-en-Bresse, July 5, 1857; *d.* Paris, Aug. 10, 1936. Musical historian and composer. He lived in Paris from 1871 and studied medicine, and later music under Massenet and César Franck at the Conservatoire, where he became assistant librarian (1883) and librarian (1910). He was professor at the École des Hautes Études Sociales and president of the Société Française de Musicologie and gave lectures on folklore in America, Belgium, Holland and Sweden. He wrote many books on musical history and folk-music, edited collections of folk-songs, worked with Saint-Saëns on the Pelletan edition of Gluck's works, contributed to various periodicals and composed works for chorus and orchestra, a suite and other orchestral works, and incidental music for a play.

Tiessen [teece′-ĕn], HEINZ: *b.* Königsberg, Apr. 10, 1887. Composer, conductor and music critic. He settled in Berlin, where he studied at the University, was music critic of the *Allgemeine Musik-Zeitung* (1912-17), worked at the Royal Opera (1917-18), was conductor of the Volksbühne (1918-21) and the University Orchestra (1920-22), founded a mixed choir (1924), was teacher of composition at the Hochschule für Musik (from 1925) and director of the State Conservatorium (1946-49). He became a member of the Academy of Arts in 1930. He has written a history of modern music and an autobiography, and has composed 2 symphonies and other orchestral works, incidental music for plays, a dance drama, choral arrangements of folk-songs and other choral works, chamber music, piano pieces and many songs.

Tigrini [tee-gree′-nee], ORAZIO: *b.* Arezzo, 16th cent. Canon at Arezzo, 1588, and *maestro di cappella* of the Cathedral, 1591. He composed a book of madrigals for 4 voices (1573) and 2 books for 6 voices (1582, 1591), and wrote a four-volume work on counterpoint (*Compendio della musica*, 1588), from which Morley quoted a number of examples, without acknowledgement, in his *Plaine and Easie Introduction* (1597; *v.* ed. by R. A. Harman, 1952, p. 241).

Tikhi Don [teekh′-ee don] (Quiet flows the Don). Opera in four acts by Dzerjinsky. Libretto from Michael

Sholokhov's novel. First performed, Leningrad, Oct. 22, 1935.

Till Eulenspiegels lustige Streiche [till oil'-ĕn-shpeeg-ĕlss loŏst'-ig-er shtry*sh*'-er] (Tyl Owlglass's Merry Pranks). Symphonic poem by Richard Strauss, Op. 28 (1895), based on a 15th-cent. German folk-tale. First performed, Cologne, Nov. 5, 1895.

Tillyard, HENRY JULIUS WETENHALL: *b.* Cambridge, Nov. 18, 1881. Classical scholar. Educated at Cambridge. Studied at the British Schools in Athens and Rome, 1904-07, and in 1912 visited Athos and Sinai. Professor, Johannesburg, 1919; Birmingham, 1922; Cardiff, 1926. He is one of the editors of the series *Monumenta Musicae Byzantinae,* and has published a number of studies in Byzantine music and musical notation, including *Byzantine Music and Hymnography* (1923), *Handbook of the Middle Byzantine Musical Notation* (1936), *The Hymns of the Sticherarium for November* (1938), *The Hymns of the Octoechus* (two parts, 1940, 1949), and *Twenty Canons from the Trinity Hirmologium* (1952).

Timbales [tan͡-bull], *Fr.* Timpani.

Timbre [tan͡br], *Fr.* (*G.* Klangfarbe). Quality of tone. Also used in English as an alternative term for TONE-COLOUR.

Time. (1) In *mensural notation,* the relation of the breve to the semibreve. In perfect time, shown by the sign O, the breve contains three semibreves; in imperfect time, shown by the sign C, two.

(2) Since *c.* 1700 time has been indicated in musical notation by bar-lines and a TIME-SIGNATURE. Time in this sense may be duple (two beats in a bar), triple, quadruple, quintuple, and so on. Each of these is called " simple " when the beat is a simple note-value, *i.e.* semibreve, minim, crotchet, etc. A " compound " time is one in which the beat is a ternary note-value, which is always represented by a dotted note; thus six quavers in a bar is compound duple time, *i.e.* two dotted crotchets in a bar, and twelve quavers in a bar is compound quadruple time. *v.* also METRE, RHYTHM.

Time-Signature. An indication in the form of a fraction of the metre of a piece or part of a piece, *i.e.* of the number of beats in each bar and of the value of each beat. The denominator gives the value of each beat in relation to the semibreve, which is represented by 1; the minim is represented by 2, the crotchet by 4, the quaver by 8, and so on. The numerator gives the number of beats in the bar. Where *n* stands for the figure 1, 2, 4, 8, 16, etc. the time-signature for simple duple time is 2-n, for simple triple time 3-n, and so on. The time signatures for the compound times are: duple, 6-n; triple 9-n; quadruple, 12-n; quintuple, 15-n.

Time-signatures are, in effect signs of proportion based on the semibreve, which was the unit of time in the 17th cent. Two signs which were a part of the time-signature system in use before 1600 and which were commonly combined with signs of proportion in the 17th cent. have survived in modern use: C as the equivalent of 4/4 time, and ¢ as the equivalent of 2/2 time, also called ALLA BREVE. *v.* also METRE.

Timpan. A string instrument used by the Irish in the early Middle Ages. It was played with the nails or a plectrum and was thus an early type of PSALTERY. In the later middle ages the strings were struck with a rod in the same way as those of the DULCIMER.

Timpani [tim'-pah-nee] (*Fr.* timbales, *G.* Pauken), *I.* Kettle-drums. The kettle-drum is a basin-shaped shell of copper across which is stretched a " head " of calf-skin, the tension of which is adjusted by screws turned by hand, or by a mechanism controlled by a pedal, so that a sound of definite pitch is produced. In the baroque period two timpani were often used with three trumpets, as almost invariably in Bach, and played the bass of their chords. In the orchestra of the classical period two timpani, tuned to the tonic and dominant of the key, were used. Beethoven wrote for timpani tuned to a fifth, a fourth, a diminished fifth (in *Fidelio*), a minor sixth (in the Scherzo of the seventh symphony), and an octave (in the eighth and ninth symphonies). Three drums became normal during the Romantic period, and four were not unusual in late 19th-cent. scores. The timpani have a range of idioms which, though not wide, can be extremely effective. Beethoven saw their possibilities as a foil to the whole orchestra, *e.g.* :

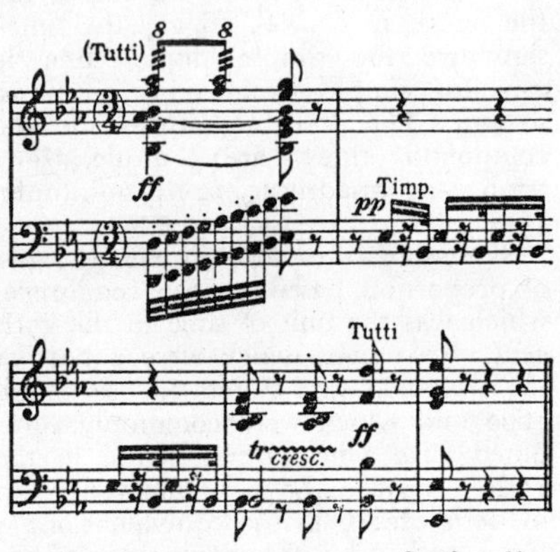

BEETHOVEN : *Symphony No. 4*

and the Scherzo of the ninth symphony; as the bearers of the rhythmic pattern of a particular passage, as in the slow movement of the first symphony; and to give support and rhythmic definition to a tutti. One of his most important works, the violin concerto, begins with a bar for a kettle-drum solo. Few later composers have used the timpani with as much insight.

J. E. ALTENBURG : *Versuch einer Anleitung zu heroisch-musikalischen Trompeter- und Pauker-Kunst* (1795 ; fascimile ed. 1911).

P. R. KIRBY : *The Kettle-drums* (1930).

Tinctoris [tink-to'-reece], JOANNES: *b.* probably at Poperinghe (nr. Ypres), *c.* 1445 ; *d.* Nivelles, Oct. 12, 1511. Theorist and composer. Studied at the University of Louvain, where he became master in 1471. By 1476 he was a chaplain and singer in the chapel of Ferdinand I in Naples, and tutor to Ferdinand's daughter Beatrice of Aragon. He died as canon of Nivelles. In the dedication to Ferdinand of his *Liber de arte contrapuncti* (1477) he remarked that no music written more than 40 years before that time was thought worth hearing, and in the preface to the *Proportionale musices* (before 1476) observed that the "fount and origin" of this new art was considered to be among the English, of whom Dunstable was the chief. In the same paragraph he pointed to the conservatism of the English composers of his own time, as compared to the French. He published (probably *c.* 1475) the first dictionary of musical terms, the *Terminorum musicae diffinitorium* (printed in Coussemaker, *Scriptores*, iv; modern edition with French translation and introduction by A. Machabey, 1951) and *De inventione et usu musicae* about 1484. Nine other treatises are printed in Coussemaker, iv, and English translations of the preface of the *Proportionale musices* and the dedication of the *Liber de arte contrapuncti* in O. Strunk, *Source Readings in Music History* (1950).

Tinel [tee-nel], EDGAR: *b.* Sinay, March 27, 1854; *d.* Brussels, Oct. 28, 1912. Composer, pianist and teacher. Studied at the Brussels Conservatoire. *Prix de Rome*, 1877. Director of the Church Music Institute, Malines, 1882; music inspector of state schools, 1889; teacher of counterpoint (1896) and director (1909), Brussels Conservatoire. He composed 2 sacred dramas, an oratorio, 2 Te Deums, a Mass, cantatas, psalms and other choral works, 2 works for solo voice, chorus and orchestra, an orchestral suite, 4 nocturnes for voices and piano, and piano pieces, and published a book on Gregorian chant (1895).

Tiorba [tee-orr'-bah], *I.* Theorbo.

Tippett, MICHAEL KEMP: *b.* London, Jan. 2, 1905. Composer. Studied at the Royal College of Music. Appointed conductor of musical educational organizations under the London County Council and in 1940 became music director at Morley College. He has composed the oratorio *A Child of our Time* (1941), the opera *The Midsummer Marriage* (1952), 2 symphonies, concerto for double string orchestra, choral works, chamber music and piano pieces.

Tirasse [tee-russ], *Fr.* A manual to

pedal coupler on the organ. *v.* COUPLER (3).

Tiré [tee-ray], *Fr.* The downward stroke of the BOW in string instruments.

Titelouze [teet-looz], JEAN: *b.* St. Omer, 1563; *d.* Rouen, Oct. 25, 1633. Organist and composer. He lived in Rouen where he was organist at St. Jean (from 1585) and organist (from 1588) and canon (from 1610) at the Cathedral. He visited Paris to inaugurate the organ at the Abbey of Saint Denis (1604) and at Notre Dame (1610). He composed organ hymns (*Hymnes de l'Église pour toucher sur l'orgue*, 1623) and Magnificats (*Le Magnificat ou Cantique de la Vierge pour toucher sur l'orgue*, 1626) and a Mass *In ecclesia*. His organ works have been reprinted in *Archives des maîtres de l'orgue* (ed. Guilmant and Pirro, i).

Titus. *v.* CLEMENZA DI TITO.

Toccata [tock-cah'-tah], *I.* (from *toccare*, to touch, play). (1) A piece for a keyboard instrument. Towards the end of the 16th cent. two types of toccata were written by Italian composers. The first, practised by A. Gabrieli, G. Gabrieli and L. Luzzaschi, and later by Frescobaldi, was in free style with a great deal of elaborate passage-work, as in the opening of the first toccata in Frescobaldi's second book of toccatas, canzonas, etc., of 1627:

The second, practised by Merulo, and later by Frescobaldi (*e.g.* the ninth toccata in his first book, 1637) and Michelangelo Rossi, used sections in this style alternating with sections in imitative style. This type, and the shorter toccatas to be played before a *ricercar* (*avanti il Ricercare*) in Frescobaldi's *Fiori musicali* (1635), may be considered two of the prototypes of the later toccata (or prelude) and fugue. The *Fiori musicali* also contain short toccatas in a quieter style to be played before Mass (*avanti la messa*) or at the Elevation.

Sweelinck and the German organists (*e.g.* Scheidt) adopted both of the Italian types, which were later cultivated by Froberger, Pachelbel and Buxtehude. One of Pachelbel's toccatas, a short piece in free style, is followed by a fugue; others were of a kind also written by Italian composers of his time (*e.g.* Pasquini) in which the free style became much less diffuse, and each piece tended to pursue one particular form of figuration. Bach's toccatas for harpsichord are of the alternating type, which he divides into three or more distinct sections. Of the organ toccatas, each of which precedes a fugue, that in F major is unique in combining the traditional characteristics of the genre with the utmost consistency of idea and clarity of design. Toccatas by later composers, *e.g.* Schumann, Widor, Ravel (in *le Tombeau de Couperin*), Prokofiev, are usually pieces in a fast tempo with a continuous rhythm based on one kind of figuration.

(2) The word was also applied *c.* 1600 to a short piece with the character of a fanfare, for brass with or without other instruments (the English "tucket"). In Italy this kind of toccata was usually played three times before a stage work, *e.g.* the toccata at the beginning of Monteverdi's *Orfeo*.

Toch [tockh], ERNST: *b.* Vienna, Dec. 7, 1887. Composer. Studied medicine and philosophy, won various prizes for composition and from 1909 studied piano at Frankfort. He was appointed teacher at the Hochschule für Musik in Mannheim (1913), where he taught composition privately after 1918. Composition teacher at the New School for Social Research in New York, 1934-36. Moved to Hollywood and in 1940 became professor of composition at the University of Southern California. He has composed 4 operas, a concerto and a symphony for piano and orchestra, a symphony for soli, chorus, organ and orchestra, an overture and other orchestral works, choral works, string quartets and other chamber music, music for plays, radio plays and films, numerous studies and other piano pieces, and has written *The Shaping Forces in Music* (1948).

Tod und das Mädchen, Der [dair tote o͝ont duss met*sh*′-ĕn], *G.* (Death and the Maiden). Song by Schubert, Op. 7, no. 3, composed in 1817. Words by Matthias Claudius. Schubert used the piano accompaniment as the subject for a set of variations in the slow movement of his string quartet in D minor, completed in 1826. For this reason the quartet is often known as the "Death and the Maiden" quartet.

Tod und Verklärung [tote o͝ont fair-clair′-o͝ong], *G.* (Death and Transfiguration). Symphonic poem by Richard Strauss, Op. 24 (completed in 1889). The poem by Alexander Ritter which is placed at the head of the score was written after the work was composed. First performed, Eisenach, June 21, 1890.

Toëschi [to-ess′-kee] (Toesca della Castella-Monte), CARLO GIUSEPPE : *b.* Romagna (Italy), 1724; *d.* Munich, Apr. 12, 1788. Composer and violinist. Studied under Johann Stamitz, became violinist (1752) and leader (1759), as successor to Stamitz, of the Mannheim Court Orchestra and went with the court to Munich (1778), where he was appointed music director (1780). He composed 63 symphonies, ballet music for operas by other composers, trio sonatas, many flute quintets and piano quintets and other chamber music. His brother, Johann Baptist, leader of the Mannheim Orchestra from 1774, was also a violinist and composer. Giuseppe's symphony in B♭ is published in *D.T.B.*, vii (2), his flute quartet in G and flute quintet in F in *D.T.B.*, xv, and his trio in G and a thematic catalogue of the chamber music of both composers in *D.T.B.*, xvi.

Tolomeo, Re d'Egitto [to-lo-meh′-o reh deh-jeet′-to] (Ptolemy, King of Egypt). Opera in three acts by Handel. Libretto by Nicola Francesco Haym. First performed, London, May 11, 1728.

Tolstoy [toll′-stoy], COUNT THEOPHIL MATVEIVICH : *b.* St. Petersburg, 1809 ; *d.* there, March 4, 1881. Composer and critic. Studied in St. Petersburg, Naples and Moscow and began work as a music critic (under the *nom de plume* Rostislav) in 1850. He composed an opera and about 200 songs and published analyses of Glinka's *Life for the Czar* (1854) and Serov's *Rogneda* (1870).

Tomášek [to′-mah-sheck] (Tomaschek), JAN VÁCLAV (Johann Wenzel): *b.* Skuč (Bohemia), Apr. 17, 1774; *d.* Prague, Apr. 3, 1850. Composer and pianist. Chorister at the monastery of Jihlava, studied music at Chrudin, philosophy and law at Prague University (1790-93), and was later in the service of Count Bucquoi von Longueval. He made many visits to Vienna and met Beethoven in 1814. He composed 3 operas, 3 Masses, 2 Requiems, cantatas, hymns, vocal scenas from works by Goethe and Schiller, a symphony, a piano concerto, chamber music, sonatas and other piano pieces, and many songs. Extracts from his reminiscences were published in *The Musical Quarterly*, xxxii (1946).

Tomasini [to-mah-zee′-nee], LUIGI : *b.* Pesaro, June 22, 1741; *d.* Esterház, Apr. 25, 1808. Violinist and composer. A member of Prince Esterházy's orchestra at Eisenstadt (1757), appointed leader by Haydn (1761) and later became chamber music director. He moved with the court to Esterház in 1766. Haydn wrote several violin concertos for him. He composed violin concertos, string quartets, duets for two violins and 24 *Divertimenti* for baryton, violin and cello. His son, Luigi, was also a violinist in the Esterházy orchestra.

Tombeau [tõ-bo], *Fr.* "Tomb, tombstone." A title used by French composers in the 17th cent. (*e.g.* Gaultier, L. Couperin, d'Anglebert) for a lament on the death of a notable person. Gaultier's *Tombeau* for lute for the lutenist de Lenclos, which is followed by a *Consolation aux amis du Sr. Lenclos*, is printed in Schering's *History of Music in Examples*, No. 215. The idea was revived by Ravel in his *Tombeau de Couperin*. *v.* also LAMENT.

Tombelle [la tōn-bell], FERNAND DE LA. *v.* LA TOMBELLE.

Tomkins, THOMAS: *b.* St. David's 1572; *d.* Martin Hussingtree, June, 1656. Composer and organist. Studied under Byrd. Organist of Worcester Cathedral, *c.* 1596-1646; one of the organists at the Chapel Royal from 1621. He composed services (*Tudor Church Music*, vii), 93 anthems, *Songs of 3, 4, 5 and 6 parts* (1622, *E.M.S.*, xviii), pieces for virginals (4 in the *Fitzwilliam Virginal Book*), an *In nomine* and 4 6-part fantasias for viols, and coronation music for Charles I (1625). His church music was published posthumously in *Musica Deo sacra* (1668). Complete keyboard works, ed. S. D. Tuttle, in *Musica Britannica*, v. He was a master equally of the polyphonic style (his third service is a fine example of the more elaborate type of setting), of the verse anthem, and of the string fantasia, in which he wrote some effective passages of expressive chromaticism. His brother John (*c.* 1586-1638), organist of King's College, Cambridge (1606) and St. Paul's Cathedral (1619), composed some anthems and a set of keyboard variations on "John come kiss me now." His brother Robert, a musician in the household of Charles I (*c.* 1633- *c.*1641), composed anthems.

I. ATKINS: *The early Occupants of the Office of Organist . . . of the Cathedral . .*, *Worcester* (1918).

D. STEVENS: *Thomas Tomkins* (1957).

Tommasini [tom-mah-zee′-nee], VINCENZO: *b.* Rome, Sept. 17, 1880. Composer. Studied at Santa Cecilia in Rome and under Bruch in Germany. He has composed 2 operas, a ballet (on music by Domenico Scarlatti), orchestral suites and symphonic poems, choral settings of poems by Dante and others, chamber music, piano pieces and songs, and has published essays on music.

Ton. (1) *Fr.* [tōn]. (*a*) Key, mode. (*b*) Pitch. (*c*)=TONE (1). *Demi-ton*, semitone. (*d*) *Ton de rechange*, crook (of a brass instrument).

(2) *G.* [tone]. (*a*) Sound. *Tondichter*, lit. "poet in sound," *i.e.* composer. (*b*) Note. (*c*) *Ganzton*=TONE (1). *Halbton*, semitone. (*d*) Quality of sound. *Tonfarbe*, tone-colour. (*e*) *Kirchenton*, church mode.

Tonal Answer. *v.* FUGUE.

Tonality. *v.* KEY, POLYTONALITY.

Tonart [tone′-arrt], *G.* Key, mode.

Tondichtung [tone′-di*sh*-tŏŏng], *G.* Tone-poem. *v.* SYMPHONIC POEM.

Tone. (1) The interval of a major second, *e.g.* between C and D, or E♭ and F, sometimes known as a whole tone. It may be subdivided into two semitones. Some 20th-cent. composers have divided it still further into quarter-tones and sixths of a tone, which can be played accurately on string instruments and the trombone but not on other instruments as normally constructed. On keyboard instruments the interval of a tone is always the same. If the major scale, however, is based on the notes of the HARMONIC SERIES there are slight differences according to the position of the notes in the scale. Thus in the scale of C major the ratio between C and D is 8:9, between D and E 9:10. The first of these intervals (C to D) is called in acoustics a major tone, the second (D to E) a minor tone. It is unfortunate that the terminology is ambiguous, "major" and "minor" being also used in quite another sense to distinguish intervals differing by a semitone, *e.g.* major third (four semitones) and minor third (three semitones), as well as the major and minor scales. *v.* KEY, MAJOR, MINOR, SCALE, SECOND.

(2) In America a musical note. In England used in this sense only in acoustics, *e.g.* a pure tone (a note without upper partials or overtones), resultant tone (a note produced by the combination of the frequencies of two other notes). *v.* ACOUSTICS.

(3) Quality of sound, *e.g.* good tone, harsh tone, brittle tone.

(4) In PLAINSONG a melodic formula used for the recitation of the psalms, canticles and other parts of the liturgy (*L.* tonus). There are eight ordinary psalm-tones, corresponding to the eight MODES, and most of them have a number

of alternative endings, *e.g.* in the SARUM RITE:

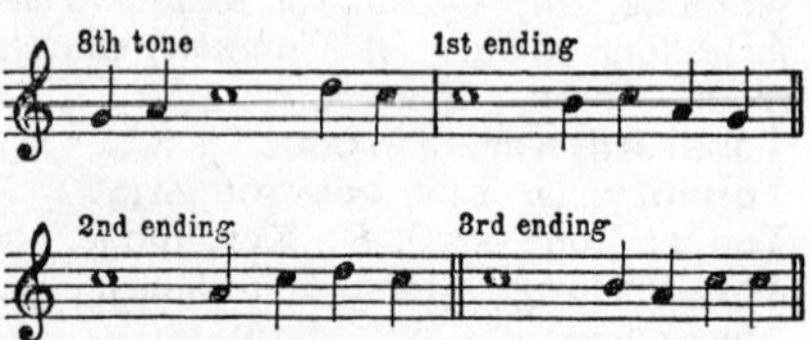

v. PSALMODY, TONUS PEREGRINUS.

(5) In the 17th cent. used also in the sense of "key," *e.g.*:

> "If wee say a lesser Third consists of a Tone, and a Semi-tone ; here by a Tone is ment a perfect Second, or as they name it a whole note : But if wee aske in what Tone is this or that song made, then by Tone we intend the key which guides and ends the whole song."
>
> (Campion, *A New Way of making fowre parts in Counter-point*, *c.* 1618, printed in *Campion's Works*, ed. P. Vivian, p. 192).

Tone Cluster. A group of notes on the piano played simultaneously with the forearm, elbow or fist. This method of performance was first introduced in 1912 by the American composer Henry Cowell.

Tone-Colour (*Fr.* timbre, *G.* Klangfarbe). The characteristic quality of tone of an instrument or voice. The effective combination of tone-colours is a chief part of the art of ORCHESTRATION. The investigation of the physical basis of tone-colour is a part of ACOUSTICS. The tone-colour of a note depends on the number, selection, and relative strengths of the overtones of which it is composed. In the flute and in the flue pipes of the organ the lower harmonics are relatively strong; the quality of reed instruments is determined by the relative strength of certain of the higher harmonics. Further, the tone quality of any individual instrument, *e.g.* a particular violin, depends on the extent to which the vibrations of the body of the instrument are in resonance with the overtones produced by the strings. The range in which these vibrations occur, which is a constant factor in each instrument, is called the "formant" of the tone quality of the instrument.

Tone-Poem. *v.* SYMPHONIC POEM.

Tone-Row. *v.* TWELVE-NOTE SYSTEM.

Tonic. The first note of a scale, which is its key-note and the centre of its tonality, and the key-note of compositions written in that tonality.

Tonic Sol-fa. A system of ear-training and sight-singing in which the notes are sung to syllables and the ear is trained to recognise and reproduce, through the syllables, the intervals between the notes of the scale and between each note and the tonic. In the English system, established and taught by John Curwen, the tonic of a major scale is always *doh*, whatever the key ("movable *doh*"), whereas in the French *solfège* (*v.* SOLFEGGIO) the syllables are fixed ("fixed *doh*"), C being always *ut*. The tonic of a "natural" minor scale is *lah*, so that the same relation of intervals to syllables holds as in a major scale, and *ba* is used for the sixth degree of the ascending harmonic minor scale. The vowel *e* is used for sharps, and the vowel *a* for flats: *e.g.* in C major-A minor :

In tonic sol-fa notation the syllables are represented by their initial letters. The idea of tonic sol-fa and its syllables are derived from SOLMIZATION.

Tonkunst [tone'-co͝onst], *G.* Lit. "art of sound," *i.e.* music. *Denkmäler deutscher Tonkunst* (*q.v.*), Monuments of German Music.

Tonleiter [tone'-lite-er], *G.* Scale.

Tono [to'-no], (also *tuono*) *I.* (1) KEY, MODE, TONE. (2) Thunder.

Tonreihe [tone'-ry-er], *G.* Tone-row.

Tonstück [tone'-shtĕĕk], *G.* A piece of music.

Tonus Peregrinus [ton'-o͝oss perr-eg-ree′-nōōss], *L.* "The strange (or alien) tone." An additional psalm-tone to the 8 regular tones (*v.* PSALMODY), which is irregular in that the second half has a different dominant (reciting note) from the first half. In its Sarum form it is :

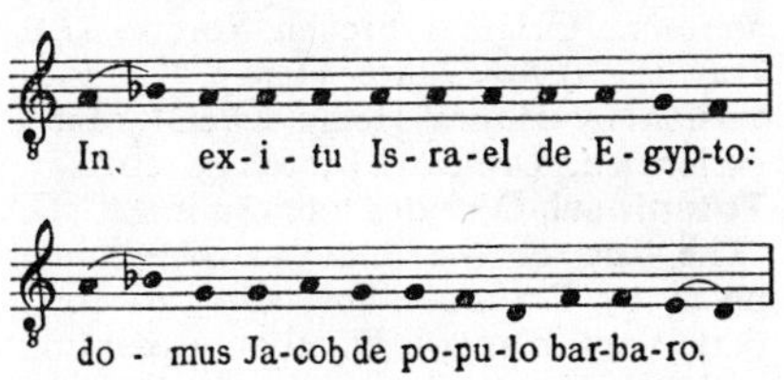

It is sung to Psalm 114 (113 in the Vulgate Bible), "In exitu Israel," and has been adapted as an Anglican chant.

Torchi [torr′-kee], LUIGI : *b.* Mondano (nr. Bologna), Nov. 7, 1858 ; *d.* Bologna, Sept. 18, 1920. Musicologist. Studied at the Liceo Musicale in Bologna, at the Royal Conservatorio in Naples and at the Leipzig Conservatorium under Reinecke and Jadassohn. He was teacher at the Rossini Conservatorio in Pesaro (1884) and at the Bologna Liceo Musicale (1891), where he also became librarian. He was founder of the *Rivista musicale italiana* (1894) and its editor until 1904. He wrote books on Wagner, and on Italian instrumental music of the 16th-18th cent., edited collections of Italian music, including *L'arte musicale in Italia* (7 vols.), and composed 2 operas, a symphony and sacred choral music.

Tordion [torrd-yōn], *Fr.* A lively French dance, current in the 15th and early 16th cent., used to form a contrast with the stately BASSE DANSE.

Torelli [to-rell′-lee] (Torrelli), GASPARO: 16th-17th cent. An Italian composer who taught at Borgo San Sepolcro, Lucca. He composed *I fidi amanti*, a pastoral fable in madrigal style for 4 voices (1600; reprinted in Torchi's *L'arte musicale in Italia*, iv), a book of madrigals for 5 voices (1598) and 4 books of *canzone* for 3 voices (1593-1608).

Torelli [to-rell′-lee], GIUSEPPE : *b.* Verona, Apr. 22, 1658 ; *d.* Bologna, Feb. 8, 1709. Composer and violinist. Violinist at the Church of S. Petronio in Bologna from 1686-95, when he visited Vienna, and leader of the court orchestra of the Margrave of Brandenburg-Ansbach from 1697-99, when he returned to Vienna. He lived in Bologna from 1701. Torelli and Corelli (*q.v.*) were the composers chiefly responsible for the development of the *concerto grosso.* In the concertos in Torelli's set of 6 sinfonias *a tre* and six concertos *a quattro* of 1692, the first publication to make this distinction between sinfonia and concerto, the two violin parts predominate, and are accompanied by simpler viola and continuo parts. This is also true of his *Concerti musicali* of 1698 for four-part strings with organ, in most of which he adopted the three-movement scheme Allegro-Adagio-Allegro. His set of *Concerti grossi con una Pastorale per il santissimo Natale*, published posthumously in 1709, contains 6 *concerti grossi* and 6 solo concertos. In the latter the themes of the violin solo are clearly contrasted with the *tutti* themes of the orchestra. The eighth concerto of this set (the third movement is reprinted in the *Historical Anthology*, No. 246) was arranged for organ by J. Gottfried Walther, a pupil of Johann Bernhard Bach ; the arrangement is published in *D.D.T.*, xxvii. Torelli also published a set of *Concerti da camera* (1686), a set of trio-sonatas (1686) and a set of sinfonias (1687).

Torrefranca [torr-reh-frahn′-cah], FAUSTO : *b.* Monteleone Calabro (now Vibo Valentia), Feb. 1, 1883 ; *d.* Rome, Nov. 26, 1955. Musicologist, originally an engineer. Lecturer in musical history, University of Rome, 1913 ; Conservatorio San Pietro, Naples, 1914. Librarian, Conservatorio San Pietro, Naples, 1915-23 ; Milan Conservatorio, 1924-40. Lecturer, Catholic University, Milan, 1930-5. Professor, Florence, 1941. In addition to numerous contributions to periodicals and composite volumes his published works include *La vita musicale dello spirito* (1910), *Giacomo Puccini e l'opera internazionale* (1912), and *Le origini italiane del romanticismo musicale* (1930).

Tosca [toss′-cah]. Opera in three acts by Puccini. Libretto by Giuseppe Giacosa and Luigi Illica (based on a play by Victorien Sardou). First performed, Rome, Jan. 14, 1900. Angelotti (an escaped prisoner) hides in a church where Mario Cavaradossi (an artist) is painting. Mario helps him to escape. When Scarpia (the chief of police) arrives on the scene he is suspicious and has Cavaradossi arrested and sent to the torture chamber. Scarpia, who has become attracted by Tosca (Cavaradossi's mistress), promises her lover's liberty in return for her favours. She finally grants pretended consent to his wishes, but as soon as he has written the orders for a mock execution of Cavaradossi she stabs him with a knife. At dawn she explains to Cavaradossi what has happened and tells him of the arrangements she has made for his escape after the mock execution. When the firing is over she hurries to his body and finds to her horror that he is dead. She realises her murder of Scarpia has been discovered. As a police agent attempts to arrest her she climbs the prison walls and leaps to her death.

Toscanini [toss-cah-nee′-nee], ARTURO: *b.* Parma, March 25, 1867; *d.* New York, Jan. 16, 1957. Conductor. Studied at the Parma Conservatorio and was appointed conductor of opera in Rio de Janeiro (1886) and of the Teatro Carignano in Turin (1886), where he later also conducted the municipal orchestra. He conducted at various European cities (1887-1898), was conductor of La Scala in Milan (1898-1903 and 1906-08) and of the Metropolitan Opera in New York (1908-15). He conducted the New York Philharmonic Orchestra (which was joined with the New York Symphony Orchestra in 1928) from 1926-36, at festivals in Bayreuth (1930 and 31) and at Salzburg (1933 and 1935-37), and was appointed conductor of the National Broadcasting Company Symphony Orchestra in 1937. One of the most eminent conductors of our time, he was renowned for the clarity and vigour of his interpretations.

H. TAUBMAN: *Toscanini* (1951).

Tosto [toss′-to], *I.* (1) Quick, rapid. *Più tosto*, faster.

(2) Quickly, soon. *Più tosto* or *piuttosto*, sooner, rather.

Toten Augen, Die [dee tote′-ĕn owg′-ĕn] (The Dead Eyes). Opera by d'Albert consisting of a prologue and one act. Original French libretto (*Les Yeux morts*) by Marc Henry (German version by Hanns Heinz Ewers). First performed, Dresden, March 5, 1916.

Toteninsel, Die [dee tote′-ĕn-in-zĕl], *G.* (The Isle of the Dead). Symphonic poem by Rachmaninov, Op. 29 (first performed in 1909), based on a painting with the same title by Arnold Böcklin. The painting has also inspired compositions by Max Reger, Andreas Hallen and other composers.

Totenmesse [tote′-ĕn-mess-er], *G.* Requiem Mass.

Totentanz [tote′-ĕn-tunts], *G.* "Dance of death." The title of a work by Liszt for piano and orchestra. *v.* DANSE MACABRE.

Tote Stadt, Die [dee tote′-er shtut] (The Dead Town). Opera in three acts by Korngold. Libretto by Paul Schott (from Georges Rodenbach's play *Bruges-la-Morte*). First performed, Hamburg and Cologne, Dec. 4, 1920.

Touch. (1) The manner in which a key on a keyboard instrument is depressed so as to produce the desired strength and quality of tone. Because the hammers of a piano are covered with felt a key which is depressed forcefully will cause the string to produce more overtones than a key which is depressed gently, thus affecting the quality of the tone. On a particular instrument the touch is governed by the weight of the action and by the depth of travel of the key. For a scientist's account of pianoforte tone and touch, see J. Jeans, *Science and Music* (1937).

T. MATTHAY: *The Act of Touch* (1926).

(2) Obsolete term for TOCCATA (*Fr.* touche).

Touche [toosh], *Fr.* (1) Key of a keyboard instrument.

(2) Fret (on a viol, lute, etc.).

(3) Fingerboard of a string instrument. *Sur la touche* (*G.* am Griffbrett, *I.* sul tasto), on the fingerboard, *i.e.* play

near, or actually above, the fingerboard, thus producing a rather colourless tone.

(4) 17th-cent. term for TOCCATA.

Tournemire [toorn-meer], CHARLES ARNOULD : *b.* Bordeaux, Jan. 22, 1870; *d.* Arcachon, Nov. 3, 1939. Composer and organist. Studied at the Paris Conservatoire and later under d'Indy. Organist of Sainte-Clotilde (1898) and teacher of chamber music at the Conservatoire. He gave many organ recitals, and composed 2 operas, 8 symphonies, choral works, chamber music, organ works, piano pieces and songs. In his organ music he was the leader of the movement of his time towards a more liturgical use of the organ, and composed in his *L'Orgue mystique* a set of pieces for the Office for 51 Sundays of the church year (*Offices de l'année liturgique*), based on their plainsong themes.

Tourte [toorrt], FRANÇOIS : *b.* Paris, 1747 ; *d.* there, Apr. 1835. Bowmaker. Studied his craft under his father, went into business with his elder brother, Xavier, and later by himself. He made many improvements in the violin bow, and was responsible for its modern form.

Tovey, DONALD FRANCIS : *b.* Eton, July 17, 1875 ; *d.* Edinburgh, July 10, 1940. Musical historian, pianist, composer and conductor. Studied under Parratt and Parry and at Balliol College, Oxford (1894-98). Played in London (1900-01), Berlin and Vienna (1901-02), and organized chamber music concerts in London. Reid professor, Edinburgh, 1914. Founded the Reid Orchestral Concerts, 1917. Knighted, 1935. He composed an opera, a symphony, a piano concerto, a cello concerto, 9 string quartets and other chamber music, anthems, piano pieces and songs. He wrote articles on music for the *Encyclopedia Britannica* (published in one volume, 1944), *A Companion to Bach's Art of Fugue* (1931), *A Companion to Beethoven's Pianoforte Sonatas* (1931), *Musical Form and Matter* (1934), *Essays in Musical Analysis* (7 vols., 1935-44), *The Main Stream of Music* (1938), *Beethoven* (1944), *Essays and Lectures on Music* (ed. H. Foss, 1949), *Normality and Freedom in Music* (1936), *The Integrity of Music* (1941) and *Musical Textures* (1941).

M. GRIERSON : *Donald Francis Tovey* (1952).

Toy. A term found occasionally in English virginal music of the 16th-17th cent. for a piece of a simple, playful character in dance rhythm.

Toye, (1) GEOFFREY : *b.* Feb. 17, 1889 ; *d.* June 11, 1942. Conductor and composer. Studied at the R.C.M. and conducted for London theatres, the Beecham Opera Company, the Royal Philharmonic Society Concerts (1918-19) and the D'Oyly Carte Opera. Manager of the opera at Sadler's Wells, 1931-34; managing director to the Royal Opera, Covent Garden, 1934-36. He composed an opera, a radio opera, 2 ballets, a masque (with his brother), a symphony and songs.

(2) JOHN FRANCIS : *b.* Winchester, Jan. 27, 1883. Music critic, composer and author. Brother of (1). From 1925 he was music critic for the *Morning Post* (later joined with the *Daily Telegraph*), from 1936-39 director of the British Institute in Florence. He returned to Florence in 1945. He has written *The Well-Tempered Musician* (1925), *Verdi* (1931), *Rossini* (1934), and a novel *Diana and the Two Symphonies* (1913). He has also composed a masque (with his brother) and songs.

Toy Symphony. An instrumental work with parts for toy instruments (cuckoo, rattle, etc.) added to the ordinary score. The earliest example, in three movements, is generally attributed to Haydn, though the music exists also as part of a *divertimento* attributed to Leopold Mozart. It is possible that the symphony as we know it is an arrangement by Haydn's brother Michael. Among later examples the best-known is that by Andreas Romberg.

Trabaci [trah-bah'-chee] (Trabacci), GIOVANNI MARIA: *b.* Montepeloso ; *d.* Naples, Sept. 1647. Composer, a pupil of Jean de Maque. Organist at the Royal Chapel in Naples (1603) and later choirmaster there. He composed motets for 5 to 8 voices (1602), 2 books of madrigals for 5 voices (1606, 1611), Masses, psalms and two books of *Ricercate* and other organ pieces (1603, 1615). 12 five-part motets, 4 six-part motets, 4 eight-part motets, and 2 Masses for double choir have been published in *Istituzioni e monumenti dell'arte musicale italiana*, v, ed. Guido Pannain (1934), and a *ricercar*, 2 *gagliarde*, two *partite*, a toccata, and a piece called *Consonanze stravaganti*, all from the *Ricercate, Canzone franzese, Caprice* . . . of 1603 in Torchi's *L'arte musicale in Italia*, iii.

Tracker. A flat strip of wood used as part of the mechanism which connected the key of an organ with the lid (" pallet ") which admitted wind to a pipe. Tracker action has now been universally replaced by some form of electric action.

Tract. A part of the Proper of the Mass, which is sung in penitential seasons at the point where the Alleluia is sung at other times, *i.e.* after the Gradual. The tracts are among the oldest part of plainsong, and are all either in the second or eighth mode. Their words are taken from the psalms, and in one case (" Qui habitabit " for the first Sunday in Lent) consist of a complete psalm. Their music may preserve the form in which psalmody was sung until the 4th-5th cent.

E. WELLESZ : *Eastern Elements in Western Chant* (1947), pp. 127-140.

Traetta [trah-et'-tah], TOMMASO MICHELE FRANCESCO SAVERIO : *b.* Bitonto (Terra di Bari), March 30, 1727; *d.* Venice, Apr. 6, 1779. Composer. Studied in Naples at the Conservatorio Santa Maria di Loreto under Durante and Porpora. *Maestro di cappella* and singing teacher at the ducal court of the Infante Felipe of Spain in Parma, 1758 ; director of the Conservatorio dell' Ospedaletto in Venice, 1765 ; and musical director at the court of Catherine II of Russia, 1768-74. He visited London and returned to Naples. He composed 42 operas, a *divertimento* for 4 orchestras, an oratorio for female choir, motets, a *Stabat Mater* for 4 voices and instruments, arias and duets. Extracts from his operas *Il Farnace* (1751), *I Tintaridi* (1760), *Ifigenia in Tauride* (1763), *Le Feste d'Imeneo* (1760), and *Antigona* (1772) are printed in *D.T.B.*, xiv (1), and from *La Sofonisba* (1762) in *D.T.B.*, xiv (1) and xvii.

Tragédie lyrique [tra-zhay-dee lee-reek], *Fr.* A 17th-cent. term for opera, especially those of Lully (also called *tragédie en musique*), all of which were settings of tragedies by Quinault and Corneille.

Tragic Overture. Brahms's *Tragische Ouvertüre*, Op. 81 (1880), a companion work to his *Akademische Fest-Ouvertüre*, Op. 80. It was not intended as the overture to any particular tragedy.

Tragic Symphony. Schubert's symphony No. 4 in C minor, composed in 1816 and entitled *Tragische Symphonie* by the composer.

Tranquillo [trahn-cweell'-lo], *I.* Calm.

Transcription. *v.* ARRANGEMENT.

Transition. (1) An incidental MODULATION.

(2) A link which involves MODULATION.

Transposing Instruments. The music for instruments whose " natural " key is not C is in some cases written as if it were, so that its written notes are higher or lower than their sounds. Such instruments are called transposing instruments, and include among common examples clarinets in B♭ and A, horns in F, cor anglais (which sounds a fifth lower than written), and trumpets in B♭. The solo for clarinet in A which begins at bar 200 of Mendelssohn's *Hebrides* overture appears thus in the score :

and sounds a minor third (A-C) lower, thus :

The reasons for this practice are historical. In the 18th cent. the technical limitations of the clarinet made it advisable to use instruments of different sizes (and hence different scales) according to the key of the piece. Since the player could hardly be expected to learn several different sets of fingering, the music was always written as for a clarinet in C, which sounds the same pitch as the written notes : clarinets of other sizes would automatically transpose the music to the appropriate pitch. Before long the clarinets in normal use were reduced to three : in C, in B♭ and in A. The superior tone of the B♭ and A instrument led to the disappearance of the C clarinet, but the system of fingering survived. Some players today, however, use only a B♭ clarinet, with an extra key which extends the compass a semitone lower to that of the A clarinet. The case of the cor anglais is similar to that of the clarinet : it is played with the same fingering as the oboe but sounds a fifth lower, so that an oboist can play it without having to learn an entirely new fingering.

Transposition in the case of horns and trumpets is effected by CROOKS or by bringing into use an extra piece of tubing. Crooks were a necessity before the invention of valves in the early 19th cent., since the instruments could play only the notes of the HARMONIC SERIES and hence were severely handicapped, if not actually helpless, in keys which were not identical with, or nearly related to, the pitch at which they were built. Crooks made available a whole series of transpositions of the harmonic series and so made available a wide range of keys. The horn in F, which is now the one in normal use, survived because of its tone-quality and general convenience. In consequence the modern horn-player is not only producing sounds a fifth lower than the written notes when playing from a part for horn in F, but in a great many classical works is also transposing as he plays. The trombone has always been written for in the orchestra as a non-transposing instrument, since its slide gives it a complete chromatic compass and no crooks were ever necessary. The practice of writing for brass instruments invented after the valve system varied. Cornets, for example, are generally written for in B♭ or A, but the bass tuba is always written for at the sounding pitch. In brass bands, however, all instruments except the bass trombone are treated as transposing instruments, and their parts are written in the treble clef (*v.* BRASS BAND).

Restoring mentally the written sounds of transposing instruments to their actual pitch is part of the training involved in reading from an orchestral SCORE. There is, however, no reason whatever why all the instruments in a score (other than the piccolo, double bassoon and double bass) should not be written for at the sounding pitch, transposition being reserved for the separate orchestral parts. The adoption of this practice, which has been favoured by Prokofiev and some other modern composers, would result in nothing more drastic than the abandonment of a pointless convention, and would enormously simplify the reading of difficult and complex works.

Transposition. The performance or writing down of music at another pitch, and therefore in a different key, from that in which it is originally written. Songs with piano are frequently published in three keys, high, medium, and low ; a good accompanist should, however, be able to transpose an accompaniment when necessary. This ability is needed also in reading the parts for TRANSPOSING INSTRUMENTS from an orchestral score. A. Schlick (1511) described an organ with movable manuals to effect transposition, and pianos with moveable keyboards were made during the 19th cent. Some of the harpsichords made by the Ruckers family between 1600 and 1650 had two manuals which differed in pitch by a fourth.

Trapassi [trah-pahss'-see], PIETRO. *v.* METASTASIO.

Trapp [trup], MAX: *b.* Berlin, Nov. 1, 1887. Composer and pianist. Studied at the Berlin Hochschule für Musik under Juon and Dohnányi and was appointed piano teacher and in 1913 a director at the Benda Conservatorium in Berlin.

He was teacher at the Hochschule (from 1920), a member of the Academy of Arts (1934-45) and became professor at the Berlin Conservatorium in 1951. He has composed 6 symphonies, a piano concerto, a cello concerto, a violin concerto, 3 orchestral concertos, 2 *divertimenti* and other orchestral works, chamber music, a cantata, incidental music for plays, songs and piano pieces.

Trauermarsch [trow′-er-marrsh], *G.* Funeral march.

Trauer-Ode [trow′-er-ode-*er*], *G.* (Funeral Ode). Cantata No. 198 by Bach (1727). Text by Johann Christoph Gottsched. Performed in Leipzig at the memorial ceremony of Christiane Eberhardine, Queen-Electress of Poland-Saxony, Oct. 17, 1727.

Trauerwalzer [trow′-er-vults-er], *G.* (Mourning Waltz). The title given by the publisher to a piano composition by Schubert, Op 9, No. 2 (1816; published 1821). It was also known as *Le Désir* and was often attributed to Beethoven, since a corrupt version of it was published under his name.

Traurig [trow′-*rish*], *G.* Sad.

Travers, JOHN : *b. c.* 1703 ; *d.* London, June 1758. Organist and composer. Chorister at St. George's Chapel, Windsor. Studied under Greene and Pepusch. Organist of St. Paul's, Covent Garden, London, *c.* 1725 ; later of Fulham Church ; Chapel Royal, 1737. He composed *The Whole Book of Psalms* for one to five voices with continuo for harpsichord (1750), anthems, services, a Te Deum, canzonets for two and three voices and voluntaries for organ or harpsichord.

Traversa [trah-vairr′-sah], *I.* 18th-cent. name for *flauto traverso,* the transverse flute (now known simply as *flauto,* flute).

Traviata, La [lah trah-vyah′-tah] (The Woman who was Led Astray). Opera in three acts by Verdi. Libretto by Francesco Maria Piave (after *La Dame aux camélias* by Alexandre Dumas the younger). First performed, Venice, March 6, 1853. (In the following synopsis the names of the characters in Dumas's play, which have been restored in E. J. Dent's English version, are printed in brackets.) Alfredo Germont (Armand Duval), having fallen in love with the courtesan Violetta (Marguerite Gautier), succeeds in persuading her to give up her life of pleasure and retire with him to the country. His father (Georges Duval), however, tells Violetta that her life with his son is a barrier to the marriage of Alfredo's sister and persuades her to leave him. Alfredo, believing that she has deliberately returned to her old life, follows her to Paris and publicly insults her at a ball. By the time he learns the truth it is too late : Violetta has been stricken by consumption and dies in his arms.

Traynour [tray-noor], *Fr.* A term referred to by the Italian 14th-cent. theorist Philippus de Caserta (*Tractatus de diversis figuris,* printed in Coussemaker's *Scriptores,* iii) as applied to the combination of different rhythmic groups, *e.g.* four notes against three, nine against two. He remarks that such combinations are commonly called *trayn* or *traynour* by the French.

Treble. (1) The highest voice in a choir, especially when sung by boys ; otherwise " soprano " is more often used. The term was first used in the 15th cent., as the equivalent of the Latin *triplex,* for the third voice above the tenor (counting the tenor itself as the first voice, as with the *triplum* of the 13th-cent. motet), the second voice being the " meane."

(2) The G clef on the second line :

is commonly called the treble clef. The C clef on the first line :

is known as the soprano clef.

Treble Viol. *v.* VIOL.

Tre corde [treh corr′-deh], *I.* " Three strings." A term used in piano music to indicate the release of the left-hand pedal. On grand pianos this normally has the effect of allowing the hammers to hit all the strings assigned to each note, instead of only one or two (*una corda*). *v.* CORDA.

Tregian, FRANCIS: *d.* Fleet Prison, London, 1619. Son of a Roman Catholic exile of the same name who had been deprived of his properties in Cornwall and died in Lisbon in 1608. The younger Tregian was educated at Eu and entered Douai College in 1586. From 1592 to 1594 he was chamberlain to Cardinal Allen in Rome. He returned to England to claim his father's lands, was convicted as a recusant in 1608-9 and committed to prison. While there he copied the manuscript of virginal music known as the Fitzwilliam Virginal Book, a manuscript (recently acquired by the British Museum and designated Egerton 3665) containing about 1200 vocal and instrumental works by English and Italian composers, and a manuscript (now in the Drexel Collection in the New York Public Library) containing motets and madrigals by English and Italian composers.

E. COLE: "In Search of Tregian," in *Music and Letters*, xxxiii (1952).

B. SCHOFIELD & THURSTON DART: "Tregian's Anthology," in *Music and Letters*, xxxii (1951).

Treibenreif [tribe'-ĕn-rife], PETER. *v.* TRITONIUS.

Tremblement [trũbl-mũ], *Fr.* Trill.

Tremolo [treh'-mo-lo], **Tremolando** [treh-mo-lahnd'-o], *I.* "Trembling." (1) On bowed instruments the rapid reiteration of a note by up and down movements of the bow (bowed tremolo), indicated thus:

or the rapid alternation of two notes of an interval (fingered tremolo), indicated thus:

or of the two notes of an interval with a movement of the bow for each (bowed and fingered tremolo), similarly indicated, but without the slur:

The bowed tremolo appeared early in the 17th cent. A famous, though not the earliest, example is in Monteverdi's *Combattimento di Tancredi e Clorinda*, composed in 1624. Schütz wrote a fingered tremolo in his "Freuet euch des Herren" in the second part of the *Symphoniae sacrae* (1647), indicating it thus:

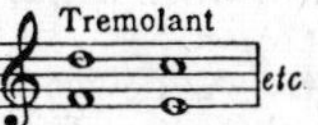

His "Von Gott will ich nicht lassen" in the same publication contains an example of an obsolete kind of tremolo (*Fr.* ondulé, *I.* ondeggiando) used in the 17th and 18th cent., and usually indicated thus:

Schütz wrote it:

(2) On the piano the tremolo is played as the rapid alternation of the notes of an interval or of a chord, *e.g.*:

from the accompaniment to Schubert's song *Die junge Nonne*, in which the right hand plays tremolando throughout.

(3) In singing, the term "tremolo" is often used of the wavering of pitch in a single note which corresponds to the VIBRATO on stringed instruments. It is properly applied to the rapid reiteration of a single note—a practice current in the 17th cent., when it was known as the *trillo* (*v.* TRILL).

Tremulant. A device used on the organ to produce an effect resembling a VIBRATO by alternately increasing and decreasing the wind pressure. Though it has recently acquired an unsavoury reputation by mixing with bad company, it has a reputable history. Scheidt considered it an asset to the organ, and imitated its effect in his *Tabulatura nova* (1624) thus:

Later it was used on organs in France and Germany. Bach's organ at Arnstadt had a tremulant, and in his specification of the work to be done on the organ at Mühlhausen (1708) he suggested that the tremulant be "made to vibrate properly."

Trent Codices. Six manuscript volumes (now numbered 87-92) of 15th-cent. music were discovered by Haberl in the chapter library of the Cathedral of Trent and a further volume (No. 93) in 1920. They form the largest extant collection of music of the period, comprising over 1500 sacred and secular pieces by some 75 French, English, Italian and German composers. Selections from them have been published in *D.T.Ö.*, vii, xi (1), xix (1), xxvii (1), xxxi and xl.

Trepak [trep-ahk']. A Cossack dance in quick 2/4 time which occasionally appears in works of Russian composers, *e.g.* in Tchaikovsky's "Invitation to the Trepak," No. 18 of the *Eighteen Pieces* for piano, Op. 72.

Trésor Musical [tray-zorr mēē-zee-cull], *Fr.* *v.* MALDÉGHEM.

Triad. A chord of three notes, the highest making the interval of a fifth (perfect, diminished or augmented) with the lowest, while the middle note is a third (major or minor) above the lowest. These intervals give their names to four different triads:

(1) Major triad (major third and perfect fifth), *e.g.*:

(2) Minor triad (minor third and perfect fifth), *e.g.*:

(3) Diminished triad (minor third and diminished fifth), *e.g.*

(4) Augmented triad (major third and augmented fifth), *e.g.*:

v. CHORD, HARMONY, INVERSION.

Trial by Jury. Comic opera in one act by Sullivan. Libretto by William Schwenk Gilbert (the only Gilbert and Sullivan opera without spoken dialogue). First performed, London, March 25, 1875.

Triangle (*G.* Triangel, *I.* triangolo). A percussion instrument consisting of a steel bar bent to the shape of a triangle, which is struck with a steel beater. It was one of the instruments adopted from JANISSARY MUSIC in the 18th cent. *e.g.*, by Mozart in *Die Entführung*. Liszt wrote for it solo in his piano concerto in E♭.

Tricinium [trick-in'-i-ŏŏm], *L.* (from *tres*, three, and *canere*, to sing). A title used in the 16th and early 17th cent. for a short three-part piece, corresponding to BICINIUM for a two-part piece, as in

Rhau's collection *Tricinia tum veterum tum recentiorum in arte musica symphonistarum, latina, germanica, brabantica & gallica* (1542). A tricinium on "Ein feste Burg" from Calvisius's *Tricinia ; ausserlesene teutsche Lieder mit dreyen Stimmen zu singen, und sonst auff Instrumenten zu üben* (1603) is printed in Schering's *History of Music in Examples*, No. 160.

Triebschener Idyll [treep'-shĕn-er ee-deel'], *G. v.* SIEGFRIED IDYLL.

Trill (*Fr.* cadence, tremblement, trille, *G.* Triller, *I.* gruppo, trillo). (1) An ornament consisting of the rapid alternation of a note with the note a second above (also known as " shake "). It occurs in English choral music early in the 16th cent. :

RICHARD DAVY, *O Domine coeli terraeque* (c. 1500)

which may be interpreted as an ornamentation of

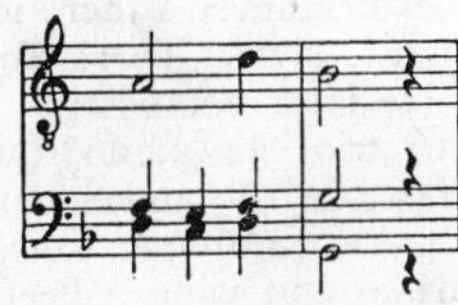

and later in instrumental music, most frequently as an ornamentation of the suspension in a cadence, *e.g.* :

JOHN BULL, *Queen Elizabeth's Pavan* (c. 1600)

In the 17th and 18th cent. the trill was begun on the upper note, and was indicated *tr* or ꟿ or 𝆖 or ⫽ (Purcell), *e.g.* :

played :

It might also begin with the upper appoggiatura, *e.g.* :

played :

with the lower appoggiatura, *e.g.* :

played :

or with a turn, *e.g.* :

played :

and might end with a turn, *e.g.* :

played :

The number of notes in a trill depended on the length of the note (it could be played as a turn if the note were very short), and the turn was frequently used to end it, whether indicated or not. This is also true of the modern trill, introduced early in the 19th cent., which is begun on the principal note, *e.g.*:

played :

unless the beginning on the upper note is indicated by a grace note.

(2) In the Italian terminology of the early 17th cent. the trill was called *gruppo* or *tremolo*, and the term *trillo* (English "plain shake") denoted the rapid reiteration of a note, given thus by Caccini (1602) :

In his *Madrigales and Ayres* of 1632 Walter Porter gave this explanation :

> "In the Songs which are set forth with Division where you may find many notes in a place after this manner
>
> 
>
> in rule or space they are set to express the *Trillo*."

v. also PRALLTRILLER, SCHNELLER.

Trillo del Diavolo, Il [eel treel′-lo del dyah′-vo-lo], *I.* (The Devil's Trill). The title of a violin sonata in G minor by Tartini (published posthumously in J. B. Cartier's *L'Art du violon*, 1798), which is supposed to have been inspired by a dream. In the dream he sold his soul to the devil, who proceeded to give a remarkable performance on the violin. When Tartini woke he attempted to write down what he heard, but the result was far inferior. The title alludes to an extended passage in the last movement.

Trio. (1) A composition for three parts, *e.g.* the trio sonata (*v.* SONATA) of the baroque period for two instruments and continuo, and Bach's trio sonatas for organ.

(2) The middle section of a minuet or scherzo after which the first section is repeated. Such a trio was written earlier in three parts, as are the first trio (for two oboes and bassoon) and the second trio (for two horns and oboes) of the minuet in Bach's first Brandenburg concerto. The title was kept after the custom of writing in three parts had been dropped.

(3) An instrumental or vocal piece for three performers. The most frequent instrumental type is the piano trio (piano, violin, cello), which in its earliest state (*e.g.* J. C. Bach's *Six Sonates, pour le Clavecin, accompagnées d'un Violon ou Flûte Traversière et d'un Violoncelle*, Op. 2, 1763) was a keyboard sonata with optional violin and cello. The main interest of Haydn's trios, although most of them were written late in his life, is in the piano part. This is less so in Mozart's trios, and in Beethoven's there is a true chamber music style. There are many examples by later composers. Haydn wrote three trios for piano, flute and cello, Mozart one trio and Schumann a set of four pieces (*Märchenerzählungen*) for piano, clarinet and viola ; Beethoven's Op. 11 is for piano, clarinet and cello, Brahms's Op. 114 for piano, clarinet and cello, and his Op. 40 for piano, violin and horn.

Other types of instrumental trio are the string trio (violin, viola and cello ; 21 or more by Haydn, 5 by Beethoven, 1, the *Divertimento*, K.563, by Mozart, 2 by Hindemith), the woodwind trio (*e.g.* Mozart's 5 *Divertimenti* for two clarinets and bassoon, K.App.229, Beethoven's Op. 87 for two oboes and English horn), and the trio for woodwind and strings (*e.g.* 9 by Haydn for two flutes and cello, 1 by Reger for flute, violin and viola, Debussy's sonata, and Bax's *Elegy* for flute, viola and harp).

Triole [tree-ole′-er], *G.*, **Triolet** [tree-oll-ay], *Fr.* Triplet.

Trionfo del Tempo e del Disinganno, Il [eel tree-on′-fo dell tem′-po eh dell deez-een-gahn′-no,] (The Triumph of Time and Enlightenment). Oratorio by Handel. Text by Cardinal Benedetto Pamfili. First performed, Rome, 1708; revised version (*Il trionfo del Tempo e della Verità*), London, Apr. 4, 1737. *v.* TRIUMPH OF TIME AND TRUTH.

Trionfo di Dori, Il [eel tree-on′-fo dee-do′-ree], *I.* (The Triumph of Doris). An anthology of 29 Italian madrigals by various composers, first published in Venice in 1592. The refrain "Viva la bella Dori" (Long live the fair Doris) is common to all the poems. The English anthology *The Triumphes of Oriana* (ed. by Thomas Morley) is presumably an imitation of the Italian publication. *v.* TRIUMPHES OF ORIANA.

Tripla. *v.* NACHTANZ.

Triple Concerto. A concerto for three solo instruments with orchestra, *e.g.* Beethoven's Op. 56 for piano, violin, cello and orchestra.

Triple Counterpoint. When three parts are so written that they may be disposed in any order, *i.e.* so that each will make a good bass to the others, they are in triple counterpoint. For example, the subject and the two counter-subjects of Bach's Fugue in C♯ minor in the first book of the *Forty-Eight* appear in these three ways in the course of bars 48-80:

Triple Croche [tree-pler crosh], *Fr.* Demisemiquaver.

Triplet (*Fr.* triolet, *G.* Triole, *I.* terzina). A group of three notes which is to be performed in the time of two: for an example *v.* HEMIOLA. For the relation of its rhythm to the rhythm of a dotted note in the 18th cent. *v.* DOT.

Triple Stop. A chord of three notes played on a bowed string instrument by using three adjacent strings.

Triple Time. Time in which the number of beats in the bar is three, *e.g.* 3/8, 3/4, 3/2. If the beats are divisible by two, the time is "simple"; if they are divisible by three, it is "compound," *e.g.*:

Simple triple time:

Compound triple time:

Triple Tonguing. A means of achieving rapid articulation on the flute and brass instruments. It is similar to DOUBLE TONGUING, but is used for groups of three notes, for which the series of consonants T-K-T is articulated in rapid succession.

Triplum [trip′-loom], *L.* The third part above the tenor, counting the tenor itself as the first part, in the organum of the late 12th cent. and in the motet of the 13th cent. For an example *v.* PEROTIN.

Tristan und Isolde [trist'-un ŏŏnt ee-zolld'-er] (Tristram and Iseult). Opera in three acts by Wagner. Libretto by the composer. First performed, Munich, June 10, 1865. Tristan, nephew of King Marke of Cornwall, has been sent to Ireland to bring back Isolde to be his uncle's bride. He is no stranger to her, since on a previous occasion she had tended him when he was severely wounded, in spite of the fact that he had killed her lover. Now, stung by what she considers to be Tristan's ingratitude and in despair at the thought of her unwelcome marriage, she proposes that both she and Tristan should drink a poisonous draught. Her attendant Brangäne, however, substitutes a love-philtre. In the palace gardens in Cornwall they declare their love, while the king is away on a hunting expedition. He returns to find them in each other's arms. A fight ensues between Tristan and Melot, one of the king's knights. Tristan, severely wounded, is taken off to Brittany by the faithful Kurwenal. While his master lies by the shore in a feverish delirium, Kurwenal waits impatiently for Isolde, whom he has summoned from Cornwall. When she arrives, Tristan is so overcome by excitement that he tears off his bandages and collapses. A second ship arrives with the king and his attendants. Kurwenal, expecting a new attack, kills Melot and himself falls dead by Tristan's side. Marke has come to offer forgiveness, but it is too late. Tristan is dead, and Isolde, having sung for the last time the melody of their love, sinks to rest on his body.

Tritone. The interval comprising three whole tones, *i.e.* the augmented fourth. In EQUAL TEMPERAMENT it is identical in sound (though not in function) with its inversion, the diminished fifth, each interval representing exactly half an octave. The difference in function can be represented by examples of resolution. Thus :

is in the key of C and resolves thus :

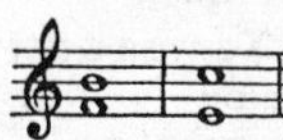

If by a change of notation it is written as a diminished fifth :

it is in the key of F♯ and resolves thus :

The tritone or its inversion occurs most often as part of a dominant seventh chord, or of the chord on the leading note, *e.g.*:

in the key of C.

The tritone and its inversion were normally avoided in plainsong and, generally speaking, in medieval polyphony, though it is not certain to what extent singers supplied accidentals (*v.* MUSICA FICTA) in the many cases where it occurs melodically in one part or as an interval between two parts.

Tritonius [trit-on'-i-ŏŏss], PETRUS (Peter Treibenreif) : *b.* Bozen, *c.* 1475. Composer. Studied in Ingolstadt under the humanist Conrad Celtes, at whose suggestion he composed four-part settings of Horace's Odes *c.* 1497. He lived in Vienna as teacher of singing and instrumental music, was director of the Latin school at Bozen from 1508 and settled in Schwatz (nr. Innsbruck) in 1521. His odes, which were composed in simple homophonic style in rhythms governed by the metre of the verse, were printed by Öglin in Augsburg in 1507. An example is reprinted in Schering's *History of Music in Examples*, No. 73.

Trittico, Il [eel treet'-tee-co] (The Triptych). A group of three one-act operas by Puccini—*Il tabarro* (libretto by Giuseppe Adami), *Suor Angelica* (libretto by Giovacchino Forzano), and *Gianni Schicchi* (libretto by Forzano). First performed, New York, Dec. 14, 1918.

Triumph of Time and Truth, The. Oratorio by Handel. Text translated by Thomas Morell from Handel's earlier work *Il trionfo del Tempo e della Verità* (1737), a revision of the still earlier *Il trionfo del Tempo e del Disinganno* (1708). Several of the movements were adapted from *Il trionfo del Tempo* and other works.

Triumphes of Oriana, The. A collection of 25 five-part and six-part madrigals, perhaps in honour of Queen Elizabeth I, edited by Thomas Morley and published in 1601. The anthology, in which each madrigal ends with the refrain :

> " Then sang the shepherds and nymphs of Diana:
> Long live fair Oriana,"

was no doubt suggested by the Italian collection *Il trionfo di Dori* (1592), in which each piece has the refrain " Viva la bella Dori." Modern ed. by E. H. Fellowes in *E.M.S.*, xxxii. *v.* TRIONFO DI DORI.

Triumphlied [tree-o͝omf'-leet], *G.* (Song of Triumph). A composition by Brahms, Op. 55 (1870-71) for chorus, orchestra and organ *ad lib.* to words from the Revelation of St. John. It was composed to celebrate the German victory in the Franco-Prussian War.

Troilus and Cressida. Opera in three acts by Walton. Libretto by Christopher Hassall. First performed, London, Dec. 3, 1954.

Trojans, The. *v.* TROYENS.

Tromba [trom'-bah], *I.* Trumpet. *Tromba cromatica*, *tromba ventile*, valve trumpet. *Tromba da tirarsi*, slide trumpet (*v.* TRUMPET).

Tromba marina [trom'-bah mah-ree'-nah], *I.* (*Fr.* trompette marine, *G.* Trumscheit, Nonnengeige). A bowed instrument, used from the 15th to the 18th cent., which was in effect a monochord with a tapering body about 6 ft. long. The string was touched so as to produce harmonics and bowed between the finger (or thumb) and the peg ; hence its notes, which had a soft trumpet-like quality, were those of the harmonic series. Their sound was accompanied by the drumming of the bridge (one leg of which was shorter than the other) against the soundboard, and by the sound of a large number of sympathetic strings which were inside the soundbox. The instrument has no traceable connection with the sea, and the reason for its name has not been definitely explained. It was used by nuns until late in the 18th cent. (hence the German name *Nonnengeige*, " nuns' fiddle "). Alessandro Scarlatti wrote a passage in his opera *Mitradate Eupatore* (1707) in which two muted trumpets with timpani are echoed by two tromba marinas with timpani. Two concertos of Vivaldi said to be for tromba marinas are actually for two violins imitating the sound of tromba marinas (*Violini in tromba marina*). Pepys records on Oct. 24, 1667 :

> " To Charing Cross, there to see Polichinelli. But it being begun, we in to see a Frenchman at the house where my wife's father last lodged, one Monsieur Prin, play on the trump-marine, which he did do beyond belief."

v. F. W. GALPIN, ' Monsieur Prin and his Trumpet Marine " in *Music and Letters*, xiv (1933), p. 18.

Trombetta [trom-bet'-tah], *I.* (diminutive of *tromba*). (1) An old name for the trumpet used by some 17th-cent. composers (*e.g.* Buxtehude).

(2) Given by Praetorius in his *Syntagma Musicum* (1618-19) as one of the Italian names for the tenor trombone (*gemeine rechte Posaune*). He also gives *trombetta piccola* as a name for the alto trombone.

Trombetti [trom-bet'-tee], ASCANIO. 16th-17th cent. Italian composer who was in the service of the Signoria of Bologna. He composed motets in 5 to 12 parts for voices and instruments (Venice, 1589), 2 books of madrigals for 4 and 5 voices (Venice, 1583, 1586) and *Napolitane* for 3 voices (Venice, 1573).

Tromboncino [trom-bon-chee'-no], BARTOLOMMEO: *b.* Verona, second half of the 15th cent. Composer, singer and lute-player. He lived at Mantua (1487-95), where he was at the ducal court, went to Venice (1495), was attached to the courts of Vicenza and Casale (1499) and lived again in Mantua from 1501-13, when he went to Ferrara. He murdered his wife Antonia and her lover in 1499.

He composed *frottole* for 4 voices, canzonets, madrigals, 9 settings of the Lamentations, and other church music. Many of his compositions were published by Petrucci. Examples of his settings of various forms of poetry (*oda*, sonnet, *canzon*, *ballata*, madrigal, *ottava rima* and *strambotto*) are printed in the third volume of A. Einstein, *The Italian Madrigal* (1949), and a *frottola* in Schering's *History of Music in Examples*, No. 69.

Trombone, *E.Fr.* [trôn-bon] *I.* [trom-bo′-neh] (*G.* Posaune). Lit. "large trumpet" (from *tromba*). A brass instrument with a cylindrical bore expanding into a bell, played with a cup-shaped mouthpiece and fitted with a "slide" in the form of a U-shaped tube drawn over the fixed tubes. The movement of the slide changes the length of the air-column to a different fundamental note in each of its seven positions. The lowest of these fundamental notes, however, are hardly practicable. The octaves (or second harmonics) of the seven fundamentals are:

Above each of these the player can produce further notes in the respective HARMONIC SERIES.

Two sizes of trombone are now used in the orchestra, forming a trio of two tenors and a bass, except in France, where three tenors are usual. The tenor trombone has a range from

plus three "pedal notes" (the fundamentals of its first three positions):

The bass trombone in F or G has a range from:

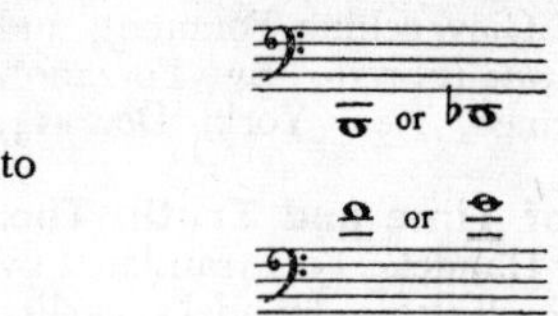

Music for the tenor trombone is written in the tenor or bass clef, music for the bass trombone exclusively in the bass clef. Being rather unwieldy, the bass trombone is now largely replaced by the tenor-bass, a compromise in the form of a tenor with a larger bore and a valve which lowers the pitch a fourth when required. The alto trombone is obsolete, though it has been revived for the performance of old music. The contrabass trombone, introduced into the orchestra by Wagner, has four parallel tubes and a double slide, and sounds an octave below the tenor.

The slide is the oldest method of changing the air-column of a brass instrument. The trombone was devised in the 15th cent., and was written for by Giovanni Gabrieli (*Sacrae Symphoniae*, *c.* 1600) and occasionally by Bach and Handel. Gluck used a group of trombones in *Orfeo*, *Alceste* and *Iphigénie en Tauride*, and Mozart in *Don Giovanni* and *The Magic Flute*. They had been used in combination with voices in 16th-cent. church music, and perhaps for that reason were associated in stage music with the supernatural, as in Monteverdi's *Orfeo*, and later in Gluck and Mozart. Since Beethoven, who used three trombones in the finale of the fifth symphony and in the ninth symphony, the group of three has been regularly included in the orchestra.

The invention of VALVES in the early 19th cent. led to the application of this system to the trombone, as well as to the trumpet and horn. But though valve trombones are still found in some military bands on the Continent, and were at one time used in orchestras (*e.g.* in Italy and Belgium), they have not succeeded in supplanting the slide trombone in normal orchestral use. The two disadvantages of the slide trombone—the absence of a complete legato (except between two related harmonics) and the distance which sometimes separates consecutive notes—are offset by its superior tone and the possibility of perfect intonation.

A. CARSE : *Musical Wind Instruments* (1939).

Trommel [trom′-ĕl], *G.* Drum. *Grosse Trommel*, bass drum ; *kleine Trommel*, side drum.

Trompete [trom-pate′-*er*], *G.* Trumpet. *Ventiltrompete*, valve trumpet ; *Zugtrompete*, slide trumpet.

Trompette [trôn-pet], *Fr.* (1) Trumpet. *Trompette à pistons*, valve trumpet.

(2) *Trompette marine.* *v.* TROMBA MARINA.

Trope. Additional words, or music and words, which preceded, were interpolated in, or followed a piece of liturgical plainsong. Many such additions were written between the 9th and the 12th cent., for example by Tuotilo (*d.* 915), a monk of St. Gall, who wrote tropes but was not their originator. When words were added, they were adapted to the existing melodies, as in the SEQUENCE, which was at first a trope of the Alleluia and afterwards became an independent form of hymn. All the parts of the Ordinary of the Mass, excepting the *Credo*, were troped. The *Kyrie*, for example, which still retains the name *Conditor Kyrie omnium* although it has been deprived of its trope since the 16th century :

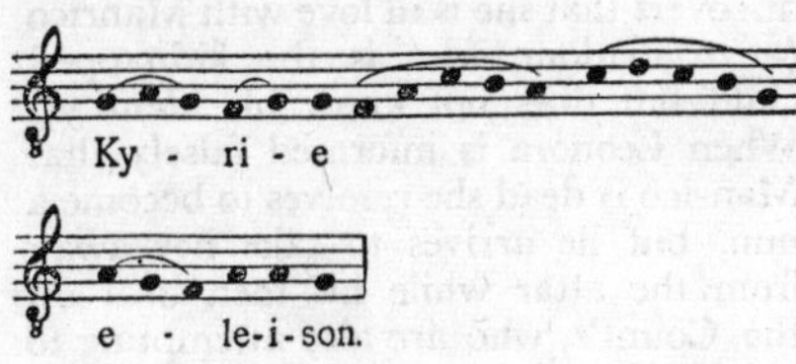

was sung at High Mass on Christmas Day in the Sarum rite in this form :

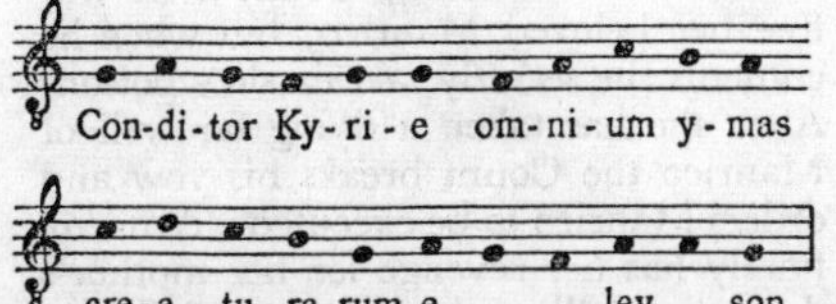

Other parts of the liturgy which were troped included the *Ite missa est*, sung at the end of Mass, and the *Benedicamus Domino* sung at the end of Mass in Lent and Advent and at the end of the offices. Many of the early examples of polyphony were settings of tropes, and may be regarded as musical tropes or elaborations, based on the liturgical chant. A trope, beginning *Virgo mater ecclesiae*, to the antiphon *Salve Regina* (*q.v.*) was customary in England from *c.* 1400 to the Reformation, and was included in virtually all the polyphonic settings of the *Salve regina* by English composers written during that period. All tropes were eliminated from the Roman liturgy by the decrees of the Council of Trent in the 16th cent.

The liturgical drama, from which the later medieval mystery plays developed, sprang directly from the trope. The trope to the Introit for Christmas, *Hodie cantandus est*, which is attributed to Tuotilo (printed in Schering's *History of Music in Examples*, No. 3) was in the form of a dialogue. In the 10th cent., while the trope to the Introit for Easter, *Quem quaeritis*, was sung (*v.* Schering, No. 8), the story of the three Marys coming to the tomb was enacted. This is considered to be the earliest liturgical play.

E. K. CHAMBERS : *The Mediaeval Stage* (2 vols., 1903).

W. H. FRERE : *The Winchester Troper* (1894).

E. WELLESZ : *Eastern Elements in Western Chant* (1947).

Troppo [trop′-po], *I.* Too much. *Allegro non troppo*, not too fast.

Troubadours [troo-ba-door], *Fr.* (*Prov.* trobadors). Poet-musicians of the early Middle Ages who lived in the south of France and wrote in the *langue d'oc* (generally called Provençal). The word *trobador* is clearly connected with the verb *trobar* (=*trouver*), " to find ": a suggested origin for both words is the Latin *tropus* (from *Gr.* τρόπος), " a song " or " tune " (which was used also in the special sense of TROPE). Many of the troubadours (though not all) were of aristocratic birth. The first whose songs have survived is Guillaume, Count of Poitiers (1071-1127), who became Duke of Aquitaine in 1087. Others who were famous were Marcabru (early 12th cent.) and Bernard de Ventadour (12th cent). The cultivation of lyrical song spread to the north of France in the late 12th cent., the word *trobador* being translated into its French equivalent *trouvère.*

The music of the troubadours and trouvères was monophonic ; but its melodic style had a considerable influence on the polyphonic motet of the 13th cent., though the actual quotation of anything more extensive than the melody of a *rondeau* is uncommon. Furthermore such poetical forms as the *ballade* and the *virelai* continued to be set as polyphonic *chansons* in the 14th and 15th cent. The majority of troubadour and trouvère melodies have come down to us in a form which gives no indication of their rhythm, no doubt because they were never sung in strict time. Most modern editors interpret the notation in the light of the rhythm of the words and transcribe the songs in one or other of the RHYTHMIC MODES. Such transcriptions, however, though practically convenient, should not be understood to imply a rigid observance of the written note-values.

The following facsimile editions of troubadour and trouvère manuscripts (in some cases with transcriptions) have been published :

P. AUBRY : *Le Chansonnier de l'Arsenal* (1909, incomplete).
J. BECK : *Le Chansonnier Cangé* (2 vols., 1927).
J. & L. BECK : *Le Manuscript du Roi* (2 vols., 1938).
A. JEANROY : *Le Chansonnier d'Arras* (1925).
P. MEYER & G. RAYNAUD : *Le Chansonnier français de Saint-Germain des Prés* (1892).
U. SESINI : *Le melodie trobadoriche nel canzoniere provenzale della Biblioteca Ambrosiana R.* 71 *sup.* (1942).

In German-speaking countries the art of the troubadours and trouvères was imitated by the MINNESINGER.

P. AUBRY : *Trouvères et troubadours* (1909; English ed., 1914).
J. BECK : *La Musique des troubadours* (1910).
T. GÉROLD : *La Musique au moyen âge* (1932).
G. REESE : *Music in the Middle Ages* (1940).
J. A. WESTRUP : "Medieval Song," in *New Oxford History of Music*, ii (1954).

Trouluffe (Truelove), JOHN. 15th-16th cent. English composer who wrote, apparently with Richard Smert, carols and other sacred pieces in two and three parts. The carols are printed in *Mediaeval Carols* (*Musica Britannica*, iv, 1952).

Trout Quintet (*G.* Forellenquintett). The popular name for Schubert's quintet in A major for violin, viola, cello, double bass and piano, composed in 1819 and published posthumously in 1829 as Op. 114. The fourth movement consists of variations on Schubert's song *Die Forelle* (The Trout).

Trouvères [troo-vair], *Fr.* *v.* TROUBADOURS.

Trovatore, Il [eel tro-vah-to′-reh] (The Troubadour). Opera in four acts by Verdi. Libretto by Salvatore Cammarano (based on a Spanish play by Antonio García Gutiérrez). First performed, Rome, Jan. 19, 1853. The story takes place in the 15th cent. in Biscay and Aragon. Believing that a gypsy had bewitched one of his sons, the Count di Luna ordered her to be burnt at the stake. Azucena (the gypsy's daughter), wishing to avenge her mother, attempts to kill the boy, but by a mistake kills her own child and so kidnaps the Count's son and brings him up as her son. Years later the young Count di Luna (the brother of the kidnapped child) falls in love with Leonora but discovers that she is in love with Manrico (a troubadour who is the kidnapped child but does not know his identity). When Leonora is informed falsely that Manrico is dead she resolves to become a nun, but he arrives to take her away from the altar while his men beat off the Count's, who are also attempting to kidnap her. The Count's men later capture Azucena and she is condemned to be burnt like her mother. When Manrico rushes to rescue her he is also captured. Leonora declares that she will give herself to the Count if he will free her beloved Manrico, but when he consents she secretly takes a slow poison. After she has taken a dying farewell of Manrico the Count breaks his vow and orders Manrico to be executed. Azucena finally has her revenge for her mother's death by telling the Count just before she dies that he has murdered his own brother.

Troyens, Les [lay trwa-yañ] (The Trojans). Opera in two parts by Berlioz (1856-8). Libretto by the composer (after Virgil). The two parts are: (1) *La Prise de Troie* (The Capture of Troy). 3 acts. First performed in German (*Die Eroberung Trojas*), Carlsruhe, Dec. 6, 1890. First performance of the original French text, Nice, Feb. 1891. (2) *Les Troyens à Carthage* (The Trojans at Carthage). 4 acts. First performed, Paris, Nov. 4, 1863. First performance of the complete work (in German), Carlsruhe, Dec. 6 & 7, 1890; first performance in French, Brussels, Dec. 26 & 27, 1906.

Trumpet. (1) A treble brass instrument with a cylindrical tube widening into a conical bell (which forms about a quarter of its length) and played with a cup-shaped mouthpiece (*Fr.* trompette, *G.* Trompete, *I.* tromba, clarino). In its natural form—*i.e.* without valves and hence able to produce only the notes of the HARMONIC SERIES based on a single fundamental—it was in use from the Middle Ages to the 19th cent. Until the 17th cent. it was restricted to ceremonial and military functions. The opening toccata of Monteverdi's *Orfeo* (1607) records in permanent form the 16th-cent. practice of beginning an entertainment with a fanfare of trumpets. With the growth of opera in the 17th cent. trumpets and timpani became orchestral instruments, used normally for scenes of a pompous and festal character. In Germany the instrument was cultivated by town musicians, who developed remarkable skill in playing in the highest register, where the harmonics make available a complete scale. The evidence of this accomplishment can be seen in Bach's elaborate, and often very difficult, trumpet parts.

In the 17th and early 18th cent. trumpets were normally made either in D or in C, or alternatively the D instrument was provided with a CROOK to lower its pitch to C (*v.* TRANSPOSING INSTRUMENTS). Hence the great mass of festal music of this period is either in C major or D major. The use of an F trumpet in Bach's second Brandenburg concerto is exceptional. With the change of style which occurred about the middle of the 18th cent. the practice of writing brilliant melodic parts for the trumpets disappeared, and they were reduced largely to reinforcing a tutti. For this purpose a wider range of keys was called for, and hence the number of crooks was increased.

The limitations of the natural trumpet led to various expedients designed to fill up the missing notes in its compass. The construction of an instrument in the shape of a horn, on which additional notes could be obtained by inserting the hand in the bell, had comparatively little success. But the slide trumpet (*Fr.* trompette à coulisse, *G.* Zugtrompete, *I.* tromba da tirarsi) was used in Germany in the early 18th cent. (*e.g.* in Bach's cantatas) and, in a slightly different form, was cultivated by English players in the early 19th cent. The nature of the slide mechanism made the instrument unsuitable for rapid passages; but it was able to play chorale melodies which would have been impossible (in a normal register) for the natural trumpet and Bach frequently used it for this purpose.

The keyed trumpet (*Fr.* trompette à clefs, *G.* Klappentrompete, *I.* tromba a chiavi), invented in the late 18th cent., was an attempt to fill up the gaps in the compass by piercing the tube with holes and fitting keys similar to those used for woodwind instruments. Haydn wrote a concerto for this instrument in 1796. It failed to survive the invention of the valve trumpet (*Fr.* trompette à pistons, *G.* Ventiltrompete, *I.* tromba ventile) in the early 19th cent. This, with certain modifications, is the instrument still in use (for the mechanism *v.* VALVE). The first composer to specify valve trumpets in a score appears to have been Halévy in his opera *La Juive* (1835). In spite of the fact that valves gave a complete chromatic compass composers continued until the end of the 19th cent. (and in some cases even later) to write for trumpets theoretically crooked in different keys. The instrument normally used in England to-day is in B♭, with a switch which lowers the pitch a semitone to A. It is (if in B♭) a minor sixth higher than the 18th-cent. D trumpet for which Bach wrote, and is therefore considerably shorter. Trumpets are also made in C, and many modern composers write for them, disregarding the fact that in most cases the parts will be played on B♭ trumpets. The compass of the C trumpet is from :

to

The compass of the B♭ trumpet is a tone lower, that of the A trumpet a minor third lower.

The success of the valve trumpet led to the construction of smaller and larger instruments. A small trumpet in D (an octave higher than the 18th-cent. trumpet in D) is widely used for the performance of the high trumpet parts in the works of Bach and other 18th-cent. composers and is popularly known as the Bach trumpet, in spite of the fact that it is completely different from the instrument for which he wrote. Wagner in the *Ring* demanded a bass trumpet, which is in all essentials a valve trombone with the following compass :

the notes being written an octave higher in the score.

J. E. ALTENBURG : *Versuch einer Anleitung zu heroisch-musikalischen Trompeter- und Pauker-Kunst* (1795 ; facsimile ed., 1911).

A. CARSE : *Musical Wind Instruments* (1939).

W. MENKE : *History of the Trumpet of Bach and Handel* (1934).

(2) Marine trumpet. *v.* TROMBA MARINA.

(3) Mock trumpet. An English name for the *chalumeau* or early clarinet. Walsh published four books for the mock trumpet between 1698 and *c.* 1707. *v.* CLARINET.

THURSTON DART : "The Mock Trumpet," in *Galpin Society Journal*, vi (1953).

Trumpet Voluntary. The popular name for a piece, falsely attributed to Purcell, which occurs among the harpsichord solos of Jeremiah Clarke (*c.* 1673-1707) under the title "The Prince of Denmark's March" (modern ed. in J. A. Fuller-Maitland, *At the Court of Queen Anne*).

Trumscheit [troŏm′-shite], *G. v.* TROMBA MARINA.

Tsarskaya Nevesta [tsahrr-sca′-ya nev-yess′-ta] (The Czar's Bride). Opera in three acts by Rimsky-Korsakov. Libretto by Lev Alexandrovich Mei. First performed, Moscow, Nov. 3, 1899.

Tschudi, BURKHARDT. *v.* SHUDI.

Tuba. (1) A brass instrument of the saxhorn type which has a conical bore and three to five valves, and uses a cup-shaped mouthpiece. There are three sizes : (a) a bass-cum-tenor size, also called EUPHONIUM (G. Barytonhorn), in B♭ with a range from

(b) a bass size a fourth or fifth lower, in F (the normal orchestral instrument) or E♭ (used in military and brass bands) with a range from

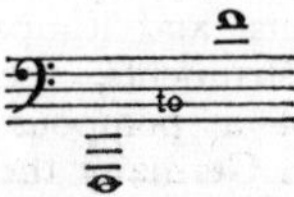

or

(c) a double-bass size an octave lower than the first, in B♭ with a range from

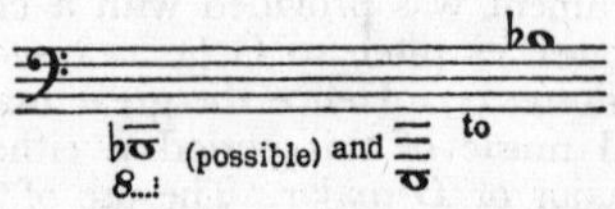

The two latter sizes are also called bombardon, or, if made in circular shape for marching, HELICON. Music for the tubas is normally written in the bass clef, with the actual sounds and key-signature (except in BRASS BAND music).

(2) The "Wagner tubas" designed for use in the *Ring* are a group of five instruments consisting of two pairs and a bass. The upper pair are modified horns, with a funnel-shaped mouthpiece, in B♭ with a range from

the lower pair similar instruments a fourth lower, in F, with a range from

to

Wagner wrote for these four as TRANSPOSING INSTRUMENTS; they are also used in Bruckner's last 3 symphonies. The bass of the group is a double-bass tuba.

A. CARSE : *Musical Wind Instruments* (1939).

(3) An organ stop of the reed type with a loud tone, chiefly used as a solo stop. The tuba of 8-ft. pitch is sometimes called *tuba mirabilis,* that of 4-ft. pitch a *tuba clarion.*

(4) *L.* [to͝ob'-a]. (a) Trumpet. *Tuba mirum,* the opening words of the verse of the *Dies irae* which begins "Tuba mirum spargens sonum" (the trumpet, spreading a marvellous sound). (b) The RECITING NOTE in the plainsong psalm tones.

Tucket. An Elizabethan term for a fanfare of trumpets (*G.* Tusch), a corruption of the Italian TOCCATA.

Tudor Church Music. An edition of church music by English composers of the 16th and early 17th cent. published in 10 vols. between 1923 and 1929. The contents are : Vol. I, Masses by Taverner ; Vol. II, English church music by Byrd ; Vol. III, Magnificats and motets by Taverner ; Vol. IV, Services and anthems by Orlando Gibbons ; Vol. V, Latin and English church music by Robert White ; Vol. VI, Latin church music by Tallis ; Vol. VII, Byrd's *Gradualia* I and II ; Vol. VIII, Responses, psalms, and services by Tomkins ; Vol. IX, Latin church music by Byrd ; Vol. X, compositions by Aston, Marbeck and Parsley. An appendix, containing supplements from sources discovered later, was published in 1948.

Tudway, THOMAS : *b. c.* 1650 ; *d.* London, Nov. 23, 1726. Chorister at the Chapel Royal under Blow from *c.* 1660 and lay vicar at St. George's Chapel, Windsor, in 1664. He was at Cambridge as organist (from *c.* 1670) and instructor of the choristers (1679-80) at King's College and organist at Pembroke College. Professor, Cambridge, 1705. For the Earl of Oxford he collected and edited 6 manuscript volumes of cathedral music by various composers (now in the British Museum). He composed a Te Deum (1720), anthems and other church music.

Tunder [to͝ond'-er] FRANZ : *b.* Burg auf Fehmarn, 1614 ; *d.* Lübeck, Nov. 5, 1667. Composer and organist. Organist at the court of Gottorp, 1632-41, and preceded his son-in-law, Buxtehude, as organist at the Marienkirche in Lübeck (from 1641), where he organized a group of instrumentalists for the church music. He composed sacred works for solo voice accompanied by one or more strings and organ, cantatas and other church music, chorale preludes, preludes, fugues and other pieces for organ. A selection of his church music was published in *D.D.T.*, iii. In the history of the Lutheran cantata his name is particularly associated with the form in which each verse of a chorale is based on the melody treated in a different way, a form sometimes called variation-cantata. An example is his setting of "Ein feste Burg" (*D.D.T.*, iii, p. 142). He also used chorale melodies as material for solo pieces accompanied by strings and organ continuo, as in his *Wachet auf* (*D.D.T.*, iii, p. 107).

Tune. *v.* MELODY.

Tuning. *v.* TEMPERAMENT.

Tuning-Fork (*Fr.* diapason, *G.* Stimmgabel, *I.* corista). A device for giving accurately the pitch of a single note, invented in 1711 by the trumpeter John Shore (*d.* 1752). The sound given by a tuning-fork is practically a pure note, without overtones.

Tunsted, SIMON: *b.* Norwich, 14th cent.; *d.* Bruisyard (Suffolk), 1369. He entered the Franciscan order at Oxford, studied theology, music and astronomy, and became head of the English branch of the Minorite Franciscans in 1360. He is the alleged author of *De quatuor principalibus musicae* (1351), a treatise on mensural music, printed in Coussemaker's *Scriptores*, iv, pp. 200-98.

Tuono [too-o'-no], *I.* *v.* TONO.

Turandot [too-rahn-doat', *E.* tew'-r'n-dot]. Opera in three acts by Puccini, completed by Alfano. Libretto by Giuseppe Adami and Renato Simoni (after Gozzi). First performed, Milan, Apr. 25, 1926. Turandot (the beautiful Princess of China) delivers a proclamation that she will marry any man of noble blood who can answer three riddles which she will ask: if he fails he will be beheaded. After the Prince of Persia has been condemned to be executed, Calaf (the disguised son of the dethroned Tatar King) announces that he will try the test. To the Princess's dismay he succeeds. Her father insists that she must marry him, but Calaf promises to release her if she can discover his identity by dawn. The Princess orders that everyone must spend the night trying to find out his name. When she discovers that Liu (a slave who is secretly in love with Calaf) knows the stranger, she demands that she be tortured until she reveals who he is. Liu stabs herself and finally Calaf himself tells the Princess that he is the enemy Tatar Prince. Turandot, overcoming her pride, suddenly realizes that she has at last fallen in love and declares to her father that his name is "Love."

Turba [toorr'-ba], *L.* Crowd. *v.* PASSION.

Turca, Alla [ahl'-lah toorr'-cah], *I.* "In the Turkish style." *v.* JANISSARY MUSIC.

Turges (Sturges), EDMUND. 15th-16th cent. composer. He composed a 3-part song celebrating the marriage (1501) of Prince Arthur and Catherine of Aragon and other secular songs, Masses, Magnificats and antiphons. Of his church music there have survived two settings of "Gaude flore virginali" (in the Eton choirbook), a particularly elaborate setting of the Magnificat (in the Caius College choirbook), and a *Kyrie* and *Gloria.*

Turina [too-ree'-nah], JOAQUÍN: *b.* Seville, Dec. 9, 1882; *d.* Madrid, Jan. 14, 1949. Composer, pianist and conductor. Studied in Seville, Madrid and in Paris under Vincent d'Indy at the Schola Cantorum (1905-14) and under Moszkowski. He settled in Madrid as teacher and critic. He composed operas, symphonic poems, incidental music for plays, chamber music, piano pieces and songs.

Türk [teerk], DANIEL GOTTLOB: *b.* Claussnitz (Saxony), Aug. 10, 1756; *d.* Halle, Aug. 26, 1813. Composer and writer on music. Studied in Dresden, and in Leipzig under J. A. Hiller, and became a violinist at the opera and in Hiller's orchestra. Cantor at St. Ulrich's, Halle, 1776; director of music at the university, 1778; organist at the Liebfrauenkirche, 1787. He published some useful text-books, including a *Klavierschule* (1789) and a treatise on figured bass (1791). His compositions include piano sonatas, symphonies, songs and church music.

F. T. ARNOLD: *The Art of Accompaniment from a Thorough-Bass* (1931).

Turn (*Fr.* doublé, double cadence, brisé, *G.* Doppelschlag, *I.* gruppetto). An ornament which makes a turn around a note, beginning with the note above. In its commonest forms it is indicated over a note thus:

and played thus:

or between two notes thus:

and played thus :

or thus :

played thus :

It may occasionally begin on the principal note, indicated by a grace note thus :

played

or be inverted, shown by the sign :

played

In music of the second half of the 18th cent. it may be more appropriate to play the first two notes of the turn more quickly than the others, in the manner preferred by C. P. E. Bach. In that case

would be played

The sign ≈, used by Couperin, means the usual form of TRILL ending with a turn.

Turner, WILLIAM: *b.* Oxford, 1651; *d.* London, Jan. 13, 1740. Composer and singer. Chorister at Christ Church, Oxford, and at the Chapel Royal. Gentleman of the Chapel Royal, 1669; vicar choral at St. Paul's and lay vicar at Westminster Abbey. He composed services, anthems, hymns, a masque, songs for plays, other songs, odes and catches.

Turnhout [tirrn'-howt], GERARD DE (Gheert Jacques): *b.* Turnhout (Belgium), *c.* 1520; *d.* Madrid, Sept. 15, 1580. Composer and singer. He was singer (1545) and *Kapellmeister* (1563) at Antwerp Cathedral, and from 1572 was attached to the court of Philip II at Madrid. He composed a book of motets for 5 and 6 voices (1568), Masses and *chansons*. His son, Jean de Turnhout, was *Kapellmeister* at the Royal Chapel in Brussels from 1618 and composed madrigals and motets.

Turn of the Screw, The. Opera in two acts by Britten. Libretto by Myfanwy Piper (after the novel by Henry James). First performed, Venice, Sept. 14, 1954.

Tusch [tŏosh], *G.* *v.* TUCKET.

Tutte le corde [toot'-teh leh corr'-deh], *I.* "All the strings." A term used in piano music to indicate the release of the left-hand pedal. On grand pianos this normally has the effect of allowing the hammers to hit all the strings assigned to each note, instead of only one or two (*una corda*). *v.* CORDA.

Tutti [toot'-tee], *I.*, now also *E.* [tŏot'-i]. "All" (pl.). Used, most often in concertos, to indicate an entrance of the full orchestra, as distinct from passages in which it is accompanying the soloist.

Twelfth. (1) The interval of an octave plus a fifth, *e.g.*:

(2) An organ stop of diapason quality and $2\frac{2}{3}$ ft. pitch. The sounds produced are an octave and a fifth above the notes played.

Twelve-Note System (*G.* Zwölftonsystem). A method of composition formulated by Arnold Schönberg about 1921 after a period of experimentation in writing music without tonality and without using the traditional ways of building chords. In it the basis of both melodies and chords of a composition is an arrangement of the twelve notes of the chromatic scale in a particular order, called a tone-row. This series is always used complete, but may be transposed to any one of the eleven other possible positions, inverted, reversed (*v.* RETROGRADE MOTION), or reversed and inverted. It thus has 48 forms, and in addition any note of the series may be used in any of its octaves. Both the melody and the chords, for example, of the last of the Five Piano Pieces, Op. 23, which begins thus:

are derived from this tone-row:

Schönberg used the method much less rigidly in his later works than in the pieces written in the 1920's. It was adopted as a working basis by his pupils Anton Webern and Alban Berg, and later by Ernst Křenek and other composers. The tone-row on which Berg based his violin concerto (1935):

is quite tonal in its implications, being a series of thirds followed by three whole tones. In the last section of the work a modified form of this series is combined with the melody of J. R. Ahle's chorale "Es ist genug" (It is enough), which begins with three whole tones, thus:

and the chorale is then continued by the woodwind in Bach's harmonisation from the cantata *O Ewigkeit, du Donnerwort*:

E. KŘENEK: *Studies in Counterpoint* (1940).
J. RUFER: *Composition with Twelve Notes* (1954).

Twelve-Tone System. An American version of the German *Zwölftonsystem.* In England the term is misleading, since it suggests the use of a scale consisting of twelve whole tones (*v.* TONE), instead of a chromatic scale in which each note is potentially equal. The logical English version is TWELVE-NOTE SYSTEM.

Twilight of the Gods, The. *v.* GÖTTERDÄMMERUNG.

Tye, CHRISTOPHER: *b. c.* 1500; *d.* 1573. Composer. Educated at Cambridge, where he was chorister and lay-clerk at King's College. Master of the choristers, Ely Cathedral, 1542-61; tutor of Edward VI from 1544. Ordained, 1560. He retired from Ely in the following year and was succeeded by his son-in-law, Robert White. He composed a four-part setting of the *Acts of the Apostles* (first 14 chapters) to a metrical translation by himself (London, 1553; reprinted in M. Frost, *English and Scottish Psalm and Hymn Tunes*, 1953, p. 346), Masses (of which two, *The Western Wynde* and *Euge bone*, have survived complete), motets, anthems, services, and In Nomines for strings. The *Euge bone* Mass has been published by G. P. Arkwright (*Old English Edition*. x).

Tyl Owlglass. *v.* TILL EULENSPIEGELS LUSTIGE STREICHE.

Tympani. Obsolete spelling of TIMPANI.

Tympanon [tan͡-pa-non͡], *Fr.* Dulcimer.

Tyrwhitt-Wilson, GERALD HUGH. *v.* BERNERS.

U

U. The abbreviation *u.c.*=UNA CORDA.

Uber [oob′-er], (1) CHRISTIAN BENJAMIN: *b.* Breslau, Sept. 20, 1746; *d.* there, 1812. Composer and lawyer. He studied law and music at Halle and became a barrister at Breslau (1774), where he held public performances of music and plays. Composed a comic opera, a cantata, trios for harpsichord, violin and cello, divertimentos, concertinos and other chamber music and harpsichord sonatas.

(2) ALEXANDER: *b.* Breslau, 1783; *d.* there, 1824. Composer and cellist. Son of (1). He toured southern Germany (1804), lived in Basle (1820) and returned to Breslau (1821), where he was *Kapellmeister* to Prince Schönaich-Carolath (from 1824). Composed cello concertos, variations for cello, overtures and vocal music.

(3) CHRISTIAN FRIEDRICH HERMANN: *b.* Breslau, Apr. 22, 1781; *d.* Dresden, March 2, 1822. Composer. Son of (1). He studied law and music in Halle, was chamber-musician to Prince Louis Ferdinand of Prussia, first violinist at Brunswick (1807), *Kapellmeister* of the Opera at Cassel (1808) and music director of Seconda's opera company at Dresden (1816). Composed operas, an intermezzo, cantatas, a Passion, a violin concerto, music for plays, and German and French songs.

Übung [ēēb′-ōōng], *G.* Study.

Uccellini [oot-chell-lee′-nee], DON MARCO: *b.* Modena, *c.* 1610. Violinist and composer. Master of instrumental music at the ducal court in Modena and *maestro di cappella* at Modena Cathedral. He composed *sonate*, *sinfonie*, *concerti*, *arie* and *canzoni* for one to four string instruments and continuo, and other chamber music (all published between 1639 and 1667), psalms and litanies for voices and instruments and a few operas. He was one of the first to extend the technique of the violin to the sixth position.

Ugolini [oo-go-lee′-nee], VINCENZO: *b,* Perugia, *c.* 1570; *d.* Rome, May 6, 1638. Composer. *Maestro di cappella,* Santa Maria Maggiore, Rome, 1592-1603; Benevento Cathedral, 1609; San Luigi dei Francesi in Rome, 1616-20 and from 1631, Cappella Giulia of St. Peter's, 1620-26. He composed Masses, motets, psalms, vespers and other church music, and madrigals.

Uhlig [ool′-i*sh*], THEODOR: *b.* Wurzen (nr. Leipzig), Feb. 15, 1822; *d.* Dresden, Jan. 3, 1853. Author, composer and violinist. Studied at Dessau. A member of the Royal orchestra at Dresden from 1841 and Wagner's friend and supporter. He wrote theoretical works and composed symphonies, *Singspiele*, chamber music and songs.

Uilleann Pipe. *v.* UNION PIPE.

Ukulele. A small Hawaiian guitar with four strings and a fretted fingerboard. Its notation is a form of TABLATURE.

Ullrich [ŏŏl-ri*sh*], HERMANN: *b.* Mödling (nr. Vienna), Aug. 15, 1888. Composer. Studied in Vienna and in Salzburg at the Mozarteum. He has composed a ballet-pantomime, a symphony, a symphonic poem and other orchestral works, *Variations on a Romantic Theme* for chamber orchestra, and chamber music.

Umlauf [ōōm′-lowf] (1) IGNAZ: *b.* Vienna, 1746; *d.* Mödling (nr. Vienna), June 8, 1796. Composer. Violinist in the court theatre orchestra, Vienna, from 1772; director of the German national *Singspiel*, which he opened with his *Bergknappen* (1778), and from 1789 assistant *Kapellmeister* (under Salieri) for the court theatre orchestra and (under Weigl) for the Opera. He composed *Singspiele*, a comic opera, and incidental music. Modern ed. of *Die Bergknappen* in *D.T.Ö.*, xviii (1).

(2) MICHAEL: *b.* Vienna, Aug. 9,

1781 ; *d.* Baden (nr. Vienna), June 20, 1842. Composer and conductor. Son of (1). Violinist at the Vienna Opera and *Kapellmeister* at the two court theatres, 1810-25 and from 1840. From 1814 he gave the beat to the orchestra in performances of Beethoven's works, while the composer (who was then growing deaf) conducted. He composed 12 ballets, a *Singspiel*, an opera, church music and piano sonatas.

Un Ballo in Maschera. *v.* BALLO IN MASCHERA.

Una corda [oo'-nah corr'-dah], *I.* "One string." A term used in piano music to indicate the use of the left-hand pedal. On grand pianos this normally shifts the whole keyboard slightly to the right, so that the hammers can strike only one or two of the two or three strings assigned to each note. For other methods of achieving a similar effect on upright pianos *v.* CORDA.

Unda maris, *L.* "Wave of the sea." An organ stop of soft tone which is tuned slightly flatter than the true pitch, or which has two ranks slightly mistuned, so that a beat results which has an effect similar to that of a vibrato. A stop of this type may also be called *voix céleste* or *vox angelica.*

Unfinished Symphony. The title given to Schubert's symphony No. 8 in B minor (1822), of which he completed only two movements, though sketches for a third have survived. It was sent to the Musical Society at Graz in return for his election as an honorary member. It was recovered in 1865 and performed for the first time in Vienna, Dec. 17, 1865, conducted by Johann Herbeck. See the articles by O. E. Deutsch, Hans Gál and T. C. L. Pritchard in *The Music Review*, i-iii (1940-2).

Unger [o͝ong'-er], GUSTAV HERMANN: *b.* Kamenz (Saxony), Oct. 26, 1886. Composer. Studied in Munich and under Reger in Meiningen. Taught in Cologne, where he became professor in 1928. He has written books on music and composed 2 operas, 2 symphonies, 3 concertos, symphonic suites and other orchestral works, choral works (some with orchestra), incidental music, chamber music, songs and piano pieces.

Union Pipe. A form of bagpipe, popular in Ireland from the early 18th cent. It is blown by a bellows and has a relatively quiet tone which makes it suitable for indoor use. The modern instrument is very elaborate. There is no foundation for the theory that the name was originally "uilleann pipe" (from the Gaelic word for "elbow").

Unison. The combined sound of two or more notes of the same pitch.

Unruhig [o͝on'-roo-i*sh*], *G.* Restless.

Unterwerk [o͝ont'-er-vairk], *G.* Choir organ.

Urban [oorb'-un], CHRISTIAN: *b.* Elbing, Oct. 16, 1778 ; *d.* Danzig, *c.* 1830. Theorist and composer. Musical director in Elbing, in Berlin and in Danzig. He wrote theoretical works, and composed an opera and music for Schiller's *Braut von Messina.*

Urhan [ĕer-u͡n], CHRÉTIEN; *b.* Montjoie, Feb. 16, 1790 ; *d.* Paris, Nov. 2, 1845. Composer, violinist, violist, and player of the *viola d'amore* and *quinton.* Sent by the Empress Josephine to Paris with a recommendation to Lesueur, under whom he studied. Became a member (1816) and Baillot's successor as leader (1831) of the Opéra orchestra. Composed string quintets, quintets for violas, cello, double-bass and drums *ad lib.*, piano solos and *Duos romantiques* for piano duet, songs and vocal duets.

Urio [oorr'-yo], FRANCESCO ANTONIO: *b.* probably in Milan, *c.* 1660. Composer and Franciscan monk. He was *maestro di cappella* of the Church of the Twelve Apostles in Rome (1690) and later of the Church of the Frari in Venice. He composed a *Te Deum* (modern ed., supplement No. 2 to Chrysander's ed. of Handel), oratorios, motets for voices and instruments, and psalms. A considerable amount of material from the *Te Deum* was used by Handel in his *Dettingen Te Deum, Saul, Israel in Egypt* and *L'Allegro.* The view, however, has been taken that Handel was himself the composer of the *Te Deum* attributed to Urio (*v.* P. Robinson, *Handel and his Orbit*).

Usper [oo-spair'], FRANCESCO SPONGIA: *b.* Parenzo, 16th century ; *d.* Venice, 17th century. Organist, composer and priest. He lived in Venice, where he was organist at San Salvatore (*c.* 1614), deputy organist at San Marco (1621-23), and director of the school of St. John the Evangelist (1627). He composed church music, madrigals, *ricercari* and other instrumental pieces. He used the tremolo for violin in his instrumental works before its appearance in Monteverdi's *Combattimento di Tancredi e Clorinda* (1624).

Ut. (1) The first note of the Guidonian hexachord. *v.* SOLMIZATION.

(2) *Fr.* [ēēt]. The note C.

Utendal [ēēt'-en-dull], ALEXANDER: *b.* in the Netherlands, *c.* 1530; *d.* Innsbruck, May 8, 1581. Composer and singer. He was in the service of the Archduke Ferdinand as chorister in his chapel at Prague, singer in his chapel at Innsbruck (from 1568), court composer (from 1573), and assistant *Kapellmeister* (from *c.* 1579). He composed Penitential Psalms, Masses, motets, Magnificats and secular French and German songs for voices and instruments (1574).

Utopia (Limited). Comic opera in two acts by Sullivan. Libretto by William Schwenk Gilbert. First performed, London, Oct. 7, 1893.

Uttini [oot-tee'-nee], FRANCESCO ANTONIO BARTOLOMEO: *b.* Bologna, 1723; *d.* Stockholm, Oct. 25, 1795. Composer and singer. Studied in Bologna, where he became a member (1743) and principal (1751) of the Philharmonic Academy. He was attached to the Danish court in Copenhagen (1753), visited Hamburg (1754), settled in Stockholm, where he became court music director (1767), and visited London (1768). He composed the first Swedish serious opera, *Thetis och Pelée* (Stockholm, 1773), and other operas in Italian and Swedish, symphonies and trio sonatas.

V

V. As an abbreviation V.=violin, voice. ℣.=verse (in Gregorian chant). Vc.=cello. Vla.=viola. Vln.=violin. V.S.=*volti subito* (turn over quickly)—an instruction frequently found in manuscripts of orchestral parts.

Vaccai [vahk-cah'-ee], NICOLA: *b.* Tolentino, March 15, 1790; *d.* Pessaro, Aug. 5, 1848. Opera composer, who studied under Paisiello at Naples. He spent a few years in Paris and London as a singing-teacher. Director of studies, Milan Conservatorio, 1838. Of his operas the most successful was *Giulietta e Romeo* (Milan, 1825), the last scene of which came to be substituted for the corresponding section of Bellini's *I Capuleti ed i Montecchi* (Venice, 1830), a setting of the same libretto (after Shakespeare's *Romeo and Juliet*). His treatise on singing, *Metodo pratico di canto italiano per camera*, had a considerable vogue.

Vaet [vaht], JAKOB: *d.* Jan. 8, 1567. Flemish composer, in the service of Maximilian, King of Bohemia, on whose accession as emperor (Maximilian II) he was appointed *Kapellmeister* in Vienna. He composed a quantity of church music, some of which was published under the title *Modulationes quinque vocum (volgo motecta) nuncupatae* (2 vols., 1562). Modern ed. of 6 motets by E. H. Meyer.

Valen [va-lehn'], OLAV FARTEIN: *b.* Stavanger, Aug. 25, 1887; *d.* Valevåg, Dec. 14, 1952. Composer. Studied at the Oslo Conservatoire and the Hochschule für Musik, Berlin, where he was a pupil of Reger. Music librarian, Oslo University, 1925-35. He received a state grant for composition, 1935. His compositions, comparatively few of which are published, are said to show the influence of Berg. They include 5 symphonies, 2 string quartets, violin concerto, choral works, piano music and songs.

Valkyrie, The. *v.* WALKÜRE.

Vallas [vull-uss], LÉON: *b.* Roanne, May 17, 1879; *d.* Lyons, May 9, 1956. Music critic and teacher, originally a student of medicine. Lecturer in the history of music, Lyons University, 1908-11; Lyons Conservatoire, 1912-31; Sorbonne, 1929-30. Founded the *Revue musicale de Lyon*, 1903 (later *Revue française de musique* and *Nouvelle Revue musicale*). He lectured frequently on French music in Europe and America. In addition to works on the history of music in Lyons he also published *Les Idées de Claude Debussy* (1927; Eng. ed., 1929), *Claude Debussy et son temps* (1933; Eng. ed. 1933) and *Vincent d'Indy* (2 vols., 1946).

Valse [vulss], *Fr.* Waltz.

Valse, la [la vulss], *Fr.* (The Waltz). *Poème chorégraphique* for orchestra by Ravel. First performed, Paris, Jan. 8, 1920.

Valses Nobles et Sentimentales [vulss nobl ay sun-tee-mun-tull], *Fr.* (Noble and Sentimental Waltzes). A set of 7 waltzes for piano solo by Ravel. The title is an allusion to Schubert's *Valses nobles*, Op. 77, and *Valses sentimentales*, Op. 50, for piano solo. First performed in Paris in 1911 at a concert where all the works in the programme were anonymous. Subsequently orchestrated and performed as a ballet under the title *Adélaïde, ou le langage des fleurs*, Paris, Apr. 22, 1912.

Valse Triste [vulss treest], *Fr.* (Sad Waltz). Orchestral piece by Sibelius, part of the incidental music to Arvid Järnefelt's play *Kuolema*, Op. 44 (1903).

Valve (*Fr.* piston, *G.* Ventil, *I.* pistone). A device enabling brass instruments to command a complete chromatic compass. Used on the cornet, trumpet, flügelhorn, saxhorns, euphonium and tuba—less frequently on the trombone, where the same result is normally achieved by means of a slide. Valves are of two kinds: (1) piston valves, (2) rotary valves. Each type consists of a cylinder, pierced with holes in the appropriate places. The first type moves vertically inside a cylindrical case ; the second rotates. The holes are so designed that when the valve is depressed the air column is compelled to pass through extra tubing : in this way the pitch of the notes of the HARMONIC SERIES is lowered by a semitone or more, according to the length of the additional tubing.

The standard number of valves is three ; the first lowers the pitch a tone, the second a semitone, the first and second together (or the third alone) a minor third, the second and third together a major third, the first and third together a perfect fourth, all three together a diminished fifth (or augmented fourth.) The following example shows a chromatic scale of one octave as played on a trumpet in C (o represents an open note, *i.e.*, without the use of valves) :

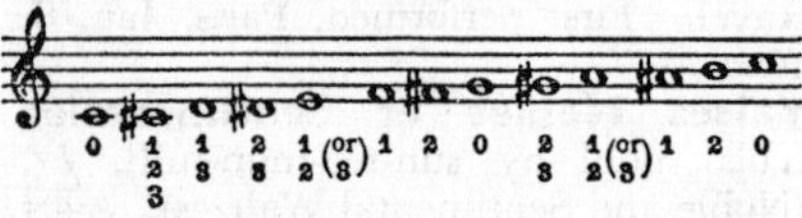

Four valves are normal on the euphonium and tuba. The fourth valve lowers the pitch a perfect fourth : by this means the tuba in F becomes a tuba in C, and the first three valves can then be used as above to lower the pitch still further. A fourth valve is also used on the so-called "German" or "double" horn. This switches the instrument from F to B♭ *alto*, and so raises (instead of lowering) the pitch a perfect fourth. On all instruments with valves there are a number of notes which can be played in more than one way. Thus the note :

on the tuba in F can be played either with valves 2 and 4, or with valves 1, 2 and 3. This convenience facilitates the fingering of awkward passages, and also offers the player alternatives differing slightly in tone quality.

Valves were invented in the early 19th cent., but it was only gradually, in the course of the century, that their use on horns and trumpets became general. Their invention made possible the invention of the CORNET, SAXHORN and similar instruments.

Valve Horn (*Fr.* cor à pistons, *G.* Ventilhorn, *I.* corno a pistoni, corno cromatico, corno ventile). *v.* HORN.

Valve Trumpet (*Fr.* trompette à pistons, *G.* Ventiltrompete, *I.* tromba cromatica, tromba ventile). *v.* TRUMPET.

Van den Borren, CHARLES. *v.* BORREN.

Van Dieren, BERNARD. *v.* DIEREN.

Vanhall, JOHANN BAPTIST. *v.* WANHAL.

Varèse [va-rez], EDGAR: *b.* Paris, Dec. 22, 1885. Composer. Studied at the Schola Cantorum, Paris, under d'Indy and Roussel, and at the Paris Conservatoire under Widor. After organizing choral concerts in Paris and Berlin he emigrated to America in 1916. Founder and conductor, New Symphony Orchestra, New York, 1919 ; founder, International Composers' Guild, 1921. His compositions, which owe nothing to tradition, include several works for large or unusual orchestras.

Variation. The process of modifying a theme, figure or passage in such a way that the resulting product is recognizably derived from the original.

(1) The simplest type of variation consists in repeating a passage with modifications, *e.g.* :

CHOPIN, *Nocturne No.* 15, *Op.* 55, *No.* 1.

(2) Extended melodic variation occurs in 15th-cent. motets in which the upper part is an embellished version of a familiar plainsong melody. In such cases the variation is heard without the theme on which it is based. Dunstable's motet "Veni, sancte Spiritus" (*D.T.Ö.*, vii, p. 203, and *The Old Hall Manuscript*, ed. A. Ramsbotham, etc., ii, p. 66), however, is an example of a piece in which the plainsong melody (of the hymn "Veni, creator spiritus") is present (a) in its original form, in long notes, (b) in a melodic variation in the treble.

(3) Variation of accompaniment is found in Spanish and French lute-songs of the 16th cent. Two versions of the accompaniment are given, one simple, the other florid; the voice-part remains the same in both. Variation of accompaniment became a familiar practice of composers of strophic songs in the late 18th and 19th cent: for an example see Osmin's first song in Mozart's *Die Entführung* (1782).

(4) Variation of contrapuntal setting occurs in 15th-and 16th-cent. compositions based on a CANTUS FIRMUS: (a) in motets in which the *cantus firmus* is stated more than once, (*b*) in Masses, where the same *cantus firmus* serves as a basis for several movements. In such cases the rhythm of the *cantus firmus* may be altered, but melodically it remains the same, while the material of the other parts which compose the contrapuntal texture is constantly varied, though their melodic material may often be derived from the *cantus firmus*.

(5) Melodic variation above a repeated bass occurs in the strophic monodies of the Florentine composers of the early 17th cent.: for an example see the prologue to Monteverdi's *Orfeo* (1607). In such cases the bass has no symmetrical structure but is used simply as a foundation for the melodies of the successive verses.

(6) Melodic variation above a symmetrical bass is represented by the GROUND or *ostinato*, which was extremely popular in the 17th cent. and has remained an element in composition down to the present day. The origin of such variation is probably to be sought in popular dance music. Examples are to be found both in instrumental and vocal music. Allied forms are the CHACONNE and PASSACAGLIA, though here the persistent theme is not necessarily restricted to the bass. *v.* also DIVISIONS.

(7) The practice of writing a sequence of instrumental variations on a theme occurs first in the Spanish lute music of the early 16th cent. Similar variations were also written by English composers for the virginals in the late 16th and early 17th cent. The themes chosen were in many cases popular songs. From that time the "theme and variations" has been a standard form of composition. As well as choosing popular songs composers have also borrowed themes from other composers (Beethoven's variations on a theme of Diabelli, Brahms's variations on a theme of Haydn, Britten's variations on a theme of Frank Bridge) or provided their own (Mendelssohn's *Variations sérieuses*, Elgar's *Enigma* variations). Since one element in variation is elaboration, it is inevitable that variations for a solo instrument (as well as for chamber music ensembles and orchestra) should make some demands on virtuosity. The temptation to make virtuosity a mere excuse for variations has proved irresistible to some composers. Beethoven's exploration of more subtle methods of presenting a theme in new guises did not put an end to this tendency. Mendelssohn's *Variations sérieuses* were in fact written as a protest against the emptiness of so much of the work of early 19th-cent. composers in this form. Later composers, *e.g.* Brahms and Elgar, have moved far away from the mere pursuit of brilliance: Elgar's *Enigma* variations have a unique psychological interest, in that they are not only variations on an original theme but also portraits in music of his friends.

(8) The basic elements to be found in a series of variations are: (1) variation of melody, (2) variation of figuration or texture, (3) variation of rhythm, (4) variation of tonality (*e.g.* minor for major, or vice versa), (5) variation of harmony. Any or all of these may be combined in the same variation.

The art of variation is, however, more complex than the mere exploitation of these basic types: it consists much more in using the theme as a source of inspiration and deriving from it suggestions which may superficially appear to have only a slight connection with it. The link is not necessarily to be sought on the surface but in the composer's imagination.

(9) Variation has also been combined with other forms. In the 17th cent. variation suites were written, in which the several dance movements were thematically related and hence were in fact variations on a basic melody. From the late 18th cent. variations have frequently figured as a complete movement in a sonata, symphony, or similar composition. Schumann combined variations on a theme with sonata form in the first movement of his piano concerto. Strauss, in *Don Quixote,* wrote a symphonic poem in the form of an introduction, theme and variations, each of which illustrates an episode in the life of his hero. In a more general sense variation is an indispensable element in all symphonic writing. DEVELOPMENT of a theme or themes consists in realizing the possibilities inherent in the material and so is itself a form of variation.

v. also DOUBLE.

Variations on a Theme of Haydn. *v.* HAYDN VARIATIONS.

Variazione [varr-yahts-yo'-neh], *I.* Variation. *Tema con variazioni*, theme and variations.

Varsovienne [varr-sov-yen], *Fr.* Short for *danse varsovienne*, Warsaw dance. A dance in fairly slow 3/4 time, in mazurka rhythm, popular in Paris in the time of Napoleon III.

Vassilenko [va-see-leng'-co], SERGEI NIKIPHOROVICH: *b.* Moscow, March 30, 1872. Composer. Studied at the Moscow Conservatoire, where he taught from 1906 to 1938. Beginning as a nationalist composer, he developed for a time a more cosmopolitan style, subsequently reverting, under the influence of Oriental melodies which he collected, to a characteristically Russian idiom. His compositions include the opera *Son of the Sun* (Moscow, 1929), the cantata *The Legend of the City of Kitezh* (later rewritten as an opera), 4 other operas, 6 ballets, 4 symphonies, the symphonic poems *The Garden of Death* (after Oscar Wilde) and *Witches' Flight* (*Hircus Nocturnus*) and other orchestral works, a violin concerto, incidental music, chamber music and songs.

Vatielli [vah-tyell'-lee], FRANCESCO: *b.* Pesaro, Jan. 1, 1877; *d.* Portogruaro, Dec. 12, 1946. Musicologist and composer, a pupil of Mascagni. Lecturer, Liceo Musicale, Bologna, 1905; librarian, 1906; temporary director, 1924-5. Editor, *La cultura musicale*, 1922-3. He published a number of important works on musical history, edited old Italian solo cantatas, and wrote intermezzi for Poliziano's *Favola di Orfeo.*

Vaudeville [vode-veel], *Fr.* (origin uncertain). (1) A popular song.

(2) In particular, a topical song to a well-known tune, sung in Paris in the early 18th cent. at the Théâtre de la Foire (Fair Theatre) and its successor the Opéra-Comique.

(3) The final *vaudeville* in such an entertainment often consisted of verses sung by each of the characters in turn. This practice was also imitated in opera, *e.g.* Mozart's *Die Entführung* (1782).

(4) With the establishment of *opéra-comique* as an independent form with original music the term *vaudeville* came to be given to comedies interspersed with songs (originally *comédies mêlées de vaudevilles* or *comédies vaudevilles*). This type of entertainment flourished in the 19th cent.

(5) In modern usage a variety entertainment.

Vaughan Williams, RALPH: *b.* Down Ampney (Glos.), Oct. 12, 1872; *d.* London, Aug. 26, 1958. Composer. Educated at Charterhouse and Cambridge. Studied at the R.C.M. with Parry and Stanford, and in Berlin with Max Bruch. He held comparatively few official appointments. He joined the R.C.M. as teacher of composition in 1918, conducted the Bach Choir, 1920-6, and became president of the English Folk Dance and

Song Society in 1932. He also for many years directed the Leith Hill Festival at Dorking. His interest in English folksong dated from the beginning of this century: he was active as a collector and discovered an affinity between the traditional melodies and his own aspirations. The influence of folksong came to colour his work more and more, but this was combined with the influence of Tudor polyphony and restrained by an independence of outlook which gave to his mature work a wholly individual flavour. He made occasional use of POLYTONALITY, *e.g.* in *Flos campi*; but more frequently this arrived naturally as the result of turning single melodic lines into sequences of chords in block harmony—a process which results in strong passing dissonance when two independent sequences of this kind are combined. The range of expression in his work is considerable: brutal violence, robust jollity and an almost mystical tranquillity which is rare in contemporary music—all these find a place, often in the same work. The contrasts between them are not contradictions but related facets of the same personality. In his published opinions on music—his own and others—he always expressed a profound distaste for shams and insincerity. His own work is the best evidence of the value of uncompromising honesty. Familiarity with its mannerisms does nothing to lessen respect for its integrity.

His principal compositions are:

(a) ORCHESTRA: *A London Symphony* (1914; rev. 1920); *A Pastoral Symphony* (1922); symphony in F minor (No. 4; 1935); symphony in D major (No. 5; 1943); symphony in E minor (No. 6; 1948); *Sinfonia Antartica* (1953); symphony in D minor (No. 8; 1956); symphony in E minor (No. 9; 1958); 3 Norfolk rhapsodies (1906-7); Fantasia on a theme by Tallis (1910); *The Lark ascending*, for violin and orchestra (1914); *Flos campi*, for viola, orchestra and voices (1925); *Concerto accademico* for violin (1925); piano concerto (1933); suite for viola and orchestra (1934); *Five Variants of "Dives and Lazarus,"* for strings and harp (1939); oboe concerto (1948).

(b) CHORAL WORKS: *Toward the Unknown Region* (1907); *A Sea Symphony* (1910); *Five Mystical Songs* (1911); Fantasia on Christmas carols (1912); Mass in G minor (1923); *Sancta Civitas* (1926); *Benedicite* (1930); 3 choral hymns (1930); *Magnificat* (1932); *Dona nobis pacem* (1936); *Five Tudor Portraits* (1936); *Te Deum* (1937); *Serenade to Music* (1938); *The Sons of Light* (1950).

(c) OPERAS: *Hugh the Drover* (1914); *Riders to the Sea* (1927); *The Poisoned Kiss* (1928); *Sir John in Love* (1929); *The Pilgrim's Progress* (1951, incorporating most of the one-act *The Shepherds of the Delectable Mountains*, 1922).

(d) OTHER STAGE WORKS: incidental music to *The Wasps* of Aristophanes (1909); ballets—*Old King Cole* (1923); *Job* (1930).

(e) CHAMBER MUSIC: piano quintet; 2 string quartets (G minor, A minor); fantasy quintet for strings.

(f) SONGS: *The House of Life* (6 sonnets by Rossetti); *Songs of Travel* (Stevenson); *On Wenlock Edge* (song-cycle; Housman); and many individual songs.

Also works for organ and piano, and film music.

He also published *National Music* (1934) and *Some Thoughts on Beethoven's Choral Symphony* (1953).

A. E. F. DICKINSON: *An Introduction to the Music of R. Vaughan Williams* (1928).
H. FOSS: *Ralph Vaughan Williams* (1950).
F. HOWES: *The Music of Ralph Vaughan Williams* (1954).
S. PAKENHAM: *Ralph Vaughan Williams: a Discovery of his Music* (1957).
P. M. YOUNG: *Vaughan Williams* (1953).

Vautor, THOMAS. English composer of the early 17th cent. who published a volume of five-part and six-part madrigals (1619), dedicated to the Marquess (later Duke) of Buckingham: modern ed. in *E.M.S.*, xxxiv.

Vauxhall Gardens. A house and grounds at Lambeth, opened to the public at the Restoration under the name "Spring Garden" and used for concerts in the 18th cent. and also for dramatic entertainments with music in the early 19th cent. The name "Vauxhall Gardens" was first used in 1786. Roubiliac's statue of Handel (now at Messrs. Novello & Co., 160 Wardour Street) was erected here in 1738.

Vecchi [veck'-kee], (1) ORAZIO: *b.* Modena, 1550; *d.* there, Feb. 19, 1605. Composer. *Maestro di cappella*, Modena Cathedral, 1583-5, 1596-1604; Reggio Cathedral, 1586; canon (from 1586) and archdeacon (1591-5), Corregio; *maestro di cappella* to the Duke of Modena, 1598-1605. He published 6 books of *canzonette*, 2 books of madrigals, Masses, motets, and 4 collections for voices entitled *Selva di varia ricreatione* (The grove of varied recreation), *Convito musicale* (Musical banquet), *Amfiparnasso* and *Veglie di Siena* (Evening parties in Siena). Of these the best known is *Amfiparnaso* (modern ed. in *Publikationen älterer praktischer und theoretischer Musikwerke*, xxvi, and L. Torchi, *L'arte musicale in Italia*, iv), in which characters from the *commedia dell' arte* are presented in a series of contrasted and frequently comic madrigalian compositions: the characterization is left to the singers, since a stage presentation would not only be impossible but is expressly excluded by the composer.

(2) ORFEO. Late 16th-cent. composer, *maestro di cappella* at the church of S. Maria della Scala, Milan. His compositions—motets, Masses, psalms, etc.—are almost exclusively for the church.

Venegas de Henestrosa [veh-neh'-gahss deh eh-neh-stro'-sah], LUYS. 16th-cent. Spanish musician who was in the service of Cardinal Juan de Tavera, archbishop of Santiago and later of Toledo. He compiled and published in 1557 *Libro de cifra nueva para tecla harpa y vihuela* (A book of new tablature for keyboard, harp and *vihuela*); modern ed. by H. Anglès, *La Música en la Corte de Carlos V* (*Monumentos de la Música Española*, ii). It contains several pieces by Cabezón.

Venetian Swell. A series of shutters, similar to the laths of a Venetian blind, used to control the volume of sound produced by a keyboard instrument. First applied to the harpsichord by Burkat Shudi in 1769, and subsequently adapted for the organ (*v.* SWELL ORGAN).

Venite, *L.* (usually pronounced in English ver-nite'-i). The first word of Psalm 95, "Venite, exultemus Domino" (O come let us sing unto the Lord), sung as a canticle before the psalms at Matins in the Anglican service. It was included in choral settings of the service by pre-Commonwealth composers (*e.g.* Tallis, Byrd, Gibbons), but since the Restoration has been sung to a chant, like the psalms.

Ventil [ven-teel'], *G.* Valve. *Ventilhorn*, valve horn. *Ventiltrompete*, valve trumpet.

Venus and Adonis. Masque with a prologue and three acts by Blow. Librettist unknown. First performed at the court of Charles II, *c.* 1682. Modern ed.: (1) by G. E. P. Arkwright, *Old English Edition*, No. xxv, (2) by Anthony Lewis.

Vêpres Siciliennes, Les [lay vepr see-seel-yen] (The Sicilian Vespers). Opera in five acts by Verdi. Libretto by Augustin Eugène Scribe and Charles Duveyrier. First performed, Paris, June 13, 1855. The story takes place in Sicily in the 13th cent. Monforte (the French governor of Sicily) offers to take Arrigo (a commoner who is really the son of Monforte) into the service of the French, but Arrigo refuses. Procida (a Sicilian patriot) tells Elena (a noblewoman) and Arrigo that foreign support awaits the Sicilians, and Elena promises to wed Arrigo if he will avenge her brother who has been executed. Arrigo is taken away by Monforte's soldiers and Monforte reveals to him that they are father and son. Arrigo, fearing for Elena, is horrified by the news. Elena, Procida and others plan to assassinate Monforte; Arrigo warns him and the conspirators are arrested. Arrigo persuades Monforte to spare Procida and Elena on condition that he will publicly recognize Monforte as his father. Arrigo and Elena are to be married with Monforte's blessing, but the Sicilians plan to massacre the Frenchmen when the wedding bells ring. Elena, knowing this, declares that she cannot go through with the ceremony, but Monforte forcibly places her hand in Arrigo's and orders that the wedding bells be rung. In the massacre that follows Monforte and all the French are slain.

Veracini [veh-rah-chee′-nee], (1) ANTONIO. Late 17th-cent. Florentine violinist and composer. He composed violin sonatas and trio sonatas.

(2) FRANCESCO MARIA: *b.* Florence, Feb. 1, 1690; *d.* Pisa, 1750. Violinist and composer. Nephew of (1). He made his reputation in Venice, came to London in 1714, was subsequently in Dresden and Prague, and returned to London in 1735. His compositions include operas, cantatas, concertos and sonatas. Several of his sonatas have been published in modern editions.

Verdelot [vaird-lo], PHILIPPE. Early 16th-cent. French composer, possibly born at Carpentras (*v.* A. Einstein, *The Italian Madrigal*, i, p. 154). He spent most of his life in Italy and probably died in Florence, *c.* 1540. One of the earliest composers of Italian madrigals. Two books of madrigals by him were published, and many more appeared together with the works of other composers. He also composed a Mass and several motets. Two specimens of his work are printed in Schering's *History of Music in Examples*, Nos. 97-8, and four in Einstein, *The Italian Madrigal*, iii, Nos. 16-19.

Verdi [vairr′-dee], GIUSEPPE: *b.* Le Roncole (Parma), Oct. 10, 1813; *d.* Milan, Jan. 27, 1901. Composer. His early experience included playing the organ at the village church and acting as assistant conductor of the Busseto Philharmonic Society. Having failed to secure admission to the Milan Conservatorio in 1832, he studied privately with Lavigna, who was on the staff of La Scala. His first opera, *Oberto, Conte di S. Bonifacio*, was successfully produced at La Scala in 1839. *Un giorno di regno* (Milan, 1840), however, was a failure, and he had decided to give up composition when he was persuaded to set *Nabucco*, which was enormously successful at Milan in 1842. From that time he devoted himself to the composition of operas, with varying success: *Rigoletto* (Venice, 1851) and *Il Trovatore* (Rome, 1853) were immediately popular, *La Traviata* (Venice, 1853) was a failure. In his later years he composed some church music, including the *Requiem* and the *Te Deum*, and also a string quartet. Married (1) Margherita Barezzi, 1836 (*d.* 1840), (2) Giuseppina Strepponi (for many years his mistress), 1859 (*d.* 1897).

Brought up in the traditions of Italian opera, which exalted the singer at the expense of the orchestra, he began by accepting them wholeheartedly and only gradually, by the light of his own genius, developed the form until he reached supreme mastery in the two operas of his old age—*Otello* and *Falstaff*. Unlike Wagner, he was not troubled by theory: he accepted, for example, the ensemble as a natural form of expression and treated it in a masterly fashion in works as diverse as *Rigoletto*, *Simone Boccanegra* and *Falstaff*. Only at the end of his life did he come to abandon aria for arioso. As he matured his work showed a steady growth of musicianship, an increased sensitivity and, in particular, a resourceful and imaginative treatment of the orchestra. His scoring, at first conventional, became highly individual and picturesque, and always achieved complete clarity. The orchestra never dominates but in his later work it becomes increasingly important and in *Falstaff* supplies a sort of continuous, connecting tissue of sound. He was at all times a dramatist, with a passion for Shakespeare which found its natural expression in *Otello* and *Falstaff*. He brought the same vivid imagination to the composition of the *Requiem*, a work which is thoroughly Italian in conception yet never deserves the conventional epithet "operatic." His principal compositions are:

(a) OPERAS: *Oberto, Conte di S. Bonifacio* (Milan, 1838); *Un giorno di regno* (Milan, 1840); *Nabucodonosor* (*Nabucco*, Milan, 1842); *I Lombardi alla prima crociata* (Milan, 1843; revised as *Jérusalem*, Paris, 1847); *Ernani* (Venice, 1844); *I due Foscari* (Rome, 1844); *Giovanna d'Arco* (Milan, 1845); *Alzira* (Naples, 1845); *Attila*

(Venice, 1846); *Macbeth* (Florence, 1847; revised, Paris, 1865); *I masnadieri* (London, 1847); *Il corsaro* (Trieste, 1848); *La battaglia di Legnano* (Rome, 1849); *Luisa Miller* (Naples, 1849); *Stiffelio* (Trieste, 1850; revised as *Aroldo*, Rimini, 1857); *Rigoletto* (Venice, 1851); *Il Trovatore* (Rome, 1853); *La Traviata* (Venice, 1853); *Les Vêpres siciliennes* (Paris, 1855); *Simone Boccanegra* (Venice, 1857; revised, Milan, 1881); *Un ballo in maschera* (Rome, 1859); *La forza del destino* (St. Petersburg, 1862); *Don Carlos* (Paris 1867); *Aida* (Cairo, 1871); *Otello* (Milan, 1887); *Falstaff* (Milan, 1893).

(b) CHORAL WORKS : *Inno delle nazioni* (1862); *Messa da Requiem* (1874); *Ave Maria* (1889); *Stabat Mater* (1898); *Te Deum* (1898).

(c) CHAMBER MUSIC : string quartet (1873).

F. BONAVIA : *Verdi* (1930).
G. CESARI & A. LUZIO : *I copialettere di Giuseppe Verdi* (1913).
D. HUSSEY : *Verdi* (1940).
A. LUZIO : *Carteggi Verdiani* (4 vols., 1935-47).
F. TOYE : *Giuseppe Verdi : his Life and Works* (1931).

Veress [verr'-ess], SÁNDOR : *b.* Kolozsvár (Hungary; now Cluj, Roumania), Feb. 1, 1907. Pianist, composer and critic. He first appeared in public as a pianist in 1916, and as a composer in 1920. Studied at the Musical Academy of Buda and the State Academy of Music, Budapest, where his teachers included Bartók and Kodaly. Teacher of composition, Academy of Music, Budapest, 1943 ; Berne Conservatorium, 1950. In addition to composition his special interests are musical education, which he has studied in foreign countries, and folk music. His music has been influenced by his activity as a collector of folk-songs, by the example of Bartók, and by Stravinsky's neo-classical style. His compositions include an opera for children, ballets, several choral works (mostly without accompaniment), 2 symphonies and other orchestral works, violin concerto, piano concerto, 2 string quartets, sonata for solo violin, sonatinas for violin and cello, piano music and songs. He has also written several articles on Hungarian folk music and on various aspects of musical education.

Verismo [veh-reez'-mo], *I.* (from *vero*, "true"). Anglicized as "verism." An artistic movement originating in the late 19th cent. which aimed at a vivid and realistic representation of contemporary life. In opera this resulted in a melodramatic treatment which tended to exploit individual moments at the expense of development or structural unity. The best known examples are Mascagni's *Cavalleria rusticana* (1890), Leoncavallo's *Pagliacci* (1892), and Charpentier's *Louise* ; in all these the participants are people of humble birth. Such realism is different from that of Bizet's *Carmen* (1875), which, though it treats a vulgar subject, is in the tradition of 19th-cent. *opéra-comique.* The influence of *verismo* is to be seen in many of Puccini's operas, though his work in general by no means shows a whole-hearted acceptance of its aims.

Verne (originally Wurm), (1) ADELA : *b.* Southampton; *d.* London, Feb. 4, 1952. Pianist, a pupil of her sister Mathilde (3). Made her first public appearance in London in 1898 and continued to play until the end of her life.

(2) MAREY. Sister of (1) and (3). *v.* WURM.

(3) MATHILDE : *b.* Southampton, May 25, 1868 ; *d.* London, June 4, 1936. Pianist and teacher, a pupil of Clara Schumann. Sister of (1) and (2). For many years she appeared in chamber music programmes at the "Tuesday, 12 o'clock" concerts, which she organized. Founded a school of piano-playing, 1909. Published her memoirs under the title *Chords of Remembrance* (1936).

Verschiebung [fair-sheeb-ŏŏng], *G.* Soft pedal (of the piano).

Verse Anthem. An anthem in which important sections are assigned to one or more solo voices with independent accompaniment.

Verset. An organ piece based on a plainsong melody and used to replace a verse of a psalm, Magnificat, etc. or a section of an item of the Mass. The performance would thus alternate between choir and organ. Numerous examples of such versets have survived by composers of the 16th, 17th and early 18th cent.: for examples see *Historical Anthology*, Nos. 117 (Mass) and 133 (psalm).

Verto [vairr'-to], *I. v.* OUVERT.

Vespers. The service preceding Compline in the series of *horae diurnae* (daily hours) of the Office in the Roman rite. It includes a series of psalms with their antiphons, a hymn and the Magnificat. Examples of elaborate settings for voices and orchestra are those by Monteverdi (modern ed. by H. F. Redlich) and Mozart (K. 321 and 339).

Vestale, La [la vess-tull] (The Vestal Virgin). Opera in three acts by Spontini. Libretto by Victor Joseph Étienne de Jouy. First performed, Paris, Dec. 16, 1807.

Viadana [vee-ah-dah'-nah], LODOVICO (Lodovico Grossi) : *b.* Viadana, *c.* 1564; *d.* Gualtieri, May 2, 1645. Composer, a pupil of Porta. *Maestro di cappella*, Mantua Cathedral, 1594-1609. He became a Franciscan in 1596. His compositions include canzonets, madrigals and church music. His *Cento concerti ecclesiastici, a una, a due, a tre, & a quattro voci* (1602, containing only the first instalment of the 100 pieces) is provided with an unfigured *basso continuo* and includes detailed instructions for its performance by the organist (*v.* F. T. Arnold, *The Art of Accompaniment from a Thorough-Bass*, pp. 2-5, 9-33).

Viardot-Garcia [vyarr-do-garrce-ya], PAULINE (originally Michelle Ferdinande Pauline): *b.* Paris, July 18, 1821; *d.* there, May 18, 1910. Soprano, daughter of the singer Manuel del Popolo Garcia [garr-thee'-ah], sister of the singing-teacher Manuel Garcia and the singer Maria Malibran. Pupil of her father for singing, Liszt for the piano, and Reicha for composition. First appeared in public at Brussels, 1837. Subsequently sang with great success in opera in London, Paris, Berlin and elsewhere. Teacher of singing, Paris Conservatoire, 1871-5. Married the music critic and impresario Louis Viardot, 1841. Among her outstanding roles was that of Fidès in Meyerbeer's *Le Prophète*, which she sang at the first performance in Paris, Apr. 16, 1849.

Vibrato [vee-brah'-toh], *I.* Lit. "shaken." A method giving expressive quality to the sound of a note by means of rapid and minute fluctuations of pitch. This is achieved in the following ways :

(1) On string instruments by oscillations of the left hand, which is used to stop the strings. Described by Leopold Mozart, *Versuch einer gründlichen Violinschule* (1756; trans. by Editha Knocker as *A Treatise on the Fundamental Principles of Violin Playing*, p. 203), as a "natural quivering on the violin." He calls it the TREMOLO, and adds : "Because the tremolo is not purely on one note but sounds undulating, so would it be an error if every note were played with the tremolo. Performers there are who tremble consistently on each note as if they had the palsy." One may assume that he would have condemned modern violin-playing, since it is now the practice to use *vibrato* more or less consistently wherever the notes are sufficiently long to make it possible.

(2) On the CLAVICHORD by repeating the pressure of the finger on a key without releasing it, the result being to vary slightly the tension, and hence the pitch, of the string. This practice is generally known by its German name, BEBUNG.

(3) On wind instruments by suitably manipulating the supply of air.

(4) In singing by a method similar to that used on wind instruments. This is often referred to as *tremolo*, a term which is properly applied to the rapid reiteration of the same note—a practice now obsolete but much cultivated in the 17th cent. and known then as the *trillo* (*v.* TRILL). *Vibrato* is even more likely to be abused by singers than by string-players, particularly as it arises naturally from incomplete control and may as easily be a sign of defective technique as a deliberate means of expression.

Vicentino [vee-chen-tee'-no], NICOLA : *b.* Vicenza, 1511 ; *d.* Rome, 1572 (or Milan, 1575). Composer and theorist, a pupil of Willaert. *Maestro di cappella* to

Duke Ercole d'Este, 1546-9. Published 4 books of madrigals (of which only the first survives), and an unscientific treatise entitled *L'antica musica ridotta alla moderna prattica* (1555), in which he argued that the DIATONIC, CHROMATIC and ENHARMONIC *genera* of Greek music should be used as the basis for composition (*v.* J. Hawkins, *A General History of the Science and Practice of Music*, 1875 ed., pp. 41-5, 392-5). In pursuit of his theory he invented a keyboard instrument called the *arcicembalo* (with 6 manuals) and another called the *arciorgano*.

Victoria [vick-tohrr'-yah] (Vitoria, Vittoria), TOMÁS LUIS DE : *b.* Avila, *c.* 1548; *d.* Madrid, Aug. 27, 1611. Composer. Student at the Collegium Germanicum, Rome, 1565. Organist, S. Maria di Monserrato, Rome, 1569. *Maestro di cappella*, Collegium Romanum, 1571 (in succession to Palestrina); Collegium Germanicum, 1573-8. Ordained priest, 1575; chaplain, S. Girolamo della Carità, 1578-85. Became chaplain to the Empress Maria (sister of Philip II of Spain), *c.* 1580, and returned with her to Spain, where he became director of music at the Convent of the Descalzas Reales, Madrid (to which she retired), 1596-1611. His compositions, exclusively for the church, appeared between 1572 and 1605, many of them in sumptuous folio editions. They include motets, Masses, Magnificats, hymns and psalms; among them are several elaborate works for 8-12 voices with organ. A master of subtle and expressive polyphony, he is one of the outstanding figures among 16th-cent. composers of church music and one of the most remarkable in the history of Spanish music. A complete edition of his works in 8 vols. was edited by F. Pedrell (1902-13).

R. CASIMIRI : *Il Vittoria : nuovi documenti* (1934).
H. COLLET : *Le Mysticisme musical espagnol au XVIe siècle* (1913).
Victoria (1914).
R. MITJANA : *Estudios sobre algunas músicos españoles del siglo xvi* (1918).
F. PEDRELL : *Tomás Luis de Victoria abulense* (1918).

Vida Breve, La [lah vee'-dah breh'-veh]. *v.* VIE BRÈVE.

Vie Brève, La [la vee brev] (Life is short). Opera in two acts by Falla. Original Spanish libretto (*La vida breve*) by Carlos Fernández Shaw; French version by Paul Milliet. First performed, Nice, April 1, 1913: first performed in Spanish, Madrid, Nov. 14, 1914.

Vielle [vyell], *Fr.* (1) The medieval fiddle (*L.* viella).

(2) 17th and 18th-cent. name for the hurdy-gurdy (*L.* organistrum, symphonia).

Vienna Philharmonic Orchestra. A self-governing body of players drawn from members of the Vienna State Opera. The first Philharmonic concert, given by the Imperial Opera Orchestra under Otto Nicolai, took place on March 28, 1842.

Viennese School. A general term for the composers active in Vienna in the late 18th and early 19th cent., notably Haydn, Mozart, Beethoven and Schubert.

Vier Grobiane, Die [dee feer grobe'-yahn-er] (The Four Boors). Opera in four acts by Wolf-Ferrari. Original Italian libretto (*I quattro rusteghi*) by Giuseppe Pizzolato (after Goldoni); German version by Hermann Teibler. First performed, Munich, March 10, 1906; first performed in Italian, Milan, June 2, 1914. The English version by Edward J. Dent is entitled *School for Fathers*.

Vierne [vyairn], LOUIS VICTOR JULES : *b.* Poitiers, Oct. 8, 1870; *d.* Paris, June 2, 1937. Organist and composer. Studied at the Paris Conservatoire under Franck and Widor. Organist, Notre Dame, 1900; teacher of organ, Schola Cantorum, 1911. His pupils included Joseph Bonnet, Marcel Dupré and Nadia Boulanger. In addition to compositions for the organ (6 large-scale works entitled "symphonies" and a large number of shorter pieces) he also wrote choral works, chamber music and a symphony for orchestra.

Viertel [feer'-těl], *G.* Crotchet.

Vieuxtemps [vyer-tũn], HENRI : *b.* Verviers (Belgium), Feb. 20, 1820; *d.* Mustapha-lez-Alger (Algeria), June 6, 1881. Violinist and composer. He showed unusual precocity as a small boy, and by the age of 13 was touring as a soloist. He studied for a time in Paris with de Bériot, but much of his excellence as a performer was due to his own industry. For many years he travelled widely in Europe and the United States. He settled in Brussels in 1871 as teacher at the Conservatoire, but was compelled to resign in 1873 in consequence of a paralytic stroke. He wrote a number of works for the violin, including several concertos, some of which are still in the repertory.

Vif [veef], *Fr.* Lively.

Vihuela [vee-oo-eh′-lah], *Sp.* (1) Originally a generic term for a string instrument. *Vihuela de arco*, viol ; *vihuela de braço*, violin (*v.* VIOLA DA BRACCIO).

(2) In particular, *vihuela de mano* (*i.e.* played with the hand), a flat-backed instrument, similar in shape to the guitar. The normal tuning of its 6 strings was similar to that of the LUTE. A considerable amount of music for it—original compositions and transcriptions—was published by Spanish composers in the 16th cent., as well as songs with *vihuela* accompaniment, the earliest collection being Luis Milan's *Libro de música de vihuela de mano intitulado El Maestro* (1535).

Village Romeo and Juliet, A. *v.* ROMEO UND JULIA AUF DEM DORFE.

Villa-Lobos [veel′-lah-lo′-boss], HEITOR *b.* Rio de Janeiro, March 5, 1887. Composer, mainly self-taught. As a young man earned his living as an orchestral player. Visited Paris with a fellowship from the Brazilian Government, 1922-6. Superintendent of Musical Education in Schools, Rio de Janeiro, 1931. Founder and director, Orfeão de Professores (a teachers' training college). His compositions, which are numerous, show the influence of Indian music, which he studied in 1912, and Brazilian folksong : they include 5 operas, 6 symphonies, symphonic poems, cello concerto, a number of *chôros* (serenades) for various media, chamber music, choral works, piano solos and songs.

Villancico [veel-lyahn-thee′-co], *Sp.* (from *villano*, rustic). (1) A type of song in a popular but sophisticated style, current in Spain in the late 15th and 16th cent. It is characterized by the fact that it begins with a refrain, which is subsequently repeated after each verse, as in the French *virelai* and the 13th-cent. *cantigas* of Alfonso el Sabio. Examples for vocal ensemble are in F. Asenjo Barbieri, *Cancionero musical del los siglos xv y xvi* (1890), R. Mitjana, *Cancionero de Upsala* (1944), and *Monumentos de la Música Española*, iv, v, viii & ix. *Villancicos* were also set in the 16th cent. for solo voice with *vihuela* accompaniment (*v.* VIHUELA).

(2) In the 17th and 18th cent. a cantata for soli and chorus with instrumental accompaniment, frequently on the subject of Christmas.

(3) In modern Spanish a Christmas carol.

Villanella [veel-lah-nell′-lah], *I.* Lit., "rustic song" (*cf.* VILLANCICO). A popular but sophisticated form of part-song in 17th-cent. Italy. It originated in Naples and was hence also known as *napolitana* (Neapolitan in English). The most popular type was for three voices, with frequent use of consecutive triads, *e.g.* :

DI MAIO (in A. Einstein, *The Italian Madrigal*, iii No. 38).

The words often parodied the elevated and sentimental style of the madrigal.

Villotta [veel-lot′-tah], *I.* A form of popular part-song of North Italian origin current in the 16th cent. and cultivated in opposition to the more serious style of the madrigal. It was normally for four voices.

Vinci [veen′-chee], LEONARDO : *b.* Strongoli (Calabria), 1690 : *d.* Naples, May 28, 1730. Composer. Studied in Naples, where he made his reputation as a composer of *opera buffa* and *opera seria.* He also wrote church music, and was one of the *maestri da cappella* at the Neapolitan court from 1725.

Viñes [veen′-yess], RICARDO : *b.* Lérida, Feb. 5, 1875 ; *d.* Barcelona, Apr. 29, 1943. Pianist. Studied in Barcelona and Paris. He gave the first performance of a number of works by Debussy and other 20th-cent. French composers.

Vingt-Quatre Violons du Roi, Les [lay vañ-cutr vyoll-oñ dēē rwa] (The King's 24 Violins). A string orchestra maintained by the French kings in the 17th and early 18th cent. The organization was copied by Charles II, who instituted a band of "24 violins." *v.* VIOLIN.

Viol (*Fr.* viole, *G.* Gambe, Kniegeige, Viole, *I.* viola da gamba, *Sp.* vihuela de arco). A family of bowed string instruments which were widely used in the 16th and 17th cent. and have been revived in modern times for the performance of music of that period. Sizes, tuning and shape varied considerably in the 16th cent., but by the 17th cent. there was some degree of standardization, in spite of local variations. Three sizes were normally used in chamber music: treble, tenor and bass. They were generally tuned :

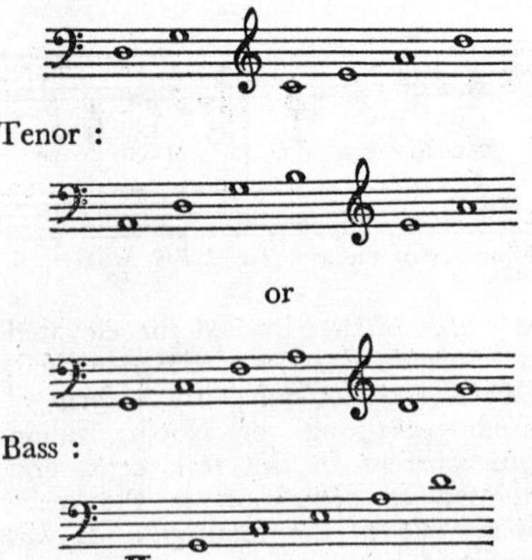

The back was normally flat and the shoulders sloping. All three sizes were played resting on, or held between, the knees (hence the Italian name *viola da gamba*, "leg viol"). The bow was held above the palm of the hand. A series of gut frets on the fingerboard gave a clear tone to each stopped note.

In England a set of viols for ensemble playing was known as a "chest of viols," from the cupboard in which they were kept : Thomas Mace, in *Musick's Monument* (1676), recommends 2 trebles, 2 tenors and 2 basses. The literature of ensemble music for viols is extensive, particularly in England in the mid-17th cent., though it was rarely published there, except in mixed collections of vocal and instrumental music. The bass viol in particular was also cultivated as a solo instrument, especially for playing "divisions" (or variations) on a GROUND. For this purpose a rather smaller instrument was used : the standard book on the subject is Christopher Simpson's *The Division-Violist* (1659), in which, it is interesting to note, he expresses a preference for a type of instrument with rounded shoulders, like the cello. A still smaller bass viol was used for playing "lyra way," *i.e.* with a variety of different tunings to facilitate hand-playing ; the problem of constantly using new fingerings was solved by writing the music in TABLATURE, as for the lute. The bass viol continued to be used as a solo instrument in the early 18th cent. Bach wrote three sonatas for it, with harpsichord, and obbligato parts for it in the *St. Matthew Passion* and the *St. John Passion.* French composers of the early 18th cent. were particularly conservative in their attitude to the viol, writing not only for the bass but also for the treble and for the *pardessus de viole*, a high treble tuned a fourth above the normal instrument.

The bass viol had also an important function as an accompanying instrument in the 17th cent. It was used to play the bass line of the continuo part (in association with the harpsichord or organ), not only in vocal music but also in violin sonatas and in trio sonatas for two violins and bass, where it was for long preferred to the cello. For the same reason the *violone* (or double-bass viol, an octave below the bass viol) was widely used in preference to the coarser double-bass violin. Monteverdi, in his opera *Orfeo* (1607), expressly writes for a *contrabasso de viola da gamba* to be used in association with an ensemble of *viole da braccio* (violins, violas and cellos). The double bass now used in the orchestra retains the shape of the *violone*, though it no longer uses frets.

G. R. HAYES : *Musi al Instruments and their Music*, 1500-1750. II. *The Viols, and other Bowed Instruments* (1930).

Viola [vee-o'-lah], *I.* (1) A generic term for any bowed string instrument : see the entries following.

(2) In particular, the alto (or tenor) member of the violin family (*Fr.* alto, *G.* Bratsche), formerly known in England as the tenor violin, or simply the tenor, and now exclusively called by its Italian name. The German name is a corruption of the Italian *viola da braccio*, the name of the violin family in the 17th cent. The instrument is larger than the violin, but not proportionately to its pitch, which is a fifth lower. The tuning is :

The range of the instrument makes it convenient to use the alto clef, except for the higher register, for which the treble clef is employed, in order to avoid leger lines.

The viola has been a member of the orchestra since the early 17th cent. Its development in chamber music, on the other hand, dates from Haydn's cultivation of the string quartet in the 18th cent. As a solo instrument it received only occasional attention before the 20th cent. : examples are a concerto by Carl Stamitz (1746-1801), Mozart's *Sinfonia concertante* for violin, viola and orchestra, and Berlioz's *Harold en Italie* for viola and orchestra. Brahms's 2 sonatas for viola are arrangements of works originally written for clarinet. Modern works include concertos by Walton and Rubbra, sonatas by Bax and Bliss, and several works by Hindemith, who is himself a viola-player.

Viola bastarda [vee-o'-lah bust-arr'-dah], *I.* The instrument known in England as the lyra viol, or the viol played " lyra way " (*v.* VIOL). It was a small-size bass viol, the tuning of which was varied to suit the player's convenience. Being so small, it might also have been regarded as a large tenor viol, in spite of its pitch : this is probably the origin of the name *viola bastarda*, which implies that it was neither one thing nor the other.

Viola da braccio [vee-o'-lah dah brah'-tcho] (viola da brazzo), *I.* Lit. " arm viol." The name of the violin family in the 16th and early 17th cent., applied equally to treble, alto (or tenor) and bass members of the family ; thus, *bassa viola da braccio* means cello, in spite of the illogicality of applying the name to an instrument which could not possibly be played on the arm. In the course of the 17th cent. the term *violino* (a diminutive of *viola*) became normal for the treble instrument. The term *violoncello* (a diminutive of *violone*) for the bass instrument was in use by the beginning of the 18th cent. The term *viola da braccio* was thus reserved for the alto (or tenor) instrument and was shortened for convenience to *viola* : the description *da braccio*, however, survives in the German name for the instrument —*Bratsche*.

Viola da gamba [vee-o'-lah dah gahm'-bah], *I.* Lit. " leg viol." The name of the viol family, referring to the fact that all the instruments in the family are held on or between the knees, in contrast to the smaller members of the *viola da braccio* family (violin and viola), which are held on the arm. In the 18th cent. the term implies the bass viol, since this was the only member of the family still in normal use, except in France. *v.* VIOL.

Viola d'amore [vee-o'-lah dah-moh'-reh], *I.* (*Fr.* viole d'amour, *G.* Liebesgeige). Lit. " love viol," possibly so called because the scroll is frequently made in the shape of a Cupid's head with the eyes blindfold.

(1) In the 17th and early 18th cent. a treble viol or violin with wire strings.

(2) From *c.* 1720 a bowed string instrument with 6 or 7 principal strings, and a number of subsidiary strings made

of wire which are not touched by the bow but vibrate in sympathy. It is played under the chin, like a viola. Tuning varies considerably. It was little used in the latter half of the 18th cent. but was revived by Meyerbeer in *Les Huguenots* (1836) and has been used by a number of 20th-cent. composers, including Charpentier, Puccini, Strauss and Hindemith.

Viola da spalla [vee-o′-lah dah spahl′-lah], *I. v.* VIOLA DI SPALLA.

Viola di bordone [vee-o′-lah dee borr-do′-neh], *I. v.* BARYTON.

Viola di spalla [vee-o′-lah dee spahl′-lah] (viola da spalla). Lit. "shoulder viol". An 18th-cent. term indicating either (1) a portable cello suitable for itinerant musicians, suspended by a strap passed over the shoulder, or (2) an ordinary cello.

Viola pomposa [vee-o′-lah pom-po′-zah], *I.* An obsolete instrument for which a few 18th-cent. compositions survive. It appears to have been a five-stringed viola, with a high E string (the same pitch as the violin's) added above the normal four. The name *violino pomposo*, which also occurs, seems to indicate the same instrument.

Viole, *Fr.* [vyoll], *G.* [vee-ole′-er]. Viol. *Viole d'amour*, viola d'amore.

Violet. Leopold Mozart gives the name "English Violet" to a type of *viola d'amore* having 7 bowed strings and 14 sympathetic strings (*A Treatise on the Fundamental Principles of Violin Playing*, trans. E. Knocker, p. 12).

Violeta [vee-o-leh′-tah], *Sp.* Mentioned by Cerone in 1613 as a name commonly given to the *vihuela de braço, y sin trastes* (arm viol without frets), *i.e.* the *viola da braccio* or violin family. *v.* VIOLETTA.

Violetta [vee-o-let′-tah], *I.* (diminutive of *viola*). (1) G. M. Lanfranco in 1533 gives the name *violetta da arco senza tasti* (little bowed viol without frets) or *violetta da braccio* (little arm viol) to an instrument with three strings which appears to be an early form of the violin.

(2) The name often given to the viola by 18th-cent. German composers.

(3) Praetorius, in his *Syntagma Musicum* ii (1619), gives *violetta piccola* as an alternative name for the violin. He also, however, gives it as an alternative name for the treble viol, as does Zacconi in his *Prattica di musica* (1592).

Violin. (1) In the 17th cent. the name of a family of bowed string instruments (*Fr.* violon, *G.* Geige, *I.* viola da braccio, *Sp.* vihuela de braço). Thus in France the King's string orchestra was called *les vingt-quatre violons du roi*, and in Restoration England the "24 violins." In both cases the name refers to treble, alto (or tenor) and bass instruments. The members of the family differ from the VIOL family in several respects, notably: (1) they have slightly rounded backs and round shoulders, (2) there are normally only four strings, which are tuned in fifths, (3) there are no frets, (4) the smaller members (violin and viola) are held on the arm (hence the Italian name *viola da braccio*). The alto (or tenor violin) is now known as the VIOLA, the bass violin as the cello (an abbreviation of VIOLONCELLO). An instrument intermediate between the viola and cello existed in the late 17th cent. but is now obsolete: it is often referred to as the "tenor violin"—a confusing nomenclature, since "tenor violin" is the old English name for the viola. A double-bass violin also existed, but the double-bass viol was preferred (*v.* DOUBLE BASS), and from this the modern double bass, though it has no frets, is derived.

The ancestry of the family is complex. A large number of bowed string instruments of various shapes existed in the Middle Ages, and from these the members of the violin family (at first with three, and soon with four, strings) were evolved in the 16th cent. From the first they were used for ensemble music, like the viols, and when orchestras became necessary for opera in the early 17th cent. the violin family were preferred on account of their more incisive, brilliant tone. From that time they have remained in all essentials the same, though such details as methods of bowing, the shape of the bridge, and the material of the strings have changed. In consequence though wind-players prefer new instruments, old violins, violas and cellos, fashioned by master-craftsmen, are much sought after and highly valued.

(2) In particular, the treble of the violin family, to which the name "violin" (*Fr.* violon, *G.* Violine, *I.* violino) is now exclusively assigned. The standard tuning is:

Other tunings were adopted in the 17th cent. to facilitate chord-playing (*v.* SCORDATURA). The violin was used early in the 17th cent. as a solo instrument and its capacity for virtuosity exploited. The solo sonata and the trio sonata for two violins and continuo developed side by side. The solo concerto appeared *c.* 1700. In view of the popularity of the form it is curious that so many 19th- and 20th-cent. composers—*e.g.* Beethoven, Mendelssohn, Schumann, Brahms, Tchaikovsky, Dvořák, Elgar, Sibelius, Bartók and Walton—should have written only one violin concerto,

(3) A smaller violin was used in the 17th and 18th cent. *v.* VIOLINO PICCOLO.

G. R. HAYES: *Musical Instruments and their Music*, 1500-1750. II. *The Viols, and other Bowed Instruments* (1930).

E. VAN DER STRAETEN: *The History of the Violin* (2 vols., 1933).

Violine [vee-ole-een′-er], *G.* Violin.

Violino [vee-o-lee′-no], *I.* (diminutive of *viola*). (1) A name used indiscriminately in the 16th cent. for members of the viol and violin families.

(2) From the 17th cent. onwards it means "violin," *i.e.* the treble of the violin family.

Violino piccolo [vee-o-lee′-no peek′-co-lo], *I.* (*G.* kleine Discantgeige, Quartgeige). A small violin used in the 17th and early 18th cent. Praetorius, in his *Syntagma Musicum* (1619), gives the following tuning:

Monteverdi's *Orfeo* (1607) has parts for two *violini piccoli alla francese* (*i.e.* on the French model). Bach wrote solo parts for it in Cantata 140 and the first Brandenburg concerto, using a tuning a tone lower than that given by Praetorius:

and writing as for a transposing instrument (*i.e.* a minor third lower than the actual sounds), so that a player accustomed to a normal violin could use the same fingering. The instrument became obsolete in the latter half of the 18th cent.

Violino pomposo [vee-o-lee′-no pom-po′-zo], *I.* *v.* VIOLA POMPOSA.

Violon [vyoll-on͡], *Fr.* (1) In the 16th cent. used, like *violino*, for members both of the viol and of the violin family.

(2) In the 17th cent. the name of the violin family—treble, tenor and bass.

(3) Now used exclusively for the treble of the violin family—the violin.

Violoncello [vee-o-lon-chell′-lo], *I.* (*Fr.* violoncelle, *G.* Violoncell, Violoncello). The bass of the violin family. The name is a diminutive of VIOLONE. The illogical but convenient abbreviation "cello" [chell′-o] is peculiar to non-Romance languages, *e.g.* English, Dutch, German and Swedish. Originally known, in the 17th cent., as *bassa viola da braccio*. It now has four strings, tuned:

but was also made with five in the 17th and early 18th cent. The last of Bach's 6 suites for unaccompanied cello is for a five-string instrument, tuned:

Alternative tunings were used for the four-string instrument, as for the violin (*v.* SCORDATURA): the fifth of Bach's suites requires the following tuning:

Music is written for the cello in the bass clef, except for the higher register, where the tenor and treble clefs are used, in order to avoid leger lines. The practice of writing in the treble clef an octave higher than the actual sounds is now obsolete, though often retained in modern editions of classical works.

For the greater part of the 17th cent. the cello was restricted to playing the bass line in the orchestra and in chamber music (though in the latter case the bass viol was often preferred). Solo music begins to appear at the end of the 17th cent. and is frequent in the 18th cent. in the form of concertos, sonatas and obbligatos in opera and oratorio. Concertos by 19th- and 20th-cent. composers include those by Schumann, Dvořák and Elgar. In Strauss's symphonic poem *Don Quixote* the solo cello represents the hero. The repertory of modern concertos is limited, since the combination of solo cello with the sonority of the modern orchestra presents problems which few composers have cared to solve.

E. VAN DER STRAETEN : *History of the Violoncello* (1915).

Violoncello piccolo [vee-o-lon-chell'-o peek'-co-lo], *I.* A small-sized cello for which Bach wrote obbligato parts in 9 of his cantatas.

Violone [vee-o-lo'-neh], *I.* (augmentative of *viola*). (1) Properly the double-bass viol (or *contrabasso da gamba*), a six-stringed instrument an octave below the bass viol. (2) Applied also in the 18th cent. to the double-bass violin: hence the diminutive *violoncello* for the bass violin. *v.* DOUBLE BASS.

Viotti [vee-ot'-tee], GIOVANNI BATTISTA: *b.* Fontanetto da Po (Piedmont), May 23, 1753; *d.* London, March 3, 1824. Violinist and composer, a pupil of Pugnani. In 1780 he embarked on a tour of Europe, visiting Switzerland, Germany, Poland and Russia. He arrived in Paris in 1782 and remained for 10 years, first as a soloist at the Concert Spirituel and later as joint director of the Italian opera at the Théâtre de Monsieur. The rest of his life, from 1792, he spent partly in London where he played at Salomon's concerts and also conducted, partly near Hamburg, and partly in Paris, where he was director of the Opéra, 1819-22. He had a great reputation as a performer, and his influence as a teacher was far-reaching. His compositions include 29 concertos: his practice of writing the first movement in march time was imitated by both Mozart and Beethoven in their piano concertos.

Virdung [feerd'-oong], SEBASTIAN. Late 15th- and early 16th-cent. musician who published at Basle in 1511 an important work on musical instruments entitled *Musica getutscht* (fascimile ed., 1931).

Virelai [veer-lay], *Fr.* A form of medieval French song, beginning with a refrain which was subsequently repeated after each verse. The same structure is found in the 13th-cent. *cantigas* of Alfonso el Sabio and in the Spanish *villanico*.

Virginal, Virginals (both singular and plural occur). A member of the harpsichord family, first mentioned and described by Sebastian Virdung in his *Musica getutscht* (1511). The name (which was used also in the Netherlands) presumably implies that it was an instrument favoured by young ladies, who are in fact constantly represented performing on it in Dutch paintings, whereas men are shown playing the lute. It belongs properly to the oblong (or rectangular) SPINET, but English usage was inconsistent, and in the Tudor and Jacobean period any instrument of the harpsichord type was called "virginal." A clear distinction between harpsichord and virginal was not made until the Restoration.

English composers of the 16th and early 17th cent. were particularly active in writing for this instrument. Their compositions include variations, dance movements, fantasias and transcriptions of vocal pieces. The only printed collection was *Parthenia* (1611; facsimile ed., 1942), containing works by Byrd, Bull and Gibbons. There are, however, several substantial manuscript collections, notably: (1) The Fitzwilliam

Virginal Book (modern ed. by J. A. Fuller Maitland and W. Barclay Squire, 2 vols., 1899), (2) My Ladye Nevells Booke, containing only pieces by Byrd (modern ed. by Hilda Andrews, 1926), (3) Will Foster's Virginal Book (in the Royal Music Library), (4) Benjamin Cosyn's Virginal Book (also in the Royal Music Library), (5) Elizabeth Rogers's Virginall Booke (British Museum), and (6) a manuscript in the New York Public Library (Drexel 5612). A complete edition of English virginal music is in course of preparation for *Musica Britannica*. Byrd's keyboard works have been published in a modernized text by E. H. Fellowes, and Orlando Gibbons's by Margaret Glyn.

C. VAN DER BORREN : *The Sources of Keyboard Music in England* (1913).

M. H. GLYN : *About Elizabethan Virginal Music and its Composers* (1924).

E. W. NAYLOR : *An Elizabethan Virginal Book* (1905).

W. BARCLAY SQUIRE : "Collections of Virginal Music," in Grove's *Dictionary of Music and Musicians*, article VIRGINAL MUSIC.

Vitali [vee-tah'-lee], (1) FILIPPO. Early 17th cent. composer. Singer in the Papal Choir in Rome, 1631, where he also enjoyed the patronage of Cardinal Barberini. *Maestro di cappella*, Florence Cathedral, 1642. His *L'Aretusa* (1620) was one of the earliest operas performed in Rome. He also published madrigals, arias for one or more voices with instrumental accompaniment, and church music.

(2) GIOVANNI BATTISTA : *b.* Cremona ; *d.* Modena, Oct. 12, 1692. Violinist and composer. Vice-*maestro di cappella* to the Duke of Modena, 1674 ; *maestro di cappella*, 1684. One of the most important composers of chamber music in the 17th cent., he published several collections of trio sonatas and dance movements for strings, as well as psalms for voices and instruments, and also composed operas and oratorios. Examples of his work are in L. Torchi, *L'arte musicale in Italia*, vii.

(3) TOMMASO ANTONIO : *b.* Bologna. Violinist and composer. Son of (2). In the service of the Duke of Modena. His surviving publications—3 sets of trio sonatas and *Concerto di sonate a violino, violoncello e cembalo*—are dated 1693, 1695 and 1701. A set of variations above an ostinato bass in G minor, for violin and continuo, described in the manuscript as "Parte del Tomaso Vitalino" (modern ed. by G. Benvenuti), was attributed to him by Ferdinand David and published in a truncated and much edited version under the title "Ciaccona" (Chaconne) in *Die hohe Schule des Violinspiels* (1867).

Vitoria. *v.* VICTORIA.

Vitry [der vee-tree], PHILIPPE DE : *b.* Vitry (Champagne), Oct. 31, 1291 ; *d.* Meaux, June 8, 1361. Composer, poet and theorist. He was a diplomat in the service of the French court and became Bishop of Meaux in 1351. Only a few compositions by him survive, but enough to show that he was a master of the isorhythmic motet (*v.* ISORHYTHM) : complete ed. in L. Schrade, *Polyphonic Music of the Fourteenth Century*, i. The title of his treatise *Ars nova* (printed in Coussemaker, *Scriptores*, iii, p. 13) has been adopted by historians as a general term for the music of the 14th cent. Among the refinements of notation advocated by, or attributed to, him are the introduction of time signatures, the use of red notes (principally to indicate modifications of rhythm), the recognition of duple time, and the precise division of the semibreve into two or three minims by analogy with the division of the breve into semibreves.

Vittoria. *v.* VICTORIA.

Vivace [vee-vah'-cheh], *I.* Lively. *Allegro vivace*, quick and lively.

Vivaldi [vee-vahl'-dee], ANTONIO : *b.* Venice, *c.* 1675 ; *d.* Vienna, July 1741. Composer and violinist, a pupil of his father, Giovanni Battista Vivaldi, and Legrenzi. Ordained priest, 1703, and familiarly known as *il prete rosso* (the red-haired priest). For many years in the service of the Conservatorio dell' Ospedale della Pietà (a music school for girls in Venice) from 1704 ; violin teacher, 1709 ; *maestro de' concerto*, 1716. He travelled extensively, but no details of his journeys are known. He was one of the most prolific composers of his time. His surviving works include concertos for a wide variety of solo instruments with orchestra (he was one of the first composers to use clarinets), chamber music, secular cantatas, church music, an oratorio and operas. A catalogue is in the second volume of Pincherle's work (cited below). A complete edition of his instrumental works, under the direction of G. F. Malipiero, is in course of publication. In spite of his tremendous output he was by no means a conventional composer, and much of his instrumental work shows a lively and fertile imagination. He was not without influence on Bach, who transcribed some of his concertos, including a concerto for 4 violins which he arranged for 4 harpsichords (*B.G.*, xliii, 1).

M. PINCHERLE : *Antonio Vivaldi et la musique instrumentale*, 2 vols. (1948).
O. RUDGE : *Lettere e dediche di Antonio Vivaldi* (1942).
A. SALVATORI : *Note e documenti sulla vita e sulle opere di Antonio Vivaldi* (1939).

Vivo [vee'-vo], *I.* Lively.

Voce [vo'-cheh], *I.* Voice. *Colla voce*, with the voice (an indication that the accompaniment must neglect strict time and follow the singer) ; *mezza voce*, medium voice, *i.e.* fairly quietly ; *sotto voce*, under the voice, *i.e.* very quietly. *v.* also MESSA DI VOCE.

Voces musicales [vo'-cace moo-si cah'-lace], *L.* "Musical notes." The notes of the hexachord, sung to SOLMIZATION syllables, often used in the 16th cent. as a *cantus firmus* in vocal and instrumental pieces.

Vogel [fogue'-ĕl], EMIL : *b.* Wriezen a.d. Oder, Jan. 21, 1859 ; *d.* Berlin, June 18, 1908. Musicologist. Studied with Spitta at Berlin University, and with Haberl in Italy. Director of the Musikbibliothek Peters, Leipzig, 1893-1901 ; founder and editor of the *Jahrbuch der Musikbibliothek Peters*, 1894-1900. He published detailed studies of Monteverdi and Gagliano, both the product of the most thorough research, a catalogue of the music of the Ducal Library at Wolfenbüttel, and *Bibliothek der gedruckten Vokalmusik Italiens aus den Jahren 1500-1700* (2 vols., 1892). The last of these is indispensable for students of the period : revisions were published by A. Einstein in *Notes*, iii-v (1945-8).

Vogelweide [fon dair fogue'-ĕl-vide-er], WALTHER VON DER. Late 12th- and early 13th-cent. MINNESINGER. Very few of his poems survive with music. His song of the crusader in Palestine, "Nu alerst leb' ich mir werde," is one of the finest of all Minnesinger melodies : it has often been printed, *e.g.* in *Historical Anthology*, No. 20b, and *New Oxford History of Music*, ii, p. 253).

Vogl [fohg'l], JOHANN MICHAEL : *b.* Steyer, Aug. 10, 1768 ; *d.* Vienna, Nov. 19, 1840. Baritone. Educated at Vienna University. Having shown promise at school as a singer and actor, he was engaged to sing at the court opera in 1794 and was a regular member of the company from 1795-1822. Among the parts which he sang were Oreste in Gluck's *Iphigénie en Tauride* and the Count in Mozart's *Figaro*. He was for several years a close personal friend of Schubert and was the first to sing "Erlkönig" in public.

Vogler [fogue'-ler], GEORG JOSEPH : *b.* Würzburg, June 15, 1749 ; *d.* Darmstadt, May 6, 1814. Composer, organist and teacher, the son of a violin-maker. Studied law at Bamberg University. Visited Italy, 1773-5 ; ordained priest in Rome, 1773. Chaplain and second *Kapellmeister*, Mannheim, 1775 ; moved with the court to Munich, 1779, where he became *Kapellmeister*, 1784. *Kapellmeister* to the King of Sweden, Stockholm, 1786-99. In spite of these official appointments he travelled extensively from 1781 onwards, visiting France, England, Holland, Russia, Denmark, and several other countries. He also directed successively music schools in Mannheim, Stockholm and Frankfort. He composed a large number of operas, as well as a quantity of church music and instrumental works, and published books on harmony, organ-playing, tuning of keyboard instruments, etc. He advanced a number of ideas for the improvement of organ-building, some of which were subsequently adopted by others, and was the inventor of the so-called Acoustic Bass stop, which produces the effect of a 32 ft. stop by utilising the COMBINATION TONES resulting from the simultaneous use of a 10⅔ ft. stop and a 16 ft. stop (*v.* ORGAN). Among his pupils were Weber and Meyerbeer. Mozart, who met him at Mannheim in 1778-9, describes him as "exceedingly conceited and rather incompetent" (*v.* E. Anderson, *The Letters of Mozart and his Family*, p. 522) and expresses several other contemptuous opinions about him: against this, however, must be set the loyalty and friendship of a great number of his pupils.

Voice. As a technical term used traditionally for an individual part in a contrapuntal composition (particularly a fugue), whether for voices or for instruments. Thus a keyboard fugue for 3 voices is a fugue in three-part counterpoint. The use of the word in instrumental music is due to the fact that contrapuntal writing for instruments was originally imitated from similar writing for voices.

Voice Leading. A literal American translation of the German *Stimmführung* (part-writing).

Voicing. The process of ensuring a good and uniform tone-quality from any particular set of organ pipes. This is done by making minor adjustments to the pipes after they have left the maker's hands, and demands not only a sensitive ear but also expert craftsmanship.

Voix céleste [vwa say-lest], *Fr.* "Heavenly voice." An organ stop. *v.* UNDA MARIS.

Volbach [foll'-buckh], FRITZ: *b.* Wipperfürth (Rhineland), Dec. 17, 1861; *d.* Wiesbaden, Dec. 6, 1941. Composer and conductor. Studied at Cologne Conservatorium and at the Königliche Institut für Kirchenmusik, Berlin (where he also taught from 1887 to 1892). Conductor of choral societies in Mainz, 1892; director of music, Tübingen University, 1907; professor, Münster, 1919-30 (and municipal director of music, 1921-5). His compositions include symphonic poems, choral works and chamber music. As a conductor he was active in reviving performances of Handel's works and published a dissertation on the subject. His other publications include books on Beethoven, the orchestra, and the accompaniment of plainsong.

Volkmann [follk'-mun], FRIEDRICH ROBERT: *b.* Lommatzsch (Saxony) Apr. 6, 1815; *d.* Pest, Oct. 30, 1883. Composer and teacher. Studied under C. F. Becker in Leipzig, where he made the acquaintance of Schumann. Teacher in Prague, 1839-41; Pest, 1841-54, 1878-83. From 1854-58 he lived in Vienna. His compositions, which were once very popular and are still in the repertory of chamber-music players, include 2 symphonies, overture to *Richard III*, 3 serenades for string orchestra, cello concerto, 6 string quartets, 2 piano trios, Masses and other choral works, songs, and a number of works for piano solo (including *Variations on a theme of Handel*).

Volkslied [follks'-leet], *G.* (1) A folk song, in the generally accepted English sense of a traditional song of unknown authorship.

(2) A popular song, whether anonymous or by a known composer. The great majority of *Volkslieder* belong to this category. Their square-cut rhythm and symmetrical structure have had a considerable influence on German composers.

Vollerthun [foll'-er-toon], GEORG: *b.* Fürstenau, Sept. 29, 1876. Composer. Opera conductor in Prague, Berlin, Barmen and Mainz, 1899-1905. For several years active as a music critic and teacher in Berlin. Teacher, Berlin Hochschule, 1933-8. In addition to choral works, orchestral pieces and songs he has composed the following operas: *Veeda* (Cassel, 1916), *Island-Saga* (Munich, 1925), *Der Freikorporal* (Hanover, 1931) and *Das königliche Opfer* (Hanover, 1942).

Volles Werk [foll'-ĕss vairk], *G.* Full organ.

Volta [voll'-tah], *I.* Lit., "turn" or "time." (1) A lively dance in 6/8 rhythm (*Fr.* volte) which was very popular in the late 16th and early 17th cent., though condemned by moralists, since the men swung the women high in the air. Often referred to in English sources as *lavolta*. The following is an example:

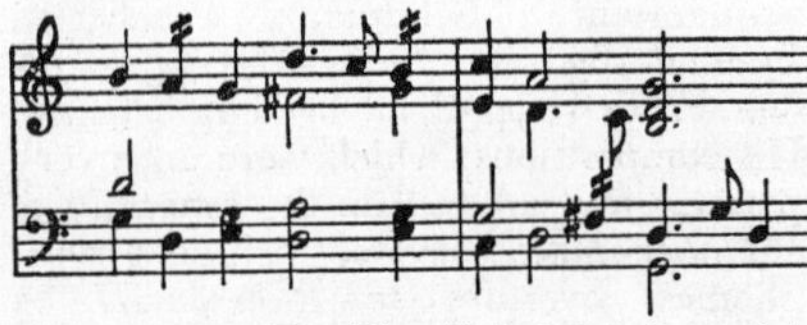

BYRD (*Fitzwilliam Virginal Book*, ii, p. 180)

(2) *Prima volta* (first time) and *seconda volta* (second time) are used when a composition, or a section of a composition, is to be repeated with some change in the concluding bar or bars. Horizontal brackets above the stave indicate the bars affected : the first time the performer plays the bar or bars marked *prima volta* (or simply " 1 ") and then goes back to the beginning, the second time he omits these bars and goes straight on to the bars marked *seconda volta* (or " 2 ").

Voluntary. (1) In general a keyboard piece in a free style.

(2) In particular an organ solo played before or after the service in the Anglican church. The earliest use of the term appears to be in the mid 16th-cent. " Mulliner Book " (*Musica Britannica*, i).

Von Bülow. *v.* BÜLOW.

Vorschlag [fohrr′-shlahk], *G.* Appoggiatura.

Vorspiel [fohrr′-shpeel], *G.* Prelude.

Vox Angelica, *L.* " Angelic voice." An organ stop. *v.* UNDA MARIS.

Vreuls [vrerlce], VICTOR: *b.* Verviers, Feb. 4, 1876 ; *d.* Brussels, July 26, 1944. Composer. Studied at the Liège Conservatoire and the Schola Cantorum, Paris, where he subsequently taught viola and harmony, 1901-6. Director, Luxemburg Conservatoire, 1906. His compositions include a symphony (with violin solo), 3 symphonic poems, chamber music, and the operas *Olivier le simple* (Brussels, 1922) and *Un Songe d'une nuit d'été* (Brussels, 1925).

Vulpius [vo͝olp′-i-o͝oss], MELCHIOR: *b.* Wasungen (Henneberg), *c.* 1560 ; *d.* Weimar, Aug. 7, 1615. Cantor at Weimar. He published several volumes of church music for 4-8 voices, settings of Lutheran chorale melodies, and a *St. Matthew Passion.* His own chorale melodies include " Christus der ist mein Leben " and " Jeus Leiden, Pein und Tod " (originally Jesus Kreuz, Leiden und Pein).

Vuota [voo-o′-tah] (fem. of *vuoto*, empty), *I.* (1) Short for *corda vuota*, open string (of a violin, etc.). (2) Short for *misura vuota*, empty bar, *i.e.* a bar in which the instruments or voices are silent (*G.* Generalpause, abbreviated G.P.).

W

Waelrant [vahl'-runt], HUBERT: *b.* Tongerloo, *c.* 1518; *d.* Antwerp, Nov. 19, 1595. Composer and singer. His compositions, which had a great reputation in his day, include *chansons*, madrigals and motets.

Waffenschmied, Der [dair vuff-ĕn-shmeet] (The Armourer). Opera in three acts by Lortzing. Libretto by the composer (based on Friedrich Julius Wilhelm Ziegler's comedy *Liebhaber und Nebenbuhler in einer Person*). First performed, Vienna, May 31, 1846.

Wagenaar [vahg'-ĕn-ahrr], (1) BERNARD: *b.* Arnhem, July 18, 1894. Violinist and composer. Studied in Holland and migrated to America, where he became a member of the New York Philharmonic Orchestra and taught at the Juilliard School. His compositions include symphonies and other orchestral works, chamber music and songs.

(2) JOHAN: *b.* Utrecht, Nov. 1, 1862; *d.* The Hague, June 16, 1941. Composer and choral conductor, a pupil of Richard Hol. Organist, Utrecht Cathedral, 1888; director, Utrecht Conservatoire, 1904; Royal Conservatoire, The Hague, 1919-37. One of the most influential of modern Dutch composers. His compositions include the opera *Pieces of Eight*, 4 symphonies, violin concerto, chamber music, piano sonata, and songs.

Wagenseil [vahg'-ĕn-zile], (1) GEORG CHRISTOPH: *b.* Vienna, Jan. 15, 1715; *d.* there, March 1, 1777. Composer to the Imperial Court, Vienna. His numerous compositions include symphonies, concertos, keyboard works, church music, oratorios and operas. Examples of his instrumental music are in *D.T.Ö.*, xv, (2).

(2) JOHANN CHRISTOPH: *b.* Nuremberg, Nov. 26, 1633; *d.* Altdorf, Oct. 9, 1708. Historian. He published in 1697 a history of Nuremberg, to which was appended a detailed account of the Meistersinger. The latter was one of the sources of Wagner's opera *Die Meistersinger* (*v.* H. Thompson, *Wagner and Wagenseil*).

Wagner [vahg'-ner], (1) PETER JOSEF: *b.* Kürenz, Aug. 19, 1865; *d.* Fribourg, Oct. 17, 1931. Historian of music. Studied at Strasbourg and Berlin. Professor, Strasbourg, 1897; Rector, 1920-1. First president of the International Musicological Society, 1927. His principal studies were in the field of Gregorian chant. His *Einführung in die gregorianischen Melodien* (1895) was subsequently re-issued in a new edition in three vols. His other publications include *Geschichte der Messe* (1914) and a large number of contributions to periodicals.

(2) RICHARD (originally Wilhelm Richard): *b.* Leipzig, May 22, 1813; *d.* Venice, Feb. 13, 1883. Composer and conductor. Probably the son of the Jewish actor Ludwig Geyer, who married Johanna Wagner nine months after the death of her first husband in November, 1813. At school in Leipzig he acquired a profound interest in drama and in Beethoven's symphonies, and before the age of 20, having had some lessons in composition, had written several orchestral works. His earliest theatrical appointments were at Würzburg as chorus-master, 1833, and as conductor at Magdeburg, 1835, where his opera *Das Liebesverbot* was unsuccessfully performed, 1836. Subsequently conductor at Königsberg, 1837, and Riga, 1837. Arrived in Paris, 1839, where he maintained himself by journalism and arrangements of other composers' works. Moved to Dresden, 1842, where he became second conductor; performances given here of *Rienzi*, 1842, *Der fliegende Holländer*, 1843, and *Tannhäuser*, 1845. Forced to leave Dresden through participation in the Revolution of 1849. His

friendship with Liszt resulted in the production of *Lohengrin* at Weimar, 1850. After more than ten years' exile, mainly spent in Switzerland, allowed to re-enter Germany, 1860. In 1864 settled in Munich under the personal patronage of Ludwig II of Bavaria; *Tristan und Isolde* produced here, 1865. Antagonism at court compelled him to leave Munich for Switzerland, though *Die Meistersinger* was performed at Munich, 1868. In spite of financial difficulties he planned the construction of a special festival theatre for his operas at Bayreuth, the foundation stone of which was laid in 1872; the theatre opened with the first performance of *Der Ring des Nibelungen* in 1876. *Parsifal* performed there, 1882. Married (1) Minna Planer, an actress, 1836 (*d.* 1866), (2) Cosima, illegitimate daughter of Liszt and formerly wife of the conductor Hans von Bülow, 1870 (*b.* Dec. 25, 1837; *d.* Apr. 1, 1930).

Wagner's whole career was characterized by a determination to succeed as an opera composer: his other compositions are few and, apart from the *Faust* overture, of minor importance. In the pursuit of this career he became aware of the necessity for creating a new type of dramatic work, in which all the arts—music, drama and spectacle—could be united in a significant whole. The fulfilment of this design necessitated the building of a special theatre at Bayreuth, which is still used for festival performances of his works. The financial difficulties which this project involved were alleviated by the persistent generosity of his friends, particularly Liszt, who continued to believe in him in spite of his irresponsibility in money matters. He showed an equal irresponsibility in his dealings with women, using for his own ends the fascination which he seems to have exercised over them.

The works which illustrate, in varying degree, his theory of operatic construction are *Der Ring des Nibelungen*, *Tristan und Isolde*, *Die Meistersinger von Nürnberg* and *Parsifal*. The principal points in that theory are briefly: (1) traditional opera was at fault in its subject matter, its verse-forms and the domination of music over drama; (2) Beethoven had shown the significance of instrumental melody, but music needs to be fructified by poetry; (3) the subject-matter must be suitable, hence legends were more suitable than the everyday commonplaces of modern opera; (4) the importance of feeling, as opposed to mere understanding, necessitated a type of verse likely to stimulate the emotions, *e.g.* by the use of alliteration, to which music could add a further stimulus; (5) operatic conventions which were opposed to the creation of such direct impressions must be abandoned, *e.g.* the operatic ensemble; (6) the orchestra should not merely accompany—it should express everything that the voice cannot, and should also make use of the powerful force of association; (7) above all, continuity was essential. These principals were carried out most consistently in the four operas which constitute *Der Ring des Nibelungen*, in which the force of association was maintained by a large number of short and reasonably simple thematic fragments, which recur constantly in varying forms, sometimes independently, sometimes in combination, and are woven together to form a continuous symphonic texture. The objection to operatic ensembles broke down in *Die Meistersinger*, which employs a large number of subsidiary characters as well as a chorus, and to a lesser degree in *Tristan und Isolde*, where a considerable part of the second act is taken up by a love duet. In general Wagner's instinctive musicianship triumphed over the limitations of his theories. All his mature works exhibit a highly developed gift for melody, an unusual inventiveness in harmony, and a mastery of orchestration which owes little to tradition. It was this awareness of sound which made him so successful as a conductor.

He wrote the following operas (words and music):

Die Feen (1834; first performed posthumously, Munich, 1888); *Das Liebesverbot* (after Shakespeare's *Measure for Measure*; Magdeburg, 1836); *Rienzi* (1840; first performed, Dresden, 1842); *Der fliegende Holländer*

(1841; first performed, Dresden, 1843); *Tannhäuser* (Dresden, 1845); *Lohengrin* (1848; first performed, Weimar, 1850); *Der Ring des Nibelungen*: (1) *Das Rheingold* (1854; first performed, Munich, 1869), (2) *Die Walküre* (1856; first performed, Munich, 1870), (3) *Siegfried* (1871; first performed, Bayreuth, 1876), (4) *Götterdämmerung* (1874: first performed, Bayreuth, 1876); *Tristan und Isolde* (1859; first performed, Munich, 1865; *Die Meistersinger von Nürnberg* (1867; first performed, Munich, 1868): *Parsifal* (Bayreuth, 1882).

His other compositions include *Eine Faust Ouvertüre* (1840) and *Siegfried Idyll* (1870) for orchestra, and *Das Liebesmahl der Apostel* (The Love Feast of the Apostles, 1843) for chorus and orchestra. His numerous prose works were published in 10 vols., translated by W. A. Ellis in 8 vols. (1892-9). The following list is a small selection from the voluminous literature on Wagner: Newman's *Life* includes detailed bibliographies.

P. BEKKER: *Richard Wagner* (1931).
J. N. BURK: *Letters of Richard Wagner: the Burrell Collection* (1951).
W. H. HADOW: *Richard Wagner* (1934).
R. L. JACOBS: *Wagner* (1935).
E. NEWMAN: *The Life of Richard Wagner*, 4 vols. (1933-46).
R. M. RAYNER: *Wagner and "Die Meistersinger"* (1940).

(3) SIEGFRIED (originally Helferich Siegfried Richard): *b.* Triebschen, June 6, 1869 (14 months before his parents' marriage); *d.* Bayreuth, Aug. 4, 1930. Son of (2) and Cosima von Bülow. Studied with Humperdinck and from 1899 onwards was active as an opera-composer. His most important work, however, was the part which he played in the direction of the festival theatre at Bayreuth (now controlled by his sons, Wieland and Wolfgang).

Wagner Tuba. *v.* TUBA (2).

Wainwright, JOHN: *b.* Stockport, 1723; *d.* Manchester, Jan. 1768. Organist of the Collegiate Church, Manchester (now Manchester Cathedral), 1767. Best known by his tune for John Byrom's Christmas hymn "Christians, awake, salute the happy morn" (*E.H.*, 21).

Wait. (1) Another name for the medieval SHAWM, presumably derived from (2).

(2) (*G.* Stadtpfeifer). A wind-player employed by a municipality (and in earlier times by the king or noblemen), so called because his original function was to act as a watchman and to announce the hours at night. Companies of waits were maintained in England from the 14th to the 18th cent. inclusive. The term "waits" is now loosely applied to itinerant musicians who play in the streets at Christmas time.

(3) A piece of music played by the waits.

G. A. STEPHEN: *The Waits of the City of Norwich* (1933).

Waldhorn [vult'-horrn], *G.* "Woodland horn." The original German name for the French horn (*I.* corno da caccia). In 19th-cent. scores it is sometimes used to distinguish the natural horn without valves from the *Ventilhorn* (valve horn), *e.g.* in Schumann's third symphony.

Waldstein [vult'-shtine] **Sonata.** Beethoven's piano sonata in C major, Op. 53 (1804), dedicated to his friend Count Ferdinand Ernst Gabriel von Waldstein (1762-1823). The slow movement (*Introduzione*) was an afterthought. The original slow movement, which it replaced, was published separately as *Andante favori*.

Waldteufel [vult'-toy-fĕl], EMIL: *b.* Strasbourg, Dec. 9, 1837; *d.* Paris, Feb. 16, 1915. Composer of highly successful waltzes. Studied at the Paris Conservatoire. For a time employed in a piano factory. Pianist to the Empress Eugénie, 1865.

Walford Davies. *v.* DAVIES (4).

Walker, ERNEST: *b.* Bombay, July 15, 1870; *d.* Oxford, Feb. 21, 1949. Composer, pianist and historian. Educated privately and at Balliol College, Oxford, where he was director of music in charge of the Sunday evening concerts, 1900-25. He also taught for musical degrees in the University. Editor, *Musical Gazette*, 1899-1902. Author, *A History of Music in England* (1907; 2nd ed., 1924; 3rd ed., edited by J. A. Westrup, 1952). His compositions include choral works, chamber music and songs.

M. DENEKE : *Ernest Walker* (1951).

Walker & Sons, J. W. A firm of organ-builders, founded in London by George England in 1740 and acquired in 1820 by Joseph W. Walker (*d.* 1870), a former apprentice in the business.

Walküre, Die [dee vull-kēēr'-er] (The Valkyrie). Opera in three acts by Wagner, the second part of the cycle *Der Ring des Nibelungen* (*q.v.*). First performed, Munich, June 26, 1870.

Wallace, (1) LUCILLE: *b.* Chicago, Feb. 22, 1898. Pianist and harpsichordist. Studied at Bush Conservatory (Chicago), Vassar College, Vienna University and the Sorbonne; also privately with Wanda Landowska, Nadia Boulanger and Artur Schnabel. Married Clifford Curzon, pianist, 1931.

(2) WILLIAM: *b.* Greenock, July 3, 1860; *d.* Malmesbury, Dec. 16, 1940. Ophthalmic surgeon, composer and writer on music. Studied at Glasgow University, where he graduated in medicine, and at Vienna. Studied music at the R.A.M., 1889. For many years secretary of the Royal Philharmonic Society. His compositions include a symphony, 6 symphonic poems (*The Passing of Beatrice, Anvil or Hammer, Sister Helen, To the New Century, Wallace, a.d. 1305-1905*, and *Villon*), choral works and songs. He published the following books: *The Threshold of Music* (1908), *The Musical Faculty* (1914), *Richard Wagner as he lived* (1925) and *Liszt, Wagner and the Princess* (1927).

(3) WILLIAM VINCENT: *b.* Waterford, March 11, 1812; *d.* nr. Vieuzos (Htes. Pyrénées), Oct. 12, 1865. Opera composer, the son of an army bandmaster. While still a boy appeared as violinist in Dublin. Left Ireland in 1835 and spent some years abroad, travelling in Australia, New Zealand, India, Mexico and the United States. His opera *Maritana* (London, 1845) brought him immediate success as a composer. He spent several more years abroad, returning to London in 1853. Of his other operas the most successful was *Lurline* (London, 1860). He also wrote a quantity of piano music.

Wallaschek [vull'-ush-eck], RICHARD: *b.* Brno, Nov. 16, 1860; *d.* Vienna, Apr. 24, 1917. Writer on aesthetics and primitive music. Lecturer, Freiburg, 1886. Research in London, 1890-5. Professor, Vienna, 1896. Several of his works were originally published in English.

Walmisley, (1) THOMAS FORBES: *b.* London, May 22, 1783; *d.* there, July 23, 1866. Composer of glees. Chorister at Westminster Abbey and a pupil of Attwood. Organist, St. Martin-in-the Fields, 1814-54.

(2) THOMAS ATTWOOD: *b.* London, Jan. 21, 1814; *d.* Hastings, Jan. 17, 1856. Organist and composer. Son of (1), godson of Attwood, under whom he studied. Organist, Trinity College and St. John's College, Cambridge, 1833. Professor, Cambridge, 1836. A volume of his church music was published after his death by his father.

Walsh. A firm of music-publishers in London, founded by John Walsh (*d.* 1736) and continued by his son, John Walsh the younger (*d.* 1766). A large number of Handel's works were published by this firm.

W. C. SMITH: *A Bibliography of the Musical Works published by John Walsh during the Years 1695-1720* (1948).

Walter [vult'-er] (originally Schlesinger), BRUNO: *b.* Berlin, Sept. 15, 1876. Conductor and composer. Studied at the Stern Conservatorium, Berlin. Successively conductor at opera houses at Cologne, Hamburg, Breslau, Pressburg (Bratislava), Riga, Berlin: Vienna Opera, 1901-12; general music director, Munich, 1913-22; Berlin Städtische Oper, 1925-33; Gewandhaus concerts, Leipzig, 1930-3; Vienna Philharmonic Orchestra, 1933-8. Assumed French nationality, 1938. Since 1940 has been active as a conductor in the United States and England. He played an important part in establishing the Salzburg Festival in the pre-war years. As a conductor he excels in the interpretation of Mozart and Mahler. His compositions include 2 symphonies, chamber works and songs. He published his reminiscences under the title *Theme and Variations* (1946) and also a book on Mahler.

P. STEFAN : *Bruno Walter* (1936).
B. WALTER : *Theme and Variations—an Autobiography* (1947).

Walther [vult'-er], (1) JOHANN: *b.* Kahla (Thuringia), 1496 ; *d.* Torgau, Apr. 1570. Singer and choirmaster. *Sängermeister* to the Elector of Saxony, 1525 ; director of the chapel of Moritz of Saxony, Dresden, 1548-54. A friend of Luther, he played a prominent part in establishing the music of the Reformed Church. His publications include the first Protestant hymn-book, *Geystlich Gesangk-Buchleyn* (1524), and a number of other collections of religious music. A number of instrumental compositions survive in manuscript. A complete edition of his works is in course of publication.

(2) JOHANN GOTTFRIED: *b.* Erfurt, Sept. 18, 1684 ; *d.* Weimar, March 23, 1748. Organist, composer and lexicographer. Organist, St. Thomas's, Erfurt, 1702 ; municipal organist, Weimar, 1707 ; court musician, Weimar, 1720. A relative of J. S. Bach, who was a godfather to his eldest son. He excelled in the composition of chorale preludes ; complete organ works published in *D.D.T.*, xxvi-xxvii. His dictionary of music, entitled *Musicalisches Lexicon oder Musicalische Bibliothec* (1732 ; facsimile ed., 1953), was for long a standard work.

(3) JOHANN JAKOB: *b.* Witterda, 1650. Violinist and composer, successively in the service of the Elector of Saxony at Dresden and the Elector of Mainz. His compositions for violin include imitations of nature and of orchestral instruments.

Walthew, RICHARD HENRY: *b.* London, Nov. 4, 1872 ; *d.* East Preston (Sussex), Nov. 14, 1951. Composer and conductor. Studied at the G.S.M. and the R.C.M. He did valuable work as conductor of the opera class at the G.S.M. and in the organization of the South Place chamber concerts. His published compositions include a number of chamber works and a setting of *The Pied Piper of Hamelin* for soli, chorus and orchestra.

Walton, WILLIAM TURNER: *b.* Oldham, March 29, 1902. Composer. Chorister at Christ Church, Oxford. Mainly self-taught as a composer. He made his reputation by a string quartet performed at the festival of the International Society for Contemporary Music, Salzburg, 1923, and by *Façade*, a series of instrumental pieces designed to be played in conjunction with the recitation of poems by Edith Sitwell. He reached maturity with his viola concerto (1929) and the oratorio *Belshazzar's Feast* (1931). His work, even when most successful, gives the impression of having been created with effort ; his later compositions have been relatively few and sometimes seem to strive to recreate artificially the atmosphere of their predecessors. He shows considerable assurance in handling boldly large masses of sound, *e.g.*, in *Belshazzar's Feast* and the symphony, but his most characteristic work exploits a nostalgic vein which is seen at its best in the viola concerto. He has occasionally flirted with modern tonality, but in essentials his work is in the English tradition represented by Elgar, whose influence is apparent in spite of an undoubtedly personal idiom. His principal compositions are :—

(a) ORCHESTRA : *Sinfonia concertante* (piano and orchestra) ; symphony ; overture, *Portsmouth Point* ; viola concerto ; violin concerto ; cello concerto ; 2 suites from *Façade* ; 2 coronation marches.

(b) CHORAL WORKS : *Belshazzar's Feast* ; *In Honour of the City of London.*

(c) CHAMBER MUSIC : Piano quartet ; 2 string quartets ; violin sonata.

(d) OPERA : *Troilus and Cressida* (London, 1954).

Waltz (*Fr.* valse, *G.* Walzer, *I.* valzer). A dance in triple time, slow or fast, with one beat in the bar. It first appeared in the late 18th cent. as a development of the older DEUTSCHER TANZ. An early example is the waltz by Diabelli, on which Beethoven published a set of variations (Op. 120) in 1823:

The development of the waltz as a dance-form in the 19th cent. was due principally to the Viennese composers Joseph Lanner and Johann Strauss, followed by Johann Strauss, the younger, composer of *An der schönen blauen Donau* (*The Blue Danube*, 1867), and his brother Joseph. Examples of waltzes by the three Strausses are in *D.T.Ö.*, xxxii (2), xxxv (2), and xxxviii (2). Sets of waltzes for piano (solo or duet) were also written by Schubert, Weber, Chopin and Brahms. Weber's *Aufforderung zum Tanz* (Invitation to the Dance) for piano solo is a programmatic piece consisting of a series of waltzes, with introduction and epilogue. The vogue of the waltz was not confined to instrumental pieces. Brahms wrote two sets of waltzes for piano duet, *Liebeslieder-Walzer* and *Neue Liebeslieder-Walzer*, with parts for four voices. The influence of the waltz is to be found in many songs and operas of the late 19th and early 20th cent. (*e.g.* the waltzes in Richard Strauss's *Der Rosenkavalier* and *Arabella*). Waltzes have also appeared as movements in symphonies, *e.g.* Berlioz's *Symphonie fantastique* and Tchaikovsky's fifth symphony. Ravel's choreographic poem *La Valse* for orchestra is an impressionistic interpretation of the Viennese waltz.

Walzer [vults'-er], *G.* Waltz.

Wanderer Fantasia. The name popularly given to a *Fantaisie* for piano by Schubert, Op. 15 (1822). It is in four linked sections. In the second section (Adagio) the composer uses part of his song "Der Wanderer," Op. 4, No. 1 (1816). Liszt arranged the work for piano and orchestra (first performed, 1851).

Wanhal [vun'-hull] (spelt Vanhall by English publishers), JOHANN BAPTIST: *b.* Nechanice, May 12, 1739; *d.* Vienna, Aug. 26, 1813. Austrian composer of Czech origin. Studied under Dittersdorf in Vienna, and subsequently in Italy. Exceptionally prolific, he wrote 100 symphonies, more than 100 string quartets, 23 Masses, and numerous other instrumental and vocal works. His reputation, considerable in his day, extended to England.

Ward, JOHN. Early 17th-cent. composer in the service of Sir Henry Fanshawe. He published a set of madrigals in 1613 (reprinted in *E.M.S.*, xix). He also wrote a number of anthems, fantasias for strings, and keyboard pieces. 10 pieces for strings are printed in *Musica Britannica*, ix.

Warlock, PETER. *v.* HESELTINE, PHILIP.

Warner, HARRY WALDO: *b.* Northampton, Jan. 4, 1874. Viola-player and composer. Studied at the G.S.M., and with Alfred Gibson and Orlando Morgan. An original member of the London String Quartet (founded 1907) and also active as an orchestral player. He wrote a number of chamber works, some of which won prizes offered by W. W. Cobbett and Mrs. Coolidge respectively, orchestral suites, and songs.

Wasielewsky [vuz-ee-lev'-ski], JOSEPH WILHELM VON: *b.* Grossleesen (nr. Danzig), June 17, 1822; *d.* Sondershausen, Dec. 13, 1896. Violinist, conductor and musical historian. Studied at the Leipzig Conservatorium, where he was a pupil of Mendelssohn and Ferdinand David. Played in the Gewandhaus Orchestra and wrote musical criticism. Leader, Düsseldorf Orchestra (under Schumann), 1850; conductor of various societies, Bonn,

1852, Dresden, 1855; director of music, Bonn, 1869-84. Of his numerous historical and biographical works the most important are *Robert Schumann* (1858), *Die Violine und ihre Meister* (1869), both of which went through several editions, and *Die Violine im 17. Jahrhundert und die Anfänge der Instrumentalkomposition* (1874, with a supplementary volume of musical examples).

Water Carrier, The. *v.* DEUX JOURNÉES.

Water Music. A suite of orchestral pieces by Handel, first published in 1740. It appears to have been associated originally with a royal occasion on the Thames, *c.* 1715. Some of the pieces have acquired popularity in an adaptation for modern orchestra by Hamilton Harty.

Watson, THOMAS. Editor of an anthology of Italian madrigals, published with English texts in 1590. Most of the pieces are by Marenzio. The collection also includes two madrigals by Byrd, written at the editor's request.

A. OBERTELLO: *Madrigali italiani in Inghilterra* (1949).

Webbe, (1) SAMUEL: *b.* 1740; *d.* London, May 25, 1816. Prolific composer of glees and catches. Librarian, Glee Club, 1787; secretary, Catch Club, 1794. He also published motets and Masses.

(2) SAMUEL: *b.* London, *c.* 1770; *d.* Liverpool, Nov. 25, 1843. Pianist, organist and composer of glees and church music. Son of (1). He held several appointments as organist at Roman Catholic churches.

Weber [vay'-ber], (1) ALOYSIA: *b.* Zell, 1760; *d.* Salzburg, 1839. Soprano. Sister of (5) and (8), 2nd cousin of (4). Married the actor Josef Lange, 1780. Mozart, who had at one time been in love with her, wrote for her the part of Constanze in *Die Entführung aus dem Serail* (Vienna, 1782) and several concert arias.

(2) BERNHARD ANSELM: *b.* Mannheim, Apr. 18, 1766; *d.* Berlin, March 23, 1821. Pianist and composer, a pupil of Vogler and Holzbauer. Became second conductor at the National Theatre, Berlin, and subsequently conductor of the united National Theatre and Italian Opera. Conducted the first performance in Berlin of Gluck's *Iphigénie en Tauride*, 1795. His numerous compositions include several operas, songs and piano sonatas.

(3) BERNHARD CHRISTIAN: *b.* Wolferschwenda, Nov. 1, 1712; *d.* Tennstedt, Feb. 5, 1758. Organist at Tennstedt and composer. His *Das wohltemperierte Clavier*, a set of preludes and fugues for organ in all the major and minor keys, which survives in manuscript at Brussels (mod. ed. by M. Seiffert), was at one time thought to have preceded Bach's first set by 33 years (*v.* WOHLTEMPERIRTE CLAVIER) but was in fact written more than 20 years after.

(4) CARL MARIA FRIEDRICH ERNST VON: *b.* Eutin, Nov. 18, 1786; *d.* London, June 5, 1826. Composer, conductor and pianist. 2nd cousin of (1), (5) and (8). Studied under his father, J. P. Heuschkel and Michael Haydn, under whom he became a chorister at Salzburg. Further study in Munich, 1798. Appeared as a solo pianist in several towns and wrote his first opera, *Das Waldmädchen* (Freiberg, 1800). Settled in Vienna, 1803, where he studied further with Vogler. Conductor at the theatre, Breslau, 1804-6. Secretary to Duke Ludwig of Würtemberg, Stuttgart, 1807-10; banished by the King of Würtemberg, 1810. Moved to Mannheim, and thence to Darmstadt. After several concert tours appointed conductor at Prague, 1813; Dresden opera, 1816. His most successful work, the opera *Der Freischütz*, was produced at Berlin in 1821. Visited London, 1826, to produce *Oberon*, written for Covent Garden Opera, and died there nearly 8 weeks after the first performance. He was virtually the creator of romantic German opera. *Der Freischütz*, a *Singspiel* with dialogue, shows the influence of German folklore and the German countryside in its two aspects, one homely, the other mysterious. *Euryanthe* (Vienna, 1823), an opera with continuous music, which suffers from an obscure libretto, recreates the atmosphere of medieval chivalry and may be regarded as the precursor of

Wagner's *Lohengrin*. Weber's piano compositions show a fertile imagination and a brilliant technical command of the instrument. He was also active as a music critic. His principal compositions are :

(a) OPERAS : *Peter Schmoll und seine Nachbarn* (1803) ; *Silvana* (1810) ; *Abu Hassan* (1811) ; *Der Freischütz* (1821) ; *Euryanthe* (1823) ; *Oberon* (1826).

(b) CHORAL WORKS : *Der erste Ton* ; *Kampf und Sieg* ; *L'accoglienza* ; *Jubelkantate* ; 3 Masses.

(c) ORCHESTRA : 2 symphonies ; overture, *Beherrscher der Geister* ; *Jubelouvertüre* ; 2 piano concertos ; *Konzertstück* for piano and orchestra; 2 clarinet concertos ; clarinet *concertino* ; bassoon concerto ; horn *concertino*.

(d) PIANO : 4 sonatas ; *Aufforderung zum Tanz* (Invitation to the Dance); variations, dances.

Also numerous songs and part-songs.

J. BENEDICT : *Weber* (1881).
A. COEUROY : *Weber* (2nd ed., 1927).
E. KROLL : *Carl Maria von Weber* (1934).
W. SAUNDERS : *Weber* (1940).

(5) CONSTANZE : *b.* Zell, Jan. 6, 1763; *d.* Salzburg, March 6, 1842. Sister of (1) and (8), and 2nd cousin of (4). Married (1) Wolfgang Amadeus Mozart, 1782 (*d.* 1791), (2) Georg Nikolaus Nissen, of the Danish diplomatic service, 1809 (*d.* 1826). She supervised the publication of Nissen's life of Mozart (1828). Translations of letters written by her will be found in E. Anderson, *The Letters of Mozart and his Family*, vol. iii.

(6) FRIEDRICH DIONYS : *b.* Velichov, Oct. 9, 1766 ; *d.* Prague, Dec. 25, 1842. Czech composer and teacher, a pupil of Vogler. One of the original founders of the Prague Conservatoire, 1811, and its first director. He rehearsed Wagner's youthful symphony in C major there in 1832. His compositions were mostly of a popular character.

(7) GOTTFRIED : *b.* Freinsheim, Mar. 1, 1779 ; *d.* Kreuznach, Sept. 12, 1839. Lawyer, composer and theorist. In his house Carl Maria von Weber (not a relation) found refuge after he had been banished from Würtemberg in 1810. His compositions include church music, songs and instrumental pieces of various kinds. He also founded a conservatoire at Mannheim. He published *Versuch einer geordneten Theorie der Tonsetzkunst* (3 vols., 1817-21), which reached a third edition in 1830-2 and was twice translated into English, and several other important works on the theory of music and acoustics.

(8) JOSEPHA : *b.* Zell, 1758 ; *d.* Vienna, Dec. 29, 1819. Coloratura soprano. Sister of (1) and (5), and 2nd cousin of (4). Mozart wrote for her the part of the Queen of the Night in *Die Zauberflöte* (Vienna, 1791). Married (1) Hofer, a violinist, (2) Meyer, a bass.

(9) LUDWIG : *b.* Nuremberg, Oct. 13, 1891 ; *d.* Borken, June 30, 1947. Composer and teacher, mainly self-taught. He taught in Nuremberg and Münster, and played a prominent part in promoting the cultivation of music by young people, particularly at the Folkwangschule at Essen. These interests are reflected in his music, which shows a deep understanding of the spirit of German folksong. His compositions include choral and dramatic works, a symphony, chamber music and songs.

Webern [vay'-bern], ANTON VON : *b.* Vienna, Dec. 3, 1883 ; *d.* Mittersill, Sept. 13, 1945. Composer and editor, a pupil of Schönberg and Adler. He began his career as a theatre conductor, and later appeared as choral and orchestral conductor at the concerts organized for workers in Vienna. In spite of these practical associations he cultivated in his own compositions a style remote from any ordinary experience. Like Schönberg he employed the TWELVE-NOTE SYSTEM and various ingenious contrapuntal devices, but went further in his attempt to create a tenuous fabric of sound, with subdued dynamics and combinations of instruments so intimate that often the melody can only be pieced together from isolated notes in the different parts.

His integrity is beyond question, but the result is often barely intelligible, even to sympathetic listeners. His compositions include a symphony for small orchestra, 3 cantatas, a string quartet, a string trio, a concerto for 9 instruments, and songs. He also edited Heinrich Isaac's *Choralis Constantinus*, part II, *D.T.Ö.* xvi, 1 (1909).

Weckerlin [veck-air-lañ], JEAN-BAPTISTE THÉODORE : *b.* Guebwiller, Nov. 29, 1821 ; *d.* Trottberg, May 20, 1910. Alsatian composer and editor. Studied at the Paris Conservatoire, but without success. Chorus master, Société de Sainte Cécile, 1850-5 ; archivist, Société des Compositeurs de Musique, 1863 ; assistant librarian, Paris Conservatoire, 1869 ; chief librarian, 1876-1909. His compositions, which include 6 operas, symphonies, church music and songs, are of minor importance, though his one-act opera *L'Organiste dans l'embarras* (Paris, 1853) was very successful when it first appeared. He published many collections of old French songs (not always well arranged) and an incomplete catalogue of the books in the reserve of the library of the Paris Conservatoire.

Weckmann [veck'-mun], MATTHIAS : *b.* Niederdoria (nr. Mühlhausen), 1619 ; *d.* Hamburg, Feb. 24, 1674. Organist and composer. Chorister under Schütz at Dresden ; studied further at Hamburg. Court organist, Dresden, 1641 ; organist to the Crown Prince of Denmark, 1642 ; returned to his post in Dresden, 1647 ; organist, St. James's, Hamburg, 1655. At Hamburg he helped to found the *Collegium Musicum*, which gave public performances. His reputation as an organist was considerable. Examples of his church cantatas are in *D.D.T.*, vi. A number of keyboard works have been edited by R. Buchmayer in *Aus Richard Buchmayers Historischen Klavierkonzerten* (1927) ; several others in M. Seiffert's collection *Organum.* See also *E.D.M.*, *Landschaftsdenkmale, Schleswig-Holstein und Hansestädte*, iv.

Wedge Fugue. The nickname given to an organ fugue in E minor by Bach, which has the following subject :

Weelkes, THOMAS : *d.* London, Nov. 30, 1623. Composer. Successively organist of Winchester College and Chichester Cathedral. His first published work—*Madrigals to* 3, 4, 5, & 6 *Voyces*—appeared in 1597. Four further volumes date from 1598-1608. A considerable amount of church music survives in manuscript, some of it incomplete. He was one of the most original and inventive of the English madrigalists, excelling particularly in the composition of works for six voices. Modern ed. of his madrigalian works in *E.M.S.*, ix-xiii. A selection from his church music is in *T.C.M.*, 8vo ed.

Wegelius [vay-gay'-li-ŏŏss], MARTIN : *b.* Helsinki, Nov. 10, 1846 ; *d.* there, March 22, 1906. Composer and conductor. After studying philosophy at the University, he turned to music and studied in Vienna and Leipzig. Became conductor at the Finnish Opera in Helsinki, 1878, and founder and first director of the Conservatoire (now the Sibelius Academy), 1882. Among his pupils were Sibelius, Järnefelt and Palmgren. In addition to a relatively small number of compositions he published works on the theory of music.

Weichsel, ELIZABETH. *v.* BILLINGTON.

Weigl [vyg'l], (1) BRUNO : *b.* Brno, June 16, 1881 ; *d.* there, Sept. 25, 1939. An engineer by profession, who turned to composition and musical criticism at the age of 43. His compositions include organ works, choral works, orchestral pieces and songs. He also published a number of books, including a history of the waltz, *Die Geschichte des Walzers* (1910).

(2) JOSEPH : *b.* Eisenstadt, March 28, 1766 ; *d.* Feb. 3, 1846. Composer, son of a cellist in Prince Esterházy's orchestra and godson of Haydn, a pupil of Albrechtsberger and Salieri. He early won recognition as a composer in Vienna, where he held various posts as

an opera conductor and at the Court. His reputation in his lifetime was high. His compositions include more than 30 operas, of which *Die Schweizerfamilie* (Vienna, 1809) was particularly popular, as well as ballets, oratorios, church music, songs and instrumental trios. An aria from the opera *L'Amor marinaro* (Vienna, 1797) was used by Beethoven as a theme for variations in the finale of his trio for clarinet, cello and piano, Op. 11 (1798).

(3) KARL : *b.* Vienna, Feb. 6, 1881 ; *d.* New York, Aug. 9, 1949. Composer, a pupil of Adler and Zemlinsky. Répétiteur at the Vienna Opera, 1904-6 ; teacher at the Neues Wiener Konservatorium, 1918. Settled in the United States, 1938. His compositions include 2 symphonies and other orchestral works, piano concerto for the left hand, violin concerto, cantata for soli, chorus and orchestra—*Weltfeier*, chamber music and more than 100 songs.

Weihe des Hauses, Die [dee vy'-er dess howz'-ĕss], *G.* (The Consecration of the House). Overture in C major by Beethoven, Op. 124, written for the opening of the Josephstadt Theatre, Vienna, 1822.

Weihnachts-Oratorium [vy'-nuckhts-oh-ra-toh'-ri-o͝om], *G.* *v.* CHRISTMAS ORATORIO.

Weill [vile], KURT : *b.* Dessau, March 2, 1900 ; *d.* New York, Apr. 3, 1950. Composer, a pupil of Humperdinck and Busoni. Left Germany in 1933 and settled in Paris, removing to New York in 1935. He won a brief reputation by the skill with which he combined modern idioms with jazz : the most successful example is the setting of Bert Brecht's version of *The Beggar's Opera*, entitled *Die Dreigroschenoper* (Berlin, 1928). In his later works he was content to employ the current idioms of musical comedy, revue and film music. In his earlier years he also wrote a number of instrumental works, including a symphony and a violin concerto.

Weinberger [vine'-bairg-er], JAROMIR : *b.* Prague, Jan. 8, 1896. Czech composer. In 1922 went to Ithaca (U.S.A.) to teach composition at the Conservatoire. Returned to Europe in 1926 and held various other teaching posts. Settled in the United States, 1938. Of his compositions the most successful has been his first opera *Švanda dudák* (Schwanda the Bagpiper) (Prague, 1927). Written in a racy, national idiom it has become immensely popular in both hemispheres. His later operas are : *Die geliebte Stimme* (Munich, 1931), *Lidé z Pokerflatu* (after Bret Harte's *The Outcasts of Poker Flat*) (Brno, 1932) and *Wallenstein* (Vienna, 1937). He has also written several orchestral works, including variations on the popular tune "Under the spreading chestnut-tree."

Weiner [vine'-er], LEÓ : *b.* Budapest, Apr. 16, 1885. Composer. Studied at the Budapest National Academy, where he was appointed teacher, 1908. He has written works for orchestra and for the stage, but his most important compositions are chamber works, of which the 2nd string quartet, Op. 13, won the Coolidge Prize in 1921.

Weingartner [vine'-garrt-ner], FELIX (originally Paul Felix) VON : *b.* Zara, June 2, 1863 ; *d.* Winterthur, May 7, 1942. Conductor and composer. Studied in Graz and Leipzig, and with Liszt in Weimar. Opera conductor, Königsberg, 1884 ; Danzig, 1885 ; Hamburg, 1887 ; Mannheim, 1889 ; Berlin, 1891 ; Munich, 1898 ; Vienna, 1908-11 ; Hamburg, 1912-14 ; Vienna Volksoper, 1919-24 ; Vienna State Opera, 1935-6. Also conductor, Royal Symphony Concerts, Berlin, 1891-1907 ; Munich, Kaim concerts, 1898-1907 ; General Music Director, Darmstadt, 1914-19 ; Vienna Philharmonic Orchestra, 1908-27 ; director, Basle Conservatoire, 1927-35. He conducted frequently in Europe and America, and excelled in the interpretation of Beethoven and Liszt. Sparing of gesture, he secured his results by the most economical means. In the opera house, where he seemed to ignore the demands of the stage, this austerity was less successful. He was a prolific composer. His compositions include 7 operas, 6 symphonies, symphonic poems and overtures, choral works, chamber music and songs. His literary works include an essay on conducting—*Über das Dirigieren* (1895), *Bayreuth 1876-96* (1896), *Die Symphonie nach Beethoven* (1897), *Ratschläge für Aufführung der Sinfonien Beethovens,* (1906), *Akkorde* (collected essays, 1912), *Lebenserinnerungen* (2 vols., 1923-9). English translations were published of *Über das Dirigieren* (*On Conducting*), *Die Symphonie nach Beethoven* (*Symphony Writers since Beethoven*), *Ratschläge für Aufführung der Sinfonien Beethovens* (*On the Performance of Beethoven's Symphonies*) and *Lebenserinnerungen* (*Buffets and Rewards,* 1 vol.). He was five times married.

Weis [vice], KAREL : *b.* Prague, Feb. 13, 1862 ; *d.* there, Apr. 4, 1944. Composer. Studied at the Prague Conservatoire and Organ School. Until 1887 held various posts as organist, teacher and conductor. He wrote several operas, including *Viola,* based on Shakespeare's *Twelfth Night* (Prague, 1892) and *Der polnische Jude* (Prague, 1901), which was very successful and was performed at a number of other opera-houses, including the Metropolitan Opera, New York. He also composed a number of instrumental works.

Weismann [vice′-mun], JULIUS : *b.* Freiburg Dec. 26, 1879; *d.* Singen, Dec. 22, 1950. Composer. Studied in Munich, Freiburg and Berlin. His life was devoted wholly to composition, in which he was extremely prolific, producing more than 140 opus nos. His compositions include 7 operas (3 based on works by Strindberg), 4 symphonies, concertos for violin (3), piano (3), cello and horn (*concertino*), 8 string quartets, numerous other chamber works, choral works, piano solos and songs. In 1934 he was one of two composers commissioned by the Nazi *Kulturgemeinde* to write new music for *A Midsummer Night's Dream,* Mendelssohn's being inadmissible as the work of a Jew.

Weiss [vice], AMALIE. *v.* JOACHIM (1).

Weissmann [vice′-mun] ADOLF : *b.* Rosenberg, Aug. 15, 1873 ; *d.* Haifa, Apr. 23, 1929. Critic. Studied at Breslau, Innsbruck, Florence and Berne. Music critic, *Berliner Tageblatt,* 1900-15 ; *Berliner Zeitung am Mittag,* from 1916. His published works include books on Bizet, Chopin, Puccini and Verdi, and *Die Musik in der Weltkrise* (1922 ; English ed., *The Problems of Modern Music,* 1925).

Weist-Hill, THOMAS HENRY : *b.* London Jan. 23, 1828 ; *d.* Dec. 25, 1891. Violinist and conductor. Studied at the R.A.M. Toured as a violinist, subsequently becoming conductor at Drury Lane and His Majesty's Theatre ; also conductor, Alexandra Palace, 1874-6, Viard-Louis concerts, 1878-9. First Principal, Guildhall School of Music, 1880. As a conductor he introduced to the public a considerable number of new and unfamiliar works, both English and foreign.

Welcome Song. A composition for soli, chorus and orchestra used in Restoration times to mark the return to London of the King or other members of the royal family. Examples by Purcell are in the Purcell Society's edition, xv and xviii.

Weldon, JOHN : *b.* Chichester, Jan. 19, 1676 ; *d.* London, May 7, 1736. Composer and organist. Educated at Eton, and subsequently a pupil of Purcell. Organist, New College, Oxford, 1694-1702 ; Chapel Royal, 1708. Composer, Chapel Royal, 1715. Also organist of St. Bride's, Fleet Street, and St. Martin's-in-the-Fields. His compositions include anthems, songs and dramatic music.

Wellesz [vell′-ess], EGON : *b.* Vienna, Oct. 21, 1885. Composer and musicologist, a pupil of Adler and Schönberg. Studied at Vienna University. Lecturer in history of music, Vienna, 1913 ; professor, 1930-8. Hon. D. Mus., Oxford, 1932. Resident in England since 1938. Lecturer, Oxford, 1943 ; Reader in Byzantine Music, 1948-56. Edited Fux's opera *Costanza e fortezza, D.T.Ö.,* xvii (1910). He has published a number of works on Byzantine music, in particular *Eastern Elements in Western Chant* (1947) and *A History of Byzantine Music and Hymnography* (1949), and is one of the editors of *Monumenta Musicae Byzantinae.* He has also written on 17th-century opera and on modern orchestration. As a composer he showed in his earlier work the strong influence of Schönberg, to whom he has devoted a biographical study (1921, English ed. 1925); his later works are marked by a considerable simplification of harmony and a ready acceptance of Romantic idioms. His principal compositions are:

(a) OPERAS: *Die Prinzessin Girnara* (Hanover, 1921); *Alkestis* (Mannheim, 1924); *Die Opferung des Gefangenen* (Cologne, 1926); *Scherz, List und Rache* (Stuttgart, 1928); *Die Bacchantinnen* (Vienna, 1931); *Incognita* (Oxford, 1951).

(b) BALLETS: *Das Wunder der Diana*; *Persisches Ballett*; *Achilles auf Skyros*; *Die Nächtlichen*.

(c) ORCHESTRA: 5 symphonies; piano concerto; *Vorfrühling* (symphonic poem); *Prosperos Beschwörungen* (symphonic suite, after *The Tempest*).

(d) CHORAL WORKS: *Mitte des Lebens* (cantata); 3 Masses; motets.

(e) CHAMBER MUSIC: octet; 7 string quartets.

Also songs and piano solos.

Well-Tempered Clavier, The. *v.* WOHLTEMPERIRTE CLAVIER.

Wendling [vent'-ling], JOHANN BAPTIST: *b.* 1720; *d.* Munich, Nov. 27, 1797. Flautist and composer, who held posts successively at Zweibrücken, Mannheim (1754-78) and Munich. He also toured Europe as a soloist and wrote works for the flute (examples in *D.T.B.*, xv-xvi).

Wennerberg [ven'-er-bair-*yer*], GUNNAR: *b.* Lidköping, Oct. 2, 1817; *d.* Leckö, Aug. 24, 1901. Schoolmaster, civil servant, poet and composer. His compositions, the fruit of his leisure hours, include several oratorios and other choral works, among them *Davids psalmer* for soli, chorus and piano. His songs of student life in Upsala, where he was educated (*Gluntarne* for two basses and piano, and *De tre* for male voices in three parts without accompaniment), are still popular in Sweden.

Werckmeister [vairrk'-mice-ter], ANDREAS: *b.* Beneckenstein, Nov. 30, 1645; *d.* Halberstadt, Oct. 26, 1706. Organist successively at Hasselfelde, Quedlinburg and Halberstadt. As a writer on the theory of music he was much respected by his contemporaries and successors. In his *Orgelprobe* (1681; 2nd ed. 1698, facsimile reprint, 1927) and *Musicalische Temperatur* (1691) he gave detailed instructions for the tuning of keyboard instruments.

Wert [vairrt], GIACHES DE: *b.* 1535; *d.* Mantua, May 6, 1596. Composer, for many years in the service of the Duke of Mantua. One of the most prolific madrigal-composers of the 16th century. His publications include 11 books of madrigals in five or more parts, one book of madrigals in four parts, *canzonette* and motets.

Werther [vair-tair]. Opera in four acts by Massenet. Original French libretto by Édouard Blau, Paul Milliet and Georges Hartmann (after Goethe). First performed in a German version by Max Kalbeck, Vienna, Feb. 16, 1892.

Wesley, (1) SAMUEL: *b.* Bristol, Feb. 24, 1766; *d.* London, Oct. 11, 1837. Organist and composer, a son of the hymn-writer Charles Wesley. He showed outstanding gifts as a child and had written a considerable amount of music, both vocal and instrumental, before the age of 20. His subsequent career was limited by the recurrent effects of an accident to his skull. His enthusiasm for the music of J. S. Bach did much to bring it to the notice of other musicians at a time when it was virtually unknown in England. In particular, he helped to produce an English edition of *Das wohltemperirte Clavier*. His best-known composition is the 8-part motet "In exitu Israel."

J. T. LIGHTWOOD: *Samuel Wesley, Musician* (1937).

E. WESLEY: *Letters of Samuel Wesley to Mr. Jacobs* (1875).

(2) SAMUEL SEBASTIAN: *b.* London, Aug. 14, 1810; *d.* Gloucester, Apr. 19, 1876. Organist and composer. Son of (1). Chorister of the Chapel Royal. Held various appointments as organist at London churches, 1826-32. Subsequently organist, Hereford Cathedral, 1832; Exeter Cathedral, 1835; Leeds Parish Church, 1842; Winchester Cathedral, 1849; Gloucester Cathedral, 1865. He also taught the organ at the

R.A.M. His compositions, which are not without individuality, are mostly for the church.

Wettergren [vet′-er-grehn], GERTRUD. *v.* PÅLSON-WETTERGREN.

Wetz [vets], RICHARD: *b.* Gleiwitz, Feb. 26, 1875; *d.* Erfurt, Jan. 16, 1935. Composer, largely self-taught. He conducted various organizations at Erfurt, from 1906 onwards, and also taught at the Landeskonservatorium there and at the Music School at Weimar. He was a strong admirer of Bruckner and Liszt, and wrote books on both these composers. His compositions include 2 operas, *Requiem*, *Weihnachts-Oratorium* (Christmas Oratorio) and other choral works (with and without orchestra), 3 symphonies, violin concerto, 2 string quartets, and more than 100 songs.

Wetzler [vets′-ler], HERMANN HANS: *b.* Frankfort, Sept. 8, 1870; *d.* New York, May 29, 1943. Conductor and composer. Studied at the Hoch Konservatorium, Frankfort, where his teachers included Clara Schumann, Iwan Knorr and Humperdinck. Settled in New York, 1892, and was active there as an organist and as conductor of concerts organized by himself. Subsequently opera conductor at Hamburg, 1904; Elberfeld, 1908; Riga, 1909; Halle, 1913; Lübeck, 1915; Cologne, 1919-23. From that time a free-lance conductor. Settled in Switzerland, 1930. His compositions, which show the influence of Richard Strauss, particularly in his handling of the orchestra, include the opera *Die baskische Venus* (Leipzig, 1928), incidental music to *As you like it*, *Assisi* (symphonic poem) and other orchestral works, and songs.

Weyse [vize′er], CHRISTOPH ERNST FRIEDRICH: *b.* Altona, March 5, 1774; *d.* Copenhagen, Oct. 8, 1842. Composer and teacher. Studied with J. A. P. Schulz in Copenhagen, where he spent the rest of his life. He wrote a number of Danish operas, of which *Sovedrikken* (The Sleeping-Draught, 1809) and *Et Eventyr i Rosenborg Have* (An Adventure in Rosenborg Gardens, 1827) were particularly successful in Copenhagen. He also wrote a number of sonatas for the piano, and some studies which were much admired in the 19th century. Among his pupils were Gade and Hartmann.

Weyssenburg [vice′-ĕn-bŏŏrk], HAINZ. *v.* ALBICASTRO.

White, ROBERT. *v.* WHYTE (2).

Whitehill, CLARENCE: *b.* Marengo (Iowa), Nov. 5, 1871; *d.* New York, Dec. 19, 1932. Operatic baritone, who excelled in Wagnerian roles. He first appeared in Gounod's *Roméo et Juliette* at Brussels, 1899, and subsequently sang at Paris, Cologne, New York, Chicago, Covent Garden, Bayreuth and Munich.

Whitehouse, WILLIAM EDWARD: *b.* London, May 20, 1859; *d.* there, Jan. 12, 1935. Cellist. Studied at the R.A.M. Toured with Joachim, and was a member of several ensembles. Also taught at the R.A.M., R.C.M. and Trinity College of Music.

Whithorne, EMERSON: *b.* Cleveland, Sept. 6, 1884. Composer. Studied in Cleveland and Vienna. Music critic and teacher in London, 1907-15. His compositions include 2 symphonies, violin concerto, symphonic poems, chamber music, piano solos, and songs.

Whittaker, WILLIAM GILLIES: *b.* Newcastle upon Tyne, July 23, 1876; *d.* Orkney Isles, July 5, 1944. Conductor, teacher and composer. After some years as a schoolmaster became lecturer in music at Armstrong College (now King's College), Newcastle-upon-Tyne. Founder and conductor, Newcastle upon Tyne Bach Choir, 1915. Professor, Glasgow, and Principal of the Scottish National Academy of Music, 1930. A lifelong campaigner for the works of Bach, many of which he edited for public performance. He also made numerous arrangements of other works (including many folksongs) for school and domestic use. His compositions, few in number, include choral works and a piano quintet.

Whole-Note. American for "semibreve."

Whole-Tone Scale. A scale consisting of a series of intervals of a tone. It may begin on any note. There is no tonic or any other implicit relationship between the notes of the series. The limitations of notation make it necessary to represent one of the intervals as a diminished third (*v.* DIMINISHED INTERVALS), but on a keyboard instrument this is identical with a tone, *e.g.* A♯ to C is the same as A♯ to B♯, or as B♭ to C. Two such scales are possible, the notation of which may vary according to convenience :

A scale starting on D is obviously part of the same series as the one starting on C, and so on.

The following passage shows the use of the whole-tone scale in an actual composition :

DEBUSSY, *Voiles* (*Preludes, Bk.* 1).

Whyte, (1) IAN : *b.* Dunfermline, Aug. 13, 1901. Conductor and composer. Studied at the R.C.M., where he was a pupil of Stanford and Vaughan Williams. Director of music to Lord Glentanar, 1923 ; B.B.C., Scottish Region, 1931. In addition to arranging a large number of Scots melodies he has composed 2 symphonies, 2 overtures, choral works and chamber music.

(2) ROBERT : *b. c.* 1530 ; *d.* London, 1574. Composer. Master of the choristers, Ely Cathedral, 1561 ; Chester Cathedral, 1566 ; Westminster Abbey, 1570. His compositions, of high quality, consist of Latin church music, a few English anthems, and instrumental music. Modern ed. of church music in *T.C.M.*, v.

Whythorne, THOMAS : *b.* 1528. Composer of two sets of partsongs for voices or instruments : (a) *Songes, for three, fower, and five voyces* (1571), (b) *Duos, or Songs for two voices* (1590). The pieces in the first set, designed for a single voice with vocal or instrumental accompaniment, were reprinted by P. Warlock.

Widerspänstigen Zähmung, Der [dair veed′-er-shpence-tig-ĕn tsame′-ŏŏng] (The Taming of the Shrew.) Opera in four acts by Goetz. Libretto by Joseph Victor Widmann (after Shakespeare). First performed, Mannheim, Oct. 11, 1874.

Widor [vee-dorr], CHARLES MARIE JEAN ALBERT : *b.* Lyons, Feb. 22, 1845 ; *d.* Paris, March 12, 1937. Composer and organist. Studied in Brussels, where he was a pupil of Lemmens and Fétis. Organist, St. Sulpice, Paris, 1870-1934. Teacher at the Paris Conservatoire, 1896. He wrote 10 large-scale works for organ, described as "symphonies." His other compositions include 3 operas, of which *Les Pêcheurs de Saint-Jean* (Paris, 1905) was the most successful, 5 symphonies (two with organ, one with final chorus), 2 piano concertos, cello concerto, *Une Nuit de Walpurgis* (chorus and orchestra), chamber works, piano solos, and songs. He also edited Bach's organ works, in collaboration with Schweitzer, and wrote a supplement to Berlioz's *Traité de l'instrumentation.*

Wieck [veek], (1) CLARA JOSEPHINE. Daughter of (2). *v.* SCHUMANN (1).

(2) FRIEDRICH : *b.* Pretzsch, Aug. 18, 1785 ; *d.* Dresden, Oct. 6, 1873. Piano-teacher. Studied theology at Wittenberg. For some time proprietor of a piano-manufacturing business and lending library in Leipzig. Settled in Dresden, 1840. He developed his own method of teaching the piano and practised it with the greatest success. His pupils included Hans von Bülow and his daughter Clara. Married (1) Marianne Tromlitz (mother of Clara), from whom he was divorced, (2) Clementine Fechner.

Wiegenlied [vee′-gĕn-leet], *G.* (*Fr.* berceuse). "Cradle song." *v.* BERCEUSE.

Wieniawski [vyain-yuff′-ski], HENRI : *b.* Lublin, July 10, 1835 ; *d.* Moscow, Apr. 2, 1880. Polish violinist. Studied at the Paris Conservatoire. Violinist to the Czar, 1860-72. Teacher, Brussels Conservatoire, 1875 (for a few years only). Toured widely as a soloist, at first with his brother Joseph, later with Anton Rubinstein. One of the outstanding violinists of his time. His compositions include two concertos and pieces of a popular kind.

Wieprecht [vee'-pre*sht*], WILHELM FRIEDRICH: *b.* Aschersleben, Aug. 8, 1802; *d.* Berlin, Aug. 4, 1872. Bandmaster of the Prussian Guards. Inventor of the TUBA and author of several improvements to wind instruments.

Wigmore Hall. A concert hall in Wigmore Street, London, W.1, suitable for chamber concerts and solo recitals. Built by the firm of Bechstein, pianomakers, and opened as the Bechstein Hall, 1901. Closed during the first part of the 1914-18 war and re-opened as the Wigmore Hall, 1917.

Wiklund [veek'-lo͝ond], ADOLF: *b.* Långserud, June 5, 1879; *d.* Stockholm, Apr. 3, 1950. Swedish composer and conductor. Studied at the Stockholm Conservatoire, and subsequently in Paris and Berlin. Répétiteur, Karlsruhe, 1907; Berlin Royal Opera (now Staatsoper), 1908. Conductor, Stockholm Opera, 1911; Konsertförening, 1925-38. His compositions include 2 piano concertos and other orchestral works, chamber works, piano pieces and songs.

Wilbye, JOHN: *b.* Diss, 1574; *d.* Colchester, Sept. 1638. Composer, in the service of Sir Thomas Kytson, Hengrave Hall, Suffolk. The only complete compositions extant are two volumes of madrigals (modern ed. in *E.M.S.*, vi and vii), which are among the finest examples by English composers, a contribution to *The Triumphes of Oriana* (*E.M.S.*, vi, also xxxii), two sacred pieces to English words (*E.M.S.*, vi) and two Latin motets (*Old English Edition*, xxi).

Wilder [veel-dair], JÉRÔME ALBERT VICTOR: *b.* Wetteren, Aug. 21, 1835; *d.* Paris, Sept. 8, 1892. Belgian poet, critic and translator. Studied law and philosophy at Ghent. Settled in Paris, 1860. Wrote musical criticism for several French papers, translated Wagner's later operas into French (and works by other composers), published *Mozart, l'homme et l'artiste* (1880) and *Beethoven, sa vie et ses œuvres* (1883). He had a considerable influence on musical life in France: his translations are highly praised.

Wilhelmj [vil-helm'-i], AUGUST DANIEL FERDINAND: *b.* Usingen, Sept. 21, 1845; *d.* London, Jan. 22, 1908. Violinist. Studied at Wiesbaden, and with F. David at the Leipzig Conservatorium. First appeared as a soloist, 1854. From 1865 onwards toured widely in Europe, America, Australia and Asia. Leader of the orchestra at the first Bayreuth Festival, 1876. Teacher, Guildhall School of Music, 1894. Outstanding as a teacher, and also took an active interest in the making of violins.

Wilkinson, ROBERT. *v.* WYLKYNSON.

Willaert [vill'-lahrrt], ADRIAN: *b.* probably Bruges, *c.* 1480-90; *d.* Venice, Dec. 7, 1562. Composer, one of the many Flemish musicians who made their career in Italy. *Maestro di cappella*, St. Mark's, Venice, from 1527 till his death. According to Zarlino he was inspired by the existence of two organs at St. Mark's to write *cori spezzati*, or compositions for two antiphonal choirs: the practice of this form of church music remained one of the characteristics of Venetian composers. He was also one of the first composers of the typical polyphonic madrigal of the mid-16th cent., and one of the first to issue collections of polyphonic *ricercari* (*v.* RICERCAR) for instrumental ensembles. His compositions include Masses, motets, madrigals, *chansons* and *ricercari*. A complete edition of his works, ed. by H. Zenck and W. Gerstenberg, is in progress.

Willan, HEALEY: *b.* London, Oct. 12, 1880. Composer and organist. Lecturer, Toronto, 1914; vice-principal, Toronto Conservatoire, 1920. His compositions include a symphony, choral works, organ music and songs.

Williams, (1) ALBERTO: *b.* Buenos Aires, Nov. 23, 1862; *d.* there, June 17, 1952. Argentine composer, pianist, conductor and poet. Studied at Buenos Aires Conservatoire and at the Paris

Conservatoire. Active in Buenos Aires as recitalist and conductor. His compositions, several of which are influenced by South American folksong, include 9 symphonies and other orchestral works, chamber music, unaccompanied choral works, many piano pieces and songs.

(2) CHARLES FRANCIS ABDY: *b.* Dawlish, July 16, 1855 ; *d.* Milford, Feb. 27, 1923. Organist and writer on music. Studied at Cambridge. After a period as organist in New Zealand and London he was for a short time in charge of the music for the Greek plays performed at Bradfield College. He made several contributions to the study of Greek music, and also published *A Short Historical Account of the Degrees in Music at Oxford and Cambridge* (1893), *Bach* (1900 ; rev. ed. 1934) and *Handel* (1901 ; rev. ed. 1935).

(3) JOSEPH, LTD. A firm of London music-publishers, founded by Lucy Williams in 1808.

(4) RALPH VAUGHAN. *v.* VAUGHAN WILLIAMS.

William Tell. *v.* GUILLAUME TELL.

Willis, HENRY: *b.* Apr. 27, 1821 ; *d.* London, Feb. 11, 1901. Organ-builder and organist, founder of the firm of Henry Willis and Sons, which has built or restored a large number of cathedral organs in this country. Among the other organs built by him were those at the Great Exhibition of 1851, St. George's Hall, Liverpool, Alexandra Palace, and Royal Albert Hall.

Wilson, (1) JAMES STEUART: *b.* Clifton, July 21, 1889. Tenor and administrator. Educated at Cambridge. Studied singing with Jean de Reszke and George Henschel. An original member of the ENGLISH SINGERS, 1920-4. Sang in several operatic performances (particularly of works by Boughton) and in oratorio. Director of music, Arts Council, 1945. Director of music, B.B.C., 1948. Deputy administrator, Covent Garden Opera, 1951. Principal, Birmingham School of Music, 1957. Knighted, 1948. Collaborated with A. H. Fox Strangways in translations of songs by Schubert, Schumann and Brahms, Haydn's *Creation* and Brahm's *Requiem.*

(2) JOHN : *b.* Apr. 5, 1595 ; *d.* London, Feb. 22, 1674. Instrumentalist, singer and composer. In his earlier years he seems to have appeared as a singer in plays ; it is at any rate certain that he set songs for stage productions. He became one of Charles I's musicians in 1635. From 1646 onwards he lived in retirement for several years. In spite of his Royalist affiliations he was made professor of music at Oxford in 1656. At the Restoration he became one of Charles II's musicians and in 1662 a Gentleman of the Chapel Royal. Many of the song collections of the Commonwealth and early Restoration periods contain pieces by him. He also published *Psalterium Carolinum,* a memorial tribute to Charles I (1657), and *Cheerful Ayres or Ballads* (printed at Oxford in 1660).

Wilt [vilt], MARIE (*née* Liebenthaler): *b.* Vienna, Jan. 30, 1833 ; *d.* there, Sept. 24, 1891. Operatic soprano. Originally a concert singer. First appeared in opera at Graz, 1865 (as Donna Anna in *Don Giovanni*). Later sang in Berlin, London (Covent Garden), Venice, Vienna, Leipzig, Brno and Budapest, with considerable success, in spite of her obesity and her lack of dramatic ability. She sang Sulamith at the first performance of Goldmark's *Die Königin von Saba* (Vienna, 1875).

Wind Band. *v.* BRASS BAND, MILITARY BAND.

Wind Instruments (*Fr.* instruments à vent, *G.* Blasinstrumente, *I.* strumenti a fiato). A generic term for all instruments in which a column of air is set in motion by the player's breath. Two subdivisions are commonly accepted : (1) BRASS INSTRUMENTS, (2) WOODWIND INSTRUMENTS. The distinction is not based simply on the material of which they are made, since " woodwind " instruments may also be made of metal, ivory, glass or plastic, but on the basic methods of tone-production.

A. CARSE: *Musical Wind Instruments* (1939).

Wind Machine (*G.* Windmaschine). An apparatus in common use on the stage to imitate wind. The sound is produced by creating friction between a hard substance and a piece of silk stretched over a revolving framework. It has occasionally been employed in the orchestra, *e.g.* by Strauss in *Don Quixote* and by Vaughan Williams in *Sinfonia Antartica.*

Windsperger [vint'-shpairg-er], LOTHAR: *b.* Ampfing, Oct. 22, 1885; *d.* Mainz, May 29, 1935. Composer. Studied in Munich, where he was a pupil of Rheinberger. For several years (from 1913) reader to the publishing firm of Schott; later director of the Music School at Mainz. His compositions include a symphony, a piano concerto, a violin concerto, a considerable number of chamber works, *Missa Symphonica*, and *Requiem.*

Wingham, THOMAS: *b.* London, Jan. 5. 1846; *d.* there, March 24, 1893, Organist and composer. Studied at the R.A.M., where he later became a teacher of the piano, 1871. As organist of the Brompton Oratory, from 1864 till his death, he played an important part in the revival of English church music of the 16th century. His compositions include 4 symphonies, 6 concert overtures, 2 Masses, and chamber music.

Winkelmann [vink'-el-mun], HERMANN: *b.* Brunswick, March 8, 1849; *d.* Vienna, Jan. 18, 1912. Operatic tenor, who excelled in Wagnerian roles. For many years at the Vienna Opera. He also sang in London in the first performances in England of *Die Meistersinger* and *Tristan.* He sang Parsifal at the first performance of that work at Bayreuth, 1882.

Winter [vint'-er], PETER VON: *b.* Mannheim, 1754; *d.* Munich, Oct. 17, 1825. Opera composer. As a boy was violinist in the Elector's orchestra at Mannheim; conductor at the court theatre, Mannheim (subsequently in Munich), 1776; vice-*Kapellmeister*, 1794; *Kapellmeister*, 1798. He also travelled widely. He wrote more than 30 operas: of these the most famous and most successful was *Das unterbrochene Opferfest* (Vienna, 1796), while *Das Labirint* (Vienna, 1798) is interesting as a setting of Schikaneder's sequel to *Die Zauberflöte* (set by Mozart, 1791). He also wrote a mass of Church music and numerous instrumental works, including concertos for clarinet and bassoon. For a thematic list of his chamber music see *D.T.B.*, xv-xvi.

Winter Journey, The. *v.* WINTERREISE.

Winterfeld [vint'-er-felt], CARL GEORG AUGUST VIVIGENS VON: *b.* Berlin, Jan. 28, 1784; *d.* there, Feb. 19, 1852. Musical historian. Studied law at Halle and pursued a legal career until his retirement in 1847. Throughout his professional life and after his retirement he pursued his studies in the history of music, to which all subsequent historians are deeply indebted. His most important works are *Johannes Gabrieli und sein Zeitalter* (3 vols., 1834), and *Der evangelische Kirchengesang und sein Verhältnis zur Kunst des Tonsatzes* (3 vols., 1843-7).

Winterreise, Die [dee vint'-er-rize'-er], *G.* (The Winter Journey). A cycle of 24 songs by Schubert (1827). Words by Wilhelm Müller, who also wrote *Die schöne Müllerin*; modern English version by A. H. Fox Strangways and Steuart Wilson. The title of the songs are:

1. *Gute Nacht* (Good night).
2. *Die Wetterfahne* (The weather-vane).
3. *Gefrorne Thränen* (Frozen tears).
4. *Erstarrung* (Numbness).
5. *Der Lindenbaum* (The lime-tree).
6. *Wasserfluth* (Flood).
7. *Auf dem Flusse* (On the stream).
8. *Rückblick* (Retrospect).
9. *Irrlicht* (Will-o'-the-wisp).
10. *Rast* (Rest).
11. *Frühlingstraum* (Dream of spring).
12. *Einsamkeit* (Loneliness).
13. *Die Post* (The post).
14. *Der greise Kopfe* (The hoary head).
15. *Die Krähe* (The crow).
16. *Letzte Hoffnung* (Last hope).
17. *Im Dorfe* (In the village).
18. *Der stürmische Morgen* (The stormy morning).
19. *Täuschung* (Illusion).
20. *Der Wegweiser* (The sign-post).
21. *Das Wirtshaus* (The inn).
22. *Muth* (Courage).
23. *Die Nebensonnen* (The mock-suns).
24. *Der Leiermann* (The hurdy-gurdy man).

Wirén [vee-rehn'], DAG IVAR: *b.* Noraberg, Oct. 15, 1905. Composer. Studied at the Stockholm Conservatoire, and in Paris with Sabaneiev. Music critic, *Svenska Morgonbladet*, 1938-46. One of the most original Swedish composers. His compositions include 2 symphonies, 2 concert overtures, a cello concerto, 3 string quartets and other chamber works, choral works, piano pieces, songs, and film music.

Wise, MICHAEL: *b.* probably Salisbury, *c.* 1648; *d.* there, Aug. 24, 1687. Organist and composer. Chorister in the Chapel Royal after the Restoration. Lay-clerk, St. George's Chapel, Windsor; organist, Salisbury Cathedral, 1668; gentleman of the Chapel Royal, 1676; master of the choristers, St. Paul's Cathedral, 1687. His compositions include anthems, services, songs and catches.

Witkowski [veet-kov-ski] (originally Martin), GEORGES MARTIN: *b.* Mostaganem (Algeria), Jan. 6, 1867; *d.* Lyons, Aug. 12, 1943. Composer. Son of a French father and a Polish mother. Entered the army, and had already produced several compositions before he studied under d'Indy at the Schola Cantorum, Paris, 1894-7. Founded at Lyons the Schola Cantorum (a choral society), 1902, and the Société des Grands Concerts, 1905. Director, Lyons Conservatoire, 1924. His compositions include the opera *La Princesse lointaine*, founded on a play by Rostand (Paris, 1934), 2 symphonies, the oratorio *Poème de la maison*, chamber works and songs (several with orchestral accompaniment).

Wittgenstein [vit'-gĕn-shtine], PAUL: *b.* Vienna, Nov. 5, 1887. Pianist. Studied in Vienna. First appeared in public, 1913. Lost his right arm in the 1914-18 war and has since devoted himself to playing compositions for left hand alone. Among the many works specially written for him are Ravel's concerto in D major and Strauss's *Parergon zur Symphonia Domestica*.

Woelfl [vurlf'l], JOSEPH. *v.* WÖLFL.

Wohltemperirte Clavier, Das [duss vole-tem-per-eer'-ter cluv-eer'], *G.* "The well-tempered keyboard." The title of two sets of preludes and fugues for keyboard by Bach, each set consisting of 24 preludes and fugues in all the major and minor keys. The first set, dating from 1722, is described as "for the use and profit of young people who are desirous of learning, as well as for the amusement of those already skilled in this study." It was also clearly designed as a practical demonstration of the advantage of tuning keyboard instruments in EQUAL TEMPERAMENT. This system, now universally employed, makes all the semitones equal. The result is that while every key is very slightly out of tune, it is possible to play as easily in one key as another; whereas with the older system of tuning some keys were virtually impossible because they were so badly out of tune. Bach was undoubtedly influenced by a collection of 20 preludes and fugues by J. K. F. Fischer, entitled *Ariadne musica neo-organoedum* and published *c.* 1700 (modern edition by E. von Werra).

The second set of *Das wohltemperirte Clavier* dates from 1744 and is more in the nature of a compilation. It is known that some of the pieces were originally in other keys than those in which they appear here. Others have the air of transcriptions. There is no indication of the instrument for which *Das wohltemperirte Clavier* was written. *Clavier* is a generic term for a keyboard instrument with strings and may equally well mean the harpsichord or the clavichord. The probability is that Bach intended the pieces to be available for either instrument.

C. GRAY: *The Forty-Eight Preludes and Fugues of J. S. Bach* (1938).

Wolf [volf], (1) HUGO: *b.* Windischgraz, March 13, 1860; *d.* Vienna, Feb. 22, 1903. Composer. Studied at the Vienna Conservatorium, 1875-7, but was compelled to leave owing to a disagreement with the director. For some years he was forced to make a precarious living by teaching and by writing musical criticism for the *Wiener Salonblatt.* In 1897 he lost his reason and had to enter an asylum, where he died. He began writing songs in 1876 and this continued to be his principal activity for the rest of his creative life. He worked irregularly: a furious spate of composition would be succeeded by a completely fallow period. A fanatical admirer of Wagner, he lost no opportunity of expressing his prejudices in his criticism. Wagner's influence appears also in the highly significant character of his song accompaniments, which often have the character of independent instrumental compositions to which a voice-part has been added. The reason for this is not that he regarded the singer as superfluous, but that a passion for exact declamation and a genius for interpreting in music the mood of the words constantly induced him to write a vocal line which, like Wagner's, is virtually recitative, sung in strict time above an accompaniment which ensures the continuity and logical development of the musical ideas. His principal compositions are:

(a) SONGS: *Nachgelassene Lieder* (youthful works, first published in 1936); 12 *Lieder aus der Jugendzeit* (1877-8); *Lieder nach verschieden Dichtern* (settings of poems by various authors, including Gottfried Keller, Ibsen, Robert Reinick and Michelangelo, 1877-97); *Mörike-Lieder* (1888); *Eichendorff-Lieder* (1888); *Goethe-Lieder* (1889); *Spanisches Liederbuch* (1890); *Italienisches Liederbuch* (1891 & 1896).

(b) OPERA: *Der Corregidor* (Mannheim, 1896).

(c) CHORAL WORKS: *Christnacht* (1889): *Elfenlied* (1891); *Der Feuerreiter* (1892); *Dem Vaterland* (1898).

(d) ORCHESTRA: *Penthesilea* (symphonic poem, 1885); *Italienische Serenade* (1892).

(e) CHAMBER MUSIC: string quartet (1884); *Italienische Serenade* (1887).

His collected musical criticisms were published by R. Batka and H. Werner (1911).

E. NEWMAN: *Hugo Wolf* (1907).
F. WALKER: *Hugo Wolf* (1951).

(2) JOHANNES: *b.* Berlin, Apr. 17, 1869; *d.* Munich, May 25, 1947. Musicologist. Studied in Berlin, where he was a pupil of Spitta. Lecturer, Berlin University, 1902; professor, 1908; honorary professor, 1922. Librarian, music section of Preussische Staatsbibliothek (Prussian State Library), 1915; director, 1928-34. Joint editor, *Sammelbände der Internationalen Musikgesellschaft*, 1899-1904. Edited the complete works of Obrecht for the Vereeniging voor Noord-Nederlands Muziekgeschiedenis (Society for the History of Music in the North Netherlands), and the following volumes of the German and Austrian *Denkmäler*: *D.D.T.*, v (selected vocal works by J. R. Ahle), *D.D.T.*, xxxiv (Georg Rhau's *Newe deudsche geistliche Gesenge*, 1544), *D.T.Ö.*, xiv (1) & xvi (1) (secular vocal and instrumental works by Isaac). He made numerous contributions to musical periodicals. His books include *Geschichte der Mensuralnotation von 1250-1460* (3 vols., 1905), *Handbuch der Notationskunde* (2 vols., 1913 & 1919), *Musikalische Schrifttafeln* (a portfolio of facsimiles illustrating the development of notation, 1923), and *Kleine Musikgeschichte* (3 vols., 1923-9) together with *Sing- und Spielmusik* (an anthology of examples, since reissued in America as *Music of Earlier Times*). A history of English music, completed but not published, was destroyed in an air raid in the last war. His edition of *Das Squarcialupi Codex* was published posthumously.

Wolff [volf], ALBERT LOUIS: *b.* Paris, Jan. 19, 1884. Conductor and composer. Studied at the Paris Conservatoire. Conductor, Opéra-Comique, 1911; chief conductor, 1922. Conductor, Lamoureux concerts, 1928-34; Pasdeloup concerts from 1934. His compositions include the opera *L'Oiseau bleu* (The Blue Bird), a setting of Maeterlinck's play (New York, 1919).

Wolf-Ferrari [volf - fair - rah' - ree], ERMANNO: *b.* Venice, Jan. 12, 1876; *d.* there, Jan. 21, 1948. Composer. Son of the painter August Wolf and an Italian mother. Studied under Rheinberger in Munich, 1893-5. Director, Liceo Benedetto Marcello, Venice, 1902-12. His principal activity lay in the field of opera. He was particularly successful in comic opera, where he adroitly adapted the idioms of the 18th cent. to the modern stage; his attempt at *verismo* (*q.v.*) in *I gioielli della Madonna* (The Jewels of the Madonna) was less convincing. His principal compositions are:

(a) OPERAS: *Cenerentola* (Venice, 1900); *Die neugierigen Frauen* (*Le donne curiose*, Munich, 1903) ; *Die vier Grobiane* (*I quattro rusteghi*, Munich, 1906) ; *Susannens Geheimnis* (Munich, 1909) ; *Der Schmuck der Madonna* (*I gioielli della Madonna*, Berlin, 1911) ; *Der Liebhaber als Arzt* (*L'amore medico*, Dresden, 1913) ; *Gli amanti sposi* (Venice, 1925) ; *Das Himmelskleid* (Munich, 1927); *Sly* (Milan, 1927) ; *La vedova scaltra* (Rome, 1931) ; *Il campiello* (Milan, 1936) ; *La dama boba* (Milan, 1939) ; *Der Kuckuck von Theben* (*Gli dei a Tebe*, Hanover, 1943).

(b) CHORAL WORKS : *Talitha kumi* (*Die Tochter des Jairus*) ; *La vita nuova* (after Dante).

(c) CHAMBER MUSIC : Piano quintet ; 2 piano trios ; string quintet ; string quartet ; 2 violin sonatas.

Also piano pieces and minor orchestral works.

Although the operas with German titles were originally composed to Italian words and are commonly referred to by their Italian titles, it was in most cases some time before they were performed in Italian, and even longer before they were given in Italy. *Die vier Grobiane* (*I quattro rusteghi*) has been performed at Sadler's Wells in an English version by E. J. Dent, under the title *School for Fathers*.

Wolf-Ferrari also published a volume entitled *Considerazioni attuali sulla musica* (1943).

A. C. GRISSON : *Ermanno Wolf-Ferrari* (1941).

R. DE RENSIS : *Ermanno Wolf-Ferrari* (1937).

E. L. STAHL : *Ermanno Wolf-Ferrari* (1936).

Wölfl [vurlf'l], JOSEPH : *b.* Salzburg, Dec. 24, 1773 ; *d.* London, May 21, 1812. Pianist and composer. Chorister, Salzburg Cathedral. Lived in Warsaw, 1791-4. Returned to Vienna, 1795, where he had some success as an opera-composer. Subsequently toured Europe as a pianist, reaching London in 1805. His reputation as a performer was high. His compositions include 2 symphonies, 7 piano concertos, 15 string quartets, 13 piano trios, 22 violin sonatas and other chamber works, 58 piano sonatas and other keyboard works, operas and songs. His famous piano sonata *Non plus ultra*, written as an exhibition of technical difficulties, provoked Dussek to the composition of his sonata *Plus ultra* (Op. 71).

R. BAUM : *Joseph Wölfl, Leben und Klavierwerke* (1928).

J. S. SHEDLOCK : *The Pianoforte Sonata* (1895).

Wolfrum [volf'-rōōm], PHILIPP : *b.* Schwarzenbach, Dec. 17, 1854 ; *d.* Samaden, May 8, 1919. Composer and organist. Studied at Altdorf and Munich. Lecturer, Bamberg, 1878 ; University director of music and organist, Heidelberg, 1884, where he founded and conducted a Bach Choir ; professor, 1898. His choral works include *Weihnachtsmysterium* (1899), performed at the Three Choirs Festival in Hereford as *A Christmas Mystery*, 1903. His organ works include 3 sonatas and a large number of chorale preludes. He also wrote chamber works, songs and part-songs, and published several books, including a study of Bach in two volumes (1906).

Wolfurt [volf'-ŏŏrt], KURT VON : *b.* Lettin, Sept. 7, 1880. Composer, of German-Baltic origin. After studying science at several universities he entered the Leipzig Conservatorium in 1901 to study music and in the following year became a pupil of Reger. Conductor, Strasbourg, 1911 ; Kottbus, 1912-13. Lived in Russia, 1914-17, and in Sweden, 1917-18. Secretary of the music section of the Akademie der Kunst, Berlin, 1932-45. Lecturer, Göttingen, 1945-50. His compositions include 3 operas, concertos for cello, organ and piano, *Sinfonia classica* and other orchestral works, chamber works, choral works and songs.

Wolkenstein [volk'-ĕn-shtine], OSWALD VON : *b.* Gröden, 1377 ; *d.* Aug. 2, 1445. Poet and composer, one of the last of the Minnesinger. His songs, some of which are in two and three parts, have certain affinities with folk-song ; modern ed. in *D.T.Ö.*, ix (1).

Wolstenholme, WILLIAM : *b.* Blackburn, Feb. 24, 1865 ; *d.* London, July

23, 1931. Organist and composer, blind from birth. Educated at Worcester College for the blind. He held various appointments as organist and had a great reputation as a recitalist. His organ works have still a certain popularity with organists; the rest—chamber music, orchestral works, piano pieces, etc.—are forgotten.

Wood, (1) CHARLES: *b.* Armagh, June 15, 1866; *d.* Cambridge, July 12, 1926. Organist and composer. Studied at the R.C.M., where he subsequently became a teacher. Organist, Gonville and Caius College, Cambridge, 1889-94. Lecturer, Cambridge, 1897; professor, 1924. His compositions include a setting of the Passion according to St. Mark and other church music, secular choral works (including *Dirge for Two Veterans*), music for Greek plays at Cambridge, string quartets and songs. He acted as joint editor (with G. R. Woodward) of *Songs of Syon*, *The Cowley Carol Book* and *An Italian Carol Book*.

(2) HENRY JOSEPH: *b.* London, Mar. 3, 1869; *d.* Hitchin, Aug. 19, 1944. Conductor. Studied composition at the R.A.M. Began his career as an opera conductor, 1889. Conducted the Promenade Concerts in London from their inauguration in 1895 until his death—in Queen's Hall until its destruction in the last war, and subsequently in the Royal Albert Hall. He also conducted innumerable other symphony concerts and festivals in England, Europe and America. He introduced to English audiences, particularly at the Promenade Concerts, a very large number of new works by English and foreign composers, and also gave many young performers the opportunity of appearing in public. His meticulous technique and business-like methods at rehearsals enabled him to give finished performances under the most adverse conditions. His numerous arrangements and re-orchestrations of older music show a passion for vivid colouring which is rarely justifiable on either historical or aesthetic grounds. Knighted 1911. Published his autobiography under the title *My Life of Music* (1938) and a collection of singing exercises, *The Gentle Art of Singing* (4 vols., 1927-8).

(3) THOMAS: *b.* Chorley, Nov. 28, 1892; *d.* Bures, Nov. 19, 1950. Composer. Studied at Oxford and the R.C.M. Director of music, Tonbridge School, 1918-24. He wrote a number of lively choral works, with and without accompaniment; several of these are concerned with the sea, to which, as the son of a master mariner, he was naturally attracted. His literary skill found expression in his autobiography, *True Thomas* (1936), and *Cobbers* (1932), a book about Australia. Throughout his life he was afflicted but not hampered by defective eyesight. In his later years he was chairman of the music-publishing firm of Stainer & Bell.

Woodwind Instruments (*Fr.* instruments de bois, *G.* Holzblasinstrumente, *I.* strumenti di legno). Wind instruments which employ the fundamental and a limited number of upper partials of the HARMONIC SERIES (on the clarinet only the odd numbers), the notes of the scale being produced by holes in the tube which, if opened, shorten the air column and so raise the pitch. Usually known in the orchestra simply as "woodwind." The name is due to the fact that wood is the normal material employed in their construction, though other substances are also used, such as metal, ivory, glass or plastic; the saxophone, which belongs to this family, is always made of metal. Woodwind instruments may be subdivided as follows:

(1) Flute, piccolo, bass flute (tubes open at both ends);
(2) Oboe, cor anglais, hecklephone, bassoon, double bassoon (double reed instruments);
(3) Clarinet, basset horn, bass clarinet, saxophone (single reed instruments).

v. the separate articles on these instruments.

A. BAINES: *Woodwind Instruments and their History* (1957).

A. CARSE: *Musical Wind Instruments* (1939).

Wooldridge, HARRY ELLIS: *b.* Winchester, Mar. 28, 1845; *d.* London, Feb. 13, 1917. Painter and musicologist. Studied painting at the Royal Academy of Art, and at the same time worked privately in libraries at the history of music. After some years as a painter of frescos and stained-glass windows became Slade Professor of Fine Art, Oxford, 1895. He published a new edition of W. Chappell's *Popular Music of the Olden Time,* under the title *Old English Popular Music* (2 vols., 1893), *Early English Harmony* (a volume of facsimiles, 1897) and *The Polyphonic Period* (vols. i & ii of the *Oxford History of Music,* 1901 & 1905 ; new ed. by P. C. Buck, 1929 & 1932). Joint editor (with Robert Bridges) of *The Yattendon Hymnal* (1899) and (with G. E. P. Arkwright) of vols. xiv and xvii (anthems) of the Purcell Society (1904 & 1907).

Worcester. *v.* THREE CHOIRS FESTIVAL.

Wordsworth, WILLIAM BROCKLESBY: *b.* London, Dec. 17, 1908. Composer. Studied privately and with Tovey at Edinburgh. His compositions, which show a respect for tradition unusual at the present day, include 4 symphonies, piano concerto, 4 string quartets, piano quartet, violin sonata, cello sonata, choral works, music for piano and organ, and songs.

Worgan, JOHN : *b.* 1724 ; *d.* London, Aug. 24, 1790. Organist and composer. Studied with his brother James and Roseingrave. Organist at St. Botolph's, Aldgate ; organist and composer, Vauxhall Gardens. His compositions include oratorios, church music, organ music and harpsichord works. One of a group of English composers who shared a strong admiration for Domenico Scarlatti (*v.* R. Newton, "The English Cult of Domenico Scarlatti," *Music and Letters,* Apr. 1939).

Wormser [vorrm-zair], ANDRÉ ALPHONSE TOUSSAINT : *b.* Paris, Nov. 1, 1851 ; *d.* there, Nov. 4, 1926. Composer. Studied at the Paris Conservatoire. *Prix de Rome,* 1875. He wrote several operas and a number of instrumental works, but is best known by his music written to accompany the wordless play *L'Enfant prodigue* (The Prodigal Son), first performed in Paris, 1890.

Wotquenne [vot-ken], ALFRED : *b.* Lobbes, Jan. 25, 1867 ; *d.* Antibes, Sept. 25, 1939. Librarian and historian. Studied at the Brussels Conservatoire ; librarian there, 1894-1919. His publications include *Catalogue de la Bibliothèque du Conservatoire de Bruxelles* (4 vols., 1898-1912), *Catalogue des livrets d'opéras et d'oratorios italiens du XVIIe siècle* (1901), and thematic catalogues of the works of Gluck, C. P. E. Bach and Luigi Rossi. He also edited a considerable amount of French and Italian vocal music of the past.

Wozzeck [vots'-eck]. Opera in three acts by Berg. Libretto from Georg Büchner's drama. First performed, Berlin, Dec. 14, 1925. Wozzeck (a German soldier) is the servant of the captain of the garrison and also of the doctor, who experiments on his body and mind and tells him that he suffers from mental aberration. The captain claims that Marie (Wozzeck's mistress, by whom he has a son) is having an affair with the drum-major. Wozzeck, enraged by the drum-major's boastful words, fights with him but is defeated. He later stabs Marie near a pond, throws his knife into the water and drowns himself. When the news of Marie's death is announced her child does not understand and goes on playing.

Wranitzky [vra-nits'-ki], (1) ANTON : *b.* Neureisch, June 13, 1761 ; *d.* Vienna, Aug. 6, 1820. Violinist and composer. Pupil of Albrechtsberger, Mozart and Haydn. *Kapellmeister* to Prince Lobkowitz in Vienna, 1808. He composed numerous instrumental works, including symphonies, violin concertos and string quartets, and also church music.

(2) KAROLINE : *b.* Vienna, 1790 ; *d.* Berlin, Sept. 4, 1872. Soprano. Daughter of (1). She sang Agathe at the first performance of Weber's *Der Freischütz* (Berlin, 1821).

(3) PAUL : *b.* Neureisch, Dec. 30, 1756 ; *d.* Vienna, Sept. 28, 1808. Violinist, conductor and composer. Brother of (1). Studied in Vienna, where he became conductor at the Court Opera. In addition to a number of instrumental works he composed several operas, which were very successful in Germany, particularly *Oberon, König der Elfen* (Vienna, 1789).

Wreckers, The. Opera in three acts

by Smyth. Original French libretto (from a Cornish drama, *Les Naufrageurs*) by Henry Brewster. First performed (in a German version, *Strandrecht*), by H. Decker and John Bernhoff, Leipzig, Nov. 11, 1906.

Wüllner [veel′-ner], (1) FRANZ : *b.* Münster, Jan. 28, 1832 ; *d.* Braunfels, Sept. 7, 1902. Pianist, conductor and composer. Studied in Münster and Frankfort with Schindler and others. Toured as a pianist, 1852-4. Teacher of piano, Munich Conservatorium, 1856. Director of music to the town of Aachen, 1858 ; court *Kapellmeister*, Munich, 1864; conductor, Munich Court Opera, 1869. Conducted the first performances of Wagner's *Das Rheingold* (Munich, 1869), and *Die Walküre* (Munich, 1870). Court *Kapellmeister*, Dresden, 1877-82 ; conductor, Berlin Philharmonic Orchestra, 1883-4; director, Cologne Conservatorium, 1884. He gave outstanding service to the Lower Rhine Festival. His compositions include a number of large-scale choral works, chamber music, piano pieces and songs.

(2) LUDWIG : *b.* Münster, Aug. 19, 1858 ; *d.* Kiel, Mar. 19, 1938. Actor and singer (at first baritone, later tenor). Son of (1). Sang the part of Gerontius in the first performances in Germany of Elgar's *The Dream of Gerontius* (1901-2), and in the first performance in London (1903).

Würfel [vĕĕr′-fĕl], WILHELM : *b.* Plaňan, 1791 ; *d.* Vienna, Apr. 22, 1832. Composer, pianist and conductor. Teacher, Warsaw Conservatoire, 1815 ; director of music, Kärntnertortheater, Vienna, 1826. His compositions include the opera *Rübezahl* (Prague, 1824), which was for long popular in Germany.

Wurm [vŏŏrrm], (1) ADELA. *v.* VERNE (1).

(2) MAREY : *b.* Southampton, May 18, 1860 ; *d.* Munich, Jan. 21, 1938. Pianist and composer. Sister of (1) and (3). Studied at the Stuttgart Conservatorium and with Clara Schumann and Raff. Mendelssohn Scholarship, 1884. First appeared as a soloist, Crystal Palace, 1882. One of the few pianists of her time to continue the 19th-cent. tradition of public improvisation. Founded a women's orchestra in Berlin, 1898. Her compositions include an opera, a piano concerto, chamber music, piano solos and songs.

(3) MATHILDE. *v.* VERNE(2).

Wurstfagott [vŏŏrrst′-fug-ot], *G.* Lit. " sausage bassoon." *v.* RACKET.

Wylkynson, ROBERT. Composer. Parish clerk at Eton, 1496-1500 ; master of the choristers, 1500-1515. His surviving compositions (all in the Eton choirbook) comprise two settings of " Salve regina," one in 9 parts, a 13-part setting of the Apostle's Creed in the form of a round, 3 incomplete antiphons and an incomplete Magnificat.

Wyzewa [vee-zay-va], TEODOR DE : *b.* Kaluszik, Sept. 12, 1862 ; *d.* Paris, Apr. 17, 1917. Musicologist, of Polish origin, who came to France at the age of 7 and spent the rest of his life there. Joint founder (with E. Dujardin) of the *Revue Wagnérienne* (1885-8). A regular contributor to periodicals, he also published *Beethoven et Wagner* (1898) and (with G. de Saint-Foix) the first two volumes of *W. A. Mozart, sa vie musicale et son œuvre* (1912), a standard work which was completed by Saint-Foix in three further volumes.

X

Xylophone (*Fr.* xylophone, *G.* Xylophon, *I.* xilofono). Lit. " wood sound " (*Gr.* ξύλον, wood, and φωνή, sound). A percussion instrument similar to the GLOCKENSPIEL, except that the bars, which are hit with beaters, are made of resonant wood instead of steel. The normal compass in England is :

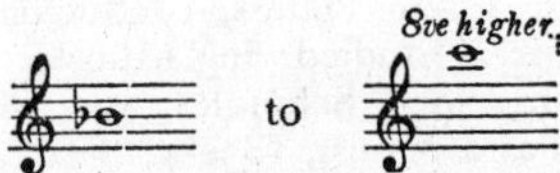

The instrument appears to be of ancient origin and, in a simpler form, is found in many primitive societies. *v.* MARIMBA.

Y

Yeomen of the Guard, The. Comic opera in two acts by Sullivan. Libretto by William Schwenk Gilbert. First performed, London, Oct. 3, 1888.

Yonge, NICHOLAS : *b.* Lewes; *d.* London, Oct., 1619. Editor of two volumes of Italian madrigals, published with English texts under the title *Musica Transalpina* (1588 & 1597). *v.* A. Obertello, *Madrigali italiani in Inghilterra* (1949).

Youll, HENRY. English madrigalist, who published a volume of *Canzonets to three voyces* in 1608. Modern ed. in *E.M.S.*, xxviii.

Young, WILLIAM : *d.* 1671. Violist and violinist. One of the king's musicians at the Restoration. Published at Innsbruck in 1653 *Sonate a* 3, 4, 5 *voci*, dedicated to the Archduke Ferdinand (modern ed. by W. G. Whittaker). The collection, which also includes dance tunes, is interesting as the earliest known set of sonatas for strings and continuo by an English composer.

Yradier [ee-rah-dee-air'], SEBASTIÁN DE : *b.* Sauciego, Jan. 20, 1809 ; *d.* Vitoria, Dec. 6, 1865. Composer of popular songs and dances. His " Habanera " was introduced by Bizet into *Carmen* (1875).

Ysaÿe [ee-za-ee], (1) EUGÈNE : *b.* Liége, July 16, 1858 ; *d.* Brussels, May 12, 1931. Violinist and conductor. Studied at Liége Conservatoire, and subsequently with Wienawski and Vieuxtemps. Teacher, Brussels Conservatoire, 1886-97. Founder and conductor of the Société des Concerts Ysaÿe, Brussels. Toured widely as a soloist and as leader of a quartet. Conductor, Cincinnati Symphony Orchestra, 1918-22.

(2) THÉOPHILE : *b.* Verviers, Mar. 2, 1865 ; *d.* Nice, Mar. 24, 1918. Pianist and composer. Brother of (1). Studied at Liége Conservatoire, and subsequently in Berlin and Paris. Appeared as a pianist with his brother, and also individually. His compositions include a *Requiem*, 2 symphonies, 2 piano concertos and a *Fantaisie wallonne* for orchestra.

Z

Zacconi [dzahk-co′-nee], LODOVICO : *b.* Pesaro, June 11, 1555 ; *d.* there, Mar. 23, 1627. Singer, composer and theorist. He was for a time a member of the court chapel at Munich, but spent most of his life in Italy. His *Prattica di musica* (2 vols., 1592 & 1619) is one of the most comprehensive treatises of its time ; the subjects dealt with include notation, counterpoint, musical form, the modes, instruments, and methods of performance. His manuscript works include a set of canons (with solutions) and *ricercari* for organ.

Zachow [tsuckh′-ow] (Zachau), FRIEDRICH WILHELM : *b.* Leipzig, Nov. 19, 1663 ; *d.* Halle, Aug. 14, 1712. Organist and composer. Organist of the Liebfrauenkirche, Halle, from 1684 till his death. Handel as a boy was his pupil. His compositions include church cantatas and organ works (modern ed. in *D.D.T.*, xxi-xxii).

Zádor [zah′-dawr], JENÖ: *b.* Bátaszék, Nov. 5, 1894. Hungarian composer. Studied at Vienna and Leipzig, where he was a pupil of Reger. Music critic, 1915-20. Teacher, Neues Wiener Konservatorium, 1922 ; Budapest Academy, 1935. He has written several operas, including *A Holtak Szigete* (The Island of the Dead; Budapest, 1928), 2 symphonies and other orchestral works, chamber music, piano solos and songs.

Zählzeit [tsell′-tsite], *G.* Beat.

Zahn [tsahn], JOHANNES : *b.* Eschenbach, Aug. 1, 1817 ; *d.* Neuendettelsau, Feb. 17, 1895. Author of a number of important collections of Lutheran hymns, particularly *Die Melodien der deutschen evangelischen Kirchenlieder* (6 vols., 1888-93). He also published some organ preludes.

Zampa [zũn-pa]. Opera in three acts by Hérold. Libretto by Anne Honoré Joseph Mélesville. First performed, Paris, May 3, 1831.

Zandonai [dzahn-do-nah′-ee], RICCARDO : *b.* Sacco, May 28, 1883 ; *d.* Pesaro, June 12, 1944. Composer. Studied at the Liceo Musicale, Pesaro. His first opera, *Il grillo del focolare*, after Dickens's *The Cricket on the Hearth*, was performed at Turin in 1908. Of his other operas the most successful were *Conchita* (Milan, 1911), *Francesca da Rimini* (Turin, 1914) and *Giulietta e Romeo* (Rome, 1922). He also composed a *Requiem* and other choral works, concertos for violin and cello, and songs.

Zandt, MARIE VAN : *b.* New York, Oct. 8, 1861 ; *d.* Cannes, Dec. 31, 1919. Operatic soprano. First public appearance, Turin, 1879. Sang regularly at the Opéra-Comique, Paris, 1880-5, where she was very popular. She sang the title role in the first performance of Delibes's *Lakmé* (Paris, 1883). She retired after her marriage in 1896.

Zarlino [dzarr-lee′-no], GIOSEFFO : *b.* Chioggia, Mar. 22, 1517 ; *d.* Venice, Feb. 14, 1590. Composer and theorist, a pupil of Willaert. *Maestro di cappella*, St. Mark's, Venice, 1565. Few compositions survive. His reputation rests on his theoretical works : *Istitutioni harmoniche* (1558), *Dimostrationi harmoniche* (1571), and *Sopplimenti musicali* (1588). The subjects treated include the mathematical basis of music, counterpoint, and the modes. The *Sopplimenti musicali* was a reply to Vincenzo Galilei, who had attacked Zarlino's theories in his *Discorso intorno alle opere di messer Gioseffe Zarlino di Chioggia* (1589), reprinted in the second edition (1602) of his *Dialogo della musica antica et della moderna* (1st ed., 1581).

Zar und Zimmermann. *v.* CZAAR UND ZIMMERMANN.

Zarzuela [tharr-thoo-eh′-la], *Sp.* A characteristically Spanish type of opera with dialogue, so called from La Zarzuela, a royal palace in the country outside Madrid, where representations were given in the 17th cent. The earliest known example appears to be *Celos aun del ayre matan* (Jealousy, even of air, is deadly) by Juan Hidalgo, produced in 1660. The popularity of the *zarzuela* declined in the 18th cent. but it was revived in the 19th cent. The Teatro de la Zarzuela, in Madrid, specially built for such performances, was opened in 1856. The modern *zarzuela* is generally either a serious work in three acts or a comic opera, satirical in character, in one act.

G. CHASE : *The Music of Spain* (1941).

Zauberflöte, Die [dee tsowb'-er-flurt-er] (The Magic Flute). *Singspiel* (opera with dialogue) in two acts by Mozart. Libretto by Emanuel Schikaneder. First performed, Vienna, Sept. 30, 1791. The work is a mixture of allegory and fantasy which conceals several references to freemasonry and the political situation in Austria at the time. The prince Tamino, having fallen in love with a picture of Pamina, daughter of the Queen of Night, sets out to rescue her from the clutches of Sarastro, High Priest of Isis and Osiris. He is given a magic flute as a protection against evil, and Papageno, a bird-catcher, who accompanies him, is given a chime of magic bells. When Tamino reaches the temple he discovers that Sarastro is wise and good and that it is the Queen of Night who is evil. Tamino and Pamina, having passed through several mysterious ordeals, are finally united, the Queen of Night being powerless to injure them. Papageno is also rewarded with a bride, Papagena.

Zeitmass [tsite'-mahss], *G.* Tempo.

Zelter [tsell'-ter], CARL FRIEDRICH : *b.* Petzow-Werder, Dec. 11, 1758 ; *d.* Berlin, May 15, 1832. Conductor and composer. Originally a mason, he studied music while still a boy and rapidly became an accomplished musician. Accompanist, Berlin Singakademie, 1792 ; conductor, 1800. Founder and conductor, Königliche Institut für Kirchenmusik, 1820. An intimate friend of Goethe, many of whose poems he set to music, and Mendelssohn, who as a boy was his pupil. He revived Bach's motets with the Singakademie. Though at first opposed to Mendelssohn's revival of the *St. Matthew Passion* in 1829, he yielded to persuasion and allowed Mendelssohn to conduct it.

Zémire et Azor [zay-meer ay a-zorr]. Opera (*comédie-ballet*) in four acts by Grétry. Libretto by Jean François Marmontel (based on Pierre Claude Nivelle de la Chaussée's comedy *Amour par amour*). First performed, Fontainebleau, Nov. 9, 1771.

Zemire und Azor [tsay-meer'-er o͝ont uts-orr']. (1) Opera in four acts by Baumgarten. Libretto translated by Karl Emil Schubert and the composer from Marmontel's libretto of *Zémire et Azor* (*q.v.*). First performed, Breslau, May 18, 1776.

(2) Opera in three acts by Spohr. Libretto by Johann Jakob Ihlee (based on Marmontel's *Zémire et Azor*). First performed, Frankfort, Apr. 4, 1819.

Zemlinsky [tsem-lince'-ki], ALEXANDER VON : *b.* Vienna, Oct. 4, 1872 ; *d.* Larchmont (New York), Mar. 16, 1942. Composer and conductor. Studied at the Vienna Conservatorium. Conductor, Vienna Volksoper, 1906 ; Vienna Opera 1908 ; Mannheim, 1909 ; Prague, 1911 ; Berlin State Opera, 1927-30. Rector, Deutsche Musikakademie, Prague, 1920-7. Settled in America, 1934. Schönberg was his pupil and married his sister ; he also wrote the libretto of Zemlinsky's first opera, *Sarema* (Munich, 1897). Zemlinsky's other operas are *Es war einmal* (Vienna, 1900), *Kleider machen Leute* (Vienna, 1910), *Eine florentinische Tragödie* (after Oscar Wilde ; Stuttgart, 1917), *Der Zwerg* (after Wilde's *The Birthday of the Infanta* ; Frankfort, 1921), and *Der Kreidekreis* (Zurich, 1933). He also composed 2 symphonies and other orchestral works, choral works, chamber music, piano pieces and songs.

Zhizn za Tsara [zheez'n za tsahrr'-ya] (A Life for the Czar). Opera in four acts, with an epilogue, by Glinka. Libretto by Baron Georgy Fedorovich Rosen. First performed, St. Petersburg, Dec. 9, 1836. It was originally called *Ivan Sussanin* (the title by which it is now known in Russia), but was renamed in honour of the Emperor Nicolas I, to whom it was dedicated by the composer.

Ziani [dzyah′-nee], (1) MARC' ANTONIO: *b.* Venice, 1653; *d.* Vienna, Jan. 22, 1715. Composer. Vice-*Kapellmeister*, Vienna, 1700; *Kapellmeister*, 1712. A prolific composer of operas (including the puppet opera *Damira placata*, Venice, 1680) and oratorios.

(2) PIETRO ANDREA: *b. c.* 1630; *d.* Naples, Feb. 12, 1684. Uncle of (1). Composer. Organist first at Venice and Bergamo; second organist, St. Mark's, Venice, 1669; in the Royal Chapel, Naples, 1676-84. Composed operas, oratorios, church music and sonatas for instrumental ensemble.

Ziehharmonika [tsee-harr-moh′-nee-ca], *G.* Accordion.

Ziehn [tseen], BERNHARD: *b.* Erfurt, Jan. 20, 1845; *d.* Chicago, Sept. 8, 1912. Theorist and teacher. Began his career as a schoolmaster in Mühlhausen and Chicago; from 1871 devoted himself wholly to music. His publications include *System der Übungen* (a piano method, 1881), *Harmonie und Modulationslehre* (1887), *Manual of Harmony* (1907), *Five and Six-Part Harmonies* (1911), and *Canonical Studies* (1912).

Zilcher [tsil*sh*′-er], HERMANN: *b.* Frankfort, Apr. 18, 1881; *d.* Würzburg, Jan. 1, 1948. Pianist and composer, son of the composer Paul Zilcher. Studied with his father and at the Hoch Konservatorium, Frankfort. He toured widely as a pianist. Teacher at the Hoch Konservatorium, 1905; Akademie der Tonkunst, Munich, 1908. Director, Würzburg State Conservatorium, 1920. His compositions, in a romantic style, include the comic opera *Doktor Eisenbart* (Mannheim, 1922), the oratorio *Die Liebesmesse*, incidental music to plays, 5 symphonies, concerto for 2 violins, violin concerto, piano concerto, and many other vocal and instrumental works, including pieces for accordion. He also prepared a new edition of Spohr's opera *Jessonda*.

Zimbalist [zim′-ba-list], EFREM: *b.* Rostov, May 7, 1889. Violinist and composer. Studied with Auer at the St. Petersburg Conservatoire. First appeared as a soloist, Berlin, 1907. Toured widely and eventually settled in America, Director, Curtis Institute, Philadelphia, 1941. His compositions include the comic opera *Honeydew* (New Haven, 1920), a violin concerto and other orchestral works.

Zimbel [tsim′-bĕl], *G.* A medieval chime-bell. *v.* CYMBALS (1).

Zimmermann, [*E.* zim′-er-man, *G.* tsim′-er-mun, *D.* zim′-er-mun, *Fr.* zee-mair-mun], (1) AGNES: *b.* Cologne, July 5, 1847; *d.* London, Nov. 14, 1925. Pianist. Lived in England from childhood. Studied at the R.A.M. First public appearance, Crystal Palace, 1863. Edited the piano sonatas of Mozart and Beethoven and the complete piano works of Schumann (Novello). Her compositions include chamber music, piano solos and songs.

(2) LOUIS: *b.* Gronigen, July 19, 1873. Dutch violinist. Studied at the Leipzig Conservatorium and with Ysaÿe in Brussels. Leader of the Concertgebouw Orchestra, Amsterdam, 1899-1904 and from 1911. Teacher, R.A.M., 1904-11. His compositions include a violin concerto and a string quartet.

(3) PIERRE JOSEPH GUILLAUME: *b.* Paris, March 17, 1785; *d.* there, Oct. 29, 1853. Pianist and teacher. Studied at the Paris Conservatoire, where he subsequently taught, 1816-48. His most important work is his *Encyclopédie du pianiste*, a treatise on piano-playing, harmony and counterpoint. His daughter married Gounod, who was one of his pupils.

Zingarelli [dzeen-gah-rell′-lee], NICOLA ANTONIO: *b.* Naples, Apr. 4, 1752; *d.* Torre del Greco, May 5, 1837. Composer. Studied at the Conservatorio Santa Maria di Loreto, Naples, where his first opera, *I quattro pazzi*, was performed, 1768. *Maestro di cappella*, Milan Cathedral, 1792; Loreto, 1794; St. Peter's, Rome, 1804-11; Naples Cathedral, 1816. Director, Real Collegio di Musica, Naples, 1813. A prolific composer, he wrote 35 operas, numerous oratorios and cantatas (including *Isaiah* for the Birmingham Festival, 1829), and an enormous number of Masses, Magnificats, motets and other church music. His refusal to perform a Te Deum in 1811 to celebrate the birth of

Napoleon's son (the King of Rome) led to his dismissal from St. Peter's.

Zingarese. *v.* ALLA ZINGARESE.

Zink [tsink], *G.* The obsolete cornett.

Zipoli [dzee′-po-lee], DOMENICO : *b.* Prato, Oct. 15, 1688 ; *d.* Córdoba (Argentine), Jan. 2, 1726. Composer. Organist of the Jesuit church, Rome. Published *Sonate d'intavolatura per organo o cimbalo* (2 vols., 1716). *A third collection of toccatas, voluntaries and fugues* is an English reprint of part of the s me collection. Examples of his keyboard works are in L. Torchi, *L'arte musicale in Italia*, iii.

Zither [tsitt′-er], *G.* (1) The English CITTERN.

(2) A plucked string instrument popular in Bavaria and Austria. It is flat and has two kinds of strings : (1) 5 melody strings of metal, passing over 29 frets arranged in semitones, which are stopped with the fingers of the left hand and played with a plectrum, (2) as many as 40 or more open strings, plucked with the fingers of the right hand and used for accompaniment.

Z mého života [zmeh′-ho zhiv′-o-ta], *Cz. v.* AUS MEINEM LEBEN.

Zöllner [tsu*r*l′-ner], HEINRICH : *b.* Leipzig, July 4, 1854 ; *d.* Freiburg, May 4, 1941. Composer. Studied at the Leipzig Conservatorium. Director of music, Dorpat (Tartu) University, 1878 ; teacher, Cologne Conservatorium and conductor of the Male Voice Choir, 1885 ; director, Deutscher Liederkranz, New York, 1890 ; director of music, Leipzig University, 1898-1906 ; teacher, Leipzig Conservatorium, 1902-6 ; conductor, Flemish Opera, Antwerp, 1907. From 1914 lived in Freiburg. He wrote 10 operas (most of them to his own librettos) : the best known is *Die versunkene Glocke* (Berlin, 1899), which has been frequently revived. He also wrote several large-scale choral works (including *Die neue Welt*, which won a prize at Cleveland), 5 symphonies and 5 string quartets.

Zolotoy Petoushok [zoll′-ot-oy p'yet-oo′-shock] (*E.* The Golden Cockerel, *Fr.* Le Coq d'or). Opera in three acts by Rimsky-Korsakov. Libretto by Vladimir Ivanovich Belsky (after Pushkin). First performed, Moscow, Oct. 7, 1909 (16 months after the composer's death). King Dodon, worried about affairs of state, is offered by an astrologer a golden cockerel which will warn him of danger. When the alarm is sounded, first Dodon's sons and then the king himself go forth to battle. The sons are killed but the king meets the beautiful Queen of Shemaka, whom he takes home to be his bride. The astrologer demands her as his reward. Dodon kills him and is himself killed by the cockerel. The queen disappears in the darkness which covers the sky.

Zoppa. *v.* ALLA ZOPPA.

Zoroastre [zorr-o-ustr] (Zoroaster). Opera in five acts by Rameau. Libretto by Louis de Cahusac. First performed, Paris, Dec. 5, 1749.

Zugtrompete [tsook′-trom-pate′-e*r*], *G.* (*I.* tromba da tirarsi). Slide trumpet. *v.* TRUMPET.

Zukunftsmusik [tsoo′-co͞onfts-moo-zeek], *G.* " Music of the future." A term originally applied satirically by the critic Ludwig Bischoff to the music of Wagner, who had written an essay entitled *Das Kunstwerk der Zukunft* (The Art-Work of the Future), and subsequently adopted by Wagner himself in his *Zukunftsmusik : Brief an einen französischen Freund* (Music of the Future : Letter to a French Friend).

Zumpe [tso͞omp′-er], (1) HERMAN : *b.* Taubenheim, Apr. 9, 1850 ; *d.* Munich, Sept. 4, 1903. Conductor and composer. Originally a schoolmaster, he assisted Wagner in preparing the score of *Der Ring des Nibelungen* for the first complete performance in Bayreuth, 1876. Subsequently conducted in various German theatres. Court conductor, Stuttgart, 1891 ; conductor, Kaim concerts, Munich, 1895 ; court conductor, Schwerin, 1897 ; court conductor, Munich, 1900 (conducting the first performance in the new Prinz Regenten Theatre). He also conducted Wagner at Covent Garden in 1898. He composed several operas, two of which were produced after his death.

(2) JOHANNES. Late 18th-cent. German employee of the piano-manu-

facturer Shudi in London. The first known maker of square pianos; the earliest extant instrument is dated 1766.

Zumsteeg [tsoo͝m'-shtake], JOHANN RUDOLF: *b.* Sachsenflur, Jan. 10, 1760; *d.* Stuttgart, Jan. 27, 1802. Composer. Son of a soldier, who became a groom of the chamber in the Stuttgart court. Court *Kapellmeister*, Stuttgart, 1792. Famous for the composition of *Balladen* (extended solo songs with contrasted sections) which formed the model for some of Schubert's earlier works. He also wrote several operas, including *Der Geisterinsel* (after Shakespeare's *Tempest*; Stuttgart, 1798), incidental music, church cantatas, and 2 cello concertos. Modern ed. of selected songs by L. Landshoff.

L. LANDSHOFF: *J. R. Zumsteeg* (1902).

Zurückhaltend [tsoo-re͞ek'-hult-ĕnt], *G.* Holding back, *i.e.* slowing down the tempo.

Zweiunddreisigstel [tsvy-o͞ont-drice'i*sh*-stĕl], *G.* Demisemiquaver.

Zwischenspiel [tsvish'-ĕn-shpeel], *G.* (1) Interlude. (2) Episode (*e.g.* in a fugue or rondo).

Zwölftonsystem [tsvu*r*lf'-tone-ze͞ece-tame'], *G.* Twelve-note system.